Poets
American and British

Poets

American and British

Ian Scott-Kilvert
(for the British Council)

George Stade
Leonard Unger
A. Walton Litz
Editors in Chief

VOLUME 1

CHARLES SCRIBNER'S SONS
An Imprint of Macmillan Library Reference
NEW YORK

Charles Scribner's Sons
An imprint of Macmillan Library Reference
1633 Broadway
New York, NY 10019

Library of Congress Cataloging-in-Publication Data

Poets : American and British / Ian Scott-Kilvert . . . [et al.], editors
in chief.
p. cm.
Includes bibliographical references and index.
ISBN 0-684-80605-3 (set : alk. paper). — ISBN 0-684-80606-1 (v. 1
: alk. paper)
1. American poetry—Bio-bibliography—Dictionaries. 2. English
poetry—Bio-bibliography—Dictionaries. 3. American poetry—
Dictionaries. 4. English poetry—Dictionaries. I. Scott-Kilvert, Ian.
PS308.P64 1998
821.009'03—dc21 98-36811
CIP

3 5 7 9 11 13 15 17 19 20 18 16 14 12 10 8 6 4 2

Printed in the United States of America

The paper used in this publication meets the minimum requirements of American National
Standard for Information Sciences—Permanence of Paper for Printed Library Materials.
ANSI Z39.48-1992.

Contents

Publisher's Note

Poets: American and British comprises seventy-two unabridged essays chosen by the publisher from Scribners' thirteen-volume *American Writers* and eleven-volume *British Writers.* The selection is based on a survey of American libraries with a view toward including those English-language poets most often studied by high school students and undergraduates.

The need to make an affordable set has limited the selections. We hope that readers will be inclined to seek out biocritical articles on other poets in the Scribner World Literature series, which also includes *African American Writers, African Writers, American Nature Writers, Ancient Writers: Greece and Rome, European Writers, Latin American Writers, Writers for Children,* and *Writers for Young Adults.*

Matthew Arnold
(1822–1888)

KENNETH ALLOTT

I

If anyone asks what is central in Matthew Arnold's achievement—a question easily prompted by the volume of his work and the range of its interests—one of two replies is probable, in accordance with what is momentarily uppermost in our minds. It may be the missionary nature of Arnold's activities:

> Therefore to thee it was given
> Many to save with thyself
> (no. 87, 140–141)[1]

he wrote approvingly of his father, Dr. Thomas Arnold, in "Rugby Chapel"—in which case we are likely to say that what is central, in the sense of being nearly omnipresent, is the moral and social passion that is the mainspring of such books as *Culture and Anarchy* and *Literature and Dogma* and a sizable element in the poems and literary criticism. Alternatively, at a tangent to this, we may be thinking of what is distinctive, what most gives the taste of Arnold in Arnold's works, in which case we shall be found paying attention to a handful of poems and some selected pages of literary criticism that embody insights with an economical freshness and liveliness, and arguing that they are central in the sense that nobody else could have written them. In this manner a looseness in the original question brings forward two main aspects of Arnold's genius that cannot always be easily separated in his writings. On the one hand, there is the disinterestedness with which objects, ideas, and experiences may be viewed by him ("to see the object as in itself it really is"): the roll call of examples includes such a poem as "Growing Old," the splendid pages on the "ways of handling nature" in *On the Study of Celtic Literature*, Arnold's opinion that the onlooker sees most of the game and that the critic should always remain a little remote from practice. On the other hand, there is the impulse to catechize and instruct, which involves him in judging ideas and even works of art partly by their relevance to apparent social needs: culture, Arnold insists, is a poor thing if it is self-regarding and, in a balanced view, "moves by the force . . . of the moral and social passion for doing good." Something is here left out. Over prose work representing both of these aspects (but not over his verse) Arnold's wit plays at times, aerating its seriousness and preventing its moderation from becoming insipid. If wit is not quite at the center of his achievement, it is an attractive accompaniment of some very characteristic writing. Max Müller speaks of Arnold's Olympian manners at Oxford. It would take a dull dog not to find endearing the Olympian impudence with which he begins an apology to Mr. Wright, a translator of the *Iliad*: "One cannot always be studying one's own works, and I was really under the impression, till I saw Mr.

1. All references for poems are to M. Allott, ed., *The Poems of Matthew Arnold*, 2nd ed. (London, 1979), which has a slightly modernized text. The text reprinted here is that of the 1885 edition. Poem numbers are submitted for titles where appropriate.

Wright's complaint, that I had spoken of him with all respect. . . ."[2]

Ideally, detachment and zeal are the two sides of a single responsibility: the critic (using the term in the convenient Arnoldian sense to cover social commentator as well as literary critic) is loyal to the whole truth, but his judgment of what the public needs at a particular moment causes him to floodlight one fragment of it rather than another. Practically, however, there are sometimes two distinct responsibilities, and an awkward strain may be set up in the critic who is trying to do justice to both of them. Some confusions and peculiarities of emphasis in Arnold's prose—occasionally in the literary criticism, but more often elsewhere—show this clearly enough. There is some truth in the generalization that in the best of Arnold's poetry and literary criticism, insight is preferred to missionary zeal and that an inverse order holds for the social and religious essays, but at best this is a rule with many exceptions. It may give us a reason for echoing the common opinion that Arnold's literary criticism and some of his poems[3] ought to be read first, or, to put it another way, that he is first and most importantly a poetic critic. But we should not in consequence think of the missionary aspect of Arnold's personality simply as a source of weakness. It was a source of both weakness and strength. It saved him from the typical solipsistic pedantries of the ivory tower critic. It seems to have supplied the motive-force for his devotion to his literary vocation: we think of Arnold rising earlier than the servants to read and write before the busy working day of a school inspector, and we recall that temperamentally by his own confession a life of fly-fishing and reading the newspapers would have made him happy. And it may be connected with the common sense that ballasts his other qualities, preventing his intelligence from feeding too much on abstractions and his finesse from becoming too ethereally fine.

"From time to time, every hundred years or so, it is desirable that some critic shall appear to review the past of our literature, and set the poets and the poems in a new order . . . Dryden, Johnson and Arnold have each performed the task as well as human frailty will allow," T. S. Eliot has said (and today we may complete this short list with his own name). There are other poet-critics—Ben Jonson, Shelley, Coleridge (for many purposes the greatest of all English critics)—but, within the exact scope of Eliot's intended meaning, only three of the highest rank before the twentieth century. They are easily recognized. Each one in his own time singles himself out from his fellow-poets by a highly developed civic sense on all matters touching the health of literature. Each, too, shows something of the flair of a public relations officer, so that he is readily accepted as the reigning king of the Sacred Wood, who personifies the unquestioned (because apparently self-evident) literary assumptions of the age. The relationship of a poet-critic to his immediate predecessor may be admiring, but it must be murderous (see Sir James Frazer's *The Golden Bough*): it has been noted that Eliot, while striving to be just, always has an edge in his voice when he speaks of Matthew Arnold. (F. O. Matthiessen calls it "deft, if inconspicuous sniping, kept up over quite a few years.") In this context Eliot's admission of the importance of Arnold's historical role is as handsome as it is convincing.

Matthew Arnold's appearance in the Victorian age at one remove from the present makes his importance much more than historical. He is nearer to us in time than other critics, and this in itself suggests that his criticism may still carry a "live" charge, but the nearness is not simply a matter of chronology: it depends on a similarity between the Victorian age and our own, which underlies all the superficial differences, and it implies the existence of a real watershed between ancient and modern somewhere in the neighborhood

2. Preface to *Essays in Criticism* (London, 1865), vol. III, p. 286. Quotations of prose works are from R. H. Super, ed., *The Complete Prose Works of Matthew Arnold*, 11 vols. (Ann Arbor, Mich., 1960–1977). Volume numbers and page numbers are given.

3. Some only, for in many pieces—notably the sonnets of *New Poems* (1867)—the "willed" or missionary element is uncomfortably strong.

of Coleridge's *Biographia Literaria* (1817)—to put it as far back as possible. All great critics have their *aperçus* (to adopt Arnold's expression), which are timeless, but it is also the critic's function to organize these perceptions, to see how they best hang together in a pattern (the *ordo concatenatioque veri* is Arnold's name for it), and in the end much of every pattern is outmoded. An effort at translation from a dead tongue is needed when we consider the treatment of some of the classical questions of criticism in a seventeenth- or eighteenth-century critic, whereas Arnold's treatment is still in the vernacular in spite of the period flavor of a few of his usages. Equally important to our appreciation of him as a "living" critic is a self-conscious approach that engages our natural sympathies. He performs and is the first spectator of his own performance, and this watchfulness smoothly dilates the reader's understanding of the meaning of critical activity:

> . . . judging is often spoken of as the critic's one business; and so in some sense it is; but the judgement which almost insensibly forms itself in a fair and clear mind, along with fresh knowledge, is the valuable one; and thus knowledge, and ever fresh knowledge, must be the critic's great concern for himself; and it is by communicating fresh knowledge, and letting his own judgement pass along with it,—but insensibly, and in the second place not the first, as a sort of companion and clue, not as an abstract lawgiver,—that he will generally do most good to his readers. Sometimes, no doubt, for the sake of establishing an author's place in literature, and his relation to a central standard (and if this is not done, how are we to get at our *best in the world?*), criticism may have to deal with a subject-matter so familiar that fresh knowledge is out of the question, and then it must be all judgement; an enunciation and detailed application of principles. Here the great safeguard is never to let oneself become abstract, always to retain an intimate and lively consciousness of the truth of what one is saying, and, the moment this fails us, to be sure that something is wrong. ("The Function of Criticism at the Present Time," in *Essays in Criticism,* vol. III, p. 283)

This is so true that in becoming obvious it has almost ceased to seem valuable, but it would not have crossed Dr. Johnson's mind to study himself so curiously or to explain himself in quite this way. It is a post-Coleridgean note.

Again, rightly considered, Arnold's tendency to stray from literary criticism into social and religious comment links him with Eliot and others among our contemporaries and distinguishes him from earlier critics—indeed, the tendency to stray seems to be a peculiar professional hazard in and after the romantic period. To seek the reason would take us far, but I suppose it to be connected with the withering of customary certainties in literary criticism (for example, the obsolescence of "kinds"), and this withering is part of a wider skepticism. When most questions are open questions, a critic may be hard put to it to deal with the propriety of a lyric's diction without raising the ghosts of moral and social issues. In Arnold and Eliot, and in a few capable modern critics on a smaller scale than either, the tendency to range widely marks the seriousness of the attention brought to bear on literature. They shoulder the same sort of burden because they belong to the same cultural phase of the European mind.

Even an incomplete description of the variety of Arnold's attachments to the present must include one further illustration. For two generations or more now, critics have discussed the dilemma of the serious writer in a democracy that is for the most part complacently unaware that the education of taste lags hopelessly behind literacy. The problem, though smaller then, existed for some Victorians. "You see before you, gentlemen," Arnold told the income tax commissioners at Edgware in 1870, "what you have often heard of, *an unpopular author.*" It was more than a joke. He did not avoid public acclaim—on the contrary he wrote delightedly to his mother when he saw men with sandwich boards in Regent Street advertising his essay on Marcus Aurelius—but he soberly realized how little excellence could mean to a mass audience. "Excellence dwells among rocks hardly accessible," he declared, "and a man must almost wear his heart out before he can reach her" (the easy, popular view that excellence was abundant had been taken by a lady from Ohio who sent Arnold a volume on American writers). He knew that his fastidiousness would appear to many both arrogant and lymphatic, but this did not deflect him from his course.[4] He also knew (sometimes with a jealous tincture) that his poetry would have to make its way slowly: general applause is perfunctory for verse that illustrates, in Henry James' words, "a slight abuse of meagreness for distinction's sake." Arnold's is an unobtrusive example of a literary integrity that a degree of isolation neither weakens nor sours: ". . . no one knows better than I do how little of a popular author I am," he writes equably to a sister in 1874, "but the thing is, I gradually produce a real effect, and the public acquires a kind of obscure interest in me as this gets to be perceived."[5]

It would have meant something to Arnold that Walter Bagehot liked his poems (and took them with him on his honeymoon), or that Gerard Manley Hopkins sprang to his defense against the more conventional Robert Bridges ("I do not like to hear you calling Matthew Arnold Mr. Kidglove Cocksure . . . I am sure he is a rare genius and a great critic"), but it never disturbed him not to be the "people's candidate." The knowledge that the Victorian public was tepid about Arnold's gifts may have helped to keep his head above water when the high tide of disapproval of Victorianism rolled in during and after World War I: more upholstered reputations sank waterlogged.

Matthew Arnold is certainly not a neglected "great Victorian" in the present decade, but in one respect his reputation as a literary critic is less settled than it was a generation ago. This is a promising fact, for it is another indication that his influence is live, and at this interval from Eliot's accession to the kingship of the Sacred Wood, it is becoming easier to see and acknowledge it. Arnold's historical position is disputed by nobody: he is a distinguished poet and a major critic, some of whose poems and literary essays are already secure English classics. What is disputed is the extent to which he can influence usefully the practice of criticism in our time. Now that Eliot's earlier critical work is in turn becoming historical, and we are less dazzled by the immediacy of his achievement as a poet and critic, Arnold's usefulness may be given broader limits and his authority may be expected to grow. This is fortunate. No two English critics complement each other so well in the whole of their critical performance; no other English critic has succeeded half so well as either in discovering the tone and temper most exactly suited to the handling of literary subjects.

II

Arnold's writings have an inner logic shaped by personality and events. There need be nothing puzzling in the variety of subject matter, style, and intention found in such works as *Empedocles on Etna, A French Eton,* and *Friendship's Garland* if we keep in mind the main stages of his career; and the tug-of-war of purposes in a particular essay makes sense more rapidly when we recognize that duality haunts Arnold's thinking (Hellenism and Hebraism, Celt and Teuton, "natural magic" and "high seriousness," and so on) and expresses something in his nature. Arnold's own diagnosis of this something cannot be disregarded.

4. "It is true that the critic has many temptations to go with the stream, to make one of the party of movement, one of these *terrae filii;* it seems ungracious to refuse to be a *terrae filius,* when so many excellent people are; but the critic's duty is to refuse, or, if resistance is vain, at least to cry with Obermann: *'Pé rissons en ré sistant'.*" ("The Function of Criticism at the Present Time," *Essays in Criticism,* vol. III).

5. G. W. E.Russell, ed., *The Letters of Matthew Arnold, 1848–1888* (London, 1895), vol. II, p. 117.

> Ah! two desires toss about
> The poet's feverish blood.
> One drives him to the world without,
> And one to solitude . . .
> ("Stanzas in Memory of the Author
> of 'Obermann,' " no. 39, 93–96)

he tells us (in a stanza that illuminates the distinction between detachment and missionary zeal made in the previous section). He is also the inventor of that striking phrase "the dialogue of the mind with itself." Certainly he did not think of his own nature as monolithic: "I am fragments," he admitted to his favorite sister, Jane,[6] in 1853. Since the change from poetry to prose and the tendency to branch out from literary criticism into social and theological comment are both intimately connected with the development of Arnold's personality, something more must be said on this subject (even at the risk of over-simplification) when we have outlined his career.

Matthew Arnold was born on Christmas Eve 1822 at Laleham-on-Thames, and died at the Dingle, Liverpool, on 15 April 1888. He went to school at Winchester and Rugby and ended his Oxford years by election to an Oriel Fellowship (1845). In 1851 he wanted to marry and obtained through Lord Lansdowne, whose secretary he had been, the position of school inspector, which he held continuously until he retired in 1886. Various attempts to find a more congenial post all ended in frustration, and when his friend John Duke Coleridge was appointed lord chief justice of common pleas in 1873, Arnold joked about the servants' hall being the right place for him if he paid a visit. He was a Balliol man, he declared sardonically, who had not "got on." A civil list pension at sixty was the only official recognition of his talents. Unlike Alfred Tennyson or Robert Browning, he had to make time for his literary work after dreary rounds of school visits and interminable report writing.

> Here is my programme for this afternoon: Avalanches, the Steam Engine, the Thames, Indian Rubber, Bricks, the Battle of Poictiers, Subtraction, the Reindeer, the Gunpowder Plot, the Jordan. Alluring is it not? Twenty minutes each, and the days of one's life are only three score years and ten. (*Letters of Matthew Arnold, 1848–1888*, vol. I, p. 281)

He was a sympathetic rather than a stringent inspector, and some of his colleagues thought of him as an amateur even after a lifetime of service. To put it euphemistically, there were jobs that would have suited him better. But against the suggestion of waste must be set whatever is valuable in the argument of *Culture and Anarchy or Friendship's Garland*: without Arnold's enforced intimacy with dissent in the persons of nonconformist school-managers and teachers, his portrait of the middle class would not have been a speaking likeness. His experiences as a school inspector helped to turn him into a critic of society.

The relief in the irksomely monotonous landscape of Arnold's official career comes from his tenure of the Oxford Chair of Poetry (1857–1867),[7] which he held along with his bread-and-butter appointment, three educational missions to the continent (which sometimes allowed him to feel pleasantly ambassadorial), and a six-month lecture-tour to America in 1883–1884. His regular "anti-attrition" was in a most affectionate family life, a diversity of friendships, solitary fishing, holidays abroad, favorite cats and dogs, including the superb Atossa—

> So Tiberius might have sat,
> Had Tiberius been a cat,
> ("Poor Mathias," 41–42)

the Athenaeum, a little botanizing, tireless letter-writing, country house visits, and wide reading in six languages. Most of the poetry was written before 1857, almost all the prose after. The late 1860's and the 1870's were the years in which Arnold was most concerned in his writings with society and religion. Obvious trigger-causes were the troubles at the

6. Known to the family as "K."

7. Arnold was the first professor to lecture in English instead of Latin. He drew enthusiastic audiences.

time of the second Reform Act (1867) and the "crisis of belief" in the early 1870's.

The man behind this brief dossier was tall and solidly built, and affected a certain dandyism of manner which does not quite sort with the strength of his face—he inherited a "Cornish" nose from his mother's side of the family—or its tinge of melancholy. As a young man he was thought handsome, and he long kept a youthful appearance and energy—it is not very fanciful to see a connection between his luxuriant black hair, hardly touched with gray in his late forties, and what Eneas Sweetland Dallas calls "the intense juvenility—a boy-power to the *nth*" of his more ebullient prose. But this confident and youthfully energetic man had had an inauspicious childhood, which included the early wearing of iron leg-braces, a succession of illnesses and accidents, and a loved and admired father's undisguised suspicion that he was lazy and irresponsible. Arnold's later wish to be "papa's continuator" is rooted in the fact of Dr. Arnold's death before his son had done anything to "justify" himself.

Probably Arnold's gaiety and fecklessness are best looked on as protective clothing for a genuine but never too sturdy poetic gift which he feared to expose to the onslaught of his father's earnestness. If so, it was also a highly effective piece of camouflage, for few of Arnold's intimates seem to have expected the seriousness of his first book of poems in 1849. Of course, they may have been shortsighted: in 1846 George Sand was not deceived and described Arnold's appearance at Nohant as that of "*un Milton jeune et voyageant.*" It is proper to assume that there was always an earnestness in the poet's nature which responded sympathetically to Dr. Arnold's fervor, but that he hid both it and his poetic seriousness behind a mask of frivolity in order to feel free enough and private enough to be a poet. This makes Dr. Arnold a more significant figure in the story of his son's development than anyone else—than even Arthur Clough, or "K," or the shadowy Marguerite.

It is interesting to notice the places that were loved by Matthew Arnold. In England, he was fondest of the Thames valley, the city of Oxford with the surrounding "scholar-gipsy" countryside, Loughrigg and the fells overlooking "Fox How," the family home by the shallow Rotha on the outskirts of Ambleside (the clear running water that was Arnold's passion belongs to all three places and escapes into much of his characteristic poetic imagery). Abroad, he was always happy in France, and a small part of Switzerland glowed in his mind. Oxford and Thun[8] are more than place-names: they are mnemonics for recalling states of happiness associated with his fullest experience of feeling before settling down.

> And yet what days were those, Parmenides!
> When we were young, when we could
> number friends
> In all the Italian cities like ourselves . . .
> ("Empedocles on Etna," 235–237)

Few poets have ever been so miserably aware of the passage of time ("How life rushes away, and youth. One has dawdled and scrupled and fiddle-faddled—and it is all over")[9] and the reiterated scoring in his notebooks of the phrase "*les saines habitudes de la maturité*" shows with what an effort at self-mastery he tried to welcome the bleakness of responsibility. Here again we seem to be close to Arnold's "secret."

The divergent impulses that determine the dichotomies of his literary and social analysis exist because he is in two minds between wholeheartedly accepting maturity (and Dr. Arnold's mission) and the partial rejection implied by an agonized regret for youth and poetry and irresponsibility (which is the other face of detachment). At Thun in 1849 Arnold had two books with him, Béranger and Epictetus, and we find him writing to Clough that Béranger appealed to him less than formerly. It comes almost too pat to symbolize the vic-

8. Thun is the scene of the love affair with the French girl known in the Switzerland poems as Marguerite. It is simplest to say that we know nothing about it.

9. H. F. Lowry, ed., *The Letters of Matthew Arnold to Arthur Hugh Clough* (Oxford, 1932), no. 37, p. 120.

tory of Stoic self-mastery over pleasure and poetry, a victory that governs Arnold's later development in the years of prose. But if poetry died, the poet in Arnold did not. He lived on to ensure the delicacy of the literary critic's insight, the social critic's unfailing contempt for optimistic claptrap. If Arnold is a good critic, it is because regret kept open a line of communication with his poetic past, because "character" was never quite free from the promptings of "temperament." When he tells us that the work of the nineteenth century in literature is work for the "imaginative reason," he is asserting that a control that is never imperiled is likely to become obtuse. Even a fifth column may be useful in keeping a government on its toes.

"They went forth to battle and they always fell," Arnold quotes in speaking of the Celts, and in the opposition he establishes between Celt and Teuton we have another avatar of the conflict between poetic temperament and moral character. "Natural magic" is Celtic and a happiness of poetic style, whereas Teutons have no sense of style in spite of being worthy, forthright, and necessary. "I have a great *penchant* for the Celtic races, with their melancholy and unprogressiveness," Arnold wrote to Lady de Rothschild, and it is curious how emphatically in this instance he repudiated any suggestion that Dr. Arnold might have shared his sentiments.[10] The Celt strained against "the despotism of fact" as the poet in Arnold's makeup struggled against accepting maturity. When Arnold insisted that his father had not really understood the Celts, he was insisting that his father had not understood him. He was also saying obliquely what he once said openly: "My dear father had many virtues, but he was not a poet." Several critics have noticed that Sohrab's death in the poem at the hands of his father, Rustum, is a type of Arnold's sacrifice of the poetic temperament so that he may identify himself more closely with his father's moral earnestness. What is also to be remarked if we are to do full justice to the situation is Sohrab's profound admiration and affection for Rustum and the poignancy of his regret for the final loss of

> . . . youth, and bloom, and this delightful
> world.
> ("Sohrab and Rustum," 856)

Matthew Arnold, as W. H. Auden said, "thrust his gift in prison till it died," but he did it out of love. Perhaps this explains why his maturity is so little cross-grained, and why he is almost incapable of a false note when he sings of renunciation and unwished necessity.

In his finest short story, "The Point of It," E. M. Forster pessimistically argues that "everyone grows hard or soft as he grows old," and Arnold himself did not have many illusions about the irony of the "gifts reserved for age." There are, I think, a few signs of hardening in the later Arnold (far fewer than in most of his contemporaries): a crotchetiness about the Irish question in the 1880's, which found fuel in his old antipathy to Gladstone; traces of personal agitation when he accuses the French of worshiping the goddess Lubricity; an ill-natured stiffness in one or two remarks about John Keats and Percy Bysshe Shelley (with the connotation of an almost reflex disapproval of sexuality); some absurdity in his ducking respect for German "higher critics of the Bible."[11] But these signs do not add up to much, and it is pleasanter to stress how open to fresh impressions, how "ondoyant et divers" as a critic, he remained to the end. He conquered regret without turning his heart into a stone, and the last pages of his letters show us a man who deserves admiration—shrewd, capable, deeply affectionate, still interested in everything about him, and honorably civilized.

10. *Letters of Mathew Arnold, 1848–1888*, vol. I, p. 279.

11. Contrast Arnold's blithe impatience with them as a younger man. In May 1850 he writes to Clough about F. W. Newman's *Phases of Faith*: "One would think to read him that enquiries into articles, biblical inspiration, etc., etc., were as much the natural functions of a man as to eat and copulate. This sort of man is only possible in Great Britain and North Germany, thanks be to God for it" (*Arnold to Clough*, no. 34, p. 115).

III

Matthew Arnold had written some verse before he went to school at Winchester, and a few pieces (including some "animal" poems and the frigid "Westminster Abbey") belong to the 1880's. But almost all the work by which he is still known was produced between 1845 and 1867. Indeed, *New Poems* of the latter year contained such a thin harvest for the second decade that it had to be filled out with "Empedocles on Etna," reprinted for the first time since 1852 at the request—as Arnold was careful to tell his readers—of a "man-of-genius, Mr. Robert Browning." But if few poems were composed between 1857 and 1867, certain of them were among Arnold's most finished work, notably "Thyrsis," considered by some to be his poetic masterpiece. It is part of Arnold's "tragedy" as a poet that he reached his fullest command of expressive power when his creative impulse was already failing—a fact noticed with laconic bitterness in "The Progress of Poesy." Arnold's first two volumes were *The Strayed Reveller* (1849) and *Empedocles on Etna* (1852). The various collections issued between 1853 and *New Poems* lean heavily on the two early books, both of which had been published pseudonymously. For example, *Poems* (1853) contains lyrics from both volumes, as well as the famous preface defending the suppression of "Empedocles on Etna," "Sohrab and Rustum" (written to illustrate—in the words of the preface—"that the action itself, its selection and construction, . . . is . . . all-important"), "The Scholar-Gipsy," and various other new pieces that are less well known. Arnold liked to play with his poems when he was unable to write many new ones, suppressing and reviving now one and now another, and tinkering with their order in different collections, so that the makeup of his successive books of verse is confusing; but these changes hardly affect our estimate of him as a poet.

It is clear from *The Strayed Reveller* that a naked ethical intention intrudes into Arnold's poems from the beginning and often does them injury. "Intrude" may seem to be an odd word in connection with an intention so typical of Arnold and so usually present in his work, but I use it advisedly to suggest that his truest note as a poet depends on qualities of feeling at war with ethical impulse. This is evident in Arnold's response to his own poems. "Empedocles on Etna" is rejected for reasons that may be summarized by saying that Arnold thought his poetic drama would dispirit rather than fortify (though we may well think him wrong in his judgment of its probable effect). There is another weak aesthetic choice for "heroic" moral reasons in a letter to Clough: "I am glad you like the Gipsy Scholar—but what does it *do* for you . . . in its poor way I think Sohrab and Rustum *animates*—the Gipsy Scholar at best awakes a pleasing melancholy. But this is not what we want."[12] Arnold was quite wrong. What his readers have always wanted from him is more poems like "The Scholar-Gipsy" or the Cadmus and Harmonia episode from "Empedocles on Etna," that is to say, more pieces in which he realizes his poetic vocation without interference. Caught faithless between two worlds and "wavering between the profit and the loss," his vocation was to sing of melancholy and indecision, to express the sad confusion of desires that find no sufficient object, to create for us the self-conscious animal whose thinking runs ahead and undermines his present experience of happiness. The best poetry is a time-haunted, dimly lit *campagna* of regret, for all Arnold's wish that it should be something different. Not that the regret is simple and unmixed. The bracing of moral intention is never completely absent from the pieces I have in mind, but in them it appears inoffensively and always as a minor constituent, to make the regret stoically tight-lipped, to produce an effect that I can describe only as one of ravaged composure. The best poetry, then, is written by a "Celt" and pierces by its understatement. When the "Teuton" shoulders aside the "Celt," and morality takes

12. *Arnold to Clough*, no. 51, p. 146.

charge, we get the priggish artificiality of "East London" or "The Second Best":

> Not here, O Apollo!
> Are haunts meet for thee . . .
> ("Empedocles," 421–422)

while in other poems, undoubtedly superior but still liable to worry us, it is impossible to say whether "Teuton" or "Celt" has gained the upper hand. "Palladium" may be cited as an example. A final class consists of poems innocent of a conscious moral intention but into whose conception too strong a willed element has entered, and we have then the blameless nullities of *Merope* and "Balder Dead."[13] "Sohrab and Rustum" is another "willed" poem, but, as I have already indicated, it managed to attach itself to Arnold's emotional life without his knowledge, and it draws whatever effectiveness it has from this source. In this brief account of the poetry it is fair to say that Arnold's deepest poetic intuition is of

> The something that infects the world
> ("Resignation," 278)

and that he never makes us anxious for him as an artist when he writes of it (for instance, in "The Sick King in Bokhara"), or nostalgically of loss, or—at his most positive—of fortitude and resignation. On the other hand, his attempts to whistle up a simple cheerfulness are invariably poetic failures—even the modified optimism at the end of "Obermann Once More" has a counterfeit ring.

When Arnold discovered how dark were his gifts as a poet, he stopped writing poetry—an action for which we are prepared after the rejection of "Empedocles on Etna." In his letters the pathos of his middle-aged regret for the loss of his Ariel, whom he had handed over to perpetual confinement in the charge of a moralist, is real and moving. But as a poet he had then done what it was in him to do. In "Empedocles on Etna," "Resignation," and "The Sick King in Bokhara," in passages from "Sohrab and Rustum" and the unequal "Tristram and Iseult," in many of the shorter lyrics, and in almost all the elegiac pieces (including "Thyrsis" and "The Scholar-Gipsy"), we have his most genuine note. "Arnold is more intimate with us than Browning, more intimate than Tennyson ever is except at moments," Eliot observes justly, and it must be of some of these pieces that he is thinking. Henry James certainly had them in mind when he spoke with his customary exactitude of Arnold's "minor magic" and of his sensitive touching of "the particular ache, or regret, or conjecture, to which poetry is supposed to address itself." In a number of these successes it must be admitted that Arnold incurs the censure that he himself pronounced on those who substitute "thinking aloud" in poetry for "making something"—in his view a tendency encouraged by Wordsworth. A too casual thinking aloud seems to be the fault of "The Future," "The Buried Life," and "The Youth of Man," which are ramshackle in structure. (We recognize the support that the pastoral convention gave Arnold in "Thyrsis" and the advantages that he found in a well-defined subject in "A Southern Night" and "Stanzas from the Grande Chartreuse.") But these structural faults weaken without disabling the poems in which they occur, and it may be claimed for these pieces, as perhaps on behalf of the greater number of Arnold's poems, that they are more satisfying at the tenth than at the first reading, and more endearing than many Victorian poems that wear their too obvious hearts on gaudier sleeves. Let us set down here a typical penny-plain passage of Arnold's verse:

> Rais'd are the dripping oars,
> Silent the boat! the lake,
> Lovely and soft as a dream,
> Swims in the sheen of the moon.
> The mountains stand at its head
> Clear in the pure June-night,

13. This conjunction is perhaps a little unfair. *Merope* is virtually unreadable, whereas "Balder Dead" has many of the secondary poetic virtues and even some emotional vitality in the exchanges between Hermod and Balder toward the end of part 3.

But the valleys are flooded with haze,
Rydal and Fairfield are there;
In the shadows Wordsworth lies dead.
So it is, so it will be for aye.
Nature is fresh as of old,
Is lovely; a mortal is dead.
("The Youth of Nature," 1–12)

These verses chosen at random are in a quiet way impressive. There is no Keats in them and little Wordsworth. The vocabulary is simple, the moonlight and water are among Arnold's most pleasing stage properties, even the hint of a mechanical quality in the rhythm (which seems to be accepted as if to slight any charge of extravagance) is, I think, effective, and the whole verse paragraph lucidly projects the constraint put upon emotion. A reader may not be attracted by these unassuming lines and still find it possible to admire "Thyrsis" or "Dover Beach," but I do not think he can be said to have understood Arnold's poetic character unless they engage his sympathies.

Clearly an informed appreciation of Arnold as a poet must recognize the severe limitations of his gift. He has little poetic *élan* (the possession of which he envied Byron), slight ease, rare incandescence, no prodigality in phrase or metaphor: he spends his poetic income thriftily. He makes too much of excellence of subject, and one has unhappy memories of Benjamin Haydon's historical paintings and the old recipes for an epic—this is not to deny the significance of his protest against the overvaluing of the poetic "moment" and poetic frills by the "spasmodic" admirers of Keats in Arnold's own day. He is completely undramatic—the banality of the dialogue in the second part of "Tristram and Iseult" is disconcerting—and lack of dramatic sense narrows his scope as a narrative poet. He is uninventive in verse forms, limited in color and vocabulary in all but a very few pieces, repetitive in theme and situation, too often seriously insensitive to the sound of his poems. Such a line as the following in a poem that is something of a showpiece—

But when the moon their hollows lights
("To Marguerite—Continued," 7)

—is far from unusual; Tennyson would have shuddered at it. Yet Arnold triumphs over his maladroitness and unobtrusively creates a presumption in his own favor by the time we are ready to sit down in judgment. He is like a handicapped man whom his disabilities have taught a distinctive spryness and resource, and for whom we are prepared to make allowances. He triumphs by a feeling for poetic decorum in which many other Victorians were exasperatingly deficient, by his intelligent command of tone and temper, by an intimidating kind of honesty, for he steadily refuses to varnish his unease. He is an unfinished Giacomo Leopardi, comfortless in the Victorian Canaan. We understand at once what Hopkins means when he says that sometimes Arnold's poems "seem to have all the ingredients of poetry without quite being it," and we agree with him again when he continues, " . . . still they do not leave off of being, as the French say, very beautiful." When the devil's advocate has done his worst, "Empedocles on Etna" remains perhaps the best long poem by a Victorian, while in "Thyrsis," "The Scholar-Gipsy," and three or four shorter pieces (which do not include the overpraised and rather vapid "Requiescat") Arnold's poetry is no longer hobbled, and he escapes from his limitations, as a stutterer may escape in dreams, into speech of unimpeded fluency.

Arnold argued that his poetry represented "the main line of modern development" in his day and that this would finally recommend it to attention. He was prepared to await his turn. There is certainly a level of approach at which we can link many of Arnold's poems with Clough's "Dipsychus" and Herman Melville's "Clarel" under the heading of Victorian "poetry of doubt"—it may be useful to think of his influence on A. E. Housman and Edwin Arlington Robinson—but I have here preferred to suggest that his complaint against

. . . this strange disease of modern life
With its sick hurry, its divided aims . . .
("The Scholar-Gipsy," no. 78, 203–204)

betrays a more fundamental discontent. As a poet he is always, it seems to me, the romantic Celt struggling against the "despotism of fact." His muted nostalgia is for a wholeness and simplicity of experience that never was. By any normal system of moral bookkeeping it may be reprehensible, and clearly the more robust comment on experience is "if you don't like it, you can lump it," but any man who has not buried his youth too deeply can understand Arnold. What evidence there is points to his being found more congenial today than any other mid-Victorian poet.

IV

In May 1853, Matthew Arnold wrote to Clough:

> I catch myself desiring now at times political life, and this and that; and I say to myself—you do not desire these things because you are really adapted to them, and therefore the desire for them is merely contemptible—and it is so. (*Arnold to Clough,* no. 44, p. 135)

Ten years later we find him writing to his mother:

> It is very animating to think that one at last has a chance of getting at the English public. Such a public as it is and such a work as one wants to do with it. (*Letters of Matthew Arnold, 1848–1888,* vol. I, pp. 233–34)

It is the gap between the self-regarding ethic of the first statement and the eager wish to interfere of the second that explains the plausibility of the late Professor E. K. Brown's *Matthew Arnold: A Study in Conflict,* the most acute study yet of Arnold as a prose writer, critic, and controversialist, in which it is argued that the objectivity of Arnold's criticism is flawed by his wish to be a moral leader, and that in the social essays detachment is often most flagrantly only a wraithlike appearance. In many places in Arnold's prose, Professor Brown held, it is proper to talk of a "strategy of disinterestedness," for the apparent candor and urbanity are almost exclusively at the service of an "interested disposition."

Once or twice already I have expressed reservations about this view. Evidently the poet speaks in the first letter quoted above, the son of Dr. Arnold in the second. But to agree with many other commentators that there is a conflict in Arnold, and that it casts a shadow over his writings, need not lead us to assume with Professor Brown that a crusading impulse is incompatible with a local and particular objectivity: if this were really so, one would expect Arnold's criticism to have some of the polemical extravagance of Ruskin's or the later Carlyle's. This view also fails to recognize how much of Arnold's most "detached" literary criticism we may owe to his missionary impulse. To put this naively, Arnold might very well have kept his *aperçus* to himself if he had not felt them to be useful when he began at the call of duty "to pull out a few more stops in that powerful but at present somewhat narrow-toned organ, the modern Englishman."

Arnold's prose works in the incomplete Macmillan collected edition run to ten volumes—this disregards his letters, and there are uncollected papers to fill two volumes more—and, within the confines of the present essay, I can hardly even signal the inclusiveness and authority of Arnold's interpretation of his age, or hope to submit Professor Brown's thesis to the examination that it deserves: instead I must say that in my opinion Arnold ordinarily succeeds in finding a third way between a limiting involvement in practical issues and a lack of interest in the social implications of his ideas. His "detachment" is more than a confidence-man's patter. If a "strategy of disinterestedness" exists in Arnold's wish to speak calmly and without rancor, the wish is in no sense Jesuitical: it stands both for the respect with which the writer approaches the truth and for the power of his writings to charm an audience. To a dispassionate reader "The Function of Criticism at the Present Time" in *Essays in Criticism*

(1865) is quite explicit on the double need for disinterestedness and moral engagement. It tells us what Arnold thought he was doing and, in nine cases out of ten, it is what he was doing.

At this point it is obvious that limited space must enforce a paralyzing generality on any attempt to survey Arnold's prose. I propose to escape from this difficulty by indicating the motivation of Arnold's criticism as a whole, selecting a few topics, mostly in the literary criticism, for a rapid closer look. Such a bias may be justified because the literary criticism is in fact more often studied than the social and religious writings, and because it is superior to them in freshness, confidence, and ease—this is more especially true of the earlier critical essays. To come to *On Translating Homer* (1861) or *On the Study of Celtic Literature* (1867) straight from the poetry, or to turn back to them after being immersed in *Literature and Dogma* (1873) or *Last Essays on Church and Religion* (1877), is to find oneself in an atmosphere with an exhilaratingly high proportion of oxygen. This mood of the early criticism (with the exception perhaps of the valuable but partly perverse 1853 preface) exhibits publicly the excitement at discovering an unexpected second vocation that is characteristic of so many of Arnold's private letters to Clough—a correspondence third only to Keats' letters and Hopkins' letters on English literature for its sharp insights and its fascinating glimpse at the elliptical gamboling of a free intelligence. A famous passage in Sainte-Beuve's *Portraits Contemporains,* in which he speaks of a critical vocation often being concealed in youth by poetry and of criticism as *"un pis-aller honorable,"* apparently came to Arnold—increasingly aware that his talent, though distinguished, was stinted—with the force of a revelation.

The most general motive of Arnold's criticism is ethical. He is almost without metaphysical passion, which may be the fundamental reason for F. H. Bradley's dislike of the religious writings, but his ethical passion is unmistakable. To Arnold metaphysical reasoning was simply methodical self-bewilderment, but he had as strongly as George Eliot the conviction that the moral law exists and speaks unequivocally in experience. On the one side, then, religion was ceremonial practices, which he supported *because* they were absurd—much as Walter Bagehot defended the decorative elements in the English constitution as "social cement." On the other side, religion was morality, which religious feeling could light up and transform into a driving force. The rest was overbelief (*Aberglaube*). In the eyes of orthodox churchmen, Arnold was "widening the rathole in the Temple," but he saw himself as a conservative. Miracles did not occur, theology was a pseudoscience, and literary tact discerned that theologians had done enormous violence to the loose figurative language of the Bible, language never meant to be precise, but thrown out at objects of consciousness not fully grasped. If the philosopher F. H. Bradley could tartly describe the God of Arnold's writings as no more than "an hypostasized copybook heading," Arnold was quite sure that the traditional idea of God arose from a failure to distinguish the scientific and poetic uses of language. Arnold believed that he was defending religion by surrendering its untenable outposts, but we are more likely to feel that he was attempting—in an adaptation of Hartley Coleridge's phrase about Wordsworth—to smuggle Spinoza into the pulpit in a curate's ragged surplice.

What made Arnold so keen to save religion from its friends was his conviction of its social importance. Numerous impulses (including the religious one), he argued, must be met for man's harmonious development:

> Money-making is not enough by itself. Industry is not enough by itself. Seriousness is not enough by itself. . . . The need in man for intellect and knowledge, his desire for beauty, his instinct for society, and for pleasurable and graceful forms of society, require to have their stimulus felt also, felt and satisfied. ("A Liverpool Address," vol. X, p. 83)

This is the master thought of Arnold's social writings. His experiences as a school inspector had made him peculiarly aware that social and political influence was passing into the hands of the middle class, which was quite unready for power and even unsuited to it. He could not turn hopefully from the Philistines to the old aristocracy. With a cool eye for a real lord and no faith in the Carlylean alternative of an industrial nobility, he confided in an ideal of democratic state action, and the state's first responsibility was to be in the field of education. The matter was urgent. The upper classes were materialized, the middle class was vulgarized, the lower classes were brutalized (the famous division into Barbarians, Philistines, and Populace). The state was the only possible source of national unity, but for a combination of reasons it was regarded with deep suspicion, and this made Arnold overemphatic and something less than disinterested in certain pages of *Culture and Anarchy* (1869).[14] The battle cry of Hebraism and Hellenism was important for all Englishmen, most important for the Philistines. Hebraism characterized the narrow life of that typical Philistine, the thrifty, earnest Dissenter who divided his time between countinghouse and chapel, sure of his solvency in this world and salvation in the next. He stood sadly in need of Hellenization; culture might woo him from his dreary tea-meetings and temperance lectures (with lantern slides), his hymnal and his balance sheets. Culture might induce him to reexamine his stock notions and habits, might broaden his religious sympathies, might ultimately shame him into dissatisfaction with a "dismal, illiberal life" in Sheffield or Camberwell. In Arnold's opinion, culture spoke most persuasively through literature.[15]

This explanation of the main motive of Arnold's social thinking does not bring in all his important social ideas—it omits, for example, his stress on equality, the subject of an essay in 1878—but it is enough to show the link between the social and the literary criticism. In "The Function of Criticism at the Present Time," the failure of the romantic poets in spite of their prodigious creative talent is ascribed to a weakness in the surrounding cultural atmosphere. For a great creative epoch "two powers must concur, the power of the man and the power of the moment." Arnold sees a critical effort in his own generation as the necessary spadework for a new creative age. It is the critic's job by making available "the best that is known and thought in the world" to produce a "current of fresh and true ideas" in society. If he fails, the poet is unable to realize all his gifts or to produce work of the first order. The critic, then, is much more than a judge. At one and the same time he is a kind of midwife to artistic genius and the mediator between the artist and the general public.

Nothing takes precedence of the critic's function to supply fresh knowledge, and in speaking of this Arnold is a European.

> But, after all, the criticism I am really concerned with . . . is a criticism which regards Europe as being, for intellectual and spiritual purposes, one great confederation, bound to a joint action and working to a common result; and whose members have, for their proper outfit, a knowledge of Greek, Roman, and Eastern antiquity, and of one another. ("The Function of Criticism at the Present Time," in *Essays in Criticism*, vol. III, p. 284)

Occasionally scholars have regretted the essays on minor figures of foreign literature (Joseph Joubert, Henri-Frédéic Amiel, et al.) as if

14. The appeal to find in the state a collective representation of the "best self" in every man has been supposed by some writers to have dangerous Hegelian overtones, but it was really no more than a political application of the religious idea of "dying to the old Adam." The state was to charge itself with supporting the "disinterested" ethical self of which every person was capable. It is quite wrong to suppose that Arnold had a sneaking weakness for authoritarianism; he came to look on Carlyle as a "moral desperado," and he was one of the few literary men who had no patience with the rowdy defense of Governor Eyre. Arnold had much the same view of the state as Dr. Arnold, and both looked back to Edmund Burke.

15. *Culture and Anarchy* (1869), *Mixed Essays* (1879), and the satirical extravaganza *Friendship's Garland* (1871) are the most valuable of the social writings.

they were a frivolous turning aside from the truly important, but Arnold has a ready answer. He is bringing to light comparatively unknown excellence, and while he is so engaged he avoids a very real danger: he runs no risk of interesting readers in his treatment of the subject at the expense of the subject itself (how much modern criticism of Shakespeare or Milton is X's judgment of Y's opinion of Z's remarks). Arnold thought the critic should explore widely and "welcome everything that is good," but this did not blur for him the distinctions between "excellent and inferior, sound and unsound and only half-sound." These distinctions were of "paramount importance." Arnold's severity can be measured by his remarks on the limiting effects of Milton's temper on his genius, or his disquiet when faced with the uneven copiousness of Shakespeare's style.

Two of the three most significant aspects that identify Arnold's critical practice have now been mentioned—namely, the concern with fresh information and the need to discriminate between what is excellent and what is less good while welcoming positive excellence even in unusual or subordinate "kinds." The third aspect has to do with his wholesome sense of the difficulty of criticism. His preference for the judgment that forms itself insensibly in the critic's mind (with its corollary that for the reader the critic's opinion should appear simply to make explicit what is implicit in the accompanying information) is clearly connected with his awareness of the delicacy of the critical act.

> To handle these matters properly there is needed a poise so perfect that the least overweight in any direction tends to destroy the balance. . . . To press to the sense of the thing itself with which one is dealing, not to go off on some collateral issue about the thing, is the hardest matter in the world. The "thing itself" with which one is here dealing, the critical perception of poetic truth, is of all things the most volatile, elusive, and evanescent; by even pressing too impetuously after it, one runs the risk of losing it. The critic of poetry should have the finest tact, the nicest moderation, the most free, flexible, and elastic spirit imaginable; he should be indeed the "ondoyant et divers," the *undulating and diverse* being of Montaigne. ("On Translating Homer: Last Words," vol. I, p. 174)

Again, the care to reach the truth exemplified in this passage is certainly not unrelated to Arnold's desire to charm. To charm meant to investigate his subject in such a way that the reader's own prejudices should not be interposed between him and what the critic had taken so much trouble to say.

Around this just and comprehensive understanding of the critic's task, the counters of Arnold's criticism—"high seriousness," "natural magic," "the grand style," "*Architectonicè*"—group themselves, not as precise meanings, but as instruments he found useful in obtaining a view of the truth and in creating for his readers an intimate sense of his critical adequacy. Arnold's prose style should be noticed in a study of his technique of persuasion. It has several modes, including the lyrical and the willfully impertinent—both are illustrated in the preface to the second edition of *Essays in Criticism* (1869)—but the usual middle style resembles Newman's prose in its subtle vitality. Perhaps the similarity is more than stylistic, and it may be right to be reminded of Newman's psychological account of what we do when we reason or believe, as we read Arnold's description of what constitutes the critical act.

In what has been said, there is a basis of justification for calling Arnold a great critic. The argument would need to be completed in a fuller discussion by an analysis of his remarks on Homer, Dante, Shakespeare, Milton, Voltaire, Thomas Gray, Dr. Johnson, Leopardi, Heinrich Heine, and the English romantic poets—to mention only a few of those to whom he paid attention. In some instances the necessary assembling of scattered references has yet to be attempted; and perhaps some modern critics have been overhasty in giving us Arnold's opinion on a particular topic without making a real effort to discover what it was. It is possible that on many of these subjects we might not express ourselves exactly as he did, but this is unimportant. Occasionally—for example, in discussing Byron as a man of feeling—I think that he misses the point, but quite often he comes very close to a reputable contemporary opinion: I would cite in evidence his parenthetic observation that Shelley's "natural magic" is almost entirely in his rhythm and hardly at all in his language; or, again, the several judgments on Goethe, which add up to a very respectable whole view (and what a triumph of detachment, in its Victorian context, his reserved attitude to *Wilhelm Meister* represents). Such successes more than cancel his too much paraded critical howlers, some of which are susceptible of a kind of defense. For example, Arnold's opinion that Dryden and Pope are "classics of our prose" shows that he failed to appreciate the Augustan achievement in poetry, but it pithily expresses that turning down of the imaginative lamps that any reader must feel as he moves from a study of the great Renaissance poets to the poetic literature of the late seventeenth and early eighteenth centuries.

In estimating Arnold's special importance as a critic today, debate about the supersession of this or that opinion is unhelpful. What matters is his example of serious critical responsibility. Literary criticism was not a matter of self-expression for Arnold. He directs attention at his subject and away from his own dexterity. He does his best to steer clear of aesthetics and general theories of literature (which fascinated Coleridge certainly but are usually the infatuation of lesser men). He commits himself unambiguously and in an unpedantic language, and he makes no secret of the relationship between his literary opinions and his views on the great questions of life and society. His candor is never ill-humored. In all these respects, T. S. Eliot is his only rival. I have already said that these two major critics complement each other in a variety of ways. No better exercise for sharpening the wits can be imagined than the setting up of one against the other on any topic on which they overlap. For several decades now we have used Eliot to correct Matthew Arnold. It is useful to remember that the process can run in reverse.

Selected Bibliography

BIBLIOGRAPHIES

Smart, T. B., *The Bibliography of Matthew Arnold,* (London, 1892) revised and expanded, in *The Works,* vol. XV (London, 1904); Wise, T. J., *Catalogue of the Ashley Library,* vol. I (London, 1922); Ehrsam, T. G., Deily, R. H., and Smith, R. M., *Bibliographies of Twelve Victorian Authors,* (London, 1936); V. L. Tollers, ed., *A Bibliography of Matthew Arnold 1932–1970,* (University Park, Pa., 1974).

CONCORDANCE

S. M. Parrish, ed., *A Concordance of the Poems of Matthew Arnold,* (Ithaca, N.Y., 1959).

COLLECTED EDITIONS

G. W. E. Russell, ed., *The Works of Matthew Arnold,* 15 vols. (London, 1903–1904) contains the poems (vols. I and II), the prose works (vols. III-XII), and the letters (vols. XIII-XV), but omits various uncollected essays.

POETRY

Poems: A New and Complete Edition, (Boston, 1856); *Poems,* 2 vols. (London, 1869) contains narrative and elegiac poems (vol. I), dramatic and lyric poems (vol. II); *Poems. New and Complete Edition,* 2 vols. (London, 1877) contains early poems, narrative poems, and sonnets (vol. I), and lyric, dramatic, and elegiac poems (vol. II); *Poems,* 3 vols. (London, 1885) contains early poems, narrative poems, and sonnets (vol. I), lyric and elegiac poems (vol. II), dramatic and later poems (vol. III); the first comprehensive ed. and the last ed. supervised by Arnold; *The Poetical Works,* (London, 1890) the Globe ed.; H. S. M.[ilford], ed., *The Poems, 1840–1867,* (Oxford, 1909) intro. by A. T. Quiller-Couch, repr. seven times until 1940, reiss. as *The Poetical Works,* (Oxford, 1942) repr. (1945) with poems written after 1867; C. B. Tinker and H. F. Lowry, eds., *Poetical Works,* (London, 1950) with critical apparatus; K. Allott, ed., *The Poems of Matthew Arnold,* (London, 1965) contains material omitted from (*Poetical Works,* 1950) and is fully annotated, 2nd ed. by M. Allott (London, 1979), among the new poems not included in the 1965 ed. are two pieces later found by K. Allott and some seven youthful poems written in the period 1836–1841, included by the second editor; other emendations include the reordering of some poems because of the first editor's fresh weighing of evidence and their dates of composition, and additional variant readings for certain poems based on the renewed study of manuscript material; K. Allott and M. Allott, eds., *Poems,* (London, 1979) the Annotated English Poets series.

PROSE

Works, 10 vols. (1883–1903) the Smith, Elder & Co. "Popular" ed., contains all the important prose vols. except *Essays in Criticism* First and Second Series, and *Discourses in America; Essays by Matthew Arnold,* (Oxford, 1914) contains *Essays inCriticism* First Series, *On Translating Homer* (with F. W. Newman's reply), *On Translating Homer: Last Words,* and five essays "hitherto uncollected" in Great Britain, four of these essays had already appeared in the American *Essays in Criticism,* Third Series (see below); R. H. Super, ed., *Complete Prose Works,* 11 vols. (Ann Arbor, Mich., 1960–1977) in chronological order with textual notes and explanatory commentary, contains *On the Classical Tradition* vol. I, *Democratic Education* vol. II, *Lectures and Essays in Criticism* vol. III, *Schools and Universities on the Continent* vol. IV, *Culture and Anarchy with Friendship's Garland and Some Literary Essays* vol. V, *Dissent and Dogma* vol. VI, *God and the Bible* vol. VII, *Essays Religious and Mixed* vol. VIII, *English Literature and Irish Politics* vol. IX, *Philistinism in England and America* vol. X, *The Last Word* vol. XI.

SELECTIONS

Selected Poems, (London, 1878) selected by Arnold himself; W. Buckler, ed., *Passages from the Prose Writings of Matthew Arnold,* (London, 1880) selected by Arnold himself; L. Trilling, ed., *The Portable Matthew Arnold,* (New York-London, 1949); J. Bryson, ed., *Matthew Arnold: Poetry and Prose,* (London, 1954) the Reynard Library ed., a comprehensive selection that includes some of Arnold's letters; A. D. Culler, ed., *Poetry and Criticism of Matthew Arnold,* (Boston, 1961) the Riverside ed.; C. Ricks, ed., *Selected Criticism,* (New York, 1972) the Signet Classics series; G. Sutherland, ed., *Arnold on Education,* (London, 1977); M. Allott, ed., *Selected Poems and Prose,* (London, 1978). *Note*: Verse and prose selections are numerous. Selections from the verse have appeared in the Temple Classics, the World's Classics, the Muses' Library, Everyman's Library. Among prose selections the following should be noted: L. E. Gates, ed., *Selections from the Prose Writings,* (New York, 1898); D. C. Somervell, ed., *Selections from Matthew Arnold's Prose,* (London, 1924); E. K. Brown, ed., *Representative Essays of Matthew Arnold,* (Toronto, 1936) which contains some reprinted passages from early eds.

SEPARATE WORKS

Alaric at Rome: A Prize Poem, Recited in Rugby School, (Rugby, 1840) a facs. was privately printed by T. J. Wise (London, 1893); *Cromwell: A Prize Poem, Recited in the Theatre, Oxford,* (Oxford, 1843); *The Strayed Reveller, and Other Poems,* by "A" (London, 1849); *Empedocles on Etna, and Other Poems,* by "A" (London, 1852); *Poems,* new ed. (London, 1853) repr. poems from 1849 and 1852, includes a critical preface and, among the new poems, "Sohrab and Rustum" and "The Scholar-Gipsy"; *Poems,* 2nd ed. (London, 1854) without five poems included in the 1st ed. but with "A Farewell," first published in 1852, and a further brief preface; *Poems,* Second Series (London, 1855) repr. poems from 1849 and 1852, includes "Balder Dead" and one other new poem; *Poems,* 3rd ed. (London, 1857) repr. of the 1854 collection with a new piece in the "Switzerland" group; *Merope: A Tragedy,* (London, 1858) verse with a preface, also annotated in J. C. Collins, ed. (Oxford, 1906); *England and the Italian Question,* (London, 1859) also in M. Bevington, ed. with "Matthew Arnold and the Italian Question," Stephen, J. Fitzjames, (Durham, N.C., 1953); *The Popular Education of France with Notices of that of Holland and Switzerland,* (London, 1861); *On Translating Homer: Three Lectures Given at Oxford,* (London, 1861) also in W. H. D. Rouse, ed. (London, 1905); *On Translating Homer: Last Words: A Lecture Given at Oxford,* (London, 1862); *A French Eton; or, Middle Class Education and the State,* (London, 1864); *Essays in Criticism,* (London, 1865) known as "First Series," the 2nd ed. (1869) has a condensed preface, the 3rd ed. contains an additional essay "A Persian *Passion* Play," also usefully annotated in C. A. Miles and L. Smith, eds. (Oxford, 1918); *On the Study of Celtic Literature,* (London, 1867) also in A. Nutt, ed. (London, 1910) repr. in Everyman's Library (London, 1977); *New Poems,* (London, 1867) includes "Empedocles on Etna," repr. for the first time since 1852, and six other pieces that had already appeared in a collection; *Schools and Universities on the Continent,* (London, 1868); *Culture and Anarchy: An Essay in Political and Social Criticism,* (London, 1869) also in J. D. Wilson, ed. (Cambridge, 1932).

St. Paul and Protestantism: With an Introduction on Puritanism and the Church of England, (London, 1870) the Popular ed. of 1887 contains a new preface and "A Comment on Christmas"; *Friendship's Garland: Being the Conversations, Letters, and Opinions of the Late Arminius, Baron Von Thunder-Ten-Tronckh. Collected and Edited, with a Dedicatory Letter to Adolescens Leo, Esq., of "The Daily Telegraph"* (London, 1871); *Literature and Dogma: An Essay Towards a Better Apprehension of the Bible,* (London, 1873) the Popular ed. of 1883 is condensed; *Higher Schools and Universities in Germany,* (London, 1874) repr. of the German chapters of *Schools and Universities on the Continent; God and the Bible: A Review of Objections to "Literature and Dogma"* (London, 1875) the Popular ed. of 1884 is condensed; *Last Essays on Church and Religion,* (London, 1877); *Mixed Essays,* (London, 1879); *Irish Essays and Others,* (London, 1882); *Discourses in America,* (London, 1885); *Education Department: Special Report on Certain Points Connected with Elementary Education in Germany, Switzerland, and France,* (London, 1886) repr. by the Education Reform League with a brief prefatory note (London, 1888); *General Grant: An Estimate,* (Boston, 1887) the two parts of this essay have not appeared as a book or been included in any collection of Arnold's essays in Great Britain; *Essays in Criticism,* Second Series (London, 1888); *Civilization in the United States: First and Last Impressions,* (Boston, 1888) contains *General Grant* and three essays on America; F. Sandford, ed., *Reports on Elementary Schools, 1852–1882,* (London, 1889) also in F. S. Marvin, ed. (London, 1908).

Matthew Arnold's Notebooks, (London, 1902) preface by the Hon. Mrs. Wodehouse, a brief selection; *Essays in Criticism,* Third Series (Boston, 1910) the essays on Renan and Tauler have not been collected in Great Britain; B. Matthews, ed., *Letters of an Old Playgoer,* (New York, 1919) these letters appear in *The Works,* vol. IV (London, 1904); H. F. Lowry, K. Young, and W. H. Dunn, eds., T*he Note-Books of Matthew Arnold,* (London, 1952) the literary contents of Arnold's notebooks and his reading lists, essential for students; K. Allott, ed., *Five Uncollected Essays of Matthew Arnold,* (Liverpool, 1953) contains Arnold's three essays on America, an uncollected essay on Sainte-Beuve, and "A Liverpool Address"; F. Neiman, ed., *Essays, Letters, and Reviews by Matthew Arnold,* (Cambridge, Mass, 1960) collects and annotates uncollected pieces by Arnold, including some anonymous items recently identified, essential for students. *Note*: For works arranged and edited by Arnold or containing contributions by him, see Smart's *Bibliography,* pp. 37–42.

LETTERS

G. W. E. Russell, ed., *Letters of Matthew Arnold, 1848–1888,* 2 vols. (London, 1895) censored by Arnold's family and the arranger, has no index; A. Whitridge, ed., *Unpublished Letters of Matthew Arnold,* (New Haven, Conn., 1923); H. F. Lowry, ed., *The Letters of Matthew Arnold to Arthur Hugh Clough,* (Oxford, 1932) contains two valuable introductory chapters; W. E. Buckler, ed., *Matthew Arnold's Books: Toward a Publishing Diary,* (Paris-Geneva, 1958) includes numerous extracts from Arnold's letters to his publishers between 1860 and 1888, with introductory chapter and brief notes; A. K. Davis, Jr. ed., *Matthew Arnold's Letters: A Descriptive Checklist,* (Charlottesville, Va., 1968) lists 2,658 letters—more than half of them unpublished—and 2,506 different correspondents.

BIOGRAPHICAL AND CRITICAL STUDIES

Rossetti, W., review of *The Strayed Reveller* in the *Germ: Thoughts Toward Nature in Poetry, Literature, and Art,* no. 2 (February 1850); *The Poems and Prose Remains of A. H. Clough,* (London, 1869) vol. I contains a review (1853) of Arnold's early poetry; Swinburne, A. C., *Essays and Studies,* (London, 1857) includes a good essay on Arnold's *New Poems,* (1867); Bradley, F. H., *Ethical Studies,* (London, 1876) contains a merciless dissection of Arnold's religious views in a clever parody of his style; Mallock, W. H., *The New Republic . . .*, (London, 1877) "Mr. Luke" is a satirical portrait of Arnold; Hutton, R. H., *Literary Essays,* 2nd ed. (London, 1877) includes an essay on Arnold's poetry; Harrison, F., *The Choice of Books,* (London, 1886) contains "Culture: A Dialogue," (1867); Robertson, J. M., *Modern Humanists,* (London, 1891) contains a useful study of Arnold (*Modern Humanists Reconsidered,* 1927); Birrell, A., *Res Judicatae,* (London, 1892) includes a short study of Arnold; Fitch, J. G., *Thomas and Matthew Arnold and Their Influence on English Education,* (London, 1897); Stephen, L., *Studies of a Biographer,* (London, 1898) vol. II contains a study of Arnold; Saintsbury, G., *Matthew Arnold,* (London, 1899).

Arnold, T., *Passages in a Wandering Life,* (London, 1900) an important source for Matthew Arnold's early life; Butler, A. G., *The Three Friends: A Story of Rugby in the Forties,* (Oxford, 1900) contains an agreeable description of Arnold in his "dandy" phase; Brownell, W. C., *Victorian Prose Masters,* (New York, 1901); Paul, H. W., *Matthew Arnold,* (London, 1902) English Men of Letters series; Russell, G. W. E., *Matthew Arnold,* (London, 1904); Coleridge, E. H., *Life and Correspondence of John Duke Coleridge,* (London, 1904) includes some interesting letters by Arnold; Dawson, W. H., *Matthew Arnold and His Relation to the Thought of Our Time,* (London, 1904); James, H., *Views and Reviews,* (London, 1908) includes a review (1865) of *Essays in Criticism,* First Series, see also the essay by James in the *English Illustrated Magazine* vol. I January (1884); Kelso, A. P., *Matthew Arnold on Continental Life and Literature,* (Oxford, 1914); Ward, Mrs. Humphrey, *A Writer's Recollections,* (London, 1918) by Arnold's niece, the author of *Robert Elsmere* (London, 1888).

Grierson, H. J. C., *Lord Byron: Arnold and Swinburne,* (London, 1921) the Warton Lecture on English Poetry for the British Academy, repr. in *The Background of English Literature . . .* (London, 1934); Ker, W. P., *The Art of Poetry,* (London, 1923); Raleigh, W., *Some Authors,* (Oxford, 1923); Houghton, R. E. C., *The Influence of the Classics on the Poetry of Matthew Arnold,* (Oxford, 1923); Murry, J. M., *Discoveries,*

(London, 1924); Kingsmill, H., *Matthew Arnold,* (London, 1928); Whitridge, A., *Dr. Arnold of Rugby,* (New York, 1928); Orrick, J. B., *Matthew Arnold and Goethe,* (London, 1928) publication of the English Goethe Society, n.s., vol. IV; Garrod, H. W., *Poetry and the Criticism of Life,* (Oxford, 1931) includes three lectures on Arnold; Harvey, C. H., *Matthew Arnold,* (London, 1931); Chambers, E., *Matthew Arnold,* (London, 1932) the Warton Lecture on English Poetry for the British Academy; Eliot, T. S., *Selected Essays,* (London, 1932) contains "Arnold and Pater" (1930); Eliot, T. S., *The Use of Poetry and the Use of Criticism,* (London, 1933) contains a brilliant, unsympathetic account of Arnold; F. J. C. Hearnshaw, ed., *The Social and Political Ideas of the Victorian Age,* (London, 1933) includes "Matthew Arnold and the Educationists," a valuable essay on Arnold's social thinking by J. D. Wilson; Bateson, F. W., *English Poetry and the English Language,* (Oxford, 1934) contains interesting remarks on Arnold's poetic diction; Brown, E. K., *Studies in the Text of Matthew Arnold's Prose Works,* (Paris, 1935); Sells, I. E., *Matthew Arnold and France,* (Cambridge, 1935) explores the influence of Senancour and includes an unpublished early poem by Arnold; Leavis, F. R., *Revaluation,* (London, 1936) contains a note on Arnold's poetry, see also Leavis' "Arnold as Critic," (*Scrutiny,* December 1938); Stanley, C., *Matthew Arnold,* Toronto (1938); Trilling, L., *Matthew Arnold,* (London, 1939) a sympathetic and penetrating study of Arnold's ideas by a liberal critic; Groom, B., *On the Diction of Tennyson, Browning and Arnold,* (Oxford, 1939) S. P. E. Tract, no. 53, useful.

Tinker, C. B., and Lowry, H. F., *The Poetry of Matthew Arnold: A Commentary,* (London, 1940) still essential for the student but now to be used with caution; Ford, G. H., *Keats and the Victorians . . . ,* (New Haven, Conn., 1945) pt. 2 is a sensitive examination of Keats' influence on Arnold; Chambers, E. K., *Matthew Arnold,* (Oxford, 1947); Bonnerot, L., *Matthew Arnold, Poète,* (Paris, 1947) scholarly and formidably detailed, an app. contains Arnold's letters to Sainte-Beuve, includes excellent bibliography; Brown, E. K., *Matthew Arnold: A Study in Conflict,* (Chicago, 1948) stimulating; Macdonald, I., *The Buried Self: A Background to the Poems of Matthew Arnold, 1848–1851,* (London, 1949) fiction but interestingly documented; Connell, W. F., *The Educational Thought and Influence of Matthew Arnold,* (London, 1950) a scholarly survey; Faverty, F. E., *Matthew Arnold the Ethnologist,* (Evanston, Ill., 1951); Tillotson, G., *Criticism and the Nineteenth Century,* (London, 1951) contains three valuable essays on Arnold; Johnson, E. D. H., *The Alien Vision of Victorian Poetry,* (Princeton, N.J., 1952) contains a section on Arnold's poetry; Holloway, J., *The Victorian Sage: Studies in Argument,* (London, 1953) includes an interesting discussion of Arnold's techniques of persuasion; Wymer, N., *Dr. Arnold of Rugby,* (London, 1953) makes use of much unpublished material, including an early poem by Arnold; Woodward, F. J., *The Doctor's Disciples,* (London, 1954); Jump, J. D., *Matthew Arnold,* (London, 1955); Tillotson, K., *Matthew Arnold and Carlyle,* (London, 1956) the Warton Lecture on English Poetry for the British Academy, scholarly and stimulating; F. L. Mulhauser, ed., *The Correspondence of Arthur Hugh Clough,* (Oxford, 1957) contains many new references to Arnold; Raleigh, J. H., *Matthew Arnold and American Culture,* (Berkeley-Los Angeles, 1957) of particular interest to readers outside America; Jamison, W. A., *Arnold and the Romantics,* (Copenhagen, 1958); Baum, P. F., *Ten Studies in the Poetry of Matthew Arnold,* (Durham, N. C., 1958); Buckley, V., *Poetry and Morality: Studies in the Criticism of Matthew Arnold, T. S. Eliot and F. R. Leavis,* (London, 1959); Robbins, W., *The Ethical Idealism of Matthew Arnold,* (London, 1959).

Bamford, T. W., *Thomas Arnold,* (London, 1960); Johnson, W. S., *The Voices of Matthew Arnold,* (New Haven, Conn., 1961); James, D. G., *Matthew Arnold and the Decline of English Romanticism,* (Oxford, 1961) a hostile look at Arnold as a critic; Fairclough, G. T., *A Fugitive and Gracious Light: The Relation of Joseph Joubert to Matthew Arnold's Thought,* University of Nebraska Studies, n.s., no. 23 (Lincoln, Nebr., 1961); Duffin, H. C., *Arnold the Poet,* (London, 1962); Gottfried, L., *Matthew Arnold and the Romantics,* (London, 1963) the best study of this subject; Cockshut, A. O. J., *The Unbelievers,* (London, 1964); Day, P. W., *Matthew Arnold and the Philosophy of Vice,* (Auckland, 1964); McCarthy, P. J., *Matthew Arnold and The Three Classes,* (London, 1964); Harding, F. J. W., *Matthew Arnold the Critic and France,* (Geneva, 1964); Alexander, E., *Matthew Arnold and John Stuart Mill,* (London, 1965); Anderson, W. D., *Matthew Arnold and the Classical Tradition,* (Ann Arbor, Mich., 1965); DeLaura, D. J., *Matthew Arnold and John Henry Newman,* University of Texas Studies in Literature and Language, vol. VI (Austin, Tex., 1965); Tillotson, G., and Tillotson, K., *Mid-Victorian Studies,* (London, 1965); Frykman, E., *"Bitter Knowledge" and "Unconquerable Hope": A Thematic Study of Attitudes Towards Life in Matthew Arnold's Poetry 1849–1853,* (Gothenberg, 1966); Culler, A. D., *Imaginative Reason: The Poetry of Matthew Arnold,* (New Haven, Conn., 1966) intelligent and lively, but sometimes fanciful in interpretation; J. Bertram, ed., *New Zealand Letters of Thomas Arnold the Younger,* (London, 1966) contains many references to Matthew Arnold and the family circle at Fox How; Strange, G. R., *Matthew Arnold: The Poet as Humanist,* (Princeton, N. J., 1967); Madden, W. A., *Matthew Arnold: A Study of the Aesthetic Temperament in Victorian England,* (Bloomington, Ind., 1967) discusses the poetry and, more summarily, the prose; S. Potter, ed., *Essays and Studies,* (London, 1968) contains a study of Arnold's "Empedocles on Etna"; Leavis, F. R., "Arnold as Critic," *A Selection from Scrutiny,* (Cambridge, 1968); C. Dawson, ed., *Matthew Arnold: The Critical Heritage,* (London, 1973); K. Allott, ed., *Matthew Arnold: A Symposium,* (London, 1975) includes Newman, F., "A Reader's Guide to Arnold," Madden, W., "Arnold the Poet: Lyric and Elegiac Poems," Allott, K., and Allott, M., "Arnold the Poet: Narrative and Dramatic Poems," DeLaura, D. J., "Arnold and Literary Criticism: Critical Ideas," Super, R. H., "Arnold and Literary Criticism: Critical Practice," Bertram, J., "Arnold and Clough," Keating, P., "Arnold's Social and Political Thought," Willey, B., "Arnold and Religion," Anderson, W., "Arnold and the Classics," Simpson, J., "Arnold and Goethe"; Robbins, W., *The Ethical Idealism of Matthew Arnold: A Study of the Nature and Sources of His Religious Ideas,* (Toronto, 1975); Trilling, L., *Matthew Arnold,* (London, 1976); Rowse, A. L., *Matthew Arnold: Poet and Prophet,* (London, 1976); M. Allott, ed., *Matthew Arnold,* (London, 1978); Simpson, J., *Matthew Arnold and Goethe,* (London, 1979); C. Dawson and J. Pfordresher, eds., *Matthew Arnold, Prose Writings: The Critical Heritage,* (London, 1979); Horan, P., *Matthew Arnold,* (London, 1979).

John Ashbery
(b. 1927)

JOHN SHOPTAW

In a 1983 interview with John Koethe, John Ashbery offered the following explanation of his poetry by way of advice: "You should try to make your poem as representative as possible." Ashbery's own poetry is representative in several ways. First, he will choose particulars for their typical or representative quality. Ashbery told Ross Labrie that *The Vermont Notebook* (1975), for example, was written largely "on buses traveling through New England, though not Vermont. Generally speaking I guess it's a catalogue of a number of things that could be found in the state of Vermont, as well as almost everywhere else." Second, he will use details characteristic of some literary or nonliterary convention. We need not know who the newlywed is in the opening lines of "More Pleasant Adventures" (from *A Wave,* 1984) in order to recognize it as oral autobiography: "The first year was like icing. / Then the cake started to show through." As the poem exclaims, "Heck, it's anybody's story." But Ashbery commonly writes of personal experiences with details drawn from other lives. In an interview with John Murphy, he described "Soonest Mended" (from *The Double Dream of Spring,* 1970), for instance, as "my 'One-size-fits-all confessional poem,' which is about my youth and maturing but also about anybody else's." Third, Ashbery's "concrete particulars" are representative because they function in relations rather than as isolated terms. In "At North Farm," the opening poem of *A Wave,* the relational, representative character of Ashbery's poetics is immediately apparent:

Somewhere someone is traveling furiously
toward you,
At incredible speed, traveling day and night,
Through blizzards and desert heat, across
torrents, through narrow passes.
But will he know where to find you,
Recognize you when he sees you,
Give you the thing he has for you?

Hardly anything grows here,
Yet the granaries are bursting with meal,
The sacks of meal piled to the rafters.
The streams run with sweetness, fattening
fish;
Birds darken the sky. Is it enough
That the dish of milk is set out at night,
That we think of him sometines,
Sometimes and always, with mixed
feelings?

This lucid but indeterminate poem, crowded with indefinites, may leave readers with a host of questions: Who or what is traveling toward "you"? Does "you" mean "us" or "me"? Where is "here"? What is this poem *really* talking about? Rather than simply maintaining that the poem means just what it says, or doesn't mean anything, we may read "At North Farm," and any Ashbery poem, by attending to terms in their relations. The key relation in "At North Farm," as the allusion to the postal carrier's motto ("Neither rain nor snow nor gloom of night . . .") suggests, is the postal system, requiring a messenger (or sender), a message, and a receiver. We generate different readings of "At North Farm" depending on what terms we plug into the relational system. We can read the poem self-reflexively as the advent of the poem or new book of poems, amorously as the approach of a new lover, theologically as the coming of Christ (as Santa), autobiographically as the warding off of death, and so on. But "At North Farm" sustains no single meaning throughout.

At a further remove, "sacks of meal" (rather than grain) echoes "sacks of mail," "mail" being strangely absent from this postal poem. Ashbery discussed this kind of cryptic revision in an interview with Richard Jackson: "I just wrote a poem this morning in which I used the word 'borders' but changed it to 'boarders.' The original word literally had a marginal existence and isn't spoken, is perhaps what you might call a crypt word." All poets compose, consciously or unconsciously, by means of underlying "crypt words," but in Ashbery's poetry the relations between missing words and those marking their absence take on an added significance. As Ashbery maintains in *Three Poems* (1972), "the word that everything hinged on is buried back there. . . . It is doing the organizing, the guidelines radiate from its control." Reading Ashbery's poetry, then, involves hearing words in relation to missing words, and taking particulars in relation to the kind of thing or language they represent.

Born on July 28, 1927, John Lawrence Ashbery was raised in Sodus, New York, a small town near Lake Ontario in western New York State. His father, Chester Ashbery, operated a fruit farm, where Ashbery worked for several summers canning cherries, a sticky job he does not remember fondly. His mother, Helen Lawrence Ashbery, had taught biology in high school before she married, and it was in her father's house that Ashbery began reading literature, primarily Victorian novels. Fascinated by a 1937 article in *Life* on the surrealist exhibit at the Museum of Modern Art, he decided to try his own hand at the visual arts and took painting classes at the art museum in Rochester from the ages of eleven to fifteen. Some still lifes from this period survive. When Ashbery was thirteen, his nine-year-old only brother died of leukemia. At fifteen, Ashbery won a *Time* current-events award, selecting for his prize Louis Untermeyer's anthology of modern American poetry, which started him writing poetry. He remembers admiring the poetry of Elinor Wylie early on, but not being able to make much of either Wallace Stevens or W. H. Auden. Before he left home in 1943 for two years at Deerfield Academy, Ashbery declared his homosexuality to his mother. He published his first poems in the *Deerfield Scroll,* but was shocked to learn, at Harvard in 1945, that two of his poems had been stolen by a supposed friend of his at Deerfield and published in *Poetry* under the name Joel Michael Symington. His first credited publication of poetry, apart from poems in the *Deerfield Scroll* and the *Harvard Advocate,* would be in *Furioso* in 1949.

At Harvard, Ashbery majored in English, and, along with Robert Creeley and John Hawkes, studied poetry with Theodore Spencer. In 1947, with the help of Kenneth Koch, Ashbery joined the editorial board of the *Harvard Advocate,* which published "Some Trees," among others of his poems. He collaborated with Fred Amory on a collage for one of the magazine's covers, and in his last semester at Harvard he met Frank O'Hara. In "A Reminiscence," in *Homage to Frank O'Hara* (1988), Ashbery recalls being struck by the uncanny similarity of their accents:

> Though we grew up in widely separate regions of the east, . . . we both inherited the same flat, nasal twang, a hick accent so out of keeping with the roles we were trying to play that it seems to me we probably exaggerated it, later on, in hopes of making it seem intentional.

Ashbery wrote his senior thesis on Auden's poetry up to *The Sea and the Mirror* (1944), a book that influenced his own *Three Poems.* He met Auden at a reading at Harvard and got to know him through a mutual friend, James Schuyler, in New York. While an undergraduate, Ashbery also heard Wallace Stevens at Harvard give one of his rare poetry readings.

After he was turned down for graduate study in English at Harvard and accepted at

Columbia, Ashbery moved to New York in the summer of 1949. Kenneth Koch, who had graduated the year before and was encouraging him to move, let him stay in his apartment for the summer. There he met Koch's upstairs neighbor, the painter Jane Freilicher, who became a lifelong friend. She introduced Ashbery to Larry Rivers, another friend for life, and to the world of abstract expressionism. Freilicher illustrated Ashbery's first, small collection of poetry, *Turandot and Other Poems* (1953). His play *The Heroes* (an Audenesque assemblage of Theseus, Patroclus, Achilles, Circe, and others in "a living room of an undeterminable period") premiered at the Living Theatre in 1952. That year, Ashbery also completed a master's thesis on the novels of Henry Green, a dialogue novelist in vogue at the time. During the same busy year, Ashbery and his constant friend James Schuyler began writing their own dialogue novel, *A Nest of Ninnies,* which they finished and published in 1969.

In comparison with the New York school of painting, the academic school of poetry seemed tame. The tradition of Robert Lowell, John Berryman, Allen Tate, and Randall Jarrell held little interest for Ashbery. His favorite poets during the late 1940's and early 1950's included Marianne Moore, Elizabeth Bishop, Wallace Stevens, William Carlos Williams, Delmore Schwartz, and F. T. Prince. Ashbery didn't care for much of Auden's self-consciously colloquial American poetry (*The Sea and the Mirror* excepted), and his taste for T. S. Eliot would not develop until later. He also began avidly reading the now-neglected poets David Schubert, Laura Riding, John Wheelwright, and the French poet and novelist Raymond Roussel, all of whom he would showcase as "An Other Tradition" in the Charles Eliot Norton lectures he was asked to deliver at Harvard in the 1989–1990 academic year. In 1956 he and O'Hara both submitted poetry manuscripts to the Yale Younger Poets competition, judged by Auden, and both were rejected in the preliminary round. When Auden complained that he did not like any of the manuscripts submitted to him, someone (possibly Auden's companion, Chester Kallman) told him about Ashbery's and O'Hara's rejected submissions. Auden asked to see the manuscripts and chose Ashbery's *Some Trees,* which O'Hara, in a typically generous review, hailed as the best first volume of poems since Stevens' *Harmonium* (1923).

Some Trees (1956), which included new work and nearly all the poems from *Turandot,* is as remarkable for what it excludes or slights as for what it presents. There is little detailed description of the world; few of the poems rely on close observation. New York passes unmentioned. Only "Some Trees" and the last section of "The Picture of Little J. A. in a Prospect of Flowers" employ anything like a lyric "I." Nor will the readers of Ashbery's later work find here the prosaic rhythms of speech or the cascading images of the purportedly indistinguishable "Ashbery poem." What we do find in *Some Trees* are poems of polished, often elevated or archaic diction, high sonic resonance, and high linear definition. Composing more by the line than by the sentence and proceeding more by sound than by sense, Ashbery creates poems that disassemble into their components, each of which collapses into itself, like a self-fulfilling prophecy. Consider the opening lines of "Two Scenes":

> We see us as we truly behave:
> From every corner comes a distinctive
>   offering.
> The train comes bearing joy;
> The sparks it strikes illuminate the table.
> Destiny guides the water-pilot, and it is
>   destiny.
> For long we hadn't heard so much news,
>   such noise.
> The day was warm and pleasant.
> "We see you in your hair,
> Air resting around the tips of mountains."

Each line echoes itself, and creates, for its duration, a distinct sonic environment. Though syntactically fragmented, the fifth line centers the Miltonic "water-pilot" within his "destiny." And the tight weave of assonance and consonance in the first line submerges the idiomatic wish to "see ourselves as others see us." This folk adage or moral injunction ("If you could see yourself!"), however garbled, nevertheless organizes this scene of being seen. The news of who or how we are arrives by rail, sea, or over the wireless as the news and weather. But as the sonic slippage of "so much news, such noise" suggests, these bulletins carry little more than the ring of truth. "But who / Knows anything about our behavior?" Ashbery will ask thirty years later in *A Wave*; neither in life nor in art does the mask or guard come down.

Some Trees is a network of echoes, silences, secrets, ambiguous signs, defenses, and imminent revelations. "The Grapevine," for instance, begins with a sonorously convoluted warning: "Of who we and all they are / You all now know." The secrecy, evasiveness, and self-protectiveness that have become a trademark of Ashbery's poetry bear some relation to his necessarily covert homosexual lifestyle throughout the 1940's. Even the often-anthologized, limpid love lyric "Some Trees," which Ashbery wrote at Harvard in 1948 to one of his male classmates, betrays the caution necessary when behavior is shadowy and unsanctioned:

> These are amazing: each
> Joining a neighbor, as though speech
> Were a still performance.
> Arranging by chance
>
> To meet as far this morning
> From the world as agreeing
> With it, you and I
> Are suddenly what the trees try
>
> To tell us we are:
> That their merely being there
> Means something; that soon
> We may touch, love, explain.

Certainly this description of imminent love (such as was prophesied in "Two Scenes") is "anybody's story." And the brilliance of Ashbery's keeping what Charles Baudelaire called a "forest of symbols" to the horizontal, emotional plane of correspondences amazes. Yet this love is unaccompanied by open gestures, even though by mutual agreement the lovers have retreated from the world. The joy of the poem consists in the lovers' being surrounded by the nonjudgmental presences of the trees. Even so, this still performance cannot last, and the guarded time of self-reflection resumes:

> Placed in a puzzling light, and moving,
> Our days put on such reticence
> These accents seem their own defense.

In the early 1950's, the United States was embroiled in the Korean War and grappling with the rise of Senator Joseph McCarthy, whose truly reductive imagination equated homosexuals with Communists. It was a time of lists, purges, drafts, and raids on suspicious bars. Ashbery told Richard Kostelanetz:

> In the early 50's, I went through a period of intense depression and doubt. I couldn't write for a couple of years. . . . It did coincide with the beginnings of the Korean War, the Rosenberg case, and McCarthyism. . . . I was jolted out of this by going with Frank O'Hara—I think it was New Year's Day, 1952—to a concert by David Tudor of John Cage's *Music of Changes*.

With Cage's changes ringing in his ears, the young Ashbery's response to this repressive climate was neither fight nor flight but a resourceful evasive action. In "The Thinnest Shadow" the poet counsels himself (with a disturbingly paternal tone) to make himself a thin, moving target: "A face looks from the mirror / As if to say, / 'Be supple, young man, / Since you can't be gay,' " advice playing on the latent meaning of "gay" that Ashbery first learned in the mid-1940's. In "A Boy," Ashbery evades both the paternal repression of gays and the patriarchal oppression of the Korean War. Written in 1951, after Ashbery saw John Huston's mangled film version of Stephen Crane's *The Red Badge of Courage,* "A Boy" ends with a dire bulletin:

> They're throwing up behind the lines.
> Dry fields of lightning rise to receive

> The observer, the mincing flag. *An unendurable age.*

The crypt phrase "the mincing fag" determines the conclusion. The decade of Ashbery's twenties, after World War II and during the Korean War (neither of which Ashbery fought in), was indeed unendurable.

One popular poem in which the artist goes his own way is the flawless sestina "The Painter," the only other Harvard poem included in *Some Trees.* As in "Some Trees," the enjambed tetrameters of "The Painter" keep to an effortless syntax and a colorless vocabulary, including the poem's end words ("buildings," "portrait," "prayer," "subject," "brush," "canvas"). It is remarkable, for instance, that the only color word appearing in "The Painter" is "white." With its fixed form and sustained irony, "The Painter" raises the issue of flawlessness. Yet the poem relies on a productive incongruity between its formal perfection and its Romantic subject matter, the painter in sublime confrontation with the ocean. No Vincent van Gogh or Jackson Pollock, Ashbery's painter is more of a Prufrockian artist who does not think the sea will sit for him. One key model for "The Painter" (as for Eliot's "The Love Song of J. Alfred Prufrock") is Robert Browning's "Andrea del Sarto (Called 'The Faultless Painter')." With its source material in Giorgio Vasari, long verse paragraphs, and extended apostrophe, and especially with its exploration of the aesthetics and psychology of perfection, "Andrea del Sarto" is also an important model for Ashbery's "Self-Portrait in a Convex Mirror," for which "The Painter" becomes the preliminary sketch. Like Ashbery's "perfectly white" sestina, Browning's Andrea del Sarto painting is colorless and finished: "All is silver-gray / Placid and perfect with my art." Andrea painstakingly paints his wife, and settles for technical excellence while chafing at the flawed soulful paintings of his rivals Michelangelo and Raphael:

> Their works drop groundward, but themselves, I know,
> Reach many a time a heaven that's shut to me,
> Enter and take their place there sure enough,
> Though they come back and cannot tell the world.

Ashbery literalized these dropping paintings, now thrown seaward by the rival painters, in the concluding tercet of "The Painter":

> They tossed him, the portrait, from the tallest of the buildings;
> And the sea devoured the canvas and the brush
> As if his subject had decided to remain a prayer.

The most malleable of the end words in "The Painter" is "subject," meaning subject matter, self, and subjection. To paint his "self-portrait," Ashbery's painter masters his ego (as he had his model wife) and dips his brush into the sea, subjecting his conscious perfections to his oceanic "soul." The paradoxically passive self-expression of abstract expressionism ("Imagine a painter crucified by his subject!") was already in Browning's post-Romantic reading of the Renaissance. "My soul," Ashbery's painter prays (with an implicit pun on "canvas" and "sail"), "when I paint this next portrait / Let it be you who wrecks the canvas." As though drawn on sand, the painting's ambiguous "subject" fails to survive:

> Finally all indications of a subject
> Began to fade, leaving the canvas
> Perfectly white.

But "The Painter" succeeds by drawing the mock-heroic proportions of the subject's subjection.

Along with "Some Trees" and "The Painter," the most anthologized poem in *Some Trees* is "The Instruction Manual," written in 1955. Unlike the collage narratives of such poems as "Popular Songs" or "A Long Novel," "The Instruction Manual" follows a single narrator and a single, simple story from the beginning to an abbreviated end. A harassed, dreamy functionary, under a deadline to "write the instruction manual on the uses of a new metal," gazes out the window and fancies he visits "dim Guadalajara! City of rose-colored flowers!/City I wanted most to see, and most did not see, in Mexico!" There is a special nostalgia, Baudelaire tells us in "Invitation to a Voyage," for the "country one does not know." But whereas Baudelaire's imaginary country is richly textured, recessed, and exotic, the "local colors" of Ashbery's Guadalajara are taken from Bishop's and Stevens' elementary palates:

> Around stand the flower girls, handing out
> rose- and lemon-colored flowers,
> Each attractive in her rose-and-blue striped
> dress (Oh! such shades of rose and blue),
> And nearby is the little white booth where
> women in green serve you green and
> yellow fruit.

In an interview with Sue Gangle in 1977, Ashbery provides a fascinating backdrop to this travelogue:

> I wrote ["The Instruction Manual"] actually when I was working for a publisher [McGraw-Hill], writing and editing college textbooks. . . . The poem . . . is probably about the dissatisfaction with the work I was doing at the time. And my lack of success in seeing the city I wanted most to see, when I was in Mexico. The long lines in the poem were suggested by Whitman. . . . Also the French poet, Raymond Roussel, whom I later studied in France.

Several things are interesting about Ashbery's retrospective sense of "The Instruction Manual." First, unlike the speaker in lyrics such as those from Lowell's *Life Studies* or Whitman's apostrophe to the Suez Canal, Ashbery's persona is as cartoonish as the characters he imagines ("And, as my way is, I begin to dream"). He takes the reader on a walking tour of Guadalajara, the Proustian place-name ("Here you may see one of those white houses with green trim / That are so popular here. Look—I told you!"), and in fact appears as little more than an embodiment of the discourse of a travelogue. The reduced narrator, his generic observations, the languid (more than ecstatic Whitmanian) long lines, and the pleasant confusion of narrative levels in which we never really leave the frame for the picture, or the world for the map, are all strongly reminiscent of Bishop, whom Ashbery had begun to read in the 1940's.

By the time Ashbery had written "The Instruction Manual," he had received a Fulbright Fellowship to write a thesis on Raymond Roussel in France, where, with some interruptions, he would spend the next decade of his life. Although he did not fulfill his intention of writing a dissertation on Roussel, Ashbery did publish a few articles on him, and even discovered the missing first chapter to Roussel's last, unfinished novel. Not long after his arrival Ashbery met Pierre Martory, an art and music critic for *Paris Match,* with whom he lived for the next nine years. Ashbery dedicated his second book of poetry, *The Tennis Court Oath* (1962), to Martory, and—in an unusual tribute—mentions his name as the fellow viewer of Parmigianino's *Self-Portrait in a Convex Mirror* in his best-known poem, of the same title: "Vienna where the painting is today, where / I saw it with Pierre in the summer of 1959." In 1957 Ashbery began writing art reviews for *Art News,* and in 1960, through the help of Frank O'Hara, Ashbery became an art reviewer for the *New York Herald Tribune* in Paris.

The next year, Ashbery and Harry Mathews, a novelist whom he had met in France, enlisted Kenneth Koch and James Schuyler as co-editors of the Francophile literary review *Locust Solus* (named for one of Roussel's novels), which ran for two years. Also in 1961, John Myers coined the term "New York school of poetry." Ashbery sees more differences than similarities in the poets of this "school" (from which he was absent at the time it was named). As he explained in 1981 to A. Poulin:

> I think that Frank O'Hara's life was the subject of his poetry in a way that mine isn't.

> Although many of his poems are about things that happened to him, people that he knew, events he experienced, these were a kind of springboard for getting into something wider, more poetic. Kenneth Koch is at the opposite extreme, I think, because his work is involved much more deeply with just words, which are the end result he's after. Really words, rather than a transcending of them, which is what I have always felt I had to do. I might stand halfway between these two, because I don't feel that words are the end of thought and yet I don't feel that experience has to be transformed by words.

And Schuyler, Ashbery told Piotr Sommer, "is really much more of a classical poet, I mean he's somebody more resembling Elizabeth Bishop whose work is very clear in structure." Though there were no qualities shared by the New York school of poetry other than a spirit of experimentation, there did exist a family relation of shared experiences, attitudes (a dislike, for instance, of the academic poetry being written in the 1950's), and projects. Ashbery collaborated with Schuyler, Koch, and O'Hara on various short plays and poems.

In 1962, to Ashbery's surprise, Wesleyan University Press (with Donald Hall on the board) agreed to publish a collection of his experimental poems written mostly in France, *The Tennis Court Oath*. The book disappointed critics, who felt shut out from its isolated words and phrases, but, significantly, this volume was singled out for praise by the "language poets" (another ill-fitting but adhesive label) for its relentless attack on conventional grammar, syntax, voice, and diction. Ashbery himself has expressed mixed feelings about this misshapen offspring. He told Richard Kostelanetz that much of the work was little more than an attempt to break away from the style of *Some Trees*: "I didn't want to write the poetry that was coming naturally to me then, . . . and I succeeded in writing something that wasn't the poetry I didn't want to write, and yet was not the poetry I wanted to write." Probably no poem of Ashbery's has sent more readers' hands into the air than his detective epic, "Europe," in which Ashbery collaged passages from a British detective novel, *Beryl of the Biplane* (1917), written by William Le Queux during World War I. Le Queux's novel, set almost entirely in England, concerns the exploits of the ace pilots Ronald Pryor and his beloved, Beryl (compare "Ash*bery*") Gaselee, who fly "The Hornet," an experimental flying machine (like Ashbery's "Europe") equipped with a top-secret "silencer," which allows the pilots to creep up on their prey undetected. The deadly couple work not for the RAF but as undercover agents to protect England from "the enemy within." The book is filled with the mechanisms of detection: Morse and other codes, disguises, and double agents. These doublings, in which the enemy looks and acts "just like you and me," produce a paranoid atmosphere most immediately resembling the McCarthyism of the early 1950's. To see how representative this repressive paranoia is, we need only substitute "Communists," "homosexuals," "Jews," or "obscene artists" for "Germans." Though McCarthy had fallen and America was now an ocean away, Ashbery must have seen poetic possibilities both in the self-reflexively detective and in the sociopolitical dimensions of Le Queux's grim little novel:

> The engine had stopped, for, half the propeller being broken, the other half had embedded itself deeply into the ground. Collins came running up, half frantic with fear, but was soon reassured by the pair of intrepid aviators, who unstrapped themselves and quickly climbed out of the wreckage. Ere long a flare was lit and the broken wing carefully examined; it was soon discovered that "The Hornet" had been tampered with, one of the steel bolts having been replaced by a painted one of wood!
>
> "This is the work of the enemy!" remarked Ronnie thoughtfully. "They cannot obtain sight of the silencer, therefore there has been a dastardly plot to kill both of us. We must be a little more wary in future, dear."

Juxtaposing the above passage from page 61 of *Beryl* (which preserves the line breaks of the original) with a few of the 111 stanzas from "Europe" will give us an idea of Ashbery's own procedures:

104.

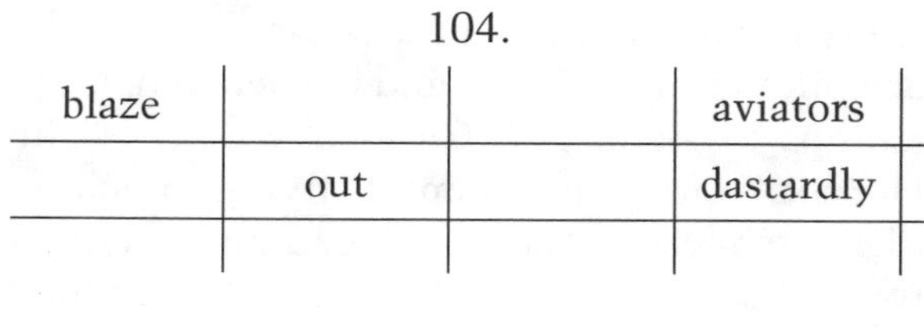

105.

We must be a little more wary in
future, dear

106.

she was trying to make sense of
what was quick laugh
hotel—cheap for them
caverns the bed

box of cereal

Ere long a flare was lit
I don't understand wreckage

107.

blue smoke?
It was as though
She had
the river
above the water

The steel bolts
having been replaced
by a painting of
one of wood!
Ronnie, thoughtfully

of the silencer

plot to kill both of us, dear.
pet
oh

it that she was there

These stanzas from "Europe" are dotted with the representative conventions of detective fiction. We know what to make of clues such as "steel bolts" or "box of cereal," signs such as "a flare" or "blue smoke?," or self-reflexive statements like "she was trying to make sense of," whether or not we know their source. We also find romantic conventions, such as Ronnie's unintentionally hilarious, patronizing caution to Beryl. The "wreckage" of Ronnie and Beryl's airplane becomes a figure for "Europe," another postwar wasteland. In stanza 104, the generically descriptive "aviators," "blaze," and "dastardly," along with the colorless "out," litter the open field of the poem in a mannered parody of William Carlos Williams or Charles Olson. In 107, the two-columned wreckage of the poem anticipates the long, double-columned "Litany" of *As We Know* (1979). On the left wing, we note that Ashbery has slightly altered Le Queux's prose to create the surrealist joke of a steel bolt being replaced by "a painting of" (rather than "a painted") one in wood. The lines "Ronnie, thoughtfully / of the silencer" duplicate the fracturing of the original prose as determined by the left margin of the published text, whose accidental features Ashbery preserves. And the final isolated words and phrases strewn about are reminiscent both of Anton von Webern's music and the erasures and splatters of Robert Rauschenberg and Jackson Pollock. Ashbery's ungrammatical fragments exceed the always grammatical experiments in "automatic writing" undertaken by surrealists such as André Breton and Guillaume Apollinaire. The problem with "Europe" is not its obscurity but its clarity. We "get the idea" of "Europe" too quickly and completely for the poem to keep satisfying us. Still, we are fortunate that Ashbery earned his wings of sustained lyric flight with "Europe" rather than, for example, with the moving but sober and essayistic "Self-Portrait in a Convex Mirror." With "Europe," Ashbery carved out an immense lyric space and dispersed a universe of poetic fragments that would take years to explore and to recollect.

The most ambitious and prospective poem in *The Tennis Court Oath* is "A Last World," which in its mythological scope rivals *The Waste Land* and anticipates Ashbery's own long poem "A Wave." The expansive, consecutive lines of "A Last World" culminate what Ashbery, in an interview with Piotr Sommer, has called "the compromise style" of *The Ten-*

nis Court Oath: the poem is more disjunct than the poems in *Some Trees* but less fragmented than poems such as "Europe." Like *The Waste Land,* "A Last World" diagnoses the sexual disorders of the Western world, in which "passions are locked away, and states of creation are used instead, that is to say synonyms are used." Yet this repressive modern world in which love cannot speak its name is the only one in which poetry, speaking in synonyms, is possible. "A Last World" ends with a wonderfully sentimental apocalypse:

> Everything is being blown away;
> A little horse trots up with a letter in its
> mouth, which is read with eagerness
> As we gallop into the flame.

Once we recognize that the crypt word for "flame" is "sunset," the genre of the western (comically apt for a poem on the Western world) with its prairie winds, its pony express, its rocking-horse young readers, and its society of men riding off together, swings into view. Within the context of the poem, the horse is also the Trojan Horse, which leads to the burning of Troy. But Ashbery's flame is not simply destruction, or even Eliotic purgation, but the flame of desire, which renews private and fuels public life. With its scope, beauty, and intelligence, "A Last World" becomes the most important poem Ashbery had written thus far in his career.

Ashbery returned to New York for good in 1965, after his father died of a heart attack. (Frank O'Hara died the following year.) Also in 1965, Ashbery became an executive editor at *Art News,* where one of his duties was to recruit other poets to do art reviews. The following year, Ashbery published his third major volume of poems, *Rivers and Mountains,* which marked a return in some ways to the poetry of his first two volumes but also paved the way for many projects to come. "The Skaters," for instance, marks a clear advance over the austere discontinuities of "Europe" and in fact has more "personality" (livelier masks) than do any of Ashbery's earlier poems. The same disquieting muses of "The Instruction Manual"—Roussel, Marcel Proust, and Bishop—watch over "The Skaters" (the desert island passage in part three seems to have influenced Bishop's "Crusoe in England" [1976]). And much of "The Skaters" is involved with Proustian places never visited, typical boyhoods never experienced. Yet in many ways "The Skaters" is a kind of farewell to the New York school, as well as to his collage poems. Other playful collages will follow, but not on this romping scale. Ashbery told Kostelanetz that with "The Skaters" he wanted to "put everything in, rather than, as in 'Europe,' leaving things out." As with "Europe," "The Skaters" reproduces passages from another book, this time a British children's book titled *Three Hundred Things a Bright Boy Can Do* (1911). But the splintered, mysterious lines and stanzas of "Europe" have been replaced by long, easygoing lines reminiscent of "The Instruction Manual." The "instruction manual" *Three Hundred Things a Bright Boy Can Do* allowed Ashbery to sketch out a representative rather than a reminiscent childhood:

> Fire Designs.—This is very simple, amusing, and effective. Make a saturated solution of nitrate of potash (common nitre or saltpetre), by dissolving the substance in warm water, until no more will dissolve; then draw with a smooth stick of wood any design or wording on sheets of white tissue paper, let it thoroughly dry, and the drawing will become invisible. By means of a spark from a smouldering match ignite the potassium nitrate at any part of the drawing, first laying the paper on a plate or tray in the darkened room. The fire will smoulder along the line of the invisible drawing until the design is complete.

With its self-reflexive imagery of secrecy, *Three Hundred Things a Bright Boy Can Do* probably appealed to Ashbery for the same reasons as did *Beryl of the Biplane*; but the way the text is adapted in "The Skaters" is quite different:

> In my day we used to make "fire designs,"
> using a saturated solution of nitrate of
> potash.

Then we used to take a smooth stick, and using the solution as ink, draw with it on sheets of white tissue paper.
Once it was thoroughly dry, the writing would be invisible.
By means of a spark from a smoldering match ignite the potassium nitrate at any part of the drawing,
First laying the paper on a plate or tray in a darkened room.
The fire will smolder along the line of the invisible drawing until the design is complete.

Ashbery does not mount or preserve this passage as a ruin of language or culture (as in "Europe" or Eliot's *The Waste Land*). Rather, he allows it to devour itself as a self-consuming, protean artifact. This temporal, more than spatial, "leaving-out business" produces here the sudden transformation from clichéd reminiscence ("In my day") to instruction manual ("ignite the potassium nitrate"). But with its discrete stanzas (verse paragraphs, quatrains, indented lyrics) and abrupt shifts in style and persona, "The Skaters" was not really well-equipped for the seamless or fluid transformations described above. Ashbery came closer in "Clepsydra," the watershed poem of *Rivers and Mountains.* "Clepsydra" was written in the spring of 1965, roughly a year after "The Skaters" was finished and a few months after "Fragment," the long poem of *The Double Dream of Spring.* The actual chronology of these three poems is important in charting Ashbery's progress as a poet. Before considering "Clepsydra," then, I will turn briefly to the ironically titled "Fragment" (not "Fragments" but a piece from a vaster puzzle).

"Fragment" is a monumentally meditative poem, composed of fifty ten-line stanzas, or dizains, inspired by Maurice Scève's *Délie* (1544; "délie" is an anagram for "l'idée" or "idea"), which apparently leaves nothing out. "Fragment" was first handsomely published by Black Sparrow Press as a volume dedicated to James Schuyler, with two dizains per page facing the "illustrations" (like the emblems of *Délie*) of the cool realist Alex Katz. The first dizain of "Fragment" illustrates both its limitations and its power:

The last block is closed in April. You
See the intrusions clouding over her face
As in the memory given you of older
Permissiveness which dies in the
Falling back toward recondite ends,
The sympathy of yellow flowers.
Never mentioned in the signs of the oblong day
The saw-toothed flames and point of other
Space not given, and yet not withdrawn
And never yet imagined: a moment's commandment.

It is helpful to place this block in the context of Ashbery's personal history. This stanza was written in December 1964, soon after Ashbery's father died. The mausoleum of "Fragment" opens with its "last block" being fitted into place. With the decorous "sympathy" of flowers, the grief that clouds the face of the mother and blots the memory of her former permissiveness from the wayward "son" (compare the "saw-toothed flames" of the child's drawn daisy "sun") commanded to honor his parents is never mentioned. This "moment's monument," as Dante Gabriel Rossetti called the sonnet form, sustains its meditative intensity for fifty stanzas, erotically extending its immediate grief with the memory of romantic separations. Yet the intensity of "Fragment" is achieved at the cost of variation. The childhood experience here is related in the same patient, ruminative language of thought as the mother's grief. Nor are the ungrieving signs of the times in the oblong daily news given in journalese. The consolatory "idea" of "Fragment," the absent yet latent moment of the past, means a lot to Ashbery. But it is difficult for the romantic momentum of "and yet not withdrawn / And never yet imagined" to overcome the inertia of "and point of other / Space not given." Or perhaps "Fragment" transcends its words and discourses too completely in its sanctuary of feelings and ideas.

Ashbery's language begins to thaw and coalesce in "Clepsydra," which Ashbery himself sees as a pivotal poem. As he told Kostelanetz:

> After my analytic period, I wanted to get into a synthetic period. I wanted to write a new kind of poetry after my dismembering of language. Wouldn't it be nice, I said to myself, to do a long poem that would be a long extended argument, but would have the beauty of a single word? "Clepsydra" is really a meditation on how time feels as it is passing. The title means a water clock as used in ancient Greece and China. There are a lot of images of water in that poem. It's all of a piece, like a stream.

This newfound style, more "synthetic" than Pablo Picasso's reconstructions, seems in fact to be one of the topics of "Clepsydra":

> The half-meant, half-perceived
> Motions of fronds out of idle depths that are
> Summer. And expansion into little
> draughts.
> The reply wakens easily, darting from
> Untruth to willed moment, scarcely called
> into being
> Before it swells, the way a waterfall
> Drums at different levels. Each moment
> Of utterance is the true one; likewise none
> are true,
> Only is the bounding from air to air, a
> serpentine
> Gesture which hides the truth behind a
> congruent
> Message, the way air hides the sky, is, in
> fact,
> Tearing it limb from limb this very
> moment: but
> The sky has pleaded already and this is
> about
> As graceful a kind of non-absence as either
> Has a right to expect: *whether* it's the
> form of
> Some creator who has momentarily turned
> away,
> Marrying detachment with respect, so that
> the pieces
> Are seen as parts of a spectrum,
> independent
> Yet symbolic of their spaced-out times of
> arrival;
> *Whether* on the other hand all of it is to be
> Seen as no luck. [italics added]

The cascading, serpentine sentence, descending from William Wordsworth's "Lines Composed a Few Miles Above Tintern Abbey" and "Ode: Intimations of Immortality," from Stevens' "The Auroras of Autumn," and from Proust, has displaced the linear integrity of *Some Trees* and *The Tennis Court Oath.* In "Clepsydra" the enjambments seem "half-meant, half-perceived" pauses along the way. Only in retrospect do the end words sound their momentous ideas (cause, being, time, truth, etc.). The language of philosophical assertion and of argument takes its place alongside that of spontaneous, stream-of-consciousness description—something that was ruled out, for example, in "The Instruction Manual." The "I," who in "The Skaters" was not ready to explain, is brimming with justifications in "Clepsydra," though the first-person "I am" is withheld for about five pages. The diction of "Clepsydra" is idiomatic ("the way," "in fact") as well as lyrical, and the tone serious. Perhaps one limitation of "Clepsydra" is that it aims too carefully at being the "Intimations Ode" of its day (Wordsworth is better known for his wisdom than his wit). The humor in "Clepsydra" is wry rather than coy and evasive. And the word-play ("whether" hides "weather," which translates "les temps") is self-effacing. A water clock, the clepsydra was used to time the arguments of lawyers in court. Ashbery's "Clepsydra" is itself a monumental argument: a philosopher's system, a lawyer's case, a plot summary, and a lovers' quarrel. The case tried is a divorce: that of the past from the present, the poem from the poet, and one lover from another. The question of "Clepsydra" may be put in romantic terms: "If our love has failed, was it false or unreal?" But the possibility that he "dreamt the whole thing," made up his past and his love, is ruled out in his wakeful end: "It is not a question, then, / Of having not lived in vain." Ashbery wakes in an uneasy assurance of the outside world: that of his apartment, and his past, which is realized in his own day and poem:

> What is meant is that this distant
> Image of you, the way you really are, is the test
> Of how you see yourself, and regardless of whether or not
> You hesitate, it may be assumed that you have won, that this
> Wooden and external representation
> Returns the full echo of what you meant
> With nothing left over, from that circumference now alight
> With ex-possibilities become present fact,
> [. . .]

In our postdeconstructive world, we may find it difficult to believe in this world poem without supplement. But at least we find it easier to understand the blind faith in the weather, the story of life in the world, to which we sooner or later return.

The lyrics of *The Double Dream of Spring,* which include a sestina, a collage poem, a ballad, and translations, match the formal variety of *Some Trees,* but also exhibit a new discursive range. Consider the antic opening from the sestina "Farm Implements and Rutabagas in a Landscape":

> The first of the undecoded messages read: "Popeye sits in thunder,
> Unthought of. From that shoebox of an apartment,
> From livid curtain's hue, a tangram emerges: a country."
> Meanwhile the Sea Hag was relaxing on a green couch: "How pleasant
> To spend one's vacation *en la casa de Popeye,*" she scratched
> Her cleft chin's solitary hair. She remembered spinach. [. . .]

With its antic shifts in diction, "Farm Implements" is a far cry from the mannered formality of Ashbery's early sestina "The Painter." Ashbery's source for "Farm Implements" was a Spanish cartoon strip of *Popeye* in which the Sea Hag, like Circe, changes Swee'pea into a pig. Here the only metamorphoses are the familiar one of Popeye, sitting like a Miltonic God in thunder, whose spinach restores his omnipotence. But the Sea Hag adjusts to Popeye's mood swings: "If this is all we need fear from spinach / Then I don't mind so much."

In "Soonest Mended," the most popular poem in *The Double Dream of Spring,* the antic mixtures of "Europe" and "The Skaters" are themselves mixed in with the meditative argumentation of "Fragment" and "Clepsydra" in a poem with an easygoing pathos that we will recognize as characteristic of many of Ashbery's best later poems. Consider the fatal recognition that we are only end words in someone else's wacky sestina, only dice thrown in the game:

> These then were some hazards of the course,
> Yet though we knew the course *was* hazards and nothing else
> It was still a shock when, almost a quarter of a century later,
> The clarity of the rules dawned on you for the first time.
> *They* were the players, and we who had struggled at the game
> Were merely spectators, though subject to its vicissitudes
> And moving with it out of the tearful stadium, borne on shoulders, at last.

The humor of this passage plays off its pathos. The counters aren't those of academic poetry, "they" and "I," the conventional world and the poet, but "they" and "we," those powers that be and "we" ordinary citizens who have little to say about our destiny. Twenty years earlier, in a review of Gertrude Stein's epic poem on "them," *Stanzas in Meditation,* the poet in exile praised the absence of the inclusive personal pronoun: "What a pleasant change from the eternal 'we' with which so many modern poets automatically begin each sentence, and which gives the impression that the author is sharing his every sensation with some invisible Kim Novak" (*Poetry,* 1957). By *The Double Dream of Spring* the middle-aged poet, once again part of the United States, has found a new interest in writing (rather than collaging) common American language and public discourses.

"Decoy," another more serious piece of resistance, begins with the "we" of the Declaration of Independence, whose own truths have divorced themselves from America's dream:

> We hold these truths to be self-evident:
> That ostracism, both political and moral, has
> Its place in the twentieth-century scheme of things;
> That urban chaos is the problem we have been seeing into and seeing into,
> For the factory, deadpanned by its very existence into a
> Descending code of values, has moved right across the road from total financial upheaval
> And caught regression head-on.

This nation under God, which still ostracizes those of different sexual orientation, has descended into its own moral chaos. Ashbery's adoption of public, nonlyrical discourse marks an important advance in the career of the repatriated American poet. This hybrid, confrontational style, which has left its mark on the language poets, makes its poetry not by reshaping the world but by reforming the clichés of its daily, official life ("looking into," "destined by its very nature to"). This democratization of language will lead to the sermonic history of Ashbery's declaration of poetic interdependence, "The System," in *Three Poems.*

Three Poems is Ashbery's favorite book. It is also his most important book both in the sense that it continues his project of revitalizing (not parodying) ordinary languages for the purposes of prose poetry and because it spells out, hesitantly, Ashbery's "philosophy of life and writing." *Three Poems* marks the poet's most extended and fruitful experiments with prose poetry. There are all kinds of speech and writing going on in these 118 pages: clichéd conversation, business diction, journalese, history, philosophy, sermon, graduation poetry, and so on. Moreover, the style moves from the Proustian Romantic narratives of "The New Spirit" to the more public history and homily of "The System" and the urgent reconciliations of "The Recital." Ashbery has mentioned Arthur Rimbaud, St.-John Perse, Thomas Traherne, Auden, Proust, Giorgio de Chirico, and the later Henry James as stylistic influences on these poems. Although these authors all developed endless, protean sentences, none of their work really prepares the reader for the particular excitement and pleasure that *Three Poems* brings.

Three Poems consists of two fifty-page works, "The New Spirit" and "The System," and a ten-page summation, "The Recital." "The New Spirit" is written in unindented prose blocks and prosaic verse, "The System" in prose blocks, and "The Recital" in prose paragraphs. Within *Three Poems* itself, there are a number of nearly resolved dialectical oppositions: new and old, part and whole, present and past, private and public, and physical and spiritual love. After an initial consideration of the problem of poetic selection, "The New Spirit" moves into reflections on a love affair. This reminiscence is itself reminiscent of "Clepsydra" and "Fragment," both in style and in subject matter, but it is more successful and diverse than either poem in that it modulates its language of private thought with the languages of public communication. Near the end of "The New Spirit," these reflections coalesce into a character called "the Ram," or simply "he," who in "The System" takes the podium, or pulpit, offering a religious history of the 1960's and a sermon on living out one's destiny. In "The Recital," which begins "All right. The problem is that there is no new problem," an insistent, dark argument resolves itself:

> The point was the synthesis of very simple elements in a new and strong, as opposed to old and weak, relation to one another. Why hadn't this been possible in the earlier days of experimentation, of bleak, barren living that didn't seem to be leading anywhere and

> it couldn't have mattered less? Probably because not enough of what made it up had taken on that look of worn familiarity, like pebbles polished over and over again by the sea. . . .

For Ashbery, the collages of *The Tennis Court Oath* perhaps announced themselves too insistently as avant-garde, to the exclusion of subsequent explorations. In *Three Poems,* the prosaic, demotic elements, such as the worn simile of the pebbles, are not erased but blended into Ashbery's argument so that it is impossible to separate the public from the individual spirit.

The "system" of *Three Poems* represents the physical, political, and discursive systems that determine our lives: computer systems, the solar system, the circulatory system, the traffic system, the system of government, a philosophical or religious system, and so on. Ashbery's response is not to drop out but to work and write within and against the system. The historian who opens "The System" tells us that there was a subversive principle at work: "There was, however, a residue, a kind of fiction that developed parallel to the classic truths of daily life. . . . It is this 'other tradition' which we propose to explore." The oratorical turns of phrase here mark the clearest departure in style of "The System" from the personally charged reflections of "The New Spirit." But no clear and safe distinction may be drawn between the languages of the establishment and that of the non-establishment poet. "The Other Tradition" democratizes the poetry of "the Tradition."

To represent the other tradition, Ashbery replaces the historian's discourse with the pastor's. Ashbery's preacher of the gospel of love makes an important distinction, virtually the only one in Ashbery's poetry, between "the frontal and the latent" forms of happiness. Frontal happiness, he tells us, "is experienced as a kind of sense of immediacy, even urgency; . . . Its sudden balm suffuses the soul without warning, as a kind of bloom or grace." We recognize this kind of happiness as the privileged or involuntary moments of Wordsworth or Proust. The problem with these moments is that they don't last. What follows, and what Ashbery ultimately comes to prefer, is latent happiness. If "frontal" suggests "frontal assault" or "frontal pose," "latent" seems drawn from the mysteriously autobiographical final lines of Roussel's "The View":

> Thanks to the intensity suddenly increased
> of a memory long-lived and hidden ["vivace
> et latent"] of a summer
> Already dead, already far from me, suddenly
> carried away.

Latent happiness means, first, the feeling that the past bliss is about to return, like summer:

> We all know those periods of balmy weather in early spring, sometimes even before spring has officially begun: days or even a few hours when the air seems suffused with an unearthly tenderness, as though love were about to start, now, at this moment, on an endless journey put off since the beginning of time.

Ashbery in fact fell in love with David Kermani, who has remained his companion, while writing "The System." This Eliotic "mid-winter spring" may also be taken as the traces and influences of the lost moment that have permeated the text of the present. In the following tumultuous rhetorical question of "The System," Ashbery's preacher presents us with his article of faith:

> For they never would have been able to capture the emanations from that special point of life if they were not meant to do something with them, weave them into the pattern of the days that come after, sunlit or plunged in shadow as they may be, but each with the identifying scarlet thread that runs through the whole warp and woof of the design . . .

The claim that "this second kind of happiness is merely a fleshed-out, realized version of that ideal first kind . . ." is borne out most strongly in *Three Poems* itself, which is a brilliantly fleshed-out version of "Clepsydra." As "the faithful reflection of the idealistic concept that started us along this path, but a reflection which is truer than the original because more suited to us, and whose shining perspectives we can feel and hold," the full-blown latent happiness points forward to Ashbery's self-portrait in the convex mirror of the globe. The superiority of this model of latent happiness, whether or not one subscribes to Proustian or Wordsworthian consolations of the past, is that it is worldly and textual, rather than visionary and hyperlinguistic. Ashbery's romanticism is a means to an encompassing realism by which we make sense of ourselves in the context of the world.

In 1972, after new owners took over *Art News,* Ashbery found himself without a job as an art critic. He took a teaching job at Brooklyn College in 1974. But the ending (or interruption) of his career as an art critic encouraged Ashbery to "realize" his art criticism into poetry. The result was his best-known long poem, "Self-Portrait in a Convex Mirror." The volume containing the title poem, dedicated to Kermani, won Ashbery three major poetry prizes upon its appearance in 1975—the Pulitzer Prize, the National Book Award, and the National Book Critics Circle Award—and moved Ashbery, in many people's eyes, from "the other tradition" into "*the* tradition." Ashbery himself does not like the poem, which he finds too conventional—the apparently clear antipodes to the apparently obscure "Europe." He began "Self-Portrait" in Provincetown in February 1973, and finished in what he told me was "three months of not very inspired writing." Nevertheless, the unemployed art critic succeeded perfectly at what he set out to accomplish.

Part of Ashbery's difficulty with the poem is its pretext or premise. "Self-Portrait in a Convex Mirror" reads like a critical essay, a reflection on a small but remarkable painting by Parmigianino, an early mannerist whose distortions anticipated the surrealists. In his *Self-Portrait in a Convex Mirror* (1523–1524), Parmigianino painted his reflection in a convex barber's mirror onto a ball of wood so that his head, at the virtual center of the round painting, is framed by the elongated hand in the foreground or at the circumference. As Parmigianino's painting mirrors his reflection, Ashbery's poem reflects Parmigianino's painting. When Ashbery first saw the painting in 1959, he was studying Roussel, whose long poem "La Vue" (The View), with its immensely detailed and extended description of a convex scene depicted in the "ball of glass" on a pen holder, must have encouraged Ashbery's elongated meditation on Parmigianino's ten-inch painting. Ashbery begins the poem as an art critic:

> As Parmigianino did it, the right hand
> Bigger than the head, thrust at the viewer
> And swerving easily away, as though to
> protect
> What it advertises.

Ashbery "does it" here by eliding his grammatical subject ("[I want to do it] as Parmigianino did it . . .") in favor of an adverb, the grammatical indicator of "manner" (from "manus": hand). "As," the manner, protects the matter, the nearly erased "As[hbery]." Unlike the erasures of "Europe," this elision passes almost undetected. The poem and painting illustrate a paradox: the head moves the hand that draws the head. All the important relations in "Self-Portrait in a Convex Mirror" align themselves around the central head and the circumferential hand: depth and surface, matter and manner, signified and signifiers, whole and parts, past and present, present and future, and self and other. In fact, we may align more of the fluid images of "Self-Portrait" with either the head or the hand: "light [head] behind windblown fog and sand [hand]"; "The city [head] falling with its beautiful suburbs [hand]"; "There is room for one bullet [head] in the chamber [hand]."

Ashbery probes the otherness, or convexity, of the self-portrait in six stanzas or globes, which cover topics deliberately, like a well-shaped essay: (1) the confining present, (2) the receding past, (3) the convex future, (4) the otherness of the painting, (5) the otherness of the city and history, (6) and the otherness of creation itself. For Ashbery, the self exists only in the convex mirror of the world, understood spatially as other people, or temporally as the history of one's frustrated projects. Each stanza break ruptures the mannered world of the poem. Consider the break between the first and second globes:

> You will stay on, restive, serene in
> Your gesture which is neither embrace nor
> warning
> But which holds something of both in pure
> Affirmation that doesn't affirm anything.
>
> The balloon pops, the attention
> Turns dully away. Clouds
> In the puddle stir up into sawtoothed
> fragments.
> I think of the friends
> Who came to see me, of what yesterday
> Was like. [. . .]

The opening stanza, which concerns the imprisonment of the self within its self-portrayals, ends with a self-reflexive doctrine of "pure poetry," that the only subject matter of a poem is itself. In *An Apologie for Poetrie,* Sir Philip Sidney said that the poet "never affirmeth" since he never makes the reader take his fictions for the truth. But with this negative affirmation the boredom of incomprehension sets in. With the introduction of a new subject, the seamless global stanza bursts. Ashbery here puns on "pop art," particularly that of Roy Lichtenstein, who enlarged, or "blew up," the comic strip with its balloons of speech and clouds of thought. Each stanza break, each new "subject" in "Self-Portrait in a Convex Mirror," means the death of the old. In this mannered, perfect world, the only changes possible are violent.

In the last, longest globe, the critical patience has run out in an exasperated, impassioned recognition of the otherness of anybody's self-image:

> Is there anything
> To be serious about beyond this otherness
> That gets included in the most ordinary
> Forms of daily activity, changing everything
> Slightly and profoundly, and tearing the
> matter
> Of creation, any creation, not just artistic
> creation
> Out of our hands, to install it on some
> monstrous, near
> Peak, too close to ignore, too far
> For one to intervene? This otherness, this
> "Not-being-us" is all there is to look at
> In the mirror. [. . .]

The adverbs of manner ("Slightly and profoundly"), one line's triplication of "creation," the pregnant end words ("otherness," "everything," "matter," "this"), the imagery ("Peak" as the hand), the wordplay ("monstrous" means "sign"), and the final response with its existential vocabulary, all charge this passage with Ashbery's tragic eloquence. Any reader skeptical of Ashbery's "merit," or convinced of his "willful obscurity," may very well be converted by "Self-Portrait in a Convex Mirror." Despite the monochromatic limits of its ironic and elegiac tone, the poem is capable of both power and subtlety, and succeeds in both its conceptions and its manners.

While there is little formal variety in the free-verse lyrics of *Self-Portrait in a Convex Mirror,* there is a pleasant range of styles, such as the following narrative from "Worsening Situation":

> One day a man called while I was out
> And left this message: "You got the whole
> thing wrong
> From start to finish. Luckily, there's still
> time
> To correct the situation, but you must act
> fast.
> See me at your earliest convenience. And
> please
> Tell no one of this. Much besides your life
> depends on it."
> I thought nothing of it at the time. Lately
> I've been looking at old-fashioned plaids,
> fingering
> Starched white collars, wondering whether
> there's a way
> To get them really white again. My wife
> Thinks I'm in Oslo—Oslo, France, that is.

The coy figure skater of "The Skaters" and the explaining prophet of "The System" are both upended by this deadpan speaker, benumbed with capitalist anxiety. Deities here communicate through answering machines rather than burning bushes. The anticonfessional poet's hilarious final confession is doubly nonreferential: both "Oslo, France" and the gay poet's "wife" are off the map. This confidentiality, much like Robinson Crusoe's wish that Friday were a woman in Elizabeth Bishop's "Crusoe in England," is as good a self-portrait as anything in the volume.

The opening poem of *Self-Portrait in a Convex Mirror,* "As One Put Drunk into the Packet-Boat" (the title is taken from Andrew Marvell), introduces a new musicality into Ashbery's verse (the accents have been added; the ellipsis is Ashbery's):

> I tríed each thíng, only sóme were immórtal
> and frée.
> Élsewhere wé are as sítting ín a pláce where
> súnlight
> Fílters dówn, a líttle át a tíme,
> Wáiting for sómeone to cóme. Hársh órds
> are spóken,
> As the sún yéllows the gréen of the máple
> trée. . . .

The delicate interweaving of two- and three-beat measures marks a departure from the prosaic cadences of *Three Poems.* In fact, Ashbery's ellipses reveal that this first stanza should be read as a written fragment of this new style, as the next lines confirm: "So this was all, but obscurely / I felt the stirrings of new breath in the pages." This documentary distancing, which Ashbery developed in "Europe," now occurs without calling too much attention to itself.

At the other stylistic extreme, "Scheherazade" begins with a shorthand, gnarled scene description:

> Unsupported by reason's enigma
> Water collects in squared stone catch basins.
> The land is dry. Under it moves
> The water. Fish live in the wells. The
> leaves,
> A concerned green, are scrawled on the
> light. Bad
> Bindweed and rank ragweed somehow forget
> to flourish here.
> An inexhaustible wardrobe has been placed
> at the disposal
> Of each new occurrence. It can be itself now.

Unlike the natural, seasonal music of "As One Put Drunk into the Packet-Boat," these lines are strikingly artificial. The sentences seem too short or too long for the lines. The discordant intrusion of "Bad / Bindweed and rank ragweed" registers its absence. The Audenesque allegorical abstractions ("Unsupported by reason's enigma" and "at the disposal / Of each new occurrence") and the minimalist enigma ("It can be itself now") suspend our visualization of the landscape. No luxurious fairy-tale kingdom, this scene offers meager fare for the reader's eyes and ears. Yet the messy style of these lines is more experimental and ambitious than the free-verse opening of "As One Put Drunk into the Packet-Boat."

Houseboat Days (1977) contains some of Ashbery's best short poems to date. "Street Musicians," which opens the book, is a moving elegy; "Wet Casements" (my own favorite) is a protest by the now-famous poet against his encroaching publicity; "The Other Tradition" supplements the history of the avant-garde given in "The System"; "Pyrography," commissioned by the U.S. Department of the Interior for its bicentennial exhibition, explores America's westward expansion, burning its way across the continent; the antic "Daffy Duck in Hollywood" sketches L-the cartoonlike world of American materialism; "And *Ut Pictura Poesis* Is Her Name" (borrowing Horace's dictum that a poem is like a painting) and "What Is Poetry" respond to creative-writing students, whom Ashbery had begun to teach, who want to know what poetry is, now, and how to write it, now. "Syringa" mythologizes the origin and the loss of song.

The only relative disappointment of the volume is, surprisingly, its long poem "Fantasia on 'The Nut-Brown Maid.' " Ashbery's "Fantasia" follows the fifteenth-century anonymous ballad stanza for stanza, often incorporating the language of its mannered debate. "The Nut-Brown Maid" is a courtly ballad in which He and She debate the legendary unfaithfulness of women by assuming the respective roles of the banished lover and his faithful nut-brown maid. The argument of "Fantasia," as in the ballad, is intricate and incremental—much like that of Ashbery's earlier amorous argument, "Fragment." It is a clear departure or retreat from the fluent mannerisms of "Self-Portrait in a Convex Mirror." A stanza from "Fantasia" will illustrate how little Ashbery is willing to trade on his patented fluid style:

> Be it right or wrong, these men among
> Others in the park, all those years in the
> cold,
> Are a plain kind of thing: bands
> Of acanthus and figpeckers. At
> The afternoon closing you walk out
> Of the dream crowding the walls and out
> Of life or whatever filled up
> Those days and seemed to be life
> You borrowed its colors, the drab ones
> That are so popular now, though only
> For a minute, and extracted a fashion
> That wasn't really there. You are
> Going, I from your thought rapidly
> To the green wood go, alone, a banished
> man.

By the time we reach the stubborn, vaguely pornographic syllables "bands / Of acanthus and figpeckers," we know we are no longer listening to the seductive rhythms of "Self-Portrait": "thrust at the viewer / And swerving easily away." It doesn't necessarily follow that "Fantasia" is inferior to "Self-Portrait," rather that it will not be preferred by the same readers or enjoyed for the same reasons. "Fantasia" is another world, a diversion from the relentless topicality of much contemporary poetry. Those who fancy the medieval and Renaissance subtleties of dialogue and argument will prefer "Fragment" and "Fantasia"; those who love propelled Romantic meditations will choose "Self-Portrait in a Convex Mirror" and "A Wave."

If no readers have thus far championed "Fantasia," many have applauded the short poems of *Houseboat Days.* The seductively resistant "Wet Casements," for instance, attracts readers by the very force of the writer's demand for privacy. The poem begins with a rare epigraph taken from Franz Kafka's unfinished story "Wedding Preparations in the Country" (1951): "When Eduard Raban, coming along the passage, walked into the open doorway, he saw that it was raining. It was not raining much." What interests Ashbery about this "passage" is that the reader sees through Raban's eyes. This voyeuristic pleasure can turn sour when the defining gaze of another is turned on us, so that we see ourselves as merely someone else's "correct impressions" of us. Many labels—"intentionally obscure," "fraudulent," "New York school poet," "canonical"—have been attached to the name Ashbery. Once an "Ashbery" poem slips out of the poet's grasp, it may be kept, read, and evaluated by any stranger who "carried that name around in his wallet / For years as the wallet crumbled and bills slid in / And out of it." Ashbery's response to this vicissitude of publication is anger and determination:

> I want that information very much today,
>
> Can't have it, and this makes me angry.
> I shall use my anger to build a bridge like
> that
> Of Avignon, on which people may dance for
> the feeling
> Of dancing on a bridge. I shall at last see my
> complete face
> Reflected not in the water but in the worn
> stone floor of my bridge.
>
> I shall keep to myself.
> I shall not repeat others' comments about
> me.

The bridge at Avignon, like Kafka's story, is unfinished. So too, the critical commentary on Ashbery will remain incomplete. For the time being, people may dance to his music.

But the "complete face," still under construction, is for Ashbery's eyes alone. Even the final, seemingly confessional couplet is in the discourse of a journal resolution in which the doubled "I" remains apart from "myself" and "me." "Wet Casements" covers the same territory as "Self-Portrait in a Convex Mirror" more briefly and with more power.

"Syringa" (compare Pan's syrinx), arguably Ashbery's best lyric, tells the story of Orpheus in the mannered style of Ovid (or Jean Cocteau) rather than in the tragic style of Virgil. The poem begins casually:

> Orpheus liked the glad personal quality
> Of the things beneath the sky. Of course,
> Eurydice was a part
> Of this. Then one day, everything changed.
> He rends
> Rocks into fissures with lament. Gullies,
> hummocks
> Can't withstand it. The sky shudders from
> one horizon
> To the other, almost ready to give up
> wholeness.
> Then Apollo quietly told him: "Leave it all
> on earth.
> Your lute, what point? Why pick at a dull
> pavan few care to
> Follow, except a few birds of dusty feather,
> Not vivid performances of the past." But
> why not?
> All other things must change too.

Eurydice is taken for granted here in this serio-comic apocalypse, which reminds one that Ovid's Orpheus, who taught men how to love young boys, was the mythical inventor not only of elegy but of homosexuality. The real test is not the absence of Eurydice but the presence of Apollo, who reminds the songster of the burden of the past. Harold Bloom had used "Fragment" in *The Anxiety of Influence* (1973) to illustrate how the Stevens of "Le Monocle de Mon Oncle" (1918) sounded more like Ashbery than vice versa, and had placed Ashbery in his canon of "strong poets" along with Whitman, Stevens, and Hart Crane. Ashbery's response, again, is that the past—whether it is a memory or a tradition—is latent in the present. The mistake is to try to recapture the past (in the manner of Orpheus or of Proust), as either a memory or a style, since the past will soon enough capture us:

> Stellification
> Is for the few, and comes about much later
> When all record of these people and their
> lives
> Has disappeared into libraries, onto
> microfilm.
> A few are still interested in them. "But
> what about
> So-and-so?" is still asked on occasion. But
> they lie
> Frozen and out of touch until an arbitrary
> chorus
> Speaks of a totally different incident with a
> similar name
> In whose tale are hidden syllables
> Of what happened so long before that
> In some small town, one indifferent
> summer.

This wonderful passage (I have quoted only a fragment) illustrates the intelligence, clarity, humor, and nostalgic mystery of Ashbery at his best. Long gone into the technologized library crypts, only a few poets surface, and even then anonymously, from oblivion: "But what about / So-and-so?" As Ashbery instructs: "You can't say it that way any more." The old songs reverberate without royalties in current numbers, as Ashbery's representative summer echoes, again, the final lines of Roussel's "The View." Canonization is arbitrary (why Ashbery and not Roussel?) and for the few. But Ashbery's work is so diverse partly because he has not confined his reading (or criticism) to those on top of the charts. We should take the same approach in our reading of his own rich work.

In 1978 "Syringa" was set to music by Elliott Carter, one of Ashbery's favorite composers. Ashbery's poem, sung by a female mezzosoprano, was scored along with various Greek fragments on the myth of Orpheus, sung by a male bass. The conversational, competitive simultaneity of this piece is characteristic of Carter's work, which influenced

Ashbery's "Litany," the opening poem of *As We Know.* "Litany" runs for seventy pages in two parallel columns. The beginning stanzas illustrate the added dimensions of this parallelism:

For someone like me	*So this must be a*
	hole
The simple things	*Of cloud*
Like having toast or	*Mandate or trap*
Going to church are	*But haze that casts*
Kept in one place.	*The milk of*
	enchantment
Like having wine	*Over the whole town,*
and cheese	
The parents of the	*Its scenery, whatever*
town	*Could be happening*
Pissing elegantly	*Behind tall hedges*
escape knowledge	*Of dark, lissome*
Once and for all.	*knowledge.*
The Snapdragons	*The brown lines*
consumed in a	*persist*
wind	
Of fire and rage far	*In explicit sex*
over	*Matters like these*
The streets as they	*No one can care*
end.	*about,*
The casual purring	*"Noone." That is I've*
of a donkey	*said it*
Rouses me from my	*Before and no one*
accounts:	
What given, what	*Remembers except*
gifts. The air	*that elf*
Stands straight up	
like a tail.	

He spat on the flowers.

The visionary obliquity of the right-hand, italicized column slants away from the upstanding, plainspoken intimacy of "someone like me" in the left column. The voices, however, soon become indistinguishable, like those of "Fantasia." The short lines of either side result in surprising, ominous pauses, as though they were running up against an invisible wall. The scene, depicted by the appearance of the poem on the page, is Main Street, U.S.A., with the town parents "pissing" (or "passing") elegantly and ritually along the middle blank space while escaping the carnal knowledge of the hedges of print on either side. The two-columned poem has various analogues or parallels: the two eyes or ears, consciousness and self-consciousness, text and commentary or translation, twin phalluses or columns of figures, newspaper or Bible columns of print, "simultaneous but independent monologues" (as Ashbery describes them in an introductory note), and so on. Ashbery told Peter Stitt, "I once half-jokingly said that my object was to direct the reader's attention to the white space between the columns." This white space at the core of the poem represents ineffable, unspeakable knowledge that keeps conversations and texts from intersecting. Following the terminology of "The System," we may think of the *"hole / Of Cloud"* as a frontal moment that has absconded like an *"elf"* (compare self) into the past but that still exerts its latent pressure. It may also mark the eclipse or absence of God. Ashbery originally titled this poem "The Great Litany," after Thomas Cranmer's Episcopal service in the Book of Common Prayer, where the minister's supplications and congregational responses are printed in italic and roman type respectively.

All the poems in *As We Know* are preoccupied with place or space. A series of one-liners, the diminutive counterpoints to "Litany," make the most of their seven-by-nine-inch pages:

I HAD THOUGHT THINGS
WERE GOING ALONG WELL

But I was mistaken.

The sobering visual and narrative humor of this poem relies on a double afterthought: that correcting one's mistaken projection about how things were going is also a mistake, since one's knowledge of "things" in the universal vacuum is so paltry that nothing can be concluded. The lyrics in *As We Know* are generally conducted in hushed tones that avoid the gregariousness of "Litany." There is a sense of time running out in these haunted poems that results in a minimalist domestic economy, as in these lines from the volume's title poem:

The light that was shadowed then
Was seen to be our lives,
Everything about us that love might wish to
    examine,
Then put away for a certain length of time,
    until
The whole is to be reviewed, and we turned
Toward each other, to each other.
The way we had come was all we could see
And it crept up on us, embarrassed
That there is so much to tell now, really now.

This intimate new style is minimal in discursive range, narration ("then," "until"), vocabulary, figure ("it crept up on us": age, a ghost), play ("reviewed" book), and revision. In this tacit manner, the smallest and commonest words take on philosophical and religious import, such as "all" for totality, "as" and "way" for our manner of speaking and behaving, and "it" for latent presence. Aside from "As We Know," there are several endearing and fascinating poems in the volume, including "Many Wagons Ago," "Haunted Landscape," "Flowering Death," "Knocking Around," "Train Rising Out of the Sea," and "This Configuration." Although the interior mode of the poems in *As We Know* makes it difficult for them to rival either the ringing periods of "Clepsydra" or "Syringa," at least one poem in this volume, "Tapestry," ranks among Ashbery's best:

It is difficult to separate the tapestry
From the room or loom which takes
    precedence over it.
For it must always be frontal and yet to one
    side.

It insists on this picture of "history"
In the making, because there is no way out
    of the punishment
It proposes: sight blinded by sunlight.
The seeing taken in with what is seen
In an explosion of sudden awareness of its
    formal splendor.

The best-known tapestry for depicting " 'history' in the making," the seventy-meter-long Bayeux Tapestry (ca. 1082), which Ashbery had seen in France, narrates the Norman Conquest, climaxing in the Battle of Hastings, where Harold is shown blinded by an arrow stitch to The eye. It is as difficult, now, to separate the Norman Conquest from its depiction as it is to separate the tapestry (and "Tapestry") from our responses to it—"The seeing taken in with what is seen." "Tapestry" is a dazzling display of Ashbery's ability to compose on several fronts simultaneously: self-reflexive, aesthetic, political, philosophical (Plato's cave), and personal. This twenty-two line poem, like the twenty-page "Self-Portrait in a Convex Mirror," examines what art means, and only a poet who has studied and written about art for years could have written it.

Ashbery resumed writing art criticism in 1979, for *New York* magazine, and in the early 1980's he also wrote for *Newsweek*. Around this time, Ashbery purchased a Victorian-era house in Hudson, a small town in his native eastern New York State. These previously inhabited rooms seem to lend their own atmosphere to his next volume, *Shadow Train* (1981), a boxlike sequence of fifty poems, four quatrains each. These *quatrains* are "frontal and yet to one side" in that, unlike the sestets of sonnet sequences, they evade closure. What was "latent happiness" now looks more like anxiety in these poems. "The Pursuit of Happiness," for instance, ominously foreshadows some event that never happens:

It came about that there was no way of
    passing
Between the twin partitions that presented
A unified façade, that of a suburban
    shopping mall
In April. One turned, as one does, to other
    interests

Such as the tides in the Bay of Fundy.
    Meanwhile there was one
Who all unseen came creeping at this scale
    of visions
Like the gigantic specter of a cat towering
    over tiny mice
About to adjourn the town meeting due to
    the shadow,

The talismanic words of *As We Know*—"It came about," "way," "one"—are still in force. What is different here is the long-shot perspective, which takes in both the "gigantic specter" of the storm cloud and the "tiny" suburban Americans pursuing shelter. This perspective results in an ironically distanced narrative in which "one," rather than "we," "you," or "I," remains aloof as the cat. The vast scale of these stanzas removes us from the intimacy of *As We Know.* The humor of the tale is similarly "overshadowed" by its ominousness, as is its political discourse. "The Pursuit of Happiness" is a chilling declaration of dependence, but it may move us no more than it has moved its narrator.

The eerie objectivity of these minimalist building blocks can sometimes produce some fascinating special effects, as in "Paradoxes and Oxymorons":

> This poem is concerned with language on a
> very plain level.
> Look at it talking to you. You look out a
> window
> Or pretend to fidget. You have it but you
> don't have it.
> You miss it, it misses you. You miss each
> other.
>
> The poem is sad because it wants to be
> yours, and cannot.
> What's a plain level? It is that and other
> things,
> Bringing a system of them into play. Play?
> Well, actually, yes, but I consider play to be
>
> A deeper outside thing, a dreamed role-
> pattern,
> As in the division of grace these long
> August days
> Without proof. Open-ended. And before you
> know
> It gets lost in the stream and chatter of
> typewriters.
>
> It has been played once more. I think you
> exist only
> To tease me into doing it, on your level, and
> then you aren't there
> Or have adopted a different attitude. And
> the poem
> Has set me softly down beside you. The
> poem is you.

It is easy to see why this wonderful poem has been frequently anthologized. Here, the mixture of discourses—pedantic, romantic, sentimental, conversational—adds dimension after dimension to its plain levels. The author himself enters the poem, paradoxically, for a brief interview. What charges this poem, however, is its playful lover's discourse. A substitution of "I" or "me" for "it" will disclose "Paradoxes and Oxymorons" for the love song it is. Ashbery is often reserved and defensive, as when addressing the "critic," but he is equally persuasive and moving when dreaming of the "reader," his erotic double. Although *Shadow Train* is dwarfed by earlier volumes such as *Three Poems* or *As We Know,* it may be the right place to begin for the reader who wants to learn Ashbery's alphabet.

In the spring of 1982 Ashbery underwent major surgery for a nearly fatal spinal infection, and for a few years afterward he walked with a cane. Around the end of that year Ashbery began "A Wave," which he finished in about two months. This long title poem helped make *A Wave* Ashbery's best book since *Self-Portrait in a Convex Mirror.* Of Ashbery's long poems, "A Wave," with its surging free-verse stanzas, resembles "Self-Portrait" most closely, but it is free from the "subject matter" that, although merely a meditative pretext, confines the tone of "Self-Portrait in a Convex Mirror" within relatively narrow parameters. A wave is a fluid convexity ("wave" and "convex" are cognates), and that fluidity circulates through recurrent phases within the poem, from wake to wave to wait to wave again, as we see from the beginning:

> To pass through pain and not know it,
> A car door slamming in the night.
> To emerge on an invisible terrain.
>
> So the luck of speaking out
> A little too late came to be worshipped in
> various guises:
> A mute actor, a future saint intoxicated
> with the idea of martyrdom;

And our landscape came to be as it is today:
Partially out of focus, some of it too near, the middle distance
A haven of serenity and unreachable, with all kinds of nice
People and plants waking and stretching, calling
Attention to themselves with every artifice of which the human
Genre is capable. And they called it our home.

No one came to take advantage of these early
Reverses, no doorbell rang;
Yet each day of the week, once it had arrived, seemed the threshold
Of love and desperation again. At night it sang
In the black trees: *My mindless, oh my mindless, oh.*
And it could be that it was Tuesday, with dark, restless clouds
And puffs of white smoke against them, and below, the wet streets
That seem so permanent, and all of a sudden the scene changes:
It's another idea, a new conception, something submitted
A long time ago, that only now seems about to work
To destroy at last the ancient network
Of letters, diaries, ads for civilization.

The poem passes through a complete cycle here, with each new phase bringing a new scene and cast. The first unfinished sentence, with its Dickinsonian infinitives, presents us with the climactic end of an affair and its immediate wake. The next stanza gives us not the "morning after" but the dawn of civilization, an allegorical fair field, or landscape painting, full of folk. With the third stanza, we find ourselves in a protracted wait, along with the lover on the rebound. When the doorbell rings, however, the wave appears not as a lover but as a conceptual revolution that swamps our current ways of seeing the world. A wave may be a new (or renewed) love, a childhood crisis, a way of thinking, a brush with death, a new president, poem, or artistic movement. Ashbery did not consciously compose "A Wave" by phases, but the second-natured phases of this rapidly written poem must have allowed him to concentrate on the differences in manner that each transition brings. As we might expect, we miss the playful wit of "The Skaters" or "Litany," but we find in its place an unparalleled adventuresomeness in Ashbery's coming to terms with art, life, and love. The swelling crest of "A Wave" contains Ashbery's most moving writing since "Syringa."

The best lyrics of *A Wave* think through American discourses and languages rather than simply parody them, as in the powerful "Down by the Station, Early in the Morning":

It all wears out. I keep telling myself this, but
I can never believe me, though others do. Even things do.
And the things they do. Like the rasp of silk, or a certain
Glottal stop in your voice as you are telling me how you
Didn't have time to brush your teeth but gargled with Listerine
Instead. Each is a base one might wish to touch once more.

Before dying.

As the only alternative to toothpaste is Listerine, there is no way out of threadbare conversations, which nevertheless may be as charged with meaning as a Proustian rasp of silk. The intimate meditative minimalism of *As We Know* ("It all wears out"; "And the things they do") is here enlivened by the idiomatic undertones of *Three Poems.* Ashbery makes the worn-out figure of touching all the bases of a topic his own with the sentimental fragment "want to touch once more" and the suddenly frank "Before dying." Like "A Wave," "Down by the Station" (the title is from a children's train song) involves a cathartic interruption, which is also (like Listerine) a purification. The purgative third and last stanza dazzles with a moving economy:

As the wrecking ball burst through the wall
with the bookshelves
Scattering the works of famous authors as
well as those
Of more obscure ones, and books with no
author, letting in
Space, and an extraneous babble from the
street
Confirming the new value the hollow core
has again, the light
From the lighthouse that protects as it
pushes us away.

The shocking rupture of the wrecking ball, after the second devastating stanza "break," upends but purifies the library with the languages of the tribe. The marker, "babble," gathers the crypt words "Babel," "bubble," "rabble," and "rubble," all of which speak their piece. The convex "hollow core," emptied by this catharsis (opening an apartment window onto the noisy street), sends out its own protective light, the "shield of a greeting," as Ashbery described Parmigianino's stylish gesture. The difficulty we have in fixing the stance of this passage—apocalyptic, moving, optimistic, and reflexive—is compounded by the split perspective of the reader / writer both inside the apartment and outside on the street. But this split perspective is characteristic of Ashbery's homey privacy. Ashbery has set us down beside him—"On the outside looking out," he says in a preceding poem ("But What is the Reader to Make of This?").

A Wave won Yale's Bollingen Prize in 1984, and the next year Ashbery received a MacArthur Prize Fellowship, which allowed him the leisure of writing for several years without teaching. Also in 1985, Ashbery published *Selected Poems,* retrieving from among nearly forty years of poetry the work he wished to be remembered by. Ashbery then sold a vanload of his surviving papers to the Houghton Library at Harvard, some of which were gathered from the basement of his recently deceased mother's home in Sodus. These cumulative savings, in the face of losses, helped fund Ashbery's next published volume, *April Galleons* (1987).

Though there is no long poem in *April Galleons,* several of its lyrics equal those of *A Wave* in the pleasure they afford the reader: "April Galleons," "Finnish Rhapsody," "Vetiver," "Dreams of Adulthood," "Winter Weather Advisory," and "One Coat of Paint." In the Thoreauvian prose poem "The Ice Storm," Ashbery finds another way to make prose new. The allegory of the [p]rose at the center of this I-storm is lucidly unassuming:

> Today I found a rose in full bloom in the wreck of the garden, all the living and sentience but also the sententiousness drained out of it. What remained was like a small flower in the woods, too pale and sickly to notice. No, sickly isn't the right word, the thing was normal and healthy by its own standards, and thriving merrily along its allotted path toward death. Only we hold it up to some real and abject notion of what a living organism ought to be and paint it as a scarecrow that frightens birds away (presumably) but isn't able to frighten itself away. Oh, no, it's far too clever for that! But our flower, the one we saw, really had no need of us to justify its blooming where it did. So we ought to think about our own position on the path. Will it ever be anything more than that of pebble? I wonder.

As the former minister Ralph Waldo Emerson said of the rhodora, "Beauty is its own excuse for being." Ashbery's message is that commentators (on roses or prose poems) are as self-reliantly transient as their subjects. This lay preacher, who (as in the later poems of Auden or Eliot) has been speaking regularly in Ashbery's later poetry, has here the garrulousness and self-betraying obstinacy of "Litany," which domesticates the Proustian character of *Three Poems.*

"Obviously," the narrator of the title poem of *April Galleons* concludes, "It was time to be off, in another / Direction." Since *April Galleons,* Ashbery has written the longest verse poem of his career, "Flowchart," and another volume's worth of short poems. He gave the Charles Eliot Norton lectures at Harvard during the 1989–1990 academic year, and also read his poetry in Japan, Sweden, and the Soviet Union. He edited an eclectic anthology of poetry, *The Best American Poetry: 1988,* which includes language poets alongside Iowa creative-writing graduates. Ashbery has resumed teaching, this time at Bard College, near his home in Hudson.

In the prose coda to "Fantasia," Ashbery offers us one good reason for living: "Always there was something to see, something going on, *for the historical past owed it toitself, our historical present.*" The historical present of Ashbery's ongoing work has been marked by changes. His less-popular books, *The Tennis Court Oath* and *Shadow Train,* were each followed by successful departures from their norms, *Rivers and Mountains* and *A Wave.* More significantly, Ashbery has resisted the temptation to reproduce his popular favorite, "Self-Portrait in a Convex Mirror." Yet nobody in American literature has written so many fine long poems. Rather than settling for an essayistic familiarity (as the later Auden often did), Ashbery has continued to experiment, and his work maintains a productive difficulty. The many changes in Ashbery's poetry, however, were not dictated merely by his own or by other poets' work. As powerfully as any poet of his generation, Ashbery has both represented and resisted postwar American history from the vantage point of someone on the outside looking out. We owe it to ourselves, in turn, to keep reading Ashbery's prospective representations.

Selected Bibliography

WORKS OF JOHN ASHBERY

POETRY

Turnadot and Other Poems, (New York: Tibor de Nagy Gallery, 1953).

Some Trees, (New Haven, Conn.: Yale University Press, 1956).

The Tennis Court Oath, (Middletown, Conn.: Wesleyan University Press, 1962).

Rivers and Mountains, (New York: Holt, Rinehart, and Winston, 1966).

The Double Dream of Spring, (New York: E.P. Dutton, 1970).

Three Poems, (New York: Viking Press, 1972).

Self-Portrait in a Convex Mirror, (New York: Viking Press, 1975).

The Vermont Notebook, (Santa Barbara, Calif.: Black Sparrow Press, 1975).

Houseboat Days, (New York: Viking Press, 1977).

As We Know, (New York: Viking Press, 1979).

Shadow Train, (New York: Viking Press, 1981).

A Wave, (New York: Viking Press, 1984).

Selected Poems, (New York: Viking Penguin, 1985).

April Galleons, (New York: Viking Penguin, 1987).

OTHER WORKS

A Nest of Ninnies, With James Schuyler (New York: E.P. Dutton, 1969).

Three Plays, (Calais, Vt.: Z Press, 1978).

The Best American Poetry, 1988, Edited by John Ashbery (New York: Macmillan, 1988).

"A Reminiscence," in *Homage to Frank O'Hara,* Edited by Bill Berkson and Joe LeSueur (Bolinas, Calif.: Big Sky Bolinas, 1988).

Reported Sightings: Art Chronicles, 1957–1987, Edited by David Bergman (New York: Alfred A. Knopf, 1989).

BIBLIOGRAPHY

Kermani, David, *John Ashbery: A Comprehensive Bibliography,* (New York: Garland, 1976).

MANUSCRIPT PAPERS

The Houghton Library, Harvard University, Cambridge, Massachusetts, is currently cataloging Ashbery's manuscripts and correspondence through 1985.

BIOGRAPHICAL AND CRITICAL STUDIES

Altieri, Charles, "John Ashbery: Discursive Rhetoric Within a Poetics of Thinking," In his *Self and Sensibility in Contemporary American Poetry* (Cambridge: Cambridge University Press, 1984) 132–165.

Auden, W. H., "Foreword," In *Some Trees* (New Haven: Yale University Press, 1956) 11–16.

Blasing, Mutlu Konuk, "John Ashbery: Parodying the Paradox," In *American Poetry: The Rhetoric of Its Forms* (New Haven: Yale University Press, 1987) 200–213.

Bloom, Harold, "The Breaking of Form," In his *Deconstruction & Criticism* (New York: Continuum, 1979) 1–38.

Bloom, Harold, "Measuring the Canon: John Ashbery's 'Wet Casements' and 'Tapestry,'" In his *Agon: Towards a Theory of Revisionism* (New York: Oxford University Press, 1982) 270–289.

Bloom, Harold, *Modern Critical Views: John Ashbery,* (New York: Chelsea House, 1985).

Bromwich, David, "John Ashbery," *Raritan* 5: 36–58 (Spring 1986).

Breslin, Paul, "Warpless and Woofless Subtleties: John Ashbery and 'Bourgeois Discourse,'" In his *The Psy-*

cho-Political Muse: American Poetry Since the Fifties (Chicago: University of Chicago Press, 1987) 211–235.

Costello, Bonnie, "John Ashbery and the Idea of the Reader," *Contemporary Literature* 23: 493–514 (Fall 1982).

Davidson, Michael, "Languages of Post-Modernism," *Chicago Review* 27: 11–22 (Summer 1975).

Donoghue, Denis, "John Ashbery," In his *Reading America: Essays on American Literature* (New York: Alfred A. Knopf, 1987) 302–319.

Fredman, Stephen, "'He Chose to Include': John Ashbery's *Three Poems*," In his *Poet's Prose: The Crisis in American Verse* (New York: Cambridge University Press, 1983) 99–133.

Holden, Jonathan, "Syntax and the Poetry of John Ashbery," In his *The Rhetoric of the Contemporary Lyric* (Bloomington: Indiana University Press, 1980) 98–111.

Hollander, John, "The Poetry of Restitution," *Yale Review* 70: 161–186 (Winter 1981).

Howard, Richard, "John Ashbery," In his *Alone with America: Essays on the Art of Poetry in the United States Since 1950* (New York: Atheneum, 1980) 25–56.

Kalstone, David, "John Ashbery: 'Self-Portrait in a Convex Mirror,'" In his *Five Temperaments* (New York: Oxford University Press, 1977) 170–199.

Keller, Lynn, "'Thinkers without final thoughts:' the continuity between Stevens and Ashbery," and "'We must, we must be moving on:' Ashbery's divergence from Stevens and modernism," In her *Re-making It New: Contemporary American Poetry and the Modernist Tradition* (New York: Cambridge University Press, 1987) 15–78.

Lehman, David, ed. *Beyond Amazement: New Essays on John Ashbery,* (Ithaca, N.Y.: Cornell University Press, 1980).

McClatchy, J. D., "Weaving and Unweaving," *Poetry* 145: 301–306 (February 1985).

Mohanty, S. P., and Monroe, Jonathan, "John Ashbery and the Articulation of the Social," *Diacritics* 17: 37–63 (Summer 1987).

Molesworth, Charles, "'This Leaving-Out Business': The Poetry of John Ashbery," In his *The Fierce Embrace: A Study of Contemporary American Poetry* (Columbia: University of Missouri Press, 1979) 163–183.

O'Hara, Frank, "Rare Modern," *Poetry* 89: 307–316 (February 1957).

Perkins, David, "Meditations of the Solitary Mind: John Ashbery and A. R. Ammons," In his *A History of Modern Poetry: Modernism and After* Vol. 2 (Cambridge, Mass.: Harvard University Press, Belknap Press, 1987) 614–633.

Perloff, Marjorie, "'Mysteries of Construction': The Dream Songs of John Ashbery," In her *The Poetics of Indeterminacy: Rimbaud to Cage* (Princeton: Princeton University Press, 1981) 248–287.

Ross, Andrew, "Doubting John Thomas," In his *The Failure of Modernism: Symptoms of American Poetry* (New York: Columbia University Press, 1986) 159–208.

Shapiro, David, *John Ashbery: An Introduction to the Poetry,* (New York: Columbia University Press, 1979).

Shoptaw, John, "Saving Appearances: On John Ashbery," *Temblor* no. 7: 172–177 (Spring 1988).

Vendler, Helen, "Making It New: *A Wave,*" (*New York Review of Books,* July 14, 1984) 32–35.

Vendler, Helen, "John Ashbery, Louise Glück," In her *The Music of What Happens: Poems, Poets, Critics* (Cambridge, Mass.: Harvard University Press, 1988) 224–261.

Von Hallberg, Robert, "Robert Creeley and John Ashbery: Systems," In his *American Poetry and Culture, 1945–1980* (Cambridge, Mass.: Harvard University Press, 1985) 36–61.

Williamson, Alan, "The Diffracting Diamond: Ashbery, Romanticism, and Anti-Art," In his *Introspection and Contemporary Poetry* (Cambridge, Mass.: Harvard University Press, 1984) 116–148.

INTERVIEWS

Bloom, Janet, and Losada, Robert, "Craft Interview with John Ashbery," *New York Quarterly* no. 9: 11–33 (Winter 1972).

Gangel, Sue, "An Interview with John Ashbery," *San Francisco Review of Books* 3:12 (November 1977).

Jackson, Richard, "The Imminence of a Revelation," In his *Acts of Mind: Conversations with Contemporary Poets* (University: University of Alabama Press, 1983) 69–76.

John Ashbery and Kenneth Koch: A Conversation, (Tucson, Ariz.: Interview Press, 1965).

Koethe, John, "An Interview with John Ashbery," *SubStance* 37–38: 178–186 (1983).

Kostelanetz, Richard, "How to Be a Difficult Poet," (*New York Times Magazine,* May 23, 1976) 18–22.

Labrie, Ross, "John Ashbery," *American Poetry Review* 13: 29–33 (May–June 1984).

Lehman, David, "John Ashbery: The Pleasures of Poetry," (*New York Times Magazine,* December 16, 1984) 62–92.

Murphy, John, "John Ashbery," *Poetry Review* 75: 20–25 (August 1985).

Osti, Louis, "The Craft of John Ashbery," *Confrontation* 9: 84–96 (Fall 1974).

Poulin, A., Jr. "John Ashbery," *Michigan Quarterly Review* 20: 243–255 (Summer 1981).

Sommer, Piotr, "An Interview in Warsaw," In *Code of Signals: Recent Writings in Poetics* Edited by Michael Palmer (Berkeley, Calif.: North Atlantic Books, 1983).

Stitt, Peter, "The Art of Poetry 33: John Ashbery," *Paris Review* no. 90: 30–59 (Winter 1983).

W. H. AUDEN

(1907–1973)

RICHARD HOGGART

THE WANDERER

MANY OF US who began our adult reading during the 1930's in England will always think of W. H. Auden with a particular warmth, with the family sense we reserve for those writers who place their fingers on the pulse of a crucial period, whose writings are interwoven with our own intellectual and imaginative maturing. We may differ in our judgments of his later work, but we agree in remaining grateful that at such a time he spoke about our common situation with intelligence and breadth, with urgency and energy and wit; that he spoke—to use a word he would probably have found congenial—memorably. Auden's middle-class and private jokes were as puzzling to some of us as they were to foreigners; but we responded to his high spirits and confidence, his novelist's interest in the details of social life, the exciting concreteness with which he captured salient features of the gray England of the raw suburbs and housing estates, the arterial roads and chromium-and-plastic cafés. With due scaling-down we can say of him what he said of Freud:

> To us he is no more a person
> now but a whole climate of opinion.
> ("In Memory of Sigmund Freud," 67–68)[1]

We are not likely to forget the apt releasing force of such poems as "Dover," "Musée des Beaux Arts," "Sir, No Man's Enemy," and "A Shilling Life," or his vivid vigorous openings, or many scattered passages, such as:

> What do you think about England, this country of ours where nobody is well?

or,

> The vows, the tears, the slight emotional
> signals
> Are here eternal and unremarkable gestures
> Like ploughing or soldiers' songs:
> ("Dover," 28–30)

or,

> May with its light behaving
> Stirs vessel, eye, and limb,
> The singular and sad
> Are willing to recover.
> ("May," 1–4)

Yet, though Auden has held a high and special place in English poetic experience since the 1930's, it is easy to feel some force in the argument that his illuminations are sometimes no more than heterogeneous surface insights, and his technical skill more often showy than profound. Auden does occasionally employ certain fashionable clichés of tone and feeling; and he has been overrated in some literary circles. Just as surely, he has been underrated in others. Both attitudes tell something about contemporary cultural conditions in Britain. They tell less about the merits of Auden himself.

1. Unless noted otherwise, quotations are from E. Mendelson, ed., *Collected Poems* (New York-London, 1976).

Auden remained intellectually and technically open and fluid (these are not polite euphemisms for "fickle") to a degree that is not evident in any of those who were once known with him as "the poets of the thirties." His technical fluidity may be seen in his exercises in various poetic forms, especially after 1940. He practiced, for instance, in terza rima, the villanelle, the sestina, and the ballade. From this point of view the long poems *New Year Letter* (1941), *The Sea and the Mirror* (1945), *For the Time Being* (1945), and *The Age of Anxiety* (1948) are all aspects of the same formal search.

Yet this technical openness probably derives in part from a more radical quality, from an intellectual quixotry and eclecticism. Auden was something of an intellectual jackdaw, picking up bright pebbles of ideas so as to fit them into exciting conceptual patterns. He was evidently aware of this tendency and of one related to it; that is, of his inadequate submission to the "this-ness," the immediate sensuous stuff, of life. More than once he refers with admiration to Rainer Maria Rilke's "acceptance," or insists that one must "bless what there is for being," or that "every poem is rooted in imaginative awe." "One must be passive to conceive the truth" he says in "Kairos and Logos"; and a fine metaphorical passage by Caliban in *The Sea and the Mirror* ("The shy humiliations . . .") treats the same theme.

We can probably carry this same line of argument even further. For the intellectual unsteadiness seems to be a function of a yet deeper force: of a profound desire to come to ordered moral terms with life, and of a profound difficulty in doing so. *The Double Man* was the American title of *New Year Letter.* It is not one of Auden's best poems, though it has some moving lyric passages; it is nevertheless the fullest exposition of his philosophical problems. The American title was a peculiarly apt image for Auden's position at the time, and might still apply, though with less stress. Throughout his career, but with special force in the period before he became a professed Christian, Auden seems to have been an unusually divided man: searching for a belief toward which he could be truly humble, and finding humility difficult; questioning constantly the tensions within his own nature as both a fallen man and a creative artist. For Auden is primarily a purposive and moral writer. He is in the best sense a teacher, one who loves to influence others; on his weaker side he can be a somewhat gawky prose moralizer. For him—the characteristic assertion indicates both a limitation and the source of much of his strength—"Art is not enough."

Thus we may think of Auden in terms of one of his favorite images—that of the Wanderer, the man on a Quest. His poetry abounds in journeys over hills and across plains, in ascents of mountains and voyages across seas. The image appears in his very early adaptation of a Middle English poem, "Sawles Warde":

> But ever that man goes
> Through place-keepers, through forest trees,
> A stranger to strangers over undried sea. . . .
> ("The Wanderer," 7–9)

Variations occur throughout the 1930's: in the Airman of *The Orators,* in poems such as "Reader to Rider" and in the central characters of the plays *The Dog Beneath the Skin* and *The Ascent of F6.* Later, the same figure appears in the group of Quest sonnets printed in one volume with *New Year Letter,* in *The Sea and the Mirror,* in *The Age of Anxiety,* and in the libretto of *The Rake's Progress.* It is the theme of Auden's one full-length book of criticism, *The Enchaféd Flood* (1951), in which the sea and the desert are considered as complex images of man's spiritual wanderings. Less sustained instances occur throughout all Auden's work, from the early "mad driver pulling on his gloves" to "A Change of Air" (in *About the House*).

In Auden's final decade the Wanderer figure was not quite so prominent. Before then we might have been justified in saying, with many qualifications, that Auden was himself the Wanderer, the Wanderer pursuing the questions outlined above—of the "double man" and, especially, of the double man as an artist.

Any one of a hundred passages could exemplify the first kind of question. The quotation below has been deliberately chosen at random from the *Collected Shorter Poems* so as to indicate the frequency of the theme:

> In my own person I am forced to know
> How much must be forgotten out of love,
> How much must be forgiven, even love.
> ("Canzone," 46–48)

The second question is raised most strikingly in Auden's elegies on other writers, as in these lines on Henry James:

> All will be judged. Master of nuance and scruple,
> Pray for me and for all writers living or dead;
> Because there are many whose works
> Are in better taste than their lives; because there is no end
> To the vanity of our calling: make intercession
> For the treason of all clerks.
>
> Because the darkness is never so distant,
> And there is never much time for the arrogant
> Spirit to flutter its wings . . .
> ("At the Grave of Henry James," 55–60)

Yet it is important to notice that the Quest is not undertaken for its own sake. That would be a romantic delusion, and Auden never had much patience with the self-regarding romantic personality. The Quest is for order, for pattern and meaning, in life.

The constant interaction of all the qualities we have briefly outlined—Auden's great technical skill (in particular his fine ear and sense of timing); his remarkably acute eye for revealing detail; his intellectual responsiveness, liveliness, and range; his search for spiritual order—all these combine to produce Auden's characteristic tones and themes:

> The earth turns over; our side feels the cold;
> And life sinks choking in the wells of trees:
> The ticking heart comes to a standstill, killed;
> The icing on the pond waits for the boys.
> Among the holly and the gifts I move,
> The carols on the piano, the glowing hearth,
> All our traditional sympathy with birth,
> Put by your challenge to the shifts of Love.
> . . .
> Language of moderation cannot hide—
> My sea is empty and its waves are rough;
> Gone from the map the shore where childhood played,
> Tight-fisted as a peasant, eating love;
> Lost in my wake the archipelago,
> Islands of self through which I sailed all day
> Planting a pirate's flag, a generous boy;
> And lost the way to action and to you.
>
> Lost if I steer. Tempest and tide may blow
> Sailor and ship past the illusive reef,
> And I yet land to celebrate with you
> The birth of natural order and true love: . . .
> ("Through the Looking-Glass," 1–8; 49–60)

1930 TO THE WAR YEARS: THE NEED FOR ORDER

THE 1930's IN ENGLAND

Few recent decades in English life have, retrospectively, so boldly defined a character as the 1930's. They seem now like a rising wave after a trough, a wave that preceded disasters.

In domestic affairs the keynote was struck in America, with the Wall Street crash of 1929. From the time this recession reached England until the rearmament boom of the decade's last years, unemployment was an ever-present feature of English life. This was the period of the "Depressed Areas," of what Auden called "the Threadbare Common Man / Begot on Hire-Purchase by Insurance," of "smokeless chimneys, damaged bridges, rotting wharves and choked canals." It was a period when shabby-genteel clerks could be found selling gimcrack Japanese household sundries from door to door. It was a gray and squalid period, especially for the millions directly affected by unemployment.

Internationally the starting point lies in earlier events, but it may be conveniently taken as Hitler's assumption of the German chancellorship in 1933. Thereafter, as is clear now, there was a giant's march to the explosion of September 1939. The crucial midway stage was the opening of the Spanish Civil War in 1936.

For most young English people with left-wing (or pacifist) interests this was a period of fervent activity, of Popular Front meetings, of milk for Spain and aid for Basque refugees, and of Victor Gollancz's Left Book Club publications. It was marked by a more than usually strong feeling that "the old gang" was appallingly unaware of the changing world situation. It was, in Auden's phrase, a "time of crisis and dismay."

Yet in the apparent simplicity of its issues and in the dramatic or even symbolic quality of its detail (unemployed men standing idle under the lamp posts at street corners; the International Brigades; Guernica) it was a peculiarly heady period. It was in a certain sense enjoyable precisely because of its comparatively clear-cut moral situations and general all-hands-on-deck air. Such a period could call out the best qualities, as well as the more naive enthusiasms, of concerned young Englishmen in all classes, and notably of that traditionally concerned group, the intelligent professional middle class at the universities.

To this class Wystan Hugh Auden belonged. Born in 1907 in York, Auden was the son of a medical officer with wide general and literary interests. His mother was a devout Anglo-Catholic. Subsequently the family moved to the great Midland city of Birmingham, and here no doubt Auden later gained much of his firsthand experience of economic depression. Here too he probably first discovered the unfailing fascination that "the soiled productive cities" had for him, the pull of the great urban sprawls of the commercial Western world (Pittsburgh, Manchester, Detroit, the Ruhr). "My heart has stamped on / The view from Birmingham to Wolverhampton," he said in a light poem he later rejected, and "Tram-lines and slag-heaps, pieces of machinery / That was, and is, my ideal scenery." "Nothing is made in this town," he said of Dover, and the implication was plainly pejorative.

At Gresham's School, Holt, Auden talked first of becoming an engineer and read technological works, chiefly on mining and geology. But in his early teens, prompted by a friend, he began to write poetry. Thomas Hardy was his first master—an admirably humane man and a magnificently varied and idiosyncratic versifier who yet is rarely so completely successful as to discourage a young practitioner. At Christ Church, Oxford, Auden had reached the stage at which he could one day tell his tutor, with an impressive confidence, that only T. S. Eliot was worth the serious consideration of poetic aspirants. But this was one necessary moment in a poet's development, and there were other influences, notably Anglo-Saxon and Middle English poetry, that continued to fascinate Auden. At Oxford, too, Wilfred Owen and Edward Thomas were admitted to the accepted canon of ancestors for his generation. Auden's friendship with Stephen Spender began (and had about it, typically, something of the English public schools' prefect-to-fag[2] relationship); and his first links were made with others who were to become writers and publicists in what has variously been called the Thirties Group, the Pylon School, and the Auden Group. Incidentally, the members were united more by common assumptions and written influence than by actual meetings. The three best-known poets of the group, Auden, Spender, and C. Day Lewis, did not meet as a trio until the late 1940's, at a cultural conference in Venice.

After a stay in pre-Hitler Berlin there followed for Auden a short period of school teaching, which he seems to have deeply enjoyed. He had, we have already implied, a strong charismatic sense, a good teacher's love and firmness, energy and fidelity. Meanwhile, his first book, *Poems,* had been pub-

2. An English public-school boy who acts as a servant to an older schoolmate.

lished in 1930 and had been followed in 1932 by *The Orators,* an acute, fantastic, and vigorous attack on the state of England and the English establishment. In 1935 he married Erika Mann. As the decade progressed he became more and more engaged, not only in his craft as a poet but in the time-consuming borderland where political affairs and the practice of writing mingle. A largely light-hearted visit to Iceland with Louis MacNeice in 1936 was followed by visits to Spain in 1937 and to China and the U.S. with Christopher Isherwood in 1938. A few months before the beginning of World War II Auden settled in America, and in due time adopted American citizenship.

POLITICS, PSYCHOLOGY, "LOVE"

Centring the eye on their essential human element

Some critics suggest that Auden is a peculiarly English poet, and that in leaving England he severed essential roots. The first suggestion is to a large extent true, in both more and less obvious senses. Local and family concerns are very dear to Auden; and his bedside book in New York was a work on the mineralogy of the Lake District. More, the cast of Auden's mind was markedly formed by some of the main elements in the English tradition. His is not a voice from the American Middle West or from Central Europe: "England to me is my own tongue."

Yet does the second suggestion—that Auden weakened his poetry by a physical removal—necessarily follow? Wherever he lived, the bent of Auden's mind, the way he approached the problems that interested him—his particular form of complicated cranky independence as well as his tough gentleness—remained recognizably English. But the nature of these problems had something to do with the decision as to where he might best live. Auden's interest was in people in urban societies, in people living through their perennial moral and metaphysical problems in megalopolitan settings. London or some large English provincial city might have provided such a setting; but England is small and domestically intimate, its cultural life demandingly homely. Auden needed a kind of anonymity within an urban mass, and this New York provided (as well as providing sufficient money and the friendships Auden needed):

> More even than in Europe, here,
> The choice of patterns is made clear
> Which the machine imposes, what
> is possible and what is not,
> To what conditions we must bow
> In building the Just City now.
> (*New Year Letter,* pt. 3)

Auden is a socially unrooted poet who could have been at home in any of the large urban centers of the Western hemisphere. Whatever he might have lost by leaving England was not central to these gifts: in America, he seemed understandably to feel, he was at the chief pressure point of forces that were changing the face of life in the West.

Auden's isolation in a crowd reflects a constant quality of his verse, a quality most plainly indicated in the early figures of the Hawk and the Airman (*The Orators*). The Airman is physically isolated from the messy, close disorder of life below and, more important, able from his post of observation to detect therein some pattern not visible to those immersed in the details of personal involvement. Similarly, Auden's is often an abstracting and generalizing intelligence. In some sense very difficult to define fairly, we may say that he is emotionally detached from much of what he describes, that he has a "clinical" quality.

Though Auden speaks to and for many in his generation, his speech commonly lacks certain kinds of intimacy. There are important areas of experience, particularly those concerned with relations between the sexes, which he either does not touch or touches in a perfunctory or stereotyped or briskly impersonal manner (falling in love, married life, some forms of insecurity, the tragic, gay, and dignified tensions in the day-to-day life of "ordinary" people). At such points he is likely to move into a detached "placing" of detail by the use of successive definite articles:

> The boarding-house food, the boarding-
> house faces,
> The rain-spoilt picnics in the windswept
> places,
> The camera lost and the suspicion,
> The failure in the putting competition,
> The silly performance on the pier . . .
> (*The Ascent of F6,* Act I, sc. ii)

A poet's weaknesses are often peculiarly revealing. There are forms of emotional wobble in, say Alfred Tennyson, or of anger and enthusiasm in Robert Browning, or of sensuous indulgence in Dylan Thomas; these weaknesses at once limit the poets and bring them closer to us. In Auden's poetry there are certainly struggles, but they are expressed through a continuous argument with the self rather than through the play of personal emotions. The "I" is there, but is rarely at a loss with itself; it may be exploring its own weaknesses but always does so with an air of control, with the implication that certain areas are sealed off and the limits of the struggle grasped. These are the roots Auden lacks and would have lacked even if he had remained in England.

This quality seems related to the fact that Auden's poems tend to be remembered not so much for their sensuous effects (apart from a few striking exceptions) as for the articulation of their phrasing and the pattern of their moral insights. His poems have little color, smell, or touch. He once said that he tended to think of them as "squares and oblongs"; that is, as geometric shapes rather than as, for example, extended images. The bare shapes are the shapes of his dialectic. Similarly, his epithets usually have a conceptual rather than a sensuous relationship to the nouns they qualify; they comment rather than describe. Where several epithets are used they do not cumulatively describe their noun so much as set up an intellectual friction with the noun and with each other:

> And the active hands must freeze
> Lonely on the separate knees.
> ("Twelve Songs," VI, 7–8)

Auden does not say "green slope" or "grassy slope" but "tolerant enchanted slope"; a lover's head on his arm is caught, beautifully, as a moral rather than a visual pattern:

> Lay your sleeping head, my love,
> Human on my faithless arm.
> ("Lullaby;" 1–2)

Again, though Auden's similes are rhetorical, often boldly rhetorical, they usually gain their effect from the yoking of an abstract idea to a vividly concrete fact, from a vivid metaphorical personification of ideas: "Problems like relatives standing," and, "Will Ferdinand be as fond of a Miranda/Familiar as a stocking?" And Auden's geography is almost always economic or political geography; thus his poem about the Chinese port of Macao opens "A weed from Catholic Europe, it took root." Or his landscapes are symbols of human dilemmas.

A varied intelligence, a congenitally pattern-making mind, and a persistent moral drive: all these place the emphases in Auden's work firmly on man rather than nature, and on man-in-the-city rather than man-in-the-fields. It was inevitable that in the 1930's Auden should pursue his psychological and social interests, should be purposively trying to create an order in his experience:

> Our hunting fathers told the story
> Of the sadness of the creatures,
> Pitied the limits and the lack
> Set in their finished features;
> Saw in the lion's intolerant look,
> Behind the quarry's dying glare,
> Love raging for the personal glory
> That reason s gift would add,
> . . .
> Who, nurtured in that fine tradition,
> Predicted the result,
> Guessed Love by nature suited to
> The intricate ways of guilt . . . ?
> ("Our Hunting Fathers," 1–8;11–14)

The bent of Auden's political interests ensured that he was often thought, mistakenly, to be a Marxist. He did find much to admire in Marxist analysis; the argument that "freedom is the recognition of necessity" alone would have won his interest. He did work, incidentally, for left-wing causes ("the expending of powers / On the flat ephemeral pamphlet and the boring meeting"). Of this kind of poem the most representative, whether by Auden or by any of the engaged poets of the 1930's, is "Spain 1937," with its characteristic refrains: "Yesterday all the past," "Tomorrow, perhaps, the future," and "But today the struggle."

But for Auden this activity was inspired chiefly by his urgent search for spiritual order and moral responsibility. At bottom his attitude had more in common with that of some conservative and right-wing intellectuals than with that of the more progressive, "free," and romantically expectant left-wing intellectuals.

And his psychological interest was deeper than his political interest. Why were so many out of love with themselves? How had we become a nation of "aspirins and weak tea"? At this stage Auden was predominantly interested in the plight of the specifically neurotic, of "the lost, the lonely, the unhappy," of "the malcontented who might have been," of the anxious and fear-ridden. The interest remained, but it widened into a concern with a more radical anxiety. In the 1930's Auden's reading of Freud and George Walther Groddeck,[3] notably, encouraged a kind of modern myth-making, since both these writers communicate an unusual imaginative excitement in their presentation of concepts themselves richly suggestive:

> Sir, no man's enemy, forgiving all
> But will his negative inversion, be prodigal:
> Send to us power and light, a sovereign
>   touch
> Curing the intolerable neural itch,
> The exhaustion of weaning, the liar's
>   quinsy,
> And the distortions of ingrown virginity.
> Prohibit sharply the rehearsed response
> And gradually correct the coward's stance:

The address to a negatively defined power was an early indication that politics and psychology were only aspects of a more central interest, of Auden's concern with the spiritual dilemmas of individuals beyond the reach of political and psychological reforms. This is, of course, a religious interest; and though it showed itself plainly only toward the end of the decade it had many earlier intimations. Particularly, Auden returns again and again to a single word, "Love"—and uses it elusively:

> O Love, the interest itself in thoughtless
>   Heaven,
>   (*The English Auden,* pt. 4:
>   "Poems 1931–1936," no. VI)

and,

> The word is Love
> Surely one fearless kiss would cure
> The million fevers . . .
>   (*Look, Stranger!,* no. XXX)

and,

> Birth of a natural order and of Love. . . .
>   (*Look, Stranger!,* no. IX)

"Love" seems to have been an undefined but powerful third force, a quality both inside man and affecting man from outside, which at once offered him hope and indicated the perennial and personal nature of his situation. The history of Auden's earlier mental journey is, roughly speaking, that of the gradual discovery of the potentialities of this word's meaning for him—from an unresolved assertion to a rich and complex ambiguity that embraces the idea of Christian love, of conscience, of charity and grace. When that moment was reached Auden was an avowed Christian. The more directly political and psychological interests had fallen into place

3. Groddeck (1866–1934) was a German psychotherapist who made a special study of psychosomatic illness.

and the first phase was over. It is easy to exercise hindsight in such matters. In Auden's development the lines are clear and expressed:

> Perhaps I always knew what they were
> saying:
> Even the early messengers who walked
> Into my life from books
> . . .
> Love was the word they never said aloud
> . . .
> And all the landscape round them pointed
> to
> The calm with which they took complete
> desertion
> As proof that you existed.
> It was true. . . .
> ("The Prophets," 1–3; 7; 18–20)

PUBLIC AND PRIVATE SPEECH

There is a small body of Auden's very early verse whose qualities are different from those we normally associate with his poetry in the 1930's. These poems are dry and gnomic:

> Love by ambition
> Of definition
> Suffers partition
> And cannot go
> From yes to no
> For no is not love, no is no . . .
> ("Too Dear, Too Vague," 1–6)

Since the impulse behind these poems is close to that which informs some of Auden's poems of the 1950's, we are reminded once more of the coherence of his intellectual development. But in the 1930's Auden was more characteristically a poet of perceptive epigrammatic verse, of various kinds of conversational meter, and of a number of remarkable lyrics.

The epigrammatic manner clearly took force from Auden's purposively ranging mind and from his insistent rhetorical inclinations. The epigrams usually enshrine memorable social and psychological observation, sometimes not so much crisp as slick, but generally intelligent and pithy:

> Steep roads, a tunnel through the downs, are
> the approaches;
> A ruined pharos overlooks a constructed
> bay;
> The sea-front is almost elegant; all this
> show
> Has, somewhere inland, a vague and dirty
> root:
> Nothing is made in this town.
>
> But the dominant Norman castle floodlit at
> night
> And the trains that fume in the station built
> on the sea
> Testify to the interests of its regular life:
> Here live the experts on what the soldiers
> want
> And who the travellers are, . . .
> ("Dover" 1–10)

Poems such as this are among the more notable instances of the way in which the climate of the 1930's could affect a well-equipped poetic mind. There were other manners of "speaking to the times" that said more for the earnestness of the poet's intentions than for their grasp of poetry's function. We may grant that society was "sick" and that the poets urgently wished to contribute usefully. Yet by the nature of contemporary culture they spoke only to a small minority. How could they speak more widely? Could they in any proper way compete with the truly popular voices?

To this aspect of Auden's work belong the two plays he wrote with Christopher Isherwood and the verse with Louis MacNeice, between 1935 and 1938. In some of their techniques for presenting social problems and for obtaining a sense of urgent participation from the audience they seem to have learned something from the early "epic theater" of the German Marxist playwright Bertolt Brecht. They made use also of hints from German expressionism, from popular songs and variety and music-hall performances. The plays are lively, intelligent, and witty. To those, out of love with a glossy commercial theater, who saw them at Rupert Doone's Group Theatre in London, they must have been unusually exciting. But they have the faults of their originating assumptions. They are lively charades with passages of striking banality and pert "knowingness." Their characters are not merely "types"—that may be true of certain good plays. But they are usually cliché-ridden or idea-ridden types, Freudian or Marxian puppets. Both plays have some good lyrics and choruses, but only *The Ascent of F6* is now worth close attention. In this play the Quest theme, because it is more deeply probed, inspires some scenes much more searching and eloquent than any in *The Dog Beneath the Skin.*

During the 1930's Auden's demotic interests best served his poetry in the practice of the epigrammatic line and of various conversational meters. In the latter he aimed at a laconic and loose-limbed, a dryly ironic or apparently offhand tone of voice. The tone had begun to appear by mid-decade, as in the unbuttoned, in medias res, colloquially reflective opening of "Musée des Beaux Arts":

> About suffering they were never wrong,
> The Old Masters: how well they understood
> Its human position; how it takes place
> While someone else is eating or opening a
> window or just walking dully along;
> . . .
> In Brueghel's *Icarus,* for instance: how
> everything turns away
> Quite leisurely from the disaster; the
> ploughman may
> Have heard the splash, the forsaken cry,
> But for him it was not an important failure;
> the sun shone
> As it had to. . . .
> ("Musée des Beaux Arts," 1–4;14–18)

For this manner (especially as it was adopted in his often admirable symbolic sonnets) Auden took much from Rilke. But the most important influence was William Butler Yeats, whose conversational meters Auden most perceptively praised. Yeats's "Easter 1916" begins:

> I have met them at close of day
> Coming with vivid faces
> From counter or desk among grey
> Eighteenth-century houses.

The echo can be plainly heard (though really in no more than a very competent imitation) in Auden's "1st September 1939":

> I sit in one of the dives
> On Fifty-Second Street
> Uncertain and afraid
> As the clever hopes expire . . .

The conversational manner was predominant in *Another Time* (1940). Subsequently, it was influenced by Auden's experience in America, where the rhythms of colloquial speech often seem more flexible than they are in England:

> The sailors come ashore
> Out of their hollow ships,
> Mild-looking middle class boys
> Who read the comic strips;
> One baseball game is more
> To them than fifty Troys.
>
> They look a bit lost, set down
> In this unamerican place . . .
> ("Fleet Visit," 1–8)

Since this is essentially a relaxed manner it sometimes encouraged Auden's characteristic technical faults, and so became slipshod rather than relaxed, slick instead of laconic, informedly glib rather than finely allusive. At its best its shrewdly loose articulation allowed it to carry very effectively the intelligent, unvatic, contemporary observations Auden often wished to make.

Most of the foregoing comments on Auden's style have a bearing on his social and psychological interests. His lyrics exist much more in their own right, and spring from simpler but very firm poetic roots. This is an aspect of Auden's work that his evident moral drive can easily lead us to underrate. Auden's admirable lyrics have been a continuous feature of his verse, from a fine group in the mid-1930's that includes such poems as "O who can ever praise enough" to "Deftly, Admiral"

(*Nones,* 1952). We remember here also the quick and witty choral songs such as "At last the secret is out," the comic and satiric poems such as "O for doors to be open," the nonsense rhyme in *Nones,* and "Willow-Wren and the Stare." The note that seems most characteristic and most impressive in the lyrics is of a kind of stillness; not a passivity nor always the stillness of menace, but a held imaginative stasis where the spirit looks steadily and often tenderly at a still moment of experience. It is all, of course, as much a matter of sound as of sense:

> Dear, though the night is gone,
> Its dream still haunts to-day,
> ("Twelve Songs," no. IV, 1–2)

and,

> Fish in the unruffled lakes
> The swarming colours wear . . .
> ("Twelve Songs," V, 1–2)

and,

> Deftly, admiral, cast your fly
> Into the slow deep hover,
> ("Five Songs," no. I, 1–2)

and,

> Now the leaves are falling fast,
> Nurse's flowers will not last;
> Nurses to the graves are gone,
> And the prams go rolling on.
>
> Whispering neighbours, left and right,
> Pluck us from the real delight;
> And the active hands must freeze
> Lonely on the separate knees.
> ("Twelve Songs," VI, 1–8)

FROM THE FORTIES TO THE MID-FIFTIES: THE EXPLORATION FORMS

"ORIGINAL ANXIETY"

From 1940 to the mid-1950's, Auden moved around the American continent fairly consistently, chiefly as a lecturer and teacher at universities and colleges. Then, from 1956 to 1961, he was professor of poetry at Oxford and so spent some time regularly in England. From 1949 to 1957 he had a spring and summer home on Ischia, an island off Naples. That yielded in 1958 to another spring and summer home in Kirchstetten, lower Austria. He died en route from there to Oxford, where, at Christ Church, he had a "grace and favour" cottage[4] in the last year of his life. But for more than thirty years—from 1939 to 1972—Auden's home base or point of rest was overwhelmingly New York.

The move to America roughly coincided with the clear and frequent appearance in Auden's poetry of a number of new influences. If Freud and Marx were the most striking and typical intellectual influences of the 1930's, then those of the 1940's were Søren Kierkegaard and Reinhold Niebuhr.

The exploration by the Danish "existentialist" theologian Kierkegaard of "original anxiety," the basic insecurity of man that marks both his fallen condition and his possible salvation—this in particular replaced for Auden, as a fruitful area of thought and a seminal metaphor, the psychologists' more scientific analysis of the nature of anxiety. "Psychotherapy will not get much further until it recognizes that the true significance of a neurosis is teleological," Auden now said.

Similarly, Reinhold Niebuhr's analysis of the moral dilemmas and social involvements of man submerged Auden's rather scrappy and qualified interest in Marxism. Niebuhr was, from 1930 to 1960, professor of applied Christianity at Union Theological Seminary, New York; the most accessible exposition of his outlook is in the two volumes of Gifford Lectures, *The Nature and Destiny of Man.* Auden's sense of continuous struggle in the will makes it easy to understand why he should have been drawn to Niebuhr's form of Protestantism—Auden was in fact a Protestant

4. A royal or church residence provided for aged retainers who have served the crown, the church, or some other important institution.

Episcopalian. We may assume that he would have been in sympathy with this statement by Niebuhr: "The Catholic emphasizes the initial act of intellectual assent; the Protestant the continuous process of voluntary assent." Nor was Auden's awareness of society likely to allow him ever to become mystical or contemplative.

Such statements are bound to oversimplify; there are obviously many other interweaving lines of force. But these were the dominant and most revealing forces at this time. Auden quoted Kierkegaard repeatedly, in his poetry and prose; and some of his poems of the 1940's are like versified paragraphs of Niebuhr.

Auden's social and psychological interests remained, but were related now to a central religious root. Man is seen as fallen yet free, and this is his paradox. He is bound by his "creatureliness" yet always tempted to deny the limitations this imposes; he is free to exercise moral choice for good or ill. Hence his "willfulness" in both the senses of "possessing free will" and "prompt to disobey." He works out his destiny here "historically" in time; his consciousness of time informs his awareness of guilt and of possible grace. This awareness marks man's unique situation and is the ground of his anxiety: "Anxiety is the inevitable concomitant of the paradox of freedom and finiteness in which man is involved," said Niebuhr.

Man is unfinished but forever has the possibility of "becoming." By contrast the animals and plants, which appear frequently in Auden's poems as images of unawareness, are perfect, finished, and forever unpromising, unconscious of identity, time, and choice:

> Let them leave language to their lonely
> betters
> Who count some days and long for certain
> letters;
> We, too, make noises when we laugh or
> weep,
> Words are for those with promises to keep.
> ("Their Lonely Betters," 13–16)

And elsewhere,

> The hour-glass whispers to the lion's paw,
> The clock-towers tell the gardens day and
> night,
> How many errors Time has patience for,
> How wrong they are in being always right.
> ("Our Bias," 1–4)

So far this description might seem to suggest an anxiety-ridden outlook that could easily become querulous or nagging. Auden is never querulous and rarely nags; his purposiveness and sense of humor both relieve him. "Accept the present in its fullness," he says in a characteristically firm and positive passage. Man is a social creature, and a sign of the individual's growing spiritual maturity is the decision not to try one of the many forms of escape from this commitment, but to stay where he is, soberly and steadily to work out his destiny with the intransigent material of human relations. To work for civility, and to build the Just City—these are favorite phrases of Auden's. The building of the Just City can never be completed, he adds, but could not be even an aspiration were there not outside man an order of which his dream of the Just City is a reflection.

In all this, "Love" is still often invoked by Auden, though now with a more complex sense of its difficulty and also of its ineluctability:

> Let no one say I Love until aware
> What huge resources it will take to nurse
> One ruining speck, one tiny hair
> That casts a shadow through the universe.
> . . .
> ("In Sickness and in Health," 25–28)

Auden's general approach is well illustrated in a vigorous and hortatory poem, "Memorial for the City." The theme is the destruction of traditional European values as they are expressed in the ancient city-architecture of the Continent, and the now more plainly exposed dilemma of fallen man immersed in time:

> The steady eyes of the crow and the
> camera's candid eye

See as honestly as they know how, but they
  lie.
The crime of life is not time. Even now, in
  this night
Among the ruins of the Post-Vergilian city
Where our past is a chaos of graves and the
  barbed-wire stretches ahead
Into our future till it is lost to sight,
Our grief is not Greek: as we bury our dead
We know without knowing there is reason
  for what we bear,
That our hurt is not a desertion, that we are
  to pity
Neither ourselves nor our city;
Whoever the searchlights catch, whatever
  the loudspeakers blare,
We are not to despair.
  ("Memorial for the City," 24–35)

In a later poem, "The Shield of Achilles," Thetis, the mother of Achilles, looks over the armorer Hephaestos' shoulder at the decorative scenes on the shield. In the sort of world represented on the shield, there is time and event; but without the sense of sin or the hope of redemption, such a world is, in the most terribly exact sense, meaningless. Auden counterpoints the description of the shield with scenes from similarly "unsaved" worlds:

A ragged urchin, aimless and alone,
  Loitered about that vacancy, a bird
Flew up to safety from his well-aimed stone:
  That girls are raped, that two boys knife a
    third,
  Were axioms to him who'd never heard
Of any world where promises were kept,
Or one could weep because another wept.
  (53–59)

The altered emphasis in Auden's preoccupations often brought with it a greater leanness and firmness of attitude. He seemed less attentive to the rich muddle of life. But we may be disproportionately fascinated, as well as seriously concerned, with the sheer detail of experience. In some ways Auden's approach in the 1940's and early 1950's was more austere than it had been, closer to the kind of promise made in his earlier poems. And in seeking to express this new pattern of interests Auden developed some sinewy and complex verse of great power and interest.

SYMBOLIC LANDSCAPE AND THE LONG LINE

For a few years after his arrival in America, Auden apparently decided that he would, predominantly, write long poems (poems occupying all or most of one volume) whose structural complexities would embody a variety of materials, tones, and intellectual approaches. Later his collections were of shorter poems, ranging from lyrics to what might be called longish short poems (from sixty to a hundred lines).

But between 1941 and 1948 Auden produced four long poems: *New Year Letter, The Sea and the Mirror, For the Time Being,* and *The Age of Anxiety.* Poetically, the first is the least interesting, though, as we noted earlier, it has some moving lyric passages and is almost everywhere lively; and the Quest sonnets that complete the volume are more than good derivatives from Rilke. The title poem draws to its close, all argument aside, with a joyful invocation to God:

O Unicorn among the cedars,
To whom no magic charm can lead us,
White childhood moving like a sigh
Through the green woods unharmed . . .
  (pt. 3)

The Sea and the Mirror is subtitled *A Commentary on Shakespeare's "The Tempest,"* and is chiefly about the relations between art, the artist, and society. For each character Auden produces a different verse form, often a highly elaborate one. The result is sometimes merely curious, though the performance is technically brilliant; and some parts (Alonso's address to Ferdinand, Miranda's villanelle) are not only brilliant but more deeply engaging.

For the Time Being, a Christmas oratorio dedicated to the memory of Auden's mother, is more emotionally harmonious than the other long poems, probably because of the greater simplicity and firmness of Auden's theme—of belief in sin and hope for humility. Here, not surprisingly, is to be found the peculiarly "still" lyric note we remarked earlier:

> Let number and weight rejoice
> In this hour of their translation
> Into conscious happiness:
> For the whole in every part,
> The truth at the proper centre . . .
> ("The Annunciation," pt. 4)

The Age of Anxiety is brilliant, perverse, disjointed, a "baroque eclogue" with all the extraneous ornamentation and deviousness that such a subtitle implies, a structural experiment that does not succeed. Yet even here, in a meter drawn from Anglo-Saxon verse, a few sections achieve an unusual gaunt beauty. A tired clerk in a New York bar nostalgically describes childhood in a city that might just as well have been Birmingham or Dortmund:

> . . . how fagged coming home through
> The urban evening. Heavy like us
> Sank the gas-tanks—it was supper time.
> In hot houses helpless babies and
> Telephones gabbled untidy cries,
> And on embankments black with burnt
> grass
> Shambling freight-trains were shunted away
> Past crimson clouds.
> (pt. 2: "The Seven Ages")

Perhaps in the last three of these long poems Auden was tackling his own form of a problem similar to that of T. S. Eliot in *The Waste Land* (though aspects of the same problem in its contemporary form can be seen at least as far back as Robert Browning's *The Ring and the Book*, 1868–1869): how to achieve a form that would embody the detail of social dilemmas, the diverse pressures of moral problems, and the necessary changes of tone, angle, and level of suggestion—in a shape somehow organic to the theme. Auden does not succeed: *For the Time Being* is comparatively harmonious but not really complex; *The Sea and the Mirror* is complex and in a sense unified, but gains its unity chiefly from the assumed background of *The Tempest*.

In his shorter poems Auden continued to use several kinds of conversational meter and seemed still to regard some of this verse as a sort of "public" utterance, though now to a public accepted as small, and sympathetic by predisposition. This is an aspect of what Auden has called "unofficial poetry" and "comic" art:

> From now on the only popular art will be comic art—and this will be unpopular with the Management. It is the law which it cannot alter which is the subject of all comic art. . . . Every poet stands alone. [But] this does not mean that he sulks mysteriously in a corner by himself.
> ("Squares and Oblongs," in *Poets at Work*)

Cheerful and debunking comic art can help to preserve self-respect in increasingly "generalized" societies. Against "the lie of Authority" a poet, as one of the few individuals—by profession—in modern society, will propose the idea of the personal life.

Auden gems to have a more deliberate and prescribed purpose in his later use of the conversational voice than he had earlier. He seems to be aiming not at a widely acceptable demotic speech but at a low-temperature verse of intelligent observation and comment:

> [We] would in the old grand manner
> Have sung from a resonant heart.
> But, pawed-at and gossiped-over
> By the promiscuous crowd,
> Concocted by editors
> Into spells to befuddle the crowd,
> All words like Peace and Love,
> All sane affirmative speech,
> Had been soiled, profaned, debased
> To a horrid mechanical screech:
> No civil style survived
> That pandemonium
> But the wry, the sotto-voce,
> Ironic and monochrome
> ("We Too Had Known
> Golden Hours," 11–24)

Verse such as this can induce its own cult snobberies and is no doubt not meant to be of the first importance in the body of Auden's work. It is "occasional" verse in a valid sense—verse written for and commenting on specific occasions—and within these limits it is usually acute and enjoyable. Inevitably, it retains some of the faults of its kind: it is sometimes slapdash and unmuscular, a versified *New Yorker* journalese that may be observant and intelligent but is too brittle to cut deep.

In his imagery Auden turns instinctively to landscape: he commonly speaks of "villages of the heart," "our landscape of pain," "suburbs of fear," and so on. We may say roughly that he has two distinctive kinds of natural imagery: that in which landscape is an illuminating backcloth to some human social activity, and that in which landscape is a symbol for an inner dilemma in human personality. Again speaking generally, we may say that the first predominates in Auden's earlier poetry, and the second later. In the present day the great industrial cities of America might provide the first kind of imagery; and the Apennine backbone of Italy, dropping to its coastal plains, might provide the second. But the scenery common to the Northern and Midland Pennines of Auden's childhood and youth continued more than any other to be drawn on for both types of imagery. The lusher scenes of southern England—or the hollyhocks and lawns of Tennyson's rectory gardens—had little appeal for him.

In the 1930's Auden was more likely than later to invoke the densely packed, intensively worked-over, huddled, and smoky industrial-revolution landscapes of the Pennines, the grim and uncompromising little towns of the foothills and valleys or the great black sprawling cities on the plains below. He did write also of the bare, stark uplands then, but was still likely to speak of them, with their abandoned workings and derelict mines, as illustrations of the same direct social interest: to use them, in short, as backcloths. And of course he loved them in and for themselves:

> Always my boy of wish returns
> To those peat-stained deserted burns
> That feed the Wear and Tyne and Tees.
> (*New Year Letter,* pt. 3)

During the 1950's landscape became for Auden more and more a means of visually symbolizing the spiritual conflicts in man, and to this need the involved geometry of the upper hills speaks best. As in so much, Rilke had guided Auden to what he sought here:

> One of the constant problems of the poet is how to express abstract ideas in concrete terms. . . . Rilke is almost the first poet since the seventeenth century to find a fresh solution . . . [he] thinks of the human in terms of the nonhuman . . . one of [his] most characteristic devices is the expression of human life in terms of landscape. It is this kind of imagery which is beginning to appear in English poetry.

Certainly Auden's use of landscape in the 1950's expresses his characteristic urge to wrest meaningful patterns from experience. But it is important to recognize that the landscapes are not being wrenched into the form of symbols. They speak to him—had indeed always spoken to him, though not always receiving his later comprehension—as symbols, as "sacred objects." They spoke to him before he could consciously decipher their language:

> . . . There
> In Rookhope I was first aware;
> Of Self and Not-Self, Death and Dread:
> Audits were entrances which led
> Down to the Outlawed, to the Others.
> The Terrible, the Merciful, the Mothers;
> Alone in the hot day I knelt
> Upon the edge of shafts and felt
> The deep *urmutterfurcht* that drives
> Us into knowledge all our lives . . .
> (*New Year Letter,* pt. 3)

The process is not a fitting of pictures to ideas, but is part of Auden's natural manner of establishing relations with the outside world, of establishing "the relations of man—as a history-making person—to nature":

> Whenever I begin to think
> About the human creature we
> Must nurse to sense and decency,
> An English area comes to mind,
> I see the native of my kind
> As a locality I love . . .

After the war Auden exercised this interest in symbolic landscape much more closely, especially in what were described earlier as longish short poems. The sequence began notably with a remarkable poem, "In Praise of Limestone," and was continued in the seven "Bucolics" in *The Shield of Achilles* (1955). The symbolic landscape and the long line that usually accompanies it combined to make one of the most important and exciting postwar developments in Auden's work.

Auden would muse before a large and varied landscape and seek to evoke from within it his sense that it symbolized an extensive pattern of human dilemmas. In the following passage the people who remain within the gregarious life of the valleys are contrasted with the exceptional few who go elsewhere:

> Adjusted to the local needs of valleys
> Where everything can be touched or reached by walking,
> Their eyes have never looked into infinite space
> . . .
> That is why, I suppose,
> The best and worst never stayed here long but sought
> Immoderate soils where the beauty was not so external,
> The light less public and the meaning of life
> Something more than a mad camp.
> "Come!" cried the granite wastes,
> "How evasive is your humour, how accidental
> Your kindest kiss, how permanent is death."
> (Saints-to-be Slipped away sighing.)
> "Come!" purred the clays and gravels.
> "On our plains there is room for armies to drill; rivers
> Wait to be tamed and slaves to construct you a tomb
> In the grand manner; soft as the earth is mankind and both
> Need to be altered." (Intendant Caesars rose and
> Left, slamming the door.) But the really reckless were fetched
> By an older colder voice, the oceanic whisper:
> "I am the solitude that asks and promises nothing;
> That is how I shall set you free. There is no love;
> There are only the various envies, all of them sad."
> ("In Praise of Limestone," 32–34; 44–60)

Here Auden is using his long line and verse-sentence, which have themselves some of the qualities of his second kind of landscape. The lines are syllabically counted (13:11 syllables, with elision of all contiguous vowels and through "h"[5]). They have a sinuous, following-through, flexible though connected movement; they follow the ideas suggested by the panorama, varying pitch easily as Auden turns to a new aspect or alters his angle of approach or branches into a side consideration. They hold always to the main thread of the thought, though directed from moment to moment by its sinuosities and qualifications.

The intention differs from that which produced the curt, epigrammatic line of the mid-1930's and probably owes most, insofar as it is indebted to Auden's earlier practice, to the conversational verse of the later 1930s. The long verse-sentence is unusually free from the more obvious demands of line-endings (as, for instance, Auden's laconic sonnets necessarily were not). It is less immediately restricting than the three- or four-beat iambic line of Yeats—though that line was so magnificently varied in Yeats's hands that its apparent limitations turned to real advantage. Auden, we know, immensely admired the Yeatsian line and had sometimes used it. But a longer and

5. The elision of an "h" when it is preceded by a vowel; for example, "the house" becomes "th'ouse."

more loosely articulated line seemed more natural to him.

Like most of the valuable developments in Auden's verse this line is frequently marred, in this case by jarring and artistically unjustified changes of tone and attitude, and especially by a tiresome overinsistence on remaining too casual. We see the point, in the passage quoted above, about "Intendant Caesars . . . slamming the door" (it echoes an assertion by Josef Goebbels), but the combination is intellectually pert. On the other hand, the verb "fetched" in the same line has a nice ambiguity, drawn from Auden's acquaintance with contemporary American vernacular. To most English readers the verb will mean "brought" or "called away"; to an American it was likely to mean also "emotionally bowled over" (as when jazz enthusiasts said that a solo performer "fetched" them). And this second association—of something slightly hysterical—does add to the ironic texture of the passage.

At its best the long verse-sentence has a beautifully easy spoken note, an attractive mixture of colloquialism and serious observation, of wit and of moral concern—all managed with a verbal and aural skill that hardly any other living poet can approach. The shape and movement of the poem acts out, as it were, the tense dialectic of the poet's will, mind, and heart. In the following passage Auden opens on a typical landscape, limestone hills above the wide plains and their towns. The landscape is both actually and symbolically moving to him:

> If it form the one landscape that we the
>   inconstant ones
> Are consistently homesick for, this is
>   chiefly
> Because it dissolves in water. Mark these
>   rounded slopes
> With their surface fragrance of thyme and,
>   beneath,
> A secret system of caves and conduits; hear
>   the springs
> That spurt out everywhere with a chuckle,
> Each filling a private pool for its fish and
>   carving
> Its own little ravine whose cliffs entertain
> The butterfly and the lizard; examine this
>   region
> Of short distances and definite places . . .
>   (1–10)

So the complex interplay of human motives for which this landscape speaks begins to be developed. The poem closes on a view in perspective of the statues man makes out of this same rock, and farther back—picking up again the wider panoramic view of the opening—of the rock in its aboriginal landscape:

> . . . In so far as we have to look forward
> To death as a fact, no doubt we are right:
>   But if
> Sins can be forgiven, if bodies rise from the
>   dead,
> These modifications of matter into
> Innocent athletes and gesticulating
>   fountains,
> Made solely for pleasure, make a further
>   point:
> The blessed will not care what angle they
>   are regarded from,
> Having nothing to hide. Dear, I know
>   nothing of
> Either, but when I try to imagine a faultless
>   love
> Or the life to come, what I hear is the
>   murmur
> Of underground streams, what I see is a
>   limestone landscape.
>   (84–94)

This kind of poetic activity is altogether less gregarious and less intellectually extensive than that normally associated with Auden's work in the 1930's. But it emerged naturally from the broad lines of his intellectual and poetic development up to that point.

FROM THE MID-FORTIES TO 1973

> Lost of course and myself owing a death

DIVIDED AIMS:
THE GAME OF KNOWLEDGE

> . . . Can I learn to suffer
> Without saying something ironic or funny

On suffering? . . .
("Prospero to Ariel," *The Sea and the Mirror*)

Auden's work after the war, especially up to *Homage to Clio* (1960), expresses some striking tensions and divisions; expresses them with unusual directness. The tensions seem to be of three main kinds, each a matter of uncertain relationships: between Auden and his audience, between the artist and the moralizer, and between the artist and the believer.

We noted earlier that Auden was at that time somewhat more "austere" and less "knowing" than he used to be. But the difference is one of degree. He was still very often unsteady in tone and taste; the excellent parts have still to be sifted from much that is merely clever-clever or spry (a poem such as "Homage to Clio" shows this as well as any). To say this is not to be academically portentous or to forget that, then as always, a part of Auden's pertness arises from a deliberate wish to flout all conceptions of artistic decorum. This particular quality is not a tough or quirky comedy so much as something would-be funny. Several kinds of instances could be cited: the raiding of the dictionary for words that are not merely odd but unhelpfully odd; the overworking of pat endings, which had persisted since the early sonnets; the drop into an affectedly colloquial manner; the showy manipulation of conceits; in short, a recurrent bright technical flurry.

These faults seem to arise in part from Auden's unsureness about his exact audience, his lack of relation to a known and fairly homogeneous group whose attitudes he habitually appreciated. He had, we know, a considerable capacity for friendship; and he was not without a good circle of admirers among poets—indeed, he has been a strong influence on American poetry for many years. Yet he was in one sense isolated, and this is partly the result of the move to America we discussed earlier and sought to justify.

We do not now retract that justification. But we need to see as sharply as possible the problems it presented Auden. The difficulty of knowing to just whom he was speaking had sometimes led him to solitary verbal pirouettes or to new versions of the "private joking in panelled rooms" of which he accused himself in the 1930's. At such times the audience seems to be either a very small "in-group" or almost hypothetical—the audience of the brighter weeklies, say, which is not really any of us but is parts of many of us on both sides of the Atlantic and which is intellectually fashionable.

But occasionally Auden could speak steadily as well as wittily and intelligently to an audience composed, we may imagine, of what he called "ironic points of light"; of people whose irony does not preclude charity, who are interested in both poetry and moral ideas, who are on the whole unambitious and who try to steer honestly between righteous indignation, contempt, and self-surrender. No doubt this is a small audience, scattered and hard to find. But it exists, and Auden's career particularly qualified him to seek it:

O every day in sleep and labour
Our life and death are with our neighbour,
And love illuminates again
The city and the lion's den
The world's great rage, the travel of young
men.
(*New Year Letter*, pt. 3)

In his vividly metaphorical, alert, and companionable conversational verse and in his landscape poetry Auden could sometimes reach out to the kind of audience he might particularly address. "In Praise of Limestone" is a fine poem and yet a poem severed from local cultures. Its unrooted, engaged intelligence sees, and sees through, the landscape. The later "Whitsunday in Kirchstetten," to which we will return, rediscovers the sense of locality and is companionable in a way that recalls some of the poems of friendship in the early 1930's (such as "Out on the lawn I lie in bed") but is less parochial.

Auden's second area of tension lies in the uneasy relationship between the purposive moralist and the creative artist—the artist who is not concerned to wrest statements from experience directly but works in the intuitive knowledge that, to use Yeats's phrase, "words alone are certain good." We referred to an aspect of this earlier. Since Auden now sees the problem more clearly, the split is not so sharp-edged. It is still there, as the disconcerting unevenness of such a poem as "Memorial for the City" shows. Auden simply will not leave the good verse of the poem's first section to work in its own way, but continues by piling up bright perceptions. He is able to quote with obvious approval "the value of art lies in its effects—not in beauty but in right action"; but he can also refer to "the devil's subtlest temptation, the desire to do good by [your] art." There need be no real contradiction there. Yet for a personality such as Auden's there is likely to be a powerful tension until the exact ways in which each statement may be true have been resolved.

The work of resolution leads directly into what we are calling Auden's third problem. Around this whole area he exercised his mind considerably for many years, and it was entirely typical that he should have devoted his inaugural lecture as professor of poetry at Oxford to aspects of it. The core of the question is the relation of the poet and his work to himself as a man (fallen, free, bound, and willful) and so to God. Its main divisions are: What are the dangers of artistic vocation? What are the justifications?

The theme of the spiritual dangers in the life of an artist has engaged several important contemporary writers, notably Eliot and Thomas Mann. There are striking similarities between the theme of Mann's story *Death in Venice* and the long second part of Caliban's vivid parody of the later Henry James (and also in the whole concept of Prospero) in Auden's *The Sea and the Mirror.* If man's life is a constant struggle in the will, how far is the artist tempted—because he is a sort of creator—to abrogate this responsibility, to get, so to speak, between himself and God? "The artist up to his old game of playing at God with words," quotes Auden from Kierkegaard, and adds a note from the same source about the need to "get out of the poetical into the existential."

Auden had, therefore, to define to his own satisfaction the justification of art. His most typical single phrase from many on the subject asserts that poetry is "a game of knowledge." First, poetry (and all art) is a *game.* It is a form of magic (the naming of "sacred objects") and of fun ("the joke of rhyme")" a release for writer and reader, inspired first not by a desire to do good or acquire fame but by a love of "playing around with words." Also as a game, it is not finally real or serious as "theology and horses" are; it "makes nothing happen." Again like a game, it has fixed rules (patterns, rituals, ceremonies, forms, "necessities"), which the players must obey if they are to enjoy. But pure luck ("the luck of verbal playing") also has a part; something is simply "given" (grace?). "Only your song is an absolute gift," Auden says of the composer" and intends the line to carry the ambiguities of both the idiomatic and the philosophic meanings. The practice of art was for Auden yet another example of the fruitful paradox of freedom and necessity.

Yet poetry is a game of *knowledge.* It is in a certain sense concerned with knowledge, and its magic is meaningful. The knowledge is, though, a product of the play and comes by indirection, as in the serious, absorbed play of a child. Aesthetic patterns and resolutions are not metaphysical patterns and resolutions ("analogy is not identity"), but can analogously point toward them: "And the hard bright light composes / A meaningless moment into an eternal fact." In art's harmony and ritual are mirrored the possibility of a greater order outside man,s power; both demand "an acknowledgement that there are relationships which are obligatory and independent of our personality."

So poetry can help to "direct us to ourselves," can "persuade" us to a form of "moral rejoicing," can point through man's "lying nature" to "love and truth." At this stage this was the fullest expression of Auden's continuing urge to irradiate daily human activity with mythical meaning and of his questioning of the relation between art and moral purpose. By the 1960's the dilemma was still not altogether resolved in Auden's personality and could create a jarring unsteadiness. To regret this unsteadiness is not to make aesthetic considerations override all others. For we may say that to the artist, in a special sense, "analogy *must* be identity," that the tense play of ambiguities which make up a poem is indeed part of the poet's "being."

PROSE

Of all Auden's varied output during the last dozen years of his life, two main elements demand to be discussed in particular: his prose criticism and his four final volumes of verse (one of them posthumous).

Actually, the earliest volume of prose criticism, *The Enchàfed Flood,* dates back to 1951. It is still interesting and indeed exciting to read; and it showed what were to be over the following twenty or so years the main characteristics of Auden's considerable prose output: his literary criticism is freely ranging, synoptic, paradoxical, aphoristic. It is not much concerned (though it can be occasionally) with close critical analysis of the words on the page; it is much more likely to muse widely on the symbolic and philosophic implications of a work, to deal in parables, recurrent themes, archetypes, myths, patterns.

The Enchàfed Flood, which began as the Page-Barbour lectures at the University of Virginia, is thus closely organized around a number of related themes, those of the romantic symbolism of the sea and of the desert. These were issues to which Auden returned again and again, notably in *The Sea and the Mirror, The Age of Anxiety,* the seven "Bucolics," and other landscape poems. He made use of a similar general approach when he delivered the 1967 T. S. Eliot Memorial Lectures at the University of Kent, Canterbury, which were subsequently published as *Secondary Worlds* (1968). Primary worlds are those of everyday social experience; secondary worlds are those of art: the phrases themselves are from his beloved J. R. R. Tolkien. Here is a typical quotation, typical not only of his manner but of one of his recurrent themes, an aspect of the relations between art and life:

> All art is gratuitous [a favorite word], so that one can never say that a certain kind of society must necessarily produce a certain kind of art. On the other hand, when we consider a certain society and the literature which it did actually produce, we can sometimes see reasons why it was possible for such a society to produce it.

Outside of these two "commissioned" volumes, Auden wrote essay after essay for all sorts of different occasions but especially as introductions to collections of other writers' work, as long reviews, and as lectures. His poetry cannot usefully be described as "literary"; there are manifestly literary elements, but they are not a major part of the poems' qualities. But he was certainly a very literary and scholarly man, and the overall impression created by his great bulk of essays is the pendulum swing from literary and historical allusion to general analysis and observation on almost any subject under the sun. The fruit of all this effort, covering about thirty years, is to be found in the more than five hundred pages each of *The Dyer's Hand* (1963) and *Forewords and Afterwords* (1973).

Here we can see in full measure Auden's main qualities as a critic and indeed as a personality, since his own style comes out, necessarily, more directly in his prose than in his poetry. He has a whole range of favorite themes and favorite approaches, ways of dealing with those themes. He also has certain favorite single notions, mild bees in his bonnet, such as the impropriety of publishing a man's letters after his death, or the virtues and the limits of English family life (really, of English upper-middle-class professional family life in the first three or four decades of this century; he never ceased, in spite of all his criticisms, to feel both a nostalgia and a moral admiration for that).

Of his major recurrent themes, one of the

two or three most dominant is, once again, the relations between art and life. He talks, at different points in these two volumes, about poems as belonging to a "limitless world of pure joy"; about art as "a mirror in which [we] may become conscious of what [our] own feelings really are; its proper effect, in fact, is disenchanting"; about poetry as "a clarification of life" concerned with two key questions "Who am I?" and "Whom ought I to become?"; and about a poem as "a dialectical struggle between the events the poet wishes to embody and the verbal system." A hundred other similar quotations could be brought forward.

Or one recalls Auden's fondness for observing animals and then for teasing out reflections on the human condition by comparing man—self-aware, having free will, using language—with animals or birds, which have none of these things. Robert Bloom, an American critic, is surely right to call the two essays collected as "Two Bestiaries" in *The Dyer's Hand,* devoted respectively to D. H. Lawrence and Marianne Moore, "masterful, learned and penetrating" and to go on to relate them to Auden's own animal poems: "in them, Auden manifests his own affection for humankind, and his sacred sense of its transcendence over the creatures. And his urgent concern with the nature and exigencies of the human predicament has from the beginning of his career testified to his unending preoccupation with the Good Life."

Yet again, these essays illustrate time after time the perceptiveness, the unusualness, often the quixotry of Auden's powers of general observation. Read only the essay in *The Dyer's Hand* called "The American Scene," which embodies an exceptional range of insights on the texture and nature of American life. Or note the incidental comments scattered throughout his essays, such as this one: "In any modern city, a great deal of our energy has to be expended in *not* seeing, *not* hearing, *not* smelling. An inhabitant of New York who possessed the sensory acuteness of an African Bushman would very soon go mad." And here is a remarkably percipient short paragraph on Rudyard Kipling:

> His poems in their quantity, their limitation to one feeling at a time, have the air of brilliant tactical improvisations to overcome sudden unforeseen obstacles, as if, for Kipling, experience were not a seed to cultivate patiently and lovingly, but an unending stream of dangerous feelings to be immediately mastered as they appear.

These two volumes show also, once again and time after time, Auden's love of myth, structure, and pattern. I am not myself a reader or a lover of the "detective story," that characteristically English form of fiction (which is to be distinguished from the gangster novel, the spy thriller, or the police novel). It was bound to appeal to Auden, and his essay on the genre is, even for one who does not read them, a fascinating exercise in elaborate pattern tracing and symbol identification. Auden never tired of this kind of exercise; here he is in the course of an essay on the brothers Grimm and Hans Christian Andersen:

> A fairy story, as distinct from a merry tale, or an animal story, is a serious tale with a human hero and a happy ending The progression of its hero is the reverse of the tragic hero's: at the beginning he is either socially obscure or despised as being stupid or untalented, lacking in the heroic virtues, but at the end, he has surprised everyone by demonstrating his heroism and winning fame, riches and love.

Or consider the perfectly typical opening of *Secondary Worlds*: "In myth, history and literature, we meet four kinds of human beings, of whom it may be said that their deaths are the most significant event in their lives, the Sacrificial Victim, the Epic Hero, the Tragic Hero and the Martyr." He then proceeds to define them one by one before beginning to play variations on the concepts. Auden's essays, for all their occasional prejudices, opinionations, and admonishings, are on the whole a source of continuous pleasure and insight—into both literature and experience.

POETRY AND COMPANIONABILITY

Auden's poetry of the 1960's and 1970's is on the whole more closely contained, more quietly ruminative than before. Technically it is as brilliant as ever, inventive, witty, and extraordinarily skillful. But there is little larger formal experiment. The predominant tones and manners are occasional, domestic, relaxed, and idiomatic rather than more largely thematic or outward-turned.

In the light of all this we can make new glosses on the three divisions in Auden's work we discussed earlier. As for the relation between Auden and his audience: the audience envisaged in this last period is, more often than not, a small group of good friends. Sometimes there is even—though partly with the tongue in the cheek—a prim, keep-your-distance manner toward outsiders. Catching familiar notes in these late poems one realizes sharply that much of Auden's poetry right from the beginning addressed itself to, found its voice in, a small, known, domestic group of friends. It seems at first glance ironic that Auden's reputation in the 1930's should have been so much that of "the conscience of his generation," which seems to imply adopting a much more public intellectual stance. But the reputation was fairly gained; at bottom there is no real contradiction between the two claims.

In talking about the tension between the artist and the moralist in Auden we discussed his description of poetry as "a game of knowledge." The stress later, both in his criticism and in his poetry, was less on the "knowledge" and more on the "game," more on poetry as verbal artifice expressing celebration, awe, or piety before experience. Third, the tension between the artist and the believer seemed less, because poetry had been put in its place as, in the last resort, a side occupation or exercise—enormously worthwhile, of course:

> . . . After all, it's rather a privilege
> amid the affluent traffic
> to serve this unpopular art . . .

but still, as the tone of the above quotation conveys, a marginal matter, secondary to the real questions of faith and the effort to serve God. That life, too, does not demand melodramatic, rhetorical, or histrionic responses. Best, without underestimating the actual melodrama of experience, to work quietly and as well as one can, where we are, trusting in God and his grace. The times may tempt us to do otherwise, and especially tempt writers to assume roles beyond their competence; these voices have to be quietly ignored.

Hence, Auden's last four volumes of verse, which cover the final dozen years of his life, show—like his prose—certain strongly marked and distinctive qualities. The volumes are *About the House* (1966), *City Without Walls* (1969), *Epistle to a Godson* (1972), and the posthumous *Thank You, Fog* (1974). They have common qualities of theme and tone that mark them off fairly decisively from the volumes that preceded them.

It is useful to read them also in conjunction with his commonplace book, *A Certain World* (1971), which, through deploying his favorite extracts from a multitude of writers of many times and nationalities, shows well once again the strange conformations of his idiosyncratic mind. The book is, he said, not an autobiography (he would never have written one of those) but "a map of my planet." Here, too, are all his favorite ideas, but put by other writers: that poetry makes nothing happen; that it is a form of pure play; that listening to the birds reminds you that man is a creature with "the right to make promises," or—as William Hazlitt is quoted as saying—"man is the only animal that laughs and weeps"; that man is haunted by the difference between what is and what might have been, the exerciser of free will, choice, commitments in speech, and so on.

In these last four volumes of poetry, in general, Auden writes less than he had used to about political or public matters; his poetry still largely lacks the kind of intimacy whose absence from his work, throughout his career, I noted earlier. But this later poetry is much more about personal matters, which is why I used the word "companionability" in the title to this section. I think it is fair to say that most critics do not think as highly of these later volumes as of the earlier ones. I do, and find they give a valuable new dimension to the body of Auden's work.

It is poetry of, first, acceptance; acceptance of creatureliness, of the real world (under God), of the temporal order. It is a poetry of celebration of that natural world, and of harmony and measure before it; it is a humane poetry. One characteristic tone and some of its basic seriousness are caught in the last lines of the last poem of *About the House*:

> . . . about
> catastrophe or how to behave in one
> I know nothing, except what everyone
> knows—
> if there when Grace dances, I should dance.
> ("Whitsunday in Kirchstetten")

It is therefore poetry that pivots around the idea of a modest, unarrogant acceptance of the self—"my personal city"—and of the body, of home (there are many poems of "place"), and of friendship. Here we need to say more about the role of that small group of friends to which I referred earlier. Look only at the dedications of many of these later poems; they are to living friends, in memoriam for dead friends, to doctors, the local priest (in Austria), relatives, a godchild. It is a small group, and the sense of it was intensified by Auden's renewed Oxford links; the pull of all that held.

All this is admirable, and we should try to take it straight and link it with Auden's continuing preoccupations; in both small and large senses he was coming home. By "small" senses I mean that this poetry could occasionally be that of a rather stiff, mandarin, Oxford man who knew he had been to the best place and who, with his friends, never quite got rid of a sense that the great body of people outside were not quite as nice as *they* were. But then Auden was always very conscious of his privacy and inviolability. He had a right to be like that. What seems to me less justifiable is the tampering with the chronology of the poetry so as to put people off tracing any lines of development (he later allowed chronological printing) and, even more, amending poems written many years ago. Auden justified this by saying: "I have never, consciously at any rate, attempted to revise my former thoughts or feelings, only the language in which they were first expressed when, on further consideration, it seemed to me inaccurate, lifeless, prolix or painful to the ear." I do not think that the full range of his later amendments is caught within the above prescription; some of them do indicate revisions of thoughts and feelings.

The tone is almost always low-keyed (and sometimes high camp). There are irritating oddities and pawkinesses, but overall I would agree with Justin Replogle that throughout this last period Auden can be called almost exclusively a comic poet and that he wrote some of his best poems in this mode. At their best these are seriously playful poems, domestic, conversational, both warm and dry.

As to their craft, they are, to use a favorite word of Auden himself in this connection, elegant "contraptions." They tend to build up a labyrinthine and complex interplay of tones and meanings; thus Richard Johnson, in a particularly subtle book on Auden's poetry—*Man's Place*—can speak of "the coherence of idea, art, organization, and tone" in these later poems.

We noted earlier that after the late 1930's Auden wrote no more very long poems. But what may be said to have taken their place—and he wrote them for more than a decade thereafter—were linked groups, series, or sequences of poems. Again I would agree with Johnson that these are among his most substantial achievements. They include, in *The Shield of Achilles,* the seven "Bucolics," a further development of that landscape poetry to which we have referred earlier, and the seven "Horae Canonicae" in the same volume, a superb sequence. Then, in *About the House,* there are the twelve poems called "Thanksgiving for a Habitat," which are capped, in the same volume, by the fluently tender "Whitsunday in Kirchstetten," from whose last lines I quoted a little earlier in this section.

Finally, there are the eight songs from "Mother Courage" in *City Without Walls.*

The harvest of these last years, in short, was a very good and a distinctive one; without it English poetry—and our understanding of Auden's own capacities as a poet—would have been the poorer.

Consistently, through more than forty years of writing, Auden rejected "the soft carpets and big desks" of the successful men of letters and stuck to his explorations with a quite unusual devotion. He made his own mistakes in his own way and, by example and precept, urged "the acceptance by every individual of his aloneness and his responsibility for it, and a willingness continually to re-examine his assumptions." We have suggested that in one sense poetry seemed less absorbing to Auden in his last decade than heretofore. Yet still poetry remained his natural way of speaking; he was always a dedicated poet for whom the practice of poetry was an activity of the moral will. He pursued his honestly persistent inquiries eagerly and hopefully. He could write: "wherever / The sun shines, brooks run, books are written / There will also be this death." But also, just as characteristically, he wrote: "After so many years the light is / Novel still and immensely ambitious."

Meanwhile, Auden's achievement is remarkable: in much pithily epigrammatic verse; in many lovely songs, lyrics, and sonnets; in a flexible, acute, and often comic conversational verse; and in his moral-landscape poetry. He helped considerably to define and make articulate our situation in the 1930's, and also in the 1950's, as this finely rhetorical passage from "The Shield of Achilles" will remind us:

> The mass and majesty of this world, all
> That carries weight and always weighs the
> same
> Lay in the hands of others; they were small
> And could not hope for help and no help
> came:
> What their foes liked to do was done, their
> shame
> Was all the worst could wish; they lost their
> pride
> And died as men before their bodies died.
> (38–44)

Later, the sense of dramatic menace receded and with it some kinds of urgency in Auden's verse. He now sought different music, other relationships; and in doing so he went back more than ever to his origins:

> Let your last thinks all be thanks:
> praise your parents who gave you
> a Super-ego of strength
> that saves you so much bother
> digit friends and dear them all,
> then pay fair attribution
> to your age, to having been
> born when you were. In boyhood
> you were permitted to meet
> beautiful old contraptions . . .
> ("Lullaby")

Of all this, the result is a considerable body of memorable speech on our times and problems, an example that contributes to the civility Auden so much admired, and a commitment that claims our respect and admiration.

Selected Bibliography

BIBLIOGRAPHY

J. P. Clancy, "A. H. Auden Bibliography, 1924–55," in *Thought,* 30 (Summer, 1955), pub. by Fordham University; *An Annotated Check List of the Works of W. H. Auden,* E. Callan, (Denver, 1958); *W. H. Auden, A Bibliography: The Early Years Through 1955,* B. C. Bloomfield, (Charlottesville, Va., 1964), 2nd ed., (1972), ed. by B. C. Bloomfield and E. Mendelson, extends through 1969.

COLLECTED AND SELECTED WORKS

Selected Poems, (London, 1938); *Some Poems,* (London, 1940), small sel. of previously published verse; *Collected Poetry of W. H. Auden,* (New York, 1945), published in the U.K. as *Collected Shorter Poems, 1930–1944,* (London, 1950), rev. versions of most of Auden's earlier poems, with excisions; *W. H. Auden. A Selection by the Author,* (London, 1958), published in the U.S. as *Selected Poetry of W. H. Auden,* (New York, 1959; 2nd ed., 1971); *Selected Essays,* (London,

1964, criticism); *Collected Shorter Poems, 1927–1957,* (London, 1966; New York, 1967), further revs. and excisions of earlier work, arranged chronologically; *Collected Longer Poems,* (London, 1968; New York, 1969); *Collected Poems,* E. Mendelson, ed., (New York-London, 1976), includes all of *Collected Shorter Poems, 1927–1957* and *Collected Longer Poems,* with some additional poems restored by Auden in later years and with the contents of his later vols. of short poems; Auden's final rev. texts, with many early poems omitted; *The English Auden. Poems, Essays, and Dramatic Writings, 1927–1939,* (London, 1977; New York, 1978), repr. the original versions, including all the poems that Auden printed in book form during his lifetime but omitted from his late collections.

SEPARATE WORKS

Poems, (London, 1930, rev. ed., 1932), includes *Paid on Both Sides,* a charade in verse; *The Orators: An English Study,* (London, 1932, rev. eds., 1934, 1966), verse and prose, last ed. includes preface by Auden; *The Dance of Death,* (London, 1933), verse and prose; *The Dog Beneath the Skin: Or, Where Is Francis?,* (London, 1935), drama, verse, and prose, with C. Isherwood; *Look, Stranger!,* (London, 1936), verse, pub. in the U.S. as *On the Island,* (New York, 1937); *The Ascent of F6,* (London, 1936, rev. ed., 1937), drama, verse, and prose, with C. Isherwood; *Spain,* (London, 1937), verse, a pamphlet poem; *Letters from Iceland,* (London, 1937), travel, verse, and prose, with L. MacNeice; *On the Frontier,* (London, 1938), drama, verse, and prose, with C. Isherwood; *Journey to a War,* (London 1939, rev. ed., 1973), travel, with C. Isherwood, includes Auden's sonnet sequence "In Time of War."

Another Time, (London, 1940), verse; *New Year Letter,* (New York; London, 1941), verse, pub. in U.S. as *The Double Man,* includes the long title poem, the sonnet sequence "The Quest", prologue, and epilogue; *Three Songs for St. Cecilia's Day,* (London, 1941); *For the Time Being,* (London, 1945), verse, also contains *The Sea and the Mirror: A Commentary on Shakespeare's "The Tempest"; The Age of Anxiety: A Baroque Eclogue,* (London, 1948), verse; *The Enchàfed Flood, or, The Romantic Iconography of the Sea,* (London, 1951), criticism, the Page-Barbour Lectures, (University of Virginia, 1949); *Nones,* (London, 1952), verse; *Mountains,* (London, 1954), a Faber Ariel poem; *The Shield of Achilles,* (London, 1955), verse; *The Old Man's Road,* (New York, 1956, verse.

Homage to Clio, (London, 1960), verse; *The Dyer's Hand and Other Essays,* (London, 1963), criticism; *About the House,* (London, 1966), verse; *Secondary Worlds,* (London, 1968), criticism, the T. S. Eliot Memorial Lectures at the University of Kent, (1967); *City Without Walls and Other Poems,* (London, 1969), verse. *Academic Graffiti,* (London, 1971), light verse; *Epistle to a Godson and Other Poems,* (London, 1972), verse; *Forewords and Afterwords,* (London, 1973), criticism, sel. by E. Mendelson; *Thank You, Fog: Last Poems,* (London, 1974, verse.

LIBRETTI

No More Peace: A Thoughtful Comedy, E. Toller, (London, 1937), trans. by E. Crankshaw, lyrics trans. and adap. by Auden; *The Rake's Progress—An Opera,* (London, 1951), music by I. Stravinsky, libretto by Auden and C. Kallman; *The Magic Flute,* (London, 1957), music by W. A. Mozart, new English libretto by Auden and C. Kallman; *Elegy for Young Lovers—An Opera,* (Mainz, 1961), music by H. W. Henze, libretto by Auden and C. Kallman; *The Bassarids,* (London, 1960), music by H. W. Henze, libretto by Auden and C. Kallman, performed at Salzburg *Love's Labour Lost,* (London, 1973), music by N. Nabokov, libretto by Auden and C. Kallman, performed in Brussels; *Paul Bunyan—An Operetta,* (London, 1976), music by B. Britten, libretto by Auden, performed at Columbia University (May, 1941).

EDITED WORKS, INTRODUCTIONS, TRANSLATIONS, AND ANTHOLOGIES

Oxford Poetry, (London, 1926), anthology, with C. Plumb; *Oxford Poetry,* (London, 1927), anthology, with C. Day Lewis; *The Poet's Tongue,* (London, 1935), anthology, with J. Garrett; *Poetry,* (Chicago), 49 (January, 1937), with M. Roberts; *The Oxford Book of Light Verse,* (London, 1938), anthology; *The American Scene,* H. James, (New York, 1946), intro. by Auden, repr. in *Horizon,* 86 (February, 1947); *Tennyson,* (London, 1946), sel. from his poems and with intro. by Auden; *Slick but Not Streamlined,* J. Betjeman, (New York, 1947), poems and short pieces sel. and with intro. by Auden; *The Portable Greek Reader,* (New York, 1948), intro. by Auden; *Intimate Journals,* C. Baudelaire, (London, 1949), trans. by C. Isherwood, intro. by Auden.

Selected Prose and Poetry of Poe, (New York, 1950), ed. and with intro. by Auden; *Poets of the English Language,* 5 vols., (London, 1952), anthology, with N. H. Pearson; *An Elizabethan Song Book,* (New York, 1955), music ed. by N. Greenberg, lyrics ed. by Auden and C. Kallman; *Kierkegaard,* (London, 1955), sel. and with intro. by Auden; *The Faber Book of Modern American Verse,* (London, 1956), anthology, *The Selected Writings of Sidney Smith,* (London, 1957); *The Complete Poems of Cavafy,* (New York, 1961), trans by R. Dalvin, intro. by Auden; *Goethe: An Italian Journey, 1786–1788,* (London, 1962), trans. and with intro. by Auden and E. Mayer; *A Choice of de la Mare's Verse,* (London, 1963), sel. and with intro. by Auden; *Markings,* D Hammarskjold and L. Sjöberg,

(London, 1964), foreword by Auden; *The Faber Book of Aphorisms: A Personal Selection,* (London, 1964), with L. Kronenberger; *Nineteenth-Century Minor Poets,* (London, 1966), ed. by Auden; *The Elder Edda: A Selection,* (London, 1969), trans. from the Icelandic by P. B. Taylor and Auden.

G. K. Chesterton: A Selection from His Non-Fictional Prose, (London, 1970), sel. by Auden; *A Certain World: A Commonplace Book,* (London, 1971), anthology, sel. by Auden; *Selected Poems of Gunnar Ekelöf,* (London, 1971), trans. by Auden and L. Sjöberg; *A Choice of Dryden's Verse,* (London, 1973), sel. and with intro. by Auden; *George Herbert,* (London, 1973), Sel. by Auden; *Evening Land,* Par Lagerkvist, (London, 1977), trans. by Auden and L. Sjöberg.

BIOGRAPHICAL AND CRITICAL STUDIES

F. R. Leavis, *New Bearings in English Poetry,* (London, 1932); *The Destructive Element,* S. Spender, (London, 1935), pt. 3 is relevant; *The Faber Book of Modern Verse,* M. Roberts, ed., (London, 1936), new ed., 1951, intro. by Roberts describes the social, political, and cultural climate of Auden's time; *Enemies of Promise,* C. Connolly, (London, 1938), contains comments on Auden; *Lions and Shadows,* C. Isherwood, (London, 1938), contains comments on Auden; *Modern Poetry: A Personal Essay,* L. MacNeice, (London, 1938); *Modem Poetry and the Tradition,* C. Brooks, (Chapel Hill, N.C., 1939); *The Present Age from 1914,* E. Muir, (London, 1939), brought up to 1950 with new survey by D. Daiches, (1957).

E. Drew, *Directions in Modern Poetry,* (New York, 1940); *Sowing the Spring,* J. G. Southworth, (Oxford, 1940), a study of the "Auden Group"; *Southern Review,* R. Jarrell "Changes of Attitude and Rhetoric in Auden's Poetry", 7, (1941); *Auden and After,* F. Scarfe, (London, 1942); *Life and the Poet,* S. Spender, (London, 1942); *The Personal Principle,* D. S. Savage, (London, 1944); *Paritisan Review,* R. Jarrell "Freud to Paul: The Stages of Auden's Ideology", 12, (1945); *Poets at Work,* (New York, 1948); *Poetry of the Present,* G. Grigson, ed., (London, 1949), valuable intro.; *Auden,* F. Scarfe, (Monaco, 1949); *The Tell-Tale Article,* G. R. Hamilton, (London, 1949).

R. Hoggart, *Auden: An Introductory Essay,* (London, 1951); *World Within a World,* S. Spender, (London, 1951), contains material on the young Auden; *The Modern Writer and His World,* G. S. Fraser, (London, 1953, rev. ed., 1964); *More Modern American Poets,* J. G. Southworth, (London, 1954); *Predilections,* M. Moore, (New York, 1955); *The Whispering Gallery,* J. Lehmann, (London, 1955), contains comments on the young Auden; *The Making of the Auden Canon,* J. W. Beach, (Minneapolis, 1957); *The Romantic Survival,* J. Bayley, (London, 1957); *The Shaping Spirit,* A. Alvarez, (London, 1958); *Vision and Rhetoric,* G. S. Fraser, (London, 1959).

R. Hoggart, *W. H. Auden: A Selection,* (London, 1961); *The Poetry of W. H. Auden: The Disenchanted Island,* M. K. Spears, (New York, 1963); *Auden,* B. Everett, (London, 1964); *Auden: A Collection of Critical Essays,* M. K. Spears, ed., (Englewood Cliffs, N.J., 1964); *The Poetic Art of W. H. Auden,* J. G. Blair, (Princeton, N.J., 1965); *Quest for the Necessary: W. H. Auden and the Dilemma of Divided Consciousness,* H. Greenberg, (Cambridge, Mass., 1968); *Changes of Heart: A Study of the Poetry of W. H. Auden,* G. Nelson, (London, 1969); *Auden's Poetry,* J. Replogle, (London, 1969).

G.W. Bahlke, *The Later Auden,* (New Brunswick, N.J., 1970); *W. H. Auden,* D. Davison, (London, 1970); *A Reader's Guide to W. H. Auden,* J. Fuller, (London, 1970); *W. H. Auden as a Social Poet,* F. Buell, (Ithaca, N.Y., 1973); *Man's Place: An Essay on Auden,* R. Johnson, (Ithaca N.Y., 19730; *W. H. Auden: A Tribute,* S. Spender, ed., (London, 1975); *The Auden Generation: Literature and Politics in England in the 1930s,* S. Hynes, (London, 1976); *W. H. Auden: The Life of a Poet,* C. Osborne, (New York, 1979).

E. Mendelson, *W. H. Auden: Nineteen Hundred Seven to Nineteen Hundred Seventy-Three,* (New York, 1980); *Early Auden,* E. Mendelson, (New York, 1981); *W. H. Auden,* G. T. Wright, rev. ed., (New York, 1981).

BEOWULF AND ANGLO-SAXON POETRY

ROBERT W. HANNING

INTRODUCTION

THE EARLIEST EXTANT epic and the first great poem in the English language is *Beowulf.* Although its availability and influence within its era (*ca.* 600–1066) seem to have been minimal, and although its scope (3,182 lines in the only extant manuscript, *Brit. Lib. Cotton Vitellius A. XV, ca.* A.D. 1000) is constricted compared with later, more self-consciously literary and derivative epics like Spenser's *Faerie Queene* and Milton's *Paradise Lost,* it has stimulated ever-increasing study and admiration during the last hundred years because of the excellence of its artistry, the nobility of its heroic vision, and its uniqueness as a primary epic within early medieval Germanic literature.

Despite the substantial attention paid to *Beowulf* by philologists, folklorists, anthropologists, and social and literary historians, we can still only guess at the circumstances of its composition and offer tentative judgments about its unity, significance, and essentially Christian or pagan outlook. Given the traditional (that is, inherited rather than created) materials, of Germanic or even Indo-European origin, from which it is largely constructed, *Beowulf* resists many types of analysis easily applied to an original narrative fiction composed by a self-conscious verbal artist for a literate audience. To begin to understand its values and perspective, we must first attempt, as much as our literacy-conditioned processes of thought and imagination will allow us, to reconstruct those processes as they might function in a preliterate, traditional culture. Then we must use all available information about the transitional (partly Germanic and traditional, partly Christian and literate) culture of Anglo-Saxon England, and other analogous civilizations, to try to place *Beowulf* within it in time and place, and to form plausible opinions about the poem's poetics, historical consciousness, and commitment (or lack of commitment) to Christianity. Finally, we must be attentive to *Beowulf's* presentation of the heroic ideal—an ideal it shares with primary, or traditional, epics from several cultures—in order to evaluate the protagonist and his battles with monstrous adversaries.

The following discussion of *Beowulf* will focus successively on its pre-insular cultural heritage; its Anglo-Saxon context; its physical state as a manuscript; and its unity, structure, significance, and art as a poem.

SUMMARY

The poem opens by recalling Scyld Scefing, founder of the Scylding dynasty of the Danish nation. God sends Scyld to the lordless Danes; he comes as a child in a boat and grows up to be a great war-king. When he dies, his followers send his body back out to sea in a treasure-laden boat. Scyld's son, Beowulf (not the hero of the poem), continues his father's reign, and the Danes prosper through generations. Hrothgar, in his kingship, builds Heorot—a great mead hall—and plans to dispense treasure within it to his war band. The joyful songs of the celebrating Danes attract and infuriate Grendel, a border-dwelling semi-human monster descended from Cain, whose lineage was banished by God from the haunts of humanity after the first murder. When the Danes are asleep, Grendel bursts into Heorot and kills and eats thirty warriors. So begins a twelve-year reign of terror: Grendel invades Heorot each night, effectively disrupting Danish social existence, and the Danes have no warrior strong enough to oust him. In their misery, they make offerings to idols; Hrothgar endures helpless, terrible grief.

In Geatland, the young hero *Beowulf,* strongest of men, hears of the Danes' plight and sets out across the sea with a small troop of companions. They arrive in Denmark and are received with courtesy by Hrothgar. Unferth, the þyle (orator? jester? official challenger?) of the Danish court, expresses doubt that Beowulf, who lost a swimming (or rowing) match to a famous warrior called Breca some time before, can now conquer Grendel. Beowulf denies the allegation of defeat and tells the true story, including how he killed nine sea monsters. He then impugns the Danes' courage, and says that he is ready to destroy Grendel or die trying. Hrothgar is pleased by the visitor's reply and leaves the Geats alone in Heorot as night falls. Grendel arrives, expecting to feast on more sleeping warriors. He devours one Geat, but Beowulf, who has disavowed the use of weapons against Grendel, takes the monster in a handgrip. A terrific battle ensues, which nearly wrecks Heorot. The terrified Grendel tries to escape; Beowulf tears his arm off, and the monster flees to his swampland home to die.

The next morning the Danes rejoice at Grendel's fate and celebrate Beowulf's deed in songs. Celebrations begin in Heorot; a *scop* (court poet) recites the story of the battle at Finnsburh between the Half-Danes under Hnaef and the Frisians under Finn. The fight was a standoff, but Hnaef was killed, and Hildeburh, his sister and Finn's wife, mourned him and her son, also a victim. Hengest, Hnaef's henchman, entered into a treaty to serve Finn with the other Half-Danes, but ultimately broke the agreement and avenged Hnaef by killing Finn. The story over, gifts are given and Wealhtheow, Hrothgar's queen, asks for support for her young sons from Beowulf and Hrothulf, Hrothgar's nephew.

After the Danes and Geats go to sleep, Grendel's mother enters Heorot seeking vengeance for her dead offspring. She seizes one Danish warrior and flees to her swamp. The Danes and Hrothgar are desolate at this new attack, but Beowulf promises to avenge the dead man and is escorted to the dreadful, fiery pool beneath which the monsters live. Armed and bearing Unferth's sword, Hrunting, Beowulf dives to the bottom, finds the monsters' hall, and does battle with Grendel's mother. The fight is difficult; Hrunting fails its user, but Beowulf sees a great old sword, too big for anyone but himself, and uses it to kill the mother and behead the body of the son, whose blood destroys the blade. The hero returns to the surface of the purged pond, finds the Danes gone and his own men despairing, and returns to Heorot with Grendel's head and the sword hilt, which he gives to Hrothgar. The old king stares at the hilt and instructs the young warrior on the shortness of life and the necessity of sharing out treasure. After an exchange of gifts and protestations of friendship between Geats and Danes (who had been feuding), Beowulf returns home and tells his king, Hygelac, of his exploits; he also indicates that the political marriage between Hrothgar's daughter, Freawaru, and Ingeld, prince of the Heathobards, will only briefly quiet the feud between the two peoples. Beowulf passes on to Hygelac the gifts he has received from Hrothgar, and Hygelac gives him a large tract of land and a hall.

Many years later, when Beowulf has been king of the Geats for fifty years, a dragon begins a feud against him because an unknown slave (or thane—the manuscript is unclear) has robbed a cup from the hoard that the dragon has guarded for 300 years. The dragon burns down Beowulf's hall with his fiery breath, and the old king sets out to fight him unaided, except for specially constructed fire-proof armor. Before the fight, Beowulf recalls the deaths of Hygelac and Hygelac's son Heardred in feuds with other nations, and recapitulates some of the battles between Geats and Swedes in earlier years. Having established an elegaic mood, Beowulf challenges the dragon, who emerges from his barrow to begin the fight. Beowulf's sword breaks (we are told that he has always been too strong for swords), and the dragon gives him a lethally poisonous wound.

All his retainers run away, terrified by the dragon, except young Wiglaf, who recalls Beowulf's munificence and vows to fight with him to the death. The two men succeed in killing the dragon, striking him in his soft belly, but Beowulf is also dying. Wiglaf brings him some of the treasure that he has fought to win for his people; placed in the dragon's barrow by the last survivor of an ancient race, it has a curse upon it, unknown to the Geats' king. Beowulf looks on the treasure and dies. Wiglaf chastises the cowardly retainers and sends a messenger to tell the Geats of their lord's demise; the messenger warns that, with Beowulf gone, the Geats can expect renewed hostility from the Swedes, Franks, and Frisians, and a bleak future. (Beowulf has no son, and Wiglaf, his apparent successor, is young and untested.) Beowulf's body is ritually burned, and the remains are placed with the gold (as useless as before, the poem says) in a barrow that the dying king instructed to be built by the sea, where passing ships can see it. The poem ends with the Geatish warriors riding around the barrow, sadly uttering the praises of the dead Beowulf.

HERITAGE

Beowulf's obvious debt to traditional culture takes four main forms: (1) its depiction of a German warrior aristocracy (in the main plot and in numerous digressions and allusions) and of the poetic practices of this society; (2) its quasi-formulaic diction, reminiscent of preliterate poetic composition; (3) the form and narrative method of its three main stories; (4) its preoccupation with a hero—a warrior whose strength and courage distinguish him from other mortals and whose dedication to glory at all costs makes him at once a savior of, and threat to, society. This section will examine each of these four aspects of the poem.

BEOWULF AND GERMANIC SOCIETY

Scholars who deal with material relating to pre-Anglo-Saxon Germanic history (classical sources of varying reliability, the most famous being Tacitus' *Germania,* and Germanic texts from the Christian era) find evidence of a society organized around a sacral kingship that functioned as the link between the tribal group and its gods. Attached to the sacral king was a tribal poet whose primary task, it would seem, was to utter the praises of the king and his ancestors in improvised, non-narrative eulogistic poetry with strong religious, even shamanistic, overtones. The purpose of such eulogies was to preserve the fame of its subjects after their deaths and thus to keep them alive in order that they might protect their royal descendants and the tribe as a whole. In addition to this "official" poetry, Germanic society would have fostered poems and songs of all kinds, improvised and memorized, recited by warriors and their womenfolk before battle to increase valor and win the favor of the gods, by peasants as they farmed their lands or watched their cattle, and by families in order to bring the living into close and fruitful contact with the tutelary spirits of their ancestors. At this stage of society, it has been argued, there would be no narrative poetry; the deeds of the great kings and warriors of the past recalled in eulogies would live on as a body of traditional stories, unfixed in form and passed on from generation to generation as the property of the entire tribe.

The causes and nature of evolution beyond the phase just described are subject to dispute. H. M. Chadwick long ago noted that many references to the past in postclassical Germanic texts are international in character—that is, kings and heroes from one nation appear in the literature of another, as in *Beowulf*, an Anglo-Saxon poem about Danes, Geats, and Swedes—and look back to a period between the fourth and sixth centuries of our era, which Chadwick calls the "heroic age" of the Germanic peoples and which coincides with their triumph over the Roman Empire in the West. Drawing on analogies between Germanic material and the Homeric poems, Chadwick posited the heroic age as a stage through which many physically mobile societies pass, perhaps as a response to the challenge of a new, superior power with which they come into contact. A warrior aristocracy comes into being, one that places comitatus, or lord-retainer, relationships above kindred ties and subordinates a primarily religious view of life to a code of heroic values centered on loyalty to ruler, bravery, and willingness to die in the pursuit of fame and glory. During this period, among the Germanic nations, a new class of bards, held in high esteem as preservers in narrative song of the deeds of heroes, moved about from nation to nation, cross-fertilizing the traditions in which the warrior aristocracy found its inspiration, ideals, and even identity as a group.

Jeff Opland, who has done pioneering work among the Xhosa and Zulu nations of southern Africa and finds among them many analogies to Germanic society in its pre- and postconversion phases, takes a different view of the extant evidence. He contends that nonnarrative eulogy remained the dominant, official form of poetry among the Germanic nations until the coming of Christianity, which, by redefining and Christianizing the office of the cultic king, deprived the tribal poet of his traditional function as eulogizer of the ruler and, through language, controller of people and gods. In Opland's view, wandering singers who lacked the special rank and privileges of the eulogizing tribal poets began to circulate among some Germanic nations, carrying with them an international fund of memorized heroic songs, the result of coming into contact with Roman traditions of public entertainment by professional performers. The fact that narrative is embryonically present in eulogy facilitated the shift in poetic genre. Later, after the Anglo-Saxons received Christianity, in good part through missionary activity originating in Rome, narrative "heroic" poetry—with *Beowulf* as an extreme example—sprang up in England as a type of nostalgic entertainment for small monastic or aristocratic communities, under the influence of classical literature, biblical stories, and militant early-medieval hagiography.

We may infer from Opland's interpretation of the evidence that Germanic heroic narrative poetry tells us little or nothing about a separate "heroic age" of Germanic society, since it reflects the conditions of a later, postconversion period and the impact of ecclesiastically fostered literacy rather than the domination of a secularized warrior aristocracy in the period between the sacral king and the Christian God.

It seems unlikely that we will ever know the development of Germanic society thoroughly enough to perceive within it the precise sequence of, or relationships among, eulogistic verse, narrative lays sung to a mixed audience by peripatetic entertainers who presumably accompanied themselves on the harp, and heroic narrative poetry intended for a secular or religious elite. We can, however, distinguish between a religious, God-centered view of the world (or cosmos) and a heroic one, in which the struggles of mortals are central and the finality of death magnifies the glory won by defying it in battle. *Beowulf* is obviously a narrative poem, and its most overt, consistently proposed values are earthbound and "heroic": loyalty to lord and, subsidiarily, kindred; bravery; generosity; and the hero's search for glory through the acceptance of challenges to combat. The presentation of the poem's kings—Hrothgar of the Danes, Hygelac and Beowulf of the Geats—has little of the overtly sacral about it, although Hrothgar does offer moral warnings and guidance to Beowulf in a passage often characterized by modern critics as a sermon (1700–1784). But, as Opland indicates, *Beowulf* contains clear elements of eulogy amid its narrative. The opening eleven lines of the poem constitute a "praise poem" of Scyld Scefing, founder of the Danish Scylding dynasty, culminating in the celebratory exclamation "þæt wæs god cyning!" (he was a good king: 11). A little later, after the construction of Heorot, while the Danes feast in the hall, a court poet sings a song that sounds much like a eulogy of God the creator (90–98; compare Caedmon's *Hymn*, discussed later in this essay). When Beowulf has mortally wounded Grendel, the Danes follow the tracks of the dying monster to his lair and then return rejoicing; along the way a wise old thane who knows many stories sings or recites the praises of Beowulf, then of the Germanic hero Sigemund, whose legendary feats provide a sympathetic context for the young Geatish warrior (853–900).

In other parts of the poem, the consistent linking of poetic utterance—including references to Germanic heroic stories such as the Finnsburh episode—to moments of communal joy in Heorot (after the hall is built; after Beowulf has cleansed it of Grendel and then of Grendel's mother) seems clearly to reflect an established tradition of songs or recited poetic entertainment, probably narrative in nature, within an aristocratic, warrior society.

Whatever conclusions one may draw about the precise stage of Germanic society that saw the nascence of *Beowulf*, the fact remains that characteristics of several evolutionary phases coexist in our text. Furthermore, the various functions of poetry during these phases—eulogy, inspirational heroic narrative, social entertainment—all seem present as well.

BEOWULF AND ORAL CULTURE

The various kinds of poetry mentioned in the preceding section would not have been conceived or preserved in writing in pre-Christian Germanic culture, since it was an oral rather than a literate culture. (Literacy, as already noted, came to the Germanic nations with their evangelization by Christian missionaries.) The differences between an oral and a written culture are numerous and profound; inhabitants of a literate culture can never fully appreciate the implications of nonliteracy for a society and its members, but much can be deduced from texts rooted in an oral culture and subsequently preserved (in however modified a form) by literates, and from observations of the world's remaining nonliterate or partially literate societies.

In an oral culture certain distinctions that we take for granted do not exist: distinctions, for example, between hearsay and fact, between history and tradition or legend. Furthermore, the division of knowledge into areas such as law, history, philosophy, and literature, each of which constitutes a separate (written) body of information, is also foreign to an oral culture. Replacing (or rather, preexistent to) all these categories is the collective memory of the group, which determines both its identity and its sense of right and wrong by keeping alive exemplary stories of great deeds and heroes of the past. The ultimate purpose of an oral culture's recollections is to link past and present, living and dead, humanity and its gods in an ongoing relationship, in order to maintain the group and inspire its individual members. The past, in other words, remains a vivid presence to be called up and shared by members of a tribal group whenever they gather together and one of them begins to recite or sing of the tribal past as it has been preserved in genealogy, eulogy, or narrative.

By contrast, writing objectifies the past so that, although it is always available (in the form of records) and not contingent upon strength or weakness of memory, it also becomes discontinuous with, and therefore remote from, the world of experience. The absence of written records to freeze information in a final, limiting form means that in an oral culture the past is fluid and constantly evolving, not because of new research or discoveries—as in a literate culture when unknown or forgotten documents are discovered that change our understanding of the past—but because, as events recede further into the past, they conform more and more to certain basic story patterns; and in the crucible of memory the deeds of one hero are confused with those of another, while people from different eras are recalled as contemporaries or vice versa.

The contemporary scholar Walter Ong has characterized the main features of an oral culture as *dynamism, polemicism,* and *traditionalism.* All relate to the function of memory in a culture without literacy and records.

Dynamism, an epistemological category, refers to the centrality of unpredictable, dynamic events, not static theories or systems, in apprehending the world. When knowledge is a function of recollection rather than abstraction, things most easily recalled—unexpected actions that have brought about change, confrontation, crisis—define the contours of what is known.

Polemicism, an evaluative and structural category, reflects the fact that the most remarkable actions, and therefore the most influential across generations, are battles between good and evil or between exemplary figures and groups in similarly definitive opposition. From this fact follows the intertwining of action and judgment in an oral culture: for any generation, the past is not a neutral record, but a challenge to identify with some characters and events and to reprobate others. Another result of polemicism is that material we might, from our literate perspective, consider extraneous—catalogs, historical allusions, gnomic or sententious utterances—tends to become attached to, and encrusted upon, memorable stories to facilitate its preservation. (Hence, for example, the ship catalogs in the *Iliad.*)

Traditionalism, a methodological category, refers to techniques of preserving and transmitting the recollections that define knowledge, values, and identity. These include fixed or highly conservative verse forms, diction, and narrative patterns. The object of traditionalism, to *preserve* rather than to innovate or to define with precision, has two important consequences. The first is the very slow evolution of poetic art, since originality would run counter to poetry's mnemonic function. The second is that, instead of narrative structure and language conforming to events as they happen, new events are made to conform to preexisting structures and diction so that they can be more easily understood and transmitted from age to age. Traditional poetry takes two distinct, though never absolutely separate, forms: improvisation and memorization. An improvising poet/singer articulates his material in a traditional, formulaic diction. The act of articulation differs somewhat from performance to performance: each retelling of a story will be a fresh act of improvisation and therefore to some extent creative. By contrast, performances of deliberately memorized poems or songs are re—creative, literal repetitions, and the singer/poet is but the passive medium through whom are transmitted the verbal patterns previously composed by another. In most traditional cultures, improvisation is the more appreciated skill.

Since an oral culture lacks the larger political systems made possible by abstractions and recordkeeping—both products of literacy—its experience tends to consist of repeated, tradition—based conflicts (or feuds) among small sociopolitical units, each held together by links of kindred and common recollection. The end of constant local warring between such fragmentary polities must await the (literate) articulation of constitutions, treaties, and theories of strong central authority and the res publica; lacking these instruments, neighboring villages or tribes in an oral culture can seek to resolve feuds only by concrete gestures: money payments to injured kin groups, intermarriage between ruling families, or de jure kinship between leaders.

Although few students of *Beowulf* would now classify the poem as in any direct way the product of an oral culture, it abounds in techniques and characteristics denoting its ultimate kinship with such a culture. In fact, *Beowulf* seems in some respects quite self-conscious about the nature and limits of an oral culture, a phenomenon suggesting its attainment of literate detachment.

The characteristic movement of *Beowulf* stresses the instability and unpredictability of life, summed up most strikingly in the sudden appearances of monsters who transform a social situation of peace, joy, and harmony into one of misery and strife. The poem's term for this depiction of the dynamism inherent in oral culture's recollective way of knowing reality is *edwenden,* a sudden, unexpected change. Hrothgar tells Beowulf of his career as victorious king, "Hwæt, me þæs on eþle edwenden cwom,/ gyrn æfter gomene, seoþðan Grendel wearð,/ ealdgewinna, ingenga min" (See how a great turnabout came to me in my homeland: grief after joy, once Grendel, the old adversary, became my invader: 1774–1776). Interestingly, the poem's insistence on the Danes' ignorance of the biblical origin of Grendel's lineage (discussed later) and of providence in general as it concerns their own history seems to be a self—conscious critique of the epistemological limitations of an oral culture. The Danes lack crucial knowledge because they lack the book that would tell them the truth—the book on which Christianity depends and which determines its literate impulse.

The polemicism of *Beowulf* is one of its most obvious features: its core comprises the three battles between Beowulf, an exemplary protagonist, and his equally exemplary monstrous antagonists. The quasi-symbolic absoluteness of the adversarial relationships—attained by identifying Grendel and his mother with Cain, the first murderer, and the dragon with devouring time—suggests the poem's self-consciousness about the polemical nature of preliterate civilization. Also, the sharp contrast between the poem's two main subdivisions, Beowulf's youth and age, constitutes a kind of displaced polemicism transferred from the hero's main battles to his life, and from characters in the poem to the poem itself. Finally, the assimilation into the poem of gnomic sayings ("Gæð a wyrd swa hio scel" [Fate always goes as it must: 455]), sententious maxims ("Sinc eaðe mæg,/ gold on grunde gumcynnes gehwone / oferhigian, hyde se ðe wylle" [Treasure, gold in the earth, can easily outdo any of humankind, whoever hides it: 2764–2766]), and historical allusions (Hama stealing the necklace of Eormenric: 1198–1201) illustrates the process of encrustation whereby such material is preserved by association with memorable conflicts such as Beowulf's heroic combats.

The traditionalism of *Beowulf* manifests itself not only in quasi-formulaic diction (see below) but in its use of traditional themes such as the presence at battles of the eagle, raven, and wolf as creatures of prey (3024–3027). The traditional folktale-like structure of the battles will be examined in the next section.

The political fragmentation and instability that mark preliterate society underlie the feuds in *Beowulf,* which are so omnipresent as to constitute a basic theme of the poem (see below). Beowulf's statement that political marriages rarely succeed in permanently settling a feud ("Oft seldan hwær/æfter leodhryre lytle hwile/bongar bugeð, þeah seo bryd duge" [Only seldom after the fall of a prince does the war spear remain at rest for any length of time, however excellent the bride: 2029–2031]) reflects wisdom that clearly derives from recollection. In fact, the processes and consequences of recollection hold a great self-conscious fascination for the poet, as two examples will demonstrate: an ancient weapon or piece of jewelry (usually called *a laf* [a relic, inheritance, survivor: 1688, 2036]), passed on from hand to hand, stimulates recollection of past events (the necklace Wealhtheow gives to Beowulf: 1195–1214), maxims whereby one generation teaches the next (the hilt Beowulf gives Hrothgar: 1677–1698; 1724–1768), or actions that reopen an old feud (the Heathobard sword worn by a Danish warrior: 2036–2069); the *laf* also stands as a metaphor for the nature and function of an oral culture's legacy of recollection. And the old man who recalls everything ("se ðe eall gemon": 1700–1701; 2042; 2427) represents with equal force the ideal of total recall, and therefore complete wisdom, toward which an oral culture must always strive.

BEOWULF AND THE TRADITIONAL STORY

As noted above, basic narrative patterns are one of the oral culture's methods for preserving and transmitting its recollected past. A traditional story is one that cannot be assigned to a particular author and that circulates widely in a variety of versions, none of which can be considered original or definitive. While many traditional stories originate in an oral culture, they have enormous longevity and can continue to exist for centuries in multiple oral and written (or transcribed) versions having the same basic plot but many variants of character and motivation.

Common forms of the traditional story include the joke, or short humorous tale; the folk or fairy tale (which looks inward, to fears and desires, for its inspiration); and the heroic tale (which looks outward, to deeds and experiences). Patterns assumed by the traditional story for purposes of recollection and clarification show remarkable persistence and invariability: in 1928 the Russian formalist critic Vladimir Propp demonstrated by studying a body of Russian folktales that the plot of a traditional story can be separated into thirty-one parts or functions that always appear in the same order, though not every tale has all the functions. These functions are the building blocks of the story; they recount the occurrence of a crisis and the stages of its eventual resolution.

The constant patterns of the traditional story take its hero through peril to final triumph or satisfaction. The many versions of a particular story will share the same pattern of events, all of which revolve around the central character(s). Other characters exist *not* independently and with their own psychological complexities, but rather only to test and define the protagonist. Hence these other characters—companions adversaries, fairy godmothers—often appear to behave inconsistently or without motivation. Indeed, even the protagonist's actions will sometimes appear arbitrary or unmotivated and his (or her) character to lack consistency. Everything is subordinated to the working out of the plot; character and motivation constitute rationalizations of the plot and vary from teller to teller. (In the mimetic tradition of the novel, by contrast, plot often seems to evolve organically from character.)

Propp's study shows that many folktales have a multiple, paratactic structure: the hero, having seen one adventure through to a happy conclusion, must face another version of the same adventure with a different antagonist. The additive principle at work here also appears in other, less structurally coherent guises in traditional stories based on historical deeds or characters. As written down, often hundreds of years after the event, such stories can be highly composite (like the Middle High German *Nibelungenlied,* for example), combining material from several versions with results that seem to us contradictory and ineffective. We see here that the impulse behind this type of traditional story is synthetic—it retains all available material about the past, adding and combining stories because all are part of its culture's memory-defined identity—rather than analytic, as is the case in a literate culture where students of the past, attempting to determine which account of an event tells "what really happened," make choices among available versions and discard the "inauthentic" ones.

A notable feature of history-based traditional stories is their lack of the surprise that depends on the audience's ignorance of the outcome. Instead, the audience is constantly reminded of the denouement in narrational asides or prophetic dreams and utterances of characters, all of which recognize and capitalize on the audience's familiarity with the obligatory traditional events recounted. The story absorbs into itself its audience's foreknowledge, translating it into an often overwhelming sense of inescapable destiny; the story's inability to avoid the denouement established for it by tradition becomes the characters' inability to avoid the denouement established for them by fate.

Beowulf conforms to the norms of the traditional story in many ways. Daniel Barnes has submitted the poem to Proppian analysis and demonstrated the considerable extent to which the hero's three battles are three repeated adventures, or "moves," comprising the same order of functions. Comparison between the *Beowulf* episodes of Grendel and his mother and two adventures involving the hero of the fourteenth-century Icelandic *Grettissaga* shows that the two works are utilizing versions of the same two-move traditional story: a double struggle between a brave, strong hero and his monstrous opponents. In the first move, the evil antagonist invades a place that should be tranquil and safe (in *Beowulf,* Heorot; in *Grettissaga,* the farmhouse of Þorhallr), dominating and terrorizing it until defeated and expelled by the hero. (The persistence even today of this plot, in "alien invasion" science-fiction films, for example, should be obvious.) In the second move, the momentum is reversed, and the hero enters an alien environment (the fiery, blood-stained swamp in *Beowulf*; a cave behind a waterfall in *Grettissaga*), risking his life to confront and extirpate the evil at its source. (Science-fiction and other types of action-adventure films fall into this category.)

The basic story shared by *Beowulf* and *Grettissaga* is rationalized in each work according to its artistic intent and the expectations of its audience. The saga writer has domesticated the struggle between good and evil by placing it in the agrarian society and known geography of Iceland. *Beowulf* by contrast, exalts the struggle by investing it with a setting in the Germanic heroic past, by linking it to the antagonism between God and Cain's kin, and by endowing the monsters' swamp home with trappings of Gothic horror closely paralleled in an Anglo-Saxon homily describing St. Paul's vision of hell.

The third move in *Beowulf* is equally traditional; fights between heroes and dragons occupy a central place in the folklore and mythology of northern Europe—Saint George and Siegfried, for example. Here again we find in *Beowulf* elements of rationalization to explain the story of the hero's death: the curse on the gold guarded by the dragon (3051–3057); the failure of Beowulf's sword because his strength has always been too great for weapons (2680–2687); the cowardice of his retainers, except for Wiglaf (2596–2601).

The inconsistencies of traditional stories grounded in history find ample representation in *Beowulf.* Perhaps the most famous instance occurs in Beowulf's recapitulation of his Danish adventures to Hygelac. Here the previously unnamed Geatish victim of Grendel is called Hondscio, and Grendel is retrospectively equipped with a *glof* (glove-shaped sack) into which he attempts to thrust Beowulf before the latter engages him in the fatal grip. Another possible inconsistency of a traditional nature comes at this point—in the reference to Beowulf's unpromising youth (2183–2189), hitherto unmentioned—relating his career to the "young slacker" folklore motif familiar from the much later tale of *Jack and the Beanstalk.*

The prediction of the outcome of battles, a characteristic of stories known to their audience, occurs before the fights with Grendel (696–700, 716–719) and with the dragon (2309–2311, 2419–2424).

As with its relation to oral culture, *Beowulf* appears to manifest, on at least two occasions, an intriguing self-consciousness about its own treatment of the traditional stories it utilizes. Both occur shortly after Beowulf arrives in Denmark. First, Hrothgar employs the technique of rationalization in interpreting Beowulf's journey to his court to fight Grendel and win glory as the result of a desire to repay Hrothgar for having settled, some years earlier, a feud involving Ecgtheow, Beowulf's father (456–472). Then, when Unferth questions Beowulf's heroic credentials by alluding to the latter's contest with Breca, he bases his challenge on a version of the adventure significantly different from the one Beowulf himself proceeds to tell. The multiple forms of the same story that mark traditional narrative here rise up to confront the hero; he can control the contest with Breca as a deed, but not its subsequent recounting as a story.

BEOWULF AND THE HEROIC IDEAL

As a poem about a hero and his heroism, *Beowulf* reflects the fascination of Indo-European civilization with the figure of the warrior who performs prodigies of strength and courage in pursuit of glory—the man who, in the words of an Icelandic saga hero, would rather die than yield. The ultimate mystery of the hero is that, fully cognizant of his mortality, he chooses to behave as though he were immortal, deliberately exposing himself to danger when the normal human response would be to opt for safety and survival. To put it another way, the hero pushes to the limits the possibilities of the human will by choosing to take risks that all the instincts of self-preservation resist. The reward of this triumph of will over the knowledge of mortality and the instinct for survival is glory: the recognition by others that there is something of the divine about the hero—hence the phrase "hero worship"—when the frenzy of action seizes him. (The unforgettable image in the *Iliad* [book 21] of Achilles, in all his fiery energy, battling the river Simois perhaps best conveys our culture's response to heroic glory.)

The hero's energy and unwavering commitment to glory, his unwillingness ever to recognize the arguments of diplomacy or prudence against heroic action, also make him a problem to those who depend on his strength—whether, like Achilles, he chooses to withdraw from the Trojan war rather than seem to lose face to Agamemnon, or, like Roland, he dooms 20,000 Frankish warriors to Charlemagne's rear guard by refusing to summon the main army with his horn, lest he seem cowardly. The hero's dread of appearing unheroic—the key to his problematic status—leads him always to choose the option in any situation that cannot possibly be interpreted as motivated by fear. Sooner or later, that choice brings his world to disaster and himself to death, since it rules out the possibility of compromise, restraint, and prudent withdrawal, which are sometimes required in every sphere of life, domestic or political.

The great medieval primary epics—*Beowulf*, the *Chanson de Roland*, the *Nibelungenlied*—celebrate the life and mourn the death of their heroes. In the climactic battles of the epic, the hero's antagonist must in some way be a match for him if he is to win glory from the encounter and the epic is to hold the interest of its audience. A subtler conflict involves the hero's relationship to the king he serves, often as a visitor from another land. The king finds his authority implicitly or explicitly threatened by the outsider hero; as a result, the epic may focus on the rituals and strategies whereby a king and a society receive a visiting hero and domesticate him.

The hero's death marks the end of an era or seals the fate of a civilization; it is accordingly an occasion for sadness and gloomy prophecies. The story of the hero's fall serves a social function as an explanation of *our* fallen, postheroic state, an etiological myth to account for our unwillingness to be heroes, as well as our continued allegiance to the heroic ideal of self-sacrifice in the interest of glory. One might also argue that the fall of the hero is a symbolic account of growing up, of coming to the realization that we are mortal and cannot, therefore, afford to behave as heroes do if we are to survive. Heroes, in their absolutism, self-absorption, and refusal to compromise, are wondrous children who haven't grown up enough to appreciate the complexities of life that render their pursuit of glory an unaffordable luxury. Yet even as we outgrow a heroic outlook, we mourn its loss within us, just as we mourn all of childhood's passing. Such an analysis may explain the continued hold on us of tales about quasi-mythical mortals who lived (if at all) eons ago; it may also provide an insight into the deep ambivalence we feel about the descendants of those heroes in our own society: much-decorated generals who charge when they should retreat, outrageously self-centered sports stars who thrive on confrontation. Magnificent self-destruction continues to attract and disturb us as few other phenomena in our experience of life.

When Beowulf first appears in his poem, his exceptional ability in the heroic mode takes precedence over his name by almost 150 lines: "se wæs moncynnes mægenes strengest/on þæm dæge þysses lifes" (he was the strongest of mankind at that time: 196–197). His words after his arrival at Hrothgar's court convey quintessentially heroic sentiments: he will fight Grendel alone (424–426) and without weapons (677–687) to maximize his chance for glory; if he fails, he is fully aware that it will mean death: "Ic gefremman sceal/eorlic ellen, oþðe endedæg/on þisse meoduhealle minne gebidan!" (I shall perform noble deeds or come to the end of my days in this mead hall: 636–638). Throughout the poem, Beowulf's rhetoric remains constant. When Hrothgar tells him that Grendel's mother has carried off Aeschere, Beowulf replies that it is better to avenge a friend than to be immobilized by mourning (1384–1385); his speech continues paradigmatically:

> Ure æghwylc sceal ende gebidan
> worolde lifes; wyrce se þe mote
> domes ærdeaþe; þæit bihelp
> drihtguman unlifgendum æfter selest.
> (1386—1389)

> Each of us must come to the end of life in the world; let each who can, obtain glory before death; that will be best afterward for the departed warrior.

The dragon episode finds the old Beowulf proclaiming to his retainers that he would rather fight the dragon without armor and weapons, if the beast's fiery breath would allow. He will not retreat, but will engage the creature singlehandedly, for it is no one's task but his:

> Ic mid elne sceall
> gold gegangan, oððe guð nimeð,
> feorhbealu frecne frean eowerne!
> (2535—2537)

> I shall bravely win the gold, or battle—terrible, deadly evil—will take away your lord.

It is Beowulf's singlemindedness about fighting the dragon alone—Wiglaf calls him *anhydig,* consistent in resolution (2667)—and his unwillingness, as is proper for heroes, to forfeit *dom,* or glory (2666), that wins him the final judgment he seeks from those who judge correctly (*sōfaestra dom*: 2820), but also brings his death and the danger of destruction to the Geats. This problematic side of Beowulf, shared by all heroes who seem too big for their worlds and their mortality, finds metaphoric expression in the fact that his strength has always been too great to allow him to use weapons well. Only his grip, the full expression of his energy and frenzy, fully represents the hero's *mana* (power)—when used not only on Grendel, but on the Huga (Frankish) champion, Dæghrefn, as well (2501–2508).

Beowulf's superhuman (and isolated from human) heroic essence underlies the verbal and imagistic equivalency between him and the monsters he fights. He and Grendel meet, equally unarmed and dependent upon a handgrip. They share feelings and status: "Yrre wæron begen, / reþe renweardas" (They were both furious, the fierce hall—guardians: 769–770). He and the dragon appear like two old kings fighting (or bargaining) over a single treasure (2413–2419), or two warring monsters (*aglæcean*: 2592). Indeed, when Beowulf dies in battle, he has a barrow built to his orders, and the treasure that the dragon has guarded is buried with him; he has become the dragon in death.

Beowulf's departure leaves a terrible sense of loss as well as danger hanging over the Geats—and the poem. The eulogistic lament uttered by the twelve warriors who ride around Beowulf's barrow not only puts the final testimony to the hero into place at the end of the poem—its last word, describing Beowulf, is *lofgeornost* (most eager for renown: 3182)—but summon up a last image of his centrality in his world, and of the emptiness now at the circle's midpoint.

THE ANGLO-SAXON CONTEXT

Anglo-Saxon England, the immediate cultural context of *Beowulf,* came into existence sometime around 550 with the Germanic settlement of the heartland of Britain and ceased with the Norman Conquest of 1066. Its civilization demonstrates with particular clarity the uneven, sometimes traumatic process of assimilation whereby three cultural traditions—classical, Christian, and Germanic—were fused into the unique indigenous culture of medieval Europe. In fact, the picture is even more crowded in England, where a fourth strand, the idiosyncratic, ascetic religious culture of Celtic Ireland, had to be woven into the tapestry. A brief consideration of some aspects of the evolution of Anglo-Saxon England will help to illuminate *Beowulf's* combination of Christian and Germanic elements. In addition, an equally abbreviated survey of the contents and techniques of Anglo-Saxon poetry will help us to understand the artistic context of *Beowulf* as a necessary preliminary to grappling with its artistic achievement.

THE CULTURAL SYNTHESIS

In 596 Pope Gregory the Great sent a mission, headed by Augustine, to convert the Germanic peoples then occupying much of Britain—Angles, Saxons, Jutes, and others, organized in small kingdoms isolated from, and often at war with, each other. The missionaries landed in Kent (whose king had a Frankish Christian wife) and set out from there. Throughout the first half of the seventh century, Christianity made uneven progress in England through the uncoordinated efforts of evangelists dispatched from Rome and Ireland; not until the Synod of Whitby in 663 did the Roman party succeed in imposing its loyalty to the pope and liturgical discipline (including the dating of Easter) on the entire English church.

Thanks to Bede's *Historia ecclesiastica gentis Anglorum (Ecclesiastical History of the English Nation,* 731), we have a richly documented, ideologically committed, and brilliant depiction of the conversion of the English. From Bede we learn that the conversion of an Anglo-Saxon kingdom usually depended upon the conversion of the prince, often the result of a confluence of factors. These included the prior conversion of his wife, the eloquent preaching of a missionary, and a calculation on his part (rooted in Germanic sacral kingship) that the new God offered him and his nation a greater chance of success in battle and overall prosperity than did the older Germanic pantheon. Conversion, in short, was a political and self-interested process, not a spiritual and self-sacrificial one.

In the famous account of the conversion of King Edwin of Northumbria, Bede shows many factors at work on the king, including letters from the pope and quasi-visionary experiences while Edwin was in exile and great danger. Bede's vivid dramatization of the council meeting at which Edwin makes his momentous decision is the masterpiece of the *Historia* (2.13): Coifi, the pagan priest, argues that the old gods have not repaid the king's efforts on their behalf, so Coifi is ready to see if the new God will show greater munificence. An unnamed counselor, also urging conversion, compares human life, surrounded by the mysteries of human origins and destiny, to a sparrow who flies into, then out of, a brightly lit hall on a dark winter night; while the bird is in the hall, it is known, but not before or after. He argues that the new religion, offering knowledge about life beyond life, should be embraced. Edwin acquiesces and is rewarded by God with victory at war until he is martyred in 632 and his kingdom is divided.

Given the political basis of many of the conversions of Anglo-Saxon rulers, frequent backsliding into paganism or syncretism was inevitable. Bede tells of several cases of reversion by sons of Christian kings or by apostatizing kings themselves. Redwald, king of the East Angles, had both pagan and Christian altars in his chapel (*Historia* 2.15) during the first quarter of the seventh century. Such combining of new and old religions could stem from an understandable desire to receive "luck" from as many divine sources as possible; in addition, it may have been inadvertently encouraged by missionaries if they followed Pope Gregory's advice to Mellitus (*Historia* 1.30) not to destroy pagan shrines but only the idols in them, substituting Christian altars and relics and thus luring the people to new worship in familiar settings.

We can see the continued attraction of traditional customs, and their partial integration with Christianity, in the magnificent seventh-century ship buried at Sutton Hoo in East Anglia and unearthed in 1939. The artifacts in the tomb (or cenotaph; there is disagreement over whether there was a body) come from Sweden and other places on the Continent as well as England; among them is a pair of baptismal spoons. In the latter part of the seventh century and thereafter, Christian monastic culture flourished in England as practically nowhere else in western Europe under the influence of Rome and (through Theodore, archbishop of Canterbury from 668) of Greek culture. Manuscripts were brought from Rome to be copied; scriptural commentaries (especially Bede's), hagiography, and scientific treatises were written in the thriving monasteries of Northumbria. There, too, the Hiberno-Saxon style of manuscript illumination evolved, combining Mediterranean representational traditions with the Germanic and Celtic love of abstract patterns and fanciful zoomorphic forms.

While integration of the various traditions vitalizing English life proceeded apace, tensions remained. Bede relates (*Historia* 3.22) that Sigeberht, king of the East Saxons, was murdered (*ca.* 660) by his two brothers; "when they were asked why they did it, they could make no reply except that they were angry with the king and hated him because he was too ready to pardon his enemies, calmly forgiving them for the wrongs they had done him, as soon as they asked his pardon." Presumably, the brothers saw Sigeberht as undermining the Germanic imperative of vengeance, against which the church set itself, but without complete success, as is shown in the famous entry in the *Anglo-Saxon Chronicle* about the slaying of King Cyneheard of Wessex as an act of vengeance in 786.

During the eighth century the English church sent missionaries to the Germanic nations on the Continent, and English monks such as Alcuin aided Charlemagne in his ecclesiastical and educational reforms. Then in 793 began the period of Scandinavian raids on Britain; though halted by King Alfred of Wessex in the late ninth century, they began again in the tenth and culminated in the rule over a joint kingdom of England and Denmark by the Dane Cnut and his sons from 1016 to 1042. The Danish invasions disrupted monastic life and Christian intellectual and educational activity. Alfred attempted to turn the tide of cultural decline by having the leaders of the Danes baptized and by translating or having translated a number of important works from Latin into English. Later in the tenth century a monastic revival, under the reforming influence of Benedictine monasticism from the Continent, led to renewed cultural achievement, especially at Eynsham Abbey under its abbot, Aelfric.

We see, then, a pattern of advance and decline in Christian culture in Anglo-Saxon England; concurrently, there were sure to be numerous survivals (if not revivals) of Germanic pagan religion and superstitions (some of which surfaced in the collections of charms from the period preserved in a manuscript). And the heroic traditions of continental Germany remained alive and were frequently rehearsed, even in monasteries; Alcuin's famous letter to the monks of Lindisfarne in 797 scolds them for their attachment to Germanic heroes and asks rhetorically, "Quid Hinieldus cum Christo?" (What has Ingeld to do with Christ?) On the other hand, Alcuin also praised a *thegn* of the murdered King Etheldred of Northumbria, who avenged his lord's blood.

We may safely conclude that the interaction of Christian and pagan-Germanic elements continued in dynamic and unsettled fashion, at least at intervals, throughout most of the Anglo-Saxon period. At almost any time, the situation depicted in *Beowulf*—a heroic civilization embracing the values of loyalty and vengeance, intermittently aware of divine providence and, with one exception, monotheistic in religious expression—could be presented and understood as an evocation of a past era denied the fullness of Christian truth yet possessed of attractive nobility and quasi-Old Testament patriarchal attitudes. Scyld Scefing's ship burial, full of parallels to Sutton Hoo (the poem was used in the 1939 inquest as evidence of who owned the hoard), is mysterious to the Danes, who do not know Scyld's destination, but not to the reader, who has been told (in line 27) that the king goes to the Lord's protection.

THE POETIC CORPUS

The greater part of extant Anglo-Saxon poetry has been preserved in four codices datable on paleographic grounds around the year 1000 (one, containing *Beowulf*, is perhaps of later compilation). Two, the Exeter and Vercelli books, are miscellanies containing religious, secular, and mixed texts of various lengths and functions. The Junius manuscript contains only religious pieces, and the *Beowulf* manuscript also contains *Judith*, based on the apocryphal Old Testament story. The late date of the codices suggests either a major revival of interest in the poetic heritage or a continuing tradition happily saved for posterity by the labors of monks in the reformed Benedictine monasteries. Several poems included in tenth-and eleventh-century entries of the *Anglo-Saxon Chronicle*, and the traditional eleventh-century heroic poem commemorating the defeat of an English force under Bryhtnoth by the Danes at Maldon in Essex, testify to the continued or renewed attraction of the Germanic poetic form and outlook well after the age of conversion in England.

The intermingling or antagonism of Christian and Germanic elements in Anglo-Saxon poetry continues to stimulate scholarly debate. As mentioned before, Jeff Opland believes that Christianity ruptured the nexus between eulogizing scop and sacral king in the early stages of conversion; bishop or priest replaced tribal poet as the interpreter of past to present, and the new touchstone (as we see in Bede's record of letters written to kings by churchmen) was biblical, not recollective and traditional. On the other hand, England's Rome-based Christianity opened the culture to Roman traditions of entertainment, which resulted in the popularity of the *gleoman*, the peripatetic entertainer who sang songs about the deeds of the past. The church may have frowned on such doings, in and out of the monasteries, or tried to capitalize on the popularity of traditional songs by adapting them to Christianity—as when Bishop Aldhelm of Sherborne (*d.* 709) supposedly disguised himself as a minstrel and lured his congregation to consider the Christian mysteries with the bait of Germanic song—but the continued attraction of the poetic legacy of the pre-Christian past can be taken for granted throughout our period.

Meanwhile, as monastic culture flourished in the seventh and eighth centuries, it attracted not only children given to monasteries by their parents early in life (as Bede was), but also warriors and rulers who sought peace and salvation within the cloister after a life of instability and violence. The resulting society would presumably take equal pleasure from Germanic heroic song and the rich deposit of native and continental hagiography in Latin that vividly portrayed the battles of ascetic saints and hermits against diabolical temptations and assaults.

Such appears to be the context within which Bede's story of Caedmon must be placed (*Historia* 4.24). Caedmon was a lay brother at the monastery of Whitby, an unlettered man who performed duties necessary to the operation of the institution. He could not sing and fled when the harp was passed around the evening table, until one night an angelic stranger appeared who instructed him to sing about creation, which the surprised Caedmon proceeded to do. Abbess Hild learned of the miraculous occurrence, and thereafter Caedmon was instructed in scriptural story, which he turned into English narrative verse.

Of Caedmon's poetry only his first song, the nine-line *Hymn,* is extant, preserved in copies of Bede's *Historia* when the latter was translated in the late ninth century. Opland points out that the *Hymn* is a praise—poem to God the creator and argues that Caedmon's first achievement was the Christian domestication of the Germanic eulogistic tradition. Thereafter, given the adumbrations of narrative present in eulogy, it was quite simple to apply traditional poetic diction and techniques to biblical narrative subjects.

Several biblical poems in Old English survive; they are marked by the more or less adroit application of Germanic concepts and diction to the sacred story. *Exodus* (early eighth century?) treats the escaping Israelites as a war band following their leader, Moses; the superb, visionary *Dream of the Rood* (late eighth century?) imagines Christ as a young hero leaping up onto the cross. Other religious poetry attributed to Cynewulf, of whom nothing is known except that his name is worked in runes into the text of four poems, has been translated more closely from Latin hagiographical material. And a poem like *Seafarer* (eighth or ninth century?), which fits no modern generic category, appears to reconceive Germanic ideas of exile and endurance as metaphors for the Christian life, letting their true meaning emerge ever more clearly as the poem moves from a description of life at sea to meditations on the afterlife.

The continuing appeal of Germanic traditions explains the preservation in the Exeter Book (copied *ca.* 1000 in Exeter, where it has remained in the cathedral library) of *Widsith* (seventh century?) and *Deor* (date unknown), poems cataloging allusively many recollections of preconversion and pre-insular nations, heroes, and events. The obscure *Wulf and Eadwacer* (date unknown) may also hide nostalgic evocations of the Germanic past, while collections of gnomes and charms are clearly rooted there.

The Danish invaders of England from the ninth century onward brought with them intact traditions of eulogy and poetic improvisation centered on the *skald,* or Scandinavian court poet. Opland perceives skaldic influence in a revived eulogistic tradition underlying some of the chronicle poems of the tenth century, most especially the *Battle of Brunanburh,* which celebrates but does not describe King Athelstan's victory over a Scandinavian army in 937, using heavily conventional diction and evoking (as does the later *Battle of Maldon* [*ca.* 10251) the traditional values of Germanic heroism.

We see then that uses of traditional poetic form and content varied widely in Anglo-Saxon England. Nothing in the corpus, however, can directly "explain" *Beowulf,* the longest extant poem in Old English and the only complete narrative based on Germanic traditions (there are fragments of an Anglo-Saxon poem on the Waltharius legend).

POETIC TECHNIQUE

The same techniques govern Anglo-Saxon poetry from Caedmon's Hymn to *The Battle of Maldon,* and the presence of these techniques in continental Germanic texts testifies to their preliterate origin. Although there is substantial agreement about the major technical norms of Anglo-Saxon versification, several questions remain unanswered and subject to debate. The problem is that we lack any handbook of poetics from Anglo-Saxon times, and the poems themselves do not discuss their techniques. (Lines 870b–871a of *Beowulf*—"word oþer fand, / sōðe gebunden"—have sometimes been read as a reference to alliterative technique, but a more probable translation would be: "he found a new subject [*word oþer*], one guaranteed to be true.") Accordingly, the rules given here have been deduced, not always without controversy, from the poetry we possess. One result is that we risk oversimplifying or overgeneralizing because our statistical sample is too small. We have but a small fraction of the poetry composed during this era; the cost of parchment and the animosity of the church would have doomed much to oblivion. Or our deductions are too restrictive, and we emend texts to remove the evidence of this fault by making them conform to our patterns.

Anglo-Saxon poetry is strongly rhythmic, in keeping with the marked tonic-vowel stress of Germanic languages. The basic unit is the half-line, comprising two stressed syllables and a varying number of unstressed syllables. Two half-lines joined by alliteration across a caesura make up the standard Anglo-Saxon poetic line. The first accented syllable of the second half-line determines alliteration; it can alliterate with either or both of the stressed syllables in the first half-line, but normally not with the other stressed syllable of the second half-line. (Double alliteration—*ab, ab*—seems exceptional, but may serve a not yet understood affective or technical function.) A consonantal sound normally alliterates only with itself (although palatalized and nonpalatalized *g* alliterate); all vowels, by contrast, form an alliterating group, and initial *h* seems not to impede vocalic alliteration. (The name printed in editions of *Beowulf* as Unferth, and alliterating with vowels, always appears in the manuscript as *Hunferth.*)

The metrical patterns into which Anglo-Saxon half-lines fall seem basically five in number, as determined by the placement of the two syllables of primary stress (and in some cases a syllable of secondary stress) in relation to the unfixed number of unstressed syllables that may precede, follow, or intervene between them. Primary stress falls on long syllables (that is, with a long vowel or blocked by a double consonant) or, as a "resolved" stress, on two consecutive short syllables; and there is a hierarchy of parts of speech that may receive stress, with nouns and adjectives generally preceding verbs and adverbs.

Anglo-Saxon poetic diction derives its characteristic effect from the fact that the halfline, rather than the word, is its basic unit. Many half-lines appear in exactly, or almost exactly, the same form more than once in the extant poetic corpus. This fact led F. P. Magoun in 1953 to apply to Anglo-Saxon poetry the oral-formulaic theories developed by Albert Lord and Milman Parry to explain the poetic techniques and origin of the Homeric epics and tested by them during the 1930's on the improvisatory oral poetry of Yugoslavian *guslars* (bards who recite poetic narratives accompanied by the *gusla,* a stringed instrument). Magoun's argument is that (1) the repeating half-lines of Anglo-Saxon verse are formulas; (2) in an oral culture, poetic diction is formulaic for mnemonic purposes; (3) only oral (that is, unlettered) poets compose in formulas; literacy and formulaic composition are mutually exclusive; therefore (4) Anglo-Saxon poetry was orally composed by illiterate improvisational poets; and (5) it follows that our extant texts are transcriptions of individual performances improvised from an extremely conservative stock of formulas, within which context the creation of new, original diction is practically impossible. If we had other texts of these works, they would manifest differences in formula consistent with the fact that different performances by the same poet will be different acts of composition, albeit drawing on the same formulaic stock.

Magoun's premises have been widely challenged. Larry Benson has shown that even Anglo-Saxon texts closely translated from Latin originals share the same formulaic diction as more obviously traditional texts. It is clear that literates can easily learn to write formulaically: Magoun's own pupil, Robert Creed, arguing for the oral-formulaic composition of *Beowulf,* "recomposed" part of it using half-lines from other texts, thereby proving that a literate, twentieth-century scholar can write Anglo-Saxon poetry. Furthermore, as Parry and Lord themselves discovered, an oral poet who knows his work is being transcribed for posterity will produce a longer, more carefully structured version of a poem showing the effects of his awareness. Thus one cannot speak of transcription as a neutral process not affecting the material transcribed.

Perhaps the most important obstacle to the Magoun-Parry-Lord thesis, as applied to Anglo-Saxon poetry, lies in its assumptions about formulas. Parry and Lord demonstrated that Homeric texts practice "formulaic economy": each fixed formula has a metric pattern that makes it fit into a certain part of the Greek hexameter line; when the concept or fact embodied in it is needed at the place in the line where it fits, *that formula only* is used, and its form never varies, no matter how frequently it appears. By contrast, in Anglo-Saxon verse, the "formula" corresponds to an entire half-line, the looser structure and alliterative requirements of which result in a wide variety of related but distinct utterances. Compare, for example, these phrases from *Beowulf: weox under wolcnum* (he grew up under the skies [i.e., on earth]: 8), *wan under wolcnum* (dark under the skies: 651), *Wod under wolcnum* (He advanced under the skies: 714), *wæer under wolcnum* (water under the skies: 1631), *weold under wolcnum* ([I] ruled under the skies: 1770); the kinship of these half-lines is clear, but the variant word is sometimes a verb, sometimes a noun or adjective. And how does one characterize the relationship between this system and *hæleþ under heofenum* (hero under the heavens: 52) or *gehedde under heofenum* ([anyone should] care for under the heavens: 505)? One system would clearly suggest the other to a poet wanting to make the kind of general statement involving "on earth" as an intensifier, and the choice would depend on alliteration, an element lacking in the Greek poetic system.

In short, the basic characteristics of the Anglo-Saxon poetic line promote dictional variety within limits imposed by the same characteristics (number of stressed syllables, alliterative patterns). Greek practice encourages the fixity and economy underlying Parry and Lord's definition of a formula—a definition that is of little use in attempting to understand the traditional norms underlying even the most indisputably literate poetry in Old English. This conclusion is doubly important for the study of *Beowulf*: we need deny its ultimate poet neither literacy nor originality in his manipulation of the flexible style and inherited content at his disposal; nor must we assume that the particular form in which we have it is the result of a chance preservation of one performance as opposed to many others, all somewhat different (and some presumably much better than ours, as dictated by the law of averages).

Two other elements of poetic style, common to Anglo-Saxon poetry but uncommonly well handled in *Beowulf*, deserve brief note. One is the technique of *variation*—the use of successive half-lines to vary the content of a preceding one, adding nuances or new information or merely saying the same thing in a different way for aesthetic effect. At its simplest, such variation substitutes a title for a proper name: "*Hroðgar maþelode, helm Scyldinga*" (Hrothgar spoke, protector of the Scyldings: 456); or expands and specifies a verb: "Beowulf *maðelode, beotwordum spræc*" (Beowulf spoke, uttered boasting words: 2510). Piling up variations slows down the forward movement of the narrative, an effect useful for giving an impression of particular solidity to a character or for conveying the sense of almost pompous solemnity appropriate for ceremonial discourse. We see both intentions in the variation technique of lines 340–346:

Him þe *ellenrof* andswarode,
wlanc Wedera leod, word æfter spræc
heard under helme: We synt Higelaces
beodgeneatas; Beowulf is min nama.
Wille ic asecgan *sunu Healfdenes,*
mærum þeodne min ærende,
aldre þinum. . . .

The man famed for courage answered him,
The bold prince of the Geats, the brave,
helmeted one,
spoke these words: We are Hygelac's
table companions; Beowulf is my name.
I wish to give my message
to Healfdene's son, the famous king,
your lord. . . .

The first three italicized lines are varied epithets for Beowulf, the warrior-leader; the last three for Hrothgar, the king whom Beowulf must approach respectfully if he is to be allowed to fight Grendel. Separating the two groups of variations and heightening our awareness of them by its stark simplicity is the poet's first mention of his hero's name. There are many more subtle and complex uses of variation in *Beowulf* contributing to our sense of poetic mastery.

The other noteworthy stylistic feature that *Beowulf* shares with Germanic poetry—and language as a whole—is the propensity for word compounding with metaphorical effect. Old English has many compounds meaning "sea," including *swanrade* (swan's road), *ganotes bæð* (gannet's bath); "ship," including *famigheals* (foamy-necked [one]), *hringedstefn* (ring-prowed [one], referring to ornaments on the ship's prow); "warrior," including *lindhæbbende* (linden[-wood shield] bearer), *hildedeor* (battle—brave [one]); and, more imaginatively, for "sword," *homeralaf* (relic of hammers, or what is left when the weaponsmith has finished beating the hot iron). Studies by Arthur G. Brodeur and others have shown *Beowulf* to be rich in compounds not elsewhere recorded in Old English. Even allowing for much verse irrevocably lost, we must conclude that ingenious and inveterate compounding distinguishes *Beowulf* among Anglo-Saxon poems.

The poetic language in which most Anglo-Saxon poetry is preserved constitutes a special speech, rich in words (presumably archaic) that do not appear in Old English prose (a later development dependent upon literacy) or that are used there with different meanings. In addition, the poetry seems to have incorporated features from various Old English dialects, so that placing a poem geographically merely from its language, as opposed to its content or external evidence, is usually impossible. The effect of this special, nonconsuetudinary language, combined with the diction and techniques just surveyed, must have been to endow Anglo-Saxon poetry with considerable affective force, quite apart from the impact made by the subject of a given poem.

MANUSCRIPT

A long-standing scholarly consensus has held that *Brit. Lib. Cotton Vitellius A. XV* comprises two separate codices joined in the seventeenth century, probably after they came into the possession of Sir Robert Cotton (1571–1631), the English antiquarian. Cotton's manuscript collection was housed in bookcases atop each of which stood the bust of a Roman emperor; "Vitellius" in the manuscript's title refers to the bust atop its case. A fire destroyed part of the Cottonian collection in 1731, but only scorched the edges of *Vitellius A. XV.* Some words were lost as the damaged pages crumbled, and this process continued until the manuscript was rebound and the pages protected in 1845. (Two late-eighteenth-century transcripts of *Beowulf,* one made by the Icelandic diplomat Grímur Jónsson Thorkelin and another commissioned by him, preserve some words subsequently lost due to crumbling.)

Beowulf's segment *of Vitellius A. XV,* called the Nowell codex because the inscription "Laurence Nouell, 1563" appears on its first page, contains five works—three in Old English prose, followed by *Beowulf* and the fragmentary poem *Judith*—written down by two scribes, the second taking over at line 1939b of *Beowulf.* As in the other three manuscripts preserving most of the extant Anglo-Saxon poetry, *Beowulf* is written out as prose.

The integrity of the Nowell codex has been universally assumed, but so has its lack of authority as a witness to the text of *Beowulf.* Proposed dates for the poem are many, but until recently all have antedated the manuscript by at least a century; in addition, the mixture of dialectal forms in the text has supported the thesis that several copyings in different parts of England stand between the composition and the extant version of *Beowulf,* a situation conducive to error and loss by scribal ineptitude. (Such a hypothesis justifies frequent editorial intervention to eliminate textual corruption.)

The earliest date proposed by modern scholars for composition of the poem is the seventh century, based on its Germanic outlook, apparently incomplete Christian overlay, and archaic linguistic forms. Parallels between the seventh-century Sutton Hoo ship burial and the sea burial of Scyld Scefing buttress the argument that some form of *Beowulf* existed as early as the era, and perhaps in the kingdom, of Redwald, the East Anglian syncretist whose sponsorship of both Christian and pagan worship might well find reflection in *Beowulf's* ambiguous presentation of the Danes' religious culture.

The next claimant as the setting for *Beowulf's* composition is Northumbria in the age of Bede (*ca.* 700–750). Support for this attribution comes again from linguistic forms, primarily from the fact that the level of culture in Northumbrian monasteries was sufficiently high to make possible the composition of the poem (in this view, a highly literate work perhaps indebted to Vergil's *Aeneid* as well as to the Bible).

Dorothy Whitelock, in *The Audience of Beowulf,* argues that certain locutions in *Beowulf* (*non dæges* [the ninth hour of the day: 1600]; *helle hæfton* [captive of hell, translating Latin *captivus inferni*: 788]) suggest a full assimilation into the English language and culture of ecclesiastical institutions and ideas by the time the poem was composed. Citing the apparent compliment to King Offa of Mercia intended in the story of Offa the Angle (1944–1962), she suggests that the poem may have originated in late-eighth-century Mercia, then the dominant Anglo-Saxon kingdom.

Eric John suggests a similar conclusion on different grounds: he interprets Hygelac's gift of land to Beowulf (2195–2196) as *folcland,* a fief belonging to Beowulf's father that reverted to the king on Ecgtheow's death until such time as Beowulf could reclaim it by honorable deeds and the payment of a fee *(heriot)*—in this case the gifts that Hrothgar had given him. Since the custom of *folcland* seems to have disappeared during the eighth century, the poem's genesis must antedate the disappearance. John also places the poem on the margins of Anglo-Saxon society where Christian and Germanic views overlap; he sees the concern with swords, feuds, and treasure throughout *Beowulf* as evidence that it was composed for an audience of retainers—men in search of honor and security—who would have especially appreciated Beowulf's Danish expedition as the great successful gamble of a young mercenary soldier who had until that point done nothing to earn back his father's land.

The positive view of the Danes offered by *Beowulf* has struck many as an argument against composition after 793, when the Danes began their incursions into the north of England. Nonetheless, a few scholars prior to 1980 had found evidence in the poem to support a ninth- or tenth-century date. One argument, by Levin Schücking, even proposed to read the poem as a "mirror for princes" composed to educate young Danish princes living in the recently captured north. Such a view would place the composition of *Beowulf* in the first half of the tenth century.

A thorough review of received opinions on *Beowulf's* date is now underway, thanks largely to a conference held in Toronto in 1980. (The proceedings were edited by Colin Chase and published in 1981.) Several scholars have pronounced in favor of a ninth- or tenth-century date of composition, basing their arguments on the poem's meter and language, its use of tribal names and royal genealogies, or its reflection of Anglo-Danish political and cultural interactions. The most striking challenge to all previous theories appears in Kevin Kiernan's 1981 study, *Beowulf and the Beowulf Manuscript.* Kiernan's examination of *Vitellius A. XV* has convinced him that the "Beowulf codex" is a separate manuscript, written very soon after the poem took its final shape during the reign of King Cnut, shortly after 1016. Originally, he argues, two separate *Beowulf* poems, one about his youthful deeds (and a tribute to Cnut's heritage) and the other about his last battle and death (a nostalgic tribute to the House of Alfred, now extirpated), were being copied by two scribes in the same Mercian monastery when Scribe B had the idea of combining them by means of the newly composed transitional section (Beowulf's return to Geatland and report to Hygelac). Differences in the construction and lineation of manuscript gatherings convince Kiernan that the original *Beowulf* projects were conceived as quite distinct from one another; the linking section offers clues that the revision of the ending of the first story ran longer than planned and had to be crowded into too little space because the rest of the newly unified poem had already been copied.

Kiernan's revisionism extends to a new explanation for the partly unreadable condition of folio 179r: it is a palimpsest (one text erased, another written over it). Scribe B returned to the manuscript some twenty years after copying the new transition with new material to make it smoother. He scraped off the apposite page and recopied the beginning of the dragon episode in its new form, but some of the ink did not take well, so he erased several places and never filled them in, which would account for the gaps on this folio. At this time, he also erased the first three lines of folio 180r, a fact hitherto unnoticed.

This summary omits much of Kiernan's argument and all of his supporting evidence. His hypothesis transforms the "Beowulf codex" (now seen as an independent manuscript) from a late, non authoritative copy into something very close to an autograph, one containing much more important evidence of the process of combinative composition of a traditional epic than can be found in any other manuscript. Further examination of the manuscript, his logic, and the poem's text will be necessary to corroborate or combat Kiernan's argument.

Meanwhile, some general judgments about *Beowulf* dating theories can be made. The main problem in attempting to date tradition-based texts is that early or archaic elements may be preserved for atmospheric or mnemonic effect long after they have ceased to have direct relevance to the poem's audience. Furthermore, episodes of varying derivation can be added to the main narrative stock at any time, out of nostalgia or a desire to preserve a record of the past. It is impossible to determine what completed material the last poet of *Beowulf* (who may or may not have been the first literate poet to assemble the poem's components in their present shape) had at his disposal, or what his compositional task may have been. We must live with this uncertainty and not press the text for genetic information that its links to traditional Germanic culture in form and content prevent it from supplying.

CRITICAL APPROACHES

The evolution and variety of this century's critical responses to *Beowulf* as the earliest English epic provide guidance—and in some cases cautionary examples—to the modern student attempting to deal with the poem.

For a long period it was customary to judge the poem by standards of decorum derived from, and appropriate to, later literature. In his edition of *Beowulf,* Frederick Klaeber speaks of the disproportion between "the main plot, three fabulous exploits redolent of folk-tale fancy" and "a number of apparently historical elements which are introduced as a setting for the former and by way of more or less irrelevant digressions." He adds, "We may well regret that those subjects of intensely absorbing interest play only a minor part in our epic, having to serve as a foil to a story which is in itself of decidedly inferior weight." Other objections to the poem included lack of suspense and the intrusion of "Christian coloring" into an essentially pagan—heroic vision. Behind such censure of *Beowulf* we can detect a class bias against (lower-class, peasant) folktale and in favor of (aristocratic) heroic digression, as well as a professional bias in favor of historical study and against the symbolic imagination.

The era of patronizing *Beowulf* ended, and the era of serious, sympathetic literary criticism began, with the publication of J. R. R. Tolkien's 1936 British Academy lecture, "*Beowulf,* the Monsters and the Critics." Tolkien defends the unity of the poem and the seriousness of its concern with monsters: the hero's three nonhuman opponents are symbolic embodiments of evil, and Beowulf himself of quintessential heroism in combating them fearlessly, even to the death. Nothing could be more timelessly noble. Tolkien argues that the poem possesses a highly self-conscious, unified two-part structure embodying a principle of balance analogous to the balanced tension of the two-part Anglo-Saxon poetic line, and illuminating the dynamic of youth and age in the life of a hero. The young Beowulf rescues old King Hrothgar; as an old king himself, Beowulf receives crucial assistance from the young hero Wiglaf in his last fight. The ultimate balance is between the triumphant life and unflinching but immeasurably sad death of the hero. With Beowulf's death, an era ends and the future darkens.

Tolkien's rehabilitation of *Beowulf* revitalized study of the poem in many ways. Successors studied the monsters for clues to their significance and for distinctions between the clearly evil Grendel lineage and the (perhaps) less theologically tinctured dragon; or they attempted to refine and support Tolkien's argument about the poem's unity. Many critics have concerned themselves with the nature of the judgment being passed on the heroic world by the poem's Christian author. Tolkien's view of the poem as noble, nostalgic, and concerned with timeless symbols of human greatness and the evil that attacks it can safely be called romantic (or romanticizing), and he falls at times into overly enthusiastic hyperbole, largely in response to the legacy of patronization that he was combating. For example: "[Beowulf's] final foe should not be some Swedish prince, or treacherous friend, but a dragon: a thing made by imagination for just such a purpose. Nowhere does a dragon come in so precisely where he should." Attempting to defend *Beowulf* against the charge of being inferior history, Tolkien lyrically (and anachronistically) evokes the ahistorical imagination as its driving force.

Several critical positions since Tolkien, and directly or indirectly influenced by him, have been less nuanced and more prescriptive or anachronistic. Adrien Bonjour, seeking the poem's unity, has submitted the many historical allusions and digressions in the work to often ingenious analysis, attempting to show their appositeness to the main plot. For other scholars, the unifying factor is thematic (the feud), modal (ironic reversals and parallels), or structural (the interweaving of motifs in a manner analogous to the interlaced patterns in the decoration of Anglo-Saxon manuscripts). Some readers have sought to explain events and characters by applying to them psychological and motivational analysis inappropriate to a traditional story that, as we have seen, presents subsidiary characters and events as reflections of or subordinate to the needs of the basic plot and the protagonist. To take one example, Unferth, the Danish court figure who challenges Beowulf, has been explained by some in terms of his earlier career, moral defects, and personality traits. Elaborate lives have been constructed for him outside the poem in a manner all too similar to the "how many children had Lady Macbeth" methodology. However unified *Beowulf* may be at its core, it cannot be criticized as if it were a carefully plotted Victorian novel.

Such rationalizing criticism coexists with a Christianizing approach to the poem that may take one of two forms: despite the relatively few Christian references in the poem and the absence of any references to Christ, the poem's pervasive Christianity shows itself in the assimilation of Beowulf to Christ or in the poem s condemnation of Beowulf as a sinner in his old age and its disapproving view of the world of Danes and Geats. Obviously, these two views are mutually exclusive. The first establishes parallels between the hero's career and the gospel or apocryphal accounts of Christ's passion and resurrection: the journey to the bottom of the swamp and subsequent return after defeating the she-monster qualify as a version of the harrowing of hell, while the Danes' departure from beside the fiery lake, when they see it welling with what they take to be Beowulf's blood, recalls the disloyalty of the disciples at Jesus' moment of betrayal. Beowulf's self-sacrifice in the final part of the poem, as he attempts to protect his people and secure treasure for them, offers final proof of his Christlike status.

The negative Christian judgment of *Beowulf* draws its support primarily from the dragon episode, where Beowulf, in this view, stands convicted of pride in attempting to fight the dragon alone, or of avarice in seeking the dragon's hoard and succumbing to its curse. The passage early in the poem that condemns the Danes for placing their trust in idols when harassed by Grendel (175–188)—a passage that Tolkien, with his more favorable view of the Danes, wished to see as a late interpolation—places the whole poem under the cloud of paganism, and a Christian author, however sympathetic to the plight of his preconversion ancestors, would have no choice but to consign the Danes to everlasting punishment.

The difficulty with the Beowulf-Christ hypothesis is that it relies on forced or imagined parallels for too much of its support; for the rest, it relies on universal narrative patterns displaced from myth into less cosmic literary genres in many cultures throughout the world. The judgmental approach stems from a misunderstanding of the accretive nature of the traditional story (Christian maxims about the joys of heaven and pains of hell [183–188] mixed with reflections on the Danes' ignorance of God [175–183] are making two different points, although they have been drawn together by a similar subject in the poem's traditional economy). It also stems from too univocal a view of Anglo-Saxon society, in which, as Benson and others have shown, Christian missionary zeal could coexist with—indeed, be inspired by—favorable attitudes toward still-heathen continental Germanic nations that shared the same heroic heritage. (The constant "marginal" overlap of Christian and Germanic values noted by John and Whitelock in areas such as loyalty and revenge also renders categorical judgments in *Beowulf* less likely, though by no means impossible.)

Finally, one should point to what might be called a demythologizing tendency in some recent assessments of the poem, attempts to strip it of some of the resonances found by previous critics and used to support, on slender evidence, one or another interpretation. One instance of this tendency has already been noted: Eric John's submission of the poem to historical scrutiny and his explanation of Beowulf's trip to Denmark not as the expression of heroic nobility but as an Anglo-Saxon retainer's search for booty and honor sufficient to claim the *folcland* that had reverted on his father's death to the lord. (Oddly, John seems to overlook the passage in *Beowulf* that most supports his argument: Wiglaf undertakes to aid Beowulf in battle because he remembers that the latter had given him "wicstede weligne Wægmundinga,/folcrihta gehwylc, swa his fæder ahte" [the rich dwelling place of the Wægmundings, every right to the *folcland* that his father had held: 2607–2608].) Similarly, John believes that an audience of retainers would condemn Beowulf as a foolhardy king for attempting to fight the dragon alone. John implicitly rejects Tolkien's lyrical symbolism in favor of hard-headed historicism.

Kenneth Sisam had earlier proposed an analogous debunking of some interpretations that stress the unity and artistic complexity of the poem, as well as its affective impact and symbolic force. In the scene of rejoicing after Beowulf has killed Grendel, the Danes carouse in Heorot; Hrothgar and his nephew Hrothulf sit together with Unferth at their feet. The text says, "Heorot innan wæs/freondum afylled; nalles facenstafas/þeod-Scyldingas þenden fremedon" (Heorot was filled with friends within; not at all did the þeod-Scyldings then engage in treachery: 1017–1019). Later, when Wealhtheow approaches Hrothgar and Hrothulf, we are told of them, "þa gyt wæs hiera sib ætgædere,/æghwylc; oðrum trywe" (their peace [or kinship] still joined them, each was true to the other: 1165–1166). Wealhtheow then expresses confidence that Hrothulf will be kind to her children if he should outlive Hrothgar, as long as he remembers her and Hrothgar's kindnesses to him when he was young (1180–1187). From these three moments and some stories in later Scandinavian chronicles, many readers have deduced that the poem here alerts its audience to the coming feud between Hrothgar and Hrothulf, in which the former's children will be victims. Sisam argues that a straightforward reading of the text, without circular arguments from distant and unconvincing analogues, shows no such future treachery being forecast. His position, if accepted, renders unacceptable the eloquent analysis of Edward Irving and others that the scene in Heorot balances present joy with future sorrow, and that the Finnsburh episode, by asserting a proleptic parallel between Hildeburh and Wealhtheow as queens tragically victimized by an intrafamilial feud, has thematic relevance at this point in the poem.

Recent years have seen a philological demythologizing of Beowulf himself in the work of Fred C. Robinson ("Elements of the Marvelous in the Characterization of Beowulf") and others. This initiative involves scrutinizing Beowulf's exploits, especially their more fantastic components, with a view to discovering their basis in the words of the text instead of the imaginations of critics. For example, Beowulf's swimming exploits against Breca and in the Geats' retreat from Friesland after Hygelac's last raid have been reinterpreted as feats of rowing or sailing, based on lexicographical evidence that words for "swim" and "swimming" had wide, metaphorical applications to all seagoing activities in Old English. Basically, this type of demythologizing has two aims: to expose and combat the tendency to derive special meanings for words from an interpretation of their context in the poem (a subjective act) and then to give these meanings objective force by enshrining them in dictionaries; and, incidentally, to make Beowulf less a superhuman or monstrous figure and more a strong but normal human being. Of these aims the first is laudable and unassailable, but the second seems at times to fly in the face of the entire Indo-European presentation of the hero as a quasi-divine figure and the consistent representation of Beowulf as peculiarly like his monstrous opponents in many ways.

Surveying these major approaches to the poem—patronizing, romanticizing, rationalizing, Christianizing, and demythologizing—we are again struck by their common unease with the techniques and cultural function of a traditional, or tradition—based, narrative. Each in its own way wants the poem to be simpler, more accessible than it is to our thoroughly literate, post-Renaissance culture, which finds *Beowulf's* outlook and method as profoundly alien as it is profoundly attractive. This is not, however, to deny the need and pleasure of coming to critical grips with the poem, nor to gainsay the contributions of each of the perspectives just rehearsed. Keeping before us the need to respect at all times the complexities inherent in dealing with a poem that is in one sense the product of a literate Christian culture and in another the legacy of a preliterate Germanic traditional culture, we offer some suggestions toward a tentative, open-ended, but useful interpretation of *Beowulf*.

INTERPRETATION

UNITY AND STRUCTURE

Kiernan's hypothesis that the "*Beowulf* codex" reveals the creation of our poem from two antecedent ones by the ex post facto composition of a hinge or transitional section recalls the waggish suggestion of many years ago that all Anglo-Saxon poetry had three authors: Germanic poets A and B and the monkish redactor who cobbled their work together and added Christian references. The lack of unity by modern standards of traditional literature has, over the years, prompted theories that *Beowulf* was constructed by stringing together three heroic lays about the same hero, each with its separate prehistory. More recently, the oral—formulaists sought proof for their theories by maintaining that *Beowulf's* inner inconsistencies could be traced to separate performances of the same work later synthesized by a literate scribe.

Most readers of the poem, however, though fully aware of its digressiveness and impulse toward inclusiveness, its penchant for explanation by accretion rather than analysis, still experience it as a profound unity. Various explanations of *Beowulf's* coherence have been offered. Barnes, following Propp, has argued that it has the paratactic unity of a folktale in three moves, each with the same structure. Other scholars in recent years have sought what may be called mechanical unity, three types of which are ring composition, envelope structure, and tectonic (numerical) structure.

Ring composition means the symmetry of subsections of the poem placed within each other, like boxes within boxes. *Beowulf* begins and ends with a funeral (Scyld's, Beowulf's), with a lordless nation (Danes before Scyld, Geats after Beowulf), and with contrasting statements about retainers (Beowulf the Dane gives treasure to his retainers so that they will support him in battle later; Beowulf the Geat, having given treasure to his retainers, finds that they flee instead of supporting him in battle). These sections will in turn enclose other, briefer segments, and so on. Cedric Whitman has performed this sort of analysis on the *Iliad,* pairing books 1 and 24, 2 and 23, etc. Although *Beowulf* is divided into forty—three *fitts* (sections) in the manuscript, they lack the autonomy of books or chapters; and two section numbers are missing, creating ambiguity in the sequence.

Envelope structure seeks to find subunits, often overlapping, within the poem by the occurrence of key words and phrases in widely separated groups. One might point here to the same phrase in 100b and 2210—"oð ðæt an ongan" (until someone began)—at the beginning of the Grendel and dragon fights, as an indication of rhetorical envelopes.

Tectonic analysis seeks to demonstrate the unity of a poem by showing the numerical proportions, organized around a few key numbers, multiples of which control the placement of all the key incidents, as revealed by repeated words that call attention to the underlying numerical structure. Impressive as some of the results obtained by T. E. Hart may be, his analysis of *Beowulf* depends completely upon our having in the extant manuscript exactly the same number of lines, in the same sequence, written by the final author—a situation that would be argued only by Kiernan, who, however, also argues definitively against tectonic composition by his insistence that the manuscript reveals two originally separate poems joined only after composition and copying.

Given the conflict inherent in all schemes of mechanical unity between their ostensible objectivity and actual subjectivity, it seems more satisfying to seek *Beowulf's* unity through frankly subjective literary analysis, however sophisticated. The subsequent discussion proposes that *Beowulf* embodies a complex unity of contrasting narrative *contents* and *methods* held together, not without tension, by the grip (to use a central image of the poem) of the hero's life. We can begin to understand this statement by comparing *Beowulf* to the other two great tradition-based medieval epics, the *Nibelungenlied* and the *Chanson de Roland.* All three are composed of linked, separate adventures, a structural scheme that has led modern critics to try to dissect them in search of "original" shorter poems. *Beowulf* is unique in ending with its hero's death, while the other two place this traumatic event in the middle and devote their final sections to recounting its consequences. The latter narrative strategy raises the theme of vengeance for the hero's death to a position of importance equal to the hero's character and achievement; by so doing, it creates a duality of focus: the hero himself while he lives, and the fate of his world after his death. In *Beowulf,* by contrast, the hero is always on hand to provide a unifying focus. But the binary structure of the poem profoundly modifies and complicates the cohesive force of the omnipresent hero by dividing his life into two segments clearly separated in time and strongly in contrast with each other. Tolkien has characterized this structure as a balance of youth and age, but this analysis, although accurate, is insufficient. In the two contrasting parts of *Beowulf,* youth versus age functions as a clarifying metaphor, along with several others, subordinate to the larger opposition between a vision of the possibilities of heroism in part 1 and the limits of heroism in part 2.

There is a strong tension at the heart of *Beowulf* between the centripetal force of the hero's life—as a testimony to human possibilities of will, bravery, and accomplishment—and the centrifugal force of its two main parts, embodying testimony to the tragic divergence in impact and result of the resolute heroic will operating amid life's multiplicity. This tension finds reflection and amplification in two other structural features of the poem: first, the alternation and opposition in each main part between an impulse toward intensity—focusing on the isolated hero and his titanic struggles with quasi-equal but monstrous antagonists—and another toward expansiveness, a movement beyond concern for the hero to a full picture of a society, the continuities and burden of history, the action of memory, and even the designs of providence; second, the construction of part 1 in two "movements," clearly related but further diverting the broad stream of narrative unity into subsidiary channels of comparison and contrast between the two monster fights.

We see, then, how precarious and contingent the concept of unity is in *Beowulf* and at how many levels it sustains pressure from strong centrifugal, diversifying forces. A brief examination of the poem's two main parts will heighten an appreciation of its parallel impulses toward the one and the many.

Part 1 comprises a two-movement structure bracketed by an introductory section taking place before the hero's arrival on the scene (1–193) and a postlude recounting Beowulf's return to Geatland and the report of his adventures to Hygelac (1888–2199). The bracketing sections contextualize the hero and his deeds in several ways, as well as provide an aesthetically satisfying beginning and end for them.

Structurally, the introduction establishes the need for the hero in the story; thematically, it demonstrates that his exploits have their ultimate origin in occurrences before his birth and establishes a broad historical and even providential level of significance for heroism. Its basic purpose is to supply the antagonist (Grendel) and the setting (Heorot) for Beowulf's first great fight, but it also provides them—and therefore the hero's deed—with far-reaching significance. Heorot's is dynastic because the hall represents the zenith of the Scyldings' power, as well as of Hrothgar's career as king, and social because it represents the ideal functioning of a heroic society. The founding of the Scylding dynasty with which the poem begins clarifies Heorot's historical importance, while Hrothgar's announced intention to share out within it all that he has won in battle (71–73, 80–81) embodies the proper use by a king of his power and possessions to ensure social harmony and cohesion.

Heorot is no sooner built than the joy within its walls—the joy of a triumphant, harmonious war band—attracts Grendel, who invades the hall, kills its occupants, disrupts its function, and possesses it nightly for twelve years while Hrothgar mourns and the helpless Danes pray to idols. Grendel opposes Heorot's social joy as an eternal, angry outsider, the lonely border walker (*mearcstapa*: 103). The elemental nature of this feud, which can never be peacefully settled (154–158), is corroborated by the information that Grendel's alienation, as a descendant of Cain, is the result of God's perpetual banishment of the first murderer and his offspring from human society. In other words, the opposition between sharing and feuding in human life is absolute; the two cannot coexist. God opposes the sowers of discord, but the legacy of discord embodied in Grendel is so strong that it can overpower even the most harmonious society. So Beowulf's resolve in undertaking to cleanse (*faelsian*: 432) Heorot is, according to the introduction, no mere youthful exploit or folktale giant killing, but the intercession of heroism, however unknowingly, into a struggle of divine intention and social aspirations against ancient forces seeking to thwart them.

The two moves of part 1 have three-part structures; the outer sections are expansive, the middle one intensive. The first section of the first move (194–661) integrates the hero into Hrothgar's court, giving in the process a sense of the court's etiquette and rituals, through Beowulf's successive encounters with the coast guard, door guard, Hrothgar, and Unferth. The narrative also expands, through Beowulf's recollection, to include his youthful contest with Breca and first monster fight. But opposing this leisurely, inclusive current is the intention to define Beowulf's heroism through his voice, his sentiments, and his response to Unferth's challenge. The modulation from diplomatic, circumlocutory rhetoric (267–285), through direct request (426–432) and the recognition of possible consequences (442–445), to the account of his lonely sea battle (559–573) makes Beowulf a more and more vivid presence in the poem. His final dismissal of Unferth's (and the Danes') courage (581–601) and his promise that Grendel is about to discover Geatish *eafoð ond ellen* (might and courage: 602) announces unmistakably that a hero has arrived in Heorot, full of the confidence and bellicosity that set him apart from other men.

In the first fight (662–836), the expansive, public, daylight world contracts to the close-up spectacle of two great hostile forces wrestling in the dark, joined together by an irresistible handgrip and, as if by a collision of matter and antimatter, nearly tearing Heorot apart as they battle (767–782). The focus of the episode shrinks at the moment of greatest intensity to the even smaller field of the grip itself: its first moment, when the two antagonists tangle in a syntactically undecipherable mingling of hands and arms (745–749), and its last, as we watch in horror, with Grendel, the violent separation of his arm from his body (815–818). (The instant of greatest collapse inward thus far in the poem comes in 76 lb: *fingras burston* [fingers burst].) The monster's frantic flight from the hall leaves Beowulf in possession (820–827), his boast fulfilled: "Hæfde East-Denum/Geatmecga leod gilp gelæsted" (The prince of the Geats fulfilled his heroic promise to the East—Danes: 828–829). The flight also marks a change of direction away from maximum centripetality and back toward expansiveness.

The last section of the first move portrays a tremendous release of tension and a strong impulse toward inclusiveness to compensate for the extreme isolation of Beowulf in the fight scene. The release takes many forms: Danish warriors race their horses (864–867), songs are sung, gifts given; there is joy again in the hall. Beowulf's deed begins to pass into history (871–874) and to be placed in the context of other exemplary, memorable events—Sigemund's dragon fight, Heremod's crimes (874–915). It provokes, or at least provides the occasion for, other acts of recollection: the Finnsburh episode, the stories prompted by the necklace that Wealhtheow gives Beowulf. This last artifact especially galvanizes the poem's centrifugal energies, driving them backward but also forward to recount Hygelac's last raid, and thus to darken, if only momentarily, the joyful mood, perhaps in preparation for the second move shortly to begin.

The attack by Grendel's mother on Heorot begins the second move and returns us momentarily to the mood of ignorance and helplessness that surrounds her son's attack in the introduction. Beowulf's earlier journey into the poem from Geatland finds a parallel in the journey to the hideous, seething, monster-infested swamp. The expansiveness here is geographical rather than social; it brings into the poem glimpses not of Beowulf's heroic past but of the hunted stag who chooses death rather than enter the poisonous waves beneath which Beowulf must now dive (1368–1372). Again, events isolate Beowulf from his fellows and provide the occasion for the cry of the hero defying mortality in quest of glory: "ic me mid Hruntinge/dom gewyrce, oþðe mec deað nimeð!" (I shall win glory with Hrunting [Unferth's sword, which in fact fails him], or death will take me: 1490–1491).

The hero enters the lair of evil for his second fight, following the pattern of reversal we have noted in this traditional story. There are elements of contrast, even deterioration, vis-à-vis the first battle: Beowulf has armor and a (useless) sword; he comes closer to death (1541–1553) than before as he once again wrestles with a monster (1533–1534; 1541–

1542, recalling 745–749). But Beowulf thinks of fame rather than survival (1534–1536) and endures the moment of supreme constriction in the fight, when Grendel's mother holds him on the floor and hacks at his armor with her knife (1545–1549). Now begins the outward movement: the hero finds the *ealdsweord eotenisc* (old sword of giants: 1558), too big for any man but him. In short order he kills the she-monster; beheads the body of her dead son, cleansing the swamp as he did Heorot (1620; compare 825: the same verb, *fœlsian,* is used); and returns to the surface, thence to Heorot for the last part of the move. The poem flows outward into expansiveness, from the claustrophobic intensity of the underwater hall, by means of its only extended simile (comparing the melting of the sword blade in Grendel's blood to the flowing of spring waters when God sets them free from their winter ice-fetters: 1607–1611).

The return to Heorot has less of the expansiveness of exaltation (as in the equivalent part of the first move) than of meditation. Hrothgar, staring at Grendel's head and the now bladeless sword hilt brought back by the hero, sets his recollections free of their fetters in order to praise Beowulf and to warn him by once again invoking Heremod (1709–1722) and urging him to learn from the wicked and stingy king's example: ðu þe lær be þon,/ gumcyste ongit!" (You learn from him; understand [the importance of] generosity: 1722–1723). Memory shades into moralizing as the old king paints the picture of a ruler who hoards his wealth, forgetful of his mortality until he is swept away by it and his successor disperses what he has so carefully gathered (another image of inflow giving way to outflow: 1748–1757). As the section ends, Beowulf and Hrothgar exchange pledges of friendship and future assistance (a beneficent version of the hostile grip that bound Beowulf and the monsters) that expand their own personal bond outward to include their two nations, and forward in time to include future generations, when Beowulf may also be a king (1822–1865).

The part 1 postlude returns Beowulf to Geatish society and shows us his deeds beginning their passage through future ages as recollected stories. (The fact that we see him beginning the transmission constitutes an implicit claim of authenticity on the part of the poem.) Two concessions to expansiveness balance each other: Beowulf's account (or prediction) of renewed feuding between Danes and Heathobards, despite Freawaru's marriage to the Heathobard prince, Ingeld (2020–2069), shows peace becoming war; the exemplary career of Offa's wife (1931–1962) reaches farther into time to show violence becoming tamed.

Part 2 offers every possible contrast with part 1. It opens with a brief prologue (2200–2210) putting Beowulf in place as an old king, paralleling Hrothgar in part 1; but while the Scylding dynasty moves from Scyld to Hrothgar in an ascending curve, imparting to the poem's opening a sense of forward movement, Beowulf gains his throne by the deaths of Hygelac and Heardred in battle, a sad, descending process. The dragon then assumes the central role (2210–2311) in a section that seems a deformed parody of the analogous introductory segment of part 1. The dragon, as scholars have suggested, is a "stingy king" who hoards his gold instead of sharing it like Hrothgar. His "Heorot," an old cave he finds rather than a new hall he builds, contains a treasure left there by the last survivor of a vanished race—the opposite of Scyld, who founds a dynasty and leaves as his treasure for posterity a son who distributes, rather than hoards, wealth (20–21). The anti-Hrothgar in his anti-Heorot is now violated by an *ingenga* (invader, trespasser)—no Grendel seeking the lives of men, but a pathetic slave who takes one cup from the hoard to use as a bribe in ending a feud with his master. (Grendel's feud with his lord, and his unwillingness to settle his feud with the Danes by payment, here find parodic echo and reversal.) The elemental attack in part 1 on the center of a living society has been transformed into a pathetic, sneaky raid on the inert remains of a dead one.

Hrothgar responds to Grendel's depredations by sitting, sad and helpless (129–134); the dragon launches into an almost comic flurry of activity (2293–2302), whirling around inside and outside the barrow looking for the trespasser. The preliminary section ends when the energy of the narrative moves out from the barrow with the dragon as he flies off at night in search of vengeance. The centripetal, inertial force of part 2 (embodied in the heavy hoard in the ground around which the dragon lies coiled), by now established, contrasts strongly with the images of intense energy—mighty handgrips and tremendous struggles—compressed at the center of the two fights in part 1 and, as it were, fighting against the act of compression.

The next section (2312–2537) parallels the hero's arrival in Denmark. It begins when the dragon burns down Beowulf's hall, an action that brings the old king into the work as a homeless exile. The dragon's deed in effect establishes his inhospitable barrow as the setting of this part of the poem, and Beowulf will succeed not in cleansing the barrow, but in getting one of his own (2802–2808) into which he transfers the still inert, still cursed, still useless hoard—an action programmatically opposed to cleansing. (We are repeatedly told that the treasure has no one to polish it: 2253, 2256, 2761.) Beowulf responds to the dragon's aggression not with a boasting speech, but with anxious, Hrothgar-like introspection (2327–2332), which the poem rightly characterizes as unusual for him, since heroes should not meditate, but act: "breost innan weoll/þeostrum geþoncum, swa him geþywe ne wæs" (within, his breast swelled with dark thoughts, as was not usual for him: 2331–2332). This inward movement, so unlike the Beowulf of part 1, gives way to a movement outward in space to the barrow, where Beowulf utters an expansive speech recalling his past battles. But recollection has gone bad in part 2: the words, even as they goad the old warrior to action against the dragon, recount moments when action and vengeance are impossible (Hæþcyn's accidental slaying of his brother; a man hanged as a criminal) and focus on would-be avengers condemned to impotent grief and decline (2435–2472). The effect of Beowulf's expansive speech is oppressive rather than liberating.

Beowulf now undertakes to fight the dragon (2538–2709) not, as in the Grendel encounter without weapons, but with a special set of armor to protect against the dragon's poisonous flames. (The hand-to-hand combat of part 1 becomes a battle in which the hero can only with difficulty approach his foe: 2546–2549.) By the end of his speech, his voice is that of the hero of old (2535–2537), promising to obtain the dragon's gold or die trying; his battle cry (2550–2552) marks, in effect, the full recovery of heroic energy and the readiness to discharge it. The battle itself, however, mocks the intensity of the encounters in part 1: the dragon puffs fire and retreats, while Beowulf strikes ineffectual blows with his sword until it finally breaks. Beowulf's mortal wound is a bite on the neck; the dragon is punctured in his soft underbelly. Only Wiglaf's intervention, prompted by the recollection of favors from Beowulf and expressed as a willingness to die with his lord (2606–2608; 2646–2660), brings the spirit of Beowulf's youth into the poem. (Even his sword, with its inheritance of attached stories, partakes of the expansive, heroic recollections of part 1 more than the doom-laden retrospection of part 2.)

The dragon's death (2697–2709) ends the central section of part 2. The next section (2710–2845) ironically pairs Beowulf's death and the violation of the treasure, some of which Wiglaf brings into the open air so that his lord can see it before dying. Wiglaf's penetration to the heart of the barrow, with its bizarre scene of rusting treasure strewn about in disarray, expands the circle of desolation, recalling and reversing the joyful trip to the swamp after Grendel's demise. The old, ravaged hoard, like a reified recollection, glosses the old king who has won it: time is the enemy. The treasure now brought to Beowulf by Wiglaf parallels the hilt brought to Hrothgar by Beowulf, but this time the recipient's vision expands only as far as his funeral barrow. The hero's last words to Wiglaf in effect rename him, in a grisly, eschatological pun, as the *endelaf* (last survivor: 2813) of the Wægmunding line; the speech constitutes a melancholy expansion of the moment's significance, for it reminds us of the treasure's own status as *endelaf* of the nation whose human *endelaf* placed it in the ground to await the dragon and Beowulf (2247–2270).

Meanwhile, the dragon's body lies coiled nearby, fallen to earth for the last time (2834). Each warrior has killed the other (2844–2845), bringing to completion the bargain (*ceap*: 2415, 2482) that the two old merchants entered into over the gold they both wanted, one to brood over, the other to pass on to his people (2413–2419). The relationship between Beowulf and his last opponent is, in effect, trivialized by the language in which it is presented—yet another contrast to the language of part 1, which elevates Beowulf's monster fights almost to the status of providential encounters (696–702; compare the description of God's battles with the giants on the hilt of the sword that Beowulf uses to kill Grendel's mother: 1688–1693).

The poem's final centrifugal movement begins inauspiciously with the return of Beowulf's cowardly retainers from the woods to which they fled when the dragon appeared (2596–2599). Wiglaf sends a messenger to tell the Geats of their lord's death; his message forms the last great expansion of the poem's vision, and what it beholds is not the promise of future allegiance, as Beowulf and Hrothgar pledged for their respective nations at the end of part 1, but the grim foreboding of unremitting hostility from the neighboring nations that Beowulf had long kept at bay. Beowulf's funeral, balancing Scyld's, ends the work; while part 1 concluded with Beowulf receiving land and honor from Hygelac, part 2 sees a dead hero buried with useless treasure "given" him by the king who also killed him. Beowulf's seaside barrow will remind his people, as well as passing shipmen, of him (2804–2808); the hero who told his own story to Hygelac in part 1 now becomes a story to be recalled by others when they see his *laf* (remains).

The pervasiveness of the contrasts between parts 1 and 2, focused by structural parallels, cannot be denied. It remains to formulate their significance for the poem as a whole.

THEMATIC CONTRASTS AND UNITY

Beowulf's life derives its form from, and imparts unity to, the clash of contrasts between the two main sections of the poem and the complex rhythms of alternating expansion and intensification within each section. This relationship between hero and structure is paralleled by another between the thematic continuities and the different forms taken by key concepts and images in the two parts. Thematic constancy and transformation hold the key to the overall meaning that we derive from our experience of *Beowulf*.

The poem's central concern is clearly the nature and uses of heroism or, in other words, the interaction of the heroic will with the social and temporal world in which it functions. Part 1 of *Beowulf* presents a positive model of this interaction, part 2 a negative one. Each model revolves around the presentation and treatment of several main themes—time or history, treasure, feuds, reversals, and recollection—which attract other subsidiary themes to them. Part 1 also has a theme of providence—the action of God in history—crucially lacking in part 2.

All the main themes appear at once, tightly interwoven, in the poem's introduction, which, as we have seen, prepares for Beowulf's arrival by establishing a feud between Grendel and the Danes, set in Heorot. Heorot represents the confluence of power and generosity in Hrothgar—power that protects the Danes from external feuds (as Hrothgar says he has done: 1769–1773), generosity that protects them from the internal misery caused by a stingy, vicious king such as Heremod (1718–1720). Heremod's banishment in fact created the lordlessness that the Danes endured until Scyld established the dynasty of which the building of Heorot stands as the crowning achievement (12–16). But God sent Scyld a son to succor the Danes, so the great reversal *(edwenden)* that begins the poem (and is paralleled by Scyld's own reversal from destitute foundling to powerful king: 4–11) has providence at its root.

The presence of Heorot attracts Grendel, who creates by his malice and violence the next reversal—sorrow in the hall after joy: "þa wæs æfter wiste wop up ahafen" (then weeping arose after prosperity: 128). Grendel presents himself as a perverse hall—thane (142) who wants—and takes—as his share of the hall's treasures one of the two things Hrothgar cannot give out: the lives of men (73). Grendel can never be part of Heorot's system of sharing, which binds the nation together—we are told he cannot approach the *gifstol* ("giftstool," or throne) from which Hrothgar dispenses treasure, even though he controls the hall at night (168–169)—because he will not come to terms with the Danes, will not settle his implacable feud (154–156). He is the perpetual outsider, banished with the rest of Cain's kin after Cain began the human feud by murdering his brother. Providence has, in effect, set the Danes and Grendel on a collision course. His advent establishes the primacy of the feud over the peaceful sharing of treasure, sours the triumph of the Scylding dynasty, and reverses the providentially guided flow of events from Scyld to Hrothgar. Grendel's effect is division (the negative version of sharing out) and deprivation among the Danes, who must abandon their hall, the symbol of their national identity, each night and sleep dispersed in the outbuildings. The poem relates the Danes' helplessness to their ignorance, another key theme of part 1, sounded at the time of Scyld's death (the Danes do not know who receives his body: 50–52) and repeated with respect to Grendel (they do not know where he lives: 162–163) and God (180–182). The cumulative force of the ignorance formulas that dot this part of the text is to induce not condemnation of the Danes but pity for them, and recognition that they will need crucial help from outside their own knowledge-deprived world to break Grendel's hold on their society and history.

The complex thematic preparation for Beowulf's arrival elevates his two battles in Denmark far above the level of folktale exploits. As he says to Hrothgar, he has come not just to kill a monster, but to cleanse Heorot (*Heorot fǣlsian*: 432) by fighting Grendel singlehandedly, an activity that the hero describes as if it were a judicial meeting: "ond nu wið Grendel sceal,/wið þam aglæcan ana gehegan/(ðing wið þyrse" (and now I shall with Grendel, alone hold a meeting with the monster: 424–426). In fact, the poem suggests that the fight will be almost a judicial combat, with God on the side of the hero, whose strength the text equates with God's grace (670). Although Beowulf is as ignorant as the Danes of God's purposes and Grendel's lineage, he makes choices here and in the later battle with Grendel's mother that suggest a profound harmony between his heroism and providence: he refuses to fight Grendel with weapons, lest he seem to be afraid of, or have an advantage over, the unarmed creature (432–440; 677–687); but, as it turns out (798–805), Grendel is immune to swords, so Beowulf's choice is the necessary one. Later, in the underwater hall, he will find the old sword, too big for any other mortal to use, just in time to kill Grendel's mother with it; when the hilt is described, we learn that it portrays God's battle against antediluvian giants, and we understand that God's protection of Beowulf against the she-monster (1553–1556) is the result of the hero's usefulness in continuing the old feud against new enemies.

Beowulf's destruction of Grendel has several salutary consequences for the Danes. The grip in which he traps the monster symbolizes another great *edwenden,* the reversal of the disruption that has driven the Danes apart by denying them Heorot as a place for socially cohesive gift-giving. The poem uses forms of the word *dǣl* ("part," "portion") and its verbal derivatives to express the paradoxes and significance of Beowulf's function as reuniter of Hrothgar's nation. Hrothgar builds Heorot to share (*gedǣlan*: 71) all his God-given treasure, thereby bringing the Danes together in harmony. Grendel, taking the forbidden share, men's lives, enters Heorot on his last visit, rejoicing in the prospect of dividing the sleeping warriors' souls from their bodies by eating them: "mynte þæt he *gedælde,* ær þon dæg cwome,/atol aglæca anra gehwylces/lif wið lice" (the terrible monster intended, before daylight came, to divide [take away] the life from each of the [sleeping] bodies: 731–733; emphasis added). The verb is the same in both cases. Furthermore, Grendel arrives at Heorot deprived of joy (*dreamum bedæed*: 721), and there he experiences departure (or division) from life (*lifgedal*: 841). His death takes the ironic form of a literal dividing-up of his body and a sharing of some of it with the Danes when he leaves his arm behind as a grisly trophy in Heorot (984–990). Against this rich verbal background, the metaphoric as well as the literal force of Beowulf's grip becomes clear: he has brought the Danes together again to experience the joy that they have lacked for twelve years and that resounds in Heorot again the following night.

The *edwenden* accomplished by Beowulf redeems time and sharing; treasure can flow again, and it does as a sign of Hrothgar's gratitude and desire to integrate Beowulf's heroism into the Danes' world. The result of the king's generous response to the hero's liberating and consolidating feat of strength is that an old feud between the Geats and Danes is settled (1855–1864), and Beowulf can now obtain his share of land from his own lord. Hrothgar's vision of a future in which boats will bring booty and tokens of friendship back and forth across the sea between the two nations (1862–1863) suggests that the cleansing power of Beowulf's heroism extends well beyond Heorot in time and space. The hero has set his strength and will against a feud between Grendel and the Danes; played an important part in prosecuting God's feud with Cain's kin; and brought about the resolution of feuds between neighboring nations. When we are told that he never killed his hearth companions (2179–2180), we can almost believe that Beowulf has singlehandedly reversed the legacy of Cain.

The main themes find in the Beowulf of part 1 a most favorable interpreter who emphasizes their positive and diminishes their negative dimensions. The connection between the efficacy of heroism and divine providence is never clarified, but it is clearly suggested, while the salutary effect of heroic endeavor on the social processes of humanity and the relations between nations cannot be doubted. In part 2, everything changes as heroism itself must endure a catastrophic reversal.

Part 2 forces Beowulf—and us—to confront the limitations, rather than the possibilities, of heroism. The hero's will has not changed, except for his one moment of doubt, but everything else in his world has, and the changes have rendered heroism either irrelevant, useless, or counterproductive. Now treasure does not lubricate the operation of society; it lies in the earth, rusting and inert, seeming to pull down with it, like some great magnet, the dragon and Beowulf. Time has become, in the absence of providence, a negative medium, bringing old age, the ending of civilizations, the rusting of treasure. History becomes a ticking time bomb, full of unsettled old scores: the messenger who enumerates them relentlessly to the Geats offers the prospect of a future completely opposed to the golden vision imagined by Hrothgar when Beowulf leaves Denmark. What has darkened history in part 2 is the feud—a legacy of strife, especially between Geats and Swedes, passed on from generations and turning kinsmen against each other. (Onela must overlook the fact that Weohstan has killed his nephew Eanmund, and reward him for the deed, because Eanmund had rebelled against his uncle: "no ymbe ða fæhðe spræc,/þeah ðe he his broðor bearn abredwade" [he didn't speak of the hostile act, even though he (Weohstan) had killed his brother's son: 2618–2619]. The word fæhð also means feud; Onela can't speak of one feud because another takes precedence.) Everyone in this part of the poem seems caught in the inescapable coil of feuds, or old age, or ill fortune that prevents fathers from avenging their sons—Hrethel because one son has accidentally killed another; the nameless old *ceorl*

(2444–2462) whose son has been hanged—or ancient, unknown curses laid on treasure hoards. The dragon's coiled shape (and other shapes curving back on themselves), kept before us by forms of the verb *bugan* (or *gebugan*) and nominal derivatives, takes on symbolic significance for this sense of futility and entrapment hanging over part 2. The curse on the gold (whether or not we read the obscure lines 3074–3075 as saying that Beowulf has been felled, even damned, by it) expresses the motif of victimization, but the curse also serves as a metaphor for the poisoned well of time and history, the compressed equivalent of the "curse" laid on history by feuds, which will sooner or later so pile up as to come tumbling down on a nation (here the Geats) and bring it to its knees.

Amid this world gone bad, Beowulf's (and Wiglaf's) heroism gleams and goes out. Given time's negative function as a bringer of age, the hero's will must eventually outlive his strength and seal his fate. Given the omnipresence of feuds, even the most heroic death of a king leaves his people vulnerable to catastrophe. Given the curse on treasure, and its inertia as well, to win it is to win something useless (*unnyt*: 3168). While Beowulf's ignorance in part 1 did not prevent him from serving providence, his ignorance of the curse on the gold may have cost him his life. Part 2's pessimism—its conviction that all activity is ultimately fated and futile—finds perhaps its purest expression in almost identical pronouncements about the dragon's hoard—guarding (recognized as involuntary in Germanic folklore) and Beowulf's use of a sword in battle: of the dragon, *ne byð him wihte ðy sel* (he is not at all the better for it: 2277); of Beowulf, *næs him wihte ðe sel* (he wasn't any the better for it: 2687).

What are we to make of the heroic diptych that glorifies Beowulf in part 1 and surrounds him with gloom, impotence, and pessimism in part 2? Perhaps, if the poem is indeed a meditation on the Germanic past and its ideals by a Christian poet, the message is that heroism, like any other human activity, is subject to God's will. Perhaps it is a "best case-worst case" analysis of heroism, suggesting its absolute as well as its pragmatic value within the range of human behavioral options. It may even be that the poem is an attempt to recapture and preserve the full range of a traditional culture's experiences, good and bad, as gathered, in the best traditional manner, around the polemic core of the hero's supreme moments of combat. We can, in any case, enjoy and learn from this great poem even while freely admitting that much of its consciousness and social institutions have become so alien as to be beyond the reach of all but the most creative recollection.

Selected Bibliography

EDITIONS

The Anglo-Saxon Poetic Records. Edited by G. P. Krapp and E. V. K. Doobie, 6 vols. (New York, 1931–1953). The standard collection of texts.

Beowulf. Edited by G. J. Thorkelin; (Copenhagen, 1815).

Beowulf. Edited by J. M. Kemble; (London, 1833); with other poems.

Beowulf. Edited by B. Thorpe; (Oxford, 1855); with other poems.

Beowulf. Edited by F. Klaeber. 3rd ed. with 1st and 2nd supplements (Boston, 1950). The standard text.

Beowulf. Edited by E. V. K. Dobbie. (New York, 1953). With Judith in *The Anglo-Saxon Poetic Records,* vol. 6.

Beowulf. Edited by C. L. Wrenn. 3rd ed. revised by W. F. Bolton. (New York, 1973).

Beowulf. Edited with translation by Howell D. Chickering. (Garden City, N.Y., 1977).

Beowulf. Edited with translation by Michael Swanton. (Manchester, 1978).

Finnsburh: Fragment and Episode. Edited by D. R. Fry. (London, 1974).

FACSIMILIES

Malone, K., ed. *The Nowell Codex, (British Museum Cotton Vitellius A. XV 2nd ms.).* (Copenhagen, 1963).

Malone, K., ed. *The Thorkelin Transcripts of Beowulf.* (Copenhagen, 1951).

Zupitza, J., ed. *Beowulf: Facsimile with Transliteration.* (London, 1882). 2nd. ed. with new reproductions of the manuscripts and an introductory note by N. Davis. (London, 1959).

TRANSLATIONS

Donaldson, E. T. *Beowulf.* (New York, 1966). The best translation.

Gordon, R. K. *Anglo-Saxon Poetry Selected and Translated.* (London, 1926).

Greenfield, S. B. *A Readable "Beowulf."* (Carbondale, Ill., 1982).

Hamer, R. *A Choice of Anglo-Saxon Verse.* (London, 1970).

Hieatt, C. B. *"Beowulf" and Other Old English Poems,* (New York, 1967).

Kemble, J. M. *Beowulf.* (London, 1837).

Kennedy, C. W. *An Anthology of Old English Poetry.* (New York, 1960).

CONCORDANCES AND BIBLIOGRAPHIES

Bessinger, J. B. and Smith, P. H. *A Concordance to the Anglo-Saxon Poetic Records,* (Ithaca, 1978).

Bessinger, J. B. and Smith, P. H. *A Concordance to Beowulf.* (Ithaca, 1969).

Fry, D. R. *Beowulf and the Fight at Finnsburh: A Bibliography.* (Charlottesville, N.C., 1969).

Garmonsway, G. N., and J. Simpson, trans. *Beowulf and Its Analogues.* (London, 1968). A collection of translations from Old English, Latin, Old Norse and other languages.

Greenfield, S. B. and Robinson, F. C. *A Bibliography of Publications on Old English Literature to the End of 1972.* (Toronto, 1980).

Short, D. D. *Beowulf Scholarship: An Annotated Bibliography to 1978.* (New York, 1980).

RELATED TEXTS

Albertson, C., trans. *Anglo-Saxon Saints and Heroes.* (New York, 1967). Studies of several Anglo-Saxon saints' lives.

Bede. *Ecclesiastical History of the English People.* Edited and translated by B. Colgrave and R. A. B. Mynors. (Oxford, 1969).

Goldin, F., trans. *The Song of Roland.* (New York, 1978).

Hatto, A. T., trans. *The Nibelungenlied.* (Harmondsworth, 1965).

Translated by R. Lattimore. *The Iliad,* Homer. (Chicago, 1951).

Sandars, N. K., trans. *The Epic of Gilgamesh.* (Harmondsworth, 1960; rev. ed., 1964).

Whitelock, D., D. C. Douglas, and S. Tucker, eds. and trans. *The Anglo-Saxon Chronicle.* (London, 1961).

BACKGROUND STUDIES

Amos, A. C. *Linguistic Means of Determining the Dates of Old English Literary Texts.* (Cambridge, Mass., 1981).

Barnes, D. "Folktale Morphology and the Structure of Beowulf." *Speculum,* 45: 416–434 (1970).

Benson, L. "The Literary Character of Anglo-Saxon Formulaic Poetry." *PMLA,* 81: 334–341 (1966).

Benson, L. "The Originality of Beowulf." *Harvard English Studies,* 1: 1–43 (1970).

Benson, L. *Old English Poetry: Fifteen Essays,* "The Pagan Coloring of Beowulf." Edited by R. Creed. (Providence, R.I., 1967) Pp. 193–213.

Blair, P. Hunter. *Introduction to Anglo-Saxon England.* 2nd ed. (Cambridge, 1977).

Blair, P. Hunter. *The World of Bede.* (London, 1970).

Bliss, A. J., "*Beowulf,* Lines 3074–75." *In J. R. R. Tolkien, Scholar and Storyteller.* Edited by M. Salu and T. Farrell. (Ithaca, N.Y., 1979) Pp. 41–63. Argues that Beowulf is damned at the end of the epic.

Bonjour, A. *The Digressions in "Beowulf."* (Oxford, 1950).

Bowra, C. M. *Heroic Poetry.* (London, 1952).

Brewer, D. S. *Symbolic Stories.* (Cambridge and Ottawa, 1980).

Brodeur, A. G. *The Art of Beowulf.* (Berkeley and Los Angeles, 1959). Especially the first two chapters on compounding and variation.

Campbell, A. "The Old English Epic Style." *English and Medieval Studies Presented to J. R. R. Tolkien on the Occasion of His Seventieth Birthday.* Edited by N. Davis and C. L. Wrenn (London, 1962) Pp. 13–26.

Campbell, J. *The Hero with a Thousand Faces.* 2nd ed. (Princeton, N.J., 1960).

Chadwick, H. M. *The Heroic Age.* (Cambridge, 1912) Reprinted 1967.

Chambers, R. W. *Beowulf: An Introduction to the Study of the Poem.* 3rd ed. (Cambridge, 1959).

Chaney, W. A. *The Cult of Kingship in Anglo-Saxon England.* (Berkeley and Los Angeles, 1970).

Chase, C., ed. *The Dating of Beowulf.* (Toronto, 1981).

Creed, R. P. "The Making of an Anglo-Saxon Poem." *Journal of English Literary History.* 26: 445–454 (1959).

DeVries, J. *Heroic Song and Heroic Legend.* Translated by B. J. Timmer (London, 1963).

Donahue, C. "*Beowulf* and Christian Tradition: A Reconsideration from a Celtic Stance." *Traditio* 21: 55–116 (1965).

Frye, N. *Anatomy of Criticism.* (Princeton, N.J., 1957).

Girvan, R. *Beowulf and the Seventh Century.* (London, 1971). This reissued edition includes a chapter on Sutton Hoo.

Godfrey, C. J. *The Church in Anglo-Saxon England.* (Cambridge, 1962).

Goldsmith, M. E. *The Mode and Meaning of Beowulf.* (London, 1970).

Greenfield, S. E. *A Critical History of Old English Literature.* (New York, 1965).

Greenfield, S. E. *The Interpretation of Old English Poems.* (London, 1972).

Haarder, A. *"Beowulf": The Appeal of a Poem.* (Aarhus, 1975). History of *Beowulf* criticism.

Hamilton, M. P. "The Religious Principle in *Beowulf.*" *PMLA* 61: 309–331 (1946).

Hanning, R. W. "*Beowulf* as Heroic History." *Medievalia et Humanistica* 5: 77–102 (1974).

Hanning, R. W. "Sharing, Dividing, Depriving: The Verbal Ironies of Grendel's Last Visit to Heorot." *Texas Studies in Literature and Language* 15: 203–214 (1973).

Hart, T. E. "*Ellen*: Some Tectonic Relationships in *Beowulf* and their Formal Resemblance to Anglo-Saxon Art." *Papers on Language and Literature.* 6: 263–290 (1970).

Hieatt, C. B. "Envelope Patterns in the Structure of Beowulf." *English Studies in Canada* 1: 250–265 (1975).

Hume, K. "The Concept of the Hall in Old English Poetry." *Anglo-Saxon England* 3: 63–74 (1974).

Irving, E. B. *A Reading of Beowulf.* (New Haven, Conn., 1968).

Jabbour, A. "Memorial Transmission in Old English Poetry." *Chaucer Review.* 3: 174–190 (1969).

Jackson, W. T. H. *The Hero and the King, An Epic Theme.* (New York, 1982).

John, E. "Beowulf and the Margins of Literacy." *Bulletin of the John Rylands University Library of Manchester* 56: 388–422 (1974).

Kiernan, K. *Beowulf and the Beowulf Manuscript.* (New Brunswick, N.J., 1981).

Lee, A. A. *The Guest-Hall of Eden: Four Essays on the Design of Old English Poetry* (New Haven, Conn., 1972). Especially pp. 171–223.

Levy, G. R. *The Sword from the Rock: An Investigation into the Origins of Epic Literature and the Development of the Hero.* (London, 1953).

Leyerle, J. "Beowulf the Hero and the King." *Medium Aevum* 34: 89–102 (1965).

Leyerle, J. "The Interlace Structure of Beowulf." *University of Toronto Quarterly* 37: 1–17 (1967).

Lord, A. B., *The Singer of Tales,* (Cambridge, Mass., 1960) Sets forth Parry and Lord's work in Yugoslavia.

Magoun, F. P., Jr. "Beowulf A: A Folk Variant," *Arv* (Journal of Scandinavian Folklore) 14: 95–101 (1958).

Magoun, F. P., Jr. "Beowulf B: A Folk Poem on Beowulf's Death." In *Early English and Norse Studies: Presented to Hugh Smith in Honour of His Sixtieth Birthday,* Edited by A. Brown and P. Foote. (London, 1963) Pp. 127–140.

Magoun, F. P., Jr. "Oral-Formulaic Character of Anglo-Saxon Poetry." *Speculum* 28: 446–467 (1953).

Niles, J. D. "Ring Composition and the Structure of Beowulf." *PMLA* 94: 924–935 (1979).

O'Loughlin, J. L. N. "Beowulf: Its Unity and Purpose." *Medium Aevum* 21: 1–13 (1952) Discussion of the feud.

Ong, W. J. "World as View and World as Event." *American Anthropologist* 71: 634–647 (1969).

Opland, J. *Anglo-Saxon Oral Poetry.* (New Haven, Conn., 1980).

Osborn, M. "The Great Feud: Scriptural History and Strife in Beowulf." *PMLA* 93: 973–981 (1978).

Pearsall, D. *Old English and Middle English Poetry,* (London, 1977) *Routledge History of English Poetry* vol. 1.

Pope, J. C. "Beowulf's Old Age." In *Philological Essays: Studies in Old and Middle English Language and Literature in Honour of Herbert Dean Meritt,* Edited by J. Rosier (The Hague, 1970) Pp. 55–64.

Pope, J. C. *The Rhythm of "Beowulf."* Rev. ed. (New Haven, Conn., 1966). Argues that the poem was sung to the accompaniment of the harp.

Propp, V. *Morphology of the Folk Tale.* Translated by L. Scott (Bloomington, Ind., 1958).

Raw, B. *The Art and Background of Old English Poetry.* (London, 1978).

Robinson, F. C. "Elements of the Marvelous in the Characterization of Beowulf: A Reconsideration of the Textual Evidence." In *Old England Studies in Honor of John C. Pope.* Edited by R. B. Burlin and E. B. Irving (Toronto, 1974). Pp. 119–138.

Robinson, F. C. "Two Aspects of Variation in Old English Poetry." In *Old English Poetry: Essays in Style,* Edited by D. G. Calder. (Berkeley and Los Angeles, 1979) Pp. 127–146.

Rogers, H. L. "Beowulf's Three Great Fights." *Review of English Studies* 6: 339–355 (1955).

Schücking, L. "Wann Entstand der Beowulf? Glossen, Zweifel und Fragen." *Beiträge zur Geschichte der deutsches Sprache und Literatur* 42: 347–410 (1917). Suggests that the poem was composed in the Danelaw during the tenth century.

Shippey, T. A. *Beowulf. Studies in English Literature, 70.* (London, 1978).

Sisam, K. *The Structure of Beowulf.* (Oxford, 1965).

Sisam, K. *Studies in the History of Old English Literature.* (Oxford, 1953). Especially pp. 29–44 on the authority of Old English poetical manuscripts.

Stanley, E. G. "*Beowulf.*" In *Continuations and Beginnings: Studies in Old English Literature.* Edited by Stanley. (London, 1941). Pp. 104–141.

Stanley, E. G. "Hæþenra hyht in Beowulf." In *Studies in Old English Literature in Honor of Arthur G. Brodeur.* Edited by S. B. Greenfield (Eugene, Ore., 1963) Pp. 136–151.

Stevens, M. "The Structure of Beowulf From Gold-Hoard to Word-Hoard." *Modern Language Quarterly* 39: 219–238 (1978).

Tolkien, J. R. R. "Beowulf, the Monsters and the Critics." *Proceedings of the British Academy* 22: 245–295 (1936). The widely anthologized Gollancz Memorial Lecture.

Wallace-Hadrill, J. M. *Early Germanic Kingship in England and on the Continent,* (Oxford, 1971).

Watts, A. C., *The Lyre and the Harp: A Comparative Reconsideration of Oral Tradition in Homer and Old English Epic Poetry.* (New Haven, Conn., 1969).

Whitelock, D. *The Audience of Beowulf,* (Oxford, 1951).

Whitelock, D. *The Beginnings of English Society.* (Harmondsworth, 1952) *Pelican History of England* vol. 2.

Whitman, C. H. *Homer and the Heroic Tradition.* (Cambridge, Mass., 1958). Reprinted New York, 1965).

Williams, D. *Cain and Beowulf: A Study in Secular Allegory,* (Toronto, 1982).

Wrenn, C. L. *A Study of Old English Literature.* (London, 1967).

COLLECTIONS OF ESSAYS

Burlin, R. B. and E. B. Irving, eds. *Old English Studies in Honor of John C. Pope.* (Toronto, 1974).

Fry, D. R., ed. *The "Beowulf" Poet.* (Englewood Cliffs, N.J., 1968). Twentieth Century Views series.

Greenfield, S. B., ed. *Studies in Old English Literature in Honor of Arthur G. Brodeur.* (Eugene, Ore., 1963).

Nicholson, L. E., ed. *An Anthology of "Beowulf" Criticism.* (Notre Dame, Ind., 1963).

John Berryman
(1914–1972)

WILLIAM J. MARTZ

Despite career-long unevenness in the quality of his work, John Berryman has become a major American poet, has achieved a permanency that places him in a group with Theodore Roethke and Randall Jarrell. Berryman, it seems to me, has taken on the whole modern world and has come to poetic terms with it. At the same time he has taken on himself, and has come to poetic terms with that too. He has seen the wreck of the modern world (or, better, the modern world insofar as it is a wreck) and the wreck of his personal self in that world. He is not a pessimist but has, rather, what we would have to call a tragic view of human life—with good reason for holding it. Yet, not surprisingly, the tragic view finds its complement in a comic view, his wild and so often devastatingly effective sense of humor. He is preeminently a poet of suffering and laughter.

To understand his achievement it is necessary to look first at the life of the man, for his poetry will emerge as strongly autobiographical, and the intensity of his personal suffering must be understood. He was born October 25, 1914, in McAlester, Oklahoma, and grew up in Anadarko, Oklahoma, a town of 3000. His father was the town banker, his mother was a schoolteacher, and he had a younger brother. His upbringing was strict Roman Catholic, which was the faith of both his parents, and, though in his last years he attended mass only occasionally, he remained a Catholic in spirit, religiously questing. Until he was ten he spent summers on a farm, throughout the year fished and hunted, and was from the beginning a bright boy in school rather than a young rebel. When he was ten the family moved to Tampa, Florida, where his mother and father had severe marital difficulties. His father, fearing that his wife was about to leave him, repeatedly threatened to drown himself and John with him. Lack of money was not the problem; in fact, young John had an allowance of $25 a week, all of which he spent on his stamp collection. His relationship with each of his parents was, moreover, close. His father, a captain in the National Guard, even took the boy with him occasionally when he went on maneuvers to Fort Sill, Oklahoma, as well as on hunting and fishing trips. But when John was twelve he suffered an ultimate trauma—his father shot himself right outside his son's window. The father was buried in Oklahoma, but the son never returned to his grave.

After the death of the father, the family settled in New York. John's mother then married a Wall Street banker named John Angus McAlpin Berryman, who formally adopted John and his younger brother. (John's father's name had been John Allyn Smith.) His mother and stepfather were divorced after ten years of marriage, but whatever the strains of their relationship the children were not adversely affected, and Berryman was good to his adopted children. John was sent to South Kent School in Connecticut, which his mother chose for him. South Kent was, in John's later words, "very muscular," that is, devoted to athletics, and very high-church Episcopalian. Though he came to feel friendly toward it later, at the time John hated South Kent with heart and soul. He was much bullied there, had many fights—usually with stand-off results—began to have literary ambitions, and rebelled because he was an intellectual and the school, as he saw it, was not sympathetic to intellectuals. At South Kent the boys were beaten regularly with a paddle, upon the command "Assume the angle." But the experience of the school was partly redeemed for John by two masters, one in English and one in history, who were sympathetic to him personally.

Following four years at South Kent, he attended Columbia, from which he took his B.A. in 1936. The teacher who inspired him was Mark Van Doren, all of whose courses he took. His development as a writer probably begins at about the age of nineteen under the close personal influence of Van Doren, whose book of poems *A Winter Diary* he reviewed, and then Van Doren got him going on other poets. He flowered at Columbia despite dismissal for half a year for flunking one of Van Doren's courses because he read only seventeen of forty-two assigned books. He returned to make A's and be elected to Phi Beta Kappa.

Following graduation from Columbia, a traveling fellowship took him to Cambridge, England, for two years. There he wrote poetry all the time and was known as a poet though he was not actually publishing at the time. He took a B.A. from Clare College in 1938 and returned to New York, where he became a close personal friend of Delmore Schwartz, then poetry editor of *Partisan Review*, a friendship renewed when both were teaching at Harvard, Berryman from 1940 to 1943 and Schwartz from 1940 to 1947. Berryman's long teaching career had begun at Wayne State in 1939. He taught at Princeton intermittently from 1943 to 1949, held a fellowship there in 1950–51, and received a Guggenheim Fellowship in 1952–53. He had been rejected for service in World War II on medical grounds. His eyesight was poor and he had recurrent serious nervous difficulties.

He married for the first time in 1942. The marriage lasted eleven years. One of the love affairs he had during this time became the basis of his *Sonnets*. It was this affair that brought him to the point of suicide, with thoughts of killing both himself and his mistress because she flatly refused to leave her husband and marry him. His wife, who was ignorant of the affair, persuaded him to undergo psychoanalysis, and he stayed under analysis from 1947 to 1953. The analysis relieved his suicidal depression and led him to renounce the affair; thereafter he still saw his analyst occasionally. At the time of his separation from his wife in 1953—his heavy drinking and the tensions accompanying the writing of *Homage to Mistress Bradstreet* acting as causes—both were hoping for reconciliation.

In 1955 he moved to the University of Minnesota, where he remained, and became a professor of humanities. He remarried in 1956, had a son by this marriage, and was divorced in 1959. Again heavy drinking and disorderly behavior acted as causes, as well as the tensions accompanying his writing, this time, of the Dream Songs. He married once more in 1961. He and his third wife, Kate, who was twenty-five years younger than he, had two daughters, Martha and Sara. Like her husband, Mrs. Berryman was also a Catholic living outside the Church because of their marriage. In his last years John Berryman was evangelistically opposed to adultery. On Friday, January 7, 1972, he jumped to his death from a bridge over the Mississippi River, landing on the west bank about 100 feet below.

Formal honors for his poetry have been awarded to Berryman throughout his career. These include the Shelley Memorial Award in 1949, the Harriet Monroe Poetry Prize in 1957, the Pulitzer Prize for poetry in 1965, the Bollingen Prize in 1968, and the National Book Award for poetry in 1969.

Throughout his career—and underlying the unevenness in the quality of his work—Berryman was beset by the problem of style. It is as if he wrestled with artistic agonies at the same time as with personal ones, or that the former were perhaps a deep reflection of the latter. Although it is safe to say that he arrived at widespread and qualitatively certain recognition with his 1968 volume, *His Toy, His Dream, His Rest,* his earlier reviewers show great consistency in recognizing the problem of style. Going back to 1948 and Berryman's first important collection of poems, we find Dudley Fitts writing that it is "somehow without the excitement that attends the transformation of a craft into a completely realized art," and Randall Jarrell saying, "Doing things in a style all its own sometimes seems the primary object of the poem, and its subject gets a rather spasmodic treatment." Stanley Kunitz, with language strongly in mind, called *Homage to Mistress Bradstreet* a failure "worth more than most successes." John Ciardi wondered whether the same poem was "a thing literary and made," and John Holmes thought that it would "fascinate the intellectuals." Louise Bogan responded to *77 Dream Songs* with the incisive phrase "this desperate artificiality." Even Berryman's biography of Stephen Crane revealed the problem of style. As Morgan Blum acutely observed, Berryman's trouble in the biography "apparently resides in an inability to reduce his insights to reasoned discourse." One could as easily say that in the biography Berryman so insisted on style, on being his own man, that he paid a price for it. Blum's summary judgment, "Flawed and distinguished," has the force of an epithet summarizing a central reaction to Berryman. But implicit in the reaction is the fact that there is only one Berryman, the Berryman of tension, agony, and struggle.

The biography of Crane, which appeared in 1950, is almost a tour de force. It is as if nothing but tension, agony, and struggle could have produced it. The closer one looks at its organization, the more one realizes the truth of Morgan Blum's comment. Despite tile fact that it must be granted in advance that the art of writing biography is extraordinarily challenging—in my own opinion the most difficult of all literary writing—there is hardly an excuse to be found for the diffuseness it displays. Even when Berryman comes to a climactic chapter on the all-important subject of Crane's art, he seems unable to pull his materials together, despite the fact that in a cumulative way, as the reader by that time knows, he has the basic resources to do it. What makes matters even more frustrating for the reader is that Berryman's purpose is clearly to make an intelligent and balanced attempt at a fair evaluation of Crane. He obviously wants to do what the academically oriented critic normally does do. He is also too honest to make excuses. Although he remarks with casualness in his preface that it is a "psychological biography," he does not use that fact as a device to mitigate his own responsibility as a critic to make judgments when judgments are called for. And yet he persistently falls short of doing what he is telling himself that he must do.

The biography of Crane represents, then, Berryman's inability to reduce his insights to reasoned discourse or, to give the matter another emphasis, a values choice of passion over reason. Trite as it sounds, the poet in him wins out. His style is vigorous and vivid, and his eloquence is the kind found in only the very finest biographies. His eye for detail, his sensitivity to the selection of detail, is acute. One of the best parts of the book, for example, is in his description of Crane's childhood, as when he describes the young Stephen's contact with the color red or the boy's terror when his hands brush a handle of his father's coffin. In broad terms Berryman communicates sympathy for his subject by means that are often poetic. He leaves the reader with a vivid picture of Crane, a man who had teeth among the worst those who knew him had ever seen, an artist dead at twenty-eight of tuberculosis. It should be emphasized, however, that the biography is a far cry from being merely a poetic outpouring. Some of its vigor of thought, which relates ultimately to a poetic talent of forceful expression and projection of a speaker's character, is similar to that distinguishing the best academic writing. Berryman wisely sees, for example, that our own period of literature has developed toward increasing absorption in style, and he emphatically sees Crane as a great stylist, particularly as an impressionist, mentioning, as one of Crane's friends recorded it, Crane's assertion that impressionism was truth. Berryman also sees Crane as a writer of will, and comes to the very sensible conclusion that the world emerging from some of Crane's early sketches was one of "perfect aloneness." Sympathy and insight give the biography a unity that counters its diffuseness. There is a pattern here, I would suggest, than anticipates Berryman's experience with "The Dream Songs," but by that time he is all poet and whatever his organizational problems with the poem, he is also far beyond the possibility of any flirtation with a tour de force.

Berryman's poetic output divides into what might conveniently and after the familiar pattern be called the early Berryman and the later Berryman. The early Berryman, whose work began appearing in such journals as *Southern Review, Kenyon Review, Partisan Review, Nation,* and *New Republic* in the late 1930's, publishes twenty poems in 1940 in the New Directions book *Five Young American Poets* and a pamphlet called *Poems* in 1942. Then in 1948 he publishes the important *The Dispossessed,* which collects, often in revised form, many previously published poems. He also writes a sonnet sequence in the 1940's but this is not published until 1967. The later Berryman publishes *Homage to Mistress Bradstreet* in 1956, *77 Dream Songs* in 1964, *His Toy, His Dream, His Rest,* which completes the poem "The Dream Songs," in 1968, *Love and Fame* in 1970, and the posthumous *Delusions, etc.* in 1972. The 1958 *His Thought Made Pockets & the Plane Buckt* is a group of thirteen poems which may be regarded as an extension of *The Dispossessed,* and the 1967 *Short Poems* merely brings together *The Dispossessed, His Thought Made Pockets,* and a rather ineffectual poem called "Formal Elegy" written in 1963 on the occasion of the death of President John F. Kennedy.

So much for orientation to the poet's life and output. The immediate basis for the division between early Berryman and later Berryman is a striking contrast in style. Indeed, *Homage to Mistress Bradstreet* is rightly regarded as a breakthrough for Berryman, though the early Berryman obviously meshes with the later Berryman and the later Berryman does not hold, as it were, to the style of his breakthrough. Always conspicuously conscious of his identity as a poet, he provides us in Sonnet 47 with the perfect epigraph for his contrasting styles when he refers to "Crumpling a syntax at a sudden need." The early Berryman tends not to crumple his syntax but to write "normal," or we could say "traditional," verse sentences such as these:

> Images are the mind's life, and they change.
> "A POINT OF AGE"

> We must travel in the direction of our fear.
> "A POINT OF AGE"

> An ultimate shaking grief fixes the boy
> As he stands rigid, trembling, staring down
> All his young days into the harbour where
> His ball went.
> "THE BALL POEM"

> I hope you will be happier where you go
> Than you or we were here, and learn to know
> What satisfactions there are.
> "FAREWELL TO MILES"

> How could you be so happy, now some thousand years
> disheveled, puffs of dust?
> "NOTE TO WANG WEI"

But in *Homage* a crumpling of syntax is typical and will be recognized as an element of the stream-of-consciousness or shift-of-association technique so common in the twentieth century—and also harking back to Gerard Manley Hopkins' sprung rhythm—that it too must be called "normal":

> So squeezed, wince you I scream?
> (19.1)

> Pioneering is not feeling well,
> not Indians, beasts.
> (23.2–3)

This technique is, of course, larger than the crumpling of the syntax of a single sentence;

since it is basically a device to dramatize the condition of the mind the crumpling in *Homage* is also a movement, often abrupt or rapid, from sentence to sentence, from thought to thought, or emotion to emotion. Quantitatively speaking, there are numerous normal verse sentences in *Homage*, but the steady effect of the poem is one of associational shift. Consider now a few examples of crumpled syntax from the Dream Songs:

> Maybe but even if I see my son
> forever never, get back on the take,
> free, black & forty-one.
> NUMBER 40

> The course his mind his body steer, poor
> Pussy-cat,
> in weakness & disorder, will see him down
> whiskers & tail.
> NUMBER 49, "BLIND"

> Henry—wonder! all,
> when most he—under the sun.
> NUMBER 52, "SILENT SONG"

But it must be said that this syntax, conspicuous as it is, does *not* dominate the Dream Songs, which are replete with normal English verse sentences. At the same time the first 77 Dream Songs do, like *Homage*, have a steady shift-of-association effect. Their crumpled language tends to be an untraditional drunken lurching consonant with the central character, Henry, and the psychic or dream world which he inhabits. To simplify a complicated matter we may say for the moment that the later Berryman writes in a style, or styles, directed toward dramatic immediacy. The early Berryman writes in a style that is ultimately dramatic but he tends to be a "speaker" of individual poems who does not become a developed character such as, for example, Frost's mythic New England Yankee or, in identity closer to the real-life poet, the Roethke who journeys to the interior in "North American Sequence." We could easily imagine the later Berryman—Mistress Bradstreet and Henry—on a stage in some kind of performance, but not the early Berryman. Clearly the early Berryman was searching for a poetic identity which could only be found by an experiment in style.

Style, however, can be a false light to follow. The pre-eminent question to ask about the early Berryman is, I think, whether or not he creates a substantial number of poems that establish not so much a style as the fact of his talent and particularly that talent as it identifies itself in terms of essential subject and theme. The question is, What does the Berryman of *The Dispossessed* care about? Though he is an individual speaker of poems rather than a developed character, is there nevertheless a certain unity to his early work, does the speaker of his poems take on a singleness of character? And to suggest the answers to these questions is naturally to anticipate his later development.

The most essential thing to say about the Berryman of *The Dispossessed* is that he offers a subjective response to the objective reality of the modern world. His early poems typically do not encounter objective reality in terms of an elaboration of the facts of that reality. He thus forgoes what we might call pure or external subject interest in favor of a focus on the individual as the individual responds to his world. It is most decidedly not an egocentric emphasis, but rather a steady and a dynamic relationship between the individual, the sensitive individual, and the world to which he *must* respond. The speaker of his early poems is typically anxious to generalize about humanity from a variety of specific experiences, but to proceed from a specific experience is not the same as to detail the specifics. The persistent concern is broad, and distinctly in the humanistic tradition. It would be fair to say that the basic character of the speaker in *The Dispossessed* is that of a sensitive and rather desperate humanist—we think too of the man who has abandoned his Catholic faith. What he cares about, broadly speaking, is our common humanity and its survival in the face of terrible threats. He cares about caring. His poetic attempt, his subject, is *how it feels* to be in a certain kind of world.

The pivot point of the world he finds himself in is World War II, the beginning of which he regards as a dark time for mankind, and as reason for feeling hatred and bitterness. It is a dark time because he finds fascism so evil and committed to destroy precious individual freedom. He sees the state as a monster of oppression, "At Dachau rubber blows forbid" ("Letter to His Brother")—this written in 1938. Or consider the terror and bitterness in these sensitive lines:

> The time is coming near
> When none shall have books or music, none
> his dear,
> And only a fool will speak aloud his mind.
> "THE MOON AND THE NIGHT AND THE MEN"

He looks out and sees "tortured continents" ("Boston Common") and becomes inwardly tortured by what he sees. His reaction to the world of the 1930's and 1940's is to take its burdens upon himself—much as Robert Lowell was shortly to do—and, as a result, to enter into the abyss of himself, which, as Yeats remarked, may show as reckless a courage as those we honor who die on the field of battle.

The early Berryman as a speaker of poems interests us, then, as a sensitive individual meditating upon and absorbing the shocks of a grim time. His perspective is broad in the sense that besides the state he sees other threats to human freedom: materialism, for example, as he calls out, "Great-grandfather, attest my hopeless need/Amongst the chromium luxury of the age" ("A Point of Age"). In a poem called "World-Telegram" he even catalogues the ordinary events of the day, and masks his horror with this reportorial matter-of-factness:

> An Indian girl in Lima, not yet six,
> Has been delivered by Caesarian.
> A boy. They let the correspondent in:
> Shy, uncommunicative, still quite pale,
> A holy picture by her, a blue ribbon.

At the end of the same poem he speaks in desperate understatement to dramatize the condition of civilization as he sees it: "If it were possible to take these things/Quite seriously, I believe they might/Curry disorder in the strongest brain." To take upon oneself the horrors of such a world as the *World-Telegram* reports is clearly to go mad. Berryman knows that we are saved, if we can be saved, by the strength of rational awareness and perhaps a final necessary refusal to accept burdens which are beyond our capacity as individuals to endure.

The Berryman of *The Dispossessed* also emerges in the poignant terms of more personal experience, as, for example, this reference to the loss of his father: "The inexhaustible ability of a man/Loved once, long lost, still to prevent my peace" ("World's Fair"). Or the reader can look at the fine poem "Farewell to Miles" on the simple subject of saying goodbye and the "ultimate loss" which that involves. But it must be said that the pessimism, the despair, and the bitterness which characterize the early Berryman are balanced by hope and such affirmation as these lines from "Letter to His Brother": "May love, or its image in work,/Bring you the brazen luck to sleep with dark/And so to get responsible delight. " And he affirms especially the life of nature, "natural life springing in May," with a healthy sense of man's mortality, "Those walks so shortly to be over" ("The Statue"). Or the reader may wish to look at another fine early poem, "Canto Amor," which tells us "Love is multiform" and sings to the end of joy.

It is clear that the early Berryman creates a substantial number of poems that establish the fact of his talent as it identifies itself in terms of essential subject and theme, or in terms of the singleness—the sheer interestingness—of the character of his speaker. What, then, qualifies praise of *The Dispossessed*? The answer to this is probably as obvious as it could be. Vagueness, obscurity, a failure to project a clear dramatic situation, characterize a number of the poems in the volume. We hear, too often, a flat academic voice, given to a kind of punchless abstraction:

Cold he knows he comes, once to the dark,
All that waste of cold, leaving all cold
Behind him hearts, forgotten when he's
  tolled,
His books are split and sold, the pencil
  mark
He made erased, his wife
Gone brave & quick to her new life.
  "SURVIVING LOVE"

Even the grammar—leaving all cold/Behind him hearts"—fails. Or we encounter a dreadful triteness, as in these opening lines: "The summer cloud in summer blue/Capricious from the wind will run" ("Cloud and Flame"), suggesting a verse exercise, an unauthentic voice. It is worth noting that any poet who lets himself become so sloppy in his craft is sure to irritate his critics, especially if it is obvious that he is intelligent and should know better.

But what is really intriguing about *The Dispossessed* is not so much its obvious weakness as a phenomenon involving the relationship between what Dudley Fitts calls *craft* and *art* and Randall Jarrell calls *subject* and *style.* I refer to poems that are very appealing in their rhythms—and generally speaking expert in their craft—but nevertheless do not finally work as poems, or fulfill the treatment of subject. "Winter Landscape," for example, transcribes skillfully from the Brueghel painting "Hunters in the Snow" but does not realize a meaningful theme about it or, as Berryman intended, about something else. Or consider the following from the title poem, "The Dispossessed":

That which a captain and a weaponeer
one day and one more day did, we did, *ach*
we did not, *They* did..cam slid, the great
  lock

lodged, and no soul of us all was near was
  near,—
an evil sky (where the umbrella bloomed)
twirled its mustaches, hissed, the ingenue
  fumed,

poor virgin, and no hero rides . . .

Not even notes or a rationalization of context can rescue lines like these from their lack of exact, or exactly suggestive, imaginative coherence. It is relatively easy to dismiss egregious verse, but here we are frustrated by a sense of talent going to waste. What is not so apparent, though perhaps hardly hidden, is that the early Berryman is seeking to find himself as a poet. His bent, I think, is toward impressionism, but in *The Dispossessed* he does not readily shape impressions into the final imaginative world we call the poem. "Winter Landcape," the first poem in the chronologically arranged volume, and the title poem, the last, are different aspects of the same problem. The general movement of the book, in terms of style, is toward a loosening of form, a syntax crumpling that distinctly anticipates *Homage to Mistress Bradstreet.* This movement is particularly apparent in sections IV and V. The temptation, at first, is to see Berryman's development as linear from traditional to modern, but this would be exactly to miss the point. His basic problem as a young poet is not so much stylistic development, important as that is, but rather discovering *how* or *to what* style is best applied. His bent toward impressionism was to become the impressionism of the mind of *Homage* and the Dream Songs. This, I believe, is the basic reason why *Homage* and the Dream Songs do not look imitative, though there is obviously nothing startling in the twentieth century about their technique. Both have their roots in the active soil of the early Berryman's struggle for poetic identity.

That struggle produced a good number of successful poems, some mellifluous misses, and a forgivable amount of weak verse. It was also a period in which Berryman produced two short stories which relate importantly—partly because they *are* short stories—to his early development. The first, and his first, "The Lovers," appears in the Winter 1945 *Kenyon Review* and is reprinted in *The Best American Short Stories 1946.* "The Lovers," which recalls Joyce's "Araby," tells of the discovery that adolescent first love cannot last. Like "Araby" it is told from the point of view of the mature man looking back over his past experience, but it is not a powerful story, chiefly because it is more expository than dramatic. It does, however, contain this comment from the narrator which implies strong awareness of personal development: "Purity of feeling, selflessness of feeling, is the achievement of maturity. . . ." Viewed as an aspect of the struggle of the early Berryman, this statement both defines his basic problem as an artist and points to his later achievement. His second story, "The Imaginary Jew," also appeared in *Kenyon Review* (Autumn 1945) and won first prize in the *Kenyon Review*—Doubleday Doran story contest. Although superior to "The Lovers," it is a cross between a fairly good short story and a beautiful essay. The speaker is a man who has gone through the harrowing experience in the late 1930's of being mistaken for a Jew. The story ends: "In the days following, as my resentment died, I saw that I had not been a victim altogether unjustly. My persecutors were right: I was a Jew. The imaginary Jew I was was as real as the imaginary Jew hunted down, on other nights and days, in a real Jew. Every murderer strikes the mirror, the lash of the torturer falls on the mirror and cuts the real image, and the real and the imaginary blood flow down together." Berryman did not go on to become a short-story writer, though he has written other stories yet unpublished. Poetic language and firm subject matter, such as may be seen in "The Imaginary Jew," were not enough to make him a wholly successful short-story writer. He needed to escape from his own intellect, his academic intelligence, in order to achieve selflessness of feeling, or the power of the truly dramatic. Mistress Bradstreet and Dream Song Henry were to become his challenge to selflessness.

Our descriptive definition of the early Berryman completes itself as we examine *Berryman's Sonnets* (1967). Except for their number, 115, they could easily be construed as a section, perhaps a later section, of *The Dispossessed.* They give us a greater sense of dealing with an objective as well as a subjective reality than is characteristic of *The Dispossessed,* probably for the obvious reason that behind them lies the story of a love affair, illicit, between "the poet" and a Danish-American blonde named Lise, but their subject, paralleling *The Dispossessed,* is preeminently *how it feels* to love, which is to say, how it feels to respond to a personal situation as opposed to more general world conditions. The singleness of situation of the sonnets and the fact that the speaker is talking directly to his lady love doubtless helps to give them a somewhat greater dramatic immediacy than the poems of *The Dispossessed,* but they fall far short of creating a speaker who is also a developed character in a developed situation, in what we would recognize as a good plot. Nevertheless, as with the speaker of the poems in *The Dispossessed,* the speaker of the sonnets does take on a singleness of character and further suggests a certain unity in Berryman's early work.

The sonnets—apparently written over a period of several months in 1946—are a sequence of emotions hinged on the ecstasy and the pain of a particular love. The speaker's epithet for himself is "The adulter and bizarre of thirty-two" (105), but the sonnets hardly make us feel much about his guilt. What they do make us feel is his energy, his humor, and his exuberance. He coins an appropriate epigraph for the affair as "knock-down-and-dragout love" (97). But this is, of course, rhetoric for an old ideal, elsewhere simply stated, "without you I / Am not myself" (94), "you are me" (27), or love's goal is "To become ourselves" (45). Though somewhat repetitious in theme, the sonnets are appealing in their sheer erotic exultation, their reveling in sex—breasts, blonde hair, soul kisses, biting and kissing, even an orgasm compared to a rumbling subway train. But the speaker, fortunately, never takes himself too seriously and can see their quarrels as funny, as when his lady breaks her knuckle in smashing objects. He has a quick wit: "In the end I race by cocky as a comb" (52), ". . . The *mots* fly, and the flies mope on the food" (53). He speaks to his lady with tender and somewhat formulaic but delightful irony: "You, Lise, *contrite,* I never thought to see" (18), or laughs wryly, laughs inside: "My glass I lift at six o'clock, my darling, / As you plotted . . . Chinese couples shift in bed" (13), a reference, of course, to the renowned particulars of Oriental lovemaking. He loves to kid his lady about her drinking, and to kid himself—"we four / Locked, crocked together" (33). What the sonnets best accomplish is finally to sing assuredly of joy: "What I love of you / *Inter alia* tingles like a whole good day" (86). The spirit of E. E. Cummings is here.

As with *The Dispossessed* there is an unevenness in the quality of the sonnets as poems. The following, for example, is conventional to the point of being banal: "I feel the summer draining me, / I lean back breathless in an agony/Of charming loss I suffer without moan, / Without my love, or with my love alone" (59). As is rhyming like this: "I grope / A little in the wind after a hope / For sun before she wakes . . . all might be well" (68). But the amount of this kind of writing over the span of the sonnets is relatively small. More difficult to assess is the difference between the sonnets that really work as poems and those that, though they may have outstanding qualities or lines, do not. In any case, style as the primary object of the poem does not characterize the sonnets, for they always have subject and are, moreover, seldom "difficult" in the sense that the poem "The Dispossessed" is difficult. But their technique often shows signs of strain, or tends to be nonfunctional, and thus they have a certain link to Berryman's preoccupation with style, his straining for effect at the price of poem quality. Berryman's typical devices in the sonnets are ellipsis and variations of normal sentence structure. He often omits connectives, such as prepositions, relative pronouns, and conjunctions, and secures an elliptical effect by an omission of punctuation, an omission which when it works creates a functional ambiguity of syntax. His variation of normal sentence structure takes such form as wide separation of a verb from its direct object, sudden interruptions and shifts from one sentence pattern to another, and inversion both for rhythmic effect and to aid in speeding the movement of the speaker's thoughts. The net intent of such technique, healthily, is better dramatization, and there is, of course, an obvious anticipation of what he is to do some years later. But the questions, as always, is not what technique is used—including devices and conventions as traditional as his Petrarchan rhyme scheme or as modern as rapid shift of association—but whether or not a chosen technique works.

A contrast will serve us well in evaluating Berryman's achievement as a sonneteer. Consider the opening octave of Sonnet 71:

> Our Sunday morning when dawn-priests were applying
> Wafer and wine to the human wound, we laid
> Ourselves to cure ourselves down: I'm afraid
> Our vestments wanted, but Francis' friends were crying
> In the nave of pines, sun-satisfied, and flying
> Subtle as angels about the barricade
> Boughs made over us, deep in a bed half made
> Needle-soft, half the sea of our simultaneous dying.

Although at first glance this might look fluid and controlled, the opening metaphor is both strained and vague. It functions to set the time of the lovers' action as simultaneous to a communion service, with an obvious ironic contrast between the sacred and the profane, the familiar Donnean paradox that profane love may be sacred. But what precisely is a "dawn-priest"? If merely a priest who gives communion at dawn, then the speaker is forcing us to make an association that offers no more than short literal mileage. Why are the priests "applying" wafer and wine? The word is ill chosen. Why "the human wound"? Such a phrase tells us nothing about the communicants and has a gravity suggesting that the speaker is a prig. Is the tongue, moreover, in some meaningful sense suggestive of "wound"? Why even bother to say "human" wound? With such a start there is little hope for the poem, but craft gets worse. The device of separating the adverb "down" from its verb "laid" helps the rhythm of the line at the price of creating a dull academicism. By line 3 we are, moreover, scarcely ready to believe that the lovers really have anything wrong with them that needs to be cured. If sin, original or recent, the premise is just too much to accept. In line 4 the reference to "Our vestments" merely belabors a contrast already made. By the time we come to the periphiasis "Francis' friends" for "birds" we suspect—perhaps with a groan—that the speaker is not only a bore but also a sentimentalist, especially if the birds are "crying" tears as well as just crying out, and it is useless to argue that since the birds are "sun-satisfied" the context excludes the suggestion of crying tears since the context is established too late for such exclusion. The phrase "Subtle as angels" is meaningless as description of how the birds are flying, nor is it, even if accepted in some metaphysical way, a phrase to which the speaker has established his right. And then, why does the speaker describe the boughs about which the birds are flying as a "barricade"? The description is arbitrary rather than in relation to the feeling of the presence of some enemy, real or imagined. Finally, the metaphor of the bed, half "Needle-soft" and half "sea," fails, for the two halves do not relate to suggest the total quality of the lovers' experience. Even the final phrase, "simultaneous dying," dying used in the Elizabethan sense of orgasm—with now a groan from English teachers—is too much. Since these are lovers, dare we not assume their simultaneity? At the end of the octave we feel nothing about either the sacred or the profane, and the sestet, which includes such miserable phrases as "Shivering with delight" and "Careless with sleepy love," is more of the same.

Here by contrast is a Berryman sonnet (9) that works:

> Great citadels whereon the gold sun falls
> Miss you O Lise sequestered to the West
> Which wears you Mayday lily at its breast,
> Part and not part, proper to balls and brawls,
> Plains, cities, or the yellow shore, not false
> Anywhere, free, native and Danishest
> Profane and elegant flower,—whom suggest
> Frail and not frail, blond rocks and
> madrigals.
>
> Once in the car (cave of our radical love)
> Your darker hair I saw than golden hair
> Above your thighs whiter than white-gold
> hair,
> And where the dashboard lit faintly your
> least
> Enlarged scene, O the midnight bloomed . .
> the East
> Less gorgeous, wearing you like a long
> white glove!

The general reason why this sonnet works is that the character of the speaker is interesting, not boring, not sentimental, not priggish, but instead honest, tender, sensuous, erotic, realistic, acutely aware, and wittily self-ironic. But there is a touch of circularity in this argument, since the character works because the craft succeeds, and the craft works because the character is well conceived—such paradox is poetry's way. The first line of Sonnet 9 is fatuously conventional and toneless, but the poet immediately establishes a personal tone that frames the impersonality in an ironic way. By line 3 he is calling his love a "Mayday lily," which ordinarily might be fatuously conventional but here has sincerity because it is touched with irony. Lovers, we feel, ought to have a sense of humor, especially about sex, because ironic self-awareness is part of love's delight. In a similar way, the bawdy pun on "balls" in line 4 falls within the frame of the speaker's irony. He earns the right to call his love a "Profane and elegant flower," a phrase which also refers back ironically to the epithet "Mayday lily." By the end of the octave we feel something about the sacred and the profane, something about delight. The sestet becomes its vivid, erotic, profane, and yet humorously sacred example. "O the midnight bloomed."

Such a fine poem as Sonnet 9 represents Berryman's achievement as a sonneteer. Many others of the 115 could be named. As a sample, I would suggest these: 12, 13, 32, 33,

37, 53, 67, 75, 104, and 115. The unevenness in the quality of *Berryman's Sonnets* seems to me patent, though opinion on individual sonnets will naturally vary. What is important is the high quality of those that succeed, which leads us to conclude that a good number of high-quality poems from *The Dispossessed* combine with a good number of high-quality poems from *Berryman's Sonnets* to establish the fact of Berryman's talent, and particularly that talent as it identifies itself in terms of *how it feels* to respond to his world. Such talent is always rare and makes us hope that it will flower into new achievement. It is, however, a talent that is distinguished only in the narrow sense of basic ability. It is a talent that typically carries a poet to a plateau of challenge. The early Berryman, at the not surprising age of approximately forty, had to make a new turn or fall back with the talented nondescript. Turn he did, and with his turn came 456 lines, 57 eight-line stanzas, called *Homage to Mistress Bradstreet.*

Homage is a poem that requires definition. It is basically an interior monologue narrative, with Anne Bradstreet revealing the story of her life in the early colonies. Born Anne Dudley in England in 1612, she married Simon Bradstreet at sixteen, crossed the Atlantic in the *Arbella* in 1630, had the first of her eight children in 1633, became the first woman in America to devote herself to writing poetry, and died in 1672 (her husband became colonial governor of Massachusetts in 1679). But *Homage,* though it functions to tell a story, is primarily concerned with a sensibility, with *how it feels* to be a sensitive individual in a certain kind of world. It is the voice of Anne that we hear, for example in a moment of peace following the delivery of her first child: "Blossomed Sarah, and I/blossom" (21.7–8). Her voice is, however, a voice that we hear only in relationship to the voice of the poet, for the poem opens with the poet rather than Anne as speaker. He imagines her in her grave:

> The Governor your husband lived so long
> moved you not, restless, waiting for him?
>   Still, you were a patient woman.—
> I seem to see you pause here still:
> Sylvester, Quarles, in moments odd you
>   pored
> before a fire at, bright eyes on the Lord,
> all the children still.
> 'Simon . .' Simon will listen while you read
>   a Song.

Because of the tenderness of the speaker toward his subject, *Homage* immediately defines itself as a poem of personal caring, and the poet takes on the character of the caring self. To this—implying, as it does, that human relation is the ultimate reality—all else, it seems to me, is eventually subordinated. As a poem of personal caring, with consequent emphasis on personal identity, *Homage* also immediately defines itself as a poem distinctly and appealingly modern in subject and in theme. But the personal identity is the *combined* identity of the poet and Anne, the union, if you will, of past and present. Although the voice of the poet opens the poem and thus provides a framing point of view for what follows, the two voices blend, modulate from one to the other, and, though often distinct, are finally one voice, a voice of passion and caring, which is the final identity sought, and an emblem of our common humanity.

This identity—emerging from a technique appropriately called fluid characterization—has to be set forth in terms that seem faithful to the complexity of human experience. To the dramatic immediacy of voice must be added substance, detail. In this respect the first stanza is particularly instructive, and reveals the later Berryman's extraordinary mastery of economy of means—sonnets were good practice. In one stanza is established (1) the character of the poet, his tenderness, his caring, his distinctive tone, (2) the character of Anne, wife, mother, intensely religious person, and would-be poet, and (3) a sense of relationship between them. In fact, it is not going too far to say that the sexual love of the sonnets is transmuted into the poet's caring for Anne, as in the simple and direct "Lie stark,/thy eyes look to me mild" (2.8–3.1), or in the question "How do we/linger, diminished in our lovers' air" (3.4–5). Or as in this explicit expression of the caring theme: "We are on each other's hands/who care" (2.7–8). Moreover, this caring later becomes a love dialogue directly between the poet and Anne, which is to say, a symbolic marriage or consummation of identity. The first stanza introduces the identity of poet as the specific link between the two. In the accurate words of the notes on the poem, Sylvester and Quarles were "her favourite poets; unfortunately." Despite her prolific output, Anne was not much of a poet at all, a fact of which Berryman makes us acutely aware. She is "mistress neither of fiery nor velvet verse" (12.8); her poems are "bald/abstract didactic rime" (12.5–6), and are "proportioned" and "spiritless" (42.6). Through her Berryman seems to be expressing by implication his own fear of not succeeding as a poet. What it means to be a poet is obviously an important theme of the poem, not, however, in the contemporary mode of self-conscious artiness but rather as an aspect and epitome of what it means to be a person.

Neither the first stanza nor the other examples thus far cited suggest that the language of *Homage* presents us with a problem, but it does. In general terms the problem is, How is the poem to be read? More specifically, the reader encounters a good deal of speech that is stylized or mannered. This is not in itself a fault. On the contrary, it is an acceptable device and even, for both Anne and the poet, an acceptable premise of character. The problem is rather one of degree.

Ciardi refers, for example, to Berryman's eccentricities in *Homage* and observes as chief among them "a constant queer inversion of normal word order." "Can be hope a cloak?" (40.8) asks Anne, and the reader rightly asks why this is not simply, "Can hope be a cloak?" One could argue from the negative and say that the latter, with its lightly accented rapid syllables between two long o's, sounds like doggerel and thus has to be avoided. But when poetry modifies actual speech for the sake of rhythm or meter, it usually manages to retain the quality of speech, as Frost does so beguilingly when his New England Yankee speaks an iambic pentameter that no New England Yankee ever spoke, or as Hopkins does when, to quote Kunitz, "however radical his deflections from the linguistic norm," he "keeps mindful of the natural flow and rhythm of speech, which serves him as his contrapuntal ground." So the question is whether or not the inversion "Can be hope a cloak?" has some relation to a quality of speech or thought that is Anne's. It would, I think, be merely a formal rationalization to say that she is a would-be poet, or even a bad poet, and thus reflects that fact in her mannered speech. But I do not think it merely a formal rationalization to relate this inversion to the meditative quality of her mind. If the short sentence is read very slowly, the inversion functions to heighten its questioning power, whereas this is not true in the doggerel-like noninverted version. My example, to be sure, is rather extreme, and if *Homage* were permeated with such extremes I suspect it would be a freak or at least would break down as a poem. But the following inversions, by contrast, are more representative of this aspect of the language of the poem and even out of context reveal a "contrapuntal ground":

Out of maize & air
your body's made, and moves. I summon,
see, from the centuries it. (3.1–3)

Winter than summer worse (9.1)

The shawl I pinned
flaps like a shooting soul
might in such weather Heaven send
(11.2–4)

Brood I do on myself naked. (27.4)

so shorn ought such caresses to us be
(30.5)

Once
less I was anxious when more passioned to
upset
the mansion & the garden & beauty of God.
(49.7–8, 50.1)

The reader's response to such lines depends desperately on how they are read. *Homage* becomes a poem that demands to be read aloud; it requires, moreover, a willingness not only to be in but to participate in a reflective or a meditative mood, to join the perceiving spirit. Whenever it seems not to be reading smoothly, the reader may find that all that is necessary is a change of pace, or a pause (sometimes a short pause, sometimes a very long one), or an accent for emphasis. There is, of course, a limit to how much of this kind of demand a poem may make on us, for a poem must draw us into an imaginative world, not shut us out. The reader's response is finally dependent upon his orientation to a paradox. Every poem stands lifeless on the page until the reader gives it life by interpreting it, and yet every poem stands on the page only with the life that it inherently contains. In *Homage* Berryman has extended the typical twentieth-century shift-of-association device to a stylizing or mannering of speech, the intent of which is to create a new dynamics of language. As Kunitz remarks, "the peculiar energy of language compels attention." In compelling attention the language also succeeds in compelling our sympathetic involvement in character, and all that that implies. In *Homage* Berryman modifies natural rhythms of speech to suggest, which is to say to dramatize, the dynamics of human thought and emotion. In doing so he often sacrifices some but far from all of the quality of natural speech, leading critics to use such terms as "peculiar" and "queer." To this I can only say that today's "peculiar" and "queer" may become tomorrow's standard, though *Homage* is the kind of poem that may require the reader to become an amateur actor to know its rewards.

Critics have tended, I think, to make too much of the language of *Homage* and as a consequence to ignore its structure, which combines with its language and characterization to give it hard dramatic impact. Berryman takes just four stanzas to establish the character of the poet as the caring self, ending with quietly powerful lines that declare the feeling of universal brotherhood poised with an awareness of our mortality (4.2–8). We then hear the voice of Anne, who describes the ocean crossing and early hardships in the New World with cinematographic immediacy—sleet, scurvy, vermin, wigwams, a tidal river, acorns, brackish water. The controlling sensibility is that of a pioneer spirit, as shown in this religious affirmation discreetly couched in lyrical understatement: "Strangers & pilgrims fare we here,/declaring we seek a City" (8.4–5). The word *city* is charged with Biblical echo, "holy city," "city of God," "they of the city shall flourish like grass" (Psalms, 72:16), "Glorious things are spoken of thee, O city" (Psalms, 87:3), "he shall build my city" (Isaiah 45:13). Specifically the reference seems to be to Hebrews 11:13–16: "These all died in faith, not having received the promises but having seen them afar off, and were persuaded of *them,* and embraced *them,* and confessed that they were strangers and pilgrims on the earth. For they that say such things declare plainly that they seek a country. . . . But now they desire a better *country,* that is, an heavenly: wherefore God is not ashamed to be called their God: for he hath prepared for them a city." This is echoed in Anne's own meditation 53: "We must, therefore, be here as strangers and pilgrims, that we may plainly declare that we seek a city above and wait all the days of our appointed time till our change shall come." At this point we should note that in *Homage* Anne speaks from a point of view that both is and is not the poet's point of view. It is not the poet's point of view in the sense that he is specifically a Christian believer. It is his point of view in the sense that his humanistic fervor is a religious phenomenon. The "city" which the poet seeks is, we feel, a heart's union, an existential consciousness of the human reality as it suggests a divine reality; it is a spiritual meaning in life urgently lived as human relationship. Such a comparison and contrast, uniting and yet separating past and present, is integral to the dramatic impact of the poem. This is another aspect of fluid characterization functioning to dramatize the dynamics of human thought and emotion.

At 12:5 the voice of Anne is interrupted by the voice of the poet, and their dialogue continues until 39.4. But the focus continues to be on Anne's description of her experiences and feelings. The distinctive characteristic of that description is that it unites soaring religious and metaphysical concerns with the raw reality of the pioneer experience. Although Anne's final concern as a Puritan woman of the seventeenth century may be for a divine reality, she is also—though the terms are not hers—an existential consciousness in the act of searching for meaning in life. Religion, for her, is not a pat answer to anything. At fourteen she was carnal, and knew it. She states flatly, "Women have gone mad/at twenty-one" (15.7–8). "O love, O love" (18.6), she exclaims, and that love is multifarious in its quality, carnal, erotic, marital (one flesh and one spirit), motherly, religious, universal, what Goethe called eternal womanly. Her consciousness is epitomized now in a long passage on the birth of her first child. It is a time of mixed emotion, of horror combined with joy, of pain and shame, until "it passes the wretched trap whelming and I am me/ drencht & powerful, I did it with my body" (20.8, 21.1). Identity: "I am me." Anne—as any psychiatrist would say—is healthily not alienated from her own body. The childbirth becomes her symbol for what it means to be human, the ultimate symbol of the caring self; also, of the continuity of past and present, and of a sense of our mortality and immortality. Everything that she is or could be seems beautifully summarized in a single line: "Mountainous, woman not breaks and will bend" (21.5).

The childbirth passage marks the end of the first third of the poem. The second third is the remainder of the love dialogue between the poet and Anne, with dialogue as dialogue receiving more emphasis and becoming quite explicit. Kunitz—in a reaction parallel to that of Jarrell commenting on an early Berryman poem called "At Chinese Checkers"—feels that it "tends to collapse into bathos somewhat reminiscent of Crashaw's extravagant compounding of religion and sex." He finds that Berryman lapses into the incongruous when the poet interrupts Anne's flights with, for example, such lines as "I miss you, Anne" (25.3), or "I have earned the right to be alone with you" (27.6). Berryman himself says that the latter line belongs to Anne, and we should also notice that it completes a couplet: "A fading world I dust, with fingers new./—I have earned the right to be alone with you." The general point, however, still has to be reckoned with. Kunitz cites, for example, Anne in reply to the poet: "I know./I *want* to take you for my lover" (32.4–5). But this, it seems to me, is to read out of context. Out of context in two senses; first, the immediate, for Anne, as is typical with her, is in a moment of self-recognition: "I am a sobersides; I know./I *want* to take you for my lover." I think too that a long reflective pause, a dramatic turning to the poet, at the end of the first line charges the lines with a quality that is anything but bathos. Secondly, the larger context should not be ignored. When Anne, whom, following the childbirth passage, we know as a woman, not a girl, speaks of such desire, it is not a cliché of romantic youth but an earned truth. What is true, of course, is that such lines as "I *want* to take you for my lover" could be out of a soap opera. In addition to context, the question is one of proportion. A powerful context has to be created; if every other line is a cliché, it never will be. Berryman's use of such lines seems to me distinctly sparing. They fall, I think, well within the framework of the poem's fidelity to the complexity of human experience, a fidelity which, of course, a soap opera never wants to have and never can have.

The dialogue following the childbirth passage functions to unite the poem's two caring selves, a marriage, symbolizing the fact that life finds its meaning in terms of human relationship. This is naturally a complement to rather than a denial of Anne's concern with obedience to the will of God. The last third of the poem is the voice of Anne except for the final three stanzas, in which the poet says his farewell. Anne continues her story, but the tones of passion, appropriately, subside. Her spirit in these last stanzas is essentially one of reconciliation. "I lie, & endure, & wonder" (51.3). We have the sense of reflecting on a whole life and all that it has meant and could mean. When the poet says farewell, we, I think, say it too. "I must pretend to leave you" (56.1). The experience of the poem has, finally, been the experience of love:

> still
> Love has no body and presides the sun,
> and elfs from silence melody. I run.
> Hover, utter, still
> a sourcing whom my lost candle like
> the firefly loves.
> (57.4–8)

And so with *Homage to Mistress Bradstreet* the early Berryman becomes the later Berryman. The move is made, at approximately the age of forty, from talent to talent best applied. With *Homage* Berryman achieves poetic maturity and becomes a poet of the first rank. The process harkens back to, of all places, his short stories. *Homage,* after all, is a modern narrative, and Berryman has the narrative bent. In his short stories, moreover, he uses poetic language, and in *Homage* he is language's daring master. In *Homage* he combines in narrative form the vivid detail of American history with the sensibility of the present. But in the short stories he does not live up to his own excellent dictum: "Purity of feeling, selflessness of feeling, is the achievement of maturity," for in the short stories he remains an academic personage. But in *Homage* he achieves purity and selflessness of feeling, he creates the caring self, paradoxically retaining his academic intelligence while yet losing it. In *Homage* he is not expository, but dramatic. And in *Homage* he combines the best elements of his early self. His language is original and his musicality, his sound, is not less than marvelous. He has depth of feeling, passion, and humane concern, combined, all, in an authentic voice, or voices, with a fidelity to the complexity of human experience that only really mature poets can show. In *Homage* he is, moreover, not really "difficult," as he is in a number of his early poems, though *Homage* requires a certain careful attention if the reader is to feel its power. In American poetry following World War II, only two long poems emerge as great. Roethke's "North American Sequence" is one, and *Homage* is the other. Allen Ginsberg's "Howl" would be a third except for the fact that it is based on a false premise, that the poet, as he says in the first line of the poem, saw the best minds of his generation destroyed by madness, whereas in fact no best minds in any sense are then forthcoming, despite the poet's elaborate and passionate effort to describe them. But from premise to dramatic power Berryman in *Homage* and Roethke in "North American Sequence" are true. With *Homage* Berryman is indelible on the American scene.

The inevitable question of what was to follow *Homage* was answered eight years later by the Pulitzer Prize-winning *77 Dream Songs,* the first installment, Parts I, II, and III, of the very long poem called "The Dream Songs," and four years after that by *His Toy, His Dream, His Rest,* the second and final installment, Parts IV VII. The total number of Dream Songs, each one eighteen lines long, is 385, thus making a poem of 6930 lines, or nearly twice the length of *Hamlet.* The arithmetic alone prompts the question, Does it all hang together? Is it finally a poem in the ideal sense of a final imaginative coherence? Does it have a single dramatic impact similar to that of *Homage*? The answer is flatly no. In plain terms, it lacks plot, either traditional or associative. In fact from an artistic point of view the Dream Songs parallel the sonnets. It is altogether appropriate that they are collected and numbered as a single poem, for as a sequence they are distinctly homogeneous, but this is not the same as to say that they have an organic structure (plot in its ultimate sense). What distinguishes them from the sonnets, however, is the range and quality of their imaginative power. They are even in their maturity, their purity and selflessness of feeling, in some ways an achievement beyond *Homage,* which is no light compliment. But they are not a poem that takes the logical step beyond *Homage,* the creation of a new masterpiece with *Homage's* exciting singleness of effect and yet in every way deeper and richer.

By what standard, then, are we to judge Berryman? If we compare "The Dream Songs" as poetic structure to *Hamlet*—that is, to any impressively long and tightly knit poetic work recognized as great—"The Dream Songs" comes off a poor second. We may ask whether or not Berryman's flaws fall reasonably within the framework of a distinguished achievement. For "The Dream Songs" the answer would, I believe, be yes, not merely because many of them are brilliantly successful as individual poems but, more important, because there is a cumulative impact, a wholeness that is distinctly short of a fully realized organic structure and yet participates in some of the final effect that organic structure is known to yield. I would say that Berryman made a serious mistake in not culling the Dream Songs more carefully, in not ruthlessly discarding those that are inferior. But even if this were done, we would end by talking about cumulative impact as opposed to organic structure.

Not that such a matter as judging a poem as long and complex as this will be settled in a day, for critics may well be puzzling over it for years to come. But even Berryman himself attests to the crucial nature of the problem of its structure: ". . . so to begin Book VII/or to design, out of its hotspur materials,/its ultimate structure/whereon will critics browse at large . . ." (293). But this is, I think, essentially Berryman the academic man—and a very good one at that—assuring himself of success merely by recognizing the existence of the problem. His assertion about structure doubtless relates to his terrible unrest over the possibility that he might not succeed wholly, in final terms, as a poet. In a word, he hungers for fame, "his terrible cry/not to forget his name" (266). This all too human hunger relates, in turn, to the depths of his own personal insecurities, as might be suggested, for example, by his repeated references to mere sexual conquests, which imply great insecurity and immaturity of personality, not that he does not recognize, simultaneously, the grief of it all and seek, as always, a mature understanding of it. Put another way, there is a strong element of defensiveness in his personality, but since this is coupled with piercing honesty he emerges as a poet who delves into life and takes us with him rather than yielding to what the critic would come to judge as tired formulas.

At the heart of the Dream Songs is the character of Henry, who, according to Berryman, "refers to himself as 'I,' 'he,' and 'you,' so that the various parts of his identity are fluid. They slide, and the reader is made to guess who is talking to whom." In a somewhat defensive note to *His Toy, His Dream, His Rest* he adds that the poem "is essentially about an imaginary character (not the poet, not me) named Henry, a white American in early middle age sometimes in blackface, who has suffered an irreversible loss. . . ." This raises the important question of how imaginary is Henry and how much the real-life John Berryman he is. This in turn raises another question, which is that of the relationship between *77 Dream Songs* and *His Toy, His Dream, His Rest.* The answer to this latter question, in general terms, is that "The Dream Songs" becomes increasingly autobiographical. But its more specific terms involve an aspect of technique, a description of which is necessary to an understanding of the relationship between imaginary Henry and the real-life poet.

In technique *77 Dream Songs* is clearly an extension or variant of *Homage,* with a movement, however, from a relatively ordered consciousness, Anne's, to a relatively disordered (dream) consciousness, Henry's. But we immediately confront the problem of the relationship between Henry's life as reality and his life as dream. It is a problem that prompts recall of Jarrell's comment, "Doing things in a style all its own sometimes seems the primary object of the poem, and its subject gets a rather spasmodic treatment." *77 Dream Songs* certainly shows us a style (mainly Henry's way of speaking) all its own and, like the sonnets, has a clear subject, Henry's, or more broadly the modern world. Nevertheless, these Dream Songs not only are difficult but remain difficult in spite of the reader's sympathetic acceptance of their dramatic situation, of their intent, and of their technique, whereas *Homage* by contrast does not remain difficult for long. What, then, is the best way to define the problem of these Dream Songs remaining difficult? Frederick Seidel calls it withdrawing "into abstraction" and "disguised personal allusion," but it is, I think, more than both of these things. It is essentially what Edmund Wilson was talking about when he made this comment in *Axel's Castle* on Symbolism: ". . . what the symbols of Symbolism really were, were metaphors detached from their subjects—for one cannot, beyond a certain point, in poetry, merely enjoy color and sound for their own sake: one has to guess what the images are being applied to." In *77 Dream Songs* Berryman persistently takes the risk of detaching metaphor, broadly construed, from subject. That he is talking about psychic reality does not change this fact. The strange thing is that any poem in the volume may seem to have the quality of simultaneously being a metaphor detached from its subject and yet realizing its subject, giving it a treatment that could not be called spasmodic. If, on the whole, the first 77 Dream Songs emerged as metaphors detached from their subjects they would be incomprehensible and fail as poems. If, on the whole, they emerged as metaphors that fully realized their subjects (and as a structure created a world) they would probably constitute the first installment of the finest long poem in the twentieth century. Instead they tend to exist in a perilous balance which puts an extraordinary demand on the reader and holds both frustration and reward.

But the Dream Songs of *His Toy, His Dream, His Rest,* as if in acknowledgment of this problem and in a desire to do something about it, tend to drop the extraordinary demand and move in the opposite direction, often becoming such flat and explicit statement that a child, or at least a young adult, could hardly mistake their meaning, their clarity as metaphor in a broad sense. Style, in other words, is distinctly no longer the primary object of the poem. Louise Bogan could never use the phrase "this desperate artificiality" in reference to *His Toy, His Dream, His Rest* as she did with *77 Dream Songs.* What this all means in simple terms is that "The Dream Songs" grows increasingly and plainly autobiographical, though aspects of the earlier technique do persist. We become, that is, increasingly aware that Henry is indeed John Berryman struggling with his own life, with the whole problem, human, spiritual, call it what you will, of his own identity. We become increasingly aware that Henry is an imaginary character simply in the sense of serving as an alter ego, a device whereby the poet may look at himself, talk about himself, talk to himself, and be a multi-farious personality. But, just as with the early Berryman, it is not an egocentric emphasis but rather a question of "how I feel" (120) in the sense of how a sensitive individual feels in response to his own psyche and to the world he inhabits. Henry is John Berryman saying, Here I am as a man, as the particular implies the universal. In this he succeeds. Henry is interesting. He has sheer interestingness, which is, of course, not to say that every Dream Song succeeds by this standard. That the poetic technique of "The Dream Songs" tends to shift from *77 Dream Songs* to *His Toy, His Dream, His Rest* is, it seems to me, a weakness, and this is true despite the flexibility gained by the device of fluid characterization. For a shift in technique must be functional, must be, in fact, part of the organic character of the poem as a structure. Henry, in sum, is a brilliant but insufficient unifying device. The question of how imaginary he is, and of how much the real-life John Berryman he is, is important only insofar as the poem creates a nonfunctional tension between the two. Who would object if Henry were wholly imaginary and one were hardly able to see or to care about a reference to the real-life John Berryman in the poem? Who would object if Berryman deliberately wrote an autobiographical and perhaps even a confessional poem? What we care about is only that the poem exists beautifully as a poem, and yet in the final analysis the device *is* the poem, and so it is unsettling to lose our sense of the fictional Henry in favor of the quasi-fictional Berryman.

In *77 Dream Songs* Henry is essentially a picaresque hero in the ironic mode, a comic type who begins as a stereotype from vaudeville and ends as distinct in his humanity and suffering. He is described as "a human American man" (13), "free, black & forty-one" (40), a man whose basic problem is clearly to bear the slings and arrows of outrageous fortune, particularly the outrageous fortune of being black in white America, though fluid characterization does enable us to accept Berryman's later statement that Henry is white, which is to say, for dramatic purposes, a white man who imagines how it feels to be black. Henry is described, often in an ironic context, by such words as *bewildered, horrible, desolate, bitter, industrious, affable, subtle, somber, savage,* and *seedy.* Or in a somewhat more extended' way: "hopeless inextricable lust, Henry's fate" (6), "with his plights & gripes/ as bad as achilles" (14), and "savage and thoughtful/surviving Henry" (75). The words used to describe him in *His Toy, His Dream, His Rest* are quite consistent with those found in *77 Dream Songs: disordered, obsessed, stricken, sad, wilful, sympathetic, lively, miserable, impenetrable, mortal, joyous, perishable, anarchic, apoplectic,* and *edgy.* But in *77 Dream Songs,* although we have a visual, a concrete sense of what he is, he is not detailed in the sense that Mistress Bradstreet is detailed. When we finish *Homage* we can recall the facts of a biography, but when we finish *77 Dream Songs* we can recall only the existence of a man. The Henry of *77 Dream Songs* is a character in a mode perhaps best described as impressionistic or mildly surrealistic. The Henry of *His Toy, His Dream, His Rest* is in the realistic mode. Although there is certainly a strain of the picaresque hero in the later Henry, Henry *as* picaresque hero gives way to the quasi-fictional John Berryman. There is a great deal of consistency in this, but significant inconsistency too.

The complexity of the problem of responding to "The Dream Songs" as a whole poem inheres, finally, in the relationship between the conception of the character of Henry and the degree of success of the individual Dream Song. It will be instructive to select a fairly representative Dream Song from *77 Dream Songs* for commentary, and then to put it next to a fairly representative autobiographical passage from *His Toy, His Dream, His Rest.* Here is Dream Song 76, "Henry's Confession":

> Nothin very bad happen to me lately.
> How you explain that?—I explain that, Mr.
> Bones,
> terms o' your bafflin odd sobriety.
> Sober as man can get, no girls, no
> telephones,
> what could happen bad to Mr. Bones?
> —*If* life is a handkerchief sandwich,
>
> in a modesty of death I join my father
> who dared so long agone leave me.
> A bullet on a concrete stoop
> close by a smothering southern sea
> spreadeagled on an island, by my knee.
> —You is from hunger, Mr. Bones,
>
> I offers you this handkerchief, now set
> your left foot by my right foot,
> shoulder to shoulder, all that jazz,
> arm in arm, by the beautiful sea,
> hum a little, Mr. Bones.
> —I saw nobody coming, so I went instead.

For purposes of analysis we can disregard the fact that the character of Henry has been previously defined and ask how this poem handles the key problem of characterization. It opens with Negro dialect, the voice of Henry, who is speaking with Mr. Bones, a friend, a vaudeville stereotype, an alter ego, a mere name suggesting death. Both characters are comic, with the comedy springing from Henry's premise that he normally expects something very bad to happen to him every day. We are at once in the world of the vaudeville skit. It is a charming and disarming world, and in its way a fit place to discuss the nature of man. But at the end of the first stanza the voice of Henry—and the vaudeville skit—is dropped, and the poet's voice enters. The handkerchief sandwich motif at the end of the first stanza continues the vaudeville joke but some of the tone of the joke is abandoned. There is nothing particularly funny in the second stanza about the death of a father or a bullet on a stoop, especially if it is read as a reference to the suicide of Berryman's father. But at the end of the second stanza we return to the voice of Henry, though the poet is also speaking the line, "You is from hunger, Mr. Bones." In the first line of the third stanza we return to the voice of Henry in his conversation with Mr. Bones, but the voice that follows seems to be more that of the poet than that of Henry, and the vaudeville humor is but slightly sustained. But if the poem is to realize its subject, which I take to be man's mortality or his isolation in the universe, then the handkerchief and the sea must become unifying symbols, must take us into the subject. This they do not do in a complete way. A fuller situation for the handkerchief offering is needed, and the relationship between the popular song phrase "by the beautiful sea" and "a smothering southern sea" is not at all clear—metaphor is detached from its subject. Part of the problem is that the reference to "a smothering southern sea" (with *bullet, stoop, island,* and *knee*) is itself vague. The referent of lines 9–11 is too personal to the speaker to have universal meaning. The "smothering southern sea" happens to be the Gulf of Mexico, but knowledge of this fact does not improve the poem as a poem. And yet the poem as a whole does have singleness of effect. ". . . hum a little, Mr. Bones" becomes Henry's sprightly understatement, right from a vaudeville skit, of self-persuasion and universal affirmation, not to mention the suggestion of darker agony as we hear the line as the poet's voice, or one could say a non-vaudevillian Henry. And the last line seems particularly effective as a summary of the human condition that the poem has been defining: "I saw nobody coming, so I went instead."

Consider now these lines from Dream Song 143 on the subject of the father's suicide:

> He was going to swim out, with me,
> forevers,
> and a swimmer strong he was in the
> phosphorescent Gulf,
> but he decided on lead.
>
> That mad drive wiped out my childhood.

It might aid our appreciation of these lines to recall the biographical fact that Berryman's father had threatened to drown himself and John with him, but the lines stand well as they are. What is being said is perfectly plain, and this plainness, this direct treatment of subject, is typical of *His Toy, His Dream, His Rest.* There are poems in *77 Dream Songs* that also treat subject directly—such as the rather conventional and quite unsuccessful 18, "A Strut for Roethke," the perfectly successful 35, "MLA," and the moving 37–39, "Three around the Old Gentleman," honoring Robert Frost—but these are more the exception than the rule.

What we have in *His Toy, His Dream, His Rest,* then, is the mature Berryman grappling in a straightforward way with the meaning of his life. One is prompted to recall the dictum of F. Scott Fitzgerald that if you begin with an individual you create a type, but if you begin with a type you create nothing. Berryman sees himself as a dying man, "in love with life / which has produced this wreck" (283). With a discreet sense of mortality he affirms his individual dignity and worth: "If the dream was small / it was my dream also, Henry's" (132). The life he looks back on is one full of wives and rages, though with typical humor he comments, "The lust-quest seems in this case to be over" (163). Though often angry and protesting, he celebrates many things, a democratic society, the sheer mystery of love, the birth of his daughter, the success of his third marriage, autumn, which seems so much to be an American season and "comes to us as a prize / to rouse us toward our fate" (385), his old friends, particularly, and elegiacally, Delmore Schwartz, the poet's ideal of perfection, "to craft better" (279), anything and everything which out of suffering he can emerge to affirm.

Taken as a whole the Dream Songs are a panoramic meditation on life and death. The title of the second volume sums them up best of all. His toy is life as a game we play (and the stakes are not less than everything), his dream is life in its psychic aspects and the poet's goal of fame, and his rest is an infinite sense of man's mortality and immortality, and finally death itself. He proclaims the value of life as a thing lived: "No, I want rest here, neither below nor above" (256), and we believe him when in Dream Song 83 he writes, "I know immense / troubles & wonders to their secret curse."

Selected Bibliography

WORKS OF JOHN BERRYMAN

POETRY

Twenty poems in *Five Young American Poets,* (Norfolk, Conn.: New Directions, 1940).

Poems, (Norfolk, Conn: New Directions, 1942).

The Dispossessed, (New York: William Sloane Associates, 1948).

Homage to Mistress Bradstreet, (New York: Farrar, Straus and Cudahy, 1956).

His Thought Made Pockets & the Plane Buckt, (Pawlet, Vt.: C. Fredericks, 1958).

77 Dream Songs, (New York: Farrar, Straus and Giroux, 1964).

Berryman's Sonnets, (New York: Farrar, Straus and Giroux, 1967).

Short Poems, (New York Farrar, Straus and Giroux 1967).

His Toy, His Dream, His Rest, (New York: Farrar, Straus and Giroux, 1968).

Love and Fame, (New York: Farrar, Straus and Giroux, 1970).

Delusions, etc., (New York: Farrar, Straus and Giroux, 1972).

PROSE

"The Imaginary Jew," *Kenyon Review,* 7: 529–39 (Autumn 1945).

"The Lovers," *Kenyon Review,* 7: 1–11 (Winter 1945) (Reprinted in *The Best American Short Stories 1946,* edited by Martha Foley, Boston: Houghton Mifflin, 1946).

"Young Poets Dead," *Sewanee Review,* 55: 504–14 (July–September 1947).

"The Poetry of Ezra Pound," *Partisan Review,* 16: 377–94 (April 1949).

Stephen Crane, (New York: William Sloane Associates, 1950) Reprinted in 1962 as a Meridian paperback with an additional preface; "Shakespeare at Thirty," *Hudson Review,* 6: 175–203 (Summer 1953).

"The Long Way to MacDiarmid," *Poetry,* 88: 52–61 (April 1956).

"Spender: The Poet as Critic," *New Republic,* 148: 19–20 (June 29, 1963).

"Despondency and Madness," (on Robert Lowell's "Skunk Hour"), in *The Contemporary Poet as Artist and Critic,* edited by Anthony Ostroff, (Boston: Little, Brown, 1964) pp. 99–106; "One Answer to a Question," *Shenandoah,* 17: 67–76 (Autumn 1965).

REVIEWS AND CRITICAL STUDIES

Blum, Morgan, "Berryman as Biographer, Stephen Crane as Poet," *Poetry,* 78: 298–307 (August 1951).

Bogan, Louise, "Verse," *New Yorker,* 40: 242–43 (November 7, 1964).

Brinnin, John Malcolm, Review of *77 Dream Songs, New York Times Book Review,* (August 23, 1964) p. 5.

Carruth, Hayden, "Love, Art and Money," *Nation,* 211: 437–38 (November 2, 1970).

Ciardi, John, "The Researched Mistress," *Saturday Review,* 40: 36–37 (March 23, 1957).

Connelly, Kenneth, "Henry Pussycat, He Come Home Good," *Yale Review,* 58: 419–27 (Spring 1969).

Cott, Jonathan, "Theodore Roethke and John Berryman: Two Dream Poets," in *On Contemporary Literature,* edited by Richard Kostelanetz. (New York: Avon Books, 1964), pp. 520–31.

Eberhart, Richard, "Song of the Nerves," *Poetry,* 73: 43–45 (October 1948).

Evans, Arthur, *Texas Studies in Literature and Language,* Evans, Catherine, "Pieter Bruegel and John Berryman: Two Winter Landscapes," 5: 310–18 (Autumn 1963).

Fitts, Dudley, Review of *The Dispossessed, New York Times Book Review,* (June 20, 1948) p. 4.

Holmes, John, Review of *Homage to Mistress Bradstreet, New York Times Book Review,* (September 30, 1956) p. 18.

Howard, Jane, "Whiskey and Ink, Whiskey and Ink," *Life,* 63: 67–76, (July 21, 1967).

Jarrell, Randall, Review of *The Dispossessed, Nation,* 167: 80–81, (July 17, 1948).

Kessler, Jascha, "The Caged Sybil," *Saturday Review,* 51: 34–35, (December 14, 1968).

Kunitz, Stanley, "No Middle Flight," *Poetry,* 90: 244–49, (July 1957).

Meredith, William, "Henry Tasting All the Secret Bits of Life: Berryman's 'Dream Songs'," *Wisconsin Studies in Contemporary Literature,* 6: 27–33, (Winter–Spring 1965).

Rosenthal, M. L., "The Couch and Poetic Insight," *Reporter,* 32: 53–54, (March 25, 1965).

Rosenthal, M. L., *The New Poets: American and British Poetry since World War II,* (New York: Oxford University Press, 1967) pp. 118–30.

Seidel, Frederick, "Berryman's Dream Songs," *Poetry,* 105: 257–59 (January 1965).

Shapiro, Karl, "Major Poets of the Ex-English Language," *Washington Post Book World,* (January 26, 1969) p. 4.

Elizabeth Bishop
(1911–1979)

JOHN UNTERECKER

It is an obvious and easy thing to say that "The Map," the first poem in Elizabeth Bishop's mistitled *Complete Poems,* anticipates the way her work will go—*North & South, Questions of Travel,* and *Geography III* neatly ticking off the principal way-stops in a body of work that is variously set in Nova Scotia, New England, New York, France, Key West, Mexico, and Brazil.

This is no great news. As she herself noted in the spring of 1976, when—at the age of sixty-five—she was awarded the Neustadt International Prize for Literature: "I know, and it has been pointed out to me, that my poems are geographical, or about coasts, beaches and rivers running to the sea and most of the titles of my books are geographical too."

On that occasion Bishop saw herself as in some ways like the sandpiper she had once used as the subject for a poem: "I begin to think: Yes, all my life I have lived and behaved very much like that sandpiper—just running along the edges of different countries and continents, 'looking for something.'"

She went into no detail, however, as to what that something was that she had spent a lifetime looking for; and it is tempting for an admirer to assign it a conventional label: "the meaning of life," say, or "wisdom" or "truth" or "affection" or something as mundane as "a home." Any of these guesses might do; but most likely the "something" one spends a lifetime looking for is more intricate and human than any abstraction: perhaps, in terms of a later poem, something one can—and must—learn, barely, to accept the loss of:

I lost my mother's watch. And look! my
last, or next-to-last, of three loved houses
went.
The art of losing isn't hard to master.
I lost two cities, lovely ones. And, vaster,
some realms I owned, two rivers, a
continent.
I miss them, but it wasn't a disaster.
—Even losing you (the joking voice, a
gesture
I love) I shan't have lied. It's evident
the art of losing's not too hard to master
though it may look like (*Write* it!) like
disaster.

Quoted out of context, as they are here, lines like these from "One Art" seem extravagant. But in the body both of the poem and of the rest of Bishop's work, they take on great precision. For the geographies she travels best are simultaneously geographies of earth and of the human heart; their poems have the breathing quality of life itself. They are tentative, yet patterned: hesitant when it comes to final answers, yet totally assured in the variations of repetition—sounds, themes, rhythms, words themselves—that distinguish living poetry from mechanical verse.

If places have accounted for much of Bishop's poetry, her New England birthplace and her mother's Nova Scotia home have to be credited as of central importance among them. Over and over she returns to the landscapes, houses, persons who shaped her childhood.

It wasn't really an easy childhood. It started with a pair of losses that she does not catalog in "One Art" but that were losses men and women more sentimental than she would certainly have cataloged as "disasters." Eight months after she was born, her father died. Her mother's mental state deteriorated over the next few years and she was hospitalized at various times. The final breakdown occurred when Elizabeth was five and she was staying with her mother's parents. "I was there the day she was taken away," Miss Bishop told me. And although her mother was to live on nearly twenty more years in a mental hospital at Dartmouth, Nova Scotia, that day in 1916 was to be the last time her daughter saw her.

Elizabeth Bishop was born in Worcester, Massachusetts, on February 8, 1911. But it was the area in and around Great Village, Nova Scotia, a quiet country settlement at the head of the Bay of Fundy, that constituted "home." Here, her grandfather Bulmer had been a tanner until chemicals replaced tanbark and the ancient trade of tanning became industrialized. Her grandmother was the daughter of the captain—or part owner—of a small ship that had been lost at sea off Cape Sable, with all hands, when she was nine years old. Three of her grandmother's brothers became Baptist missionaries in India. (One of them was later president of Acadia College, in Nova Scotia.) A fourth brother, George, left home at fourteen as a cabin boy, then later sailed for England, where eventually he became a painter whose childish work is commemorated in the poem "Large Bad Picture" and late work in "Poem" from *Geography III*.

At home, there was Bishop's grandmother ("laughing and talking to hide her tears" in the poem "Sestina"). And, of course, her Grandfather Bulmer, recollected in the poem "Manners" for his politeness to man and crow alike and in the short story "Memories of Uncle Neddy" for his uncomplaining gentleness.

In the outdoor world there were wagon rides with grandfather, out into the farm country or down along the Bay of Fundy, where extraordinary tides—the second-highest in the world—twice a day race threateningly across the mudflats.

People drowned in those tides. But closer to home there were also deaths, among them the "First Death in Nova Scotia," that of "little cousin Arthur," who, "very small" in his coffin, seemed "all white, like a doll / that hadn't been painted yet." He had been "laid out" beneath chromographs of the ruling family of England: "my mother laid out Arthur."

This Nova Scotia childhood, full of laughter and tears, tugged toward the crisis point that is the heart of the short story "In the Village."

It is important, of course, to realize that none of Elizabeth Bishop's "autobiographical" poems and stories—although they have been called that—are in any literal sense autobiographies. They are works of art, not histories. The "facts" in them are adjusted to the needs of poem and story. "Arthur," for example, in "First Death in Nova Scotia," is an invented name. And the conversations in the stories, as many of the names of townspeople and relatives, are by and large inventions. The sequence of dreamlike events that take place in the story "In the Village" are not in exact chronology; the words spoken in "The Moose" are, obviously, not literal transcripts of conversations on a bus.

What the "autobiographical" works do project is not, therefore, private anecdote but rather a remembered lost world: the vivid yet time-blurred world that all readers trying to reconstruct the feel of childhood are likely to share.

If we are to read these poems and stories accurately, we must consequently read them as if they were indeed true; yet at the same time we must realize that it is the quality of the past, the quality of an experience, that is being offered us, not "reality." Although what I have called the "crisis point" of "In the Village" clearly relates to Elizabeth Bishop's experiences shortly before and soon after her mother was taken away from her grandparents' home, the story itself fictionalizes such "real" events as are touched on. The story—like several of the poems—interweaves adult and child viewpoints. Distanced by brilliantly manipulated images, it gives us the illusion of being participants in a dream of childhood that is part nightmare and part idyllic pastoral romance. Because the story is fictionalized so well, we accept it as truth. Because it is a story, we are able to extract from it some sense of the rich complexity of experience—not so much Elizabeth Bishop's as our own. For every successful first-person fiction demands the reader's collaboration, the projection of his own remembered past onto the fictionalized past of the author. Out of the semblance of Elizabeth Bishop's childhood, we are—if we are lucky—better able to deal with our own early years.

Perhaps the best approach to "In the Village" is a structural one. The story—in many ways more poem than story—is suspended from three sounds: a mother's sudden scream during a dress fitting; the lovely, pure clang of a blacksmith's hammer during a different fitting—that of a horseshoe; and a Presbyterian church bell that maddingly, mercilessly clangs during a fire ("Noise! I can't hear myself think, with that bell!").

These sounds balance and counterbalance each other, and echo in strange places. The pitch of the scream is "the pitch of my village," yet it can be apprehended best through the steeple of the church: "Flick the lightning rod on top of the church steeple with your fingernail and you will hear it." The "pure and angelic" note of the blacksmith's hammer shapes red-hot metal into horseshoes that "sail through the dark like bloody little moons." In the middle of the night, the church bell "is in the room with me; red flames are burning the wallpaper beside the bed. I suppose I shriek."

Like a mother's scream, like the blacksmith's lovely clanging hammer and the pounding of a harsh church bell, the flames that seem to burn wallpaper are echoes: reflections of a burning barn that in its own destructive way echoes the blacksmith's lovely forge.

Other echoes: "It's probably somebody's barn full of hay, from heat lightning." But the lightning rod above the Presbyterian church protects from fire the clanging bell in the steeple that is "like one hand of a clock pointing straight up." Despite the warning bell and the horsedrawn wagons hauling water, "All the hay was lost." In the morning, the child visits the burned barn, "but the smell of burned hay is awful, sickening." On the day that the mother had been fitted for a new dress, "The dressmaker was crawling around and around on her knees eating pins. . . . The wallpaper glinted and the elm trees outside hung heavy and green, and the straw matting smelled like the ghost of hay."

The smell of hay—and in other places of horse manure and "cow flops"—roots the story in the rural earth of the village. On the other hand, water reminds us that this is a tidal world—"the long green marshes, so fresh, so salt," "the Minas Basin, with the tide halfway in or out," the "wet red mud," "the lavender-red water": "We are in the 'Maritimes' but all that means is that we live by the sea."

Other water imagery serves a different but related function: the blacksmith's tub of "night-black water," a big kitchen dipper full of rusty, icy water, a mint-bordered brook, the backyard watering trough, the morning dew gray on the village grass, swampy places in the fields, the town's river and the bridge that crosses it, the barrels of river water pumped onto the burning barn, the gurgle of the river, even the cow flops "watery at the edges" all bind water to earth. But water also appears in the pathos of tears: "Now the dressmaker is at home, basting, but in tears." "'Don't cry!' my aunt almost shouts at me, 'It's just a fire. Way up the road. It isn't going to hurt you. Don't *cry!*'" "My grandmother is crying somewhere, not in her room." "My grandmother is sitting in the kitchen stirring potato mash for tomorrow's bread and crying into it. She gives me a spoonful and it tastes wonderful but wrong. In it I think I taste my grandmother's tears; then I kiss her and taste them on her cheek."

Fire, earth, water, and, of course, air: "those pure blue skies, skies that travellers compare to those of Switzerland, too dark, too blue, so that they seem to keep on darkening a little more around the horizon"; air that on hot summer afternoons carries the odor of honeysuckle and horse and cow, the odor of straw matting in a mother's bedroom or the sickening odor of burned hay after a fire, the odor of brown perfume spilled among the unpacked mourning clothes of a mother now sent permanently off to a sanatorium; air that once vibrated to the sound of a hammering church bell and a scream that hangs over the village "forever" but that becomes entangled in memory with the beautiful pure sound of a hammer shaping a horseshoe:

> *Clang.*
>
> And everything except the river holds its breath.
>
> Now there is no scream. Once there was one and it settled slowly down to earth one hot summer afternoon; or did it float up, into that dark, too dark, blue sky? But surely it has gone away, forever.
>
> *Clang.*
>
> It sounds like a bell buoy out at sea.
>
> It is the elements speaking: earth, air, fire, water.
>
> All those other things—clothes, crumbling postcards, broken china; things damaged and lost, sickened or destroyed; even the frail almost-lost scream—are they too frail for us to hear their voices long, too mortal?

Much of the art of Elizabeth Bishop's writing is in her shaping of frail, "almost-lost" things into works of extraordinary power. Never "confessional," her poems and stories are sensitive arrangements of significant life.

I want to pause on that notion, for, although the phrase is not hers, I think she would accept its validity. Let me put it this way:

Each of us, I think, recognizes the paradox that, as a consequence of our being alive only from moment to moment, we cannot be alive last week, yesterday, or even five seconds ago; similarly, none of us can, this second, be alive both now and a few seconds from now, now and tomorrow, or now and sometime next week. There is no way for any man literally to live either in the past or in the future. Your beingness, my beingness, exists only in the fraction of a second that it takes to get from this *now* to the immediately following one. My "being" ceases constantly, constantly comes into existence. And it ceases and comes into existence only on the treadmill of time. I run from *now* to *now* to *now* in order not to be swept back into *was*. My "progress" can never move me further forward than *is*, no matter how fast I run.

Yet we also all have the illusion, except in moments when we are bludgeoned with passion or with mortality, that from minute to minute we exist without change. So long as the body stays alive, the thousands and thousands of little births and deaths of being seem inconsequential.

But there is another equally important paradox. Although the body is alive only in the moment, almost all of it is still left over from what it had been a moment before. The bit of skin that sloughs off is already replaced by new skin. Our leftover body knows very well how to keep going, surviving second by second thanks to habits imprinted during the course of a lifetime.

The miracle of our staying alive is almost entirely a consequence of the imprint circuitry within our minds and the ingenious chemistry of our bodies that lets it operate effectively. The circuitry, prodded by that chemistry, tells us what to do without "thinking." But it also lets us think, marvelously, as all of the little synapses go on testing out connections while we move from this *now* to that *now*. Consequently, although I lose being, I do not lose memories or ideas—at least not readily. The circuitry of the brain stays fundamentally unchanged as I slide through being; it even allows, instant by instant, new, tentative material to be manipulated by the clicking dendrons that say "put on hold," "retrieve," "cancel," and sometimes "add."

One final paradox: Though our experience is that of living only in a continually evolving *now*, everything we think or imagine seems ultimately to come out of the great kitchen midden of memory: the dump of our own past.

Those memories that we must have if we are to function are nothing more than an echoing substratum of images and words: images glimpsed, forgotten, and retrieved by a habit or an accidental overlap of pattern. A name or place name overheard in a bar or a classroom or on a street corner triggers a retrieval system more ingenious than IBM's.

Bishop's story resounds to a scream and the clang of a bell and a hammer. I hear the word "elm," and I am offered a bedroom, a street, two houses, a family, a place at a kitchen table, a fork in my hand, a glint of recognition in an eye across the table, a word hesitating in my mouth. And, of course, I am simultaneously offered loss, a house vanished, the trees diseased and broken, nothing left where hands touched real hands but bare lawn and a flagstone: the stone in front of three vanished steps that had once led to a kitchen door. Absence calls me by my name.

Such significant moments from the evoked, almost-lost world feed art. For one of our most basic drives is the effort to rescue—to "understand"—the past. Some of us content ourselves with faded photographs and time-yellowed letters. An artist like Elizabeth Bishop, on the other hand, shapes "almost-lost" memories into satisfying forms. She manipulates them until private value is transformed into something that has value for the reader as well. The significant past of one writer—the "almost-lost" *now* as intense as a scream—abruptly becomes part of your constantly changing present, and of mine. It becomes the *is* of literature that holds out against slippery years.

Consider, for example, "Poem" from the collection *Geography III*. A response to one of her Great-Uncle George's paintings ("about the size of an old-style dollar bill"), it projects a minor drama in which Elizabeth Bishop and the reader jointly discover that the landscape of the much earlier painting is the landscape of Bishop's own childhood.

Integrated by an imagery borrowed from the old-style "American or Canadian" dollar bill itself ("Mostly the same whites, gray greens, and steel grays"), the painting and poem gain power because they are "free" yet "collateral." (The painting, which "has never earned any money in its life," has "spent" seventy years, "useless and free," in being handed along "collaterally" from one owner to the other.) Perhaps because their real values cannot be measured in terms of cold cash, both painting and poem, by the end of the poem, represent "the little that we get for free, / the little of our earthly trust. Not much." Their real value—like that of the landscapes they display—has to be calculated in terms not of the dollar bills they resemble (if the painting is the size of one of them, the poem—not much bigger—is a bit over the size of three) but in terms of "life itself," the "memory" of life, and "love"—the fact that both life and the memory of it are "loved" enough to make two artists seventy years apart feel compelled to "compress" what they have seen and experienced into art.

Part of that compression—as in a great deal of Elizabeth Bishop's poetry—is accomplished by sheer repetition. The "steel grays" of the dollar bill reappear as "steel-gray" storm clouds. "(They were the artist's specialty.)" Its dollar-bill whites show up in terms of white houses, white geese, a white and yellow wild iris, and a farmer's white barn. ("There it is, / titanium white, one dab.") Houses, the Presbyterian church steeple, cows, the iris, elm trees, and the geese interlace the sixty-four lines of the poem.

Repetitions of this sort assert the "reality" of a scene, but they also account for the drama of discovery that is at its core. For this is not just an observed scene but a shared one. And we are made aware of its shared nature as uncertainties become certain. At first the painting is something that its various owners "looked at . . . sometimes, or didn't bother to." Bishop herself at first approaches it casually. It's a painting all right, but maybe it's less than what it might have been. (Is it "a sketch for a larger one?")

In being (perhaps) a sketch, it's a little like the poem itself. "I had begun the poem some years earlier," Miss Bishop told me. "It started out much less serious." By mid-poem, the painting that *might* be a sketch for a larger one is definitely a sketch: "a sketch done in an hour, 'in one breath.'" The quoted phrase is a key to the freshness, the *momentary* freshness, of both poem and painting.

But by this time, the scene of the painting has been far more accurately defined. In the second stanza, it is located in a rough geography:

> It must be Nova Scotia; only there
> does one see gabled wooden houses
> painted that awful shade of brown.

In the third, although we aren't given the name of Great Village, we are clearly in Elizabeth Bishop's childhood world:

> Heavens, I recognize the place, I know it!
> It's behind—I can almost remember the
>   farmer's name.
> His barn backed on that meadow. There it is,
> titanium white, one dab. The hint of steeple,
> filaments of brush-hairs, barely there,
> must be the Presbyterian church.

By now, however, another kind of repetition has taken place, for we have no choice but to remember the Presbyterian church steeple that in the story "In the Village" threatens to echo an insane mother's scream, the same steeple from which the raw hammering of the bell has roused a frightened child to the burning of a neighbor's barn.

These kinds of overlap add power both to story and to poem. They force us to acknowledge that places are valuable not just for the beauty they can offer but for the intensity of experience that they carry. Both poem and story, of course, stand alone. Each also reinforces and complicates the other.

In a most sensitive essay, Helen Vendler comments on Elizabeth Bishop's almost habitual linkage of "the domestic and the strange." And though Vendler never pinpoints "the strange," she makes clear that it frequently has something to do with a disconcerting peculiarity in the domestic world. "The fact that one's house always *is* inscrutable," Vendler says, "that nothing is more enigmatic than the heart of the domestic scene, offers Bishop one of her recurrent subjects." The overlap linkage between "In the Village" and "Poem"—although Vendler does not point it out—is a first-rate example of what she is talking about.

Vendler does talk of some of the strangeness of "Poem," but, oddly, not about the appearance of the word "strange" itself. It occurs when Bishop realizes that she and her great-uncle, despite their "years apart," had looked at a common landscape "long enough to memorize it." The landscape that they each saw, she realizes, "must have changed a lot" between the time one stopped looking and the other started ("I never knew him")—and a lot more between the time she memorized the landscape as a child and the *now* in which, as a middle-aged woman, she tries to reconstruct an "almost-lost" child's world out of a dead relative's pictured world that, except for the luck of his being a painter, would have been totally lost.

These *nows*, separated from each other by two generations (and from us by three or more), are by the strange miracle of art superimposed—and coincide! They coincide because life, love, and the memory of life—despite superficial changes—are trapped into art: "How strange," Bishop says. And we, of course, add, "how significant." The whole passage is worth looking at, both for its precision and for its very serious consideration of the relationship between art and what I've chosen to call "significant life":

> I never knew him. We both knew this place,
> apparently, this literal small backwater,
> looked at it long enough to memorize it,
> our years apart. How strange. And it's still
>   loved,
> or its memory is (it must have changed a
>   lot).
> Our visions coincided—"visions" is
> too serious a word—our looks, two looks:
> art "copying from life" and life itself,
> life and the memory of it so compressed
> they've turned into each other. Which is
>   which?

Life and the memory of it cramped,
dim, on a piece of Bristol board,
dim, but how live, how touching in detail
—the little that we get for free,
the little of our earthly trust. Not much.

We notice, of course, the familiar echoing language: "knew"/ "knew"; "memorize"/ "memory"/ "memory"/ "memory"; "visions"/ "visions"; "looks"/ "looks"; "life"/ "life"/ "life"/ "Life"/ "live"; "dim"/ "dim"; "little"/ "little"—all in fifteen lines.

But we notice more: that art is validated by "detail" that "touches" us into feeling, a feeling different from but related to the "love" both painter and poet felt for a "literal small backwater" named Great Village. The meticulous detail that love imprinted once on mind is translated into technique: the painter's handling of his materials (a "gray-blue wisp" of paint, "two brushstrokes" that become "confidently cows," a wild iris "fresh-squiggled from the tube," the "titanium white" barn) and the writer's handling of the words that constitute her own materials:

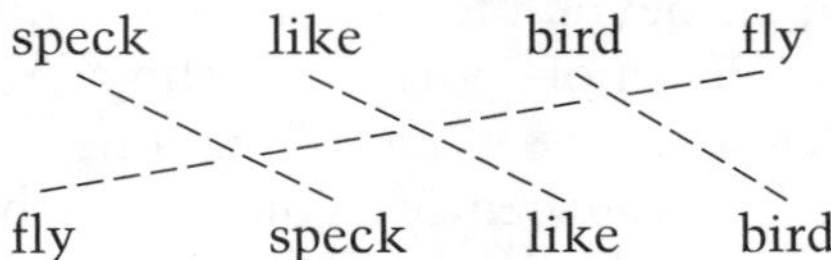

inconspicuous but efficient in the role of statement and question:

A specklike bird is flying to the left.
Or is it a flyspeck looking like a bird?

As "fly" flies left and the other repeated words drift right, we feel, if we are reasonably sensitive to language, a tingle of amused admiration. For flecks of color and line, patterns of repeated words and of rhyme and partial rhyme are what we call art.

What art accomplishes, however, is totally different from its materials. Out of art's technical compression of "life and the memory of it" into "dim" paint "on a piece of Bristol board," into words disposed ingeniously on a page, something refreshing emerges. On the "dim" board, "almost-lost" life emerges into present life: seventy-year-dead cows and iris, water long since dried up, and broken elms are not just vivid but vividly alive—even animate. At the end of the poem, in the last lines, they are "*munching* cows," iris that is "*crisp* and *shivering,*" water "*still standing* from spring freshets," and "yet-to-be-dismantled" elms (emphasis added).

They come to life because, given vitality through technique, they move us emotionally; "touching in detail," they offer us "the little that we get for free, the little of our earthly trust." If that little is "Not much," it is what we have and can live by.

In speaking of Elizabeth Bishop's life, I have tried so far to be chronological. In speaking of her work, I've chosen to roam freely from old material to new and back again, in no particular order. My choice has been deliberate, for it seems to me that, unlike many poets, she found her literary voice early. Her developments are not primarily in the areas of style and technique but, rather, in areas that have to do with theme and, perhaps, wisdom.

It has been unpopular until very recent years to ask poets to be concerned with such matters as wisdom and truth, but it seems evident that wisdom and truth are of interest to most writers (and their real audiences) and that despite a criticism focused largely on manner rather than matter—on decorative effects rather than on poetic statements—major poets have always, in fact, wanted to say something. Here, it seems to me, chronology is useful in examining Bishop's work.

But before I talk about the kind of developments I'm especially interested in, let me briefly dispose of a few stylistic matters.

I said that Bishop's dominant style is established very early—and it is. I've already talked exhaustively about her use of repetition and at least mentioned in passing her interest in rhyme and partial rhyme. All of these matters are part of the aspect of style that is usually labeled "form." And Bishop, it seems to me, is a "formal" poet.

But she is a formal poet with a difference. That is, she recognized early in her career what many other poets waited until early middle age to discover: that form is most interesting when stretched, when pulled almost (but not quite) out of shape. It is as if our ears are not always content with such neat structures as the endlessly symmetrical lines of *Hiawatha,* for instance, or the metronome regularity of Shakespeare's earliest work or the first version of *The Wanderings of Oisin.* Not that there are not fine passages to be found in such places. There are. But Yeats, who spent years in cleaning up his poem by roughening rhythms and varying rhymes, learned late what luckier poets—Gerard Manley Hopkins among them—recognized near the beginnings of their careers: You can do almost anything to a poem so long as you satisfy the ear's complex and contradictory need for order and diversity.

I think it was this that Bishop initially responded to when she first read the second edition of Hopkins, in 1928, whom she found fascinating not just for his sound effects but also for his strategy of abrupt self-address ("Fancy, come faster.") and his complex handling of tense. At approximately age twelve, she had begun to read Emily Dickinson, whom she did not much care for (probably because she was reading an inadequate early edition) and Walt Whitman, whom she did like. ("I also went through a Shelley phase, a Browning phase, and a brief Swinburne phase," she told Ashley Brown in an especially informative 1966 interview for the winter issue of the magazine *Shenandoah.*)

She learned from a great many poets, but the last thing Elizabeth Bishop should be called is an "influenced" poet, if by "influenced" we mean that she sounds like somebody else.

It is possible, of course, to pick out parallels. Once in a while her special kind of repetitions, as we shall soon see, seem a little like those of Wallace Stevens, who, in *Notes Toward a Supreme Fiction,* had defined the master poet as "he that of repetition is most master." A phrase in "Wading at Wellfleet" sounds to my ear not far from one by Robert Frost, and a phrase in "Chemin de Fer" ("The pet hen went chook-chook") could perhaps have been written by John Crowe Ransom, although Miss Bishop says she was at the time ignorant of his work. The third poem of "Songs for a Colored Singer" seems to me similar to Yeats's "Lover's Song" (from the "Three Bushes" sequence); and none of them, as Bishop has several times observed, might have been written at all had she not heard Billie Holiday sing "Strange Fruit," in fact all her early songs. (Actually, the fourth song echoes a bit of William Blake's "Tiger" as well.)

Bishop has learned a good deal from the metaphysical poets. "Conceits" that remind one of John Donne and Andrew Marvell show up frequently in the early poetry and, somewhat more toned down, all through her work. George Herbert, she told Ashley Brown, was particularly important to her (for poems that seemed "almost surrealistic"); and she mentioned that her poem "The Weed" was "modelled somewhat on 'Love-Unkown.'" It is equally important, however, to remember that she praises Herbert for his "absolute naturalness of tone," a much less conspicuous characteristic that she also shares with him.

But minor echoes of line or manner never extend far beyond the phrases in which they appear. No whole poem of Bishop's really resembles a whole poem by anyone else. Her "voice" is as authentic a voice as can be found anywhere in American poetry.

Since I have been focusing on poetry associated with her family and particularly on the very late poem about her great-uncle's little painting, it might be worth turning to her very early poem on his "Large Bad Picture" for some examples of what I mean by "form stretched almost out of shape." (I do not, needless to say, want to suggest that she is incapable—when she wants to—of structuring tight conventional patterns.)

Even a glance at the poem identifies it as "formal"—eight rhymed quatrains in lines that are neither extraordinarily short nor extraordinarily long. The "stretch" shows up on the second glance, when one tries to calculate the rhythm and the rhyme.

Rhymes are more conspicuous, so almost immediately one becomes aware of a glaring oddity. The rhyme scheme of each stanza is in one way or another different from every other stanza—although often, because of slant rhymes, a scheme is difficult to detect.

Look at stanza 1:

Remembering the Strait of Belle Isle or
some northerly harbor of Labrador,
before he became a schoolteacher
a great-uncle painted a big picture.

Do we, paying attention to heavily accented sounds only, call the "rhymes" a/b/c/d, or do we plot the rhyme as a repeated full sound in the unaccented last syllables of lines one and two (a/a) and as a slant rhyme in the unaccented last syllables of lines three and four (b/b′)—or do we throw caution to the wind and say that all four lines end in an *r* sound and therefore should be heard as a/a/a′/a′? But then internal rhymes come leaping in as we notice a whole family of *or*'s and *er*'s: *or*, *nor*therly, har*bor*, Labra*dor*, be*fore*; Remem*ber*ing, north*er*ly, teach*er*, pic*ture*. By this time we have probably heard the internal *a* rhymes in *Strait* and *great* and the slant rhyme in *pai*nted—and the even more conspicuous chiming pattern of terminal *l*'s in the first line's Be*lle* Is*le* that goes echoing on through the entire poem (schoo*l*, mi*le*s, sti*ll*, pa*le*, litt*le*, lev*el*, sma*ll*, sai*l*s, ta*ll*, occasion*al*, anim*al*, sma*ll*, ro*ll*ing, ro*ll*ing, perpetu*al*, conso*l*ing). Dizzying! Every stanza a different rhyme scheme and the whole poem a construct of echoing sound.

Rhythms are complex. The poem can be scanned, no question of it—but with line lengths that range from four syllables to fourteen (both in stanza 7), a rhythmic pattern shows up that is even more variable than the sound pattern we have just looked at.

Why is it all going on? One answer, I think, is a variant on Hopkins' answer when he tried to explain the function of sprung rhythm. Our ear, as I suggested earlier, really wants two different things at once: a "poetic" rhythm (all the variations on ta *tum*, ta ta *tum*, *tum* ta, *tum* ta ta, *tum tum*, ta ta, ad nauseam) and, opposing it, running against it in a counterpointing way, a proselike "sentence" rhythm (the irregular rhythm of ordinary talk). Similarly, our ears like full rhyme (sky/high), but we like it best when it is accompanied by a very strict meter. A mix of full and partial rhyme (sky/high in areas of regular rhythm and, to a *tum* ta ta final beat in lines of loose rhythm, Bellé Isl̄e or̄/ Labrādor̄/ schoól-teac̄her̄/bíg pic̄tur̄e) can, in a poem as light and amusing as "Large Bad Picture," startle us into careful attention both to what the poem is saying and to what it is doing.

What we get from this sort of rhyme and rhythm is a flexibility, a range of effects, that can go from the extraordinarily songlike regularity of the fifth stanza's

– / – / – / – – / /
And high above them, over the tall cliffs'
/ – – / – /
semi-translucent ranks,
– / – / – – / / /
are scribbled hundreds of fine black birds
/ – / – –
hanging in *n*'s in bańks.

to the vast, thudding shift in the sixth stanza's rhyme and rhythm when the "huge aquatic animal" of the last line comes gasping to the surface:

– – / – / – / –
One can hear their crying, crying,
– /– / – /
the only sound there is
– / – – / – – / –
except for occasional sighing
– – / – / – /– – /
as a large aquatic animal breathes.

(It is impossible not to digress for a moment to comment on the fine, funny effect of that string of six *n*'s in the line that sees the birds as *n*'s in the sky or to remark on the fact that the birds are as lyrical as they are because they have picked up the sound of their "crying, crying" from stanza five's buried *i* rhymes of *high* and *fine*, which in turn go back most conspicuously to stanza two's end rhymes of *high* and *sky* and slant rhymes of *mi*les and *si*de.)

But a poem—particularly a poem as cheerful, ironic, tender, ingenious, and complex as this one—can explain itself only by the reader's getting used to it. A few notes, however, might be helpful.

We are, of course, once again back in Elizabeth Bishop's childhood world and, as Lloyd Schwartz points out in his excellent commentary, "One Art: The Poetry of Elizabeth Bishop, 1971–1976," the poetic version of that world is almost always immensely intricate: "Changes in levels of diction shift the point of view. There is the child's naivete and candidness. . . . And yet there are perceptions about the child's reactions only an adult could articulate." He is speaking of "In the Waiting Room," but he might well have been considering this slighter, more casual poem.

The voice in that first stanza is pretty much a little girl's voice. She's not quite sure where the "picture" (not painting) is supposed to be set, but she knows it's either on the Strait of Belle Isle or at some northerly harbor of Labrador; she also knows that her great-uncle must have seen it "before he became a schoolteacher." (He had, in fact, painted several large works on his return from his first cabin-boy voyage to the north. "I loved them," Bishop told Ashley Brown. "They're not very good as painting." Years after he had become a fairly successful painter in England, he came back to Great Village for a summer's visit—several years before Elizabeth's birth—and conducted art classes for his nieces and their friends. It was, indeed, during this time that the sketch was done that Bishop uses in "Poem.")

If the first stanza of "Large Bad Picture" belongs primarily to the child, by the second stanza the child's admiration for the "big picture" begins to mingle with an adult's analysis of it. (Its cliffs, seen with a child's enlarging eye, are "hundreds of feet high"; but the bases of the cliffs, "fretted by little arches," are described in the diction of an adult.) From this point on, the adult and child voices are intermingled. Only in the last stanza does the adult voice become totally dominant.

Often there are transformations in a Bishop poem, and some of the most interesting in this one occur when the child/adult observer shifts stance in order literally to enter the scene. In the beginning of the poem, she is looking at the painting. Suddenly the painting fills with sound. She is no longer the observer, but a participant in the action of the painting. She is able really to hear the crying of the birds and the sighing of an invisible "large aquatic animal." But precisely as the painting comes to life, time stops! A "perpetual sunset" begins, a stopped *now,* that, something like a few of the stopped-time actions in Wallace Stevens, involves everything in fixed action. The sun goes "rolling, rolling,/ round and round and round." But for all its rolling, it isn't going anywhere. This sunset, trapped just before it disappears, is literally perpetual; and the ships—which now join the child and adult and adult/child as observers—"consider it," presumably forever.

Meaning—any meaning—is, however, ambiguous; and no one knows that better than Elizabeth Bishop. If she is a poet of echoes, she is also a poet of options. Her favorite word must be *or*. It dominates her poetry. The scene here (that is *either* the Strait of Belle Isle *or* a Labrador harbor) achieves, finally, a stasis. But even then doubt arises. The ships are fixed in a fixed harbor under a permanently fixed, permanently setting sun. But the most one can say of them is that "*Apparently* they have reached their destination" (emphasis added). No one can really know the destination of anyone or anything.

And not only can we not know destinations, we have no way of determining motives. Why have these ships come to this harbor? They're ships, so perhaps they have come for "commerce." They're in a work of art; and, like us, they "consider" this sun that cannot set. Perhaps they have come, therefore, for "contemplation." Options, even in a work of art (especially in a work of art), tease us, like Keats's Grecian urn, out of thought.

I said earlier that I saw little "development" in Elizabeth Bishop's technique. "The Map," which was written in 1934 or 1935 and opens her first book and *Complete Poems,* is as assured as "One Art," the villanelle with which, she told me, she had hoped to end her 1976 collection, *Geography III.* The "voice" that asserts "Land lies in water; it is shadowed green" anticipates the very similar "voice" that asserts "The art of losing isn't hard to master."

On the other hand, the late poetry has changed, it seems to me, considerably in *tone*. It is far more willing to risk statement than the early poetry. And though many of its assertions are still tentative, they seem driven by more open feeling than Bishop allowed herself to display in the earliest work.

To put it another way, though almost all of Bishop's best poems are shot through with both strong personal feeling and strong intellectual conviction, in the early poems style is used to mask feeling and conviction and in the later works to uncover them.

This is certainly no novel idea. Most critics of Bishop's early work praised it for its immaculately "cool" surface, its wit, and its meticulous attention to detail.

Selden Rodman, for example, writing in the New York *Times* of October 27, 1946, said: "If the author of the thirty-two remarkable poems in this book used paint she would undoubtedly paint 'abstractions.' Yet so sure is her feeling for poetry that in building up her over-all watercolor arrangements she never strays far from the concrete and the particular."

When her second book of poems was published, Richard Eberhart, also writing in the *Times* (July 17, 1955), said that he found "the same detached, deliberate, unmoved qualities in the new work as in her old. . . . She is devoted to honest announcements of what she knows, to purity of the poem, to subtle changes in scope and intention."

But not until *Questions of Travel* was published were many critics ready to notice, as Lisel Mueller did in an August 1966 review in *Poetry,* that

> she still has the eye for detail, the capacity for detachment, the sense for the right word and the uncanny image, and the mental habit that imposes order, balance, and clarity on everything she sees. But this third book holds more yet: a greater richness of language, a grasp of proportion and progression that makes every poem appear flawless, and an increased involvement between the "I" of the traveler and the "it" and "thou" of landscape and stranger.

I like Mueller's adaptation of Martin Buber's analysis of the I/Thou relationship in art to the poetry of Elizabeth Bishop. But, as I've just suggested, it seems to me that that relationship exists in all of Bishop's poetry. It does not so much "increase" in the later work as simply become more visible.

In order to trace the evolution of what might be called gradually unmasked feeling and conviction, chronology is useful. And so is a bit more in the way of biographical information.

All of the work I've focused on so far is associated with Bishop's mother's family in Great Village. But from the age of seven until she was ready to enter college, she lived—except for summer visits to Great Village—in Boston suburbs with her mother's older sister. At thirteen, she started going to summer camp at Wellfleet. At sixteen, she went to boarding school outside Boston. These were essentially Boston/Cape Cod years.

For a very brief interval, however, for half a year just after she left Great Village, she lived with her paternal grandparents. John W. Bishop, her grandfather, had originally come with his family from White Sands, Prince Edward Island (off the coast of Nova Scotia), first to Providence, Rhode Island, and then to Worcester, where he founded the firm of J. W. Bishop and Son. He was an ambitious and most successful man. By the time Elizabeth was born, his firm of builders was responsible for constructing many public buildings in Boston and college and university buildings in other parts of the country. Her father, William Thomas Bishop, joined the firm soon after his high school graduation. He remained single almost all of his life, not marrying until he was thirty-seven. (Elizabeth's mother was twenty-seven.) About two years later, Elizabeth was born.

If her Canadian years were, in retrospect, full of a tangle of joy and anxiety, her return to Massachusetts and the years before her admission to Vassar were, on the whole, complicated by illness and some loneliness. Her abrupt transfer from the warmth and generosity of her Canadian grandparents to the very different world and life of her father's parents was hard on the six-year-old, and a sudden onslaught of ailments—bronchitis, eczema, severe chronic asthma, and what was diagnosed as early symptoms of chorea—made her brief time in Worcester a dismal one.

Although her illnesses moderated when Bishop was sent to Boston to live with her Aunt Maud, most of the next eight years were relatively lonely. She had a playmate or two, but she was too ill to attend school with any regularity. Instead, she devoted her time to piano lessons and reading—a good deal of the reading done while propped up in bed, wheezing with asthma.

Summers, however, were frequently pleasant. Bishop regularly visited her grandparents in Great Village until she was in her late teens—until her grandfather died and her grandmother went to live with a daughter in Montreal. (Through her entire life, she has continued to return to Nova Scotia to visit an aunt.) Another activity was also important to her, for between her twelfth and sixteenth years, she was enrolled for two months each summer at the Nautical Camp for Girls in Wellfleet, where she discovered sailing and, meeting other girls who were interested in books and poetry, began to break down the shyness that had characterized her childhood.

Finally, in 1927, she had her first real school experience. She was sent to a boarding school, Walnut Hill, in Natick, Massachusetts. Here, studying Latin and English under very good teachers, she continued to write the poetry that she had first begun at the age of eight. She also, however, had real opportunities to talk about writing. "The teaching was of very good quality," she told Ashley Brown:

> I only studied Latin then. I didn't take up Greek till I went to Vassar. I now wish I'd studied nothing but Latin and Greek in college. In fact I consider myself badly educated. Writing Latin prose and verse is still probably the best possible exercise for a poet.

After Walnut Hill, she entered Vassar where, with Mary McCarthy and other friends, she started a literary magazine. (It was started because the college literary magazine refused to print their work. After three numbers had appeared, the college magazine gave in and some of the group were asked to become its editors.) Toward the end of her college career, her poetry was beginning to appear in little magazines. But perhaps the most significant event of that time was her meeting with Marianne Moore, who became a lifelong friend.

The winter following her graduation was spent alone in Greenwich Village in New York. In 1935–36 and again in 1937–38, she lived some months in Paris and later traveled in Italy; but for the ten years from 1938 on—except for nine months in Mexico in 1943—Bishop lived principally in Key West, Florida. She wrote much and published less (much less), so that it was not until 1946, when she was thirty-five, that her first book, *North & South,* was published as the winner of the Houghton Mifflin Poetry Award.

Many of the themes and preoccupations, as well as much of the imagery, of Bishop's later work show up in that first book. When I spoke to her in the summer of 1977, I mentioned that I'd been particularly struck by the quantity of water imagery, the number of poems set at a time of divided light (dawns and dusks), the frequent appearances of birds in the poems. "I don't think I notice things like that," Miss Bishop said. "After *North & South* was published, an aunt remarked that there was a lot of water in my poems; until then, I hadn't been conscious of it." Nevertheless, more than two-thirds of the thirty poems in the present version of that first book have explicit water references and most of those that don't—all but two, in fact—offer either mud, mermaids, snow, spit, tears, dew, or washing. There are precious few deserts in Elizabeth Bishop's early poetry.

One might expect a lot of water and birds—and even sunrises and sunsets—in a poetry that moves this way and that on the map of the world. On the other hand, in view of the later strong focus on the landscapes of childhood, it is a little surprising that in her first book there is no explicit reference to Nova Scotia—not one that I can locate—and only one direct reference to Massachusetts ("Wading at Wellfleet," which, with its "back shore" location, is founded on memories not of early childhood but of summer camp and later, and which is certainly dominated by an adult point of view). It is as if the places and persons of childhood are still too painfully close to be tackled as subject matter or as if not quite enough perspective has yet been gained to value them accurately.

But if Nova Scotia does not show up at all, and Massachusetts appears only once, that does not mean childhood has been neglected. The child and the child's point of view (and the child's extreme sensitivity to wonder and to pain) are still very much with us. The place names are missing. Sometimes even the child is superficially missing (as in "Large Bad Picture," which, I suppose, should properly be called a Nova Scotia poem, since the painting, if not its subject or its painter, was in Nova Scotia when Bishop was there). Yet the literary function of the child's wide-eyed approach to reality is demanded in much of this poetry, and Elizabeth Bishop finds a variety of ways to provide it.

What happens most often is that the child puts on an adult's disguise (as in "From the Country to the City"), or peeps out from behind poetry read in childhood and "revised" from an adult's point of view (as in "The Gentleman of Shalott"), or tells—with neither place nor time specified—an anecdote that could or should have been experienced in childhood (as in the walk along the railroad track in "Chemin de Fer"—in fact, a summer camp "adolescence" memory—when, "with pounding heart" the protagonist discovers "the ties were too close together/ or maybe too far apart"), or suddenly finds herself dragged abruptly into an adult world (her "childish snow-forts, built in flashier winters" suddenly intruding on "Paris, 7 A.M."), or discovers herself reflected in the echoing mirror of a remembered fairy tale ("the crumbs . . . clever children placed by day/ and followed to their door/ one night, at least" in "Sleeping Standing Up"), or seems to show something like a lost child's face in a homemade fairy tale ("The Man-Moth," for example), or is forced on us in a child's toy observed by an adult ("Cirque d'Hiver"), or is terribly, universally with us in the third of the "Songs for a Colored Singer," the "Lullaby" that lets "Adult and child/ sink to their rest" in precisely the same way "the big ship sinks and dies" during a war, and that announces with casual matter-of-factness, "The shadow of the crib makes an enormous cage."

We are, of course, all entrapped—all caged—by the secret child who is caged within us, whose tear, like that of the Man-Moth, is "his only possession" and, "like the bee's sting," the defense that keeps him alive:

> Slyly he palms it, and if you're not paying
> attention
> he'll swallow it. However, if you watch,
> he'll hand it over,
> cool as from underground springs and pure
> enough to drink.

If we see this moving poem as having something to do with the secret child, the shy self we all carry with us, some of its mystery disappears but none of its mysterious power.

In order to talk about this poem, however, it is useful to put it into the context of its book. It is the tenth poem in *North & South*. "The Map," which opens the book with water (and to which I want to turn next), sets up the geography image that dominates not just this first book but all of Bishop's poetry. "The Imaginary Iceberg" sails us from the literal North Atlantic of "The Map" to the North Atlantic of the imagination, and we have a chance to study a natural object that reminds us a little of the soul ("both being self-made from elements least visible"). We see the imaginary iceberg from the deck of a ship;

"Casabianca" sets that lonely ship of the soul burning ("Love's the boy stood on the burning deck"). "The Colder the Air," in direct opposition to the "burning boy" of love, presents a winter huntress whose shooting gallery freezes not just birds and boats but time as well ("ticking loud/ on one stalled second"). When this "clock" later falls "in wheels and chimes of leaf and cloud," we are prepared for the central image of "Wading at Wellfleet," which offers waves that are like the "sharp blades" around the wheels of an Assyrian war chariot. "Chemin de Fer" reduces the waves of Cape Cod Bay to ripples on a "little pond." The subject, like the subject of "Casabianca," is love; but here it is the incomplete love of an old hermit who keeps people away from him while shooting his shotgun and screaming, "Love should be put into action!" (That this is an incomplete love is insisted on in the last lines, where we learn that "across the pond an echo/ *tried and tried* to confirm it" (emphasis added). If the hermit has an incomplete love, "The Gentleman of Shalott," who follows, is incompleteness itself, a man who is half mirror:

> If the glass slips
> he's in a fix—
> only one leg, etc. But
> while it stays put
> he can walk and run
> and his hands can clasp one
> another. . . .

The mirror-moral of the poem is, perhaps, contained in the last line and may apply to many of these poems: "Half is enough." "Large Bad Picture" offers a mirror of a different kind: the mirror of art that reflects a natural landscape in such a way as to stop time and invite us to enter the painted world for the sake, possibly, of "contemplation." The "perpetual sunset" of "Large Bad Picture" moves us quickly on to the not-quite-darkness of "From the Country to the City." Here, too, there are mirrors not altogether unlike those in "The Gentleman of Shalott," who had worried about the effect on thought "if half his head's reflected." In "From the Country to the City," the "glittering arrangement" of the city's brain consists of "mermaid like,/ seated, ravishing sirens, each waving her hand-mirror," the glitter flashing out toward the country as "vibrations of the tuning-fork" that the city holds and strikes "against the mirror frames." This ominous, dark, and glittering city leads directly to the nighttime subway world of "The Man-Moth."

Threading such a diagram of interconnected images and themes distorts the poems; but it does, I think, suggest something of the workings of what Hart Crane liked to call "the logic of metaphor." Neither logical nor illogical, such alogical linkages work like those synapses in the brain that make metaphor, and so poetry, possible. "Resemblance" leads us to a shock of insight as unrelated things put on mirroring costumes. Certainly the title of "The Man-Moth," the lucky newspaper misprint for "mammoth" that had offered Elizabeth Bishop a way into her poem, is a lovely illustration of the process I'm talking about.

What happens in that poem, however, is of far more interest. We are again in a world where the principal viewpoint seems to be that of a most precocious child who adopts an adult's vocabulary while at the same time retaining her own myth-making way of looking at things. Under a full moon, she notices, "The whole shadow of Man is only as big as his hat./ It lies at his feet like a circle for a doll to stand on."

But we soon learn that the poem is not about Man but, rather, about a fabulous, if timid, creature, the "Man-Moth," whose appearances in the light are "rare." (I'm suggesting, of course, that he bears in many ways a speaking likeness to that secret child I mentioned earlier. He is both timid and brave. He is filled with illusions that are more satisfying than reality. And the tear that is "his one possession" is "pure enough to drink." Since he lives in a subway, he is also literally the underground man.)

One thing that the secret child notices is that Man, though he feels the "queer light" of the moon on his hands, "does not see the moon." The Man-Moth, on the other hand, sees it but doesn't know what it is. (He thinks it is a hole at the top of the sky; "Man, standing below him, has no such illusions.") Despite his fears, the Man-Moth "nervously," "fearfully" must climb the facades of the buildings in order to "push his small head through that round clean opening." What Bishop stresses is what every sensitive child has always known: "what the Man-Moth fears most he must do." We call this compulsion "growing up," I suppose, or perhaps "education." Like any child, however, who never quite learns to cope with failure, the Man-Moth "fails, of course, and falls back scared but quite unhurt." Immediately, he returns underground, "to the pale subways of cement he calls his home." He rides backward on those subways, each night forced to "dream recurrent dreams."

As I've said, this Man-Moth seems to me another version of the secret child, here apprehended in a mix of adult and child diction by the secret child from the past. It is as if the author looks into her own eye at the end of the poem to discover that the mirroring Man-Moth's eye is "all dark pupil,/ an entire night itself." He is, as it were, not only himself/herself but also the recurrent dream as well as its dreamer. The tear that is forced from his eye, "his only possession," is both his life (the bee sting analogy insists on it) and his innocence, "pure enough to drink," that we—as observers—are perpetually forcing him to give up.

That loss of innocence is central to many poems by Elizabeth Bishop, and I'd like to track it through several of them. Because I want to see that loss in terms of geographies, it is important to begin with "The Map," where it is not especially prominent but where geographies certainly are.

I've spoken of Miss Bishop as a poet of options and echoes; and the echoing lands, waters, weeds, names, shadows, and maps of this poem are as conspicuous as the five *or*s that keep us suspended until the final line's statement: "More delicate than the historians' are the map-makers' colors." The mapmakers' colors are more delicate, of course, because historians—inevitably distorting the tangled maps of love and fear and friendship—force us away from "shadows" into the glare of bare red, yellow, and blue: the fictions that result from oversimplified biography.

I think for most readers that last line comes as a considerable surprise. The "subject" of the poem, after all, is the map, not "history." Yet once we realize that it is a most subjective world that Bishop is mapping (no one more emphatically denies the validity of John Ruskin's "pathetic fallacy" than she), the surprise disappears and admiration replaces it. For it is the world's body she is interested in and its analogous relationship with the human one. As a result the land can "*lean down* to lift the sea from under,/ drawing it *unperturbed* around itself" (emphasis added), as if the sea were a kind of live shawl. "Is the land tugging at the sea from under?" she asks herself. Similarly, when we see the map's materials as living ones, we have no difficulty with the notion that we can "stroke" a bay, not just by rowing on it but by petting it as well. Living peninsulas, in such a world, are able to "take the water between thumb and finger/ like women feeling for the smoothness of yard-goods."

A poet who translates feeling into topography deals metaphorically with primitive emotions, the emotions that govern the child/adult; and it is right, therefore, that the map offer us both "agitation" and "quiet," and that its most telling pronouncement has to do with the "excitement" we all experience "when emotion too far exceeds its cause." (We remember the extravagant tears of a grandmother.) The kind of analysis that occurs in this statement (even if it is attributed to the printer of the map rather than to the author or the reader of the poem) is, it seems to me, the kind that comes not from innocence but from experience—that comes, indeed, precisely from loss of innocence. But because we are apprehending the world in many of these poems with the bifocal vision of the child/adult, it is important that we recognize that such answers can come only because the innocent questioner in us asks the right questions: "Are they assigned?" for example, "Or can the countries pick their colors?" Lurking behind the naive question is the much larger one of determinism and free will. But it takes the innocent questioner to insist that we cope with problems of this sort. Though Bishop makes no explicit answer to the question of how a country's "color," its personality, is achieved, she does, in the last line, manage to say that the historian's notion of reality is different from that of the mapmaker (the evolving individual, if we see this as a poem about the "delicate" ways in which the individual self is achieved; the artist, if we see the poem as about the differences between the artist's "delicate" way of presenting truth and the gross, heavy-handedness of historian, biographer, or—in an essay like this one—critic).

If "The Map" concerns itself obliquely (via free will and determinism) with the nature of the soul, "The Imaginary Iceberg"—another North Alantic poem—deals explicitly with that question. Like the iceberg, "self-made" and cutting its facets from within, the soul "saves itself perpetually and adorns only itself." Although isolated and perhaps lonely, the iceberg/soul is valuable: "We'd rather have the iceberg than the ship."

Behind the poem and important to all of Bishop's work is another complex relationship—what Mueller, paraphrasing Buber, had called the "I/Thou" relationship. In this poem, although "we" and the ship sail off to a "warmer sky," it is not before acknowledging the importance of that separate "breathing plain of snow," the "other" we would like to, and cannot, "own." "Good-bye, we say, goodbye" to any important "other."

Another variant on the I/Thou relationship is worked out in Bishop's "metaphysical" poem "The Weed." A dream poem, its opening reminds us a little of "The Imaginary Iceberg," for from the cold heart of the "dead" speaker a "frozen" final thought extends "stiff and idle" as the body under it. Suddenly, a weed begins its growth within the heart and awakens the sleeper. Eventually, the "rooted heart" splits apart and produces a double river. The weed is almost swept away. However, as it struggles to lift its leaves out of the water, a few drops are splashed on the eyes of the speaker, who thinks that each drop is a "small, illuminated scene" and that the "weed-deflected stream" is made up of "racing images." In place of frozen thought, the weed now stands in "the severed heart." Its role, it explains, is "but to divide your heart again."

Once more—as in "Sestina," "In the Village," and "The Man-Moth," to mention only those works I have focused on—tears are of central importance. For the stream that springs from the heart is, of course, a stream of tears that are occasioned both by lost love and by new love. We learn to cry early; but when childhood innocence is gone, our tears—like our loves—are more desperate and more necessary than in childhood.

Though there are no children in "The Weed" (unless we count the "slight young weed" itself with its "graceful head," who seems more adolescent than child and more "young adult" than adolescent), nevertheless the poem does manage to make its statement about the continuity of life from earliest childhood on; for the "racing images" of the drops of water/blood/tears that constitute the stream flowing from the heart are explained in terms of such continuity:

> (As if a river should carry all
> the scenes that it had once reflected
> shut in its waters, and not floating
> on momentary surfaces.)

These are—to use a phrase from the beginning of this essay—images of "significant life," the stopped *now*s that can be drawn from childhood, from adolescence, from maturity, the *now*s that memory must constantly retrieve and that we must examine, reexamine, and evaluate if we are to be able to function in any useful present. Here we are offered only the process itself abstracted into an image: the "frozen" thought above a "cold" heart giving way to the weed of feeling and love that brings both tears and an insight into the meaning of life. As in many other early poems, the example of brokenheartedness is not offered nor really needed. For beneath the witty surface, private pain, we know, powers the poem. The roots of such pain are important not to us but to Elizabeth Bishop.

The preoccupations of *North & South,* despite its superficial focus on travel, have to do with the sense of an isolated self and that self's relationships to various "others," whether those relationships (as in "The Weed" and "Late Air") deal with love, or (as in "Quai d'Orléans") shared experience, or (as in "Roosters") "unwanted love," denial, and "forgiveness." But there are also several poems (particularly "The Monument" and, of course, "Large Bad Picture") that concern themselves with the nature and value of art and still others (often dream poems like "Sleeping Standing Up" or dawn poems like "Paris, 7 A.M.") that draw on reveries of childhood to project a sense of meaningless, undefined loss.

During the nine years between her first book and her second, Elizabeth Bishop accumulated honors but not a wide readership. Literary friends such as Randall Jarrell, Robert Lowell, Marianne Moore, and Pablo Neruda admired and praised her work; but despite the fact that she was granted a Guggenheim Fellowship in 1947 (and another in 1978), in 1949 acted as consultant in poetry at the Library of Congress, in 1950 was given the American Academy of Letters Award, in 1951 was awarded the first Lucy Martin Donnelly fellowship from Bryn Mawr College, and in 1952 was granted the Shelley Memorial Award, she was neither widely anthologized nor really widely acclaimed.

Part of the reason for her delayed popularity has to do, I suspect, with her travels; for during much of her life she has been abroad. For fifteen years, beginning in 1951 and interrupted by infrequent visits to New York and a summer's travel in 1964 to Italy and Spain, she shared a house in the mountains of Brazil (near Petrópolis) and an apartment in Rio de Janeiro with Lota Costellat de Macedo Soares, a Brazilian friend whom she had met in New York in 1942.

Not even the publication in 1955 of *Poems: North & South—A Cold Spring,* although it won her the 1956 Pulitzer Prize for poetry and a *Partisan Review* fellowship, made Bishop a "popular" poet. For one thing, of course, her new book added only nineteen poems to the previously published thirty of *North & South*—giving her an average production of a little more than one poem for each year of her life! But, more importantly, the poems made no aggressive claims, not even to their own chiselled elegance.

What the new poems did do, however, was to explore somewhat more openly than before both "real" landscapes (New York's "Varick Street," for example) and recollected but "fictionalized" ones ("The Prodigal") for areas of private feeling or, in poems like "Over 2000 Illustrations and a Complete Concordance," to contrast the significant landscapes of history with the jumbled—even more significant—ones of memory. Their major opening out, however, comes in a set of four "Nova Scotia" poems that not only are set firmly on the landscape of Miss Bishop's childhood but that very delicately—almost imperceptibly—contrast what *is* with what *was* (especially "At the Fishhouses").

One of the principal accomplishments of all of these poems, however, is their steady, unsentimental insistence that we see reality not as it ought to be but as it is. Literature, history, theology, she suggests, are always deceiving us by promising more than they can deliver. We read the Great Book—it really doesn't matter which—and we are offered a coherent universe. We contrast that with experience, and we discover that in the real world everything is "only connected by 'and' and 'and.'" Reality never gives us—as a book subtitled "Over 2000 Illustrations and a Complete Concordance" cheerfully does—the happy miracle of domesticity crossed on virgin birth:

Open the heavy book. Why couldn't we
    have seen

this old Nativity while we were at it?
—the dark ajar, the rocks breaking with
light,
an undisturbed, unbreathing flame,
colorless, sparkless, freely fed on straw,
and, lulled within, a family with pets,
—and looked and looked our infant sight
away.

This is, of course, how the poem ends: with our "infant" sight focused on the Nativity's infant and his "family," the Bethlehem cattle reduced to "pets," and the miracle made casual yet still properly miraculous (the dark come "ajar" and the rocks "breaking with light"). What the 2,000 illustrations offer is reassurance that the world, for all its sadness and strangeness, makes sense.

Bishop's strategy is to begin and end with the illustrations, sandwiching reality between them. The initial illustrations are not quite so grand as the final one, but all of them testify to a world that has meaning built into it: a group of Arabs, "plotting, probably,/ against our Christian Empire,/ while one apart, with outstretched arm and hand/ points to the Tomb, the Pit, the Sepulcher." All of the engravings "when dwelt upon . . . resolve themselves."

The transition to reality—Elizabeth Bishop's own reality, her own travels—is accomplished by water. The reader's eye "drops, weighted, through the lines/ the burin made" until "painfully, finally," it reaches lines "that ignite/ in watery prismatic white-and-blue." Suddenly—in much the same way that she steps *into* the scene in "Large Bad Picture"—she steps *out of* the engraving and onto the deck of a ship that is passing along the coast of Newfoundland:

Entering the Narrows at St. Johns
the touching bleat of goats reached to the
ship. We glimpsed them, reddish, leaping
up the cliffs among the fog-soaked weeds
and butter-and-eggs.

What may be worth a moment's thought is that when we leave the concordance, we enter reality to the *touching* bleat of goats. We are moved by the real world and its lovely, fragile landscapes, the free leap of animals that will die (that are not, as those in the biblical landscapes, everlasting "pets" and that do not inhabit the silence—"always the silence"—of the engravings). As opposed to the ordered, labeled "significance" of the engravings—the outstretched arms and hands that point to Tomb, Pit, and Sepulcher—the real world, connected by *and*s ("And at St. Peter's . . . And at Volubilis . . . And in the brothels of Marrakesh") seems filled instead with significant but frightening disorder. (The poem, of course, reorders it to make its own satisfactions: it is no accident that our travels take us to St. Peter's after St. John's, for example, or that the concordance sepulcher is echoed in the Mexican Easter lilies.) Reality offers a jumble of meaningless life and death:

In Mexico the dead man lay
in a blue arcade; the dead volcanoes
glistened like Easter lilies.
The jukebox went on playing "Ay, Jalisco!"

The dead man, the dead volcano, and the noisy jukebox coexist. Similarly, "a golden length of evening" in Ireland illuminates "rotting hulks" while an Englishwoman, pouring tea, explains that "the Duchess" is going to have a baby. ("Nativity" chimes in our minds!) Prostitutes in Marrakesh do belly dances and fling themselves "naked and giggling against our knees,/ asking for cigarettes." But "somewhere near there" a grave "open to every wind from the pink desert" is more frightening than anything previously cataloged:

. . . It was somewhere near there
I saw what frightened me most of all:
A holy grave, not looking particularly holy,
one of a group under a keyhole-arched stone
baldaquin
open to every wind from the pink desert.
An open, gritty, marble trough, carved solid
with exhortation, yellowed
as scattered cattle-teeth;

half-filled with dust, not even the dust
of the poor prophet paynim who once lay
there.
In a smart burnoose Khadour looked on
amused.

It is frightening, not because its holiness has been violated, or even because the guide "in a smart burnoose" finds the whole scene amusing; it is not even especially frightening because, open-mouthed in silent "exhortation," its yellowed trough is the color of scattered cattle teeth (our minds leap forward to the peaceful cattle of the Nativity scene). Its real cause for terror, it seems to me, is that it means *nothing*. And suddenly we realize that this scene is not the only frightening one, but only the one that "frightened me most of all." For all of the travels have been frightening: the travels to Newfoundland, to Rome, to Mexico, to Volubilis, to Ireland, to Marrakesh: the "beautiful poppies," the "touching bleat of goats," the giggling little prostitutes, the Englishwoman pouring tea are all frightening. They are alive, vulnerable, trapped in mortality. No wonder the concordance attracts and repels us! It offers us innocence regained. But innocence is what we have all lost. In a frightening and beautiful world, we must make do with the tangible real: the goats, some "fog-soaked weeds and butter-and-eggs," a fat old guide who makes eyes at us—even an amused guide to the empty graves. When "infant sight" is gone, we look out on and accept frightening reality.

What satisfies us in a poem of this sort is a double integrity: an honesty of feeling and—something I have not especially stressed here—an honesty of craft. (I mentioned a few of the image links, but the links of sound are brilliant: the hidden rhymes, for example, in "some*where* near *there*" or—after a grand total of eleven *ands* in the long first stanza—the casual comment that everything is connected by "'and' and 'and'" ironically adding three more, or the remarkable design that places "a *holy* grave, not looking particularly *holy*" under a "key*hole*-arched" baldaquin, or the ingenious use of *open* to link the grave "*open* to every wind"—a grave that is nothing more than "an *open* . . . trough"—to the command that we reexamine the concordance: "*Open* the book," "*Open* the heavy book." The poem is not just a moral but also a technical triumph.)

The Nova Scotia poems, although I do not want to examine them here, show the same qualities. "At the Fishhouses" concludes that the sea, "cold dark deep and absolutely clear," "is like what we imagine knowledge to be:/ dark, salt, clear, moving, utterly free,/ drawn from the cold hard mouth/ of the world, derived from the rocky breasts/forever, flowing and drawn, and since/ our knowledge is historical, flowing, and flown." In "Cape Breton," a man carrying a baby gets off a bus to enter a landscape indifferent both to life and to death. ("Whatever the landscape had of meaning appears to have been abandoned,/ unless the road is holding it back, in the interior,/ where we cannot see." What we can see—and sense—is that "an ancient chill is rippling the dark brooks.")

To accept, as I think Elizabeth Bishop does, a world that in point of fact is not disordered but that is certainly nontheologically ordered—that is indifferent not only to man but to everything else as well—does not mean that one feels life is without value. In fact, it means exactly the opposite: life is the only value there is. The function of the artist is to see it honestly, to record its intensity, to find a way—for a while at least—to preserve its unique fragile/tough, tearful/comic, tender/brutal qualities.

This is the area of "knowledge"—and, I'm inclined to add, of "wisdom"—that Bishop drives toward in her later poetry. It is a cold knowledge, but it is inevitably shot through with intense feeling. (What poet wouldn't give his eye teeth to have written the superb love sequence "Four Poems" and the related lyrics "Varick Street" and "Insomnia," or the delicate lyric "The Shampoo"?)

"The Prodigal," a central poem in the 1955 volume, concerns the exile who takes "a long time/ finally to make his mind up to go home." The title poem in *Questions of Travel*

(1965) questions where home is and, implicitly, what it is.

Between the two books lies much work: the 1956 assistance in the translation of Henrique Mindlin's *Modern Brazilian Architecture*; the 1957 translation and publication of *The Diary of "Helena Morley"* (Alice Brandt); the 1962 publication of *Brazil*, a book commissioned by Time-Life and rather heavily revised by its editors ("Maybe two-thirds of it is mine," Miss Bishop once ironically remarked); and the translation of a number of poems by major Brazilian poets.

There were also more honors: the 1957 Amy Lowell traveling fellowship, the 1962 Chapel-brook fellowship, the 1964 Academy of American Poets fellowship.

And there were important travels—including a 1961 trip down the Amazon that, along with a 1972 trip to the Galápagos Islands and Peru, remains in Bishop's mind as among the most satisfying of her life.

But "travels" during the Brazilian years take on a different quality from the travels that preceded them. Almost all of the "short" trips are within the huge country of Brazil. And Bishop's work itself takes on a different quality—not a difference in tone or technique so much as in an attitude toward herself as "subject" of her own poetry—a quality that isn't easy to define but that has something to do, I think, with that "strange" domesticity Vendler notices. Perhaps, like anyone who writes from a congenial but very foreign country, Bishop during these years settles down, as if—granted a home, friends, and an occupation—she is freed by her foreignness to be most herself. The important qualifications in the last statement are, of course, "granted a home, friends, and an occupation." In Brazil, Bishop was lucky: for more than fifteen years, she found all three.

Her literary occupation needs no further documentation. The apartment in the Leme section of Rio and the home above Petrópolis have been well described by Ashley Brown; but we already know a good deal about the apartment, its neighborhood, and one of its views onto the steep hill or peak of Babilonia (with its climbing slums) from the poems "House Guest," "Going to the Bakery," and, particularly, "The Burglar of Babylon." As far as the home near Petrópolis is concerned, it has for years been radiantly with us in "Electrical Storm," "Rainy Season; Sub-Tropics," "The Armadillo," and "Song for the Rainy Season," the last of which I wish to discuss not because I think it is one of Bishop's major works but because it is one of three poems (the other two, both from *Geography III*, both stronger poems and both in subtle ways related to this one, are "One Art" and "Crusoe in England") for which I feel unqualified love.

It is difficult for a reader—any reader, but perhaps most difficult for a reader pretending to be a literary critic—to say in all honesty just why he not only admires but loves one poem more than another. Maybe it is all accident—private resonance that has nothing to do with the craft he can sometimes seem ingeniously to account for, syllable by interwoven syllable. Or maybe, more accurately, the love for a particular poem is a consequence of private resonance (my own memories of three lost houses) and the way a poem catches fire in the larger context of an author's work, or perhaps even in the still larger context of a whole genre. A single poem simultaneously lights up a blaze of totally public and totally private "meaning." For me "Song for the Rainy Season" does just that.

It is a song, of course, and a brilliant one: six intricately rhymed ten-line stanzas. The short lines sing to us and to each other a love song not to a person or even to a home (though I've called it that) but to a "house" that, like everything valuable that we know, is doomed to eventual destruction. (I think of the lost elms of "Poem," the lost elms of my own childhood, perhaps of yours; I think of the lost houses—surely this is one of them—of "One Art.")

Though it is an "open" house, it is also "hidden, oh hidden." (I think of the early nightmare poem "Sleeping Standing Up" in which, unlike Hansel and Gretel, the dreamer—searching all night—never finds out "where the cottage [is]." But this house is hidden only from the world, not from its proper inhabitants. It is "the house we live in.") It is hidden in high fog.

Even the fog is homemade, a "private cloud" invented by an almost-human brook that "sings loud/from a rib cage/of giant fern." Vapor climbs up the fern and then turns back to achieve the hidden privacy of a house in a fog cloud, a house beneath a magnetic rock that is "rain-, rainbow-ridden," and where, "familiar, unbidden," the natural world's owls, lichens, and bromeliads cling—not precariously—but at ease. (Even the vapor climbs the fern's rib cage "effortlessly.")

For the house is open to everything—"white dew," "silver fish, mouse,/ bookworms,/ big moths," even "the mildew's/ ignorant map." (Phrases and memories of other works echo, not just conspicuous ones like the opening scene of "Memories of Uncle Neddy," where the related molds and mildews of Rio return us to the child world of Nova Scotia, or "The Map" itself that fails to anticipate Brazil, but memories of poems that touch on the animal world threatened by man, a world that is still almost miraculously—just barely—able to refresh us and momentarily give us the illusion of freedom. "The Moose" is the most vivid example of such a poem but, pointing a more painful moral, "The Armadillo" comes also to mind.)

Hidden, private, open, the house is "cherished," for it has been "darkened and tarnished/ by the warm touch/ of the warm breath" of its inhabitants. Surrounded by "the forgiving air," serenaded by "the fat frogs that,/ shrilling for love,/ clamber and mount" (despite the brown owl that will pursue them), the house lives in a balance of life where even the "milk-white sunrise" can be "kind to the eyes."

Open, private, and hidden, the house, like the poem—like its author—is full of a generosity of spirit that reminds one of the phrase from Luís de Camões, the sixteenth-century Portuguese poet-traveler-adventurer, that is used to dedicate *Questions of Travel* to Lota de Macedo Soares: ". . . O dar-vos quanto tenho e quanto posso,/ Que quanto mais vos pago, mais vos devo." (I give you everything I have and everything I can,/ As much as I give you, I owe you.)

If the poem celebrates a beautiful place where friendship is possible, a place in casual harmony with the natural world, it also acknowledges how fragile such a place is. (One thinks here of other poets—particularly Hopkins, who, in "Binsey Poplars," makes a parallel observation, that "country is so tender/ To touch, her being so slender,/ That, like this sleek and seeing ball/ But a prick will make no eye at all,/ Where we, even where we mean/ To mend her, we end her.") The fact of joy does not abolish loss. Our project—and the project of the house we can save only in a work of art—is therefore to "rejoice" in the face of certain—absolutely certain—destruction:

darkened and tarnished
by the warm touch
of the warm breath,
maculate, cherished,
rejoice! For a later
era will differ.
(O difference that kills,
or intimidates, much
of all our small shadowy
life!) Without water
the great rock will stare
unmagnetized, bare,
no longer wearing
rainbows or rain,
the forgiving air
and the high fog gone;
the owls will move on
and the several
waterfalls shrivel
in the steady sun.

In 1966, shortly before her fifty-fifth birthday, Elizabeth Bishop's teaching career began: two short semesters at the University of Washington in Seattle. (Later she would teach for seven years at Harvard and for a semester at New York University.) In 1967, she began restoring a colonial house in Ouro Preto, Minas Gerais, and for a number of years spent parts of each year at it. In 1969, *The Complete*

Poems earned her the National Book Award. In the same year she was given the Order of Rio Branco by the Brazilian government. In 1972, her *Anthology of Twentieth-Century Brazilian Poetry* (coedited with Emanuel Brasil) was published. In 1974, she moved most of her possessions from Brazil to an apartment on the Boston waterfront. In 1976, *Geography III*, her most brilliant book, was published.

Themes that in earlier works are obscured by shimmering technique are in *Geography III* boldly highlighted by it. "In the Waiting Room" stops time on the *now* of a single instant of "the fifth/ of February, 1918," three days before Bishop's seventh birthday, the instant of her discovery in a Worcester dentist's office that she is a part of humanity—simultaneously an "I," an "Elizabeth," and a "them" that includes not just the aunt whose cry of pain seems to come from Elizabeth's mouth, but also the people in the waiting room and the strange natives in a 1918 issue of the *National Geographic*.

Another poem, "The Moose," captures a different hallucinatory moment from the other side of her childhood's split Boston/ Nova Scotia world, a confrontation between a busload of travelers headed south toward Boston and a free life from the woods, a moose that has wandered onto a New Brunswick road to stop, inspect, and finally ignore the machine full of people.

Some of these remarkable poems—"One Art," "Poem"—I have already discussed. "The Moose," "In the Waiting Room," and "Crusoe in England" are so rich and so rewarding as each to deserve a separate essay. To try to compress them into a few paragraphs would be a pointless exercise.

I felt, when I agreed to write this essay, that it was important for me to talk to Elizabeth Bishop. And it was important, but not in ways that I could possibly have anticipated. I had planned to ask her a little about her working methods. We did talk about them—the quantity of poems that never reach print, the kinds of revision that go into those that do, the processes by which finished poems are sequenced into a book. She corrected a few biographical facts that had previously been misreported. It was all information that I might have gathered—probably more accurately—in a letter.

My visit must have complicated her life, slowed down her work in one way or another, for I was traveling with a friend, the poet Roger Conover. Our afternoon arrival on the Maine island where she had rented a summer house meant that we had to be not just fed but housed overnight.

I saw firsthand a little of the domesticity Helen Vendler talks about. "I'm considered a good cook," Miss Bishop told me, as I helped make a salad while she assembled a dinner that seemed effortless but that was superb. There were five of us there that evening, and our conversation was almost wholly about life on the island. Earlier, we had walked some of the beaches, studying seabirds through binoculars. I had brought along a tape recorder and two cameras. I didn't use the tape recorder at all. I used one of the cameras only to photograph dried seaweed on two beach pebbles.

When, several months later, I read Helen Vendler's remarks about the relationship between the domestic and the strange in Bishop's work, I made a note to myself:

—the domestic and the strange *and the civilized,*
—a careful writer who is a good cook and a meticulously accurate observer of nature,
—a woman who sees life as a balance between loneliness and communion (see "The Moose"),
—a poet able to accept the jumble of cruelty and affection in the natural world (see the prose poems in *Geography III*).

That didn't seem good enough to me, and on another day I tried again:

Civilized: Try to see Bishop as the changing, valued, and valuing person. The element of integrity has everything and nothing to do with her biography and her poetry: her remarks about Latin ("I'm not a 'Latinist.' I wish I were. But I have forgotten a lot of it"), her modesty about being a good cook ("I'm not proud of my cooking; I know lots of people equally good or better at it"), the loyalty and richness of her friendships, her "shyness," her reticence about religious "problems." The facts of her life account in part for her poetry and her personality—the childhood that is at first evaded but used and later literally studied. But there has to be a point in her life when the half-created person takes over and begins shaping her own life. The integrity comes in at this point: the sense of responsibility as the half-created personality becomes both self-creating and a contributor to the personalities of other people. It is the same thing with her writing: the debts not so much of style as of insight picked up from others; the gift of her own writing, her own private insights extended toward others. Her sense of self/other/the indifferent natural world: the separate value of that insight to me and each one of her other readers who is receptive to it. Her value not to "the public" but to each reader separately: "I/Thou" relationship. For me, her great gift is her capacity to love and be frightened of and moved by an alien "outside" world that has no responsibility to love her in return. The special excellence of "Crusoe in England" and "Song for the Rainy Season" and "One Art" is in their acknowledgment of a significant "other" in a world that must, not because it wants to but because it is caught up in time and so has to, destroy that "other." At its best, her art is almost always an art of stopped time: an art that acknowledges loss but that uses loss to define the power of love, a love that forces the artist to commemorate the loved and lost ("almost-lost") person, place, thing: in the largest sense, my own loss—yours—as well as hers. Perhaps, finally, her integrity can be measured by her accuracy and that accuracy by its function in creating a stoical, joyous, valuing and—major element—*modest* wisdom. She is at once responsive to the domestic and the strange, as well as one of our most civilized and—in the heart of her work—most civilizing poets.

Selected Bibliography

WORKS OF ELIZABETH BISHOP

BOOKS

North & South. Boston: Houghton Mifflin, 1946.

Poems: North & South—A Cold Spring. Boston: Houghton Mifflin, 1955.

Poems. London: Chatto and Windus, 1956.

The Diary of "Helena Morley." Translated and edited by Elizabeth Bishop. New York: Farrar, Straus and Cudahy, 1957; reprinted with new forward, New York: Ecco Press, 1977.

Brazil. New York: Time Inc., 1962. (In Life World Library.)

Questions of Travel. New York: Farrar, Straus and Giroux, 1965.

Selected Poems. London: Chatto an? Windus, 1967.

The Complete Poems. New York: Farrar, Straus and Giroux, 1969.

An Anthology of Twentieth-Century Brazilian Poetry. Edited, with introduction, by Elizabeth Bishop and Emanuel Brasil. Middletown, Connecticut: Wesleyan, 1972.

Geography III. New York: Farrar, Straus and Giroux, 1976.

PRINCIPAL UNCOLLECTED PROSE

"Gerard Manley Hopkins: Notes on Timing in His Poetry," *Vassar Review,* 23: 5–7 (February 1934).

"The Sea and Its Shore," *Life and Letters To-day,* 17, no. 10: 103–08 (Winter 1937).

"In Prison," *Partisan Review,* 4, no. 4: 4–10 (March 1938); reprinted in *The Poet's Story,* edited by Howard Moss. New York: Macmillan, 1973. Pp. 9–16.

"Gregorio Valdes, 1879–1939," *Partisan Review,* 6, no. 4: 91–97 (Summer 1939).

"The Housekeeper" (by "Sarah Foster"), *New Yorker,* 24, no. 29: 56–60 (September 11, 1948).

"Gwendolyn," *New Yorker,* 29, no. 19: 26–31 (June 27, 1953).

"On the Railroad Named Delight," *New York Times Magazine* (March 7, 1965), pp. 30–31, 84–86.

"Memories of Uncle Neddy," *Southern Review,* 13, no. 4: 11–29 (Autumn 1977).

INTERVIEWS

Brown, Ashley. "An Interview with Elizabeth Bishop," *Shenandoah,* 17, no. 2: 3–19 (Winter 1966).

Starbuck, George. "'The Work!' A Conversation with Elizabeth Bishop," edited by Elizabeth Bishop, *Ploughshares,* 3, no. 3–4: 11–29 (1977).

CRITICAL AND BIOGRAPHICAL STUDIES

Ashbery, John. "The Complete Poems," New York *Times* Book Review (June 1, 1969), pp. 8, 25.

Bloom, Harold. "Books Considered," *New Republic,* 176, no. 6: 29–30 (February 5, 1977).

Brown, Ashley. "Elizabeth Bishop in Brazil," *Southern Review,* 13, no. 4: 688–704 (Autumn 1977).

"Elizabeth Bishop," *Current Biography,* 38, no. 9: 15–17 (September 1977).

Hollander, John. "Questions of Geography," *Parnassus,* 5, no. 2: 359–66 (Spring/Summer 1977).

Ivask, Ivar, ed. "Homage to Elizabeth Bishop," *World Literature Today,* 61, no. 1: 3–52 (Winter 1977).

Jarrell, Randall. "The Poet and His Public," *Partisan Review,* 13, no. 4: 488–500 (September–October 1946); reprinted in his *Poetry and the Age.* New York: Farrar, Straus and Giroux, 1972. Pp. 234–35.

Kalstone, David. *Five Temperaments.* New York: Oxford University Press, 1977.

Lowell, Robert. "Thomas, Bishop, and Williams," *Sewanee Review,* 55: 493–503 (Summer 1947).

———. "For Elizabeth Bishop," in his *History.* New York: Farrar, Straus and Giroux, 1973. Pp. 196–98.

McClatchy, J. D. "The Other Bishop," *Canto,* 1, no. 4: 165–74 (Winter 1977).

Mizener, Arthur. "New Verse," *Furioso,* 2, no. 3: 72–75 (Spring 1947).

Moore, Marianne. "Archaically New," in her *Trial Balances.* New York: Macmillan, 1935. Pp. 82–83.

———. "A Modest Expert," *The Nation,* 163, no. 12: 354 (September 28, 1946).

Paz, Octavio. "Elizabeth Bishop, or the Power of Reticence," *World Literature Today,* 61, no. 1: 15–16 (Winter 1977).

Schwartz, Lloyd. "One Art: The Poetry of Elizabeth Bishop, 1971–1976," *Ploughshares,* 3, no. 3–4: 30–52 (1977).

Spiegelman, Willard. "Elizabeth Bishop's 'Natural Heroism,'" *Centennial Review,* 22, no. 1: 28–44 (Winter 1978).

Stevenson, Anne. *Elizabeth Bishop.* New York: Twayne, 1966. (Twayne's United States Authors Series 105.)

Vendler, Helen. "Domestication, Domesticity and the Otherworldly," *World Literature Today,* 61, no. 1: 23–28 (Winter 1977).

The author wishes to extend thanks to Lloyd Schwartz for his work in compiling this bibliography.

William Blake

(1757–1827)

F. B. BEER

SINCE WE REMEMBER AGES by their positive achievements, we tend to think of the eighteenth century as a time of elegant furniture and well-proportioned buildings in the midst of highly cultivated landscapes, a time of moderation and decency in the home, but also of uproarious life and broad humor in the streets: the age of Thomas Gainsborough and William Hogarth, of Alexander Pope and Henry Fielding. So indeed it was, but there was another side to the picture. Poverty was rife in town and country, with little to cushion the deprived against starvation and death, while disease could strike at all levels in society, cutting down the children of well-to-do as well as of the poor. The law took its course, often oppressively and mercilessly, mirroring the popular religious conception of a God who, while favoring those who kept his commandments, would have not pity on those who resolutely disobeyed them.

When we look at this harsher side to the century, the dominating images are of imprisonment. Eighteenth-century prisons were notoriously grim: it was a time when even the modest reforms instigated by John Howard were only just beginning, and criminals could hope for little remission. The most notorious prison of the age, the Bastille in Paris, moved William Cowper (a poet not given to very radical sentiments) to declare that there was not an Englishman would not be delighted if it were to be torn down.

It was not only the harshness of physical incarceration that fostered this atmosphere of oppressive enclosure. John Locke's view of the human mind, which inspired the dominant philosophy of the time, likened the understanding to "a closet, wholly shut from light, with only some little opening left, to let in external visible resemblance, of *ideas* of things without." The image of the mind itself was thus transformed into something dangerously resembling a prison cell. The guilt-ridden religious teaching of the time, similarly, would make any sensitive listener think of the body as a containing power, imprisoning the will, which tried to overcome its urges. Pope, a central spokesman for the contemporary intellectual view, could write.

> Most souls, 'tis true, but peep out once an age,
> Dull sullen pris'ners in the body's cage . . .
> ("Elegy to the Memory of an Unfortunate Lady")

Isaac Watts, the hymn writer, similarly, could count it a blessing that

> Shortly this prison of my Clay
> Must be dissolv'd and fall
> ("There Is a House Not Made with Hands")

William Blake, born on 28 November 1757, the son of a successful London hosier, was a man who might have found it difficult to fit into any human society, but whose nature rebelled particularly against accepting one such as this. Endowed with unusually strong imaginative powers, he found the darker side of eighteenth-century life more oppressive than did most of his fellows. When he was only four years old, he said later, God "put his head to the widow" and set him screaming. All his life he was haunted by images of prisons: images of human beings in gloomy, confined places appear throughout his designs, and he illustrated Dante's account of Count Ugolino and his sons in the Tower of Hunger several times over. Blake also had direct experience of the prisons of his time: during the Gordon riots in 1780 he was carried along at the front of the mob, and so saw the storming of the Newgate jail and the release of three hundred prisoners; more than once in his later life he was in danger of imprisonment when he fell under suspicion of treason. But he was also aware that imprisonment did not stop with buildings; most of the men and women he saw as he walked the streets of London had to him the air of captives, held by invisible bonds. Jean Jacques Rousseau's memorable saying, "Man is born free, and everywhere he is in chains," only deepened the mystery. Could it be that the chains were manufactured not by "society" but by human beings themselves?

Reflections such as this were intensified by an imaginative power that all too easily found fuel for its nightmares. Blake once said that he could look at a knot in a piece of wood until he felt frightened by it. Yet this capacity for fear was matched by an equally strong power of ecstatic vision that could transform the world into a place of joy and beauty. As a child he once saw a tree full of angels, spangling every bough, and on another occasion saw angelic figures walking among haymakers. On the first of these occasions he just escaped a thrashing from his father for telling a lie, being saved only by his mother's intercession. Blake evidently enjoyed the power of eidetic vision, a condition in which human perception projects physical images so powerfully that the projector cannot easily tell the difference between them and images of the natural world. Such a power is occasionally found among children, but it seldom persists beyond the age of twelve; in Blake it lasted all his life. In older age he would often sketch visionary heads "from the life" sitting at his table and looking at his sitters as if they were actually in the room.

The strong visionary capacity thus manifested resulted also in a proneness to states of enthusiasm and fear: later Blake was to tell how the great events of his time (particularly the American and French revolutions) took the form for him of visions so powerful that he felt he could hardly "subsist on the earth." Those who met him sometimes had an impression of mental abnormality. Joseph Farington said in 1796 that Blake had something of madness about him; a decade later William Hayley, speaking of a "nervous irritation, & a too vehement desire to excel" said that Blake had often appeared to him to be on the verge of insanity. To those who knew only his works, the impression of madness could be even stronger, but those who had the opportunity of more intimate acquaintance denied such an implication indignantly. "I saw nothing but sanity" said Edward Calvert. "He was not mad, but perverse and wilful; he reasoned correctly from arbitrary, and often false premises" said Francis Oliver Finch. Another friend (perhaps Frederick Tatham) declared that his extravagance was "only the struggle of an ardent mind to deliver itself of the bigness and sublimity of its own conceptions." The time when Blake came closest to insanity was in the first decade of the nineteenth century, when he was most deeply at odds with those around him. Some of the writings produced then hint at paranoia. But most often what we witness is a vehement energy that refuses to be bound by the demands of convention. In *The Marriage of Heaven and Hell* (ca. 1790) he spoke of himself as "walking among the fires of hell, delighted with the enjoyments of Genius, which to Angels look like torment and insanity."

In youth Blake's independence.of mind was nurtured by the fact that he did not go to a conventional school, being first sent to Henry Pars's drawing school in the Strand and then apprenticed to James Basire, an engraver. But he was drawn not only to the visual arts; he loved music and poetry as well. To a person of his imaginative powers, the arts of the time seemed impoverished by comparison with their flourishing condition in, say, the Elizabethan period. His first book of poems, *Poetical Sketches* (1783), contained a lament for the current state of things:

Whether on Ida's shady brow,
Or in the chambers of the East,
The chambers of the sun, that now
From antient melody have ceas'd;

Whether in Heav'n ye wander fair,
Or the green corners of the earth,
Or the blue regions of the air,
Where the melodious winds have birth;

Whether on chrystal rocks ye rove,
Beneath the bosom of the sea
Wand'ring in many a coral grove,
Fair Nine, forsaking Poetry!

How have you left the antient love
That bards of old enjoy'd in you!
The languid strings do scarcely move!
The sound is forc'd, the notes are few![1]
("To the Muses," 10–11)

Blake not only honored but also practiced all the arts. Apart from his progress in drawing and engraving, he wrote poems such as "To the Muses" and accompanied them on the harp to airs of his own composing. So impressed was the company at the home of the Reverend Anthony Mathew, where he sometimes performed, that he was encouraged to publish a collection of his poems; some people there took down the tunes to which he had set them. Blake evidently won favor at this time for an air of inspiration; yet there was also a side to his nature that resisted any kind of adulation, particularly when it might impinge on his independence. He did not take easily to patronage at any time of his life; at the Mathews, he was after a time discouraged from continuing his attendance because of his "unbending deportment."

This alternation between visionary ardor and firm independence corresponds to a feature of Blake's personality that shows itself again and again. Not only was he unusually subject to contrary moods, he seems to have cultivated them actively, believing (in the words of his favorite advice to others) that "Truth is always in the extremes—keep them." The maxim, however unwelcome in a century that valued the "golden mean" and sought to dissuade people from extremes of any kind, was one to which he firmly adhered. Even in his earliest lyrics Blake tended to proceed by evoking contrary states of mind: two consecutive poems in *Poetical Sketches*, for example, each entitled "Song," give opposing versions of a village love. The first describes the pleasures of going to visit his beloved ("Each village seems the haunt of holy feet") and concludes:

But that sweet village, where my black-ey'd maid
Closes her eyes in sleep beneath night's shade,
Whene'er I enter, more than mortal fire
Burns in my soul, and does my song inspire.

The second song describes the torments of jealousy, culminating in a fear lest some other youth should walk with his love and concluding:

O should she e'er prove false, his limbs I'd tear,
And throw all pity on the burning air;
I'd curse bright fortune for my mixed lot,
And then I'd die in peace, and be forgot.

Blake's ability to see the same situation from varying points of view, his recognition that in different moods all the lights of a scene could be changed, was to come into its own in his later writing, notably in the *Songs of Innocence and of Experience* (1794). Already

1. All quotations from Blake are taken from G. Keynes, ed., *The Complete Writings* (London, 1966–), the Oxford Standard Authors series; references are to page numbers. For Blake's original punctuation D. V. Erdman, ed., with commentary by H. Bloom (New York, 1965) should be consulted. Sources for most of the biographical statements will be found in G. E. Bentley, Jr., ed., *Blake Records* (London, 1969); see bibliography.

in *Poetical Sketches,* though, there was much that looked to the future, including an image of winter ("O Winter! bar thine adamantine doors") that had the lineaments of his cold deity Urizen, and a characteristic image of imprisonment, wrought unexpectedly into what might appear at first sight to be a pleasant little love poem:

How sweet I roam'd from field to field,
And tasted all the summer's pride,
'Til I the prince of love beheld,
Who in the sunny beams did glide!

He shew'd me lilies for my hair,
And blushing roses for my brow;
He led me through his gardens fair,
Where all his golden pleasures grow.

With sweet May dews my wings were wet,
And Phoebus fir'd my vocal rage;
He caught me in his silken net,
And shut me in his golden cage.

He loves to sit and hear me sing,
Then, laughing, sports and plays with me;
Then stretches out my golden wing,
And mocks my loss of liberty.
("Song," 6)

So far as one can trace Blake's intellectual life as a young man (the evidence is mostly indirect), he read intensely in certain books, including both the most imaginative English poets, such as Edmund Spenser and William Shakespeare, and works of imaginative philosophy ranging from occult writers such as Paracelsus and Jakob Boehme to the writings of Plato and the Neoplatonists, which were being rediscovered and translated in his time by Thomas Taylor. The Bible and John Milton, which were especial favorites, he read by the light of his own intuition, valuing their passages of imaginative vision or fiery prophecy, while turning aside from those that represented God as a lawgiver bound by his own conception of justice.

At the same time his feeling for works of strong imagination made Blake impatient at the dominating thought of his time, which for all its progress in the applied sciences struck him as often trifling and uninspired. His attitude emerges briefly in *An Island in the Moon* (1787), in which he presents a group of cultured individuals, each wrapped in his or her own pursuits. Joseph Priestley, a man notable for the range of his intellectual interests, is probably the original of the character Inflammable Gas, while Thomas Taylor the Platonist seems to be satirized as Sipsop the Pythagorean. But it should not be thought that such caricatures were altogether intended to belittle the originals. These were some of the leading thinkers of the time, discussing issues and making discoveries that were exciting in their implications. Blake's satire seems, rather, to poke fun at an ultimate ineffectuality, an unwillingness to think even more boldly. They remained in confinement, though on a pleasant enough island.

An Island in the Moon is an amusing piece of satire, but it has an unfinished quality that seems to betray Blake's uneasiness at the time he was writing it. Was there really any point in satirizing his contemporaries in this way? Was it not more important to find a bold line of his own and lead the way to a more genuine art? Some such reasoning would seem to lie behind the change from the inspired pastiches of *Poetical Sketches* and the gentle, probing satires of *An Island in the Moon* to the clear, incisive line of his subsequent work. From now on, he would follow a particular line with energy and determination at any one time—even if he might strike out in a quite new direction immediately afterward.

By 1787, Blake was in an unusual state of mind. In February his favorite brother, Robert, died, appearing to him as he did so to pass through the ceiling of his bedroom, clapping his hands for joy. It was a vision that Blake, who had been watching over him, and who then collapsed, exhausted, into sleep for three days and three nights, was never to forget. It led him to believe more firmly in the existence of a spiritual world surrounding and infusing the world of nature, not to be identified with it but not to be ignored either.

This was no simple "spiritualism" of the kind that was to become popular in the middle of the nineteenth century. So far as one can reconstruct Blake's state of mind during these years, he was moved by the discovery that his own psyche was not a simple entity, but changed according to his physical state. He was not the same man when he was exercising himself in energy as when occupied in rational study; he was a different man again when surrounded by affection, especially sexual love. It is necessary to grasp this triple distinction if one is to understand the distinctive features of his work, since it gave him an uncommon view of the world and even an unusual vocabulary.

When he speaks at this time of science and reason, Blake is thinking of the state of nature as it presents itself when contemplated and studied passively; when he speaks of wisdom, intellect, and the "spiritual" on the other hand, he is thinking primarily of the mind and imagination in a state of energy; and when he speaks of love and innocence, he is thinking of the state of affection. (In later years the distinctions are less clear, but are still touched by this early ferment of thought.) From such distinctions he developed his idea of the man of spirit as a "mental traveler" who in walking through the world of experience or laboring at his creative work develops "intellect" thus discovering true wisdom. His own ideal of passivity, similarly, submits him not to the world of sense perception but to the inner illuminations of innocent vision mediated by affection.

As he developed these ideas, Blake was assisted by a number of contemporary developments. In 1787, Thomas Taylor published "Concerning the Beautiful," a short translation from Plotinus that was the harbinger of many further translations from the Neoplatonist writers. In that pamphlet a number of unusual words occur with a charge of particular meaning: the "study" of "particulars," "non-entity," "indefinite." In particular Taylor distinguishes between "the corporeal eye" and "the intellectual eye"—a distinction that Blake was to take over in his own way. His "intellectual eye" belongs to the energetic human being who is a mental traveler and a maker.

Plotinus' philosophy was not simply a quietist or passive one, since he regarded matter as being "neither soul nor intellect, nor life, nor form, nor reason nor bound, but a certain indefiniteness"; this left the way open for an artist such as Blake to assert that his true activity lay in creating definite outlines and living forms. From this time forward, one of his most distinctive features as artist and poet—his love of the distinct and vibrant image, visual or verbal—is to be traced. Good as some of Blake's previous works are, they do not have quite this decisive line or dramatic directness of statement.

His move in this direction was assisted by his friendship with Henry Fuseli, an Anglo-Swiss painter noted for his flamboyant behavior and vehemence of expression. Blake, though a quieter man in demeanor, was attracted by such qualities in a man who must often have seemed to him to have "all the fury of a spiritual existence." A further stimulus, though of a quite different kind, was the establishing of the Swedenborgian Church in Britain. To those who were oppressed by a sense of gloomy imprisonment in the teachings of the eighteenth-century dissenting sects, the writings of Emanuel Swedenborg opened new windows by reasserting the power of visionary knowledge and insisting on a reading of the Bible according to its "internal sense." Nature was seen not as the intricately wrought machine of eighteenth-century rationalism, but as a world in which were to be traced correspondences with a God who was most himself when most human.

Blake was at first deeply drawn to teachings that ran in such close parallel with his own visionary leanings, and when the New Church was established by a general conference in London in 1789, he and his wife, Catherine, were among those who put their signatures to its manifesto. The influence of Swedenborg's ideas can be found here and there in the *Songs of Innocence* (1789) where, in exploring the new world that opened for him after the death of his brother, Blake subdues the more satirical and sardonic side of his personality to an art that is the medium of direct, light-filled vision. In particular he draws on his belief that childhood is the time when the imaginative powers are at their most intense.

From this account of Blake's progress it will be seen that the idea, still sometimes to be found in criticism, that the succession from *Songs of Innocence* to *Songs of Experience* (1794) corresponds to a dramatic change in Blake's view of the world as he passed from the innocence of youth to the bitterness of maturity, will hardly bear serious examination. It ignores, among other things, the fact that Blake was more than thirty when he put together the Songs of Innocence. The case seems, rather, to be that Blake felt drawn to press a particular point of view to its extreme, allowing its contrary then to emerge and shape a new way of writing. Some of the *Songs of Innocence,* such as "The Little Boy Lost" and "Nurse's Song" first appeared, in fact, in *An Island in the Moon.* In their new setting, though, they are not subdued to a general tone of amusement, but are free to transmit their vision in a pure form. No doubt there were shifts in Blake's attitudes, corresponding to the dominant tone of the work he was producing at any given time, but his personality cannot be contained within them. As with many great artists, he had the gift of concentrating himself into one point of view at a time while leaving much in reserve, ready to generate further changes when they were ready to emerge.

By the time he put together *Songs of Innocence,* Blake was already deeply read in many authors and points of view. The indications are that in the wake of his early enthusiasms, he had embarked on a long study of the significance of human nature in the light of his own experiences, turning particularly to authors (usually flourishing before the eighteenth century) who had explored the relationship between nature and the imagination. The fruits of his thought can be found, before *Songs of Innocence,* in the little collections of aphorisms entitled *There Is No Natural Religion and All Religions Are One* (both ca. 1788), in which he launched his first open attacks on contemporary intellectual attitudes.

For many eighteenth-century philosophers, following in the wake of Francis Bacon, John Locke, and Isaac Newton, the human body seemed to be a highly appropriate instrument for dealing with nature, the five senses being finely attuned to all that it had to offer. The task of the intellectual was simply to investigate the relationships between man and nature until they were brought into harmony. Blake could not agree. For him the idea that there was nothing in the universe that could not be perceived by the five senses was imprisoning. He would have agreed with Andrew Baxter, who argued that "the body, in its present constitution, *limits* and *confines* the perceptions of the soul, but no way effects them." Locke had, as we have seen, suggested that there might be other faculties locked up in man for want of an organ by which they could be perceived, likening the understanding to "a closet, wholly shut from light, with only some little opening left."

Blake took over from both Locke and Baxter the point that if we had only three senses, we should not have the means to know of the sense experiences we lacked, and used it in *There Is No Natural Religion,* concluding with the reflection: "If it were not for the Poetic or Prophetic character the Philosophic & Experimental would soon be at the ratio of all things, & stand still, unable to do other than repeat the same dull round over again." For him such a vision of science was nightmarish, since the necessary limits to knowledge that it implied must abandon human beings to the dull fate of continually contemplating the same limited mechanism. The "Poetic or Prophetic character," on the other hand, liberated them by invoking a vision that transcended the sum of sense experiences. They no longer need feel themselves trapped within the confines of their own physical bodies, but could know a sense of true freedom. That sense of freedom is implicit in the vision that informs *Songs of Innocence.*

But to paint such a state in vivid colors was to invoke (almost automatically, perhaps, in so spirited a man) a complementary sense of ways in which children were oppressed from their earliest years and subtly assisted to grow into practices of deceit and submission to secret, self-enclosed pleasures.

Blake's movement toward a collection of poems based on this alternative, more cynical vision no doubt gained impetus from the current political situation. A few months after the meeting that established the Swedenborgian New Church, the French Revolution had broken out: an event that, following so soon after the American War of Independence, appeared to mark a decisive movement forward in human affairs. For a time Blake was a fervent supporter, and is said to have worn the emblem of the revolutionaries openly in the streets of London. The sense that a new era was opening in human affairs, already prophesied in the writings of Swedenborg, must for a time have been compelling. At this time Blake was also producing engravings for the publisher Joseph Johnson, who brought out books by a number of forward-looking writers, including Richard Price, Joseph Priestley, Henry Fuseli, William Godwin, Thomas Paine, and Mary Wollstonecraft. Blake, who is said to have met some of these figures at Johnson's weekly dinners, would have heard much talk of new ideas, not only in politics but also in social affairs. His enthusiasm for the French Revolution is said to have come to an abrupt end at the time of the September massacres in 1792, when he tore off his white cockade and never wore it again.

It is to this event, the disappointing culmination—at least in political terms—to the intellectual ferment that he had known over the previous few years, that the increasing bitterness of his writings around 1793 may be attributed. Blake could not renege on the excitement and enthusiasm he had felt during the previous years; he was forced to admit, on the other hand, that his fellow citizens showed few signs of allowing themselves to be possessed by new ideals in the future shaping of their society. On the contrary, since they remained largely at the command of those who wished to manipulate them, the future looked bleak. Early in 1795 his friend George Cumberland wrote of fears that England would soon be living under an absolute government or be plunged into a civil war. Neither prospect would be inviting to Blake; either would intensify the imprisoned state from which his fellows seemed powerless to escape.

The poems written into his notebook a short time before, many of which were to find a place in his *Songs of Experience,* are redolent of his mood at this time. Among other things Blake was haunted by a sense of sexual failure and restriction, of potentialities of fulfillment that were thwarted, almost inexplicably, among his fellows:

> Thou hast a lap full of seed,
> And this is a fine country.
> Why dost thou not cast thy seed
> And live in it merrily?

The reply is hopeless:

> Shall I cast it on the sand
> And turn it into fruitful land?
> For on no other ground
> Can I sow my seed
> Without tearing up
> Some stinking weed.
> (untitled, 168)

Yet Blake could not believe that human beings fully assented to this situation: "What is it men in women do require?" he asked in "Several Questions Answered" and went on to answer his own question: "The lineaments of Gratified Desire." He then put the same question and answer in relation to women. His thoughts on the matter often look forward to those associated with Sigmund Freud's conclusions:

> Abstinence sows sand all over
> The ruddy limbs & flaming hair,
> But Desire Gratified

Plants fruits of life & beauty there.
(verse fragment, 168)

In opposition to this vision of a free and happy gratification of sexual desire, Blake saw about him the secret indulgence of a lust that had no pleasure. The chapels in which abstinence was preached were caricatures of the true dwelling of sexual desire, and their adherents reaped a cruel crop:

I saw a chapel all of gold
That none did dare to enter in,
And many weeping stood without,
Weeping, mourning, worshipping.

I saw a serpent rise between
The white pillars of the door,
And he forc'd & forc'd & forc'd,
Down the golden hinges tore.

And along the pavement sweet,
Set with pearls & rubies bright,
All his slimy length he drew,
Till upon the altar white

Vomiting his poison out
On the bread & on the wine.
So I turn'd into a sty
And laid me down among the swine.
(verse fragment, 163)

Blake did not include this or some of the other, more bitter poems in *Songs of Experience.* Since it was still intended, evidently, as a book that might be read by children, he perhaps wished to omit poems that presented too dispiriting a view of the world that awaited them. Among the poems that remain, though, a similar trend is to be traced: a despair when he looked about him in society, coupled with a belief that the ultimate truth behind things was not what his fellows might suppose it to be as they listened to the preachings in their chapels and followed the discussions of contemporary scientists and philosophers.

The modern reader coming to these poems for the first time will soon pick up the underlying bitterness, but is likely to be seized even more immediately by the extraordinary simplicity and directness of the writing. This is all the more striking if one reads Blake's verses alongside others that were being written in his time. "London" one of his best poems, has been compared with one of Isaac Watts's poems for children, which begins:

Whene'er I take my Walks abroad,
How many Poor I see?
What shall I render to my God
For all his Gifts to me?
("Praise for Mercies, Spiritual and Temporal")

"London" opens:

I wander thro, each charter'd street,
Near where the charter'd Thames does flow,
And mark in every face I meet
Marks of weakness, marks of woe.
(216)

Despite their obvious similarity the difference between the two poems is revealed immediately as that between formally "taking a walk" and informally "wandering." Watts's stanza consists primarily of two exclamations, the first dominated by the second. We hardly have time to see the poor before the speaker is counting his blessings in not being of their number. Blake, by contrast, makes a single factual statement. We have an immediate impression of a man walking the streets, reflecting on the civilization about him, peering intently into the faces of all whom he meets to see what is to be read there, and finding primarily two bleak qualities: weakness and woe.

The purposes of the two poets are different, of course. Watts is writing a hymn for children: like all hymn writers his first aim is to lead those who sing it into suitable sentiments that all can share. He is the spokesman for a society of shared beliefs. Blake is a lonely figure, offering to speak for no one but himself. His is an adult poem: we are not sure whether even the speaker of the poem knows of a more positive vision, or whether he too does not bear the marks of weakness and woe.

The directness of "London" carries on into the reining stanzas:

In every cry of every Man,
In every Infant's cry of fear,
In every voice, in every ban,
The mind-forg'd manacles I hear.

How the Chimney-sweeper's cry
Every black'ning Church appalls;
And the hapless Soldier's sigh
Runs in blood down Palace walls.

But most thro' midnight streets I hear
How the youthful Harlot's curse
Blasts the new born Infant's tear,
And blights with plagues the Marriage
hearse. (216)

This is one of Blake's greatest poems; it has the quality, which shapes his most characteristic utterances, of describing the world as if one were looking at it for the first time. There is nothing naive about the vision, moreover; we need only turn back to the first stanza to see two very complex effects at work. "And mark in every face I meet/Marks of weakness, marks of woe": there is something awkward in the repetition of the word "mark." The observer "marks" but the marks "marks." Yet the awkwardness is in no way inept; by that dulling repetition Blake reinforces the effect of being dragged into an imprisoned world, where nothing radiates from the faces he sees: he marks them, but they do not seem to mark him in return. The arrow of his perception finds its mark, but finds itself fixed there, no longer at liberty.

The word "charter'd" repeated in the second line, also draws the reader's attention by its suggestion of irony. The word "charter" was originally associated with liberty. Magna Charta, signed by King John in 1215, was traditionally one of the foundations of British liberty, and was one of many such charters over the centuries. But these charters were freedoms granted to particular classes of people: they automatically involved a loss of liberty for those who did not belong; and by Blake's time it was hard to walk around London without feeling that the whole city had been parceled out among different groups of this kind, leaving no freedom for the human beings they excluded. "It is a perversion of terms to say that a charter gives rights" wrote Thomas Paine in *The Rights of Man* (1791–1792); "it operates by a contrary effect—that of taking rights away." Even the Thames, which might be thought by definition to be free, was so given over to the uses of commerce as to lose all identity except as a trade route. One of Shakespeare's characters describes the air as a "chartered libertine"; used in connection with the Thames, the word reads more like "shackled" looking forward to the "mind-forg'd manacles" of the second stanza.

Not all Blake's poems are as straightforward in their effect as this one. In "London" there is a sense of accumulating power gathering strength from the dramatic use of certain words, such as "appalls" (which draws into itself the sense of "pall"), and culminating in the final stanza. In many of his most typical poems, on the other hand, there is something that resists interpretation. It is a feature all the more unexpected in view of the directness of the language, which carries the reader along in assent. Only when one tries to make out and paraphrase the sense of what has just been read may it be discovered that the poem is less simple than was thought. A good example is one of his most simple lyrics, "The Fly":

Little Fly,
Thy summer's play
My thoughtless hand
Has brush'd away.

Am not I
A fly like thee?
Or art not thou
A man like me?

For I dance,
And drink, & sing,
Till some blind hand
Shall brush my wing.

If thought is life
And strength & breath,
And the want
Of thought is death;

Then am I
A happy fly,
If I live
Or if I die.
(213)

The poem has some clear antecedents in eighteenth-century poetry, notably in Thomas Gray's "Ode on the Spring":

Methinks I hear in accents low
The sportive kind reply:
Poor moralist I and what art thou?
A solitary fly!
Thy Joys no glittering female meets,
No hive hast thou of hoarded sweets,
No painted plumage to display:
On hasty wings thy youth is flown;
Thy sun is set, thy spring is gone—
We frolick, while 'tis May.

Whereas Gray's point is simple enough, Blake's "Fly" involves a strange shift of subject: the poem does not end as we might have expected. In the conclusion we discover that we can be happy whether we live or die—which might suggest, logically, that it does not matter very much whether we treat flies kindly. Yet there is a clear moral, connected with the lines in *King Lear*: "As flies to wanton boys, are we to the gods;/They kill us for their sport." We should not like to be treated in the way that boys treat flies, and this might be thought a good reason for being kind to insects. There is also an implication that those who show cruelty to living things are more likely to be cruel to their fellow human beings. To encourage kindness to animals and insects is to encourage habits of mind that may be beneficial to human society generally.

All this is in the vein of late eighteenth-century humanitarianism; there is little to criticize—apart, perhaps, from a veiled anthropocentrism. But Blake's interest in such closed systems of amoral approbation is limited. Their basis is ultimately an enlightened self-interest that has more to do with interest than with light. And behind this scene of moral instruction there remains a disturbing further implication from the *Lear* quotation: that however we treat flies or each other, we must eventually die in circumstances over which we shall have no control. Across the questions of kindness to others or otherwise there falls the shadow of a recognition that nature certainly entertains no such feeling for human beings.

It is this further shadow that seems to be responsible for a shift in "The Fly" after the third stanza (accurately signaled in the illuminated version by the existence of branches and a tendril that discreetly cut off the last two stanzas from the rest). The effect is of a strange conjuring, whereby we find ourselves, at the end of the poem, in an unexpected place, having passed through a subterranean transformation of meaning that cannot easily be unraveled into ordered sense, but that has changed the terms of the discussion from the question of kindness to that of life and its significance.

In these years Blake's poetic and literary powers reached their peak. The quality of his writing at this time is all the clearer when one looks at the notebook drafts and sees the process by which he reached his final versions. The ruthless parings and bendings into place are undeniably improvements. In "The Tyger" for instance, the early draft ran:

And what shoulder & what art
Could twist the sinews of thy heart?
And when thy heart began to beat
What dread hand & what dread feet

Could fetch it from the furnace deep
And thy horrid ribs dare steep
In the well of sanguine woe?
In what clay & in what mould
Were thy eyes of fury roll'd?
(172)

In the final version the second stanza is omitted, so that the last line of the first turns into a more indefinite, but at once more vivid, question:

What dread hand? & what dread feet?
(214)

Blake's revisions do not work only by way of dramatic contractions. An instructive example of another kind may be found in the notebook poem that begins "I heard an Angel singing." The angel's theme, "Mercy, Pity, Peace/Is the world's release," is followed by another:

I heard a Devil curse
Over the heath & the furze,
"Mercy could be no more,
If there was nobody poor,

And pity no more could be
If all were as happy as we."
At his curse the sun went down,
And the heavens gave a frown.

Down pour'd the heavy rain
Over the new reap'd grain,
And Mercy & Pity & Peace descended
The Farmers were ruin'd & harvest ended.
(164)

The swift and sardonic conclusion of the last stanza was deleted by Blake; and when he came to draw upon the draft for "The Human Abstract" he took nothing but the four lines of the Devil's song, which formed, with slight changes, the opening stanzas of his new poem. He then moved from this piece of sophistic logic to further examples ("mutual fear brings Peace" for instance). The result of the process emerges in the growth of a Tree of Mystery, nurtured by cruelty with the aid of humility. He concludes:

The Gods of the Earth & Sea
Sought thro' Nature to find this Tree;
But their search was all in vain:
There grows one in the Human Brain.
(217)

This brilliant use of the eighteenth-century image of the upas tree (the tree that in contemporary mythology was said to poison the atmosphere for miles around) exemplifies a characteristic working of Blake's mind during these years. When faced with the effects and processes of social injustice, his first impulse was to speak out in indignation, sullen resentment, or simple sardonic statement; in the longer term, though, he was looking for deeper causes. If his society allowed itself to build great mills in which human beings were imprisoned most of the day, that must be because dark satanic mills in their own minds screened from them the incongruity and inhumanity involved. If they swallowed the spurious logic of contemporary spokesmen for the status quo, similarly it must be because their minds were so overshadowed by self-imprisonment that they could not detect the false reasonings that they would be only too swift to spot in a matter affecting their own material interests.

It is germane to Blake's own mental honesty, as well as to his desire to rouse his fellows to think for themselves, that he does not try totally to refute the writers with whom he disagrees. If there is a positive energy or illumination to which he can respond, he will respect that, while subtly subverting those elements he believes false. A good example is found in his dealings with Swedenborg, who interpolated into his writings passages that he called "Memorable Relations." One of these, as Kathleen Raine has pointed out, throws a direct light on the chimney sweep of *Songs of Innocence*: "There are also Spirits among those from the Earth Jupiter, whom they call Sweepers of Chimnies, because they appear in like Garments, and likewise with sooty Faces . . ." (*Earths in Our Solar System,* sect. 79). Swedenborg is informed that these figures will later, when they form part of the Grand Man, or Heaven, "constitute the province of the Seminal Vessels." This implication that the chimney sweep is a symbol of sexual activity can draw also upon popular traditions, such as that of the chimney sweep kissing the bride to give her good luck. Heather Glen has given a number of such instances. But for Blake the chief importance of the symbolism might well lie in the suggestion that the practice of forcing boys to climb chimneys to sweep them was tolerated as part of the social system because sexual activity itself was thought of as secret and dirty; he would also have liked Swedenborg's further assertion that it was the burning intensity of the sweeper's desire to be in heaven that led to his being called upon to cast off his clothes with a promise of new and shining raiment—an incident that resembles the dream of Tom Dacre in Blake's first "Chimney Sweeper" poem.

But although Blake could draw directly upon Swedenborg's visions, he must have found the "Memorable Relations" in general to be long and rambling, just as he found Swedenborg's philosophy, for all its imaginative promise, to be simply another way of presenting conventional teachings. So in *The Marriage of Heaven and Hell* he presents several "Memorable Fancies" the second of which is of a more quizzical kind and begins:

> The Prophets Isaiah and Ezekiel dined with me, and I asked them how they dared so roundly to assert that God spake to them; and whether they did not think at the time that they would be misunderstood, & so be the cause of imposition.
>
> Isaiah answer'd: "I saw no God, nor heart any, in a finite organical perception; but my senses discover'd the infinite in every thing, and as I was then perswaded, & remain confirm'd, that the voice of honest indignation is the voice of God, I cared not for consequences, but wrote."
>
> Then I asked: "Does a firm perswasion that a thing is so, make it so?"
>
> He replied: "All poets believe that it does, & in ages of imagination this firm perswasion removed mountains; but many are not capable of a firm perswasion of any thing." (153)

It is well to bear this narrative in mind when reading some of the anecdotes that are told about Blake himself, since it has a strong bearing on his own practice. Even while Blake is asking whether Isaiah and Ezekiel thought they might be misunderstood when they said that God spoke to them, he knows perfectly well that he is in danger of being misunderstood for saying that Isaiah and Ezekiel dined with him. The defense they offer is also his own: the poet can be effective through the statement of firmly held convictions, which will also, if asserted powerfully enough, carry conviction back into his own mind.

The Marriage of Heaven and Hell provides the best example of Blake's dramatic power—a power that also emerges at times in *Songs of Experience.* "The Voice of the Devil" is not to be taken as Blake's own in more than a limited sense, as a reader with an ear for self-contradictions will soon detect. To say that "everything that lives is holy" is one thing; but when we read elsewhere in the book that "As the catterpiller chooses the fairest leaves to lay her eggs on, so the priest lays his curse on the fairest joys" we may find ourselves asking whether the life of caterpillars, then, is not, after all, holy. Blake's purpose in the book is not to proclaim the holiness of life or the gospel of energy as such but rather to allow room for voices not commonly heard in his society: to look at the world through the eyes of a human being exalted by the exercise of energy, for example, and to ask whether the resulting picture is not more attractive than the view projected by the eye of a containing and self-contained reason.

In one sense the enterprise was successful almost beyond Blake's expectations. His wit found room for full play in his little sketches of life in hell, and his assertion that Milton "wrote in fetters when he wrote of Angels & God, and at liberty when of Devils & Hell, is because he was a true Poet and of the Devil's party without knowing it" turned out to be true of himself in ways that he would hardly have acknowledged. Indeed, as he begins to enumerate the "Proverbs of Hell" they turn into a rhapsodic poetry on their own account:

> The pride of the peacock is the glory of God.
> The lust of the goat is the bounty of God.
> The wrath of the lion is the wisdom of God.
> The nakedness of woman is the work of God.
> Excess of sorrow laughs. Excess of joy weeps.
> The roaring of lions, the howling of wolves,
> the raging of the stormy sea, and the
> destructive sword, are portions of
> eternity, too great for the eye of man.
> (151)

The change of line length at the end is one that no poet of his time could easily have tolerated, yet it works triumphantly, looking forward to the large rhythm shifts of later writers.

Although much in *The Marriage of Heaven and Hell* is to be ascribed to Blake's dramatic invention, there are places where it is possible to misread him because of a failure of communication that he seems not to have foreseen. If it is the price he pays for not having submitted himself to a formal education, it is a small price, in view of his liberation from the constraints imposed by an overly formal grammar and syntax; it needs to be recognized, nevertheless. Some years ago a well-known American critic declared that in spite of his admiration for Blake, he must invite his readers to consider soberly the injunction in *The Marriage of Heaven and Hell*: "Sooner murder an infant in its cradle than nurse unacted desires." Vigorous and positive this might be, but was it not also a highly immoral statement? How would they defend it if asked to do so?

It is inconceivable that the Blake of *Songs of Innocence and of Experience* could ever have thought that the murder of a child was justifiable. On the contrary, he probably felt so sure that his readers would share his revulsion against such acts that he felt free to ignore such a possible reading of his remark. What he was urging, rather, was that desires are like infants: if you allow them to remain unacted, the action is like murdering an infant in its cradle. Instead of being repressed in this way, desires should be treated with the respect and delight that are equally appropriate to children: in that way they will grow up humanized. Unacted desires, on the other hand, like children stunted through lack of affection, are likely to turn to destruction: it is indeed (and ironically) such desires that might end in a crime so inhuman as child murder.

Possibilities of self-contradiction are bound to exist in such a philosophy, nevertheless, and Blake seems sometimes to have been conscious of them. Reading once about a meanness of mind that he disliked, he wrote in the margin, "To hell till he behaves better!" then added hastily, "Mark that I do not believe there is such a thing litterally, but hell is the being shut up in the possession of corporeal desires which shortly weary the man, *for* ALL LIFE IS HOLY" (annotation to J. C. Lavater, *Aphorisms* on *Man*, 74). He is not calling for a transvaluation of values, but for recognition of a dialectic between different views of the world—a dialectic that may in turn point back to a hidden harmony that could contain what are now warring elements. When he asserts that the Devil's version of events is that the Messiah fell, not himself, he is not saying that the Devil is right, but simply pointing to the impoverishment of reason once it is deprived of connection with energy. His book is not called *The Supremacy of Hell*, but *The Marriage of Heaven and Hell*; and it is that marriage, in the form of a reconciliation between reason and energy within a larger human vision, that he seeks to promote.

It was because he was dissatisfied with simple versions of the world and unwilling to proceed simply by inverting them that the quest for a viable mythology came to play such an important part in Blake's developing thought. Already in his youth, as we have seen, he seems to have engaged himself with mythologies and allegories of all kinds, ranging from alchemy and Greek tragedy to Shakespeare, Milton, and symbolic interpretations of the Bible, in order to discover a reading of human nature more optimistic than the conventional one. The first results are found in the rather turgid manuscript poem "Tiriel" in which the sources are comparatively near the surface of the poem and where many of the names of the characters can be traced to actual sources.

Later, though, Blake evolved his own mythology, in which the names (while still reflecting traditional themes) are purely his own, bearing the stamp of his distinctive thought. At some point the reader has to decide whether to follow Blake into this idiosyncratic world—and if not, where to stop. There is one figure so dominant in the writings and so absorbing in significance, however, that most readers find him fascinating.

This is Urizen, best known from the design in which he leans down with compasses into darkness from a blank disk of a sun. When Blake looked at the behavior of human beings in his world and asked himself what kind of God they really worshiped, this was the answer he found. They believed themselves to be in a world where their fate was to be overwhelmed by the darkness and death that surrounded all human existence; the only possible course, therefore, seemed to be to build an ordered world that might protect them from the vision of such a dire end. Urizen, in Blake's designs, is not an ugly figure, but graceful, and even majestic; he is often depicted with his eyes closed, on the other hand, to suggest his lack of true vision.

When Blake is confronting the effects of such a rule in his own society, he is moved to indignation and even abuse, calling its originator by the belittling name of "Nobodaddy." His favorite form then is the pithy rhyme or epigram;

> Why art thou silent & invisible;
> Father of Jealousy?
> Why dost thou hide thyself in clouds
> From every searching Eye?
>
> Why darkness & obscurity
> In all thy words & laws,
> That none dare eat the fruit but from
> They wily serpent's jaws?
> Of is it because Secresy gains
> females' loud applause?
> ("To Nobodaddy" 171)

Elsewhere Nobodaddy enters some of Blake's more powerful political poems, as when he attacks the French monarch's tyranny in the poem that begins "Let the Brothels of Paris be opened":

> Then old Nobodaddy aloft
> Farted & Belch'd & cough'd,
> And said, "I love hanging & drawing & quartering
> Every bit as well as war & slaughtering.
> Damn praying & singing,
> Unless they will bring in
> The blood of ten thousand by fighting or swinging." (185)

Although Blake's indignation against the effects of social oppression found natural vent in such language, the object of his more sustained effort was an inquiry into why Urizen achieved such dominance if, as he believed, the ultimate reality in the universe was one of light and energy, color and music. In the long run, he concluded, Urizen was enabled to stay in power through some deep failure in human beings themselves.

Seen in these terms, the story of Urizen is one of tragedy rather than evil; he could, indeed, be seen as a rather noble figure, pioneering a means of survival for all human beings who shared his dark sense of the world, rather in the way that Milton's Satan set out on his heroic journey when the other fallen angels had refused. This view of Urizen dominates *The First book of Urizen* (1794), one of the darkest of the prophetic books and written as a conscious pastiche of the biblical book of Genesis. Creation here is seen not as a sublime creation out of darkness and chaos, but as the result of a withdrawal from the true state of eternity.

In creating Urizen, Blake evidently had in mind some of the more lurid portraits of God the Father that were current in his time. "Thinking as I do that the Creator of this World is a very Cruel Being," he once said, "& being a Worshipper of Christ, I cannot help saying: 'The Son, O how unlike the Father!' First God Almighty comes with a Thump on the Head. The Jesus Christ comes with a balm to heal it" ("A Vision of the Last Judgment," 617). Such a portrait was recognizable in the teachings of some Christian denominations, particularly gloomier ones; and it may be relevant that although the Blake children were baptized in an Anglican church (St. James's in Piccadilly), their father seems to have joined the Baptists, at least for the time. It is possible, therefore, that Blake was forced to read their hymns while attending chapel services with his father.

In any case, he could hardly have escaped acquaintance with the works of Isaac Watts, one of the most popular hymn writers in the eighteenth century. As we have seen, the *Songs of Innocence and of Experience* read in places like satirical versions of Watts's *Divine and Moral Songs for Children.* The God whom Watts paints likewise is a recognizable version of the "Cruel Being" whom Blake disliked. The fact that Watts was not a very subtle poet should not blind us to the impact that his descriptions of divine justice would have on an imagination so vivid as Blake's. It is easy to imagine him turning Watts's pages and reacting indignantly to the idea of the universe conveyed here, a universe in which men are invited to pursue their pleasure if they wish, but in which nevertheless a day of judgment awaits them. One of the hymns begins

Adore and tremble, for our GOD
Is a *Consuming Fire.*
His jealous Eyes his Wrath inflame
And raise his Vengeance higher.
("Divine Wrath and Mercy")

This is a prototype of the "jealous god" whom Blake conveys in Urizen; another of Watts's portraits comes even closer to the cold power that is stored in Blake's figure:

God has a Thousand Terrors in his Name,
A thousand Armies at Command
Waiting the signal of his Hand,
And Magazines of Frost, and Magazines of Flame.
Dress thee in Steel to meet his Wrath
His sharp Artillery of the *North*
Shall pierce thee to the Soul, and shake thy mortal Frame.
("Divine Judgments")

Imagery such as this, along with that of a God with "Stores of Lightning" seems to have been at the back of Blake's mind as he depicted Urizen in *The Four Zoas* as basing himself in the north, or in *America* (1793) described how

. . . his jealous wings wav'd over the deep;
Weeping in dismal howling woe, he dark descended, howling
Around the smitten bands, clothed in tears & trembling, shudd'ring cold.
His stored snows he poured forth, and his icy magazines
He opened on the deep, and on the Atlantic sea white shiv'ring
Leprous his limbs, all over white, and hoary was his visage. . . .
(203)

In Blake's work Urizen is always a cold god, working through snow, ice, and cold plagues. The fire and lightning are reserved for his opponent Orc, the uprising spirit of energy that cannot find humanized form.

There are many other places in which Watts's images can be discerned in Blake's writings, particularly during the early period, betraying his horror at the workings of such a God.

Long ere the lofty Skies were spread,
Jehovah fill'd his Throne,
Or Adam form'd, or Angels made,
The Maker liv'd alone . . .
("God's Eternity")

wrote Watts, who also painted a vivid picture of God making the human body, heart, brains, and lungs, in turn, and writing out his promise of redemption for men:

. . . His Hand has writ the sacred Word
With an immortal Pen.
Engraved as in eternal Brass
The mighty promise shines . . .
("The Faithfulness of God in the Promises")

Blake, translating this language into its visual imagery, could have gained some strong hints toward his depiction of Urizen, who turned aside from the light, color, and harmony of the Eternals to brood in solitude, "A self-contemplating shadow,/In enormous labours occupied" and wrote out his laws with an iron pen. When he eventually reports on his activities, it is in the words

Lo! I unfold my darkness, and on
This rock place with strong hand the Book
Of eternal brass, written in my solitude.
(*The First Book of Urizen,* 224)

That "Book,' contains all the Christian virtues, but reduced to laws: "Laws of peace, of love, of unity,/Of pity, compassion, forgiveness." Everything is reduced to standardization, in the hope of imposing permanence.

Blake, by contrast, believes the human quest for permanence to be mistaken. In a world of life, fixity is impossible to achieve; the task of human beings is to learn how to live in a world where changes, shifts, and transformations are part of the essential process. "We are born to Cares and Woes" writes Watts gloomily in one of his hymns; Blake's version sees the human condition as one of necessary alternations:

> Man was made for Joy & Woe;
> And when this we rightly know
> Thro, the world we safely go.
> Joy & Woe are woven fine,
> A Clothing for the Soul divine;
> Under every grief & pine
> Runs a joy with silken twine.
> ("Auguries of Innocence," 432)

He did not wish to deny the existence of griefs and sorrows, but believed that a view of the world that made them central was at once mistaken and dangerous, fostering a defensive attitude in individuals and a desire for permanence that was Urizen's great mistake, reflected in the mental captivity of his eighteenth-century subjects.

Looking closely at Urizen's activities, we see that, as elsewhere, Blake's purpose was not simply to attack his predecessor. In one sense he was on the side of Watts, whose work possessed a grandeur, and even visionary power, that he could respect deeply. The questions that were agitating him, on the other hand, deeper than any faced by Watts, related to his own vision. How was it that the beauty and delight that he discovered everywhere in the world seemed not to be noticed at all by his fellows? Why did they persist in disregarding not only their own imaginative faculties but also the psychic experiences induced by terror or the free exercise of energy?

At one level Blake found it easy to locate humanity's enemies. They formed the alliance of church and state attacked by eighteenth-century radicals such as Jean Messelier, who in his will, published by Voltaire, desired to see the last king strangled with the guts of the last priest. Looked at from a hostile point of view, the eighteenth-century church could be seen as lending supernatural backing to the authority of a law that was in fact no more than the will of an entrenched ruling class needing to secure its power more firmly.

Some of Blake's most memorable writings were spurred on by his sense of the social iniquities resulting from such an imposition. But, as has been said, he seems to have suspected also that there was something in the human psyche that allowed complicity in such conspiracies. It was hard to believe that the whole human race would have allowed itself to be hoodwinked for so long if some power in the mind were not assenting to the enforcement of law. From another point of view, it was hard to see how the rule of a solid law had come to be established against the setting of an eternity that consisted of "visionary forms dramatic." In such terms it was possible to take a much more sympathetic view of the ruling powers, seeing them as representatives of a blinded humanity that sought security in a world it did not understand and in which it felt constantly threatened by dangers of all kinds. So he moved toward the development of a mythology of his own that might help resolve some of these puzzles.

Urizen, in this larger view, is not just a "jealous god" whose purposes are inexplicably malignant, but a being who is bewildered, having lost his way in eternity and turned away from its light and energy to become wrapped in dark ruminations of his own. This view entails a total retelling of the Creation story as found in the Hebrew and Christian Scriptures. The creative "brooding" of the Spirit on the face of the waters in Genesis is replaced by the self-enclosed "brooding" of Urizen; the biblical Creation, a positive making on a firm basis in the midst of darkness and nonentity, by a work of desperation in the face of loss. Urizen begins to create the world we know, but in the hope of establishing ramparts against chaos in a universe where he has lost his bearings. Because he has turned away from eternity, where vision and energy are harmonized, he must continue to suffer the despair of a darkened imagination and the fears of a thwarted energy that returns to threaten his standing.

It was his interest in these questions that led Blake away from the short lyrics in which he excelled to the longer enterprise that we now think of as the prophetic books. A comment is needed on the word "prophetic." Blake's use of it did not mean that he claimed to be foretelling the future in any detailed sense. A better guide to his attitude is found in one of his own statements on the subject:

> Prophets, in the modern sense of the word, have never existed. Jonah was no prophet in the modern sense, for his prophecy of Nineveh failed. Every honest man is a Prophet; he utters his opinion both of private & public matters. Thus If you go on So, the result is So. He never says, such a thing shall happen let you do what you will. A Prophet is a Seer, not an Arbitrary Dictator. . . . (annotation to Richard Watson's *Apology for the Bible,* 392)

He was looking, in other words, for the patterns of significance underlying human events. By comparison with the Bible, where the common assumption was that human ills were due to transgression of the divine law and that the God behind the universe was a great and gloomy lawmaker, Blake believed many of the ills of the world to result from a loss of imagination and an unwillingness to cultivate human energies in freedom. A mythology conceived in those terms provided, he thought, a more convincing interpretation of human existence than those normally derived from the Bible; if universally accepted, moreover, it would offer greater possibilities of human amelioration.

The resulting enterprise began with two poems, "Tiriel" and *The Book of Thel,* where Blake reorders well-known mythical narratives such as that of the Garden of Eden; it proceeded with the Lambeth books, such as *America* and *Europe* (1794), in which he offered his own interpretations of recent history; and it came to a climax in *Vala, Or the Four Zoas* (1797), in which he attempted to set out a total mythical pattern that could be applied to the whole of human history as well as to every individual human life.

The poem that resulted is one of the most interesting and extraordinary in English literature. It takes its form from Edward Young's *Night Thoughts* (1742–1745), which is, like this poem, organized in "nights" rather than "books"; but it is in most respects different from Young's poem, which has a very recognizable figure, that of the narrator, at the center of its reflections. It resembles *Night Thoughts* further only at the deepest level: its serious concern with life, death, and immortality. Since Blake rejects the normal Christian expectation of an immortality after death in favor of an eternity that lies about us all the time if we could only see it, he adopts a different approach, which takes some coloring from *Paradise Lost.* In Milton's poem we are made to feel not only that Satan has fallen from heaven but also that he is gradually forgetting what it was like, to be reminded only when he glimpses light in the distance or meets one of its inhabitants again. The characters of Blake's poem are in a similar state, moving about in a world they resent, yet haunted by the sense that things were once otherwise. From time to time one of the characters will have a dream in which some part of the story of their disruption is recaptured, so that the reader can gradually build up, through these flashbacks, a full picture of what that state was like.

These characters are not fully formed human beings, since it is a part of Blake's contention that what has been lost is the presence of an integrating power that should work in the human psyche and harmonize its various functions. Each Zoa embodies one of these conflicting functions, Urizen being associated with the head, Luvah with the heart, Tharmas with the genitals, and Urthona with the shaping powers generally. At times it may seem that Urizen is to blame for the disruption, with his substitution of eighteenth-century mathematical rationality for a more creative and imaginative kind of reasoning. At times it is the lost genital innocence of Tharmas that seems responsible. At times the other two Zoas are frightened by the unbridled energy of the figure Orc, a burning boy who threatens them with destruction from the region of the heart. In the course of the work, though, it becomes clear that these three are diminished by some deeper catastrophe: that Urizen's rationality, Tharmas, lost innocence, and Orc's uprising are the result of a deeper failure, to be localized, if anywhere, in the heart, Orc's bursting out there being the result of Luvah's impotence.

Gradually, moreover, the flashbacks make it clear that the failure does not rest even there, but with the Eternal Man, who allowed himself to be deluded by an illusion of impossible purity and holiness, and so failed in the noonday sun, sinking into a sleep within which all these events are nightmares. The implication is that if the Eternal Man awakens again, his self-recall will be felt first and foremost in the heart, and then almost simultaneously in a revival of vision in the reasoning powers and a regaining of sexual innocence.

One power has not been discussed so far. Urthona, associated with the earth forces, has been rendered even more impotent than the others by the failure of the Eternal Man. His powers can be expressed only by his representative Los, who lives primarily in his hands and feet, and can use them either to express his rage and frustration in a mad dance or to create into form anything that comes within reach. His is a visionless creativity, to be valued for its positive energy but powerless by itself to redeem the situation.

Eventually, in the last Night, an apocalypse takes place. In a rending of the universe, the Zoas find themselves pitched into a turmoil through which they recover a sense of their lost significance. Subsequent scenes of reconciliation are followed by a conclusion in which they are all seen and heard working in their ancient harmony, for the service of a restored humanity.

In certain respects this has the makings of a successful modern epic. It substitutes for the idea of a fall of man into states of sin and guilt the sense of a lost integration of the personality that many psychoanalysts, particularly those of the Jungian school, would later see as a valid account of the human condition. It is also unique in its time for the honesty of its representations of behavior, regarding sexual deviation (a theme still more evident in the illustrations) and sexual fulfillment as important factors when considering psychic health.

Blake's decision not to publish the poem suggests that he was not fully satisfied with it—a feeling that may be associated with the form he had chosen. What he had not seen in advance, perhaps, was that any attempt at a mythical interpretation for the whole of experience might in itself be a work of Urizen. In any case, such a form was bound to run into difficulties. To have main characters who were not full human beings was to make for shadowy forms of action; even more difficult was the task of writing in terms of a mythology that the reader needed to discover (or even invent) as he went along. By comparison with Milton, who could take it for granted that his reader would know the basic story of the Creation and the Fall of man from the Bible and other accounts, Blake tells a story that is founded largely in his own ideas about the meaning of human existence. The central conception—that of finding an interpretation of human civilization that would also interpret the history of every individual human being—is a brilliant one, but the structural difficulties turn out to be immense. As the poem proceeds, Blake seems to become steadily more confined within the terms he has set himself.

But if there is in one sense a failure here, it is the kind of failure that reaches above most poetic successes. One cannot read *The Four Zoas* without a sense of a strong intelligence and imagination at play. In the early Nights the depiction of Urizen trying to construct a permanent world in the midst of a desolate space and time that he does not comprehend is particularly brilliant. For the general reader the most memorable passages of all are likely to be the cries of the main victims as they describe their deprivations. Blake knew well that to those who are comfortably situated the world looks very different from the way it looks to those who are suffering from injustice and need. In the early Nights of the poem the victim's view is expressed in several passages of unforgettable poignancy:

"What is the price of Experience? do men buy it for a song?
Or wisdom for a dance in the street? No, it is bought with the price
Of all that a man hath, his house, his wife, his children.
Wisdom is sold in the desolate market where none come to buy,
And in the wither'd field where the farmer plows for bread in vain.

"It is an easy thing to triumph in the summer's sun
And in the vintage & to sing on the waggon loaded with corn.
It is an easy thing to talk of patience to the afflicted,
To speak the laws of prudence to the houseless wanderer,
To listen to the hungry raven's cry in wintry season
When the red blood is fill'd with wine & with the marrow of lambs.

"It is an easy thing to laugh at wrathful elements,
To hear the dog howl at the wintry door, the ox in the slaughter house moan;
To see a god on every wind & a blessing on every blast;
To hear sounds of love in the thunder storm that destroys our enemy s house;
To rejoice in the blight that covers his field, & the sickness that cuts off his children,
While our olive & vine sing & laugh round our door, & our children bring fruits & flowers.

"Then the groan & the dolor are quite forgotten, & the slave grinding at the mill,
And the captive in chains, & the poor in the prison, & the soldier in the field
When the shatter'd bone hath laid him groaning among the happier dead.

"It is an easy thing to rejoice in the tents of prosperity:
Thus could I sing & thus rejoice: but it is not so with me."
("Night the Second," 290)

Leaving behind the much revised *Four Zoas,* Blake went on to engrave two poems of looser structure, *Milton* (1804–1808) and *Jerusalem* (1804–1820). Each of these develops themes inherent in the earlier poem but without attempting a fully coherent narrative. *Milton* is primarily about inspiration, a manifesto for the role of the poetic genius in his time. The Milton who is Blake's model is a Milton appropriate to the new age, subduing the spectrous Puritan morals and rational devotion to law that rendered poems such as *Paradise Lost* inadequate for the future, and so releasing himself into the full vigor and self-giving illumination that Blake regards as his underlying qualities. The eighteenth-century world is seen as dominated by thinkers who wish to reduce it finally to quantitative measurement and the rule of law; it is the work of the poetic genius, by contrast, to explore the moment of illumination that can never be organized into any time scheme, to enter into the timelessness of certain sensuous experiences (the lark pouring out its song as it ascends the sky, the flower with its power to overwhelm the senses with its scent) and find in them the true significance of the world.

This is the point of some of the more mysterious sayings in *Milton*:

There is a Moment in each Day that Satan cannot find,
Nor can his Watch Fiends find it; but the industrious find

This Moment & it multiply, & when it once
is found
It renovates every Moment of the Day if
rightly placed. (526)

We may compare William Wordsworth's "There are in our existence spots of time/ That with distinct preeminence retain/A renovating virtue. . . . Or, again:

Every Time less than a pulsation of the
artery
Is equal in its period & value to Six
Thousand Years,

For in this Period the Poet's Work is Done;
and all the Great
Events of Time start forth & are conceiv'd
in such a Period,
Within a Moment, a Pulsation of the Artery.
(516)

The poem, though not easy reading, is full of brilliant ideas and images of this kind, reordering the world in the image of a nature full of momentary inspirations. *Jerusalem,* by comparison, is a more patient work, devoted to Blake's belief that the long-term work of the artist is to continue making, giving forms to things, since this is the only true work of redemption that is possible in the world. Los is now the hero.

In these later prophetic books there are many references to Christianity—so many that at first sight Blake might appear to have been converted back to the established religion of his fellow Englishmen. Many of his paintings, similarly, are devoted to biblical subjects, and there was certainly a shift in his attitude somewhere about the turn of the century. He seems to have decided that for all its shortcomings Christianity was the religion by which the forces of imagination had been most successfully nurtured. For the rest of his life, therefore, he supported it, though still very much on his own terms. The Bible was to be read not, as was common in his time, for its promulgation of the moral law, but for its dreams and visions and for its accounts of visionaries and prophets who had suffered for their beliefs. Like many religions, Christianity was to be seen as constantly dominated by priests intent on maintaining the existing order; it was also, on the other hand, founded in the life of a supreme visionary, Jesus of Nazareth, who had had little respect for either priests or conventions.

Blake's mature attitude to the Christian religion is set out in a poem entitled "The Everlasting Gospel" a fragmentary piece devoted to the theme that Jesus fulfilled the law by destroying it: he was not particularly humble, he forgave the woman taken in adultery—indeed, as the Devil in *The Marriage of Heaven and Hell* had pointed out, he broke most of the Ten Commandments at one time or another, because he "acted from impulse, not from rules." In many respects he could be seen as proclaiming Blake's own religion, which, in contradistinction to that preached by the church, set man at the center of things—but man interpreted through his powers of energy and imagination:

Thou art a Man, God is no more,
Thine own Humanity learn to adore. . . .
(750)

Jerusalem belongs to the same strain of thought, and the references to Christianity there must be read with that in mind. When Blake uses names and places from the Bible, it is not in order to refer the reader back to Christianity as commonly accepted, but to encourage a new interpretation. (He may also have hoped to make his poem more readily comprehensible by using familiar names and terms, though such names, when not used with their normal connotations, can be more, rather than less, bewildering at first sight.)

The reader should not expect to find a single, coherent narrative. The indications are that various of the single plates and sequences of plates were engraved over many years and then assembled into the four chapters of the final version. There is a general theme, the sleep and ultimate awakening of the Eternal Man; there is also some special motif for each chapter, announced in the preface. But there are many other themes and ideas at work; the reader will do best not to worry about unusual names and terms in the first instance, but to read the poem steadily with a sense of Blake's general themes and his loftiness of approach. If there is a list of English counties, with their equivalents among the tribes of Israel, this may be not an attempt to make a series of detailed parallels but a hint to the reader that if the poets and prophets of Israel could find splendor and sublimity in the provinces and landscapes of their native land, there is no reason why an English reader should not find similar qualities in the landscapes and cities of the British Isles. The more radical ideas at work in the poem are subtly deployed, sometimes surfacing choose to ignore them and read at a more general in a particular name or unusual word. Readers who level will find much to admire, but investigation of them will increase their respect for Blake's intelligence and imaginative power still further.

Looking at the high visionary intent of such a poem, we may well ask what had happened to the more satirical and dramatizing Blake of earlier years. There are touches of wit in *Jerusalem,* and some good dramatic moments, but the work as a whole is not pitched for an audience that would put such qualities in the forefront. During the 1790's Blake hat shifted from his ingenious advocacy of extremism in *The Marriage of Heaven and Hell* to an extremist practice of his own, offering suggestions of illuminations and inspiration that his readers were free to follow or not, as they chose:

> I give you the end of a golden string,
> Only wind it into a ball,
> It will lead you in at Heaven's gate,
> Built in Jerusalem's wall.
> (*Jerusalem,* 716)

Despite his self-dedication in carrying forward his enterprise, Blake was too human not to feel the effects of opposition and neglect. On the one hand he pressed firmly on, asserting in private the lasting quality of his work:

> Still admir'd by Noble minds,
> Follow'd by Envy on the winds,
> Re-engrav'd Time after Time,
> Ever in their youthful prime,
> My designs unchang'd remain.
> Time may rage but rage in vain.
> For above Time's troubled Fountains
> On the Great Atlantic Mountains,
> In my Golden House on high,
> There they Shine Eternally.
> ("The Caverns of the Grave I've Seen," 558)

When he felt himself driven too far by the patronizing attitudes of others, he could set down his feelings—again in private: the sardonic power of the early writings would then reemerge in a more virulent form. William Hayley, who befriended him and gave him commissions, was unappreciative of his individual genius, Blake in turn considered him passive and basically uninspired. His feelings found vent in pithy epigrams:

> Thus Hayley on his Toilette seeing the sope,
> Cries, "Homer is very much improv'd by Pope." (556)

> Of Hayley's birth this was the happy lot
> His Mother on his Father him begot.
> (539)

T. S. Eliot praised Blake for his "terrifying honesty" and Samuel Palmer called him "a man without a mask." Neither of these characterizations ought to be taken too literally, as the private notebooks make clear. William Hayley can hardly have known some of the things that Blake thought of him, or he would not have continued to refer to him (with continuing patronization) as "our good Blake." What is being referred to is, rather, the sincerity of his major art, resulting from a determination to say what he feels, when he chooses to say it, without curtainings of Augustan decorum or concessions to the demands of propriety.

When Blake did make more public statements of his bitterness, they were often in aid of the depressed arts of his time, as in his *Public Address and Descriptive Catalogue,* where he campaigned for his own kind of visionary art. In private marginal comments on Sir Joshua Reynolds, first *Discourse,* he attacked the rich men of England, who, he said, "form themselves into a Society to Sell and Not to Buy Pictures":

> When Nations grow Old, The Arts grow
> Cold
> And Commerce settles on every Tree,
> And the Poor & the Old can live upon Gold,
> For all are Born Poor, Aged Sixty three.
> (452)

The social criticism inherent in *Songs of Experience* evidently remained very much alive in his mind, and from one point of view it is to be regretted that his former free-playing intelligence, ready to direct itself toward satire or vision in alternate breaths, did not survive more vigorously in his later works.

It is impossible not to honor the single-mindedness and determination with which Blake pursued his unusual view of the world, on the other hand, and the reader who engages with them will discover their peculiar rewards—particularly if one or two guidelines are followed. The first is that when one is puzzled by a piece of the text or by an unusual design, it is often helpful to look both for the point of imaginative illumination and for the moment of energy. These can take innumerable forms. Sometimes they may be simply stylized, as when a figure with long, flowing locks of hair is connected with imagination, while one with closely coiled curls has to do with energy (a bald figure being, by the same token, devoid of both). Or vision and energy may work through alternating poems, as with those lyrics in *Songs of Innocence* that find their counterparts in *Songs of Experience.* It is in the interplay of the two qualities that a central key to Blake's complexities is most often found. Second, it is always important to keep in mind Blake's most vivid statements, whether in his poetry or in his designs. Obscure passages sometimes reveal their significance when considered in the light of his powerful positive images, whether of enthrallment (as in the illustrations to *The Book of Urizen*) or of human potentiality—figures running through fire, angels singing for joy, faces bearing the lineaments of desire. These are the images and statements by which he lived and for which he was content to work in isolation and obscurity.

From 1818, Blake enjoyed a time of increasing serenity. This was partly due to his friendship with John Linnell, who introduced him to a wider circle of friends. His chief influence was now upon the young painters of the time, including Samuel Palmer, Frederick Tatham, Edward Calvert, and George Richmond, who formed a group called the Ancients. Another young disciple, Francis Finch, declared that Blake "struck him as *a new kind of man,* wholly original, and in all things." He was widely respected; but except for one or two grants from benevolent funds, little was done to assist his poverty.

In these years Blake could still be mercilessly satirical and teasing when in the company of devotees of rationalism, but was equally noted for his kindness and consideration to the young. Little poetry was written, but he occupied himself with further illustrations, including the well-known Job designs and a beautiful series of watercolors to illustrate Dante's *Divine Comedy.* The old alternation between vision and vehemence continued to move him, as may be seen from the memories of people who met him at this time. One, a lady, was taken to him as a young girl:

> . . . he looked at her very kindly for a long while without speaking, and then stroking her head and long ringlets said "May God make this world to you, my child, as beautiful as it has been to me." She thought it strange at the time, she said, that such a poor old man, dressed in such shabby clothes, could imagine the world had ever been so beautiful to him as it must be to her, nursed in all the elegancies and luxury of wealth; but in after years she understood well enough what he meant. . . . (*Blake Records,* 274–275)

This reminiscence may be set in contiguity with one by the young Samuel Palmer, who found Blake at work on his Dante drawings:

"He said he began them with fear and trembling. I said 'O! I have enough of fear and trembling.' 'Then,' said he, 'you'll do'" (ibid., 291). Whether he was opening himself to the beauties of the world about him or working in the realm of energy that stretched from states of fear and trembling to states of ecstatic freedom, Blake retained his sturdy independence to the last. In one of his final letters, he can be seen facing death with equanimity, and with a sense that he is at last to be released from the body's cage. The images of the prison that haunted his early work have gradually been exorcised, but Blake still looks forward to death for a final release:

> Flaxman is Gone & we must All soon follow, every one to his Own Eternal House, Leaving the Delusive Goddess Nature & her Laws to get into Freedom from all Law of the Members into The Mind, in which every one is King & Priest in his own House. God send it so on Earth as it is in Heaven. (letter to George Cumberland, 12 April 1827)

Earlier in the letter he inveighs against his fellow countrymen who, since the French Revolution,

> . . . are all Intermeasurable by One Another, Certainly a happy state of Agreement to which I for One do not Agree. God keep me from the Divinity of Yes & No too, The Yea Nay Creeping Jesus, from supposing Up & Down to be the same Thing as all Experimentalists must suppose.

Because he had remained so firmly independent of his fellows, Blake had cut himself off from some of the resources of communication that would have facilitated reception of his work. To this day a full appreciation of it calls for unusual efforts—not simply an empathizing with Blake's various states of vision, but a willingness to enter into the strenuous dialectic of mind involved. We need to understand both the moods in which he could remain passive to the visitations of imaginative experience and those in which he committed himself to the harmonies and energies of creative work. Yet in all his works there are taproots to the vividness of the works to which the general reader responds first of all.

Blake might seem in his later years to have shut himself off deliberately from the world about him. But as one penetrates further into his life and work, one comes to see that his firm independence, baffling at first sight to the aspiring reader, was really the defense for his belief in a bounding line of freedom and a capacity for illumination that he believed to be the inner condition of all human beings, if they could only find their way back to it. Stubborn and self-assertive he might be, but he was still serving the cause of human freedom.

Selected Bibliography

BIBLIOGRAPHIES

Keynes, G., *A Bibliography of William Blake,* (New York, 1921) rev. ed., (1953) originally a lim. ed. printed for the Grolier Club and since extended, by the first major biographer of Blake; Bentley, G. E., Jr. *Blake Books: Annotated Catalogues of Blake's Writings, Designs, Engravings, Books He Owned and Critical Works About Him,* (Oxford, 1977).

COLLECTED WORKS

Ellis, E. J., and Yeats, W. B., *The Works, Poetic, Symbolic, and Critical, Edited with Lithographs of the Illustrated "Prophetic Books" and a Memoir and Interpretation* 3 vols. (London, 1893) largely of historical interest; G. Keynes, ed. *Writings (in Verse and Prose),* 3 vols. (London, 1925) with reproductions and a portrait; Keynes, G., *The Complete Writings,* (London, 1957) a new ed. of that of 1925, with variant readings; rev. continually and repr. from 1966 onward in the Oxford Standard Authors series, the best plain text for the general reader; D. V. Erdman, ed. *The Poetry and Prose of William Blake,* (New York, 1965) commentary by H. Bloom, less complete than Keynes but reproduces Blake's idiosyncratic punctuation more precisely; W. H. Stevenson, ed. *The Poems of William Blake,* (London, 1971) the only fully annotated ed., uses Erdman's text; D. V. Erdman, ed. *The Illuminated Blake,* (London, 1975) reproduces in monochrome all the works in illuminated printing; Bentley, G. E., Jr. *William Blake's Writings,* 2 vols. (Oxford, 1977) the most fully edited text in bibliographical terms, illuminations to the text reproduced in line.

SEPARATE WORKS

Note: Entries marked * were engraved, printed, and published in small eds. by Blake himself as specimens of "illuminated printing"; those marked +' have since been reproduced in facs. eds. by the Trianon Press. Additional facs. eds. are N. Bogen, ed., *The Book of Thel* (Providence, 1971), and the K. P. Easson and R. R. Easson, eds., *The Book of Urizen and Milton,* K. P. Easson and R. R. Easson, eds. both Boulder, Colo. (1978).

Poetical Sketches, (London, 1783) verse; * + *All Religions Are One,* (London, ca. 1788) prose, 10 plates, only one copy recorded; * + *There Is No Natural Religion,* (London, ca. 1788) prose, 19 plates, no complete copy recorded; * + *Songs of Innocence,* (London, 1789) verse, 31 plates; * + *The Book of Thel,* (London, 1789) verse, 8 plates; *Tiriel,* (London, ca. 1789) verse, not printed in Blake's lifetime, first complete and accurate text, from the MS in the British Museum, in the Nonesuch eds. of 1925 and 1927; facs. and transcript of the MS, reproductions of the drawings, and a commentary on the poem by G. E. Bentley, Jr. (Oxford, 1967); * + *The Marriage of Heaven and Hell and A Song of Liberty,* (London, ca. 1790) prose, 27 plates; *The French Revolution. A Poem in Seven Books,* (London, 1791) verse, the first book not published in Blake's lifetime, the only recorded copy is probably a proof; Blake completed only the first book; * + *Visions of the Daughters of Albion,* (London, 1793) verse, 11 plates;* + *America. A Prophecy,* (London, 1793) verse, 18 plates; * + *Songs of Innocence and of Experience, Showing the Two Contrary States of the Human Soul,* (London, 1794) verse, 54 plates, facs. ed. reproduced from the original first ed. by G. Keynes (London, 1967); * + *Europe. A Prophecy,* (London, 1794) verse, 18 plates; * + *The First Book of Urizen,* (London, 1794) verse, 28 plates; + *The Song of Los,* (London, 1795) verse, 8 plates; + *The Book of Los,* (London, 1795) verse, 5 plates; *Vala, Or the Four Zoas,* (London, 1795–1804) verse, not printed in Blake's lifetime, first complete and accurate text, from the MS in the British Museum, in the Nonesuch eds. of 1925 and 1927; also by H. M. Margoliouth, ed. (London, 1956) an attempted reconstruction of one of its early states, and the facs. by G. E. Bentley, Jr., ed. (Oxford, 1963) includes all illustrations; * + *The Book of Ahania,* (London, 1795) verse, 6 plates, only one copy recorded; * + *Milton,* (London, 1804–1808) verse, 45 plates; * + *Jerusalem. The Emanation of the Giant Albion,* (London, 1804–1820) verse, 100 plates, not completed until 1820; *Blake's Chaucer: The Canterbury Pilgrims,* (London, 1809) a prospectus by Blake for an engraving of his fresco of the Canterbury pilgrims; *A Descriptive Catalogue of Pictures, Poetical and Historical Inventions. Painted in Water Colours, Being the Ancient Method of Fresco Painting Restored: and Drawings for Public Inspection,* (London, 1809) comp. by Blake for an exhibition of his works; + *For the Sexes: The Gates of Paradise,* (London, ca. 1818) emblems, 21 plates, a rev. ed. of *For Children: The Gates of Paradise* (London, 1793) with text added.

Blake also designed and engraved illustrations for a number of books. The most important of these are Edward Young's *Night Thoughts* (London, 1797) Blair, Robert, *The Grave,* (London, 1808) Thornton's, Robert, *The Pastorals of Virgil,* (London, 1821) *The Book of Job,* (London, 1825).

LETTERS AND NOTEBOOKS

Letters from William Blake to Thomas Butts, 1800–1803, printed in facs. with an intro. note by G. Keynes, (Oxford, 1926); *The Note Book of William Blake Called The Rossetti Manuscript,* G. Keynes, ed., (London, 1935) with a facs. of the Note Book, the verbal contents of this sketchbook and commonplace book used by Blake in 1793–1818 are included in the Nonesuch eds. of 1925 and 1927; D. V. Erdman and D. Moore, eds., *The Notebook of William Blake; A Photographic and Typographic Facsimile,* (Oxford, 1973) more fully edited than Keynes's ed.

CRITICAL STUDIES

Swinburne, A. C., *William Blake: A Critical Essay,* (London, 1868); Yeats, W. B., *Ideas of Good and Evil,* (London, 1903) contains "William Blake and His Illustrations to the Divine Comedy"; Wicksteed, J. H., *Blake's Vision of the Book of Job,* (London, 1910) rev. ed., 1924, see also his *Blake's Innocence and Experience* (London, 1928); Saurat, D., *Blake and Milton,* (Bordeaux, 1920) rev. ed. (1935), see also his *Blake and Modern Thought,* (London, 1929); Damon, S. F., *William Blake: His Philosophy and Symbols,* (Boston, 1924); Plowman, M., *An Introduction to the Study of Blake,* (London, 1927) new ed. (1967); Murry, J. M., *William Blake,* (London, 1933); Percival, M. O., *William Blake's Circle of Destiny,* (New York, 1938); Lowery, M. R., *Windows of the Morning. A Critical Study of "Poetical Sketches," 1783* (New Haven, Conn., 1940); Bronowski, J., *A Man Without A Mask: William Blake, 1757–1827,* (London, 1944) reiss. as *William Blake and the Age of Revolution,* (New York, 1965); Preston, K., *Blake and Rossetti,* (London, 1944); Schorer, M., *William Blake: The Politics of Vision,* (New York, 1946); Todd, R., *Tracks in the Snow. Studies in English Science and Art,* (London, 1946) contains a study of Blake and the eighteenth-century mythologists; Frye, N., *Fearful Symmetry. A Study of William Blake,* (Princeton, N.J., 1947); Davies, J. G., *The Theology of William Blake,* (Oxford, 1948);

Keynes, G., *Blake Studies. Notes on His Life and Works,* (London, 1949) contains a bibliography of Keynes's writings on Blake; Blackstone, B., *English Blake,* (London, 1949); Margoliouth, H. M., *William Blake,* (London, 1951); J. H. Wicksteed, ed., *William Blake's "Jerusalem,"* (London, 1953) a commentary on the facs. published by the William Blake Trust; Gardner, S., *Infinity or the Anvil: A Critical Study of Blake's Poetry,* (Oxford, 1954); Erdman, D. V., *Blake—Prophet Against Empire,* (London, 1954) rev. eds. (1969, 1977); Adams, H., *Blake and Yeats. The Contrary Vision,* (Ithaca, N.Y., 1955); V. de Sola Pinto, ed., *The Divine Vision,* (London, 1957) contains essays on Blake by various hands; Morton, A. L., *The Everlasting Gospel: A Study in the Sources of William Blake,* (London, 1958); Glechner, R. F., *The Piper and the Road: A Study of William Blake,* (Detroit, 1959); Bowra, C. M., *The Prophetic Element,* (London, 1960) presidential address to the English Association; Fisher, P. F., *The Valley of Vision: Blake as Prophet and Revolutionary,* N. Frye, ed., (London, 1961); Harper, G. M., *The Neo-Platonism of William Blake,* (Chapel Hill, N. C., 1961); Bloom, H., *Blake's Apocalypse: A Study in Poetic Argument,* (New Haven, Conn., 1963); W. R. Hughes, ed., *Jerusalem,* (London, 1964) with commentary and notes by Hughes, a simplified ed.; Hirsch, E. D., Jr., *Innocence and Experience: An Introduction to Blake,* (New Haven, Conn., 1964); Ostriker, A., *Vision and Verse in William Blake,* (Madison-Milwaukee, 1965); Gillham, D. G., *Blake's Contrary States: The "Songs of Innocence and of Experience" as Dramatic Poems,* (Cambridge, 1966); Altizer, T. J. J., *The New Apocalypse: The Radical Christian Vision of William Blake,* (Ann Arbor, Mich., 1967); Holloway, J., *Blake: The Lyric Poetry,* (London, 1968); Beer, J. B., *Blake's Humanism,* (Manchester, 1968); Lister, R., *William Blake: An Introduction to the Man and to His Work,* (London, 1968); Raine, K., *Blake and Tradition,* 2 vols. (New York, 1968; London, 1969), Andrew Mellon Lectures, 1962, reiss. in shorter form as *Blake and Antiquity* (London, 1970); A. H. Rosenfeld, ed., *William Blake: Essays for S. Foster Damon,* (Providence, 1969); Beer, J. B., *Blake's Visionary Universe,* (Manchester, 1969); Dorfman, D., *Blake in the Nineteenth Century: His Reputation as a Poet from Gilchrist to Yeats,* (New Haven, Conn., 1969); Paley, M. D., *Energy and the Imagination: A Study of the Development of Blake's Thought,* (Oxford, 1970); Paley, M. D., and Phillips, M., *William Blake: Essays in Honour of Sir Geoffrey Keynes,* (Oxford, 1973); Wagenknecht, D., *Blake's Night: William Blake and the Idea of Pastoral,* (Cambridge, Mass., 1973); S. Curran and J. A. Wittreich, Jr., eds. *Blake's Sublime Allegory: Essays on The Four Zoas, Milton, and Jerusalem,* (Madison, Wis., 1973); Nurmi, M. K., *William Blake,* (London, 1974); Frosch, T., *The Awakening of Albion,* (Ithaca, N.Y., 1974); Ault, D. D., *Visionary Physics: Blake's Response to Newton,* (Chicago, 1974); Fox, S., *Poetic Form in Blake's "Milton,"* (Princeton, N.J., 1976); R. N. Essick and D. Pearce, eds., *Blake in His Time,* (Bloomington, Ind., 1978); M. Phillips, ed., *Interpreting Blake,* (Cambridge, 1978); Raine, K., *Blake and the New Age,* (London, 1979).

COLLECTIONS OF CRITICAL ESSAYS

Grant, J. E., *Discussions of William Blake,* (Boston, 1961); Frye, N., *Blake: A Collection of Critical Essays,* (Englewood Cliffs N.J., 1966); Paley, M. D., *Twentieth Century Interpretations of Songs of Innocence and Experience,* (Englewood Cliffs, N.J., 1969); O'Neill, J., *Critics on Blake: Readings in Literary Criticism,* (London, 1970); Bottrall, M., *William Blake: Songs of Innocence and Experience: A Casebook,* (London, 1970).

BIOGRAPHICAL STUDIES

Palmer, A. H., *The Life and Letters of Samuel Palmer,* (London, 1802); Malkin, B. H., *An Account of Blake's Early Life,* preface to *A Father's Memoir of His Child* (London, 1806); Gilchrist, A., *The Life of William Blake,* 2 vols., rev. ed. (London, 1863) the best ed. of this classic biography is by R. Todd, ed., in the Everyman's Library; Swinburne, A. C., *William Blake: A Critical Essay,* (London, 1868); Tatham, F., *Life,* (London, 1906) preface to A. G. B. Russell, ed., *The Letters of William Blake* (London, 1906); Wilson, M., *The Life of William Blake,* (London, 1927), rev. ed. with additional notes (London, 1948), the standard biography; G. E. Bentley, Jr., ed., *Blake Records,* (London, 1969) an invaluable collection of the biographical records upon which other biographies are based, including lengthy reproduction of the nineteenth-century records.

VISUAL WORKS: REPRODUCTIONS AND DISCUSSIONS

William Blake, facs. ed. (London, 1902) intro. by L. Binyon, all of Blake's woodcuts are photographically reproduced; G. Holme, ed., *The Drawings and Engravings of William Blake,* (London, 1922) intro. text by L. Binyon; *William Blake's Designs for Gray's Poems,* (London, 1922) intro. by H. J. C. Grierson; Figgis, D., *The Paintings of William Blake,* (London, 1925); Binyon, L., *The Engraved Designs of William Blake,* (London, 1926); *Illustrations to Young's "Night Thoughts,"* (Cambridge, Mass., 1927) intro. essay by G. Keynes; G. Keynes, ed., *Pencil Drawings,* (London, 1927); *Illustrations of the Book of Job,* facs. ed. (New York, 1935) intro. by L. Binyon and G. Keynes; *Illustrations of the Book of Job,* facs. ed. (New York, 1937) notes by P. Hofer; *Blake's Grave: A Prophetic Book,* (Providence, 1953) with a commentary by F. S. Damon; Roe, A. S., *Blake's Illustrations to "The Divine Comedy"* (Princeton, N.J., 1954); G. Keynes, ed., *Blake's Pencil Drawings,* 2nd ser. (London, 1956); G. Keynes., ed., *William Blake's Illustrations to the Bible,* (London, 1957); Digby, G. W., *Symbol and Image in William Blake,* (Oxford, 1957); Blunt, A., *The Art of William Blake,* (Oxford, 1960); Hagstrun, J. H., *William Blake, Poet and Painter: An Introduction to the Illuminated Verse,* (Chicago, 1964); Keynes, G., *A Study of the Illuminated Books of William Blake, Poet, Printer and Prophet,* (London, 1965); *The Book of Urizen,* (Miami, 1966) intro. by C. Emery; *Blake's Job,* (Providence, 1966) with a commentary and intro. by S. F. Damon; Butlin, M., *William Blake,* (London, 1966) 32 plates, some in color, of paintings in the Tate Gallery; D. V. Erdman and J. T. Grant, *Blake's Visionary Forms Dramatic,* eds. (Princeton, N.J., 1970); Easson, R. R., and Essick, R. N., *William Blake: Book Illustrator,* (Normal, Ill., 1972); G. Keynes, ed., *William Blake's Water-colour Designs for the Poems of Thomas Gray,* (London, 1972) facs. of Blake's illustrated copy of "Poems by Mr. Gray" (London, 1790); Lindberg, B., *William Blake's Illustrations to the Book of Job,* (Abo, 1973) the fullest study of these designs; Essick, R. N., *The Visionary Hand: Essays for the Study of William Blake's Art and Aesthetics,* (Los Angeles, 1973); Mellor, A. K., *Blake's Human Form Divine,* (Berkeley, 1974) discusses form in both the visual and verbal art of Blake; Lister, R., *Infernal Methods: A Study of William Blake's Art Techniques,* (London, 1975); G. Keynes, ed., *The Complete Portraiture of William and Catherine Blake,* (London, 1977); Bindman, D., *Blake as an Artist,* (Oxford, 1977); R. N. Essick and D. Pearce, eds., *Blake in His Time,* (Bloomington, Ind., 1978); Mitchell, W. J. T., *Blake's Composite Art,* (Princeton, N.J., 1978); Bindman, D., *The Complete Graphic Works of William Blake,* (London, 1978), *Note*: Studies of the visual art of Blake can also be found in many books listed under CRITICAL STUDIES.

CATALOGS OF WORKS IN PUBLIC COLLECTIONS

M. Butlin, ed., *William Blake (1757–1827): A Catalogue of the Works of William Blake in the Tate Gallery,* (London, 1957); Willard, H. D., *William Blake: Water-color Drawings,* (Boston, 1957) the collection at the Boston Museum of Fine Arts, *William Blake: Catalogue of the Preston Blake Library,* (Westminster, 1969); Wells, W., *William Blake's "Heads of the Poets,"* (Manchester, 1969) the collection at the Manchester City Art Gallery; Bindman, D., *William Blake: Catalogue of the Collection in the Fitzwilliam Museum,* (Cambridge, 1970); Morgan, R., and Bentley, G. E., Jr. *"A Handlist of Works by William Blake in the . . . British Museum"* V, (1972) *Blake Newsletter,* pp. 223–258.

FINDING LIST

Essick, R. N., "Finding List of Reproductions of Blake's Art," *Blake Newsletter,* V (1971) 1–160.

PERIODICALS

Blake Newsletter, (1967–1977) continued as *Blake: An Illustrated Quarterly* (1977–); *Blake Studies,* (1967–).

REFERENCE WORKS

Damon, S. F., *A Blake Dictionary: The Ideas and Symbols of William Blake,* (Providence, 1965); D. V. Erdman, ed., *A Concordance to the Writings of William Blake,* 2 vols., (New York, 1967); Bentley, G. E., Jr., *William Blake: The Critical Heritage,* (London, 1975) repr. all the early reviews and essays;

A variety of audiovisual material is also available on Blake. See G. E. Bentley, Jr., *Blake Books: Annotated Catalogues . . . ,* under BIBLIOGRAPHIES.

ELIZABETH BARRETT BROWNING

(1806–1861)

ALETHEA HAYTER

I

WHEN WORDSWORTH DIED, just halfway through the nineteenth century, and a successor for him as poet laureate had to be found, the claims of Elizabeth Barrett Browning to succeed him were seriously canvassed. It was suggested that a female poet laureate would be particularly suitable when a woman was on the throne of England, but the influential *Athenaeum* flatly stated that in any case no living poet of either sex had a higher claim than Mrs. Browning's. This seems to us a startling pronouncement to have been made on the same day—1 June 1850—on which *In Memoriam* was published. Tennyson in fact got the laureateship, to Mrs. Browning's satisfaction, though she had thought Leigh Hunt ought to have it; not even she had thought of Browning as a possible candidate.

The suggestion that a female sovereign should have a female poet laureate seemed foolish enough to Mrs. Browning. She thought of herself as a poet, not a poetess; she considered that poetry should be judged by its merits, not by the sex of its writers. "When I talk of women, I do not speak of them . . . according to a separate, peculiar, and womanly standard, but according to the common standard of human nature, " she said. But it has never been possible for critics to disentangle Mrs. Browning from her sex. She was always being classed by her contemporaries as the top woman poet (generally bracketed with Sappho), not simply as a good, or very good, or fairly good poet. No such woman writer would probably come again for a millennium, wrote Sydney Dobell unprophetically in 1850; but he went on to say that no woman writer, not even Mrs. Browning, would ever write a great poem. "She was a woman of real genius, I know; but what is the upshot of it all? She and her sex had better mind the kitchen and the children," said Edward FitzGerald. Elizabeth Barrett Browning was as much obscured as a poet by her sex and her personal legend as Byron was by his. It is therefore difficult to assess her achievement as objectively as that of other nineteenth-century poets such as Coventry Patmore, or Arthur Hugh Clough, or George Meredith, with whom she might reasonably be classed; but she has in fact much more in common with them than with Christina Rossetti or Emily Brontë .

II

Elizabeth Barrett was born on 6 March 1806 at Coxhoe Hall in Durham. She was the eldest of the twelve children of Edward Moulton Barrett and his wife Mary. When she was three years old, the family moved to Hope End in Herefordshire, and she spent the next twenty-three years of her life in this minareted country house overlooking a lake and deep in a wooded park. Here she produced her juvenilia: *The Battle of Marathon,* an epic poem written when she was thirteen and privately printed by her father in 1820; *An Essay on Mind, with Other Poems,* published in 1826; a number of poems published in magazines; and a good deal of verse, including one long poem, "The Development of Genius," which remained unpublished in her lifetime. Encouraged by two neighbors, the scholars Hugh Stuart Boyd and Uvedale Price, she made a thorough study of classical and Byzantine Greek literature, and of prosody. Apart from a severe but unidentified illness in 1821, she led a normal social and family life during all these years.

In 1832 financial losses forced her father to sell Hope End and move with his children (his wife had died in 1828) first to Sidmouth, in Devonshire, and then in 1835 to London. In 1833, Elizabeth Barrett published a volume containing a translation of the *Prometheus Bound* of Aeschylus, and some short poems, but neither this nor her earlier volumes (all published anonymously) attracted much notice. Her first real success was achieved with *The Seraphim, and Other Poems,* published in 1838 under her own name, which was given long and mainly favorable reviews in the leading journals.

The literary scene on which Elizabeth Barrett entered in the late 1830's was comparatively empty—an undistinguished pause between two great periods of creative writing. Wordsworth, Leigh Hunt, and Walter Savage Landor were the patriarchs of the day, but their best work was past; Tennyson, Browning, Dickens, Carlyle had published their first works, but their great achievement and fame were still to come; Thackeray, Ruskin, and the Brontës were still just below the literary horizon. The admired writers of the day were Field Talfourd, Harriet Martineau, Harrison Ainsworth, Mary Russell Mitford, Thomas Hood, Edward Bulwer-Lytton, Barry Cornwall, Felicia Hemans, Letitia Landon, and Sheridan Knowles. Among these writers Elizabeth Barrett began to make friends and a place for herself. Her ill health and her family circumstances prevented her from going out much into the social life of London, but she embarked on exchanges of letters with literary figures which were to influence both her writing and her life. Among her correspondents were Wordsworth, Edgar Allan Poe, Carlyle, Harriet Martineau, Mary Russell Mitford (who gave her Flush, her spaniel), John Kenyon, R. H. Horne, and the painter Benjamin Robert Haydon. They exchanged criticisms and appreciations of each other's work, discussed other writers of the day and the ethics and techniques of their profession; Elizabeth Barrett was at last enjoying the stimulus of intellectual equality which had been missing from her secluded childhood and adolescence.

In 1837 her health broke down, her lungs were affected, and she was sent from London to the milder climate of Torquay. Her family took it in turns to stay with her there; and while her eldest brother Edward, nicknamed Bro, was prolonging his stay at Torquay at her entreaty, he went out sailing and was drowned. His sister's lasting grief altered and in some ways strengthened her character.

She came back to London in 1841, still very much of an invalid, and plunged into literary work—book reviews, articles, translations, contributions to symposia. This productive period culminated in the two-volume *Poems* of 1844, the most popular of all her works until *Aurora Leigh* with both the critics and the public. One poem in this collection, "Lady Geraldine's Courtship," referred favorably to the work of Robert Browning, and he wrote to Elizabeth Barrett to thank her. So began, on 10 January 1845, a correspondence which led to their first meeting four months later. On the day after he had first seen Elizabeth Barrett, Browning sent her a declaration of love, which disturbed her so much that he had to disclaim it before she would consent to receive him again; and it was only gradually, with devoted patience, that he was able to convince her of the reality of his love, to make her avow hers, and to get her consent to an engagement. For a whole year they wrote to each other almost daily, sometimes twice a day, and he called on her every few days. More frequent visits would have aroused suspicion. Mr. Barrett's immovable objection to the marriage of any of his children enforced secrecy on Browning and Elizabeth Barrett until they had left for Italy, a week after their marriage on 12 September 1846.

After some months in Pisa, the Brownings moved to Florence, which was to be their base for the rest of Mrs. Browning's life; from 1848 they kept a permanent residence there, Casa Guidi, though they were often away from it for many months at a time, on visits to Rome, to Lucca, to Siena. In 1849 the poets' only child, a son christened Wiedeman, but afterward nicknamed Pennini or Pen, was born. The Brownings visited London four times during the 1850's, and renewed their friendships in its literary world. They also spent two winters in Paris, where they got to know many French writers, and were witnesses of some of the most striking events in the rise to power of Napoleon III. Mrs. Browning became increasingly absorbed in European politics, particularly the political development of Italy and France, and this preoccupation was reflected in the poetry which she wrote in the last ten years of her life. She also became deeply, almost obsessively, interested in spiritualism, though her credulity was tempered by occasional flashes of common sense.

In the 1840's and 1850's Elizabeth Barrett Browning's poetic reputation was at its height, and made her a serious candidate for the poet laureateship. The four books of poetry which she published between 1846 and 1861 were: the first collected edition of her poetry, published in 1850 and including, as well as the best of the 1838 and 1844 poems, some new lyrics and the celebrated "Sonnets from the Portuguese," addressed to her husband; *Casa Guidi Windows,* a partly political poem about Italy, which appeared in 1851; *Aurora Leigh,* a modern epic or "novel in verse," as she called it, which was published in 1857 and won immense acclaim; and *Poems Before Congress* (1860), again political in inspiration and deservedly less popular than any other work of her maturity. This was the last book which she published in her lifetime. Her health, which had greatly improved with the happiness and the change of climate which her marriage and her move to Italy brought her, weakened again after she had reached the peak of her achievement in *Aurora Leigh,* and she died in Florence on 29 June 1861.

Last Poems, containing some of her most famous lyrics, was published posthumously in 1862. Since then many of her unpublished poems, especially her juvenilia, have appeared in small collections, and many volumes of her letters have been published in England and in America, where most of the surviving original letters are now. The most famous of these volumes of correspondence is her exchange of love letters with Robert Browning, a unique interplay of genius and passion. The best of the other collections of Elizabeth Barrett Browning's letters are those to R. H. Horne, Mary Russell Mitford, and Benjamin Robert Haydon, full of comment on contemporary literature, art, and social problems; the letters to H. S. Boyd, chiefly concerned with Greek scholarship and metrical experiments; and the letters to her sister Henrietta and her brother George, which give a picture of her family and daily life. The best selection from her general correspondence is still Frederic Kenyon's two-volume one, published in 1897, though it necessarily omits a good deal of interesting biographical material which has appeared since then.

Even the baldest statement of the main events in Elizabeth Barrett Browning's life reveals an exceptional character and destiny. She was a fortunate woman. She had a happy childhood and, even after she grew up, a family life in which she never lacked affection, companionship, and admiration for her talents, however much she was deprived of sympathetic understanding and of freedom. She experienced keen pleasure from the study of languages and literature, and had the leisure to indulge the taste fully. In middle life, when she seemed a confirmed invalid, she met and married a great poet who devotedly loved her. She had a charming and intelligent child; she lived in the most beautiful cities of Italy; she never experienced any real want of money; she had many devoted friends, who included most of the great writers of the day. She was convinced that she herself was born to be a poet, she was intensely happy writing poetry, and she had splendid success with her poems when they were published. She died without pain or lingering.

Her good fortune was due to the strength and integrity of her character as much as to her innate talents and her social and economic advantages. She had to overcome crippling ill health, the loss of a dearly loved brother, and the unforgiving tyranny and hardness of her father. To achieve this, and to make such a success of her personal and professional life, required a toughness of will, a generosity of heart, a healthiness of mind which have not always been recognized in Elizabeth Barrett Browning, whose willpower and fierce mental energy have been somewhat obscured by her legend of invalidism and ringlets.

III

"A genuine poetess of no common order," said the *Examiner* of Elizabeth Barrett when reviewing *The Seraphim, and Other Poems,* which was published in 1838 and widely praised. The title poem, a lyrical drama on the Crucifixion as seen through the eyes of two mourning archangels, is an ambitious, uneven work full of imagination, of mystical visions of the red primeval heats of creation still forever burning from the heavenly Throne and casting fiery shadows on the crystal sea; of the whole hierarchy of Heaven attendant on the hill of Golgotha:

> Beneath us sinks the pomp angelical,
> Cherub and seraph, powers and virtues, all,
> The roar of whose descent has died
> To a still sound, as thunder into rain.
> Immeasurable space spreads magnified
> With that thick life, along the plane
> The worlds slid out on.[1]
> (*The Seraphim*, pt. I, 18–24)

The volume also contained several shorter poems, such as "The Deserted Garden," "The Sleep," and "Cowper's Grave," which have always been popular with the anthologists. In this volume, too, appeared the first of the ballads which Elizabeth Barrett Browning's contemporaries loved best of all her works. Poems such as "The Romaunt of Margret," "Isobel's Child," and "The Lay of the Brown Rosary" (the last was published in 1844), in which the challenge between Love and Death is played out over and over again, with Death always triumphing, have a haunting Gothic strangeness and necromancy which is a persistent mood in nineteenth-century English poetry; from "Christabel" and "La Belle Dame sans Merci" and "The Lady of Shalott," it runs through Mrs. Browning's ballads, and on from them to influence Dante Gabriel Rossetti's "Sister Helen" and William Morris' "The Blue Closet."

Most of Elizabeth Barrett Browning's religious poetry also dates from the volume of 1838: not only "The Seraphim" but also such lyrics as "The Soul's Travelling," "The Virgin Mary to the Child Jesus," and "Cowper's Grave," in which she meditated on mystical experiences and on the problem of reconciling belief in Divine Love with the suffering and the evils of the world—the problem which tormented so many of her contemporaries, above all Tennyson as he wrote *In Memoriam.* Most of these early religious poems of Mrs. Browning's, though intense in feeling, are diffuse and undisciplined in expression; but in a few of the lyrics written at this time she achieved an economy of words which startles the reader by its fineness, as in "My Doves," her poem about the imprisonment of city streets and the longing for escape. Most of the poem is musically sweet, rather than strong, as when she describes the cooing of the doves who share her imprisonment:

> . . . Of living loves
> Theirs hath the calmest fashion,
> Their living voice the likest moves
> To lifeless intonation,

1. All quotations from the poetry are from the *Poetical Works*, with *Two Prose Essays* (London, 1920).

The lovely monotone of springs,
And winds, and such insensate things.
(st. 4)

Then she surprises the reader with the unadorned fitness of her conclusion, in which, renouncing the hope of airy shores and silent, dewy fields, she says:

My spirit and my God shall be
My seaward hill, my boundless sea.
(st. 14)

This concentration is rare in her work; she achieved it in "A Sabbath Morning at Sea," in "A Seaside Walk," in snatches of "The Poet's Vow" and "Night and the Merry Man," but most completely in "A Reed":

I am no trumpet, but a reed;
Go, tell the fishers, as they spread
Their nets along the river's edge,
I will not tear their nets at all,
Nor pierce their hands, if they should fall:
Then let them leave me in the sedge.
(st. 3)

Elizabeth Barrett's next volumes of poems, published in 1844, showed a development and hardening of her character and style. Illness, bereavement, approaching middle age had made her less dreamy and more confident, even aggressive in her mannerisms. The 1844 volumes include her most advanced prosodic experiments, some of which seemed barbarous innovations to her contemporaries, but have many parallels in mid-twentieth-century poetry. Her political and social opinions were also growing more definite. Two poems in the 1844 volumes, "The Cry of the Children" and "The Cry of the Human," were militant attacks on the employment of child labor in factories, and on the protectionists who kept up the price of bread; the poems were widely commented on, and influenced public opinion in favor of reform. There is more intellect, and a more individual character, in the 1844 *Poems* than in Elizabeth Barrett Browning's earlier works, and the volumes had a considerable success with the critics and the public; but in a good many of them there is a note of wildness and exaggeration which has caused subsequent literary historians to class Mrs. Browning with the poets who were nicknamed the Spasmodic School, and were attacked for their overstrained hyperbole, subjectivism, and lack of discipline. Two of the longer poems in Elizabeth Barrett's 1844 volumes—"A Drama of Exile," a strange, cloudy work on the expulsion of Adam and Eve from Paradise, and "A Rhapsody of Life's Progress"—do almost justify her classification as a Spasmodic. But these same uneven volumes also contain some of her finest and most disciplined sonnets. Some, like "Futurity" or the lapidary "Grief," commemorate her brother's death and her struggle to accept her loss of him; some, like "The Soul's Expression" and "The Prisoner," are analyses of the workings of poetic inspiration:

I count the dismal time by months and years,
Since last I felt the green sward under foot,
And the great breath of all things summer-
mute
Met mine upon my lips. Now earth appears
As strange to me as dreams of distant spheres,
Or thoughts of Heaven we weep at. Nature's
lute
Sounds on behind this door so closely shut,
A strange, wild music to the prisoner's ears,
Dilated by the distance, till the brain
Grows dim with fancies which it feels too
fine:
While ever, with a visionary pain,
Past the precluded senses, sweep and shine
Streams, forests, glades,—and many a
golden train
Of sunlit hills, transfigured to Divine.
("The Prisoner")

One poem in the 1844 volumes, "Catarina to Camoens," was a particular favorite with Robert Browning; he identified Elizabeth Barrett with the Portuguese girl Catarina, the beloved of the poet Camoens, and when his wife's sonnets to him were eventually published, the Brownings chose to call them

"Sonnets from the Portuguese," an ambiguous title which was a disguise from the world but full of secret meaning for the Brownings themselves. These sonnets were published in 1850, four years after the Brownings' marriage, in the first collected edition of Mrs. Browning's works. The "Sonnets from the Portuguese" are her best-known poems, but not her best. The dramatic story of her marriage has given the sonnets something of the fascination of a roman à clef; but considered simply as poetry, they are uneven and sometimes embarrassing. Individual lines are strong and shapely:

> Beholding, besides love, the end of love,
> Hearing oblivion beyond memory;
> As one who sits and gazes from above,
> Over the rivers to the bitter sea.
> (Sonnet xv)

or

> Yet love, mere love, is beautiful indeed
> And worthy of acceptation. Fire is bright,
> Let temple burn, or flax. An equal light
> Leaps in the flame from cedar-plank or
> weed. . . .
> (Sonnet x)

And there are some whole sonnets, notably xxii and xliii, which sustain an unforced strength of music. But it is impossible to say of the "Sonnets from the Portuguese" as a whole, as one can say of the greatest sonnet sequences, that their beauty and interest are self-sufficing, independently of their personal reference. The abiding attraction of these sonnets is the psychological interest of tracing the evolution in love of a thirty-nine-year-old invalid, who at first cannot believe that a brilliant poet, six years younger than herself, can really love her and want to marry her; then, when she begins to believe it, is held back by conscientious scruples at burdening him with her melancholy and ill health; then is brought to confess her own passion, and to see that he knows what he needs, and loves her for what she really is; then grows happy, and luxuriates in the tokens and catchwords and secrets of acknowledged lovers; and at last looks forward to a lifetime, an eternity, of enduring love.

Elizabeth Barrett Browning's marked individuality of style and personality makes all her poetry distinctive, but she was at various times much influenced by other poets. Pope was her model in her juvenilia; Thomas Campbell, Byron, Wordsworth lent forms and themes to her early lyrics; and after her marriage to Browning, she acquired something of his powers of vivid, ironic characterization and comment, an element in her poetry which had been latent since her earliest work but first came to the surface, under Browning's influence, in *Casa Guidi Windows*, published in 1851. This poem, written in a modified terza rima, is a reflection on recent political events in Florence and on the character and destiny of the Italians, about whom she is sympathetic but unsentimental:

> We chalked the walls with bloody caveats
> Against all tyrants. If we did not fight
> Exactly, we fired muskets up the air
> To show that victory was ours of right.
> We met, had free discussions everywhere
> (Except perhaps i' the Chambers) day and
> night.
> We proved the poor should be employed . . .
> that's fair,—
> And yet the rich not worked for anywise,—
> Pay certified, yet payers abrogated,—
> Full work secured, yet liabilities
> To over-work excluded. . . .
> (part II, 153–163)

Six years later, in 1857, she published her masterpiece, *Aurora Leigh*. This immense nine-book poem, longer than *Paradise Lost*, contains the finest passages that Elizabeth Barrett Browning ever wrote; but they are imbedded in an implausible story of a woman poet, a philanthropist who loves her, and a series of misunderstandings and catastrophes which keep them apart until the happy ending. The poem traces the parallel careers of Aurora Leigh, the successful but lonely and dissatisfied poet, convinced that man's salvation must come through the inspired individual, and her cousin Romney Leigh, the social reformer, who believes in progress organized for the people as a whole. He sets up a phalanstery on his ancestral estate, and decides to marry a poor seamstress as a precedent for a classless society. Romney's schemes fail—his bride is tricked away before the wedding, and entrapped into a brothel; the destitute people for whom he set up his phalanstery destroy it; and he loses his sight in the holocaust. When he and Aurora are finally reunited, they conclude that both were partly wrong: he had failed to recognize that to raise men's bodies, one must first raise their souls; she had not seen that one must work with, as well as for, humanity.

Mrs. Browning took various elements of the story of *Aurora Leigh* from Charlotte Brontë , George Sand, and other novelists; but the best way to appreciate the poem is to disregard its story, and to read it—like Wordsworth's *Prelude,* which is perhaps its nearest affinity—not for the narrative, but for the reflections occasioned by the events in the narrative, for the glimpses of distant mountains, for the moments of intense feeling. Elizabeth Barrett Browning said that *Aurora Leigh* contained her highest convictions on life and art, and in it she was above all concerned with the poet's responsibilities, his call to be a witness to the values of humanity. She was an early propagandist for *la littérature engagée,* maintaining that the sole work of poets is

. . . to represent the age,
Their age, not Charlemagne's,—this live throbbing age,
That brawls, cheats, maddens, calculates, aspires,
And spends more passion, more heroic heat,
Betwixt the mirrors of its drawing-rooms,
Than Roland with his knights at Roncesvalles.
To flinch from modern varnish, coat or flounce,
Cry out for togas and the picturesque
Is fatal,—foolish too. King Arthur's self
Was commonplace to Lady Guenevere;
And Camelot to minstrels seemed as flat
As Fleet Street to our poets.
(*Aurora Leigh,* bk. V, 203–214)

Aurora Leigh is rich in unusual and glowing imagery, mature and often witty in its comments on contemporary society, compassionate over injustices and the sufferings of the poor, and written in a vigorous and agile blank verse. It had a great and immediate success, though some readers were shocked by its frank sexual references to prostitution and even to rape. Mrs. Browning was not a prude; she thought that social evils were more likely to be abolished by plain speaking about them than by pretending they did not exist.

The last volume of poems which Mrs. Browning published in her lifetime, *Poems Before Congress,* which appeared in 1860, was a disappointment. It was a small collection of mainly political poems about France and Italy, too much imbued with her obsessive and often faulty judgments on contemporary political events and personalities. A year after her death, a further small volume, *Last Poems,* was published; it contained two lyrics, "A Musical Instrument" and "The North and the South," which have found their way into many anthologies, and one remarkable poem, "Bianca Among the Nightingales," which has a story and a refrain like some of the ballads of her youth, but a passion and a sophistication which are quite new.

"*Last Poems* is the last title which anyone could desire to read on a book which bears the name of Elizabeth Barrett Browning," began the *Athenaeum* review of her posthumous volume, and it went on to call her "the greatest English poetess that has ever lived" and to say that she had "the heart of a lion, the soul of a martyr, and the voice of a battle-trumpet. Hers was a great genius, nurtured alike on study of the ancients and instinct for the moderns." Now, more than a century later, no one would claim "great genius" for Elizabeth Barrett Browning, but there are qualities in her poetry which still have power to move and interest us.

IV

Perhaps the best approach to the poetry of Elizabeth Barrett Browning is to note first the thorough training and preparation she underwent in the techniques of her profession. It was a profession to her; she worked full-time, all her adult life, at the business of poetry, and she took seriously the skills and the responsibilities of her trade. In writing of its responsibilities, she sometimes lapsed into a shrill didacticism; but at its best her vocation emerges as a genuine poetic impulse to show life, and enable others to see it, as it really is, unobscured by prejudice, self-interest, or self-deception. Poets, she said, are "the only truth-tellers still left to God"; and they must speak out against tyranny, against unjust wars, against the exploitation of women and children, against want and slavery, against complacency and ignorance. They must make human beings think for themselves, must help them to be honest about their emotions, must teach them to outgrow narrow nationalism and sectarianism.

But if poets are to have the power to move men's minds in this way, they must learn the skills which give such power to poetry. She herself gave much time and study to the science of versification; she experimented in many different meters, and was a pioneer in the use of assonantal double rhymes. Her very thorough reading of English poetry, from the earliest to the latest, had convinced her that not enough use was made of the possibilities of rhyme. Double rhymes were almost entirely confined to comic poetry; in any case, regular double rhymes were rare in English. Her innovation was to introduce such assonantal double rhymes as "trident/silent" and "benches/influences," or still more extreme ones, matching neither in vowel nor in consonant, such as "angels/candles" or "burden/disregarding." These are commonplaces in English poetry of the 1930's and 1940's; but in Mrs. Browning's day, and for half a century afterward, they were considered utterly lawless. Her metrical experiments were less extreme. She used a very wide variety of meters, from the most regular rhymed couplets and Petrarchan sonnets to the loosest accentual verse, approximating to sprung rhythm.

Her prosodic experiments were often more daring than successful, but they were the result of much exploration of classical and Byzantine Greek literature and of early English poetry. She published a modernized version of a Chaucer poem, and translations of Aeschylus, Theocritus, Apuleius, Nonnus, and Anacreon; she also wrote a critical study, illustrated by many translations, of Byzantine poetry from the fourth to the fourteenth centuries. Greek was the language she loved best; but she also knew Latin, French, Italian, and some German, Spanish, and Hebrew, and was so widely read in the literature of these languages that she could trace an image from Lucretius through Saint Basil to Tasso, and draw a parallel between *The Choephoroe* and *Macbeth,* or between an ode of Anacreon and *Romeo and Juliet.* Some of the best-known passages in her poetry are her roll calls of other poets: in *An Essay on Mind*; in "A Vision of Poets," where she dashes off some notable sketches, such as

. . . bold

Electric Pindar, quick as fear,
With race-dust on his cheeks, and clear
Slant startled eyes that seem to hear

The chariot rounding the last goal,
To hurtle past it in his soul.
(st. 104–106)

and

Lucretius—nobler than his mood;
Who dropped his plummet down the broad
Deep universe, and said "No God",

Finding no bottom: he denied
Divinely the divine, . . .
(st. 112–113)

and in *Aurora Leigh,* where she analyzes the young poet's reactions to his predecessors, how he loves and imitates them and then finds his own inspiration, and how sometimes there comes a poet like Keats, to whom none of the generalizations about young poets apply; and then she wrote the lines on Keats with which Edmund Blunden chose to sum up Keats's achievement:

> the life of a long life
> Distilled to a mere drop, falling like a tear
> Upon the world's cold cheek to make it burn
> For ever.
> *Aurora Leigh,* bk. I, 1007–1010)

Mrs. Browning's knowledge of comparative literature gave her an acute ear for style and the boldness to refute, on internal stylistic evidence and in an astonishing metaphor, the theory of the multiple authorship of Homer. She possessed a handsome edition of Friedrich Wolf's *Prolegomena ad Homerum,* on thick, white paper with wide margins, and she wrote these memorably indignant lines about "the kissing Judas, Wolf":

> Who builds us such a royal book as this
> To honour a chief-poet, folio-built,
> And writes above, "The house of Nobody!",
> Who floats in cream, as rich as any sucked
> From Juno's breasts, the broad Homeric
> lines,
> And, while with their spondaic prodigious
> mouths
> They lap the lucent margins as babe-gods,
> Proclaims them bastards. Wolf's an atheist;
> And if the Iliad fell out, as he says,
> By mere fortuitous concourse of old songs,
> Conclude as much too for the universe.
> (*Aurora Leigh,* bk. V, 1149–1159)

The metaphor of the printed lines sucking the milk of the white page margins is a good example of another of Elizabeth Barrett Browning's special poetic qualities—her command of striking and original imagery. The richness of her imagination is all the more surprising in view of how few opportunities she had to observe either mankind or nature. She spent the first twenty-six years of her life in the seclusion of a remote countryside, and most of the next fourteen years shut up in a London house, meeting very few strangers and ill in bed for whole years. But she made the fullest use of what experience she had—of the conversation and letters of her literary friends, of her long explorations and adventures of the mind between the covers of books, even of her own ill health and its accompaniments. There is in her work a whole image cluster derived from her illness—from insomnia, from states of trance, from night silences and transfigurations, from opium visions, from fainting, from the vibrations of a galloping pulse. These made the landscape of her mind; they were to her what external nature was to Wordsworth or Tennyson. She lived in the country as a child, and she traveled widely after her marriage, but it was mostly from one sofa to another. She led an indoor life, and she writes like an indoor poet. Her descriptions of nature often have the freshness of delighted surprise; trees and hills and fresh air were to her not a necessity but a delicious occasional stimulus, like going to the theater. The spaciousness and dewy greenness of some of her landscape descriptions:

> The mythic oaks and elm-trees standing out
> Self-poised upon their prodigy of shade
> (*Aurora Leigh,* bk. I, 1089–1090)

remind one of the close, dark room in which they were written. What she actually saw from the window of her room was the texture of the London skies—in winter "wrapped like a mummy in a yellow mist," in summer "a thick mist lacquered over with light"; the sunsets which "startle the slant roofs and chimney pots/With splashes of fierce colour"; and the classic Dickensian spectacle, watching

> the great tawny weltering fog
> Involve the passive city, strangle it
> Alive, and draw it off into the void,
> Spires, bridges, streets, and squares, as if a
> sponge
> Had wiped out London,
> (*Aurora Leigh,* bk. III, 180–184)

surely a deliberate and ironic echo of Wordsworth's

> Ships, towers, domes, theatres and temples
> lie
> All bright and glittering in the smokeless
> air.

Mrs. Browning's semantic studies often gave a special turn to her imagery, an interlocking, punning ambiguity, as in her description of a man trying to rid himself of the ghost of a dead love:

> He locks thee out at night into the cold
> Away from butting with thy horny eyes
> Against his crystal dreams,
> (*Aurora Leigh,* bk. V, 1104–1106)

where the adjective "horny" is used in a double sense: the eyes of the little ghost are horns to butt against a fragile complacency, but also dim horn windows through which an icy memory peers in. Mrs. Browning concentrates and interweaves her images so closely that they sometimes defy analysis, and yet have a fierce impact:

> Ten nights and days we voyaged on the deep;
> Ten nights and days without the common
> face
> Of any day or night; the moon and sun
> Cut off from the green reconciling earth,
> To starve into a blind ferocity
> And glare unnatural; the very sky
> (Dropping its bell-net down upon the sea
> As if no human heart should 'scape alive)
> Bedraggled with the desolating salt.
> (*Aurora Leigh,* bk. I, 239–247)

This passage describes how the orphan child, carried away from her home on a miserable voyage to a sad destination, sees all nature turned into the famished wild beasts of some cosmic circus, glaring through the net which has become man's prison, not his protection.

Another of Elizabeth Barrett Browning's special qualities, at once a virtue and a vice, is her great variety. She could plunge from heights of beauty to depths of bathos, sometimes within the same poem. But not all her good work is in one manner, and all her bad in another; even her best work is in several different manners. She could write with classic economy, as in her sonnet on hopeless grief:

> Most like a monumental statue set
> In everlasting watch and moveless woe,
> Till itself crumble to the dust beneath.
> Touch it: the marble eyelids are not wet;
> If it could weep, it could arise and go
> ("Grief")

or in her description of Michelangelo's statue of Lorenzo de' Medici:

> With everlasting shadow on his face,
> While the slow dawns and twilights
> disapprove
> The ashes of his long-established race,
> Which never more shall clog the feet of men.
> *Casa Guidi Windows,* pt. I, 94–97)

Both these passages are inspired by sculpture, which was always one of Mrs. Browning's most potent images; to her, as to Wordsworth, a statue was a "marble index" of long voyages of the mind. But though she could write marmoreally, much of her most vivid poetry is more like a modern sculptor's conglomeration of *objets trouvés*—mechanisms and reptilian forms welded together in flowing or glutinous structures—as in some passages from *Aurora Leigh*:

> This social Sphinx
> Who sits between the sepulchre and the
> stews,
> Makes mock and mow against the crystal
> heavens,
> And bullies God
> (bk. IV, 1184–1187)

or

> That June-day
> Too deeply sunk in craterous sunsets, now
> For you or me to dig it up alive,—
> To pluck it out all bleeding with spent flame

At the roots, before those moralizing stars
We have got instead
(bk. VIII, 489–494)

a passage which may recall to readers the poetry of Christopher Fry, rather than of any nineteenth-century writer.

Mrs. Browning's learning and many interests, enriched by the influence of her husband's still greater erudition, give her poetry a very wide reference. Religion, philosophy, politics, social reform, education, classical literature, and scientific discovery all gave impulse to her poetic inspiration. Indignant at the chicanery of the great powers who concluded the Peace of Villafranca, she dreams of

the grand solution
Of earth's municipal, insular schisms,
Statesmen draping self-love's conclusion
In cheap, vernacular patriotisms,
Unable to give up Judaea for Jesus.
("Italy and the World," st. 8)

She draws a vivid image from the excavations at Pompeii, from Alexander's project to carve Mount Athos into a colossal statue, from the holy ox of Memphis, from the mixture of gall and potash on a painter's palette, from the valves of a dissected hyacinth bulb. She reads Lyell's *Principles of Geology* and Chambers' *Vestiges of the Natural History of Creation,* and is prompted to the reflection that

Good love, howe'er ill-placed,
Is better for a man's soul in the end,
Than if he loved ill what deserves love well.
A pagan, kissing for a step of Pan
The wild-goat's hoof-print on the loamy
down,
Exceeds our modern thinker who turns back
The strata . . . granite, limestone, coal and
clay,
Concluding coldly with "Here's law!
where's God?"
(Aurora Leigh, bk. V, 1113–1120)

Often the imagery in her poetry can be traced back to references in her letters. These are now more read than her poetry, and would be more popular still if they were easily accessible in an up-to-date chronological arrangement. They are a barometer of the intelligent liberal public opinion of her times. Was it true that Newman had gone over to Rome? How long would it be before manhood suffrage was universal? Was Florence Nightingale really making the best use of her powers by being a hospital nurse? Could not prosperous Britain afford schools for all her children? In a letter of 7 April 1846, she argues with Browning over the ethics of dueling. He has agreed with her in condemning capital punishment, and in opposing war, yet he maintains that "honourable men are bound to keep their honours clean at the expense of so much gunpowder and so much risk of life—*that* must be, ought to be—let judicial deaths and military glory be abolished never so!" For her part, setting aside Christian principle, and on merely rational gounds, she

> cannot conceive of any *possible combination of circumstances* which could—I will not say *justify,* but even excuse, an honourable man's having recourse to the duellist's pistol, either on his own account or another's . . . His honour! Who believes in such an honour—liable to such amends, and capable of such recovery! *You* cannot, I think—in the secret of your mind. Or if *you can—you,* who are a teacher of the world—poor world—it is more desperately wrong than I thought.[2]
> (vol. 11, p. 41)

When one finds Browning defending the principle of dueling as late as 1846, Pushkin's death in a duel only nine years earlier seems less strange.

Elizabeth Barrett Browning knew, in person or by correspondence, nearly all the eminent writers of her day, and read all the new books of any merit as they came out; and in her letters one can trace the rise and fall of reputations, the literary mysteries and controversies

2. Quotations from the letters to Browning are from *Letters of* Robert Browning *and Elizabeth Barrett, 1845–46,* 2 vols. (London, 1899).

of the day. Could the author of *Adam Bede* really be a woman? How could anyone think Casimir Delavigne's poetry superior to Lamartine's, or Monckton Milnes's to Browning's? Could it possibly be true that *Jane Eyre* was by the governess of Thackeray's daughters? New names begin to rise in her literary firmament—Trollope's *Framley Parsonage* is "really superb"; she is "thunder-struck" by *Madame Bovary*; she had no idea that Thackeray had such intellectual force as *Vanity Fair* revealed; Matthew Arnold and Clough seem to her full of promise. In her letters one can also chart the rising temperature of her own fame; fan letters addressed to her simply as

Miss Elizabeth Barrett
Poetess
London

find their way to her in Wimpole Street; the terrible arbiters of the *Quarterly Review* and the *Examiner* begin to treat her with respect; her fellow poets write to congratulate her. But how was she to reply to a letter from Edgar Allan Poe hailing her as "the noblest of her sex"? Perhaps she might say,"Sir, you are the most discerning of yours."

This little joke, mocking herself as well as others, is typical of the personal style which makes Mrs. Browning's letters, over and above the interest of many of their topics, so delightful. She had trained herself to write letters naturally, as though she were talking; they were indeed her only means of conversation for much of her life, when she was imprisoned by ill health. And she had a rare ear and memory for the few face-to-face conversations which she did have, such as the misadventure of the Leeds poetess and the dropped H, which she recounted to Browning in a letter of 6 May 1846.

Ellen Heaton had come to call, and had told Miss Barrett that "the poetess proper of the city of Leeds was '*Mrs A*' ":

> "Mrs A?" said I with an enquiring innocence. "Oh" she went on, (divining sarcasm in every breath I drew) "oh! I dare say, *you* wouldn't admit her to be a real poetess. But as she lives in Leeds and writes verses, we call her our poetess! and then, really, Mrs A is a charming woman. She was a Miss Roberts—and her 'Spirit of the Woods', and of the 'Flowers' has been admired, I assure you". Well, in a moment I seemed to remember something,—because only a few months since, surely I had a letter from somebody who was once a spirit of the Woods or ghost of the Flowers. Still, I could not make out *Mrs A*! "Certainly" I confessed modestly, "I never did hear of a Mrs A.—and yet, and yet—" A most glorious confusion I was in, when suddenly my visitor thought of spelling the name. "H-E-Y" said she. Now conceive that! The Mrs Hey who came by solution, had both written to me and sent me a book on the Lakes quite lately "by the author of the Spirit of the Woods". *There* was the explanation! And my Leeds visitor will go back and say that I denied all knowledge of the charming Mrs A. the Leeds poetess, and that it was with the greatest difficulty I could be brought to recognize her existence. Oh, the arrogance and ingratitude of me! (vol. I, pp. 133–134)

This anecdote brings out the personality of Elizabeth Barrett—her ability to see herself as others saw her, her compassionate fear to wound competing with her irresistible sense of the absurd; a complex of qualities that made Henry James say, "There is scarce a scrap of a letter of Mrs Browning's in which a nameless intellectual, if it be not rather a moral, grace . . . does not make itself felt." Elizabeth Barrett Browning's personality, as expressed in her writing, could be maudlin and overexcited; at other times she could be astringent and satirical; but she was not mean or sly. She had that magnanimity which, though it cannot be a substitute for talent, adds a grace to it. She was magnanimous in her freedom from all religious, national, class, or sex prejudices, and magnanimous in her personal relationships. The greatest wrong she ever had to suffer was the selfish tyranny of her father, and here is what she said of it:

> After all, he is the victim. He isolates himself—and now and then he feels it . . . the

> cold dead silence all round, which is the effect of an incredible system. If he were not stronger than most men, he could not bear it as he does. (vol. I, p. 436)

The complement to Elizabeth Barrett Browning's magnanimity, the final quality which distinguishes her poetry—and makes her resemble an Elizabethan poet such as Webster, or a modern one such as Dylan Thomas—is her outrageousness, the fearless unconcern with which she shouts and shocks and exaggerates. In real life she was a quiet-voiced, gentle woman, a good listener rather than a good talker, but on paper she would say anything. Christian as she was, she would compare a waltz to the Mass, the unification of Italy to the Resurrection; no squeamishness prevented her from using scalps and tortures and rotting corpses as symbols; no prudery deterred her from talking of the smell of brothels. Like her prosodic experiments, these were deliberate attempts to create a new kind of poetic language which would startle the reader into full participation. She often overdosed her poetry, and produced a lassitude rather than a stimulus in the reader. Her poems are not tasteful or aristocratic, and will never be appreciated by those who value restraint as a necessary element in good poetry. In thinking of her work, one is reminded of Roy Campbell's memorable lines:

> You praise the firm restraint with which
> they write—
> I'm with you there, of course;
> They use the snaffle and the curb all right,
> But where's the bloody horse?

Elizabeth Barrett Browning was not very handy with the snaffle or the curb, but the horse was there—a snorting and muscular charger, very liable to do a bolt.

V

In 1856 Ruskin said that Elizabeth Barrett Browning's poetry was "unsurpassed by anything but Shakespeare." In 1932, Virginia Woolf said that the only place in literature assigned to Mrs. Browning was with Eliza Cook and Alexander Smith and other totally forgotten poets. Today, more than a century after Elizabeth Barrett Browning's death, her true worth as a poet is still unfixed between these extremes of critical inflation and deflation. Her poetry is very much out of favor with the academic critics and historians of literature. You will not find it in the syllabuses of British university courses in English literature, nor in the latest anthologies. There is not a single poem of hers in John Hayward's *Penguin Book of English Verse,* and Helen Gardner's *New Oxford Book of English Verse* includes only a few of the "Sonnets from the Portuguese." Not every public library in Britain has a copy of her works; and where copies do exist, they are not very often borrowed. No edition of the collected works is in print in Britain, though new editions of "Sonnets from the Portuguese" appear from time to time. Elizabeth Barrett Browning's memory is kept alive at present more by the plays, films, and musical comedies concerned with her private life than by readers of her poetry.

It is still too soon to say whether her fame as a poet will ever return. She may have to wait 200 years, as Ford and Webster did, till Charles Lamb brought them back to life. English literary taste moves in a circle, from extravagance to elegance and round again. It is possible that Elizabeth Barrett Browning's poetry will have a revival of favor at some future time when taste has followed its wonted cycle, and the terms "Gothic" and "enthusiastic" have once again become terms of praise, not of abuse.

Selected Bibliography

BIBLIOGRAPHY

Wise, T. J., *Bibliography of the Writings in Prose and Verse of E. B. Browning,* (London, 1918) includes texts of some letters not published elsewhere, but lists as authentic Wise's forged "Reading, 1847" edition of

"Sonnets"; Wise, T. J., *A Browning Library. A Catalogue of Printed Books, Manuscripts etc. of R. and E. B. Browning,* (London, 1929) the catalog of Wise's Browning collection, now in the British Museum; Ersham, T. G., and Deily, R. H., *Bibliographies of Twelve Victorian Authors,* (New York, 1936) supplement by J. G. Fucilla in *Modern Philology* 37, (1939) 89–96; Taplin, G. B., *The Life of Elizabeth Barrett Browning,* (London, 1957) contains a list of principal manuscript sources and of contributions to annuals, almanacs, periodicals, and series; Barnes, W. J., *The Browning Collection at the University of Texas,* (Austin, Tex., 1966); Kelley, P., and Hudson, R., *The Brownings' Correspondence: A Checklist,* (New York, 1978).

COLLECTED WORKS

Poems, new ed., 2 vols. (London, 1850) 3 vols. (1856) 4 vols. 1864 the 1844 *Poems* with the addition of "Sonnets from the Portuguese" (here first published; the "Reading, 1847" edition is a forgery), a revision of *Prometheus Bound* and 35 other sonnets and lyrics not previously published in book form; *Poems,* 5 vols. (London, 1866) 6 vols. (1889) with a prefatory note by R. Browning; *The Poems,* (London, 1893) with a memoir by Mrs. D. Ogilvy; F. G. Kenyon, ed., *The Poetical Works,* (London, 1897); *The Poetical Works,* (Oxford, 1904) first ed. in the Oxford Standard Authors series; *Complete Poetical Works of Elizabeth Barrett Browning,* 2 vols. (New York, 1919) with intro by L. Whiting; *Poetical Works, with Two Prose Essays,* (London, 1920).

SELECTED WORKS

A Selection from the Poetry, 2nd series (London, 1866–1880) with a prefatory note by R. Browning; *Poems,* London (1903) with intro. by A. Meynell; E. Lee, ed., *Selected Poems,* Boston (1904) with intro. and notes by Lee; *Poems,* London (1912) the World's Classics ed.; *Poems,* London (1948) selected and with intro. by S. J. Looker; C. Kaplan, ed., *Aurora Leigh and Other Poems,* London (1978).

SEPARATE WORKS

The Battle of Marathon, a Poem, London (1820) published anonymously; *An Essay on the Mind, with Other Poems,* (London, 1826) published anonymously; *Prometheus Bound, Translated from the Greek of Aeschylus, and Miscellaneous Poems,* (London, 1833) also with intro. by A. Meynell (London, 1896); *The Seraphim, and Other Poems,* (London, 1838); *The Poems of Geoffrey Chaucer Modernized,* (London, 1841) to which she contributed a modernized version of "Queen Annelida and False Arcite"; R. H. Horne, ed., *A New Spirit of the Age,* (London, 1844) to which she contributed a number of essays and parts of essays; *Poems,* 2 vols. (London, 1844) the ed. used as the basis for subsequent eds. of her collected works produced in her lifetime and immediately after her death—new ed. (1850) included much new material; also 3rd ed. (1853), 4th ed. (incorporating *Casa Guidi Windows,* 3 vols., 1856), 5th ed. (1862), 6th ed. (incorporating *Aurora Leigh,* 1864), 7th ed. (1866); *Casa Guidi Windows, A Poem,* (London, 1851); *Aurora Leigh,* (London, 1857) also with intro. by A. C. Swinburne (London, 1898); *Poems Before Congress,* (London, 1860) repr. as *Napoleon III in Italy and Other Poems,* (New York, 1860).

Last Poems, (London, 1862); *The Greek Christian Poets and the English Poets,* (London, 1863) articles repr. from the *Athenaeum* (1842) *English Poets* being a review of an anthology titled *The Book of the Poets; Psyche Apocalypté, a Lyrical Drama,* (London, 1876) written by R. H. Horne, an earlier draft printed in *Hitherto Unpublished Poems* (see below); *The Enchantress, and Other Poems,* (London, 1913); E. Gosse, ed., *Epistle to a Canary,* (London, 1913); *Leila, a Tale,* (London, 1913); H. B. Forman, ed., *Hitherto Unpublished Poems and Stories, with an Unauthorized Autobiography,* 2 vols. (Boston, 1914); F. G. Kenyon, ed., *New Poems by Robert Browning and Elizabeth Barrett Browning,* (London, 1914); H. B. Forman, ed., *The Poet's Enchiridion,* (Boston, 1914); F. Ratchford, ed., *Sonnets from the Portuguese,* (New York, 1950) centennial variorum ed., with intro by Ratchford and notes by D. Fulton—the 1856 text as finally rev. by E. B. Browning, but with variant readings from MS texts in the British Museum, Morgan Library, and Houghton Library.

LETTERS AND DIARIES

S. R. T. Mayer, ed., *Letters Addressed to Richard Hengist Horne,* 2 vols. (London, 1877); *Kind Words from a Sickroom: [Four] Letters Addressed to Allan Park Paton,* (Greenock, 1891) privately printed; F. G. Kenyon, ed., *Letters of Elizabeth Barrett Browning,* 2 vols. (London, 1897) with biographical editions by Kenyon; *Letters of Robert Browning and Elizabeth Barrett, 1845–46,* 2 vols. (London, 1899); Lubbock, P., *Elizabeth Barrett Browning in Her Letters,* (London, 1906) a selection of the letters with critical commentary; *The Religious Opinions of Elizabeth Barrett Browning: Three Letters Addressed to William Merry,* (London, 1906) originally printed privately (1896); *The Art of Scansion: Letter to Uvedale Price,* (London, 1916) with intro. by A. Meynell; *Letters Reprinted by T. J. Wise,* (London, 1916) (1919); T. J. Wise, ed., *Letters to Robert Browning and Other Correspondents,* (London, 1916) privately printed; L. Huxley, ed., *Elizabeth Barrett Browning: Letters to Her Sister 1846–1859,* (London, 1929); *Twenty-Two Unpublished Letters of Elizabeth Barrett Browning and Robert Browning, Addressed to Henrietta and Arabella Moulton-*

Barrett, (New York, 1935); W. R. Benét, ed., *From Robert and Elizabeth Browning: A Further Selection of the Barrett-Browning Family Correspondence,* (London, 1936); M. H. Shackford, ed., *Letters to Benjamin Robert Haydon,* (New York, 1939).

B. Weaver, ed., *Twenty Unpublished Letters to Hugh Stuart Boyd,* (London, 1950); B. Miller, ed., *Elizabeth Barrett to Miss Mitford: Letters to Mary Russell Mitford,* (London, 1954) with intro. by Miller; S. Musgrove, ed., *Unpublished Letters of Thomas De Quincey and Elizabeth Barrett Browning,* (Auckland, 1954); B. P. McCarthy, ed., *Elizabeth Barrett to Mr. Boyd: Unpublished Letters to Hugh Stuart Boyd,* (London, 1955) with intro. by McCarthy; P. Landis and R. E. Freeman, eds., *Letters of the Brownings to George Barrett,* (Urbana, Ill., 1958); G. R. Hudson, ed., *Browning and His American Friends: Letters Between the Brownings, the Storys and James Russell Lowell, 1841–1890,* (London, 1965); V. E. Stack, ed., *The Love Letters of Robert Browning and Elizabeth Barrett,* (London, 1969) selected with intro. by Stack; E. Kintner, ed., *The Letters of Robert Browning and Elizabeth Barrett, 1845–1846,* 2 vols. (Cambridge, Mass., 1969); W. B. Pope, ed., *Invisible Friends: The Correspondence of Elizabeth Barrett Browning and Benjamin Robert Haydon,* (Cambridge, Mass., 1972); E. Berridge, ed., *The Barretts at Hope End: The Early Diary of Elizabeth Barrett Browning,* (London, 1974); P. N. Heydon and P. Kelley, eds., *Elizabeth Barrett Browning's Letters to Mrs. David Ogilvy,* (London, 1974).

BIOGRAPHICAL AND CRITICAL STUDIES

R. H. Horne, ed., *A New Spirit of the Age,* (London, 1844) contains a chapter on "Miss E. B. Barrett and Mrs. Norton"; Taine, H. A., *Notes sur l'Angleterre,* (Paris, 1872) includes a brief and important study of E. B. Browning's poetry; Bayne, P., *Two Great Englishwomen: Mrs. Browning and Charlotte Brontë,* (London, 1881) critical study with a useful analysis of *The Seraphim* and "A Drama of Exile"; des Guerrois, C., *Etude sur Mistress Elizabeth Browning,* (Paris, 1885) analysis of her aesthetic theory and trans. of some of the poems; Sarrazin, G., *Poètes modernes de l'Angleterre,* (Paris, 1885) critical study; Ingram, J. H., *Elizabeth Barrett Browning,* (London, 1888) the first biography, inaccurate as to some dates and facts, but sensible on poetry; E. C. Stedman and G. E. Woodbury, eds., *Works of Edgar Allan Poe,* (Chicago, 1895) vol. VI contains an 1845 essay "Miss Barrett's *A Drama of Exile, and Other Poems*"; A. Meynell, intro to *Prometheus Bound . . . , and Other Poems,* (London, 1896) her first trans., first published in 1833; A. C. Swinburne, intro to *Aurora Leigh,* (London, 1898); James, H., *William Wetmore Story and His Friends,* (Edinburgh, 1903) includes some short but penetrating references to E. B. Browning; Gould, E. P., *The Brownings and America,* (Boston, 1904) contains a survey of American reviews of her poetry; Merlette, G. M., *La vie at l'oeuvre d'E. B. Browning,* (Paris, 1905) contains summaries and analyses of all principal poems and a study of prosodic experiments.

Whiting, L., *The Brownings, Their Life and Art,* (London, 1911) the first authoritative biography, includes many facts obtained from the Brownings' son; Trevelyan, G. M., *English Songs of Italian Freedom,* (London, 1911) assesses her influence on political opinion; Nicati, R. B., *Femme et poète: Elisabeth Browning,* (Paris, 1912) critical study which includes analysis of her religion; Viterbi, B., *Elisabetha Barrett Browning,* (Bergamo, 1913) biography; Trevelyan, G. M., *Englishmen and Italians: Some Aspects of Their Relations Past and Present,* (London, 1919) assesses her influence on political opinion; Burdett, O., *The Brownings,* (London, 1928) critical study; Boas, L. S., *Elizabeth Barrett Browning,* (London, 1930) biography; Woolf, V., *The Common Reader,* 2nd ser. (London, 1932) the most important critical study by a twentieth-century creative writer; Woolf, V., *Flush,* (London, 1933) ostensibly a biography of E. B. Browning's dog, but contains biographical material on her; Carter, J., and Pollard, G., *An Enquiry into the Nature of Certain Nineteeth Century Pamphlets,* (London, 1934) exposes the 1847 edition of *Sonnets from the Portuguese* as a forgery; Shackford, M. H., *Elizabeth Barrett Browning: R. H. Horne: Two Studies,* (Wellesley, Mass., 1935) critical study; Marks, J. A., *The Family of the Barrett,* (New York, 1938) history of the Barrett family in Jamaica, with a section on E. B. Browning's opium addiction.

Winwar, F., *The Immortal Lovers,* (London, 1950) biography; Hewlett, D., *Elizabeth Barrett Browning,* (London, 1953) biography and critical study; Maurois, A., *Robert et Elizabeth Browning,* (Paris, 1955) the best representative of the disillusioned view of the Brownings' story; Treves, G. A., *The Golden Ring: The Anglo-Florentines,* (London, 1956) section on the Brownings' lives and friends in Florence; Taplin, G. B., *The Life of Elizabeth Barrett Browning,* (London, 1957) biography incorporating much new material, valuable bibliography; Tompkins, J. M. S., *Aurora Leigh,* (London, 1961) the Fawcett Lecture, analyzes E. B. Browning's ideas on women as writers; Hayter, A., *Mrs. Browning: A Poet's Work and Its Setting,* (London, 1963) critical study; Hayter, A., *A Sultry Month: Scenes of London Literary Life in 1846,* (London, 1964); Hayter, A., *Opium and the Romantic Imagination,* (London, 1968) contains ch. on E. B. Browning as an opium taker; Pickering, G., *Creative Malady,* (London, 1974) also discusses E. B. Browning as an opium taker; Mander, R., *Mrs. Browning: The Story of Elizabeth Barrett,* (London, 1980).

Important material on E. B. Browning is contained in Robert Browning's letters and in biographies of him:

Lady Ritchie (Anna Isabella Thackeray), *Records of Tennyson, Ruskin and Browning* (London, 1892); Chesterton, G. K., *Robert Browning,* (London, 1903); Orr, Mrs. S., *Life and Letters of Robert Browning,* (London, 1908); Griffin, W. H., and Minchin, H. C., *Life of Robert Browning,* (London, 1910); T. L. Hood, ed., *Letters of Robert Browning,* (London, 1933); R. Curle, ed., *Robert Browning and Julia Wedgwood. A Broken Friendship as Revealed in Their Letters,* (London, 1937); E. C. McAleer, ed., *Dearest Isa. Robert Browning's Letters to Isabelle Blagden,* (Austin, Tex., 1951); W. C. de Vane and K. L. Knickerbocker, eds., *New Letters of Robert Browning,* (London, 1951); Miller, B., *Robert Browning, a Portrait,* (London, 1953); Duffin, H. C., *Amphibian: A Reconsideration of Browning,* (London, 1956); Ward, M., *Robert Browning and His World; the Private Face,* (London, 1968); Irvine, W., and Honan, P., *The Book, the Ring and the Poet: A Biography of Robert Browning,* (London, 1975).

ROBERT BROWNING
(1812–1889)

PHILIP DREW

LIFE

I only knew one poet in my life:
And this, or something like it, was his way.

BROWNING WROTE THESE lines in one of his finest poems, "How It Strikes a Contemporary." It is a monologue spoken by a carefree young man, and the whole point of it is his total inability to reconcile the dull humdrum routine of the poet, who lives humbly in the world, with the conventional picture of the excitements of artistic life:

I found no truth in one report at least—
That if you tracked him to his home, down lanes
Beyond the Jewry, and as clean to pace,
You found he ate his supper in a room
Blazing with lights, four Titians on the wall,
And twenty naked girls to change his plate!
Poor man, he lived another kind of life
In that new stuccoed third house by the bridge,
Fresh-painted, rather smart than otherwise!
The whole street might o'erlook him as he sat,
Leg crossing leg, one foot on the dog's back,
Playing a decent cribbage with his maid
(Jacynth, you're sure her name was) o'er the cheese
And fruit, three red halves of starved winter-pears,
Or treat of radishes in April. Nine,
Ten, struck the church clock, straight to bed went he.[1]
(72–87)

Many close observers remarked on the contrast between the ordinariness of Browning's own life, especially in his later years when he lived in London, and the exuberant products of his imagination. Perhaps there has never been a poet whose private life was more carefully insulated from his published works. Therefore, in setting out the simple facts of his career, I do so with a double warning—first, that they are not of especial interest in comparison with the really important events of his life, his poems; and secondly, that Browning himself bitterly denounced any attempt to establish a connection, in either direction, between his personal opinions and the ideas he handled in his poetry.

Robert Browning was born on 7 May 1812 in Camberwell, one of the southeastern suburbs of London. His father, a clerk in the Bank of England who had broad and varied tastes in art and literature, owned a large collection of books (chosen on catholic principles), which Browning was encouraged to read. "My first dawn of life," he wrote later, in *Pauline,* "Passed alone with wisest ancient books/All halo-girt with fancies of my own." There is little doubt that this exceptionally wide but

1. Quotations from all poems published through 1864 (except "Memorabilia," of which the first edition of 1855 has been used) are from I. Jack, ed., *Browning. Poetical Works, 1833–1864* (London, 1970). All later poems are from A. Birrell, ed., *The Complete Poetical Works,* 2 vols. (New York, 1915).

unsystematic reading, especially of plays and works of curious scholarship, laid the foundation for the extraordinary diversity of interests that was to mark his poetry throughout his life. At the same time he was keenly interested in the writing of his contemporaries. In 1826, his father's cousin gave him a volume of Shelley's lyrics, which influenced Browning at once. He declared himself, if only temporarily, a vegetarian and an atheist like Shelley; but the literary effect went far deeper, for the book led Browning to read Keats and the other romantic poets and to recognize that poetry was to be his life's work. In a later poem, "Memorabilia" (1855), he recorded the enduring impression of this first encounter with Shelley:

> Ah, did you once see Shelley plain,
> And did he stop and speak to you?
> And did you speak to him again?
> How strange it seems, and new!
>
> But you were living before that,
> And you are living after,
> And the memory I started at—
> My starting moves your laughter!
>
> I crossed a moor with a name of its own
> And a use in the world no doubt,
> Yet a hand's-breadth of it shines alone
> 'Mid the blank miles round about—
>
> For there I picked up on the heather
> And there I put inside my breast
> A moulted feather, an eagle-feather—
> Well, I forget the rest.

Browning's mother, Sarah Anne Wiedemann, was born in Scotland of a German father and Scottish mother. She was a devout Congregationalist, and saw to it that her son's religious education was thorough; otherwise he depended on a local school and his father's tuition in the classics. Since he had been brought up as a Nonconformist, the older English universities were not open to him. (It is perhaps worth noting that he and Keats were the only major poets of the nineteenth century not to be enrolled at either Oxford or Cambridge.) His father was one of the original subscribers to the new foundation on nonsectarian principles of University College, London, and in return for his money he was allowed to claim a place at the college for his son. Browning entered classes in 1828 in German, Latin, and Greek, but left after a very short time. Thereafter he lived at home with his parents, at first in Camberwell and, after 1840, in Hatcham, two or three miles farther out of town. He made a journey to St. Petersburg in 1834 with George de Benkhausen, at that time the Russian consul general, and paid two short visits to Italy in 1838 and 1844.

It was in this period, from 1832 to 1846, that he wrote his early poems, long and short, and most of his plays. His first published work, *Pauline: A Fragment of a Confession* (1833), appeared anonymously. It is ostensibly a dramatic monologue addressed to an imaginary Pauline, but most of its early readers assumed that it was a naked revelation of the poet's own adolescent passions and preoccupations. John Stuart Mill, for instance, wrote scornfully of the poet's exposure and indulgence of his own emotions and his "intense and morbid self-consciousness." There is a persistent tradition that it was Mill's critique which determined Browning never again to write poetry which would leave him open to attacks of this kind. Certainly almost all of his subsequent works were more objective—either unmistakably in the person of a fictitious character or specifically designed to be performed on the stage.

In 1835, he published *Paracelsus* and in 1840, *Sordello,* both long and elaborate poems dealing with men of extraordinary gifts trying to express in words their strivings with the complexities of the world of the Renaissance. *Paracelsus* was on the whole favorably received, but *Sordello* was generally declared unreadable and became a byword for incomprehensibility. It made exhausting demands on the reader's knowledge of an obscure period of history, employed an immense vocabulary of unusual words, and presumed a readiness to master long sentences of great syntactical difficulty. It is hard to exaggerate the derision with which the poem was greeted or the damaging effect on the young poet's reputation of these two long and unyielding poems. This was especially unfortunate, since *Sordello* in particular contained many passages in which a new poetic voice could be clearly heard:

> "Not any strollings now at even-close
> Down the field-path, Sordello! by thorn-rows
> Alive with lamp-flies, swimming spots of fire
> And dew, outlining the black cypress' spire
> She waits you at, Elys, who heard you first
> Woo her, the snow-month through, but ere she durst
> Answer't was April. Linden-flower-time-long
> Her eyes were on the ground; 'tis July, strong
> Now; and because white dust-clouds overwhelm
> The woodside, here or by the village elm
> That holds the moon, she meets you, somewhat pale,
> But letting you lift up her coarse flax veil
> And whisper (the damp little hand in yours)
> Of love, heart's love, your heart's love that endures
> Till death. . . ."
> (III.103–117)

Browning himself perhaps wanted, like Sordello, to talk in "'brother's speech'" "'in half-words, call things by half-names,'" and did not realize how difficult it was for the reader to decipher these intimate communications. Nevertheless, the poem was much talked of, and Browning soon found himself on friendly terms with many of the leading poets, editors, and artists of the day.

Meanwhile, his lively interest in the theater continued, and he was persuaded to write a number of verse dramas, mainly for the famous actor-manager William Charles Macready. Although these plays were not as spectacularly unsuccessful as Browning liked to pretend in later years, not all of them were staged, and those that were did not run for long. Browning enjoyed writing for the theater, because it safeguarded the impersonality of the author and yet gave him an immediate response from the audience, but his strength lay, as he observed himself, in depicting "Action in Character, rather than Character in Action."

Of his eight works written in the form of plays, only *Pippa Passes* (1841) has any real dramatic life. It is ingeniously constructed in four parts, in each of which the singing of the little mill-girl Pippa is of crucial effect, as she passes by on her one day's holiday of the year, unconscious of the part she is playing in the lives of others. Between 1841 and 1846, Browning published under the title *Bells and Pomegranates* a series of eight pamphlets that included all the plays that he had written for the theater. These, like most of his earlier works, were printed at the expense of his family. The third and the seventh pamphlets in the series (1842, 1845) were devoted to short poems. They include "My Last Duchess," "Soliloquy of the Spanish Cloister," "Waring," "The Pied Piper of Hamelin," "'How They Brought the Good News from Ghent to Aix (16—),'" "Pictor Ignotus, Florence 15—," "The Lost Leader," "Home Thoughts from Abroad," "The Bishop Orders His Tomb at St. Praxed's Church," and "The Flight of the Duchess." They were distinguished by their liveliness and strong feeling and by a firm incisiveness that led a contemporary reviewer to comment, "They look as though already packed up and on their way to posterity," while the poet Walter Savage Landor wrote:

> . . . Since Chaucer was alive and hale
> No man has walked along our road with step
> So active, so inquiring eye, or tongue
> So varied in discourse. . . .

One of Browning's most distinguished admirers was the poet Elizabeth Barrett, who included in her *Poems* (1844) some lines in praise of him. When he wrote to thank her, a voluminous and passionate correspondence followed. They met in May 1845 and soon discovered that they were deeply in love. Miss Barrett, however, had been treated for many years as an incurable invalid. Her father was a dominant and possessive man, profoundly attached to his daughter, who depended equally on his love. She was ordered to Italy for her health; when her father refused to allow her to travel, Robert and Elizabeth decided to wait no longer. They were married secretly in London in September 1846, and left for Pisa a week later, arriving there safely in spite of Browning's notable incompetence in reading a timetable.

Mrs. Browning was never forgiven by her father, who returned her letters unopened, but in every other way the clandestine marriage was strikingly happy and successful. Elizabeth's health improved in Italy and a son, Robert Wiedemann Browning ("Pen"), was born in 1849. The Brownings spent holidays in France and in England, but regarded Italy as their home, living mainly in Florence in a flat in Casa Guidi (the flat is now owned by the Browning Institute. It has been carefully restored and is open to visitors). At first they lived on a fairly small income, but after Pen's birth, John Kenyon, Mrs. Browning's cousin, made them an allowance of (pounds) 100 a year; when he died in 1856 he left them (pounds) 11,000. They lived a pleasant life, not mixing very much in Florentine society, but enjoying the company of English and American writers and artists. Mrs. Browning was an ardent supporter of the unification of Italy, a cause with which Browning sympathized more temperately; but both of them were at one in a love of Italy and the Italians. "Italy was my university," Browning wrote, and one of his most famous poems concludes as follows:

> What I love best in all the world
> Is a castle, precipice-encurled,
> In a gash of the wind-grieved Apennine.
> Or look for me, old fellow of mine,
>
> . . .
>
> In a sea-side house to the farther South,
> Where the baked cicala die of drouth,
> And one sharp tree—'tis a cypress—stands,
> By the many hundred years red-rusted,
> Rough iron-spiked, ripe fruit-o'ercrusted,
> My sentinel to guard the sands
> To the water's edge. For, what expands
> Before the house, but the great opaque
> Blue breadth of sea without a break?
> While, in the house, for ever crumbles
> Some fragment of the frescoed walls,
> From blisters where a scorpion sprawls.
> A girl bare-footed brings, and tumbles
> Down on the pavement, green-flesh melons,
> And says there's news today—the king
> Was shot at, touched in the liver-wing,
> Goes with his Bourbon arm in a sling:
> —She hopes they have not caught the
> felons.
>
> Italy, my Italy!
> Queen Mary's saying serves for me—
> (When fortune's malice
> Lost her—Calais)—
> Open my heart and you will see
> Graved inside of it, "Italy".
> Such lovers old are I and she:
> So it always was, so shall ever be!
> ("'De Gustibus—,'" 14–17; 21–46)

A reviewer in *Chambers Journal* commented tartly in 1863: "He has chosen to make his dwelling in Italy. His preference for that spot is undisguised, and, to Englishmen, almost repulsive."

Not surprisingly, many of Browning's most spirited poems at this time dealt with Italian subjects and scenes, but the first poem of his married life, *Christmas-Eve and Easter-Day* (1850), is firmly based on British themes. After a review of the various modes of religious life open to men at the time, Browning affirms his own decision to continue to worship in the tradition of Protestant dissent. We may perhaps detect here the influence of the circumstances of his own life, for his mother, his earliest guide in religious matters, had recently died, and Elizabeth was herself a devoted churchwoman.

In 1852, Browning was asked to write an introduction to a volume of letters by his early hero Shelley. The letters proved to be spurious, but the introduction survives as Browning's only considerable work in prose and an invaluable introduction to his opinions about the nature of poetry. In one of his letters at about this time, he told his French friend Joseph Milsand, "I am writing—a first step towards popularity for me—lyrics with more music and painting than before, so as to get people to hear and see" (24 February 1853). The sentiment is echoed in a letter to John Forster: "I hope to be listened to this time" (5 June 1854). The result was his best-known and most popular work, *Men and Women* (1855). It contained fifty-one poems, most of which are now to be found dispersed under other headings in complete editions of his works. Some of them are short dramatic pieces, such as "Memorabilia," "Love Among the Ruins," "A Toccata of Galuppi's," " 'Childe Roland to the Dark Tower Came,' " and "Two in the Campagna," continuing the vein of his earlier lyrics, but with an even more powerful combination of technical assurance and warmth of feeling. Other poems in the volume are among Browning's most celebrated extended dramatic monologues, such as "Karshish," "Cleon," "Andrea del Sarto," "Fra Lippo Lippi," "A Grammarian's Funeral," and "Bishop Blougram's Apology." In addition, there were a very few poems in which Browning for once spoke about himself and his love for his wife, either obliquely as in "By the Fire-side," or openly as in "One Word More":

> Love, you saw me gather men and women,
> Live or dead or fashioned by my fancy,
> Enter each and all, and use their service,
> Speak from every mouth,—the speech, a
> poem.
> Hardly shall I tell my joys and sorrows,
> Hopes and fears, belief and disbelieving:
> I am mine and yours—the rest be all men's,
> Karshish, Cleon, Norbert and the fifty.
> Let me speak this once in my true person,
> Not as Lippo, Roland or Andrea,
> Though the fruit of speech be just this
> sentence:
> Pray you, look on these my men and women,
> Take and keep my fifty poems finished;
> Where my heart lies, let my brain lie also!
> (XIV. 129–142)
>
> . . .
>
> God be thanked, the meanest of his
> creatures
> Boasts two soul-sides, one to face the world
> with,
> One to show a woman when he loves her!
> (XVII.184–186)

It was a fine collection of poems, fit to stand comparison with any in the nineteenth century; but it did not find a large number of readers, except among young people. The reviews were mainly uncomprehending and unsympathetic, and eight years after it appeared his publisher still had copies unsold. Browning was more than a little disappointed by the reception of his work; his letters at this period show his bitterness and resignation. He took refuge in drawing and modeling in clay and in the society of his friends, but soon a graver concern occupied his days. Mrs. Browning, although she had been remarkably restored by living in Italy, had never been strong, and her health began to fail. She died on 29 June 1861 with her husband at her side. Browning was heartbroken. He at once decided to "go away, break up everything, go to England, and live and work and write." In the autumn he left Florence, never to return, and slowly traveled back to England with his young son.

He undertook to prepare Elizabeth's *Last Poems* for the press, unselfishly pleased as ever that the sales of her work much exceeded those of his own. Gradually he began to accept invitations and to move in society, eventually becoming much in demand as a guest. His next book of poems, *Dramatis Personae* (1864), included some of his most intricate argumentative monologues, such as "A Death in the Desert," "Caliban upon Setebos," and "Mr. Sludge 'the Medium,' " yet it proved unexpectedly popular, a second edition being called for during the same year. This, taken together with the encouraging sales of a collected edition and a volume of selections (both 1863), showed that Browning was at last beginning to overcome the mistrust of the British public. On the death in 1866 of Browning's father, who had lived in Paris since 1852 as a consequence of a mildly scandalous court case, the poet's sister Sarianna came to live with him in Warwick Crescent, London. She kept house for him and was his companion in his many holidays abroad.

In four monthly volumes (1868–1869) Browning published his longest and most ambitious work, *The Ring and the Book,* which is over 21,000 lines in length. He had been working on it at intervals since 1860, and had devised a method of telling the story that allowed him full use of his dramatic and speculative gifts. The execution was equally authoritative. The poem's reception was mixed, but the major reviews were full of praise for its vigor, scope, and originality. Once more the sales were encouraging, with a second edition appearing in 1872.

By this time Browning was established as a prominent and high-spirited member of London society, to the point where many people found his unaffected enjoyment of dinner parties hard to reconcile with any very intense inner life. He spent much of his time in London planning his son's education or trying to help him in his career as an artist, and usually spent the summer with friends in France or Switzerland or Scotland. In one of his poems of the 1870's we can catch a pleasant glimpse of Browning on holiday on the French coast; his simple physical enjoyment is as characteristic as his sharpness and specificity of observation:

> Meek, hitherto un-Murrayed bathing-place,
> Best loved of sea-coast-nook-ful Normandy!
> That, just behind you, is mine own hired
> house:
> With right of pathway through the field in
> front,
> No prejudice to all its growth unsheaved
> Of emerald luzern bursting into blue.
> Be sure I keep the path that hugs the wall,
> Of mornings, as I pad from door to gate!
> Yon yellow—what if not wild-mustard
> flower?—
> Of that, my naked sole makes lawful prize,
> Bruising the acrid aromatics out,
> Till, what they preface, good salt savours
> sting
> From, first, the sifted sands, then sands in
> slab,
> Smooth save for pipy wreath-work of the
> worm:
> (Granite and mussel-shell are ground alike
> To glittering paste,—the live worm troubles
> yet.)
> Then, dry and moist, the varech[2] limit-line,
> Burnt cinder-black, with brown uncrumpled
> swathe
> Of berried softness, sea-swoln thrice its size;
> And, lo, the wave protrudes a lip at last,
> And flecks my foot with froth, nor tempts
> in vain.
> *Red Cotton Night-Cap Country,* I.20–40)

It was while he was staying in Scotland in 1869 that he proposed marriage to Louisa, Lady Ashburton, a rich and attractive widow, explaining candidly to her that his heart lay buried with his wife in Florence and that for him the real attraction of the match would be the advantages to his son Pen. When Lady Ashburton not unreasonably declined the offer, there followed much recrimination and unpleasant gossip, which distressed Browning more than his rejection.

By now Browning wrote with great fluency and was able to produce with comparatively little effort a series of long poems, some narrative, some dramatic, mainly dealing with subjects of contemporary interest. *Prince Hohenstiel-Schwangau* (1871), for example, described obliquely the career and political philosophy of Napoleon III of France. It was followed by *Fifine at the Fair* (1872), a prolonged monologue by a modern Don Juan about constancy in love in a world of shifting values; *Red Cotton Night-Cap Country, or Turf and Towers* (1873), set in Normandy and based on a recent cause célèbre; *The Inn Album* (1875), based on a story current in the clubs of London; and the two series of *Dramatic Idyls* (1879, 1880). Throughout his life Browning was interested, as an accomplished amateur, in the study of Latin and, even more, of Greek. He wrote in the 1870's a number of long poems on classical themes, including *Balaustion's Adventure* (1871), which contains a version of Euripides' *Alcestis,* and Aristopha-

2. seaweed.

nes' *Apology* (1875), which contains a version of Euripides' *Herakles.* He also made a translation of *The Agamemnon of Aeschylus* (1877), which is so hard to follow—it was said that it could be understood quite easily with the help of the original Greek—that Browning has been suspected of deliberately making it obscure and unattractive in order to score a point in his argument with Matthew Arnold about the nature of poetry.

Browning continued to write with undiminished energy. He produced many collections of shorter poems—*Pacchiarotto and How He Worked in Distemper: With Other Poems* (1876), *Jocoseria* (1883), and *Ferishtah's Fancies* (1884)—and two poems of more than usually close personal interest—*La Saisiaz* (1878), in which the poet moves from an elegy for his friend Anne Egerton Smith to a sustained meditation on the need for belief in life after death, and *Parleyings with Certain People of Importance in Their Day* (1887), in which he conducts imaginary dialogues with dead and forgotten writers and artists whose ideas had influenced him at varying stages of his life and who are ingeniously made to contribute to the discussion of some of the major controversial issues of Victorian England. This series of poems is as near as Browning ever ventured to writing an intellectual autobiography.

Browning and his sister continued to take holidays abroad, visiting Italy after 1878, and Browning eventually bought the Ca' Rezzonico in Venice. While staying there in 1889 he caught a cold and became seriously ill. His last book of poems, *Asolando: Fancies and Facts,* had just been published; he had time to learn that it had been favorably received before he died on 12 December. His popularity had been increasing slowly but steadily since the mid-1860's, and had been denoted by honorary degrees from the University of Oxford, an honorary fellowship of Balliol College, and presentation to the queen. Public recognition of his distinction was fittingly completed by his burial in Westminster Abbey. So much for the facts of a life which, apart from the decisive central episode, is little more than a tale of devotion to a demanding and financially unrewarding profession.

This section must conclude as it began, with a warning that Browning himself strenuously objected to any attempt to establish connections between his life and his poetry, between the public and the private face. As he wrote to his publisher in 1887, "I am so out of sympathy with all this 'biographical matter' connected with works which ought to stand or fall by their own merits quite independent of the writer's life and habits that I prefer leaving my poems to speak for themselves." He expresses the same position pungently in poems such as "House" and "At the 'Mermaid.' " Every biographer of the poet must hear the voice of Browning's Shakespeare demanding indignantly:

> Which of you did I enable
> Once to slip inside my breast,
> There to catalogue and label
> What I like least, what love best,
> Hope and fear, believe and doubt of,
> Seek and shun, respect—deride?
> Who has right to make a rout of
> Rarities he found inside?
> ("At the Mermaid,' " V)

We have then to observe particular discretion in relating the poems and the life, bearing constantly in mind the advertisement that Browning put before his first collection of short poems: "Such poems as the following come properly enough, I suppose, under the head of 'Dramatic Pieces', being, though for the most part Lyric in expression, always Dramatic in principle, and so many utterances of so many imaginary persons, not mine."

THE DRAMATIC MONOLOGUE

Browning exploited the dramatic mode at every period of his career, and is the most ambitious and successful writer of the dramatic monologue in English. Indeed it is hardly possible to read Browning at all without some understanding of what the dramatic monologue is and of the different purposes it can be made to serve in the hand of a master.

In its simplest form, the dramatic monologue is a poem purporting to be the words of an imaginary or historical character, not the poet. Nothing is provided by way of context beyond the title and the words of the poem, but from these it is generally possible for the reader to infer the circumstances in which the monologue is delivered, who the listener or listeners are and how they are receiving what they hear, and something of the earlier history of the speaker. Of all this the speaker is aware. But expertly handled, the monologue can also reveal a great deal that the speaker does not realize he is betraying, particularly of course about his own character and motives, his accuracy as a narrator of events, and his trustworthiness as a judge of other people. In this indirect way the reader is put in possession of the material he needs to assess the speaker and thus to come to a conclusion about the issues that are raised in the poem. Since this is a process that continues throughout the monologue, it is difficult to illustrate compactly; examples in which it can be seen operating fairly obviously are the early poems "Porphyria's Lover," "Johannes Agricola in Meditation," "My Last Duchess," and "Soliloquy of the Spanish Cloister," or the much later "A Forgiveness."

Formally, of course, we see the entire action from the point of view of the speaker, but it is nevertheless a mistake to suppose that we are therefore committed entirely to the speaker's position, for, as I have said, we are often able to decide whether his view is comprehensive or in some way limited. A simple and straightforward example of this is "Up at a Villa—Down in the City" (1855); the main point of the poem is that the contrasts drawn by the speaker, with his exaggerated ideas of the only fashionable way to live, are all reversed by the reader, so that the arguments advanced in favor of the town are seen to be superficial, while the speaker's complaints about the countryside only show his blindness to its beauty:

What of a villa? Though winter be over in
 March by rights,
'Tis May perhaps ere the snow shall have
 withered well off the heights:
You've the brown ploughed land before,
 where the oxen steam and wheeze,
And the hills over-smoked behind by the
 faint grey olive-trees.
(V)

The major monologues, however, do not yield their meaning to a simple reversal of values. Consider, for example, the poem "Cleon" (1855). The speaker is a Greek poet, heir to all the riches of Hellenic civilization, yet unhappy and troubled in his mind. He debates with himself the question of the immortality of the soul and the inevitability of death, which, he says,

. . . is so horrible.
I dare at times imagine to my need
Some future state revealed to us by Zeus,
Unlimited in capability
For joy, as this is in desire for joy,
. . .
. . . But no!
Zeus has not yet revealed it; and alas,
He must have done so, were it possible!
(323–327; 333–335)

In the last paragraph of the poem Cleon refers slightingly to an inquiry after the apostle Paul:

. . . we have heard his fame
Indeed, if Christus be not one with him—
I know not, nor am troubled much to know.
Thou canst not think a mere barbarian Jew
As Paulus proves to be, one circumcized,
Hath access to a secret shut from us?
Thou wrongest our philosophy, O king,
In stooping to enquire of such an one,
As if his answer could impose at all!
He writeth, doth he? well, and he may write.
O the Jew findeth scholars! certain slaves
Who touched on this same isle, preached
 him and Christ;
And (as I gathered from a bystander)
Their doctrine could be held by no sane man.
(340–353)

So the monologue concludes. The irony of the poem very plainly resides in the fact that Cleon longs for some promise of personal immortality, yet when he has the opportunity to hear Christian teaching, he dismisses it on hearsay evidence because he cannot bring himself to admit that a Greek has anything to learn from a barbarian. The reader is conscious of Cleon's inadequacy and can use this knowledge to arrive at a judgment of him that is not one of simple moral approval or disapproval but rather an assessment of him and his subject.

A similar technique may be observed in "Karshish," in which an Arab physician refuses to accept the testimony of Lazarus himself because his scientific learning and his intellectual caution forbid him to take miracles seriously, yet he too, as we learn, longs for the all-loving God of Christianity. Thus in these two poems, though they are presented dramatically, with no voice heard but that of Cleon or Karshish, we do not rest content with the experiences they describe. Browning forces us to recognize each speaker's limitations, and is able in this way not only to control our opinions of his character but also to suggest fresh ways of thinking about Christianity, both as it was in the days of the early church and as it is in our own time. We can see that the pride that prevents Cleon from accepting the faith for which his heart is yearning and the intellectual scruples that prevent Karshish from acknowledging the true nature of his strange experiences have their counterparts in the nineteenth century and the twentieth.

It is clear that in many of his monologues, including some of the most notable, Browning is challenging the reader to appraise the value of the first-person narrative and to pronounce it and the speaker to be defective in some way. In others he does not invite the same scrutiny, but is, as far as one can tell, "lending his voice out" in an endeavor to allow a speaker to express a point of view that is not ironically exhibited. Poems such as " 'How They Brought the Good News' " and "The Flight of the Duchess" fall into this category, as do "Andrea del Sarto" and "Fra Lippo Lippi." We are provided with no reason to suppose that the speaker's words are not to be taken at face value, even though we know, of course, that we are receiving one man's version of events, which is necessarily incomplete.

Most of Browning's monologues fall, as one would expect, somewhere between these two extremes, either because we can sense an ironic undercurrent but cannot be quite sure whether or not it is directed against the speaker, as in "Pictor Ignotus" and "A Grammarian's Funeral," or because the speaker successfully attacks one set of ideas while revealing at the same time that his own position is even less tenable. Such is "Bishop Blougram's Apology," which is worth a closer examination as an outstanding example of Browning's skill in manipulating the single voice of the speaker to produce dramatic and dialectic effects of great complexity.

A few economical phrases serve to establish the setting: a great dignitary of the Roman Catholic church in Britain has for a whim entertained to dinner an insignificant journalist, Gigadibs, who has written critically of the bishop's religious position. As they sit over their wine, the bishop embarks on a long examination of the nature of faith, which is simultaneously an assault on Gigadibs' skepticism and a defense of his own selected compromises. Blougram is a man of the world with a well-stocked mind and a copious supply of witty and ingenious arguments. Wherever he attacks the sterile reductive arguments of Gigadibs he is victorious, but the reader eventually perceives that for all his worldly charm and intellectual flexibility many, if not all, of the points he puts forward in his own favor are disingenuous or evasive, especially his calculating avowal of belief in popular superstitions and his false public professions of complete freedom from religious doubt.

At the conclusion of the poem, Blougram states with great condescension and complacency his conviction that the only possible alternative to Gigadibs' mean and sheeplike existence is one of luxury and secular influence like his own. Browning then adds an unexpected *coda* in which the monologue form is abandoned and he simply narrates, without comment, the effect of the bishop's words on Gigadibs, who has given close attention to everything he has heard. Routed from his position of complete unbelief, and—convinced by Blougram's blatant dishonesty of the falsity of any compromise, he is seized with "a sudden healthy vehemence," renounces his life in Britain, and decides to lead, with his family, a simple, practical life in Australia, where,

> . . . I hope,
> By this time he has tested his first plough
> And studied his last chapter of St. John.
> (1012–1014)

The whole effect of the monologue is thus to convert Gigadibs from disbelief to Christianity. But the judgment involved is not a simple one, for Blougram is by no means presented as an entirely unsympathetic figure. He is intelligent enough to see the implications of his own arguments, but lacks the courage to take them to their logical conclusion. He can only shelter behind defenses whose hollowness is evident even to himself, although he has at times painful glimpses of a world of belief he can never reach. It is because of this self-frustrated desire for faith that the reader, even while he observes the feebleness of Blougram's sophistries, sympathizes with him, just as he does with Karshish and Cleon. But to say that we feel sympathy for the speaker and at the same time condemn his evasiveness is not to say that the two impulses cancel out, leaving us indifferent. On the contrary, the poem is a powerful affirmation not just of faith but of the need for belief, made even more moving by being put into the mouth of a man who is not himself able to sustain the demands of Christianity.

The purpose of that extended account of "Bishop Blougram's Apology" is to illustrate the point that there are two mistaken ways of reading a dramatic monologue—the first, naive way is to suppose that the words spoken are to be taken at their face value as a literal expression of Browning's own sentiments; the second way, scarcely less naive, is to suppose that the only alternative to the first way is to accept that we can never go behind the words of the monologue and infer Browning's opinion of the speaker. This may sometimes be true, but in general the central performance of the monologue is that of putting the reader in a position to judge the speaker.

The most celebrated example of this is *The Ring and the Book* (1868–1869), a poem of great length based on the proceedings in a late seventeenth-century Italian court case. Book I explains how Browning came across an account of the trial as he strolled through a square in Florence, and book XII concludes the story; but books II-XI are all massive monologues, many of them over 2,000 lines long, each recounting a different version of the same set of events as they appeared to the participants, to their lawyers, and to members of the public. It might seem that such a procedure would produce a relativist poem, in which the reader was handed, bewildered, from one narrator to another, each offering an account of the facts that can be neither proved nor disproved and must therefore lead in the end to a complete suspension of judgment. Yet nothing could be further removed from the experience of reading the poem. As each monologue makes its contribution to the reader's knowledge, a central body of truth is gradually established. The entire structure of *The Ring and the Book* implies that there is an objective truth, variously refracted though it may be, and that this truth, once it is perceived, is available for judging the honesty of each speaker. As Browning says, his object is to enable his readers to come at the true facts: "There's nothing in nor out o' the world/Good except truth" (I.698–699). He insists, however, that it is by the oblique exercise of his art, which is itself the mirror of creation, that the writer must make the truth available:

> So write a book shall mean beyond the facts,
> Suffice the eye and save the soul beside.
> (XII.866–867)

In conclusion it must be emphasized that the dramatic monologue was not, as some have suggested, a refuge to Browning, a mask behind which he could hide instead of writing poetry in his own person, nor was it a predetermined form that permitted only a limited range of effects. On the contrary, it was in Browning's hands, as I have tried to show, an infinitely flexible mode of expression, allowing him to exercise his mimetic and dramatic gifts to present characters with varying degrees of sympathy or satire; to lay stress on action or on "incidents in the development of a soul"; to handle matters from the past in a way that made them seem live and immediate or to handle issues of his own day with ironic detachment; and to involve the reader in the active process of discriminating truth from falsehood, of discovering the answer to Browning's constant question—"What say you to the right and wrong of that?"

It is at all times an intimate form, designed to entertain and instruct the reader by allowing him to hear the voices of men and women speaking about the matters that lie closest to their hearts: "what I imagine the man might, if he pleased, say for himself." Browning describes Gigadibs listening patiently "While the great bishop rolled him out a mind/Long crumpled, till creased consciousness lay smooth." When we read the great monologues, we can see that the man who fashioned them had nothing to learn from later novelists about the technique of displaying a stream of consciousness or from psychologists about the devious recesses of the human personality.

BROWNING AND CHRISTIAN TEACHING

Browning once defined his own interests with memorable brevity as "Man's thoughts, loves, hates," and of the thoughts none engaged him more constantly than the various attempts to comprehend and explain the relation of God and his creation. Having learned from the previous section that Browning had perfected the art of the dramatic monologue to a point where he could, if he wished, control the reader's response to the speaker and hence to the views he puts forward, we shall realize that once we understand the mechanism of the dramatic monologue, it is possible to construct a general sketch of the values that emerge from the poems as normally receiving the poet's approval. Although the religious and philosophical ideas that Browning was prepared to entertain and endorse changed fairly radically during his life, some central points remain constant. Browning never, for example, handles unkindly those who preserve a simple unquestioning faith in God, even though we may sense that he sometimes envies and sometimes pities their innocence. The most celebrated, indeed notorious, example come, from the play *Pippa Passes,* when the young mill-girl on her annual holiday sings happily as she goes on her way through the town of Asolo in the Trevisan:

> The year's at the spring
> And day's at the morn;
> Morning's at seven;
> The hill-side's dew-pearled;
> The lark's on the wing;
> The snail's on the thorn:
> God's in his heaven—
> All's right with the world!
> (I.222–229)

The whole action of the play is designed to show that Pippa is quite unconscious of the evil that is abroad in the town, and even the terms of her happy song are called in question in the concluding scene: "Ah Pippa, morning's rule is moved away,/Dispensed with, never more to be allowed!/Day's turn is over, now arrives the night's." Nevertheless, her artless faith, although it is shown to be naively blind to the darker side of life, is certainly not derided, and at the end of the play her trust in Providence is vindicated by events.

Browning never disparages those who with a clear heart and mind are lucky enough to be able to live by an uncomplicated set of religious or moral ideals, yet his own varieties of religious experience are by no means simple. A convenient place to begin the account is with *Christmas-Eve and Easter-Day* (1850). Technically this double poem can be read as an elaborate structure of monologues and dialogues, but Browning drops frequent hints that the arguments he is handling are not purely fictitious or hypothetical, but rather correspond to episodes in his own history and to positions that were in fact available to him and to his contemporaries. The poem, although dramatic in form, is thus not devoted to the manipulation of imaginary characters but to the clash and conflict of real arguments. The speaker reviews various modes of worship—the dissenting sect in " 'Mount Zion' with Love-lane at the back of it," the congregation at St. Peter's, the audience in the lecture hall of a German higher critic—and is tempted to say complacently, "This tolerance is a genial mood," and to pride himself on his broadmindedness. But he is violently shaken out of this "Lazy glow of benevolence,/O'er the various modes of man's belief," and forced to choose "one way, our chief/Best way of worship." He decides to stand fast in the dissenting chapel, as representing the sort of faith in which he has been brought up. It is the most difficult and demanding way of life, lacking the firm supporting dogma of Catholicism and the rational reassurances of the higher criticism.

> Thank God, no paradise stands barred
> To entry, and I find it hard
> To be a Christian, as I said!
>
> . . .
>
> . . . But Easter-Day breaks! But
> Christ rises! Mercy every way
> Is infinite,—and who can say?
> (XXXIII.1029–1031; 1038–1048)

So the poem ends. The concluding words epitomize its speculative, inquiring, anxious approach to matters of faith, and also the kind of Christian Browning had to be if he was to be a Christian at all—earnest, plain, strenuous, committed but undogmatic. Although the poem gives a not unsympathetic voice to an easier kind of religious life, its tenor is to expose the inadequacy of this looser faith, which ultimately appears to be no more than "a condiment/To heighten flavours with." Yet if the path of primitive Christianity is too hard, or, more pertinently, if it calls for an absolute faith in Christ that can no longer be commanded, Browning must face the teasing question of whether the laxer forms of belief are really any better than outright skepticism. *Christmas-Eve and Easter-Day* provides a masterly exposition of the issues at stake, which were to play their part in Browning's poetry for the rest of his life.

From the volumes of *Men and Women* (1855) I need mention only "Saul," "Cleon," "Karshish," and "Bishop Blougram's Apology" by way of example and illustration. These are all poems that are designed to bring home to the reader the power and hope of the dedicated Christian life and the loving promise of the incarnation:

> ". . . O Saul, it shall be
> A Face like my face that receives thee; a
> Man like to me,
> Thou shalt love and be loved by, for ever: a
> Hand like this hand
> Shall throw open the gates of new life to
> thee! See the Christ stand!"
> ("Saul," XVIII.309–312)

Yet in all of these poems great weight is also given to the difficulties and obstacles that lie in the way of faith. Browning never ceases to engage with this insoluble question. It is true that in his later years he wrote fewer poems that discuss Christian doctrines as such, but the central concerns of Christianity were his concerns also. In this sense Browning, though never neglecting "earth's common surface, rough, smooth, dry or damp," was always a religious poet. It is plain that by 1864, the year of *Dramatis Personae,* it was becoming more difficult for him to rely on biblical testimony as a defense against loss of faith, and correspondingly more difficult to rely on his Christian faith to confirm the value of his ethical insights.

In "A Death in the Desert," for example, a long monologue spoken by John the Evangelist on his deathbed, the central issues are the evidences for Christianity, especially the miracles, and the argument of critics like Ludwig Feuerbach that the love, might, and will of God are merely projections of human qualities. This last, in particular, is an argument that John sees to be sincere and worth answering; in doing so he uses arguments that Browning was to find attractive for many years. John reasons as follows: life is not static but a progression. Knowledge of God is a vital stage in man's progress: it leads him, among other things, to a consideration of his own stature in the universe. Now, however, he has not unreasonably concluded that if he is the only being in whom love, power, and will combine, he is himself the "first, last, and best of things," that is, God. If man reaches this conclusion, nobody can prove to him that he is wrong, but "his life becomes impossible, which is death."

> "How shall ye help this man who knows himself,
> That he must love and would be loved again,
> Yet, owning his own love that proveth Christ,
> Rejecteth Christ through very need of Him?"
> (508–511)

If, on the other hand, men will only admit in humility that they cannot know God's nature or their own with certainty, they will find their proper place in the world, for it is man's unique nature that he

> "Finds progress, man's distinctive mark alone,
> Not God's, and not the beasts': God is, they are,
> Man partly is and wholly hopes to be."
> (586–588)

Such progress is possible only because of man's ignorance and his consequent desire for knowledge. "He learns/Because he lives, which is to be a man."

It is sometimes objected that the language of "A Death in the Desert" is as drab and as arid as the wasteland in which it is set: it is fairer to say that Browning is working in deliberately neutral tones. Colorful rhetoric would be improper in the mouth of a dying man pondering the meaning of human life, and the issues are too delicately balanced to be settled by a passionate assertion of belief. In any case, Browning had not, at this point in his life, any straightforward solution to offer. To distinguish his own position from that of the higher critics, who were expertly scrutinizing the whole status of Holy Writ, he had to make ever more subtle discriminations. His language is consequently circumspect and hesitant, rather than bold and picturesque. By 1864, this constant questioning and sifting of his faith had left Browning far from the safe harbor of any church. Indeed, even the idea of God's love of man being made manifest in the incarnation of Christ, which had animated so many of his poems, is found much more rarely in his later work. Once Browning began to doubt the fundamental revealed truths of Christianity, he was confronted with two alternative ways of proceeding. To put the case crudely, he could either demythologize Christian doctrine and liberalize it until it no longer required an act of faith to assent to it, or he could analyze man's nature, hoping to discover there some elements of the absolute which would provide a stable principle in life. The difficulty is that Browning was always conscious that the first way might be a hypocritical compromise, as it was for Blougram, while the second might issue in the most blatant self-projection, as it did for the misguided Caliban in the monologue "Caliban upon Setebos."

In moving away from anything that might be termed orthodox Christianity, he moved very far also from any poetic tradition that might have helped him. After 1864, one of his chief technical problems was to discover a strategy for developing a poem of analysis and speculation; his chief achievement was the creation of a large number of long poems that were based not on a story or on a system of belief, but on the exploration of an important and difficult question. The clearest example of this is the fine poem *La Saisiaz* (1878). The occasion of the poem was the sudden death of an old friend of Browning's, Anne Egerton Smith, while she was staying with Browning and his sister near Geneva in a villa called "La Saisiaz." During the summer of 1877, Miss Smith and Browning had followed with great interest a symposium in the *Nineteenth Century* on "The Soul and Future Life," in which various writers discussed the question of the immortality of the soul, for the most part without appeal to revelation.

In the central part of *La Saisiaz* Browning makes his own contribution, as it were, to the debate, meditating on the possibility of establishing eternal life by reasoning from first principles and on the moral implications of the conclusions he reaches. Throughout the poem Browning observes the prior conditions of the symposium and does not rely on Christian evidences. He considers earnestly the critical questions that arise: whether he can convince himself of the immortality of the soul simply from an inspection of his own existence; what the purpose is of gaining experience in this world if it is not to be put to use elsewhere; and how a man would have to behave on earth if he knew for certain that there was a life to come. He explores these and other positions with some acuteness and great honesty, deciding at last that no certainty is available in such matters. All man's soul can do on earth is

> . . . pass probation, prove its powers, and exercise
> Sense and thought on fact, and then, from fact educing fit surmise,
> Ask itself, and of itself have solely answer, "Does the scope
> Earth affords of fact to judge by warrant future fear or hope?"
> (521–524)

The argument hinted at here, especially in the use of the terms "probation" and "exercise," is one that Browning made great use of throughout his career. It runs: only if we have limited knowledge can we view this life as one of probation; but only if we view this life as one of probation can we postulate a future life. Thus the imperfections of man's knowledge, far from being a source of despair, become the necessary condition for the immortality of man's soul. "Life is probation and this earth no goal/But starting-point of man." This device, by which human defects are seen to be positively welcome if they guarantee a life of constant striving toward an unattainable perfection, was memorably expressed in "Abt Vogler": "On earth the broken arcs; in the heaven, a perfect round"—and lies behind many later poems such as "Jochanan Hakkadosh," "Rephan," and "Reverie." He applies the idea very movingly to his own life in the poem "Development," remembering how gently his father had introduced him to the world of classical learning through the medium of plays based on Homer. Truth is never easy and sometimes it can be arrived at only through fictions, and yet it has its own unique value, which no fiction can ever have: "Truth ever, truth only the excellent." The particular religious issue that lies behind the poem is the problem of demythologizing: if you dispense with the historical evidences of Christ's existence in favor of an imaginative conviction of the truth of his ministry, is there any point short of total skepticism at which you can arrest the process?

"Development" appeared in *Asolando* (1890), Browning's last book of poems, in which he gives us the reflections of a man who does not claim to have found a final solution to problems of this kind, but is content to remember that at least he never gave up the fight to discover a position where a man might stand without sacrificing either his honor or his hope. The idea of human responsibility, of the duty to keep trying to do whatever it is right for a man to do, is never absent long from Browning's poems on religious subjects. When the framework of religious observance is stripped away, as it was in the poems of his old age, the responsibility remains and indeed becomes even heavier. Although he grew progressively less able to accept the literal truth of the incarnation and progressively less concerned with forms of worship, he was never less insistent that one of man's chief ends is to think earnestly about his place in creation and his corresponding duties.

A man who is living as he should be, doing his best to use his powers in a world that offers no possibility of absolute attainment, will be distinguished by his activeness and resilience:

> Though I do my best I shall scarce succeed.
> But what if I fail of my purpose here?
> It is but to keep the nerves at strain,
> To dry one's eyes and laugh at a fall,
> And, baffled, get up and begin again,—
> So the chace takes up one's life, that's all.
> ("Life in a Love," 10–15)

To discriminate between beneficial and harmful kinds of human energy, Browning's great touchstone is love. Characters who are in love or who act through love are almost always treated with affection and admiration. Love is the master passion, more powerful than evil and stronger than death:

> Love which endures and doubts and is oppressed
> And cherished, suffering much and much sustained,
> And blind, oft-failing, yet believing love,
> A half-enlightened, often-chequered trust. . . .
> (*Paracelsus,* V.702–705)

Thus, letting love slip, either through laziness or timidity, is unforgivable. Poems such as "Too Late" and "Dis aliter visum; or, Le Byron de nos Jours" illustrate Browning's general attitude to those who are afraid to accept the challenge of loving, while "The Statue and the Bust" is a more extreme example. On the whole, Browning presents favorably in his poems men and women who act intuitively as the heart dictates: "Let him rush straight, and how shall he go wrong?" the pope asks rhetorically. Conversely, he implies his dislike and contempt for those who behave cautiously and calculatingly, contrasting them unfavorably with those who boldly aim at a high mark even though they know that they cannot hope to reach their target. "Andrea del Sarto," with its carefully subdued register of gray and silver tones, shows how coolly Browning felt toward the man who aspired only to what he was certain he could achieve. In contrast, the scholar in "A Grammarian's Funeral," although to a superficial eye he has retreated from the real business of life, has in fact set his goal so high that it is perfectly plain that it cannot be achieved in this world. Therefore he must rely on a life to come, and his renunciation of the possibility of worldly success is in itself a testimony of faith. He is "still loftier than the world suspects,/Living and dying," and is saved because he has perceived that failure through attempting too much is in itself a kind of heroism. Human successes, by definition, are at best trivial compared with the works of God, but when he fails man is doing what God himself cannot do. "The incomplete,/More than completion, matches the immense." This idea can be found in many different places in Browning's work:

> But what's whole, can increase no more,
> Is dwarfed and dies, since here's its sphere.
> ("Dis aliter visum," XXIX.141–142)

> Manhood—the actual? Nay, praise the potential!
> . . .
> What *is*? No, what *may* be—sing! that's Man's essential.
> ("Apollo and the Fates," 211; 213)

> "Man's work is to labour and leaven—
> At best he may—earth here with heaven;
> 'Tis work for work's sake that he's needing:
> Let him work on and on as if speeding
> Work's end, but not dream of succeeding!
> Because if success were intended,
> Why, heaven would begin ere earth ended."
> ("Of Pacchiarotto," XXL.368–374)

> No, Man's the prerogative—knowledge once gained—

To ignore,—find new knowledge to press
  for, to swerve
In pursuit of, no, not for a moment:
  attained—
Why, onward through ignorance! Dare and
  deserve!
As still to its asymptote speedeth the curve,
So approximates Man—Thee, who,
  reachable not,
Hast formed him to yearningly follow Thy
  whole
Sole and single omniscience . . .
  ("Fust and His Friends," 421–428)

And what is our failure here but a triumph's
  evidence
For the fulness of the days? Have we
  withered or agonized?
Why else was the pause prolonged but that
  singing might issue thence?
Why rushed the discords in but that
  harmony should be prized?
  ("Abt Vogler," XI)

If to this brief summary of positions that Browning presents with favor we add the statement that he never doubted that human freedom was real and that men could if they chose attain a sufficient knowledge of truth, we have sketched in the main constants in Browning's thought. In this abstract formulation they may appear a primitive, perhaps even a barbarous, set of values, but when we encounter them as active forces in the poems they are much less naive. Browning realizes the moral lives of his speakers with singular richness and complexity. He portrays his casuists, for example, with great insight, and endows them generously with intellectual resourcefulness. But behind all the equivocations and all the sophistries, the reader is always aware of the presence of equally subtle moral standards which he will ultimately be expected to use himself to assess the worth of the speaker. I do not think that Browning has anywhere expressed these positive values more straightforwardly than in his essay on Shelley, where he wrote: "I call Shelley a moral man, because he was true, simple-hearted and brave, and because what he acted corresponded to what he knew."

BROWNING AS A POET OF VICTORIAN LIFE

So far I have discussed Browning as though his poems were distinguished by nothing more remarkable than an ingenious narrative technique and an uncompromising but basically uncomplicated view of human responsibility. Yet to many readers the essence of Browning lies quite elsewhere—in the exuberant freedom of his language and in the fertility of his invention of unusual situations and subjects for poems. He chose his topics freely from the classical world, from rabbinical lore, from the Middle Ages and the Renaissance, from the world of the Augustans, and from nineteenth-century life in Europe and America. His speakers are equally diverse in character. The experience of reading Browning is thus infinitely varied—from the pathos of "A Woman's Last Word" to the malicious hypocrisy of "Soliloquy of the Spanish Cloister," from the energetic heroism of "Hervé Riel" to the close argument of "A Death in the Desert," from the coarse jollity of "Holy-Cross Day" to the subtle casuistries of "Fifine at the Fair," from the slow unwinding of "The Inn Album" to the rapid easy narrative of "The Pied Piper of Hamelin," a list that could be extended without difficulty. It is worth remembering that at this time there was continuous and heated debate about the role of the poet in the modern world, and in particular about the proper subject matter of Victorian poetry. Browning, by his example no less than by his essay on Shelley, was a major force on the side of pluralism. He rejected alike any supposed romantic requirement to reveal his own commitment in his poems and any suggestion that the poet had a duty to lose himself in the remote classical impersonality of his subjects. Similarly he resisted with equal vigor those who thought that nineteenth-century life was not suitable material for poetry and those who thought that nothing else was. Browning always celebrates the diversity of human characters and activities:

He stood and watched the cobbler at his
trade,
The man who slices lemons into drink,
The coffee-roaster's brazier, and the boys
That volunteer to help him turn its winch.
He glanced o'er books on stalls with half an
eye,
And fly-leaf ballads on the vendor's string.
And broad-edge bold-print posters by the
wall.
He took such cognizance of men and things,
If any beat a horse, you felt he saw;
If any cursed a woman, he took note;
Yet stared at nobody,—you stared at him,
And found, less to your pleasure than
surprise,
He seemed to know you and expect as much.
("How It Strikes a Contemporary," 23–35)

He writes always with his eye on the object, determined to render it fully and specifically:

The swallow has set her six young on the rail,
And looks sea-ward:
The water's in stripes like a snake, olive-pale
To the leeward,—
On the weather-side, black, spotted white
with the wind.
. . .
Our fig-tree, that leaned for the saltness, has
furled
Her five fingers,
Each leaf like a hand opened wide to the
world
Where there lingers
No glint of the gold, Summer sent for her
sake . . .
("James Lee's Wife," III.54–58; 61–65)

I wonder, does the streamlet ripple still,
Outsmoothing galingale and watermint
Its mat-floor? while at brim, 'twixt sedge
and sedge,
What bubblings past Baccheion, broadened
much,
Pricked by the reed and fretted by the fly,
Oared by the boatman-spider's pair of arms!
(*Aristophanes' Apology,* 199–204)

Never mind! As o'er my punch
(You away) I sit of evenings,—silence, save
for biscuit-crunch,
Black, unbroken,—thought grows busy,
thrids each pathway of old years,
Notes this forthright, that meander, till the
long-past life appears
Like an outspread map of country plodded
through, each mile and rood,
Once, and well remembered still. . . .
("Clive," 9–14)

In the argument about poetic diction Browning once again stands quite apart from the conventional positions, insisting this time on the poet's right to use in his poetry whatever elements of the language he chooses, however exotic or recondite, however homely or prosaic. The sort of broad-minded charity he shows to men and women he exercises also in his choice of words. Thus we find in Browning not simply a very large vocabulary (38,957 words, we are told, as against Shakespeare's 19,957) but a remarkable lexical diversity. He claims for the poet the right of a man in ordinary conversation to choose the suitable word for the occasion, whether it happens to be vulgar ("higgledy piggledy") or technical ("asymptote" or "abductor"), newly coined ("calotypist") or old-fashioned ("thill-horse" or "hacqueton"), familiar ("dirt-cheap") or unfamiliar ("olent" [odorous]), prosaic ("candlestick-maker" or "ginger-pop") or fanciful ("rose-jacynth"). Again, in a randomly chosen group of poems we find such strikingly "unpoetical" nouns as shrub-house, window-pane, weevil, geraniums, slide-bolt, cut-throat, proof-mark, moustache, flap-hat, beer, tar, rocket-plant, rubbish, cheese, blister, slug, trousers, dry-rot, parsley, and many others. The unselfconscious use of exact words simply because they are the ordinary way of referring to the things they name is a distinctive feature of Browning's idiom. It makes no small contribution to the crisp concreteness of description which is one of the characteristic pleasures of reading his poetry, and is to be observed whether he is writing about such unpromising material as geological changes:

The centre-fire heaves underneath the earth,

And the earth changes like a human face:
The molten ore bursts up among the rocks,
Winds into the stone's heart, outbranches
 bright
In hidden mines, spots barren river-beds,
Crumbles into fine sand where sunbeams
 bask
 (*Paracelsus,* V.653–658)

or small living creatures:

 . . . this kingdom, limited
Alone by one old populous green wall
Tenanted by the ever-busy flies,
Grey crickets and shy lizards and quick
 spiders,
Each family of the silver-threaded moss—
Which, look through near, this way, and it
 appears
A stubble-field or a cane-brake, a marsh
Of bulrush whitening in the sun . . .
 (*Paracelsus,* I.36–43)

or about everyday life in Italy:

As to-night will be proved to my sorrow,
When, supping in state,
We shall feed our grape-gleaners (two dozen,
Three over one plate)
With lasagne so tempting to swallow
In slippery ropes,
And gourds fried in great purple slices,
That colour of popes.
Meantime, see the grape bunch they've
 brought you:
The rain-water slips
O'er the heavy blue bloom on each globe
Which the wasp to your lips
Still follows with fretful persistence:
Nay, taste, while awake,
This half of a curd-white smooth cheese-ball
That peels, flake by flake,
Like an onion, each smoother and whiter;
Next sip this weak wine
From the thin green glass flask, with its
 stopper,
A leaf of the vine;
And end with the prickly-pear's red flesh
That leaves thro' its juice
The stony black seeds on your pearl-teeth.
Scirocco is loose!
 ("The Englishman in Italy," 93–116)

In addition, Browning makes free use of the contractions that represent the normal elisions of informal speech, especially of course in his dramatic monologues. For example, in "Mr. Sludge the Medium' " we find, "He's the man for muck," "I'd like to know," "I'll try to answer you," "I can't pretend to mind your smiling," and "It don't hurt much." These colloquial licenses are common in Browning: they are one of the more obvious ways in which he deliberately rejects a formal rhetorical structure in favor of a much less ceremonious and balanced way of putting his sentences together, full of loose qualifying phrases. This has the effect of making the speaker seem matter-of-fact and reliable, even though he is using a metrical form.

Ours is a great wild country:
If you climb to our castle's top,
I don't see where your eye can stop;
For when you've passed the cornfield
 country,
Where vineyards leave off, flocks are
 packed,
And sheep-range leads to cattle-tract,
And cattle-tract to open-chase,
And open-chase to the very base
Of the mountain where, at a funeral pace,
Round about, solemn and slow,
One by one, row after row,
Up and up the pine-trees go,
So, like black priests up, and so
Down the other side again
To another greater, wilder country,
That's one vast red drear burnt-up plain,
Branched through and through with many a
 vein
Whence iron's dug, and copper's dealt;
Look right, look left, look straight before,—
Beneath they mine, above they smelt,
Copper-ore and iron-ore,
And forge and furnace mould and melt,
And so on, more and ever more,
Till at the last, for a bounding belt,
Comes the salt sand hoar of the great sea-
 shore,
—And the whole is our Duke's country.
 ("The Flight of the Duchess," II.6–31)

Browning's ability to write verse in current English was put to many other uses. In "Too

Late," for example, he preserves the realistic surface of the poem, making the extraordinary situation of the speaker, a man at the point of death addressing the woman that he has loved and lost, at once more credible and pathetic by his deliberate reining in of language. Again, colloquial idiom and contemporary speech patterns can suggest the topicality of a monologue set in a remote time or place, as in "Fra Lippo Lippi," or they can operate as touchstones of the heroic attitude, as in *Prince Hohenstiel-Schwangau, Saviour of Society* (1871). Perhaps the faithfulness of Browning's language to its basis in everyday speech is most strikingly shown in those numerous poems that are a conversation or half a conversation between a man and a woman who are, or have been, in love with one another. Dramatic romances such as "Love Among the Ruins," "Two in the Campagna," "A Light Woman," "James Lee's Wife," "The Worst of It," "Dis aliter visum," "Youth and Art," and "St. Martin's Summer" are representative of the great range of Browning's love poetry: they all depend to some extent on registering the accents of the speaking voice, so that the emotion, whether of ardent love or regret for love lost, is always tested against the language of the real world. Conventional exaggeration and compliment are exposed at once, and so is the kind of love poetry that depends on substituting for a real woman an abstraction built up of traditionally charming cliches. "The Lost Mistress" is a compact example:

All's over, then: does truth sound bitter
As one at first believes?
Hark, 't is the sparrows' good-night twitter
About your cottage eaves!

And the leaf-buds on the vine are woolly,
I noticed that, to-day;
One day more bursts them open fully
—You know the red turns grey.

To-morrow we meet the same then, dearest?
May I take your hand in mine?
Mere friends are we,—well, friends the merest
Keep much that I resign:

For each glance of the eye so bright and black,
Though I keep with heart's endeavour,—
Your voice, when you wish the snowdrops back,
Though it stay in my soul for ever!—

Yet I will but say what mere friends say,
Or only a thought stronger;
I will hold your hand but as long as all may,
Or so very little longer!
(st. I-V)

The falling rhythm and unaffected vocabulary reinforce the poem's impression of powerful feelings held in check reluctantly and with difficulty. Henry James, not in general given to overpraising Browning, puts the case finely when he observes that Browning's "treatment of the special relation between man and woman [is] a complete and splendid picture of the matter, which somehow places it at the same time in the region of conduct and responsibility."

A poet as various as Browning not surprisingly provokes contradictory critical responses. Thus he is sometimes spoken of as one of the most exotic of British poets, always escaping to the past or to Italy, sometimes as the most committed of poets, always engaged with the problems of depicting the multitudinous modern world. *The Ring and the Book,* for instance, may be regarded as deliberately removed in time and place from Browning's own readers or alternatively as the only epic poem in which the chief characters are modern men and women, living in cities and swayed by passions like our own. Similarly, Browning's long poems of the 1870's seemed to some readers contrived and novelettish, while others found them topical and realistic.

Consider the poem *The Inn Album,* which was first published in the *New York Times* in 1875, and was, like its predecessor *Red Cotton Night-Cap Country,* based on a true story of Victorian life. The encounter it describes is the culminating event in the lives of two men and two women, but much of the early part of the poem is spent in recapitulation. This is designed to bring to light the unresolved incident from the past that has drawn these four characters on a summer day to the parlor of a country inn. The narration is full of topical references and the setting is deliberately prosaic:

> Two personages occupy this room
> Shabby-genteel, that's parlour to the inn
> Perched on a view-commanding eminence;
> —Inn which may be a veritable house
> Where somebody once lived and pleased
> good taste
> Till tourists found his coign of vantage out,
> And fingered blunt the individual mark
> And vulgarized things comfortably smooth.
> On a sprig-pattern-papered wall there brays
> Complaint to sky Sir Edwin's dripping stag;
> His couchant coast-guard creature
> corresponds;
> They face the Huguenot and Light o' the
> World.
> Grim o'er the mirror on the mantelpiece,
> Varnished and coffined, *Salmo ferox* glares
> —Possibly at the List of Wines which,
> framed
> And glazed, hangs somewhat prominent on
> peg.
> (I.26–41)

Since the story is one of meanness and greed and unhappiness and its conclusion brings two unnatural deaths, *The Inn Album* puzzled those of its early readers who approached it with fixed ideas about what poetry should do, but many perceptive critics, including Swinburne, recognized that Browning, without ceasing to write poetry, was staking a claim to a new territory, that of novelists like Balzac. This is perhaps the most helpful parallel to the many poems in which Browning began from an incident or an episode in Victorian life. The amplitude of the nineteenth-century novel, its opportunities for leisurely description and careful analysis of action and motive, its impression of a lavishness that is closer to the prodigality of life than to the economy of art, all these features, which distinguish the novel from the short story, are denied to poetry except in the medium of the long poem. The successes of the nineteenth century in this form were few, and mostly Browning's.

Nor is this an admission that Browning is in some way limited by the period in which he lived and about which he wrote. Like the novelists, he realized his age so thoroughly and completely that it survives in him. If we go to Browning expecting neither romantic nor twentieth-century poetry, but simply Victorian poetry, we shall not come away unrewarded. It is very difficult to set up any other expectations in advance. He is exceptionally versatile in his use of meter and equally prolific in devising new stanza forms, while his fondness for unusual and unorthodox rhymes is well known:

> A tune was born in my head last week
> Out of the thump-thump and shriek-shriek
> Of the train, as I came by it, up from
> Manchester;
> And when, next week, I take it back again,
> My head will sing to the engine's clack
> again,
> While it only makes my neighbour's
> launches stir. . . .
> (*Christmas-Eve,* IV.249–254)

Unlike some of his contemporaries, Browning had a robust sense of verbal humor and a keen eye for human absurdities: poems as different in tone and setting as "The Bishop Orders His Tomb at St. Praxed's Church," "Caliban upon Setebos," and "Ned Bratts" are equally rich in well-developed comic detailing. The reader's access to a poem is very often by way of a character whose way of thinking is unfamiliar to the point of being eccentric. Browning frequently chooses for his speaker a man or woman with an extraordinary combination of blindness and sharpness of observation, rather as he was said himself to have one eye very long-sighted and the other very shortsighted. What we notice about his speakers is how clearly they see some things, in the simple sense of keen perception of physical fact, and how blind they are, in a metaphorical sense, to other facts in their world. A poem of Browning's can be relied on for one thing: to exact from the reader this totally distinctive combination of physical response to a series of brilliantly accurate sense perceptions, and inferential response to a succession of inaccurate intellectual formulations. This is not true, it must be admitted, of Browning's holy old men, such as Abt Vogler and Rabbi Ben Ezra and the pope, but it is true in the main, and goes some way to explain the characteristic activeness, almost aggressiveness, of the monologues.

The range of effects that Browning commanded is perhaps most effectively suggested by a passage from *Pippa Passes.* Jules, an artist, is speaking:

> But of the stuffs one can be master of,
> How I divined their capabilities!
> From the soft-rinded smoothening facile
> chalk
> That yields your outline to the air's
> embrace,
> Half-softened by a halo's pearly gloom;
> Down to the crisp imperious steel, so sure
> To cut its one confided thought clean out
> Of all the world. . . .
> (II.93–100)

Browning's sympathies were wide enough to include the age of Raphael and the age of Disraeli, without using one as a refuge from the other. On the contrary, more than any other poet of his century, more even than Wordsworth, he labored to bring poetry

> Down to the level of our common life,
> Close to the beating of our common heart.
> (Aristophanes' *Apology*)

William Sharp records the following anecdote: "On another occasion I heard him smilingly add, to someone's vague assertion that in Italy only was there any romance left, 'Ah, well, I should like to include poor old Camberwell.' "

BROWNING'S REPUTATION

As Henry James observed:

> Browning is "upon" us, straighter upon us always, somehow, than anyone else of his race . . . as if he came up against us, each time, on the same side of the street and not on the other side, across the way, where we mostly see the poets elegantly walk, and where we greet them without danger of concussion.

Many years earlier, Matthew Arnold had perceived the same immediacy and the same bristling actuality in Browning, but had found them much less congenial. In a letter to Arthur Hugh Clough he wrote, ". . . Browning is a man with a moderate gift passionately desiring movement and fulness, and obtaining but a confused multitudinousness." Although this was written in 1849, and is therefore based on only a small fraction of Browning's work, it does point to a permanent point of critical divergence.

The predominant impression derived from reading Arnold's poetry is that of a man of great sensibility attempting in vain to discover ideal certainties in a utilitarian age with which he is quite out of sympathy. Renunciation, resignation, and patient suffering are the only attitudes he can adopt in a world from which the traditional supports of life have been withdrawn, leaving the individual in isolation. Browning, as I have tried to show, shares Arnold's sense that his is a particularly exploratory and unsettled age. He is not a heedless or blinkered optimist; his constant endeavor is to start with the facts of experience, the "petits faits vrais," and to use them as a basis to proceed to a longer view, which may also be more hopeful:

> Nothing is prominently likeable
> To vulgar eye without a soul behind,
> Which, breaking surface, brings before the
> ball
> Of sight, a beauty buried everywhere.
> If we have souls, know how to see and use,
> One place performs, like any other place,
> The proper service every place on earth

Was framed to furnish man with: serves
alike
To give him note that, through the place he
sees,
A place is signified he never saw,
But, if he lack not soul, may learn to know.
(*Red Cotton Night-Cap Country,* I.54–64)

It is true that in his less successful poems, Browning's vigor, rapidity, and raciness desert him and we are left with harshness, coarseness, or flatness. He seldom achieves a classic economy of effect—hence Arnold's disapproval.

In Browning's lifetime his reputation was dimmed by that of Tennyson, who began publishing earlier, was established by 1842, and was appointed poet laureate in 1850. In the same year he published *In Memoriam,* a moving and intricate series of poems which furnished all classes of reader with poetic pleasure of one kind or another. Thereafter, Tennyson was accepted as one who voiced the sentiments of his age, and his later volumes commanded an audience comparable with that of a popular novelist. It is true that some Victorian critics complained that Tennyson varied between an official optimism and a private pessimism and never produced the major poem of modern life for which the age stood in wait, but his public remained faithful to him. Browning, on the contrary, was never to attract a mass readership. By the 1860's he had begun to live down the reputation for unintelligibility which had dogged him since *Sordello,* and to receive recognition as a more experimental, more speculative, and more adventurous poet than the laureate. The Browning Society of London, which was founded in 1881, did much to enlist support for him in his later years by discussing papers on his poetry and by providing a series of useful aids to the reading of it. Unluckily, it concentrated on one side of his work and insisted on his value as a philosophical and religious teacher in terms that deterred many people. The prospectus contained the significant sentence "Browning's themes are the development of Souls, the analysis of Minds, Art, Religion, Love, the Relation of Man and Nature to God, of Man to Man and Woman, the Life past, present, and to come." The capital letters were particularly ominous. Edward Berdoe, one of the society's most enthusiastic supporters, wrote, "Browning was not born a mere man, but a Buddha on the highest peak of the Himalayas of thought," while W. G. Kingsland recorded, "Going out from his presence this Sabbath morning, I felt that I had been in the company of a man of God, of a denizen of another sphere, of one who lived in the world, yet was out of it."

To some readers, evidently, Browning was the most profound and philosophical of poets, to others the most dramatic and immediate. This double-sidedness has fascinated and disconcerted his critics and admirers from James to Maisie Ward. If there are, as it is tempting to suppose, two Robert Brownings, one of them is the Browning who has been known and loved for a century and a half, the ventriloquial genius whose greatest poems are "My Last Duchess," "The Bishop Orders His Tomb," and similar condensed dramas. It is of this Browning that Charles Stringham remarked, "He always gives the impression of writing about people who are wearing very expensive fancy dress." The other Browning is much less easy to depict, although he can perhaps be approached by way of Shelley and his insistence on the duty of the poet to be also a prophet. This implies a Browning who valued his dramatic gifts primarily because they enabled him to objectify his arguments. The arguments themselves, however, are what constitute the poem: the endeavor to "get truth and falsehood known and named as such" is the poem's active principle, not the endeavor to reproduce the sound of another man's voice. This is true even of his more obviously grotesque and high-spirited poems. He makes his own reply to critics of his method at the end of *Christmas-Eve*:

. . . if any blames me,
Thinking that merely to touch in brevity
The topics I dwell on, were unlawful,—
Or worse, that I trench, with undue levity,

On the bounds of the holy and the awful,—
I praise the heart and pity the head of him,
And refer myself to THEE, instead of him
Who head and heart alike discernest,
Looking below light speech we utter,
When frothy spume and frequent sputter
Prove that the soul's depths boil in earnest!
May truth shine out, stand ever before us!
(XXII.1343–1354)

Browning's obstinate insistence that poetry is a medium of expression has affected his reception in our own time, when, one might have thought, the surface difficulty that handicapped him during his life would be no deterrent to a modern reader accustomed to tolerating and welcoming in contemporary poets much greater degrees of obscurity and abruptness. Yet Browning is not very well suited by current definitions of poetry, especially those which are implied in the lines "A poem should not mean/But be." Browning constantly resists any attempt to treat his poems in this way; his voice is insistently heard, saying:

It is the glory and the good of Art,
That Art remains the one way possible
Of speaking Truth.

Browning has always demanded alert, informed reading. Poems such as "A Death in the Desert" or "Caliban upon Setebos" cannot be received in any fullness except by a willing reader prepared to follow the poet's thought, to understand the positions in a debate and evaluate them, and to respond not simply to the patterns of the poem but to the pressures of the argument. In short, Browning must be read not with the easygoing collaboration that is all that many contemporary poets get, and all that they seem to expect, but with the same attention and concentration that we accord to, say, Donne or Marvell.

Since James referred to Browning as "a tremendous and incomparable modern," it has been fashionable to call him the most modern of the Victorian poets, often with the suggestion that he had a direct influence on the poetry of the twentieth century. Edward Lucie-Smith, for example, has drawn attention to Browning's use of an imaginary speaker to some extent detached from the action; his habit of incorporating quotations into his poems with an effect of collage; his display of an impressive erudition, perhaps not all genuine; his free use of proper names and sobriquets; his use of the objects of every day, even of rubbish and miscellaneous refuse, as materials of lists and catalogs; and his willingness to shift abruptly from the sordid to the sublime, achieving particular effects by the juxtaposition. To these devices, which will no doubt be reminiscent of similar features in, for example, Pound and Eliot, one might add other distinctive innovations, in particular the use of a specific oblique objective correlative—an apparently remote and forgotten person or event or scene, which by its very singularity is presented as a unique image of a more immediate general situation. This audacious confidence in his own power to find a previously unimagined point of view on a continuing problem Browning shares with many later poets, though it is perhaps too strong to say that they were influenced by him.

If we are to describe Browning as a modern poet at all, we must do so within limits and with careful qualifications. As I have been at pains to emphasize, he is in many important ways an antimodernist, most obviously in his insistence on the significance of content, not as an accidental motivator of poetic language, but rather as that for which the poem exists. Yet it remains true that when we look at the Victorian age, his is the face that is turned most openly toward us. The firmness and freshness of his language; the inventiveness of his dramatic imagination; his curiosity about the extraordinary workings of the human mind; his resolute inquiry into human purposes and responsibilities; and his refusal to be satisfied either with a traditional formula or with a cynical evasion of the question or with resignation to defeat; all these mark Browning as a modern poet in the only sense that is of importance—as a poet who wrestled for himself with the problems of his art and solved them sufficiently to produce a great series of works of authentic power and originality, and who transmitted to his successors a tradition of poetry as a living and powerful force in the life of urban industrial man.

Browning's lifetime of labor in the service of his art for small reward brings to mind his own description of a dedicated poet:

> I'd like now, yet had haply been afraid,
> To have just looked, when this man came to die,
> And seen who lined the clean gay garret-sides
> And stood about the neat low truckle-bed,
> With the heavenly manner of relieving guard.
> Here had been, mark, the general-in-chief,
> Thro' a whole campaign of the world's life and death,
> Doing the King's work all the dim day long,
> In his old coat and up to knees in mud,
> Smoked like a herring, dining on a crust,—
> And, now the day was won, relieved at once!
> ("How It Strikes a Contemporary," 99–109)

Selected Bibliography

BIBLIOGRAPHY

Orr, Mrs. S., *A Handbook to the Works,* (London, 1885) an "authorized" handbook, the 6th ed. (1892) and later reprs. contain a bibliography; Broughton, L. N., and Stelter, B. F., 2 vols. *A Concordance to the Poems of Robert Browning,* (New York, 1924–1925); Broughton, L. N., Northrup, C. S., and Pearsall, R., *Robert Browning: A Bibliography, 1830–1950,* (Ithaca, N.Y., 1953) Cornell Studies in English 39; DeVane, W. C., *A Browning Handbook,* 2nd rev. ed. (New York, 1955) indispensable; F. E. Faverty, ed. 2nd ed. *The Victorian Poets: A Guide to Research,* (Cambridge, Mass., 1968) ch. on Browning by P. Honan gives a full description of Browning studies up to 1966; *English Poetry, Select Bibliographical Guides,* A. E. Dyson, ed. (London, 1971) ch. on Browning by I. Jack, good critical and bibliographical survey; Crowell, N. B., *A Reader's Guide to Robert Browning,* (Albuquerque, N.M., 1972) includes bibliographies of Browning scholarship in the period 1945–1969, reading lists, surveys 23 of Browning's short poems; Peterson, W. S., *Robert and Elizabeth Barrett Browning: An Annotated Bibliography, 1951–1970,* (New York, 1974) continued in the annual bibliography of *Browning Institute Studies,* the 1971 bibliography was published in vol. I, (1973); other annual bibliographies can be found in *Browning Society Notes* and *Studies in Browning and His Circle.*

COLLECTED WORKS

Poems, 2 vols. (London, 1849); *The Poetical Works,* 3 vols. (London, 1863); *The Poetical Works,* 6 vols. (London, 1868); *The Poetical Works,* 17 vols. (London, 1888–1894) this ed. represents Browning's final arrangement and rev. of his poems; vols. I–XVI ed. by Browning himself, vol. XVII by Dr. Berdoe; C. Porter and H. A. Clarke, eds. 12 vols. *The Complete Works,* (New York, 1898) the Florentine ed., with prefatory essay, biographical intro., and bibliography; A. Birrell, ed. *The Complete Poetical Works,* 2 vols. (New York, 1907) intro. by Birrell, new ed. with additional poems (1915) subsequent rev. reprs.; F. G. Kenyon, ed. *The Works,* 10 vols. (London, 1912) the Centenary ed.; *Poems and Plays,* J. Bryson and M. M. Bozman, eds. 5 vols. (London, 1956–1964) Everyman Library nos. 41, 42, 502, 964, 966; R. A. King, Jr., gen. ed. *The Complete Works,* (Athens, Ohio, 1969-) Variorum ed., the last vol. to appear was vol. IV (1973); *The Complete Poems,* 3 vols.: R. Altick, ed. *The Ring and the Book* (Harmondsworth, 1971) and J. Pettigrew, ed. *Robert Browning: The Poems* 2, vols. (Harmondsworth, 1981) Penguin Poets series.

SELECTIONS

Selections, (London, 1863); S. Nowell-Smith, ed. *Browning: Poetry and Prose,* (London, 1950) reiss. (1967) the Reynard Library ed.; *A Choice of Browning's Verse,* E. Lucie-Smith, ed. (London, 1967) interesting intro. on Browning's use of the dramatic monologue; I. Jack, ed. *Browning: Poetical Works, 1833–1864,* (London, 1970) Oxford Standard Authors series; J. F. Loucks, ed. *Robert Browning's Poetry: Authoritative Texts, Criticism,* (New York, 1979) texts, criticism, interpretations, essays, etc.

SEPARATE WORKS

Pauline: A Fragment of a Confession (London, 1833) also in N. H. Wallis, ed., *Pauline: The Text of 1833 Compared with That of 1867 and 1888* (Philadelphia, 1978), repr. of the 1931 ed., with intro. and notes by Wallis; *Paracelsus* (London, 1835), also in M. L. Lee and K. B. Locock, eds., *Browning's Paracelsus* (London, 1909), useful annotated ed.; *Strafford: An Historical Tragedy* (London, 1837); *Sordello* (London, 1840), also in A. J. Whyte, ed. (London, 1913), helpfully annotated; *Bells and Pomegranates* (London, 1841–1846): no. 1, *Pippa Passes* (1841); no. 2, *King Victor and King Charles* (1842); no. 3, *Dramatic Lyrics* (1842); no. 4, *The Return of the Druses. A Tragedy* (1843); no. 5, *A Blot in the Scutcheon. A Tragedy* (1843); no. 6, *Colombe's Birthday. A Play* (1844); no. 7, *Dramatic Romances and Lyrics* (1845); no. 8, *Luria: and a Soul's Tragedy* (1846); each part was published separately in paper wrappers under its own title, the complete series of eight parts was issued in cloth boards under the title *Bells and Pomegranates; Christmas-Eve and Easter-Day. A Poem* (London, 1850); "An Essay on Percy Bysshe Shelley" (London, 1852), written as the introductory essay to the *Letters of Percy Bysshe Shelley,* the book was withdrawn from publication when the letters were found to be spurious, the essay has been frequently repr.; a particularly useful repr. by H. F. B. Brett-Smith, ed. (Oxford, 1921), includes Peacock's *Four Ages of Poetry* and Shelley's *Defense of Poetry; Men and Women,* 2 vols. (London, 1855), also in F. B. Pinion, ed. (London, 1963), the English Classics series, an annotated ed., and P. Turner, ed. (London, 1972), intro., notes, and selected bibliography; *Dramatis Personae* (London, 1854), also F. B. Pinion, ed., *Robert Browning: Dramatis Personae* (Glasgow, 1969), Collins Annotated Student Texts; *The Ring and the Book,* 4 vols. (London, 1868–1869), also in F. B. Pinion, ed. (London, 1957), the Scholar's Library, an abridgement with intro. and notes, R. Altick, ed. (Harmondsworth, 1971), text of the 1st ed., brief intro., bibliography, and notes; *Balaustion's Adventure* (London, 1871); *Prince Hohenstiel-Schwangau, Saviour of Society* (London, 1871); *Fifine at the Fair* (London, 1872); *Red Cotton Night-Cap Country, or Turf and Towers* (London, 1873); *Aristophanes' Apology Including a Transcript from Euripides, Being the Last Adventure of Balaustion* (London, 1875); *The Inn Album* (London, 1875); *Pacchiarotto and How He Worked in Distemper: With Other Poems* (London, 1876); *The Agamemnon of Aeschylus* (London, 1877), translation; *La Saisiaz: The Two Poets of Croisic* (London, 1878); *Dramatic Idyls* (first series) (London, 1879); *Dramatic Idyls Second Series* (London, 1880); *Jocoseria* (London, 1883); *Ferishtah's Fancies* (London, 1884); *Parleyings with Certain People of Importance in Their Day . . .* (London, 1887); *Asolando: Fancies and Facts* (London, 1890); D. Smalley, ed., *Browning's Essay on Chatterton* (Cambridge, Mass., 1948), convincing attribution to Browning of an article in the *Foreign Quarterley Review,* 29 (July 1842), 465–483.

LETTERS

F. G. Kenyon, ed., *Robert Browning and Alfred Domett* [1840–1877] (London, 1906); T. J. Wise, coll., *Letters of Robert Browning* [1830–1889], T. L. Hood, ed. (New Haven, Conn., 1933); R. Curle, ed., *Robert Browning and Julia Wedgwood: A Broken Friendship as Revealed in Their Letters* [1864–1869] (London, 1937); W. C. DeVane and K. L. Knickerbocker, eds., *New Letters of Robert Browning* [1835–1889] (New Haven, Conn., 1950); E. C. McAleer, ed., *Dearest Isa: Robert Browning's Letters to Isabella Blagden* [1857–1872] (Austin, Tex., 1951); P. Landis and R. Freeman, eds., *Letters of the Brownings to George Barrett* [1861–1889] (Urbana, Ill., 1958); G. R. Hudson, ed., *Browning to His American Friends: Letters Between the Brownings, the Storys and James Russell Lowell, 1841–1890* (London, 1965), with an intro. and notes by Hudson; E. C. McAleer, ed., *Learned Lady: Letters from Robert Browning to Mrs. Thomas Fitz-Gerald, 1876–1889* (Cambridge, Mass., 1966); E. Kintner, ed., *The Letters of Robert Browning and Elizabeth Barrett Barrett, 1845–1846,* 2 vols. (Cambridge, Mass., 1969); P. Kelley and R. Hudson, *The Brownings' Correspondence: A Checklist* (New York, 1978), a comprehensive listing of the Brownings' correspondence; W. S. Peterson, ed., *Browning's Trumpeter, The Correspondence of Robert Browning and Frederick J. Furnivall, 1872–1889* (Washington, D.C., 1979).

BIOGRAPHICAL STUDIES

G. K. Chesterton, *Robert Browning* (London, 1903), lively and perceptive, there are later reprs.; H. James, *William Wetmore Story and His Friends, from Letters, Diaries, and Recollections,* 2 vols. (Boston, 1903), contains an interesting and vivid account of Browning as he appeared to those who knew him; Mrs. S. Orr, *Life and Letters of Robert Browning* (London, 1908), a new, rev. ed. by F. G. Kenyon; B. Miller, *Robert Browning: A Portrait* (London, 1952), a psychological study of Browning that tends to be unsympathetic; M. Ward, *Robert Browning and His World:* vol. I, *The Private Face* [1812–1861] (London, 1968); vol. II, *Two Robert Brownings?* [1861–1889] (London, 1969), sympathetic to Browning; W. Irvine and P. Honan, *The Book, the Ring, and the Poet: A Biography of Robert Browning* (London, 1975), a comprehensive and fully documented biography with much critical analysis of the poetry; J. Maynard, *Browning's Youth* (Cambridge, Mass., 1977).

CRITICAL STUDIES

A. Symons, *An Introduction to the Study of Browning* (London, 1886); H. Jones, *Browning as a Philosophical and Religious Teacher* (Glasgow, 1891); *The Old Yellow Book* (London, 1911), trans. with an intro. by C. Hodell, Browning's main source for *The Ring and the Book;* A. K. Cook, *A Commentary Upon Browning's "The Ring and the Book"* (London, 1920); W. C. DeVane, *Browning's "Parleyings": The Autobiography of a Mind* (New Haven, Conn., 1927); W. O. Raymond, *The Infinite Moment and Other Essays on Robert Browning* (Toronto, 1950; 2nd ed., 1965); E. D. H. Johnson, *The Alien Vision of Victorian Poetry: Sources of the Poetic Imagination in Tennyson, Browning, and Arnold* (Princeton, N.J., 1952), Princeton Studies in English no. 34, for Browning see pp. 71–143; H. C. Duffin, *Amphibian: A Reconsideration of Browning* (London, 1956); R. Langbaum, *The Poetry of Experience: The Dramatic Monologue in Modern Literary Tradition* (London, 1957); R. A. King, Jr., *The Bow and the Lyre: The Art of Robert Browning* (Ann Arbor, Mich., 1957); P. Honan, *Browning's Characters: A Study in Poetic Technique* (New Haven, Conn., 1961); H. S. Davies, *Browning and the Modern Novel* (Hull, 1962), the St. John's College, Cambridge, Lecture, 1961–1962; N. B. Crowell, *The Triple Soul: Browning's Theory of Knowledge* (Albuquerque, N.M., 1963); J. H. Miller, *The Disappearance of God: Five Nineteenth Century Writers* (Cambridge, Mass., 1963), interesting section on Browning; W. J. Whitla, *The Central Truth: The Incarnation in Robert Browning's Poetry* (Toronto, 1963); B. Litzinger, *Time's Revenges: Browning's Reputation as a Thinker, 1889–1962* (Knoxville, Tenn., 1964); P. Drew, ed., *Robert Browning: A Collection of Critical Essays* (London, 1966); T. J. Collins, *Robert Browning's Moral-Aesthetic Theory, 1833–1855* (Lincoln, Nebr., 1967); B. Litzinger and K. L. Knickerbocker, eds., *The Browning Critics* (Lexington, Ky., 1967), includes a detailed bibliography, 1951–1965; I. Jack, *Robert Browning* (London, 1968), the Warton Lecture on English Poetry, 1967; N. B. Crowell, *The Convex Glass: The Mind of Robert Browning* (Albuquerque, N.M., 1968); R. A. King, Jr., *The Focusing Artifice: The Poetry of Robert Browning* (Athens, Ohio, 1968); W. D. Shaw, *The Dialectical Temper: The Rhetorical Art of Robert Browning* (Ithaca, N.Y., 1968); B. Melchiori, *Browning's Poetry of Reticence* (Edinburgh, 1968); R. D. Altick and J. F. Loucks, *Browning's Roman Murder Story: A Reading of "The Ring and the Book"* (Chicago, 1968); R. A. King Jr., ed., *Victorian Poetry: An Issue Commemorative of the Centennial of the Publication of "The Ring and the Book"* (Morgantown, W. Va., 1968), a repr. in book form of *Victorian Poetry,* 6, nos. 3–4 (1968), an interesting collection of essays on *The Ring and the Book;* C. R. Tracy, ed., *Browning's Mind and Art* (Edinburgh, 1968), useful critical anthology; M. R. Sullivan, *Browning's Voices in "The Ring and the Book"* (Toronto, 1969); I. Armstrong, ed., *The Major Victorian Poets: Reconsiderations* (London, 1969), contains four important essays on Browning; B. Litzinger and D. Smalley, eds., *Browning: The Critical Heritage* (London, 1970); P. Drew, *The Poetry of Browning: A Critical Introduction* (London, 1970); D. S. Hair, *Browning's Experiments with Genre* (Edinburgh, 1972); I. Jack, *Browning's Major Poetry* (Oxford, 1973); W. E. Harrold, *The Variance and the Unity: A Study of the Complementary Poems of Robert Browning* (Athens, Ohio, 1973); J. R. Watson, ed., *Browning: "Men and Women" and Other Poems: A Casebook* (London, 1974), useful anthology of critical studies on Browning; I. Armstrong, ed., *Robert Browning: Writers and Their Background* (London, 1974), contains a reader's guide to Browning by P. Keating; E. Cook, *Browning's Lyrics: An Exploration* (Toronto, 1974); C. De L. Ryals, *Browning's Later Poetry, 1871–1889* (Ithaca, N.Y., 1975); B. S. Flowers, *Browning and the Modern Tradition* (London, 1976); B. Brugière, *L'Univers Imaginaire de Robert Browning* (Paris, 1979).

William Cullen Bryant
(1794–1878)

DONALD A. RINGE

THE POETRY OF William Cullen Bryant has always been difficult to place in an appropriate context. Because he was a poet of nature who found in the commonplace things of the natural world a source for reflection, critics often have sought to compare him with earlier poets who, like him, had developed their themes in descriptive poems of a philosophic cast. When his mature poetry was first published in pamphlet form in 1821, it was compared at once with that of William Cowper and, when a much enlarged edition was printed in 1832, with that of, among others, James Thomson and William Wordsworth. In the early nineteenth century this attitude was perhaps understandable. No poet of Bryant's stature had yet appeared in America, and critics were unsure of how to judge him. The persistence of this view into the twentieth century, however, does Bryant a serious injustice. Aside from the fact that no one poet could possibly bear close resemblance to writers so different as those with whom he has been compared, Bryant deserves to be seen on his own terms and valued for his accomplishments, however limited they may sometimes seem to be.

Every poet learns from the works of his predecessors. He imitates what he has read as he learns to write; and even when he has achieved his distinctive voice, he sometimes echoes lines or images from other poets that have stuck in his mind. Bryant is no exception. As a young man he was especially fortunate to have had at his disposal the volumes of English poetry that his father, Peter Bryant, himself the author of Augustan verse, had brought to their isolated home in western Massachusetts. They ranged from William Shakespeare, John Milton, and John Dryden through the major and minor poets of the eighteenth century—including such "graveyard" figures as Robert Blair, Beilby Porteus, and Henry Kirke White—to Wordsworth and the early Byron. The aspiring poet read much of it. We know from both his critical essays and his poetry that the range of Bryant's knowledge was broad. Illustrations and examples in his critical prose are drawn from Shakespeare and Milton, and certain lines in his verse echo familiar ones by Alexander Pope, Thomas Gray, and William Cowper. There are verses in "Thanatopsis" that resemble Blair's *The Grave,* and some in "A Winter Piece" that are unmistakably Wordsworthian.

The point is not, however, that such passages exist. They are always to be expected, and too much must not be made of them. Although they illustrate well the range of verse from which, under his father's tutelage, the young Bryant learned his craft, they are merely the last vestiges of those poetic masters from whom the young man quickly established his independence. Bryant was no imitator. Whatever he learned from his predecessors, the content and form of his poems are unmistakably his own. If he affirms an ordered world in his verse, it is not the deistic order of Thomson's *The Seasons*; if his poetic vision is fundamentally religious, it is not the evangelical Christianity of Cowper; if he maintains a close relation to nature and to nature's God, the two never merge into the pantheistic system of Wordsworth. Although Bryant no doubt learned to handle the blank verse form from reading the works of these and other poets who had made it an effective vehicle for contemplative poetry, his own blank verse does not resemble theirs in either movement or tone. Eclectic in his taste, he developed a point of view and mode of expression only partially conditioned by the poets he read.

At least as important were other elements in Bryant's education and training, especially the beliefs of two strong men who left an indelible impression upon him. One was his maternal grandfather, Ebenezer Snell, the stern Calvinist with whom the Bryant family lived for a number of years. The religious training the young boy received at his hands left such a mark upon him that Bryant the mature poet has sometimes been called a Puritan. This influence was strongly countered, however, by that of the poet's father. Peter Bryant, a medical man, was a much more liberal thinker and strongly influenced the boy toward the Unitarian thought that the poet eventually accepted. Both men, moreover, influenced his reading and writing. Bryant read the Scriptures and, at his grandfather's prompting, attempted to turn parts of the Old Testament into English verse. But he also read the classics, and under his father's guidance he began at an early age to write a kind of Augustan verse. It is almost as if, in the village of Cummington, Massachusetts, the budding poet was undergoing in small something of the intellectual experience of American society as a whole in the opening years of the nineteenth century.

As Bryant prepared to enter Williams College in 1810, he encountered yet another important intellectual system, Scottish associationist philosophy. Among the books he read were three by members of that "common sense" school: Dugald Stewart, Thomas Reid, and, most important, Archibald Alison, the aesthetician of the group. Unlike some earlier eighteenth-century thinkers, these philosophers accepted the external world as both real and knowable by the human mind. Because of its constitution, the mind, acting upon the impressions that came to it through the senses, could discern the qualities of that world and exert upon it the various modifications of thought. When disposed in the proper fashion, moreover, the mind could also perceive and be moved by the beauty and sublimity of the material world. The philosophy did not, of course, limit itself to nature; but examples drawn from the natural scene, from landscape gardening, and from landscape art are so important in Alison's *Essays on the Nature and Principles of Taste* as to make quite clear the aesthetician's deep interest in that aspect of material reality.

Because the aesthetic laid such stress not solely on the beauty and sublimity of the material world, but also on the essential truth to be found in it, the poet had of necessity to be a close observer of the external scene. The representation of nature in his verse had to be accurate. In no other way could he be sure that the meaning he perceived was true, or that he had been able to communicate it effectively to his reader. Since knowledge comes to the mind through sensory experience—primarily through sight and secondarily through hearing—visual and, to a lesser extent, auditory images must make up the bulk of the poem. The mind of the poet, then, acting upon the landscape, re-creates his vision in the poem; and if his sight be true and if his mind interpret the sensory images properly, he will draw from the natural scene a meaning that he will embody in his poem. Readers of that poem, moreover, will have the description before them expressed in suggestive language. If the poet has done his work well, they will perceive both the beauty and the truth he has discovered for them.

Such an aesthetic quite naturally had a profound effect on Bryant's poetry. The theory demanded that his material be drawn not from the poets he had read, but from what he had personally experienced among the hills and valleys of western Massachusetts. It gave him a point of view, that of a sensitive observer who consciously sought the beauty and truth to be found in the natural scene; and it gave him a source for his imagery in the sights and sounds he had witnessed in his rambles around his native countryside. Not all of Bryant's subjects, of course, are drawn from the natural landscape. His poems supporting the struggle for freedom in Greece and his long philosophic poem "The Ages" are obvious exceptions. But these and a few similar ones aside, the bulk of Bryant's poetry does indeed record his direct and continuing encounter with the natural world; and these are the poems by which his accomplishment must be judged today. In the best of this verse, he frees himself from his poetic masters, creates a vision of reality that bears little resemblance to theirs, and speaks in a poetic voice that is unmistakably his own.

Born November 3, 1794, in Cummington, Massachusetts, a village that had been settled for only some twenty-five years, William Cullen Bryant grew up in much the same fashion as most other boys in America. With his older brother, Austin, he attended the district school, where he received an education of the most elementary kind; and, although somewhat frail, he learned to work in his grandfather's fields as soon as he was able to handle the farm tools. Both winter and summer he rambled among the neighboring hills, and became from his earliest days, he later wrote, a keen observer of nature in all its various forms. During the stormy days and long evenings of winter, Bryant and his brother read the books in their father's well-chosen library, especially the *Iliad* in Pope's edition and, when they tired of Pope, the works of Sir Edmund Spenser, Cowper, and other English writers of verse and prose. Cullen, as he was called, was different from most boys, however, in showing signs of a strong intellectual bent. He began to compose verse as early as 1802, and wrote a poem for declamation at school in 1804 that attained such currency in the neighborhood that it was published in the Hampshire *Gazette* on March 18, 1807.

By that time the budding poet had written a goodly amount of juvenile verse—some, like his poem "On the Late Eclipse," in pentameter couplets, but at least one, a version of David's lament over Saul and Jonathan, in blank verse. His skill increased markedly; and when his father saw some satiric lines of his on Thomas Jefferson, occasioned by the Embargo Act of 1807—an act that particularly hurt the commerce of New England—he encouraged his son to write more. The result was Bryant's first book, *The Embargo,* a satiric poem of 244 lines in heroic couplets, "By a Youth of Thirteen." Peter Bryant arranged for its publication at Boston in 1808. The pamphlet was favorably reviewed by Alexander Hill Everett in the *Monthly Anthology* in June; and since the uproar over the embargo continued as supplementary acts were passed, the book quickly sold out. At his father's direction Cullen prepared a second edition, enlarged to 420 lines and including seven additional poems that he had written in 1807 and 1808. The new edition was published in February 1809, and this time the young man's name appeared on the title page.

Although only a piece of juvenile verse that Bryant never included in any collected edition of his poems, *The Embargo* merits at least a glance for what it tells us about its author in 1809. While the original poem was retouched by his father and another gentleman in Boston, it remains nonetheless a remarkable performance for so young a poet and illustrates well both the native talent he possessed and the degree to which it had already been disciplined. Its Federalist politics and Augustan style reveal the bent of mind and poetic taste of the young man, attitudes he would abandon during the period of intellectual and artistic growth that quickly ensued. And the revised edition clearly shows the skill with which Bryant was already able to criticize and improve his verse. The second edition smooths or removes some infelicities of language, expands his treatment of the sufferings of New England workers under the embargo, and sharpens and extends the satire on Jefferson and his supporters. Both versions attack Napoleon and France as the enemies of freedom, but in the second edition the title poem is followed by another, "The Spanish Revolution," that makes an additional attack on the French.

Because his son had shown such intellectual and artistic talent, Peter Bryant decided, despite his limited means, to give Cullen a college education. From November 1808 to October 1809, the young man studied the classics, first Latin with his uncle, Thomas Snell, in North Brookfield, and then Greek with Rev. Moses Hallock in Plainfield, Massachusetts. Cullen was a ready scholar and prepared himself so well in these languages, in mathematics, and in more general studies that he entered the sophomore class at Williams College in October 1810. He did not stay the year. Although he seemed to have enjoyed the literary society—the Philotechnian—to which he belonged, he was disappointed at the level of instruction; and, following the lead of his roommate, John Avery, he obtained an honorable dismissal during his third quarter so that he might prepare himself to enter Yale. His father's finances, however, would not permit the transfer. Although Austin was committed to farming, there were three boys and two girls younger than Cullen; and Peter Bryant had also to think of them. Instead of attending Yale, therefore, the young poet was put to the study of the law, first with Samuel Howe at Worthington and later with William Baylies at West Bridgewater.

As always, Bryant worked diligently, completed his studies in four years, and was admitted to practice law in August 1815. He settled in Plainfield in December of that year but, a better opportunity presenting itself, he formed a partnership with George H. Ives at Great Barrington the following fall. Bryant remained there for almost nine years, pursuing a career that he did not really like. Yet he seems to have been successful. By May 1817 he was able to buy out his partner; his solitary practice succeeded; and over the next few years he held a number of elected or appointed offices, including town clerk and justice of the peace. It was in Great Barrington, too, that he met and courted Frances Fairchild. They were married on January 11, 1821; and the first of their two daughters, Frances, was born the following year. Bryant felt isolated in western Massachusetts, however; and although he met and associated with the Sedgwick family in nearby Stockbridge, he longed for more literary company than was available in Berkshire villages. What made its absence the more keenly felt was the rapid development of his poetic career.

Throughout the years of his education and legal training, Bryant had never stopped writing verse. As he mastered Latin and Greek, he tried his hand at translating Virgil, and later Sophocles and the Greek lyric poets. Indeed, the earliest of his poems, much reworked, that he included in his collected editions was "Version of a Fragment of Simonides," written while he was at Williams College. Bryant wrote a number of verse letters: to his brother Austin, to the Philotechnian Society at Williams, and later to his friend Jacob Porter (on the occasion of his marriage and, shortly thereafter, on the death of his wife). Most interesting of all, however, is a group of poems written while he was studying law. Many seem to record the vicissitudes of a romance between Bryant and a young lady from Rhode Island who had visited Cummington, while others, probably composed under the influence of the "graveyard" poets, show the young man s concern with and fear of death. Bryant was gradually freeing himself from his Augustan models. Under the influence of the associationist philosophers and of the Romantic poets, especially Wordsworth, that he had begun to read, he soon developed the mature voice of his best-known poetry.

The dates of Bryant's first important poems cannot be established precisely. The writing of "Thanatopsis" has been placed as early as 1811 and as late as 1815, and both the date and the occasion for the writing of "To a Waterfowl" have been the subject of some discussion. But if William Cullen Bryant II is correct in his arguments, we may reasonably consider 1814–1815 as the period of the poet's coming of age. During this time he composed initial versions of some of his best-known poems: the central section of "Thanatopsis,"

"The Yellow Violet," "To a Waterfowl," "Inscription for the Entrance to a Wood," and "I Cannot Forget with What Fervid Devotion." The difference between these and his earlier verses is marked. They clearly indicate the relation he had discovered between the mind of the poet and the natural world he observes, and they record the meanings that the discerning eye can discover in the external scene. Both "The Yellow Violet" and "To a Waterfowl" illustrate the analogical method by which, according to the Scottish philosophers, the mind could discover meaning through the impressions it received from the external world; and "Thanatopsis" and "Inscription" show the reflective mind deriving knowledge and comfort from its contemplation of nature.

In language and imagery, too, these poems mark a real advance over the juvenile verse. Although some of the poems were later much revised to clarify the thought and remove some roughness in movement and tone, even the earliest versions indicate the progress Bryant had made in poetic diction. Never colloquial in his poetry, Bryant writes with an idiomatic freedom that does no violence to the natural patterns of educated language. Words like "russet," "illimitable," "primal," or "dissembled" sound natural in his verse; but he did learn from the new Romantic poets—specially Wordsworth and Robert Southey—to be, for the most part, precise and concrete in his imagery. Thus, although he may be guilty of such eighteenth-century diction as "the winged plunderer" in "Inscription," he also includes, in the early version of the poem, some sharply detailed descriptions of the external scene:

> here from tree to tree
> And through the rustling branches flit the birds
> In wantonness of spirit;—theirs are strains
> Of no dissembled rapture—while below
> The squirrel with rais'd paws and form erect
> Chirps merrily.

Once he had achieved his characteristic voice, the way was open for him to develop his vision of the world in language well suited to its expression.

Bryant matured as a poet just at the time he was admitted to the practice of law; and at first he did nothing to advance his literary career, preferring to establish himself as a lawyer in Great Barrington. His father, however, acting upon the request of Willard Phillips, sent several of Bryant's poems to the *North American Review.* In September 1817 there appeared in the journal a four-stanza poem and a blank-verse fragment under the title "Thanatopsis," a name coined by one of the editors, and a "Fragment" that was later to become "Inscription for the Entrance to a Wood." These poems created a stir. Richard Henry Dana, who became Bryant's life-long friend, could not believe that they had been written in America; and through some mistake "Thanatopsis" was attributed for a time to the poet's father. Early the next year Cullen sent the Simonides fragment and "To a Waterfowl" to the magazine, and the two appeared in March 1818. Although all the poems were published anonymously, Bryant had been introduced to some of the literati of Boston; and during the next few years he contributed some prose pieces to the review.

Despite this initial success, Bryant published no more poems at this time in the *North American Review.* He had also sent them "The Yellow Violet," but the poetry section was discontinued for lack of verse of sufficient quality and the poem was not printed. During the next few years, however, literary opportunities opened up for him. At Catharine Sedgwick's request Bryant contributed a group of five hymns to a Unitarian collection, in 1820, and he continued to write a few new poems. In the spring of 1821, he was surprised to learn that he had been elected to Phi Beta Kappa four years earlier, and was now invited to deliver the Phi Beta Kappa poem at the Harvard commencement in August. While he was writing this poem, moreover, he learned from Edward T. Channing that Dana was about to publish his own journal, *The Idle Man.* During the summer of 1821, Bryant completed and delivered a poem, "The Ages," on the cyclical vision of history; and during the summer and fall he sent Dana four poems for his journal: "Green River," "A Walk at Sunset," "A Winter Piece" (then called "Winter Scenes"), and "The West Wind."

But, most important of all, his friends in Boston—Channing, Dana, and Phillips—helped Bryant to publish a collection of his poems. The book is hardly more than a pamphlet, containing only eight poems in its forty-four pages: "The Ages," "To a Waterfowl," "Translation of a Fragment of Simonides," "Inscription for the Entrance to a Wood," "The Yellow Violet," "Song" (later entitled "The Hunter of the West"), "Green River," and "Thanatopsis." This is the version of "Thanatopsis" that everyone knows, for while he was in Boston, Bryant wrote the introduction and conclusion that surround the now-revised section that had appeared in the *North American Review.* Slight as the book is, however, the publication of *Poems* (1821) was as significant an event in American literature as the appearance of Washington Irving's *The Sketch Book* (1819–1820) and James Fenimore Cooper's *The Spy* (1821). A truly American poetic voice joined theirs in prose; and if the book did not receive a wide circulation outside Boston, it was well reviewed by Willard Phillips in the *North American Review* and by Gulian C. Verplanck in the New York *American.* Bryant's reputation was spreading not only in America but also in England, where the eight poems were reprinted in *Specimens of the American Poets* (1822) and reviewed in *Blackwood's Edinburgh Magazine.*

Although Bryant had thus received considerable recognition both in the United States and abroad, he did not immediately pursue his poetic career. Quite the contrary. He remained in Great Barrington, practicing law. He may even have attempted, as he wrote in one of his poems, to break the spell of poetry and devote himself entirely to his profession. He did begin a satirical farce and a long narrative poem, but his output of poetry over the next two years was very slight. Late in 1823, however, yet another unexpected opportunity opened for him. In December of that year, Theophilus Parsons, editor of the *United States Literary Gazette,* asked him to contribute poetry on a regular basis. Since the payment offered—$200 a year—would increase his income substantially, Bryant readily accepted; and over the next two years he published some two dozen poems in that journal, including such important pieces as "The Rivulet," "An Indian at the Burial-Place of His Fathers," "Monument Mountain," and "A Forest Hymn." In January 1826, moreover, a volume of poems selected from the pages of the *Gazette* and including Bryant's verses was published in Boston, thereby giving the poet added visibility in the literary world.

These years, 1824–1826, were a very important period in Bryant's life. They were undoubtedly the most productive that Bryant the poet ever had, but they also marked a crucial turning point for Bryant the man. Although well-established in Great Barrington, Bryant disliked the narrow community and was restive in his—to him—distasteful profession. He needed a larger arena for his talents, and his friends the Sedgwick brothers helped him find one. In April 1824 he visited Henry and Robert Sedgwick in New York, where he met James Fenimore Cooper, Fitz-Greene Halleck, Robert Sands, and Jared Sparks. During the following months, he considered the possibility of moving to that city. In January, Henry Sedgwick urged him to come down since a new literary review was under discussion and the owners wanted Bryant to be associated with it. Bryant made two trips, in February and March, but the negotiations took time; and it was not until May that he moved permanently to New York to be editor, with Henry J. Anderson, of the newly organized *New-York Review and Atheneum Magazine.* The first issue was dated June 1825.

Like most contemporary journals, the *New-York Review* was short-lived, lasting only a year. By the spring of 1826, Bryant was already making plans to merge it with the *United States Literary Gazette.* But before negotiations were complete, he took, in July, what he thought was to be a temporary job as editorial assistant on the New York *Evening Post,* an important city newspaper. Even after the merger of the magazines, which resulted in the *United States Review and Literary Gazette,* he divided his time between newspaper and magazine. Bryant was responsible for only half of the literary journal. He selected the poetry and supplied the reviews of books from New York and points south, while Charles Folsom, in Boston, handled the material from New England. The *United States Review* was thus an attempt to establish a national magazine, published simultaneously in the two cities; but it, too, failed, the last issue appearing in September 1827. Thereafter, Bryant cast his lot with the *Evening Post.* He became joint editor in December, bought a one-eighth share in the firm, and began an editorial career that ended at his death, more than half a century later.

Bryant's first years in New York broadened his experience in ways that he could not have foreseen. He was soon caught up in the intellectual life of the city and began to associate with its leading writers and painters. In November 1825 he was elected to membership in Fenimore Cooper's Bread and Cheese Club, where he joined such writers as Halleck, Verplanck, and Sands, and such painters as Samuel F. B. Morse, Asher B. Durand, and Thomas Cole. Bryant was quick to support the young painters in their attempt to establish the National Academy of Design, where he later lectured on mythology. In the spring of 1826, moreover, he delivered a series of four lectures on poetry at the New York Athenaeum. Bryant had long been interested in the criticism of poetry. He had criticized Solyman Brown's *Essay on American Poetry* in 1818; he had published his famous essay "On the Use of Trisyllabic Feet in Iambic Verse" in 1819; and he had reviewed books of poetry. The lectures, however, gave him the opportunity to make a comprehensive aesthetic statement based on his knowledge of the Scottish philosophers, his wide reading in poetry, and his own poetic practice.

These years also provided Bryant with additional publishing opportunities. The two literary journals required a large amount of material; and in addition to his reviews, Bryant printed a number of poems, both old and new, in them. He even tried his hand at fiction, publishing three of his thirteen prose tales in these magazines. The journals were not, however, his only outlets. He joined his friends in a number of cooperative ventures. With Verplanck and Sands he helped to write a series of Christmas annuals, called *The Talisman,* published under the pseudonym Francis Herbert, in December 1827, 1828, and 1829. Bryant contributed poetry and prose, including short fiction, to all three, printing such well-known poems as "The Past" and "To Cole, the Painter, Departing for Europe." In 1830 he contributed to *The American Landscape,* a book of paintings by his artist friends, engraved by Durand and with letterpress by the poet; and in 1832 he joined with Sands, William Leggett, Catharine Sedgwick, and James Kirke Paulding to publish *Tales of Glauber-Spa,* for which Bryant wrote two stories, "The Skeleton's Cave" and "Medfield," his last attempts in the genre.

By far the most important event of these years, however, was the publication of the first collected edition of Bryant's works. The 1821 *Poems* had been merely a pamphlet. Now, ten years later, he selected eighty-nine poems, most of which had already appeared in print; revised them carefully, although not extensively; and published them in January 1832, in a book of 240 pages. Readers and critics were thus for the first time given the opportunity to read all of Bryant's mature poetry in one collection, and the book confirmed his position as the leading American poet of his time. Bryant wanted his book to be published in England and wrote to Washington Irving, then still living abroad, to enlist his help. Irving placed the work with a London publisher, added his own name as editor, and dedicated it to Samuel Rogers, the well-known British poet—all necessary, Irving wrote to Bryant, to call attention to the book in a depressed literary market. Bryant was pleased, and grateful to Irving for what he had done. *Poems* (1832) was now before the entire English-speaking literary world, and the reviews on both sides of the Atlantic were generally favorable.

The publication of this volume marked the culmination of Bryant's career as a poet. Although the last edition of his works in 1876 contained more than double the number of poems of the 1832 volume, most of his best work was already behind him. An occasional later poem is worthy of note. "The Prairies," written after his visit to Illinois in the spring of 1832 and published the following year, is probably the best. But poems like "Earth" and "To the Apennines," written in Europe during his first trip abroad, and three blank-verse poems of the late 1830's and early 1840's—"The Fountain," "Noon," and "A Hymn of the Sea"—are also significant and should be mentioned. There were few years after 1832, however, in which Bryant wrote as many as six or eight poems; and as time passed, his annual production became very small. As new editions of his works appeared, Bryant incorporated into them the poems of the intervening years—four new poems in 1834, twelve in 1836, and only one in 1839—but since the bulk of each volume was essentially the same as that of 1832, there was little more to be said about his verse as a whole than had been elicited by the appearance of that volume.

Bryant did publish three completely new books of poetry: *The Fountain and Other Poems* (1842), a small collection of poems including parts of an unfinished long work; *The White-Footed Deer and Other Poems* (1844), ten new poems including both "Noon" and "A Hymn of the Sea"; and *Thirty Poems* (1864), a small gathering that includes some of his Civil War verse. The poems from these volumes were also collected in the enlarged editions of his poetical works that appeared in 1847, 1855, 1858, 1871, and 1876, the last that Bryant himself brought out. None of these collections, it is fair to say, is so important as that of 1832, for none of them added appreciably to a poetic reputation that had peaked around then and was soon to be surpassed by that of the extraordinarily popular Henry Wadsworth Longfellow. The later books, including *Thirty Poems*, were well received; but it was Bryant the well-known, established figure who was being praised. He made no new departures in these books, remaining a poet of the early nineteenth century who lived to become an important newspaper editor who also occasionally wrote verse.

By 1832, Bryant was firmly established on the *Evening Post*. Editor in chief since 1829, he bought an increasing share in the business over the years, and soon found himself in comfortable circumstances. Bryant was not always happy in the editorial profession, but it supported him well and eventually brought him wealth. It also drew him deeply into politics. He had long since given up his youthful Federalist views to become an outspoken advocate of liberal causes, first among the Jacksonian Democrats and later, as the Civil War approached, with the newly founded Republican Party; and he wrote vigorous editorials in support of the positions that, under his guidance, the paper advocated. Moreover, Bryant's success on the *Evening Post* gave him the opportunity to indulge his love for travel. Over a period of some forty years, he made six voyages to Europe and the Near East; he traveled in the United States, to Illinois and the South; and he went to Cuba and Mexico. On most of these trips he wrote letters back to the *Evening Post*, many of which were collected in three volumes: *Letters of a Traveller* (1850), *Letters of a Traveller, Second Series* (1859), and *Letters from the East* (1869).

His position as editor of an important daily kept Bryant much in the public eye and, especially in his later years, he was frequently asked to deliver speeches on public occasions of both literary and civic importance. As well-known members of his generation died, Bryant was called upon to deliver memorial addresses for them: for Cole in 1848, Cooper in 1852, Irving in 1860, Halleck in 1869, and Verplanck in 1870; and he spoke on such occasions as the Burns centennial celebration in 1859, the laying of the cornerstone at the National Academy of Design in 1863, and the fiftieth anniversary of the Mercantile Library in 1870. A small collection of his speeches was published in 1873 as *Orations and Addresses,* a volume noteworthy mainly for gathering in one place the five major addresses on his friends in literature and the arts. Those on Cole, Cooper, and Irving are undoubtedly the most important. The poet felt called upon to comment on their works as well as their lives, and his critical judgments are of value both for what they say about the subjects themselves and for what they reveal about the poet's critical standards.

In his last years, too, Bryant engaged in several large projects. He wrote the introduction and helped select the material for a massive anthology of poetry, *The Library of Poetry and Song.* Bryant had earlier published a smaller collection, *Selections from the American Poets* (1840); but the new volume, published in 1871, included British as well as American works and soon attained a wide popularity. He also wrote introductions for both *Picturesque America; or, the Land We Live In,* published in two volumes (1872 1874), and the multivolume *Popular History of the United States* (1878), written by Sydney Howard Gay. The most important work of Bryant's last years, however, was translation. From his earliest days he had translated Greek and Latin poetry, and his collected works contain a number of poems translated mainly from Spanish and German. In his old age he turned to Homer, making blank-verse translations of the *Iliad* (1870) and the *Odyssey* (1871–1872). Bryant found he could do this work without the strain that original composition entailed, and he sought in it a means to occupy himself after the death of his wife in 1866 had left him feeling like "one cast out of paradise."

Bryant remained active until the last weeks of his life. Strong of body and alert in mind, he kept busy not only with his newspaper work but also with his many other activities. Occasionally he would write poetry; and it is a testimony to his intellectual vigor that one of his last poems, "The Hood of Years," an imaginative treatment of life and death written in 1876, remains memorable. Bryant had lived a long and productive life. Although forced to earn his living by what he considered the drudgery of both law and journalism, he managed to keep his poetic fire alive and contributed both to the intellectual life of his city and to American literature as a whole. In his later years, of course, the exigencies of his profession forced him to mute his poetic voice: and he never completed the long poem he apparently attempted in the early 1840's. His accomplishment in poetry, however, is nonetheless significant. When Bryant died on June 12, 1878, in his eighty-fourth year, an important American poetic voice was stilled, one that had spoken truly of native things and, in its quiet way, had demonstrated to the English-speaking world that a distinctively American poetry had been born.

What is there in Bryant's verse that can be called specifically American? Certainly not the form. Although in his later years he experimented successfully with a number of lyric stanzas, Bryant was never an innovator in verse. He believed, as he wrote in his "Lectures on Poetry," that every apprentice in the art learns his craft from reading the works of those who have gone before him. Like the mathematician, the poet takes up his art at just the place where his predecessors left off; and if he has genius enough, he advances it just as far as he is able. Such a theory places great emphasis on both tradition and continuity in poetry. It leaves little room for the kind of originality that breaks with the past and launches the art in a new direction. Those critics were right, therefore, who in the early reviews of his poems observed his relation to the English poets of the immediate past; and even though more perceptive ones also made it clear that he did not imitate those poets, knowledgeable readers have always recognized that Bryant's roots lie deep in the British poetry he had read and loved as a young man.

Both Bryant's philosophic stance and his aesthetic theory derive from a foreign source: Scottish associationist philosophy. Works by Dugald Stewart and Archibald Alison were extremely popular in the United States in those days: they were used as textbooks in the colleges, and they helped to form the aesthetic views of the first generation of American Romantic artists and writers. Along with other members of that generation, Bryant accepted as a matter of course both their realistic philosophy and its aesthetic corollaries. Their sensationalist view provided him with an epistemology that he never questioned, and he followed them in the moral and religious aspects of their belief. He found in Alison's treatment of the sublimity and beauty of nature an adequate explanation of the human response to the natural world, and he formed his taste around those aesthetic categories as they were illustrated and explained by Alison's treatment of both descriptive poetry and landscape art. Bryant even constructed his poems in accordance with those intellectual processes that the Scottish school had shown to be the means by which one learned from his impressions of external reality.

One finds the influence of these beliefs throughout Bryant's poetry. The sensationalist basis of his thought is apparent in the numerous images of sight, sound, and even smell that are everywhere in his verse. Most, of course, are visual. But the sounds of birds and insects, of rippling water and rustling trees are also present, as is the fragrance of those flowers that occasionally appear. Like the philosophers, Bryant believed that through the senses, the sympathetic observer could establish a proper relation with external reality. Not everyone, of course, would react in the same way to the natural scene, nor would the individual relate to it in the same fashion on different occasions. Although nature answers to the requirements of the mind, the mind itself, as Bryant wrote in "An Invitation to the Country," must actively participate in the process. The sights and sounds of the springtime are beautiful only when the observer "fondly" looks and listens. One must gaze at the world with "a loving eye" and breathe "with joy" the fragrance of April breezes, or the beauty and glory of nature will not be perceived.

On the properly disposed mind, therefore, the beauty and sublimity of the external world could have a salutary effect, answering, as the need might arise, to the gay or solemn mood with which one viewed the landscape. This was not, however, the only function of nature. Through correct perception of the external scene, the healthy rational mind could be led to an understanding of its meaning. Like the philosophers, of course, Bryant knew that sense impressions could sometimes be deceptive; and he occasionally included in his poems such phenomena as the delusive images of glittering light that so attract the dreamy youth in "Catterskill Falls" that he almost perishes, or the dim and misty landscape that leads the weary hunter to misinterpret reality and plunge to his death in "The Hunter's Vision." Indeed, the poet even plays fancifully with the concept in "A Day-Dream," where, gazing at rays of light quivering across the ocean floor, he imagines that sea nymphs rise from the waves and, in the murmuring of the waters, speak to him of the times when men believed in their existence. In all three poems, deceptive visual images, playing upon the imagination, influence the mind to perceive what is not actually there.

Such incidents are rare in Bryant's poetry. He more usually bases his themes on the philosopher's fundamental position that the objects of the world are both real and knowable. He can perceive the yellow violet and the fringed gentian, for example, not only as ephemeral flowers but also as entities that have certain specific and verifiable characteristics. In his part of the world, the yellow violet is a flower of April, blooming alone in the woods before the other flowers of spring appear; the fringed gentian is the last flower of autumn, blossoming when all others have died. Each has certain demonstrable qualities that help the poet to identify and place it in the general order of things. Bryant was an accomplished botanist, and sought to be scientifically exact in his descriptions of such plants. He saw no conflict between his scientific and poetic approaches to nature. Both were premised upon the belief that the natural world was real, that it could be reached and understood by the minds of men, and that reliable knowledge could be drawn from it of the utmost value to both the physical and the moral well-being of men.

It is precisely because he acted upon such beliefs that Bryant developed into a truly American poet. Once he had accepted the epistemological and aesthetic views of the Scottish philosophers, he found himself in a complex relation with nature; and the interaction between his mind and the objects that he perceived formed the intellectual and aesthetic basis for his poetry. The world Bryant observed could not be anything but American, for before his first trip to Europe in 1836, he had experienced no other; and the mind with which he perceived it, though necessarily influenced by the education he had received in Scripture, in classical and English poetry, and in Scottish philosophy, remained fundamentally American in its view both of external nature and of men and their institutions. This is not to say that Bryant and other Americans of his generation were totally different from their British contemporaries. But the process of change that had begun to work on the American character with the arrival of the first colonists had proceeded so far by the beginning of the nineteenth century that a distinctly American cast of mind had formed, and men born on these shores saw things through American eyes.

What they saw, moreover, was uniquely their own. The American landscape of the 1820's was markedly different from that of Europe, and Bryant sought to catch its quality and meaning in his art. The point is not that he wished to be nationalistic. He was willing to include European views in his work after he had experienced them, but his heart and mind were always with American nature because of what he had felt and learned in its presence. As he wrote in his sonnet "To Cole, the Painter, Departing for Europe," there is a brightness and a wildness in the American landscape, an expansiveness in its wide savannas and boundless groves, a solemnity in the uninhabited reaches of the wilderness that cannot be matched in Europe, where the hand of man, working through time, is seen in the houses, graves, and ruins of a thoroughly domesticated landscape. Bryant does not insist on the superiority of either; he stresses only the difference. But a man whose mind and art were formed in response to the wild, bright nature of his expansive country must always create an art that will reflect the values he derived from his experience.

This view of nature was not, of course, his only one, nor did Bryant rule out the presence of man in the American landscape. Most often, however, the human agents include such typically American characters as hunter, Indian, or independent farmer—there are no Wordsworthian leech gatherers or old Cumberland beggars in his verse—and his less expansive scenes frequently include some specific American locality or precisely described flora that the poet had observed. Yet it is not so much the presence of American things as the broad vision of reality that is important in Bryant's verse. Each poem presents some aspect of it, but no poem contains it all. No one could, since each records an individual perception, a unique encounter between the mind of the poet and the external world. What Bryant might perceive one day was necessarily different from what he might see the next, for his mood would inevitably change and different aspects of the material world would catch his attention. Nonetheless, his fundamentally American bent of mind gave him a point of view that enabled him to maintain a consistent moral vision throughout his many poems.

To understand that vision, we must begin where Bryant did, with man's relation to nature. In composing his poems he sought, as he writes in his "Lectures on Poetry," "to shape the creations of the mind into perfect forms according to those laws which man learns from observing the works of his Maker," and to reveal to his readers "those analogies and correspondences which [poetry] beholds between the things of the moral and of the natural world." From the poet's point of view, he stands in a complex relation to nature and, through it, to God. Nature thus stands between the poet and the Deity, reveals to the former the moral truths of God, and provides the means through which the poet communicates those truths to his readers. The poet must first perceive those qualities in the natural landscape that have led him to his belief, and then re-create in his verse not merely a detailed description of the scene, but an evocation of its meaning. This he does by presenting a few suggestive touches and glimpses to awaken the imagination of the reader and fill his mind with delight. By this means the poet leads him to a perception of those truths that God has instilled in the natural scene.

Such a process must be premised upon a fundamentally innocent nature that does not itself deceive, and Bryant goes out of his way to establish the point. Though he believes in a fallen world, he writes, in "Inscription for the Entrance to a Wood," that "the primal curse / Fell" on an "unsinning earth," which, since it remains guiltless, still contains qualities that can ease the mind and heart of those who come to it from the "sorrows, crimes, and cares" of the world of guilty men. "The calm shade" brings "a kindred calm, and the sweet breeze" carries a balm to the "sick heart." Bryant is seldom so explicit in developing the basis for his view. More usually he simply asserts the fact of an innocent nature. In "A Summer Ramble," for example, he describes the beautiful calm of a summer day, leaves his desk, and goes out amid "the sinless, peaceful works of God" to share the season's calm; and in "The Firmament" he carries the theme one step further by looking away from the earth to the "calm pure sphere" of the skies, where he perceives "seats of innocence and rest."

An innocent nature is a reliable one that can be depended upon in its communication of moral truth. It teaches, at times, by analogy. Simple flowers like the yellow violet and the fringed gentian, or birds like the waterfowl, lead the poet to an understanding of human behavior or to a perception of his place in the cosmos. Although he welcomes the yellow violet when he sees it blooming alone in the April woods, he ignores it when the gorgeous flowers of May appear; and the poet recognizes in this experience the sin of pride, which makes one forget his early friends when he climbs to wealth and social position. In a similar fashion the fringed gentian, blooming late in the year, when the woods are bare and the frost has come, makes him wish that when death draws near to him, he will similarly find hope blossoming in his heart. The famous "To a Waterfowl" illustrates the same relation. The poet, like the bird, is moving through space to a new destination; and, perceiving his own situation reflected in its flight, he draws the moral conclusion that the God who directs the waterfowl unerringly to its destination will lead his steps aright.

Nature teaches in other ways as well. It is, for example, the measure of man and his accomplishments. Bryant does not always describe such small natural phenomena as wildflowers and birds. Sometimes he stresses the expansiveness of nature in both space and time. The opening lines of "Monument Mountain" depict a spacious scene of rocky precipice and beautiful valley where the habitations of men are dwarfed to insignificance; those of "The Prairies" describe a vast landscape that, stretching to the horizon, makes the lone man on horseback seem small indeed. "The Rivulet," on the other hand, measures man on a scale of time, for the little stream dances along its way unchanged, while the poet who played as a child along its banks already finds himself a grave man whose youthful visions have faded, and can foresee the day when he, "trembling, weak, and gray," will be an aged man. Indeed, after his death other children will mature and age near the spot, while the unchanging stream, "singing down [its] narrow glen, / Shall mock the fading race of men." In the presence of nature, man should perceive how small he is and how short his existence.

Man may react to this knowledge in a number of different ways. His initial response may be one of humility. The poet who feels "almost annihilated" when he stands beside a "mighty oak" in "A Forest Hymn" reacts in a perfectly appropriate fashion, for the size and density of the centuries-old trees can only convince him of his own weakness and mortality and the vanity of human striving. On other occasions, however, the opposite response is proper. When the poet stands for the first time on the Illinois prairies and his "dilated sight / Takes in the encircling vastness," his "heart swells" with the experience; when one looks out over the landscape from a lofty peak, as in "Monument Mountain," his "expanding heart" feels kindred to the higher world to which he has been translated; and he experiences an "enlargement of [his] vision." All these reactions occur because the sensitive observer recognizes in nature the presence of an enormous power that, from one point of view, threatens to overwhelm him yet, from another, raises his spirit above the physical and gives him a glimpse of a brighter, happier sphere.

Both responses to nature derive from the poet's recognition that behind the spacious world lies the source of those truths to be discerned in it. Bryant's conception of God has always been the subject of some discussion. The poet's relation to Wordsworth might lead one to expect that he, like the English poet, would take a pantheistic view. But what one finds in his poems is something quite different. To be sure, in "A Forest Hymn" there is a brief passage that seems to imply that the forest flower may be

> An emanation of the indwelling Life,
> A visible token of the upholding Love,
> That are the soul of this great universe.

But lines like these are rare in Bryant's poetry. His typical vision of God is that of a Creator who stands somewhat apart from His creation and reveals Himself not in, but through, it. The opening lines of the second section of "A Forest Hymn" are more typical. Here he addresses God as the "Father" who reared the massive trunks and wove the verdant roof above them, who looked "upon the naked earth" and raised forthwith all the "fair ranks of trees."

Precisely the same view appears in "The Prairies." As the poet looks across the "boundless and beautiful" unshorn fields, his mind turns to their Creator:

> The hand that built the firmament hath
> heaved
> And smoothed these verdant swells, and
> sown their slopes
> With herbage, planted them with island-
> groves,
> And hedged them round with forests.

Even when Bryant considers the physical world in terms of the geological processes that have formed its various features over eons of time, he sees as the ultimate cause of physical change that same God who initially created it. Thus, he begins "A Hymn of the Sea" with the lines:

> The sea is mighty, but a mightier sways
> His restless billows. Thou, whose hands
> have scooped
> His boundless gulfs and built his shore, thy
> breath,
> That moved in the beginning o'er his face
> Moves o'er it evermore.

Bryant goes on to describe the changes that occur as the shores are worn away by waves and both coral reefs and volcanic islands form new land. Here too the hand of God is at work; and in a second echo of Genesis, Bryant writes: "Thou dost look / On thy creation and pronounce it good."

In Bryant's vision of reality, nature is both separate from and dependent upon a still-creating, still-sustaining Deity; but because the Creator may be known through His creation, God's qualities can be discerned in the physical world. The broad sweep of both space and time to be perceived' in the universe bespeaks the infinity and eternity of Him who created it; the beauty and majesty of the natural landscape suggest the similar, though greater, qualities that He possesses. The light of God is revealed through the stars of the firmament, in "Song of the Stars," and His majesty in the mountains in "To the River Arve." The "grandeur, strength, and grace" of the trees, in "A Forest Hymn," suggest in small the similar qualities of God; and man, perceiving God's greatness in the surrounding forest, feels his spirit bowed "with the thought of boundless power / And inaccessible majesty." Indeed, once Bryant had established in his verse this fundamental vision of the external world as revealing the nature of God, any description of beauty or grandeur would carry with it the suggestion that the infinitely greater qualities of God were also being revealed.

But if the nature of God is made manifest in the external world, so too is His will, which, perceived by men, should lead them to moral action. For Bryant this is a crucial function of nature. He believes that fallen man, left to himself, is an easy prey to his passions, and that man as a whole in society creates endless conflict. While still a young man in Great Barrington, he had complained, in "Green River," that his occupation as lawyer had forced him to "mingle among the jostling crowd, / Where the sons of strife are subtle and loud"; and in "Autumn Woods" he longed to

> leave the vain low strife
> That makes men mad—the tug for wealth and power—
> The passions and the cares that wither life,
> And waste its little hour.

Later, in New York, Bryant returned to the same idea. His heart is oppressed with sadness, in "A Rain-Dream," because of the strifes and "tumults of the noisy world" where Fraud deceives and Strength overpowers his adversary. Evil, in Bryant's view, derives from the passions of men, which, if left unchecked, cause untold misery.

On a larger scale the same cause leads to war. As an early nineteenth-century American, Bryant was inclined to attribute aggressive war to the passions and greed of kings; and his poems on Europe frequently stress the horror of war and oppression that have characterized the past. Thus, in "Earth" he surveys the valleys of Italy that since early times have been the fields of war, where nations vanished, "driven out by mightier," and where free men fought each other until "strange lords" placed the yoke of servitude on all. To point up the folly of such struggles, and to affirm the peace that God wills for the world, Bryant sometimes juxtaposes a description of violent conflict and one of peaceful nature. In "To the Apennines" he recapitulates the long history of violence that has beset the Italian peninsula and pictures the shouting armies that have rushed together at the base of the Apennines. Beleaguered cities were destroyed, realms were torn in two, and commonwealths rose against each other and engaged in fratricidal war. Meanwhile, "in the noiseless air and light that flowed" around the mountain peaks, "eternal Peace abode."

The point of the contrast is not lost on some men. The poet recognizes, and tries to communicate to others, not only the folly of conflict but also its cure. He returns to the woods, in "A Forest Hymn," to reassure his "feeble virtue" in the presence of God; and he steals "an hour from study and care," in "Green River," to reestablish his peace of mind. In the peaceful stream he finds once again "an image of that calm life" he had previously found in his experience with nature. Many elements in the natural landscape can serve the same function. In "A Summer Ramble" the poet seeks peace in the calm of a summer day, while in "Lines on Revisiting the Country" he finds in the mountain wind a kind of "health and refreshment" that seems to come from heaven's own gates. Nature is thus an appropriate retreat from the conflicts of the world; but it is not merely an escape, nor does the poet seek only some vague influence from the natural scene. While it does provide an emotional calm, it also has a higher function in affirming the moral order that, in Bryant's view, is everywhere apparent in the harmony of nature.

Bryant was well aware that to most observers, the world did not appear to be a place of order and harmony. Even nature, unchanging as it may seem to be in comparison with human life, has undergone convulsive alterations in the geologic past; and wherever one looks in the present world, "eternal change," as Bryant wrote in "The Evening Wind," is clearly the law of nature. Like many another thinking man in the early nineteenth century, Bryant was fascinated with the problem of time and change, illustrated wherever he turned by the cycles of days, seasons, and years. And like many others, too, he sought some principle by which he might reconcile the endless manifestations of mutability that he perceived around him. He turned in one poem to the North Star as an apparently fixed element that could be read as a sign of "that bright eternal beacon" by which man might guide his life; but he needed some more general principle than this, some aspect of the external scene that, discernible throughout the natural world, could serve as an effective restraint on the passionate actions of men.

Bryant found that principle in the concept of ordered change. However mutable the world may be, change moves through constant patterns. The evening wind blows from sea to shore, but later returns from shore to sea; and the perceptive man will emphasize not the change, but the stable principle according to which change occurs. Thus, in "The Fountain" the poet writes of the many changes that have taken place around a woodland spring, itself a symbol of constant change. Yet something more than mutability may be seen in the flowing water. "Here the sage," Bryant writes,

> Gazing into [the] self-replenished depth,
> Has seen eternal order circumscribe
> And bound the motions of eternal change,
> And from the gushing of [the] simple fount
> Has reasoned to the mighty universe.

Universal order is as apparent in the world as is the principle of mutability, and is more significant in that it reflects the unchanging nature of God. The lesson for man is obvious. He must learn to conform the order of his life to the order that lies at the heart of nature.

Some men, however, fail to perceive or heed the lesson that is writ large on the natural landscape. They continue their passionate struggle, unmindful of God or the message of peace and harmony He imparts to them through the ordered calm of nature. But if they will not learn from the milder aspects of the natural world, they may be influenced by the harsher. Bryant knew full well that nature could be frightening as well as reassuring, and he occasionally included its violent aspects in his work. In "A Forest Hymn" he depicts a tempestuous scene of thunder and lightning, of whirlwinds, and of pounding tidal waves that inundate the shore and destroy the cities. In scenes like these, he continues, prideful man lays by "his strifes and follies," recognizes his own incapacity, and acknowledges the power of God, Who rules the elements. The sublime aspects of the natural world are as important as the beautiful ones in leading men to a knowledge of how they should act, and the poet prays at the end of the poem that he may be spared the sterner aspects of God's power and learn from His "milder majesty" to order his life properly.

Yet even such warnings, Bryant believed, were sometimes not enough. In "A Hymn of the Sea" he carries the theme one step further by making a storm at sea the instrument of God's justice. Here an armed fleet is royally sailing to carry aggressive war to some unsuspecting realm, when "the fierce tornado" descends upon it. In a highly evocative passage filled with discord and violence, Bryant describes the destruction of the fleet, the vast ships whirled like chaff, sails rent, masts snapped, cannon thrust overboard, and the invading army whelmed / By whirlpools or dashed dead upon the rocks." The instruments of power, violence, and oppression are utterly destroyed by the overwhelming force of the storm at sea; but the elements themselves are, after all, merely the instruments of a yet greater Power, who, in Bryant's view, may use them to teach a lesson to erring men. It ought to be a salutary one, and for a time it may be effective. But the poet offers scant hope that nations will change because of it.

Although they stand in awe of what has happened to the invading fleet, they pause for only "a moment, from the bloody work of war."

The history of the world, as Bryant understood it, certainly justified his conclusion. The record of the past was for the most part only a long series of wars and conflicts, as states and empires rose and fell, leaving only their ruins scattered across the landscape. His Phi Beta Kappa poem, "The Ages," recapitulates much of the record. He describes the ancient despotisms that flourished in the East, only to fall and leave behind a few monuments and tombs in the desert; he includes the decay of Rome as it sank, under the empire, into a state of guilt and misery; and he mentions the many nations that were "blotted out from earth, to pay / The forfeit of deep guilt." In "The Ruins of Italica," moreover, a poem Bryant translated from the Spanish of Francisco de Rioja, he presents the remains of the Roman city in Spain as an eloquent testimony to the emptiness of past glory. The palaces and gardens were all swept away with the Caesars, and Roman grandeur vanished from the earth as Trojan and Greek had disappeared before it. Such a record ought to be doubly instructive to men, to convince them that the glories of the world have always been, and still are, perishable, and to teach them that they should place their trust in other things.

This "ruins of empire" theme was a favorite among nineteenth-century writers and painters, both in the United States and abroad; and it so fascinated Bryant that he even developed it in an American context. The clearing of the forest and the supplanting of the Indian may have left no decaying monuments to past glories; but the historical process was, in a sense, little different from that recorded in Europe. The present American civilization was rising from the destruction of an earlier culture; and those involved in the process ought to be aware not only of what had happened in the past, but also of what might develop in the future. Bryant wrote several important poems on this theme. He imagines, in "The Fountain," the unrecorded history that has taken place around a woodland spring that once flourished in the virgin forest. The Indian waged war in its vicinity, and hunters built their lodges near the spot. Then, after centuries passed, the white man came, cut the trees and plowed the ground; since that time a whole society has grown up around it. But change does not end with the present, and the poet muses on what additional changes—caused by man or nature—might lurk in the future.

Bryant depicts an even grander history, one more closely approximating the European version of the theme, in "The Prairies," where he tells of yet a third race, supplanted during the historical process in America—the Mound Builders, whom contemporary historians took to be a pre-Indian race. The mounds they left scattered across a large number of the eastern states were thus considered to be true ruins of a great historical past. Bryant describes their builders as "a disciplined and populous race" who constructed the mounds while the Greeks were erecting the Parthenon. He depicts their civilization as a relatively high one, brought down by the "warlike and fierce" redmen, who attacked and destroyed them. Now the Indians, too, have been driven away; and the white man is about to cultivate the fields where two previous cultures had once flourished. "Thus change the forms of being," Bryant writes:

> Thus arise
> Races of living things, glorious in strength,
> And perish, as the quickening breath of God
> Fills them, or is withdrawn.

The course of history in America resembles that in Europe, and contemporary men should heed the lesson it teaches.

That lesson involves both the present and the future. Men should not take pride today in what they know, from history, must eventually perish; but since men are by no means helpless in the world, what they do today can have some effect on the future. The basic question, of course, is whether the pattern must be continued unendingly, whether men must always succumb to their passions and forever repeat, as Bryant states in "Earth," "the horrid tale of perjury and strife, / Murder and spoil, which men call history." To Americans in the early nineteenth century, this question was crucial, for they saw their country as a young democratic state standing almost alone in a despotic world; and poets from Bryant to Walt Whitman viewed the United States as the hope of the future. America could serve that function only if it learned to avoid the mistakes of the past; but since, in Bryant's view, those mistakes had derived from the passionate nature of man, it remained an open question whether men in his day could acquire the self-control that would enable them to live in harmony, avoid conflict, and escape the age-old process of war and desolation that had overtaken all former people.

In his early poem "The Ages" (1821), Bryant had seemed hopeful that man in his time could change. "He who has tamed the elements," he writes, will not remain "the slave of his own passions"; he who can trace the course of celestial bodies will see God's will in His "magnificent works . . . / And love and peace shall make their paradise with man." Indeed, he ends the poem with the vision of a free and progressive America throwing off the last fetters of mankind and looking forward to a happy future. In later poems, however, Bryant sometimes appears to be less optimistic. In "Earth," for example, written in Europe some thirteen years later, he considers all the horrors that men have perpetrated and asks the obvious question of his "native Land of Groves" across the sea:

> a newer page
> In the great record of the world is thine;
> Shall it be fairer? Fear, and friendly Hope,
> And Envy, watch the issue, while the lines,
> By which thou shalt be judged, are written
> down.

There is an ominous tone to these last lines that contrasts sharply with the optimism of the earlier poem.

Bryant's uneasiness about the future derived, apparently, from his perception of what the historical process in America entailed. He knew, of course, that men of affairs in law and commerce were bound to be aggressive and contentious; and he always prescribed the untouched natural scene as the cure for passionate involvement in what are essentially trivial matters. But change in America involved the destruction of the wilderness; and by the early nineteenth century, American writers were beginning to warn their countrymen of the possible consequences of their actions. In "An Indian at the Burial-Place of His Fathers," Bryant makes a telling commentary on what had been happening. The Indian, who speaks the poem, visits the ancient burial ground of his tribe, from which they have long been driven; and in a series of contrasted pictures, he reveals the changes that the white man has made. In the first part of the poem, the contrast seems merely to indicate the two ways of life that the cultures created, the white man preferring the domesticated landscape of wheat fields and pasturage, while the Indian longs for the woods in which the warriors hunted. But there is more to the contrast than this.

The Indian sees a sign that the white man cannot perceive, and he predicts a future that resembles the European past:

> Their race may vanish hence, like mine,
> And leave no trace behind,
> Save ruins o'er the region spread,
> And the white stones above the dead.

Because the white men have cut the trees and farmed the soil, the springs have dried up, and the rivers run "with lessening current." Hence, if the process continues, the lands for which the Indians were crushed may one day become "a barren desert." Although the words are placed in the mouth of an Indian, there can be no doubt that Bryant himself was aware of the danger. Toward the end of "The Fountain," after he has depicted all the changes that have taken place around the woodland spring, he considers the future and wonders whether, in historic time, men will not "seek out strange arts to wither and deform / The pleasant landscape which [the spring makes] green." If they do, the very aspect of the natural scene that could preserve them from their follies will have been destroyed.

Bryant thus faced a dilemma. Like many in his generation, he found value both in the untouched wilderness and in the strong democratic society that must come from its destruction; he lamented the passing of the Indian and foresaw the consequences that the despoliation of nature might entail, yet he could not condemn the rapid process of change that his generation of Americans, perhaps more than any other, was destined to experience. Bryant was well aware that the historical process could not be reversed. The continent would be settled and the face of the landscape would change. Yet, in the final analysis, his faith in America's future was so strong that he could face it with confidence. Even in "The Crowded Street," a poem that depicts the tide of humanity in all of its various aspects flowing through the city, he ends with the belief that however self-concerned these people may be and however aimless and wayward their course of action may seem, God holds them in His boundless love and guides "the mighty stream," of which they are but eddies, "to its appointed end." The providential view of history, in other words, informs Bryant's vision and gives him the faith that the process of change works ultimately for good.

For Bryant, as for many in his generation, the progress of history was toward human freedom; and since the United States was in the forefront of that movement, he could indeed look forward with confidence toward a time when God's will for man would be fulfilled. The basis for this belief was manifest in nature. Bryant saw in the unrestrained movement of the winds that spirit of freedom that must one day inspire the multitudes of Europe to throw off their chains, and he found in the mountains—both Alps and Apennines—an image of the liberty that had freed the Switzerland of William Tell and that would someday liberate Italy. Indeed, in "The Antiquity of Freedom," the poet finds in the peaceful woods of his native land a sign that the natural condition of man was originally freedom. Tyranny is later-born and, though powerful, "shall fade into a feebler age" while freedom waxes stronger. The battle is not yet over, for tyranny has become more subtle as it weakens; but the poet never doubts that the time will come when freedom shall triumph and a "new earth and heaven" be born.

Throughout his life Bryant supported the cause of freedom in his verse. He had celebrated the Spanish victory over the invading French in "The Spanish Revolution" (1808); and in "The Massacre at Scio," "Song of the Greek Amazon," "The Greek Partisan," and "The Greek Boy," he supported, like many a poet in his generation, the Greek struggle for independence. Although, unlike John Greenleaf Whittier and James Russell Lowell, he wrote little verse in support of the antislavery cause, there is "The African Chief," which details the destruction of the proud black man when he is captured and sold into slavery. The Civil War, of course, elicited Bryant's support of the federal government, "the gentlest sway / That Time in all his course has seen"; and he celebrated the emancipation of the slaves with an ode, "The Death of Slavery." The God "who marks the bounds of guilty power" had struck the shackles from the slave, who now "stands in his native manhood, disenthralled," while slavery itself, in these "better years that hasten by," is buried in the "shadowy past, with all those former wrongs of suffering and oppression from which so much of the world has been freed.

Bryant also counted on the ties of free trade to destroy the barriers that had arisen between men, and thus to unite the earth in one brotherhood. In "The Path" he imagines how a simple woodland path is linked to other paths and roads to make a vast network that binds all men together, and he praises the "mighty instinct, that dost thus unite/Earth's neighborhoods and tribes with friendly bands." Like many another American in the nineteenth century, he sees in the physical links between men a sign of the higher association that will follow from them. Further, in "The Song of the Sower" Bryant pictures all the types of men who look to the sower's work for sustenance, and ends his poem with a vision of the grain going across the earth wherever "roads wind and rivers flow," to fill the marts of the ancient East and the tropical South. The image of peace and plenty that Bryant creates in this poem suggests the benefits that will flow when all men enjoy the blessings of liberty and neither barriers nor strife, caused by pride or spite, stand in the way of the peaceful interchange of goods between nations.

Bryant's philosophy of nature thus provided him with a comprehensive vision of reality that enabled him to write significantly about the American experience. Since close observation of nature could provide fallen man with the knowledge he needed to live successfully in the world, and since America was particularly blessed with broad expanses of forested hills and valleys that embodied the meanings that God intended for men to discern, Americans could learn from their native landscape the self-discipline necessary to control the pride and passions of their fallen nature and, thus, to live in freedom and peace. In building their country, of course, Americans incurred some risk that the result might differ little from the experience of the past; and that prospect had to be faced. Time and change, however, could not be stopped. The westward expansion would go on at the expense of the Indian and of that wild, bright nature that Bryant valued so highly. Nonetheless, the poet found reason to hope that the change was being directed in such a way that a free American society would result and lead the world to that liberty and peace that he discerned in the natural landscape.

Bryant was not always so broadly philosophical in his verse. Although most of his important poems do develop one aspect or another of his vision, in a very few poems he wrote on highly personal subjects. Bryant was a man of strong emotions who kept them so firmly in check as to appear rather cold and severe, but he sometimes allowed his personal feelings to show through the medium of his verse. Of the several poems he wrote recording his youthful love for Frances Fairchild, he published only "Oh, Fairest of the Rural Maids," a poem in which he associates the beauty and innocence of the young girl with the analogous qualities of the natural scene in which she has lived. He also composed a few poems about her during his later years. In "The Life That Is," for example, written at Castellammare, Italy, in 1858, Bryant rejoices in her recovery from a serious illness that had threatened to take her life; and in "October, 1866," he expresses his grief and sense of loss at her death, which had occurred in July.

Bryant also treats the deaths of several members of his family. While composing "Hymn to Death" in 1820, he was shocked to learn of the death of his beloved father; he ended the poem with a tribute to the man who had taught him the art of writing verse and who had read and criticized all of his previous attempts at poetry. A few years later, in 1824–1825, he wrote two poems on his favorite sister, Sarah Bryant Shaw. In the first, "Consumption," he reconciles himself to the fact that his sister is dying; and in the very popular poem "The Death of the Flowers," he pays tribute to her after her death. Finally, in 1849, Bryant wrote "The May Sun Sheds an Amber Light" to commemorate his mother, who had died two years before in Illinois. In most of these poems—"Hymn to Death" may be an exception—Bryant exerts a firm control over the emotion he has experienced; and one feels that he published them not because of the personal meaning they had for him, but because he was satisfied that in each poem, the emotion had been given proper poetic expression.

The poems on the deaths of his wife and beloved members of his family are, moreover, important contributions to a subject that had fascinated the poet since his youth. Bryant had apparently had a real fear of death as a young man, had written a number of juvenile poems on the subject, and had read the British "graveyard" poets, who had dealt with it. One of his earliest poems—"Thanatopsis"—and one of his later—"The Flood of Years"—discuss the problem; and between these two there are many that, in one way or another, touch upon it. Poems on death, therefore, represent a significant part of Bryant's poetic output and deserve consideration both for themselves and for what they contribute to an understanding of his philosophy. From the latter point of view, the subject of death presented him with something of a problem. Because he based his philosophic position on the direct observation of nature and constructed his system of belief around it, Bryant would necessarily turn first to the material world for an understanding of the meaning of death. This he did, of course, in "Thanatopsis," where the voice of nature gives one aspect of that meaning.

What nature can say of death, however, must be limited to the physical. Since death is the natural end of all living things, it must simply be accepted as a matter of course. Beyond that, nature can say nothing about the ultimate significance of death; and the only comfort it can give is that all who have ever lived lie together equally in the common grave of earth. Critics have made much of the fact that no hint of immortality is given in the poem, and the omission is sometimes taken as a sign of Bryant's religious position at the time. It may well be. But Bryant himself had trouble identifying the voice that speaks the central section of the poem. In an early manuscript version of the introductory lines, he had made it his "better genius"; but this he rejected in favor of the present reading, in which the "still voice" comes from nature. The effect is to give a partial treatment of the subject, as if the poet would say: Here is the view that nature takes of the common fate of man, one that should give the observer courage to accept his personal end.

Seen from other points of view, however, death appears quite different. In human terms, as Bryant writes in "Hymn to Death," it can be seen as a deliverer who frees the oppressed and crushes the oppressor, or as the great leveler without whom the powerful of the earth would have enslaved the weak forever. Seen in yet other terms, as Bryant has it in "A Forest Hymn," death is not so triumphant as it sometimes appears to be. Though "all grow old and die," youth, "ever-gay and beautiful youth / In all its beautiful forms," perpetually presses on the faltering footsteps of decay." Life mocks at death because it comes from God, Who has no end. From this intellectual position it is but a step to the affirmation of human immortality. Belief in an afterlife appears in some of the earliest of Bryant's poems—"Hymn to Death," for example—and is repeated in such later works as "Consumption," "The Past," and "The Future Life." In all of these poems, Bryant looks forward to another life, in which he hopes to meet again those whom he loved on earth.

As Bryant grew older, he turned increasingly to allegory to express his view of death and the afterlife, most frequently using the rather conventional image of passage down a road or stream into the unknown. In "The Cloud on the Way" he suggests the mystery of death by an image of mist into which all travelers disappear, and in "Waiting by the Gate" he depicts death as a portal through which everyone must pass. Both of these poems, moreover, show the strong Christian affirmation that appeared in Bryant's work as he grew older, for both suggest that on the other side one shall meet not only his departed loved ones but also "the Sinless Teacher" who died for men. In one of his last poems, "The Flood of Years," Bryant gave his final thoughts on death. The passing generations rise and fall on the crest of the flood of time, only to be overwhelmed and disappear in the ocean of the past. But all that is good and valuable shall be restored in an eternal present in which the process of change so familiar on earth will at last be reconciled in everlasting harmony.

Bryant, of course, was not alone in his intellectual position, nor was his mode of expression unique. Other writers and painters of his generation—James Fenimore Cooper and Thomas Cole are but two important examples—shared his religious vision of nature and expressed their related themes in strikingly similar ways. Both Cooper and Cole depict the beauty and sublimity of the American scene and suggest the moral meaning to be derived from its observation; they also take precisely the same view of human history and include the "ruins of empire" theme in their works. Bryant may thus be seen as both drawing upon a body of thought generally accepted by literate Americans in his generation, and addressing his works to an audience who shared many of his assumptions, approved the themes of his poetry, and took pleasure in their expression. From the historical point of view, therefore, Bryant must be considered an important member of the first generation of American Romantic artists; and his poetry may profitably be read as a significant statement of those intellectual, artistic, and moral values that characterized the cultural life of early nineteenth-century America.The success that Bryant achieved as a spokesman for his generation, however, may stand in the way of a proper appreciation of his poetic achievement today. His vision of nature was rapidly superseded by those of the transcendentalists, the symbolists, and the realists—for all of whom he had helped to pave the way—and to many readers of poetry in the twentieth century, both the themes he develops and his mode of expression may seem old-fashioned. Some will object, for example, to the touches of sentimentality that appear in a number of Bryant's poems or to the use of analogy in the development of his themes. To many readers today the analogies he draws will seem like moral tags appended to his verse, and it must be admitted that some of his analogies do not derive so closely from the descriptions that inspired them as one might wish. Finally, we may also note that Bryant's range was narrow and his development relatively slight. Once he had established his intellectual position and found his poetic voice, he wrote a body of verse that explored that position fully; but he did not often venture onto new ground.

Bryant's limitations as a poet are real, and cannot be gainsaid. He is not a major poet, but a very good minor one who can still be read with pleasure. In his favorite forms, the short lyric and reflective blank-verse poem, he is quite effective. At their best, as in "To a Waterfowl," his poems of analogy develop naturally and convincingly from observed phenomenon to philosophical conclusion; and his rolling blank-verse rhythms often strike the ear as most appropriate for his reflections upon the natural scene. These poems record the play of the mind across the external landscape; and as we read, we can watch the theme develop as the poet considers the meaning he finds in his observation. Bryant's mood changes, moreover, from poem to poem; and he evokes both gaiety and awe, peace and exhilaration in the movement of his verse, depending upon his bent of mind at the moment. Each poem is, after all, a new experience of nature: and since both he and the landscape change, it is natural that the tone of the poetry should vary. To Bryant's credit, he was often able to capture these changing moods well in his verse. In content, too, Bryant remains a poet of some significance. Although his celebration of untouched nature comes from the preindustrial age of America, many of his themes are by no means out of date. He knew the cost that the settlement of the continent would entail—the destruction of the Indian and the despoliation of nature that would come with the westward expansion; and while he celebrated the democratic society that should result from the process, his knowledge of history and of the universal destruction of past civilizations made him aware that this nation, too, could perish. He depicted the passion, greed, and strife that he saw developing in the American cities; and he stressed the horrors that come from the selfishness and pride of human beings, especially in the form of war. He knew that the only cure was for men to recognize a power beyond their reach and strength, and he wrote of the need for humility if men were to lay by their follies. These are not minor themes. They were pertinent to the age in which he was writing and, considering what has happened since then, they cannot be considered irrelevant today.

Selected Bibliography

WORKS OF WILLIAM CULLEN BRYANT

POETRY

The Embargo, (Boston: printed for the purchasers, 1808). (Enlarged version with additional poems published 1809).

Poems, (Cambridge, Mass.: Hilliard and Metcalf, 1821).

Miscellaneous Poems Selected from the United States Literary Gazette, (Boston: Cummings, Hilliard and Co., and Harrison Gray, 1826). Contains twenty-three poems by Bryant.

Poems, (New York: Elam Bliss, 1832). (Republished, with new poems added, in 1834, 1836, 1839, 1847, 1855, 1858, 1871).

The Fountain and Other Poems, (New York: Wiley and Putnam, 1842).

The White-Footed Deer and Other Poems, (New York: I. S. Platt, 1844).

Thirty Poems, (New York: D. Appleton and Co., 1864).

Hymns, No place; no publisher (1864).

Poems, (New York: D. Appleton and Co., 1876). The final collection in Bryant's lifetime.

PROSE

Tales of Glauber-Spa, 2 vols. (New York: J. and J. Harper, 1832) Contains two stories by Bryant; other contributors were Robert Sands, William Leggett, Catharine Sedgwick, and James Kirke Paulding.

Letters of a Traveller, (New York: George P. Putnam, 1850).

Letters of a Traveller, Second Series, (New York: D. Appleton and Co., 1859).

Letters from the East, (New York: G. P. Putnam and Son, 1869).

Orations and Addresses, (New York: G. P. Putnam's and Son, 1873).

MISCELLANIES

The Talisman for MDCCCXXVIII, (New York: Elam Bliss, 1827).

The Talisman for MDCCCXXIX, (New York: Elam Bliss, 1828).

The Talisman for MDCCCXXX, (New York: Elam Bliss, 1829) Bryant contributed poetry and prose to all three.

TRANSLATIONS

The Iliad of Homer, 2 vols. (Boston: Fields, Osgood and Co., 1870).

The Odyssey of Homer, 2 vols. (New York: James R. Osgood and Co., 1871–72).

COLLECTED EDITIONS

The Poetical Works of WilliamCullen Bryant, edited by Parke Godwin. 2 vols. (New York: D. Appleton and Co., 1883; Russell and Russell, 1967).

Prose Writings of William Cullen Bryant, edited by Parke Godwin. 2 vols. (New York: D. Appleton and Co., 1884).

The Poetical Works of William Cullen Bryant, (New York: D. Appleton and Co., 1903) The Roslyn ed..

LETTERS

The Letters of William Cullen Bryant, edited by William Cullen Bryant II and Thomas G. Voss. Vol. 1: 1809–1836. (New York: Fordham University Press, 1975). Other volumes in progress.

BIBLIOGRAPHIES

Blanck, Jacob, "William Cullen Bryant," *Bibliography of American Literature,* (New Haven: Yale University Press, 1955).

Phair, Judith T., *A Bibliography of William Cullen Bryant and His Critics 1808–1972,* (Troy, N.Y.: Whitston Publishing Co., 1975).

Rocks, James E., "William Cullen Bryant," *Fifteen American Authors Before 1900,* edited by Robert A. Rees and Earl N. Harbert (Madison: University of Wisconsin Press, 1971).

Sturges, Henry C., *Chronologies of the Life and Writings of William Cullen Bryant, with a Bibliography of His Works in Prose and Verse,* (New York: D. Appleton and Co., 1903). Printed also in the Roslyn edition of the *Poetical Works.*

CRITICAL AND BIOGRAPHICAL STUDIES

Allen, Gay Wilson, *American Prosody,* (New York: American Book Co., 1935).

Arms, George W., *The Fields Were Green,* (Stanford, Calif.: Stanford University Press, 1953).

Bigelow, John, *William Cullen Bryant,* American Men of Letters Series (Boston: Houghton, Mifflin, 1890).

Bradley, William A., *William Cullen Bryant,* English Men of Letters Series (New York: Macmillan, 1905).

Brown, Charles H., *William Cullen Bryant,* (New York: Charles Scribner's Sons, 1971).

Callow, James T., *Kindred Spirits: Knickerbocker Writers and American Artists 1807–1855,* (Chapel Hill: University of North Carolina Press, 1967).

Conner, Frederick W., *Cosmic Optimism: A Study of the Interpretation of Evolution by American Poets from Emerson to Robinson,* (Gainesville: University of Florida Press, 1949).

Duffey, Bernard, "Romantic Coherence and Romantic Incoherence in American Poetry," *Centennial Review,* 7: 219–36 (Spring 1963); 8: 453–64 (Fall 1964).

Godwin, Parke, *A Biography of William Cullen Bryant, with Extracts from His Private Correspondence,* 2 vols. (New York: D. Appleton and Co., 1883; Russell and Russell, 1967).

Johnson, Curtiss S., *Politics and a Belly-Full,* (New York: Vantage Press, 1962).

McDowell, Tremaine, *William Cullen Bryant: Representative Selections,* American Writers Series (New York: American Book Co., 1935).

McLean, Albert F., Jr., *William Cullen Bryant,* Twayne's United States Authors Series (New York: Twayne Publishers, 1964).

Nevins, Allan, *The Evening Post: A Century of Journalism,* (New York: Boni and Liveright, 1922).

Pearce, Roy Harvey, *The Continuity of American Poetry,* (Princeton: Princeton University Press, 1961).

Pritchard, John P., *Return to the Fountains: Some Classical Sources of American Criticism,* (Durham, N.C.: Duke University Press, 1942).

Ringe, Donald A., *The Pictorial Mode: Space and Time in the Art of Bryant, Irving and Cooper,* (Lexington: University Press of Kentucky, 1971).

Waggoner, Hyatt H., *American Poets from the Puritans to the Present,* (Boston: Houghton, Mifflin, 1968).

Williams, Stanley T., *The Spanish Background of American Literature,* 2 vols. (New Haven: Yale University Press, 1955).

Robert Burns
(1759–1796)

DAVID DAICHES

I

ROBERT BURNS IS the national poet of Scotland. Every year on the anniversary of his birth thousands of Scotsmen at home and abroad attend celebratory "Burns suppers" and indulge in sentimental oratory extolling his poems, of which they often know only a few of the most hackneyed. Books about his life and loves are still written and read; every relic that has been associated with him is passionately treasured; and any odd piece of information that can be connected with Burns is eagerly sought by a host of amateur antiquarians. In this national worship of Burns there is a great deal that offends the literary critic, who complains that the Burns cult, as it is often called, obscures the true nature of Burns's literary achievement and perpetuates a quite unreal and preposterously sentimentalized picture of the man and the poet. The modern Scottish poet Hugh MacDiarmid has complained that the Burns cult "has denied his poetry to laud his amours. It has preserved his furniture and repelled his message."

Yet, however much we may agree that this sort of national worship of a poet is not conducive to the discriminating appreciation of his poetry, the fact remains that the cult developed spontaneously, soon after Burns's death, and there must be something about his poetic achievement that accounts for it. Scotland has no other national figure to compare with Burns. Not even Robert the Bruce, who led Scotland in the successful Wars of Independence against the English, holds a place in the hearts of Scotsmen that can begin to compare with that held by Burns. There is a universal feeling that Burns was a "real" person, that he understood men and their weaknesses, that he really knew what life was about, that he spoke for his fellow men in a unique way and to a unique degree. The English worship of William Shakespeare is a wholly different sort of thing; it reflects wonder and admiration before the almost godlike achievement of Shakespeare's genius. Shakespeare is not the great popular hero in England that Burns is in Scotland. Indeed, no country has made a poet into a national hero in quite the same way that Scotland has with Burns.

There are two principal reasons for the special place Burns has achieved in the affections of the ordinary folk of Scotland. The first is his humble origin. He was the son of a small tenant farmer and was a working farmer for most of his life. The second reason is the way in which Burns in his songs identified himself with the Scottish folk tradition and, by rescuing, completing, refurbishing, rewriting, or recreating hundreds of items from the vast but fragmentary mass of Scottish popular songs, came to symbolize the popular voice of Scotland. There are other reasons, too—social and economic as much as literary—why a rustic poet should have maintained a special appeal in an industrialized urban Scotland nostalgic for a lost pastoral rhythm of life. There is also the fact that Burns was, in a remarkable way, the poet of humanity's "unofficial self" (to borrow a phrase from George Orwell), the poet of realized experience in the individual instance. Many of his songs represent an abandonment to the emotional moment, a passionate acceptance of the reality and validity of the given situation:[1]

As fair art thou, my bonie lass,
So deep in luve am I;
And I will luve thee still, my Dear,
Till a' the seas gang[2] dry.

This kind of poetry is never reflective, but always isolates the individual experience to make it, for the moment, the sum of all life:

But a' the pleasures e'er I saw,
Tho' three times doubled fairly,
That happy night was worth them a',
Amang the rigs o' barley.

Or again:

Green grow the rashes O,
Green grow the rashes O;
The sweetest hours that e'er I spend,
Are spent amang the lasses O!

I am not claiming that this represents the greatest kind of poetry—in any case, these are parts of songs, which must be sung to their proper tunes to be properly appreciated. But such verse does illustrate a strain in Burns that accounts for his special kind of appeal.

In this respect Burns is the opposite of a poet such as Percy Bysshe Shelley. He does not try to find in his individual emotional experiences or moments of physical passion any symbol of the Platonic idea of love or any proof of anything except the reality and zest of the experience. His love songs are not, for the most part, about "Love"; they are about two people (or one person) in a state of physical and emotional excitement. There is something refreshing and appealing about this. And popular instinct turns readily toward the unromantic love poetry of the folk tradition.

1. All quotations are taken from James Kinsley, ed., *The Poems and Songs* (Oxford, 1968).

2. Go.

Popular instinct also turns to the kind of sentimental glorifications of rustic poverty that we find in that very unequal poem, "The Cotter's Saturday Night." Burns, who was much influenced by the sentimental tradition in late eighteenth-century English and Scottish literature, sometimes postured deliberately in order to attract the attention of the genteel sentimentalists of his day. He paraded himself before them as a "Heaven-taught ploughman," pretending that he was much less educated than he in fact was and playing the part of the simple "natural man" that philosophers of the period were fond of discussing in their theoretical works. It is on this side of Burns, unfortunately, that the orators at Burns suppers prefer to concentrate, with the result that they often present a picture of a rustic philosopher turning out edifying genteel platitudes about the life of the peasant.

There is yet another Burns, besides the unromantic love poet and the posturing sentimentalist, and that Burns, though largely ignored by the Burns cult, has a strength and a subtlety that the others wholly lack. This is the satirical poet, the ironic observer of contemporary men and manners, the shrewd and humorous critic of religion and politics, of human character, of the Scotland of his day. This is the Burns who wrote "Holy Willie's Prayer," "The Ordination," "The Twa Herds," "The Holy Fair," and other satirical poems in which he worked with assurance, technical brilliance, and originality in a Scottish literary tradition that goes back to the Middle Ages.

To understand how Burns's achievement was split in this way, and indeed how his character both as man and as poet was torn in different directions, we must have some appreciation of the nature of the Scottish literary tradition and of Burns's relation to it. Burns's relation to the Scottish literary past and to the situation of Scottish culture in his own day accounts for his split personality. The latter half of the eighteenth century was not a propitious time for a Scottish poet, and Burns's achievement becomes all the greater when one realizes the conditions, both personal and national, under which he worked.

II

In the Middle Ages, Scotland was an independent country with a vigorous culture of its own. The literary language of the medieval Scottish poets was what is known as "Middle Scots," originally a northern form of English but, as a result of independent development and of its use in a flourishing Scottish literature, now a language in its own right, though closely akin to English and in large measure intelligible to Englishmen. The great fifteenth-century Scottish poets, Robert Henryson and William Dunbar, had exercised and enriched the Scottish literary language, and their successors in the sixteenth century worked largely in the tradition they did so much to establish. The fifteenth- and early sixteenth-century Scottish poets had not only a national literary tradition and a literary language of their own, they were also European in their perspective, with close cultural links with the Continent, especially France. They drew in their own way on the common European storehouse of literary themes and modes, and they made their own use, too, of material drawn from the Latin and Greek classics. Gavin Douglas' translation of Vergil's *Aeneid* into Middle Scots verse early in the sixteenth century is the earliest rendering of Vergil into any branch of the English language. Unfortunately, the stability and integrity of Scottish culture was threatened by a series of events beginning in the latter part of the sixteenth century. The Reformation came to Scotland more violently than it came to England and precipitated more than a century of bitter controversy and sometimes sharp civil conflict. The Puritan suspicion of secular literature blighted Scottish drama and drove much folk literature underground. Further, once Scotland had officially become a Protestant country (though there remained a considerable Roman Catholic area in the Highlands), its destiny became more closely linked with Protestant England and separated from Catholic France, Scotland's traditional ally. English translations of the Bible were read by Scottish Protestants, and more and more English forms came into the Scottish literary language. Then, in 1603, King James VI of Scotland inherited the English throne and moved his court to London to become James I of England. This "Union of the Crowns," by removing the court—which had been the focus of Scottish culture—from Edinburgh and encouraging many of the Scottish poets to go south and write English courtly poetry, was a damaging blow to Scottish arts and letters. And when, in 1707, the Union of Crowns was succeeded by the Union of Parliaments and Scotland lost its own parliament to become simply the northern part of "Great Britain," the Scottish cultural situation became even more confused.

What happened was that standard southern English became more and more the language used by Scotsmen in writing, although they continued to speak their native Scots in daily conversation. Thus Scots as a living literary language disintegrated, for the literary language was now generally English. But if the Scotsman's ordinary language was conducted in Scots and his formal utterances were made in English, this meant that he spoke what was becoming more and more a provincial dialect no longer capable of use in complex literary works, while he wrote a somewhat stilted artificial language that he learned at school. Neither Scots nor English was therefore capable of being employed as a medium in which the whole man could express himself in Scotland. Once there ceased to be a living Scots literary language, drawing nourishment from spoken Scots but transcending it in richness of vocabulary, and there was no longer a literary norm against which written Scots could be set, Scots degenerated into a series of local dialects, to be transcribed phonetically by antiquaries or regional humorists as interesting or amusing variations of standard English.

Frustrated Scottish national feeling manifested itself about the time of the Union of Parliaments in a deliberate attempt on the part of certain poets, editors, and publishers to preserve what could be collected of older Scottish poetry and to use Scots (in the form either of regional dialects or of deliberate imitations of the older literary language) in new verse of their own. This work was highly successful on the editorial side, and collections such as Allan Ramsay's *Tea-Table Miscellany* (1724) achieved great popularity. But the success was mostly with folk song and imitation folk song, much less with reprints of the complex and artful poetry of the medieval Scottish poets. As for Allan Ramsay's original work, though he occasionally captured the mood and tone of earlier Scottish poetry and sometimes produced a poem of considerable colloquial vigor and vitality, the greater part of his poetry in Scots shows clearly the dilemma of a Scottish poet working with one eye turned to a genteel London audience and the other to the rustic vulgarities of his own country. Scots verse became a dialect verse used for humorous or sentimental purposes, in a patronizing or an exhibitionist manner. Most serious poets turned to English, and left their country behind, often physically and literally as well as metaphorically. Thus James Thomson, author of *The Seasons,* is not generally thought of as a Scottish poet: he wrote in English for an English audience. And the prose writers all wrote in English. David Hume, Adam Smith, William Robertson, and other Scottish philosophers, historians, and men of letters whose work was known all over Europe, wrote in English, though their speech was often a broad Scots. David Hume was not the only eighteenth-century Scotsman to have his manuscripts carefully corrected by an English friend in order to make sure that all "Scotticisms" would be removed.

One eighteenth-century Scottish poet before Burns made a notable effort to produce a native Scottish poetry that was something more than merely rustic or bacchanalian or humorous, that was both fully Scottish and fully contemporary. This was Robert Fergusson, whose descriptive poems of Edinburgh life have a quality that most of Ramsay's verse lacks. Fergusson wove together the spoken dialects of Edinburgh, where he was born and lived, Aberdeenshire, where his parents came from, and Fife, where he attended St. Andrews University, with elements from Scotland's literary past to produce a richer Scots poetic idiom than had been seen for some time; but he died at the age of twenty-four, leaving only a handful of promising Scots poems. Burns, whose ambitions as a poet in Scots were nourished by his reading of Ramsay and, to a greater extent, of Fergusson (he wrote in one of his letters of "the excellent Ramsay and the still more excellent Fergusson") imitated the latter frequently. Indeed, it was emulation of Fergusson that sent him back to Scots poetry after his first youthful impulse had flagged. As he later put it, "Meeting with Fergusson's Scotch Poems, I strung anew my wildly-sounding rustic lyre with emulating vigour."

Meanwhile Scottish folk music was enjoying a revival. Collections of folk airs appeared in large numbers, sometimes with words, sometimes as dance tunes. It became a fashionable pastime among ladies and gentlemen to write new words to old folk airs—the words were generally English and sentimental, but sometimes they were in a rather self-conscious Scots dialect. Antiquarians such as David Herd collected every fragment of older Scottish song poetry that they could lay hands on. The combination of interest in Scottish music and antiquarian interest in Scottish folk poetry did something to keep Scottish national feeling alive, but it must be remembered that the arbiters of literary taste in Edinburgh in the middle and late eighteenth century—the "literati," as they liked to call themselves—had no use for Scottish verse and believed that Scottish literary culture could vindicate itself only by producing literature in English as good as the English themselves could produce. They looked for "elegance" and "sensibility." They had in large measure adopted the cult of feeling represented by that archsentimental novel, Henry Mackenzie's *The Man of Feeling.* They liked to reflect how "a cultivated taste increases sensibility to all the tender and humane passions." James Macpherson's *Ossian* had prepared them to find the tenderest sensibilities in primitive poets. They were also for the most part genteel, highly respectable, moralistic, optimistic, and inclined to confuse poetry with rhetoric. It is not in the least surprising that they approved Burns's "Cotter's Saturday Night" and "To a Mountain Daisy," but not "Holy Willie's Prayer" or the more abandoned of the songs. What is surprising is that a plowman poet from Ayrshire should have had the independence of mind and the confidence in his own judgment to reject in large measure the advice of the Edinburgh literati and turn to more genuine Scottish traditions for inspiration, thus saving himself from turning into a minor English sentimental poet and achieving single-handed a remarkable Indian summer for Scottish poetry.

III

Burns was born in 1759 in the village of Alloway, Ayrshire, in a clay cottage that his father had built with his own hands. His father had come to Ayrshire from the other side of Scotland, in an endeavor to improve his fortunes, but though he worked immensely hard, first on the farm of Mount Oliphant, which he leased in 1766, and then on that of Lochlie, which he took in 1777, ill luck dogged him continuously, and he died in 1784, worn out and bankrupt. It was watching his father being beaten down by overwork and economic misfortune that helped to make Burns both a rebel against the social order of his day and a bitter satirist of all forms of religious and political thought that condoned or perpetuated inhumanity. Like so many Scottish peasants, the elder Burns was ambitious for his children, and Robert received a certain amount of formal schooling from a teacher hired cooperatively by the farmers of the district, as well as sporadic education from other sources. He learned to read French and acquired a smattering of Latin, and he read most of the important eighteenth-century English writers as well as Shakespeare, John Milton, and John Dryden. Indeed, his formal education was oriented entirely toward England. His knowledge of Scottish literature was, in his childhood, confined to orally transmitted folk songs and folktales together with a modernization of the late fifteenth-century poem *Wallace,* which dealt rather naively with the life of Sir William Wallace, the Scottish hero in the Wars of Independence against Edward I of England. This last work, one of the first he ever read by himself, "poured a Scottish prejudice in my veins which will boil along there till the floodgates of life shut in eternal rest." Burns also studied biblical history, world geography, and English grammar, and he learned some physics, astronomy, and botany from such books as William Derham's *Astro-Theology* and John Ray's *Wisdom of God Manifested in the Works of the Creation,* which presented scientific facts as arguments for the existence of God as benevolent designer. Burns's religion throughout his adult life seems to have been a humanitarian deism.

Proud, restless, and full of a nameless ambition, the young Burns did his share of hard work on the family farm, while bitterly resenting the fact that others whom he met in town and country were born to higher destinies than his. "I formed many connections," he wrote later, looking back on his youth, "with younkers who possessed superior advantages, the youngling actors who were busy with the rehearsal of parts in which they were shortly to appear on that stage where, alas, I was destined to drudge behind the scenes." After his father's death, Burns, the oldest of seven children, was left head of the household and tenant of the farm of Mossgiel, to which the family moved. But he had already started writing poetry, in which the tone of Scottish folk song and that of eighteenth-century sentimental and meditative poetry were strangely mingled. Early in 1783 he began to keep a commonplace book, which began grandiosely, "Observations, Hints, Songs, Scraps of Poetry &c., by Robert Burness [the old spelling of his name, which he later dropped], a man who had little art in making money, a great deal of honesty, and unbounded goodwill to every creature rational or irrational." In April 1783 he entered his first poem (a song, written for a specific folk tune), preceded by the comment, "There is certainly some connection between Love and Music and Poetry . . . I never had the least thought or inclination of turning Poet till I once got heartily in love, and then rhyme and song were, in a manner, the spontaneous language of my heart." The poem is an unpretentious, lilting piece, written in an English tipped with Scots, but it becomes pure neoclassic English in the final stanza. Shortly afterward he entered in the commonplace book sentimental, melodramatic, or melancholy pieces whose thought reflected the family misfortunes of the time and whose vocabulary and manner derived from minor eighteenth-century English poets. He was reading Thomas Gray, William Shenstone, Thomson, Mackenzie's *The Man of Feeling,* Sterne's *Tristram Shandy,* and Macpherson's *Ossian* and cultivating, in a heavily self-conscious way, a gloomy sensibility. But suddenly we come across a lively, swinging piece deriving from the Scottish folk tradition rather than from contemporary English sentimentalists:

My father was a Farmer upon the Carrick border O,
And carefully he bred me in decency and order O. . . .

This was entered in the commonplace book in 1784, with an apologetic note that it was "miserably deficient in versification." Meanwhile his father's death freed him to seek male and female companionship where he would. He took sides against the dominant extreme Calvinist wing of the church in Ayrshire and championed a local gentleman, Gavin Hamilton, who had got into trouble with the Kirk Session (the local ecclesiastical authority) for sabbath breaking and other evidences of contempt for the strict observances demanded by the orthodox. Burns had an affair with a servant girl at the farm, Elizabeth Paton, who bore his first illegitimate child, and on the child's birth, he welcomed her with a lively poem that was part swagger and part the expression of genuine paternal affection and delight:

Thou's welcome, wean[3]! mishanter[4] fa' me,
If aught o'thee, or of thy mammy,
Shall ever daunton[5] me or awe me,
My sweet wee lady,
Or if I blush when thou shalt ca'me
Tit-ta or daddy. . . .

His eye was not on Gray or Shenstone here. The stanza form is one that had had a long history in Scottish—indeed, in European—poetry and had been used by Ramsay and Fergusson, while the language is the spoken language of Ayrshire, enlarged by words from southern English and by others from the older Scots literary tradition. Even more purely in the Scottish literary tradition is "The Death and Dying Words of Poor Mailie," entered in his commonplace book in June 1785. This is a "mock testament" put into the mouth of a dying sheep, done with shrewd ironical humor and considerable technical adroitness. By now Burns had available to him not only the Scottish folk tradition but also some of the traditions of Scottish "art" poetry, both as they came to him through Fergusson and as he found them for himself in collections of older Scottish poetry. Though some significant areas of earlier Scottish poetry had not been made available by eighteenth-century editors, Burns was nevertheless in contact with the main tradition, and his development as a poet clearly shows how the eighteenth-century antiquarian movement fed the creative impulse.

Burns developed rapidly throughout 1784 and 1785 as an "occasional" poet who more and more turned to verse to express his emotions of love, friendship, or amusement, or his

3. Child.
4. Mishap.
5. Discourage.

ironic contemplation of the social scene. But these were not spontaneous effusions by an almost illiterate poet. Burns was a very conscious craftsman; his entries in the commonplace book reveal that, from the beginning of his activity as a poet, he was interested in the technical problems of versification. If he never learned to distinguish emotional control from emotional self-indulgence in eighteenth-century English poetry (his critical sense remained uncertain in this area of literature), he did learn to appreciate economy, cogency, and variety in the work of Alexander Pope and others. Most important of all, he learned from older Scots literature to handle traditional Scottish literary forms and stanza patterns, particularly in descriptive and satirical verse, with assurance and cunning. From the oral folk tradition he learned a great deal about song rhythms and the fitting of words to music. And out of his own Ayrshire speech, his knowledge of older Scots, and his reading in standard English, he fashioned a flexible Scots-English idiom, which, though hardly a literary language in the sense that Henryson's or Dunbar's language was, proved time and time again to be an effective medium for at least one man's kind of Scottish poetry.

Though he wrote poetry for his own amusement and that of his friends, Burns remained restless and dissatisfied. He won the reputation throughout the countryside of being a dangerous rebel against orthodox religion, and when in 1786 he fell in love with Jean Armour, her father refused to allow her to marry Burns, even though a child was on the way and, under Scots law, mutual consent followed by consummation constituted a legal marriage. Jean was persuaded by her father to go back on her promise, and Robert, hurt and enraged, took up with another girl, Mary Campbell, who died shortly afterward, while Jean bore him twins out of wedlock. Meanwhile, the farm was not prospering, and Burns, harassed by insoluble emotional and economic problems, thought of emigrating to Jamaica. But he first wanted to show his country what he could do. In the midst of his troubles with the Armours (and they were serious, for Mr. Armour threatened to sue him to provide for the upkeep of the twins), he went ahead with his plans for publishing a volume of his poems at the nearby town of Kilmarnock. It was entitled *Poems Chiefly in the Scottish Dialect,* and appeared on 31 July 1786. Its success was immediate and overwhelming. Simple country folk and sophisticated Edinburgh critics alike hailed it, and the upshot was that Burns, leaving his native county for the first time two months before his twenty-eighth birthday, set out for Edinburgh on 27 November 1786, to be lionized, patronized, and showered with well-meant but dangerous advice.

IV

The Kilmarnock volume was an extraordinary mixture. It included a handful of first-rate Scots poems—"The Twa Dogs," "Scotch Drink," "The Holy Fair," "Address to the Deil," "The Death and Dying Words of Poor Mailie," "To a Mouse," "To a Louse," and some others, including a number of verse letters addressed to various friends. There were also a few Scots poems in which Burns was unable to sustain his inspiration, or that were spoiled by a confused purpose (such as "The Vision"); and one ("Hallowe'en") that was too self-consciously rustic in its dogged descriptions of country customs and rituals and its almost exhibitionist use of archaic rural terms. There were also six gloomy and histrionic poems in English with such titles as "Despondency, an Ode" and "Man was Made to Mourn, a Dirge." There were four songs: "It Was Upon a Lammas Night" (to the tune of "Corn Rigs Are Bonie"); two insipid love songs in English, to Scottish tunes; and a farewell to his fellow Freemasons of Tarbolton, Ayrshire, to the tune of "Goodnight and Joy Be Wi' You A' " (the traditional Scottish song at parting until Burns's "Auld Lang Syne" replaced it), an unsuccessful combination of familiar Scots and pretentious English. The final pages were padded out with a handful of poor epigrams and epitaphs. There were also what seemed to contemporary reviewers the stars of the volume, "The Cotter's Saturday Night" and "To a Mountain Daisy."

"The Twa Dogs" is a cunningly wrought dialogue between a gentleman's dog and a humbler example of the species. Its immediate inspiration was probably a poem of Fergusson's, but the dialogue is in fact in an old Scottish tradition, which Burns handles with complete assurance. Caesar, the aristocratic dog, begins by pitying the life of a poor dog such as his companion Luath, and Luath replies that poverty has its drawbacks, but there are compensations. Caesar, anxious to maintain his superiority, answers this by pointing out how contemptuously the poor are treated by the rich (a favorite theme of Burns's) and gives a brief but vivid description of the insults to be endured by "poor tenant bodies" at the hands of landlords. Luath replies with a sharply etched picture of the bright side of rustic life, wholly unsentimental and quite free from the synthetic pieties of "The Cotter's Saturday Night." The real turn in the poem comes when Luath, admitting that after all the poor are often ill-treated by the rich, talks about a member of Parliament giving up his time "for Britain's gude." Caesar interrupts him:

Haith,[6] lad, ye little ken about it;
For Britain's gude—guid faith! I doubt it!
Say rather, gaun[7] as Premiers lead him,
And saying *ay* or *no's* they bid him!
At operas and plays parading,
Mortgaging, gambling, masquerading.
Or maybe, in a frolic daft,
To Hague or Calais taks a waft,
To mak a tour, an'tak a whirl,
To learn *bon ton* an' see the worl'.
   There, at Vienna or Versailles,
He rives his father's auld entails;
Or by Madrid he taks the rout,
To thrum guitars an' fecht wi' nowt;[8]
Or down Italian vista startles,
Whore-hunting amang groves o myrtles; . . .

6. Faith.
7. Going.
8. Fight with cattle.

For Britain's gude!—for her destruction!
Wi' dissipation, feud, and faction!

This is adroitly done. Caesar, the defender of the rich, is so anxious to display his knowledge of them to the ignorant Luath that the bitter truth about them comes from his mouth, not from Luath's. It is now Luath's turn to express pained surprise, and he goes on to ask demurely:

But will ye tell me, Master Caesar
Sure great folk's life's a life o' pleasure?

In order to show how foolish Luath is in making this presumption, Caesar is led into a vivid picture of the bored and hypochondriac rich that by insensible degrees turns into a bitter denunciation of their wickedness. This is not mere abuse; it is successfully controlled satire. The tone of contempt for the amusements of the idle rich is brilliantly conveyed in such a phrase as "To thrum guitars an' fecht wi' nowt," where the homely Scots word for cattle reduces at once the ritual splendor of bullfighting to a meaningless brawl with a beast. Further, putting the dialogue into the mouths of dogs is not simply a humorous trick; the dog's-eye view of man is carefully manipulated so as to enhance the satire without in the least idealizing or sentimentalizing the dogs. They go off at the end, "rejoic'd they were na *men* but *dogs.*"

"The Twa Dogs" is not by any means Burns's greatest poem, but it is a good example of his technical competence in a traditional Scottish mode. Burns here knows exactly what he is doing; he is absorbed in his job as he writes, and does not look up at intervals to see whether Henry Mackenzie or some other member of the Edinburgh literati approves of his sentiments. In the "Epistle to Davie," on the other hand, which opens magnificently with a vivid description of the January scene in a complex traditional Scottish stanza, the poet suddenly remembers the genteel audience he is hoping for, and we get this:

All hail, ye tender feelings dear!
The smile of love, the friendly tear,

The sympathetic glow!
Long since, this world's thorny ways
Had number'd out my weary days,
Had it not been for you!
Fate still has blest me with a friend,
In every care and ill;
And oft a more endearing band,
A tie more tender still.
It lightens, it brightens
The tenebrific scene,
To meet with, and greet with
My Davie or my Jean.

Burns found the word "tenebrific" in Edward Young's *Night Thoughts* and adopted it in this exhibitionist piece of rhetorical sentimentality. It is as well to bear in mind the temptation Burns was constantly under to cater to the educated taste of his day.

"The Holy Fair" is one of the finest poems in the collection. Written in the old Scottish tradition of poems describing popular festivities and adopting an old Scottish stanza form that came down to Burns through Fergusson (whose "Leith Races" is his model here), "The Holy Fair" describes with ironic humor the goings-on at one of the great outdoor "tent preachings" that were held annually in connection with the communion service. The poet describes himself as sauntering forth on a summer Sunday morning and meeting three young women, one of them Fun and the other two Superstition and Hypocrisy. Fun explains that she is off to Mauchline Holy Fair and asks the poet to accompany her. The tone is thus humorous rather than bitter, and Burns's Brueghelesque account of the noisy, bustling, many-colored scene, with rival preachers thundering to indifferent or drunken audiences, and drinking, roistering, lovemaking, and other profane activities going on all around, emphasizes the human weaknesses, follies, passions, and appetites that indulge themselves at the Holy Fair. There is no moral indignation in the poem, only an ironical amusement at the thought that human nature will have its way even in the midst of Calvinist thunderings on the one hand and less orthodox "moderate" pleading for good works on the other. The concluding stanza, with its deliberate confusion of theological, biblical, and amorous imagery, sums up the meaning of the poem:

How mony hearts this day converts
O' Sinners and o' lasses!
Their hearts o' stane, gin night[9], are gane[10]
As saft ony flesh is.
There's some are fou[11] o' love divine,
There's some are fou o' brandy;
An' mony jobs that day begin,
May end in houghmagandie[12]
Some ither day.

The notion of converted hearts is applied equally to sinners and to lasses, and the biblical image of replacing a heart of stone by one of flesh (signifying turning to God in repentance) is employed with mischievous ambiguity. Again, the conjunction of "fou o' love divine" and "fou o' brandy" further emphasizes the theme, while the popular Scots word describing the probable end of it all is a calculated shock to those who, following the religious images in the stanza, expect the word to be either "Heaven" or (more likely) "Hell." This is not satire on religion, but observation, both comic and ironic, of the way in which the claims of the flesh assert themselves in the midst of all the paraphernalia of religious celebration.

The "Address to the Deil," drawing on the devil of folklore rather than of Calvinist theology, uses a tone of amused familiarity in order to diminish the devil's stature from that of the terrifying father of evil to that of a mischievous practical joker. The poem is a fine example of Burns's technique of implicitly criticizing theological dogmas by translating them into the daily realities of ordinary experience. The ending is masterly:

An' now, auld Cloots, I ken ye're thinkin',
A certain Bardie's rantin,[13] drinkin',

9. By nightfall.
10. Gone.
11. Full.
12. Fornication.
13. Roistering.

Some luckless hour will send him linkin'[14]
　　　　To your black pit;
But faith! he'll turn a corner jinkin',[15]
　　　　An' cheat you yet.
But fare you weel, auld Nickie-ben!
O wad ye tak a thought an' men'!
Ye aiblins[16] might—I dinna ken—
　　　　Still hae a stake:
I'm wae[17] to think upo' yon den,
　　　　Ev'n for your sake!

The familiar titles of "auld Cloots" and "auld Nickie-ben" successfully reduce the devil's stature; the poet's genially penitent reference to himself includes the conventional religious reproof in a context of casual cheerfulness; and the concluding suggestion, that perhaps the devil himself might repent (again made with deliberate casualness), implicitly includes the devil among weak and sinful humanity, the final step in his dethronement and dismissal.

Some notion of the different degrees of skill and integrity displayed by Burns in the Kilmarnock volume can be obtained by setting side by side "To a Louse," "To a Mouse," and "To a Mountain Daisy." The first is easily the best, a bright, lively, humorous poem moving adroitly toward a conclusion expressed with the gnomic pithiness of a country proverb. It begins with a sudden projection into the heart of the situation, as Burns addresses the louse he sees crawling on a lady's bonnet in church:

Ha! wh'are ye gaun, ye crowlin'[18] ferlie[19]!

The lady, unconscious of the "ugly, creepin', blastit wonner" crawling on the back of her bonnet, is full of airs and graces, and the poet chides the louse for daring to set foot on her:

How dare ye set your fit upon her,
　　Sae fine a lady?

14. Hurrying.
15. Dodging.
16. Perhaps.
17. Sad.
18. Crawling.
19. Wonder.

The contrast between the vulgarity of the insect and the social pretentiousness of the lady is developed with humorous irony until suddenly Burns drops his pose of outraged observer and addresses the lady herself:

O Jenny, dinna toss your head,
An' set your beauties a' abread[20]!
Ye little ken what cursed speed
　　　　The blastie's makin'!

At once, in calling her by the simple country name Jenny, the poet has changed her from a proud beauty to an ordinary girl whom he is warning, in friendly fashion, about an accident that might happen to anybody. Her airs and graces are stripped away, but not in the least savagely; the note of amusement is still there, but it is kindly now. The lady is restored to common humanity from whom she was distinguished earlier in the poem. And the conclusion has a simple proverbial note:

O wad some Pow'r the giftie gie us
To see oursels as others see us!
It wad frae mony a blunder free us,
　　　　And foolish notion:
What airs in dress an' gait wad lea'e us,
　　　　And ev'n devotion!

"To a Mouse," one of Burns's most charming and best-known poems, nevertheless lacks the tautness and the skillful manipulation of irony and humor that we get in "To a Louse." The poet expresses his regret to the "wee, sleekit, cow'rin', tim'rous beastie," on turning her up in her nest with the plow, and goes on to reflect that, just as the mouse's provision for winter has been brought to nothing by this accident, so

The best laid schemes o' mice an' men
　　　　Gang aft a-gley.[21]

and he himself is in an even worse situation. The fellow feeling for the little creature is

20. Abroad.
21. Go often awry.

spontaneous and engaging and conveyed in a cleverly controlled verse, and the introduction of the proverbial note, as in "To a Louse," is most effective, but the emergence of self-pity at the end as the real theme seems somewhat forced, and there is a touch of attitudinizing about the poem. This attitudinizing runs right through "To a Mountain Daisy," a forced and sentimental poem, in which he laments the fate of the crushed flower (also turned down with the plow) and compares it to that of a betrayed maiden. Burns was here posturing as a man of feeling. It is significant that he wrote to a friend, enclosing the poem, as follows: "I am a good deal pleased with some sentiments myself, as they are just the native querulous feelings of a heart which, as the elegantly melting Gray says, 'Melancholy has marked for her own.' " A similar fault mars "The Cotter's Saturday Night," a grave descriptive poem in Spenserian stanzas evoking with pious approval an evening in the life of a Scottish peasant family. The poem is modeled on Fergusson's "The Farmer's Ingle,"[22] but Burns is more pretentious than Fergusson and displays too clearly his object of showing off the Scottish peasantry for the approval and edification of men of feeling in Edinburgh. The poem contains some admirable descriptive passages and shows considerable technical accomplishment in the handling of the stanza, but the introduction of hollow sentimentalities and rhetorical exclamations at critical moments spoils the work as a whole.

V

Burns selected the Kilmarnock poems with care—he was anxious to impress a genteel Edinburgh audience. In his preface he played up to contemporary sentimental views about the natural man and the noble peasant, exaggerated his lack of education, pretended to a lack of technical resources, which was ridiculous in the light of the careful craftsmanship his poetry displays, and in general acted a part. The trouble is, he was only half acting. He was uncertain enough about the genteel tradition to accept much of it at its face value, and though, to his ultimate glory, he kept returning to what his own instincts told him was the true path for him to follow, far too many of his poems are marred by a naive and sentimental moralizing.

The real Burns is revealed in his satiric and humorous poems and in the abandonment to the moment of experience that we find celebrated in many of his best songs. Burns the songwriter was hardly represented in the Kilmarnock edition. Most of his songs were still unwritten, but in any case the Edinburgh literati did not consider songs as one of the higher kinds of poetry. Burns the satirist was revealed in some degree, but the greatest of his satiric poems he deliberately omitted from the Kilmarnock volume in order not to shock his genteel audience. He omitted "The Ordination," a brilliant satire on Ayrshire church politics composed in the same stanza as "The Holy Fair" and done with greater verve and dexterity. He omitted the "Address to the Unco Guid," a somewhat pedestrian attack on Puritan hypocrisy that might have been included without offense. He omitted the amusing and skillful "Death and Doctor Hornbook" and the rollicking satire "The Twa Herds," an early poem that Burns himself described as a "burlesque lamentation on a quarrel between two reverend Calvinists." And he omitted "Holy Willie's Prayer," the greatest of all his satiric poems and one of the great verse satires of all time. Burns is here concerned to attack the Calvinist view of predestination and of salvation by predestined grace regardless of "good works" (for, according to this view, no works of fallen man can possibly be good in God's sight), and he makes the attack by putting a prayer in the mouth of a strict Calvinist who is convinced that he is predestined to salvation by God's grace. A solemn, liturgical note is maintained throughout the poem, and the creed damns itself in the process of its expression. It opens with a

22. Fireside.

calmly expressive statement of the view that man's salvation or damnation is decreed by God without any reference to man's behavior; it is the very quietness and assurance of the statement that conceals at first its preposterousness and then suddenly reveals it when we least expect it:

O thou wha in the Heavens does dwell,
Wha, as it pleases best Thysel',
Sends ane to heaven and ten to hell,
A' for thy glory,
And no for ony guid or ill
They've done afore Thee!

I bless and praise Thy matchless might,
Whan thousands Thou has left in night,
That I am here before Thy sight,
For gifts an' grace
A burnin' an' a shinin' light,
To a' this place.

As the poem proceeds in this stately liturgical manner, the speaker's appalling complacency and egotism, disguised, even to the speaker himself, as humility, are cumulatively revealed. Holy Willie is not a conscious hypocrite. When be attributes his lust to God's protective desire to remind him that, however gifted and elect, he is still a man, he is revealing the moral horrors that, for Burns, lay beneath any claim by any individual that he had inner assurance of predestined salvation. When he asks God's vengeance on his personal enemies, he really believes that his will and God's cause are one. And when he asks for economic prosperity in this world in addition to his assured reward in the next, it is in order to demonstrate to the heathen that God protects and favors those whom he has elected. As the poem proceeds it becomes increasingly impossible to disentangle godliness from the most abandoned self-indulgence, and in the confusion the creed of election and predestination becomes monstrous. The poem ends in the same stately organ tones with which it began:

But, Lord, remember me and mine
Wi' mercies temp'ral and divine,
That I for gear[23] and grace may shine
Excell'd by nane,
And a' the glory shall be thine,
Amen, Amen!

Burns also omitted from the Kilmarnock volume his remarkable anarchist cantata, "The Jolly Beggars," in which he assembled a group of social outcasts and put into their mouths roaring songs of social defiance and swaggering independence. There was always a streak of pure anarchism in Burns, and here he associates it with conviviality in a characteristic way. All institutions, all conventions, anything that limits the freely chosen association of friends and lovers with one another, are hence abandoned in roaring professions of antisocial independence. It is not a mature or a complex attitude, but it does touch a fundamental human drive, and "The Jolly Beggars" gives brilliant expression to man as outcast and vagabond. Complete independence of social order implies poverty, squalor, and vice, but Burns does not shrink from that. He is not romanticizing independence from society, but simply bodying it forth, motivated less by doctrinaire anarchism than by sheer high spirits.

VI

Edinburgh unsettled Burns, and after a number of amorous and other adventures there and several trips to other parts of Scotland, he settled at a farm in Ellisland, Dumfriesshire, leased to him by an admirer who was nevertheless a shrewd landlord. At Edinburgh he had arranged for a new and enlarged edition of his poems, but little of significance was added to the Kilmarnock selection. Substantially, it was by the Kilmarnock poems that Burns was known in his lifetime. He found farming at Ellisland difficult, though he was helped by Jean Armour, with whom he had been reconciled and whom he had finally married; she remained loyal to him throughout. At Edin-

23. Wealth.

burgh he had met James Johnson, a keen collector of Scottish songs who was bringing out a series of volumes of songs with music and enlisted Burns's help in finding, editing, improving, and rewriting items for his collection. Burns was enthusiastic about the project and soon became virtual editor of Johnson's *Scots Musical Museum.* Later he became involved with a similar project for George Thomson, but Thomson was a more consciously genteel person than Johnson, and Burns had to fight with him continuously to prevent him from "refining" words and music and so ruining their character. He did not always succeed. The latter part of Burns's life was spent largely in assiduous collecting and writing of songs, to provide words for traditional Scottish airs and to keep Johnson and Thomson going. He regarded this work as service to Scotland and quixotically refused any payment. The only poem he wrote after his Edinburgh visit that showed a yet unsuspected side of his poetic genius was "Tam o' Shanter," a magnificently spirited narrative poem based on a folk legend associated with Alloway Kirk. The poem is in octosyllabic couplets, and in variations of speed and tone, in unfolding the details of the story and in creating the proper atmosphere for each part, Burns showed himself a master of a form that, unfortunately, he never attempted again.

Meanwhile, Burns corresponded with and visited on terms of equality a great variety of literary and other people who were considerably "above" him socially. He was an admirable letter writer and a brilliant talker, and he could hold his own in any company. At the same time, he was still a struggling tenant farmer, and the attempt to keep himself going in two different social and intellectual capacities was wearing him down. After trying for a long time, he finally obtained a post in the excise service in 1789, and in 1791 he moved to Dumfries, where he lived until July 1796, when he died of rheumatic heart disease, contracted in his youth as a result of too much physical exertion on an inadequate diet. (The myth that Burns died of drink has long since been exploded. Burns liked his glass, but he was not a heavy drinker for the time, and drink had nothing to do with his death.) His life at Dumfries was active until the end. He wrote numerous "occasional" poems on contemporary political and other events and did an immense amount of work for the two song collections, in addition to carrying out conscientiously his duties as exciseman. He remained defensive and sensitive about his social position, for the slightest suggestion of condescension on the part of a social "superior" infuriated him. He never found a way of life that really solved his social and intellectual problems.

Burns was the greatest songwriter Britain has produced. In refurbishing old songs, making new ones out of fragmentary remains, using an old chorus as a foundation for a new song, and sometimes simply touching up a set of characterless old words, as well as providing entirely new words to traditional airs and dance tunes, he was of course going far beyond the editorial and improving tasks he undertook for Johnson and Thomson. If he had not been an original poet himself and uncannily in tune with the folk tradition, he would have been execrated by later scholars for spoiling original material with false improvements. His work as a songwriter was a unique blend of the antiquarian and the creative. He took the whole body of Scottish folk song and, in a passion of enthusiasm for his native culture, brought it together, preserved it, reshaped it, gave it new life and spirit, speaking with the great anonymous voice of the Scottish people and uttering that voice with an assurance, a technical skill, and a poetic splendor that cannot be matched in the literature of any other country. And he not only rescued and preserved the words; he also took the mass of song tunes and dance tunes and saw to it that they each had words properly fitted, if necessary altering the pace and movement of a melody in order to bring out a quality that had been lost in speeding it up for dance purposes. He could sing the songs of either sex. No other man has ever captured the feminine delight in prospective motherhood combined with the feminine joy in sexual surrender as

Burns did in the song he wrote for Jean when she was about to bear his child:

O wha my babie-clouts[24] will buy?
O wha will tent[25] me when I cry?
Wha will kiss me whare I lie?
The rantin' dog the daddie o't. . . .

Nor has any other poet so powerfully and simply expressed the combination of tenderness and swagger, which is a purely male attitude toward love, as Burns did in "A Red, Red Rose." Nor has the note of male protectiveness sounded so poignantly as in the poem that Burns wrote for Jessie Leward, the girl who helped to nurse him in his final illness. With a supreme effort of the imagination, Burns, as he lay dying, reversed their roles and wrote, to one of Jessie's favorite old Scottish airs,

O, wert thou in the cauld blast,
On yonder lea, on yonder lea,
My plaidie to the angry airt,[26]
I'd shelter thee, I'd shelter thee. . . .

Nor has the note of remembered friendship ever been so movingly expressed as in "Auld Lang Syne," Burns's rewriting of an older song, which he never claimed as his own. It must always be remembered that these are songs and should never be ludged without their tunes, for Burns thought of words and music as part of a single whole.

VII

Burn's influence on Scottish poetry has not been happy, for he was canonized partly for the wrong reasons and had his weaknesses imitated and his great strength ignored. That was not his fault but his posthumous misfortune. Thus modern Scottish poets have preferred to go back to Dunbar rather than to Burns, for they object not to Burns but to what has become of the Burns tradition. A coyly self-conscious emphasis on sensibility as such, a cloying coziness of tone, a false sugaring over of the realities of experience with stock sentimental situations, all done in a vernacular whose main feature is the adding of diminutive endings in "-ie" to as many words as possible—this is what later generations too often made of Burns. His faults rather than his virtues were praised and imitated. This was all the easier because Burns was a rustic poet who wrote when Scotland was on the verge of the Industrial Revolution, after which the temptation to sentimentalize over an idealized country life was irresistible. Burns did not—and could not have been expected to—help Scottish literature to come to terms with the Industrial Revolution.

But the real Burns is coming back. Modern readers recognize more and more that he is neither a minor figure in the English "romantic movement" nor a heaven-taught plowman artlessly warbling under the stress of his simple emotions, nor a naive idealizer of rustic life, nor a harmless rhetorical exhibitionist whose works are a storehouse of pious platitudes to be quoted from platform and pulpit. The real Burns—Burns using his full strength and genius as a poet—was the heir of Henryson in his humorous tenderness and of Dunbar in his technical brilliance, the heir of the sixteenth-century Scottish poet Alexander Montgomerie in his feeling for the shape and movement of a stanza, of Ramsay in his relish of humanity caught in the act, of Fergusson in his ability to render the color and absurdity of human behavior. And he was also the heir of the people, of the lost authors of Scotland's folk songs, whose fragments he gathered in, like a god gathering the remnants of a shattered world to recreate them and send them abroad again with new life and meaning. Songwriter, satirist, narrative poet, celebrator of friendship, of love, and of hate, Burns was also a brilliant talker, an intelligent observer, and a fascinating and sometimes dangerous personality. It was his fate to be born into a Scotland suffering from national schizophre-

24. Clothes.
25. Look after.
26. Direction.

nia, torn between a superficial genteel tradition and a deeper but frustrated national culture. It was not his fault that he was caught in the midst of these crosscurrents and sometimes carried off his true course. The remarkable fact is that he never left his true course for long, in spite of the many pressures on him, and that he spoke so often with an authentic voice.

Selected Bibliography

BIBLIOGRAPHY

Ewing, J. C., *Bibliography,* (London, 1909) privately printed; *Cambridge Bibliography of English Literature,* vol. II, (London, 1940) the most complete short-title list of books, etc., by and about Burns; Egerer, J. W., *A Bibliography,* (Edinburgh, 1964) the most complete listing of Burns's poetical and prose works between 1786 and 1802 and of all "formal" eds. after 1802, includes a list of translations and a section of "original material first published in periodicals."

COLLECTED AND SELECTED WORKS

The following list contains only the most important of the very large number of eds. of Burns's works published from 1800 onward. *Poems Chiefly in the Scottish Dialect,* (Kilmarnock, 1786; Edinburgh, 1787), 2 vols. (1793), the latter being the last ed. with which Burns himself was directly concerned; *The Works,* J. Currie, ed., 4 vols., (London, 1800) with an account of his life in which the editor overemphasizes Burns's proneness to drink and paints a melodramatic picture of his last years; 8th ed. contains some new material by Gilbert Burns, the poet's brother; an explanation and defense of Currie's attitude is presented in R. D. Thornton, *James Currie "The Entire Stranger" and Robert Burns,* (Edinburgh, 1963); *Poems,* J. Walker, ed., 2 vols., (Edinburgh, 1811) with an account of Burns's life that is largely dependent on Currie's biography, also includes "The Jolly Beggars," "Holy Willie's Prayer," and other poems omitted in earlier eds.; *The Life and Works,* A. Peterkin, ed., 4 vols., (Edinburgh, 1815) a revision of Currie's ed., with an attempt to free Burns from the misrepresentations of earlier biographers, includes letters; *The Works [and] Life,* A. Cunningham, ed., 8 vols., (London, 1834) the editor was a notorious inventor of biographical "facts" and the life is quite unreliable, but his account of Burns had great influence, includes letters; *The Works,* J. Hogg and W. Motherwell, eds., 5 vols., (Glasgow, 1834–1836) vol. V contains Hogg's life of Burns, much of which is the sheerest invention; *The Life and Works,* R. Chambers, ed., 4 vols., (Edinburgh, 1856–1857), rev. ed. Wallace, W., (1896), the library ed., based on careful research, this remained the standard ed. and life until its revision; poems and letters in chronological order, interspersed with biographical material, the monumental Chambers-Wallace ed. of 1896 is still the most comprehensive of all works on Burns; *The Works,* W. S. Douglas, ed., 6 vols., (Edinburgh, 1877–1879) a variorum ed. of the poems and letters with important notes and other apparatus; *Poems and Songs,* A. Lang and W. A. Craigie, eds., (London, 1896) with intro., notes, and glossary, a useful ed. with the poems arranged in chronological order and biographical and explanatory notes at the foot of the page; *The Poetry,* W. E. Henley and T. F. Henderson, eds., 4 vols., (Edinburgh, 1896–1897) the centenary ed., a carefully edited text of the poems with important notes giving for the first time evidence of how Burns rewrote old songs, until 1968 the standard ed. of the poems; the biography, though full of brilliant insights, perpetuates the old errors about Burns's debauchery and degeneration (now out of print); *The Poetical Works,* J. L. Robertson, ed., (London, 1904) in the Oxford Standard Authors series; *Poems of Robert Burns,* L. Brander, ed. and sel., (London, 1950) in the World's Classics series, this and the World's Classics selection of Burns's letters described below together provide an admirable intro. to Burns as man and poet; *Poems and Songs,* J. Barke, ed. (London, 1955) contains a number of uncollected poems and a few previously unpublished ones; *Selected Poems of Robert Burns,* G. S. Fraser, ed., (London, 1960); *The Poems and Songs,* J. Kinsley, ed., 3 vols., Oxford (1968) the authoritative modern ed., vols. I and II contain the text together with all the identifiable airs for the songs in their eighteenth-century form, vol. III contains the commentary.

SONGS

The bulk of Burns's songs first appeared, often anonymously, in the five vols. of James Johnson's *Scots Musical Museum,* (Edinburgh, 1787–1797) and in the four vols. of George Thomson's *Select Collection of Original Scottish Airs,* (Edinburgh, [1793]–1805); *The Songs,* (Glasgow, 1896) with symphonies and accompaniments by J. K. Lees and intro. and historical notes by H. C. Shelley, the historical account of Scottish music is quite out of date; *The Songs,* J. C. Dick, ed., (London, 1903) repr. (Hatboro, Pa., 1962) with bibliography, an important scholarly ed. of the songs, with the airs to which they were originally set, with historical and critical notes on both the words and the music, repr. together with the same editor's *Notes on Scottish Song,* (London, 1908) and D. Cook, *Annotations of Scottish Songs by Burns,* (London, 1922).

LETTERS

The Letters, J. De L. Ferguson, ed., 2 vols., (Oxford, 1931) edited on modern scholarly principles from the original MSS, the standard ed.; *Selected Letters,* J. De L. Ferguson, ed., (London, 1953) in the World's Classics series, text based on Ferguson's complete ed. but a few letters have original texts from MSS that had not been recovered at the time of the complete ed.

BIOGRAPHICAL AND CRITICAL STUDIES

There is much biography and criticism in the collected eds. listed above. There is also a mass of miscellaneous material in the *Burns Chronicle,* published annually since 1892. The biographies listed below are the most important that have appeared independently of eds. of the works. Cromek, R. H., *Reliques of Robert Burns,* (London, 1808) not strictly a biography but contains some important biographical material; Lockhart, J. G., *Life of Robert Burns,* (London, 1828) long popular but very inaccurate; Thomas Carlyle's famous review that first appeared in *Edinburgh Review* 48 (December 1828) is an important study of the man and his work, though it accepts Lockhart's misinformation about the man; Angellier, A., *Robert Burns: La Vie, les oeuvres,* 2 vols. (Paris,, 1893) an important work of original scholarship and criticism, with a comprehensive bibliography; Hecht, H., *Robert Burns: Leben und Wirken des Schottischen Volksdichters,* (Heidelberg, 1919), trans. (Edinburgh, 1936), 2nd ed. (1950) translated by J. Lymburn; Carswell, C., *The Life of Robert Burns,* (London, 1930) a lively and sympathetic study by a writer who knew all the relevant facts but interpreted them sometimes rather arbitrarily; Snyder, F. B., *The Life of Robert Burns,* (New York, 1932) a scholarly study scrupulously documented; Ferguson, J. De L., *Pride and Passion: Robert Burns,* (London, 1939) an excellent study of Burns the man by a sound scholar and perceptive critic; Daiches, D., *Robert Burns,* (New York, 1950; London, 1952) rev. ed. (1966), primarily a detailed critical study of the poems but includes an intro. chapter on the Scottish literary tradition and considerable biographical material; Lindsay, M., *Robert Burns: The Man, His Work, the Legend,* (London, 1954); Lindsay, M., *The Burns Encyclopedia,* (London, 1959) contains articles about people whom Burns met or referred to in his letters and his poems and descriptions of many of the places he visited; *Burns as Others Saw Him,* W. L. Renwick, ed., (Edinburgh, 1959) compiled for the Saltire Society, a useful collection of accounts of Burns by twelve people who met him; Crawford, T., *Burns: A Study of the Poems and Songs,* (Edinburgh, 1960) a critical and scholarly study; Dent, A. H., *Burns in His Time,* (London, 1966); Butterworth, L. M. A., *Robert Burns and the Eighteenth Century Revival in Scottish Vernacular Poetry,* (Aberdeen, 1969); *Robert Burns: The Critical Heritage,* D. Low, ed., (London, 1974).

George Gordon, Lord Byron
(1788–1824)

MALCOLM KELSALL

INTRODUCTION

George gordon, Lord Byron, was born on 22 January 1788, and died of fever on 19 April 1824, at Missolonghi, in Greece, where he had gone to fight for the patriot cause against Turkish imperialism. His life has exercised a magnetic attraction for generations of biographers. The personality is inextricably bound up with the poetry, and the confusion between the two was at times deliberately exploited by Byron, who posed as the real-life hero of his own romances. The sardonic misanthrope with a sublime imagination; or the guilty soul with a wellspring of scarcely concealed feeling: such characterizations in particular spoke to the nineteenth century of the essence of Byronism. The political and social rebel, the aristocratic outsider, the offspring of Satanism: these provide another nexus of Byronic ideas. More recently taste has responded rather to the comic than to the tragic aspects of the poet and his works. The wit, the good companion, the amiable, ill-used gentleman, "more sinned against than sinning," has emerged as a truer characterization both of the real man and of his personality as developed in his masterpiece *Don Juan* (1819–1824).

It is not a pertinent question to literary study to consider how far the poetry may be used as a key to the psychology of the man. But some knowledge of the man and the myth is required to understand the poetry because Byron utilized his experiences and reputation as the raw material for his creativity. He described his work at one time as the lava of the imagination, which implies that it was the uncontrolled outpouring of his mind. There are elements of symbolic suggestion and dark introspection in some of the poems that hint at inexplicable and uncoordinated self-revelation. But such elements are also common technical devices in much romantic art. They can be discussed in literary terms just as readily as narrative structure or verse form. Common sense indicates that no spontaneous eruption of the imagination ever found immediate utterance in verse. The following sketch of Byron's life, therefore, is an account of source material that the artist used.

Byron was not born the heir to a great title or a rich estate. The early years suggest more the origins of some picaro, the rogue hero of a novel by Henry Fielding, Tobias Smollett, or William Thackeray, rather than the English milord of European fame he was to become. His father, Captain John Byron, was a sexual adventurer, who, having run out of wives, money, and health, died in France in 1791 at the age of thirty-six. The infant Byron—lame from birth—was brought up in provincial obscurity in Aberdeen by a mother whom he found vulgar, and at the hands of servants and tutors who seem to have inducted him at early years to the gloom of Calvinistic Christianity and the dubious pleasures of premature sexuality.

At the age of ten he succeeded to the title of sixth Baron Byron of Rochdale and to an encumbered estate. Although he was to embark on the *cursus honorum* (career ladder) of the great—Harrow School; Trinity College, Cambridge; the House of Lords—there is at no time about him that complacent security of expectation not to be disappointed that characterizes many of the British ruling class. He was a parvenu, an upstart, "born for opposition." His first literary success was *English Bards and Scotch Reviewers* (1809), which is in the satiric tradition of Pope and the Latin poet Juvenal, poets who attacked society from without. The ultimate cantos of the uncompleted *Don Juan* castigate the British "establishment" from a personal position of exile, and in narrative terms, through the introduction of a hero who belongs to no social order: a Byronic alter ego, the wandering figure of "Donny Jonny."

Byron's grand tour of 1809–1811 took him through Portugal, Spain, Greece, and Turkey. It was a usual part of a gentleman's education, but it may also be seen as an act of symbolic liberation and exile rather than one fitting him for a patrician destiny in the classic way by the study of men, manners, and government. His meeting with the warlord Ali Pasha may have provided him with the inspiration for the heroes of his romances; the traditions and culture of the Mediterranean peoples fertilized his imagination for the rest of his life; his admiration for the ideal liberties of Greece found culminative expression in his death. His literary reputation was established by the works deriving from this tour: *Childe Harold's Pilgrimage* (cantos I and II, 1812) and the Turkish tales: *The Giaour* (1813); *The Bride of Abydos* (1813); *The Corsair* (1814); *Lara* (1814); and *The Siege of Corinth* (1816).

On his return to England, he found himself instantly famous. But fame as a writer was not the pathway to success associated with a lord. A great man of state might be an amateur of letters or a connoisseur of the arts, but he would not be a professional literary man like Pope, the son of a linen draper, or Johnson, a bookseller's son. For a time Byron affected to be in the Restoration tradition of "the mob of gentlemen who write with ease"; he refused, initially, payment for his work, and looked, in vain, for a role in politics or in military adventure, which would be a more appropriate field of endeavor for a great man. He became acquainted with the leaders of the Whigs and spoke three times in the House of Lords in the service of that party, attacking the repressive measures of the Tories against industrial unrest and speaking in favor of Catholic emancipation and some degree of parliamentary reform. His later association with movements for national self-determination in Europe—the Carbonari in Italy and the insurrectionists in Greece—represents a practical extension of Whig politics into military action.

One result of this patrician tradition was to lead Byron sometimes to write carelessly and to devalue the craft of the "scribbler." He has none of the sustained sense of a dedicated spirit called to a high, prophetic mission we find in his contemporary Wordsworth or his friend Shelley. Yet his very hastiness and prolixity seem to have prepared the way for the emergence of his mature style from *Beppo* (1818) onward. The sequence of great comic poems, *The Vision of Judgment* (1822) and the sixteen cantos of *Don Juan,* remind one of *The Canterbury Tales.* The verse bears the impress of a speaking voice, a brilliant conversationalist and anecdotal narrator, a strong and experienced personality.

The reasons for Byron's permanent departure from England in 1816 are too complex psychologically to be guessed at. Simple practical reasons were debts and sexual scandal. England was too expensive for an impoverished lord, though later he set himself up financially by cheap living in Italy, parsimony, and payment, now accepted, for his writing. The sexual scandals have provided endless speculative fascination. On 2 January he had married Anne Isabella Milbanke, a prude, but loved his half-sister Augusta Leigh. He may have had sexual intercourse with her. Buggery may have added variety to the marriage bed. The salacious gossip of his ex-mistress, Lady Caroline Lamb, who may not have been sane, poured oil on the flames. There are those who have read Byron's metaphysical tragedy *Manfred* (1817) as a confession to all Europe of incestuous passion.

He traveled through Germany and Switzerland to Italy, completing a third canto of *Childe Harold* (1816) and a fourth (1818). He had settled for a while at Lake Geneva with Shelley and Shelley's wife Mary(the daughter of William Godwin, the political philosopher), and a certain Claire Clairmont, Godwin's stepdaughter, who bore Byron a child, Allegra. Through Shelley he was exposed both to the metaphysical ideas of romanticism and a more radical political philosophy than would have been practical for the Whig party in London. Later, in Pisa, the conjunction of Leigh Hunt with Byron's entourage was to lead to an abortive venture into political journalism, the *Liberal* (1822–1823); but the death by drowning of Shelley, in 1822, removed an important catalyst. Byron, in any case, was shortly to turn his mind to Greece.

Byron's years in Italy are dull biographically. There was a period of sexual debauchery in Venice and a long period as *cavalier servente* (publicly accepted lover) to another man's wife, the prettily pedestrian Teresa Guiccioli. The Austrian police kept him under surveillance, but the nationalist secret society, the Carbonari, had neither the means nor the will to fight a war of liberation. Yet, in the period from 1818 onward, Byron produced what are now regarded as his comic masterworks: *Beppo, The Vision of Judgment,* and *Don Juan.* Enforced idleness, maturing years, a more assured social role in a tolerant society, a stable and undemanding sexual liaison with an agreeable woman, even "emotion recollected in tranquillity": these factors may have contributed to the development of his technique. In the later poems he frequently plays with the roles adopted in his earlier verses and his reputation or notoriety. Like the novels of Marcel Proust, these works go searching back into lost time, and in *Don Juan* he takes as one of his major motifs the waste and flight of years.

The embarkation for Greece in 1823, like the self-imposed exile of 1816, may be seen as a symbolic act. Eighteen-sixteen is the rejection of the insularity of English society; 1823 is the finding, at last, of a European role: as philhellene and champion of liberty. It is also recognized in the poetry that death would be welcome (though not by his shrewd and practical letters). To die for Greece would be to confirm a role that life denied. But the reality of the situation lacked all romance. The "patriots," Alexander Mavrokordatos, Odysseus Androutsos, and the rest, were divided against themselves. The Greek committee in London, on which Byron's friend John Cam Hobhouse served, at first dispatched a printing press to aid a cause that needed munitions. Byron himself never saw battle. He caught a fever, and died under the hands of his doctors in wretched circumstances. As a cynic he would have appreciated the irony of his fate. It is typical of the many situations in *Don Juan* that devalue human endeavor and pride. Yet the romantic side of his character longed for fame, and by dying he secured idealization as a hero and martyr. His reputation as a great man has been confirmed by posterity. Nothing is more typical of the man and artist than that the same act may be seen in terms of the grotesque and of the highest valor, an example of the vanity of human wishes, and of the power of the human imagination to strive, to seek, to find, and not to yield.

THE TURKISH TALES

Byron's Turkish tales enjoyed a popular success. The versification is facile; the settings exotic; the staple fare the ever popular ingredients of sex and violence; the protagonists a stagy assortment of Byronic heroes, Gothic-satanical, sentimental-piratical. *Parisina* (1816), *Mazeppa* (1819), and *The Island* (1823) are later exercises more or less in the same mode but with different settings.

Beneath the racy sentimental melodrama there are suggestions of mythic ideas struggling for some form of representation. The poems have been seen as reiterative treatments of the theme of "the misery and lostness of man, the eternal death of love, and the repetitive ruin of paradise" (R. F. Gleckner, *Byron and the Ruins of Paradise*). If this is so, then the subject finds a more appropriate treatment in the metaphysical and symbolic dramas *Manfred* (1817) and *Cain* (1821). The romances carry strong political overtones also, not only to the oppression of Greece but also to matters nearer home. The dedication of *The Corsair* expresses strong sentiments about the "wrongs" of Ireland, and it is easy to read into *Lara* echoes of the French Revolution. The impact of these slight poems upon European romanticism enhances the suggestion that important themes blend with naive matter. The imaginative ideas were reworked by Hector Berlioz and Eugène Delacroix. The Byronic hero was naturalized on the Yorkshire moors in the figure of Emily Brontë's Heathcliff. Byron himself plundered these early poems. *Don Juan* would not have its present form without the heroes of the Turkish romances to change and burlesque.

Sir Walter Scott wrote of the Byronic hero:

> almost all, have minds which seem at variance with their fortunes, and exhibit high and poignant feelings of pain and pleasure; a keen sense of what is noble and honourable; and an equally keen susceptibility of injustice or injury, under the garb of stoicism or contempt of mankind. The strength of early passion, and the glow of youthful feeling, are uniformly painted as chilled or subdued by a train of early imprudences or of darker guilt, and the sense of enjoyment tarnished, by too intimate an acquaintance with the vanity of human wishes. (cited in Byron's *Works* [1833], x.24)

The literary origins of this figure have been traced by P. L. Thorslev, Jr., in *The Byronic Hero: Types and Prototypes* and precisely analyzed in their various manifestations. The villain-hero of Elizabethan and Jacobean drama, John Milton's Satan, Friedrich von Schiller's *The Robbers (Die Räuber)* (1781), William Godwin's *Caleb Williams* (1794), Ann Radcliffe's *The Italian* (1797), the cult of sensibility—one may track the origins of the figure everywhere. But the effect in the earliest of the Turkish tales of the first appearance of Byron's Giaour (infidel) defies sober analysis. To respond to the verse is to yield to a wild intoxication:

> Who thundering comes on blackest steed,
> With slackened bit and hoof of speed?
> Beneath the clattering iron's sound
> The caverned Echoes wake around
> In lash for lash, and bound for bound;
> The foam that streaks the courser's side
> Seems gathered from the Ocean-tide:
> Though weary waves are sunk to rest,
> There's none within his rider's breast;
> And though to-morrow's tempest lower,
> 'Tis calmer than thy heart, young Giaour!
> I know thee not, I loathe thy race,
> But in thy lineaments I trace
> What Time shall strengthen, not efface:
> Though young and pale, that sallow front
> Is scathed by fiery Passion's brunt;
> Though bent on earth thine evil eye,
> As meteor-like thou glidest by,
> Right well I view and deem thee one
> Whom Othman's sons should slay or shun.[1]
> (180–199)

The speaker is a Turkish fisherman. The character is unimportant in himself, but the device enables Byron to enhance the mystery of the galloping figure by telling the tale in fragments of an onlooker's discourse: we have to guess at what has happened and what the characters feel. Equally important is the removal of the moral viewpoint outside Christendom. It is the European who is the infidel, and it is his romantic moral code of love that, in the Turkish setting, precipitates the tragedy. The passionate force of love is normally destructive in Byron, and the Byronic hero is already a prey to the canker of remorse, which neither revenge nor repentance will alleviate. The associative force of the trains of imagery enhance the significance of the figure. The image of the unbridled horse as symbolic of the danger of passion is one of the oldest European archetypes; the blackness of the steed suggests the powers of night, death, and the devil. The echoes that wake "beneath" the

1. All quotations from Byron's poems are from E. H. Coleridge, ed., *The Poetical Works*, (London, 1905).

steed's "iron" hooves are "caverned," thus suggesting an affinity with the underworld, while "iron" is traditionally the metal associated with the worst of the seven ages of the world. The imagery then reaches out to embrace more elemental forces: ocean, tempest, meteor. Perhaps these are too easily conventional to be fully effective, but the words suggest that the infidel passions are eternally part both of the human psyche and the nature of things. Less commonplace in the portrayal may be the expression "What Time shall strengthen, not efface." Time cannot heal, repentance will not reform. Like Godwin's Falkland, Byron's Giaour corrodes inwardly with his crime. In the monastery where ultimately he seeks refuge, he seems at times like Satan, at times like a vampire: one of those who, though dead, cannot die.

Although it would be absurd to seek to read too much into stories that never pretend to naturalism and are exotic and sensational in action and description, nonetheless the effectiveness of art does not always depend either on truth or craft. The mind feeds upon romance and delights in liberated images of other selves. Compare with the dark image of the Giaour the hero of *The Bride of Abydos* (1813), young Selim, about to die fighting for love against tyranny:

> His robe of pride was thrown aside,
> His brow no high-crowned turban bore,
> But in its stead a shawl of red,
> Wreathed lightly round, his temples wore:
> That dagger, on whose hilt the gem
> Were worthy of a diadem,
> No longer glittered at his waist,
> Where pistols unadorned were braced;
> And from his belt a sabre swung,
> And from his shoulder loosely hung
> The cloak of white, the thin capote
> That decks the wandering Candiote;
> Beneath—his golden plated vest
> Clung like a cuirass to his breast;
> The greaves below his knee that wound
> With silvery scales were sheathed and bound.
> But were it not that high command
> Spake in his eye, and tone, and hand,
> All that a careless eye could see
> In him was some young Galiongée.
> (613–632)

Such an image suggests Lawrence of Arabia. The combination of youth, rebellion, simplicity, and exoticism is erotic. That erotic element I find ambivalent, combining the heterosexual and homosexual. Both qualities have been seen as present in Byron; his readers confused the man and his verse; many women were as ready to prostitute themselves to their image of the poet as the heroines of the poems adore with bovine submission their sexual masters. The image of Selim is potentially complex and disturbing.

The element of sexual politics implicit in this kind of character has been little examined. Yet the heroes of the romances are generally both lovers and rebels. Selim is the least corrupted of these figures because he is most justified. His father has been murdered.

He has come to carry away from an oppressor the woman he loves. The typical political situation of the poems is that the evils of despotism produce criminals or outlaws but that crime, though not condoned, is less wicked, less hypocritical, than the society which produces it. Such an argument is political dynamite, and if such were Byron's serious view, it was a subject that could be safely treated only in a remote setting and romantic form. Only *Lara* begins to come close to home when the serfs, rebelling against feudalism, take up the cry that they "dig no land for tyrants but their graves."

Yet Byron's robber chiefs are themselves as tyrannical as the forces they oppose. Young Selim's eye speaks "high command." So too does his hand. War is his medium. Force meets force destructively. The *Führerprinzip* (authoritarian principle) is most clearly obvious in *The Corsair.* "I form the plan, divide the spoil," he comments; "And all obey, and few enquire his will." His other self in *Lara* is always the "chieftain" of his serfs. When Selim's pirate band considers "equal rights, which man ne'er knew," he dismisses this talk as "prate," and cries, "I have a love for freedom too." For the Byronic hero freedom is the exercise of his will, and, in a sense, the existence of an opposing will is welcome, because it provides a force against which the hero may exercise himself. To the rebel leader men, militarily, and women, sexually, submit voluntarily. It is this voluntariness that distinguishes Selim or Conrad from tyrants. Their symbolic garb as common men appeals to democratic forces, but men know their masters even in the guise of a galiongee (Turkish sailor).

The outcome for the leader and his men is disastrous. At times Byron is moralistic about the evils of rebellion:

> And they that smote for freedom or for sway,
> Deemed few were slain, while more
>   remained to slay.
> It was too late to check the wasting brand,
> And Desolation reaped the famished land;
> The torch was lighted, and the flame was
>   spread,
> And Carnage smiled upon her daily dead.
> (*Lara,* 921–926)

Such Augustan sententiousness is not what the world recognized as Byronic. It is the fateful dash upon the reef of disaster—better to expire in a storm than rot in the torpor of stagnation—or the sentimental gesture at the critical instant, when blood and cunning were the only ways to success: these are the ways in which Byronic heroes are destroyed. Yet that destruction, paradoxically, is symbolic of the very freedom of the spirit to take what path it will. The pirate, free to wander over the tempestuous sea as his feelings direct, is the reiterated symbol. The beginning of *The Corsair,* though imaginatively far from the most exciting passage of the romances, provides a clear enunciation of the motif:

> O'er the glad waters of the dark blue sea,
> Our thoughts as boundless, and our souls as
>   free,
> Far as the breeze can bear, the billows foam,
> Survey our empire, and behold our home!
> These are our realms, no limits to their
>   sway—
> Our flag the sceptre all who meet obey.
> Ours the wild life in tumult still to range
> From toil to rest, and joy in every change.
> Oh, who can tell? not thou, luxurious slave!
> Whose soul would sicken o'er the heaving
>   wave;
> Not thou, vain lord of Wantonness and Ease!
> Whom Slumber soothes not—Pleasure
>   cannot please—
> Oh, who can tell, save he whose heart hath
>   tried,
> And danced in triumph o'er the waters wide,
> The exulting sense—the pulse's maddening
>   play,
> That thrills the wanderer of that trackless
>   way?
> That for itself can woo the approaching fight,
> And tub what some deem danger to delight;
> That seeks what cravens shun with more
>   than zeal,
> And where the feebler faint can only feel—
> Feel—to the rising bosom's inmost core,
> Its hope awaken and its spirit soar?
> No dread of Death—if with us die our foes—
>
> Save that it seems even duller than repose;
> Come when it will—we snatch the life of
>   Life—
> When lost—what recks it by disease or
>   strife?
> (1–26)

CHILDE HAROLD'S PILGRIMAGE III AND IV

Byron initially describes Harold as "the wandering outlaw of his own dark mind." The image relates him, therefore, to the pirate or brigand heroes of the romances. As with *The Corsair* the sea is an important defining motif. The third canto of the pilgrimage opens with the poet upon the ocean, and a grammatical solecism confuses the speaker with the natural element: "Awaking with a start, / The waters heave around me." The fourth canto concludes with the invocation: "Roll on, thou deep and dark blue Ocean —roll!" For the corsairs, the sea was the place where they found freedom; the danger of their condition was the very stimulus of pleasure by which they "snatch the life of life"; "the wanderer of that trackless way" thrills to the exultation of his endless movement; energy is eternal delight. Harold, on the other hand, is the victim of that pessimistic weariness of life to which German romanticism has given the name *Weltschmerz.* He is upon the sea because society has exiled him, and he in turn has rejected the world to wrap himself in his own proud solitude, his sense of alienation, grief, and wrong. The waters are an emblem of trackless wandering—"I am as a weed, / Flung from the rock" (III.ii)—and he is hence the victim of circumstance rather than the master of his fate. At the end of the fourth canto the ocean is seen as "The image of Eternity" that subsumes all human endeavor and hence forever reminds the man of philosophical sensibility that all is vanity.

In these cantos the poet has chosen all the darker and more passive elements of the Byronic hero—his solitude, gloom, remorse, and excessive parade of feeling—and adopted them as his own. Hamlet brooding over a skull would be an appropriate emblem (and Byron's skull-cup is notorious). The dramatic being of Harold is of little importance. In the prentice work of the first two cantos the poet had attempted in vain to create a separate protagonist, but now the evocation "Long absent HAROLD reappears at last" is a mere ritual gesture. All pretense at distinguishing narrator from narrative persona soon dissolves. The cantos are Byron's journal of his physical and spiritual pilgrimage to the eternal city of Rome. This is, for him, *not* an emblem of a life and empire continuing to the end of time but a perpetual memento mori, a reminder of death and decay in which his blighted spirit may stand "a ruin among ruins."

There are obvious dangers in Byron's decision to adopt as his own, characteristics of romantic heroes who belong only in exotic fantasy. Fact and psychological fiction become strangely entwined. Much of the verse has a melodramatic and histrionic tone, and the ejaculations of feeling are often perilously close to rant. Yet this declamatory oratory has an extraordinary and insistent force that batters the sensibility:

> There are some feelings Time can not benumb,
> Nor Torture shake, or mine would now be cold and dumb.
>
> But from their nature will the Tannen grow
> Loftiest on loftiest and least sheltered rocks,
> Rooted in barrenness, where nought below
> Of soil supports them 'gainst the Alpine shocks
> Of eddying storms; yet springs the trunk, and mocks
> The howling tempest, till its height and frame
> Are worthy of the mountains from whose blocks
> Of bleak, gray granite into life it came,
> And grew a giant tree;—the Mind may grow the same.
>
> Existence may be borne, and the deep root
> Of life and sufferance make its firm abode
> In bare and desolated bosoms: mute
> The camel labours with the heaviest load,
> And the wolf dies in silence—not bestowed
> In vain should such example be; if they,
> Things of ignoble or of savage mood,
> Endure and shrink not, we of nobler clay
> May temper it to bear,—it is but for a day.
> (IV.xix–xxi)

The sentiments are in the noblest tradition of European philosophy: the Stoic. The image of the wolf dying in silence was to inspire one of the finest of Alfred de Vigny's poems. Psychologically the fascination of the lines lies in the paradoxical struggle between feeling and "apathy" (ἀπάθεια); between the deep-seated human need to communicate and the ideal of that integrity which expresses itself in silence. Poetically the images suggest rich ambiguities. The invocation of the power of the mind to overcome "Time" and "Torture" suggests the sufferings of Prometheus and hence Titanic or Satanic rebellion or punishment, now seen, through the Alpine imagery, like a force in nature. This has rich mythic potential and may well have been inspirational for Shelley's *Prometheus Unbound* (1820). The use of the wolf as an emblem to raise the aspiration of the human mind is unusual, a beast of prey suggesting, in human terms, a figure like the Giaour or Conrad. Conversely, the comparison of social utility with the ignoble camel in some measure devalues the mundane with backhanded praise. The Stoic tradition in which Byron writes, therefore, is changed both under the pressures of acute personal sensibility and subtle poetic imagery.

The poet, throughout *Childe Harold,* is seeking to transform his own condition into some mythical representation of the eternal suffering of the human mind. At times, looking back into that Calvinistic tradition in which he was reared, he describes unhappiness as arising from the "uneradicable taint" of "sin"; or, in more modern and Freudian terms, he calls the mind "sick" and sees its disease arising from the alienation of man: "Our life is a false nature—'tis not in/ The harmony of things" (IV.cxxiv–cxxvi). These ideas are more centrally Byronic than the poet's occasional excursions into nature mysticism by way of consolation, especially in canto III, which are bastard Wordsworthianisms arising from Shelley's influence.

This pessimism is profoundly disturbing if true, yet its universal force is continually vitiated by the poet's posing like the protagonist of one of his own romances. He presents himself as immensely suffering from some dark secret—which *cannot* be told, he repeatedly *tells*—and he parades the scowl of nervous anguish as the badge of courage:

> But I have lived, and have not lived in vain:
> My mind may lose its force, my blood its fire,
> And my frame perish even in conquering pain;
> But there is that within me which shall tire
> Torture and Time, and breathe when I expire. . . .
> (IV.cxxxvii)

The "there is that within me" is no more specified than the "some feelings" of the earlier passage quoted. Again the ambiguous Titanic image is repeated, though now this figure, we shall be told, will move "In hearts all rocky now the late remorse of Love." This vague self-dramatizing utterance and self-pity have, in fact, a simple and mundane cause: Byron had quarreled with his wife. Should this be recalled, for instance as Thomas Peacock recalled it in *Nightmare Abbey,* it is difficult not to reject the grandiose pretensions of Byronism on the commonsense ground that the subject and the sentiments are ludicrously disproportionate. Shelley moved the matter into myth with Prometheus, and Byron was to explore something of the same line of development. In the metaphysical speculations of *Manfred* we find suggestions of the monstrous crime of incest, and in *Cain* there is overt Satanic speculation. Byron exploited these matters to add a heightened dramatic dimension to his tempest-riven mind. A domestic quarrel between a man and his wife is not large enough motivation for a poet to become the Titanic hero of his own poetry. There must be some great crime, the feelings must be intenser, the dark intellectual vision more daring. Byron will pile Pelion upon Ossa until suddenly the sublime topples into the ridiculous and he emerges with the domestic comedy of *Beppo.*

Granted these limitations in *Childe Harold,* cantos III and IV, nonetheless the oratorical vigor of utterance is united with an extraordinary synthesizing power of the imagination to interpret natural or artistic scene, present or historical character or event, in terms of the sensibility of the narrator, and yet always to find new variations upon the poem's themes. One of the usual "purple" passages may readily provide an example. The stanzas inspired by the statue of the dying gladiator follow shortly after the lines quoted above, which ended with a reference to "the late remorse of Love":

> I see before me the Gladiator lie:
> He leans upon his hand—his manly brow
> Consents to death, but conquers agony,
> And his drooped head sinks gradually low—

And through his side the last drops, ebbing
slow
From the red gash, fall heavy, one by one,
Like the first of a thunder-shower; and now
The arena swims around him—he is gone,
Ere ceased the inhuman shout which hailed
the wretch who won.

He heard it, but he heeded not—his eyes
Were with his heart—and that was far
away;
He recked not of the life he lost nor prize,
But where his rude hut by the Danube lay—
There were his young barbarians all at play,
There was their Dacian mother—he, their
sire,
Butchered to make a Roman holiday—
All this rushed with his blood—Shall he
expire
And unavenged?—Arise! ye Goths, and glut
your ire!
(IV.cxl–cxli)

The gladiator is another Byronic hero. The phrase "Consents to death, but conquers agony" goes straight to the heartland of Stoic tradition and is memorably terse. At the same time he is a man of feeling who recalls his children and his wife as he dies. So Byron in exile had recalled both his wife and daughter at the inception of the third canto. In a sense the poet has been butchered in reputation to make entertainment in England, just as the gladiator has been killed to amuse the Romans. Yet from these personal correlations a truth of more general importance arises, the more effective because of the poet's empathy with his subject. The gladiator is a type of all colonial peoples oppressed by imperialism. The scene arouses both pity and indignation as imagery and expectation are subtly modulated. After the lines on children and mother one might expect tears to rush," but it is blood instead, and the expression "rushed with his blood" is used in two senses: to describe the literal death of the man but also with the usual metaphorical implication of the expression, a surge of angry emotion. That blood, earlier, had been described as falling like the first drops of a thundershower, proleptic thus of a storm to come: the storm of anger and of retribution on imperial Rome. Hence the cry to the barbarians: "Shall he expire/ And unavenged?—Arise!" One need only compare Byron upon the gladiator's statue with Keats on the Grecian urn to appreciate the immeasurably greater kinetic energy of Byronism, despite whatever way one might judge the two poets' diverse verbal skills.

Yet the call to liberty is strangely placed within the structure of the poem. It follows on the passage ending with the expression of "the late remorse of Love" and leads into a meditation on the Coliseum that takes as its theme that all is vanity, and the ruins reecho with a sense of universal void (IV.cxlii–cxlv). The poem, therefore, is always modulating, tending to modify or even to contradict its own sentiments: love or hate, silence or impassioned utterance, universal vanity or passionate concern for human wrongs, selfhood or general typology. This complexity, or contradiction, is intrinsic in the poem's lack of structural principle. It flows in open-ended form on the stream of the poet's own life. Blake claimed that without contraries there is no progression, but he was a system builder, while we shall find that the essence of Byronism, as it comes to maturity, is to deny all system. One might rephrase Blake's aphorism for Byron: without contraries there is no life. Stasis is death.

It is difficult to illustrate without disproportionately long quotation. Consider another famous sequence, that on the battle of Waterloo, beginning III.xvii and ending perhaps around stanza xlv. The modulations here are continual from the confident eighteenth-century generalities of the lines "There was a sound of revelry by night" (xxi) to the personalized, even psychotic, introspection of the description of the broken heart like a mirror, "The same—and still the more, the more it breaks" (xxxiii); from the excitement of "And wild and high the 'Cameron's Gathering' rose!" (xxvi) to the bold gesture of the pathetic fallacy "Grieving, if aught inanimate e'er grieves,/Over the unreturning brave" (xxvii); the whole leading to the presentation of Napoleon as a real-life Byronic hero, a "Spirit antithetically mixed," greater, yet less than man, conqueror and captive, "sedate and all-enduring" whose "breath is agitation" and whose life a storm.

Byron condemned Wordsworth and his fellow "Lakers" for dabbling in a puddle while his own bark was driven over the ocean of eternity. It is a large claim, but the stanzas on Waterloo and Napoleon confront the major events of history in all their emotional complexity and endeavor to move from the local event to philosophical generality about the human condition. Local analysis is unjust because the part cannot be detached from the whole without interrupting the effect of the rhetorical flow; and verse that is conceived in terms of public oratory will not stand the rigorous scrutiny of petty detail.

> Their childrens' lips shall echo them, and say—
> "Here, where the sword united nations drew,
> Our countrymen were warring on that day!"
> (III.xxxv)

In lines like these, in a sequence such as this, Byron has broken free from the fictional stance of the Byronic hero to find, in history, an objective subject and a European voice and audience. It is a development that was to lead to the great passages of public commentary in the dedication of *Don Juan* and in *The Vision of Judgment.* That is a matter more readily seen in retrospect than apparent at the time. But the compulsive attraction for Byron of the Byronic hero as an alter ego was still strong, as the plays *Manfred* (1817) and *Cain* (1821) show.

THE PLAYS: MANFRED *AND* CAIN

Byron's interest in the drama was consistent. He had joined the management committee of the Drury Lane Theatre in 1815; he was the friend of Richard Brinsley Sheridan; his poems and letters are thickly sown with quotations from playwrights. His own dramas are of two main kinds: historical tragedies written on neoclassical principles such as *Marino Faliero* (1821), *Sardanapalus* (1821), and *The Two Foscari* (1821); and metaphysical fantasies such as *Manfred, Cain,* and *Heaven and Earth* (1823). None of the plays was written for performance, although in the historical dramas Byron wished to set an example to the times of the traditional virtues of seriousness and truth in subject, unity of time and place in structure. Certain Byronic themes reemerge in different form. *Sardanapalus* attacks imperialistic tyranny through a hero usually condemned by history as a swinish sensualist and whose tragic fault, when he commits himself to necessary violence, is an excess of sentimental kindness for his enemies. *Marino Faliero* shows an aristocratic hero conspiring against a corrupt oligarchy. The treatment of the themes demonstrates little practical command of stagecraft in word or action, and the pieces inspired little theatrical interest.

The position of the two major metaphysical plays is different. *Cain* provoked the greatest intellectual scandal of Byron's career, and the amount of controversy that gathered around the piece has required major critical and editorial attention, notably Truman Guy Steffan's edition (1968) for the University of Texas. It has also attracted the interest of major practical craftsmen. The Moscow Art Theater and Jerzy Grotowski's Theatre Laboratory have both produced the play in this century because of the modernism of its theme and its symbolic form. *Manfred* achieved a respectable place in the nineteenth-century repertory because of its potentialities for "total theater," blending spectacle, music, and dance with the action. The boldness of its conception suggests analogies with Ibsen's *Peer Gynt*. By writing for a theater of the imagination, Byron helped, paradoxically, to enlarge the capabilities of the real stage.

Manfred has analogies with the first part of Goethe's *Faust,* which Byron knew through translation. The first scene in which the hero is discovered alone pondering in his study at midnight recalls, in general, the opening of Goethe's play. The hero is representative of human wisdom, which, having explored all earthly things, finds in them no solid joy or lasting treasure. "Sorrow is knowledge," Manfred concludes, a sentiment that the philosopher Nietzsche was to admire as immortal. There is no clear indication in the play of what spheres of learning Manfred has explored. He is a sage whose wisdom has given him direct contact with supernatural beings. He is also another typically Byronic hero, haunted by remorse for some dark crime (incest is suggested, and the "destruction" of his sister), alienated from human society, a rebel against the established order of things.

The treatment of the hero is different from that in the poems so far considered because Byron moves the story onto a metaphysical and allegorical level, suggesting the mode of later works like Shelley's *Prometheus Unbound* or the second part of Goethe's *Faust.* Lyric and dramatic elements are combined; dance and song are suggested by the text; the effects of light described would not only be scenically beautiful in performance but they are also interwoven with the allegory. The signification of these elements is not easily described and the ultimate meaning of the text is obscure. Like *Prometheus Unbound,* the play can be interpreted as a subjective and psychological work concerned with the powers and operations of the mind. What is represented as external is often internal. Allegory sometimes gives way to the kind of symbolism we find in dreams. We know that the images and words are important; they haunt us, but there are parts of the processes of our imaginations that we experience without ever fully understanding.

Not all the text is on this level. The chamois hunter, the witch of the Alps, and the abbot may all be easily interpreted allegorically in Manfred's quest for his lost sister, Astarte. The chamois hunter, who saves Manfred from suicide, is a romantic variant on the "happy husbandman": the simple man who finds contentment in his organic relationship with nature. The abbot, manifestly, represents the Christian religion. The witch of the Alps is less simply categorized but is described as the spirit of the place and of beauty and seems to represent something of the inspirational force of natural loveliness and of the power of pantheism.

The interpretative crux of the play is Astarte, Manfred's dead sister. To take her as merely being Augusta Leigh reduces the work at a stroke to absurdity. To read the play in terms of story—that is, as about incest—renders the metaphysical apparatus irrelevant. Astarte, therefore, must possess a symbolic signification, but what that is has proved mysterious. The original Astarte was a Phoenician fertility goddess and Byron may have chosen this form of the name rather than the biblical Ashtaroth because it suggests also *astra* (the Latin word for star). So Shelley was to combine the mythical Adonis and the Judaic word *Adonai* (a name for God) in *Adonais.* Seven stars appear to Manfred at the beginning of the play, the last of which seems to be an image of Astarte, for he faints with emotion on seeing her. She may represent something of the spirit of love and beauty with which the mind of man has so often been rapt, though it would be unwise to turn the play into a Platonic allegory. In earlier centuries the philosophy of Plato might have provided a framework for Byron, but for the romantic poet the thing sought is unknown and indefinable. To change to a Christian image: he is searching for the holy grail but does not know what it looks like.

The grail, according to the myth, was only for the pure in heart. The Byronic hero is impure, yet he still searches. After the vision of Astarte vanishes, an incantatory curse is spoken over the unconscious body of Manfred—possibly this indicates the workings of the unconscious mind:

> By thy cold breast and serpent smile,
> By thy unfathomed gulfs of guile,
> By that most seeming virtuous eye,
> By thy shut soul's hypocrisy;
> By the perfection of thine art
> Which passed for human thine own heart:

By thy delight in others' pain,
And by thy brotherhood of Cain,
I call upon thee! and compel
Thyself to be thy proper Hell!
(I.i.242–251)

The paradox of the play is that the mind both creates the vision of love and beauty, and yet destroys it by its innate and inescapable mental corruption. The incest theme is a metaphor for this process. When Manfred eventually finds Astarte again she is a spirit in hell who cannot reply intelligibly to his passionate pleas. He cries:

. . . cannot rest.
I know not what I ask, nor what I seek:
I feel but what thou art, and what I am. . . .
(II.iv.130–132)

One recognizes the desire, but the lines indicate that it is not possible to put a name to it. Possibly at this stage the vision of Astarte is contaminated. Since the scene is hell, if the Faust myth were still running in Byron's mind, the analogous figure here would be the visionary Helen of Troy, who destroys the hero by turning his mind to sensuality when he should think of God—so Marlowe: "Her lips suck forth my soul! See where it flies!"

Byron's hero also comes to die after this vision, though no logical reason is offered. But the play is not working within a theological system like Marlowe's *Dr. Faustus.* Instead it seems to be following a train of psychological causation: if Astarte is irredeemably in hell, then aspiration is in vain (such might be one interpretation). Yet Manfred dies defying the demons, just as he rejects the panacea of the Christian religion represented by the abbot. But, paradoxically, the ultimate demon declares that he is Manfred's "genius." Thus, the evil force which one believed was outside is revealed at the end as being within. The demonic agencies that the hero opposes even unto death may be his own creation. In support of this interpretation: precisely the same image dominates Werner Herzog's reworking of another fundamental romantic motif, the vampire myth in *Nosferatu.* Jonathan Harker creates Count Dracula by his own imagination and then becomes the vampire himself. His innocent wife (the Astarte figure) sacrifices herself in vain to the vampire's lust. This myth does not deny that innocence and beauty exist and that they are admired. But the darker and indestructible forces of the human mind always destroy them.

This is difficult and problematical ground. Byron complained of Coleridge's metaphysics: "I wish he would explain his explanation." Possibly *Manfred* is too obscure. But there is much in the working of the mind which is necessarily difficult to explain, and Byron observed that he was half-mad while writing the piece. At this time the props of Freudian imagery were not available as part of the subjective writer's stock in trade, and Byron was progressively exploring complex inner forces. The Byronic hero of a poem like *The Giaour* had become deliberately involved with the personality of the poet in the last cantos of *Childe Harold.* Now, in *Manfred,* the drama of the mind's *psychomachia* (spiritual war) shuts out more and more the objective scene. About this time Byron composed *The Prisoner of Chillon* (1816). The hero there is incarcerated so long in a dungeon below the level of the lake, scarcely able to glimpse anything of the outside world, that eventually he comes to love his own despair, and when liberty is eventually granted him, he is discontented with his freedom. The prisoner may be seen as a symbolic figure representing a mind entirely shut in upon itself.

Byron had returned to a more objective mood by 1821, when he came to write *Cain.* The extraordinary and famous change of direction in his writing after arriving in Italy seems, in retrospect, something like a self-willed therapeutic process to escape from the prison of his own subjectivity. But this is mere speculation. Although *Cain* has much in common with the earlier poetry thematically, the manner is markedly different. It is an intellectual and dialectical play built around formal arguments about theological ideas. Although these ideas are Byronic, there is little or no sense in the play that the poet himself is present in the characters. *Cain* argues about Manichaeism, or the "two principles" of good and evil, in the baldest of verse. The very directness of the iconoclasm was instrumental in causing contemporary outrage.

> *Lucifer.*
> Evil and Good are things in their own
> essence,
> And not made good or evil by the Giver;
> But if he gives you good—so call him; if
> Evil springs from *him,* do not name it *mine,*
> Till ye know better its true fount; and judge
> Not by words, though of Spirits, but the
> fruits
> Of your existence, such as it must be.
> *One good* gift has the fatal apple given,—
> Your *reason*:—let it not be overswayed
> By tyrannous threats to force you into faith
> 'Gainst all external sense and inward
> feeling:
> Think and endure,—and form an inner
> world
> In your own bosom— . . .
> (II.ii.452–464)

The intellectual ideas of the play may be traced to the skepticism of Pierre Bayle and Voltaire. The cosmology of Cain's flight through space with Lucifer owes much to Fontenelle's *Entretiens sur la pluralité des mondes* (1686), and the vision back into the pre-Adamite world of long geological time derives from Cuvier's *Essay on the Theory of the Earth.* There have been other kinds of being in this world before man, and they have become disastrously extinct. There are other worlds in the infinity of space. What then of the special claims of the Christian revelation? If we must be skeptical about biblical truth, what will we conclude concerning the nature of God from the evidence of the creation? If God were good, all that we are and behold would be good. But since evil, death, and suffering are inextricably part of nature, then they are part of God's nature.

Lucifer's description of his relationship to God suggests a possible source in the philosopher William Godwin's account in *Enquiry Concerning Political Justice* (1793). Jehovah is a gloomy tyrant who demands submission from his sycophants:

> . . .he is alone
> Indefinite, Indissoluble Tyrant;
> Could he but crush himself, 'twere the best
> boon
> He ever granted. . . .
> (I.i. 152–155)

To rebel against such a figure of political oppression is in itself an act of justice. This situation is similar to that of the rebel heroes of Byron's early romances; but now, not shrouded in the charms of exotic fiction, the idea is applied to the religious tenets of contemporary European society. Byron's pessimism makes the act of rebellion itself as evil as the system that provokes it. Lucifer is not like Shelley's Prometheus, who changes the world through sacrificial love. He is just as much a tyrant as God, and on this argument there would seem to be only one, not "two principles," in the universe. As in *Manfred,* knowledge of the nature of things brings sorrow. When Cain returns from his universal journey he brings with him death into the world by killing Abel in a fit of rage because Abel's blood sacrifice is acceptable to God, while his own innocent offering of fruits made without servility is rejected:

> . . . If a shrine without victim,
> And altar without gore, may win thy favour,
> Look on it! and for him who dresseth it,
> He is—such as thou mad'st him; and seeks
> nothing
> Which must be won by kneeling. . . .
> (III.i.266–270)

Byron, when attacked, claimed that the ideas of the piece were not his but appropriate only to the characters who uttered them: the evil figures Lucifer and Cain. This argument must be weighed. It may be granted that neither being seems to be an alter ego in the manner of Childe Harold, who merges with Byron, or of Manfred, who seems a projection of the poet's own deep mental disturbance. The characters in *Cain* are embodiments of ideas, for instance in the manner of the very similar modern morality plays of Edward Bond, and the great imaginative visions of the second act are objective in the sense that they represent what the universe is or was like. The myth also is traditionally given, whereas *Manfred* creates its own myth as an act of sublimated and darkly introspective self-revelation.

But the case for God is never put with the force of Lucifer's. Cain has already gone over to the other side intellectually before the devil appears and is distinguished from Lucifer only by his human sentiments, not by his principles. The "good" characters are loving to one another but totally submissive to a divinity who shows little sign of being anything but as Lucifer describes him, a gloomy tyrant who denies man knowledge and imposes submission by ignorance. That Cain is forced into murder by opposition to God merely shows that evil produces evil. Lucifer's interpretation of the universe appears to be the true one.

One may compare another parable for the modern world, Bertolt Brecht's *Galileo.* There the scientist (the Lucifer figure) disturbs the humble faith of the peasantry, which alone makes their poverty tolerable, by challenging the union of autocracy with ignorance that the Church (God) represents. In the process Galileo, by making himself unacceptable to authority, destroys the happiness of his daughter, who is prevented from marrying (Brecht's equivalent to the murder of Abel). But in Brecht's view such partial evil is justified by the greater good that will come from the advance of science in the service of humanity. He is in the tradition of philosophers such as Francis Bacon, Godwin, and Karl Marx, and believes in the essential union of science and reason with good. In Byron the disturbing thing about the vision of history that *Cain* represents is that "grief is knowledge" (I.354). Man's unconquerable mind burns to know truth and refuses to submit to evil, but the nature of things, and our own nature, always turns potential good to ill. Perhaps this is Byron's sense of original sin coming from Calvinism. A Brechtian answer (in the "enlightened" tradition of Lucretius) would be that Byron has simply not freed himself from superstitious guilt. But it can be seen from Byron's debates with Shelley, especially as presented in Shelley's *Julian and Maddalo,* that he has much more fundamental objections to optimism. They are based on observation of the processes of the mind and on the empirical data of history: plants, sick at germination, produce bad fruit. In *Cain* the Byronic hero has become an established literary type by which the poet can illustrate this intellectual proposition through myth and formal debate. The dramatic beings are no longer subsumed into his own personality like Harold or Manfred, but the iconoclastic ideas that they utter are centrally Byronic.

BEPPO

In *Beppo* (1818) Byron found the manner and form of the comic masterworks of his last years. The development is a surprise. His racy, vivid, and high-spirited letters are the only substantial evidence that there had long existed, in potential, a comic poet behind the mask of the satirist, sentimentalist, and misanthrope he had hitherto adopted. The new style was found almost by accident while he was still working in the vein of *Childe Harold* and *Manfred* and when, critically, his mind had seemed to be turning rather to Pope as an alternative poetical model. *Beppo* was no more than a hasty bagatelle offered to his publisher John Murray as a gift.

Two factors combined in the poem's inception. One is biographical. It had been a therapeutic experience for Byron to settle down to a life of comfortable promiscuity in Italy. His fraught nerves healed. His letters to Murray were so entertaining that the publisher asked him for some verse in the same manner. Murray wrote in January 1817: "Give me a poem,—a good Venetian tale describing manners formerly from the story itself, and now from your own observations, and call it 'Marianna.' " In the same year John Hookham

Frere published two cantos of *Prospectus and Specimen of an Intended National Work, by William and Robert Whistlecraft, of Stowmarket, in Suffolk, Harness and Collar-Makers,* a work familiarly known as *Whistlecraft* or, from its later title (1821), as *The Monks and the Giants.* This is an unfinished Arthurian burlesque written in the octave stanza (*ottava rima*) in the manner of the fifteenth-century Italian poet Luigi Pulci's tale of Charlemagne, the *Morgante Maggiore.* Byron's new style was given to him ready-made by Frere; witness the second stanza from Frere's first canto:

> Poets consume exciseable commodities,
> They raise the nation's spirit when
> victorious,
> They drive an export trade in whims and
> oddities,
> Making our commerce and revenue glorious;
> As an industrious and pains-taking body 'tis
> That Poets should be reckon'd meritorious:
> And therefore I submissively propose
> To erect one Board for Verse and one for
> Prose.

The facetious whimsicality of the narrator, the outrageous rhymes and enjambment, and the easy conversational tone are exactly the new Byronic mode. Other literary sources may have contributed: Giovanni Battista Casti's *Novelle Galanti,* which Byron had acquired in 1816 (his *Animali Parlanti* and *Poema Tartaro* also show parallels with Byron's subsequent work); later Byron turned to Francesco Berni and the "parent" of this kind of writing, Pulci himself, whom he began to translate. But "*Whistlecraft* was *my* immediate *model,*" he declared in a letter to Murray of 25 March 1818.

Frere's poem lacks both the deeper biographical resonances and the social immediacy of *Beppo.* Byron had all the literary expectations of the Byronic hero to exploit and his own notoriety. The tale he tells, although set a few years back, is about Venetian society vividly observed as he knew it now, and continually set in contrast with English society for satirical purposes. Frere, by going back to Arthur's days, usually loses connection with the actual and often writes what is little more than an amusing spoof of a chivalric poem.

Byron's new pose is of "a nameless sort of person,/ (A broken Dandy lately on my travels)" (lii). He *was* a cynical man of fashion more concerned with the superficiality of society than with deep issues of emotion, morality, or philosophy, but he now is out of English society, perhaps even a little out-of-date (for fashions swiftly change). The word "nameless" contains a double meaning. It may refer to the difficulty of defining what sort of person an English gentleman "gone native" in Italy might be—"broken Dandy" is only one suggestion. It may also refer to Byron's abominable reputation in England. His is not the kind of name mentioned in polite society. This kind of persona was to be richly developed in *Don Juan,* but one should beware of defining the new role too precisely. The poet can change the mask through which he speaks, and the role played can vary from moment to moment from self-revelation to full dramatization of another being. The "broken Dandy" is a burlesque form of the Byronic hero, and like the tragic type it is not constant in its manifestations or its use.

The old form of Byronic hero appears momentarily as the dark Turk in the carnival, the alienated and mysterious figure of the husband whom we learn in his *Wanderjähre* (years of travel) has been slave, pirate, and renegade to his religion. But no tragic figure is likely to be called Beppo by a nagging wife. The poem works often by disappointing expectation:

> How quickly would I print (the world
> delighting)
> A Grecian, Syrian, or Assyrian tale;
> And sell you, mixed with western
> Sentimentalism,
> Some samples of the *finest Orientalism.*
> (li)

The reader would expect a hot-blooded Mediterranean male to be jealous of his wife's lover, and Byron reminds his reader of the most famous of Venetian love tragedies, that "sooty devil" Othello, who "smothers women in a bed of feather." But this is the Venice of the carnival and of Carlo Goldoni, and when the husband returns after long years to find his wife unfaithful he merely strikes up a friendship with her lover, and she is merely curious about her husband's Turkish sexual and domestic life:

"Are you *really, truly,* now a Turk?
With any other women did you wive?
Is't true they use their fingers for a fork?
Well, that's the prettiest Shawl—as I'm
alive!
You'll give it me? They say you eat no pork.
And how so many years did you contrive
To—Bless me! did I ever? No, I never
Saw a man grown so yellow! How's your
liver?"
(xcii)

Insofar as the poem has a story, the tale is told with dramatic brilliance and a lively eye to social detail. But the anecdote is no more than a peg on which to hang the digressions. In this Byron resembles Laurence Sterne in *Tristam Shandy*. Anything that happens will set off a train of associated ideas, which beget fresh ideas, until by this process the most heterogeneous elements are yoked together. In *Don Juan* the method is used philosophically to satirize the pretensions of the human mind to build systems, especially systems of moral and metaphysical philosophy. In *Beppo* Byron is trying little more than to find a poetic speaking voice—as it were, a way of stretching his legs out before the fire and chatting a little facetiously upon anything that is likely to come into his head, especially what it is like to be an Englishman in Italy.

Yet the very act of comparison between the manners and climate of two societies begins to engender a far-reaching humorous skepticism:

This feast is named the Carnival, which
being
Interpreted, implies "farewell to flesh:"
So called, because the name and thing
agreeing,
Through Lent they live on fish both salt and
fresh.
But why they usher Lent with so much glee
in,
Is more than I can tell, although I guess
'Tis as we take a glass with friends at
parting,
In the Stage-Coach or Packet, just at
starting.
(vi)

The poet has picked up the paradox of Venetian Catholicism represented by the feast of joy that is the prelude to the days of contrition and penance set aside by the church to mark Jesus's forty days fasting in the wilderness. He goes on to recommend that the English traveler should bring ample stock of sauces with him "if your religion's Roman/And you at Rome would do as Romans do" but concludes that no man

If foreign, is obliged to fast; and you,
If Protestant, or sickly, or a woman,
Would rather dine in sin on a ragout—
Dine and be d—d! I don't mean to be coarse,
But that's the penalty, to say no worse.
(ix)

Byron's satire is so tolerant of the human follies he mocks that he ends by reconciling the reader to his own folly. Human nature will have its way, and the flesh, if repressed in one fashion by the church, will have its Carnival another time. In any case, if the Lenten fish is so elaborately dressed with "ketchup, Soy, Chili-vinegar, and Harvey," what sort of contrition is this, and what is human nature that it can be so easily disturbed by the absence of ketchup? Perhaps even the church itself strives in every way to mitigate its own severities to the sick, to women (the weaker sex!), and as for Protestants, the word "d—d" has lost all its force in Byron's colloquialism (as well as all its middle letters). Do Christians really dispatch their fellow religionists to hell for not eating fish? Possibly. But the bantering tone of the lines never settles to anything of moral certainty. The broken Dandy's pose is that of a man who finds the reason for things "more than I can tell." Philosophically it is the pose of Socrates; in English verse it is closest to the technique of Chaucer. The Dandy merely reports on the surface of society as a naive Englishman abroad. It is for the reader to make what he will of the paradoxes and contradictions of the human situation the truth of which he is laughingly compelled to recognize.

The Dandy turns his mind back to the land he has left:

> "England! with all thy faults I love thee
> still,"
> I said at Calais, and have not forgot it;
> I like to speak and lucubrate my fill;
> I like the government (but that is not it);
> I like the freedom of the press and quill;
> I like the Habeas Corpus (when we've got
> it);
> I like a Parliamentary debate,
> Particularly when 'tis not too late. . . .
> (xlvii)

Like the ideals of Lent, the virtues of England slide away in this and subsequent stanzas, but are not totally devalued though never directly stated. On the contrary, the list of the good things is introduced by the phrase "with all thy faults," quoted from William Cowper's *The Task* (the sentiment is not Byron's), and "love" slides swiftly to "like," and the catalog ends in stanza xlix with Byron "forgiving" and "forgetting" unemployment, riots, bankruptcies, "Our cloudy climate, and our chilly women." Yet it was proper to recall in Italy, a land repressed by foreign domination, English freedom of speech and of the press, and parliamentary democracy. But when Byron writes "I like the government" one should recall that he was a strong opponent of the Tory regime, hence the caveat "but that is not it"; and that same Tory government, faced with substantial domestic disorder, was fast dismantling the very English freedom that Byron "likes"—hence the aside on habeas corpus. In parliamentary debate Byron had spoken with passion on some of these issues. Now he admits to no more than liking debate "when 'tis not too late." Is the Dandy a lazy man, or is he suggesting that such debates are a waste of time? Byron's indignation, coiled like a spring, was shortly to fly out in the dedicatory stanzas to *Don Juan*; witness the lines on Robert Stewart Castlereagh:

> Cold-blooded, smooth-faced, placid
> miscreant!
> Dabbling its sleek young hands in Erin's
> gore. . . .
> (xii)

But here, in *Beppo,* such a declamatory outburst would offend against comic decorum. The subversive possibilities of the comic mode were to prove a much more subtle and flexible tool than the devices of grand rhetoric, as *The Vision of Judgment* will show.

THE VISION OF JUDGMENT

Byron was provoked by the Poet Laureate Robert Southey's *A Vision of Judgement* (1821). The quarrel between the poets had been festering for some time. Byron believed that Southey had accused him of living in Switzerland in "a league of incest," and in his preface to *A Vision* Southey had attacked the works of Byron and his "school" as being fit for a "brothel" and "Satanic" in their morality. The poet laureate had reneged on his earlier liberal sympathies expressed in poems like *Wat Tyler* (which he endeavored in vain to suppress) and had become the spokesman for high Toryism. In Southey's *Vision* the author is rapt into the skies from the Lake District and sees the recently dead king, George III, ascend to judgment. George is welcomed to heaven by the reactionary Prime Minister Spencer Perceval and is vainly accused by opposition speakers of the party of Satan like John Wilkes and the anonymous pamphleteer "Junius." Then he ascends to a blissful reunion with his family, helped on his way by figures like George Washington (who had fought against the king for the independence of America) and John Milton (who repents of his regicide opinions). The verse form is the Latin hexameter, which Byron called "spavined dactyls." The verse is as bad as the subject is silly; witness the account of the angel summoning the king's "absolvers":

> Ho! he exclaim'd, King George of England standeth in judgment!
> Hell hath been dumb in his presence. Ye who on earth arraign'd him,
> Come ye before him now, and here accuse or absolve him!
> For injustice hath here no place.
>
> From the Souls of the Blessed
> Some were there then who advanced; and more from the skirts of the meeting—
> Spirits who had not yet accomplish'd their purification,
> Yet being cleansed from pride, from faction and error deliver'd,
> Purged of the film wherewith the eye of the mind is clouded,
> They, in their better state, saw all things clear; and discerning
> Now, in the light of truth, what tortuous views had deceived them,
> They acknowledged their fault, and own'd the wrong they had offer'd. . . .
> (VI.1–12)

Southey, then, was more than a personal enemy. He stood as a type of the forces Byron opposed: a bad poet, a political apostate, a high Tory, above all an organ of what was for Byron one of the major ills of English society, cant: "in these days the grand '*primum mobile*' of England is *cant*; cant political, cant poetical, cant religious, cant moral."[2]

Byron had already attacked Southey and his circle of lakeland poets (Wordsworth and Coleridge) in "dedicating" *Don Juan* to him:

> And now my Epic Renegade! what are ye at?
> With all the Lakers, in and out of place . . .

2. From R. E. Prothero, ed., *Letters and Journals,* (London, 1893–1904), vol. V, p. 542.

but had chosen to let the lines remain unpublished. Now he had public as well as private cause for quarrel with the laureate. Byron's *The Vision of Judgment* was published in the first number of the opposition journal the *Liberal* with which Byron, Shelley, (now dead), and Leigh Hunt were editorially concerned.

The structure of Southey's poem is parodied. Satan, John Wilkes, and "Junius" reappear, and Wilkes even shows something of a Southeylike backsliding in forgiving a man he "beat . . .hollow" politically on earth—as the devil remarks, Wilkes "turned to half a courtier" before he died. But Junius remains fearless in his support of liberty and constant in his opposition to the king. The archangel Michael puts a Southeyian case to him:

> "Repent'st thou not," said Michael, "of some past
> Exaggeration? something which may doom
> Thyself if false, as him if true? Thou wast
> Too bitter—is it not so?—in thy gloom
> Of passion?"—"Passion!" cried the phantom dim,
> "I loved my country, and I hated him.
>
> "What I have written, I have written: let
> The rest be on his head or mine!"
> (lxxxiii–lxxxiv)

The liberal reader's sympathy is meant to lie with "Junius." A passionate love for one's country in the teeth of an enemy of liberty is a real good, but it is typical of Byronism, and of the Byronic Satanism which Southey attacked, that "Junius" is a witness summoned by the devil; and his courageous declaration "What I have written, I have written" was also the expression of Pontius Pilate crucifying Christ as king of the Jews.

The major attack on the king is made by Satan himself in the guise of a disinherited nobleman called by his sense of duty to be an advocate. Compare Southey's Christian description of the devil accusing the king:

> . . . a Demon came at the summons.
> It was the Spirit by which his righteous reign had been troubled;

Likest in form uncouth to the hideous Idols whom India
(Long by guilty neglect to hellish delusions abandon'd)
Worships with horrible rites of self-immolation and torture.
Many-headed and monstrous the Fiend; with numberless faces,
Numberless bestial ears erect to all rumours, and restless,
And with numberless mouths which were fill'd with lies as with arrows.
(V.8–15)

with the Byronic:

But bringing up the rear of this bright host
A Spirit of a different aspect waved
His wings, like thunder-clouds above some coast
Whose barren beach with frequent wrecks is paved;
His brow was like the deep when tempest-tossed;
Fierce and unfathomable thoughts engraved
Eternal wrath on his immortal face,
And where he gazed a gloom pervaded space.
(xxiv)

Byron's Satan is a figure of far greater power than Southey's. His original is the ruined archangel of Milton's *Paradise Lost*: the heroic and tragic antagonist of God. When he and Michael meet it is with a high, immortal, proud regret" as if it were "less their will/ Than destiny" for them to be engaged in eternal warfare (xxxii). The highest of the angelic powers recognizes another manifestation of himself in Satan, as it were, like Caesar shedding tears over the body of Pompey. This is a demonic entity as worthy of serious regard as Lucifer in *Cain* and another variation upon the Byronic hero: the man outcast because he will not submit to tyranny. The imagery associates him with thunder, traditionally seen as the instrument of the wrath of God. The Satanic, in this poem, comes close to being a voice that one might call, in another context, the justice of God.

The values that Satan expounds in his great piece of forensic oratory are such as he expects highest heaven to respond to with sympathy. Just as Southey expected heaven to be the home of the Tory party, so Byron turns the tables by expecting heaven to be liberal: to condemn tyranny, to oppose religious intolerance, and to reject wars waged to further those ends:

"He ever warred with freedom and the free:
Nations as men, home subjects, foreign foes,
So that they uttered the word 'Liberty!'
Found George the Third their first opponent. . . .
(xlv)

Selective quotation cannot do justice to the skill with which the attack spares the person of the "old, blind, mad, helpless, weak" octogenarian king rotting in his golden coffin—indeed, even acknowledges his personal virtues—and yet remorselessly reveals the public and political vice his reign occasioned. Such balance convinces that what is said is true more than mere polemic would do. Nor can short quotation reveal how dramatically in character is the devil's speech. It is appropriate that the first rebel should speak for liberty and claim as his own the shades of the tyrant-hater Junius Brutus and the insurrectionist George Washington. He also blatantly speaks to manipulate his audience. Although he addresses Michael as an equal, he cunningly works upon the prejudices of the silly Roman Catholic bigot St. Peter in revealing George as "The foe to Catholic participation/ In all the license of a Christian nation" (xlviii). Even in the most serious passages the derisive spirit of Byronic laughter mocks and subverts the cherished cant of society.

Byron himself appears in the poem as the sinning, tolerant, almost buffoonlike figure that is a development of the mask first adopted in *Beppo*. Even amid the condemnation of George III we find Byron, surprisingly, uttering the sentiment "God save the king!" but then subverting it with unusual reasons:

. . . It is a large economy
In God to save the like; but if he will

Be saving, all the better; for not one am I
Of those who think damnation better still:
I hardly know too if not quite alone am I
In this small hope of bettering future ill
By circumscribing, with some slight
restriction,
The eternity of Hell's hot jurisdiction.

. . .

God help us all! God help me too! I am,
God knows, as helpless as the Devil can
wish. . . .
(xiii[v])

From behind the comic mask one hears the voice of charity. We are asked to recognize the weakness of our common humanity. The lines are a mutation on the Calvinistic pessimism of the sense of original sin that is a constant quality of Byronism. "God save the king!" because the king is a sinner who needs to be saved; "God help us all!" because we are all sinners; "God help me too!" for we should not exclude ourselves when we condemn the wickedness of the world and delude ourselves with complacent pride—which is one of Southey's many failings. "God help me too!" has an additional resonance because it is Byron writing: notorious in his public capacity for "incest" and "Satanism" and a man who had deliberately involved his own poetic personality with that of his dark heroes.

The philosophical tradition that blends with Calvinism here I shall call "enlightened humanism" —there is no convenient critical shorthand for it. Eighteenth-century liberal philosophy had set itself constantly against Christian claims of exclusive revelation and of the universality of damnation for the infidel. Intellectual skepticism and comparative history had combined to undermine Christian doctrines, producing as their fruits deism, liberalism, and toleration. Byron always carried his learning lightly, but he had read in this enlightened school, and his charity is the product of the humane skepticism which that reading engendered.

Hence the salvation of George III in the poem. As in Southey's *Vision* the king gets into heaven, though merely through inadvertence on the part of the deity in Byron's story. To damn a man would be as wrong —and as arrogant in intellectual presumption—as Southey's claim that all good Tories go to God. In any case, since fellows like St. Peter are rather silly, and much of the best company seems to be in hell, Southey's Tory heaven is not so much of a reward after all. In Byron, George learns the 100th psalm because he must learn to enter heaven's gates with thanksgiving: "For the LORD *is* good; his mercy *is* everlasting." It is that quality of mercy that mankind most needs.

The real villain of the piece is Southey. Byron follows his original by having the "Laker" indeed rapt into the sky from Derwentwater, but the "truth" of the tale as *The Vision* recounts it is very different from what the lying renegade has reported in *A Vision*:

. . . here's my 'Vision'!
Now you shall judge, all people—yes—you
shall
Judge with my judgment! and by my
decision
Be guided who shall enter heaven or fall."
(ci)

No case needs to be made against the poet laureate. He is condemned from his own mouth. Byron, though he invents speech for him, does not have to invent the grounds of his condemnation. The list of the man's own works speaks for itself:

He had written praises of a Regicide;
He had written praises of all kings
whatever;
He had written for republics far and wide,
And then against them bitterer than ever;
For pantisocracy he once had cried
Aloud, a scheme less moral than 'twas
clever;
Then grew a hearty anti-jacobin—
Had turned his coat—and would have
turned his skin.
(xcvii)

For great political crimes Byron had, at moments, allowed his style to rise to declamatory grandeur. Ridicule is enough for this sort of thing. He will never strike harder than he needs to achieve his end, but the ridicule is merciless in a way that the treatment of the king is not. Southey has nothing to redeem him. On the other hand, not even he is damned eternally. He is given the treatment Dante reserved for intellectual cowardice in the *Divine Comedy*: neither heaven nor hell will accept him. He is hurled back into the English lakes.

> He first sank to the bottom—like his works,
> But soon rose to the surface—like himself;
> For all corrupted things are buoyed like
> corks,
> By their own rottenness. . . .
> (cv)

A reader familiar with Pope will recognize that Byron is drawing upon the earlier poet's attacks on bad, hireling poetasters in *The Art of Sinking in Poetry* and *The Dunciad*. There was, Pope claimed, a profound depth in bad writing just as there is a sublime of the good. Poets diving in mud and excrement in the Fleet ditch were his imaginative illustration of this. Southey now joins another laureate, Pope's butt Colley Cibber, as a type of bad writer. He too "sinks" but like all rotten things "soon rose to the surface." George III is in heaven; his poet laureate, on top on earth. The satiric poet recognizes that no practical effect has been achieved by his protest. Byron the satirist, like the Byronic hero, is an outsider who fails in his war with corrupt society.

DON JUAN

Byron began *Don Juan* in the summer of 1818 and continued work on it spasmodically until May 1823, when events in Greece made him lay it aside. His progress was checked by uncertainty about his purpose in the poem, the hostility with which the work was received by members of his circle—Teresa Guiccioli, Hobhouse, Moore—and the poor sales of the early cantos. For a time in 1821–1822 he abandoned the poem, which had progressed as far as canto V, but then, in the spring of 1822, he began work again in a sustained burst of creativity. Even then it is not certain in what way he intended to complete the poem, if at all.

While at work he issued several accounts of his purposes. Like the poem, they are self-contradictory. At one time he claimed, "Do you suppose that I could have any intention but to giggle and make giggle?" (letter to Murray, 12 August 1819), yet at other times he seriously defended the morality of his intention, calling the work "*a satire* on *abuses* of the present *states* of Society" (letter to Murray, 25 December 1822). Sometimes he claimed to have no plan or described the major part of the poem as merely prefatory to what he was about to write. But on another occasion he told Murray of his hero:

> I meant to take him the tour of Europe—with a proper mixture of siege—battle—and adventure—and to make him finish as *Anacharsis Cloots*—in the French revolution . . . I meant to have made him a Cavalier Servente in Italy and a cause for a divorce in England—and a Sentimental "Werther-faced man" in Germany—so as to show the different ridicules of the society in each of those countries —and to have displayed him gradually gaté and blasé as he grew older—as is natural.—But I had not quite fixed whether to make him end in Hell—or in an unhappy marriage,—not knowing which would be the severest. (16 February 1821)

This was about the time he laid the poem aside for a year, but it is not far removed in general from what he eventually accomplished. Juan travels widely; at the end a divorce seems likely; and an anarchic view of the French Revolution would provide a fitting climax to a work which so often mixes idealism and cynicism.

Although it is impossible to categorize this vast, sprawling, ragbag of a poem, some general indications may be offered. At the beginning of the fourth canto Byron wrote:

As boy, I thought myself a clever fellow,
And wished that others held the same opinion;
They took it up when my days grew more mellow,
And other minds acknowledged my dominion:
Now my sere Fancy "falls into the yellow
Leaf," and Imagination droops her pinion,

And the sad truth which hovers o'er my desk
Turns what was once romantic to burlesque.

And if I laugh at any mortal thing,
'T is that I may not weep; and if I weep,
'T is that our nature cannot always bring
Itself to apathy. . . .
(IV.iii–iv)

The poem is a form of self-confession. As in *Beppo* the digressions frequently take over the story entirely, but the character of the narrator is now more fully developed and inextricably linked with Byron the man, poet, and public myth. The poem is about looking back. The "boy" he refers to is both his youthful self and the "Childe" of *Childe Harold's Pilgrimage*; the ideas are his early romantic conceptions, which experience now turns to burlesque. That growth of experience is not represented as intellectual progress. He has changed because "imagination" has declined, and what might be good for the philosopher may be deleterious for the poet. Nor has he rejected his pose as hero of his own romances. The quotation about the sere and yellow leaf is from *Macbeth.* Byron identifies himself with a regicide and a villain who, when he contemplates life, sees it as "a tale told by an idiot . . .signifying nothing." It is Macbeth as moral philosopher rather than man of action of whom he thinks. Beneath this is a more fundamental philosophic and satiric tradition. Byron refers to himself as sometimes laughing, sometimes weeping. It is an allusion to a famous commonplace in the Roman satirist Juvenal, who linked his work to the sages Democritus and Heraclitus: the former laughed at human follies, the other wept for them. The same tradition had inspired one of Byron's favorite poems: Johnson's imitation of Juvenal, *The Vanity of Human Wishes.* These stanzas, then, explain on biographical and moral grounds the tensions in the poem between the idealistic (romantic) and the comic (burlesque), between sorrow and mirth, that everywhere inform the writing.

A few lines later he acknowledges Pulci as the father of the burlesque, which is a clear connection between the inspiration of *Don Juan* and *Beppo.* More usually in the poem Byron refers to his genre as "epic." This has often been regarded as mockery. Obviously *Don Juan* is not in the least like the *Iliad* or *Aeneid.* Yet its story line is not dissimilar to that of the *Odyssey*: after many wanderings over land and sea the poet turns to his own land in his cantos on English society, and a divorce would be a burlesque reversal of the chastity of Homer's Penelope. In addition, the open-ended form and the emphasis in the story on love and war are reminiscent, in general, of the Italian chivalric epic of the school of Ludovico Ariosto. To descend later in a developing tradition: the sharp, satiric eye that the poet shows for social manners recalls the work of Henry Fielding, who argued that generically his new form of fiction, which we now call the novel, was a "comic epic poem in prose." If one comes closer to our own age and relates *Don Juan* to James Joyce's *Ulysses,* then it is easy to see that Byron's poem is part of a continuing process of evolution by which classical epic has remained alive for the modern world.

Renaissance tradition had emphasized the encyclopedic learning and educative function of the epic. *Don Juan* preserves both of these. The poem is about a modern-style hero's education in the chivalric topics of love and war. A common man like Juan is the proper representative of our age (so Joyce chooses an Irish Jew, Leopold Bloom, as his wandering Ulysses). His unheroic role is a comment by the poet on traditional themes: the uncertain nature of fame and the unworthy subjects of human renown. Cicero's *Somnium Scipionis* ("The Dream of Scipio") or the concluding stanzas of Chaucer's *Troilus and Criseyde* are *loci classici* (classic examples) that make the same general comment on the heroic life seen in the light of eternity. The difference between Byron and these earlier writers is that they view life from a serious religious viewpoint, whereas the Byronic universe is an absurd one in which even religion is belittled. This is the tragicomedy of the position of modern man.

The encyclopedic tradition provides the basis both for the action of the poem containing so much and for the poet's commentaries upon everything. It is an idea that Byron mocks even as he uses, just as he burlesques the heroic. Homer, it was claimed, was the master of all arts and sciences, which he incorporated into the structure of his epics, vatically inspired. Our modern poet is "A wanderer from the British world of Fashion,/ Where I, like other dogs, have had my day" (II.clxvi), who has "picked up" bits of experience and knowledge of "no matter what" along the way. His usual pose is one of skepticism or ignorance, and his mind is in a state of constant mobility inspired as much by the state of his health or his bowels as by profound gazing into the heart of light; witness the modern Homer or Milton on how illness brought him to religion:

> The first attack at once proved the Divinity
> (But *that* I never doubted, nor the Devil);
> The next, the Virgin's mystical virginity,
> The third, the usual Origin of Evil;
> The fourth at once established the whole
> Trinity
> On so uncontrovertible a level,
> That I devoutly wished the three were
> four—
> On purpose to believe so much the more.
> (XI.vi)

The inspired poet of old was seen to have brought his worldwide knowledge into great structural order, uniting diversity in the heroic theme of his poem, uttering his vision in the loftiest style. Byron's poem, in contrast, is constructed on the principle of the "medley" where all kinds of his earlier poetry, including even lyric verse, are hung around the adventures of his hero with no pretense at any unity beyond that of the continuing authorial presence manipulating Juan. The style is that of the *improvvisatore*: "I rattle on exactly as I'd talk/With anybody in a ride or walk" (XV.xix), and it is this sense of easy spontaneity and flowing conversational invention that is the highest achievement of Byron's art. It is the very opposite of the great tradition of epic: "Hail, Muse! *et cetera* . . ."(III.i), and it is a deliberate attack on that now decadent tradition as a form of cant.

His burlesque mode is different from the mock-heroic intention of a writer like Pope, who also could not find a hero in the modern world. But Pope's heroes exist in the past in the great writers like Homer and Milton, and the captains, sages, and statesmen of antiquity with whom he liked to identify himself. It has frequently been said that Byron lacks these "positive" standards, and his verse wants the assurance of Pope's, which comes, partly, from these received traditions. But a poet's first moral duty is to truth; and if there is no firm assurance in anything past or present, then it is dishonest to take refuge behind an idealized antiquity or in the pretense that a true heroic style is still possible if only one chose to write it. There is nothing wanting in the confidence of craftsmanship in a stanza like this:

> What are the hopes of man? Old Egypt's
> King
> Cheops erected the first Pyramid
> And largest, thinking it was just the thing
> To keep his memory whole, and mummy
> hid;
> But somebody or other rummaging,
> Burglariously broke his coffin's lid:
> Let not a monument give you or me hopes,
> Since not a pinch of dust remains of
> Cheops.
> (I.ccxix)

These lines still have about them suggestions of public rhetoric now subverted. The poet is a figure who orates as a wise man for us and our posterity. Equally typical of the Byronic mode of *Don Juan* is this stanza from the shipwreck canto on the sinking of the cutter:

> Nine souls more went in her: the long-boat
> still
> Kept above water, with an oar for mast,
> Two blankets stitched together, answering ill
> Instead of sail, were to the oar made fast;
> Though every wave rolled menacing to fill,
> And present peril all before surpassed,
> They grieved for those who perished with
> the cutter,
> And also for the biscuit-casks and butter.
> (II.lxi)

This is quite outside the range of a mock-heroic stylist like Pope. It is verse trying to be prose, a deliberate antistyle that is evolved because it is appropriate to the nature of the subject. At one extreme historically are the great shipwrecks in Homer and Vergil, at the other the ditched aircraft of Joseph Heller's *Catch-22.* In the modern world death by drowning has lost all religious or heroic significance; it matters to no one except those who are not quite drowned yet. The extraordinary thing about such acts is that the artist, because he cannot make them tragic, turns them to comedy. The last couplet is horrible, true, and funny. It is what is now called by the cliché "black comedy."

Lines like those were one of the principal causes of the outcry against the poem. Against the criticism of Francis Cohen, Byron defended himself in the well-known letter to John Murray of 12 August 1819 on the theme of "scorching and drenching" (mixing incompatible things):

> did he [Cohen] never inject for a Gonorrhea?—or make water through an ulcerated Urethra?—was he ever in a Turkish bath—that marble paradise of sherbet and sodomy?

The stylistic twists in the poem from tragedy to comedy, from the sentimental to the vulgar, from high to low, are an assertion by the poet concerning the multiplicity of simultaneous human experience. A single stylistic decorum, such as the traditional lofty utterance of epic, falsifies. Something far more flexible is necessary to respond to the true, the experiential, nature of subjects like love and war. Once again Byron is part of a continuing process of literary evolution of old forms. One may compare Miguel de Cervantes' *Don Quixote,* which blended the sentimental and the comic, the idealistic and the vulgar, in a tale long, rambling, digressive, and irresistible. *Don Juan* is stylistically midway between a rejection of the Homeric epic and Cervantes' inception of the modern novel. When Byron wrote that his earlier cantos were merely prefatory to the story in England, he had, carelessly, hit on a central truth about his poem. His epic turns into a novel. The English cantos especially are far closer to Thackeray or Dickens than they are to eighteenth-century mock heroic, and they settle into an easy conversational style that is for long periods far more assured in tone and secure in attitude than the initial burlesque cantos:

> Thrice happy he who, after a survey
> Of the good company, can win a corner,
> A door that's *in* or boudoir *out* of the way,
> Where he may fix himself like small "Jack
> Horner,"
> And let the Babel round run as it may,
> And look on as a mourner, or a scorner,
> Or an approver, or a mere spectator,
> Yawning a little as the night grows later.
> (XI.lxix)

Unfortunately, in the years during which the poem evolved and Byron was finding this style, he was inclined to wobble like a would-be cyclist who cannot combine velocity with balance. At times he seems to be fighting a guerrilla war both with the epic and his own earlier romantic styles. He will be deliberately funny out of place. The story of the siege of Ismail, for example, is one of the most severe and graphic indictments of the true nature of war to be found in "epic" poetry, yet, notoriously, it collapses into mere vulgarity in the account of the rape that follows the capture. The idyll of Juan and Haidée shows flashes of the finest sentimental poetry conjoined with the sinister in the person of Lambro, who is a Byronic hero become real pirate. Yet for no intrinsic reason the poet will sidetrack into the jocular at the most inappropriate moments as though he does not trust his own ability to inspire pathos. These are severe faults. Yet, all the time, despite the wobbling, as the ramshackle poem evolves, unpredictably the diverse elements continually fuse creatively in new combinations. The poem is not a finalized object "out there" that we are invited to admire, but something with which the reader is involved in its endless development:

> But Adeline was not indifferent: for
> (*Now* for a common-place!) beneath the
> snow,
> As a Volcano holds the lava more
> Within—*et cetera.* Shall I go on?—No!
> I hate to hunt down a tired metaphor,
> So let the often-used Volcano go.
> Poor thing! How frequently, by me and
> others,
> It hath been stirred up till its smoke quite
> smothers!
>
> I'll have another figure in a trice:—
> What say you to a bottle of champagne?
> Frozen into a very vinous ice,
> Which leaves few drops of that immortal
> rain,
> Yet in the very centre, past all price,
> About a liquid glassful will remain;
> And this is stronger than the strongest grape
> Could e'er express in its expanded shape. . . .
> (XIII.xxxvi–xxxvii)

The poem is like the process of life itself. There is no over-all plan except catholic inclusiveness. For these reasons any illustrative quotation of a part is not true of the whole. It interrupts the flow, and when we look again, everything is different. For instance, compare in the first canto the style of Julia's letter (where she so manifestly finds pleasure as well as pathos in her own sentimental tragedy) with the comic tirade with which she greets her husband hunting for Juan in the bedroom; or, in the English cantos, compare the tone of Byron the satirist of society with the fascinated regret of the exile recording his own graphic memories of the "Paradise of Pleasure and *Ennui.*"

The great life-force of the poem remains the poet himself, and it is his life experience as man and artist, and all the mobility and richness of his temperament, that continually renews the narrative. He claims even the freedom of an old friend to bore his acquaintances with anecdote, recollection, and essay. These elements cannot be systematized into a structure of ideas. As William Parry observed in his account of Byron's *Last Days*: "His opinions were the results of his feelings" and these continually fluctuate. But through all the multiplicity of the experience of *Don Juan* three major themes might be picked out in the poet's pursuit of truth. One is the relativity of all systems and ideas and the inextricable confusion of the ideal with the physical in human behavior. The baseness of the flesh tests and devalues all abstract conceptions. Another is a burning commitment to the ideals of personal and political liberty. Inevitably this cannot be expressed as a positive system. It is the negative pathway of the man 'born for opposition" (XV.xxii). Then there is the sense of the hurry of the years that carry all men, societies, and systems away. The fullest formal expression is in the famous *Ubi sunt* stanzas beginning XI.lxxvi: " 'Where is the World' cries Young, at *eighty* . . ." and ending in the traditional advice of Epicurean philosophy to enjoy each day, for each day flies:

> But "*carpe diem,*" Juan, "*carpe, carpe*!"
> To-morrow sees another race as gay
> And transient, and devoured by the same
> harpy.
> "Life's a poor player,"—then "play out the
> play. . . ."
> (XI.lxxxvi)

The guarantee of the authenticity of these sentiments in the poem is Byron the man.

The truth of which he writes is known because he has himself experienced it. He is no better or wiser than other men, but he has lived fully and he is honest about his own life. The extraordinary culmination of Byron's poetic career is that a writer who began by posing as the fictional hero of his own improbable romances now, by process of evolution, has found the way of revealing himself as a type of Everyman through his art:

> But now at thirty years my hair is grey—
> (I wonder what it will be like at forty?
> I thought of a peruke the other day—)
> My heart is not much greener; and, in short, I
> Have squandered my whole summer while 'twas May,
> And feel no more the spirit to retort; I
> Have spent my life, both interest and principal,
> And deem not, what I deemed—my soul invincible.
>
> . . .
>
> Ambition was my idol, which was broken
> Before the shrines of Sorrow, and of Pleasure;
> And the two last have left me many a token
> O'er which reflection may be made at leisure:
> Now, like Friar Bacon's Brazen Head, I've spoken,
> "Time is, Time was, Time's past:"—a chymic treasure
> Is glittering Youth, which I have spent betimes—
> My heart in passion, and my head on rhymes.
> (I.ccxiii; ccxvii)

Selected Bibliography

BIBLIOGRAPHY

Noel, R., *The Life of Lord Byron,* (London, 1890), includes a bibliography by U. P. Anderson, containing extensive lists of magazine articles about Byron and of musical settings; E. H. Coleridge, ed. *The Works of Lord Byron. Poetry, vol. VII: A Bibliography of Successive Editions and Translations,* (London, 1904), the best general bibliography of the poems; Chew, S. C., *Byron in England,* (London, 1924), contains an extensive list of Byroniana; R. H. Griffith and H. M. Jones, eds. *A Descriptive Catalogue of . . . Manuscripts and First Editions . . . at the University of Texas,* (Austin, Tex., 1924); *Bibliographical Catalogue of the First Editions, Proof Copies and Manuscripts of Books by Lord Byron. Exhibited at the First Edition Club, January 1925,* (London, 1925); *Byron and Byroniana. A Catalogue of Books,* (1930), an important sale catalog, valuable for reference, issued by Elkin Mathews, the London booksellers; Wise, T. J., *A Bibliography of the Writings in Verse and Prose of George Gordon Noel, Baron Byron. With Letters Illustrating His Life and Work and Particularly His Attitude Towards Keats,* 2 vols. (London, 1932–1933), the standard technical bibliography, incorporates the material of the same author's *A Byron Library,* (1928), the privately printed catalog of the Byron Collection in the Ashley Library, now in the British Museum; *The Roe-Byron Collection, Newstead Abbey,* (Nottingham, 1937), the catalog of the collection at Byron's ancestral home.

COLLECTED WORKS

The Poetical Works, 2 vols. (Philadelphia, 1813), the first collected ed., followed throughout the nineteenth century by numerous other collected eds. in several vols., published in London, Paris, New York, and elsewhere; *The Works,* 4 vols. (London, 1815, new eds.: 8 vols. 1818–1820, 8 vols. 1825, 6 vols. 1831); J. Wright, ed. *The Works, with His Letters and Journals, and His Life, by Thomas Moore,* 17 vols. (London, 1832–1833); *The Poetical Works. New Edition, with the Text Carefully Revised,* 6 vols. (London, 1857); *The Poetical Works, Edited, with a Critical Memoir by W. M. Rossetti. Illustrated by Ford Madox Brown,* 8 vols. (London, 1870); *The Works. A New, Revised, and Enlarged Edition with Illustrations, Including Portraits,* 13 vols. (London, 1898–1904), comprising *Poetry,* E. H. Coleridge, ed. 7 vols. and *Letters and Journals,* R. H. Prothero, ed. 6 vols.; *The Poetical Works. The Only Complete and Copyright Text in One Volume. Edited with a Memoir, by E. H. Coleridge,* (London, 1905), the standard ed., often repr.; J. J. McGann, ed. *The Complete Poetical Works,* vol. I (Oxford, 1980), full textual apparatus and notes, will include many previously unpublished poems and fragments.

SELECTIONS

A Selection from the Work of Lord Byron, edited and prefaced by A. C. Swinburne, (London, 1866); *Poetry of Byron,* (London, 1881), chosen and arranged by M. Arnold; H. J. C. Grierson, ed. *Poems,* (London, 1923); E. Rhys, ed. *The Shorter Byron . . . ,* (London, 1927); R. A. Rice, ed. *The Best of Byron,* (New York, 1933);

L. I. Bredvold, ed. *Don Juan and Other Satiric Poems,* (New York, 1935); S. C. Chew, ed. *Childe Harold's Pilgrimage and Other Romantic Poems,* (London, 1936); J. Bennett, ed. *Satirical and Critical Poems,* (Cambridge, 1937); *Byron, Poetry and Prose,* (London, 1940), with essays by Scott, Hazlitt, Macaulay, intro. by A. Quiller-Couch, and notes by D. N. Smith; P. Quennell, ed. *Selections from Poetry, Letters and Journals,* (London, 1949); J. Barzun, ed. *The Selected Letters of Lord Byron,* (New York, 1953).

SEPARATE WORKS

Fugitive Pieces, [Newark, 1806], privately printed and anonymous; facs. repr., H. B. Forman, ed. (London, 1886); *Poems on Various Occasions,* (Newark, 1807), privately printed and anonymous; *Hours of Idleness: A Series of Poems Original and Translated,* (Newark, 1807), 2nd. ed. *Poems Original and Translated,* (Newark, 1808), contains five new pieces; *English Bards and Scotch Reviewers: A Satire,* (London, 1809), the early eds. of this poem were frequently counterfeited; *Address Written by Lord Byron. The Genuine Rejected Addresses, Presented to the Committee of Management for Drury Lane Theatre: Preceded by That Written by Lord Byron and Adopted by the Committee,* (London, 1812); *Childe Harold's Pilgrimage: A Romaunt,* 2 vols. (London, 1819, previously published cantos I and II, 1812, III, 1816, and IV, 1818); *The Curse of Minerva: A Poem,* (London, 1812); *Waltz: An Apostrophic Hymn by Horace Hornem, Esq.,* (London, 1813); *The Giaour: A Fragment of a Turkish Tale,* (London, 1813); *The Bride of Abydos: A Turkish Tale,* (London, 1813); *The Corsair: A Tale,* (London, 1814); *Ode to Napoleon Buonaparte,* (London, 1814), published anonymously; *Lara: A Tale,* (London, 1814).

Hebrew Melodies, Ancient and Modern with Appropriate Symphonies and Accompaniments, (London, 1815), also in T. L. Ashton, ed. (Austin, Tex., 1972); *The Siege of Corinth: A Poem and Parisina: A Poem,* (London, 1816), published anonymously; *Poems on His Domestic Circumstances,* (London, 1816), these two poems "Fare Thee Well" and "A Sketch from Private Life" had been privately printed and separately printed in the same year; various eds. of this collection with additional poems were published in (1816); *Poems,* (London, 1816); *The Prisoner of Chillon and Other Poems,* (London, 1816); *Monody on the Death of the Right Hon. R. B. Sheridan. Written at the Request of a Friend, to Be Spoken at Drury Lane,* (London, 1816); *The Lament of Tasso,* (London, 1817); *Manfred: A Dramatic Poem,* (London, 1817); *Beppo: A Venetian Story,* (London, 1818, published anonymously; 4th ed., with additional stanzas, London, 1818); *Mazeppa: A Poem,* (London, 1819).

Don Juan, cantos I-II (1819), III-V (1821), VI-VIII (1823), IX-XI (1823), XII-XIV (1823), XV-XVI (1824), originally published anonymously; first collected ed., 2 vols. (Edinburgh, 1825), the fullest ed. is that of T. G. Steffan and W. W. Pratt, 4 vols. (Austin, Tex., 1957), and vol. I contains a detailed study of the composition of the poem; *Marino Faliero, Doge of Venice: An Historical Tragedy and The Prophecy of Dante: A Poem,* (London, 1821); *Sardanapalus: A Tragedy, The Two Foscari: A Tragedy,* and *Cain: A Mystery,* (London, 1821), also in T. G. Steffan, ed. (Austin, Tex., 1968); *The Vision of Judgment,* (London, 1822), a product of Byron's feud with Southey, first printed in the *Liberal,* (1822), an ephemeral paper promoted by Byron and Leigh Hunt, and published as *The Two Visions* with Southey's "Vision of Judgement" in the same year; *Heaven and Earth: A Mystery,* (London, 1823), published anonymously, first printed in the *Liberal,* (1823); *The Age of Bronze: Or, Carmen Seculare et Annus Haud Mirabilis,* (London, 1823), published anonymously; *The Island: Or, Christian and His Comrades,* (London, 1823); *Werner: A Tragedy,* (London, 1823); *The Parliamentary Speeches of Lord Byron. Printed from the Copies Prepared by His Lordship for Publication,* (London, 1824); *The Deformed Transformed: A Drama,* (London, 1824).

DIARIES AND LETTERS

Letter to [John Murray] on the Rev. W. L. Bowles' Strictures on the Life and Writings of Pope, (London, 1821); A. R. C. Dallas, ed. *Correspondence of Lord Byron with a Friend, Including His Letters to His Mother in 1809–11,* 3 vols. (Paris, 1825); *Letters and Journals of Lord Byron, with Notices of His Life, by T. Moore,* 2 vols. (London, 1830, rev. ed. 1875); R. E. Prothero, ed. *Letters and Journals,* 6 vols. (London, 1898–1904); Carlton, W. N. C., *Poems and Letters, Edited from the Original Manuscripts in the Possession of W. K. Bixby,* (Chicago, 1912), privately printed; J. Murray, ed. *Lord Byron's Correspondence, Chiefly with Lady Melbourne, Mr. Hobhouse, the Hon. Douglas Kinnaird, and P. B. Shelley,* 2 vols. (London, 1922); *The Ravenna Journal, Mainly Compiled at Ravenna in 1821, with an Introduction by Lord Ernle,* [Prothero, R. E.], London (1928), printed for the members of the First Edition Club; P. Quennell, ed. *Byron Letters and Diaries: A Self Portrait,* 2 vols. (London, 1950); E. J. Lovell, ed. *Byron: His Very Self and Voice: Collected Conversations of Lord Byron,* (London, 1954); L. A. Marchand, ed. *Byron's Letters and Journals,* (London-Cambridge, Mass., 1973), the definitive ed.

BIOGRAPHICAL AND CRITICAL STUDIES

Hobhouse, J. C., *A Journey Through Albania and Other Provinces of Turkey,* (London, 1813); Shelley, P. B., *History of a Six Weeks' Tour,* (London, 1817); Watkins, J., *Memoirs of the Life and Writings of the Rt.*

Hon. Lord Byron, with Anecdotes of Some of His Contemporaries, (London, 1822); Medwin, T., *Journal of the Conversations of Lord Byron: Noted During a Residence with His Lordship at Pisa, in the Years 1821 and 1822,* (London, 1824), also in E. J. Lovell, ed. (Princeton, N.J., 1966); Murray, J., *Notes on Captain Medwin's Conversations of Lord Byron,* (London, 1824), privately printed, and repr. in *Works,* (1898–1904); Dallas, R. C., *Recollections of the Life of Lord Byron, from the Year 1808 to the End of 1814,* (London, 1824); Hazlitt, W., *The Spirit of the Age,* (London, 1825), contains an essay on Byron; Gamba, P., *A Narrative of Lord Byron's Last Journey to Greece,* (London, 1825); Kilgour, A., *Anecdotes of Lord Byron from Authentic Sources,* (London, 1825); Parry, W., *The Last Days of Lord Byron: With His Lordship's Opinions on Various Subjects, Particularly on the State and Prospects of Greece,* (London, 1825); E. Blaquière, ed. *Narrative of a Second Visit to Greece, Including Facts Connected with the Last Days of Lord Byron, Extracts from Correspondence, Official Documents, etc.* (London, 1825); *The Life, Writings, Opinions and Times of the Rt. Hon. George Gordon Noel Byron, Lord Byron, by an English Gentleman in the Greek Military Service, and Comrade of His Lordship. Compiled from Authentic Documents and from Long Personal Acquaintance,* 3 vols. (London, 1825), ascribed to the publisher, Matthew Iley; Hunt, L., *Lord Byron and Some of His Contemporaries,* (London, 1828).

Galt, J., *The Life of Lord Byron,* (London, 1830); Kennedy, J., *Conversations on Religion with Lord Byron and Others,* (London, 1830); Millingen, J., *Memoirs of the Affairs of Greece, with Various Anecdotes Relating to Lord Byron, and an Account of His Last Illness and Death,* (London, 1831); Gardiner, M., *Conversations of Lord Byron with the Countess of Blessington,* (London, 1834), also in E. J. Lovell, ed. (Princeton, N.J., 1969); Macaulay, T. B., *Critical and Historic Essays,* (London, 1842), includes a review of *Letters and Journals of Lord Byron; with Notices of His Life by T. Moore,* (1830); Hazlitt, W., *Lectures on the English Poets,* (London, 1858); Trelawny, E. J., *Recollections of the Last Days of Shelley and Byron,* (London, 1858), repr. E. Dowden, ed. (1906), see also the same author's *Records of Shelley, Byron, and the Author,* 2 vols. (London, 1878, new eds. 1887, 1905) in D. Wright, ed. (Harmondsworth, 1973), the Penguin English Library; Guiccioli, T., *Lord Byron jugé par les témoins de sa vie,* 2 vols. (Paris, 1868), also in English trans. (London, 1869); Leigh, E. M., *Medora Leigh: A History and an Autobiography,* C. Mackay, ed. (London, 1869); Hobhouse, J. C., *A Contemporary Account of the Separation of Lord and Lady Byron: Also of the Destruction of Lord Byron's Memoirs,* (London, 1870), privately printed, repr. in Hobhouse's *Recollections of a Long Life,* see below; Nichol, J., *Byron,* (London, 1880), in the English Men of Letters series; Jeafreson, J. C., *The Real Lord Byron: New Views of the Poet's Life,* 2 vols. (London, 1883); Smith, W. G., *Byron Re-Studied in His Dramas. An Essay,* (London, 1886); Arnold, M., "Byron," *Essays in Criticism,* 2nd ser. (London, 1888); Noel, R., *The Life of Lord Byron,* (London, 1890); Graham, W., *Last Links with Byron, Shelley and Keats,* (London, 1898).

Journal of Edward Ellerker Williams, Companion of Shelley and Byron in 1821 and 1822. With an Introduction by R. Garnett, (London, 1902); Millbanke, R., *Astarte: A Fragment of Truth Concerning Lord Byron,* (London, 1905, privately printed, enl. ed., London, 1921); Murray, J., *Lord Byron and His Detractors: Astarte. Lord Byron and Lord Lovelace,* (London, 1906) and Prothero, R. E., *Lord Lovelace on the Separation of Lord and Lady Byron,* (London, 1906), both privately printed for members of the Roxburghe Club; Edgcumbe, R. J. F., *Byron: The Last Phase,* (London, 1909); Hobhouse, J. C., *Recollections of a Long Life,* 6 vols. (London, 1909–1911); Rossetti, W. M., *The Diary of Dr. John William Polidori, Relating to Byron . . . ,* (London, 1911); Fuess, C. M., *Lord Byron as a Satirist in Verse,* (London, 1912); Mayne, E. C., *Byron,* 2 vols. (London, 1912, new ed. 1924), see also the same author's *The Life and Letters of Lady Noel Byron,* (London, 1929); Fletcher, W., *Lord Byron's Illness and Death as Described in a Letter to the Hon. Augusta Leigh, Dated from Missolonghi April 20, 1824,* (Nottingham, 1920), privately printed; Trelawny, E. J., *The Relations of Lord Byron and Augusta Leigh. With a Comparison of the Characters of Byron and Shelley,* (London, 1920), privately printed; Chew, S.C., *Byron in England: His Fame and After Fame,* (London, 1924); Nicholson, H., *Byron: The Last Journey, April 1823–April 1824,* (London, 1924, new ed. 1948); Symon, J. D., *Byron in Perspective,* (London, 1924); W. A. Briscoe, ed. *Byron, the Poet. A Centenary Volume,* (London, 1924), contains essays by Haldane, Grierson, and others; Grierson, H. J. C., *The Background of English Literature,* (London, 1925), contains "Byron and English Society"; Praz, M., *La fortuna di Byron in Inghilterra,* (Florence, 1925), see also *The Romantic Agony,* A. Davidson, trans. (London, 1933); Gordon, A. C., *Allegra: The Story of Byron and Miss Clairmont,* (New York, 1926); Railo, E., *The Haunted Castle,* (London, 1927); Du Bos, C., *Byron et le besoin de la fatalité,* (Paris, 1929), English trans. by E. Colburn Mayne, (London, 1932); Richter, H., *Lord Byron: Persönlichkeit und Werk,* (Halle, 1929).

Maurois, A., *Byron,* 2 vols. (Paris, 1930), English trans. by H. Miles (London, 1930); Quennell, P., *Byron: The Years of Fame,* (London, 1935); Origo, I., *Allegra,* (London, 1935); Calvert, W. J., *Byron: Romantic Paradox,* (London, 1935); Leavis, F. R., *Revaluation,* (London, 1936), contains his influential essay "Byron's Satire"; B. Dobrée ed., *From Anne to Victoria,* (London, 1937), contains "Byron," by Eliot, T. S., repr. in *On Poetry and Poets,* (London, 1957); Marjarum, E. W., *Byron as Skeptic and Believer,* (Princeton, 1938); Paston, G. and Quennell, P., *To Lord Byron: Feminine Profiles, Based upon Unpublished Letters 1807–1824,* (London, 1939); H. Davies, W. C. de Vane, and R. C. Bald, eds. "Byron and the East: Literary Sources of the Turkish Tales," *Nineteenth Century Studies,* (London, 1940); Quennell, P., *Byron in Italy,* (London, 1941); Boyd, E. F., *Byron's Don Juan,* (London, 1945); Borst, W. A., *Lord Byron's First Pilgrimage,* (New Haven, Conn., 1948); Lovell, E. J., *Byron: The Record of a Quest,* (Austin, Tex., 1949); Origo, I., *The Last Attachment. The Story of Byron and Teresa Guiccioli,* (London, 1949); Butler, E. M., *Goethe and Byron,* (London, 1951); Read, H., *The True Voice of Feeling,* (London, 1951), contains an essay on Byron; Knight, G. W., *Lord Byron, Christian Virtues,* (London, 1952); Spencer, T., *Fair Greece, Sad Relic: Literary Philhellenism from Shakespeare to Byron,* (London, 1954); E. J. Lovell, ed. *His Very Self and Voice: Collected Conversations of Lord Byron,* (New York, 1954); Butler, E. M., *Byron and Goethe,* (London, 1956); Escarpit, R., *Lord Byron, un temperament littéraire,* 2 vols. (Paris, 1956–1957); B. Ford, ed. *The Pelican Guide to English Literature,* vol. V, (London, 1957), contains "Lord Byron," by Jump, J. D.; Knight, G. W., *Lord Byron's Marriage,* (London, 1957); C. D. Thorpe, ed. *Major English Romantic Poets,* (London, 1957), includes "Irony and Image in Byron's Don Juan"; Marchand, L. A., *Byron,* 3 vols. (London, 1957), the standard biography; Weinstein, L., *The Metomorphoses of Don Juan,* (London, 1959); Eliot, T. S., *On Poetry and Poets,* (London, 1957), contains an essay on Byron, first published in 1937.

West, P., *Byron and the Spoiler's Art,* (London, 1960); Ridenour, G. M., *The Style of Don Juan, Yale Studies in English,* vol. 144 (New Haven, Conn., 1960); Moore, D. L., *The Late Lord Byron,* (London, 1961); Rutherford, A., *Byron,* (London, 1961); Blackstone, B., *The Lost Travellers,* (London, 1962), contains a ch. expanded from "Guilt and Retribution in Byron's Sea Poems," in *Review of English Literature* 2, (January 1961); Elwin, M., *Lord Byron's Wife,* (London, 1962); Thorslev, P. L., Jr., *The Byronic Hero: Types and Prototypes,* (Minneapolis, 1962); Marshall, W. H., *The Structure of Byron's Major Poems,* (Philadelphia, 1962); P. West, ed. *Byron: A Collection of Critical Essays,* (Englewood Cliffs, N.J., 1963); Joseph, M. K., *Byron the Poet,* (London, 1964); Marchand, L. A., *Byron's Poetry,* (London, 1965); Knight, G. W., *Byron and Shakespeare,* (London, 1966); Robson, W. W., "Byron as Poet," *Critical Essays,* (London, 1966); McGann, J. J., *Fiery Dust: Byron's Poetic Development,* (Chicago, 1968); M. K. Stocking, ed. *The Journals of Claire Clairmont,* (Cambridge, Mass., 1969); Gleckner, R. F., *Byron and the Ruins of Paradise,* (Baltimore, 1967); E. Bostetter, ed. *Twentieth Century Interpretations of Don Juan,* (Englewood Cliffs, N.J., 1969); Cooke, M. G., *The Blind Man Traces the Circle,* (Princeton, N.J., 1969); A. Rutherford, ed. *Byron. The Critical Heritage,* (London, 1970); Jump, J. D., *Byron,* (London, 1972); *The Byron Journal,* (1973–); Moore, D. L., *Lord Byron Accounts Rendered,* (London, 1974); Blackstone, B., *Byron. A Survey,* (London, 1975); J. D. Jump, ed. *Byron. A Symposium,* (London, 1975); McGann, J. J., *Don Juan in Context,* (London, 1976); Robinson, C. E., *Shelley and Byron,* (Baltimore, 1976).

THE CAVALIER POETS

ROBIN SKELTON

INTRODUCTION

THE LYRICAL POET in the reign of Elizabeth I was not very much concerned with actuality. His job was to make delightful verbal patterns filled with ideal sentiments, and, very frequently, addressed to some impossibly chaste and beautiful lady. She, turning a deaf ear to all his protestations, could be relied upon to accept some suitable gift from time to time, or to rouse him to ecstasies of happiness by a word of encouragement, or plunge him into despair with a frown. Of course this caricature is hardly fair; the better poets saw that there was more in lyrical poetry than this. Shakespeare rebelled in one sonnet to the extent of admitting that "My Mistress's eyes are nothing like the sun," and even Sir Philip Sidney went so far as to end one mellifluous complaint with an accusation of ingratitude. Sir Walter Raleigh, Ben Jonson, and others, too, made vital poetry from the Petrarchan convention, and managed to give their readers an impression that something of real importance was going on. Nevertheless, even their poetry often had an air of existing largely because they enjoyed being ingenious in compliment, witty in description, and musical in speech.

There can be no objection to this. It is a poor heart that never rejoiceth, and it would be stupidly puritanical to object to a poem because it was beautiful and ingenious but little else. Still, once the poetry of an age becomes simply an exercise in the purely decorative use of language, trouble is bound to occur. Someone is going to try to go further.

John Donne was not alone in trying to make lyrical poetry have a more direct impact, but he was the most successful of the rebels. He could rebel because he, unlike many of the previous generation, did not think of lyrical poetry as being either in a formal Petrarchan sonnet tradition, or as being accompanied by music. Donne was philosophical, but it isn't his introduction of rugged thinking into the lyrical tradition that must delay us now so much as his introduction of a new tone of voice. He threw aside the implication of "high poetic style" that a poet is a special kind of person with a special vocabulary and sensitivity, and wrote with colloquial directness. By so doing he gave his lyrics a highly personal tone; you could feel that it was not the representative of an aesthetic master race but a quite ordinary, though obviously intelligent, man who cried "For God's sake hold your tongue, and let me love," or who said, simply and directly, "Sweetest love I do not go, For weariness of thee." It could be said now that the poem became moving and pleasing largely because of the reader's or hearer's sense of an individual personality behind it.

This personality was, in Donne's case and in the case of George Herbert, Henry Vaughan, Henry King, and the other metaphysicals, just as ingenious as the more corporate personality of the contributors to the Elizabethan song books, but it was ingenious with a difference. Instead of feeling that the surprising comparisons and the bizarre metaphors are purely decorative, we feel that they have arisen naturally from the pressure of the poet's passionate intelligence. Obsessed with his situation, his ideas become as powerful and disturbed as his feelings; the passionate heart and the formidable intelligence cannot be divorced from one another. We hear, indeed, the accents of the complete man, concerned to explore, by way of his poetry, all that most interests and disturbs him. When Herbert writes of a "rope of sands" we know that this perception is at the heart of him. When Donne writes:

> Only our love hath no decay:
> This no to-morrow hath nor yesterday;
> Running, it never runs from us away,
> But truly keeps his first, last, everlasting
> day,

we feel that the riddling complexity is born of intense personal feeling.

It is a far cry from the exquisite prosody of Thomas Campion, the elegance of Sidney, or even that of Jonson, who, though tolerably ingenious at times and even crudely forthright, so often gives us the impression that his lyrics are a leisure activity, like writing letters or taking a sketch pad out on Sundays. Indeed, Jonson has several verse letters to his friends which have just that air of happy improvisation and enjoyment of ingenuity which one might expect. Donne wrote verse letters too, and many of his poems also seem casual products, but he can never avoid a passionate statement. Every conversation is a manifesto with Donne, even if it is one about the general advantages of having more than one mistress. There is none of that affectionate ease of speech, that elegance, of which Jonson is a master.

Though the cavalier poets only occasionally imitated the strenuous intellectual conceits of Donne and his followers, and were fervent admirers of Jonson's elegance, they took care to learn from both parties. In fact, reading the work of Thomas Carew, Sir John Suckling, Richard Lovelace, Lord Herbert of Cherbury (elder brother of George), Aurelian Townsend, William Cartwright, Thomas Randolph, William Habington, Sir Richard Fanshawe, Edmund Waller, and the marquess of Montrose, it is easy to see that they each owe something to both styles. The common factor that binds the cavaliers together is their use of direct and colloquial language, expressive of a highly individual personality, and their enjoyment of the casual, the amateur, the affectionate poem written by the way. They are cavalier in the sense not only of being royalists (though Waller changed sides twice) but in the sense that they distrust the overearnest, the too intense. They accept the ideal of the Renaissance gentleman, who is at once lover, soldier, wit, man of affairs, musician, and poet, but abandon the notion of his also being a pattern of Christian chivalry. They avoid the subject of religion, apart from making one or two graceful speeches. They attempt no plumbing of the depths of the soul. They treat life cavalierly, indeed, and sometimes they treat poetic conventions cavalierly too. For them life is far too enjoyable for much of it to be spent sweating over verse in a study. Their poems must be written in the intervals of living, and are celebratory of things that are much livelier than mere philosophy or art. A mistress is no longer an impossibly chaste goddess to be wooed with sighs, but a woman who may be spoken to in a forthright fashion. Though the poems written to her may be more important to the writer than she is herself, there is no pretense that this is not the case. Poetry need not be a matter of earnest emotion or public concern. Dick might like to have a ballad, so Dick gets one. Lady X gave an admirable party, and so here is a thank-you poem. On the other hand, a wedding or a funeral deserves a line or two. And why not upbraid a girl for her coldness or point out to a young man that the world won't end simply because he has been jilted?

It may all sound rather trivial, and much of it no doubt is; but the cavaliers made one great contribution to the English lyrical tradition. They showed us that it was possible for poetry to celebrate the minor pleasures and sadnesses of life in such a way as to impress us with a sense of ordinary day-to-day humanity, busy about its affairs, and, on the whole, enjoying them very much.

THOMAS CAREW
(*ca.* 1595–1639)

Thomas Carew was the son of Sir Matthew Carew. He was educated at Merton College, Oxford, and received his bachelor of arts in 1611. For about a year he studied law in the Middle Temple, and from 1613 to 1615 he acted as secretary to Sir Dudley Carleton, the ambassador to Italy. Carew was a favorite of Charles I and was notorious for his dissipation. His masque, *Coelum Britannicum,* was performed in the banquet hall at Whitehall in February 1634. He died in 1639.

Carew's life is not untypical of the cavaliers. He was a courtier, a wit, a rake, in casual employment as an aide to traveling diplomats. His masque, *Coelum Britannicum,* appeared in 1634, but otherwise only ten of his poems reached print during his lifetime, and all were commendatory verses attached to someone else's book. This is not an infrequent situation in the seventeenth century, but it indicates that the poet could not be very much concerned with the public value or reception of his works. Manuscripts were, of course, circulated; the poet's friends and patrons read them and commented upon them; reputations were made in the small literary and court circles, where verses were always a social asset, indicating that the man concerned had a certain intelligence, education, and wit. Carew was very highly valued. His wit was loved by Aurelian Townsend and by Thomas Randolph; Lord Herbert called him "that excellent wit," and "my witty Carew"; Sir William Davenant concurred, finding his verses "smooth." Others wagged a minatory finger at his loose living, but did not fail to admit his excellence as a lyricist.

Carew himself was clearly aware of his own poetic character. Suckling tells us that he wrote with great care, and, indeed, with some pain. Carew reveals his interest in his craft in his "Elegie upon the Death of . . . Dr. John Donne," in which he praised his "deepe knowledge of dark truth," his "Giant phansie," and "imperious wit," and said:

> Thou hast redeem'd and open'd Us a Mine
> Of rich and pregnant phansie, drawne a line
> Of masculine expression. . . .

One can see traces of Donne in his poems. The elaborate conceits are now a mere decorative grace rather than a passionate thought. Nevertheless the masculine note is striking. Where earlier poets implied an abandonment to sensual pleasure that was almost entirely passive—the receiving of a divine sanction and an overwhelming sacrament—Carew describes sexual "rapture" in active and impulsive terms. He does not adopt the rough accents of the young Donne, however, but the classical vocabulary of the learned Jonson, for Jonson, whose "terser Poems" he admires, is another of his masters.

> I will enjoy thee now my *Celia,* come
> And flye with me to Loves Elizium:
> That Gyant, Honour, that keepes cowards
> out,
> Is but a Masquer.
> ("A Rapture")

The ensuing lines with their high spirits and witty use of sexual imagery retain the masculine fervor, without losing the fanciful dexterity. The consequence is that we feel Carew is greatly enjoying his poem and kicking over the moral traces; but we are not convinced that a real Celia is in question. Such poems are exercises in wit, which contrive, if not to sound sincere as expressions of emotion, to amuse us as accurate portrayals of masculine sexuality. They are vigorous, sensual, witty, and objective. There is a sharp eye glinting from the carnival mask.

It is this sense of controlled and contrived passion which gives the poems their urbanity and poise. Indeed, passion is always to be suspected as a disguise for the less high-flown, but more intelligible, emotion of lust; the passionate statement is a lure or an amusement; affection is a more serious, because more balanced, emotion. Friendship and hospitality are as important to Carew as to Jonson, and the younger poet's "To Saxham" celebrates the "inward happiness" of the country house, with its good cheer and simplicity, with as sure a touch as his elder's "To Penshurst." The most important things in life are not hectic or hysterical, but based firmly upon old and well-tried values. It is not really as odd as one might at first suppose that Carew should write metrical versions of the psalms as well as amusing and wanton songs: the divine and the secular moods have each their place. There is no place, however, for pretentious affectation, and thus, when Carew imitates the pastoral eclogue, writes a complaint to his mistress for denying him her favors, or enjoys himself with a hyperbolic compliment, absurdity is never far away.

In "The Complement" he piles epithet upon epithet, each one more inventive than the last, in an effort to describe the beauty of his mistress, and then, just as we are beginning to believe that such a creature could hardly be expected to love in any earthly fashion, he introduces a sly double-entendre, an admission that all his words have only one purpose. The high rhetoric crumples. It is as much as to say "Fine words butter no parsnips; let us admit that a good deal of this is simply an elaborate disguise for a simple lust." Yet the poem ends with a curiously tender verse—a compound of conventional compliment, admitted as simply a tactic in the sex conflict, and an honest indication of affectionate admiration. The catalog of his mistress' attractions has become perfunctory and reveals itself as simply a device toward an end, but the dropping of the mask also gives us a hint of the real and tender smile behind the painted and professionally seductive one.

I love not for those eyes, nor haire,
Nor cheekes, nor lips, nor teeth so rare;
Nor for thy speech, thy necke, nor breast,
Nor for thy belly, nor the rest:
Nor for thy hand, nor foote so small,
But wouldst thou know (deere sweet) for all.

The last line, the culmination of so many verses, places the reader at last in a real human relationship. The poet has been teasing her, and now the joke is done.

This is an instance of the true cavalier tone—the careless ease, the humor, the subtle inflections of the voice. Carew is a master in this manner. "Epitaph on the Lady Mary Villers" makes use again of the revelatory last line. Here, after a series of conventional, though delicately balanced lines, in which direct address to the reader gives an effect of the poet's friendly intimacy, the final statement has an ambiguous ring:

The Lady *Mary Villers* lyes
Under this stone; with weeping eyes
The Parents that first gave her birth,
And their sad Friends, lay'd her in earth:
If any of them (Reader) were
Knowne unto thee, shed a teare,
Or if thyselfe possesse a gemme,
As deare to thee, as this to them,
Though a stranger to this place,
Bewayle in theirs, thine owne hard case;
For thou perhaps at thy returne
Mayest find thy Darling in an Urne.

The intimacy is broken. The wry humor is too obvious for the mask of pretended concern to conceal it. The friend that buttonholed you at the graveside is a damned odd fellow, insolent almost, if one could put one's finger on it.

Sometimes one can identify the insolence as a deliberate breaking of the rules of nice conduct, a controlled unexpectedness, which alters the mood of the poem completely. More frequently, however, it appears only as a part of Carew's general presentation of casual wit. In "Good Counsel to a Young Maid" two adjacent verses read:

Love, that in those smooth streames lyes,
Under pitties faire disguise,
Will thy melting heart surprize.

Netts, of passions finest thred,
Snaring Poems, will be spred,
All, to catch thy maiden-head.

This element of unexpectedness is, of course, a powerful aid to the giving of an impression of spontaneity; the surprise remark has the air of having just occurred to the mind of the speaker while he was in full flow. Nevertheless, few if any of Carew's poems lack an air of delighted contrivance which, at first sight, might seem to rule out any impression of spontaneity. We must distinguish, perhaps, between the artless spontaneity of the emotional, outpouring, overflowing heart and the sudden lucky "inspiration" of the quick intelligence. The romantics, generally speaking, aimed at moving us with the former; the cavaliers entertain us with the latter. Thus, while we accept the literary flavor and the self-conscious and self-mocking wit as evidence of a witty personality engaged in contriving something for his own (and incidentally our) entertainment, we also accept, in the same breath, the colloquial directness, the casual parentheses, and the sudden alterations of tone, as evidence that this adroit person is, after all, a man among men and inclined to be properly suspicious of too much formal attitudinizing. Sometimes he lets a careless arrogance, a take-it-or-leave-it attitude, appear just when we are expecting some sample of high seriousness. In other words, we are presented with an interesting, complex character and with a sense of insecurity.

Carew does his best to make us feel insecure. "To A. L." is a flawless specimen of aesthetic skating on thin ice. The poem's job is the traditional one of persuasion to love. We can expect the usual arguments derived from nature and classical mythology in favor of fruition. We can also expect from Carew a touch of impudence, possibly even a risqué joke or two. In fact we get a poem written in firm, colloquial octosyllabic couplets that begins with a direct and racy appeal to reason and self-interest.

Thinke not cause men flatt'ring say,
Y'are fresh as Aprill, sweet as May,
Bright as is the morning starre,
That you are so, or though you are
Be not therefore proud, and deeme
All men unworthy your esteeme.
For being so, you loose the pleasure
Of being faire. . . .
("To A. L.")

The raciness and directness, however, do not increase as the poem gathers momentum. The illustrations of the argument are formal devices, and their conventional status is clearly admitted by the use of words that remind us of the no-nonsense beginning of the poem. For example:

For that lovely face will faile,
Beautie's sweet, but beautie's fraile;
'Tis sooner past, 'tis sooner done
Than Summers raine, or winters Sun:
Most fleeting when it is most deare,
'Tis gone while wee but say 'tis here.
These curious locks so aptly twined,
Whose every haire a soule doth bind,
Will change their abroun hue, and grow
White, and cold, as winters snow.
That eye which now is *Cupids* nest
Will proue his grave, and all the rest
Will follow; in the cheeke, chin, nose
Nor lilly shall be found nor rose.

Here the commonplace "cheeke, chin, nose" not only contrast with the "curious locks," and "lilly" and the "rose," in order to emphasize the idea of the fading of the poetically beautiful young lady into the plain woman, but also indicate the shrewd, matter-of-fact observation that lies behind the strategic verbal gestures. One might say, indeed, that Carew is the poet of normality. He suspects the overelaborate and the exaggerated expression of emotion as being no more than a game on the part of the speaker. Admittedly, he himself could play the game, and play it well, but hardly ever without an ironic half-smile, a quiet glee. He presents his sense of values to us clearly enough in "Disdaine Returned":

Hee that loves a Rosie cheeke,
Or a corall lip admires,
Or from star-like eyes doth seeke
Fuell to maintaine his fires;
As old *Time* makes these decay,
So his flames must waste away.

But a smooth and stedfast mind,
Gentle thoughts, and calme desires,
Hearts, with equall love combind,
Kindle never dying fires.
Where these are not, I despise
Lovely cheekes, or lips, or eyes.

Behind the mockery, the gaiety, the enjoyment of ingenious description, the erotic trivialities, and the light, casual songs lies the firm belief in honesty, sympathy, steadfastness, and affection. This is the driving force behind the delicate description of spring, at once elaborate and tender.

Now that the winter's gone, the earth hath lost
Her snow-white robes, and now no more the frost
Candies the grasse, or castes an ycie creame
Upon the silver Lake or Chrystall streame:
But the warm Sunne thawes the benummed Earth,
And makes it tender, gives a sacred birth
To the dead Swallow; wakes in hollow tree
The drowzie Cuckow, and the Humble-Bee.
. . .
("The Spring")

The speaker of these lines may not be possessed by any great imaginative vision, but he is simply and movingly affected by natural beauty. Such a man will never really lose his emotional balance; he may pretend passion in order to tease or amuse, or to gain his masculine ends, but he is perfectly prepared to admit and ridicule his own duplicity. If he ever loses his temperate voice, it will be because he is angry and, probably, because his normal male vanity has been disturbed.

When thou, poore excommunicate
From all the joyes of love, shalt see
The full reward, and glorious fate,
Which my strong faith shall purchase me,
Then curse thine owne inconstancie.

A fayrer hand than thine, shall cure
That heart, which thy false oathes did wound;
And to my soule, a soule more pure
Than thine, shall by Loves hand be bound,
And both with eguall glory crown'd.

Then shalt thou weepe, entreat, complaine
To Love, as I did once to thee;
When all thy teares shall be as vaine
As mine were then, for thou shalt bee
Damn'd for thy false Apostasie.
("To My Inconstant Mistris")

It is not a cry de profundis. It is not even very original, for it reminds us immediately of Donne's "The Curse." It has, however, the immense virtue of vitality and ease, and in these cavalier lines we can easily perceive the presence of a man feeling as most men feel at one time or another, and putting it down in language most men will accept. The perception is not an extraordinary one, but it is absolutely faithful to the psychology of the male animal. It is this fidelity to the emotional and intellectual perceptions of ordinary masculinity which makes Carew so rewarding a writer. Unlike so many of our greater poets he is no more, and no less, than a man.

SIR JOHN SUCKLING
(1609–1642)

Sir John Suckling was born at Whitton, in Twickenham, Middlesex. He attended Trinity College, Cambridge, but did not take a degree. As a young man, he traveled on the Continent and fought in the Thirty Years' War under Gustavus II. Upon his return to England in 1632, he joined the court, where he became known as a wit and a rake. He took part in the expedition against Scotland in 1639. In 1641 he played a part in the conspiracy to free the earl of Strafford, but fled to France when the plot was discovered. He died in Paris in 1642.

Sir John Suckling was, like his friend Carew, very much a man about town. A royalist, a rake, a part-time soldier more attracted, John Aubrey suggests, by the panoply of war than by any love of action, he treated literature lightly. His plays, *Aglaura, The Goblins, The Tragedy of Brennoralt,* and *The Sad One* (unfinished), are carelessly put together and slackly written. The characters are stock puppets from the playbox of the period, and only occasionally does a passage of blank verse or, more frequently, a passage of prose surprise us with its vigor, if not with its sense. The language is at once pedestrian and pretentious, as if the intention to write a play had arisen from motives other than those of creative excitement and had been carried out simply as an exercise in the fashionable arts.

It is this quality of careless pastiche which spoils a great deal of Suckling's writings. He has not the ability of Carew to imitate an accepted manner or form in such a way as to present an ironic comment upon it, and so extend its range. The self-consciousness is that of the lazily ingenious amateur rather than that of the professional who is aware of the tricks of the trade.

It is, however, the amateur's zest that accounts for Suckling's successes. There is a wholehearted vigor of movement in those of his lyrics that are not crippled by any pretense of literary style. He is able to throw aside all decorum and achieve a bold and direct colloquialism, both cruder and more jovial than that of Carew.

Why so pale and wan, fond lover?
Prithee, why so pale?
Will, when looking well can't move her,
Looking ill prevail?
Prithee, why so pale?

Why so dull and mute, young sinner?
Prithee, why so mute?
Will, when speaking well can't win her,
Saying nothing do't?
Prithee, why so mute?

Quit, quit, for shame, this will not move:
This cannot take her.
If of herself she will not love,
Nothing can make her:
The devil take her!
(Song from Act IV of *Aglaura*)

This song is even more in opposition to the Petrarchan attitude than are the songs of Donne, for the language is that of the street, not the study. The affair does not even, it appears, merit that passionate thinking which derives from intensity of feeling. It has a backslapping heartiness, a brusque common sense.

Donne is, however, one of Suckling's masters, and echoes of his work appear frequently. Sometimes the whole method of the poem derives from Donne in its ingenious working out of an extended metaphor.

'Tis now, since I sat down before
That foolish fort, a heart,
(Time strangely spent), a year and more,
And still I did my part,

Made my approaches, from her hand
Unto her lip did rise,
And did already understand
The language of her eyes;

Proceeded on with no less art—
My tongue was engineer:
I thought to undermine the heart
By whispering in the ear.

When this did nothing, I brought down
Great cannon-oaths, and shot
A thousand thousand to the town;
And still it yielded not. . . .

The poem goes on to describe the siege, but as we read it we feel that the speaker is far more interested in his own wit than in anything else. This wit, however, does little to engage our emotions; the deliberately contrived imagery does not imply either a passionately ironic detachment from a deeply felt experience of bodily attraction, or an intelligence wrought to a new intensity and complexity by the operations of emotion. It is a game. Nevertheless, the siege called off, and the retreat begun, the speaker appears to be forced by a momentary burst of feeling into a savage directness of expression.

To such a place our camp remove,
As will no siege abide:
I hate a fool that starves her love
Only to feed her pride.
[Love's Siege]

This epigrammatic element takes the place of the metaphysical conceit in the poems of several of the cavaliers, in that it is a sudden passionate perception, in terms of the intelligence, of an emotional attitude or truth. It is, usually, however, the climax of the poem, and stands almost apart from it, being the resolution of the problem, rather than its motive center.

Suckling's poems often end with a pseudodidactic moral statement:

Spare diet is the cause love lasts;
For surfeits sooner kill than fasts,

ends the poem "Against Absence."

They who know all the wealth they have,
are poor,
He's only rich that cannot tell his store

sums up the argument of "Against Fruition."

As good stuff under flannel lies, as under
silken clothes

is the conclusion of "Love and Debt Alike Troublesome."

This last-named poem, with its jocose and swinging meter, reveals clearly where Suckling's strength lies:

This one request I make to him that sits the
clouds above,
That I were freely out of debt, as I am out of
love.
Then for to dance, to drink and sing, I
should be very willing,
I should not owe one lass a kiss, nor ne'er a
knave a shilling. . . .

It would be an exaggeration to suggest that the language and attitude of this poem are those of the common people, but they are certainly not those of the court and gentry alone. The words are commonplace, and the rhythm is that of many a street ballad, while the view of the man-woman relationship is free of any literary brand of elaboration. In another poem "The Careless Lover" sings:

When I am hungry, I do eat,
And cut no fingers 'stead of meat;
Not with much gazing on her face
Do e'er rise hungry from the place:
She's fair, she's wondrous fair,
But I care not who know it,
Ere I'll die for love, I'll fairly forego it.

This view of the sexual relationship is unashamedly predatory and selfish and extremely refreshing and lively. In "Proferred Love Rejected" the tone is more cynical and almost brutal.

It is not four years ago,
I offered forty crowns
To lie with her a night or so:
She answered me in frowns.

Not two years since, she meeting me
Did whisper in my ear,
That she would at my service be,
If I contented were.

I told her I was cold as snow
And had no great desire;
But should be well content to go
To twenty, but no higher.

This presentation of the economics of lust springs from the same source as the jibe on "T(homas) C(arew) having the P(ox)," the obscene verse upon the functions of the candle for the "female crew," and the lines on "The Deformed Mistress," in which the speaker gloats over the nauseating and the decayed. There is a dark strand in Suckling's imagination. It appears also in "Against Fruition," where he speaks with the voice of dissolute satiety:

Fruition adds no new wealth, but destroys,
And while it pleaseth much the palate,
cloys;
Who thinks he shall be happier for that,
As reasonably might hope he might grow fat
By eating to a surfeit; this one past,
What relishes? even kisses lose their taste.

The skepticism and the disillusionment expressed in these lines add a certain strength to many of the sweeter love lyrics, in that, because of the frequent use of down-to-earth words and commonplace locutions, we sense behind the delighted anticipation the shadow of futility and emptiness. Not that this despair is in any way cosmic; there is no Swiftian melancholy here; it is rather the half-comic, half-bitter knowingness of the experienced male.

Out upon it! I have lov'd
Three whole days together;
And am like to love three more,
If it prove fair weather.

Time shall moult away his wings
Ere he shall discover
In the whole wide world again
Such a constant lover.

But the spite on't is, no praise
Is due at all to me:
Love with me had made no stays,
Had it any been but she.

Had it any been but she,
And that very face,
There had been at least ere this
A dozen dozen in her place.
("A Poem with the Answer")

Here Suckling has rejected the use of obvious ingenuity in order to present an apparent straightforwardness that is much more subtle in its effect. The use of common expressions such as "whole wide world" and "the spite on't" and the deliberate avoidance of unusual and highly emotive adjectives in such phrases as "constant lover" and "that very face" make us feel that the speaker is using no contrivance, but is more concerned with his feelings than his art. Yet, because of the very simplicity of the expression, we also feel slightly superior to the speaker, recognizing the "unliterary" quality of his verse. In the case of this song our superiority leads us towards affectionate amusement at the speaker's frank self-revelation; and in every case in which this method is used we find ourselves observing the speaker's ideas and feelings rather than becoming ourselves involved in them.

Suckling clearly knew what he was about in writing in this way, for, though he was often tempted to be fashionably elaborate, in "A Ballad upon a Wedding" he not only uses a commonplace vocabulary and a naive style once again but places the poem in the mouth of a fictional character, who speaks in near-dialect and in a conversational tone:

I tell thee, Dick, where I have been;
Where I the rarest things have seen,
O, things without compare!
Such sights again cannot be found
In any place on English ground,
Be it at wake or fair.

At Charing Cross, hard by the way
Where we (thou knows't) do sell our hay,
There is a house with stairs;
And there did I see coming down
Such folk as are not in our town,
Forty at least, in pairs.

Amongst the rest, one pest'lent fine
(His beard no bigger though than thine)
Walkt on before the rest:
Our landlord looks like nothing to him:
The King (God bless him!), 'twould undo
him,
Should he go still so dressed.

We smile amusedly at a man who prizes wakes and fairs so highly and who is not used to seeing houses with stairs in them, even while we enjoy (and envy perhaps) his capacity for simple wonder and his unself-consciousness. Once we have been led into this attitude towards the speaker, we read on with an affectionate discernment that allows Suckling to vary the direction of the narrative in several ways. We feel just sufficiently superior to the speaker to accept simple jokes as part of the poem's portrayal of character, and yet we envy his innocent wonderment so much that we want to accept his description of beauty as more than a tribute to his own impressionability. The images and phrases used continually remind us of the character of the speaker also, so that we are never in danger of changing our relationship with him. Thus, the bride is described in homely terms:

Her finger was so small, the ring
Would not stay on, which they did bring;
It was too wide a peck:
And to say truth (for out it must)
It lookt like the great collar (just)
About our young colt's neck.

Her feet beneath her petticoat,
Like little mice, stole in and out,
As if they fear'd the light:
But O, she dances such a way!
No sun upon an Easter-day
Is half so fine a sight.

He would have kist her once or twice;
But she would not, she was so nice,
She would not do't in sight:
And then she lookt as who should say,
"I will do what I list to-day,
And you shall do't at night."

Even the occasional forced rhyme, and the sometimes subtly lame, sometimes aggressively jog-trot, rhythm are appropriate to the character of the narrator, who interrupts his own story every now and then with an aside:

Now hats fly off, and youths carouse,
Healths first go round, and then the house:
The bride's came thick and thick;
And, when 'twas nam'd another's health,
Perhaps he made it hers by stealth;
(And who could help it, Dick?)

Suckling's talents were perfectly adapted to this poem, for in it his merely fanciful (rather than imaginative) mind, and his amateur's careless vigor can be seen as part of the poem's "personality." Suckling's real contribution to English poetry was, indeed, this outspoken zest and this adoption of the language as well as the attitude of everyday masculinity. He is nowhere near as important a poet as Carew, but he developed one aspect of Carew's concern with the presentation of masculine attitudes in a startlingly vigorous manner. Much of his work is merely fashionable, much quite simply bad, but in his best work he followed his own prescription in "A Session of the Poets" that "A laureat muse should be easy and free," and his ease and freedom three hundred years later are still immensely enjoyable.

RICHARD LOVELACE
(*ca.* 1618–1657)

Richard Lovelace was born at his father's house in Woolwich. He was educated at Charterhouse and Gloucester Hall, Oxford, where he took his master of arts in 1636. He took part in the Scottish expedition of 1639 and was imprisoned for supporting the Kentish Petition in 1642. But he joined Charles I at Oxford, in 1645, to fight for the royalist cause. After fighting in the siege of Dunkirk in 1646, he was again imprisoned by Parliament in 1648 and released the following year. After having exhausted his patrimony, mostly through various attempts to serve the crown, he died in poverty in 1657.

The tone of the elegies on the death of Richard Lovelace is very different from the tone of those upon Suckling and Carew. The two older poets are praised as "wittie"; but Lovelace is regarded as "honourable," and the "beauty" of his soul is referred to, not infrequently. It all reminds one rather of Sir Philip Sidney. Lovelace was, clearly, much more than either Suckling or Carew, the model of a Renaissance gentleman, being a soldier, lover, wit, and pattern of chivalry. Nevertheless, as one reads his poems, one notices that something is missing. The expected "careless ease" is there, and something of the expected vigor, but the poems are much less personal. Though the superbly balanced love songs are neatly passionate, and appropriately conversational, they do not put us into a familiar relationship with the speaker:

Tell me not (Sweet) I am unkinde
That from the Nunnerie
Of thy chaste breast, and quiet minde,
To Warre and Armes I flie.

True a new Mistresse now I chase,
The first Foe in the Field;
And with a stronger Faith embrace
A Sword, a Horse, a Shield.

Yet this Inconstancy is such,
As you too shall adore;
I could not love thee (Deare) so much,
Lov'd I not Honour more.
("To Lucasta, Going to the Warres")

The statements are lucid, grave, and temperate. It is a sweetly reasonable poem that manages to avoid smugness because of the tender note in the personal appeal to his "Sweet" and "Deare." There is a love of symmetry here, however, which seems almost to be stronger than the love of the mistress. This is perhaps the real difference between Lovelace and his predecessors. Both Carew and Suckling have a good conceit of themselves. They prize their wit above their honesty, maybe, but, at their best, one feels this wit is a part of the animal spirit, which makes the pursuit of a mistress desirable. Lovelace's wit has a more withdrawn, impersonal, almost abstract air about it. Moreover, his moralizing is earnest rather than gay, and sometimes he finds it necessary to give dignity to his verses by the inclusion of a good deal of classical drapery. "Gratiana Dancing and Singing" has as its last verse:

So did she move; so did she sing
Like the Harmonious spheres that bring
Unto their Rounds their musick's ayd;
Which she performed such a way
As all th'inamoured world will say
The *Graces* daunced, and *Apollo* play'd.

This is pleasant and tuneful. It is at once relaxed and entertaining, and no irony is allowed to prevent our accepting the ideal description. Lovelace is, indeed, an enemy to irony. His strong suit is the lucid and dignified presentation of sentiment in lines of restrained rhythm which are given force by the use of parallelism, antithesis, and paradox. Thus his "An Elegie. Princesse Katherine" opens with a beautifully controlled set of balanced opposites:

You that can aptly mixe your joyes with
cries,
And weave white Ios with black Elegies,
Can Caroll out a Dirge, and in one breath
Sing to the Tune, either of life or death;
You that can weepe the gladnesse of the
spheres,
And pen a Hymne in stead of Inke with
teares,
Here, here, your unproportion'd wit let fall
To celebrate this new-borne Funerall,
And greete that little Greatnesse, which
from th' wombe
Dropt both a load to th' Cradle and the
Tombe.

This is the poetry of ceremony rather than spontaneity, and in Lovelace one feels continually that sense of the inner dignity of humanity which is so lacking in Carew and Suckling. Even when lighthearted, his humor leads him toward gentle absurdity rather than raillery, and his slightest and most casual lines have an air of sweetness about them. His is not a questioning mind. He accepts the fashionably elaborate compliment at its face value, and continually praises his mistress in highsounding terms, using vast cosmic similitudes or pastoral and idyllic language. As a result of this we feel the poetry to be "amateur" in a fashion very different from that of Suckling or Carew. With them one feels that their amateur status existed in their vigor and careless ease; their impertinence, their air of not really minding very much if the poem, as a literary object, were not in the best taste, or flawlessly made. Lovelace, however, gives the impression that he wishes his verse always to be in the best of taste and beautifully contrived, but is not really involved emotionally in his subject matter. His verse only occasionally appears to be anything more than a wellmannered and graceful diversion for the cultured reader. These diversions can, however, have a musical purity, a formal elegance that the wilder poems of Carew or Suckling never have.

Amarantha sweet and faire,
Ah brade no more that shining haire!
As my curious hand or eye,
Hovering round thee let it flye.

Let it flye as unconfined
As it's calme Ravisher, the winde;
Who hath left his darling th'East,
To wanton o're that spicie Neast.

Ev'ry Tresse must be confest
But neatly tangled at the best;
Like a Clue of golden thread,
Most excellently ravelled.

Doe not then winde up that light
In Ribands, and o're-cloud in Night;
Like the Sun in's early ray,
But shake your head and scatter day.
("To Amarantha, That She Would Dishevell Her Haire")

This is a poem of the ideal, and the ideal and the idyllic are Lovelace's pet themes. He adopts the pastoral manner more than once, and in his long pastoral, "Aramantha," moves completely away from any sense of actuality into a world of dream.

Into the neighbring Wood she's gone,
Whose roofe defies the tell-tale Sunne,
And locks out ev'ry prying beame;
Close by the Lips of a cleare streame
She sits and entertaines her Eye
With the moist Chrystall, and the frye
With burnisht-silver mal'd, whose Oares
Amazed still make to the shoares;
What need she other bait or charm
But look? or Angle, but her arm?
The happy Captive gladly ta'n,
Sues ever to be slave in vaine,
Who instantly (confirm'd in's feares)
Hasts to his Element of teares.

Poetry becomes, in such lines, simply a matter of charm, good humor, and pretty fancy. The poet's status is reduced to that of the drawing room entertainer, who takes great care not to offend the ladies by any too brutal reference to life's coarser realities. Nevertheless, it would be unfair to dismiss such work as entirely valueless, for as we read we are impressed by the delicacy of the sentiment and the description, and appreciate the writer's simple enjoyment of whatever is ingenious, musical, and well made. Moreover, behind the facade of fashionable artifice we suspect the presence of a strong sensibility and a sturdy common sense. These qualities emerge clearly in others of Lovelace's poems. His good-humored portrait of "The Ant," with its mock heroic reverence and deliberate use of familiar and commonplace images, is in the great tradition of good-humored and sensible fables:

Forbear thou great good Husband, little Ant;
A little respite from thy flood of sweat;
Thou, thine owne Horse and Cart, under this Plant
Thy spacious tent, fan thy prodigious heat;
Down with thy double load of that one grain;
It is a Granarie for all thy Train.

Cease large example of wise thrift a while,
(For thy example is become our Law)
And teach thy frowns a seasonable smile:
So *Cato* sometimes the nak'd Florals saw.
And thou almighty foe, lay by thy sting,
Whilst thy unpay'd Musicians, Crickets, sing.

Later in the poem he refers, delightfully, to the Ant's enemies:

Hovering above thee, Madam, *Margaret Pie,*
And her fierce Servant, Meagre, *Sir John Daw*

and the same touch of absurdity and humor appears in his two poems on "The Snayl," where it is addressed as "Compendious Snayl," and told that

. . . in thy wreathed Cloister thou
Walkest thine own Gray fryer too;
Strickt, and lock'd up, th'art Hood all ore
And ne'r Eliminat'st thy Dore.

In these poems Lovelace comes closer to Suckling and Carew than in most others, for here his use of the mock heroic implies a degree of detached amusement at the earnestly inflated solemnities of so much conventional verse. We can recognize that the speaker is a complex human being, caught between sheer enjoyment of fine-sounding words and the suspicion that the splendor of these may be a little pretentious and artificial. We can detect, too, the moralist, intent upon teaching, who is sufficiently aware of his audience to poke a little quiet fun at his own earnestness. Once we contrast these fables with "Aramantha," or with such tangled and high-falutin expressions of serious passion as "To Night," which begin by being pretentious and end by becoming absurd: once we compare the Lovelace of the charming and decorative poems of good taste with the Lovelace of "The Vintage to the Dungeon," or "To Althea from Prison," we can see clearly that all his work expresses a dichotomy. He doesn't know whether the poet in him is an aesthetic decorator with a penchant for complicated cornices, or merely one aspect of a civilized gentleman who enjoys good food, wine, laughter, music, and women, but who also has a serious moral side to his make up. Is the poet in fact a pose or a person, a couturier or a character?

This is really the question that all the cavalier poets had to face. Insofar as they enjoyed Jonsonian elegance and the ingenuity of Donne, they saw themselves as entertainers, but insomuch as they reverenced the strong masculine quality and the satirical bent of Jonson, and Donne's tremendously effective projection of a passionate personality, they felt they should be more critical, idiosyncratic, and personal. Careless ease must always be characteristic of their work, but must this lead toward a smooth and polished expression, devoid of dramatic vitality, or toward an almost insolent flouting of good taste and a carefully contrived freedom of meter?

In both Suckling and Lovelace the dilemma is obvious, but whereas Suckling's best poems come down successfully on the side of vigor and abandon, Lovelace's successes are, generally, of the other party. True, he can, every now and then, adopt a careless and light-hearted tone:

For Cherries plenty, and for Coran's[1]
Enough for fifty, were there more 'on's;
For Elles of Beere,[2] Flutes of Canary
That well did wash downe pasties-mary;[3]
For Peason,[4] Chickens, Sawces high,
Pig, and the Widdow-Venson-pye; . . .
Whether all of, or more behind-a
Thanks freest, freshest, Faire *Ellinda*:
("Being Treated, to Ellinda")

He can also retain the strong masculine note, even when his poems are elaborate and artificial:

Ah me! the little Tyrant Theefe!
As once my heart was playing,
He snatcht it up and flew away,
Laughing at all my praying.

Proud of his purchase he surveyes,
And curiously sounds it,
And though he sees it full of wounds,
Cruell still on he wounds it.

And now this heart is all his sport,
Which as a ball he boundeth
From hand to breast, from breast to lip,
And all it's rest confoundeth.
("A Loose Saraband")

It is, however, when he contrives a gracefully tender poem, full of gentle ceremony and musical balance, and when he allows his fancy free play within the confines of a decorously rigid meter that he is most himself. Indeed, his most "cavalier" poems are his least typical ones. We do not often get work with the controlled strength, the strong personal touch, and the gaiety and courage of "To Althea from Prison":

When Love with unconfined wings
Hovers within my Gates;
And my divine *Althea* brings

1. Currants.
2. A linear measure slightly greater than a yard; portions of beer and wine were sometimes described in such terms since they were often served in tall glasses resembling flutes.
3. Meat pies.
4. Peas.

To whisper at the Grates:
When I lye tangled in her haire,
And fettered to her eye;
The *Gods* that wanton in the Aire,
Know no such Liberty.

When flowing Cups run swiftly round
With no allaying *Thames,*
Our carelesse heads with Roses bound,
Our hearts with Loyall Flames;
When thirsty griefe in Wine we steepe,
When healths and draughts go free,
Fishes that tipple in the Deepe,
Know no such Liberty.

When (like committed Linnets) I
With shriller throat shall sing
The sweetness, Mercy, Majesty,
And glories of my KING;
When I shall voyce aloud, how Good
He is, how Great should be;
Inlarged Winds that curle the Flood,
Know no such Liberty.

Stone Walls doe not a Prison make,
Nor Iron bars a Cage;
Mindes innocent and quiet take
That for an Hermitage;
If I gave freedome in my Love,
And in my soule am free;
Angels alone that sore above,
Injoy such Liberty.

The last verse is perhaps Lovelace's finest achievement in poetry. In it we do sense a degree of personal feeling, and suspect that, at this point, the writer felt poetry alone could say what had to be said. That is, after all, the justification of poetry; it must appear to be a compulsion rather than a choice of a pleasing mode of expression.

Lovelace's sheer enjoyment of words and music is often sufficient to make us feel he had a general compulsion to play with words, ideas, and sounds, but it is rare for us to feel that any particular poem was a necessity, even if only a necessity of the moment. Nevertheless, Lovelace added poems to the language that we would not willingly miss, and if his soul is not aflame with the brightest genius, it does possess its own gentle radiance.

EDMUND WALLER
(1606–1687)

Edmund Waller was born on 3 March 1606, the eldest son of Robert and Anne Waller. He received his education at Eton and King's College, Cambridge, though there is no record of his taking a degree. He became a member of Parliament in 1621 and was a favorite of the king. In 1643 Waller was arrested and imprisoned for conspiracy by Parliament, and he narrowly escaped hanging. He toured Italy with John Evelyn in 1646. He wrote a panegyric on Oliver Cromwell in 1655 and, later, a poem of praise for Charles II on his Restoration in 1660; and he became a member of Parliament again in 1661. He died on 21 October 1687.

There was never any doubt in Edmund Waller's mind as to the poetry he wished to write. Aubrey has a story that "When he was a briske young sparke, and first studyed poetry, 'Me thought,' said he, 'I never sawe a good copie of English verses; they want smoothness; then I began to essay." Aubrey's stories may not always be factually correct, but they are often psychologically illuminating, and this particular anecdote hits off Waller perfectly. We may, in reading Lovelace, feel occasionally that the stylist has got the better of the artist in him; with Waller we only rarely feel otherwise. His thoughts are commonplace, without having the extenuating characteristic of being expressed with force. His epithets are pleasingly conventional. His verses are smooth to the point of being soporific. Moreover, while he can be regarded as a cavalier in that his work always has the air of having been written "by the way," and his verses flow with "ease," he certainly does not appear to be careless of his audience, or in any way inclined to flout the gods of social usage. It might be said that whereas Carew, Suckling, and Lovelace celebrated whatever took their fancy or aroused their passions, Waller wrote of whatever he could possibly fit a verse to, being more interested in displaying his craftsmanship and flattering the influential than in exploring his perceptions.

This is a harsh judgment, but one forced upon any reader of the collected poems who becomes dazed with the multitude of such titles as "To Vandyk," "To the King," "On a Brede of Divers Colours Woven by Four Ladies," "On the Head of a Stag," "On the Discovery of a Lady's Painting," "To My Lord Northumberland upon the Death of His Lady." One title at least reminds one more of the vast canvases of the nineteenth-century academicians, with their acres upon acres of deftly anecdotal oil paint, than of anything else. This is his "Instructions to a Painter for the Drawing of the Posture and Progress of His Majesty's Forces at Sea, under the Command of His Highness-Royal: Together with the Battle and Victory Obtained over the Dutch, June 3, 1665." There are 310 lines, beginning:

First draw the sea, that portion which
between
The greater world and this of ours is seen;
Here place the British, there the Holland
fleet,
Vast floating armies! both prepared to meet.

It is perhaps unfair to mock Waller for the thunderous banality of his failures, but such poems as the "Advice to a Painter" do reveal a difference between him and the other cavaliers. A kind of professionalism has replaced the zest of the amateur; the poet considers it to be a part of his job to comment upon matters of national importance and to offer his poems to the public, not as amusing and ingenious expressions of personal feeling, which his readers may, perhaps, enjoy, but as public statements of which his readers should approve.

He could express, or perhaps imply, a nation's grief in a series of deft lines "Upon Our Late Loss of the Duke of Cambridge," and he could, as a good politician, representative of the "top people," present His Majesty, as a birthday present, with "A Presage of the Ruin of the Turkish Empire." The elegant rectitude of the style is, in fact, as worthy of praise as the moral and social propriety of the statements.

We are nowadays so conscious of the notion that a poet writes "for posterity" that it is hard for us to believe that Waller wrote ephemeral poetry from choice rather than by accident. Yet in his lines "Of English Verse," he clearly tells us that English is inferior to Latin or Greek for the expression of important matters, and is only suitable as an aid to the seduction of a mistress, or for the making of a poem that will retain its vitality as long as the poet retains his:

Poets that lasting marble seek,
Must carve in Latin, or in Greek;
We write in sand, our language grows,
And, like the tide, our work o'erflows.

Chaucer his sense can only boast;
The glory of his numbers lost!
Years have defaced his matchless strain;
And yet he did not sing in vain.

The beauties which adorned that age,
The shining subjects of his rage,
Hoping they should immortal prove,
Rewarded with success his love.

This was the generous poet's scope;
And all an English pen can hope,
To make the fair approve his flame,
That can so far extend their fame.

Verse, thus designed, has no ill fate,
If it arrive but at the date
Of fading beauty; if it prove
But as long-lived as present love.

This is, of course, a not uncommon opinion of the period, but while these verses faithfully express the cavalier's view that Latin and Greek poetry were important and could usefully serve as models for writers in English, and to some extent explain their passion for translation, they also explain Waller's own deliberate pursuit of the flawlessly made heroic couplet, for this, to him, was the English equivalent of the Latin discipline he so admired. In his lines "Upon the Earl of Roscommon's Translation of Horace," he reveals more of his views:

Though poets may of inspiration boast,
Their rage, ill-governed, in the clouds is lost.
He that proportioned wonders can disclose,
At once his fancy and his judgement shows.
Chaste moral writing we may learn from
hence,
Neglect of which no wit can recompence.
. . .

It is worth commenting upon the emphasis upon judgment and morality in these lines. The poet is no gay dog, but a conscientious corrector of public taste:

The Muses' friend, unto himself severe,
With silent pity looks on all that err;
For where a brave, a public action shines,
That he rewards with his immortal lines.
Whether it be in council or in fight,
His country's honour is his chief delight;
Praise of great acts he scatters as a seed,
Which may the like in coming ages breed.

Such a picture of the poet is one we expect rather of the eighteenth than the late seventeenth century. It is with something of a shock that one turns to his lyrics and reads:

Go, lovely Rose!
Tell her that wastes her time and me
That now she knows,
When I resemble her to thee,
How sweet and fair she seems to be.

Tell her that's young,
And shuns to have her graces spied,
That hadst thou sprung
In deserts, where no men abide,
Thou must have uncommended died.

Small is the worth
Of beauty from the light retired;
Bid her come forth,
Suffer herself to be desired
And not blush so to be admired.

Then die! that she
The common fate of all things rare
May read in thee;
How small a part of time they share
That are so wondrous sweet and fair!
("Go, Lovely Rose!")

This possesses that direct and personal vitality which we have come to expect of the cavaliers, and while its language has a touch of the ceremonious about it, largely because of its inversions, this adds dignified restraint to the straightforward appeal to the lady in question. There is also a carefully delicate touch of pathos in the closing lines immediately following the sudden dramatic injunction "Then die!" As with Lovelace, however, one feels that a certain kind of vigor is missing, though it is perhaps compensated for by the superb balance of the phrases and the strong economy of the language. "Go, Lovely Rose!" is, of course, Waller's most anthologized poem, and it is untypical. Waller's forte is neat charm rather than controlled passion. His "Written in My Lady Speke's Singing Book" runs:

Her fair eyes, if they could see
What themselves have wrought in me,
Would at least with pardon look
On this scribbling in her book:
If that she the writer scorn
This may from the rest be torn,
With the ruin of a part,
But the image of her graces
Fills my heart and leaves no spaces.

These lines are suitable for any young lady's autograph album, and if their wit totters upon the edge of the bathetic, this is one of the risks a poet must take who is determined never to offend by originality, but always to give pleasure with a neat version of an expected and acceptable compliment. An occasional liveliness of speech adds vigor to some of Waller's trivia, as when he writes "Under a Lady's Picture":

Some ages hence, for it must not decay,
The doubtful wonderers at this piece, will say
Such Helen was! and who can blame the boy
That in so bright a flame consumed his Troy?
But had like virtue shined in that fair Greek,
The amorous shepherd had not dared to seek
Or hope for pity; but with silent moan,
And better fate, had perished alone.

The colloquial vitality of "who can blame the boy," added to the concise force of the following line, with its suggestion of heroic passion, succeeds in giving the whole poem a certain degree of intensity. Though the thought of the following lines may be conventional, the craftsmanship holds our attention. The verbs "shined" and "had" occur precisely at the centerpoint of the lines in which they appear, as do the pauses in the two concluding lines. It is Waller's strength that he could almost always make an acceptable conventionality appear pleasingly ingenious and original by obtruding his craftsmanship upon us. This craftsmanship was most often employed in arranging a smooth metrical regularity, given a restricted degree of variety by the careful use of pauses and occasional abrupt statements. These abrupt statements never have the take-it-or-leave-it brusqueness of Suckling or Carew; they only momentarily alter the speed with which the poem runs, and never quite reach that note of real vigor that we can hear in the splendidly disciplined lines of Dryden:

He that alone would wise and mighty be,
Commands that others love as well as he.
Love as he loved!—How can we soar so
  high?—
He can add wings, when he commands to fly.
Nor should we be with this command
  dismayed;
He that examples gives, will give his aid;

This fragment from "Of Divine Love" is a clear indication of Waller's transitional position as a poet. His heroic couplets look forward to those of the eighteenth century. Like many poets from Dryden to Samuel Johnson, he is fond of the epigrammatic moral statement:

Man's boundless avarice his want exceeds,
And on his neighbours round about him feeds.

Though justice death, as satisfaction, craves,
Love finds a way to pluck us from our graves.

Waller's lyrics, too, remind one more of later than of earlier poets. Though there is immense charm, and sometimes liveliness, there is no highly personal idiosyncracy to give them any real human immediacy. Carew and Suckling may have written their songs as games, but it is impossible to mistake the one's style of play for the other's. This is no longer true with the Restoration wits. It is possible to mistake a Dryden song for one by Sir Charles Sedley, Sir George Etherege, or even (sometimes) the incomparable Rochester. The song is no longer part of the perception of an individual singer, but an exercise in a conventional genre. The examples are often delightful, but they are basically anonymous.

Waller must be held as to some extent responsible for the anonymous style. He took over the highly personalized careless ease of the cavaliers, and, with great care, gave it more ease, and less personality. The strong masculine tone of Suckling, Carew, and Lovelace, and of so many of the minor figures—Randolph, Townsend, Montrose, and others—is replaced by a mild decisiveness of style. Even at the close of one of his most successful lyrics, where there is an attempt at the passionate exuberance of the lover, Waller only achieves a hollow gesture:

That which her slender waist confined,
Shall now my joyful temples bind;
No monarch but would give his crown
His arms might do what this has done.

It was my heaven's extremest sphere,
The pale which held that lovely deer.
My joy, my grief, my hope, my love,
Did all within this circle move!

A narrow compass! and yet there
Dwelt all that's good, and all that's fair;
Give me but what this ribband bound,
Take all the rest the sun goes round.
  ("On a Girdle")

It is charming, it is not without vigor, but it pales beside the cry of Donne, whom Carew thought so worthy of reverence. The period of the aggressively individual style and of the highly personal tone is over. Egos are out of favor, and will remain out of favor in any real sense until the romantics give the eccentric wheel another twist. Only Swift in the eighteenth century really employs the carelessly and insolently idiosyncratic style which is so enlivening in Carew and Suckling. Dryden and Pope and their followers (not forgetting Dr. Johnson, who occasionally out-Wallers Waller) went on a different tack. There is still zest, but it is of a different kind. One no longer quite expects the colonel of the cavalry to be a poet of the first rank. The complete gentleman, once a soldier, statesman, courtier, and sportsman, effortlessly accomplished in versifying and playwriting, and casually brilliant as a musician, architect, and philosopher, is becoming more of a specialist. The ideal man of the Renaissance, universally gifted, and educated in all branches of knowledge, who could lead a battle, design a mansion, dispute with bishops, compose a song, govern a province, and win a mistress, all with an equally careless dexterity and poise, is dying. In 1711 Alexander Pope wrote of Crashaw:

> I take this Poet to have writ like a Gentleman, that is, at leisure hours, and more to keep out of idleness, than to establish a reputation; so that nothing regular or just can be expected from him . . . no man can be a true Poet, who writes for diversion only.

It is the judgment of a later generation than Waller's, but it is in Waller's poetry that we can see the amateur being edged off the stage by the busy professional, the man of letters with a reputation to earn, and matters of public concern to talk about.

CONCLUSION

Although the poetry of the cavaliers is only a part of the poetry written in England between the death of Shakespeare and the Restoration, it combines almost all the poetic characteristics of the period. The so-called metaphysical poets (George Herbert, Vaughan, King, Crashaw) may have been more thorough in their allegiance to Donne and his strong personal exploration of emotional and intellectual states of mind in terms of elaborate conceits, and poets like William Strode, Thomas Stanley, Sir William Davenant, and James Shirley may have adopted a more completely Jonsonian manner, but the cavaliers partook of both schools. Even the minor religious moralists, with their penchant for biblical paraphrases and their love of didactic epigrams, are like the cavaliers in being fond of translations and direct colloquial language. The great Milton, moreover, shows in his earlier work a truly cavalier sensuality and wit (though the careless ease is missing), and Cowley's "The Mistress," though often described as metaphysical, has more in common with Carew and Lovelace than with Herbert, Vaughan, and their fellows.

Just as the cavalier poets stand at the center of the poetic sensibility of the time, so do they show us the way in which poetry was changing generally throughout the period, from an expression of personal attitudes to a statement of public truth. When the cavalier considers an affair of public importance he considers his own personal reaction to it. This is even the case with Waller and with Sir John Denham, who ranks alongside Waller in establishing the smooth heroic couplet as the main medium of poetic expression for the years to come. The poet of the Restoration, however, is more obviously moved by a sense of social responsibility, and his satirical verses are as likely to be the result of political conviction as of personal spleen or amusement. Perhaps the most striking example of the cavaliers' attitude in this respect is the marquess of Montrose's "An Excellent New Ballad." Here the political viewpoint is used to illuminate the private emotions of the lover, and the references to royalism and Puritanism are deliberately frivolous. It is as much as if to say (as Yeats said in one of his poems), "What is the value of these political notions compared with the value of human relationships?"

> My dear and only love, I pray
> That little world of thee

Be governed by no other sway
Than purest monarchy;
For if confusion have a part,
(Which virtuous souls abhor,)
And hold a *synod* in thine heart,
I'll never love thee more.

Like Alexander I will reign,
And I will reign alone;
My thoughts did evermore disdain
A rival on my throne.
He either fears his fate too much
Or his deserts are small,
That dares not put it to the touch
To gain or lose it all.

And in the empire of thine heart,
Where I should solely be,
If others do pretend a part,
Or dare to view with me,
Of if *committees* thou erect,
And go on such a score,
I'll laugh and sing at thy neglect,
And never love thee more.

But if thou wilt prove faithful then,
And constant of thy word,
I'll make thee glorious by my pen,
And famous by my sword;
I'll serve thee in such noble ways
Was never heard before;
I'll crown and deck thee all with bays,
And love thee more and more.

James Graham, marquess of Montrose, typifies the cavalier spirit. He was a dedicated statesman and a brilliant military tactician, who spent all his maturity in war and the planning of war. He helped the Scottish covenanters to free themselves from the domination of the bishops, and then, when the covenanters threatened to rebel against the crown, he led the wild Gordons and Macdonalds of the Highlands into battle for the king's cause. He was captured at last, during the Commonwealth, leading another army for the royalists, and was hanged before he was forty. His poems all have that careless brilliance which the age expected of the verses of its "compleat gentlemen," and this song illustrates particularly clearly the way in which the cavalier lyric combines casual ease and forceful expression in such a way as to give an impression of real and vital humanity. The poem is always more than the sum of its parts, but this is particularly true of the work of the cavaliers. From even the most trivial verses of Lord Herbert, William Cartwright, William Habington, Aurelian Townsend, Thomas Randolph, Sidney Godolphin, Sir Richard Fanshawe, and their fellows we derive a far from trivial impression of intense curiosity, zest, and sensitivity. The poems may or may not indulge in some philosophical or moral statement, but their general effect is always to impress upon us the importance of honest skepticism, uninhibited enjoyment, freedom of thought, and moral candor. Life should be enjoyed on many levels. There is a place for the merely fanciful, as for the deeply imaginative. One should not make a fool of oneself by being over pretentious, or pretending always to be devoted to the profoundest moral problems. On the other hand, one should not be afraid of making a fool of oneself by confessing one's own enjoyment of the trivial or one's occasional spasms of simple masculine animality. Life, viewed through the thick lens of philosophy, may appear to be in the service of God or Truth, but looked at with the eyes of everyday it seems at once less important and more amusing. Life was made for man to use, not man for life to discipline into some creature of a narrow dogma.

Whether or not this attitude is just, it is certainly invigorating, for it throws the Muse's doors wide open to all comers. Nothing that is experienced can be inappropriate to poetry. The cavaliers, indeed, released poetry from the various bondages of previous fashions and, as a consequence, the writers of the eighteenth century were able to develop new techniques and explore new subjects. The value of the cavaliers is not only historical, however. They gave us something that no one else has given us since—a strong masculine poetry that is continually life-enhancing, and always courageous, vigorous, and charming. The style is debased in Waller's work, admittedly, but in that of Carew, Suckling, Lovelace, and a host of others it provides us with tremendous pleasure and much wise instruction, and as we shut the book we cannot help recalling the words of a much later poet who was, in some ways, a cavalier at heart. "A man's a man for a' that," said Robert Burns, and it might well have been said by his fellow countryman Montrose.

Selected Bibliography

A list of the separate works of the poets discussed in this essay is given in the Grolier Club's *A Catalogue of . . . English Writers from Wither to Prior* 3 vols. (New York, 1905).

THOMAS CAREW

BIBLIOGRAPHY

A list of all the manuscripts printed and sources for the establishment of the authoritative text is printed in *The Poems of Thomas Carew,* (Oxford, 1949).

COLLECTED WORKS

[T. Maitland], ed. *The Works,* (Edinburgh, 1824); W. C. Hazlitt, ed. *The Poems,* (London, 1870); J. W. Ebsworth, ed. *The Poems and Masque,* (London, 1893); A. Vincent, ed. *The Poems,* (London, 1899) in the Muses' Library; G. Saintsbury, ed. *Minor Poets of the Caroline Period,* 3 vols. (Oxford, 1905–1921); R. G. Howarth, ed. *Introduction to Minor Poets of the Seventeenth Century,* (London, 1931) repr. (1953) an anthology containing the work of Carew, Lovelace, Suckling, and Lord Herbert of Cherbury, in Everyman's Library; R. Dunlap, ed. *The Poems with His Masque "Coelum Britannicum,"* (Oxford, 1949) the definitive ed., intro. includes a biography of Carew.

SEPARATE WORKS

Coelum Britannicum. A Masque at Whitehall in the Banquetting-House, on Shrove-Tuesday-Night, the 18 of February, 1633, (London, 1634); *Poems,* (London, 1640) other eds. (1651, 1653, 1671) additional poems in the later eds.

SOME CRITICAL STUDIES

Quiller-Couch, A. T., *Adventures in Criticism,* (London, 1896); Powell, C. L., "New Material on Thomas Carew," *Modern Language Review* 11 (1916); Duncan-Jones, E. E., "Carew and Guez de Balzac," *Modern Language Review* 46 (1951).

SIR JOHN SUCKLING

COLLECTED WORKS

The Works, (London, 1676) repr. (1696); W. C. Hazlitt, ed. *The Poems, Plays and Other Remains,* 2 vols. (London, 1874) rev. ed. (1892); A. H. Thompson, ed. *The Works,* (London, 1910) reiss. (1965); H. Berry, ed. *Sir John Suckling's Poems and Letters from Manuscript,* (London-Ontario, 1960).

SEPARATE WORKS

Aglaura, (London, 1638); *The Discontented Colonel,* (London, 1640) retitled *Brennoralt in Fragmenta Aurea* (London, 1646); *A Coppy of a Letter Written to the Lower House of Parliament,* (London, 1641); *Fragmenta Aurea. A Collection of All the Incomparable Peeces Written by Sir John Suckling,* (London, 1646) 2nd ed. (1648) 3rd ed. (1658) 3rd ed. included for the first time *Letters to Several Persons of Honor* and *The Sad One, A Tragedy.*

RICHARD LOVELACE

BIBLIOGRAPHY

A list of all the manuscripts printed and sources for the establishment of the authoritative text is printed in *The Poems,* (Oxford, 1925).

COLLECTED WORKS

S. W. S[inger], ed. *Lucasta: in Two Parts,* (London, 1817–1818); W. C. Hazlitt, ed. *Lucasta,* (London, 1864) rev. ed. (1897) also in H. Child, ed. (London, 1904) and W. L. Phelps, ed., 2 vols. (Chicago, 1921); C. H. Wilkinson, ed. *The Poems,* (Oxford, 1930) the definitive ed., intro. includes a biography of Lovelace, also in a limited, deluxe ed., 2 vols. (London, 1925).

SEPARATE WORKS

Lucasta: Epodes, Odes, Sonnets, Songs, &c., To Which Is Added Amarantha, A Pastorall, (London, 1649); *Lucasta: Posthume Poems,* (London, 1659).

EDMUND WALLER

COLLECTED WORKS

E. Fenton, ed. *The Works in Verse and Prose,* (London, 1729) repr. (1730, 1758); *The Works in Verse and Prose, with Life,* (London, 1772); G. Thorn-Drury, ed. *The Poems,* (London, 1893) the best ed., in the Muses' Library; *The Poems,* (London, 1977) the Scolar Press ed.

SEPARATE WORKS

Speech Against Prelates Innovations, (London, 1641); *Mr. Waller's Speech in the Painted Chamber,* (London, 1641); *Speech. 4 July 1643,* (London, 1643); *The Workes of Edmund Waller in This Parliament,* (London, 1645); *Poems,* (London, 1645) repr. (1664) (1668) (1682) etc.; *A Panegyrick to My Lord Protector,* (London, 1655); *Upon the Late Storme, and of the Death of His Highnesse,* (London, 1658); *To the King, upon His . . . Happy Return,* (London, 1660); *To My Lady Morton,* (London, 1661); *A Poem in St. James's Park,* (London, 1661); *To the Queen, upon Her . . . Birthday,* (London, 1663); *Upon Her Majesty's New Buildings,* (London, 1665); *Of the Lady Mary,* (London, 1679); *Divine Poems,* (London, 1685); *The Maid's Tragedy, Alter'd,* (London, 1690); *The Second Part of Mr. Waller's Poems,* (London, 1690) repr. (1705, 1711) etc. with anonymous biography.

BIOGRAPHICAL AND CRITICAL STUDIES

Stockdale, P., *Life of Waller,* (London, 1772); Johnson, S., *Lives of the Poets,* (London, 1791) later in G. B. Hill, ed. (Oxford, 1905); Cartwright, J., *Sacharissa,* (London, 1893); Lloyd, C., "Waller as a Member of the Royal Society," (*PMLA* 43, 1928); Allison, A. W., *Towards an Augustan Poetic: Edmund Waller's "Reform" of English Poetry,* (Lexington, Ky., 1962); Cherniak, W. L., *The Poetry of Limitation,* (New Haven, 1968).

OTHER CAVALIER POETS

WILLIAM HABINGTON (1605–1654)

H. C. Combs, ed. *Castara,* (Evanston, Ill., 1939); K. Allott, ed. *The Poems,* (Liverpool, 1948).

THOMAS RANDOLPH (1605–1635)

W. C. Hazlitt, ed. *Poetical and Dramatic Works,* 2 vols. (London, 1875); G. Thorn-Drury, ed. *Poems,* (London, 1929).

LORD HERBERT OF CHERBURY (1583–1648)

G. C. Moore Smith, ed. *Poems,* (Oxford, 1923); Herford, C. H., *Autobiography,* (London, 1928); H. R. Hutcheson, trans. and ed. *Religio laici,* (New Haven, 1944); Rossi, M. M., *La vita, le opere, i tempi . . . ,* 3 vols. (Florence, 1947).

SIDNEY GODOLPHIN (1610–1643)

W. Dighton, ed. *The Poems,* (Oxford, 1931).

SIR JOHN DENHAM (1615–1669)

T. H. Banks, ed. *The Poetical Works,* (New Haven, 1928).

JAMES GRAHAM, MARQUESS OF MONTROSE (1612–1650)

J. L. Weir, ed. *Poems,* (London, 1938).

WILLIAM CARTWRIGHT (1611–1643)

G. B. Evans, ed. *The Plays and Poems,* (Madison, Wisc., 1951).

GENERAL CRITICISM

Emperor, J. B., "The Catullan Influence in English Lyric Poetry, 1600–90," (*University Studies* 3, 1928); McEuen, K. A., *Classical Influence upon the Tribe of Ben,* (Cedar Rapids, Ia., 1939); Miles, J., *The Primary Language of Poetry in the 1640's,* (Berkeley, 1948); Walton, G., *Metaphysical to Augustan,* (Cambridge, 1935); B. Ford, ed. *From Donne to Marvell,* Pelican Guide to English Literature, vol. III (London, 1956) contains G. Walton, "The Cavalier Poets."

SOCIAL AND LITERARY BACKGROUND

Trevelyan, G. M., *England under the Stuarts,* (London, 1904); Grierson, H. J. C., *The First Half of the Seventeenth Century,* (London, 1906); Coate, M., *Social Life in Stuart England,* (London, 1924); Grierson, H. J. C., *Cross Currents in English Literature of the Seventeenth Century,* (London, 1929); Willey, B., *The Seventeenth-Century Background,* (London, 1934) reiss. (1963); Pickel, M. B., *Charles I as Patron of Poetry and Drama,* (London, 1936); Thompson, J. A. K., *The Classical Background of English Literature,* (London, 1948); Morpurgo, J., *Life under the Stuarts,* (London, 1950); Wedgwood, C. V., *Seventeenth-Century English Literature,* (London, 1950); Bethell, S. L., *The Cultural Revolution of the Seventeenth Century,* (London, 1951); Bush, D., *English Literature in the Early Seventeenth Century, 1600–1660,* (London, 1962).

Geoffrey Chaucer
(ca. 1340–1400)

NEVILL COGHILL

A shilling life will give you all the facts.
W. H. Auden

In what his father and mother would have regarded as his career—for it was they who had the wit, and the luck, to launch him upon it—Geoffrey Chaucer did remarkably well. His successive appointments, missions, and awards, achieved in the administrative service of three kings, were something better than a mediocre success; and who could have foreseen that his marriage, prudent and suitable as it was—romantic, too, for all we know to the contrary—would ultimately make him brother-in-law to his own best patron, John of Gaunt—that is, to the fourth son of Edward III, the uncle of Richard II and the father of Henry IV, the poet's chief employers?

But it was not as a poet that they employed Chaucer; his poetry was an extra, so far as they were concerned. His career was that of a courtier, as his father and mother had intended; and it was that career that gained him his place in the official records of the time. Except for those records, we should probably know as little about him as we do of the other great poets of his age, the authors of *Piers Plowman* and of *Sir Gawain*.

Yet the recorded facts of this courtier's life, remote from poetry as they may seem, are those upon which the styles of his poetry turn; they mark its progress from his first beginnings, step by step, to his maturities. Being a courtier made a European of Chaucer, and more than that; he became the first great English poet in the general tradition of Christendom, the heir of Ovid, of Vergil, of Boethius, of Saint Jerome, of Guillaume de Lorris and Jean de Meung, of Dante and Boccaccio.

He was not the first great English Christian poet; Langland was before him. But he was the first English poet in the high culture of Europe, then breaking out all over England in a glorious profusion of creative power. There are moments in the lives of nations when they declare their genius: the life of Geoffrey Chaucer fell in the middle of the first such moment in England.

In every art then known, and in some now lost—in architecture, sculpture, carving, and stained glass; in the work of goldsmiths and armorers and the makers of robes for ceremonial and daily use; in manuscript illumination, painting and portraiture, music and dancing—sudden perfections were being achieved all over England. Moreover, they were harmonious, as if they were the particular manifestations of a personal style flowering freely in every field. Grace, strength, freshness of invention, clarity, richness, and a sense of the humane, as well as of the divine, characterize this breeding time of England's first civilization.

Out of the multitude of masterpieces I will name a few to show these qualities: the central tower of Wells Cathedral and the breathtaking inverted arch that supports it, the work of William Joy about the year of Chaucer's birth (*ca.* 1340), and the great octagonally fashioned vault over the transept of Ely Cathedral, the work of Alan of Walsingham and William Hurley not long before—miracles, both, of strength and ingenuity; and the nave of Westminster Abbey, grove of slender stone, built by the greatest English architect before Wren, Henry Yevele. Chaucer, late in his life, knew and worked with him. It was Yevele who, with Hugh Herland, master carpenter, built Westminster Hall (1394).

In portraiture, an art then dawning and of which Chaucer became a master, one may recall the tragic alabaster face of Edward II that haunts the visitor to Gloucester Cathedral, or the knowingly practical visage of Henry IV, carved in Canterbury; less tragic than Edward, more humane than Henry, the painted effigy of Edward le Despenser, kneeling in his chantry roof in Tewkesbury Abbey. Illumination and painting could show pieces as fine as these: for instance, the Wilton diptych that presents the young Richard II to the Blessed Virgin and a host of angels, himself hardly less angelical in beauty, or the greater portrait of him that hangs in Westminster Abbey and shows him against a gold background, in a robe the color of dried blood. From his face, he seems to be thinking Shakespearean thoughts.

In glass the antechapel windows of New College by Thomas of Oxford, with their canopied saints and patriarchs in soft greens and porphyries and blues, seem a silent reproach to the baroque-souled figures and inharmnonious tints of a neighboring window by Sir Joshua Reynolds that was somehow allowed to be put there in an age that knew no better. In the same chapel is the crozier of William of Wykenham, a masterwork of the goldsmiths, silversmiths, and enamelers of the fourteenth century.

Harp and flute and social song were part of a gentleman's education, and song was gracefully combined with dance in the "carol"; the art of conversation was so much esteemed that Andreas Capellanus gave it third place among the requirements for a girl worthy to be loved; and Chaucer, in his first considerable poem, ensured that it would be known to have graced the dead patroness he was celebrating, Blanche, duchess of Lancaster:

And which a goodly, softe speche
Had that swete, my lyves leche![1]
So frendly, and so well ygrounded,
Up al resoun[2] so wel yfounded,
And so tretable[3] to alle goode . . .

In poetry (our chief concern in this essay) the age was richer than in all else, except architecture. There were the three great poets I have mentioned, of whom Chaucer was chief; there was John Gower, too, and the makers of the miracle plays, then coming to their first fullness in York and elsewhere. *Troilus and Criseyde, The Canterbury Tales, Piers Plowman, Sir Gawain, The Pearl,* and the Townley or Wakefield Plays may speak for the great achievements of those times in poetry; but there was also a first pouring forth of lyrical writing, by many anonymous hands and one-poem men, of whose work a fragment follows:

Bytuene Mersh and Aueril,
When spray biginneth to springe,
The lutel foul hath hire wyl
On hyre lud to synge.
Ich libbe in loue-longinge
For semlokest of alle thynge;
[S]he may me blisse bring—
Icham in hire baudoun.

An hendy hap ichabbe yhent;
Ichot from heuene is it me sent;
From alle wymmen mi loue is lent,
And lyht on Alysoun.

[Between March and April, when the spray begins to spring, the little bird has its pleasure to sing in its language. I live in love-longing for the seemliest of all things; may (s)he bring me joy; I am in her power. I have grabbed a lucky chance. I know it has been sent me from Heaven; from all women my love has turned away, and lights on Alison.].[4]

And here is another, in a more "metaphysical" vein:

1. My life's physician.
2. Upon all reason.
3. So tractable.
4. Kenneth Sisam, ed., *Fourteenth Century Verse and Prose* (London" 1937).

Gold & al this werdis wyn
Is nouth but cristis rode;
I woulde ben clad in cristis skyn,
That ran so longe on blode,
& gon t'is herte & taken myn In—
Ther is a fulsum fode.

[Gold and all the glory of this world is nought, save Christ's cross; I would be clad in Christ's skin, that ran so long with blood, and go to his heart and make my Inn there, where there is a bounteous food.][5]

This was a mystical age, the age of Richard Rolle of Hampole and Juliana of Norwich; her writings are like the writings of a lover:

I saw his sweet face as it were dry and bloodless with pale dying. And later, more pale, dead, languoring; and then turned more dead unto blue: and then more brown-blue, as the flesh turned more deeply dead. For his Passion shewed to me most specially in his blessed face, and chiefly in his lips: there I saw these four colours, though it were afore fresh, ruddy, and liking, to my sight. (*Revelations of Divine Love*)

It was also an age that loved learning, a founding time of colleges. Nine new ones were added within the century, four at Oxford and five at Cambridge.

Paradoxes are to be understood as best they can. This same age of the first, and in some ways the finest, English culture was also an age preeminent for plague, poverty, rebellion, war (both international and civil), political murder, heresy, and schism. Fissures seemed to be opening in the Catholic church with the "Babylonish" captivity of the popes at Avignon, followed by a great schism and war between pope and antipope. To Langland it seemed like the day of Antichrist. Heresies were also raising their terrible heads; the chronicles tell the story of a knight who snatched the consecrated host out of his priest's hand and fled away with it, to devour it with oysters and mustard, thinking (in some obscure way) that this disproved transubstantiation.

There were secular terrors too: the black death began its repeated visitations in 1348, when Chaucer was a child.

Ther cam a privee theef men clepeth
Deeth,[6]
That in this contree al the peple sleeth.
(*The Pardoner's Tale*)

The tyrannies of nature were matched by the tyrannies of man. Mob madness and xenophobia filled London with the shouts and shrieks of massacre when the rebels of the Peasants' Revolt, entering London, fell upon the Fleming there in 1381; Chaucer, in later years, passed it off as a joke, a farmyard flurry:

Certes, he Jakke Straw and his meynee[7]
Ne made nevere shoutes half so shrille,
Whan that they wolden any Flemyng kille,
As thilke day was maad upon the fox.
(*The Nun's Priest's Tale*)

This revolt, which was also an attack upon church and law, was suppressed as savagely as it had arisen, with hanging in chains for many a deluded peasant. Their betters were also liable to liquidation; the intrigues that stewed within and seethed outside the court and government led often enough to the scaffold:

The ax was sharpe, the stokke was harde
In the xiiii yere of Kyng Richarde.
(Sisam, *Fourteenth Century Verse and Prose*)

As a sort of ground bass to all these disturbances, there was an unstanched issue of blood—bitter, barbarous, and futile—in the feuds with France that are now called the Hundred Years' War. No doubt it was conducted with great panache and had moments of thrilling, heraldic heroism; it certainly dazzled the eyes of its chronicler, Jean Froissart,

5. Carleton Brown, ed., *Religious Lyrics of the XIVth Century* (London, 1924; 2nd ed., by G. V. Smithers, 1957).

6. There came a secret thief that men call death.

7. And his gang.

who could write of it in the *Chroniques* with the kind of romantic feeling that stirs in us when we read Chaucer's *The Knight's Tale*:

> Thus the knights and squires sparkled abroad in the plain and fought together . . . (Froissart, 1364)
>
> It was great joy to see and consider the banners and the penons and the noble armoury . . . the Prince himself[8] was the chief flower of chivalry of all the world, and had with him as then right noble and valiant knights and squires . . . (1367)
>
> The men of arms beat down the Flemings on every side . . . and as the Flemings were beaten down, there were pages ready to cut their throats with great knives, and so slew them without pity, as though they had been but dogs . . . (1382)

What with Jack Straw and the men of arms, the Flemings met with small mercy, but nationalism knows no restraint and soldiers cannot expect a ransom from a Flemish burgher.

Into this age of extremes, which in every direction forces superlatives from its astonished student, Geoffrey Chaucer, most equable of men, was born.

He was born in the middle of the century and in the middle of society, toward the year 1340, in a middle-class cockney home. No record was kept of the event. Round the corner, and half a street away from his father's house, flowed the Thames; a little above towered old Saint Paul's, whose chapter house and cloister, the work of William Ramsey, stood in their brand-new perpendicular beauty. A new style had been born.

EDUCATION IN RHETORIC

> *The noble rethor poete of brytayne*
> John Lydgate, *Life of Our Lady,*
> referring to Chaucer

Not far away, in the Vintry, stood Saint Paul's Almonry; and if it is not a fact, it is a likely conjecture, that young Geoffrey was sent there daily to learn his letters and his Latin, through the medium of French:

> Children in scole, ayenst the vsage and manere of alle othere naciouns beeth compelled for to leue hire owne langage, and for to construe hir lessouns and here thynges in Frensche, and so they haueth seth the Normans come first to Engelond. Also gentil men children beeth i-taught to speke Frensche from the tyme that they beeth i-rokked in here cradel . . . And vplondisshe men wil likne hym self to gentil men, and fondeth with greet besynesse for to speke Frensche, for to be i-tolde of. (Ranulf Higden, *Polychronicon,* 1363)

As might be expected from the above, Chaucer's Squire in *The Canterbury Tales,* being of "gentil" birth, was accustomed to speaking French, and confesses:

> Myn Englissh eek is insufficient.

And the Franklin, an "vplondisshe" or country-bred man if ever there was one, loudly regrets that his own son lacks the gentle breeding of the Squire, in such a way as to unleash the mockery of the Host, who could see at a glance that there was a penny short in the shilling of the Franklin's gentility:

> "Straw for youre gentillesse!" quod oure
> Hoost.

What was it like to be at school in those days? Children were sent very young: *enfantz* they were called, and their instruction began like that of Chaucer's "litel clergeon" in *The Prioress's Tale,* with the singing of Latin hymns, the easiest way into the difficult language of heaven:

> ". . . I lerne song, I kan but smal
> grammeere."
> (*The Prioress's Tale*)

At Westminster School, and probably at Saint Paul's, too, a boy who knew Latin and presumed to speak English, or even French, had

8. The Black Prince.

a cut of the cane for every word so spoken. Rod and birch were frequently applied to the seat of learning and accepted as a rueful joke by the little victims. There is, for instance, a late fifteenth-century poem by—or at least about—a boy who had dared to excuse himself for being late for school on the ground that his mother had told him to go out and milk the ducks:

> My master lokith as he were madde:
> "wher hast thou be, thow sory ladde?"
> "Milked dukkis, my moder badde":
> hit was no mervayle thow I were sadde.
>   what vaylith it me thowgh I say nay?
> My master pepered my ars with well good
>   spede
> . . . He wold not leve till it did blede,
> Myche sorow haue he for his dede!
>   (*Babees Book*)[9]

Discipline, if rough, was ready. The day began with prayer, then a recitation of the Creed, the Lord's Prayer, a salutation to the Blessed Virgin, and some psalm singing, which was called "dinging on David." And so to class to learn letters, to do sums with counters, to grammar, to logic, to rhetoric, and to the classic authors: Ovid, Vergil, Lucan, Cicero, Statius, Dionysius Cato, and the rest.

Rhetoric has come to mean a windy way of speech, marked by a pompous emptiness and insincerity, and trotted out as a trick on any occasion calling for solemn humbug. It did not mean this to the Middle Ages. It meant then the whole craft of writing, the arts and devices by which whatever you had to say could best be varied, clarified, and elaborated; it even included the study of appropriate gesture:

> And, for his tale sholde seme the bettre,
> Accordant to his wordes was his cheere,
> As techeth art of speche hem that it leere.

> [He suited his action to his words, as the art of speech teaches those that learn it, to do.]
> (*The Squire's Tale*)

The word *rethor* had come to be used as the simple equivalent of "good poet"; so Chaucer used it in *The Squire's Tale*, to underline the skill needed to describe the beauty of his heroine:

> It moste been a rethor excellent
> . . .
> If he sholde hire discryven every part.
> I am noon swich, I moot speke as I kan.

So it was used of Chaucer by Lydgate and other poets:

> O reverend Chaucere, rose of rethoris all,
> As in oure tong ane flour imperiall . . .
>   (William Dunbar, *The Golden Targe*)

The rules of rhetoric are now, for the most part, forgotten; and the enormous effect they had on the formation of Chaucer's style is therefore often not perceived, even by good Chaucerists. Every educated person in the fourteenth century knew them and admired those who knew how to use them, of whom Chaucer was chief. It would be fair to say that an anthology of the finest things in Chaucer could be employed to demonstrate the nature and use of these rules.

They had come down from Roman times, and reached a second flowering in the twelfth and thirteenth centuries. The scholars of that time, notably Matthieu de Vendôme (*ca.* 1170) and Geoffrey de Vinsauf (*ca.* 1210), had assembled all the traditions of rhetoric in a number of prose treatises and illustrative verses; the general heading under which particular devices of style were recommended was that of *amplificatio*, the art of enlarging and embellishing your matter. There were eight or ten principal ways of doing so, each with its high-sounding name, and some with as many as four subdivisions. For instance, there was *circumlocutio*, the art of making a simple statement in a roundabout and decorative way:

9. *The Babees Book (Early English Poems and Treatises on Manners and Meals in Olden Time)*. F. J. Furnival, ed., Early English Text Society, original ser., XXXII (London, 1868).

The bisy larke, messager of day,
Salueth in hir song the morwe gray,
And firy Phebus riseth up so bright
That al the orient laugheth of the light,
And with his stremes dryeth in the greves[10]
The silver dropes hangynge on the leves.
(*The Knight's Tale*)

The simple statement underlying this lovely and lively passage is "The sun rose brightly." That Chaucer was perfectly conscious of this, and sometimes also amused by it, can be seen from the following:

But sodeynly bigonne revel newe
Til that the brighte sonne loste his hewe;
For th'orisonte hath reft the sonne his lyght,—
This is as muche to saye as it was nyght!—
(*The Franklin's Tale*)

The first twelve magical lines of *The General Prologue* is a simple *circumlocutio* for "In April, people go on pilgrimages."

Another figure of rhetoric, much used by Chaucer, was *interpretatio*; this consisted in repeating an idea in other words: *varius sis et tamen idem.*[11]

A plain example of this would be

Soun ys noght but eyr ybroken,
And every speche that ys spoken,
Lowd or pryvee, foul or fair,
In his substance ys but air . . .
(*The House of Fame*, II)

The last three lines are an *interpretatio* of the first. But the figure could also have a subtler form, as when the idea was not only repeated, but given a new twist. For instance:

Ful swetely herde he confessioun,
And pleasaunt was his absolucioun:
He was an esy man to yeve penaunce,
Ther as he wiste to have a good pitaunce.
(*The General Prologue*)

The last two lines repeat the sense of the first with a dagger thrust of meaning added.

In like manner examples of every figure of rhetoric can currently be found in Chaucer: of *digressio* in its two forms, namely, when you digress to matter outside your story in order to illuminate it (as when the Wife of Bath tells the story of Midas to illustrate a point in her own tale) and when you digress by developing an idea within your story, in a manner directly arising from it (as when the Merchant, describing the garden that old January had made, digresses to thoughts of the *Roman de la rose*, Priapus, and Proserpine). Or of *occupatio*, when you explain that you are too busy to go into details; this can be used either to shorten your tale:

I coude folwe, word for word, Virgile,
But it wolde lasten al to longe while.
(*The Legend of Good Women*)

or to lengthen it, by saying you have no time to describe the things that you then proceed to describe:

And eek it nedeth nat for to devyse
At every cours the ordre of hire servyse.
I wol nat tellen of hir strange sewes,[12]
Ne of hir swannes, ne of hire heronsewes,[13]
Eeek in that lond, as tellen knyghtes olde,
Ther is som mete that is ful deynte holde,
That in this lond men recche of it but smal;[14]
Ther nys no man that may reporten al.
(*The Squire's Tale*)

The Squire's use of *occupatio* is tame, however, compared with that of his father, the Knight, who perforrns a dazzling cadenza of some fifty lines toward the end of his tale, enumerating all the features of Arcite's funeral, which (he says) he has no time to mention. It is a real tour de force.

But Chaucer's favorite rhetorical device was certainly *apostrophatio.* This figure had four subdivisions, of which the commonest

10. Groves.

11. Be various and yet the same (Vinsauf, *De poetria nova*).

12. Strange broths.

13. Their young heron (like the swans, a dish to eat).

14. In this country people think little of it.

was *exclamatio,* a simple exclamation of feeling, of whatever kind; the second and third, *subjectio* and *dubitatio,* were forms of rhetorical question; and the last, *conduplicatio,* was a series of exclamations, each beginning with the same phrase (this Chaucer uses only in his most serious invocations):

Lo here, of payens corsed olde rites,[15]
Lo here, what alle hire goddes may availle!
Lo here, thise wrecched worldes appetites!
Lo here, the fyn and guerdoun for travaille[16]
Of Jove, Appollo, of Mars, of swich rascaille!
(*Troilus and Criseyde,* V)

Chaucer sparkles with apostrophes; he is ever ready to exclaim in sympathy, wonder, indignation, pathos, prayer, and irony, to address his audiences personally with a question not meant to be answered, but that brings them into the story:

Woot ye nat where there stant a litel toun
Which that ycleped is Bobbe-up-and-doun,
Under the Blee, in Caunterbury Weye?
(*The Manciple's Prologue*)

Or they may be asked to picture an incident in a tale by reminding them of something similar in their own lives, as when Chaucer asks them to imagine the plight of his heroine by recalling the sight of some unhappy criminal on his way to execution:

Have ye nat seyn somtyme a pale face,
Among a prees,[17] of hym that hath be lad
Towards his deeth, wher as hym gat no grace,
And switch a colour in his face hath had,
Men myghte knowe his face that was bistad,[18]
Amonges all the faces in that route?
So stant Custance, and looketh hire aboute.
(*The Man of Law's Tale*)

15. Behold the accursed, ancient rites of pagans.

16. Behold the end and the reward for your labors (given by Jove, etc.).

17. Crowd.

18. Set round (with enemies).

These are rhetorical questions, not exactly of the kinds named above, but of a kind to vary, by an apostrophe to his hearers, Chaucer's means of engaging their attention. Often he will pause in midstory to ask what sort of a universe it can be where such things happen, or to make a general comment on life:

Allas! allas! that evere love was sinne!
(*The Wife of Bath's Prologue*)

These were things that Chaucer began to learn in his school days, and in his hands the rules of the pedants became the instruments of a living and natural style; as with any great virtuoso, the technical rule or accomplishment, artificial and laborious as it may seem, can become the means of a greater freedom of expression, can even prompt a thought that might have been lost without it, for

. . . Nature is made better by no mean
But Nature makes that mean: so, over that art
Which you say adds to Nature, is an art
That Nature makes.
(*The Winter's Tale*)

Above all, Chaucer's training in rhetoric sharpened his perception of character; no one was his equal in this, because no one had his touch with the rhetorical figure of *descriptio.* This is a figure to which we must return later. At the moment let us pass on from Saint Paul's Almonry (if that indeed was where he had his early schooling) and follow him to the next phase of his upbringing. It was the decisive phase, the true beginning of his career as a courtier and as a poet.

EDUCATION IN COURTESY

Let me see if Philip can
Be a little gentleman.
Heirlrich Hoffman, *Struwwelpeter*

At some unknown date, but certainly when he was still a boy, Geoffrey was taken from school and put out to service in the household of Elisabeth, countess of Ulster. She was the wife of Lionel, third son of Edward III and later duke of Clarence. For Geoffrey this was an almost unimaginable stroke of good fortune; his parents, no doubt through their slender court connections, had somehow pulled it off.

The countess kept household books on parchment. These books were later torn up and the parchment used to line a manuscript of poems by Lydgate and Hoccleve. A nineteenth-century scholar examining the manuscript discovered the lining. It was found to contain the first known reference to Geoffrey Chaucer. It is dated April 1357 and records that the countess laid out seven shillings on a cloak and a pair of red-and-black breeches for the lad. He had taken the first step in courtiership and was a page in a royal household.

This did not mean that Chaucer's education was interrupted; on the contrary, it was widened, intensified, and given a practical turn. We know almost exactly of what it consisted, thanks to another household book, the *Liber niger* of Edward IV, in which is laid down the traditional curriculum for lads in his position, rising from page to squire. They were known as henxmen or henchmen, a word derived from the older word *hengest,* meaning a horse, for all chivalry (to which Chaucer was now apprenticed) arose from the cult of the horse (*cheval*), as the word implies. It tamed and civilized the lust of battle much in the way that courtly love tamed and civilized the lust of the body; the tournament was the meeting place of both, and it did what it could to impart to the natural Yahoo some qualities of the Houyhnhnm.

Edward IV arranged for "young gentylmen, Henxmen, VI Enfauntes or more, as it shall please the Kinge" to be placed under the tuition of a "Maistyr of Henxmen"

> to shew the schooles[19] of urbanitie and nourture of Englond, to lerne them to ryde clenely and surely; to drawe them also to justes [jousting]; to lerne them were theyre harneys [to teach them how to wear their equipment, armor, etc.]; to have all curtesy in wordes, dedes and degrees [i.e., to know who ranks above or below whom, as Griselda did in *The Clerk's Tale,* welcoming her lord's guests "everich in his degree"]. . . . Moreover to teche them sondry languages, and othyr lerninges vertuous, to harping, to pype, sing, daunce, and with other honest and temperate behaviour and patience . . . and eche of them to be used to that thinge of vertue that he shall be moste apt to lerne [i.e., to be encouraged in any personal talent], with remembraunce dayly of Goddes servyce accustumed. This maistyr sittith in the halle, next unto these Henxmen . . . to have his respecte unto theyre demeanynges [attend to their behavior], and to theyre communication [conversation]. . . .

The best results of such a system can be seen in Chaucer's Knight and Squire—and, I think, in Chaucer too.

Courtesy, it will be noticed, is the first thing to be stressed in this schedule of breeding, after the military essential of horsemanship. Courtesy is behavior proper to a court; and the masters in courtesy fixed their standards by the highest court they knew of, which was the court of heaven. That was the court, they claimed, in which courtesy had its origin:

> Clerkys that canne the scyens seuene,
> Seys that curtasy came fro heuen
> When gabryell owre lady grette,
> And elyzabeth with here mette.
> All vertus be closyde in curtasy,
> An alle vyces in vilony.

> [Learned men that know the seven sciences say that courtesy came from Heaven when Gabriel greeted Our Lady and Elizabeth met with her. All virtues are included in courtesy, and all vices in rusticity.[20]] (*Babees Book*)

19. Scholars?

20. *Vilony* is a difficult word to translate. It is here intended to mean a condition of primitive rustic malice, ignorance, and crudity, to be presumed of a countryman in a savage, semianimal state. *Villanus* means someone living in the wilds, as opposed to *civis,* a city dweller versed in "urbanitie" (*urbs* = a city).

Of all English poets, Geoffrey Chaucer is the most courteous to those who read or listen to him; he seems ever-conscious of our presence and charrned to be in such perceptive company. He never threatens or alarms us, as Milton can, intent upon his great theme; nor does he ignore us, as Wordsworth can, intent upon himself. He addresses his readers as if he could wish for none better, he exchanges experiences with them, consults them, and begs them not to take offense at what he is about to say, touching his show of courtesy with an elegant but ironic wit:

But first I pray yow, of youre curteisye,
That ye n'arette[21] it nat my vileynye,
Thogh that I pleynly speke in this mateere,
To telle yow hir wordes and hir cheere,

. . .

Whoso shal telle a tale after a man,
He moot reherce as ny as evere he kan
Everich a word, if it be in his charge,
Al speke he never so rudeliche and large,
Or ellis he moot telle his tale untrewe,
Or feyne thyng, or fynde wordes newe.
He may nat spare, althogh he were his
  brother;
He moot as wel seye o word as another.
Crist spak hymself ful brode[22] in hooly writ,
And wel ye woot no vilenynye is it.
  (*The General Prologue*)

Chaucer learned his manners not only from those with whom he came in contact, but also from cautionary rhymes, of which there survive a great number, specially written for the education of children. They are too long to quote in full, for they enter into details of table manners, right down to versified instructions for the washing of spoons and the laying of cloths, freely interrningled with moral advice:

. . . Loke thyne hondis be wasshe clene,
That no fylthe on thy nayles be sene.
Take thou no mete tylle grace be seyde,
And tylle thou see alle thyng arayede . . .
And at thy mete, yn the begynnyng,
Loke on pore men that thow thynk,
For the fulle wombe without any faylys
Wot fulle lytyl what the hungery aylys.[23]
Ete not thy mete so hastely,
Abyde and ete esily . . .
  (*The Lytylle Childrnes Lytil Boke or Edyllys be*, in *Babees Book*)

Perhaps the best of these poems is the one called *The Babees Book*; it is addressed to children of the blood royal and, like other poems in this vein, gives precise instructions how to behave:

Youre heede, youre hande, your feet, hold
  yee in reste
Nor thurhe clowying your flesshe loke yee
  nat Rent;[24]
Lene to no poste whils that ye stande
  present
Byfore your lorde . . .

And so forth. It ends thus:

And, swete children, for whos love now I
  write,
I yow beseche withe verrey lovande herte,
To knowe this book that yee sette your
  delyte;
And myhtefulle god, that suffred peynes
  smerte,
In curtesye he make yow so experte,
That thurhe your nurture and youre
  governaunce
In lastynge blysse yee mowe your self
  avaunce!

In opening a window upon the Middle Ages, there is always the danger that it may turn into a stained glass window. Nevertheless, I am forced by all these cautionary verses to believe that the reason for being courteous was a religious reason, namely, that it was pleasing to God and would advance your soul; it was the application of Christianity to social behavior, a practical way of learning to love

21. Impute it not.
22. Very broadly.
23. For the full stomach, without fail, knows very little of what the hungry one is suffering.
24. See that you do not tear yourself by scratching.

your neighbor as yourself. Manners makyth Man.

The simple piety of this approach to courtesy was no doubt dinned into the little bourgeois boy from the moment he entered the Ulster household. Although there were rules of thumb for courtesy, the underlying theory had been worked out by the philosophers and poets. Indeed, when he grew up, Chaucer himself, as we shall see, made a significant contribution to it.

The problem was one with which the age was profoundly concerned. What is nobility? How does one become noble? Has it to do with wealth or heredity?

> Whan Adam dalf and Eve span
> Who was tho the gentilman?

This watchword of the Peasants' Revolt had come to them (though they knew it not) from Dante, who had devoted an entire treatise to the subject:

> If Adam himself was noble, we are all noble, and if he was base, we are all base. (*Convivio,* IV, xv)

Dante was arguing that nobility was not inherited. In this he was echoing Boethius, who some eight hundred years before had said:

> . . . yif thou ne have no gentilesse of thiself . . . foreyn gentilesse ne maketh thee nat gentil. (*De consolatione philosophie,* III, vi, translated by Chaucer)

Nor, said Dante, had nobility anything to do with wealth. It was wholly a matter of virtue, he argued, following Aristotle in his argument:

> . . . this word "nobleness" means the perfection in each thing of its own proper nature . . . everything is most perfect when it touches and reaches its own proper virtue . . . So the straight path leads us to look for this definition . . . by way of the fruits; which are moral and intellectual virtues whereof this our nobleness is the seed. . . . (*Convivio,* IV, XVI)

Chaucer had read, and alludes to, this discussion in the *Convivio*; but in giving his own account of "gentillesse" (or, as we would say, of "nobility") he appeals to higher authority than Dante or Aristotle. To be "gentil," he says, is to imitate Christ, for that is the perfection of our proper natures:

> But, for ye speken of swich gentillesse
> As is descended out of old richesse,
> That therfore sholden ye be gentil men,
> Swich arrogance is nat worth an hen.
> Looke who that is moost vertuous alway,
> Pryvee and apert,[25] and moost entendeth ay
> To do the gentil dedes that he kan;
> Taak hym for the grettest gentil man.
> Crist wole we clayme of hym our
> gentillesse,
> Nat of oure eldres for hire old richesse.
> (*The Wife of Bath's Tale*)

This, the root of all things, was for Chaucer the root from which the flowers of charity and courtesy both sprang. And, like sainthood, they might be met in every rank of life. The roughmouthed Host himself was capable of it:

> . . . and with that word he sayde,
> As curteisly as it had been a mayde,
> "My lady Prioresse, by youre leve,
> So that I wiste I sholde yow nat greve,
> I wolde demen that ye tellen sholde
> A tale next, if so were that ye wolde.
> Now wol ye vouche sauf, my lady deere?"

But the finest figure of courtesy in *The Canterbury Tales* is the Knight. Chaucer was very careful to make this noble figure as realistic as any of his rogues; half the details of his career, as it is epitomized in *The General Prologue,* were fresh in Chaucer's mind from the Scrope-Grosvenor trial of 1386, in the course of which the Scrope family, bearing the disputed arms (*azure a bend or*), had been seen in "the great sea," at Satalye, at Alexandria, in Spain, Prussia, and Lithuania (Lettowe). All these place names occur in *The General Prologue,* written in the same year,

25. In private and public.

in the description of the Knight's military career. Nothing said of him could have sounded more likely or authentic to Chaucer's first hearers; his "character" would have sounded equally so, formed as it was on the principles of Christian courtesy dinned into everyone day in and day out from childhood. The entire knightly caste had been brought up thatway for some two centuries, and was to be brought up so for at least a century more.

Chaucer's Knight is the embodiment of a whole way of life, a creation whose importance I cannot measure or state; it is the first image of the idea of a gentleman in the language that has given that idea to the world. Chaucer's Knight is to his Plowman as a fourteenth-century cathedral is to a fourteenth-century parish church, and all four of them were the products of the same great style and civilization.

Many things are mocked in Chaucer, but never courtesy; it was the great ideal of his age, upheld by every writer. The poet of *Sir Gawain* builds his poem upon it, to maintain in honor the court of Arthur and the order of chivalry. If the idea was, in its origins, aristocratic, it spread outward and downward through society to a universal acceptance, so that the peasant Langland could think and speak of the Incarnation as the courtesy of Christ.

COURTIER-SOLDIER-SCHOLAR-POET

> *The courtier's, soldier's, scholar's eye,*
> *tongue, sword . . .*
> William Shakespeare, *Hamlet*

Like many another henxman before and since, Chaucer was presently sent to the wars. It was a foul campaign, bitterly cold, utterly inept, a military fiasco; but it had one important result: it struck a blow for civilization by putting the young genius into direct touch with France and its poetry. For Chaucer's luck held; he was taken prisoner almost at once. We get a glimpse of this over his shoulder, as it were, for he tells us about it in the Scrope-Grosvernor trial already mentioned; he was one among the many witnesses. Indeed, so many and so distinguished were those called on to give evidence, a *Who's Who* for 1386 could easily be compiled from them. Chaucer deposed:

> Geffray Chaucer Esquier del age de xl ans & plus armeez p xxvii ans pduct pr la ptie de mons Richard Lescrop jurrez & examinez demandez si lez armeez dazure ove un bende dor appteignent ou deyvent appteigner au dit mons Richard du droit & de heritage, dist q oil qar il lez ad veu estre armeez en Fraunce devant la ville de Retters . . . & . . . p tout le dit viage tanq le dit Geffrey estoit pris. . . .
>
> [Geoffrey Chaucer Esquire, of the age of forty years and more, having borne arms for twenty-seven years, produced by Sir Richard Le Scrope's party, swom and examined, asked if the arms of azure with a bend or belonged or should belong to the said Sir Richard by right and inheritance. Said that yes, for he had seen them being armed in France before the town of Retters (probably Rhetel, near Rheims) . . . and . . . during the whole campaign when the said Geoffrey was taken prisoner . . .] (*The Scrope and Grosvenor Roll*, Vol. I, edited by Sir N. H. Nicolas, 1879).

His captivity did not last long; he was no Flemish burgher only fit to have his throat cut, but a negotiable prize. On 1 March 1360, the king paid £16 toward his ransom. It is an old joke among the biographers of Chaucer that this was slightly less than he paid to ransom Sir Robert de Clinton's charger.

From then on, Chaucer led three interweaving kinds of life: a courtier's, a scholar's, and a poet's. Some chronological shape can be given to at least the first of these, the events of which help to date some of his poems, and the accessions of strength, style, and subject to be discerned in them. Many are the subjects he handles; we have already touched upon one, the idea of a gentleman, and I mean to restrict myself in this essay to two more (his greatest, I think) for somewhat detailed consideration, rather than attempt in so small a space to touch on every aspect of his genius. The subjects I have chosen are love and men and women; but before I may come to them, there is the outline of a triple life to be sketched.

For the next seven years there is no record of Chaucer as a courtier, save that he carried letters for the king to Calais at least once. But his poet's life was beginning; he was at work on a translation of the *Roman de la rose,* transplanting an aristocratic and French philosophy of love and a French way of poetry to England. He was also engaged in formal studies at the Inner Temple, if we may believe a late tradition reported by Thomas Speght in his edition of Chaucer (1598), which also asserts that he was "fined two shillings for beatinge a Franciscane Fryer in fletestrete."

Chaucer was growing to manhood; all of a sudden we find him married to a lady-in-waiting to Queen Philippa, perhaps her goddaughter, Philippa de Roet; she became Philippa Chaucer in 1366. Were they in love? We do not know; he has left us no poem to her, though he once refers to her in jest. He compares her voice awakening him in the mornings to the scream of an eagle (*The House of Fame*).

In 1369, Queen Philippa died; the Chaucers went into service with Blanche, duchess of Lancaster, first wife of John of Gaunt. With that began (if it had not begun even earlier) the firm friendship and steady patronage that the duke gave Chaucer ever after. Philippa Chaucer's sister, Catherine, was to become the governess of the duke's children, then his mistress, and at last his wife; thus the duke ended brother-in-law to the poet.

If the duke did much for Chaucer, Chaucer did more for him. He made him a central and romantic figure in his first masterpiece, *The Book of the Duchess,* an elegy on the lady Blanche, who also died in 1369.

It is the first elegy in the English language, drenched in a leisured melancholy that begins with a dream and moves out into a great forest, to the sound of far-off hunting homs; under a tree the poet meets a sorrowful figure in black, singing a lament for his dead lady. It is John of Gaunt, mourning the loss of Blanche, his wife. Though the poem is an elegy, it is imagined as a love story; narrative instinct and a feeling for sexual passion (let it take what form it may) are things we learn to expect in Chaucer. This slow and dreamy poem keeps the memory of Blanche in her living grace, heroine of a tale of courtship and untimely death; the courtier and rhetor has put forth all his young art for his patron and sometime patroness.

Chaucer's career as a man of affairs was now beginning; he was being used as something between a king's messenger and a royal nuncio to France in 1370. But the great events of this kind were his missions to Italy in 1372 and 1378, for it was from these that his poetry took much of its greatest strength.

It is worth pausing on the voyage of 1372; Chaucer went to Genoa and Florence *in nuncio regis in secretis negociis.* He was away for six months, and it is a reasonable conjecture (doubted, however, by some scholars) that he spent a part of them on a private poetical pilgrimage of his own, to visit Petrarch, the most famous living poet of the day, in Padua. It would have been a rough journey, a hundred and fifty miles off course across the Apennines in the cold and windy month of March, through a war-stricken countryside. But all that would have been nothing to a young poet (he was in his early thirties) eager to snatch a chance of meeting the greatest literary figure of his time.

What prompts readers to believe that he did are the lines that Chaucer was later to put into the mouth of the Clerk of Oxford as he broaches the tale of Griselda:

> I wol yow telle a tale which that I
> Lerned at Padowe of a worthy clerk,
> As preved by his wordes and his werk.
> He is now deed and nayled in his cheste,
> I prey to God so yeve his soule reste!
> Fraunceys Petrak, the lauriat poete,
> Highte this clerk, whos rethorike sweete
> Enlumyned al Ytaille of poetrie, . . .
> (*The Clerk's Prologue*)

Now it is a question whether what an imaginary character says in imagined circumstances is evidence of anything that happened to his imaginer in the actual world. So many authors can be shown to have used their own lives to create the lives of their characters that it is not unreasonable to believe that Chaucer did so on this occasion, that he had indeed heard the story of Griselda from Petrarch's lips and recorded the occasion in this oblique manner. The text of the tale, from which he came to fashion his own version, must have been subsequently acquired by him in some other way, for its date has been established as June 1374, the year of Petrarch's death. For all these possibilities, we have no proof that the two poets ever met, and it may be wisest to say, with the Sage of Cambridge:

> Wovon man nicht sprechen kann, daruber
> muss man schweigen.[26]

In between these Italian journeys Chaucer was promoted; he became comptroller of the customs and subsidies of wools, skins, and tanned hides in London, and had to keep the books in his own fair hand.[27] It was a busy life, and all his recreation was to read:

> For when thy labour doon al ys,
> And hast mad alle thy rekenynges,
> In stede of reste and newe thyngs,
> Thou goost hom to thy hous anoon;
> And, also domb as any stoon,
> Thou sittest at another book
> Tyl fully daswed ys thy look,[28] . . .
> (*The House of Fame*)

So spoke the admonishing eagle (with a voice like his wife's); and what the bird said need not surprise us, for Chaucer read enormously—smatteringly, perhaps, but rememberingly. Almost everything that he read seems to have left its trace upon his poetry, for he delighted in allusion and quotation (whether acknowledged or not) from his favorite authors. He drew easily on the Latin classics: Ovid, Vergil, Statius, Boethius; he was at home in the poetry of France: Deguilleville, Machault, Froissart, Deschamps, and the authors of the *Roman de la rose.* In Italian he was a reader of Dante and of Petrarch; above all he had come to know at least two of Boccaccio's poems, *Filostrato* and *Teseide.* Of these he made two of his own noblest works, *Troilus and Criseyde* and *The Knight's Tale.*

Chaucer was also a considerable student of the sciences, especially of astronomy and mathematics; he was widely read in medicine, psychology, and other natural sciences, including the pseudo science of alchemy. His theology he did not so readily parade, though there is an amusing passage on God's uses for fiends in *The Friar's Tale.* He read Saint Jerome and Saint Bernard, and could quote from almost every book in the Bible and the Apocrypha. Though he may not have been the most learned, he was perhaps the most widely read man of his day; he seems never to have lost the habit and delight of reading:

> On bokes for to rede I me delyte, . . .
> (*The Prologue to The Legend of Good Women*)

There is a passage in Boswell's *Life of Johnson* describing the special powers of mind enjoyed by the doctor; they describe Chaucer's equally well:

> . . . His superiority over other learned men consisted chiefly in what may be called the art of thinking, the art of using his mind; a certain continual power of seizing the useful substance of all that he knew and exhibiting it in a clear and forcible manner; so that knowledge, which we often see to be no better than lumber in men of dull understanding, was, in him, true, evident and actual wisdom. His moral precepts are practical; for they are drawn from an intimate acquaintance with

26. Ludwig Wittgenstein, *Tractntus Logico-Philosophicus*: "What one cannot speak about, one has to keep quiet about."

27. And a fair hand it was, if D. J. Price is right in conjecturing that a late fourteenth-century manuscript, *The Equatorie of the Planetis,* brought to light by him at Peterhouse, Cambridge, is a Chaucer holograph.

28. Till thy look is fully dazed.

> human nature. His maxims carry conviction; for they are founded on the basis of common sense, and a very attentive and minute survey of real life. . . .

It is not surprising that Boswell adds:

> His mind was so full of imagery that he might have been perpetually a poet.

To return to Chaucer's life as a courtier: he had had a windfall in the customs in 1376; he caught a man named John Kent evading duty on an export of wool to Dordrecht, and the culprit was fined for it to the tune of £71 4s. 6d. The whole of this sum (worth £2,000 or £3,000 in modern money) was paid to Chaucer as a reward. He was becoming almost affluent. Foreign missions continued now and then to come his way, as well as civil appointments; in 1382 he was made comptroller of petty customs; in 1385 he was allowed to appoint a deputy and was made a justice of the peace. In October of the following year, he sat in Parliament at Westminster as knight of the shire for Kent.

Then, suddenly, in 1386, fortune deserted him:

> For whan men trusteth hire, thanne wol she
> faille,
> And covere hire brighte face with a clowde.
> (*The Monk's Tale*)

John of Gaunt was out of the country; and Chaucer, deprived of his patron, was deprived of his offices. He must live on his pension and on his savings until better times. In the next year Philippa died; he was now a widower with nothing to do. If this was sad for him, it was lucky for us; he began to compose *The Canterbury Tales.*

To take brief stock of Chaucer's career as a writer up to the time of his wife's death, it had produced several long or fairly long poems, ambitiously different from anything ever written before in English, as well as a prose translation of Boethius' *Consolation of Philosophy* and a work of instruction in mathematics—*A Treatise on the Astrolabe*—for "Lyte Lowys, my sone." There is no agreement among scholars about the dating, and little agreement about the order in which his poems were composed. We may be certain that *The Book of the Duchess* was written in 1369–1370 and *The Legend of Good Women* in 1385–1386; it is also sure that *Troilus and Criseyde* and such parts of his translation of the *Roman de la rose* as have survived were written before *The Legend of Good Women,* because it mentions them; it also mentions *The Parliament of Fowls,* "al the love of Palamon and Arcite" (later *The Knight's Tale*), the translation of Boethius, and the *Life of Saint Cecilia* (later *The Second Nun's Tale*).

The Canterbury Tales (it is agreed) were begun as such toward 1386–1387, and remained Chaucer's "work in progress" until the end of his life, never completed. It would seem that toward the end he tired of writing:

> For elde, that in my spirit dulleth me,
> Hath of endyting al the subtilte
> Wel nygh bereft out of my remembraunce;
> . . .
> (*The Complaint of Venus*)

We need not, however, take this confession too seriously; it had always been Chaucer's way to make fun of himself.

Of his longer poems it only remains to mention *The House of Fame,* of which it can only be said with certainty that it was written after Chaucer had read the *Divine Comedy*; that is, at some time after his first or second visit to Italy.

His very last poem, perhaps, was addressed on the accession (1399) of the new king—*The Complaint of Chaucer to His Purse*:

> I am so sory, now that ye been lyght; . . .

It need not be taken too tragically; the poem is almost as light as the purse.

According to the inscription on his tomb, put there by a Tudor admirer, Nicholas Brigham, in 1556, Chaucer died on 25 October 1400. He was buried in Westminster Abbey;

it is not known why. Saint Margaret's, Westminster, was his parish church, and that would have been his natural resting-place; perhaps they put him in the Abbey because he had been clerk of the works, or perhaps he slipped in by some oversight when the tumult of the new reign dwindled to a calm, much as George III, according to Lord Byron, slipped into heaven. It was, anyhow, not Chaucer's fame as a poet that made him head of the Poets' Corner; it was not until the late sixteenth century that a corner in the Abbey began to belong to the poets.

THE POET OF LOVE

For I, that God of Loves servantz serve, . . .
Troilus and Criseyde, I

From the beginning, as we have seen, Chaucer revealed himself as a love poet and a teller of tales; to commemorate the Duchess Blanche he imagined a story about her death, told by her mourning lover in a dream forest.

Now, in truth, this "lover" represented John of Gaunt, Blanche's widower; they had been married ten years. In the poem, however, they are seen as courtly lovers and the "Man in Black" voices his desire on that ideal courtly plane, in full troubadour style:

"To love hir in my beste wyse,
To do hir worship and the servise
That I koude thoo, be my trouthe,
Withoute feynynge outher slouthe[29]; . . ."
(*The Book of the Duchess*)

Troilus was later to declare his passion in the same key:

"And I to ben youre verray, humble, trewe,
Secret, and in my paynes pacient,
And evere mo desiren fresshly newe
To serve, and ben ay ylike diligent, . . ."
(*Troilus and Criseyde,* III)

For a long time, true to the convention, the "Man in Black" dares not confess his love; and when he at last summons the courage to say the hard word, he uses the favorite in the whole vocabulary of courtly love, mercy:

"I seyde 'mercy!' and no more."

He is refused; it is only after a conventional year of "service" that she understands and is willing to reward his sufferings:

"So when my lady knew al this,
My lady yaf me al hooly
The noble yifte of hir mercy,
Savynge hir worship, by al weyes,—"[30]

All that was young and romantic in Chaucer had swallowed the dream allegories of France and the philosophy of courtly love in long draughts from the *Roman de la rose,* the *Fontaine amoureuse,* the *Jugement du roi de Behaingne,* and other poems of the sort; and he was trying to do extreme honor to this ordinary Christian marriage by representing it as an idealized amour. All the conventions are beautifully there—the golden hair, the gentle eyes, the neck like a tower of ivory, the long body, the white hands, the round breasts, the tints of her cheek:

"But thus moche dar I sayn, that she
Was whit, rody, fressh, and lyvely hewed,
And every day hir beaute newed."

It was this way of imagining love and of writing poetry that Chaucer brought back from France. Much has been written about "courtly love" and of its sudden appearance in the courts of the nobles of Languedoc in the eleventh and twelfth centuries; some have explained it as a degenerated form of Plato's ideal affection, passed on through Arab hands to France from Africa and, in the process, het-

29. That I then could, by my truth, without pretence or sloth.

30. My lady gave me all wholly the noble gift of her mercy, saving her honor, of course.

erosexualized and allowed the gratification of the body. Be that as it may, this elegant, illicit amorism took all Christendom for its province; and our world began to ring with ballades, rondels, virelays, aubades, and complaints such as the "Man in Black" was singing when Chaucer came upon him in the dream forest.

If in his youth Chaucer thought it a compliment to a bereaved husband to speak of his wife as if she had been a mistress, he came ultimately to change his perspective; his maturest expression of courtly love, *Troilus and Criseyde,* ends in the knowledge of its insufficiency.

Troilus and Criseyde was the greatest yield of Chaucer's Italian journeys; he learned from Boccaccio how to abandon dream and build a story of the waking world with clarity and realism, yet retain within it the delicacies of feeling and convention that prevailed in the visionary, allegorical world of the *Roman de la rose;* the new poem was undergirt by the philosophy of Boethius, who taught Chaucer the shape of tragedy and filled him with thoughts of fortune and free will. For the lovers and their mentor Pandarus, however free they may seem in a thousand decisions, and indecisions, move to the calls of courtly love as surely as they move under fatal stars. On the way to their still-distant doom, they pass through an ecstasy of high sexual passion; and Chaucer rises effortlessly to the great poetry of their long night of first union, which I do not know where to find equaled, except in Shakespeare, for intimacy, tenderness, and noble quality. He reveals himself as engaged by the love he is describing:

> O blisful nyght, of hem so longe isought,
> How blithe unto hem bothe two thow
> weere!
> Why nad I swich oon with my soule
> ybought,
> Ye, or the lesste joie that was theere?[31]

31. Why had I not bought one such night at the price of my soul, yes, or the least joy that was there?

Yet he retains his typical attitude of spectator:

> This Troilus in armes gan hire streyne,
> And seyde, "O swete, as evere mot I gon,[32]
> Now be ye kaught, now is ther but we
> tweyne!
> Now yeldeth yow, for other bote is non!"[33]
> To that Criseyde answerede thus anon,
> "Ne hadde I er now, my swete herte deere,
> Ben yold, ywis, I were now nought heere!"[34]
>
> O, sooth is seyd, that heled for to be
> As of a fevre, or other gret siknesse,
> Men moste drynke, as men may ofte se,
> Ful bittre drynke; and for to han gladnesse,[35]
> Men drynken ofte peyne and gret distresse;
> I mene it here, as for this aventure,
> That thorugh a peyne hath founden al this
> cure.
>
> And now swetnesse semeth more swete,
> That bitternesse assaied was byforn;
> For out of wo in blisse now they flete;
> Non swich they felten syn that they were
> born.[36]
> Now is this bet than bothe two be lorn.
> For love of God, take every womman heede
> To werken thus, if it comth to the neede.
>
> Criseyde, al quyt from every drede and tene,[37]
> As she that juste cause hadde hym to triste,
> Made hym swich feste, it joye was to
> seene,[38]
> Whan she his trouthe and clene entente
> wiste;
> And as aboute a tree, with many a twiste,
> Bytrent and writh the swote wodebynde,[39]
> Gan ech of hem in armes other wynde.
>
> And as the newe abaysed nyghtyngale,
> That stynteth first whan she bygynneth to
> synge,

32. "As ever I may go (thrive)."
33. "There is no other remedy."
34. "Had I not been yielded before now, my dear, sweet heart, indeed I would not now be here."
35. To have gladness.
36. None such they felt since they were born.
37. Quite free of fear and distress.
38. Made such a feast (welcome) for him.
39. The sweet honeysuckle engirdles and writhes about.

Whan that she hereth any herde tale,
Or in the hegges any wyght stirynge,
And after siker doth hire vois out rynge,
Right so Criseyde, whan hire drede stente,[40]
Opned hire herte, and tolde hym hire
entente.

. . .

Hire armes smale, hir streghte bak and
softe,
Hire sydes longe, flesshly, smothe, and
white
He gan to stroke, and good thrift bad ful ofte
Hir snowisshe throte, hire brestes round and
lite:[41]
Thus in this hevene he gan hym to delite,
And therwithal a thousand tyme hire kiste,
That what to don, for joie unnethe he
wiste.[42]

. . .

"Benigne Love, thow holy bond of thynges,
Whoso wol grace, and list the nought
honouren,[43]
Lo, his desir wol fle withouten wynges."
(*Troilus and Criseyde* III)

But from this exaltation the poem has to turn; the fatal moment must come, the lovers must part. Once parted from her lover, Cryseyde lacks the strength to return to him; lacks the strength to resist Diomed; is faithless. Chaucer does not reproach her; he says he would excuse her, "for routhe," that is, for pity. At last Troilus is killed by the fierce Achilles.

Swich fyn hath, lo, this Troilus for love!
Swich fyn hath al his grete worthinesse!
Swich fyn hath his estat real above,[44]
Swich fyn his lust, swich fyn hath his
noblesse!
Swich fyn hath false worldes brotelnesse!

40. And as the newly abashed nightingale, that stops, as she begins to sing, when she hears any shepherd speak, and afterwards rings her voice out, just so Criseyde, when her fear ceased.

41. And begged a blessing on her snowy throat, her breasts, round and small.

42. He hardly knew what to do for joy.

43. Whoso desires grace, and cares not to honor thee.

44. Such an ending had his royal estate above (the earth, after death).

It is the insecurity of human love in a world ruled by chance that made Chaucer see the brittleness of the courtly code. Fortune can untie the holy bond of things in human affairs; and if we seek a lasting love, we must look elsewhere, to a region beyond fortune's power:

O younge, fresshe folkes, he or she,
In which that love up groweth with youre
age,
Repeyreth hom fro worldly vanyte,
And of youre herte up casteth the visage
To thilke God that after his ymage
Yow made,[45] and thynketh al nys but a faire
This world, that passeth soone as floures
faire.

And loveth hym, the which that right for
love
Upon a crois, oure soules for to beye
First starf, and roos, and sit in hevene above;
For he nyl falsen no wight, dar I seye,
That wol his herte al holly on hym leye.
And syn he best to love is, and most meeke,
What nedeth feynede loves for to seke?

[And love him who, exactly because of love, first died upon a cross, to buy our souls, and (then) rose and sits in heaven above; for he will not prove false to any, I dare affirm, that will wholly lay his heart upon him. And since he is the best and meekest to love, what is the need to seek a pretended love?] (*Troilus and Criseyde* V)

What the court held to be love, the church held to be sin. It had a contrary love system of its own. Of absolutely sovereign value in the church's scale of sex was virginity; there was no higher kind of life than to be a virgin for the love of God. Saint Jerome expressed the idea in one of his startling epigrams:

Nuptiae terram replent, virginitas
paradisum.

45. Repair home (i.e., to heaven) from wordly vanity and cast up the countenance of your heart to that God that made you after His image.

> [Marriages replenish the earth, virginity replenishes Paradise.] (*Epistola adversus Jovinianum*)

The preeminence of virginity is asserted by Chaucer in *The Parson's Tale*:

> Another synne of Leccherie is to bireve a mayden of hir maydenhede; for he that so dooth, certes, he casteth a mayden out of the hyeste degree that is in this present lyf . . . And forther over, sooth is that hooly ordre [holy orders] is chief of al the tresorie of God, and his especial signe and mark of chastitee . . . which that is the moost precious lyf that is.

It is again asserted by the Prioress, in her apostrophe to the martyred chorister:

> O martir, sowded to virginitee,[46]
> Now maystow syngen, folwynge evere in
> oon[47]
> The white Lamb celestial—quod she—
> Of which the grete evaungelist, Seint John,
> In Pathmos wroot, which seith that they
> that goon
> Biforn this Lamb, and synge a song al newe,
> That nevere, flesshly, wommen they ne
> knewe.[48]
> (*The Prioress's Tale*)

It is even asserted by the Wife of Bath.:

> Virginitee is greet perfeccion
> (*The Wife of Bath's Prologue*)

And again:

> Crist was a mayde, and shapen as a man,
> And many a seint, sith that the world bigan;
> Yet lyvved they evere in parfit chastitee.
> I nyl envye no virginitee.

Next to virginity, the church esteemed the condition of wedded chastity, which Shakespeare was later to celebrate allegorically in the *Threnos* of his most metaphysical poem, *The Phoenix and the Turtle*; it is a condition to which the Wife of Bath refers, with approval, as

> continence with devotion . . .

And one of the first stories Chaucer ever wrote, the story of Saint Cecilia (later *The Second Nun's Tale*), celebrates her sanctity in having persuaded her young and noble husband, on their wedding night and forever after, to forgo the consummation of his love. The same idea is at the back of Chaucer's mind when, in *The Man of Law's Tale*, he feels it incumbent on him to defend his holy-hearted heroine, Constance, for yielding her body to her husband. The passage rings in my ear with a note of comedy; but I am not sure if Chaucer intended it so, for it comes from his most pious period as a writer:

> They goon to bedde, as it was skile and
> right;[49]
> For thogh that wyves be full hooly thynges,
> They moste take in pacience at nyght
> Swiche manere necessaries as been
> plesynges
> To folk that han ywedded hem with rynges,
> And leye a lite hir hoolynesse aside,
> As for the tyme,—it may no bet bitide.[50]

Griselda is another chaste and patient wife; her story, enormously popular in the Middle Ages, found its fullest eloquence in Chaucer's telling of it. It was an earlyish work of his; and when he came back in later life to shape it as *The Clerk's Tale* for inclusion in *The Canterbury Tales*, he modified the effect of this marriage sermon by adding an ironic tailpiece:

> It were ful harde to fynde now-a-dayes
> In al a toun Grisildis thre or two; . . .

Still, virginity and chastity and married love of the kind approved by the church were ap-

46. O martyr, soldered to virginity.
47. Continually following.
48. That never knew women after the manner of the flesh.
49. As it was reasonable and right.
50. And lay aside her holiness a little for the moment, one can do no better.

proved in these and other of Chaucer's poems, and with no less poetry than he had celebrated courtly love. It is true that there is no sexual ecstasy recorded of the unions of Griselda and of Constance with their husbands; but then, sexual ecstasy, even in marriage, was held suspect:

> And for that many man weneth that he may nat synne for no likerousnesse that he dooth with his wyf, certes that opinion is false. (*The Parson's Tale*)

Over against what the church taught and what the troubadours taught about women, there were the opinions of the celibate misogynists. They reached in a long tradition from Saint Jerome to Walter Map, and the extremes to which they went in vilifying the fair sex almost outdistanced the extremes of the gynecolaters in the opposite direction; as I have said before, it was an age of extremes.

The Wife of Bath knew all about these scholars, the children of Mercury, the natural enemies of the children of Venus:

> The clerk, whan he is oold, and may noght do
> Of Venus werkes worth his olde sho,
> Thanne sit he doun, and writ in his dotage
> That wommen kan nat keepe hir mariage!

But, for all her low opinion of them as lovers, she admired them as debaters, and put on the whole armor of their abuse to subdue her first three husbands; her method was to anticipate the worst that could be said of women—and here she helped herself freely to Saint Jerome—and fling it back scornfully at her men:

> Thou seist to me it is a greet meschief
> To wedde a povre womman, for costage;
> And if that she be riche, of heigh parage,[51]
> Thanne seistow that it is a tormentrie
> To soffre hire pride and hire malencolie.
> And if that she be fair" thou verray knave,
> Thou seyst that every holour wol hire have;[52]
>
> . . .
>
> And if that she be foul, thou seist that she
> Coveiteth every man that she may se,
> For as a spanyel she wol on hym lepe,
> Til that she fynde som man hire to chepe.[53]
> Ne noon so grey goos goth ther in the lake
> As, seistow, wol been withoute make.[54]
>
> Thus seistow, lorel,[55] whan thow goost to bedde;
> And that no wys man nedeth for to wedde,
> With wilde thonder-dynt and firy leven
> Moote thy welked nekke be tobroke![56]

All this, and much more, that she had to say came, almost word for word, from Saint Jerome's *Epistola adversus Jovinianum* and from other "celibate" sources.

She met her match in her fifth husband, a pretty-legged lad half her age called Jankyn (Johnnykin), with whom she was reckless enough to fall in love; this lost her the initial advantage and it was soon he, not she, who was studying the misogynists; they became his favorite reading.

> He hadde a book that gladly, nyght and day,
> For his desport he wolde rede always;
>
> . . .
>
> At which book he lough alway ful faste.

It was a composite volume full of anecdote, proverb, and abuse against women; and the Wife gives us long extracts from it. Here, for instance, is an anecdote borrowed from Walter Map:

> Thanne tolde he me how oon Latumyus
> Compleyned unto his felawe Arrius
> That in his gardyn growed swich a tree
> On which he seyde how that his wyves thre

51. High lineage.

52. That every lecher will have her.

53. Some man to make a bid for her.

54. Will be without a mate.

55. Thus you say, you wretch.

56. With a wild thunderbolt and fiery lightning, may your withered neck be dashed in pieces!

Hanged hemself for herte despitus.[57]
"O leeve brother," quod this Arrius,
"Yif me a plante of thilke blissed tree,
And in my gardyn planted shal it bee."

It was in these ways that Chaucer chose to voice the views of the *tertium quid.*

If the wonderful Wife of Bath seems, when we first meet her, to have drawn her philosophy from some Cartesian well of *Copulo ergo sum,* we soon get to know her better and appreciate the complexities of her character; she can hold contradictory beliefs without the slightest inconvenience to herself, such as that virginity is a great perfection and celibacy a thing contemptible. Her bullying methods with her husbands seem at first a matter of mood and idiosyncrasy, but turn out to be employed on principle; and it is this that puts her in a central position in the great sex war of *The Canterbury Tales.* It is fought on the issue "Who is to have the mastery in marriage, husband or wife?"

How she handled her husbands is a lesson to every knowing woman (as she says herself) and to every man about to marry, as Chaucer said in the poem to his friend Bukton, in that momentous situation:

The Wyf of Bathe I pray yow that ye rede. . . .

In her view, it was right and proper that husbands should submit to their wives; this is not only the moral of her long preamble (the *Prologue* to her tale) but also of the tale itself. The point of the story is to discover what it is that women most wish for, and the surprising answer is:

"Wommen desiren have sovereyntee
As wel over hir housbond as hir love,
And for to been in maistrie hym above."

Women, that is, wish for the same sovereignty over their husbands that they exercise over their lovers—a tall order.

57. Hanged themselves, out of the spite in their hearts.

The challenge thus flung down by the Wife of Bath is taken up by the Clerk of Oxford with his tale of patient Griselda and her exemplary obedience to her husband. Other aspects of marriage come before us too: *The Merchant's Tale* of January and May shows what can happen between husband and wife when an old man marries a young girl. *The Shipman's Tale* presents us with the well-known truth that there are always half a dozen things a woman absolutely needs, to keep up with the neighbors, that she cannot very well tell her husband about:

And well y woot that wommen naturelly
Desiren thynges sixe as wel as I:
. . .
For his honour, myself for to arraye, . . .

And so she is driven to tell someone else:

Thanne moot another payen for oure cost,
Or lene us gold,[58] and that is perilous.

Perhaps the liveliest domestic scene is that between Chanticleer and Pertelote, when with husbandly self-importance he debates the prophetic meaning of a dream he has had that his wife ascribes to constipation.

These are the variations on the theme proposed by the Wife of Bath to which we return for a final statement by the Franklin; his story voices that wise equability and kindliness that is so great an attribute of Chaucer's mind. The Franklin's hero and heroine are married lovers; they had begun their attachment by falling in love in the best courtly manner:

And many a labour, many a greet emprise[59]
He for his lady wroghte, er she were wonne.
. . .
But atte last she, for his worthynesse,
And namely[60] for his meke obeysaunce,
Hath swich a pitee caught of his penaunce
That pryvely she fil of his accord
To take hym for hir housbonde and hir lord,

58. Lend us gold.
59. Enterprise.
60. Especially.

Of swich lordshipe as men han over hir
wyves.

This fourteenth-century Millamant and her Mirabell had, however, laid down certain provisos and counterprovisos before they agreed to marry; he was to exercise no "maistri" over her:

But hire obeye, and folwe hir wyl in al, . . .

And she was to allow him "the name of soveraynetee," so that he should not in public suffer the disgrace of his surrendered authority.

That wolde he have for shame of his degree.

And, on this happy compromise, the Franklin stops his story for a moment to address the company with a Chaucerian wisdom suiting his sanguine temperament:

For o thyng, sires, saufly dar I seye,
That freendes everych oother moot obeye,[61]
If they wol longe holden compaignye.
Love wol nat been constreyned by maistrye.
Whan maistrie comth, the God of Love
anon
Beteth his wynges, and farewel, he is gon!
Love is a thyng as any spirit free.
Wommen, of kynde, desiren libertee,[62]
And nat to been constreyned as a thral;
And so doon men, if I sooth seyen shal.

There was still one other attitude to lovemaking ambient in those times for Chaucer to voice and grace: the attitude of the fabliaux, the lowlife oral tales of animal grab[63] that in all ages circulate from person to person, like a limerick. In the typical fabliau, copulation seems to thrive in its cold-blooded way, borne along on strong undercurrents of guilt and hatred. Priests and millers (the most powerful and therefore the most-to-be-humiliated men in the village) are generally the victims; and the very sexuality of the story, which, at one level, they are supposed to enjoy, at another level seems to be a part of their vileness, even of their punishment. The laugh at the end is bitter with triumphant malice.

Chaucer took two such sow's-ear stories and turned them into the silk purses of *The Miller's Tale* and *The Reeve's Tale.* Here, at the bottom of the social scale, the clerical students of Oxford and Cambridge, happy-go-luckies of a saucy sexuality, are seen aping the adulteries of the aristocracy with all the cant of courtly love on their tongues. Nicholas in *The Miller's Tale* woos Alison with

" . . . Lemman, love me al at ones,
Or I wol dyen, also God me save!"

It is the argument that Pandarus uses on behalf of Troilus. Absalom, in the same story, goes on his knees (as Troilus did) to receive a kiss. That he got more than he bargained for cured him forever, we are told, of love *par amour,* that is, of courtly love. But Chaucer does more than this to rescue his fabliaux from their beastly dullness. The whole life of the village springs up before us—the rustic conversation, the superstition, the cunning; the impudence and bravado of the young in their gallantries; the rascality of the Miller, the gullibility of the Carpenter; the cottages they live in; and the vivid wenches

With buttokes brode, and brestes round and
hye

of whose portraits Alison's is the most convincingly fresh and seductive that Chaucer, or anyone else, ever painted.

If, then, we ask ourselves what this "servant of the servants of Love" knew about his masters, and about their Master, a short answer would be that he knew everything; everything that was known and felt on the subject at that time in Christendom. He voiced the whole thought of the Middle Ages, speaking as eloquently for courtly as for Christian love, and as much an expert in marriage as in misogyny; everything came within the power

61. Friends must obey one another.
62. Women, by nature, desire liberty.
63. A children's card game

of his pen, right down to the antics of John and Alan, Nicholas and Absalom and their "popelotes." No other English author has a comparable range in such matters. But it is not only a question of range, variety, and subtlety in his art of love; it is the sympathy. Chaucer is all things to all men and women in all their moods and modes of love, able to write as easily of the lowest as of the highest:

O mooder Mayde! O mayde Mooder free!
O bussh unbrent, brennynge in Moyses
  sighte,
That ravyshedest doun fro the Deitee,
Thurgh thyn humblesse, the Goost that in
  th'alighte,
Of whose vertu, whan he thyn herete lighte,
Conceyved was the Fadres sapience, . . .

[. . . O bush unburnt, burning in the sight of Moses, thou that didst ravish down, from the Deity, the Spirit that alighted in thee, by thy humbleness; by whose power, when He illumined thy heart, the Sapience of the Father was conceived . . .] (*The Prioress's Prologue*)

The reason he can do so is that he takes joy in the created world, grasps life affirmatively, and calls nothing that God has made unclean.

MEN AND WOMEN

For the eye altering alters all.
William Blake, *The Mental Traveller*

Chaucer thought the work of a writer to be something like that of a reaper; and it is with a wondering smile that we hear him say that all the corn of poetry has been reaped already, and that only the gleanings are left for him after the great poets of the past have done their work:

For wel I wot that folk han here-beforn
Of makyng ropen, and lad awey the corn;[64]
And I come after, glenynge here and there,
And am ful glad if I may fynde en ere[65]
Of any goodly word that they han left.
(*The Prologue to The Legend of Good Women*)

The fields that he is thinking of are the fields of "auctoritee," that is, of the ancient writers that he loved so much for their poetry, philosophy, and learning, whence all new learning came:

For out of olde feldes, as men seyth,
Cometh al this newe corn from yer to yere,
And out of olde bokes, in good feyth,
Cometh al this newe science that men lere.[66]
(*The Parliament of Fowls*)

But there was another immense field, the field of experience, which Chaucer himself was wont to contrast with "auctoritee." It was the "fair field of folk" of which his great contemporary, Langland, had written, the busy London world of men and women, with whom, whether he was at court or in the customs house, it was his profession and his pleasure to deal.

No one had ever looked at people in the way Chaucer did; it was his eye that altered everything, for it knew what to look for. His was not only an observant, but also an instructed, eye through which he looked out on the world of experience. The instruction had, however, come to him from authority.

There are at least three kinds of books that we can observe directing Chaucer's discovery of human nature: books on rhetoric, books on medicine, and books on astrology. From each of these he learned something that helped to train his eye. To demonstrate this (as I shall now try) is not to offer an explanation of his genius, but to show it at work.

Other men may perhaps have known as much as he about rhetoric, medicine, and astrology; but Chaucer knew how to use his knowledge, how to put his knowledge (so to

64. For well I know that folk before now have reaped (the field of) poetry and carried away the corn.

65. Find an ear (of corn).

66. Learn.

speak) at the disposal of his eyes and ears. The result can be seen in the descriptions of the characters in *The General Prologue.*

The rhetoricians were perfectly clear on the subject of how to present a human being; it was a technique or figure known to them as *descriptio,* of which there were at least three equally explicit doctrines current in the Middle Ages. The first was Cicero's.

> Ac personis has res attributas putamus; nomen,
> naturam, victum, fortunam, habitum, affectionem,
> studia, consilia, facta, casus, orationes.
>
> [We hold the following to be the attributes of persons: name, nature, manner of life, fortune, habit, feeling, interests, purposes, achievements, accidents, conversation.] (*De Inventione,* I, XXIV)

As Cicero goes on to paraphrase these eleven attributes, we are able to gloss them, where necessary, as follows:

Name.
Nature. Includes sex, place of origin, family, age, bodily appearance, whether bright or dull, affable or rude, patient or the reverse, and all qualities of mind or body bestowed by nature.
Manner of Life. Includes occupation, trade, or profession, and the character of the person's home life.
Fortune. Includes whether rich or poor, successful or a failure, and rank.
Habit. Includes special knowledge or bodily dexterity won by careful training and practice.
Feeling. A fleeting passion, such as joy, desire, fear, vexation.
Interests. Mental activity devoted to some special subject.
Purposes. Any deliberate plan.
Achievements. What a person is doing, has done, or will do.
Accidents. What is happening to a person, has happened, or will happen.
Conversation. What a person has said, is saying, or will say.

I suppose many readers will agree that the most strikingly described character in *The General Prologue* is that of the Wife of Bath. In some thirty natural, easy lines of seemingly casual observation, she appears in startling completeness. For all that air of unconcern, Chaucer has worked his miracle by remembering his Cicero:

A good Wif was ther of biside Bathe,	*Nature* (sex, place of origin)
But she was somdel deef, and that was scathe.	(bodily quality)
Of clooth-makying she hadde swich an haunt,	*Manner* of Life (trade)
She passed hem of Ypres and of Gaunt.	*Habit* (dexterity)
In al the parisshe wif ne was ther noon	*Fortune* (rank)
That to the offrynge bifore hire sholde goon;	
And if ther dide, certeyne so wrooth was she,	*Feeling* (vexation)
That she was out of alle charitee.	
Hir coverchiefs ful fyne weren of ground;	*Nature* (appearance)
I dorste swere they weyeden ten pound	
That on a Sonday weren upon hir heed.	
Hir hosen weren of fyn scarlet reed,	
Ful striete yteyd, abd shoes ful moyste and newe.	
Boold was hir face, and fair, and reed of hewe.	
She was a worthy womman al hir lyve:	*Fortune* (rank)
Housbondes at chirche dore she hadde fyve,	*Manner of Life* (home life)
Withouten oother compaignye in youthe,—	
But thereof nedeth nat to speke as nowthe.	
And thries had she been at Jerusalem;	*Achievements* (past doings)
She hadde passed many a straunge strem;	and *Accidents*

At Rome she hadde been, and at Boloigne,
In Galice at Seint-Jame, and at Coloigne.
She koude muchel of wandrynge by the weye. *Habit* (special knowledge)
Gat-tothed was she, soothly for to seye. *Nature* (bodily quality)
Upon an amblere esily she sat, *Achievements* (what doing)
Ywympled wel, and on hir heed an hat *Nature* (appearance)
As brood as is a bokeler or a targe;
A foot-mantel aboute hir hippes large,
And on hir feet a paire of spores sharpe.
In felaweshipe wel koude she laughe and carpe. *Conversation*
Of remedies of love she knew per chaunce. *Interests*
For she koude of that art the olde daunce.

The only points demanded by Cicero that are omitted are her name and purposes. We learn later that her name was Alison; as for her purposes, one of them could go without saying—to seek the shrine of Saint Thomas with the other pilgrims. We may perhaps infer another:

Yblessed be God that I have wedded fyve!
Welcome the sixte, whan that evere he shal.
(*The Wife of Bath's Prologue*)

Ciceronian as her portrait is, Cicero cannot claim it all. There is the hint of something learned from Geoffrey de Vinsauf in it, too. Vinsauf's teaching was that a description must start at the top of the head and inch its way downward, detail by detail, to the feet—*poliatur ad unguem,* let it be polished to the toenail. To follow this counsel slavishly would lead to what, in another context, Chaucer calls the "fulsomness of his prolixitee"; but he follows it selectively, beginning with the ten-pound headdress. His eye is then drawn for an instant from the boldness of her face to her all-too-striking hose, but returns to her face and wimple, glides to her hips, and falls to her spurs.

A third doctrine of *descriptio* was that of Matthieu de Vendôme, who held that a writer must first describe the moral nature and then the physical appearance of his subject. Chaucer moved easily among all these prescriptions, allowing each to point in some direction where the discerning eye could pause, the attentive ear listen. So it comes about that the description of the Prioress in *The General-Prologue* begins in the Ciceronian manner (name, sex, profession, social position, special skill, and her prevailing study, "to been estatlich of manere"), then follows Matthieu with an account of her moral sensibilities, her amiable carriage, her charity and tenderness of heart, her charming sentimentality over her pets (which, as a nun, she of course had no business to own), and at last comes to her appearance; here he follows Vinsauf, starting with her wimple and thence to nose, eyes, and mouth, moving downward to the telltale wrist with its ambiguous brooch inscribed *Amor vincit omnia.* Her portrait is a perfect example of how rules obey a genius.

There was also a medical approach to character. Medicine had evolved a theory that the human constitution was fashioned of the four elements: earth, air, fire, and water. Earth had the quality of being cold and dry; air, hot and moist; fire, hot and dry; water, cold and moist. According to the particular proportion and mixture of these elements in the individual man, he was thought to have a predominating "complexion" or temperament. Too earthy, he would be melancholy; too airy, he would be sanguine; too fiery, he would be choleric; too watery, he would be phlegmatic.

To each of these "complexions" or "humors" were attached a number of subsidiary qualities and predispositions, so well known as to be enshrined in popular mnemonic verses, both Latin and English. Here, for instance, is a popular rhyme to remind you what to expect of a sanguine man:

Or yiftes large,[67]
in love hath grete delite,
Iocunde and gladde, ay of laughyng chiere,
Of ruddy colour meynt somdel with white;[68]
Disposed by kynde[69] to be a champioun,
Hardy I-nough, manly, and bold of chiere.
Of the sangwyne also it is a signe
To be demure, right curteys, and benynge.
(Robbins, *Secular Lyrics of the XIVth and XVth Centuries*[70])

The General Prologue tells us that the Franklin was a sanguine man, and that one word is intended to carry all the qualities listed in the rhyme. They fit him very well, not only as we first see him but also as we see him later, during his colloquy with the Squire, and in the tenor of his tale. The Reeve, we are told, was choleric; all that he says and does is in keeping with what medical lore asserted of such men, who were held to be refractory, deceitful, given to anger, full of ruses, lustful, hardy, small and slender, dry of nature, covetous and solemn. Indeed, the Host rebukes him for solemnity in the prelude to his tale. The Pardoner's moral and physical nature are described in terms from which any doctor (as W. C. Curry[71] has made clear) could at once have diagnosed him as a eunuch from birth, and this fact about him explains much in his subsequent adventures on the pilgrimage. Chaucer helped himself to medical lore in much the way a modern novelist might use his knowledge of Freud or Jung.

Astrology offered yet another approach to the imagining of a character. Curry has also shown that the characters of King Emetrius and King Lycurgus in *The Knight's Tale* are imagined as "personal representatives, in the lists, of the astrological forces" that are involved in the story—namely of Saturn and/or Mars, respectively—and he quotes Ptolemy to show that the description of these kings by Chaucer follows almost exactly the physical details attributed to men born under those planets. Astrology is explicitly invoked by the Wife of Bath to account for the contradictions in her character; they were dictated by the position of the heavenly bodies at her birth:

For certes, I am al Venerien
In feelynge, and myn herte is Marcien.
Venus me yaf my lust, my likerousnesse,
And Mars yaf me my sturdy hardynesse;
Myn ascendent was Taur, and Mars therinne.
Allas! allas! that evere love was synne!
(*The Wife of Bath's Prologue*)

Instructed in such ways as these by *auctoritee,* Chaucer looked out with sharpened eyes upon experience, and saw not only how to grasp the essentials of a personality posed for a portrait, but also how to make use of what is latent within a given personality and to draw it forth with a surprising touch of individual or local color. For instance, in *The Miller's Tale,* when the superstitious old carpenter living at Osney, just outside Oxford, peeps into the room of his lodger, Nicholas, to find out what is wrong with him, he sees Nicholas lying gaping on his back on the floor:

This carpenter to blessen hym bigan,
And seyde "Help us, seinte Frydeswyde!"

In other words, he crossed himself and invoked Saint Frideswide, the local Oxford saint. One can tell that the carpenter was an Oxford man simply from that.

In like manner, in *The Reeve's Tale* the Miller's wife, awakened by the battle between Alan and the Miller, and feeling the sudden weight of her husband's body falling on top of her, cries out:

"Help! hooly croys of Bromeholm" . . .

This relic, the holy cross of Bromeholm, was preserved in East Norfolk, where the Reeve came from. No one else in Chaucer invokes

67. Large in his giving.

68. Mingled somewhat with white.

69. Disposed by nature.

70. R. H. Robbins, ed., *Secular Lyrics of the XIVth and XVth Centuries* (London, 1952; 2nd ed., 1955).

71. W. C Curry, *Chaucer and the Medieval Sciences.*

Saint Frideswide or the holy cross of Bromeholm; they are pinpoints of local color latent in the people he was creating, and perceived by him.

This power of seeing the implications in a character or a situation, so as to give a sudden twist or flavor, depth or tone, to his tale is one of the important things that make Chaucer immeasurably superior as a storyteller to his friend and contemporary John Gower, and indeed to all writers of English narrative poetry. The perceptiveness of which I am speaking is continuously, sensitively present throughout *Troilus and Criseyde,* in which there is never a false move or impulse of feeling; and the whole is sensed to be deploying humanly, freely, and yet inevitably under the compulsions latent in the characters, in their struggle with destiny.

On a smaller scale, we may see the operation of this kind of insight in *The Merchant's Tale,* perhaps his most masterly short story. It is characterized by Chaucer's usual moral lucidity. Nothing could be clearer than the never stated motive of rebellious lust present in its three main characters. These are old January, whose senile sexuality is hallowed by matrimony and encouraged by aphrodisiacs; young Damian, with his treacherous animalism; and the "faire fresshe May," who is ready to climb a tree to gratify her desires.

With rarest comment by the narrator, all three are presented through their own eyes, that is, with all the sympathy and self-approval that they all separately feel for the fantasy lives latent within them, which Chaucer elicits. January sees himself as a dear, kind, wise old gentleman, penitent for his past, eager to sin no more, and seeking the delicious safety and sancity of wedlock; his earnest care in consulting his friends in the choice of a wife (but insisting that she be under twenty), his tender apprehensions lest she be too delicate to endure his amorous heats, his solicitude for the sick squire Damian (who is about to cuckold him) and for the soul of his wife (about to collaborate with the squire) are all presented from the old man's point of view. In his own opinion, he is a generous, romantic figure; his wife will wear mourning forever after his death. We even hear his doting use of troubadour language to entice his wife into the priapic garden of the rose that he had designed for their summery encounters; like Absalom and Nicholas, he would be a courtly lover too, and borrow from the Song of Songs:

"Rys up, my wyf, my love, my lady free!
The turtles voys is herd, my dowve sweete;
The wynter is goon with alle his reynes
weete.
Com forth now, with thyne eyen
columbyn![72]
How fairer been thy brestes than is wyn!"

At the end of this dithyramb, Chaucer (or his persona, the Merchant) permits himself the remark:

Swiche olde lewed wordes used he.

But the irony does not consist in the bare contrast between this fantasy of courtly love and the nastiness of the old lecher who utters it; he is nothing so simple as a rich, dirty old man— perhaps no one is. He *is* considerate, affectionate, and generous—humble, even ready to admit his dislikable qualities to his girl-wife:

"And though that I be jalous, wyte me
noght.[73]
Ye been so depe enprented in my thoght
That, whan that I considere youre beautee,
And therwithal the unlikely elde of me,[74]
I may not, certes, though I sholde dye,
Forbere to been out of youre compaignye
For verray love; this is withouten doute.
Now kys me, wyf, and lat us rome aboute."

In all the irony, there is pathos; and in the pathos, irony. That January should go blind (as he does in the course of the story) is pathetic, but it is ironic too. He had been blind all along:

72. With they dove's eyes.
73. Blame me not.
74. My dislikable old age.

O Januarie, what myghte it thee availle,
Thogh thou myghte se as fer as shippes
saille?
For as good is blind deceyved be
As to be deceyved whan a man may se.[75]

In like manner, young Damian, the seducer, is, in his own esteem, a lover-poet; he wears the verses that he writes to May in a silk purse upon his heart, and May, who reads and memorizes his lines in a toilet (down the drain of which, for safety, she consigns them) is a heroine of romance to herself:

"Certeyn," thoghte she, "whom that this
thyng displese
I rekke noght, for heere I hym assure
To love hym best of any creature,
Though he namoore hadde than his sherte!"

Again the ironical narrator allows himself to intrude:

Lo, pitee renneth soone in gentil herte!

No moral is pointed at the end of this story; by a perfection of irony, they all lived happily ever after.

There is one character in Chaucer that neither realistic observation nor the authority of ancient books can wholly account for. He comes from some unknown half-world, a visiting presence that some have thought to be the figure of Death, some of the Wandering Jew, some of the old Adam seeking renewal. It may be better to leave him wholly mysterious and unexplained; it is the ancient, muffled man who directs the three rioters of *The Pardoner's Tale* to the heap of gold when they ask him if he knows where Death is to be found. To their rough language, and the question why he is so old, he gives this strange reply:

"For I ne kan nat fynde
A man, though that I walked into Ynde,
Neither in citee ne in no village,
That wolde chaunge his youthe for myn age;
And therefoce moot I han myn age stille,
As longe tyme as it is Goddes wille.
Ne Deeth, allas! ne wol nat han my lyf
Thus walke I, lyk a restelees kaityf,[76]
And on the ground, which is my moodres
gate,
I knokke with my staf, bothe erly and late,
And seye 'Leeve mooder, leet me in!
Lo how I vanysshe, flessh, and blood, and
skyn!
Allas! whan shul my bones been at reste?' "

It is a shock to meet with so haunting a figure in the bright Chaucerian world, a figure so loaded with suggestions of supernatural meaning. With slow gravity, he rebukes the three rioters for their discourteous behavior:

"But, sires, to yow it is no curteisye
To speken to an old man vileynye. . . ."

And that is the reader's link with this strange phantom and the shadowy world to which he belongs—the huge importance of courtesy. We are never told who our instructor is, nor has he been found in any book that Chaucer studied, save for a few hints in the obscure Latin poet Maximian; the essential creation is all Chaucer's, and it was his "cyclopean eye" that discerned this eerie figure, tap-tapping his invisible way through the crowds at Queenshithe or by the Custom House, and among the courtiers of Richard II at the palace of Eltham or of Shene.

ENVOI

I am sure you are become a good Chaucerist.
Ralph Winwood, *Letter to Sir Thomas Edmondes, 1601*

The intention here has been to present Chaucer's career as a courtier and to suggest its ef-

75. For it is as good to be deceived when blind as when you have your sight.

76. Like a restless captive.

fect on his career as a poet, rather than to write an all-embracing "honeysuckle life." If this approach leaves much unsaid that needs saying, there are many other studies to supply my deficiencies. More can always be said of any great poet.

Chaucer's greatness was a little impugned by Matthew Arnold, in a celebrated passage, where Chaucer is accused of lacking "high seriousness." It is clear, however, that Arnold knew very little about Chaucer; he shows only a slight acquaintance with *The Canterbury Tales* and does not appear to have read *Troilus and Criseyde* at all. It need not, therefore, surprise us that he did not perceive Chaucer's moral stature, or that he could not find high seriousness in high comedy; he did not know where to look for it.

There is so much fun in Chaucer, and so little reproof, that his appeal to moralists (who are seldom quite happy about pleasure) is not immediate. Yet he is one of those rare poets who can strongly affect not only our passions and intelligence, but our wills too; he creates generosities in them. A sense of welcome to the created world, to men and women, and to the experience of living flows from his pen.

Chaucer can reach out to a supernal world too; and if, to do so, he has borrowed a little from Dante, he knew what to borrow and how to borrow it:

> Thow oon, and two, and thre, eterne on
> lyve,
> That regnest ay in thre, and two, and oon,
> Uncircumscript, and al maist circumscrive,
> Us, from visible and invisible foon,
> Defende, . . .

[Thou one and two and three, that livest eternally and reignest ever in three and two and one, uncomprehended, and yet comprehending all things, defend us from visible and invisible foes . . .] (*Troilus and Criseyde,* V)

> Withinne the clositre blisful of thy sydis
> Took mannes shap the eterneel love and
> pees, . . .

[Within the blissful cloister of thy womb, the eternal love and peace took human shape, . . .] (*The Second Nun's Prologue*)

> Victorious tree, proteccioun of trewe,
> That oonly worthy were for to bere
> The Kyng of Hevene with his woundes
> newe,
> The white Lamb that hurt was with a spere,
> . . .

[Victorious tree, the protection of all true (souls), that alone wert worthy to bear the King of Heaven . . .] (*The Man of Law's Tale*)

But it is the mortal world that most exercised his poetical gift, and there he is nearest to Shakespeare as the poet of humane understanding; like him, Chaucer begets a *caritas* in the imagination of his readers. His vision of earth ranges from one of amused delight to one of grave compassion; these are his dawn and his dusk. His daylight is a lively April of fresh goodwill and kindly common sense, and if, here and there, there is a delicate frost of irony, warmth is his great characteristic. He takes deep joy in what we think of as the simple things of nature—birdsong, sunlight, gardens, daisies in the grass, the "ayerissh bestes" of the sky (the ram, the bull, and other signs of the zodiacal zoo), and even in a timid hound puppy, met in a wood:

> And as I wente, ther cam by mee
> A whelp, that fauned me as I stood,
> That hadde yfolowed, and koude no good.
> Hyt com and crepte to me as lowe
> Ryght as hyt hadde me yknowe,
> Helde doun hys hed and joyned hys eres,
> And leyde al smothe doun hys heres.
> I wolde have kaught hyt, and anoon
> Hyt fledde, and was from me goon, . . .
> (*The Book of the Duchess*)

The joy Chaucer seems to experience, he can communicate, or create in others, and that is to create a kind of goodness, or a mood that makes goodness easier; he forges a basic sense of, and desire for, harmony. His universe is not off course, but on the way to a perhaps distant but happy and Christian fulfillment, in which men and women have their generous share. There are plenty of rascals among them, to be sure; he gazes at them evenly with unembarrassed, uncondemning delight, limiting his aspirations to *tout comprendre* and leaving *tout pardonner* to higher authority.

All this is done with laughter not left behind, nor music either. If Matthew Arnold was a little blind where Chaucer was concerned, at least he was not deaf; and he wrote with wonderful discernment and eloquence on the sound of Chaucer's verses:

> of Chaucer's divine liquidness of diction, of his divine fluidity of movement, it is difficult to speak temperately. They are irresistible, and justify all the rapture with which his successors speak of his "gold dewdrops of speech."

Chaucer's music was not unrelated to his courtiership. The *Liber niger* of Edward IV ordains that young henxmen shall be encouraged to "harping, to pype and sing." Squires of his household

> of old be accustomed, winter and summer, in afternoons and evenings, to draw to Lordes Chambres within Court, there to keep honest company after there Cunninge, in talking of Cronicles of Kinges and other Pollicies, or in pipeing or harpeing, songinges and other actes marcealls, to help to occupie the Court, and accompanie estrangers . . .

In afternoons and evenings, Chaucer's music would be heard in his own voice ("after his cunning[77]), when he read out his poems. In winter, in a lord's chamber or in the great hall; in summer, in the garden below, where he would "help to occupie the Court, and accompanie estrangers," Jean Froissart, perhaps, among others.

The College of Corpus Christi, Cambridge, owns a fifteenth-century manuscript of *Troilus and Criseyde*; in it there is a full-page illumination of just such a scene. Against a sky of afternoon gold rise the trees and towers of a royal palace—Shene, it may be, or Windsor, or Eltham; a company of young lords and ladies in the richly simple robes of those times are moving down the garden slopes toward a dell where a small pulpit has been set up. It is surrounded by the gathering court: the queen is seated on the grass before it, with her ladies about her. King Richard stands in cloth of gold, a little to the left of her; to the right there stands an older man in blue, with a gold girdle. It might be John of Gaunt. In the pulpit, at which this older man is gazing, Geoffrey Chaucer is reading from a book; he seems to be a youngish man. The hair and eyes are still brown; the eyes also have something of a sad look.

He is reading from his greatest completed poem, the first tragedy in the English language, *Troilus and Criseyde*:

> Go, litel bok, go, litel myn tragedye,
> Ther God this makere yet, er that he dye,
> So sende myght to make in som comedye!
> But litel book, no makyng thow n'envie,
> But subgit be to alle poesye;
> And kis the steppes, where as thow seest pace
> Virgile, Ovide, Omer, Lucan, and Stace.
>
> [Go, little book, go my little tragedy, to that place whence may God likewise yet send thy maker power to make something in the manner of a comedy, before he dies! But, little book, envy no other poetry, but be subject to all poesy, and kiss the steps where thou seest Vergil, Ovid, Homer, Lucan, and Statius pacing.]

The "litel bok" did its errand and the "myght" was duly sent; it gave us our first and freshest comedy, *The Canterbury Tales.*

77. skill

Selected Bibliography

COLLECTED WORKS, ANTHOLOGIES, AND EDITIONS

W. W. Skeat, ed. 6 vols., *The Complete Works of Geoffrey Chaucer,* (Oxford, 1894)); R. K. Root, ed., *The Book of*

Troilus and Criseyde, (Princeton, 1926; 3rd printing, corrected, 1945); F. N. Robinson, ed., *The Complete Works of Geoffrey Chaucer,* (Boston, 1933; 2nd ed., 1957), the source of the quotations from Chaucer in the above text; J. M. Manly, et al., eds., *The Text of the Canterbury Tales,* 8 vols. (Chicago, 1940), the basic textual ed.; E. T. Donaldson, ed., *Chaucer's Poetry: An Anthology for the Modern Reader,* (New York, 1958); D. S. Brewer, ed., *The Parlement of Foulys,* (London, 1960; corrected 2nd ed., Manchester, 1972); A. C. Baugh, ed., *Chaucer's Major Poetry,* (New York, 1963); R. A. Pratt, ed., *The Tales of Canterbury,* (Boston, 1974).

CONCORDANCE, SOURCES AND ANALOGUES, DICTIONARIES

Tatlock, J. S. P., and A. G. Kennedy, *A Concordance to the Complete Works of Geoffrey Chaucer and to the Romaunt of the Rose,* (Washington, D.C., 1927); Gordon, R. K., *The Story of Troilus as Told by Benoît de Sainte-Maure, Giovanni Boccaccio [translated into English prose], Geoffrey Chaucer and Robert Henryson,* (New York, 1934); W. F. Bryan and G. Dempster, eds., *Sources and Analogues of Chaucer's Canterbury Tales,* (Chicago, 1941); Magoun, F. P., Jr., *A Chaucer Gazeteer,* (Chicago, 1961); Ross, T. W., *Chaucer's Bawdy,* (New York, 1972); Dillion, B., *A Chaucer Dictionary: Proper Names and Allusions,* (Boston, 1974).

REPUTATION

Spurgeon, C. F. E., *Five Hundred Years of Chaucer Criticism and Allusion 1357–1900,* 3 vols. (Cambridge, 1925), first issued in parts by the Chaucer Society between 1914 and 1924, the basic work; J. A. Burrow, ed., *Geoffrey Chaucer: A Critical Anthology,* (Harmondsworth, 1969); Miskimin, A., *The Renaissance Chaucer,* (New Haven, 1975); Brewer, D., *Chaucer: The Critical Heritage,* 2 vols. (London, 1978).

FACSIMILES

The Works 1532: With Supplementary Material from the Editions of 1542, 1561, 1598, and 1602, (London, 1969); *The Canterbury Tales,* (London, 1972). Caxton's 2nd ed. of *The Canterbury Tales,* 1484; *Boecius Translated by G. Chaucer,* (Norwood, N.J., 1974).

BIOGRAPHICAL AND GENERAL STUDIES

Lounsbury, T. R., *Studies in Chaucer,* 3 vols. (New York, 1892), a pioneering work that remains valuable on the early false biographical accounts and the learning of Chaucer; Kittredge, G. L., *Chaucer and His Poetry,* (Cambridge, Mass., 1915), reiss. with intro. by B. J. Whiting (1970), classic account by a great scholar; Manly, J. M., *Some New Light on Chaucer,* (New York, 1926), identifies pilgrims with real people, with varying degrees of certainty; Manly, J. M., "Chaucer and the Rhetoricians," in *Proceedings of the British Academy,* 12 (1926), the pioneer work, although Manly's conclusions are now largely qualified; French, R. D., *A Chaucer Handbook,* (New York, 1927; 2nd ed., 1947), includes many summaries and versions of analogues; Lowes, J. L., "The Art of Geoffrey Chaucer," in *Proceedings of the British Academy,* 16 (1930), distillation of a lifetime's work by a great scholar; Dempster, G., *Dramatic Irony in Chaucer,* (Stanford, 1932); Lowes, J. L., *Geoffrey Chaucer,* (Boston, 1934), contains much valuable intellectual and literary background; Whiting, B. J., *Chaucer's Use of Proverbs,* (Cambridge, Mass., 1934); Patch, H. R., *On Reading Chaucer,* (Cambridge, Mass., 1939); Chambers, R. W., *Man's Unconquerable Mind,* (London, 1939), contains an important essay; Bennett, H. S., *Chaucer and the Fifteenth Century,* (Oxford, 1947; repr. with corrections, 1948); Coghill, N., *The Poet Chaucer,* (Oxford, 1949; 2nd ed., 1967); Malone, K., *Chapters on Chaucer,* (Baltimore, 1951); Speirs, J., *Chaucer the Maker,* (London, 1951; 2nd ed., 1960); Gerould, G. H., *Chaucerian Essays,* (Princeton, 1952); Brewer, D. S., *Chaucer,* (London, 1953; 3rd ed., largely supplemented, 1973); Schaar, C., *The Golden Mirror: Studies in Chaucer's Descriptive Technique and Its Literary Background,* (London, 1955; repr. with index, 1967); Muscatine, C., *Chaucer and the French Tradition,* (Berkeley–Los Angeles, 1957), the outstanding critical work; Bronson, B. H., *In Search of Chaucer,* (Toronto, 1960); Davis, Norman, *English and Mediaeval Studies: Presented to J. R. R. on His 70th Birthday,* (Wrenn, C. L., London, 1962); Robertson, D. W., Jr., *A Preface to Chaucer: Studies in Medieval Perspectives,* (Princeton, 1962)—for discussion of the critical issues involved in the methods of Robertson (and of Huppé and Koonce, listed below) see "Patristic Exegesis in the Criticism of Medieval Literature," in D. Bethurum, ed., *Critical Approaches to Medieval Literature,* (New York, 1960); Crane, R. S., "On Hypothesis in 'Historical Criticism': Apropos of Certain Contemporary Medievalists," in *The Idea of the Humanities and Other Essays Critical and Historical,* II (Chicago, 1967); and F. L. Utley's review of D. W. Robertson's, *Preface,* in *Romance Philology,* 19 (1965).

See also Wolfgang Clemen, *Chaucer's Early Poetry,* (London, 1963); Payne, R. O., *The Key of Remembrance: A Study of Chaucer's Poetics,* (New Haven, 1963); Bowden, M., *A Reader's Guide to Geoffrey Chaucer,* (New York, 1964); Corsa, H. S., *Chaucer: Poet of Mirth and Morality,* (South Bend, Ind., 1964); Spearing, A. C., *Criticism and Medieval Poetry,* (Cambridge, 1964; rev. ed., 1972); Kane, G., *The Autobiographical Fallacy in Chaucer and Langland Studies,* (London, 1965); D. S. Brewer, ed., *Chaucer and Chaucerians,* (London, 1966); M. M. Crow and C. C. Olson, eds., *Chaucer Life-Records,* (Oxford, 1966), the fundamental work of scholarship on the records of Chaucer's life; John Lawlor, ed., *Patterns of Love and Courtesy,* (London, 1966); Jordan, R. M., *Chaucer and the Shape of Creation,* (Cambridge, Mass., 1967); Lawlor, J., *Chaucer,* (London, 1968); Mogan, J. J., *Chaucer and the Theme of Mutability,* (The Hague, 1969); Bloomfield, M., *Essays and Explorations: Studies in Ideas, Language and Literature,* (Cambridge, Mass., 1970), reprints some important studies; Donaldson, E. Talbot, *Speaking of Chaucer,* (London, 1970), a collection of essays, some already published and classic, by an outstandingly witty and penetrating critic and scholar; Rowland, B., *Blind Beasts: Chaucer's Animal World,* (Kent, Ohio, 1971); Hussey, S. S., *Chaucer, an Introduction,* (London, 1971); Burrow, J. A., *Ricardian Poetry: Chaucer, Gower, Langland and the Gawain Poet,* (Boston, 1971), "the style of the age"; Muscatine, Charles, *Poetry and Crisis in the Age of Chaucer,* (South Bend, Ind., 1972) refers also to *The Pearl* poet and Langland, and "the relation of poetry to history"; Kean, P. M., *Chaucer and the Making of English Poetry,* 2 vols. (Boston, 1972); Knight, S., *Ryming Craftily: Meaning in Chaucer's Poetry,* (Sydney, 1973); Norton-Smith, J., *Geoffrey Chaucer,* (London, 1974); Bennett, J. A. W., *Chaucer at Oxford and at Cambridge,* (Oxford, 1974); Brewer, D. S., "Towards a Chaucerian Poetic," in *Proceedings of the British Academy,* 60 (1974); Brewer, D. S., *Chaucer and His World,* (London, 1978).

CRITICAL ESSAYS

E. Wagenknecht, ed., *Chaucer: Modern Essays in Criticism,* (New York, 1959), reprints some classic studies; R. J. Schoeck and J. Taylor, eds., *Chaucer Criticism* 2 vols.: *I, The Canterbury Tales,* (South Bend, Ind., 1960), *II, Troilus and Criseyde and the Minor Poems,* (South Bend, Ind., 1961); M. Hussey et al., *An Introduction to Chaucer,* (Cambridge, 1965); D. S. Brewer, ed., *Chaucer and Chaucerians: Critical Studies in Middle English Literature,* (London, 1966); B. Rowland, ed., *Companion to Chaucer Studies,* (Toronto, 1968), essays on different aspects of Chaucer including biography, meter, learning, rhetoric, with valuable bibliographies; A. C. Cawley, ed., *Chaucer's Mind and Art,* (Edinburgh, 1969); L. D. Benson, ed., *The Learned and the Lewed: Studies in Chaucer and Medieval Literature,* (Cambridge, Mass., 1974); G. Economou, ed., *Geoffrey Chaucer,* (New York, 1975) critical articles with bibliographies.

LANGUAGE, VERSIFICATION

Brink, B. ten, *The Language and Metre of Chaucer,* M. Bentinck-Smith, trans., 2nd rev. ed. (London, 1901); Mersand, J., *Chaucer's Romance Vocabulary,* (London, 1939); Kokeritz, H., *A Guide to Chaucer's Pronunciation,* (Stockholm, 1954), excellent elementary guide (see also intros. to eds. by Skeat, Robinson, etc.; Baum, P. F., *Chaucer's Verse,* (Durham, N.C., 1961); Masui, M., *The Structure of Chaucer's Rime Words,* (Tokyo, 1964); Robinson, I., *Chaucer's Prosody,* (Cambridge, 1971); Elliott, R. W. V., *Chaucer's English,* (London, 1974)

STUDIES OF *THE CANTERBURY TALES*

Bowden, M., *A Commentary on the General Prologue to the Canterbury Tales,* (New York, 1948; 2nd rev. ed., 1967); Lawrence, W. W., *Chaucer and the Canterbury Tales,* (New York, 1950); Lumiansky, R. M., *Of Sondry Folk: The Dramatic Principle in the Canterbury Tales,* Austin, (Texas, 1955); Huppé, B. F., *A Reading of the Canterbury Tales,* (Albany, N.Y., 1964); Craik, T. W., *The Comic Tales of Chaucer,* (London, 1964); Ruggiers, P. G., *The Art of the Canterbury Tales,* (Madison, Wis., 1965); Bartholomew, B., *Fortuna and Natura: A Reading of Three Chaucer Narratives,* (The Hague, 1966); Hoffman, R. L., *Ovid and the Canterbury Tales,* (Philadelphia, 1966); Richardson, J., *Blameth Nat Me: A Study of Imagery in Chaucer's Fabliaux,* (The Hague, 1970); Mann, J., *Chaucer and Medieval Estates Satire,* (Cambridge, 1973), discussion of the pilgrims as literary-social types; T. D. Cooke and B. L. Honeycutt, eds., *The Humor of the Fabliaux,* (Columbia, Mo., 1974); Howard, D. R., *The Idea of the Canterbury Tales,* (Berkeley–Los Angeles, 1976).

STUDIES OF *TROILUS AND CRISEYDE*

Kirby, T. A., *Chaucer's Troilus: A Study in Courtly Love,* (Baton Rouge, La., 1940); Gordon, I. L., *The Double Sorrow of Troilus,* (Oxford, 1970); Steadman, J. M., *Disembodied Laughter,* (Berkeley–Los Angeles, 1972); Kelly, H. A., *Love and Marriage in the Age of Chaucer,* (Ithaca, N.Y., 1975); Rowe, D. W., *O Love O Charite,* (Carbondale Ill., 1976).

STUDIES OF *THE LEGEND OF GOOD WOMEN*

Frank, R. W., Jr., *Chaucer and The Legend of Good Women,* (Cambridge, Mass., 1972).

THE SHORTER POEMS

Bennett, J. A. W., *The Parlement of Foulys: An Interpretation,* (Oxford, 1966); Heiatt, C. B., *The Realism of Dream Visions,* (The Hague, 1967); Bennett, J. A. W., *Chaucer's Book of Fame: An Exposition of "The House of Fame,"* (Oxford, 1968); Wimsatt, J., *Chaucer and the French Love Poets,* (Chapel Hill, N.C., 1968) *The Book of the Duchess;* Winny, J., *Chaucer's Dream Poems,* (London, 1973).

GEOFFREY CHAUCER

GENERAL LITERARY BACKGROUND

Ker, W. P., *English Literature Medieval,* (Oxford, 1912), inevitably dated but a classic brief account; E. Faral, ed., *Les arts poétiques du XII*^{e} *et du XIII*^{e} *siècle,* (Paris, 1924), collection of medieval treatises on the arts of rhetoric (see also Nims, 1967); Lewis, C. S., *The Allegory of Love,* (Oxford, 1936; repr., 1938), an influential and brilliant book; Curtius, E. R., *European Literature and the Latin Middle Ages,* (New York, 1953, first published in German, 1948), a work of major significance in medieval literary history; Lewis, C. S., *The Discarded Image,* (Cambridge, 1964), how medieval men thought of the world; Howard, D. R., *The Three Temptations: Medieval Man in Search of the World,* (Princeton, 1966); M. F. Nims, trans., *Poetria Nova of Geoffrey of Vinsauf,* (Toronto, 1967), translation of one of the medieval arts of poetry; Mehl, D., *The Middle English Romances of the Thirteenth and Fourteenth Centuries,* (Boston, 1968; rev. and trans. of German ed., 1967); H. Newstead ed., *Chaucer and His Contemporaries: Essays on Medieval Literature and Thought,* (Greenwich, Conn., 1968); Gradon, P., *Form and Style in Early English Literature,* (London, 1971); D. S. Brewer, ed., *Geoffrey Chaucer,* Writers and Their Background series, (London, 1974; Athens, Ohio, 1975), essays on Chaucer's life, fourteenth-century English manuscripts, French, classical, and medieval Latin, Italian, scientific, religious and philosophical, and artistic backgrounds; Spearing, A. C., *Medieval Dream Poetry,* (Cambridge, 1976), discusses general tradition, and Chaucer's dream poems in detail; Pearsall, D., *Old English and Middle English Poetry,* (Boston, 1977).

HISTORICAL, CULTURAL, AND SOCIAL BACKGROUND

Jusserand, J. J., *English Wayfaring Life in the Middle Ages,* Eng. trans., (London, 1889; 4th ed., 1950); Thrupp, S. L., *The Merchant Class of Medieval London,* (Ann Arbor, Mich., 1948); E. Rickert, comp., *Chaucer's World,* C. C. Olson and M. M. Crow, eds., *Chaucer's World,* (New York, 1948), trans. of interesting contemporary records, contemporary illustrations; A. L. Poole, ed., *Medieval England,* (Oxford, 1958); McKisack, M. M., *The Fourteenth Century 1307–1399,* (Oxford, 1959), the standard historical work; Holmes, G., *The Later Middle Ages 1272–1485,* (London, 1962), a masterly brief account; Brewer, D. S., *Chaucer in His Time,* (London, 1963; New York, 1973); Loomis, R. S., *A Mirror of Chaucer's World,* (Princeton, 1965), richly illustrated; J. Evans, ed., *The Flowering of the Middle Ages,* (London, 1966), historians' essays, splendid illustrations; Hussey, M., *Chaucer's World: A Pictorial Companion,* (Cambridge, 1967); Robertson, D. W., Jr., *Chaucer's London,* (New York, 1968), excellent historical account of London closely related to Chaucer; Cottle, B., *The Triumph of English 1350–1400,* (London, 1969); McFarlane, K. B., *Lancastrian Kings and Lollard Knights,* (Oxford, 1972), historian's study of the Lollard knights, some of whom were Chaucer's friends.

ART AND SCIENCE

Hauser, A., *The Social History of Art,* vol. I (Boston, 1951); Henderson, G., *Gothic,* (Harmondsworth, 1967); Martindale, A., *Gothic Art,* (London, 1967). See also Jordan, Muscatine, and Robertson, above; Curry, W. C., *Chaucer and the Mediaeval Sciences,* 2nd ed. (New York, 1960); Wood, C., *Chaucer and the Country of the Stars, Poetic Uses of Astrological Imagery,* (Princeton, 1970)

RECORDINGS

General recordings include *Music of the Gothic Era,* 3 records (DGG Archive 2723045); *The Art of Courtly Love,* 3 records (HMV SLS 863). Readings in the original pronunciation include *Chaucer Readings,* (EVA Lexington LE 5505B); *Troilus and Criseyde,* abridged (Argo ZPL 1003–4); *The General Prologue,* (Argo PLT 1001); *The Knight's Tale,* (Argo Stereo ZPL 1208–10); *The Miller's Prologue and Tale,* (CUP Cassette 211859); *The Wife of Bath,* (CUP Cassette 212197); *The Merchant's Prologue and Tale,* (CUP Cassette 211875); *The Pardoner's Tale,* (Argo Stereo ZPL 1211); *The Nun's Priest's Tale,* (Argo RG 466).

BIBLIOGRAPHIES

Hammond, E. P., *Chaucer: A Bibliographical Manual,* (New York, 1908); Wells, J. E., *A Manual of the Writings in Middle English 1050–1400,* (New Haven, 1916)—the 9th and last supp. was issued in 1952, and a revision is in progress for the period 1050–1500, (Hamden, Conn., 1967); Griffith, D. D., *Bibliography of Chaucer 1908–53,* (Seattle, 1955); Crawford, W. R., *Bibliography of Chaucer 1954–63,* (Seattle, 1967); Baugh, A. C., *Chaucer (Golden Tree Bibliography),* (New York, 1968). For articles and annual bibliographies and reports, see *The Chaucer Review,* (1966–) and *The Year's Work in English Studies,* (Chaucer section) (1901–).

Samuel Taylor Coleridge

(1772–1834)

R. L. BRETT

So coleridge passed, leaving a handful of golden poems, an emptiness in the hearts of a few friends, and a will-o-the wisp light for bemused thinkers. With these words E. K. Chambers, ended his *Samuel Taylor Coleridge: A Biographical Study* (1938), and this, perhaps, is the way the general public still regards Coleridge: as the author of "The Ancient Mariner," "Kubla Khan," and "Christabel," a poet *manqué* whose gifts were dissipated in abstruse speculation and whose will was undermined by drug addiction. On this view, Coleridge was a brilliant failure, who after a few years of virtuosity burned himself out.

One charge that has been decisively dismissed since Chambers' biography is that of Coleridge's indolence. The picture of Coleridge as a broken man, sponging on his friends, and accomplishing nothing but "a handful of golden poems," has been demolished by modern editions of his writings. The *Collected Works* (not yet completed) will run to some twenty-two volumes; the *Collected Letters* (many of them more like essays), completed in 1971, totals six large volumes, and the *Notebooks* another five large volumes of text and five more of commentary. The sheer bulk of this work challenges the idea of Coleridge as ineffectual and lazy and presents a picture of sustained industry, but sustained often against great odds and threatened by personal misfortunes. But what of the contents of this work? No one would challenge Coleridge's claim to be one of England's greatest poets, not only for "The Ancient Mariner," "Kubla Khan," and "Christabel" but also for his conversational poems such as "This Lime Tree Bower My Prison," "Frost at Midnight," and "Dejection," which were novel combinations of meditative reflection and a sensitive appreciation of landscape. But now we recognize in Coleridge England's greatest philosophical critic, who analyzed in *Biographia Literaria* the workings of the poetic imagination and used this analysis as an instrument of fine critical discrimination in his lectures on Shakespeare and the other English poets. More than this, his *Confessions of an Inquiring Spirit* and *On the Constitution of the Church and State* add to these roles those of religious philosopher and political theorist. Such works are now seen as classics of English literature and have caused us to revise the estimates of his contemporaries, for Coleridge's own generation never doubted that he was a man of prodigious gifts. Even William Hazlitt, who first gave currency to the notion of Coleridge as the "lost leader," as one who had betrayed his ideals and dissipated those gifts, was ready to acknowledge the genius of Coleridge as a young man. In his *Lectures on the English Poets* (1818) he could write,

> I may say of him here, that he is the only person I ever knew who answered to the idea of a man of genius. . . . He was the first poet I ever knew. His genius at that time had angelic wings, and fed on manna. He talked on for ever; and you wished him to talk on for ever. . . . His voice rolled on the ear like the pealing organ, and its sound alone was the

> music of thought. His mind was clothed with wings; and raised on them, he lifted philosophy to heaven. (lecture VIII, "On the Living Poets")

But as Hazlitt looks back over the years, he qualifies his admiration. "And shall I, who heard him then, listen to him now?" he asks. "Not I! . . . That spell is broke; that time is gone for ever!" William Wordsworth, Thomas De Quincey, Charles Lamb (who had been at Christ's Hospital with Coleridge and who was his friend for fifty years), and many others were all united in their conviction that in Coleridge they had known a man of genius. But others began to echo the reservations Hazlitt had expressed, and in time it was the reservations alone that were heard. The most influential of these critics was Carlyle, who, though he owed him so much, wrote the most maliciously damaging account of Coleridge's last years in his *Life of Sterling*:

> Coleridge sat on the brow of Highgate hill, . . . looking down on London and its smoke-tumult, like a sage escaped from the inanity of life's battle. . . . His express contributions to poetry, philosophy, or any specific province of human literature or enlightenment, had been small and sadly intermittent. (ch. 8, p. 63)

Carlyle describes Coleridge's physical appearance:

> . . . the face was flabby and irresolute. . . . The whole figure and air, good and amiable otherwise, might be called flabby and irresolute. (*ibid.*, p. 65)

And then he dismisses him in a sentence that was to become the judgment of the majority:

> To the man himself Nature had given, in high measure, the seeds of a noble endowment; and to unfold it had been forbidden him. (*ibid.*, p. 72)

No doubt a superficial account of Coleridge's career can be used to project this image of a broken and irresolute figure whose early promise was never fulfilled, but it is one that does not stand up to scrutiny.

Coleridge was the youngest child of the Reverend John Coleridge, vicar of Ottery St. Mary in Devon. He was born on 21 October 1772, the tenth child of a second marriage and the youngest of thirteen children. As the youngest, he was petted and made much of; and his father, especially, fostered his precocious talents. His imagination was stimulated at an early age by tales from the *Arabian Nights* and other stories of the supernatural—overstimulated, in fact, for he developed a morbid fascination for stories that frightened him, until his father realized what was happening and threw the books on the fire. His precocity did not always endear him to his elder brothers. In a letter written on 16 October 1797, one of a series of autobiographical letters to his friend Thomas Poole, he recalls a childhood incident with such graphic detail that one feels it must have left its mark on an already sensitive personality. He relates how in the course of a fight he seized a knife and ran at his brother Frank, but was stopped by their mother, who had just entered the room. He dashed from the house in panic and stayed out all night. Filled with fear and remorse, he wandered in the meadows by the river Otter until, overcome by fatigue, he sank down in the wet grass to sleep. When he woke he was crippled with rheumatism and lay there helpless, listening to the distant search party, which could not hear his cries. He was found, of course, and restored to his anxious parents, but one can discern in this incident the origins of much that went to the making of Coleridge the man. He himself traced to this experience the beginnings of the so-called rheumatic attacks he suffered in later life and which drove him to seek relief in opium. It is likely that some of these attacks were partly psychosomatic and connected with the deep sense of guilt that pervaded his personality, and, if so, we can see why the story of Cain had such a hold on his imagination and why he made it the subject of a poem he abandoned, but of which he said "the Ancient Mariner was written instead."

Certainly Coleridge had a personality plagued by self-doubt, was unassertive, dependent, and at times self-indulgent. Nevertheless, he combined these traits with an acute power of self-analysis, which helped him to combat his shortcomings, but which in turn could also lead to an obsessional and paralyzing habit of introspection. His adult personality owed something not only to his early childhood but also to his removal at the age of nine from the security of home to the harsh life of Christ's Hospital. Coleridge left Devon on his father's death and spent the next nine years at school in London. He recorded in his notebooks in later life the nightmares he suffered and described how many of them took him back to Christ's Hospital. We also get a vivid account of Coleridge's feelings at the time from Lamb's essay "Christ's Hospital Five-and-Thirty Years Ago," written in the assumed person of Coleridge:

> I was a poor friendless boy. My parents, and those who should care for me were far away. . . . O the cruelty of separating a poor lad from his early homestead! The yearnings which I used to have towards it in those unfledged years! How, in my dreams, would my native town (far in the west) come back, with its church, and trees, and faces!

From Christ's Hospital Coleridge went to Jesus College, Cambridge, where he became a Unitarian and a "democrat"; that is, a member of the student Left of his day. However intellectually sophisticated Coleridge's views may have been, he was innocent in the ways of the world, and in his third year he fell in debt to the tradesmen of the town. This, coupled with the rejection of his love for Mary Evans, the sister of a school friend, perhaps caused him to leave the university and enlist in the Light Dragoons. He joined the colors in December 1793 under the assumed name of Silas Tomkyn Comberbacke, and it was some time before he was tracked down and bought out by his brothers. Coleridge made a poor soldier, and no doubt it was with some relief that he found himself back in Cambridge the following April. But he remained unsettled and at odds with the university and left at the end of the year without taking his degree. Wordsworth had left Cambridge as Coleridge arrived and the two men did not meet until 1795, when they were both in Bristol. Coleridge had gone there to join forces with Robert Southey in launching partisocracy, a utopian scheme to found a community of a few families on the banks of the Susquehanna; Wordsworth was staying in the city with his friends the Pinneys. It was not until 1797, however, when Coleridge visited Wordsworth and his sister Dorothy at Racedown in Dorset, that they became close friends. Wordsworth recalled the visit over forty years later and how Coleridge ". . . did not keep to the high road, but leaped over a gate and bounded down a pathless field by which he cut off an angle."[1] Coleridge stayed for three weeks and was soon back again with a chaise to transport the Wordsworths to Nether Stowey, in the Quantock Hills in Somerset, where his friend Thomas Poole had found him and his wife a cottage. A fortnight later Wordsworth and his sister moved to nearby Alfoxden, and the two men became neighbors and collaborators.

It was a critical period in the lives of both men. Wordsworth had been in France during the Revolution and had been caught up in the intoxication of great political events. He had fallen in love with a French girl, Annette Vallon, and was the father of her child. At the time it had seemed the beginning of a new life, and he later described his feelings in *The Prelude* in the famous lines:

> Bliss was it in that dawn to be alive,
> But to be young was very heaven.

But family disapproval had brought him home just as England declared war against France. His political hopes had turned to a deep sense of betrayal when the Revolution turned into the Terror and the collapse of his personal

1. From E. de Selincourt, ed., *The Letters of William and Dorothy Wordsworth, the Later Years* (Oxford, 1935–1939), vol, III, p. 1584.

plans and public aspirations had left him in a state of emotional turmoil on his return. Five years passed before Wordsworth recovered his mental equilibrium in the quiet countryside of the Quantocks, with the companionship of his sister Dorothy and the encouragement of Coleridge.

Wordsworth had tried to cure his breakdown by rational control, a doctrine he had met in the pages of William Godwin's *Political Justice,* but Coleridge taught him "to keep alive the heart in the head," for to repress the emotions was to deny an important part of oneself. Coleridge himself was passing through a difficult time. He had married, rather reluctantly, Southey's sister-in-law, Sarah Fricker, but only because pantisocracy would not accept bachelors. The scheme itself had never materialized, but now he was faced with the responsibility of earning a living not only for himself but for his wife and baby. The only weapons he had to fight what he called the two giants, "Bread and Cheese," were his journalism and his poetry. Little wonder, perhaps, that he was suffering from depression and anxiety.

When he met Wordsworth, Coleridge was a disciple of David Hartley, whose psychological theory saw human personality as the product of environment rather than innate forces. Hartley confirmed what Coleridge had come to believe from his own experience: that emotional health was not a matter of rational control but of allowing the mind to develop in natural surroundings away from the corruptions of city life. This conviction, which he shared and explored with Wordsworth, inspired the memorable poetry they produced together in that annus mirabilis of 1797.

When Coleridge moved to Nether Stowey he was already developing a new and simpler style of poetry. After leaving Cambridge he had continued his interest in radical politics and combined with it the ambition to be a poet. While in Bristol he had delivered lectures in 1795 attacking the government and its policy of war against France, and in the following year had started his own radical journal, the *Watchman.* Also in 1796 he had published a collection entitled *Poems on Various Subjects,* which contained sonnets first published in the *Morning Chronicle,* such as "To William Godwin" and "To Lord Stanhope." These, together with "Religious Musings," express his strong political and religious beliefs (and the two are not really separate). Others such as "Lines Composed While Climbing the Left Ascent of Brockley Combe" show an interest in landscape. Much of his early poetry had been in the manner of the eighteenth-century imitators of Milton, written in an inflated and artificial diction owing more to books than nature; but his interest in landscape now led him toward writers such as Shenstone, Goldsmith, Gray, and Cowper, whose verse used the description of nature as an occasion for reflection. We see how Coleridge began to experiment with this form in his poem on Brockley Combe and how he took it further in his "Reflections on Leaving a Place of Retirement," as he prepared to leave Clevedon, where he and his wife had started their married life, to return to Bristol in 1795. The poem begins with a description of their cottage on the shores of the Bristol Channel:

> Low was our pretty Cot: our tallest Rose
> Peep'd at the chamber-window. We could hear
> At silent noon, and eve, and early morn,
> The Sea's faint murmur.
> (1–4)

Coleridge sees Clevedon as a "Valley of Seclusion" that he and his bride must leave so that he can take up the fight for justice and freedom. He then surveys the scene from the hill above their home; in front of him the sea, behind the countryside stretching in the far distance to the spires of Bristol. The end of the poem returns to the cottage and expresses his belief that the memory of the scene will sustain him in the days to come:

> Yet oft when after honourable toil
> Rests the tir'd mind, and waking loves to dream,
> My spirit shall revisit thee, dear Cot!

Thy Jasmin and thy window-peeping Rose,
And Myrtles fearless of the mild sea-air.
And I shall sigh fond wishes—sweet Abode!
(63–68)

The poem provides a procedure that he was to develop into a new and successful poetic form in "This Lime Tree Bower My Prison" and "Frost at Midnight," written after his move to Nether Stowey in 1796. It starts with natural description, embraces the realization of a reciprocity between the mind and what it perceives, and expresses the conviction that the experience it recounts will be stored in the memory to enliven the mind in times of depression or adversity. This poetic procedure served as a model for Wordsworth's "Lines Composed . . . above Tintern Abbey," which was indebted to Coleridge not only for its poetic form but for its content. Especially, one can hear Coleridge's confident assertion in "This Lime Tree Bower My Prison":

Henceforth I shall know
That Nature ne'er deserts the wise and pure

echoed in Wordsworth's affirmation

that Nature never did betray
The heart that loved her.

The best of Coleridge's poems in this kind is "Frost at Midnight," written in 1798; in the same year and perhaps under its influence, Wordsworth wrote his Tintern poem traveling from the Wye Valley to Bristol, where he was just in time to include it in their joint venture *Lyrical Ballads,* about to be published by Joseph Cottle, the Bristol bookseller. In the poem Coleridge speaks to his infant son (named Hartley after the philosopher) of his own childhood at Christ's Hospital, "In the great city, pent 'mid cloisters dim," and promises him an upbringing close to nature:

. . . so shalt thou see and hear
The lovely shapes and sounds intelligible
Of that eternal language, which thy God
Utters, who from eternity doth teach
Himself in all, and all things in himself.
(58–62)

In much the same language Wordsworth addressed his sister on the banks of the Wye.

The other kind of poetry Coleridge made especially his own, but which he did not share with Wordsworth, was the poetry of the supernatural. His most famous poems, "The Ancient Mariner," "Kubla Khan," and "Christabel," all belong to this kind and, although the last of them was added to later, they were all composed at this time. Writing many years later in chapter 14 of *Biographia Literaria* about his collaboration with Wordsworth in *Lyrical Ballads,* Coleridge describes the difference between their contributions to the collection:

> The thought suggested itself that a series of poems might be composed of two sorts. In the one, the incidents and agents were to be, in part at least, supernatural; and the excellence aimed at was to consist in the interesting of the affections by the dramatic truth of such emotions as would naturally accompany such situations, supposing them real . . . for the second class, subjects were to be chosen from ordinary life; the characters and incidents were to be such as will be found in every village and its vicinity where there is a meditative and feeling mind to seek after them, or to notice them when they present themselves.

"With this view I wrote the 'Ancient Mariner,' " he continues, but although "The Ancient Mariner" was the only one of the three poems mentioned above to appear in *Lyrical Ballads,* the passage applies to all three.

In *Biographia Literaria* Coleridge recounts the story of his early allegiance to the philosophy of associationism and his growing dissatisfaction with it. It was only later, after he had moved to Keswick, that he began to construct a system of thought more congenial to his mind than the empiricist tradition of the eighteenth century. But much earlier than this, he tells us, when he was only twenty-three, that is, in 1795–1796, he heard Wordsworth read the manuscript of his poem "Guilt and Sorrow" and was impressed by

> . . . the union of deep feeling with profound thought; the fine balance of truth in observing with the imaginative faculty in modifying the objects observed; and above all the original gift of spreading the tone, the *atmosphere* and with it the depth and height of the ideal world, around forms, incidents and situations of which, for the common view, custom had bedimmed all the lustre, had dried up the sparkle and the dewdrops. (ch. 4)

In December 1794 he had written to Southey,

> I am a compleat Necessitarian—and understand the subject as well almost as Hartley himself—but I go farther than Hartley and believe the corporeality of thought,—namely, that it is motion.

But prolonged reflection about the experience of listening to Wordsworth, he tells us, had led to a new development in his thought. Wordsworth's poetry showed an awareness that marked it off from the devitalized writings of the eighteenth century; it had a quality of poetic genius that caused Coleridge to give an important place to the imagination when he came to construct his own philosophy. His discipleship of Hartley had brought him into a state of paralysis, religious doubt, and a darkness of mind from which he had been partly delivered by a reading of the early Neoplatonic writers Plotinus, Proclus, and Gemistus Pletho, from whom he had progressed to the seventeenth-century mystics George Fox, Jacob Boehme, and Boehme's English disciple William Law. "They contributed," he wrote in chapter 9 of *Biographia Literaria,*

> to keep alive the heart in the head; gave me an indistinct, yet stirring and working presentiment, that all the products of the mere reflective faculty partook of death, and were as the rattling twigs and sprays in winter into which a sap was yet to be propelled. . . . If they were too often a moving cloud of smoke to me by day, yet they were always a pillar of fire throughout the night, during my wanderings through the wilderness of doubt, and enabled me to skirt, without crossing, the sandy deserts of utter unbelief.

His meeting with Wordsworth brought him the friendship of a man whose vision of life confirmed the "working presentiment" of these mystics and whose poetry brought the heart and the head together in "the union of deep feeling with profound thought" that so attracted Coleridge.

The story Coleridge recounts in *Biographia Literaria* strikes the reader by its religious overtones and images; it tells us how he was lost in the wilderness of doubt but eventually reached the promised land of renewed faith and how he passed through darkness into light. After meeting Wordsworth he became convinced that this salvation could be identified with an imaginative awareness that saw the world of nature as more than matter in motion but as possessing a spiritual significance. Later he was to make this conviction part of his philosophy of religion, but the poetry that was inspired by it sits rather loosely to dogmatic Christianity. "The Ancient Mariner" uses biblical and even medieval Catholic imagery, but naturalizes it in a narrative that becomes an internalized and psychological version of redemption; nevertheless, few can doubt that it deals with a profound spiritual experience that haunts the mind with a compulsive power.

The creation of the old seaman was a great triumph in Coleridge's construction of the poem, for he gives the poem dramatic force and credibility. Because we accept him, we accept his story and grant it that "willing suspension of disbelief for the moment" the poem demands. Criticism of the poem has been endless. At the start it was seen as a narrative in the Gothic and romantic style of Gottfried August Bürger, the German poet whose poems in the translations by Sir Walter Scott and others enjoyed such a vogue in the 1790's. Southey, when he reviewed *Lyrical Ballads* soon after its appearance, thought it a poor specimen even of this kind and called it "a Dutch attempt at German sublimity," adding, "Genius has here been employed in producing a poem of little merit." Even Wordsworth, in a letter to Joseph Cottle on 24 June 1799, maintained that it had been "upon the whole . . . an injury to the volume, . . . the old words and the strangeness of it have deterred readers from going on." Since then, and especially in the last few decades, interpretations of the poem have increased in number and in ingenuity. The albatross, for instance, has been seen as a representation of Coleridge himself, of his imagination, of Mrs. Coleridge, and of God's creation. Many have ignored Coleridge's distinction between allegory, which he def-ned as a one-to-one relation, and "the Symbolical," which, he said in lecture VIII of his 1818 lectures,

> cannot, perhaps, be better defined in distinction from the Allegorical, than that it is always itself a part of that, of the whole of which it is the representation.[2]

This is important when we come to consider the shooting of the albatross, for it implies that this central act, the pivot on which the action turns, is not an arbitrary token of something else, nor something whose significance has been obscured or repressed by the censorship of the poet's superego. It is a representative example of a whole class of actions. This suggests that those critics are correct who see it as a violation of the principle of the "one-life" that Coleridge proclaimed in lines he later added to "The Eolian Harp," and which begins:

> O! the one Life within us and abroad,
> Which meets all motion and becomes its
> soul.
> (26–27)

An essential element of the crime is its motivelessness. The poem goes out of its way to isolate it and show it as an act of gratuitous cruelty without any advantage to the Mariner or his shipmates; only after the killing do they hold the albatross responsible for the bad weather. In this respect the crime is like man's original disobedience. Some readers think the Mariner's crime too petty to have had such tremendous consequences, but again the eating of the apple in Eden, insignificant in itself, had catastrophic results. By relating it to the Fall we are made aware of the mystery surrounding the action of the poem. Why should men act wantonly and cruelly, why should they violate the principle of the "one-life," when there is no advantage to themselves? The mystery of evil puzzled Coleridge for most of his life and some would say he had a pathological sense of guilt. Certainly "The Ancient Mariner" cannot be interpreted in clear conceptual terms. Its story is close to the story of mankind as told in the biblical narrative, and this itself parallels the religious experience of the individual believer. The hero of the poem is a kind of Adam, unreflective, proud in the assumption that he is master of nature rather than part of it. His disobedience is followed by a journey through the wilderness until he is rescued by God's grace. The grace of God is given and not won, and this seems to be so in the poem when the Mariner is moved by the beauty of the water snakes and "blessed them unawares." The Christian echoes and references throughout the poem are undeniable. It is difficult, but certainly not impossible, to accommodate the figures of Death and Life-in-Death to a Christian framework, just as Milton in *Paradise Lost* brought the figures of pagan mythology within a biblical dispensation. To those who say that the Mariner's redemption is incomplete we can point to the doctrine of purgatory, a state, like heaven and hell, that one can inhabit here and now.

Coleridge's preoccupation with the Fall of man can also be seen in "Kubla Khan," probably written in 1798 just after "The Ancient Mariner," or in the autumn of 1797, although it was not published until 1816, when it was printed with a note informing the reader that it appeared at Lord Byron's request. The note also described it as "a psychological curiosity" and explained that it had been written at a farmhouse between Porlock and Linton where Coleridge had retired in ill health and fallen asleep after taking "an anodyne." He

2. From T. M. Raysor, ed., *Coleridge's Miscellaneous Criticism* (London, 1936), p. 99.

had been reading the account in *Purchas's Pilgrimage* of how the Khan Kubla had ordered the building of a palace within a walled garden. After three hours he woke and started to write the "two to three hundred lines" he had composed during his profound sleep, but as he wrote he was disturbed by "a person on business from Porlock." This interruption lasted "above an hour" and when the interview was over he found that the rest of the poem had vanished from his mind. A manuscript version of the poem was acquired by the British Museum in 1962, and attached to this was a short note of Coleridge's that added a few more details. In this he specifically mentions that the anodyne was "two grains of Opium taken to check a dysentry," and he describes his sleep as "a sort of Reverie." For many years the poem was regarded as a meaningless fragment, a congeries of images and memories from Coleridge's unconscious mind, the product of automatic writing. A moment's reflection reminds us, however, that not all drug-takers are poets and that even if opium had a necessary part in the genesis of the poem, it is not sufficient to explain its marvelous character. Coleridge not only took opium, he was also a poet of genius, and the poem bears all the marks of his artistry.

Modern scholarship and criticism from J. L. Lowes's *Road to Xanadu* onward have laid bare the influence of Coleridge's wide reading upon the poem; less attention has been paid to the influence of landscape and the part played by the memory images of places Coleridge had visited. Coleridge was not only "a library cormorant (to use his own description of himself), but also a keen observer and recorder of natural scenery. It is likely, then, that the language and imagery of the poem would show a conflation not only of literary sources but also of remembered scenes. One cannot be certain of these, but the combe in which the farmhouse stands where Coleridge fell asleep would probably have been in his mind, and not far away was the rocky gorge through which the river Lyn dashes down to the sea. Even closer to the descriptive language of the poem is Wookey Hole in the Mendip Hills, which Coleridge must have visited when he walked from Cheddar to Bridgwater. Here the river Axe plunges underground from the Ebbor gorge and runs through a great cavern in which the stalagmites and stalactites have the appearance of a fairy palace made of ice. Closest of all to the poem was the fabulous estate at Hafod, near Aberystwyth, which Coleridge visited during his walking tour of North Wales in 1794. Geoffrey Grigson, in an article in the *Cornhill* magazine for 1947, first drew attention to the similarity between the landscapes of "Kubla Khan" and Hafod. Hafod, by the Devil's Bridge in Cardiganshire, was laid out by its owner, Thomas Johnes, in the 1780's to be a recreation of the Happy Valley described in Samuel Johnson's *The History of Rasselas Prince of Abyssinia* (1759), an earthly paradise enfolded in the steep hills that descend to the river Ystwyth. Johnes had the advice of the two great landscape artists of the time, Richard Payne Knight and Uvedale Price, but the idea of creating a paradise was his own, as was the little Garden of Eden that lies within it, hidden in woods and overshadowed by a great cedar tree above the river and approached by a stone gateway bearing the figures of Adam and Eve. The house itself (later destroyed by fire) was finished in 1788, only a few years before Coleridge's visit,Wand was an exercise in romantic Gothic architecture. It stood at the head of the valley and the river flowed before the lawns in front of its windows. After its completion the owner added a large octagonal library, which was built on the roof and was surmounted by a beautiful dome in the style of a Mogul palace. Not only did Coleridge see this elaborate and fantastic representation of an earthly paradise but his memory of it was probably revived by *An Attempt to Describe Hafod,* published in 179A and written by George Cumberland, who was a friend of Joseph Cottle, the publisher of *Lyrical Ballads.*

J. L. Lowes demonstrated that "The Ancient Mariner" in several places owed something to Coleridge's visit to Wales and it seems very likely that the same was true of

"Kubla Khan," that here, too, the literary memories merge with the topographical ones. Coleridge's readings of Purchas, Bartram's *Travels,* Bruce's *Travels to Discover the Sources of the Nile,* Maurice's *History of Hindostan,* and of several classical writers, were brought together and given a focus by the passage in *Paradise Lost* where Milton describes the false paradise at Mount Amara near the source of the Nile in Abyssinia. Just as several remembered landscapes coalesce to form the scenery of "Kubla Khan" so the names *Ebbor, Ab*erystwyth, *Ab*yssinia, and *Amara* come together in Coleridge's invention of "Abora."

No genetic account can determine the meaning of a poem; and Lowes himself, although he laid bare so many of its literary sources, thought "Kubla Khan" lacked unity. Most critics now would argue that the elements that come together in the poem form a whole with a discernible meaning. The first two sections of the poem describe the creation of an earthly paradise. Like the Garden of Eden, it is built by the side of a river. "Alph," which is close to the first letter of the Greek alphabet, suggests the beginning of things, but also brings to mind the river Alpheus (another river supposed to run underground), which in ancient legend was often associated with the Nile. But unlike the Garden of Eden this paradise has been built by an earthly potentate. It is another of those follies that try to make a new heaven on earth, like Milton's false paradise, or the Happey Valley of Johnson's *Rasselas,* or Johnes's palace at Hafod. Its impermanence is foreshadowed by the "Ancestral voices prophesying war."

The third section moves toward Plato's doctrine of Ideas, which informs the rest of the poem. We know Coleridge was reading intensively in Plato and the Platonists when he wrote the poem, and an entry in one of his notebooks at the end of 1796 (vol. 1, p. 204) copies a sentence from book VII of Plato's *Republic.* This comes from the beginning of the allegory of the cave, where Socrates tells Glaucon that ordinary men cannot perceive the absolute directly, that only after a gradual progression from the shadows into the light of day can they "look at the sun and observe its real nature, not its appearance in water." The fountain and the cave both symbolize time and eternity: the waters of the fountain are always changing while its shape remains the same, and the cave in Plato's allegory, where the prisoners discern only the shadows of the world outside, represents this earthly life where we see only the appearances of things. In this section of the poem we no longer perceive the dome itself; all we catch is its reflection on the surface of the river:

> The shadow of the dome of pleasure
> Floated midway on the waves.
> (31–32)

The sun, which in Coleridge's poetry generally symbolizes God's presence, casts its light upon the dome, but this too is only a reflection and the icy interior of the shadow palace is as cold as the water it floats on. And yet our vision of the dome is not an illusion since it gives us a glimpse of perfection, and as we contemplate it we can hear Plato's cosmic harmony:

> . . . the mingled measure
> From the fountain and the caves.
> (33–34)

The last section of the poem takes up the theme of music in the figure of the Abyssinian maid, whose song brings before us the paradise hidden in her native mountains. She inspires the poet to believe that he, too, through his poetry could build "That sunny dome! those caves of ice!" The picture of the poet with his "flashing eyes" and "floating hair" comes from Plato's *Ion,* in which Socrates presents a more ambiguous opinion of poets than in the *Republic,* and speaks of them as not in their right minds but as ". . . like Bacchic maidens who draw milk and honey from the rivers when they are under the influence of Dionysus." This Platonic echo also leaves an ambiguity at the end of "Kubla Khan," for we do not know whether the poet is claiming for himself an Orphic power or whether he regards poetry as a divine madness, whether he regards poetry as an access to ultimate truth or whether, as Plato argued, it deals only with appearances. We do not even know whether Coleridge himself is speaking in the poem, but it was a question he was to return to when he came to assess the powers of the imagination.

The other great poem that was started at this time was "Christabel." The first part was written in Somerset in 1797–1798, the second at Keswick in 1800, but when it was published in 1816 it still remained uncompleted. Coleridge was persuaded by Byron and Scott, both of whom read the poem in manuscript, to publish it along with "Kubla Khan" and "The Pains of Sleep." Scott had adapted its meter for *The Lay of the Last Minstrel* (1805), and Coleridge felt that others were beginning to plagiarize his work. There is a marked difference between the two parts of "Christabel," and this goes further than the change of landscape that parallels the removal from Nether Stowey to Keswick. The first part is dramatic and, since drama can only live in the present, Coleridge employs the historic-present tense and the device of question-and-answer to give the action immediacy. In the second part the dramatic is replaced by narrative and the poem becomes less effective. The poem starts successfully with its evocation of unexplained horror, but as the story unfolds this sense of inexplicable dread is dispelled. In "The Ancient Mariner" Coleridge takes the kind of supernatural story made fashionable by the translations of Bürger and gives it "the depth and height of the ideal world." "Christabel" starts out with this quality, but fails to sustain it, and it was the realization of this, perhaps, that prevented him from finishing it.

Like "The Ancient Mariner," "Christabel" is concerned with the theme of evil and guilt. The heroine, Christabel, whose innocence is symbolized by the image of a dove, meets at midnight in the woods that surround her father's castle the sorceress Geraldine, who is likened to a snake. Christabel is defenseless; her mother is dead and her father is bewitched by Geraldine's charms. The action of the poem suggests that Christabel will pass from unreflecting innocence to a knowledge of good and evil; but through grace and her own faith, in acquiring the wisdom of the serpent she will retain the innocence of the dove.

There were three contemporary accounts of how Coleridge planned to complete it, two of them by James Gillman, the physician with whom he lived from 1816 until his death, the other by his son Derwent. The shorter of the two accounts by James Gillman and that by Derwent Coleridge suggest vicarious suffering as the central theme of the poem and that Christabel's trial would be revealed as a means of saving "her lover that's far away." The remaining account, without contradicting this, reads like the synopsis of a Gothic horror story, but this does not necessarily discredit it, for a prose sketch of "The Ancient Mariner" would be equally unconvincing; nevertheless, Coleridge's inability to finish the poem suggests that it was turning into a work of fancy rather than imagination.

In 1798 Coleridge and Wordsworth left *Lyrical Ballads* with Joseph Cottle and set off with Dorothy Wordsworth for Germany. The Wordsworths settled at Goslar, in the Hartz mountains; Coleridge spent the time at the University of Göttingen, where he was a considerable success and made much of by the professors. Following their return the next year, the two families settled in the Lake District. Coleridge moved his family to Keswick in July 1800, and less than two years later, in April 1802, he wrote the saddest of all his poems, "Dejection." It was published in a shortened version the following October, but in its original and more private form it was addressed to Wordsworth's sister-in-law, Sara Hutchinson. By this time Coleridge's fortunes were at a low ebb. His wife had resented the move to the north and was jealous of the intimate circle of friends at Grasmere, and more especially of Sara Hutchinson, with whom Coleridge had fallen in love. The recriminations and strife of his own home contrasted sadly with the happiness at Grasmere, and his misery was increased by rheumatic illnesses brought on by the damp climate. He now began to seek relief from pain, depression, and guilt in ever increasing doses of opium. He could look from his windows at Greta Hall on the splendor of the mountains, but in vain, for now he discovered that nature could betray the heart that loved her. He had lost all sense of joy and with it the capacity for creative work. It was no good turning to nature, for as he cried out in despair:

> I may not hope from outward forms to win
> The passion and the life, whose fountains
> are within.

Nature cannot act on a blank mind; it needs a ready and active cooperation for its healing power to work:

> O Lady! we receive but what we give,
> And in *our* life alone does Nature live
> Our's is her Wedding Garment, our's her
> Shroud—

To the outside world and often to his friends, Coleridge's life from then on seemed to be a story of decline and even degradation, broken from time to time by achievements that fell below his real capacity. In 1804 he left for Malta, where he acted as private secretary to Sir Alexander Ball, the high commissioner, who thought so highly of him that he persuaded Coleridge to stay on some months beyond the departure date he had set himself. He returned home in 1806, but it was ten weeks before the Wordsworths saw him in October, almost three years since they had parted at Grasmere. His appearance shocked them, as Dorothy Wordsworth reported in a letter to Catherine Clarkson on 6 November 1806:

> Never, never did I feel such a shock as at first sight of him. . . . He is utterly changed; and yet sometimes, when he was animated in conversation . . . I saw something of his former self. . . . He did not complain of his health, . . . but that he is ill I am well assured, and must sink if he does not grow more happy. His fatness has quite changed him—it is more like the flesh of a person in dropsy than one in health.

They failed to realize at first that Coleridge had not freed himself from opium and that he was beginning to drink brandy to overcome the depression that followed his use of the drug. Coleridge had decided to live apart from his wife, but it was not until the next year that the separation came about. He now turned once more to lecturing and journalism, the two activities he could always fall back on and that at his best he did superbly well. But he was not at his best in the lectures on poetry he delivered at the beginning of 1808 at the Royal Institution. De Quincey, who attended the lectures and knew something of opium addiction himself, described him in terms curiously like those Coleridge had used for his own Ancient Mariner:

> His appearance was generally that of a person struggling with pain and overmastering illness. His lips were baked with feverish heat, and often black in colour; and, in spite of the water which he continued drinking . . . he often seemed to labour under an almost paralytic inability to raise the upper jaw from the lower.

Coleridge had worked for the *Morning Post* as early as 1797, when England was renewing its war against Napoleon. At that time he had been anti-Pitt and antiwar, but when he returned from Germany in 1799 he realized the dangers that could come about if Napoleon were to dominate Europe. It was this change of mind that caused William Hazlitt to charge him with apostasy, but Coleridge maintained that he had been consistent and that it was the revolutionaries who had forsaken their principles. It was at this time that he started to use the signature made up from the initials of his name to rebut the charge of apostasy. "Esthse signifies—," he wrote to William Sotheby in September 1802, "*He hath stood*—which in these times of apostasy from the principles of Freedom, or of Religion in this country . . . is no unmeaning Signature." On returning from Malta, Coleridge moved to the *Courier,* an evening paper to which he contributed some 140 pieces spread over fourteen years. Reading these pieces one is struck by their liberalism rather than their reactionary opinions. Whether he is writing on the rights of women, the place of Jews in society, child labor in the factories, the cotton operatives of Lancashire, or Quakers and military service, he shows a deep humanitarianism; and on the tortuous questions of Irish independence and Catholic emancipation, he has a far better grasp of the issues than most of his contemporaries. Although these essays were occasional pieces, they were informed by the philosophical approach to politics that he worked out in the *Friend,* the periodical he decided to launch in 1808.

In September of that year Coleridge went to stay with the Wordsworths at Grasmere, and it was here that he drew up the plans for his new periodical. The first number did not appear until June 1809, but it ran until March 1810, when it closed after the publication of the twenty-seventh number. The financial and practical arrangements for the publication of the periodical were complicated and troublesome and would have created problems even if Coleridge had been in better health. As it was, they became too much for him and it was this, coupled with Sara Hutchinson's departure to join one of her brothers in Wales, that brought the venture to an end. Coleridge had dictated the contents to her and most of these were his own contributions. They were the product of an impressive and sustained program of work, much of it involving original thought. But with Sara Hutchinson gone, Coleridge rapidly deteriorated, and it was then that the notorious quarrel with Wordsworth occurred. It came as the culmination of a long worsening in their relationship. Coleridge was a difficult person to have living for so long in their house, but the Wordsworths put up with his apathy, depression, and unsocial habits with forbearance, until at last they could take no more. The break finally came in October 1810, and the effect on Coleridge was catastrophic. The breach was finally closed, but their relationship was not quite the same; and after 1812 Coleridge never again visited the Lakes. He moved to London, spent some time in Bristol and then with his friends the Morgans at Calne, where he dictated *Biographia Literaria* in 1815. He finally settled at the house of Dr. and Mrs. Gillman in Highgate, where he spent the last eighteen years of his life. It was only then that he gained some control of his opium addiction and achieved peace of mind. It was, and still is, easy enough to condemn Coleridge for his lack of will, but in his day laudanum could be bought across the counter of any apothecary's shop and was regarded much as we now regard alcohol, something to be condemned only when it has done its worst, and then with a varying mixture of censure and pity for its victim.

To Hazlitt, to Carlyle, and to many others Coleridge seemed a failure, but there were some, and these more far-sighted even in his own generation, who recognized his genius and the importance of what he was still able to achieve; not merely the brilliance of his youth, but his lasting importance. Chief among them was John Stuart Mill, who in the memorable essay "Coleridge" in the *Westminster Review* in 1840, called him one of the two great "seminal minds" of the century. The other, according to Mill, was Jeremy Bentham, who carried on the eighteenth-century tradition of thought Coleridge sought to overthrow. Mill's tribute is even more impressive because his own philosophy finally came down on the side of Bentham rather than Coleridge.

When Coleridge wrote "Dejection" he faced the ruin of his own personal fortunes, and could find no answer to his problems in the philosophy of Hartley and eighteenth-century empiricism. He had already been reading deeply Plato and the English Platonists of the seventeenth century, and while in Germany he had acquired a knowledge of German philosophy, in particular that of Kant, who, he declared in *Biographia Literaria,* took hold of him "as with a giant's hand." It was at this time of depression and blighted hopes that he opened the box of books he had brought back with him from Germany and began the work of constructing a system of thought that would provide an answer to his intellectual, spiritual, and moral problems. He never completed this task, but what strikes the modern reader who has the hindsight to appreciate his achievement is not the failure but the heroic struggle to wrest, out of personal unhappiness, a faith to meet not only his own needs but also the challenges to religious belief in the century to come.

Coleridge's starting point was his dawning conviction that empiricism was wrong in its view of the mind as a tabula rasa, or an empty receptacle fed by sense experience, in which knowledge is built up by the association of ideas. Writing to his friend Thomas Poole in 1801, he declared:

> If the mind be not *passive,* if it be indeed made in God's Image, and that, too, in the sublimest sense—the Image of the *Creator*—there is ground for suspicion, that any system built on the passiveness of the mind must be false as a system.

Coleridge came to believe that the mind is active in perception, turning the raw material of sensation into objects by a power that he called the "primary imagination." Alongside this in Coleridge's thought ran a vitalistic conception of nature that matched his view of the mind as creative in knowledge. As God created the world out of chaos and gave it order and form, so the human mind imposes order and form upon the manifold data of sensory experience. The world was not created by God and left to run in accordance with the laws of Newtonian physics; it is sustained in being by God's spirit and is, to use a phrase of Coleridge's, *natura naturans* and not *natura naturata.* So by analogy, though in a real sense too, the human mind creates the world it perceives. Coleridge described the primary imagination in *Biographia Literaria* as "a repetition in the finite mind of the eternal act of creation in the infinite I AM."

This creative process applies to art as well as to perception. The eighteenth century accounted for the poetic imagination in terms of memory images associated in the mind under the influence of the emotions. Coleridge admitted that some poetry could be explained in this way, but described it as the poetry of fancy, and the poet who composed it, the poet of talent. The poet of genius, on the other hand, is endowed with a creative power that can form from the materials of sensation a new world; one like the everyday world, but reorganized and raised to a higher level of perception. This secondary or poetic imagination creates a world of "seeming objects," a world like the world of our ordinary experience, but one whose features carry a weight of meaning and significance. So the world of *Hamlet* or *King Lear* is not the world of the chronicler or historian and even the characters and events in Shakespeare's history plays are more universal than those we meet in Holinshed's *Chronicles*; they "may be termed ideal realities."

> They are not the things themselves, so much as abstracts of the things, which a great mind takes into itself, and there naturalizes them to its own conception.[3]

Coleridge's work on Shakespeare marks the beginning of a new period in the history of Shakespearean criticism and, indeed, of literary studies generally in England. His admiration and understanding of Shakespeare informed the development of his critical theory, and this in turn led to a new and greater discrimination when he came to analyze and discuss the plays. His criticism of Shakespeare is both inductive and deductive. Although Coleridge is rightly called a philosophical critic and some of his Shakespearean criticism echoes the writings of the German critics, it was his own poetic sensibility that formed the threshold to this achievement. Just as his reading of Wordsworth's poems when a young

3. From T. M. Raysor, ed., *Coleridge's Shakespearean Criticism,* vol. II (London, 1930; rev. ed., 1960), p. 125.

man, he tells us in *Biographia Literaria,* led to his growing conviction that a distinction must be made between fancy and imagination, so his poetic insight into Shakespeare's mind gave him a new appreciation of the plays. It was this rare combination of the poet and philosopher that made Coleridge the great critic he was. It enabled him to recognize, before anyone else, the promise of genius in Wordsworth and to reassess the achievement of Shakespeare, free from neoclassical restrictions.

Unfortunately, much of Coleridge's Shakespearean criticism comes to us in incomplete or corrupt form, from lectures that were often given extemporaneously and for which no accurate or full record remains. When still a young man, Coleridge had lectured in Bristol on political and theological topics, but it was not until 1808, two years after his return from Malta, that he gave, at the invitation of Humphry Davy, the course of lectures on literature at the Royal Institution, which has already been mentioned. Apart from De Quincey's brief account of these we know little, but certainly Shakespeare was included in the syllabus. From November 1811 to January 1812, he gave a series of seventeen lectures in London, which Byron attended. Southey arranged for a shorthand transcript to be made, so that they would not be lost, as those at the Royal Institution had been. Remains of two such reports survived: one by a Mr. Tomalin, who was probably employed by Southey; the other by John Payne Collier, whose literary dishonesty later became well known, but whose account agrees substantially with others, including that of Henry Crabb Robinson. *The Diary, Reminiscences and Correspondence of H. Crabb Robinson* (1869) furnishes us with the commentary of a cultivated man who was friendly to Coleridge, but who had a capacity for objective criticism. According to him the level of the lectures was uneven; at times brilliant and perceptive, but at others digressive and prolix. Later in the year, after some postponements, Coleridge gave a further course of five or six lectures, of which the last at least was devoted to Shakespeare and the contents of which were probably incorporated in the lectures he was to give in Bristol, of which Coleridge's own notes survived. Further lectures followed at the Surrey Institute in 1812–1813, and those at Bristol in 1813–1814. We learn from Robinson's diary that those at the Surrey Institute concentrated on Shakespeare and Milton and that Coleridge's performance was uneven, that he improvised and wandered into digressions. Those at Bristol, according to Joseph Cottle, were a great success and the report of the second lecture in the *Gazette* said that the lecture room was filled to overflowing. The six lectures on Shakespeare in this series were discovered in Bristol much later and published in 1883 in the Bohn edition of Coleridge's *Lectures on Shakespeare.* It was only when he needed money for the university expenses of his son Derwent that he returned to the lecture room and in 1818 gave another course of fourteen lectures on literature, three of which were on Shakespeare. Again, in 1818–1819 he gave some lectures on Shakespeare as a parallel series to a course he gave on the history of philosophy. The philosophy lectures were fully reported and have since been edited by Kathleen Coburn, but the only record of the literature lectures are the brief comments in the *Champion,* which have now been published along with the rest of this Shakespeare material in T. M. Raysor's edition.

In the prospectus to these last lectures Coleridge described Shakespeare as "the great Philosophic Poet." From Ben Jonson to Samuel Johnson all the critics had regarded Shakespeare as a writer whose fancy outran his judgment. Coleridge realized that what the eighteenth century called judgment and fancy were in Shakespeare, two sides of the same coin; that Shakespeare's genius, like Wordsworth's, combined deep feeling and profound thought. This was the focus of all his lectures on Shakespeare, in which, he said, his object was

> to prove that in all points from the most important to the most minute, the judgement of Shakespeare is commensurate with his

> genius—nay, that his genius reveals itself in his judgement, as in its most exalted form. (*Coleridge's Shakespearean Criticism,* vol. I, p. 114)

The genius and the judgment were united in a power of the imagination that revealed itself not in mechanically contrived plots but in works of art that had an organic life of their own, understood not by their correspondence to outside rules but by the recognition of an inner coherence.

Coleridge was, then, a philosophical critic. He believed that his distinction between the fancy and the imagination

> would in its immediate effects furnish a torch of guidance to the philosophical critic; and ultimately to the poet himself. In energetic minds, truth soon changes by domestication into power; and from directing in the discrimination and appraisal of the product, becomes influencive in the production. (*Biographia Literaria,* ch. 4)

In other words, Coleridge was not concerned with formal criticism, with the application of rules, or the attempt to assess how far a literary work conformed to a norm. Historically speaking, he hastened the end of neoclassicism and the notion that there are fixed literary kinds to which all works must belong. For him the task of the literary critic is to discover how a work of art realizes the laws implicit in its own nature. In every work there is an organic principle giving it shape and form. A work of art is not an assemblage of bits and pieces put together by mechanical rules; it is the embodiment of the creative force of the poet's imagination.

The poet "in ideal perfection," he tells us in chapter 14 of *Biographia Literaria,* "diffuses a tone and spirit of unity," which comes about by

> the balance or reconciliation of opposite or discordant qualities; of sameness, with difference; of the general, with the concrete; the idea, with the image; the individual, with the representative; the sense of novelty and freshness, with old and familiar objects; a more than usual state of emotion, with more than usual order; judgement ever awake and steady self-possession, with enthusiasm and feeling profound or vehement.

This chimes in with his earlier argument in chapter 9 that "all symbols of necessity involve an apparent contradiction." They bring together especially the two qualities he admired so much in Wordsworth's poetry: "the fine balance of truth in observing" and "the imaginative faculty in modifying the objects observed."

The creations of the poetic imagination are symbols, and Coleridge maintains in chapter 9 of *Biographia Literaria* that "An IDEA in the *highest* sense of the word cannot be conveyed but by a symbol." To grasp the significance of this one needs to appreciate the distinction he draws between the understanding and the reason. The understanding is that power of the mind which frames concepts, that is concerned with abstract and discursive knowledge derived from the world of perception. The reason goes beyond this; it is the "source and substance of truths above sense" that have their evidence in themselves. The reason is concerned with principles that, although not empirically verifiable, have to be accepted if experience itself is to make sense. It is significant that Coleridge called the secondary imagination "the agent of the reason, " for the constructions of the poet's imagination go beyond discursive and conceptual knowledge to explore a world that can be represented only in symbols.

Kant, too, believed that the reason could go beyond the understanding, but he discounted the notion that it could reach more than what he called "phenomenal knowledge" or that it could know the noumena or "things in themselves." Coleridge was reluctant to accept this and even refused to believe that this is what Kant had meant. Coleridge's earlier attraction to Neoplatonism might have led him at this point to elaborate a philosophy which claimed that art can penetrate the world of perception and apprehend the supersensuous.

The difference between Kant and the Neoplatonists was that one saw art as the representation of an idea in the artist's mind whereas the others saw it as a representation of reality itself. In places Coleridge flirted with Schelling, who tried to bring these two viewpoints together; but as he carried forward his philosophical speculation he abandoned this line of inquiry, and the imagination, though it retained its importance, ceased to hold the central place in his thinking.

Coleridge always looked to philosophy to meet the needs of his own personal life, and one of these needs was his longing for forgiveness and the lifting of his sense of guilt over missed opportunities—the waste of his own great gifts, his broken marriage, and his addiction to opium. This is given plangent expression in a brief entry in one of his notebooks:

> But O! not what I understand, but what I *am*, must save or crush me! (*Notebooks of Samuel Taylor Coleridge*, vol. III, item 3354)

And so from the time of *Biographia Literaria* onward he increasingly devoted his energies to the construction of a philosophy of religion in which the will rather than the imagination played the central part.

When Coleridge's *Aids to Reflection* was published in 1825 natural theology was at a low ebb. Of the traditional arguments for God's existence only the argument from design commanded any intellectual conviction, but this was tied to a deism that had been bled white from the wounds inflicted by skeptics like Hume. Revealed religion, which had rested upon the twin authorities of the church and the Bible, had also been weakened; the church was still suffering from the onslaughts of Gibbon, and the authority of the Bible had been undermined by the Higher Criticism from Germany. For Coleridge the truth of Christianity is a living thing, and he develops the existential approach to religious belief he had advanced in the final chapter of *Biographia Literaria*, where he wrote, ". . . we can only *know* by the act of *becoming. Do the will of my Father, and ye shall KNOW I am of God.*"

In *Confessions of an Inquiring Spirit*, published posthumously in 1840, he outflanked the attacks of the German critics on the Scriptures by claiming that the Bible carried the evidence of its own truth. "The Bible and Christianity," he declared, "are their own sufficient evidence." He rejected the crude literalism that thought the Bible had been "dictated" by God, and he distinguished between revelation and inspiration. Not everything the biblical authors wrote is revealed truth, for they were men of their own times with patterns of thought and even prejudices that influenced their narrative; but they were inspired. Every part of Scripture is inspired, but not every part is revealed truth. We can only leap what Lessing had called "the wide and ugly ditch" between the events of the Gospel narrative and the claims of the evangelists by an act of faith that starts with a recognition of our own need. Our realization of the weakness of our wills and inability to meet the demands of a moral imperative are met in the Bible with the promise of forgiveness and grace. The two come together as a key fits a lock.

Coleridge's vitalistic view of nature was matched by his conviction that society is best understood in organic rather than atomistic terms. He had started by supporting the French Revolution, but changed his mind, though not his principles, when it turned into a tyranny. He came to believe that it was wiser to change institutions than to overthrow them, for society is not a machine to be scrapped at will for a new model, but something with a life of its own. This was also Edmund Burke's reaction to eighteenth-century notions, but Coleridge goes beyond Burke in his Christian and Platonic theory of the state. The state should act not merely as a referee in the conflict of self-interests between individuals and groups, nor simply to formulate a contract between government and the governed. It has a more positive role; it should encourage and should provide opportunities for the self-fulfillment of all members of society. In *On the Constitution of the Church and State* (1830), he discerned two opposed principles in society, one of progression and the other of permanence, and he saw them embodied in his own day in the landed classes and the commercial interests. The balance of power today may be different, but the analysis itself remains valid. Coleridge also recognized a mediating and balancing force in society, embodied in what he called the "clerisy" and consisting of the educators, especially the clergy and teachers. This modern version of Plato's Guardians he termed a National Church, a body that embraced but was not identical with the Church of England. Its duty was

> to preserve the stores, to guard the treasures of past civilization, and thus to bind the present with the past; to perfect and add to the same, and thus to connect the present with the future. (ch. 5)

When Coleridge settled with the Gillmans at Highgate, the turbulence of his earlier years was over. He was never free of dependence upon opium, but his use was controlled and limited. He became the center of an admiring circle of disciples who, from 1822 on, visited Highgate for their "Thursday-evening class." This was a group of five or six young men to whom Coleridge lectured on philosophy. But there were less formal gatherings that included the Gillmans and old friends such as Lamb, as well as younger friends like Joseph Henry Green, who was to become his literary executor, and John Sterling, who was to transmit Coleridge's thought to F. D. Maurice and J. C. Hare, the leaders of the Broad Church movement. Hazlitt's tribute to Coleridge's power as a talker has already been quoted, and he was still able to hold an audience spellbound by his eloquence. Even as a young man he was better as a monologuist than as a conversationalist, and Caroline Fox recounts in her *Journal* how (probably at one of the Highgate evenings) Coleridge appealed to Lamb with the question "You have heard me preach, I think?", to be met with the reply "I have never heard you do anything else." At the end this habit of soliloquizing became a little disconcerting to the visitors who made their way to Highgate. Ralph Waldo Emerson, who was one of several Americans to visit him, recalled in his *English Traits* (1856) how

> . . . the visit was rather a spectacle than a conversation, of no use beyond the satisfaction of my curiosity. He was old and pre-occupied, and could not bend to a new companion and think with him.

But that was in 1833, at the end of Coleridge's life. Before that, in 1828, he and Wordsworth had managed a visit to the Continent that lasted a few weeks, though both men seemed very old for such an expedition. There were disappointments, some of them severe, as when his son Hartley failed to have his Oriel fellowship renewed. There was a sadness that flowed from his hopeless love for Sara Hutchinson, whom he saw only a few times after they parted in 1810, but who made several visits in 1834 when she knew his death was near. Highgate was a safe harbor after the stormy seas he had crossed. Like the wedding guest in his own "Ancient Mariner" he found himself "a sadder and a wiser man" at the end of his voyage. Although he had not thought of his great poem in autobiographical terms when he wrote it, he came increasingly to see it as a prophecy of his own life, and it was in his mind when he composed the epitaph that adorns his grave in Highgate Church. When he wrote the following lines, which form part of that epitaph, he was thinking not of his reputation but of his immortal destiny; and yet in one sense at least his prayer has been answered, for his reputation today is very much alive.

> Beneath this sod
> A poet lies, or that which once seem'd he.
> O, lift one thought in prayer for S.T.C.;
> That he who many a year with toil of breath
> Found death in life, may here find life in
> death!

Selected Bibliography

Detailed bibliographical information can also be found in the appropriate volumes of *The New Cambridge Bibliography of English Literature* and *The Oxford History of English Literature.*

BIBLIOGRAPHY

T. J. Wise, *A Bibliography of the Writings in Prose and Verse* (London, 1913; supp., 1919), also reiss. with Coleridgeana (London, 1970); T. J. Wise, *Two Lake Poets: A Catalogue of Printed Books, Manuscripts and Autograph Letters by W. Wordsworth and S. T. Coleridge* (London, 1927), a section of the Ashley Library in the British Museum; V. W. Kennedy and M. N. Barton, *Samuel Taylor Coleridge: A Selected Bibliography of the Best Available Editions of His Writings, of Biographies and Criticisms of Him, and of References Showing His Relations with Contemporaries* (Baltimore, 1935), contains a useful list of critical and biographical studies; R. Haven, J.Haven, and M. Adams, eds., *Samuel Taylor Coleridge: An Annotated Bibliography of Criticism and Scholarship,* vol. I, *1793–1899* (Boston, 1976), vol. II will bring this to 1975; J. D. Caskey and M. M. Stapper, eds., *Samuel Taylor Coleridge: A Selective Bibliography of Criticism, 1935–1977* (Westport, Conn., 1977).

COLLECTED WORKS

The first collected ed. of the works of Coleridge is in progress under the general editorship of K. H. Coburn (see below). Until this is finished the only complete ed. is W. Shedd, ed., *The Complete Works of Samuel Taylor Coleridge,* 7 vols. (New York, 1853).

The Poetical Works, 3 vols. (London, 1828; 2nd ed., 1829; rev. ed., 1834), published originally by W. Pickering in an ed. of 500 copies, includes the dramas *Wallenstein, Remorse,* and *Zapolya*—2nd ed. is the basis of J. D. Campbell's ed. and E. H. Coleridge used the rev. ed.; *The Poetical Works of Coleridge, Shelley and Keats* (Paris, 1829); D. Coleridge, ed., *The Dramatic Works* (London, 1852); D. and S. Coleridge, eds., *Poems* (London, 1852; 1870), the latter includes an intro. essay by D. Coleridge and repr. the 1798 text of "The Ancient Mariner"; W. M. Rossetti, ed., *The Poetical Works* (London, 1872), with a critical memoir by Rossetti; R. H. Shepherd, ed., *The Poetical and Dramatic Works,* 4 vols. (London, 1877); J. D. Campbell, ed., *The Poetical Works* (London, 1893), contains valuable explanatory notes and biography; J. D. Campbell and W. H. White, eds., *Coleridge's Poems. A Facsimile Reproduction of Proofs and MSS* (London, 1899).

E. H. Coleridge, ed., *The Complete Poetical Works,* 2 vols. (Oxford, 1912), the definitive ed. of the poems, the only complete text, with full textual and biographical notes, also repr. in 1 vol., with minor omissions; H. W. Garrod, ed., *Coleridge: Poetry and Prose. With Essays by Hazlitt, Jeffrey, DeQuincey, Carlyle, and Others* (Oxford, 1925), a substantial selection; S. Potter, ed., *Coleridge: Select Poetry and Prose* (London, 1933); K. H. Coburn, *Inquiring Spirit: A New Presentation of Coleridge from His Published and Unpublished Prose Writings* (London, 1951); K. Raine, comp., *Poems and Prose* (London, 1957), with an intro. by Raine; J. Beer, ed., *Poems* (London, 1963; 174), the latter has a new intro.; K. H. Coburn, gen. ed., *Collected Works* (London, 1969–), in progress, will include 16 titles in 22 vols. plus an index vol.; vol. I: L. Patton and P. Mann, eds., *Lectures, 1795,* on politics and religion; vol. II: L. Patton, ed., *The Watchman;* vol. III (in 3 pts.): D. V. Erdman, ed., *Essays on His Times;* vol. IV (in 2 pts.): B. E. Rooke, ed., *The Friend;* vol. VI: R. J. White, ed., *Lay Sermons;* vol. X: J. Colmer, ed., *On the Constitution of the Church and State.*

LETTERS

T. Allsop, ed., *Letters, Conversations and Recollections of S. T. Coleridge,* 2 vols. (London, 1836; 2nd ed., 1858; 3rd ed., 1864); *Unpublished Letters from Samuel Taylor Coleridge to the Rev. John Prior Estlin, Communicated by H. A. Bright* (London, 1884); W. Knight, ed., *Memorials of Coleorton,* 2 vols. (Edinburgh, 1887), letter to Sir George and Lady Beaumont; *Letters from the Lake Poets to Daniel Stuart* (London, 1889); A. H. Japp, ed., *De Quincey Memorials . . . with Communications from Coleridge* "and others", 2 vols. (London, 1891); E. H. Coleridge, ed., *Letters,* 2 vols. (London, 1895); R. B. Litchfield, *Tom Wedgwood: The First Photographer* (London, 1903), contains Coleridge's letters to the Wedgwoods; E. Betham, *A House of Letters* (London, 1905), contains Coleridge's letters to Matilda Betham; A. Turnbull, ed., *Biographia Epistolaris: Being the Biographical Supplement of Coleridge's Biographia Literaria with Additional Letters,* 2 vols. (London, 1911); E.L. Griggs, ed., *Unpublished Letters, Including Certain Letters Republished from Original Sources,* 2 vols. (London, 1932); S. Potter, ed., *A Minnow Among Tritons* (London, 1936), Mrs. Coleridge's letters to Thomas Poole, 1799–1834; M. K. Joseph, *Charles Aders . . . with Some Unpublished Letters by S. T. Coleridge* (Audkland, 1953); E. L. Griggs, ed., *Collected Letters, 1785–1834,* 6 vols. (Oxford, 1956–1971).

SEPARATE WORKS IN VERSE

The Fall of Robespierre: An Historic Drama (Cambridge, 1794), Act I by Coleridge, (Bristol, 1796); *Poems on Various Subjects* (Bristol, 1796), includes poems by C. Lamb and C. Lloyd; *Fears in Solitude . . . To Which*

Are Added "France, an Ode" and "Frost at Midnight" (London, 1798); *Lyrical Ballads* (Bristol, 1798; 2 vols., London, 1800), written with Wordsworth, the 1800 ed. includes change in Coleridge's contribution and a rev. of "The Ancient Mariner"; in R. L. Brett and A. R. Jones, eds. (London, 1963; rev. ed., 1965); *The Piccolomini, or, The First Part of Wallenstein: A Drama in Five Acts. The Death of Wallenstein: A Tragedy in Five Acts* (London, 1800), a trans. of Schiller's *Die Piccolomini* and *Wallenstein's Tod; Remorse: A Tragedy in Five Acts* (London, 1813); *Christabel. Kubla Khan: A Vision. The Pains of Sleep* (London, 1816); *Sibylline Leaves: A Collection of Poems* (London, 1817); *Zapolya: A Christmas Tale, in Two Parts* (London, 1817); *The Devil's Walk: A Poem* (London, 1830), written with Southey, first published anonymously in the *Morning Post* in 1799, later enlarged by Southey.

SEPARATE WORKS IN PROSE

Conciones ad Populum, or, Addresses to the People (Bristol, 1795); *A Moral and Political Lecture* (Bristol, 1795); *The Plot Discovered, or, An Address to the People Against Ministerial Treason* (Bristol, 1795); *The Watchman,* 10 numbers (1976); *The Friend: A Literary, Moral and Political Weekly Paper,* 28 numbers (1809–1810), also reiss. with supplementary matter (1812) and with new matter, 2 vols. (London, 1818); R. Southey, ed., *Omniana, or Horae Otiosiores,* 2 vols. (London, 1812), with many articles by Coleridge; *The Statesman's Manual, or, The Bible the Best Guide to Political Skill and Foresight: A Lay Sermon* (London, 1816); *Biographia Literaria, or, Biographical Sketches of My Literary Life and Opinions,* 2 vols. (London, 1817), the best ed. is J. Shawcross, ed., 2 vols. (Oxford, 1907), also recommended is G. Watson, ed. (London, 1956); *"Blessed Are Ye That Sow Beside All Waters": A Lay Sermon* (London, 1817); *Treatise on Method* (London, 1818), first published as *General Introduction "to the Encyclopaedia Metropolitana", or, Preliminary Treatise on Method*—definitive ed. is A. D. Snyder, ed. (London, 1934); *Aids to Reflection in the Formation of a Manly Character* (London, 1825); *On the Constitution of the Church and State* (London, 1830); H. N. Coleridge, ed., *Specimens of the Table Talk of the Late Samuel Taylor Coleridge,* 2 vols. (London, 1835); H. N. Coleridge, ed., *The Literary Remains,* 4 vols. (London, 1836–1839).

Confessions of an Inquiring Spirit (London, 1840; 2nd ed., 1849; 3rd ed., 1853; reiss., 1956, 1971); S. B. Watson, ed., *Hints Towards the Formation of a More Comprehensive Theory of Life* (London, 1848); S. Coleridge, ed., *Essays on His Own Times: Forming a Second Series of "The Friend,"* 3 vols. (London, 1850); *Notes on English Divines* (London, 1853); D. Coleridge, ed., *Notes Theological, Political and Miscellaneous* (London, 1853), partly repr. from *The Literary Remains,* the rest new; J. P. Collier, ed., *Seven Lectures on Shakespeare and Milton* (London, 1856), edited from Collier's shorthand notes; T. Ashe, ed., *Lectures and Notes on Shakespeare and Other English Poets* (London, 1883), from *The Literary Remains* with Collier's notes and reports of lectures; T. Ashe, ed., *Miscellanies, Aesthetic and Literary; to Which Is Added the Theory of Life* (London, 1885); W. F. Taylor, ed., *Critical Annotations: Being Marginal Notes Inscribed in Volumes Formerly in the Possession of Coleridge* (Harrow, 1889); E. H. Coleridge, ed., *Anima Poetae: From the Unpublished Notebooks* (London, 1895); J. W. Mackail, ed., *Coleridge's Literary Criticism* (London, 1908); T. M. Raysor, ed., *Coleridge's Shakespearean Criticism,* 2 vols. (London, 1930; 2nd ed., 1960); R. R. Brinkley, ed., *Coleridge on the Seventeenth Century* (Durham, N.C. 1935), includes previously unpublished material; T. M. Raysor, ed., *Coleridge's Miscellaneous Criticism* (London, 1936), K. H. Coburn, ed., *The Philosophical Lectures of S. T. Coleridge, Hitherto Unpublished* (London, 1949); K. H. Coburn, ed., *The Notebooks* (London, 1957–), vol. I: *1794–1804* (1957); vol. II: *1804–1808* (1961); vol. III: *1808–1819* (1973); each vol. in 2 pts., 5 vols. in 10 pts. plus index vol. are projected.

BIOGRAPHICAL AND CRITICAL STUDIES

W. Hazlitt, *Lectures on the English Poets* (London, 1818; 2nd ed., 1819; 3rd ed., with additional material, 1841); C. Lamb, *Essays of Elia* (London, 1822); W. Hazlitt, *The Spirit of the Age, or, Contemporary Portraits* (London, 1825), in the 2nd ed. (1835) the material on Coleridge was amplified; T. Allsop, ed., *Letters, Conversations and Recollections of S. T. Coleridge,* 2 vols. (London, 1836); J. Cottle, *Early Recollections, Chiefly Relating to the Late Samuel Taylor Coleridge, During His Long Residence in Bristol,* 2 vols. (London, 1837), rev. in 1 vol. as *Reminiscences of S. T. Coleridge and R. Southey* (London, 1847; reiss. 1970); J. Gillman, *The Life of Samuel Taylor Coleridge* (London, 1838); J. S. Mill, "Coleridge," in *Westminster Review,* vol. XXXIII (March 1840), repr. in *Dissertations and Discussions* (London, 1857); *The Autobiography of Leigh Hunt with Reminiscences of Friends,* 3 vols. (London, 1850), best ed. by J. Morpurgo (London, 1949); J. S. Mill, *Dissertations and Discussions: Political, Philosophical and Historical,* 4 vols. (London, 1859–1875); J. H. Green, *Spiritual Philosophy, Founded on the Teaching of S. T. Coleridge,* J. Simon, ed., 2 vols. (London, 1865); H. Crabb Robinson, *Diary, Reminiscences and Correspondence,* T. Sadler, ed., 3 vols. (London, 1869); *Memoir and Letters of Sara Coleridge, Edited by Her Daughter "S. Coleridge",* 2 vols. (London, 1873); A. C. Swinburne, *Essays and Studies* (London, 1875); H. D. Traill, *Coleridge* (London, 1884), in the English Men of Letters series; T. H. H. Caine, *Life of Samuel Taylor Coleridge* (London, 1887) with a bibliography by J. P. Anderson; Mrs. H. Sandford, *Thomas Poole and His Friends,* 2 vols. (London, 1888), a valuable biographical source book; W. Pater, *Appreciations* (London, 1889).

J. D. Campbell, *Samuel Taylor Coleridge: A Narrative of the Events of His Life* (London, 1894); A. W. Gillman, *The Gillmans of Highgate, with Letters from S. T. Coleridge etc.* (London, 1895); T. De Quincey, *Reminiscences of the English Lake Poets* (London, 1907), later selections include E. Sackville-West, ed. (London, 1948) and D. Wright, ed. (London, 1970); J. M. Murry, *Aspects of Criticism* (London, 1920); E. J. Morley, ed., *Blake, Coleridge, Wordsworth, Lamb, etc.: Selections from Crabb Robinson's Remains* (London, 1922); H. W. Garrod, *The Profession of Poetry* (Oxford, 1924; repr. with other lectures, 1929, 1970); L. E. Watson, *Coleridge at Highgate* (London, 1925); J. L. Lowes, *The Road to Xanadu* (London, 1927; enl. ed., 1930), a study of the sources of Coleridge's poetic inspiration; E. J. Morley, ed., *Correspondence with the Wordsworth Circle,* 2 vols. (Oxford, 1927); J. H. Muirhead, *Coleridge as Philosopher* (London, 1930); M. H. Abrams, *The Milk of Paradise* (Cambridge, Mass., 1934), a study of opium dreams and their bearing on the poetry of Coleridge (among other subjects); E. Blunden and E. L. Griggs, eds., *Coleridge: Studies by Several Hands* (London, 1934), commemorating the centenary of Coleridge's death; I. A. Richards, *Coleridge on Imagination* (London, 1934; 2nd ed., 1955; 3rd ed., 1960); S. Potter, *Coleridge and S.T.C.* (London, 1935); E. K. Chambers, *S. T. Coleridge: A Biographical Study* (Oxford, 1938); L. Hanson, *The Life of S. T. Coleridge* (London, 1938); E. L. Griggs, ed., *Wordsworth and Coleridge: Studies in Honor of G. M. Harper* (Princeton, N.J., 1939); A. H. Nethercott, *The Road to Tryermaine* (Chicago, 1939; repr. New York, 1962); G. McKenzie, *Organic Unity in Coleridge* (Berkeley, 1939).

B. Willey, *Coleridge on Imagination and Fancy* (London, 1946), the Warton Lecture before the British Academy, 1946; W. L. Kennedy, *The English Heritage of Coleridge of Bristol* (New Haven, Conn., 1947); H. Read, *Coleridge as Critic* (London, 1949); T. M. Raysor ed., *The English Romantic Poets: A Review of Research* (New York, 1950); H. House, *Coleridge* (London, 1953), the Clark Lectures at Cambridge, 1951–1952; H. M. Margoliouth, *Wordsworth and Coleridge, 1795–1834* (London, 1953); H. Read, *The True Voice of Feeling: Studies in English Romantic Poetry* (London, 1953); G. Whalley, *Coleridge and Sara Hutchinson and the Asra Poems* (London, 1955); J. V. Baker, ed., *The Sacred River: Coleridge's Theory of the Imagination* (Baton Rouge, La., 1957); W. F. Kennedy, *Humanist Versus Economist: The Economic Thought of Samuel Taylor Coleridge* (Berkeley-Los Angeles, 1958); J. B. Beer, *Coleridge the Visionary* (London, 1959); J. A. Colmer, *Coleridge: Critic of Society* (Oxford, 1959); I. A. Richards, *Coleridge's Minor Poems: A Lecture* (Missoula, Mont., 1960); M. Suther, *The Dark Night of Samuel Taylor Coleridge* (New York, 1960); J. D. Boulger, *Coleridge on Religious Thinker* (New Haven, Conn., 1961); C. R. Woodring, *Politics in the Poetry of Coleridge* (Madison, Wis., 1961); R. H. Fogle, *The Idea of Coleridge's Criticism* (Berkeley–Los Angeles, 1962); P. Deschamps, *La Formation de la pensée de Coleridge, 1772–1804* (Paris, 1963); M. F. Schultz, *The Poetic Voices of Coleridge* (Detroit, 1964).

J. A. Appleyard, *Coleridge's Philosophy of Literature* (Cambridge, Mass., 1965); M. Suther, *Visions of Xanadu* (New York-London, 1965); D. P. Calleo, *Coleridge and the Idea of the Modern State* (New Haven, Conn.-London, 1966); G. G. Watson, *Coleridge the Poet* (London, 1966); P. M. Adair, *The Waking Dream: A Study of Coleridge's Poetry* (London, 1967); M. H. Coburn, ed., *Coleridge: A Collection of Critical Essays* (Englewood Cliffs, N.J., 1967); G. Yarlott, *Coleridge and the Abyssinian Maid* (London, 1967); W. Walsh, *Coleridge: The Work and the Relevance* (London, 1967); A. C. Hayter, *Opium and the Romantic Imagination* (London, 1968); J. R. Barth, *Coleridge and Christian Doctrine* (Cambridge, Mass., 1969); W. J. Bate, *Coleridge* (London, 1969); R. L. Brett, *Fancy and Imagination* (London, 1969); G. N. Giordano-Orsini, *Coleridge and German Idealism: A Study in the History of Philosophy. With Unpublished Materials from Coleridge's Manuscripts* (Carbondale, Pa., 1969); J. R. de J. Jackson, *Method and Imagination in Coleridge's Criticism* (London, 1969); T. MacFarland, *Coleridge and the Pantheist Tradition* (Oxford, 1969); D. Sultana, *Samuel Taylor Coleridge in Malta and Italy* (Oxford, 1969); A. S. Byatt, *Wordsworth and Coleridge in Their Time* (London, 1970); J. R. de J. Jackson, ed., *Coleridge: The Critical Heritage* (London, 1970); B. Lawrence, *Coleridge and Wordsworth in Somerset* (Newton Abbot, 1970); A. T. S. Prickett, *Coleridge and Wordsworth: The Poetry of Growth* (Cambridge, 1970); W. Heath, *Wordsworth and Coleridge: A Study of Their Literary Relations in 1801–1802* (Oxford, 1970); R. L. Brett, ed., *S. T. Coleridge* (London, 1971), a collection of critical essays with a useful bibliography by G. Whalley; O. Barfield, *What Coleridge Thought* (London, 1972); N. Fruman, *Coleridge the Damaged Archangel* (London, 1972); G. H. Hartman, ed., *New Perspectives on Coleridge and Wordsworth* (London-New York, 1972); B. Willey, *Samuel Taylor Coleridge* (London, 1972); M. M. Badawi, *Coleridge: Critic of Shakespeare* (Cambridge, 1973); A. R. Jones and W. Tydeman, eds., *"The Ancient Mariner" and Other Poems; A Casebook* (London, 1973); J. B. Beer, ed., *Coleridge's Variety: Bicentenary Studies* (London, 1974); K. H. Coburn, *The*

Self-Conscious Imagination: A Study of the Coleridge Notebooks in Celebration of the Bicentenary of His Birth (London, 1974); A. J. Harding, *Coleridge and the Idea of Love* (London, 1974); R. Parker, *Coleridge's Meditative Art* (Ithaca, N.Y.–London, 1975); S. Prickett, *Romanticism and Religion: The Tradition of Coleridge and Wordsworth in the Victorian Church* (Cambridge, 1976); J. R. Barth, *The Symbolic Imagination: Coleridge and the Romantic Tradition* (Princeton, N.J., 1977); J. B. Beer, *Coleridge's Poetic Intelligence* (London, 1977); K. H. Coburn, *In Pursuit of Coleridge* (London, 1977); L. S. Lockridge, *Coleridge the Moralist* (Ithaca, N.Y., 1977); G. Dekker, *Coleridge and the Literature of Sensibility* (London, 1978); J. S. Hill, ed., *Imagination in Coleridge* (London, 1978).

E. E. Cummings

(1894–1962)

EVE TRIEM

OBEDIENT TO THE world spirit of change, in the early decades of the twentieth century a group of notable poets, by diverging from traditional practices, transformed American poetry. The most thorough "smasher of the logicalities" among them was a transcendentalist: one who views nature as a state of becoming rather than as a stasis and who believes that the imaginative faculty in man can perceive the natural world directly. He was also a troubadour who said: "enters give/whose lost is his found/leading love/whose heart is her mind." He was not only poet but novelist, playwright, and painter. In following his vision he roused hostility in academic critics and readers, apparently repelled by his idiosyncratic typographical and stylistic devices, but he was from the beginning admired by his fellow innovators, William Carlos Williams, Marianne Moore, Ezra Pound, and T. S. Eliot—and eventually he won the esteem of his critics.

"I am someone," remarked E. E. Cummings late in his career, "who proudly and humbly affirms that love is the mystery-of-mysteries . . . that 'an artist, a man, a failure' is . . . a naturally and miraculously whole human being . . . whose only happiness is to transcend himself, whose every agony is to grow." In a world oriented to dehumanized power, transcendentalism is a synonym for absurdity. Cummings recognized this early. In an address at his Harvard commencement in 1915, he had said, "we are concerned with the natural unfolding of sound tendencies. That the conclusion is, in a particular case, *absurdity,* does not in any way impair the value of the experiment, so long as we are dealing with sincere effort." The manifesto he issued then was that of one man to himself. He would experiment, and he would not fear being absurd; he would use the absurdity principle to the limit of its usefulness. As he worked at his trade of wordsmith, the implications of what he had said in 1915 were clarified in a remarkable stream of poems. From the start he used absurdity to leaven the commonplace, to startle readers into "listening" instead of merely hearing. In his later years he discovered a new significance in the concept: experimental living and the practice of his craft had redefined absurdity; it came to mean the truth of earthly living and a promise of eternity.

Edward Estlin Cummings, son of the Reverend Edward Cummings (lecturer at Harvard and Unitarian minister) and of Rebecca Haswell Clarke Cummings, was born at Cambridge, Massachusetts, on October 14, 1894. His parents had been brought together by their mutual friend William James. Dr. Cummings was a woodsman, a photographer, an actor, a carpenter, an artist—and talented in all that he undertook. Mrs. Cummings was a shy woman who overcame conventional influences to respond joyously and effectively to life. The son was educated in public schools and at Harvard University where he received an A.B., *magna cum laude,* and an M.A. for English and classical studies.

While Cummings was in graduate school he helped to found the Harvard Poetry Society. He and some of his friends in the society put together *Eight Harvard Poets* (published in 1917). In it, by a printer's error, according to one story, Cummings' name and the "I's" as well were set in lowercase letters. He seized upon this as a device congenial to him and later had "e. e. cummings" legalized as the signature to his poems.

After Harvard, Cummings went to New York. In this city he held his first and only job, three months with P. F. Collier Son, Inc., mail-order booksellers. He was twenty-one at the time. In mid-1917 he went to France to serve as a volunteer ambulance driver. There he was interned for a minor military offense—what happened was that he refused to say he hated Germans; instead, with typical Cummings care for precision, he repeated: "I like the French." From his experiences at La Ferté Macé (a detention camp) he accumulated material for his documentary "novel," *The Enormous Room* (1922), one of the best war books by an American.

Upon his release, he returned to the United States, but when the war ended he went back to Paris—this time to study art. He made the acquaintance of the poet Louis Aragon and of Picasso and their circle of poets and painters; he became friendly with many visiting writers such as Archibald MacLeish and Ezra Pound. On arriving back in New York in 1924 he found himself a celebrity—for his documentary novel and for *Tulips and Chimneys* (1923), his first book of poems. The next year he won the *Dial* Award for "distinguished service to American Letters." A roving assignment from *Vanity Fair* in 1926 permitted him to go abroad again, where he established a routine he was to follow most of his life: he painted in the afternoons and wrote at night.

From his experiences in the two cities he loved, New York and Paris, came the material for scintillating or extravagant essays on burlesque, the circus, modern art, and the foibles of the day, later collected into *A Miscellany* (1958) and *A Miscellany, Revised* (1965). He wrote forewords to books and brochures for art exhibits, and he sold sketches and paintings. Three volumes of poetry appeared in quick succession: (*And*) and *XLI Poems* in 1925, *Is 5* in 1926. The play *Him*, a phantasmagoria in 21 scenes, which was a forerunner of what is now called the Theater of the Absurd, was published in 1927 and produced by the Provincetown Players in 1928 and was acclaimed by avant-garde critics. In 1931 he published a collection of drawings and paintings, *CIOPW*, which took its title from the initial letters of the materials used: charcoal, ink, oil, pencil, watercolor. In that same year came *W (ViVa)*, a thick book of poems. A travel journal published in 1933, *Eimi* (I Am), recorded his revulsion against an even more "enormous room" than the military detention camp: the collectivized Soviet Union.

After 1930, although Cummings continued to travel abroad, he divided most of his time between a studio apartment in Greenwich Village, at 4 Patchin Place, and the family farm at Silver Lake, New Hampshire. This yearly contact with New England soil occasioned one of his finest poem-portraits: "rain or hail/sam done/the best he kin/till they digged his hole." A similar earthy wisdom is in a poem that may be a comment on himself: "my specialty is living said/a man(who could not earn his bread/because he would not sell his head)."

Because he had in common with T. S. Eliot not only a New England Unitarian background but also cosmopolitan traits, it is stimulating to observe the differences between them. Eliot became a British citizen. Cummings, responding to French art, always admiring the French civilization, nonetheless spent most of his life in the United States. He was a goldfinch needing a native tree to sing from. Through the years, from his perch, he continued to pour forth his songs: *No Thanks* (1935), *50 Poems* (1940), *1 x 1 (One Times One,* 1944), *Xaipe* (1950). *A Collected Poems* appeared in 1938. The ballet *Tom* was published in 1935 and the plays *Anthropos* and *Santa Claus* were published in 1944 and 1946.

Honors and rewards came with frequency—now. In 1950, for "great achievement," he was given the Fellowship of the Academy of American Poets. In 1952 he was invited to give the Norton Lectures at Harvard (published as *I: Six Nonlectures* in 1953), an urbane but lively analysis of the Cummings quest to discover "Who as a writer am I?" These lectures could have been subtitled "And who as a person are you?" because—like Walt Whitman with his phrases addressed to future generations who would cross on Brooklyn Ferry—Cummings was always reaching out from the persona, the neutral "i," to the "you" out there. In 1955 he received a special citation from the National Book Awards for *Poems 1923–1954* (1954) and in 1957 he received both the Bollingen Prize for Poetry and the Boston Arts Festival Poetry Award. A year later the last of his poetry collections to appear during his lifetime was published, *95 Poems.* Cummings the painter was also honored: he had one-man shows in 1944 and 1949 at the American-British Art Centre, and in 1945 and 1959 at the Rochester Memorial Gallery. His wide-ranging interest in the visual arts was reflected in *Adventures in Value* (1962), on which he collaborated with his third wife, photographer Marion Morehouse.

Cummings died on September 3, 1962, in New Hampshire. He left a manuscript of poetry published the following year as *73 Poems.*

"The artist's country is inside him," said Cummings. This was another way of saying that he would abide only by the laws of his own mind. His formalities—the literary devices he developed—were intended to show how the outer appearance reinforces the inner vision. His disordered syntax and typographical disarrangements were intended, not to bewilder, but to heighten the understanding. He described what he was trying to do in the 1926 Foreword to *Is 5*: "my theory of technique, if I have one, is very far from original; nor is it complicated. I can express it in fifteen words, by quoting The Eternal Question And Immortal Answer of burlesk, viz. 'Would you hit a woman with a child?—No, I'd hit her with a brick.' Like the burlesk comedian, I am abnormally fond of that precision which creates movement." One of his methods to achieve this was tmesis (the separation of parts of words by intervening words). It became almost like a signature for him. As Karl Shapiro put it in his *Essay on Rime,* Cummings was concerned with the "Integers of the word, the curve of 'e',/Rhythm of 'm', astonishment of 'o'/And their arranged derangement." By the analysis of words into their parts, both syllables and individual letters, and by considered use of space and punctuation marks, as well as by "arranged derangement," Cummings hoped to extend meaning beyond traditional limits.

Cummings used space in his typographical rhetoric to indicate tempo of reading: single words may have spaces within them to force the reader to weigh each syllable, as in "can dy lu/minous"; or words may be linked, as in "eddieandbill," to convey the act of boys running. A comma may be used where a period is expected, within a poem or at the end of it, to produce a pause for the reader to imagine what the next action might be. Or commas, colons, and semicolons may be used within a word to arouse new sensations and intuitions. In examining the poem beginning "as if as" (*No Thanks*) the reader disentangles from the typography the idea that it is a poem about sunrise. But it is not like other accounts of sunrise, nor, probably, does it reflect the reader's own experience. Toward the end of the poem the word "itself" is fractured into "it:s;elf." The "s" suggests the sun as well as the viewer. "Elf," relating to an earlier phrase, "moon's al-down," is a hint, in this instance, of the supernatural impact of dawn. The daily sun is no longer a habit but a miracle. In a later work (Number 48 in *73 Poems*), the word "thrushes" is divided into "t,h;r:u;s,h;e:s" so that the reader may perceive, with the poet, the individual sleepy birds gripping a branch at moonrise and, by implication, the transcendental relationship between all living things. Of the exclamation point beginning the first poem in *50 Poems,* "!blac," Cummings himself said that it might be called an emphatic "very"; the unpronounceable "?" and ")" are often similarly used. To focus the reader's attention a capital letter may be thrust into the middle of a word. In the opening poem of *No Thanks* capitals are used to imitate the roundness of the moon and to imply the eternity of the circle:

mOOn Over tOwns mOOn
whisper
less creature huge grO
pingness

In "i will be" (*And*) the word "SpRiN,k,LiNg" is manipulated to make a visual representation of sunlight filtering through wing feathers. In this poem, too, a parenthesis is used in the middle of the word "wheeling" to place simultaneously before the reader's mind the flutter of the pigeons and their effect on the sunlight:

whee(:are,SpRiN,k,LiNg an in-stant with
  sunLight
then)l-
ing . . .

Cummings made varied use of parentheses: for an interpolated comment or to split or combine words as a guide to his thought. Frequently they occur, in poem-parables, to clarify the relationship between two sentences that run simultaneously through the poem. In "go (perpe)go," published in *No Thanks,* we have a typical Cummings juxtaposition. The parenthetical sentence is a surrealist collection of "perpetual adventuring particles" describing the action of a disturbed ant heap and an anteater getting his dinner. The sentence outside the parenthesis, "go to the ant, thou anteater," is an allusion to Proverbs 6:6: "Go to the ant, thou sluggard." The poem is description and social comment, disguised as a joke. Critic Norman Friedman analyzed it succinctly: "Cummings is satirizing a certain kind of worldly and prudential wisdom. The ant's activity represents for Cummings merely busy work rather than a model of industry, and he who is advised to 'go to the ant' is the one creature who can possibly profit from such a visit—the anteater. In thus reducing the proverb to its simply 'realistic' aspects—by refusing to make the metaphorical transference intended—Cummings deflates the whole implied point of view."

Some of Cummings' poems utilize the "visual stanza" in which lines are arranged in reference, not to rhyme and meter, but to a shape reflecting the poet's thought. This kind of typographical design, with poems contrived in the form of roses, diamonds, and hourglass figures, was in fashion during the Elizabethan age and continued to be used in the seventeenth century. With changes in taste and technical practice in the last two centuries, this device fell into disuse, although it has been revived occasionally, as when Lewis Carroll used it for his mouse's "long and sad tale." More recently it appeared in the *Calligrammes* of Guillaume Apollinaire and in the "quaint" patterning of Dylan Thomas' poem "Vision and Prayer." However, the visual appearance of Cummings' poems can be largely accounted for by his interest in contemporary art forms, rather than by influence from other writers. From artists like Picasso who were bringing new vitality to painting, he learned the effectiveness of distorting lines and reshaping masses; and he juxtaposed words as they did the pigments (in John Peale Bishop's apt phrasing)—to bring perception of things into sharper focus. Cummings specifically disclaimed any stylistic influence from Apollinaire's mimetic typography, and as Gorham B. Munson observed very early, Cummings' typographical design, unlike that of the *Calligrammes,* reinforces the literary content of his poems. Some of Cummings' poems are designed to be read vertically; in others, stanzaic structures are balanced for mass, as are certain colors in painting. Effective examples of Cummings' use of the visual stanza are the poem "!blac" and the ironic dedication to *No Thanks,* which lists in the shape of a wineglass all the publishers who had rejected the manuscript. In *XLI Poems* there is a poem, "little tree," that visually suggests a Christmas tree, and another that on the page resembles smoke puffing out of a locomotive:

the
   sky
      was
can dy lu
minous

Another important device by which Cummings intended to enlarge the reader's comprehension was word coinage. He kept already existing root words, joining to them new affixes. In such compounded words the prefixes are familiar enough, but his use of the suffixes *-ly, -ish, -est, -ful* and adverbs (such as less) in unexpected combinations, a dimension natural to classical and romance languages, produces in English an intensifying of perception. Introduce one or two of these words—*riverly, nowly, downwardishly, birdfully, whichful, girlest, skylessness, onlying, laughtering,* etc.—into a verse of recognizable words and the reader has to explore possibilities in a creative way. In reading creatively a phrase like "on stiffening greenly air" he will cross the threshold of transcendence. Articles and particles were rearranged by Cummings for the same purpose—"some or if where." One part of speech may be used for another, as in the first line of a much-anthologized poem from *And,* "Spring is like a perhaps hand." The charm of this line is due in large part to the use of an adverb when an adjective is expected, to emphasize the tentative nature of springtime. This is reinforced by an image of the window dresser who moves things and changes things "without breaking anything," in contrast to the destruction of winter.

In all of these ways Cummings broke language from its conventionalized mold; it became a nourishing soil through which "faces called flowers float out of the ground" (*Xaipe*). Cummings' virtuosity was directed to capture in words what the painter gets on canvas and what children, violently alive in response to objects and seasons, display in their street games. His poems are alive on the page, as he told the printer when he instructed him not to interfere with the "arrangement." Any change would be an injury to living tissue. In discontinuous poems he tried to pin down the "illuminated moment," to ransom from oblivion the fleeting present, in words seasonal, contemporary, and timeless—like a writer of haiku. To get at the realities, Cummings smashed the logicalities, an idea in harmony with Oriental art and philosophy, with which he had acquaintance, as shown by a quotation from the Tao that appears near the end of *Eimi*: "he who knoweth the eternal is comprehensive . . . therefore just; just, therefore a king; a king, therefore celestial; celestial, therefore in Tao; in Tao, therefore enduring." Cummings' perpetual concern with transcendental ideas led to the shining leaps on the page that make his work unique.

One needs to remember, however, that this innovating poet was practiced in conventional Western literary tradition. The young Cummings learned from Elizabethan song and eighteenth-century satire, as well as from the Pindaric ode. He was rooted in the same soil as Thoreau, Emerson, and Emily Dickinson. Intermittently he read Aeschylus, Homer, and the French troubadours—as evidenced by his quotations in the *Six Nonlectures.* He cut his literary teeth on the strict rules of villanelle, roundel, and ballade royale. Nonetheless his genius led him to quite different patterns: a poem in *ViVa,* for example, records phonetically not only a conversation but a revelation of the hearts of lost men: "oil tel duh woil doi sez/dooyah unnurs tanmih essez pullih nizmus tash,oi/dough un giv uh shid oi sez. Tom." The emphasis is deliberate and made with care.

Cummings said that Josiah Royce (who appears in one of the poem-portraits) directed his attention to Dante Gabriel Rossetti, especially to Rossetti's sonnets, and that made him a sonneteer. Certainly Cummings wrote some of the finest sonnets of our century: celebrating love, savagely ridiculing human stupidity, and recording his pilgrimage to the transcendental. From the somewhat conventional, Cummings' sonnets developed, as Theodore Spencer has said, to achieve "specific gravity." Yet the only discernible influence of the Pre-Raphaelite school is in the early lyrics and might as easily have been been picked up direct from a reading of the sonnets of Dante. There is internal evidence that Shakespeare was the dynamic influence in his sonnet-making: sensory details, the absence of hypocrisy, even the rhythm of the snap at the end, as in a couplet from "being to timelessness as it's to time" in *95 Poems*: "—do lovers love?Why then to heaven with hell./ Whatever sages say and fools,all's well." In an interview with Harvey Breit in 1950 Cummings said: "Today so-called writers are completely unaware of the thing which makes art what it is. You can call it nobility or spirituality, but I should call it intensity. Sordid is the opposite. . . . Shakespeare is never sordid . . . because his poetry was the most intense."

Cummings' experimentation was clearly within Western literary tradition, as was Eliot's, but, finally, whatever he did resulted in poems that could not have been written by anyone else. He has had no sucessful imitators. And because of its nature Cummings' work cannot be held within the bounds of conventional literary analysis. The critic must stretch his own powers to find the significant new insights waiting to be revealed by this poet's language in action. What is required is "intelligence functioning at intuitional velocity"—Cummings used the phrase to characterize a work of the sculptor Lachaise but it admirably describes the approach a perceptive critic-reader must take to Cummings' writing.

For a study of Cummings' philosophy and of his devices to achieve art in motion and at a peak of excitement, the play *Him,* called by the critic Edmund Wilson "the outpouring of an intelligence, a sensibility, and an imagination of the very first dimension," is especially useful.

The action is divided between "exterior" and "interior" happenings that develop the love story of a man and the predicament of an artist. The satirical exterior scenes are presented before a garish curtain like that used in carnival shows. The deliberate lack of a third dimension is one of the poet's "absurdities"; it symbolizes the "unworld." The curtain and the parodies of circus and burlesque in the play's action reflect his interest in folk amusements. The interior scenes explore the psyche of the creative temperament. Connecting the two phases is the chorus: the three Fates, Atropos, Clotho, Lachesis. They are disguised as the Misses Weird and are nicknamed "Stop," "Look," and "Listen." They sit with their backs to the audience, rocking and knitting, as they swap a nonsensical version of backfence talk and advertising slogans. The stage directions integrate the themes and devices of the play.

In the complex design of *Him,* described by one commentator as "a play of lucid madness and adventurous gaiety," Cummings sets up a confrontation: man, a social being, versus the artist. In the *Six Nonlectures* he repeats: "Nobody else can be alive for you; nor can you be alive for anybody else. . . . There's the artist's responsibility. . . ." Yeats knew this human instinct to fulfill strenuous conditions for the sake of an ideal: writing of the Irish playwright J. M. Synge, he said, ". . . to come out from under the shadow of other men's minds . . . to be utterly oneself: that is all the Muses care for." At first glance Yeats's statement seems callous but when it is illustrated in the creative life it leads to service for the community. In the poems beginning "i sing of Olaf glad and big" (*ViVa*) and "a man who had fallen among thieves" (*Is 5*), Cummings is urging awake the sleeping conscience of his fellows. And in *Him* Cummings develops a metaphor, found with varying emphasis in his poetry, that strikingly illustrates his view. The artist is likened to a circus performer who sits astride three chairs stacked one on top of the other and balanced on a high wire. He explains to his lover, "Me," that the three chairs are three facts: "I am an Artist, I am a Man, I am a Failure."

The label on the top chair, "Failure," is disconcerting but acceptable when the reader becomes familiar with the paradoxes of Cummings' vocabulary. To distinguish true accomplishment from the disappointing successes of the salesman-politician-warmongering world, he uses words that for him state the ultimate emptiness of the prizes the crowd pursues and often captures. Throughout Cummings' poems occur the words *failure, nothing, nobody, zero* and the prefixes *non-* and *un-*. They are also scattered through the prose of *The Enormous Room* and *Eimi.* By these negatives he separated his ideals from the pleasures of a conformist world and showed his condemnation of "mobs" and "gangs" and his concern for the individual. The phrase "you and i" dominates his response to relationships: lovers, mother and child, a man and a city, a man and a tree.

The other two "chairs" of *Him* have a subordinate but vital function in the metaphor. The experiences of the man are limited to the senses until they are fused with the perceptions of the artist. It is from the artist and his transcendental realizations that the reader or viewer learns to distinguish the genuine from the pinchbeck. The artist is also dependent on the report from his five senses to actualize his ideas. So Cummings found spiritualities in "facts" and celebrated them in his poems of love and compassion. The significance that Cummings assigned to "failure" is further evident in a sonnet from *Is 5,* "if i have made, my lady, intricate/imperfect various things . . ." And a study of the Foreword to *Is 5* will reveal affirmations of the themes of *Him*: that the poet knows he is "competing" with reality and therefore "failure" is predestined. What is increasingly noticeable in the play and in the volumes of poems that follow it is the changing concept of love and the frank presentation of the artist's self-doubt. He insists on finding out who he is before he can be either artist or lover. Cummings' belief that the artist's total attentiveness to an object or subject should result in simultaneity for his audience—which was also the aim of the Imagist movement in poetry and of Cubism in painting—was not completely realizable. He therefore began to think of art as a series of mirrors reflecting the "object" in various lights and not as the thing-in-itself. So, with a sense of the "awful responsibility" of the poet, he regarded his extraordinary successes in putting on the page a flying bird, a grasshopper, a falling leaf as "failures" and called himself a nonhero.

The falling leaf poem is the first of the *95 Poems.* It is not a complete sentence and there are only four words. The form has the narrowness of a needle. In a time when novels tell no story and music is not melodic—relatively speaking—this pictogram brings new insights, which have been perceptively set forth by Norman Friedman and Barry A. Marks in their critical studies of Cummings; their lead is followed here.

l(a

le
af
fa

ll

s)
one
l

iness

Each of the first four lines has but one consonant and one vowel: two *l*'s, three *a*'s, one *e,* and two *f*'s. This suggests the fluttering pattern of a falling leaf. The next line, treated as a stanza, is a double *l,* extending meaning as the reader waits for the necessary completion. The poem ends on a shifting note which accentuates the import of "alone," "one," and "oneliness" (defined as "own").

The mind of the reader seizes the two ideas: loneliness and the parenthetical interjection of the fall of a leaf. In splitting "loneliness" Cummings shows by variations on a word blurred by indiscriminate use that it is, as Marks noted, "quite a singular word." Cummings strips the sheath from the ordinary, and the extraordinary is revealed. The "le/af/fa/ll" involves both sound and visual values; the musical relation echoes the meaning emerging from "le" and "af."

The *l* in "leaf" repeats the first *l* in "loneliness" and helps the reader keep in mind simultaneously the material inside and outside the parentheses. His old typewriter played an important role here in Cummings' idea of form as it affects thought: in the first line *l* can be either the digit "one" or the letter "el." A parenthesis separating it from *a* suggests that while the idea of doubling up on "oneness" is attractive, it is not plausible. Following the trail of the parenthesis, the reader discovers a "verse" that reinforces the necessity that *l* be "el" in the fourth stanza. The word "one" and an apparent digit reflect back to the initial *l* and in their interplay the digit vanishes into the letter.

The reader is pleased with his success in working out the "puzzle"; casually he has participated in the dance of the poet's mind. Then he arrives at the last line, "iness." The isolation and the desolation of the individual, the I alone with the I, be it a leaf or a man, have been established. Forgotten are the secondary ideas of oneness with the universe or the intimations of autumn: the reader now knows he has misunderstood the form if he accepted it as a needle stitching together all created things. However, as Henry James asserted by implication in *The Wings of the Dove,* the tragic element is art and art is delight. Yet another idea is added to the possibles of interpretation: man's unhappy isolation comes from self-loving activities and trivial goals. Self-forgetfulness is the reward of the disciplined athlete and of the artist, with the result an unblemished performance. The ever-evolving devices of Cummings are a witness to his profoundly moral nature in conflict with an imperfect world, and to his vision that it *could* be perfected.

The "puzzle" of the following lines from *No Thanks* is similarly rewarding to the reader willing to work it out:

```
                    r-p-o-p-h-e-s-s-a-g-r
               who
a)s w(e loo)k
upnowgath
               PPEGORHRASS
                                    eringint(o-
aThe):l
          eA
               !p:
S                                          a
```

The poet, through spacings of word and letter and the unorthodox use of capitals, presents a grasshopper living in his muscles. At first he is invisible, coming from the grass to us only in the sounds reverberating from earth or pebbles. But as Lloyd Frankenberg pointed out in his study of modern poetry, *Pleasure Dome*: "These sounds—some soft, some loud, some intermittent—are rearrangements of his name; just as he rearranges himself to rub forewing and hind leg together. Then he 'leaps!' clear so that we see him, 'arriving to become, rear-rangingly, grasshopper.' " The reader has been, briefly, the grasshopper and that has extended his capacity for being alive. Note that in this poem Cummings used a device resembling Cubistic painting: "r-p-o-p-h-e-s-s-a-g-r" and "PPEGORHRASS" and ".gRrEaPsPhOs" (which appears after the lines quoted above) record the "realization" of experiences that he wished to share with his readers.

In other poems which demonstrate his delight in the natural world, Cummings often used mimicry. Cummings had a talent like that of the Greek comic playwright Aristophanes, who in his oft-quoted line "Brekekekéx koáx koáx" sought to reproduce the sound of frogs. A similar mimicry is found in such unlikely Cummings poems as the colloquial "buncha hardboil guys from duh A.C. fulla" (*ViVa*) and "joggle i think will do it although the glad" (*Tulips and Chimneys*). In a punning poem, "applaws)" *(One Times One*), the "paw" is a kind of mimicry and a reminder that fundamentally we are animals.

Another aspect of the "creaturely" life that interested Cummings is to be found in his poems about horses, those animals now vanishing from sight, except in parades or circuses. In the lines below from a poem in *No Thanks* the scene is set by "crazily seething of this/ raving city screamingly street." What opens the windows to be "sharp holes in dark places" is the light from flowers. And what do the "whichs" and "small its," the half-alive, half-asleep people see?

what a proud dreamhorse pulling(smooth-
   loomingly) through
(stepp)this(ing)crazily seething of this
raving city screamingly street wonderful

flowers And o the Light thrown by Them
   opens

sharp holes in dark places paints eyes
touches hands with newness
and these startled whats are a(piercing
clothes thoughts kissing
wishes bodies)squirm-of-frightened shy are
whichs small
its hungry for Is for Love Spring thirsty for
happens
only and beautiful

Through the raucous sounds of a city street a horse is pulling a load of flowers. In that setting his movements have a grace such as is found in dreams. The horse establishes his reality as we watch him "stepp . . . ing"—the poet has plowed with horses his family's fields; he has watched milk wagons in the city. However, as Lloyd Frankenberg has suggested, the horse, "whose feet almost walk air," brings to mind Pegasus. That wingèd steed of the Muses is associated in legend with Hippocrene, the fountain of inspiration, which supposedly sprang from the earth at a blow from his forehoof. In one legend the Greek hero Bellerophon, with the aid of Pegasus, slew the Chimaera, a ravaging beast. Then he tried to fly to heaven, thereby offending the gods, and fell to earth. A poet is often trying to fly and often he fails. So we come back to the name that Cummings gave himself, "nonhero."

In another city sonnet, from *And* ("my sonnet is A light goes on in"), we meet the dray horses that sleep upstairs in a tenement stable. "Ears win-/k funny stable. In the morning they go out in pairs." Implied in the poet's words is the ancient horse sacrifice to the sun, to encourage the sun to rise again. So the sonnet comes to a climax on a line of life and beauty: "They pull the morning out of the night." There is the same fidelity to sensory perception in poems that include references to rain: "the rain's/pearls singly-whispering" (from "the moon is hiding in," *Tulips and Chimneys*) and "i have found what you are like/the rain" (*And*).

The opening lines of an early poem, from *Tulips and Chimneys,* show both Cummings' delight in the natural world and his ability to respond freshly to it:

stinging
gold swarms
upon the spires
silver

chants the litanies the
great bells are ringing with rose
the lewd fat bells

The poet avoided the obvious ideas that cluster around the subject of sunset: the timeworn meanings of silver and gold are freshened by the adroit combination of "stinging" and "swarms"; sound and image suggest the flight of a young queen and the creation of a new hive. "Spires" is echoed later in the poem in the phrase "a tall wind," and the poem concludes with an image of a dreamy sea. In an experiment Laura Riding and Robert Graves converted the pattern of this poem, the last part of which imitates a retreating wave, into conventional stanzas and concluded, rightly, that in the process the significance as well as the poetry was lost.

Informed critics, among them Barry A. Marks and the poet William Carlos Williams, have directed attention to "nonsun blob a" as probably the most difficult of Cummings' poems and yet as one containing very useful clues for the reader. It has a regularity of stanza, an Elizabethan tone, and a simplicity that might place it among the poet's charming verses for children. However, it offers a severe challenge to the mind: to put away old habits of associative thinking and to examine each stanza, line by line and word by word, for the relationships the poet has evoked. It also sums up Cummings' innovations and ideas to a remarkable degree. The emphasis Cummings himself placed upon it is evident in its position as the opening poem of the volume *One Times One.*

nonsun blob a
cold to
skylessness
sticking fire

my are your
are birds our all
and one gone
away the they

leaf of ghosts some
few creep there
here or on
unearth

Here the senses become elements of thought and the emotions are objectified to an extreme degree. The first stanza has neither verb nor expected sequences nor is it broken up to be reassembled, like an anagram. Each word compresses experiences from years of winter days; it is demanded of the reader that he be alert at all points so he may follow the clues in this celebration of bare, daunting specifics of a northern winter. Look at a winter sky: sunlessness is its chief characteristic but there is a gray waver, a "blob," sending out an almost invisible shine. The closing line, "sticking fire"—in which some critics observe a sexual connotation—brings into focus a dumb fear of being lost in a glacial world and paradoxically suggests all the physical and moral efforts to bring life-giving warmth to man, from Prometheus to nuclear industrial activities.

As we move on to a consideration of the second stanza, an observation made by Marks in his *E. E. Cummings* is especially illuminating. He noted: "the words of the first two lines . . . form two mathematical equations. One says, 'my + your = our.' The other, based on the phonetic pun, 'our' and 'are,' says, 'my = your'; 'my + your = birds'; 'my + your + birds = all.' " Intimations of what concerned Cummings—that the nature of unity is love—occur in the merging of the possessive pronouns: "mine" into "yours" into "ours" into "all." This unity is felt on repeated readings of the poem. But a Cummings poem is always in motion; the second stanza ends with the unity destroyed, the bird flock scattered in quest of a vanished leader.

The "a" which ends the first line of the poem is significant for an understanding of the third stanza. In its isolation it is related to autumn leaves creeping like crippled birds on a cold earth as indifferent as the cold sky recorded in the third stanza. Unfriendliness deprives the earth of its nourishing function; therefore Cummings used the prefix *un-* to modify the word *earth.* What is to be made of a typical Cummings inversion: "leaf of ghosts"? A remnant of birds or leaves in the increasing cold is described in the first stanza; later, birds reduced to creeping are non-birds, and cold earth is heartless as cold sky; both environments when deprived of their function as givers and nourishers, and therefore of their reality, are also ghosts. What Henry James called "perception at the pitch of passion" is involved in this "circular" poem. The implication is that of Greek tragedy: the helplessness of the alive, be it leaf or bird or a man and a woman. Yet there is joy in the contemplation of the real: a sun so clouded it may have burned out centuries ago; the relationship between the afflicted birds, leaves, and lovers—and the reader of the poem. Cummings, keeping his agonies to himself, nearly always ends on a note of joy.

This poem in twelve lines anticipates the essence of the nine stanzas of a later poem, "rosetree,rosetree" (*95 Poems*). The last stanza of "rosetree,rosetree" tells us again what the poet believes and hopes for:

lovetree!least the
rose alive must three,must
four and(to quite become
nothing)five times,proclaim
fate isn't fatal
—a heart her each petal

The reader may wonder why this master of experimental form chose rhymed stanzas for this piece. It is another instance of Cummings' sensitivity to choice among the formalities—an Elizabethan song brimming with transcendental ideas although the rose is a literal rose in a sizzle of bees. Traditional form attracts simple ideas: tree-bird, mob-war, flower-death-love. In this poem it serves as a counterweight to the complex ideas of a mystic, the poet "dreaming-true." Norman Friedman in a reasoned study of 175 worksheets of "rosetree, rosetree," rescued by Marion Morehouse Cummings from the usual destruction of preliminary work, reveals Cummings as a craftsman perfecting his materials over a long period of time. Throughout the fifty-four lines of the poem—in the adjustment of negative to positive, the victory in the final stanza over darkness and fatality—the cerebral element is always in play.

A poem that relates to this one—by melodic form and a transformation of abstracts so that they are vivid images—is the remarkable "what if a much of a which of a wind" (*One Times One*). Its rhythm perhaps reflects the influence of a ballad (attributed to Thomas Campion) which begins with "What if a day or a month or a year." But there the similarity ends. In the Cummings poem we have a deeply felt comment on the plight of universal life—nature and man—communicated by pairs of opposites: "gives the truth to summer's lie"; "when skies are hanged and oceans drowned,/the single secret will be man." In this "song" there are combinations that are reminiscent of Cummings' intriguing phrase "the square root of minus one" which he employed in at least three different contexts, notably in the Introduction to his *Collected Poems* where he wrote: "Mostpeople have less in common with ourselves than the squarerootofminusone." When he says, "Blow soon to never and never to twice/(blow life to isn't:blow death to was)/—all nothing's only our hugest home," he has made eloquent poetry of his abstract idea.

William Troy has commented that certain pages of Cummings' Russian travel journal, *Eimi,* are as good as all but the best of his poetry. Certainly there is a relation between the prose and poetry in theme and technique.

In *Eimi* Cummings' words are positioned logistically to establish the impact of viewing Lenin's tomb. Others had written, according to their political bias, of that tomb. Cummings presented what his senses reported: the smells and sounds of the never-ending line of humanity descending into the bowels of the earth to get a glimpse of the corpse of a small man with a small face, their Messiah—as secret in death as he was in life. Cummings had gone to Russia to find out what the socialistic experiment was doing to help man toward being more alive. He found men and women with "a willingness not to live, if only they were allowed not to die," in John Peale Bishop's words. In some circumstances apathy is a means of survival, but for the poet this was too little—or so it seemed to the young man of Harvard and New Hampshire. Vivid, even gay, portraits of Russians lighten the record but the following passage—illustrative of his firming style, that "specialization of sensibility"—is what he understood at Lenin's tomb:

facefacefaceface
    hand-
        fin-
            claw
    foot-
        hoof
    (tovarich)
        es to number of numberlessness (un
    -smiling)
    with dirt's dirt dirty dirtier with others'
      dirt of themselves
dirtiest waitstand dirtily never smile
    shuffle-budge dirty pausehalt
    Smilingless.

Francis Fergusson has referred to this passage as the beginning of "a sleepwalking deathrite." Cummings' deliberate abandonment of conventional syntax, which is based on an arrangement of thoughts and sensations already completed, makes the "instantaneous alone . . . his concern," as Troy put it, and he takes the reader into "an unworld of unmen lying in unsleep on an unbed of preternatural nullity."

Sensory awareness has been a dominant theme of Cummings' work discussed so far. A second primary theme in his work, both poetry and prose, is the integrity of the individual. The last lines of a sophisticated little poem about a Jewish tailor in Greenwich Village, "i say no world" (*50 Poems*), put his view succinctly: "unsellable not buyable alive/one i say human being)one/goldberger." Beginning with *The Enormous Room* and *Tulips and Chimneys,* Cummings celebrated individuals, perceiving the transcendental under the ephemeral disguise. Some of his poem-portraits focused on the famous: Buffalo Bill ("Buffalo Bill's/defunct," *Tulips and Chimneys*), the tragicomic dancer Jimmy Savo ("so little he is," in "New Poems" of *Collected Poems*), Picasso ("Picasso/you give us Things," *XLI Poems*). In others he turned a clear but sympathetic eye on burlesque queens, circus clowns, "niggers dancing," the Greenwich Village "Professor Seagull." He wrote too of bums—and caught the spirit of their search for a "self" even as they scoured the gutters for a cigarette butt.

It follows that anything threatening individuality would be the object of his hatred. War, for example:

> you know what i mean when
> the first guy drops you know
> everybody feels sick or
> when they throw in a few gas
> and the oh baby shrapnel
> or my feet getting dim freezing or
> up to your you know what in water or
> with the bugs crawling right all up
> all everywhere over you all . . .

In these lines from "lis/-ten" (*Is 5*) Cummings conveys—through the agonized, almost hysterical, words of a soldier who was there—his deep-felt indignation against the senseless destruction of individuals. And the poet's skill transforms the ephemeral statistic of a newspaper battle account into transcendental man.

The threats to the integrity of the individual posed by a mechanized society are many and pervasive. "Progress is a comfortable disease," commented Cummings in "pity this busy monster, manunkind" (*One Times One*), but a disease nonetheless. The attempts of man to identify with his inventions—to become the turbines and computers he developed—stir Cummings to remark: "A world of made/is not a world of born." And so "when man determined to destroy/himself he picked the was/of shall and finding only why/smashed it into because" ("when god decided to invent," *One Times One*).

In the morality *Santa Claus* Cummings speaks sharply against the blighting forces that keep a man from knowing his spontaneous self. "Knowledge has taken love out of the world/and all the world is empty empty empty . . . joyless joyless joyless." The Child in the morality, however, can "truly see," as in Hans Christian Andersen's story "The Emperor's New Clothes." And when the Woman calls for death and Santa dressed as Death enters, she sees through the disguise because she looks with the eyes of the heart. Ironies of belief and unbelief are frequent in *Santa Claus*; the interchange of mask and costume is reminiscent of Shakespeare, and even more of the melodramatics of tent shows that toured the hinterland of the United States, and these again are related to the comedia dell'arte which began as skits performed on a wooden cart pulled by a donkey—to amuse Italian peasants. Cummings, writing to Allen Tate in 1946, said that the whole aim of *Santa Claus* was to make man remove his death mask, thereby becoming what he truly is: a human being.

In his concern to remove the death mask Cummings often employed satire. The satirist, it has been said, needs both irreverence and moral conviction. Cummings had both. His satire is like that of Swift; it comes from conviction that something is awry, as when he declared that this world is all aleak and "i'd rather learn from one bird how to sing/than teach ten thousand stars how not to dance" ("New Poems," *Collected Poems*).

In the successful satires the penetration is trenchant, underlined by a cheerful ribaldry. At other times his intention is mislaid in a junk pile of name calling and irrelevant detail. Indignation sometimes results in an absence of poetic statement and a series of stereotypes. As Philip Horton has noted, Cummings is at times guilty of bad puns and satires that miss their mark ("a myth is as good as a smile" from "little joe gould"; "obey says toc,submit says tic,/Eternity's a Five Year Plan" from "Jehovah buried,Satan dead," both in *No Thanks*). However, in a notable example of the satiric, "A Foreword to Krazy"

(1946; collected in *A Miscellany*), Cummings explained the symbolism of George Herriman's comicstrip characters and at the same time he defined his own position as a satirist. The cast is made up of Ignatz Mouse, a brick-throwing cynic, Offissa Pupp, a sentimental policeman-dog, and the heroine, "slightly resembling a child's drawing of a cat." On the political level Offissa Pupp represents the "will of socalled society" while Ignatz Mouse is the destructive element. The benevolent overdog and the malevolent undermouse, as Cummings saw it, misunderstood Krazy Kat. Not only is she a symbol of an ideal democracy but she is personal—she transforms the brick into a kiss; the senses aided by the spirit produce joy.

These ideas ran counter to those expressed in T. S. Eliot's essay "Tradition and the Individual Talent" which for so long after its publication made the personal in literature suspect. But the swing of the pendulum through the centuries from the formalized prosaic (classic) to the formalized romantic is always rectifying the errors of critics. Poets like John Berryman and Robert Lowell have carried on experiments in the personal that Cummings would have found in his vein.

In two poems, "anyone lived in a pretty how town" and "my father moved through dooms of love" (both in *50 Poems*), Cummings very effectively worked the personal into a universal application. He used for one a contemplative narration of ideal lovers and for the other a portrait of the ideal man. The maturity of the poet's insights is displayed by his bold use of regular, rhymed stanzas to control a considered emotion and to weld it to his opinions, now sufficiently explored, of the social dilemma. The refrains are a charming blend of nursery rhyme ("sun moon stars rain" and "with up so floating many bells down") and sophisticated observation ("My father moved through theys of we").

Barry Marks has pointed out that as contemporary painters (like Juan Gris and Picasso) ambiguously employed a single curve for the neck of a vase and the edge of a guitar, so Cummings often deranged his syntax in order that a single word would both intensify a statement and question its validity; an example is the "how" in "anyone lived in a pretty how town." This word suggests, among other things, that the townspeople ask how and why about things from an emptiness of mind and an incapacity for simultaneity and the intuitive grasp. The direct vision of the painter-poet is similar to a child's delight in believing that a rain puddle is the ocean; it is a transcendental conception.

In the pretty how town "anyone" and "noone" are lovers; they live and love and die in a landscape of changing seasons, among children growing into adults and forgetting the realities and adults, "both little and small," without love or interest in life—from Cummings' penetrative view. The lively series of contrasts reinforces the ballad form; emotion and thought are strictly held to the development of the charade: "anyone" versus "someones," the individual opposed to the anxious status-seekers who "sowed their isn't" and "reaped their same." Children guessed the goodness of love between anyone and noone, because children are close to the intuitive life, but living things grow by imitation, so the children forgot as they imitated their "someones.

In the last line of the third stanza, "that noone loved him more by more," the word "noone" is emphasizing the public indifference as well as providing the identification of the "she" in the next stanza:

> when by now and tree by leaf
> she laughed his joy she cried his grief
> bird by snow and stir by still
> anyone's any was all to her

A compression of meanings is achieved in "when by now," "bird by snow," "tree by leaf," and they in turn are manipulated by repetitions suggested by later rhyme and alliteration: "all by all and deep by deep/and more by more . . ." The climax of the ballad is in the line "and noone stooped to kiss his face." In the second to the last stanza the poet states the triumph of the individual way of life, as the lovers go hand in hand into eternity:

> noone and anyone earth by april
> wish by spirit and if by yes

Cumming's testament for his father, "my father moved through dooms of love," is a ballad only by stanza and innerly varied refrain; intertwined are seasonal references, as in "septembering arms of year extend," which gives individuality to the general term "harvest." It is heroic by virtue of lines that paraphrase the Prophets: "his anger was as right as rain/his pity was as green as grain." The poem is distinguished by some fine couplets: "and should some why completely weep/my father's fingers brought her sleep," and "if every friend became his foe/he'd laugh and build a world with snow," which describes pretty accurately the poet himself. There is no narrative as such, but the poem is held together by the feeling of compassion toward humble or unfortunate people.

In contrast to the abstract quality of "my father moved through dooms of love," a sequence of colorful details characterizes an early poem for Cummings' mother, "if there are any heavens" (*ViVa*). The opening lines establish clearly the heroic light in which Cumming's viewed this woman who said of herself after a remarkable recovery from an automobile accident, "I'm tough":

> if there are any heavens my mother will(all
>   by herself)have
> one. It will not be a pansy heaven nor
> a fragile heaven of lilies-of-the-valley but
> it will be a heaven of blackred roses

Cummings' virtuosity in the management of his mechanics may especially be noted in several poems revealing his intense concern with the individual. In one, the free-form poem beginning "5/derbies-with-men-in-them" (*XLI Poems*), the reader is presented with a charade. With the poet he has entered a café that, like the Englishman's pub, seems more a social club than a restaurant: the customers play games such as backgammon and read and discuss the news while drinking coffee. Identity of place is established in the fourth stanza when one of the customers buys the Bawstinamereekin from a paperboy. But Cummings builds up an un-Yankee atmosphere with carefully chosen details: the men smoke Helmar cigarettes, one of them uses the word "effendi" and "swears in persian," two speak in Turkish, an Armenian record is played on the phonograph. This is, then, a Near Eastern café in Boston. Far from the feuds of the Old Country, proprietor and customers are united by homesickness. The men are not named; instead Cummings identifies them by lowercase letters:

> a has gold
> teeth b pink
> suspenders c
> reads Atlantis

And x beats y at backgammon. This device permits Cummings both to control his flood of feeling for the men and to stress their brotherhood. When two of them—the man with the gold teeth and the winner at backgammon—leave, Cummings says "exeunt ax"; and the coupled "by" follow. Cummings' characteristic use of space and capitals to underscore meaning is also to be found in this poem: "the pho/nographisrunn/ingd o w, n" and then "stopS."

Capital letters (not meant to be pronounced) serve as an organizing and emphasizing device in "sonnet entitled how to run the world)" (*No Thanks*), which begins:

> A always don't there B being no such thing
> for C can't cases no shadow D drink and
>
> E eat of her voice in whose silence the
>   music of spring
> lives F feels opens but shuts understand
> G gladly forget little having less
>
> with every least most remembering
> H highest fly only the flag that's furled

Here we have a commentary on the existence of "mostpeople." This satire on the "unworld" employs the comparatives "less" and "least" to emphasize the triviality and sterility of that world, while the clause "in whose silence the music of spring/lives" indicates what, for Cummings, is one of the symbols of the real world, the transcendental world. There is a flash of mocking humor in the repetition of the pedantic "entitled" in the ninth line of the poem, "(sestet entitled grass is flesh . . ." but even this line has a serious purpose: to reinforce the idea of a world where people merely exist. It is followed by a richly thought-provoking statement, "any dream/ means more than sleep as more than know means guess)," which prepares the way for the masterly concluding line, "children building this rainman out of snow." In this poem Cummings uses for the most part simple words but combines them so that the repetitions and contrasts of sound add a fresh dimension to the theme and subtly contribute to the feeling of empathy evoked for the individuals trapped in the "unworld."

Where in these two poems Cummings used, variously, lowercase and capital letters as controlling devices, in "there are 6 doors" (*ViVa*), it is repetition of the phrase "next door" that governs the orderly sequence. "Next door(but four)" lives a whore with "a multitude of chins; next door/but three" a ghost "Who screams Faintly" is the tenant and "next/Door but two" a man and his wife who "throw silently things/Each at other." Then Cummings tells what happens to some men who have been jettisoned by society.

,next door but One
a on Dirty bed Mangy from person Porous
sits years its of self fee(bly
Perpetually coughing And thickly spi)tting

Finally, "next door nobody/seems to live at present . . . or,bedbugs." The reader is left to ponder several kinds of waste of human life. Emerson wrote in his essay "Self-Reliance," "This one fact the world hates, that the soul *becomes*"; Cummings recorded in poem after poem instances of the world preventing the action of the soul—but with the purpose of rousing the transcendental spirit latent in his readers.

The individuals pictured in "mortals)" (*50 Poems*) are very different from those in the rooms "next door" and so are the technical devices used. Cummings here turns to highly skilled acrobats and puts them into motion on the page:

mortals)

climbi
ng i
nto eachness begi
n
dizzily
swingthings
of speeds of
trapeze gush somersaults
open ing
hes shes
&meet&
swoop
fully is are ex
quisite theys of re
turn
a
n
d
fall which now drop who all dreamlike

(im

"Eachness" is a critical word in this poem: as George Haines IV has pointed out, the individuality of the performers is emphasized by the separation of "climbi" and "begi" from the end letters "ng" and "n"; the swinging of the trapeze is in the line repetition "of speeds of." The reader discovering a similar pattern in "&meet&" by this time is responding with a jump of his muscles, as occurs in watching ballet or circus. As the "fully" continues into "is are ex," movement has entered the area of the unknown; the symbol *x* ("ex") is equal to the mystery of the encounters of the "is" and "are," "the "hes" and "shes." The use of "a/n/d" permits visualization of the trapeze.

The fortunate climax of "who all dreamlike" brings together the specific skills and the hovering mystery of art, whose function is to redeem what otherwise would vanish from the earth like a dream. In another sense, the acrobats are a congruent image since even the most skilled is in peril at every performance (mortals, Cummings called them), yet they are completely and happily themselves in the exercise of their art. From the final line to the first one in this "circular" poem—"im" plus "mortal"—the poet justifies his contention that precision makes motion which makes life, and that the "dark beginnings are his luminous ends."

Why did Cummings choose the symbol of acrobats for a metaphysical statement? He may have been inspired, as was Rilke, by "Les Saltimbanques" of Picasso. More likely, his enjoyment of folk amusements dictated the vehicle for his fundamental belief: mortals, by devotion to a skill, an art, become immortal.

Before leaving this aspect of Cummings' work, we may appropriately turn back to his prose to find a revealing conjunction of theme and technique. In *The Enormous Room* Cummings had used a phrase of John Bunyan's, the "Delectable Mountains," to refer to certain individuals—physically mistreated, spiritually mutilated, and yet triumphantly overcoming their situations. Of one example, whom he christened The Zulu, he said, "His angular anatomy expended and collected itself with an effortless spontaneity. . . . But he was more. There are certain things in which one is unable to believe for the simple reason that he never ceases to feel them. Things of this sort—things which are always inside of us and in fact are us and which consequently will not be pushed off or away where we can begin thinking about them—are no longer things; they, and the us which they are, equals A Verb; an IS. The Zulu, then, I must perforce call an IS." Thus, using one of his typical devices, substitution of one part of speech for another, Cummings converted one way of seeing and of thinking into another to emphasize a theme that would be meshed in all of his writings. Whenever *is,* the verb, is turned into a noun, it becomes even more of a verb; it is dramatized, it gains—as Lloyd Frankenberg put it—the force of the colloquial "He is somebody." In other words, the quality of being becomes an active principle, the individual becomes a whole person, responding to the totality of experience.

A third major theme in Cummings' work, already touched upon, is the revelation of what it means *truly* to love. In his experiments with the idea of love Cummings assigned to the word the multiple connotations inherent in it: sexual, romantic, platonic. The most intense love, paradoxically, must function with the greatest objectivity; subjective impressions must be corrected by intent observation of objects, human or otherwise. Dante could write of his ideal Lady; Cummings addressed to a platonic vision a bawdy valentine that is revelatory of his stance toward life and art ("on the Madam's best april the," *Is 5*).

In the era following World War I and acceleration of industrial growth, disregard of an earlier generation's restraints on sex became a means of protesting against the increased restrictions of the national life. In literature, Sherwood Anderson, Ernest Hemingway, Eugene O'Neill, and Henry Miller emphasized the necessity for sexual freedom. Cummings participated in this critique of the dehumanizing forces dominating the modern scene. Frankly rejoicing in sexuality as a nourishing element in an integrated life, a bond between man and the cosmos, or satirizing customs based on habit and fear of public opinion, he wrote "O sweet spontaneous" (*Tulips and Chimneys*) and "she being Brand" (*Is 5*) and "i will be/Moving in the Street of her" (*And*). A poem on Sally Rand, "out of a supermetamathical subpreincestures" (*No Thanks*), is not only a celebration of the fan dancer of the 1930's but also a transcendental view of the wonder of life. And it is a significant contrast to "raise the shade/will youse dearie?" (*And*), a realistic piece exposing the joylessness in the pursuit of "pleasure."

Cummings eventually went "beyond sex as a critique of society and . . . beyond self-indulgence to self-discipline based on a new understanding of love," as Barry Marks put it. Cummings believed that morality depends on whether there is genuine giving on both sides. Sexuality is an ingredient of any I-you relationship, in the impersonal way that there is a trace of sugar in all vegetable and animal tissues, even if they taste salty or bitter. He illustrated insights into giving in a philosophical poem, "(will you teach a/wretch to live/ straighter than a needle)," and in a comment on poverty that moves in nursery-rhyme couplets from realistic deprivations to a more desperate psychological dilemma, "if you can't eat you got to/smoke and we ain't got/nothing to smoke" (both in *50 Poems*). And a poem (from *No Thanks*) with neat stanzas to control his vehemence tells the reader from what a distance the poet has come, smiling in a wry wisdom:

be of love(a little)
More careful
Than of everything
guard her perhaps only
. . . .

(Dare until a flower,
understanding sizelessly sunlight
Open what thousandth why and
discover laughing)

Lloyd Frankenberg, in his introduction to a London reprint of *One Times One,* said that, in effect, all of Cummings' poems were love poems. A neat summation, but then an "anatomy" of love is also necessary. Conventional behavior in love is related to conventional punctuation in prosody. And for a poet who lived on the tips of not only his nerves but also his mind, love covers all of existence: in one aspect it is involved with spit on the sidewalk and in another with moonlight on the thighs of his lady; the value of a thing or an experience is its revelation of an involvement with life. Finally, in *95 Poems* and *3 Poems*, Cummings came to a position whose simplicity may have surprised him: a filial relation to the Divine So this was what it meant, the witty comment he made on his own struggles in *Is 5*:

since feeling is first
who pays any attention
to the syntax of things
will never wholly kiss you;
. . . .

for life's not a paragraph

And death i think is no parenthesis

In his critical studies T. S. Eliot repeated his view that the entire output of certain writers constitutes a single work similar to an epic (*The Divine Comedy* or Williams' *Paterson*) and that individual pieces are endowed with meaning by other pieces and by the whole context of the work. This view may assist to an understanding of Cummings: fragmentation dissolves in the continuity of recurrent themes; interrelated images and symbols by their organizing force reflect and echo each other with cumulative effect. Cummings would have said it more specifically: in the here and now we can be happy and immortal if we use our wits and our will. Even if evil and death are the co-kings of this world, love is my king, and in-serving him is my joy.

It is a leap into faith when a man casts off the customary motives of humanity and ventures to trust himself as taskmaster; he will need courage and vision "that a simple purpose may be to him as strong as iron necessity is to others"—so Emerson thought. From *Tulips and Chimneys* to *Poems 1923–1954*—a constellation of refracted and repeated images—to the posthumous *73 Poems,* Cumings led a succession of readers to accept his declaration: "I have no sentimentality at all. If you haven't got that, you're not afraid to write of love and death."

The metaphysical cord on which Cummings' sonnets are threaded was in evidence in the early "a connotation of infinity/sharpens the temporal splendor of this night" (*Tulips and Chimneys*), in "put off your faces,Death:for day is over" (*ViVa*), and in

"Love/coins His most gradual gesture,/and whittles life to eternity" ("it is so long since my heart has been with yours," *Is 5*). The efficacy of love in its multiple aspects pervades the notions of death until death becomes a gate to life. Dying is a verb as opposed to a deathly noun: "forgive us the sin of death." In another early poem, "somewhere i have never travelled,gladly beyond/any experience" (*ViVa*), the abstraction "spring" is personified and its essential mystery is presented through the adverbs *skilfully, mysteriously, suddenly,* used as in the later poetry are *miraculous, illimitable, immeasurable*: adjectival aspects of natural phenomena capable of being perceived but incapable of being truly labeled or measured.

The concern of Cummings, even in his Sitwellian phase, with juxtaposed improbables—locomotives with roses—was an effort to get at the quintessence of an apparently trivial subject. Its mystery could be reached successfully only by the evolution of devices he had scrupulously crafted. In his war against formal "thinking" he was not against study or ideas; it was an opposition to the conformity which the accumulation of "knowledge" is inclined to impose. To discover the true nature of the world—to know it; to act in it; for the artist, to depict it—is the Cummings metaphysic, his politics, and his aesthetic. The world of cyclical process is for him a timeless world. He does not deny either the past or the future; rather he denies that hope or regret should warp the living moment. In this way he is related to Coleridge and to Blake (related doubly to the latter by reason of his sensitive drawings, such as the celebrated sketch of Charlie Chaplin). His eyes are fixed on fulfillment, consenting to the perpetuation of life through death, as in "rosetree, rosetree." The individual rose dies that a hundred roses may be born; true lovers will be reborn into perfect love.

The antithesis between the false routine world and the true world is seen with icy clarity by a poet who feels mortality sitting on his shoulder. The result is a complexity of vision. That it should have cost so much to get there does not trouble the poet of transcendence; he is a compeer of all seekers, including a tramp on the highway. A poet's function is to embody in a poem the dynamics of nature (including his own response), which is primarily a mystery. Heightened awareness leads to a new dimension that leads into transcendentalism supported by specific detail: in "luminous tendril of celestial wish" (*Xaipe*), the cyclical moon is regarded as evidence of process leading to death and rebirth; the poet's humility is indicated by "teach disappearing also me the keen/illimitable secret of begin."

In *95 Poems* the poetic argument rises into an intense clarity. The affirmative transcending the negative as in "All lose,whole find" ("one's not half two," *One Times One*) and in "the most who die,the more we live" ("what if a much of a which of a wind," *One Times One*) has entered a final phase. The poet has now realized that the transcendental cannot abolish the "fact" of death but he proves the worth of the affirmative as the polarizing element of his philosophy. The former devices of making nouns into verbs and shifting the placement of antitheses are less in evidence; the reality of "appearances" is acknowledged: "now air is air and thing is thing:no bliss/of heavenly earth beguiles our spirits,whose/miraculously disenchanted eyes/live the magnificent honesty of space." This is a reminder of the early "let's live suddenly without thinking/under honest trees" (*And*). The poet, however, has come into the higher turn of the spiral of mystical development where the phenomenal world is transfigured and a tree is really understood.

In this volume Cummings has collected all of his phases: (1) look at what is happening around you; (2) the imagination is more real than reality; (3) the search for life and self brings you back to a transformed reality that is shared with a grasshopper on a flowering weed. As S. I. Hayakawa wrote in *Language in Thought and Action,* the only certainty and security is within the disciplined mind; so when Cummings says in "in time of daffodils(who know"

and in a mystery to be
(when time from time shall set us free)
forgetting me,remember me

the troubadour is telling his lady to forget his life *in* time; to remember that his mortal love always looked toward lovers in immortality. Just so did his preoccupation with twilight reach beyond mist and the "dangerous first stars" to a world new to the senses.

Begin as you mean to go on. The English proverb may explain why the young Cummings was attracted to a statement of Keats: "I am certain of nothing but the holiness of the Heart's affections, and the truth of Imagination." The innovative devices that the young Cummings developed to implement this idea were a successful means of communication in the modern world. But the Cummings of *73 Poems* has traveled farther than that: into the realm of transcendence. The poet who said "—who'll solve the depths of horror to defend/a sunbeam's architecture with his life" ("no man, if men are gods," *One Times One*) has earned the right to explain time by timelessness. In total compassion he declares, in the last poem in *73 Poems*:

(being forever born a foolishwise
proudhumble citizen of ecstasies
more steep than climb can time with all his years)

he's free into the beauty of the truth;

and strolls the axis of the universe
—love. Each believing world denies, whereas
your lover(looking through both life and death)
timelessly celebrates the merciful

wonder no world deny may or believe.

Growing from poem to poem—shedding skin after skin—Cummings emerges as really himself, and therefore as everyone: that is the true definition of transcendence. The artist's formalities have become clear as a washed windowpane, or the purity of a flower upturned to receive a heavenly dew—the canticles of a mystic.

Selected Bibliography

WORKS OF E. E. CUMMINGS

For convenience of reference the capitalization of book titles in this essay follows conventional form rather than the typographical style of the title page in each book, which often reflected Cummings' own preference for lowercase letters.

Eight Harvard Poets: E. Estlin Cummings, S. Foster Damon, J. R. Dos Passos, Robert Hillyer, R. S. Mitchell, William A. Norris, Dudley Poore, Cuthbert Wright (New York: Laurence J. Gomme, 1917) Contains eight poems by Cummings.
The Enormous Room, (New York: Boni and Liveright, 1922).
Tulips and Chimneys, (New York: Seltzer, 1923).
& (And), (New York: Privately printed, 1925).
XLI Poems, (New York: Dial Press, 1925).
Is 5, (New York: Boni and Liveright, 1926).
Him, (New York: Boni and Liveright, 1927).
Christmas Tree, (New York: American Book Bindery, 1928).
[No title], (New York: Covici, Friede, 1930).
CIOPW, (New York: Covici, Friede, 1931).
W (ViVa), (New York: Horace Liveright, 1931).
Eimi, (New York: Covici, Friede, 1933).
No Thanks, (New York: Golden Eagle Press, 1935).
Tom, (New York: Arrow Editions, 1935).
1/20 (One Over Twenty), (London: Roger Roughton, 1936).
Collected Poems, (New York: Harcourt, Brace, 1938).
50 Poems, (New York: Duell, Sloan and Pearce, 1940).
1 x 1 (One Times One), (New York: Henry Holt, 1944).
Anthropos: The Future of Art, (Mount Vernon, N.Y.: Golden Eagle Press, 1944).
Santa Claus: A Morality, (New York: Henry Holt, 1946).
Puella Mea, (Mount Vernon, N.Y.: Golden Eagle Press, 1949).
Xaipe, (New York: Oxford University Press, 1950).
I: Six Nonlectures, (Cambridge, Mass.: Harvard University Press, 1953).
Poems 1923–1954, (New York: Harcourt, Brace, 1954).
E. E. Cummings: A Miscellany, edited by George J. Firmage (New York: Argophile Press, 1958).
95 Poems, (New York: Harcourt, Brace, 1958).
100 Selected Poems, (New York: Grove Press, 1959).
Selected Poems 1923–1958, (London: Faber and Faber, 1960).

Adventures in Value, with photographs by Marion Morehouse (New York: Harcourt, Brace and World, 1962).

73 Poems, (New York: Harcourt, Brace and World, 1963).

E. E. Cummings: A Miscellany, Revised, edited by George J. Firmage (New York: October House, 1965).

LETTERS

Selected Letters of E. E. Cummings, edited by F. W. Dupee and George Stade (New York: Harcourt, Brace and World, 1969).

BIBLIOGRAPHIES

Firmage, George J., *E. E. Cummings: A Bibliography,* (Middletown, Conn.: Wesleyan University Press, 1960).

Lauter, Paul, *E. E. Cummings: Index to First Lines and Bibliography of Works by and about the Poet,* (Denver: Alan Swallow, 1955).

CRITICAL COMMENTS AND STUDIES

Abel, Lionel, "Clown or Comic Poet?" *Nation* 140: 749–50 (June 26, 1935).

Baum, S. V., "E. E. Cummings: The Technique of Immediacy," *South Atlantic Quarterly* 53: 70–88 (January 1954).

———. *ESTI: E. E. Cummings and the Critics,* (East Lansing: Michigan State University Press, 1962) Good bibliography.

Blackmur, R. P., "Notes on E. E. Cummings' Language," *Language as Gesture* (New York: Harcourt, Brace, 1952) pp. 317–40.

Bode, Carl, "E. E. Cummings and Exploded Verse," *The Great Experiment in American Literature* (New York: Praeger, 1961) pp. 79–100.

Breit, Harvey, "The Case for the Modern Poet," *New York Times Magazine,* (November 3, 1946) pp. 20, 58, 60–61.

———. "Talk with E. E. Cummings," *New York Times Book Review,* (December 31, 1950) p. 10.

Davis, William V., "Cummings' all in green went my love riding," *Concerning Poetry* 3: 65–67, (Fall 1970).

———. "Cummings' next to of course god america i," *Concerning Poetry* 3: 14–15 (Spring 1970).

Deutsch, Babette, *Poetry in Our Time,* (New York: Henry Holt, 1952) pp. 111–18.

Dickey, James, "E. E. Cummings," *Babel to Byzantium: Poets and Poetry Now* New York: Farrar, Straus and Giroux (1968) pp. 100–06.

Fergusson, Francis, "When We Were Very Young," *Kenyon Review* 12: 701–05, (Autumn 1950).

Frankenberg, Lloyd, *Pleasure Dome: On Reading Modern Poetry,* (Boston: Houghton Mifflin, 1949) pp. 157–94.

Friedman, Norman, *E. E. Cummings: The Art of His Poetry,* (Baltimore: Johns Hopkins Press, 1960).

———. E. E. Cummings: *The Growth of a Writer,* (Carbondale: Southern Illinois University Press, 1964).

Gunter, Richard, "Sentence Poem," *Style* 5: 26–36 (Winter 1971).

Haines, George, IV, "::2:1—The World and E. E. Cummings," *Sewanee Review* 59: 206–27, (Spring 1951).

Hart, J., "Champion of Freedom and the Individual," *National Review* 21: 864 (August 26, 1969).

Harvard Wake, No. 5 (Spring 1946). A special Cummings number.

Hollander, John, "Poetry Chronicle," *Partisan Review* 26: 142–43 (Winter 1959).

Honig, Edwin, " 'Proud of His Scientific Attitude,' " *Kenyon Review* 17: 484–90, (Summer 1955).

Horton, Philip, and Mangan, Sherry, "Two Views of Cummings," *Partisan Review* 4:58–63, (May 1938).

Marks, Barry A., *E. E. Cummings,* (New York: Twayne, 1963).

Metcalf, Allan A., "Dante and E. E. Cummings," *Comparative Literature Studies* 7: 374–86, (September 1970).

Moore, Marianne, "People Stare Carefully," *Dial* 80: 49–52, (January 1926).

———. "One Times One," in *Predilections* (New York: Viking Press, 1955) pp. 140–43.

Munson, Gorham B., "Syrinx," *Secession* 5: 2–11 (July 1923).

Norman, Charles, *E. E. Cummings: The Magic-Maker,* (New York: Macmillan, 1958).

Riding, Laura, and Graves, Robert, *A Survey of Modernist Poetry,* (London: Heinemann, 1927) pp. 9–34.

Shapiro, Karl, *Essay on Rime,* (New York: Reynal and Hitchcock, 1945) pp. 20–21.

Sitwell, Edith, *Aspects of Modern Poetry,* (London: Duckworth, 1934) pp. 251–57.

Spencer, Theodore, "Technique as Joy," *Harvard Wake* 5: 25–29 (Spring 1946).

Tate, Allen, "E. E. Cummings," *Reactionary Essays on Poetry and Ideas* (New York: Scribners, 1936) pp. 228–33.

Time, (September 14, 1962). A full-page obituary.

Troy, William, "Cummings's Non-land of Un-," *Nation* 136: 413, (April 12, 1933).

Untermeyer, Louis, "Quirky Communications from an Exuberant Hero," *Saturday Review* 52: 25–26, (July 5, 1969).

Voisin, Laurence, "Quelques poètes américains," *Europe: Revue Mensuelle* 37: 36–37, (February–March 1959).

Von Abele, Rudolph, " 'Only to Grow': Change in the Poetry of E. E. Cummings," *PMLA* 70: 913–33, (December 1955).

Wegner, Robert E., *The Poetry and Prose of E. E. Cummings,* (New York: Harcourt, Brace and World, 1965).

Williams, William Carlos, "E. E. Cummings' Paintings and Poems," *Arts Digest* 29: 7–8, (December 1, 1954).

Wilson, Edmund, "*Him*," *New Republic* 70: 293–94, (November 2, 1927).

EMILY DICKINSON

(1830–1886)

SUZANNE JUHASZ

EMILY DICKINSON IS at once the most intimate of poets, and the most guarded. The most self-sufficient, and the neediest. The proudest, and the most vulnerable. These contradictions, which we as her readers encounter repeatedly in her poems, are understandable, not paradoxical, for they result from the tension between the life to which she was born and the one to which she aspired. Language was where she both expressed this tension and sought to mediate it, using words to create her own identity. Language was Dickinson's salvation and her surrogate, as it gave her a place in which to come alive and a way in which to encounter the world outside her self. Language was undoubtedly power for Emily Dickinson; but it was not, nor could it be, *everything*. A life invented in words is real, but it lives only in the imaginations of the one who writes it and those who read it into existence.

Emily Dickinson's greatness, as both poet and person (for they are inexorably linked), has to do with the creation of such a life—a life of purpose, authority, and achievement—in the teeth of everything that her culture put in her way to deny it to her. Her significance has to do with the creation of 1,775 poems—brilliant, extraordinary, endlessly rewarding poems—that represent her life, there to be read by that same world. Emily Dickinson's misfortune is that her words were used as a substitute, not a supplement, for another sort of life, one for which she always yearned even as she protected herself from it: that of personal closeness, literal intimacy. Not sex so much as love. Neither of these statements cancels out the other. Taken together, they tell us something about who Dickinson was and what she means to us.

Dickinson's construction of a self was particularly focused on issues connected with power, authority, and control. In fact, we could say that for Dickinson, identity was consistent with authority, to the extent that having a self meant being able to define, to interpret, to construct meaning. The most fundamental way in which she understood gender identity as an aspect of the self, and the difference that it confers in all social relationships, was that being male equaled possession of this authority, and being female equaled its lack. Consequently, her own intelligence, articulateness, and ambition presented a difficulty regarding identity, since these qualities signified "male," not "female," in the culture into which she was born.

Dickinson's attempts to create herself, therefore, have to do with finding a way to be a woman who has authority and authenticity in relation to all that is external to her: the world. Someone who can define it, know it. But there are grounds for much conflict and ambiguity in this ambition. On the one hand, Dickinson finds herself attracted to those already in possession of that power: to strong male figures like fathers, husbands, judges, generals, editors, clergymen, and, of course, God. Their love and admiration would give her power by proxy, or so a part of her (a part she has in common with many women, both before and since) believes. On the other hand, she understands full well that their power negates and denies her own. She can have no separate identity if she gives herself over to them. And so she struggles to make a new space for herself. That struggle usually results in denying them access: keeping herself inviolate.

But the self needs something more than authority, which constitutes a form of control over experience. It needs as well the connection to experience: relationship, on all levels of existence. As a woman trained from birth to value connection rather than separation, a woman who was, however, denied that most basic connection of all—the nurture of a mother who loves her for being exactly who she is (in this case, an intelligent, articulate, ambitious female)—Dickinson sought this kind of fulfillment as well. She sought it repeatedly and hungrily all her life, even while it was at odds with her battle for control. These two apparently contradictory impulses determined the kind of self she would create, one neither traditionally "female" nor traditionally "male." Unlike a traditional woman, she did not marry, bear children, or satisfy affiliative needs in the social world of her community. Unlike a traditional man, she did not seek or achieve power over others in the public world of professional enterprise. Instead she sought to create herself, in private, as a writer whose words would reach out for her and do the deeds she yearned to do, deeds that included both taking charge of experience and connecting herself to it: belonging.

Language was Dickinson's means for accomplishing these ends. In 1,775 poems, as well as in the letters she sent with unflagging energy to the people she wanted for her own, she defined herself and her world. Endlessly exploring the meaning of emotional, intellectual, and spiritual existence, she found words that would bring into being what she thought, saw, and knew. Hers is a language that not only tells but also invites, so that we cannot understand its meanings unless we participate in it. Join her, in other words, where she herself is: located in this very space of words. The features of Dickinson's distinctive language—its startling metaphors and images, its strange ambiguities and missing parts (deletions both recoverable and not), its singular precision and eager haste, its general applicability and peculiar idiosyncrasy, the chances it takes with syntax and diction that are so pronounced and so characteristically her own—all work to accomplish these ends. These are poems that alert us to the presence of an intelligence and a passion unsurpassed in literature, poems that cause us, in turn, to feel intensely for the person who comes alive in them. And these are poems that tease us, escape us, distance us from that person, that consciousness, both frustrating and challenging us. In its complexity, richness, and volatility, Dickinson's language creates her poetry and her self.

Emily Elizabeth Dickinson was born on 10 December 1830, the middle child of Emily Norcross Dickinson and Edward Dickinson. Her older brother, Austin, was born in 1829; her younger sister, Lavinia (Vinnie), in 1833. Hers was one of the leading families in Amherst, Massachusetts. Her father was a prominent lawyer and the treasurer of Amherst College, which her grandfather, Samuel Fowler Dickinson, had been instrumental in founding. Her mother, as was customary, centered her world on her devotion to husband and children.

It is not surprising that Dickinson first recognized the patriarchal power to which she was so drawn in her strong-willed father, and that she extrapolated from this relationship the one in which she would find herself over and over again with other men, with God, and with all institutionalized authority. "His heart was pure and terrible, and I think no other like it exists," she sums him up in a letter to Thomas Wentworth Higginson. Both her father's absolute power over the household and his aloofness contributed to her attraction: "Father, too busy with his Briefs—to notice what we do." Along with the appeal, however, comes a spirit of rebellion that is, significantly, couched in terms of language, writing, and books "My father only reads on Sunday—he reads *lonely & rigorous* books."

"He buys me many Books—But begs me not to read them—because he fears they joggle the Mind." "We do not have much poetry, father having made up his mind that its pretty much all *real life*. Fathers real life and *mine* sometimes come into collision, but as yet, escape unhurt!"

Language is associated with her father, not her mother, a woman who "does not care for thought," as Dickinson predates the Lacanian notion of language as "Name-of-the-Father": the form in which culture reifies itself. But at the same time, she sees language as something she can wrest from him and revise to suit herself. If Father is real life, Emily is poetry. She could not be a lawyer to get him to take notice; but she could, she thought, be a writer.

Dickinson's relations with other men in her life were similar to the one with her father: a tense combination of adoration and competition. With Higginson, the editor to whom she sent her poems for criticism (and recognition), she is at once obsequious and proud. "Would you have time to be the 'friend' you should think I need? I have a little shape—it would not crowd your Desk—nor make much Racket as the Mouse, the dents your Galleries." However, when her requests for "improvement" are met with suggestions that are well meant but all-too-conservative, she simply refrains from following his directives: "You say I confess the little mistake, and omit the large." In a series of love letters to a mysterious person addressed as "Master," she is at her most subservient. "Master—open your life wide, and take me in forever, I will never be tired—I will never be noisy when you want to be still. I will be your best little girl—nobody else will see me, but you—but that is enough—I shall not want any more." At the same time, she challenges the way he abuses the power he possesses by virtue of his gender: "If I had the Beard on my cheek—like you—and you—had Daisy's petals—and you cared so for me—what would become of you? Could you forgive me in fight, or flight—or the foreign land?" For Dickinson, love for men, on patriarchal terms, always brought suffering and loss, but it also occasioned her attempts to renegotiate those terms so that she might acquire some of the power, and with it, the love.

In her weakness and inarticulateness, Emily Norcross Dickinson could not be a model of authority for her daughter. But the need and blame that Dickinson directed at her mother were for something else entirely: for the love and nurture that her mother, she believed, never gave her. "I never had a mother. I suppose a mother is one to whom you hurry when you are troubled," she told Higginson. "I always ran home to Awe when a child, if anything befell me. He was an awful Mother, but I liked him better than none." Instead of a real mother, she depicts herself with the abstract idea of a parent who is gendered male—that is, a father—with qualities of grandeur but not of care. In the place of Mother there is nothing, a gap or hole.

Later in her life Dickinson described the reconciliation that came while she nursed Mrs. Dickinson through her final illness. "We were never intimate Mother and Children while she was our Mother—but Mines in the same Ground meet by tunneling and when she became our Child, the Affection came." The daughter can become close to her mother by reversing their roles, but when the never-nurtured child becomes "Mother," it is her authority, not her dependence and vulnerability, that gives her access to a situation of care. This does not replace the missing mothering, and it is clear from Dickinson's letters and poems that her yearning for the unconditional love of the mother-child relationship remained powerful throughout her life: "Could you tell me what home is?"

Dickinson's friendships with women, especially with Susan Gilbert, who later became her brother's wife, are characterized by her demand for such love. Against the trajectory of their lives away from Amherst, as they moved toward schooling (and sometimes work), courtship, and marriage, she sought to hold them and keep them in the bonds of her affection—to remain the most important, the most desirable one. That it was a losing battle only increased the deep and dreaded sense of loss that love always provoked in her. These words to Susan are echoed over and over in her letters and poems to women:

> I need you more and more, and the great world grows wider, and dear ones fewer and fewer, and every day that you stay away—I miss my biggest heart; my own goes wandering round, and calls for Susie—Friends are too dear to sunder, Oh they are far too few, and how soon they will go away where you and I cannot find them, *dont* let us forget these things. (Letter 94, 11 June 1852, *Letters*, vol. 1, p. 211)

With female friends Dickinson seems to have been acting over and over the drama of her relationship with her mother: asking for and never getting the support and recognition of being first and always in the affection of a warm and loving woman.

Some women, however, did serve as models for Dickinson, women she identified with the power of language if not with the comfort of unconditional love. Dickinson was a great reader, and among her favorite writers the Englishwomen Elizabeth Barrett Browning, the Brontës, and George Eliot stand out. "What do I think of *Middlemarch*?" she wrote, "What do I think of glory—except that in a few instances 'this mortal has already put on immortality.' George Eliot is one." Dickinson idolized these "women, now, queens, now," as her frequent tributes to them attest; and that intense appreciation and affection had much to do with the way in which each represented a self defined in relation to language. "The look of the words as they lay in the print I shall never forget" is how she memorialized George Eliot. These are women who prove that a life in literature is possible. They are not traditional women like her mother; instead they represent a power and significance toward which she herself strives. Her relationship with them is important and compelling, for it is a connection created entirely in the imagination and by means of language, the kind of connection that she will try to establish for herself with other people.

From 1840 to 1847 Dickinson attended Amherst Academy, where she received an education as demanding as that of many colleges today. Amherst Academy was closely connected with Amherst College; many of its teachers were professors at the college, and students of the academy often attended lectures there. Dickinson studied languages, philosophy, and science. Under the aegis of Edward Hitchcock, professor of geology and moral theology, she received a thorough grounding not only in the most modern scientific thought of the day but also in its direct connection with religion, for Hitchcock believed that truth in every branch of learning manifested God's nature and will as revealed in the Bible. He encouraged revivals, as did Mary Lyons, the founder of Mount Holyoke Female Seminary in nearby South Hadley, which Dickinson attended for two terms, for moral instruction and secular learning were not viewed as separate categories.

Dickinson, however, found herself incapable of the commitment to Christ that her friends and family were making. Although conversion was necessary in order to become an "established Christian," she never did make a profession of faith. Her strong religious interest took the form, rather, of constant challenges to a patriarchal God whom she could believe in but never obey. In her poetry she contends with God and what he stands for, seeking a space for her independent identity and inquiry: "The name They dropped upon my face / With water, in the country church / Is finished using, now" (Poem 508). Dickinson's many poems about the issues that concerned the most dedicated theologians—from the purpose and role of faith to the existence of immortality—endlessly tease received doctrine to see what truths it might hold or conceal, and what different or "slant" truths might be wrested from it.

With the exception of three trips to Boston (in 1851, 1863, and 1864) and a visit to Washington, D.C., with stops in Baltimore and Philadelphia (in 1855), Dickinson never left Amherst and its environs. Her life was centered on her home and family—father, mother, and sister, Vinnie, who also never married. Vinnie served as Emily's practical and loyal helpmeet, taking the largest responsibility for household affairs. (Dickinson gardened and baked—"people must have puddings"—and wrote, though few realized it, many poems.) Her adored brother, Austin, a lawyer like his father, settled next door with his wife, Susan.

Dickinson's status as a recluse—"I do not cross my Father's ground to any House or town"—was gradual but effective. Seeing fewer and fewer people within the confines of her own home except her immediate family, eliminating the wider world of visits, church, and social events, gave her in their stead an intense and resonant private life. In her relationships with only those with whom she was truly intimate, in her richly mined relationship with her own mind and soul, Dickinson explored with both passion and discipline the emotional, psychological, and spiritual facets of existence lived at its most fervent. Her extreme privacy was at once protective and liberating. It gave her control over her experience, especially beneficial to someone so sensitive to every nuance of every event, and it freed her to experiment with and invent that existence along lines that would not have been possible in a more public arena. It gave her the time and the opportunity to write: to find the words that could express a self at odds with the culture that had bred her.

Aside from her immediate family, Dickinson developed friendships of an ardent nature with people with whom she did not as a rule come into personal contact. Instead, she used letters both to create these relationships and to regulate them. She corresponded with girlhood friends like Abiah Root Strong and Kate Turner Anthon; relatives like her cousin Lavinia Norcross and her daughters, Louise and Frances; and friends from public life—the editor and writer Josiah Gilbert Holland and his wife, Elizabeth; the editor Thomas Wentworth Higginson; the writer Helen Hunt Jackson; the editor Samuel Bowles and his wife, Mary; the Reverend Charles Wadsworth; and Judge Otis Lord. She also engaged in extensive correspondence with her brother, Austin, before he settled in Amherst, and with her sister-in-law, Susan, both before she married Austin and even after she lived in the house next door. Her attachment to all of these people was strong, and she loved many of them, women and men, romantically and fervently. Bowles, Wadsworth, and Lord, as well as Susan Gilbert and Kate Anthon, have been proposed by one or another advocate as Dickinson's lovers. Lovers they clearly were, but these relationships probably did not extend to any sort of physical consummation. Both from preference and from situation, Dickinson kept her erotics in the mind and on the page. When Judge Lord actually proposed marriage to Dickinson after the death of his wife, she refused him: "Dont you know that 'No' is the wildest word we consign to Language?"

In language Dickinson sought and often won the affection of people who became the recipients of her words for all occasions—words as pungent, precise, cryptic, and seductive as her poems. Dickinson's letters are in fact very like her poems, their elliptical phrasing and excessive figuration growing more and more condensed over the years, their hymn rhythms forming sentences that, punctuated by dashes, are prose only insofar as they are not divided into verse lines. (Because she both enclosed poems with and appended poems to her letters, it is easy to understand why editors have always had trouble determining exactly which parts of the letters are prose and which are poetry.) Not only do her letters look like her poems, but they function like her poems, those "letter[s] to the World": they create herself to the audience she is imagining, they engage that audience with all the attractiveness of her wit and wisdom (as well as the lure of her need), and they draw that audience into intimacy, to the best of her ability.

Although her family and friends knew that Dickinson wrote poetry, no one had any idea of the extent of her writing. Ten of her poems appeared in print during her lifetime, but the poet who sought out Higginson to tell her if her poems were "alive," to teach her "how to grow," ultimately did not try for, and even refused, publication, it was "so foul a thing" (Poem 709). There is a real contradiction between her statement that "Publication—is the Auction / of the Mind of Man" (Poem 709) and her concern to "find the rare Ear / not too dull" (Poem 842). Higginson's conservative response to her work and the editing of the few published poems to fit conventional standards must have affected the poet who resolutely hung on to her own language, no matter how "wayward." If it were necessary for the fox to fit the hound, as she put it in Poem 842, this hound soon discovered that there were not that many foxes to be found.

After Dickinson died of Bright's disease on 15 May 1886, her sister discovered hundreds of poems in her desk drawers, many of them carefully copied and sewn together into small booklets, or fascicles. Others were less systematically organized, written on scraps of paper, the backs of recipes—on anything, it seems, that had been at hand. Although Dickinson had stipulated that her letters and papers be burned after her death, Vinnie decided that the poems were exempt from this mandate. Subsequently she made it her business and her life's goal to have them published. The history of the publication of Dickinson's poetry is worth an essay in itself, for it is the story of a war between women that continued, through their daughters, well into the twentieth century.

When Susan Dickinson turned down Vinnie's request for help, Vinnie approached Mabel Loomis Todd, the wife of David Peck Todd, an astronomer at Amherst College. Mabel Todd was a woman of literary aspirations whose long-standing love affair with Austin Dickinson was an ill-kept Amherst secret. In turn, Mrs. Todd enlisted the aid of Higginson. The project, which involved transcribing the poems from Dickinson's difficult handwriting, along with making editorial decisions about punctuation, line arrangement, and even word choice (for Dickinson preferred to provide alternatives for words and phrases), took several years. *Poems by Emily Dickinson* was published in 1890. Thereafter, for over fifty years, subsequent volumes of poems and then letters were published not only by Mrs. Todd and Higginson and Mrs. Todd's daughter, Millicent Todd Bingham, but also by Susan Dickinson's daughter Martha Dickinson Bianchi, for Susan had in her possession hundreds of poems and letters that she would never relinquish to Vinnie. In this way the women who were her heirs competed to present *their* Emily Dickinson to the world that she had coveted as much as avoided.

In 1955 the scholar Thomas H. Johnson published, in approximately chronological order, a complete edition of Dickinson's poems that seeks to replicate, at last, the form in which they were originally written. Johnson also published the collected letters in 1958. In 1981 R. W. Franklin published *The Manuscript Books of Emily Dickinson*, a manuscript edition that arranges the poems in fascicle order. Today even greater attention is being paid to the manuscripts, the form in which Dickinson achieved her particular version of "self-publication."

To read in the volume that contains Dickinson's 1,775 poems is to be constantly delighted and surprised. There is no way to remember each and every poem. Rather, every reader finds the ones that speak most powerfully to her one day, one year—and often an entirely different set that speak in similar personal and enlightening terms at the next reading. In this essay a few of the many poems have been selected for discussion in some detail because the close look that follows the original response is what is most rewarding about reading Dickinson. On closer reading the poems become more, not less, complicated; but in that complexity lies the richness of Dickinson. A Dickinson poem cannot be skimmed: it must be entered, and the reader must be prepared for an extended visit. Yet no one poem determines or summarizes the poet's position about anything. Rather, the poems approach and surround a theme like points on a circle, a circumference, offering complements and alternatives. Reference to other poems demonstrates how singularity is embedded in the content that the rest of the poems comprise. The poems chosen here show Dickinson in relation first to another person; then to the world outside her, to nature; and then, of course, to us, her readers, a relationship created through our own interactions with the words with which she engages us.

Dickinson characteristically understands love as a relationship about power. As the lover she is often all too ready to find that power in the one she loves:

> You constituted Time—
> I deemed Eternity
> A Revelation of Yourself—
> 'Twas therefore Diety
>
> The Absolute—removed
> The Relative away—
> That I unto Himself adjust
> My slow idolatry—
> (Poem 765)

This poem is addressed to an unidentified "You," conceived of as so all-encompassingly powerful that everything else becomes an aspect of him. As Time can be understood as the force in which all existence operates, the space in which everything exists, so the "You" can be understood as "constituting" time. Eternity and even God are a part of time; thus they are included within this person, the poetic conceit maintains. Such power becomes the idea of power itself, its absolute, and everything else is therefore relative to it and accordingly less significant. The "You" turns into "Himself" by the end of the poem, the capital *H* that is usually reserved for God now allotted to the one to whom love has given the superior or, rather, the ultimate power. In a case such as this, "love" constitutes "idolatry," as even the lover understands. Many of Dickinson's poems express this attitude, which, as it offers the most hyperbolic of compliments to the beloved, may be understood as a form of courtship. Subsuming her identity in his is flattery in accordance with cultural conventions. He is the absolute to her tiny relative: "Least Rivers—docile to some sea. / My Caspian—thee" (Poem 212).

The docility is not, however, the whole story. For Dickinson cannot give up her identity, however much she thinks she ought to or says she will. The very act of saying so in a carefully structured poem attests to the energy of a self-consciousness that undermines the willingness to lose it. Many of her poems are about the struggle to maintain that identity at all costs:

> It might be lonelier
> Without the Loneliness—
> I'm so accustomed to my Fate—
> Perhaps the Other—Peace—
>
> Would interrupt the Dark—
> And crowd the little Room—
> Too scant—by Cubits—to contain
> The Sacrament—of Him—
>
> I am not used to Hope—
> It might intrude upon—
> Its sweet parade—blaspheme the place—
> Ordained to Suffering—
>
> It might be easier
> To fail—with Land in Sight—
> Than gain—My Blue Peninsula—
> To perish—of Delight—
> (Poem 405)

"The Sacrament of Him" could be a reference to God, so that this poem, with its vocabulary of "blaspheme" and "ordained," could be read as addressing the speaker's struggle with religious authority. Or it could be, as in Poem 765, about her relationship with a person she has deified, out of love. The point is that these relationships are profoundly similar, so that Dickinson's "religious poems" and her "love poems" not only overlap but also are variations on the same theme. Reading this one as a love poem or, rather, an anti-love poem, does not annul our awareness of its other connotations.

The contrast between "lonelier" and "loneliness" with which this poem begins turns out to be a contrast between "delight" and "loneliness," or psychic death versus psychic life. Self-appointed loneliness, the self alone, or solitude is not as *lonely* as the closeness of relationship, that delight—for one can die of the latter. The poem is about the unraveling of this paradox, for paradox it is, antisocial and antitraditional: that a person would choose solitude over relationship, especially when that person happens to be a woman. In a succession of parallel images that accumulate to explain, describe, and expand the opening statement (Dickinson's poems tend to develop not chronologically or narratively, but according to a principle of accrual, like snowballs rolling through the snow, growing fatter and denser), the poem defines the meaning of both "loneliness" and "lonelier."

Loneliness is "my Fate," "the Dark," "the little Room," and "the place—Ordained to Suffering." If loneliness is a mental condition, it is imaged as a physical space: a tiny room in which this soul is living. Lonelier, on the other hand, is equivalent to "the Other," "Peace," "The Sacrament—of Him," "Hope," and a "sweet parade." For the first three stanzas of the poem the contrast seems to be between something attractive and appealing—peace, hope, and sweet parade—and something restricting, constricted, and negative—dark, scant, and suffering.

However, as we look more closely, especially at the verbs of the poem, the action as it is being imagined (for the whole poem is set in the subjunctive mood, as a hypothetical or imaginary event), we get a different sense of the contrast. "Interrupt," "crowd," "intrude," and "blaspheme": we understand that something is happening in the little room, something valued by its occupant, no matter the pain of it; that, in fact, the pain is a part of its significance. If an other—bigger, grander, more powerful—entered, it would suck the life of the little room away. The second stanza shows this happening in physical terms, as he takes up all the air in her small space. The phrase "interrupt the Dark" changes "Dark" from a condition into an activity: in the dark, we assume, something is going on. The third stanza shifts to an emotional plane. Hope is out of place in the emotional environment of suffering. Now we understand that a challenge is being mounted between his sanctity and *hers*, for his sacrament turns into blasphemy when encountering her "ordination." The religious vocabulary heightens the sense of spiritual significance in these choices. It is this contrast of identities that prepares us for the startling final stanza.

Suddenly, the image pattern shifts. We are out of the little room—suffocatingly small or liberatingly private, as we choose to think of it—and in the world, on the seashore. The change in locale is disconcerting, even confusing. In what way is the small room of the soul equivalent to the outside world? Yet there is clearly parallelism with the opening stanza: "It might be lonelier" and "It might be easier." The stanzas stand back to back, like bookends buttressing the rest of the poem, balancing one another. But how?

One way to read the stanza is to say that if his presence would be lonelier than the loneliness of her solitude, lonelier in that she would be cut off from her self, then by the same token, "failure" might be preferable to "gain," or success. Success is winning him, the "Blue Peninsula" that is contrasted to "Land in Sight," the beckoning, faraway, beautiful promontory out there on the horizon, as contrasted with what is known and close by. The blue peninsula is equivalent, as well, to delight; and delight resonates with all the other words of pleasure that have accumulated during the poem, like "peace" and "hope."

Gaining delight means, however, death: death by drowning. Pleasure is frequently aquatic in Dickinson's canon. "Rowing in Eden— / Ah, the Sea!" begins the last stanza of one of her best-known love poems (Poem 249); but we remember the Caspian Sea of Poem 212 that will consume a small river, an image that recurs in these lines: "The Drop, that wrestles in the Sea— / Forgets her own locality— / As I—toward Thee" (Poem 284).

Clearly delight is *dangerous*. Why, then, is its opposite, failing with land in sight, such a failure? It is failure in exactly the same terms that solitude is deemed loneliness: because society says so. Why would a woman give up the sacrament of him, that romantic and exciting blue peninsula? Giving him up is failure in societal terms. But the poem has taken great pains to show us why there is danger in this kind of love. Thus, the so-called failure is really success, because it is keeping her—her own self—alive.

On the other hand, the ambiguity in the imagery as well as the parallel structure of this stanza and its indeterminate dashes make it possible to read it, and therefore the rest of the poem, differently. "Easier to fail": there is so much fear, timidity, and even masochism in this poem. The speaker could easily be accused of cowardice and a failure of nerve, of wanting to keep things safe and small, and of being hopeless, afraid to confront the marvelous totality of "perishing" of delight. If the final stanza opposes "fail" to "gain," why shouldn't we take it literally? She starts out on her quest for the blue peninsula, but she can't reach it. She drowns before, not when, she gets there. Her life in the little room is the living death; "the Sacrament of Him," a salvation that she will not, cannot accept.

Although the first reading is the more attractive, the second one is altogether possible—not only because there are readers who cannot understand the need to save the self from greater powers, who cannot imagine any felicity to life in a tiny, dark room ordained to suffering, but also because the language itself, in significant moments, is ambiguous. The last stanza, in particular, can be read as accepting cultural norms or as challenging them. Which is right? Maybe both are. That is, if both readings are based on what is *there,* then what is there is Dickinson's tension around these very issues and her need to say it both ways, at the same time. This not only protects her rebellion but also contains it in the same layers of social conformity that surround her own private life in her own private room in Amherst. The doubleness ought not be overlooked or simplified. It is an aspect of Dickinson's language, as it is an aspect of her self.

Interpersonal relationships are one arena for the encounter with authority and culturally designated power. Encounter with the external world is but another version of it. In Dickinson's struggle for the power to grant meaning to experience, language again becomes the agent and the answer. The world may have a name for it, but language is infinitely flexible; as poet, she can name it differently. She can especially do so with metaphor and figurative language, which counters the literal, the norm, with words that tell lies in order to come closer to the truth—the emotional as well as the analytic, subjective as well as objective components of experience:

They called me to the Window, for
"'Twas Sunset"—Some one said—
I only saw a Sapphire Farm—
And just a Single Herd—

Of Opal Cattle—feeding far
Upon so vain a Hill—
As even while I looked—dissolved—
Nor Cattle were—nor Soil—

But in their stead—a Sea—displayed—
And Ships—of such a size
As Crew of Mountains—could afford—
And Decks—to seat the skies—

This—too—the Showman rubbed away—
And when I looked again—
Nor Farm—nor Opal Herd—was there—
Nor Mediterranean—
(Poem 628)

This whimsical treatise on the meaning of the word "sunset" is not a particularly complex poem, so it is a good way to begin our look at Dickinson's nature poems. Culture's word "sunset" does not suffice, in this speaker's opinion, for her experience. It is abstract and general, while the event is particular, synesthetic, and dynamic. Against abstraction she poses metaphor, bringing out her words with a flourish, showing off her skill at creating meaning. A sapphire farm, a herd of opal cattle grazing—the image is simple but spectacular, as colors and shapes take on recognizable identities that exist in the imagination. Soon this vision dissolves into another: an enormous sea, sailed by ships so immense that mountains serve for crew and skies for passengers. This is one way to incarnate verbally the feeling of grandeur we get from the evening sky: its colors, shapes, and movement.

However, this poem concludes with a reminder not of her own power but of the struggle that underlies it. For her verbal performance is suddenly outclassed by another, that of the "Showman" who rubs away her farm and cows and seas like a teacher erasing a student's efforts on the blackboard. *He* is in control, not she. She may have named the shapes, but he put them there—and he can take them away. Yes, this is a clever way for her poem to announce the coming of night, the end of sunset's fireworks display, but her words reveal her awareness of an antagonist other than ordinary language. Is the Showman God? Nature? The poem does not say. But it does show how, for Dickinson, the quest for authority informs even her most "universal" or "humanistic" poems—the nature poems. As they seek to define external phenomena (so many of her poems begin with a definition, like "Presentiment—is that long Shadow—on the Lawn" [Poem 764]), they often send up the brilliance of her own flamboyant imagery in the context, the teeth of, another power that got there first and is supposed to take precedence:

The name—of it—is "Autumn"—
The hue—of it—is Blood—
An Artery—upon the Hill—
A Vein—along the Road—

Great Globules—in the Alleys—
And Oh, the Shower of Stain—
When Winds—upset the Basin—
And spill the Scarlet Rain—

It sprinkles Bonnets—far below—
It gathers ruddy Pools—
Then—eddies like a Rose—away—
Upon Vermilion Wheels—
(Poem 656)

Such a tour de force is this definition of "Autumn," which, as does Poem 628, offers metaphor, a growing crescendo of it, in place of the abstract term. Dickinson replaces "Autumn" with "Blood" to invoke the feeling of the season, and blood starts her on a series of synesthetic associations that result in a macabre landscape where the inside of a body is splayed upon the New England hills and roads. Blood is color (red) and it is substance (wet). In veins and arteries blood begins to turn into rain and stain, a storm that inundates the world with brilliance and death and then departs, like a great red wheel of a flower, for roses are also red. Dickinson's rendition of the seasonal confrontation between life and death is like a painting by Van Gogh, a swirling palette of intensity that reveals not only the potency of the season but also her own somewhat histrionic skill. Some people have a terrible time with this poem, as the images overlap one another in a way that is as illogical as it is startling and disturbing. However, what Dickinson demonstrates here is that emotion is not particularly reasonable or logical, and that there is an autumn which we feel within as well as the one in the weather report. Nonetheless, what she is also doing in this poem is showing off, pitting her skill against the Showman's:

I send Two Sunsets—
Day and I—in competition ran—
I finished Two—and several Stars—
While He—was making One—
His own ampler—but as I
Was saying to a friend—
Mine—is the more convenient
To Carry in the Hand—
(Poem 308)

Here Dickinson's subjects are her "competition" with the Showman and, because they are integrally associated, the power of poetry. However, this little poem manifests a different spirit and a different resolution from the other nature poems discussed here: a concern for connection and belonging rather than for control. It is so charming because, while admitting to the presence and power of a force outside her, here identified as "Day," it allows for different but equal authority. Reality need not be either/or; it can be relational. Day's sunsets are real enough, but so are hers, created in the words of her poem, exactly as we have watched her do in Poem 628. His are ampler, true; but hers are convenient. The *comfort* of relationship is at the heart of this valorization of relative experience—not only the poet's with nature but also the poet's with her reader.

"I send two sunsets," her poem begins: sunsets we can hold in the hand, sunsets that come to life only in the relationship between her words and our reading them. From her hand to ours: the imagery of touch is poignant. Perhaps day is that much less of an antagonist here because the reader is that much more acknowledged. When the poet sends her words, and we hold them, so convenient, in our hand, the poet is aware of the electricity and the care produced by her words as they form a conduit between us. In this poem the words function less as protection or as challenge than as bridge. They validate connection rather than conquest, so that the poem actually revises the word "competition," with which it began to establish a different manner of relating, more "maternal" in its spirit than "paternal." This is not physical touch, but the words come close to it:

Good to hide, and hear 'em hunt!
Better, to be found,
If one care to, that is,
The Fox fits the Hound—
Good to know, and not tell,
Best, to know and tell,
Can one find the rare Ear
Not too dull—
(Poem 842)

This is a quintessential Dickinson poem, as it refers to her relationship with others. The Dickinson who hides and hears them hunt, knows and does not tell, is the person in the little room too scant by cubits; the person who has to cut herself off and protect herself from a hound that does not fit, that seeks out the fox to *kill* it. Solitude is good because it gives power as well as life to the self, inasmuch as it provides a space that may be literally small but is nonetheless conceptually large: the space of the imagination, where words and poems can come into being. But solitude is a response to the problem of a world that would negate the existence of one self for the authority of another, all in the name of love.

"Best, to know *and* tell" (italics added). This would be possible if there were another, less like a father and more like a mother, who would "fit" and therefore be able to hear the words, to recognize and understand. If no one like that comes along—a mother, a friend, a lover, an editor, a reader—well, one can get along without her or him. "If one cares to, that is." This vulnerability can be controlled. There is self-protection and self-defense: words can be veil as well as window. But words can be an invitation as well as a barricade. A rare ear: this poem does not give up the hope and the search, even as Emily Dickinson probably never did.

It is telling that the other is imaged here as an ear and in the sunset poem as a hand: a hand to hold the poems, an ear to hear the words. Only through language could the connection be made. Dickinson did not count on there being a real person, in the flesh, in the room. In this way the pressures of her culture in all its manifestations—from a father who could not admire her for who she was, and a mother who could not love her for who she was, to editors who did not want her words the way she wrote them, to a society that did not want her alone in the room and writing—hurt her irrevocably. But by the same token, those pressures brought out the best in her, the genius in her—her ability to defend and to fight for her right to have a self and to send it forth into the world for posterity. "If fame belonged to me, I could not escape her," she told Higginson when he advised her not to publish. To take the language, the words for reifying normative values and behavior, and turn them into a vision of the world and a vision of herself—that was something. If today the best we can give her is an ear, many ears, that, too, is something: something remarkable, to be with her in this way.

Selected Bibliography

PRIMARY WORKS

POETRY

Poems of Emily Dickinson. Edited by Thomas H. Johnson. 3 vols. Cambridge, Mass.: Harvard University Press, 1955. Variorum edition.

The Complete Poems of Emily Dickinson. Edited by Thomas H. Johnson. Boston: Little, Brown, 1957.

The Manuscript Books of Emily Dickinson. Edited by R. W. Franklin. 2 vols. Cambridge, Mass.: Harvard University Press, 1981.

LETTERS

The Letters of Emily Dickinson. Edited by Thomas H. Johnson. 3 vols. Cambridge, Mass.: Harvard University Press, 1958.

The Master Letters of Emily Dickinson. Edited by R. W. Franklin. Amherst, Mass.: Amherst College Press, 1986.

BIOGRAPHICAL AND CRITICAL STUDIES

Anderson, Charles R. *Emily Dickinson's Poetry: Stairway of Surprise.* New York: Holt, Rinehart, and Winston, 1960.

Benfrey, Christopher E. G. *Emily Dickinson and the Problem of Others.* Amherst: University of Massachusetts Press, 1985.

Bianchi, Martha Dickinson. *Emily Dickinson Face to Face: Unpublished Letters with Notes and Reminiscences.* Boston: Houghton Mifflin, 1932.

Bingham, Millicent Todd. *Ancestors' Brocades: The Literary Discovery of Emily Dickinson.* New York: Harper, 1945.

Cody, John. *After Great Pain: The Inner Life of Emily Dickinson.* Cambridge, Mass.: Harvard University Press, 1971.

Diehl, Joanne Feit. *Dickinson and the Romantic Imagination.* Princeton: Princeton University Press, 1981.

Eberwein, Jane. *Dickinson: Strategies of Limitation.* Amherst: University of Massachusetts Press, 1985.

Frankling, R. W. *The Editing of Emily Dickinson.* Madison: University of Wisconsin Press, 1967.

Gelpi, Albert J. *Emily Dickinson: The Mind of the Poet.* Cambridge, Mass.: Harvard University Press, 1965.

Juhasz, Suzanne. *The Undiscovered Continent: Emily Dickinson and the Space of the Mind.* Bloomington: Indiana University Press, 1983.

Johnson, Thomas H. *Emily Dickinson: An Interpretative Biography.* Cambridge, Mass.: Harvard University Press, 1955.

Keller, Karl. *The Only Kangaroo Among the Beauty: Emily Dickinson and America.* Baltimore: Johns Hopkins University Press, 1979.

Leyda, Jay. *The Years and Hours of Emily Dickinson.* 2 vols. New Haven: Yale University Press, 1960.

Lindberg-Seyersted, Brita. *The Voice of the Poet: Aspects of Style in the Poetry of Emily Dickinson.* Cambridge, Mass.: Harvard University Press, 1968.

Longsworth, Polly. *Austin and Mabel: The Amherst Affair and Love Letters of Austin Dickinson and Mabel Loomis Todd.* New York: Farrar, Straus & Giroux, 1984.

Martin, Wendy. *An American Triptych: Anne Bradstreet, Emily Dickinson, Adrienne Rich.* Chapel Hill: University of North Carolina Press, 1984.

Miller, Cristanne. *Emily Dickinson: A Poet's Grammar.* Cambridge, Mass.: Harvard University Press, 1987.

Mossberg, Barbara. *Emily Dickinson: When a Writer Is a Daughter.* Bloomington: Indiana University Press, 1982.

Pollack, Vivian R. *Dickinson: The Anxiety of Gender.* Ithaca, N.Y.: Cornell University Press, 1984.

———, ed. *A Poet's Parents: The Courtship Letters of Emily Norcross and Edward Dickinson.* Chapel Hill: University of North Carolina Press, 1988.

Porter, David T. *The Art of Emily Dickinson's Early Poetry.* Cambridge, Mass.: Harvard University Press, 1966.

St. Armand, Barton Levi. *Emily Dickinson and Her Culture: The Soul's Society.* New York: Cambridge University Press, 1984.

Sewall, Richard B. *The Life of Emily Dickinson.* 2 vols. New York: Farrar, Straus & Giroux, 1974.

Weisbuch, Robert. *Emily Dickinson's Poetry.* Chicago: University of Chicago Press, 1975.

Wolff, Cynthia Griffin. *Emily Dickinson.* New York: Knopf, 1986.

BIBLIOGRAPHIES

Buckingham, Willis J., ed. *Emily Dickinson: An Annotated Bibliography.* Bloomington: Indiana University Press, 1970. Covers over 2,600 items through 1968.

Clendenning, Sheila T., ed. *Emily Dickinson: A Bibliography.* Kent, Ohio: Kent State University Press, 1968. Includes an essay on the history of Dickinson scholarship.

JOHN DONNE
(1572–1631)

FRANK KERMODE

TO HAVE READ Donne was once evidence of a curious taste; now (though the vogue may be fading) it is a minimum requirement of civilized literary talk. We have seen the history of English poetry rewritten by critics convinced of his cardinal importance. This change was partly the effect of the reception into England of French symbolist thought and its assimilation to the native doctrines of Blake, Coleridge, and Pater. Poets and critics were struck by the way Donne exhibits the play of an agile mind within the sensuous body of poetry, so that even his most passionate poems work by wit, abounding in argument and analogy; the poetry and the argument cannot be abstracted from each other. And this was interesting because the new aesthetic was founded on a hatred for the disembodied intellect, for abstract argument, for what the French called *littérature.* A series of poets, culminating in T. S. Eliot, proclaimed their affinity with Donne. They also searched the past in order to discover the moment when the blend of thought and passion that came so naturally to Donne, and with such difficulty to themselves, developed its modern inaccessibility. One answer was that this occurred during the lifetime of Milton, who helped to create the difficulties under which modern poetry labors. This very characteristic symbolist historical myth is usually called by the name that Eliot gave it, the "dissociation of sensibility." Eliot altered his views on Donne and Milton, but his later opinions have been less successful in the world than his earlier ones; and it remains true that to write of the fortunes of Donne in the past seventy years is, in effect, to write less about him than about the aesthetic preoccupations of that epoch.

Donne has been distorted to serve this myth; but it is true that earlier criticism had treated him harshly. As Ben Jonson suggested, his kind of poetry runs the risk of neglect, especially in periods that value perspicuity. Dryden thought of him as a great wit, rather than as a poet, and a normal late seventeenth-century view of Donne was that this "eminent poet . . . became a much more eminent preacher." Dr. Johnson's brilliant critique occurs more or less accidentally in his *Life of Cowley.* Coleridge and Lamb, Browning and George Eliot admired him—indeed he enjoyed a minor vogue in the middle of the last century—but Edmund Gosse, in what was, until the publication in 1970 of R. C. Bald's *Life,* the standard biography, is patronizing about the poetry and calls Donne's influence "almost entirely malign." The revaluation of Donne has certainly been radical. The present is probably a favorable moment for a just estimate. The past half-century has provided the essential apparatus, and though the time for partisan extravagance has gone, so has the time for patronage.

LIFE

Donne was born early in 1572, in the parish of St. Olave, Bread Street, in the City of London, of Roman Catholic parents. His mother was of good family; and since she numbered among her kinsmen Mores, Heywoods, and Rastells, Donne could well claim, in his *apologia* at the beginning of the anti-Jesuit *Pseudo-Martyr,* that his family had endured much for the Roman Catholic doctrine. His own brother was arrested for concealing a priest and died in prison. His father, a prosperous City tradesman, died when Donne was not yet four, leaving him a portion of about (pounds) 750. A more enduring legacy was his early indoctrination by Jesuits. To his intimate acquaintance with their persecution under Queen Elizabeth he attributes his interest in suicide (*Biathanatos*) and his right to characterize as mistaken the Jesuit thirst for martyrdom by the hostile civil power (*Pseudo-Martyr*). In fact, his whole life and work were strongly affected by this circumstance of his childhood. He suffered materially; for example, as a Roman Catholic he was disabled from taking a degree at Oxford. But, more important, his mind was cast in the mold of learned religion. We know that during his years at the Inns of Court, in the early 1590's, he read much besides law; that he explored many fields and many languages; and—though described as a great visitor of ladies—rose at four every morning and rarely left his chamber before ten. Much, if not most, of this reading must have been theological in character.

Donne traveled in Italy and Spain, and in 1596 and 1597 took part in naval expeditions. In 1598 he became secretary to the influential Sir Thomas Egerton; but his secret marriage to Lady Egerton's niece, Ann More, in December 1601, put an end to his hopes of worldly success. Her father had Donne imprisoned and dismissed from his post; he even tried to have the marriage annulled. Donne's dignified apologies prevailed, but he did not achieve reinstatement, and for some years lived somewhat grimly and inconveniently in what he called "my hospital at Mitcham," burdened and distracted by illness, poverty, and a growing family. A letter describes him writing "in the noise of three gamesome children; and by the side of her, whom . . . I have transplanted into a wretched fortune." He complained, in dark and memorable phrases, of his hated inactivity. He sought patronage, and had it of the countess of Bedford, of the king's favorite, Carr, and of Sir Robert Drury. He worked as assistant to Morton, later bishop of Durham, in anti-Romanist polemic, but refused to take orders when Morton requested it. The belated payment of his wife's dowry gave him a period of relief, in which he wrote more and published for the first time—*Pseudo-Martyr* in 1610, *Ignatius His Conclave* in 1611, and the two poems for Elizabeth Drury's death in 1611 and 1612. *Biathanatos,* which he forbade "both the press and the fire", belongs to this time, and the *Essays in Divinity* were written in 1614.

When James I had made it plain that he would advance Donne only within the Church, the poet finally took orders (January 1615). In 1616 he was appointed reader in divinity at Lincoln's Inn, where, over the years, he both gave and received great satisfaction. A learned audience suited Donne, although this one must have been well informed about those youthful indiscretions concerning which the lack of evidence has never impeded warm speculation; he was accepted as the penitent he claimed to be, and the audience would remember St. Augustine. Donne had found his true genre.

His wife died in 1617, her memory celebrated by a fine sonnet and a great sermon; Donne was left with seven children. He was made dean of St. Paul's in 1621 and became the most famous of preachers, invested with a somber sanctity and happy in the rejection of "the mistress of my youth, Poetry" for "the wife of mine age, Divinity." In 1623 he was seriously ill, and during his illness wrote *Devotions Upon Emergent Occasions,* a series of religious meditations on the course of his disease that is striking evidence of his continuing ability to be witty on all topics; with all its solemnity it has a macabre playfulness and hospital wit.

His sermons are often surprisingly personal; we learn of his family anxieties (the death of a daughter, a son missing in action, his own departure abroad in 1619) and his remorse for past sins. In the end he brought his own death (on March 31, 1631) into the pulpit (having wished to die there) and preached the appalling sermon called *Death's Duel* before Charles I in Lent, 1631. His ordering of the monument which survived the Fire and is still in St. Paul's, and his almost histrionic composure on his deathbed, Walton has made famous. This aspect of Donne has perhaps been overstressed; he and death are a little too closely associated. This can be corrected only by prolonged reading in the sermons, or perhaps by reminding oneself of his marked interest in life: his desire for success, which made him the dependent of the dubious Carr, or his rich and varied friendships—with Goodyere, with the scientist earl of Northumberland, with Lady Danvers and her sons, George and Edward Herbert, with Jonson and Wotton—many of them central to the intellectual life of their time. But it is still true that he was a somber man, a melancholic even, at a time when this quality was associated with the highest kind of wit.

CONCEPTS AS "CONCEITS"

Wit is a quality allowed Donne by all critics, of all parties. In his own time people admired his "strong lines," and perhaps the best way of giving a general account of his wit is to try to explain what this expression meant. Donne is notoriously an obscure poet—in fact his obscurity is often overestimated, but he is never easy—and this is often because his manner is tortuous and, in his own word, "harsh." Thomas Carew's famous tribute emphasizes the strain he put on language: "to the awe of thy imperious wit Our stubborn language bends." Carew speaks of his "masculine expression"; Donne himself of his "masculine persuasive force." There was a contemporary taste for this kind of thing, related probably to an old tradition that it was right for some kinds of poetry to be obscure. And Donne was not writing for the many. He expected his readers to enjoy difficulty, not only in the scholastic ingenuity of his arguments, but in the combination of complicated verse forms and apparently spontaneous thought—thought that doubled back, corrected itself, broke off in passionate interjections. This kind of writing belongs to a rhetorical tradition ignored by much Elizabethan poetry, which argued that language could directly represent the immediate play of mind—style as the instantaneous expression of thinking. And this is why Donne—if I may translate from Mario Praz what I take to be the best thing ever said about Donne's style—will always appeal to readers "whom the *rhythm of thought* itself attracts by virtue of its own peculiar convolutions."

Obviously this is a limited appeal. Ben Jonson, himself not a stranger to the strong line, was only the first to accuse Donne of overdoing it. He recommended a middle course between jejune smoothness and a manner conscientiously rough. But for a while "strong lines"—applied to prose as well as verse—was a eulogistic term; so Fuller could praise those of Cleveland, saying that "his Epithetes were pregnant with metaphors, carrying in them a difficult plainness, difficult at the hearing, plain at the considering thereof." But there was opposition to what Walton called "the strong lines now in fashion"; witness, for example, Corbet's good nonsense poem *Epilogus Incerti Authoris,* a heap of paradoxes beginning "Like to the mowing tone of unspoke speeches" and ending

> Even such is man who died, and yet did
>   laugh
> To read these strong lines for his epitaph—[1]

which not only parodies Donne, but foretells the fate of the strong line: it degenerated into a joke and until recently recurred only in comic poetry. Hobbes, legislating for a new poetry in the 1650's, called strong lines "no better than riddles." The taste for them is not

1. All quotations, in modern spellings, are from A. J. Smith, ed., *The Complete English Poems of John Donne* (Harmondsworth, 1971).

universal, nor are the powers they require of poets.

As strong lines directly record mental activity, they contain concepts, or, in the contemporary form of the word, "conceits." The meaning we now attach to this word is a specialization directly due to the vogue for strong lines. The value of such lines obviously depends on the value (and that is almost the same thing as the strangeness) of the concepts they express, and these were usually metaphors. A high valuation was placed on metaphor, on the power of making what Dr. Johnson, who understood without approving, called the *discordia concors.* The world was regarded as a vast divine system of metaphors, and the mind was at its fullest stretch when observing them. Peculiar ability in this respect was called *acutezza* by the Italians and, by the English, wit. But although the movement was European in scope, it is unnecessary to suppose that Donne owed much to its Spanish and Italian exponents; they were known in England, but they conspicuously lack Donne's colloquial convolution, and his argumentativeness. Johnson's mistake in reporting Marino as a source has often been repeated. Marino has strength but not harshness, not the masculine persuasive force. We cannot think of Donne without thinking of relentless argument. He depends heavily upon dialectical sleight of hand, arriving at the point of wit by subtle syllogistic misdirections, inviting admiration by slight but significant perversities of analogue, which reroute every argument to paradox. Still, in view of the lack of contemporary English criticism on these points, it is wise to learn what we can from Continental critics of witty poetry; and the most important lesson, brilliantly suggested by S. L. Bethell, is that they regarded the conceit of argument—making a new and striking point by a syllogism concealing a logical error—as the highest and rarest kind of conceit. This is Donne's commonest device. Of course we are aware that we are being cleverly teased, but many of the love poems, like *The Ecstasy* or *The Flea,* depend on our wonder outlasting our critical attitude to argument. Consider the progression of ideas in *The Flea*:

Mark but this flea, and mark in this,
How little that which thou deny'st me is;
Me it sucked first, and now sucks thee,
And in this flea our two bloods mingled be;
Confess it, this cannot be said
A sin, or shame, or loss of maidenhead,
Yet this enjoys before it woo,
And pampered swells with one blood made of two,
And this, alas, is more than we would do.

Oh stay, three lives in one flea spare,
Where we almost, nay more than married are.
This flea is you and I, and this
Our marriage bed, and marriage temple is;
Though parents grudge, and you, we'are met,
And cloistered in these living walls of jet.
Though use make you apt to kill me,
Let not to this, self murder added be,
And sacrilege, three sins in killing three.

Cruel and sudden, hast thou since
Purpled thy nail, in blood of innocence?
In what could this flea guilty be,
Except in that drop which it sucked from thee?
Yet thou triumph'st, and say'st that thou
Find'st not thyself, nor me the weaker now;
'Tis true, then learn how false, fears be;
Just so much honour, when thou yield'st to me,
Will waste, as this flea's death took life from thee.

This poem, which was enormously admired by Donne's contemporaries, is cited here merely as an example of his original way of wooing by false syllogisms. So in *The Ecstasy*: the argument, a tissue of fallacies, sounds solemnly convincing and consecutive, so that it is surprising to find it ending with an immodest proposal. The highest powers of the mind are put to base use but are enchantingly demonstrated in the process.

Part of Donne's originality lies precisely in the use of such methods for amorous poetry.

Properly they belong to the sphere of religion (of course there is always much commerce between the two). This human wit suggests the large design of God's wit in the creation. It is immemorially associated with biblical exegesis and preaching, sanctioned and practiced by St. Ambrose and St. Augustine, and blended in the patristic tradition with the harshness of Tertullian, as well as with the enormous eloquence of Chrysostom. The Europe of Donne's time had enthusiastically taken up witty preaching; but the *gusto espagnol,* as it was called, though associated with the Counter-Reformation, is essentially a revival of what Professor Curtius would call the "mannerism" of the patristic tradition. Now this tradition was venerated by the Church of England, a learned Church that rejected the Puritan aphorism "so much Latin, so much Flesh." And the Fathers could provide not only doctrine but examples of *ingenium,* that acuity of observation by which the preacher could best illustrate and explicate the Word. Donne's youthful examination of "the whole body of divinity controverted between the churches of England and Rome" provided him not only with a religion but with a style. Some aspects of his Jesuit training would help him in the business of analogy; but primarily the conceit of his secular poetry is derived from his later religious studies. It is, in fact, a new, paradoxical use, for amorous purposes, of the *concetto predicabile,* the preacher's conceit. As usual, we see him all of a piece, yet all paradox; Donne the poet, with all his "naturalist" passion, knowingness, obscenity indeed, is *anima naturaliter theologica.* What made him a poet also made him an Anglican: the revaluation of a tradition.

NATURAL AND DIVINE KNOWLEDGE

It is for this reason that the old emphasis on the "medieval" quality of Donne's thought, though in need of qualification, is more to the point than the more recent stress on his modernity. A great deal has been made of his interest in the "new philosophy," and the disturbance supposed to have been caused him by such astronomical discoveries as the elliptical movement of planets, the impossibility of a sphere of fire, the corruptibility of the heavens, the movement of the earth, and so on. Certainly, as we know from *Ignatius* and elsewhere, Donne was aware of such developments, aware that it was no longer humanly satisfactory to look at the heavens through the spectacles of Ptolemy. But it is the greatest possible misunderstanding of Donne to suppose that he took this as any more than another proof, where none was needed, of the imperfection of human intellect. Mutability reached higher toward heaven than one had thought; but this only shows how unreliable human knowledge must always be. In *Ignatius,* Donne does not recount the new discoveries for their own sakes, but only as part of the sneering. "Kepler . . . (as himself testifies of himself) ever since Tycho Brahe's death, hath received into his care, that no new thing should be done in heaven without his knowledge." Kepler himself called this "impudent," not "flattering." When the devil sees that he can find no worthy place in hell for Ignatius, he decides to get Galileo to draw down the moon (an easy matter for one who had already got close enough to see its imperfections) so that the Jesuits can get on to it—they will "easily unite and reconcile the *Lunatic Church* to the *Roman Church,*" and a hell will grow in the moon, for Ignatius to rule over. At times Donne uses "new philosophy" more seriously, to illustrate some moral or theological assertion. The new astronomy, for example, is "applicable well" because it is right that we should move toward God, not He to us. Or, the Roman church is like Copernicanism—it "hath carried earth farther up from the stupid Center" but carried heaven far higher. When he wants, for the sake of some argument, to disprove the sphere of fire, he does not use the new scientific argument from optics, but the old-fashioned opinion of Cardan (God would not make an element in which nothing could live). In a serious mood he often forgets that the earth moves: "the Earth is not the more constant because it lies still continually" (*Devotions*); or, it is a wonderful thing that "so vast and immense a body as the Sun should run so many miles in a minute" (sermon of 1627). The famous passage in *The First Anniversary*:

> And new philosophy calls all in doubt,
> The element of fire is quite put out;
> The sun is lost, and the earth, and no man's
> wit
> Can well direct him where to look for it,

is merely part of the demonstration of "the frailty and decay of this whole World" mentioned in the title of the poem—a theme enforced by many illustrations taken from a wide variety of subjects, including the "old" philosophy. And this is Donne's way with new or old knowledge. It would be very unlike him to be much affected by the new philosophy; "if there be any addition to knowledge", he says in a sermon of 1626, "it is rather new knowledge, than a greater knowledge." For, if you know as much as Socrates, you know nothing, and "S. Paul found that to be all knowledge, to know Christ." There is always an antithesis, in Donne, between natural and divine knowledge, the first shadowy and inexact, the second clear and sure. New philosophy belongs to the first class. What we really know is what is revealed; later we shall know in full:

> up unto the watch-tower get,
> And see all things despoiled of fallacies:
> Thou shalt not peep through lattices of eyes,
> Nor hear through labyrinths of ears, nor
> learn
> By circuit, or collections to discern.
> In heaven thou straight know'st all,
> concerning it,
> And what concerns it not, shalt straight
> forget.

THE AMOROUS POEMS

A mind habituated to such discriminations between the light of nature and "light from above, from the fountain of light," as Milton calls it, may, in some spheres of knowledge, earn the epithet "skeptical." Donne deserted a church that, as he and Hooker agreed, had mistaken mere custom for law. Liberated from the tyranny of custom, he turns, in his erotic poetry, a professionally disenchanted eye on conventional human behavior. We may speak confidently of a "libertine," or "naturalist" Donne only if we use the terms as applying to literature and thought rather than to life; but it remains true that the *Songs and Sonnets* are often (though without his shocking coolness) akin to the franker pronouncements of Montaigne. Consider, for example, his essay *Upon Some Verses of Virgil,* where he professes his contempt for "artised" love; he prefers the thing itself and, in accordance with his preference, argues that amorous poetry also should be "natural," colloquial, "not so much innovating as filling language with more forcible and divers services, wrestling, straining, and enfolding it . . . teaching it unwonted motions." This is Donne to the life:

> Who ever loves, if he do not propose
> The right true end of love, he's one who
> goes
> To sea for nothing but to make him sick.

Donne openly depises the ritual and indirection of Platonic love; he will follow nature and pluck his rose (or roses; for love's sweetest part is variety). The enemies of nature are such fictions as honor; in the good old times, before custom dominated humanity, things were very different: see *Love's Deity* and *Elegy xvii:*

> How happy were our sires in ancient time,
> Who held plurality of loves no crime!
>
> . . .
>
> But since this title honour hath been used,
> Our weak credulity hath been abused;
> The golden laws of nature are repealed,

This is the sense in which Donne often celebrates the passion of love—as immediate and natural, but constricted by social absurdities:

Love's not so pure and abstract, as they use
To say, which have no mistress but their
muse.

But of course we must allow for an element of formal paradox. Donne found this very congenial—it is in a way a theological, a liturgical, device—and his *Juvenilia* contain such joke paradoxes as a defense of woman's inconstancy, an argument that it is possible to find some virtue in women, and so on, worked out with the same half-serious, half-ribald ingenuity that we find in some of the *Songs and Sonnets:*

Go, and catch a falling star,
  Get with child a mandrake root,
Tell me, where all past years are,
  Or who cleft the Devil's foot,
Teach me to hear mermaids singing,
  Or to keep off envy's stinging,
    And find
    What wind
Serves to advance an honest mind.

If thou be'est born to strange sights,
  Things invisible to see,
Ride ten thousand days and nights,
  Till age snow white hairs on thee,
Thou, when thou return'st, wilt tell me
All strange wonders that befell thee,
    And swear
    No where
Lives a woman true, and fair.

If thou find'st one, let me know,
  Such a pilgrimage were sweet;
Yet do not, I would not go,
  Though at next door we might meet,
Though she were true, when you met her,
And last, till you write your letter,
    Yet she
    Will be
False, ere I come, to two, or three.

To take these poems too seriously, as moral or autobiographical pronouncements, is to spoil them; though some are clearly more serious than others.

THE SECULAR POEMS

This may suggest the possibility of dividing the secular poems into groups other than their obvious genres; but it is a highly conjectural undertaking. There is a similar difficulty about their chronology; attempts to determine this depend on hypothetical links with events (and women) in Donne's life. We can say that the *Satires* were written in the 1590's; we can place many verse letters over a twenty-year period; epithalamia and obsequies are datable; one or two references in the love poems hint at dates. But in these last the evidence is scanty. Jonson's testimony, that Donne did his best work before he was twenty-five, depends on what he thought good—all we know is that he admired *The Calm* and *The Storm* (verse letters) and *Elegy xi,* a frantically witty poem but not among the most admired today. Only exceptionally can we say with certainty that this poem is addressed to his wife, that to another woman; this is witty with a stock situation (*The Flea,* for example, or *The Dream*), while that is drawn from life. Gosse actually invented a disastrous affair to explain some poems and absurdly supposed *Elegy xvi* to be addressed to Donne's wife; another critic has argued passionately that *The Ecstasy* is a husband's address to his wife. Even Herbert Grierson supposes that the *Nocturnal* must be connected with the countess of Bedford, whose name was Lucy; and a whole set of poems, some of them full of racy double entendre, has been associated with Lady Danvers, ten years Donne's senior and the mother of his friends the Herberts. All we may be sure of is that Donne, with varying intensity, passion, and intellectual conviction, exercised his wit on the theme of sexual love, and that he was inclined to do this in a "naturalist" way. We need not concern ourselves with dates or with identities of mistresses celebrated, cursed, or mourned.

The *Songs and Sonnets* were read only in manuscript in Donne's lifetime, and by a small and sophisticated circle. They certainly exhibit what Donne, in the little squib called *The Courtier's Library,* calls "itchy outbreaks of far-fetched wit"; and the wit is of the kind that depends both upon a harsh strangeness of expression and upon great acuity of illustration and argument. We are asked to admire, and that is why the poet creates difficulties for himself, choosing arbitrary and complex stanza forms, of which the main point often seems to be that they put tremendous obstacles in his way. Without underestimating the variety of tone in these poems, one may say that they all offer this kind of pleasure—delight in a dazzling conjuring trick. Even the smoothest, simplest song, like "Sweetest love, I do not go", is full of mind. Donne would have despised Dryden's distinction between poets and wits. True, some of these poems deserve the censure that when we have once understood them they are exhausted: *The Indifferent, The Triple Fool,* and a dozen others fall into this class. Others, like *The Flea* and "A Valediction: of my name, in the window," are admired primarily as incredibly perverse and subtle feats of wit; yet others, like *The Apparition,* as examples of how Donne could clothe a passion, in this case hatred, in a clever colloquial fury. This is the inimitable Donne; sometimes, as in *The Broken Heart,* we might be reading Cowley's sexless exercises.

One should here dwell at rather more length on one or two poems. I almost chose *The Damp,* a fine example of Donne's dialectical wit (the main argument is attended by a ghost argument, supported by slang double meanings); and *Farewell to Love,* which would have pleased Montaigne by its grave obscenity; and, for its wide-ranging metaphor and brilliant farfetched conclusion, *Love's Alchemy. Lovers, Infiniteness* has the characteristic swerving argument, its stanzas beginning "If . . . Or . . . Yet . . ."; compare *The Fever,* with its "But yet . . . Or if . . . And yet . . . Yet . . ." For his best use of "the nice speculations of philosophy", *Air and Angels* and *The Ecstasy* commend themselves:

Where, like a pillow on a bed,
 A pregnant bank swelled up, to rest
The violet's reclining head,
 Sat we two, one another's best;
Our hands were firmly cemented
 With a fast balm, which thence did
  spring,
Our eye-beams twisted, and did thread
 Our eyes, upon one double string;
So to intergraft our hands, as yet
 Was all the means to make us one,
And pictures in our eyes to get
 Was all our propagation.

. . .

But O alas, so long, so far
 Our bodies why do we forbear?

. . .

As our blood labours to beget
 Spirits, as like souls as it can,
Because such fingers need to knit
 That subtle knot, which makes us man:

So must pure lovers' souls descend
 T'affections, and to faculties,

Which sense may reach and apprehend,
 Else a great prince in prison lies.

To our bodies turn we then, that so
 Weak men on love revealed may look;
Love's mysteries in souls do grow,
 But yet the body is his book.

But *The Curse* is both characteristic and neglected, and *A Nocturnal upon S. Lucy's Day* is Donne's finest poem; so there follow some scanty remarks on these.

The Curse has the usual complex rhyme scheme and rather more than the usual energy in that Irish ingenuity of malediction which reminds us that Donne was one of the early satirists:

Whoever guesses, thinks, or dreams he
  knows
Who is my mistress, wither by this curse;
  His only, and only his purse
  May some dull heart to love dispose,
And she yield then to all that are his foes;
 May he be scorned by one, whom all else
  scorn,
 Forswear to others, what to her he hath
  sworn,
 With fear of missing, shame of getting,
  torn:

The syntactical conciseness of lines 3–5 is remarkable: "May he win only a mercenary love, yet may he have to spend all he has to get her (and may she be dull in the bargain). Then, wretched mistress though she be, let her betray him—and do so with everybody who dislikes him (presumably a large number of people)." This only begins the cursing. "May he suffer remorse, not of conscience because he has sinned (too noble a passion for him), but because the reputation of the only woman he was able to get makes him everybody's butt" . . . and so on. The poem ends with an inventory of hatred and poison, provisions for further additions to the curse as they may occur to the poet, and finally—as often in Donne—a light, epigrammatic couplet to place the poem on the witty side of passion: you can't curse a woman more than she is naturally "cursed" (forward, fickle, uncertain of temper) already:

> The venom of all stepdames, gamesters' gall,
> What tyrants, and their subjects interwish,
> What plants, mines, beasts, fowl, fish,
> Can contribute, all ill which all
> Prophets, or poets spake; and all which shall
> Be annexed in schedules unto this by me,
> Fall on that man; for if it be a she
> Nature before hand hath out-cursed me.
> (lines 25–32)

So much of the effect depends on the control of syntactical and rhythmic emphasis, on devices like the repeated "all" (28–29), on the impressive catalog, the compression of meaning in line 26 that calls forth the neologism "interwish," the formal streak of legal diction, and the minatory solemnity of "Fall on that man"—that paraphrase breaks down into inoffensive jesting a poem that gets its effect by an impression of qualified but dangerous loathing. This is pure Donne; as a matter of opinion good, as a matter of fact unique.

This last is true, a fortiori, of the *Nocturnal,* which has the additional interest of involving some of his known intellectual problems and convictions. The imagery is predominantly alchemical; the argument goes in search of a definition of absolute nothingness; yet the cause of the poem is grief at the death of a mistress. This is the most solemn and difficult of Donne's poems, superficially slow in movement, but with a contrapuntal velocity of thought. It begins as a meditation on the vigil of his saint; St. Lucy's day is chosen because it is the dead day of the year, as midnight is the dead hour of the day:

> 'Tis the year's midnight, and it is the day's,
> Lucy's, who scarce seven hours herself unmasks,
> The sun is spent, and now his flasks
> Send forth light squibs, no constant rays;
> The world's whole sap in sunk:
> The general balm th'hydroptic earth hath drunk,
> Whither, as to the bed's-feet, life is shrunk,
> Dead and interred; yet all these seem to laugh,
> Compared with me, who am their epitaph.

That which preserves life, the "general balm," is shrunk into the frozen earth. Darkness, which is Nothing to light's All, and death, which is Nothing to life's All, reign in the great world; yet the little world, the poet, is far deader and darker, an abstract of death, an epitaph. The world will be reborn in spring, and there will be lovers; but he is "every dead thing." His deadness is enforced by a remarkable alchemical figure, based on the idea that the alchemist deals in the quintessence of *all things,* "ruining" (abstracting form from) metals in order to reconstitute them as gold, by means of the quintessence. But this "new" alchemy, on the contrary, works with a quintessence of *nothing,* privation, and imposes on the poet's "ruined" matter the "form" of absolute nothingness—" absence, darkness, death." Alchemical and theological figures come as it were naturally to Donne; he uses alchemy to push the notion of absolute privation beyond human understanding. The poet has less being than the primordial Nothing that preceded Chaos, which preceded Creation; he is a quintessence of Nothing: "I am none." The internal rhyme with "sun" (meaning light, and All, as well as the woman responsible for his state of nonbeing) brings us back, at the end, to the commonplace lovers whose activity will be restored in spring, when the commonplace sun returns:

> But I am none; nor will my sun renew.
> You lovers, for whose sake, the lesser sun
> At this time to the Goat is run
> To fetch new lust, and give it you,
> Enjoy your summer all;
> Since she enjoys her long night's festival,
> Let me prepare towards her, and let me call
> This hour her vigil, and her eve, since this
> Both the year's, and the day's deep midnight is.

The witty sneer about the object of the sun's journey to the Tropic of Capricorn helps to distance these inferior loves; and we return to darkness, the perpetual sleep of the other sun, and the propriety of this saint's day as the type of darkness and lifelessness.

This is a very inadequate account of a marvelous poem. My main object is to make a point about Donne's use, in poetry, of ideas that he clearly regarded as important. The general balm, the alchemical ruin, the violent paradoxes on All and Nothing, belong to Donne's mental habit. There is, for instance, a fine examination of the All-Nothing paradox in the exegetical passages on Genesis in *Essays in Divinity,* and it occurs in the sermons. As he extracted the notion of absolute privation in alchemical terms, Donne must have been thinking of the cabalistic description of God as the nothing, the quintessence of nothing; here a keen and prejudiced ear might discover one of his blasphemies. But it is more interesting, I think, that Donne the poet is claiming what Donne the theologian calls impossible; he constantly recurs to the point that the man cannot desire annihilation. So the wit of the poem (using the word in its full sense) really derives from its making, by plausible argument, the impossible seem true. And he does it by the use of figures from alchemy, an art traditionally associated with the resurrection of the body, the escape from annihilation—he spoke in his own last illness of his physical decay as the alchemical ruining of his body before resurrection; here, with vertiginous wit, he uses the same analogy to prove the contrary. It is not inappropriate that the finest of the *Songs and Sonnets* should also be the most somberly witty and the most difficult.

Of Donne's twenty *Elegies* I have room to say little. They are love poems in loose iambic pentameter couplets, owing a general debt, for tone and situation, to the *Amores* of Ovid; the Roman poet loses no wit but acquires harshness, masculinity. These poems are full of sexual energy, whether it comes out in frank libertinism or in the wit of some more serious attachment. *The Anagram (ii)* is an example of the wit that proved all too imitable, all too ready to degenerate into fooling—it is a series of paradoxes on somebody's foul mistress, a theme current at the time. *Elegy viii* is a similar poem, comparing one's own and another's mistress, with plenty of unpleasant detail. But the *Elegies* have a considerable variety of tone, ranging from the set pieces on change and variety (*iii* and *xvii*) which are paralleled by several of the *Songs and Sonnets,* to the passionate *xvi* and the somber *xii,* on the theme of parting:

> Nor praise, nor dispraise me, nor bless nor curse
> Openly love's force, nor in bed fright thy nurse
> With midnight's startings, crying out, "Oh, oh
> Nurse, O my love is slain, I saw him go
> O'er the white Alps alone;

The *Elegies* have always had a reputation for indecency, and they certainly exploit the sexual puns so much enjoyed by Elizabethan readers. Among the poems excluded from the first edition is the magnificently erotic *Elegy xix, Going to Bed:* too curious a consideration of some of the metaphors in this poem (such as the passage about "imputed grace") has led critics to charge it with blasphemy, a risk Donne often runs by the very nature of his method. Montaigne might have complained that Donne here substitutes a new mythology and metaphysics of love for those he had abandoned, new presbyter for old priest. But it is impossible not to admire the translation of sexual into mental activity. *Elegy xix* was later regarded as the poet's own epithalamion, a fancy as harmless as it is improbable, except that it has perhaps resulted in the acceptance of a very inferior reading in line 46.[2] One beautiful and exceptional poem is *Elegy ix, The Autumnal* to lady Danvers; but even this would not, I think, quite escape Herbert Grierson's criticism, that Donne (especially in the *Elegies*) shows "a radical want of delicacy"; for it has the wit and fantastic range of reference that mark the erotic *Elegies*.

The *Satires* belong to the same phase of Donne's talent as the work I have been discussing. They are, as Elizabethan satire was supposed to be, rough and harsh, written in that low style that Donne so often used, though here it is conventional. *Satire iii* I shall discuss later; of the others we may say that they have the usual energy, a richness of contemporary observation rather splenetic, of course, in character. Pope thought them worth much trouble; but it is doubtful if, except for *iii,* they play much part in anybody's thinking about Donne. The same may be said of the epicedes and obsequies, funeral poems that in this period were often, when they were not pastoral elegies, poems of fantastically tormented wit. So Donne proves, in the elegy on Prince Henry, that "we May safelier say, that we are dead, then he." The form suited him only too well. The same cannot be said of the epithalamion; Spenser is the poet to thrive here. Yet there are fine things in Donne's poem for the marriage of the Princess Elizabeth in 1613:

Up, up, fair Bride, and call,
Thy stars, from out their several boxes, take
Thy rubies, pearls, and diamonds forth, and
make
Thyself a constellation, of them all,
And by their blazing signify,
That a great Princess falls, but doth not die;

Donne could not speak without wit; it is this naturalness that often redeems him.

Of the occasional verse included under the title *Letters to Several Personages* a word must suffice. There is a mistaken view that they are negligible because they occasionally flatter. They were written over many years, and not all for profit; notice the little-known verses to Goodyere (Grierson, I,183), which have the strong Jonsonian ring; and the charming "Mad paper, stay" to Lady Herbert before her remarriage. The best, probably, are to the countess of Bedford, dependant though Donne may have been; and the poem beginning "You have refined me" is a great poem, certainly no more "blasphemous" in its compliment than *Elegy xix* in its persuasions.

This matter of blasphemous allusion comes to a head in the two *Anniversaries,* written for Sir Robert Drury on the death of his daughter Elizabeth, and published in 1611 and 1612. These are amazingly elaborate laments for a girl Donne had never seen. The first he called *An Anatomy of the World,* announcing in his full title that the death of Elizabeth Drury is the occasion for observations on the frailty and decay of the whole world, and representing the dead girl as Astraea, as the world's soul, as the preservative balm, and so on; her departure has left it lifeless, and he dissects it. The second, describing "the Progress of the Soul" after death, is similar: "By occasion of the religious death of Mistress Elizabeth Drury, the incommodities of the soul in this life, and her exaltation in the next, are contemplated." From Jonson forward, critics have complained of the faulty taste of such hyperbolical praise of a young girl, and Donne defended himself more than once, though without much vigor; he would have little patience with this kind of misun-

2. "There is no penance due to innocence," the reading of 1669, is represented in most manuscripts by "There is no penance, much less innocence." The received reading makes the poem slightly more appropriate if the woman is a bride. But clearly she is no more innocent than she is penitent, and ought not to be wearing the white linen that signifies either innocence or penitence.

derstanding. All we may say here is that these poems—now known to be planned in a highly original way as a series of formal religious meditations—are essential to the understanding of Donne; they come near to giving us a map of the dark side of his wit. The deathbed meditation in the second poem is comparable with the *Holy Sonnets* on the same topic:

> Think thyself laboring now with broken
> breath,
> And think those broken and soft notes to be
> Division,[3] and thy happiest harmony.
> Think thee laid on thy death-bed, loose and
> slack;
> And think that, but unbinding of a pack,
> To take one precious thing, thy soul, from
> thence.

The *Anniversaries* lead us into a consideration of Donne's religious life. But we shall find that the poet and the religious were the same man.

ACCEPTANCE OF ANGLICANISM

Donne's acceptance of the established church is the most important single event of his life, because it involved all the powers of his mind and personality. His youthful sympathies must have been with the persecuted Romanists, and his *Satires* contain bitter allusions to "pursuivants," tormentors of Jesuits; the odious Topcliffe is mentioned by name in some manuscripts. But he was familiar with the fanaticism as well as with the learning of Jesuits; and he later decided that the first of these was the hardest affliction of Christendom, though the second was to serve him well. No one can say exactly when he left one church for the other; it was a gradual process. According to Walton, he was about nineteen when, "being unresolv'd what religion to adhere to, and, considering how much it concern'd his soul to choose the most Orthodox," he abandoned all studies for divinity. Donne himself, in *Pseudo-Martyr,* claims to have done this with "an indifferent affection to both parties." Particularly, he consulted Bellarmine, "the best defender of the *Roman cause*" (Walton), and Hooker, whose *Laws of Ecclesiastical Polity* appeared in 1593, when Donne was twenty-one—though his famous sermon *Of Justification,* which must have appealed to all moderate Romanists, had long been available. Hooker triumphed; but as late as 1601 the unfinished satirical extravaganza, *The Progress of the Soul,* treats the queen as the last of a line of archheretics, and more dubious references suggest that Donne's recusancy persisted in some form up to the time of *Pseudo-Martyr.* When Walton says he treated the problem as urgent, he is paraphrasing the remarkable *Satire iii,* which must belong to the 1590's. What makes this poem odd is the brisk impatience of its manner, an exasperated harshness proper to satire but strange in a deliberative poem about religion. It has often been misunderstood. The main theme is simply the importance of having a religion; without it, one is worse off than "blind [pagan] philosophers":

> shall thy father's spirit
> Meet blind philosophers in heaven, whose
> merit
> Of strict life may be imputed faith, and hear
> Thee, whom he taught so easy ways and
> near
> To follow, damned?

But which religion? Rome is loved because true religion was once to be found there; Geneva out of a perverse love for the coarse and plain; the English church from inertia. Such divisions encourage on the one hand abstinence from all, and on the other a mistaken belief that they are all true. It is necessary to choose one; and the best course is to "Ask thy father which is she, Let him ask his." Above all, do not rest; no business is as important as this. This is a tentative assertion of the Catholic tradition invoked by all Anglicans—the true, not the Roman, Catholicism. Donne had

3. A musical term, meaning a variation on a melody, made by dividing each of its notes into shorter ones.

in fact to choose only between these two churches; though he was to develop a great respect for Calvin, he was never concerned with extreme Protestantism. Of the two communions—"sister teats of his graces" he called them, "yet both diseased and infected, but not both alike"—he was to choose the one truer to the Catholic tradition as he understood it. Like his learned contemporary Casaubon, he found this to be the Church of England—episcopal and sacramental, but divested of the Romanist accretions. *Satire iii* is a poem about his search, not about its end. He still had much to do before he could think of "binding his conscience to a local religion."

One consequence of this deliberation was that Donne was unusually moderate in later allusions to Rome. In *Pseudo-Martyr* he speaks frankly of its long hold over him and is charitable to "all professors of Christian Religion, if they shake not the Foundation." All his animus is against the Jesuits, for a false doctrine of martyrdom and inculcating for opening up, by their intransigence, deplorable breaches in the church. He attacks and satirizes them as enemies of tolerance: "that Church," he says in *Essays in Divinity,* "which despises another Church, is itself no other than that of which the Psalm speaks, *Ecclesia Malignantium.*" Here we are at the heart of his religious position. Donne had convinced himself that reform had made the English church more truly Catholic than any other. It was not only a middle way but the ground on which, he hoped, the longed-for reunion of the churches might be accomplished. Given tolerance, given an abatement of "that severe and unrectified zeal of many, who should impose necessity upon indifferent things, and oblige all the world to one precise form of exterior worship, and ecclesiastic policy," Donne saw a chance of ending the division of the church.

In this aspiration he was at one with James I, though the prospect of success was much smaller than it had been when the Gallican party in France hoped for something from the Council of Trent. With the king, and his friend Wotton, Donne had expected much of the dispute between Venice and the papacy in 1606; Wotton, as English ambassador in Venice, had played an active part, and for a while there was excited speculation about the chance of Venice turning to a sort of Anglicanism. Wotton was acquainted with Paolo Sarpi, the canonist who conducted the Venetian case; and Sarpi's *History of the Council of Trent* was published first in London. In it he deplores the rigidity and extremism of that council and, as Frances Yates has said, "indirectly suggests that if the right course had been pursued at Trent, the Church as a whole would have been reformed somewhat on the model of the Anglican reform." Wotton sent home several portraits of Sarpi for his English admirers; and it was presumably one of these that hung, as Donne's will testifies, in his study. It was an emblem of his hopes, and Donne completely accepted Sarpi's view of Trent. Preaching before Charles I in April 1626, on the text "In my Father's house are many mansions," he deplores its intolerance, its coming "to a final resolution in so many particulars"; as a result the Scriptures themselves are slighted and reduced in authority, and men are the readier to call each other heretics, "which is a word that cuts deep, and should not be passionately used." Both these consequences are disastrous. The priest is ordained to preach the Word—Donne's favorite quotation is St. Paul's *vae mihi si non,* "woe unto me if I do not so." "Nothing," he says in 1618, "is to be obtruded to our faith as necessary to salvation, except it be rooted in the Word," and he constantly complains that Rome "detorts" the Word, as the Puritans do. As for the frequent charges of heresy, he warns his own congregation to "be not apt to call opinion false, or heretical, or damnable, the contrary whereof cannot be evidently proved." Early and late, Donne the preacher insists upon the prime importance of the Word and on the great need for tolerance; only thus may the church in England be the matrix of a new universal church. So, in an early sermon: "For all this separation, Christ Jesus is amongst us all, and in his time will break down this wall too, these differences among

Christians, and make us all glad of that name." And in 1627 he prays that God "in his time bring our adversaries to such moderation as becomes them, who do truly desire, that the Church may be truly *Catholic, one flock in the fold, under one Shepherd,* though *not all of one color,* of one practice in all outward and disciplinary points." This last was after the setback to the cause in 1626, when the defeat of the elector of Bohemia elicited from Donne the sonnet "Show me, dear Christ, thy spouse."

Donne, then, accepted the Church of England because it was truly Catholic. He rejoiced to discover a Reformed church that cultivated the Fathers and was slow to come "to a final resolution" in "particulars." He wanted tradition but without its errors: Aquinas, but not the Scholastic nonsense; the Fathers, but not their mistakes. The Catholic heritage was enormously more important to him than any "new" knowledge, theological or physical, and he has little distinction as a speculative theologian, though his age is one of dogmatic controversy. He detested, for instance, the Calvinist teaching on predestination, which had the intellectual presumption to dishonor God by suggesting that He could "make us to damn us"; when it was necessary to pronounce on the matter he fell back on Aquinas ("God has appointed all future things to be, but so as they are, that is necessary things necessarily, and contingent things contingently") but he disliked the whole argument: "*Resistibility,* and *Irresistibility,* of grace, which is every Artificers wearing now, was a stuff that our Fathers wore not, a language that pure antiquity spake not." "The best men," he says, "are but Problematical, only the Holy Ghost is Dogmatical." Though by no means a complete skeptic, he knew the limits of reason and often defined its relation to faith (in *Essays in Divinity, Biathanatos,* a verse letter to the countess of Bedford, the Christmas sermon for 1621). His position is not dissimilar from Hooker's (e.g. *Laws* I, 8). The limitations of human learning he sets forth in the famous *Valediction Sermon* of 1619, and the contrast between natural and heavenly knowledge (see the passage quoted earlier from *Anniversaries*) is developed in a splendid passage of the 1622 Easter sermon: "God shall create us all Doctors in a minute." Obviously the fierce certainties of some contemporaries were not for Donne. "It is the text that saves us," he says. "The interlineary glosses, and the marginal notes, and the *variae lectiones,* controversies, and perplexities, undo us." He was content with his church's restoration of a good, lost tradition, just as, in his capacity as poet, he had used a traditional but neglected style that had its roots in the same great body of learning, the teaching of the Fathers.

THE SERMONS

No one, then, will read Donne for theological novelties; even in the *Essays,* which are full of curious applications, Donne's regard for authority puts him at the opposite pole from the radically speculative Milton. And whatever may be offered by the vast array of sermons, it is not that kind of excitement.

It is not easy to give a general account of the sermons. They were preached on all manner of occasions, over fifteen years, and they take their color from the audience, and from Donne's mood, as well as from the text and from the ecclesiastical occasion. Some were for a great audience, some for a small; some for lawyers, some for the court; some for Lent and some for Easter; some were preached when the preacher had private reason for joy, some when he was miserable. The tone varies widely. There is truth in the often repeated charge that Donne was preoccupied with sin and death; he confesses his melancholy temperament (calling it "a disease of the times") and constantly quotes St. Paul's *cupio dissolvi* (Phil. 1 : 23), "having a desire to depart and be with Christ." "If there were any other way to be saved and to get to Heaven," he says, "than by being born into this life, I would not wish to have come into this world." There are terrible sermons on death, full of the poetry of charnel house and worm. There are lamentations for the sins of youth: "I preach the sense of Gods indignation upon mine own soul." There are even rather grim sermons on apparently joyous occasions; a wedding sermon for personal friends is a forbidding, though orthodox, account of the church's teaching on marriage, with many gloomy strictures on women. But one can overdo this aspect of the sermons. Death and sin are fully presented, but perhaps not inordinately. And, to balance them, there is a massive insistence on the theme of resurrection and far more humanity than one is led to expect; see, for example, the moving passages on the death of Augustine's son, and that of his own daughter, in the superb Easter sermon for 1627:

> He was but a heathen that said, if God love a man, *Iuvenis tollitur,* He takes him young out of this world; and they were but heathens that bestowed that custom, to put on mourning when their sons were born, and to feast and triumph when they died. But thus much we may learn from these heathens, that if the dead, and we, be not upon one floor, nor under one story, yet we are under one roof. We think not a friend lost, because he is gone into another room, nor because he is gone into another land; and into another world, no man is gone; for that heaven, which God created, and this world, is all one world. If I had fixed a son in court, or married a daughter into a plentiful fortune, I were satisfied for that son and that daughter. Shall I not be so, when the King of heaven hath taken that son to himself, and married himself to that daughter, for ever? I spend none of my faith. I exercise none of my hope, in this, that I shall have my dead raised to life again.
>
> This is the faith that sustains me, when I lose by the death of others, or when I suffer by living in misery myself, that the dead, and we, are now all in one Church, and at the resurrection, shall be all in one choir.

It could be well argued that the sermon suited Donne's talents perfectly. That patristic learning which had settled his Anglican convictions and given him his style as a poet equipped him also with the matter and the manner of his preaching; and for the style that he adopted he needed all his mastery of the techniques of wit. The preacher's basic duty was simply, as Augustine said, "to teach what is right and refute what is wrong, and in the performance of this task to conciliate the hostile, and rouse the careless." This was to be done according to a general scheme that both preacher and congregation took for granted. But within this scheme there could be enormous variation. Donne was of the party that cultivated "the learned manner of preaching"; not for him the doctrinal plainness of the Puritan. He was, as hostile witnesses put it, "a strong-lin'd man" and "a bad edifier."

How did "strong lines" go with the preaching of the Word? First, their cultivation did not mean that the Word was neglected. It was stated, divided, illuminated, fantastically explicated. For example, Donne makes much of the expression "let us make man" (Gen. 1: 26): no other act of creation involved a conference; therefore, the Trinity was concerned in this one alone. Secondly, the Word itself gives warrant for all the devices of the learned preacher. The style of the Scriptures is "artificial"; indeed the Psalms are poems. "There are not in the World so eloquent Books as the Scriptures . . . they mistake it much, that think, that the Holy Ghost hath rather chosen a low, and barbarous, and homely style, than an eloquent, and powerfull manner of expressing himself." The Scriptures use metaphor of "infinite sweetness, and infinite latitude," though they have, when necessary, concision as well as eloquence, simplicity as well as highly wrought wit. All these qualities are found in the Fathers whom the Reformed church revived. Ambrose and Augustine—to whom Donne owed most—are ancestors of mannerist wit; Tertullian Christianized the Latin strong lines of Seneca. Nearer in time to Donne was the Continental revival of witty preaching, which, as I have said, had much to do with the new poetic wit; but ultimately all depended on the Fathers and on the wit and eloquence of the Holy Ghost in Scripture.

One famous and passionate page must serve to illustrate Donne's habitual eloquence:

Let me wither and wear out mine age in a discomfortable, in an unwholesome, in a penurious prison, and so pay my debts with my bones, and recompense the wastefulness of my youth, with the beggary of mine age; let me wither in a spittle under sharp, and foul, and infamous diseases, and so recompense the wantonness of my youth, with that loathsomeness in mine age; yet if God withdraw not his spiritual blessings, his grace, his patience, if I can call my suffering his doing, my passion his action, all this that is temporal, is but a caterpillar got into one corner of my garden, but a mildew fallen upon one acre of my corn; the body of all, the substance of all is safe, as long as the soul is safe. But when I shall trust to that, which we call a good spirit, and God shall deject, and impoverish, and evacuate that spirit, when I shall rely upon a moral constancy, and God shall shake, and enfeeble, and enervate, destroy and demolish that constancy; when I shall think to refresh myself in the serenity and sweet air of a good conscience and God shall call up the damps and vapours of hell itself, and spread a cloud of diffidence, and an impenetrable crust of desperation upon my conscience; when health shall fly from me, and I shall lay hold upon riches to succour me, and comfort me in my sickness, and riches shall fly from me, and I shall snatch after favour, and good opinion, to comfort me in my poverty; when even this good opinion shall leave me, and calumnies and misinformations shall prevail against me; when I shall need peace, because there is none but thou, O Lord, that should stand for me, and then shall find that all the wounds that I have come from thy hand, all the arrows that stick in me, from thy quiver; when I shall see that because I have given myself to my corrupt nature, thou hast changed thine; and because I am all evil towards thee, therefore thou hast given over being good towards me; when it comes to this height, that the fever is not in the humours, but in the spirits, that mine enemy is not an imaginary enemy, fortune, nor a transitory enemy, malice in great persons, but a real, and an irresistible, and an inexorable, and an everlasting enemy, The Lord of Hosts himself, the Almighty God himself, the Almighty God himself only knows the weight of this affliction, and except he put in that *pondus gloriae,* that exceeding weight of an eternal glory, with his own hand, into the other scale, we are weighted down, we are swallowed up, irreparably, irrevocably, irrecoverably, irremediably.

But in addition to such tremendous sentences we find a hopping Latin wit, as of Tertullian: "He came, and *venit in mundum,* He came into the world; it is not *in mundam,* into so clean a woman as had no sin at all, none contracted from her parents, no original sin . . . yet *per mundam in mundum,* by a clean woman into an unclean world." And we find startling conceits and paradoxes. Can man be the enemy of God, even as the mouse is of the elephant? Man is nearly nothing, but God is "not only a multiplied elephant, millions of elephants multiplied into one, but a multiplied World, a multiplied All. . . . Man cannot be allowed so high a sin, as enmity with God." But Donne can also be simple, like the parables. So on irresistibility of grace: "Christ beats his drum, but he does not press men; Christ is served with voluntaries." For "no metaphor, no comparison is too high, none too low, too trivial, to imprint in you a sense of God's everlasting goodness towards you." To such a preacher the "metaphysical conceit" was a natural mode of thought. Laud, addressing from the scaffold a hostile crowd, spoke of "going apace . . . towards the Red Sea . . . an argument, I hope, that God is bringing me into the land of promise." Here, at such a moment—though the conceit has a long history—we have precisely those qualities of deliberate false argument essential to the wit of Donne's poems.

As a preacher Donne is guilty, by modern standards, of pedantry. His style is artificial; he would have been angry to have been told otherwise. The pedantry was partly a matter of fashion, but also a token of his confidence in a truly Catholic tradition. The sermons are inconceivable without it; so is Donne himself. And if he makes our flesh creep, that was still part of his duty; if he almost ignores the ecstatic religion that flourished in his day, that was a defect of his central merit. If we want Donne as a modern poet we may find it tiresome that he was capable of so much archaic quibbling, so much jargon and flattery. But, while it is perfectly proper to read the *Songs and Sonnets* and ignore the sermons, it is improper to construct an image of Donne without looking at them; and many such caricatures still circulate.

THE DIVINE POEMS

It was Donne's habit, in later life, to speak slightingly of his poetry; and although he considered, for a brief moment before his ordination, the possibility of publishing his poems, it seems he did not even possess copies of them. There are signs that it was regarded as slightly improper, after his ordination, for "a man of his years and place" to be versifying, and indeed Donne wrote little verse as a priest. The *Elegies* on his death often allude to the exercise of his great wit in both secular and religious spheres—"Wit He did not banish, but transplanted it"—but Chudleigh, in these lines, has in mind not verse but sermons:

> Long since, o poets, he did die to you,
> Or left you dead, when wit and he took
> flight
> On divine wings, and soared out of your
> sight.
> Preachers, 'tis you must weep.

In fact it now appears that the bulk of the divine poems belongs to 1607–1615. These years produced the *Corona* sequence, most of the *Holy Sonnets,* the *Litany, Upon the Annunciation and Passion, Good Friday, 1613,* and probably *The Cross.* The poem addressed to Tilman, the *Lamentations of Jeremy,* the lines on Sidney's *Psalms,* the three great *Hymns,* three Sonnets, and *An hymn to the Saints, and to Marquess Hamylton,* which Donne wrote reluctantly in 1625, make up the extant poetical work of the priest. Most of the religious poetry, therefore, belongs to the period of many of the verse letters, and the *Anniversaries.*

It is verse of remarkable originality. *Satire iii* shows that even in his youth Donne considered the language of passionate exploration and rebuke appropriate to religious themes; and even when he is working in strict forms like the sonnet, and on devotional topics, we recognize at once that turbulent diction which spontaneously records the pressure of fervent and excited thought. But though he rejected some of the formalities in his secular poetry, Donne was habituated in matters of devotion to certain schematic disciplines. He had been taught to pray; and when his poems are prayers they are formed by this early training. When he undertook "a serious meditation of God," he tended to do so by employing these meditative techniques.

Here a learned man committed to the reformed religion occupies himself with papist devotion; but we should not exaggerate the paradox. Donne's church did not reject what it found good in the tradition; many devotional practices were retained, and some were revived. Donne's *Corona* sonnets are an ingenious adaptation of an old Dominican system of meditation, based on an obsolete type of rosary called the *corona.* A Puritan might condemn this, but to Donne it was, theologically, an indifferent matter and good in that it concentrated the devotional powers of a man easily distracted from prayer. More remarkable, perhaps, is the fact that some of the *Holy Sonnets,* and the *Anniversaries,* are indebted to meditative techniques defined and propagated by Ignatius Loyola and the Jesuits; yet these were so widely disseminated, and apparently so fruitful, that it was by no means exceptional for enemies of the order to adopt them.

The *Corona,* with its linked sonnets and carefully balanced ingenuity, may strike us as "mixt wit"; the Ignatian method is more interesting. The purpose of the technique is to concentrate all the powers of the soul, including the sensual, in the act of prayer. So a man might present as vividly as possible to himself the scene of the Nativity or the Crucifixion, or his own deathbed. There is no doubt that this technique, the most considerable contribution of Jesuit piety to European art, affects the *Holy Sonnets*; Helen Gardner presents twelve of them as a sequence, the first six being a formal meditative series on the Last Things. The method is to achieve a vivid image, enforce it with appropriate similitudes, and then to pray accordingly. So, in "O my black Soul! now thou art summoned," Donne imagines his deathbed in the octave and compares the sinful soul to an exile afraid to return to his country, or a prisoner afraid to be freed; then in the sestet he prays for grace to repent, so that death may not, after all, be like such miseries. The meditation is here forcefully assimilated to the sonnet form, which Donne uses with virtuosity; and the complexities of the form coexist with that sense of immediate and poignant spiritual effort, that tormented natural diction, which was his great, and sometimes abused, discovery. The sonnets are not reports of spiritual exercises; they are the exercises themselves. There is little sense of contrivance, "artificial" though the form is; Donne reconciles the prescribed form with the true word, just as he reconciles ecclesiastical tradition with the supremacy of Scripture. It is true that the wit of these poems occasionally ventures where we are reluctant to follow, as in "Show me, dear Christ, thy spouse." This last complaint for the division of the church is couched in terms of a traditional image carried to the point where we feel uneasy about its taste:

> Betray kind husband thy spouse to our
> sights,
> And let mine amorous soul court thy mild
> dove,
> Who is most true, and pleasing to thee, then
> When she' is embraced and open to most
> men.

Perhaps we dislike this metaphor (Christ as *mari complaisant*) because the image of the church as the Bride is no longer absolutely commonplace; but having accepted the image we are still unwilling to accept its development, even though we see that the main point is the *glorious* difference of this from a merely human marriage. Something is asked of us that we can no longer easily give. Many of the *Holy Sonnets* have this perilous balance; their wit is always likely to seem indelicate as well as passionate. So in one of the greatest, "Batter my heart, three-personed God":

> Batter my heart, three-personed God; for, you
> As yet but knock, breathe, shine, and seek
> to mend;
> That I may rise, and stand, o'erthrow me,
> and bend
> Your force, to break, blow, burn and make
> me new.
> I, like an usurped town, to another due,
> Labour to admit you, but oh, to no end,
> Reason your viceroy in me, me should
> defend,
> But is captived, and proves weak or untrue,
> Yet dearly I love you, and would be loved
> fain,
> But am betrothed unto your enemy,
> Divorce me, untie, or break that knot again,
> Take me to you, imprison me, for I
> Except you enthrall me, never shall be free,
> Nor ever chaste, except you ravish me.

This is a great poem, certainly; but what, we wonder, has "three-personed" to do with the passion of the opening? Yet the poem is another of Donne's exercises in the paradoxes of his religion, and the Trinity is one of the greatest of them. The epithet is obliquely justified by the intensity of the rhythmical conflicts throughout; in the opposition between the heavy "Batter" and the weak, cadential "knock, breathe, shine, and seek to mend"; in the divine absurdity of heaven troubling to take the sinner by storm, laying him low that he may stand; finally, by the imagery of rape. Love is figured as lust because it is to be rough and irresistible; God is a monster of mercy (but the Scripture compares him to a thief). The powerful paradoxes of the last couplet suggest an infinite series of such: God as infant, God as malefactor, justice as mercy, death as life, and so forth. We respond crudely to this kind of challenge, and such a reading as this is clumsy and overly explicit. Similarly we are inclined to think of a poem that celebrates the coincidence of Lady Day and Good

Friday as a toy; but for Donne it was a motive to reverence, a piece of calendar wit that challenged a Christian poet to prayer. We are usually content to be more clever about the love of women than the love of God; therefore the *Songs and Sonnets* keep better. But Donne was clever about both, and sometimes in much the same way; our awkwardness here leads us to charge *Elegy xix* with blasphemy, and "Show me, dear Christ" with indelicacy. Donne himself was not blind to some of the dangers of his method; in the *Litany* he writes, "When we are moved to seem religious Only to vent wit, Lord deliver us."

The finest of the other preordination poems is *Good Friday, 1613.* Here too Donne starts from a paradox; on this day of all days he is turned away from the east. This plunges him into that paradoxical series where he moves with such assurance; and his wit binds up the paradoxes, with just the neatness and passion of the love poems, in a fine conclusion:

I turn my back to thee, but to receive
Corrections, till thy mercies bid thee leave.
O think me worth thine anger, punish me,
Burn off my rusts, and my deformity,
Restore thine image, so much, by thy grace,
That thou mayst know me, and I'll turn my
face.

Of the poems written after ordination, only the sonnets of the Westmoreland manuscript and the three *Hymns* are of the best of Donne. The little group of sonnets includes the moving poem about the death of his wife, and "Show me, dear Christ." The *Hymns* are justly admired. "A Hymn to Christ, at the Authors last going into Germany" records a moment of intense personal feeling and is a companion to the beautiful *Valediction Sermon* of 1619. The other two belong to the period of Donne's serious illness in 1623, when he also wrote *Devotions.* "Thou art a metaphysical God," he says in that work, "full of comparisons." And although these poems abjure harshness in favor of the solemnity proper to hymns, they nevertheless live by their wit. "A Hymn to God, my God, in my sickness" is founded on a favorite conceit; the poet is a map over which the physicians pore.

As west and east
In all flat maps (and I am one) are one,
So death doth touch the resurrection.

The "Hymn to God the Father" contains the famous play on the poet's name (but so does the inscription on the portrait of the author in his shroud, prefixed to *Death's Duel*); what in our time would be only a puerile joke is thrice repeated in this solemn masterpiece.

Donne's wit, of course, depends on the assumption that a joke can be a serious matter. Wit, as he understood it, was born of the preaching of the Word, whether employed in profane or in religious expression. "His fancy," as Walton says, "was unimitably high, equalled only by his great wit. . . . He was by nature highly passionate." It will never be regretted that the twentieth century, from whatever motive, restored him to his place among the English poets, and wit to its place in poetry.

Selected Bibliography

BIBLIOGRAPHY

Keynes, G. L., *Bibliography of the Works of Dr. John Donne,* (Cambridge, 1914); rev. 1932, 1957).

COLLECTED AND SELECTED EDITIONS

Poems J. D[onne]. With Elegies on the Author's Death, (London, 1633), repr. with additions (some spurious) and alterations, 1635, 1639, repr. with some alteration 1649, 1650, 1654, repr. with alterations and important additions 1660; H. J. C. Grierson, ed., *Poems,* 2 vols. (Oxford, 1912); J. Hayward, ed., *Complete Poetry and Selected Prose,* (London, 1929; rev. 1936); H. Gardner, ed., *The Divine Poems,* (Oxford, 1952); G. R. Potter and E. M. Simpson, eds., *Sermons,* 10 vols. (Berkeley, Calif., 1953–1962); F. Manley, ed.,*The Anniversaries,* (Baltimore, 1963); H. Gardner, ed., *The Elegies, and the Songs and Sonnets,* (Oxford, 1965); W. Milgate, ed., *The Satires, Epigrams and Verse Letters,* (Oxford, 1967); E. M. Simpson, ed., *Selected Prose,* (Oxford, 1967); A. J. Smith, ed., *The Complete English Poems,* (Harmondsworth, 1971).

LETTERS

Letters to Severall Persons of Honour, (London, 1651); E. W. Grosse, ed., *The Life and Letters of John Donne,* 2 vols. (London, 1899).

BIOGRAPHICAL AND CRITICAL STUDIES

Walton, Izaak, "The Life and Death of Dr. Donne," in *The Lives of Dr. John Donne, Sir Henry Wotton, Mr. Richard Hooker, Mr. George Herbert . . .* (London, 1640; enl. 1658), many modern reprints; Ramsay, M. P., *Les doctrines medievales chez Donne,* (London, 1917; 2nd ed. 1924); Simpson, E. M., *A Study of the Prose Works of John Donne,* 2nd ed. (Oxford, 1948); Praz, M., *Secentismo e marinismo in Inghilterra; John Donne-Richard Crashaw,* (Florence, 1925); Legouis, P., *Donne the Craftsman,* (Paris, 1928); Williamson, G., *The Donne Tradition,* (Cambridge, Mass., 1930); T. Spencer, ed., *A Garland for John Donne,* (Cambridge, Mass., 1931); Mitchell, W. F., *English Pulpit Oratory from Andrewes to Tillotson,* (London, 1932); White, H. C., *The Metaphysical Poets: A Study in Religious Experience,* (New York, 1936); Coffin, C. M., *John Donne and the New Philosophy,* (New York, 1937); Sharp, R. L., *From Donne to Dryden: The Revolt Against Metaphysical Poetry,* (Chapel Hill, N.C., 1940); Tuve, R., *Elizabethan and Metaphysical Imagery: Renaissance Poems and Twentieth Century Critics,* (Chicago, 1947); Nicolson, M. H., *The Breaking of the Circle: Studies in the Effect of the "New Science" Upon Seventeenth Century Poetry,* (Evanston, Ill., 1950); Martz, L. L., *The Poetry of Meditation,* (New Haven, 1954; rev. 1962); Duncan, J. E., *The Revival of Metaphysical Poetry,* (Minneapolis, 1959); Alvarez, A., *The School of Donne,* (London, 1961); H. L. Gardner, ed., *John Donne: A Collection of Critical Essays,* (Englewood Cliffs, N.J., 1962); F. Kermode, ed., *Discussions of John Donne,* (Boston, 1962); Smith, A. J., *John Donne, the Songs and Sonnets,* (London, 1964); Andreasen, N. J. C., *John Donne, Conservative Revolutionary,* (Princeton, 1967); Bald, R. C., *John Donne: A Life,* (Oxford, 1970); Smith, A. J., *John Donne, the Critical Heritage,* (London, 1975); J. R. Roberts, ed., *Essential Articles for the Study of John Donne's Poetry,* (Hamden, Conn., 1975).

T. S. ELIOT
(1888–1965)

M. C. BRADBROOK

INTRODUCTION

When T. S. Eliot celebrated his sixtieth birthday on 26 September 1948, tributes that he received from the country of his birth and the country of his adoption, from Europe, and indeed from all over the world made it plain that he was very generally acknowledged as the greatest living poet of the English language. Nevertheless, his poetry at first provoked strong disagreement, and the reviews of his later work, especially his dramas, show that his continued development and intellectual growth could still give rise to new misunderstanding.

Eliot's literary career illustrates in a striking manner the controlling force of the poetic impulse. He was born in St. Louis, Missouri, where his father held an important position in the business world. But he was descended on both sides from New England families of the early settlements: his ancestor Andrew Eliot went to Massachusetts from the Somerset village of East Coker in 1670, and his mother was a descendant of Isaac Stearns, who went out in 1630 as one of the original settlers of the Massachusetts Bay Colony. Among his forebears, T. S. Eliot numbered many distinguished scholars, clergymen, and men of letters; in his early poems there are a number of sketches, not always entirely dutiful, of Boston relatives and of that Puritan society, earnestly intellectual and highly exclusive, which still in some measure survives, although it no longer centers on the city of Boston. In *Four Quartets* (1943), Eliot has described both East Coker, the village from which his family emigrated more than three hundred years ago, and, in "The Dry Salvages," the Massachusetts coast that he knew in his childhood.

Eliot's family tradition connected him with Harvard, where he received his education. At Harvard there is now a collection of material relating to Eliot's early life, together with much of his juvenilia. He spent four undergraduate years at this university, being especially interested in the study of philosophy. In 1910 he went to the Sorbonne, to read literature and philosophy, subsequently returning to Harvard for further study. Afterward he studied in Germany and at Oxford. During World War I he stayed in England, working first as a schoolmaster, then as a banker, and finally as an editor and publisher. It was during this period that his poetic work began to appear in various magazines, and between 1917 and 1920 in small volumes. But it was in 1922, with the publication of *The Waste Land,* that Eliot assumed that commanding position in English poetry which he ever after retained. In 1927 he became a British subject and announced in the preface to a book of essays that he was now a classicist in literature, a royalist in politics, and an Anglo-Catholic in religion, a statement that caused some disturbance in literary circles, where none of these tenets was very prominently advocated.

During the next decade he published some important poetry, wrote and lectured on a wide variety of subjects connected with literature and society, and, through his editing of the *Criterion,* a quarterly magazine, exercised considerable influence on the literary world. During the war he published what many people consider his greatest poem, *Four Quartets,* and then turned quite deliberately to the stage; but the *Criterion* had ceased publication in 1939, and Eliot tended to write less criticism than formerly. His authority and reputation had, however, grown steadily, and while in the early 1920's he was known chiefly to the young and enthusiastic students of the universities and to the younger literary generation in London, he became gradually accepted during the course of the next decade by the more traditional and conservative guardians of literary reputations. He is now treated with the greatest respect by even the crustier old gentlemen of the clubs and academies, and accorded the reverence (which he would have found somewhat embarrassing) of literary ladies and provincial clerics. He received from King George VI the Order of Merit; that most rare and coveted of honors, the Nobel Prize for Literature, in 1948; and the highest American civilian honor, the Medal of Freedom, in 1964. His double task was the interpretation of the age to itself, "holding the Mirror up to Nature," as the greatest poet of all proclaimed, and maintaining the standards of strict literary excellence, "purifying the dialect of the tribe," as he himself, quoting Stéphane Mallarmé, declared his aim to be. As Eliot said of another poet, in his own work the reader will find "a record of the spiritual struggles of a man of intellectual power and emotional intensity who gave much toil to perfecting his verses. As such, it should be a document of interest to all who are curious to understand their fellow men."

THE POET OF THE WASTE LAND

Eliot's early poetry, published during World War I, depicts in ironic and epigrammatic terseness the little anxieties, social embarrassments, and unacknowledged vacuity of polite society in Boston and London. The world he displays is the world of Henry James's novels, where frustrated society ladies breathe their invitations and deprecations by a faint nuance, where corrupt financiers and decayed nobility drive their social bargains, where the final reckoning discloses only that "I have measured out my life with coffee spoons."

In "T. S. Eliot" (*Abinger Harvest,* 1936), E. M. Forster described the relief with which he discovered a little volume of Eliot during a period of convalescence in Cairo:

> For what, in that world of gigantic horror, was tolerable except the slight gestures of dissent? He who measured himself against the war, who drew himself to his full height, as it were, and said to Armadillo-Armageddon "Avaunt!" collapsed at once into a pinch of dust. But he who could turn aside to complain of ladies and drawing rooms preserved a tiny drop of our self-respect, he carried on the human heritage.

Yet behind the hesitancies, the ironic wit of a young man trying to protect himself against *faux pas* in the society of the Old World, behind the futilities and the boredom of the middle-aged unsuccessful Prufrock, or the middle-aged unsuccessful lady of "Portrait of a Lady," with its reminiscence of Henry James in the very title, Eliot would occasionally show a glimpse of horror or of glory. In a single phrase—joined with some sardonic self-depreciatory gesture—he can call up a vision of lyric beauty, alien but poignantly felt. This very simple device, the juxtaposition of the lovely and the squalid, or the passionate and the trivial, so that they make their own comment on one another, is the basis of his poetic structure:

> I grow old . . . I grow old . . .
> I shall wear the bottoms of my trousers
> rolled.
>
> Shall I part my hair behind? Do I dare to
> eat a peach?
> I shall wear white flannel trousers, and walk
> upon the beach.

I have heard the mermaids singing, each to each.

I do not think that they will sing to me.

I have seen them riding seaward on the waves
Combing the white hair of the waves blown back
When the wind blows the water white and black.

We have lingered in the chambers of the sea
By sea-girls wreathed with seaweed red and brown
Till human voices wake us, and we drown.
("The Love Song of J. Alfred Prufrock")

Here are not only echoes of John Keats's "magic casements opening on the foam/Of perilous seas," of the chambers of the sea where the forsaken Merman of Matthew Arnold lingered—the situation, it will be noted, is reversed—but the fresh stiff drive of a lively off-shore breeze. This seascape may be compared with those of "Mr Apollinax" and "Gerontion," "Marina," the last poem of *Ash-Wednesday* (1930), and "The Dry Salvages," the third of the *Four Quartets.* Eliot has a few strong and central symbols, as he has a few strong and central themes, and the sea as the source of primal life and energy is one of the most important. Hence even in the lovely fourth movement of *The Waste Land,* "Death by Water"—a passage adapted from the French of his poem "Dans le Restaurant"—Phlebas, the drowned Phoenician sailor, appears as one who has lived a full, simple natural life and died a clean death. In the land of drought, Death by Water holds more beauty than terror; for both the present scene and the recollections are of beauty:

Gentile or Jew,
O you who turn the wheel and look to windward,
Consider Phlebas, who was once handsome and tall as you.

To the generation that wasted its youth in that earlier war, the shock of discovering the instability of their world was more severe than anything the generation of 1939 had to meet. Political and religious skepticism, already an intellectual fashion, was strengthened by general disillusion, and the temper in England during the war years and the following decade was one of cynicism, irony, and a protective, defensive toughness of mind. A. E. Housman, Lytton Strachey, Aldous Huxley, and the Sitwells were the fashionable reading of the intellectuals; the poetry of John Donne and other difficult seventeenth-century poets enjoyed a vogue that was partly created by the critical writings of Eliot himself. Social conventions were by general consent taboo: and while it could be considered by serious critics a virtue in Eliot to achieve "a complete severance between his poetry and *all* beliefs," it was held that experience should be as wide, unrestricted, and uninhibited as possible. The juvenile naughtiness of the neurotic 1920's takes on in retrospect a certain pathos. It was the reaction from a shattering experience and the refuge of those who did not wish to remember, because they could not attempt to organize or control their memories of the war years. Eliot's early poetry, with its subtle deflation of feelings ("Conversation Galante"), its shocking juxtapositions in the manner of Donne ("Whispers of Immortality" and "Mr Eliot's Sunday Morning Service"), is summed up in the Sweeney poems, "Sweeney Erect" and "Sweeney Among the Nightingales." The lovely world of Renaissance art, classic legend, and natural beauty is superimposed on the squalors of tavern and brothel. There is no comment, no explanation, and no attempt to connect the two. Instead the sharp hard lines of the verse, the alternation of magnificence and familiarity in the words, and the startling incongruity of the images are left to make their own effect. The reader has to complete the work within his own experience. Here is to be seen one of Eliot's principal poetic weapons—his use of *implication,* of statements that carry a weight far beyond their ostensive meaning. These "re-echo, thus, in your mind" by their evocative resonance inviting legitimate variation of response. For Eliot always wrote with a very strong sense of his readers. He made demands on them without which the poems are incomplete. It is no use approaching Eliot in a state of wise passiveness. You have to use your wits.

This method of ironic implication is clearly of the greatest value in an age when there are in fact no longer any generally accepted standards of belief the poet may take for granted. It enables the poet to escape or evade the kind of direct statement with which his reader may not agree—and which the poet himself will not feel capable of providing. For Eliot never claimed to speak with authority, as his later admirers suggest. He declared that some of his earlier essays "in spite of, and partly because of, their defects preserve in cryptogram certain notions which if expressed directly would be destined to immediate obloquy, followed by perpetual oblivion."

In this ironic disclaimer may be read something of the difficulties that the contemporary climate of opinion imposed on a lyric poet. The Sweeney poems are in a sense poems in cryptogram, but each reader is invited to provide his own solution. This does not mean that they are ambiguous. They are merely condensed. The single scene, the grand vista opened by an evocative phrase, the impartial and controlled movement of the verse impose a direction even while they decline to state it:

> Gloomy Orion and the Dog
> Are veiled; and hushed the shrunken seas;
> The person in the Spanish cape
> Tries to sit on Sweeney's knees.
>
> Slips and pulls the table cloth
> Overturns a coffee-cup. . . .
>
> The host with someone indistinct
> Converses at the door apart,
> The nightingales are singing near
> The Convent of the Sacred Heart,
>
> And sang within the bloody wood,
> When Agamemnon cried aloud,
> And let their liquid siftings fall
> To stain the stiff dishonoured shroud.
> ("Sweeney Among the Nightingales")

The lovely song and the birds' droppings, the squalid intrigue in the tavern and the murder of a king, are not merely contrasted in ironic equivalence. They are somehow seen as having at least so necessary a relation as to be inseparable. Here is the source of the gratitude his contemporaries feel toward Eliot. He has interpreted the chaos of their world, so that it no longer presents itself as chaotic:

> *Erhebung* without motion, concentration
> Without elimination, both a new world
> And the old made explicit, understood
> In the completion of its partial ecstasy
> The resolution of its partial horror.
> ("Burnt Norton," II)

While the Sweeney poems sum up Eliot's achievement at this time, there are two others that point forward to his later work. These are "La Figlia che Piange" and "Gerontion." It has been said, on good authority, that "La Figlia che Piange" is written about a statue of a weeping girl that the poet hoped to see in Italy but never located. Even the word of Eliot himself would not convince me that a poem beginning

> Stand on the highest pavement of the stair—
> Lean on a garden urn—
> Weave, weave the sunlight in your hair—
> Clasp your flowers to you with a pained
> surprise—
> Fling them to the ground and turn
> With a fugitive resentment in your eyes:
> But weave, weave the sunlight in your hair.

had very much to do with marble. The curious shifts between second and third person in the address, the hint of a Henry James situation at the end of the second stanza, and the summing up, "I should have lost a gesture and a pose," indicate clearly that the very substance of the poem is the relation between life and art—particularly between those moments when life falls into the ordered pattern of art; but the beautiful movement, the alternation of longing and control, conveys most poignantly a human situation that reechoes through all the poetry down to *The Family*

Reunion (1939). "Gerontion," "the old man," whose soliloquy stands at the head of the *Poems* of 1919, is a dramatic figure not unlike Tiresias, the old blind seer of *The Waste Land.* Both are voices rather than persons—the voices of representative Man, as he contemplates a decaying civilization, and the pitiable fragments of humanity that inhabit this "decayed house." Mr. Silvero, Hakagawa, Madame de Tornquist, and Fräulein von Kulp are only names, but the mixture of nationalities, the suggestions of various kinds of international hocus-pocus, artistic, or occult, accords with the description of the "owner of the house," the Jew

> Spawned in some estaminet of Antwerp,
> Blistered in Brussels, patched and peeled in
> London.

All, including Gerontion, are displaced, homeless persons, whose spiritual desolation is symbolized in the traditional religious metaphor of drought. There is no apparent sequence of thought or logical arrangement in the poem, only the broken fragmentary recollections and meditations of the old man, as he recalls those heroic deaths in battle, suggestive of Homeric war, that he did not share:

> I was neither at the hot gates[1]
> Nor fought in the warm rain
> Nor knee deep in the salt marsh, heaving a
> cutlass,
> Bitten by flies, fought.

In the meditation that follows, not only contemporary society but the inner world of the individual is seen to be crumbling:

> These with a thousand small deliberations
> Protract the profit of their chill delirium,
> Excite the membrane, when the sense has
> cooled,
> With pungent sauces, multiply variety
> In a wilderness of mirrors.

By a technique not unlike that of the early Russian films, Eliot gives a series of "shots" that when put together form a single sequence. The unity lies in the mood and tone, the flat, listless accents of the old man whose vision may have the inconsequence of a dream, because, as Eliot says in the quotation from Shakespeare that heads the poem,

> Thou has nor youth nor age,
> But as it were an after dinner sleep,
> Dreaming of both.

The poem is full of echoes of Shakespeare and of other Elizabethan dramatists. These literary echoes have often caused apprehension in the minds of readers, who feel that without an ability to recognize such allusions, they may lose the point of the poem. This fear is, I think, without foundation. A successful poem does not rely upon anything but itself for the essential core of its meaning. Eliot's use of literary allusions is part of his technique of implication. As in the Sweeney poem he could evoke the majesty of Greek tragedy in the images of Agamemnon and the nightingales, could summon up a whole train of associations in contrast to what the rest of the poem suggests, so, in his many echoes of the French symbolists, Donne, and the metaphysical poets, Dante and the poets of the *dolce stil nuovo,* which occur throughout *The Waste Land,* he sets his vision of desolation and spiritual drought in implicit contrast with the visionary worlds of the elder poets, his masters. Sometimes the contrasts are ironic, as the echoes of Shakespeare's *Antony and Cleopatra* in the second movement of *The Waste Land,* which describes the boudoir of a neurotic fine lady of the present day and her rasping quarrel with an almost silent figure, her husband or her lover. Sometimes literature consoles and supports by reminding a distraught generation that it is not alone—in recognizing the right words for the present situations, it marks the first step toward control; to accept such a definition in terms of another time and another place marks also the first step toward integration. Eliot used the words of the *Inferno* to describe the city crowd that "flowed up the hill and down King William

1. Thermopylae.

Street" because only a Dante could define for him the depth of their desolation. The poet accepts the personal suffering that such a vision entails, and the two utterances that give it most clearly are the cry of Arnaut Daniel from his purgatorial flames, "Sovegna vos" (Be mindful), which is not uttered but recalled:

> Poi s'acose nel foco che gli affina
> (*Purgatorio* 26, 147)
>
> Then he hid himself in the fire that refines
> them

and St. Augustine on the drowned Phoenician sailor. Each marks a renunciation, and each had echoed through Eliot's poetry for some time. There are indeed many familiar figures who appear momentarily—the old German princess; the damp and depressed figure of Lil, as described in the public-house scene; the typist, who might have been one of Sweeney's girl friends, and the three Thames daughters, her sisters; Mme. Sosostris, the famous clairvoyant; and Mr. Eugenides, the Smyrna merchant. All are seen through the blind eyes of old Tiresias, the seer, who has "foresuffered all"; for as Eliot says: "The poem is what he sees." The lesser characters are not clearly distinguished; they melt into each other, for they are phantoms inhabiting an unreal city. Such is Eliot's vision of the postwar world, a land by no means fit for heroes to live in, and that in any case most of his friends did not live to inhabit. It is a cosmic vision, seen on a small scale. While Joyce took seven hundred pages to describe a single day in the life of Dublin, Eliot concentrated his vision in four hundred lines. The whole poem, but especially its last lines, employs the technique of ironic juxtaposition, which has already been described, in a deeper and more tragic manner. The "wild and whirling words" of a mind unstrung, clutching desperately at the fragmentary and disintegrating remains of the world of literature, shored against its ruin, are suddenly broken in upon by the tolling magnificence of the Sanskrit benediction:

> Datta. Dayadhvam. Damyata.
> Shantih shantih shantih

The contemporary public was of course bewildered by *The Waste Land,* but after half a century of exposition there should be little difficulty for the reader who has been given the right line of approach, and who has at his disposal a large number of commentaries, some of which ascribe to the poem depths of significance its author modestly disclaimed. The quickest means of reaching its meaning is probably to listen to a reading by someone who is familiar with the work or, better still, to hear Eliot's own recorded reading, made for the Library of Congress.

The form of the poem has received a good deal of attention: it is divided into five movements, and each movement has a certain completeness in itself. The musical analogy has been much stressed by critics, the different recurring themes of drought and rain, sterility and violation, ruin and social trivialities being compared with musical themes. While the analogy is a useful one, it should be used with caution. It may suggest to the reader the kind of attention he should give and the kind of design he should look for, but it must not be pressed further.

Nor should the poem be read as a vision of despair. It has been called Eliot's *Inferno,* but even in the *Inferno* there are gleams that recall another world. Here in the first movement the vision of beauty and love is not completely shut out:

> —Yet when we came back, late, from the
> Hyacinth garden
> Your arms full, and your hair wet, I could
> not
> Speak, and my eyes failed, I was neither
> Living nor dead, and I knew nothing.
> Looking into the heart of light, the silence.
> *Oed' und leer das Meer.*

Again, in the final movement, in "the awful daring of a moment's surrender/Which an age of prudence can never retract" and in the picture of guided happiness:

The boat responded
Gaily, to the hand expert with sail and oar
The sea was calm, your heart would have
responded
Gaily. . . .

there is a momentary escape from the kingdoms of sterility and drought. Moreover, though the world depicted is one of disorder and decay, the poem contains within itself a subtle and implicit order that makes the vision bearable, if only just bearable. It has several times been pointed out that those recurrent images which are repeated throughout the poem "release markedly different shades of feeling according to their special contexts." The subtle variation between the different images of the river, for instance, or the fading of Philomel to a mere entablature in the second movement, contrasted with the violent emphasis of the third movement on the seduction of the typist, implies some order, some principle of organization within this apparently haphazard scheme of things. The repetition with modifications of the same image cannot yield any *statement* to set against the many gestures of weariness, confusion, and despair; perhaps their pattern is as arbitrary as that of the suits of a pack of cards, and indeed the symbols of the Tarot pack are in the first section identified with most of the leading symbols of the poem. Yet arbitrary as the pack of cards may be, its conventions are orderly.

As the vision of the Hyacinth girl conferred eternity upon a moment, so at the end of *The Waste Land* there is a strange sense of expectancy, of quiet, that recalls Cleopatra's line:

My desolation does begin to make
A better life.

Nothing explicit warrants this feeling, except possibly the mysterious Sanskrit benediction, but it can be felt through the rhythm, which becomes stronger, more emphatic, as though a pulse were beginning to beat after the hurried staccato movement of the "nightmare" passage at the beginning of the last movement. The words of the thunder, "give, sympathize, control," have been fulfilled for the reader in the poem itself. The sincerity and penetration with which it renders the vision of desolation console and demand response; while the power to project such a vision in the form of words, to objectify and realize it, implies the highest measure of control.

If it is not his greatest poem, *The Waste Land* is certainly Eliot's most influential poem. The generation that grew up in the later 1920's took it to themselves, absorbed it so that it became part of their habit of mind. As Auden said in his verses for Eliot's sixtieth birthday:

it was you
Who, not speechless with shock but finding
the right
Language for thirst and fear, did most to
Prevent a panic.

Moreover, the depth and violence of the contrasts in the poem, the sense that the poet is wrestling with the problems of his outer and inner world is stronger here than in the later poetry. Even in The *Four Quartets* we do not feel that "Spinoza and the smell of the cooking" (to use Eliot's formula) have been brought into relation with each other. It is the smell of the cooking that tends to disappear. The later poems are concerned more exclusively with inner experience.

THE WASTELAND

The mysterious Quinn Manuscript—the original draft of T. S. Eliot's *The Waste Land,* with nine satellite poems—was published just fifty years after its completion in the latter part of 1921. It had long been known that Ezra Pound drastically edited this first draft, cutting down to 433 lines what, because of its concentration, he termed "the longest poem in the Englisch langwidge." The version that first appeared in the first number of the *Cri-*

terion (October 1922) represented about two thirds of the draft.

What has been recovered and printed is:

(a) a single typescript of section I, "The Burial of the Dead";
(b) a typescript, with one carbon copy added, of the next two sections, both extensively annotated by Pound, and section II annotated by Vivien Eliot also;
(c) manuscripts of the last two sections, with typed copies made on Pound's typewriter;
(d) nine satellite poems, some manuscript, others typed.

Eliot told John Quinn, a New York lawyer and collector of literary manuscripts, that for much of the typescript "no manuscript, except scattered lines, ever existed"; he composed on the typewriter. The last two sections were probably written at Margate in October and at Lausanne in December 1921; later he said the poem had been written "mostly at Lausanne (*Transcript,* p. *xxii*).[2] Following a complete breakdown, he was there on leave from his employment as confidential clerk in the foreign department of Lloyd's Bank in the City.

In a broadcast to introduce the new edition, given on 7 November 1971, Valerie Eliot confirmed that the passage in Eliot's essay on Pascal (1928) referred to the composition of *The Waste Land*:

> it is a commonplace that some forms of illness are extremely favourable, not only to religious illumination, but to artistic and literary composition. A piece of writing meditated, apparently without progress, for months or years, may suddenly take shape and word; and in this state long passages may be produced which require little or no retouch. I have no good word to say for the cultivation of automatic writing as the model of literary composition; I doubt whether these moments *can* be cultivated by the writer; but he to whom this happens assuredly has the sense of being a vehicle rather than a maker. . . . You may call it communication with the Divine, or you may call it a temporary crystallization of the mind. (*Selected Essays,* enl. ed., p. 405)

Eliot had mentioned the poem two years earlier in a letter to Quinn; the struggle is described by Conrad Aiken, a friend from Eliot's Harvard days, who, in spite of some inconsistencies about dates, has no doubt recalled the essentials:

> In the winter of 1921–2 I was in London, living in Bayswater, and Eliot and myself lunched together two or three times a week in the City, near his bank . . . he always had with him his pocket edition of Dante . . . discussing also the then-just-beginning possibility of *The Criterion,* through the generosity of Lady Rothermere. And it was at one of these meetings, in midwinter, that he told me one day, and with visible concern, that although every evening the went home to his flat hoping that he could start writing again, and with every confidence that the material was *there* and waiting, night after night the hope proved illusory: the sharpened pencil lay unused by the untouched sheet of paper. ("A Reviewer's ABC," in *T. S. Eliot, "The Waste Land": A Casebook*, pp. 91–92)

When told of this at second-hand, an analyst said, "all that's stopping him is his fear of putting anything down that's short of perfection. He thinks he's God." The foreseeable result was that, when told of it, Eliot became speechless with rage:

> The *intrusion,* quite simply, was one that was intolerable. But ever since I have been entirely convinced that it did the trick, it broke the log jam. A month or two later he went to Switzerland, and there wrote *The Waste Land.*

Eliot may still have been affected by his father's death in January 1919, for he had hoped to justify his desertion of America—which

2. V. Eliot, ed., *The Waste Land: A Facsimile and Transcript* (London, 1971). The Quinn Manuscript was sold to the New York Public Library in April 1958, but its whereabouts were announced only in 1968.

had estranged his father—by publishing; *The Sacred Wood* (1920) had been inscribed to his father's memory.[3] A sensitive and overdriven man, with a desperately sick wife, shifting from one home to another and with no funds to meet the expenses of illness, Eliot's scrupulous conscience may well have inhibited his writing. The lifting of inhibitions associated with general disturbance may have contributed, with the effects of a good holiday, to bring about a release; whatever the cause, by Christmas Eve Pound was writing enthusiastically of "the Poem," now evidently in shape, for he says, "The thing runs from April to Shantih without a break," and gives advice on the "superfluities." On his way home, Eliot in early January stopped in Paris to see Pound; perhaps this was when the last part was typed.

One fact is immediately clear: the "missing links" are not links. Their elimination did not make the poem less, but rather more, coherent; the excision did not cut out logic, copulatives, or argument, but deleted subsidiary episodes, weaker versions of the pub scene, the typist's seduction, and the death of Phlebas. Their recovery makes the work seem less unified, less integrated. "I think it was just as structureless, only in a more futile way, in the longer version" was a characteristic sally of Eliot.

Certain traces of release and of the lifting of inhibitions are suggested in the structure of the drafts. Sections I, III, and IV are introduced by long narratives, which all turn out to be false starts, of an autobiographical or quasi-autobiographical character. These were the parts that Pound cut out, and their presence would have certainly turned the single poem into a series.

Section II, heavily worked over in collaboration, also trails a satellite entitled "The Death of the Duchess"—possibly an already discarded false start to the boudoir scene that replaced it. Moreover, section IV also trails a satellite entitled "Dirge," so that this section is really a triad of one lengthy sequence and two brief ones.

Then suddenly, and as it would seem subliminally ordered, the final section "came." Even here there are some discarded opening lines, themselves highly elucidative, which Mrs. Eliot would date very early from the handwriting.

> After the turning of the inspired days,
> And the praying and the silence and the
>   crying
> And the inevitable ending of a thousand
>   ways
> And frosty vigil kept in withered gardens
> After the life and death of lonely places
> After the judges and the advocates and
>   wardens
> And the torchlight red on sweaty faces. . . .
>   (*Transcript*, p. 109)

The several internal censors, judges, and advocates and wardens have been dethroned, but the speaker is identified with Jesus, the Hanged Man. The original title, "He do the Police in different Voices" (applied to reading newsprint in Dickens' *Our Mutual Friend*) would be applicable to some of the excised stories; the riotous scene in Boston might have fed a newspaper column, the heroic deaths of the fishermen certainly would; and the Lady Fresca must have featured in gossip columns. Eliot's failure at once to recognize the weakness of these lines is a strong proof of his disturbance. The last section, the one that was "given," had at first no title at all; but Pound added "O.K. from here on, I think" above the opening line.

In August 1923 Eliot wrote to Ford Madox Ford that there were about thirty "good" lines in *The Waste Land* and "the rest is ephemeral"; later he explained that these were the twenty-nine lines of the water-dripping song in the last section. He also told Bertrand Russell at this time that section V was not only the best part but "the only part that justifies the whole, at all" (*Transcript*, p. 129).

It is not uncommon for a writer to find the shaping impulse of his work revealed only

3. Compare his determination to finish his philosophical thesis for Harvard, to meet his obligations: "this return at least I owed to Harvard."

when he completes it. Here the special power of release that impelled the work forward was also a unifying power. The poem grew into unity.

After Pound had brought Eliot to Quinn's notice, he financed the little booklet that Eliot wrote in 1917 in praise of Pound to introduce *Lustra* to the American public; he placed Pound, at Eliot's suggestion, as Paris correspondent of the *Dial.* Acting as Eliot's attorney, he placed Eliot's *Poems* of 1919 and placed *The Waste Land* with Boni and Liveright, the New York publishers. Since the poem had already been accepted by the *Dial* and was also to appear in the *Criterion,* this involved some delicate negotiation. In gratitude, Eliot gave Quinn the original draft of *The Waste Land* together with a small collection of unpublished poems, for which Quinn insisted on making payment. These manuscripts were dispatched in October 1922 and acknowledged by Quinn in February 1923.

Eliot wrote to Quinn in September 1922: "I am quite overwhelmed by your letter [an eleven-page letter of fatherly advice], by all you have done for me, the results that have been effected and by your endless kindness. . . ." Pound had written to Quinn that Eliot's new poem is "about enough to make the rest of us shut up shop" and, more soberly to his former professor at Philadelphia, "Eliot's *Waste Land* is I think the justification of the 'movement,' of our modern experiment, since 1900" (*Letters,* p. 248).

LATER POETRY

"The Hollow Men" (1925) marks the sharpest break in Eliot's poetry; it may be looked on as a kind of prologue or antechamber to *Ash-Wednesday.* They have in common a new kind of image, a new kind of rhythm, and a new mood.

The world depicted in "The Hollow Men" is a gray, phantasmal country, featureless and nameless—"death's dream kingdom." The London of *The Waste Land* had been as vividly realized as Charles Baudelaire's Paris, but now the outer world is left behind. Some lines from *Four Quartets* seem best to sum up the experience conveyed in "The Hollow Men," and its relation to *The Waste Land*:

> . . . the strained time-ridden faces
> Distracted from distraction by distraction
> Filled with fancies and empty of meaning
> Tumid apathy with no concentration
> Men and bits of paper, whirled by the cold wind
> That blows before and after time. . . .
> Driven on the wind that sweeps the gloomy hills of London,
> Hampstead and Clerkenwell, Campden and Putney,
> Highgate, Primrose and Ludgate. Not here
> Not here the darkness, in this twittering world.
>
> Descend lower, descend only
> Into the world of perpetual solitude,
> World not world, but that which is not world,
> Internal darkness, deprivation
> And destitution of all property,
> Desiccation of the world of sense,
> Evacuation of the world of fancy,
> Inoperancy of the world of spirit. . . .
> ("Burnt Norton," III)

"The Hollow Men" marks the dead center in Eliot's poetry: it records the experience of utter destitution where there are no forms, not even the forms of nightmare. The "hollow men" who are also the "stuffed men," that is, scarecrows, straw dummies, whisper together only with the voice of the wind over dry grass. This image is taken from the last movement of *The Waste Land,* the approach to the Chapel Perilous, but it is very differently used. The stone images, the "cactus land," and the "beach of the tumid river" on which the hollow men gather in the twilight of death's kingdom (an image taken from the *Purgatorio* II. 100–102) are unredeemed by any vision of beauty. That has been left behind in the world of the living:

> Eyes I dare not meet in dreams
> In death's dream kingdom

These do not appear:
There, the eyes are
Sunlight on a broken column
There, is a tree swinging
And voices are
in the wind's singing
More distant and more solemn
Than a fading star.
(II)

There is a distant, barely expressed hope that the eyes, like Beatrice's *"occhi santi,"* may reappear

As the perpetual star
Multifoliate rose
Of death's twilight kingdom
The hope only
Of empty men.
(IV)

but the poem ends with a broken disconnected attempt at phrases from the Lord's Prayer and with the empty jingle of a child's nursery rhyme.

From the passages that have just been quoted it will be seen that the rhythm of "The Hollow Men" depends on short, nerveless lines, with occasional, rather haphazard rhyming. The effect conveyed is one of peculiar exhaustion, flatness, and remoteness. The voice moves in a thin and mechanical way through the repetition of phrases and of words ("death's dream kingdom," contrasted with "death's twilight kingdom" and "death's other kingdom"). This mood seems to be described dramatically in the speeches of Harry in *The Family Reunion,* when he recalls to Mary, and later to Agatha, some phases of his wanderings.

Compared with "The Hollow Men," *Ash-Wednesday* shows a movement toward recovery, a turning toward life. Whereas "The Hollow Men" would seem to be a personal poem, recording the effects of some disaster at the moment when the shock was most severe, *Ash-Wednesday* depicts reemergence into a new and strange world, which can be described only by formal and highly stylized images, so that the effect is still rather remote. Eliot was clearly at this time most strongly under the influence of Dante's poetry. He wrote a monograph on Dante (reprinted in his *Selected Essays*), which provides incidentally the best comment on his own poetry. Speaking of the Divine Pageant at the end of the *Purgatorio*—the scene in which Dante for the first time reencounters Beatrice—he says:

> It belongs to the world of what I call the *high dream,* and the modern world seems capable only of the *low dream.* I arrived at accepting it, myself, only with some difficulty. There were at least two prejudices, one against Pre-Raphaelite imagery, which was natural to one of my generation, and perhaps affects generations younger than mine. The other prejudice—which affects this end of the *Purgatorio* and the whole of the *Paradiso*—is the prejudice that poetry not only must be found *through* suffering but can find its material only *in* suffering. Everything else was cheerfulness, optimism, and hopefulness; and these words stood for a great deal of what one hated in the nineteenth century. It took me many years to recognize that the states of improvement and beatitude which Dante describes are still further from what the world can conceive as cheerfulness, than are his states of damnation.

This passage not only directly recalls the lines from *Ash-Wednesday,* IV, where the Lady is restored, a vision sheathed with white light:

. . . Redeem
The time. Redeem
The unread vision in the higher dream
While jewelled unicorns draw by the gilded
hearse

but it also points to the lines in the opening poem:

Consequently I rejoice, having to construct
something
Upon which to rejoice

to the image of the purgatorial stairs in *Ash-Wednesday,* III (originally published under the title "Al Som de l'Escalina," a phrase from the speech of Arnaut Daniel), and of course to the quotation that comes almost at the end of the poem, "In la sua voluntade è nostra pace":

> Suffer us not to mock ourselves with
> falsehood
> Teach us to care and not to care
> Teach us to sit still
> Even among these rocks,
> Our peace in His will. . . .

These lines embody the theme of the whole poem: "Teach us to care and not to care" suggests the mingled impulses of regret, renunciation, and redirection of the will that are interwoven throughout the sequence. The poem is strictly formal and makes use of the traditional formulas of the church as well as the more personal symbols drawn from Dante and from Eliot's own earlier work. Rarefied and elusive and deeply personal as it is, though its power has always been recognized, the quality of its themes and style has made it something of a connoisseur's piece among Eliot's writings.

About the same time as *Ash-Wednesday*, Eliot wrote a number of single poems, published in the series *Ariel Poems* or in magazines. "The Journey of the Magi" and "A Song for Simeon" may be compared with "Gerontion" as dramatic lyrics presenting a picture of a whole life, seen from the end by an old man looking back and meditating on its significance; with the difference that the significance is now found in the Incarnation. But the poems are Songs of Experience and not religious verse, in the sense that George Herbert or Henry Vaughan wrote religious verse; that is to say, the references are oblique and implicit. There are touches of irony—especially in "The Journey of the Magi," where the petty humiliations and discomforts of the journey stick in the mind of the Old Man and seem far clearer to him than the mysterious conclusion, which he does not understand.

The most important of the *Ariel Poems* is "Marina," the dramatic monologue of old King Pericles, the hero of Shakespeare's play of that name, who meditates on the recovery of his daughter, miraculously returned from the dead, like the Lady of *Ash-Wednesday*. This poem, one of Eliot's most beautiful and moving, is prefaced by a line from Seneca's *Hercules Furens*, the cry of the hero as he emerges from the darkness of Hell to the light of day:

> Quis hic locus, quae regio, quae mundi
> plaga?
>
> What place is this, what kingdom,
> what shore of the world?

The sense of wonder, of the gradual return of life restored to a mind numbed by sorrow, is presented in images of tenderness, in a hesitant, delicate movement of the verse, that seem to capture the moment of the old king's awakening from his trance:

> What seas what shore what grey rocks and
> what islands
> What water lapping the bow
> And scent of pine and the woodthrush
> singing through the fog
> What images return
> O my daughter. . . .
>
> What is this face, less clear and clearer
> The pulse in the arm, less strong and
> stronger—
> Given or lent? more distant than stars and
> nearer than the eye.

The moment of beatitude and of recognition, which is the complementary and opposite experience to that of "The Hollow Men," is given in terms of a landscape such as we have already seen in the last poem of *Ash-Wednesday* and are to meet again in "The Dry Salvages"—the misty coast with granite rocks and islands, which is part of the landscape of the poet's childhood. Here, in this poem, as the images of life return, the threatening shapes of what was thought to be life "become unsubstantial" and are seen to be a form of death. The poem transmits an extraordinarily intimate and deeply felt state of being, in accents of remote and unearthly serenity.

Two other poems rely on Shakespeare for their background, the two jointly entitled "Coriolan" —"Triumphal March" and "Difficulties of a Statesman." These brilliant ironic monologues of the new political regime are given first from the mob's point of view and second from the politician's—the unwilling politician confronted with a "situation of great delicacy and difficulty." In the anxious period of the early 1930's, before Hitler had really got going, these two poems provided a remarkable forecast of the political scene as it was to unfold itself. In "Coriolan" Eliot projected the helplessness of the statesmen and of the crowd alike, swept toward war and conscious only dimly and in a lost, unfocused way of what they had abandoned or betrayed. The language and rhythm of these poems show a greater variety than the preceding ones; there are free colloquialisms, such apparently unpoetic material as the catalogue of armaments in "Triumphal March," yet also the dramatic flexibility of the speaking voice and occasional lines of grand and reverberating weightiness:

> Stone, bronze, stone, steel, stone, oakleaves,
> horses' heels
> Over the paving.

In these two poems the two leading speakers of Eliot's drama seem to emerge—the Hero and the Chorus. Neither is exempt from satire; neither is wholly satirically drawn. The worried politician, trying to reconcile the conflicting interests of various parties, and the humble spectators of the triumphal procession, whose "Please, will you give us a light?" is given such unexpected depths of implication by the repetiton of the last word

> Light
> Light

were to be followed by the more fully dramatic studies of *The Rock* (1934) and *Murder in the Cathedral* (1935). Eliot set a fashion for verse drama in the middle 1930's that was followed by W. H. Auden, Stephen Spender, Louis MacNeice, and others whose attempt to write drama, and political drama especially, produced some lively occasional verse but nothing that is highly likely to survive. Eliot himself eschewed political drama, though there are implications of a political kind in *The Rock* and *Murder in the Cathedral,* in the speeches of the Tempters and the Knights in particular. During this period Eliot also wrote a number of books and articles on social and religious questions, such as *After Strange Gods* (1934) and *The Idea of Christian Society* (1939). His second drama, *The Family Reunion,* appeared in 1939. It is probable that in turning to the stage he was not merely working out his own bent but was putting into practice the ideas he expressed in *The Use of Poetry and the Use of Criticism* in 1933:

> The most useful poetry, socially, would be one which could cut across all the present stratifications of public taste—stratifications which are perhaps a sign of social disintegration. The ideal medium for poetry, to my mind, and the most direct means of social "usefulness" for poetry is the theatre. In a play of Shakespeare you get several levels of significance. For the simplist auditors there is the plot, for the more thoughtful the character and conflict of character, for the more literary the words and phrasing, for the more musically sensitive the rhythm, and for auditors of more sensitiveness and understanding a meaning which reveals itself gradually.

This passage indicates those aspects of the drama that Eliot himself was likely to find most congenial, and the last phrase suggests that method of implication and gradual exploring of the full significance of an image that has been described already as one of the leading features of his style. In *Ash-Wednesday* he had further deepened his power to explore and unfold traditional liturgical symbols. His reliance on the liturgy, the creeds, the great public affirmations is a sign of coordination between the public and the private worlds. In the plays he uses historic or mythological material. Finally, in his last and, by general agreement, his greatest poem, *Four*

Quartets, which was worked out slowly between 1935 and 1942, he achieves both a new depth and a new clarity. This work (like *Ash-Wednesday* and *The Waste Land*) consists of a number of poems complete in themselves yet also forming a unity. Each single poem is divided into five movements, and each is also named from a place: Burnt Norton—an old house in Gloucestershire, at Aston-sub-Edge under the lip of the Cotswold Hills; East Coker—the Somerset village from which Eliot's family originally came; The Dry Salvages, named from three small islands off the coast of Cape Ann; and Little Gidding, a village in Huntingdonshire where, in the early seventeenth century, Nicholas Ferrar retired with his family to live a life of ordered devotion in his "Protestant nunnery." It was to be known and loved by George Herbert, to give shelter to the defeated King Charles after Naseby, and to remain as perhaps the most perfect example of that exquisite blend of piety, learning, decency, and comeliness of life which distinguished the religious life of the seventeenth century at its best.

In these poems, Eliot meditates upon a wide diversity of material: his personal experiences as they have shaped themselves into a pattern; the pattern of history, including the beginning of the war and the London blitz; the difficulties of a poet and the nature of language. Such diversity is far greater than that of *The Waste Land,* yet it is as strictly organized as *Ash-Wednesday.* The method is again *solvitur ambulando* (solution is found in performance). Phrases are repeated from poem to poem: experiences that are recognizably related, if not the same, reappear in different contexts. There are numerous echoes of the early poems, which do not have the effect of repetition, but rather of older partial statements reintegrated and completed. There is a kind of finality and mastery about the work; the ease and boldness of the transitions are coupled with a manner still tentative and exploratory, especially in the first poem. By the time the last poem is finished, the symbols have been fully unfolded, and the accent is one of assurance and power. In spite of the apparent lack of progression, by the restatement and redefinition of the symbols "a meaning reveals itself gradually," which is then seen to have been latent, though unrecognized, in the earlier parts. This particular use of implication is assisted by various formal devices, some of which are in the nature of scaffolding and are relatively unimportant. For instance, each of the poems is concerned with one of the four elements—"Burnt Norton" with air, "East Coker" with earth, "The Dry Salvages" with water, and "Little Gidding" with fire. The four elements are brought together at the beginning of the second movement of "Little Gidding," where they are seen to be symbols of multiple meaning. The water and fire are not only those of the raids on London—firemen's or bomber's elements—they are the water of baptism and the fire of purgatory, the water that is a symbol of natural life (as in *The Waste Land*) and the fire that is a symbol both of destruction and of renewal. In medieval interpretations of poetry, each statement could have three, four, or sometimes even seven meanings—Dante, for instance, offers the interpretations of his own poems in this way in the *Vita nuova.* Each of Eliot's poems moves on several planes simultaneously, and can be both topical and timeless in its implications. Commentaries on the meaning of the *Four Quartets* are almost as plentiful as commentaries on *The Waste Land,* and almost as divergent; but the best of all has been provided by Eliot himself:

> Trying to learn to use words, and every
>   attempt
> Is a wholly new start, and a different kind of
>   failure
> Because one has only learnt to get the better
>   of words,
> For the thing one no longer has to say, or
>   the way in which
> One is no longer disposed to say it. . . .
>
>   Home is where one starts from. As we
>   grow older
> The world becomes stranger, the pattern
>   more complicated
> Of dead and living. Not the intense moment

Isolated, with no before and after,
But a lifetime burning in every moment,
And not the lifetime of one man only
But of the old stones that cannot be
deciphered. . . .
("East Coker," V)

It seems, as one becomes older,
That the past has another pattern, and
ceases to be a mere sequence— . . .
The moments of happiness—not the sense
of well-being,
Fruition, fulfilment, security or affection,
Or even a very good dinner, but the sudden
illumination—
We had the experience but missed the
meaning,
And approach to the meaning restores the
experience
In a different form, beyond any meaning
We can assign to happiness.
("The Dry Salvages," II)

We shall not cease from exploration
And the end of our exploring
Will be to arrive where we started
And know the place for the first time.
("Little Gidding," V)

"The intense moment" (which is also called "the moment of the rose" and "the moment of the yew tree" had been present in *The Waste Land* as part of an emerging but still implicit order; in all the subsequent poetry, it is present as remembered experience to be recovered only through approach to the meaning." The struggle to renounce "the infirm glory of the positive hour" without denying its glory creates the tension of *Ash-Wednesday.* By these movements only we have existed, Eliot says in *The Waste Land.* In *The Family Reunion* Agatha looks back to the moment when

I only looked through the little door
When the sun was shining on the rose-
garden
(II.2)

yet in a sense she no longer lives by it, and has even rejected it.

There are hours when there seems to be no
past or future,
Only a present moment of pointed light
When you want to burn. When you stretch
out your hand
To the flames. They only come once,
Thank God, that kind. Perhaps there is
another kind,
I believe, across a whole Thibet of broken
stones,
That lie, fang up, a lifetime's march.
(II.2)

However different the experience in these different contexts, it is the same *quality* of experience that is presented in each; and it is the reconciliation of these moments of illumination with the pattern of daily living that is the theme of the later works in general and of the *Four Quartets* in particular:

I can only say, *there* we have been; but I
cannot say where
And I cannot say, how long, for that is to
place it in time.
("Burnt Norton," II)

"The point of the intersection of the timeless with time" is the theme of the dramas, and is stated most explicitly in the choruses to *The Rock.* Throughout Eliot's poetry these words reecho, but not with the meanings they would have in prose or in philosophic discourse. The words are there to be explored, as in the passage on different sorts of time in the first movement of "The Dry Salvages" or the passage from the second movement quoted above, or that in the fifth movement, which concludes:

For most of us, there is only the unattended
Moment, the moment in and out of time,
The distraction fit, lost in a shaft of
sunlight, . . .
These are only hints and guesses,
Hints followed by guesses; and the rest
Is prayer, observance, discipline, thought
and action.
The hint half guessed, the gift half under-
stood, is
Incarnation.

What Eliot is trying to say cannot be paraphrased, reduced to a prose equivalent, or made into a message. For it is in the relationship of all the different fields of experience that are brought together in the poem that its full significance lies, and these different fields of experience cannot be related by any instrument less delicate, fine, and complex than Eliot's own language. The variety of styles in *Four Quartets* ranges from epigrammatic brilliance to such beautiful lyric interludes as the sestines of "The Dry Salvages," or the fourth movement of "Little Gidding," in which the nature of fire is finally defined as the flame of that Third Person of the Trinity to Whom Love is appropriated as His title:

> Who then devised the torment? Love.
> Love is the unfamiliar name
> Behind the hands that wove
> The intolerable shirt of flame
> Which human power cannot remove.
> We only live, only suspire
> Consumed by either fire or fire.

In this use of a very simple and elemental symbol—which had moreover been one of the leading symbols of his own earlier poetry—Eliot seems to provide that satisfying and perfected embodiment of a long-sought truth that gives at once the impression of recognition and of discovery. Eliot himself said elsewhere: "A man who is capable of experience finds himself in a different world in every decade of his life; as he sees it with different eyes, the material of his art is continually renewed." In his essay on "Tradition and the Individual Talent," he observed that the production of a new work of art makes "something happen simultaneously to all the works of art that preceded it. The existing monuments form an ideal order among themselves which is modified by the introduction of the new (the really new) work of art among them." Whether or not this is true of European literature as a whole, it is certainly true of Eliot's own work, which forms a closely related whole. The later work has modified, illuminated, and developed the significance of the earlier work: the strict sense of pattern that can be felt in *Four Quartets* can also be felt throughout the body of the poetry. "East Coker" opens with the motto of Mary Stuart reversed: "In my beginning is my end," and concludes with the motto itself: "In my end is my beginning." In the "contrapuntal" juxtaposition of themes, the use of implication and irony, Eliot controlled and related an unusually wide range of experience; and by the precision and conscious artistry of his style he was able to subdue and unify it. Toward the end of the last poem in *Four Quartets* he writes:

> And every phrase
> And sentence that is right (where every word is at home,
> Taking its place to support the others,
> The word neither diffident nor ostentatious,
> An easy commerce of the old and the new,
> The common word exact without vulgarity,
> The formal word precise but not pedantic,
> The complete consort dancing together)
> Every phrase and every sentence is an end and a beginning,
> Every poem an epitaph.

Such a trained and disciplined way of writing is not common in English; and Eliot might have given the impression, in his less happy moments, of keeping too tight a rein. But in these later poems the commerce of old and new is indeed more easy and familiar; the transitions subtler and more gracious; so that such bold modifications of language as appear in describing the last of the four seasons in accents of the fourth Evangelist become perfectly natural:

> Midwinter spring is its own season
> Sempiternal though sodden towards sundown,
> Suspended in time, between pole and tropic,
> When the short day is brightest, with frost and fire,
> The brief sun flames the ice, on pond and ditches,
> In a windless cold that is the heart's heat,
> Reflecting in a watery mirror

A glare that is blindness in the early
afternoon.
("Little Gidding," I)

This landscape, at once the country around Little Gidding and that landscape of the heart where the flames reappear after the long march "across a whole Thibet of broken stones," recalls, with the matter-of-fact conclusion about "the early afternoon," that the poet is talking of a physical journey, though the spring he sees—the hedgerow blanched with snow as with blossom—is "not in time's covenant." This use of everyday things to mirror the sublime, as well as the formal ordering of the whole poem, is reminiscent of Dante in a deeper, though less obvious, way than the structure of *Ash-Wednesday.* Eliot uses his personal symbols to give that kind of relationship between one realm of discourse and another, which in Dante is provided both by the formal structure of the journey and also by the Thomistic structure of belief. Very rarely in the poems does Eliot make use of religious terminology, although anyone acquainted with devotional writing will recognize the background of such passages as that on the virtue of detachment ("Little Gidding," III) or the dark night of the soul ("East Coker," III), which is also a description of how things felt at the beginning of the war:

O dark dark. They all go into the dark,
The vacant interstellar spaces, the vacant
into the vacant. . . .
As, in a theatre,
The lights are extinguished, for the scene to
be changed
With a hollow rumble of wings, with a
movement of darkness on darkness,
And we know that the hills and the trees,
the distant panorama
And the bold imposing facade are all being
rolled away—

The autobiographical passage in which the poet encounters the shade of the dead master at the end of a night's fire-watching is written in a modified terza rima, and the shade is more like Dante's than anyone else's. Here surely Eliot is speaking directly in the ironic account of the gifts reserved for age. But the "I" of the poem is perhaps no more to be identified with the poet speaking in his own person than are the passages in the first person in *The Waste Land,* spoken through the lips of Tiresias. The speakers in the early dramatic monologues were often subjected to implicit satire. In "The Hollow Men" the "I" has become a "we"—for in the sheer pain of that poem the sense of personality has lapsed. Eliot's growing interest in the drama had been exercised on material very similar to that which is the basis of *Four Quartets.* Several rather severe warnings were in any case issued by Eliot against the personal interpretation of his writing. "Honest criticism and sensitive appreciation is directed not upon the poet but the poetry," he observed in "Tradition and the Individual Talent," and, a little later, "Poetry is not a turning loose of emotion but an escape from emotion; it is not the expression of personality but an escape from personality. But of course only those who have personality and emotions know what it is to want to escape from these things."

Yet *Four Quartets* remains a poem of inner experience. The house of Burnt Norton is empty and deserted, and only the vision of children seen in the garden suggests the possible existence of other human forms. In "East Coker" the ghosts of the village merrymakers are seen dancing in a field at midnight; in "The Dry Salvages" the fishermen setting and hauling, the travelers and the women

who have seen their sons or husbands
Setting forth, and not returning

are more substantial; and in the final movement appears Eliot's old enemy, the Fortune Teller, dealer in past and future. "Little Gidding" is filled with a sense of historic characters—Milton, Charles I, the Ferrars, Julian of Norwich, whose words are quoted. The "familiar compound ghost" who appears at the end of the air raid speaks only when the poet, "assuming a double part," hails him; his words are mordant, sympathetic, instructive;

the accent by no means unfamiliar; the effect at once of an echo and a messenger.

THE DRAMATIST

Eliot's interest in the drama long preceded his experiments in dramatic form, and so his early essays on dramatic theory can be applied only with some caution to the consideration of his plays. But we have Eliot's own word that he had from the first wished to write plays, as well as the fragmentary *Sweeney Agonistes* (1932) by way of witness.

The essays "Rhetoric and Poetic Drama," "Four Elizabethan Dramatists," and the "Dialogue on Dramatic Poetry," which are all reprinted in Eliot's *Selected Essays,* were written during the 1920's. In the first of these essays, which should be taken in conjunction with the essay on Ben Jonson, Eliot is concerned to defend rhetoric and the "artificial" style in drama. Jonson's rhetoric is "the careful precise filling in of a strong and simple outline, and at no point does it overflow the outline . . . there is a definite artistic emotion which demands expansion at that length." Characters are seen not in terms of individual roles, recalling figures of real life, but in "their combination into a whole. And these figures are not personifications of passions: separately, they have not even that reality, they are constituents." He might be describing the Tempters and the Knights of his first play, *Murder in the Cathedral,* or the uncles and aunts who form the chorus of *The Family Reunion.* Eliot sees Jonson as the follower of Christopher Marlowe, whose tragic "farce" he succeeds with "something falling under the category of burlesque or farce."

In the essay "Four Elizabethan Dramatists" Eliot defends convention and regrets only that the Elizabethans were not more consistent in their use of it. He praises the impersonal art of the ballet:

> The difference between a great dancer and a merely competent dancer is in the vital flame, that impersonal, and, if you like, inhuman force which transpires between each of the great dancer's movements. . . . No artist produces great art by a deliberate attempt to express his personality. He expresses his personality indirectly through concentrating upon a task which is a task in the same sense as the making of an efficient engine or the turning of a jug or a table-leg.

In "A Dialogue of Dramatic Poetry" Eliot again suggests that drama should approximate to the formality of the ballet, that verse drama is preferable to prose because "if we want to express the permanent and the universal we tend to express ourselves in verse. Poetry and drama are not separable elements in such a play. The most successful of Elizabethan dramatists are the most successful poets.

Eliot's own attempt to create a new drama began with the rhythms of the music hall. The jazz songs in *Sweeney Agonistes,* the simple caricatures who form the dramatis personae, and the lurid story of murder combine into a tragic farce.

The world of *Sweeney Agonistes* is rather like the world of Graham Greene's early novels or Harold Pinter's plays. The gangsters, toughs, prostitutes, and dumb businessmen are all pursued by hidden fear. This fear is suggested by the ominous pounding rhythms and the heavy repetitions and echoes. The movement is a very simple echoing chime of two or three voices. It starts:

> *Dusty.* How about Pereira?
> *Doris.* What about Pereira?
> I don't care.
> *Dusty.* You don't care!
> Who pays the rent?
> *Doris.* Yes he pays the rent
> *Dusty.* Well some men don't and some men do
> Some men don't and you know who
> *Doris.* You can have Pereira
> *Dusty.* What about Pereira?
> *Doris.* He's no gentleman, Pereira:
> You can't trust him!
> *Dusty.* Well that's true.

The sinister echoes are continued when Doris cuts the cards and draws the coffin (two of spades), and when Sweeney later breaks into the party with his story of the man who "did a girl in" and kept her body in a bath:

> Nobody came
> And nobody went
> But he took in the milk and he paid the rent.

The play ends with a nightmare chorus in a rapid triple rhythm: "When you're alone in the middle of the night and you wake in a sweat and a hell of a fright"; and a slow crescendo of knocks on the door, which presumably herald the arrival of the dangerous Pereira.[4]

This little fragment could never have been extended into a play of any length; the rhythm is too violent and the caricature too broad. But it is the first work to introduce Eliot's dramatic style—a very free, heavily stressed irregular verse, with emphatic rhymes and an almost unvaried accent of ominous foreboding. The piece is prefaced by the words of Orestes: "You don't see them, you don't—but I see them: they are hunting me down, I must move on.

Eliot has said that there is nothing more dramatic than a ghost, and all his plays have a potent flavor of the supernatural. His first piece of dramatic writing, a pageant called *The Rock,* was written for the Building Fund of London diocese. The choruses alone are reprinted in his *Collected Poems* and, while they are of interest as technical exercises, their chief significance is to show how wide the difference is between an adequate statement of Eliot's philosophical themes and his genuine poetry. These choruses are necessarily very much more simplified in rhythm and in language than his lyric poetry. They are designed to fulfill that social function of drama which he described in *The Use of Poetry and the Use of Criticism.* The whole work is built on the theme of religion and society. There are a few epigrammatic lines, satiric and admonitory:

> In the land of lobelias and tennis flannels
> The rabbit shall burrow and the thorn
> revisit,
> The nettle shall flourish on the gravel court,
> And the wind shall say: "Here were decent
> godless people:
> Their only monument the asphalt road
> And a thousand lost golf balls."

This is the world of "Coriolan," with the chorus of unemployed as background, the world of the slump and of the rise of the dictatorships in Europe. *The Rock* is frankly propaganda and has the merits and limits of propaganda. The seventh chorus, "In the beginning God created the world," contains in an early form some of the themes of *Four Quartets;* and the influence of biblical rhythms, especially those parts of the Bible that form part of the public services of the church, anticipates the use of these rhythms in the later plays.

Murder in the Cathedral, The Family Reunion, and *The Cocktail Party* (1950) form a closely related group; all retain something of the pageant, or the ballet, and are built on a contrast between the Hero and the Chorus, between the man who sees and the rest who are blind. Eliot is a dramatist in a very special and limited sense; but he recognized and used his limitations, so that his particular form of drama, though very restricted, is coherent, self-consistent, and extremely actable. Like the plays of Ben Jonson, these dramas are two-dimensional but not superficial. They are plays of the surface, but the implications go far below the surface. The characters exist only in relation to each other: they fit in with each other and are constituent parts, distorted to scale, of the main theme. The action is of the slightest. A single moment of choice, the Kierkegaardian choice, is set before the main character; the rest of the play leads up to and leads away from this moment. There are no subplots, minor interests, or digressions. The

4. An unpublished final scene was given at the Globe Theatre on 13 June 1965, in a program entitled "Homage to T.S. Eliot."

moment of choice is the same for all. There is often actual repetition from one of these plays to another. As Eliot observed in *Four Quartets*:

> You say I am repeating
> Something I have said before. I shall say it again.
> ("East Coker," III)

The main theme is the relation of "the moment in time" to "the moment out of time"—the moment of decision for Thomas of Canterbury, the moment of recognition for Harry Monchensey, the moment of blind choice for Celia. In all three plays the central character has literally to choose between life and death—their own deaths for Thomas and Celia. Harry, the hero of *The Family Reunion,* who is based on the Orestes figure that had haunted Eliot so long, makes the choice that kills his mother and goes forward to an unknown future. The choice lies between two kinds of action; the result is in each case a resolution of the dilemma. These plays are not tragedies; they are the kinds of plays that are written when the tragic experience—necessarily a temporary, though an inevitable, state for each individual—has been left behind. Eliot's tragedy, had he written one, would have belonged to the period of "The Hollow Men."

The plays reflect, then, in simplified but nonetheless genuine form, the same experience as *Four Quartets,* scored for brass rather than strings. *Murder in the Cathedral* is quite popular. *The Family Reunion,* which would appear to be too personal, too imperfectly projected (to contain, in short, the kind of difficulties Eliot attributed to *Hamlet*), does in fact act extremely well. *The Cocktail Party* is technically the most developed of the three; in this play, Eliot seems to have succeeded in finding the appropriate formula (the "objective correlative," to use his own phrase) for which he has been looking.

The assassination of Thomas à Becket is an important event in English history; the story of the *Oresteia* is one of the great myths common to Europe; the nervous breakdown, legacy of World War II, was for some years a determining factor of the social scene, a kind of modem equivalent of the Black Death. Eliot has firmly rooted his plays in these external grounds, but they are essentially plays of inner experience.

> . . . people to whom nothing has ever happened
> Cannot understand the unimportance of events
> (I.1)

says Harry in *The Family Reunion,* and the Fourth Tempter describes to Thomas a time when

> men will not hate you
> Enough to defame or to execrate you,
> But pondering the qualities that you lacked
> Will only try to find the historical fact.
> (I)

The choice made by Thomas is not "for the lifetime of one man only." It is seen as part of the pattern of timeless moments: seen as such for a moment only, for as Thomas says (echoing a line from "Burnt Norton"): "Human kind cannot bear very much reality." But in the light of such moments the common man lives out his life.

In *Murder in the Cathedral,* there are three levels of character: Thomas, who speaks with the full consciousness of the Hero; the Tempters; and the Chorus of the poor women of Canterbury, who sense the "supernatural evil" that is descending upon the place but who try to live out their humble lives as unobtrusively as possible:

> We do not wish anything to happen.
> Seven years we have lived quietly,
> Succeeded in avoiding notice,
> Living and partly living.
> (I)

As the "small folk who live among small things" they are rather unwillingly faithful, compelled to wait and bear witness, conscious at the end of the guilt of their weakness:

> Forgive us, O Lord, we acknowledge
> ourselves as type of the common man,
> Of the men and women who shut the door
> and sit by the fire. . . .
> (II)

Thomas knows that in returning he is choosing his death, and in the scene with the Four Tempters he makes his decision to stay. He rejects the bribes of power—even the spiritual power offered by the choice of martyrdom that the Fourth Tempter proffers:

> The last temptation is the greatest treason:
> To do the right deed for the wrong reason.
> (I)

The figures of the Tempters are paralleled by the Four Knights, who, after they have murdered Thomas, come forward with good watertight explanations of the necessity and high-mindedness of the act. They, like the Tempters, are given a modern colloquial idiom, and they speak in the phrases of the modern politician. They come from the land of lobelias and tennis flannels as well as from Aquitaine, and the ingenuity of the final plea—that Thomas was deliberately courting death and was therefore really responsible for what happened ("I think, with these facts before you, you will unhesitatingly render a verdict of Suicide while of Unsound Mind")—does not even sound particularly farfetched in the light of totalitarian practices.

Satire, epigram, and social caricature alternate with the poetic choruses in which the sense of supernatural evil is given in verse of a free and irregular sort, based on the biblical rhythms, dropping sometimes into biblical phrases, at other times colloquial, and always highly repetitive. The ritualistic quality of the speech, the stylized characters, and the very limited action contrast sharply with the complex language (the play has long passages in prose, including a sermon from the Archbishop). The sardonic note suggested in the title (which might be that of a detective story) is maintained to the last in the treatment of the Knights, who may be reminiscent in some ways of the comic devils of morality plays but are in others rather like a music-hall turn. In one production, one of the Tempters carried a golf club, with which he made practice shots in the intervals of his speech.

The Family Reunion does not employ Christian terminology, nor does *The Cocktail Party.* This certainly does not mean that they are allegories and that as one reviewer of the latter play remarked, "We see that the doctor *is* a priest, that his patients *are* the church. . . ." The use of a modem secular setting enables Eliot to relate his material more exactly and closely; the satire is less superficial, the integration more complete. In *The Cocktail Party* there is a very noticeable return to the rhythms of *Sweeney Agonistes*:

> *Julia.* But how did he come here?
> *Edward.* *I* don't know.
> *Julia.* *You* don't know! And what's his name?
> Did I hear him say his name was Riley?
> *Edward.* I don't know his name.
> *Julia.* You don't know his *name*?
> *Edward.* I tell you I've no idea who he is
> Or how he got here.
> (I.1)

The bright conversation that opens this play might sound as if it were being merely too faithful to the banalities of social chatter were it not for this extremely ominous rhythm, which sounds its echoing chime all round the circle of the symmetrically grouped characters. In *The Family Reunion,* there is a chorus of four uncles and aunts who are used for similar purpose; they are stupid people, who do not understand what is wrong with Harry, and who are torn reluctantly away from their clubs and vicarage tea parties to participate in the drama of the Eumenides.

The hero of *The Family Reunion* is haunted by a crime, and he dwells in a shadowy and terrifying world until he returns to his home. Here the guilt is lifted from him by the revelation of the past—not his own past but that of his father and mother. His father's desire to murder his mother has been projected into a belief that he himself had murdered his wife:

> *Harry.* Perhaps my life has only been a dream
> Dreamt through me by the minds of others.
> Perhaps
> I only dreamt I pushed her.
> *Agatha.* So I had supposed. What of it?
> What we have written is not a story of detection,
> Of crime and punishment, but of sin and expiation
> It is possible.
> You are the consciousness of your unhappy family,
> Its bird sent flying through the purgatorial flame. . . .
> (II.2)

The suffering of Harry, and in a lesser degree of Mary, the woman who had loved him but had not been noticed ("It's just ordinary hopelessness"), and Agatha, who had loved and renounced his father, form the core of the play. Here the play is closest to the lyric poems, and sometimes more moving in its simplicity. The social setting and the blind dominating figure of the mother are there to contrast with this core of suffering. They are not related to it. Thus the play moves on two levels—the social and the supernatural—like the two worlds of *The Waste Land.*

In *The Cocktail Party* the two worlds are more closely related. It begins with an unsuccessful party and ends with a successful one. In the interval the trivialities of social exchange have all been explored and their implications fully brought to light. The four main characters have reached three different solutions: the solution of work and social success; the solution of accepting the limits of "the human condition" and maintaining the common routine, learning to avoid excessive expectation; and the other solution of a difficult vocation and a violent death.

The minor characters, who had at first seemed so tiresome—the interfering old woman, the helpful man of the world—turn out to be in benevolent league with the doctor who effects the cures, and all work together for good.

In a sense these plays are not at all realistic. It has been said that Agatha would not be likely to be elected the principal of a women's college, but I do not think anyone who was would fit in very comfortably to *The Family Reunion.* It has been said that Celia would not be sent straight out to a difficult country by any religious order, but her sudden exit and her violent death are not to be read on the level of "historical fact." There are on the other hand some scenes of quite excruciating realism, such as the quarrel between Lavinia and Edward, a full-length study of the scene suggested in *The Waste Land,* II. But this is a scene that has internal significance; it is not a mere event. There is a good deal of mordant humor that is sometimes taken amiss by inattentive readers—a tone of mock dignity and assumed gravity, which Sir Henry Harcourt-Reilly shares with Agatha and the First Priest of *Murder in the Cathedral.* It is a tone that belongs to Eliot himself:

> *Julia.* Oh, Henry!
> Lavinia is much more observant than you think.
> I believe that she has forced you to a show-down.
> *Reilly.* You state the position correctly, Julia.
> (II)

The epigrammatic comments recall the earliest poems. The central scene, that in which Celia states her case and makes her choice, belongs to a different mode. But this scene reflects back on her earlier scene with Edward, her lover. In this play the past is altered by the present, and a technique of retrospective illumination enables even the frivolities of the opening lines to be recalled quite naturally at the close.

After *The Cocktail Party,* Eliot's main dramatic impulse spent itself, although in the following decade *The Confidential Clerk*

(1954), *The Elder Statesman* (1959), and two lectures, *Poetry and Drama* (1951) and *The Three Voices of Poetry* (1953), extended his theory and practice of drama. The first lecture treats of the nature of dramatic writing, and of the relation between author and audience. Eliot thinks that "the chief effect of style and rhythm in dramatic speech, whether in prose or verse, should be unconscious"; therefore there should be no disturbing transitions from one to the other:

> We should aim at a form of verse in which everything can be said that has to be said. . . . But if our verse is to have so wide a range that it can say anything that has to be said, it follows that it will not be "poetry" all the time. It will only be "poetry" when the dramatic situation has reached such a point of intensity that poetry becomes the natural utterance, because then it is the only language in which the emotions can be expressed at all.

In the second part of the lecture, Eliot describes his own experiments, the search for a form that would establish communications between the three collaborators in dramatic art—authors, actors, and audience: "In the theatre, the problem of communication presents itself immediately. . . . You are aiming to write lines which will have an immediate effect upon an unknown and unprepared audience, to be interpreted to that audience by unknown actors, rehearsed by an unknown producer." Eliot makes it clear that he is not satisfied with any of his own experiments and critically examines their shortcomings. Yet he captured an audience not confined to poetry readers: both *The Cocktail Party* and *The Confidential Clerk* succeeded in the West End and on Broadway. In *The Three Voices of Poetry,* Eliot notes the slight shock thereby produced among those of his admirers who prefer to be among the sweet, selected few: "It may be that from the beginning I aspired unconsciously to the theatre or as the critics might say, with more asperity, to Shaftesbury Avenue."

The three voices of poetry, as distinguished by Eliot, are that of the poet talking to himself; that of the poet talking to an audience; and that of the poet speaking through another character—or meditative, rhetorical, and dramatic poetry. The comparative simplicity and directness of vocabulary, syntax, and content that he demands for the third voice are certainly exemplified in his own work. The story of *The Confidential Clerk* may be based on the *Ion,* but at a London theater I have sat behind what appeared to be the mothers' meeting of some suburban church and heard them commend act III as being "almost like a whodunit." Eliot would probably have approved. The central theme of the drama, which seems to be a search for identity, the hero's need to establish a true self, is clothed in a fantastic tale of mistaken identity involving three babies (one of them, like Betsy Trotwood Copperfield, not being forthcoming), designed to appeal to simple tastes. The moments of poetry in this play are very few; for the most part it is merely verse. Eliot sacrificed the finer qualities of his writing to the needs of communication. One moment of poetry occurs when the hero and his supposed father approach each other through their common experience as frustrated artists; another is that in which the hero and a young woman are led by the power of music to that enkindled sympathy in which mind begins to play in and out of mind. But the moment of inspiration and the moment of love are alike renounced at the end of the play, in a scene where all the characters get their wishes, only to find that the fulfillment of a wish, since choice means elimination, involves a kind of death as well as a rebirth. The Cumaean Sybil from Teddington who effects this is the hero's long-lost mother: but she has deliberately forfeited her claim to him, and he in turn now renounces all relationships:

> Let my mother rest in peace. As for a
> father—
> have the idea of a father.
> It's only just come to me. I should like a
> father
> Whom I had never known and couldn't
> know now,

> Because he would have died before I was
> born
> Or before I could remember; whom I could
> get to know
> Only by reports, by documents. . . .

Perhaps some light is cast upon this Father when the former confidential clerk says to the hero, whom he has taken under his protection and who replaces his own dead son, "You'll be thinking of reading for orders"; for Colby, like Celia, has awakened to his vocation.

Perhaps also it is not a coincidence that there are echoes of the two climaxes of this play in *The Three Voices of Poetry*—especially in view of Eliot's determination to say in that lecture something he had *not* said before. Sir Claude describes the "secret moment" of the artist:

> That state of utter exhaustion and peace
> Which comes in dying to give something
> life. . . .

and in the lecture Eliot describes the satisfactory imposition of form upon the psychic material that has struggled to find it, in terms significantly new: "a moment of utter exhaustion, of appeasement, of absolution and of something very near annihilation which is in itself indescribable." Yet a poem is handed over to the unknown audience to shape and reform for themselves, and this "seems to me the consummation of the process begun in solitude without thought of the audience, the long process of gestation of the poem, because it marks the final separation of the poem from the author. Let the author rest in peace."

If a classical model is to be found for *The Elder Statesman, Oedipus at Colonus* would serve. Hiding private failure behind public success, the hero learns to live with his ghosts—himself little more than a ghost. Cherished by his Antigone, rejected by his son, he dies under a beech tree, having exorcised the shadows of moral turpitude—inward fears, though outwardly represented by two figures from his past.

This work stands to ordinary plays rather as oratorio to opera: it lacks the dimension of outward action. The language has that sententious finality usually associated with a chorus. Exploration of the connection between private and public worlds may justify the dramatic form: the only concession to a popular audience is a variation on the comic landlady. This is an attempt to transpose themes from poetry of the first voice into poetry of the third voice. As a perceptive critic observed, it is more effective when read than when acted; a personal note of confession and of valediction is heard in the last lines:

> Age and decrepitude can have no terrors for
> me,
> Loss and vicissitude cannot appal me,
> Not even death can dismay or amaze me,
> Fixed in the certainty of love unchanging.

Since the late 1950's, a revival of drama has paradoxically produced the most vigorous writing of the period by exploiting the physical conditions of the living theater, using flat writing as part of a collaborative production. However far removed from Eliot, Samuel Beckett, Edward Albee, Harold Pinter, and their contemporaries are exploring possibilities that he as a critic was the first to point out. In *The Birthday Party,* Pinter by the very title resembles Eliot; this comedy of menace, in which the hero is kidnapped by a pair of diabolic guardians, seems like a shadow-image of Eliot's play of redemption. But unlike Eliot's work, it has little validity on the written page and exists for production.

THE CRITIC AND MAN OF LETTERS

Had he not become the most famous poet of his time, Eliot would have been known as its most distinguished critic. This statement must be qualified by adding that it is really impossible to distinguish the poet and the critic; for his criticism springs from his poetic sensibility, and his poetry is best explained in terms of his criticism. Among English critics the most memorable are those who have also been creative artists—Philip Sidney, Ben Jonson, John Dryden, Samuel Johnson, Samuel Taylor Coleridge, and Matthew Arnold. Indeed Eliot once ventured upon the statement that he thought "the *only* critics worth reading [were] the critics who practised and practised well, the art of which they wrote." This extreme view he does not attempt seriously to sustain; but his definition of the function of criticism, as of the perfect critic, assumes that "the two directions of sensibility are complementary; and as sensibility is rare, unpopular and desirable, it is to be expected that the critic and the creative artist should frequently be the same person" ("The Perfect Critic").

Eliot's conception of the true critic is that he should be impersonal, instructed, and without either the unfulfilled creative impulses that make some criticism an imperfect form of creation or the desire to use literature as a substitute for other things, for example, religion. The first type of "imperfect critic" is exhibited by Eliot in the person of Arthur Symons: "the reading sometimes fecundates his emotions to produce something new which is not criticism, but is not the expulsion, the ejection, the birth of creativeness." The second type of "imperfect critic" is discerned in Matthew Arnold: "The total effect of Arnold's philosophy is to set up Culture in the place of Religion and to leave Religion to be laid waste by the anarchy of feeling."

The task of the critic is defined in the words of Rémy de Gourmont: "Ériger en lois ses impressions personelles, c'est le grand effort d'un homme s'il est sincère" (To build a code of law from personal experience is the supreme objective of the clear-sighted man). Taking for granted that the critic is a man of natural sensibility, the impressions of his reading will "tend to become articulate in a generalized statement of literary beauty" since "perceptions do not, in a really appreciative mind, accumulate as a mass, but form themselves into a structure; and criticism is the statement in language of this structure: it is a development of sensibility."

The work of a good critic will therefore appear cold and impersonal to the reader in search of a stimulus; for it is not the business of the critic to stimulate, but to put the reader in possession of the necessary facts—not, of course, simply external facts, but the presentation of the work of art itself, by commentary or reading, which is one of the subtlest forms of interpretation: "But in matters of great importance the critic must not coerce and he must not make judgements of better and worse. He must simply elucidate; the reader will form the correct judgement for himself."

In "Tradition and the Individual Talent," the process of poetic creation itself is described as "a continual self-sacrifice, a continual extinction of personality," and the poet is compared with a catalytic agent, whose part in a chemical reaction is simply to induce the reaction and not to participate. Later, as we have seen, this moment of creation was redefined.

It follows that the emotional critic is almost necessarily a bad critic; and while scholars or dealers in facts cannot corrupt, "the real corruptors are those who supply opinion or fancy; and Goethe and Coleridge are not guiltless—for what is Coleridge's *Hamlet*: is it an honest inquiry as far as the data permit, or is it an attempt to present Coleridge in an attractive costume?"

Reserve, self-suppression, and the search for structural principles by submission to experience are not only the virtues of the critic, they are the most striking features of Eliot's early poetry. His method of juxtaposing two scenes, or two worlds, and leaving them to make their comment on each other, his reliance on implication and what he himself called the contrapuntal method has been described earlier: it is the exact equivalent of his advocacy of the Socratic, or maieutic method, in criticism. The ironic concentration of his poetic style is likewise paralleled by the terse, epigrammatic, and almost equally concentrated style of his prose. He himself described it in an ironic little poem:

> How unpleasant to meet Mr Eliot!
> With his features of clerical cut,
> And his brow so grim,

And his mouth so prim,
And his conversation, so nicely
Restricted to What Precisely
And If and Perhaps and But.
("Lines for Cuscuscaraway . . .")

Eliot's style is indeed stripped and neutral, though not without powerful resources of tone and inflection. It works much in terms of negatives, qualifications, and restrictions:

> It is not so easy to see propriety in an image which divests a snake of *winter weeds*. . . .
> ("John Dryden," *Selected Essays*)

> We are baffled by the attempt to translate the quality indicated by the dim and antiquated term wit, into the equally unsatisfactory nomenclature of our own times. . . .
> ("Andrew Marvell," *Selected Essays*)

Precisely this lack of a general critical terminology was responsible for much of his nervous stiffness and defensive irony, and the "pontifical" tone for which Eliot was later to apologize. Like the poet, the critic of the early 1920's found himself in a wasteland and had little on which he could rely in the way of equipment. Eliot was indebted principally to the French critics of the late nineteenth and early twentieth centuries, and perhaps also to the critical prefaces of Henry James. He was engaged upon an exploration of the principles of criticism as well as an examination in detail of the work of those poets to whom he as a poet was most particularly indebted. His general theory of literature is set forth in "The Perfect Critic," "Imperfect Critics," "Tradition and the Individual Talent," and "The Function of Criticism." The first three appeared in *The Sacred Wood* (1920) and the last in *Selected Essays* (1932). These brief works exercised an influence out of all proportion to their scale; and the Cambridge school of criticism, as it has come to be called (without perhaps very much justification), is based largely on the early critical writings of T. S. Eliot and of I. A. Richards, which also form the basis of the "new criticism" in America.

Eliot's work on individual writers was even more influential in redirecting the taste of the day. Based on his experience as a poet, he attempted to "reopen old communications" and "to bring back the poet to life—the great, the perennial task of criticism." In a definition of the twofold function of criticism he remarked that there are two theoretical limits of criticism, at one of which we attempt to answer the question "What is poetry?" and at the other, "Is this a good poem?" He goes on: "No theoretical ingenuity will suffice to answer the second question because no theory can amount to much which is not founded upon a direct experience of good poetry; but on the other hand our direct experience of poetry involves a good deal of generalizing activity" (*The Use of Poetry and the Use of Criticism*, p. 16).

In Eliot's writings on individual poets, the precise quality of their work is shown by carefully placed and exactly chosen quotation. The quotations are made to do the critic's work, and the reader is made to work on them. They are more than happy quotations in the usual sense: frequently they constitute the critic's main statement. In this way they recall the use of quotation in Eliot's poetry. The reader is obliged to work over these particular lines, to respond actively to them, to relate them to all his past experience of the writer under discussion. Hence the strength with which Eliot's quotations stamp themselves on the mind of the reader and the frequency with which they pass into general circulation.

His earliest critical essays, *The Sacred Wood* and *Homage to John Dryden* (1924), contain, besides the essays on general subjects, the studies of Ben Jonson, Christopher Marlowe, and Philip Massinger, the metaphysical poets, Andrew Marvell, and John Dryden. In these, Eliot set the fashion for a whole decade. The complex, ironic, and skeptical poetry of Donne and of Marvell was very much to the taste of the age; while the poetry of rhetorical writers, who maintained a surface approach but implied the depths they did not directly explore, was almost equally suited to a generation that avoided all fundamental questions, denied the validity of metaphysics, and found refuge in a bright and brittle disillusionment. The Elizabethan poets and the metaphysical poets—Donne, Herbert, Herbert of Cherbury, Marvell, and the rest—were of course among the strongest shaping influences on Eliot's own poetry. His revaluation of their work indicates what he learned from them; the famous passage about "wit" in the essay on Andrew Marvell might have been written of his own verse:

> Wit is not erudition; it is sometimes stifled by erudition, as in much of Milton. It is not cynicism, though it has a kind of toughness which may be confused with cynicism by the tender-minded. It is confused with erudition because it belongs to an educated mind, rich in generations of experience; and it is confused with cynicism because it implies a constant inspection and criticism of experience. It involves, probably, a recognition, implicit in the expression of every experience, of other kinds of experience which are possible.

The contrasts with poetry of the nineteenth century, such as William Morris' *Song of Hylas,* or that between Dryden and Milton, served not only to define the quality of the poets from whom Eliot learned so much but also to define those qualities of which he disapproved. His attitude toward Milton has become notorious; in a lecture given before the British Academy in 1947, Eliot achieved a delicate and diplomatic recantation on the grounds that while Milton was a bad influence in the 1920's, when the need was for flexibility, variety, and experiment, he had now ceased to be a bad influence for young practitioners, who were rather in need of restraint:

> It was one of our tenets that verse should have the virtues of prose, that diction should become assimilated to cultivated contemporary speech, before aspiring to the elevation of poetry. Another tenet was that the subject-matter and the imagery of poetry should be extended to topics and objects related to the life of a modern man or woman: that we were to seek the non-poetic, to seek even material refractory to transmutation into poetry, and words and phrases which had not been used in poetry before. And the study of Milton could be of no help: it was only a hindrance.
>
> We cannot in literature, any more than in the rest of life, live in a perpetual state of revolution. . . . Poetry should help, not only to refine the language of the time, but to prevent it from changing too rapidly: a development of language at too great a speed would be a development in the sense of a progressive deterioration, and that is our danger to-day.

It cannot be denied that when Eliot uttered these words, the attitude of the aged and distinguished academicians who formed the audience was rather reminiscent of the Inquisition listening to the recantation of a dangerous and influential heretic. One of them even cried out (although the whole performance was being broadcast), "A little louder, please!" But Eliot never recanted on the subject of the nineteenth-century poets. It is true that he edited an anthology of Kipling, with an introduction in which he paid tribute to Kipling's technical powers. But Matthew Arnold and the Pre-Raphaelites remain unreprieved.

One or two of Eliot's critical phrases have attained a popularity that, he says, was "astonishing to their author." The "dissociation of sensibility" he described as setting in with Milton and Dryden is one of them. In the later seventeenth century, the peculiar unification of thought and feeling he discerned in Donne and Marvell was broken up:

> A thought to Donne was an experience: it modified his sensibility. When a poet's mind is perfectly equipped for its work, it is constantly amalgamating disparate experience: the ordinary man's experience is chaotic, irregular, fragmentary. The latter falls in love, or reads Spinoza, and these two experiences have nothing to do with each other, or with the noise of the typewriter or the smell of cooking; in the mind of the poet these experiences are always forming new wholes.

It is the forming of new wholes, the *relating* of experience, that Eliot learned from the Elizabethans and from the metaphysicals, and this was what he particularly valued in their work. His account of the poetic experience is clearly based on the great definition by Coleridge of the Poetic Imagination from the fourteenth chapter of *Biographia Literaria.* Eliot quotes this passage in his essay on Marvell. The poet who is least represented in this phase of Eliot's criticism is Shakespeare himself. The essay on *Hamlet* is a document more revealing of Eliot's own difficulties than of Shakespeare's: it might stand, for instance, in part at least, as a commentary on *Sweeney Agonistes.*

During the later 1920's Eliot published a number of essays, but the little monograph on Dante (1929) marks the next phase in his critical development. It coincides with the change in his poetic style already described. At this time he also wrote an essay comparing Dante and Donne, to the great advantage of the former. The poetry of Dante remained the greatest single discernible influence in the writing of Eliot, and his interest in medieval literature, like his earlier interest in the seventeenth century, promoted a general taste for the period. Later contributions took the more informal mode of public lectures, in one of which, *The Frontiers of Criticism* (1956), he summed up the merits and defects of his own earlier "work-shop criticism." In his last work, a study of George Herbert, Eliot took a point of view opposite to that of "Tradition and the Individual Talent," for he saw Herbert's poetry as a personal record," and, some may feel, a record with a certain likeness to Eliot's own.

CONCLUSION

Eliot's death on 4 January 1965 seemed to come as the end of the long farewell that gave to his last play its deeply personal poignancy: "He has gone too far to return to us." In his line of traditional and civilized poetry, he has left no successor. His unique position of authority, comparable only with that of Samuel Johnson, derived from a variety of causes. In the first place, the particular consistency and coherence of his writing made it a structural whole; indeed in his later work, the interest of its place in the whole sometimes predominated over the effect of the particular part. The risk of overdetermination has not always been avoided, although a constant development of theme can also be followed, the early themes of the City and the Garden giving way to those of identity and relationship, communication and solitude.

The range of Eliot's output and literary concerns also conferred authority; during the decade and a half that he edited the *Criterion,* this quarterly journal was one of the most influential literary publications of its time, and in its editorials appeared some of Eliot's best occasional writing, trenchant and invigorating. The publishing firm of which he was a director, Faber and Faber, specialized in poetry, and the work of many younger poets appeared under its imprint.

But Eliot did not enjoy the atmosphere of academies, literary societies, or intellectual good causes, and some of his tastes were even unliterary. He published an extremely lively book of comic verse about cats, written originally for children, but designed to appeal to all who appreciate the naturally lawless behavior, intellectual superiority, and strong business instincts of cats. "Old Possum"—Pound's nickname for Eliot—remained an elusive jester, whose taste for practical jokes was known in private, but whose peculiar (and rather American) brand of irony was liable to be misunderstood in public. The Broadway success of *Cats* would have invited Eliot's satiric wit.

The title of one book describes him as *The Invisible Poet.* In the last few years, when his health became precarious, Eliot tended to withdraw more and more from the literary scene; yet at the same time, relaxing the impersonality of his earlier position, he gradually conceded some elements of an intellectual autobiography. His mischievous confession, that the notes to *The Waste Land* were originally supplied to fill out the bulk of a slender volume, was perhaps a half-truth combining ironic self-deflation with mockery of his more pedantic followers. But publication of his forty-eight-year-old Harvard thesis, *Knowledge and Experience in the Philosophy of F. H. Bradley,* as a "curiosity of biographical interest" provided a new and much more extended commentary on the poem. As philosophy, the work of the man whom Bertrand Russell described as "my best pupil at Harvard" shows little trace of Russell's influence; it is written in terminology that philosophers no longer employ and that Eliot confessed in 1964 he was no longer able to think in—"Indeed, I do not pretend to understand it." Originally composed only because "Harvard had made it possible for me to go to Oxford for a year; this return at least I owed to Harvard," its sustained argument confirms that the cryptic style of Eliot's other early prose was assumed for a purpose. Parts of the conclusion reveal something of the poet behind the philosopher; this constitutes its interest:

> If you will find the mechanical anywhere, you will find it in the workings of mind; and to inspect living mind, you must look nowhere but in the world outside. (p. 154)

> Our first step is to discover what experience is not, and why it is essentially indefinable. (p. 157)

> The world, as we have seen, exists only as it is found in . . . experiences so mad and strange that they will be boiled away before you boil them down to one heterogeneous mass. (p. 168)

In 1968, the long-lost first draft of *The Waste Land* came to light in New York, and proved, as was known, much longer than the final version. The drowned sailor began as a fisherman from the coasts of Eliot's boyhood, lost in the northern ice; other passages suggest *Sweeney Agonistes* in their tone of ironic jest. Pound's advice to cut the work seems to have made it more consistent and more powerful, as well as more classical. It is clear also from Martin Browne's account of collaboration with Eliot that even at the end of his career he was ready to take advice from his friends, for the plays were many times redrafted and their significance altered.

Now that his achievement is completed, those who have lived with Eliot's work, and felt it changing and growing while remaining a unity, can absorb its final form. The power to grow and change will remain with it, however, as it develops within the minds of its readers, at those deeper levels where "words, after speech, reach / Into the silence."

On the red stone that commemorates Eliot at East Coker, where he lies buried, are carved only the words "Remember Thomas Stearns Eliot, Poet," the dates of birth and death, and the two phrases "In my beginning is my end" and "In my end is my beginning."

Selected Bibliography

BIBLIOGRAPHY

Gallup, D., *T. S. Eliot: A Bibliography,* (London, 1925; rev. ed., 1969), a complete and accurate record, including contributions to periodicals and translations into foreign languages; Martin, M., *A Half Century of Eliot Criticism: An Annotated Bibliography of Books and Articles in English, 1916–1965,* (Lewisburg, Pa., 1972); M. Frank, H. P. Frank, and K. P. S. Joachum, eds., *A Supplementary Bibliography to Mildred Martin,* (Edmonton, 1978).

COLLECTED WORKS

Ara Vos Prec, (London, 1920), lim. ed., includes contents of *Prufrock, Poems,* and additional poems including "Gerontion"; *Poems 1909–1925,* (London, 1925), includes contents of *Ara Vos Prec, The Waste Land,* and "The Hollow Men"; *Collected Poems 1909–1935,* (London, 1936), includes the contents of *Poems 1909–1925,* together with *Ash-Wednesday, Ariel Poems,* "Unfinished Poems," "Minor Poems," Choruses from *The Rock,* and "Burnt Norton"; *The Complete Poems and Plays,* (New York, 1952); *Collected Plays,* (London, 1962); *Collected Poems 1909–1962,* (London, 1963); *Complete Poems and Plays,* (London, 1969).

SELECTED WORKS

Selected Essays 1917–1932, (London, 1932), enl. ed. (London, 1951), omitting dates from title, contains essays from *The Sacred Wood, For Lancelot Andrewes,* and other sources; *Essays Ancient and Modern,* (London, 1936), supersedes *For Lancelot Andrewes,* omitting some essays Eliot did not wish to preserve, and incorporates additional ones including prefaces to Pascal's *Pensées* and Tennyson's *In Memoriam; The Waste Land and Other Poems,* (London, 1940), selections from *Collected Poems 1909–1935; Later Poems 1925–1935,* (London, 1941), selections from *Collected Poems 1909–1935;* J. Hayward, ed., *Selected Prose,* (London, 1953; pprbk. repr., 1963); *On Poetry and Poets,* (London, 1957), contains essays, lectures, and addresses from various sources written and separately printed with one exception after 1932; *Selected Poems,* (London, 1961); *To Criticize the Critic,* (London, 1965) lectures and essays from various periods collected by Eliot but published posthumously; *Poems Written in Early Youth,* (London, 1967), reiss. of ed. collected by J. Hayward and privately printed (1950) under supervision of Eliot; F. Kermode, ed., *Selected Prose,* (London, 1975).

SEPARATE WORKS

Prufrock and Other Observations, (London, 1917), verse; *Ezra Pound: His Metric and Poetry,* (New York, 1917), criticism, pub. anonymously; *Poems,* (Richmond, Surrey, 1919), hand-printed by Leonard and Virginia Woolf at the original Hogarth Press; *The Sacred Wood: Essays on Poetry and Criticism,* (London, 1920), contains essays and reviews originally contributed to the *Times Literary Supplement,* the *Athenaeum,* the *Egoist* (of which Eliot was assistant ed., 1917–1919); *The Waste Land,* (New York, 1922), verse, first printed in first no. of the *Criterion,* (October 1922); first English ed. (Richmond, Surry, 1923), hand-printed by Leonard and Virginia Woolf (lim. ed., London (1962); first French ed., *Poemes 1910–1930,* P. Leyris, trans. (Paris, 1947), contains additional notes by J. Hayward, facs. and transcript of original drafts including annotations of Ezra Pound, ed. by V. Eliot, original MSS, in the Berg collection of the New York Public Library, obtained in 1968 as part of the collection of John Quinn, to whom Eliot sent it in 1922; *Homage to John Dryden: Three Essays on Poetry of the Seventeenth Century,* (London, 1924), contains "John Dryden," "The Metaphysical Poets," and "Andrew Marvell"; *Journey of the Magi,* (London, 1927), no. 8 of publisher's series of *Ariel Poems* (single poems issued as pamphlets), subsequently including "A Song for Simeon," no. 16 (1928), "Animula," no. 23 (1929), "Marina," no. 29 (1930), "Triumphal March," no. 35 (1931), "The Cultivation of Christmas Trees," new series (1954); *For Lancelot Andrewes: Essays on Style and Order,* (London, 1928), criticism, permanently out of print, see *Essays Ancient and Modern* above; *Dante,* (London, 1929), criticism.

Ash-Wednesday, (London, 1930), verse, signed lim. ed. of 600 copies pub. simultaneously in New York and London preceded regular ed. by five days; *Anabasis: A Poem by St. J. Perse with a Translation by T. S. Eliot,* (London, 1930; rev. eds., New York, 1938, 1949); *Thoughts After Lambeth,* (London, 1931), pamphlet containing observations on ecclesiastical policy discussed at Lambeth Conference; *John Dryden: The Poet, the Dramatist, the Critic,* (New York, 1932), criticism; *Sweeney Agonistes; Fragments of an Aristophanic Melodrama,* (London, 1932), poetic drama; *The Use of Poetry and the Use of Criticism: Studies in the Relation of Criticism to Poetry in England,* (London, 1933), essays originally delivered as lectures during Eliot's tenure as Charles Eliot Norton Professor of Poetry, 1932–1933, at Harvard; *After Strange Gods: A Primer of Modern Heresy,* (London, 1934), Page-Barbour Lectures delivered at the University of Virginia, 1933; *The Rock: A Pageant Play,* (London, 1934), verse libretto, "Written for Performance at Sadler's Wells Theatre May 28–June 9, 1934, on behalf of the Forty-Five Churches Fund of the Diocese of London"; *Elizabethan Essays,* (London, 1934), collected essays on Elizabethan and Jacobean drama, all previously published except essay on John Marston, later added to *Selected Essays,* (London, 1951); *Murder in the Cathedral,* (London, 1935; rev. eds., 1936, 1937, 1938), poetic drama, film script (London, 1951), contains considerable additions, ed. with notes and intro. by N. Coghill (London, 1965); *The Family Reunion,* (London, 1939), poetic drama; *Old Possum's Book of Practical Cats,* (London, 1939), verse biographies of fanciful cats written for children and published under pseudonym coined by Ezra Pound; *The Idea of Christian Society,* (London, 1939), sociology.

The Music of Poetry, (London, 1942), 3rd W. P. Ker Memorial Lecture delivered at the University of Glasgow, February 24, 1942; *The Classics and the Man of Letters,* (London, 1942), presidential address delivered to the Classical Association, April 15, 1942; *Reunion by Destruction,* (London, 1943), "Reflections on a Scheme for Church Union in South India, addressed to the Laity"; *Four Quartets,* (New York, 1943; London, 1944; lim. ed., 1961) each Quartet previously published separately: "Burnt Norton," in *Collected Poems 1909–1935,* "East Coker," (London, 1940), "The Dry Salvages," (London, 1941), "Little Gidding," (London, 1942), French version, *Quatre Quattuors,* P. Leyris, trans. (Paris, 1950), contains notes by J. Hayward; *What Is a Classic?* (London, 1945), address delivered to the Vergil Society, October 16, 1944; *Milton,* (London, 1947), Master Mind Lecture for 1947 delivered to the British Academy; *Notes Towards the Definition of Culture,* (London, 1948), sociology.

The Cocktail Party, (London, 1950; pprbk. repr., 1958), poetic drama; *Poetry and Drama,* (Cambridge, Mass.,

1951), 1st Theodore Spencer Memorial Lecture, delivered at Harvard, November 21, 1950; *An Address to Members of the London Library,* (London, 1952), presidential address, lim. to 500 copies; *American Literature and the American Language,* (St. Louis, 1953), centenary address at Washington University; *The Three Voices of Poetry,* (London, 1953), 11th annual lecture of the National Book League; *The Confidential Clerk,* (London, 1954; 2nd ed., 1967), poetic drama; *Goethe as Sage,* (Hamburg, 1955), German and English text of lecture delivered at Hamburg on receiving the Hanseatic Goethe Prize, 1954; *The Frontiers of Criticism,* (Minneapolis, 1956), Gidea-Seymour Memorial Lecture at the University of Minnesota, 1956; *Essays on Elizabethan Drama,* (New York, 1956), new selection of essays on Elizabethan and Jacobean drama; *The Elder Statesman,* (London, 1959), poetic drama; *George Herbert,* (London, 1962), essay; *Knowledge and Experience in the Philosophy of F. H. Bradley,* (London, 1964), dissertation completed in 1916, published "only as a curiosity of biographical interest"; V. Eliot, ed., *The Waste Land A Facsimile and Transcript,* (London, 1971).

Note: Eliot made contributions of prose and verse to over a hundred books or pamphlets by other writers; his contributions in prose or verse to periodicals (including numerous book reviews, broadcast lectures, and the "commentaries" written for the *Criterion* during his editorship, 1922–1939) number close to six hundred. The majority of these contributions have not been reprinted or collected. In addition, Eliot edited and introduced Ezra Pound's, *Selected Poems,* (London, 1928), Marianne Moore's, *Selected Poems,* (London, 1935), *A Choice of Kipling's Verse,* (London, 1941), *A Selection of Joyce's Prose,* (London, 1942), and *Ezra Pound's Literary Essays,* (London, 1953).

BIOGRAPHICAL AND CRITICAL STUDIES

Pound, E., "The Love Song of J. Alfred Prufrock," in *Poetry* (Chicago), 10 (1917), the first understanding criticism of Eliot's work to appear in print; Dobrée, B., *The Lamp and the Lute,* (Oxford, 1929), contains a critical essay on Eliot's early work, 2nd ed. (London, 1964), includes additional essay on his last two plays; Wilson, E., *Axel's Castle,* (New York, 1931), contains first important critical estimate of Eliot's work; MacGreevy, T., *Thomas Stearns Eliot,* (London, 1931), a short study but the first book entirely devoted to Eliot's work; Leavis, F. R., *New Bearings in English Poetry,* (London, 1932), contains a penetrating critique; Oras, A., *The Critical Ideas of T. S. Eliot,* (Tartu [Dorpat], 1932), comprehensive survey in English by an Estonian critic; Lewis, W., *Men Without Art,* (London, 1934), contains a long critique by one of Eliot's earliest and most intelligent critics; Matthiessen, F. O., *The Achievement of T. S. Eliot,* (London, 1935; rev. enl. ed., 1947), the most comprehensive and important study of the interwar years, 3rd ed. (1958) includes additional ch. on Eliot's later work and an appreciation of Matthiessen, both by C. L. Barber; M. Praz, "T. S. Eliot and Dante," in *Southern Review,* II, iii, (1937); *Harvard Advocate,* 125, 3 (1938), contains tributes by such leading American poets and critics as Conrad Aiken, R. P. Blackmur, Richard Eberhart, Archibald Macleish, F. O. Matthiessen, Wallace Stevens, Allen Tate, Robert Penn Warren, William Carlos Williams.

Bodkin, M., *The Quest for Salvation in an Ancient and a Modern Play,* (London, 1941), analogizes the *Oresteia* and *The Family Reunion*; Leavis, F. R., "T. S. Eliot's Later Poetry," in *Education and the University,* (London, 1943); Preston, R., *Four Quartets Rehearsed: A Commentary,* (London, 1946), an essay in interpretation; Rajan, B., ed., *T. S. Eliot: A Study of His Writings by Several Hands,* (London, 1947), contains 8 critical essays by Cleanth Brooks, E. E. Duncan Jones, H. Gardner, M. C. Bradbrook, and others, and a bibliographical checklist; L. Unger, ed., *T. S. Eliot: A Selected Critique,* (New York, 1948), 31 extracts from important critical studies, contains an extensive checklist of books and articles in English about Eliot's work up to 1948, the year in which he received the Nobel Prize; March, R., and Tambimuttu, *T. S. Eliot: A Symposium,* (London, 1948), a tribute to Eliot on his 60th birthday, contains 47 contributions, including poems, essays, and personal reminiscences; Wilson, F., *Six Essays on the Development of T. S. Eliot,* (London, 1949), an excellent introduction to Eliot's poems and poetic dramas; Drew, E., *T. S. Eliot: The Design of His Poetry,* (New York, 1949), a Jungian interpretation; Smidt, K., *Poetry and Belief in the Works of T. S. Eliot,* (Oslo, 1949; rev. ed., London, 1961), a study of the philosophic affiliations of Eliot's thought.

Williamson, G., *A Reader's Guide to T. S. Eliot,* (New York, 1953); Nott, K., *The Emperor's Clothes,* (London, 1953), contains a spirited attack on Eliot's orthodoxy; Smith, G., Jr., *T. S. Eliot's Poetry and Plays,* (Chicago, 1956), an exhaustive study of Eliot's literary sources; Alvarez, A., *The Shaping Spirit,* (London, 1958); N. Braybrooke, ed., *T. S. Eliot: A Symposium,* (London, 1958), contributions by some fifty authors in honor of Eliot's 70th birthday; Buckley, V., *Poetry and Morality: Studies on the Criticism of M. Arnold, T. S. Eliot and F. R. Leavis,* (London, 1959).

Kenner, H., *The Invisible Poet: T. S. Eliot,* (London, 1960); Jones, D. E., *The Plays of T. S. Eliot,* (London, 1960); Unger, L., *T. S. Eliot,* (Minneapolis, 1961); Harding, D. W., *Experience into Words,* (London, 1963); Bradbrook, M. C., *English Dramatic Form,* (London, 1965), contains a ch. on Eliot's drama; Howarth, H., *Notes on Some Figures Behind T. S. Eliot,* (London, 1965); Unger, L., *T. S. Eliot: Moments and Patterns,* (Minneapolis, 1966); Gardner, H. L., *T. S. Eliot and the*

English Poetic Tradition, (Nottingham, 1966), the Byron Lecture, Nottingham, 1965; A. Tate, ed., *T. S. Eliot, The Man and His Work,* (London, 1967), a collection of 26 essays, including personal recollections of I. A. Richards, Herbert Read, Stephen Spender, Ezra Pound, Frank Morley, E. Martin Browne, Robert Speight, originally published in the *Sewanee Review;* C. B. Cox and A. P. Hinchcliffe, eds., *T. S. Eliot: "The Waste Land." A Casebook,* (London, 1968); Browne, E. M., *The Making of T. S. Eliot's Plays,* (London, 1969), an account of the composition and production of the plays based on recollections of their director and his private memoranda and letters; Leavis, F. R., *English Literature in Our Time and the University,* (London, 1969) the Clark Lectures, 1967.

G. Martin, ed., *Eliot in Perspective: A Symposium,* (London, 1970), essays by F. W. Bateson, Donald Davie, and others; Kojecky, R., *T. S. Eliot's Social Criticism,* (London, 1971), an account of Eliot's membership in the Moot, with new work by Eliot; Patterson, G., *T. S. Eliot: Poems in the Making,* (Manchester, 1971); Kenner, H., *The Pound Era,* (London, 1972), considers Eliot in relation to modernism; Margolis, J. D., *T. S. Eliot's Intellectual Development, 1922–1939,* (Chicago, 1972); Serpieri, A., *T. S. Eliot; Le strutture profonde,* (Bologna, 1973), the best account of Eliot's transformational activity; S. Sullivan, ed., *Critics on T. S. Eliot,* (London, 1973); Ward, D., *"Between Two Worlds": A Reading of T. S. Eliot's Poetry and Plays,* (London, 1973); Leavis, F. R., *The Living Principle,* (London, 1975), the last third is a long essay on *Four Quartets;* Schneider, E., *T. S. Eliot: The Pattern in the Carpet,* (London, 1975); Rajan, B., *The Overwhelming Question: A Study of the Poetry of T. S. Eliot,* (Toronto, 1976); Spender, S., *T. S. Eliot,* (New York-London, 1976); Traversi, D. A., *T. S. Eliot: The Longer Poems,* (London, 1976); Freed, H., *T. S. Eliot: Aesthetics and History,* (London, 1977); Gordon, L., *Eliot's Early Years,* (Oxford, 1977); D. Newton-DeMolina, ed., *The Literary Criticism of T. S. Eliot: New Essays,* (Atlantic Highlands, N.J., 1977); Miller, J. E., *T. S. Eliot's Personal Waste Land: Exorcism of the Demons,* (Philadelphia, 1977); Bergonzi, B., *T. S. Eliot,* (London, 1978), Masters of World Literature series; Gardner, H., *The Composition of "Four Quartets,"* (Oxford, 1978); Rosenthal, M. L., *Eliot, Yeats and Pound: Sailing into the Unknown,* (Oxford, 1978); B. Southam, ed., *Gerontion, Ash Wednesday and Other Shorter Poems: A Casebook* , (London, 1978); Moody, A. D., *T. S. Eliot, Poet,* (Cambridge, 1979); Lee, B., *Theory and Personality: The Theory of T. S. Eliot's Criticism,* (London, 1979); Thomas, C. J., *Poetic Tradition and T. S. Eliot's Talent,* (London, 1979).

Frye, N., *T. S. Eliot: An Introduction,* (Chicago, 1981); Gray, P., *T. S. Eliot's Intellectual and Poetic Development, 1909–1922,* (Brighton, 1981); Lobb, E., *T. S. Eliot and the Romantic Critical Tradition,* (London, 1981); M. Grant, ed., *T. S. Eliot, The Critical Heritage,* 2 vols., (London, 1982), the first vol., which ends with 1930, is of special interest.

Note: The John Hayward collection bequeathed to King's College, Cambridge, in 1965 contains an almost complete assemblage of printed works by and about Eliot as well as an extensive group of MSS and typescripts. Those who wish to consult unpublished material should write to T. S. Eliot's Literary Executrix, c/o Faber and Faber Ltd., London.

LIST OF COLLECTED ESSAYS

(The titles in italics indicate the volumes in which the essay is contained; essays marked with an asterisk were added to the enlarged edition of *Selected Essays,* 1951.)

"The Age of Dryden," *The Use of Poetry and the Use of Criticism;* "The Aims of Education," *To Criticize the Critic;* "American Literature and the American Language," *To Criticize the Critic;* "Andrew Marvel," *Homage to John Dryden, Selected Essays;* "Apology for the Countess of Pembroke," *The Use of Poetry and the Use of Criticism;* "Arnold and Pater," *Selected Essays;* "Beaudelaire," *Selected Essays, Selected Prose;* "Beaudelaire in Our Time," *For Lancelot Andrewes, Essays Ancient and Modern;* "Ben Jonson," *The Sacred Wood, Selected Essays, Elizabethan Essays;* "Blake," *The Sacred Wood, Selected Essays;* "Byron," *On Poetry and Poets;* "Catholicism and International Order," *Essays Ancient and Modern;* "Charles Whibley," *Selected Essays;* "Christopher Marlowe," *The Sacred Wood, Selected Essays, Elizabethan Essays;* "The Classics and the Man of Letters," *Selected Prose;* "Cyril Tourneur," *Selected Essays, Elizabethan Essays.*

"Dante" (1920), *The Sacred Wood;* "Dante" (1929), *Selected Essays;* "A Dialogue on Dramatic Poetry," *Selected Essays;* "Euripides and Professor Murray," *The Sacred Wood, Selected Essays;* "Ezra Pound, His Metric and Poetry," *To Criticize the Critic;* "Four Elizabethan Dramatists," *Selected Essays, Elizabethan Essays;* "Francis Herbert Bradley," *For Lancelot Andrewes, Selected Essays, Essays Ancient and Modern;* "From Poe to Valéry," *To Criticize the Critic;* "The Frontiers of Criticism," *On Poetry and Poets;* "The Function of Criticism," *Selected Essays.*

"Goethe as Sage," *On Poetry and Poets;* "Hamlet," *The Sacred Wood, Selected Essays, Elizabethan Essays, Selected Prose;* "The Humanism of Irving Babbitt," *For Lancelot Andrewes, Selected Essays, Essays Ancient and Modern;* "Imperfect Critics," *The Sacred Wood;* *"In Memoriam" [by Tennyson], *Essays Ancient and Modern;* "John Bramhall," *For Lancelot Andrewes, Selected Essays, Essays Ancient and Modern;* "John Dryden," *Homage to John Dryden, Selected Es-*

says; "John Ford," *Selected Essays, Elizabethan Essays;* "John Marston," *Elizabethan Essays;* "Johnson as Critic and Poet," *On Poetry and Poets.*

"Lancelot Andrewes," *For Lancelot Andrewes, Selected Essays, Essays Ancient and Modern;* "The Literature of Politics," *To Criticize the Critics;* "Marie Lloyd," *Selected Essays;* "Matthew Arnold," *The Use of Poetry and the Use of Criticism;* "The Metaphysical Poets," *Homage to John Dryden, Selected Essays, Selected Prose;* "Milton" (I and II), *Selected Prose, On Poetry and Poets;* *"Modern Education and the Classics," *Essays Ancient and Modern;* "Modern Mind," *The Use of Poetry and the Use of Criticism;* "The Music of Poetry," *Selected Prose, On Poetry and Poets;* "Niccolò Machiavelli," *For Lancelot Andrewes;* "A Note on Richard Crashaw," *For Lancelot Andrewes.*

*"The Pensées of Pascal," *Essays Ancient and Modern, Selected Prose;* "The Perfect Critic," *The Sacred Wood;* "Philip Massinger," *The Sacred Wood, Selected Essays, Elizabethan Essays;* "Poetry and Drama," *Selected Prose, On Poetry and Poets;* "The Possibility of a Poetic Drama," *The Sacred Wood;* "Reflections on Vers Libre," *To Criticize the Critic;* "Religion and Literature," *Essays Ancient and Modern, Selected Prose;* "Rhetoric and Poetic Drama," *The Sacred Wood, Selected Essays;* "Rudyard Kipling," *On Poetry and Poets;* "Second Thoughts About Humanism," *Selected Essays;* "Seneca in Elizabethan Translation," *Selected Essays;* "Shakespeare and the Stoicism of Seneca," *Selected Essays, Elizabethan Essays;* "Shelley and Keats," *The Use of Poetry and the Use of Criticism;* "Sir John Davies," *On Poetry and Poets;* "Social Function of Poetry," *On Poetry and Poets;* "Swinburne as Poet," *The Sacred Wood Selected Essays.*

"Thomas Heywood," *Selected Essays, Elizabethan Essays;* "Thomas Middleton," *For Lancelot Andrewes, Selected Essays, Elizabethan Essays;* "Thoughts After Lambeth," *Selected Essays;* "The Three Voices of Poetry," *On Poetry and Poets,* "To Criticize the Critics," *To Criticize the Critics;* "Tradition and the Individual Talent," *The Sacred Wood, Selected Essays, Selected Prose;* "Virgil and the Christian World," *On Poetry and Poets;* "What Dante Means to Me," *To Criticize the Critic;* "What Is a Classic?," *On Poetry and Poets;* "What Is Minor Poetry?," *On Poetry and Poets;* "Wordsworth and Coleridge," *The Use of Poetry and the Use of Criticism;* "Yeats," *On Poetry and Poets.*

Robert Frost
(1874–1963)

WILLIAM DORESKI

In 1959 Lionel Trilling, then one of America's most prominent literary critics, spoke at a banquet given by Henry Holt and Company on the occasion of Robert Frost's eighty-fifth birthday. After reviewing Frost's laudatory critical reception and nearly mythical status, Trilling startled some of his audience by commenting that he thought of Frost as "a terrifying poet." Trilling was referring to the dark side of Frost's poetic vision, which is skeptical, sometimes nihilistic, though more stoic than despairing, and nearly always leavened with irony, wit, or play. Frost most deliberately explores a somber view in poems like "The Most of It," "Desert Places," "Design," and "Neither Out Far nor In Deep." But his poetry cannot easily be divided into dark and light motifs. With a late couplet from *In the Clearing* (1962) he reminds us that "It takes all sorts of in and outdoor schooling/ To get adapted to my kind of fooling." Fooling—play—underlies every emotional stance in the poems, and while the consequent ambiguity sometimes underscores Frost's skepticism it mainly serves to keep his language flexible and witty—and intense.

Several years before Trilling's speech, Randall Jarrell in "The Other Frost" and "To the Laodiceans"—both of which appear in Jarrell's *Poetry and the Age* (1953)—explored the grimmer and more challenging aspects of Frost's poetry. Jarrell points out in "To the Laodiceans" that a great source of pleasure in Frost's work is the range from "the most awful and most nearly unbearable parts of the poem, to the most tender, subtle, and loving," which the poet treats with "so much humor and sadness and composure, with such plain truth" and "a joy strong enough to make us forget the limitations and excesses and baseness that these days seem unforgettable." Understanding and appreciating its full emotional, psychological, and aesthetic range remains the pleasure and critical challenge of Frost's work.

Most of Frost's best-known poetry is set in the landscapes of New Hampshire and Vermont, particularly around the Derry, New Hampshire, farm where he lived for several years attempting to support his family as a chicken farmer and a part-time teacher at Pinkerton Academy. The Derry farm families provided the voices Frost would inscribe in *North of Boston* (1914) in poems such as "Blueberries," "The Death of the Hired Man," "The Code," and "The Mountain." Frost was not by birth a New Englander but a Californian, and he wrote at least some of his quintessentially New England poems while living in England. These apparent anomalies should not come as a surprise: Frost approached rural New England with fresh eyes and ears. Moreover—as William Wordsworth's poem "I Wandered Lonely as a Cloud" reminds us—we must bear in mind the role that memory always plays not only in re-creating but in intensifying experience. One of Frost's favorite New Englanders was Henry David Thoreau who, although a native of Concord and sometimes social in his way, spent his brief life estranged by intellect and sensibility from ordinary New Englanders. Despite assuming the mask of the farmer, Frost also stood outside rural society not to criticize but to reinvent it in what in a letter to John Bartlett he called the "dramatic accent" of poetry.

Only a few poems return to Frost's California childhood, but two of them are revealing. "Auspex," a late poem (in *In the Clearing*), satirizes the same Frost myth Trilling noted seriously:

> Once in a California Sierra
> I was swooped down upon when I was small
> And measured, but not taken after all
> By a great eagle bird in all its terror.

The bird, the boy's parents claim, rejected him because he "would not make a Ganymede": that is, model himself on the Trojan boy who was carried off by an eagle because of his beauty to be Zeus's cupbearer. (During the Middle Ages Ganymede embodied homosexual love.) In "Auspex" Frost resists the presumption that there was something he could not become, and indeed his career demonstrated he could make a great deal of himself. But his parents were correct as far as the allegory in the poem goes: Frost could not be a cupbearer for Zeus or any other god; he distanced himself from homosexuality; and although unquestionably a handsome man he would never have claimed to possess great beauty. The wit in the poem exists in the protest "I have remained resentful to this day/ When any but myself presumed to say/ That there was anything I couldn't be." The lines suggest that though the choice of Ganymede as the metaphor for Frost's potential is inappropriate, his parents took the actual event involving an eagle literally and, based on a misapplication of the Ganymede myth, both they and Frost himself came to unlikely conclusions.

If "Auspex" deals humorously with a childhood memory, "Once by the Pacific"—in *A Witness Tree* (1942)—takes a harsh Old Testament view of the origin of life and the future of humanity. The title suggests that this poem, too, derives from Frost's childhood memories, but the prophecy the poem offers, as it ironically personifies a nature antithetical to the human, is based on the adult perception that God's creation is fundamentally hostile.

> The shattered water made a misty din.
> Great waves looked over others coming in,
> And thought of doing something to the
> shore
> That water never did to land before.
> The clouds were low and hairy in the skies,
> Like locks blown forward in the gleam of
> eyes.

The second-person voice resists identity and even responsibility for its perceptions by shrugging them off on the reader:

> You could not tell, and yet it looked as if
> The shore was lucky in being backed by
> cliff,
> The cliff in being backed by continent.

This skeptical "as if" rhetorical construct is typical of Frost in his darker moments. The skepticism is rooted in uncertainty, and even the perception that leads to this doubt is veiled in uncertainty or ambiguity ("You could not tell"). The second "as if" of the poem leads to a resounding if frightening closure, in which nature gives way to the rage of the Old Testament God at his harshest:

> It looked as if a night of dark intent
> Was coming, and not only a night, an age.
> Someone had better be prepared for rage.
> There would be more than ocean water
> broken
> Before God's last *Put out the Light* was
> spoken.

With grim humor Frost refrains from identifying the "someone" and explaining how that mortal could possibly prepare for such a cataclysm. To moderate his gloomy poem, Frost wields his sense of play, invoking and reworking the biblical phrase "And God said let there be light" to leaven the most terrible of prophecies.

ROBERT FROST

EARLY LIFE

Frost's complex mixture of humor and foreboding, his respect for knowledge, and his sometimes anti-intellectual approach to learning reflect his equally complex family background. Born in San Francisco on March 26, 1874, Robert Lee Frost was the first child of William Prescott Frost Jr. and Isabelle Moodie. Frost's father was a Harvard graduate, an extroverted journalist, editor, and politician, while his mother, who had been born in Scotland, was a teacher, a poet, and sometimes a visionary. His father's excessive drinking and gambling at one point caused the parents to separate, and Isabelle took Robert, then two years old, east to visit his Frost grandparents in Lawrence, Massachusetts. When in 1885 William Prescott Frost Jr. died of tuberculosis, leaving nothing to his family, Isabelle and her two children (Jeanie was born in 1876) went back to live in Lawrence. William Prescott Frost Sr., like his son, disciplined the children with sternness and severity and displayed no generosity toward the widowed Isabelle, whom he blamed for the death of William Prescott Frost Jr. Robert, despite his grandfather's various acts of generosity, never entirely forgave him.

To free herself from the oppression of the elder Frosts, Isabelle took her children to Salem Depot, New Hampshire, only a few miles from Lawrence, and taught in the district school. This was Frost's first experience with rural New England life, which brought with it his first extended period of formal schooling. Salem and Derry, where Robert and Elinor would later spend the early years of their marriage and where their children would be born, were similar farm towns, stony-soiled, moderately hilly, neither prosperous nor impoverished. In 1888 Frost entered Lawrence High School, where while working his way to the head of his graduating class he developed an interest in astronomy, earning a telescope by selling subscriptions to the *Youth's Companion*. He later commemorated this interest in the poem "The Star-Splitter," in which he subjects his youthful pursuit to an ironic adult skepticism. He writes of "Brad McLaughlin's" telescope (obtained by burning down his house for insurance money): "It's a star-splitter if there ever was one/ And ought to do some good if splitting stars/ 'Sa thing to be compared with splitting wood." The narrator of this poem finds little use for a telescope himself. In "Desert Places" Frost reinforces the notion that we need not look to the stars to understand the extremities of the human condition:

> They cannot scare me with their empty
> spaces
> Between stars—on stars where no human
> race is.
> I have it in me so much nearer home
> To scare myself with my own desert places.

Frost's first published poem, "La Noche Triste," derived from William Prescott's *History of the Conquest of Mexico* (1843), is in a very different mode. The poem, which appeared in the *Lawrence High School Bulletin* in 1890, is a grim but uncritical celebration of a heroic conquest by "freemen" who "live, and rule, and die/ Where they [the Aztecs] ruled alone." Frost would rarely again write so unskeptical or uncomplicated a poem, but in "La Noche Triste," a minor epic, he was already displaying considerable skill in the use of both full and half rhyme; he also showed a generally firm control (with a few lapses) of a rhythmic impetus reminiscent of Henry Wadsworth Longfellow.

Frost was an excellent student. He gained a solid grasp of Latin, Greek, and history, which enabled him to pass the entrance examinations for Harvard College. As editor of the *Bulletin* in his senior year he published several of his own editorials and articles, including the fanciful "Petra and Its Surroundings," describing in colorful detail a place he would never see. More important is "A Monument to After-Thought Unveiled," which presents a miniature program for himself: "Aggressive life is two-fold: theory, practice; thought, action: and concretely, poetry, statesmanship; philosophy, socialism—infinitely." Though Frost would later reject socialism he retained an interest in statesmanship, and in old age used a goodwill trip to the Soviet Union to test his skills. Poetry would later divide itself into theory and practice; in the course of what he called "barding around," in a letter to Louis Untermeyer, he would bring an aggressive energy to promoting and publicizing his work and himself that would almost equal the effort he expended on writing.

More important than this early attempt at theorizing his life's work was meeting and falling in love with Elinor Miriam White, his co-valedictorian, whom he would pursue and eventually marry. First, however, he had to establish himself as some sort of breadwinner. He began by entering Dartmouth College, which was cheaper than Harvard and approved by his grandfather, who thought Harvard had ruined Frost's father. The most important intellectual discovery Frost made at Dartmouth was Francis Turner Palgrave's *Golden Treasury of Best Songs and Lyrical Poems in the English Language* (1861), which exposed him to a wider variety of English poetry than he had previously experienced. Otherwise Dartmouth failed to interest him, and he dropped out (or may have been expelled, suggests his biographer Jeffrey Meyers) at the end of his first semester. After attempting a variety of teaching, factory, and newspaper jobs, he finally persuaded Elinor to marry him in 1895.

Before that, however, a curious episode took place. Frost had published his first poem in a professional journal, the *Independent*, in 1894. "My Butterfly," which would eventually appear in *A Boy's Will* (1913), is a competent though stilted fin de siècle poem of longing, languor, and death written in an aloof and deliberately anachronistic style. Frost arranged to have it and four other poems published in a little book; he had only two copies of the book printed. In the fall he took one copy of the book to Elinor at St. Lawrence University and received a cool reception. Distraught, he threw away the second copy and wandered down to the Dismal Swamp on the Virginia–North Carolina border. His poem "Kitty Hawk," written and published late in life, tells one version of the adventures he had then among boatmen and hunters. He had gone off, he sometimes claimed, to lose himself in the swamp, but in the end he seems to have had an amusing trip and to have forgotten his thoughts of suicide, if he ever had any.

DERRY: 1901–1912

For the first seventeen years of his marriage, till he moved to England, Frost supported his growing family by a variety of efforts, mostly chicken farming and teaching. He made another attempt at college, attending Harvard for two years while teaching part-time. In 1901 his grandfather died and left Frost the farm in Derry on which he and his family were living. Many of Frost's most famous poems germinated during the Derry years; all four of his surviving children would remember the farm in Derry as their childhood home. The first child, Elliott, did not live beyond his fourth year. His death of cholera in 1900 and, in the same year, Frost's mother's death from cancer, was the cause of serious depression for both Frost and Elinor. The terrible strain between them at this trying time finds voice in "Home Burial," in which a mother who has recently lost her first child accuses her husband of indifference. He actually suffers not from indifference but from the inability to express emotion, a distinction she is in no mood to make. In the climax of the poem, frustrated by their mutual lack of communication, she finds herself driven to "cry out on life" (as Frost puts it in "The Most of It") for its general indifference, complaining that

> The nearest friends can go
> With anyone to death, comes so far short
> They might as well not try to go at all.
> No, from the time when one is sick to death,
> One is alone, and he dies more alone.
> Friends make pretense of following to the
> grave,

> But before one is in it, their minds are
> turned
> And making the best of their way back to
> life
> And living people, and things they
> understand.
> But the world's evil. I won't have grief so
> If I can change it. Oh, I won't, I won't!

Of course the woman's husband cannot adequately answer her great Shakespearean lament, no more than anyone could. The death of Elliott, and the later deaths of Elinor, his son Carol, and his daughter Marjorie, would haunt and scar Frost's life to the end. But though "Home Burial" offers no consolation, no hope for the flayed marriage, no poem has more fully and honestly responded to the terrible death of a child and the emotional turmoil that ensues.

Though one of his finest, "Home Burial" is only one of many blank verse narratives, dramatic poems, lyrics, and monologues Frost composed during the years in Derry and immediately after in England as he looked back on those years. In his small southern New Hampshire farm town Frost read a great deal of literature, but much of the impetus for the development of his poetics derived from listening to the speech of neighboring farmers, a pungent colloquial talk Ralph Waldo Emerson had also admired.

The plain-spoken voice Frost derived from this speech first found public expression in a series of articles he wrote for the *Poultryman*, *Farm-Poultry*, and the *Eastern Poultryman* in 1903–1905, but it soon began to appear in the poems he was occasionally publishing in magazines and newspapers.

Writing to his former student John Bartlett in 1914 while in England, Frost explained his notion of the sentence as a structural and sonic device: "A sentence is a sound in itself on which other sounds called words may be strung." To write without a sense of the "sentence-sounds" preceding the actual placement of the words courts failure, he explains in a letter published in *Selected Letters of Robert Frost* (1964). These sentence-sounds are

> apprehended by the ear. They are gathered by the ear from the vernacular and brought into books. . . . A man is all a writer if *all* his words are strung on definite recognizable sentence sounds. The voice of the imagination, the speaking voice must know certainly how to behave how to posture in every sentence he offers.
>
> A man is a marked writer if his words are largely strung on the more striking sentence sounds.

Or as Frost put it in a December 1914 letter to Sidney Cox, which also appears in *Selected Letters*:

> The sentence as a sound in itself apart from the word sounds is no mere figure of speech. . . . I shall show the sentence sound opposing the sense of the words as in irony. And so till I establish the distinction between the grammatical sentence and the vital sentence. The grammatical sentence is merely accessory to the other and chiefly valuable as furnishing a clue to the other.

The sentence-sound (an ironic opposition to grammar and a way of catching the vernacular of speech through its own sound and rhythm), rather than the sentence (an accumulation of sounds and senses of particular words), forms the basis of Frost's original and deceptively simple poetics. In poems like "A Servant to Servants" (in *North of Boston*) the sentence-sound imitates speech with precision but renders speech compatible with the strong traditional rhythm of blank verse:

> You take the lake. I look and look at it.
> I see it's a fair, pretty sheet of water.
> I stand and make myself repeat out loud
> The advantages it has, so long and narrow,
> Like a deep piece of some old running river
> Cut short off at both ends. It lies five miles
> Straight away through the mountain notch
> From the sink window where I wash the
> plates,
> And all our storms come up toward the
> house,
> Drawing the slow waves whiter and whiter
> and whiter.

The vernacular voice, the Shakespearean rhetorical effects (for example, the repetition of "whiter"), and the comfortable invocation of an unusual but clarifying simile mark this passage indelibly as being by Frost.

But the great flexibility of Frost's apparently casual voice shows up not only in his blank verse poems, where we would expect it, but also in more formally constructed poems, like his sometimes astonishing sonnets. In "Design," for example, at the close of a virtuoso performance, a sonnet rhymed *abbaabba acaacc*, Frost undermines the argument of his poem with a characteristic dropping of the voice, turning on the key word "if":

> I found a dimpled spider, fat and white,
> On a white heal-all, holding up a moth
> Like a white piece of rigid satin cloth—
> Assorted characters of death and blight
> Mixed ready to begin the morning right,
> Like the ingredients of a witches' broth—
> A snow-drop spider, a flower like a froth,
> And dead wings carried like a paper kite.
>
> What had that flower to do with being white,
> The wayside blue and innocent heal-all?
> What brought the kindred spider to that
>   height,
> Then steered the white moth thither in the
>   night?
> What but design of darkness to appall?—
> If design govern in a thing so small.

Several of Frost's poems have this skeptical type of closure. An argument about some large issue—here the presence or role of a plan or design in the universe—is carefully constructed, made seemingly persuasive, and then cast into doubt by the final lines. The satisfaction expressed by this poem's discovery of the minute scale on which cosmic questions may occur is subtly expressed but prevents the poem from seeming pointlessly ominous, though its view of the creation is undeniably a cruel one. "For Once, Then, Something," "In a Disused Graveyard," "An Old Man's Winter Night," and "After Apple-Picking" are among the other poems that use the freedom and flexibility of Frost's grasp of vernacular sentence-sound to introduce in their closures fresh notes of doubt, unexpected rationality, wit, or even cynicism.

"The Tuft of Flowers," published first in 1906 in the Derry *Enterprise* when Frost began teaching part-time at Pinkerton Academy, offers in graceful couplets an early example of Frost's grasp of the sentence-sound and his insistence that "all poetry is a reproduction of the tones of actual speech":

> I went to turn the grass once after one
> Who mowed it in the dew before the sun.
>
> The dew was gone that made his blade so
>   keen
> Before I came to view the leveled scene.

Not every couplet constitutes a complete sentence, but this opening pair establishes the movement of the poem. The ease of the couplets enables the poem to embrace an internal dialogue, in which the speaker asserts that

> I must be, as he had been,—alone,
>
> "As all must be," I said within my heart,
> "Whether they work together or apart."

However, the discovery of a tuft of unspecified flowers engenders a reversal by alerting the speaker to the bond of love that at least sometimes exists between humans and nature, and this insight becomes empathy:

> And dreaming, as it were, held brotherly
>   speech
> With one whose thought I had not hoped to
>   reach.
> "Men work together," I told him from the
>   heart,
> "Whether they work together or apart."

With three daughters and a son to support—Lesley (born in 1899), Carol (a son, born in 1902), Irma (born in 1903), and Marjorie (born in 1905); a sixth child, Elinor (born in 1907) lived only two days—the Derry years, however productive for Frost's poetry, were trying. Frost's chicken farming came to nothing, and though his position at Pinkerton Academy (part-time for a term, then full-time) was rewarding, it was not the career he envisioned for himself. It did, however, offer the opportunity to refine his pedagogical ideas, which would serve him well later, and the pleasure of directing student productions of plays by Christopher Marlowe, John Milton, Richard Brinsley Sheridan, and William Butler Yeats, which he did with gusto. His revision of the Pinkerton English curriculum and the year he spent teaching at the State Normal School in Plymouth (subsequently renamed Plymouth State College) helped him develop the conversational and informal pedagogy for which later, at Amherst College and the University of Michigan, he became famous. Frost imagined that he could achieve personal success and also support his family as a poet, though he saw that it would require drastic action to make this happen.

ENGLAND: 1912–1915

The dramatic move to England, financed by selling the Derry farm, succeeded partly through luck and partly through Frost's tactful use of new and important acquaintances in the London literary world. Frost was lucky in that the widow of David Nutt decided to publish his first book, *A Boy's Will*, in 1913 and his second, *North of Boston*, in 1914. He was tactful in his dealings with a wide variety of literary people, some of whom he genuinely liked and some of whom he found less congenial. In various ways F. S. Flint, Harold Monro, Ezra Pound, Lascelles Abercrombie, and Edward Thomas stimulated or encouraged Frost. Pound reviewed *A Boy's Will* and introduced Frost to Richard Aldington, Ford Madox Ford (then Hueffer), and William Butler Yeats, who told him that his book was "the best poetry written in America for a long time." Frost formed his closest friendship with Edward Thomas, whom he encouraged to turn from travel writing (at which Thomas excelled) to poetry. Thomas' death in World War I in 1917 grieved Frost perhaps only slightly less than the deaths in his own family.

Frost entered the literary world as a mature artist: *A Boy's Will* is a carefully ordered sequence of lyric poems. Somewhat like James Joyce's *A Portrait of the Artist as a Young Man* (1914–1915) it traces the development of a young man's sensibility from boyhood to early maturity. To help guide the reader along this progression, Frost originally added glosses in the table of contents but later dropped them. The intended development is reasonably clear without the glosses; their primary effect, as Frost may have come to realize, was to add an air of dreaminess at odds with the sharply drawn effects of the strongest poems. Poems such as "Into My Own," "A Late Walk," "Storm Fear," "Rose Pogonias," "The Tuft of Flowers," and "A Line-Storm Song" display a command of the established conventions of lyric poetry and Frost's well-developed ear for sentence-sounds. They justify Yeats's praise. But one of the best and now most famous poems in the volume is "Mowing"; this sonnet, written in hexameters, introduces a plain grace and colloquial movement that carries the reader in a new direction, toward the eclogues and dramatic poems of *North of Boston*. "Mowing" echoes the mower poems of Andrew Marvell; and Mark Scott has claimed in a 1991 essay that Andrew Lang's "Scythe Song" was Frost's source. But the voice in "Mowing" is distinctly Frost's, illustrating the perfection of his colloquial, sentence-based rhetoric:

> There was never a sound beside the wood but one,
> And that was my long scythe whispering to the ground.
> What was it it whispered? I knew not well myself;
> Perhaps it was something about the heat of the sun,
> Something, perhaps, about the lack of sound—
> And that was why it whispered and did not speak.

It was no dream of the gift of idle hours,
Or easy gold at the hand of fay or elf:
Anything more than the truth would have
seemed too weak
To the earnest love that laid the swale in
rows,
Not without feeble-pointed spikes of flowers
(Pale orchises), and scared a bright green
snake.
The fact is the sweetest dream that labor
knows.
My long scythe whispered and left the hay
to make.

Rejecting the fairies and elves and dreaminess common to much of the poetry written in the years before World War I, Frost demonstrates how graceful the voice of actual experience can be. The world of work, in which so much of his poetry centers, contains in its actuality all the dreams available, desirable, or necessary. Frost insists not only on the material beauty and grace of the world but also on its adequacy for the poet. Although Frost's poems offer some genuinely transcendent moments, they suggest that transcendence typically comes through accepting the material actuality and adequacy of this world.

North of Boston, Frost's second book, perhaps the most important of his long career, appeared in May 1914 while he was living near Dymock, Gloucestershire. (He had moved his family there in order to be closer to the poets Wilfrid W. Gibson and Lascelles Abercrombie.) *North of Boston* contains many of Frost's most famous poems, including "Mending Wall," "The Death of the Hired Man," "Home Burial," "After Apple-Picking," and "The Wood-Pile." Unlike the lyrics of *A Boy's Will*, most of these poems are blank verse dramatic poems or monologues (or eclogues or pastorals, as some critics have called them). They most fully demonstrate how Frost's use of sentence-sound, his ear for colloquial syntax, and his powerful sense of irony can empower a poem that lacks or avoids the rhymes and other sonic devices of the lyric.

Thematically the poems in *North of Boston* cover a wide range, including the isolation of the individual and the difficulty of communication ("Home Burial," "The Fear," "A Servant to Servants," "The Code"); the weight and oppression of the past ("Mending Wall"); the relationship between nature and culture ("The Wood-Pile"); the possibilities of human communion ("The Death of the Hired Man," "Blueberries," "A Hundred Collars," "The Generations of Men," "The Black Cottage"); and death and transcendence ("After Apple-Picking"). The subject matter derives mostly from Frost's observations of his fellow farmers in Derry; the poems catch not only the rhythms of the farmers' speech but also a sense of their relationship to the land. Frost is far from being a merely regional poet, but the stony northern New England landscape embodies a physical isolation that corresponds to the mental isolation that plays so large a role in these poems. Frost's vision is not necessarily bleak: some of the poems in *North of Boston* are about successfully overcoming isolation, and others, especially "The Wood-Pile," illustrate the opportunities for self-discovery created by isolation.

"The Wood-Pile" opens with an echo of Dante's picture of the traveler lost in the wilderness of life:

Out walking in the frozen swamp one gray
day,
I paused and said, "I will turn back from
here.
No, I will go on farther—and we shall see."

The brief indecision, the abrupt resolve, and the Emersonian insistence on *seeing* characterize Frost's poems about entering or envisioning the wilderness, including such famous ones as "Stopping by Woods on a Snowy Evening" and "Desert Places." Here the swamp with its frozen and featureless landscape resists naming or definition and reminds Frost that he is in the world of nature, not of human culture:

The hard snow held me, save where now
and then
One foot went through. The view was all
in lines

Straight up and down of tall slim trees
Too much alike to mark or name a place by
So as to say for certain I was here
Or somewhere else: I was just far from
home.

A small unidentified bird attracts Frost's eye and he imagines it suspects him of trying to steal a feather. But after watching for a few moments Frost discovers a woodpile neatly cut and stacked, and this sign of human life returns him to human concerns. Impressed and comforted by this mark of civilization in the wilderness, he places a positive construction on its being abandoned, assuring himself that the woodcutter, instead of having died, has busied himself with other projects:

only
Someone who lived in turning to fresh tasks
Could so forget his handiwork on which
He spent himself, the labor of his ax,
And leave it there far from a useful fireplace
To warm the frozen swamp as best it could
With the slow smokeless burning of decay.

Yet the sheer uselessness of the woodpile decaying where it stands provokes an ironic closure that returns the poem to the picture of wild desolation suggested at the beginning by the view of "tall slim trees," an inimical, featureless landscape indifferent to human needs and concerns.

Several of Frost's poems present the natural world as a grim, desolate landscape indifferent or hostile to his presence, but usually, as in "Desert Places," "The Census-Taker," and "The Most of It," the mind of the poet compensates by offering refuge, an ironic retort, or an assertion of selfhood. In some of the dramatic poems, however, the discovery of comparable indifference, hostility, or sheer otherness in another person generates a terrifying scenario. "Home Burial" dramatizes the cruel disaffection in an uncommunicative marriage. The death of the couple's first child brings about the crisis. The husband sees the wife standing on the stairway looking out through a small window and brusquely questions her:

"What is it you see
From up there always—for I want to know."
She turned and sank upon her skirts at that,
And her face changed from terrified to dull.
He said to gain time: "What is it you see,"
Mounting until she cowered under him.
"I will find out now—you must tell me,
dear."

Finally he realizes that she is looking out upon the tiny family plot in which he recently buried their child. As the poem develops, it becomes increasingly clear that the sexual hierarchy suggested by the phrase "Mounting until she cowered under him" defines a key aspect of the agonizing relationship in which husband and wife are unable to apprehend each other's emotional needs. The husband, habitually silent about his emotions, expresses himself so indirectly the wife believes him to be without feeling, while she expresses herself as vehemently as a Shakespearean heroine, befuddling her husband with rhetorical absolutes. They cannot agree upon the mutuality of their grief because they differ too much in how they express it. The wife reproaches the man for having dug the child's grave and, moments later, spoken with seeming indifference about farm matters, she quotes him: "Three foggy mornings and one rainy day/ Will rot the best birch fence a man can build." She is unable to read her husband's indirection; if she had actually understood the birch fence metaphor, she would have found it cruel. Her husband, on the other hand, finds her grief excessive, self-defeating, and inimical to their relationship:

"What was it brought you up to think it the
thing
To take your mother-loss of a first child
So inconsolably—in the face of love.
You'd think his memory might be
satisfied—"

There can be no reconciliation. The wife, after expanding her grief to indict the world, threatens to take her emotional needs elsewhere, and the husband responds by threatening force. The death of the child has brought out the worst or the weakest in each of them, and the poem closes without hope.

Though "Home Burial" surely draws upon the emotional circumstances of the death of Elliott, which deeply grieved both Frost and his wife, it is not an autobiographical poem. Frost did not suffer from emotional inarticulateness; if anything, he may have sometimes expressed himself all too volubly. Nonetheless, great suffering is as likely to drive people apart as to bring them together. The death of Elliott and later of Marjorie surely generated enormous pain for both Frosts. By 1938 when Elinor died, inflicting the worst of all losses on her husband, the couple had suffered enough for several lifetimes, though Frost would have to suffer more, alone, with the insanity of Irma and the suicide of his only son, Carol.

Most of *North of Boston* is concerned with less dramatic aspects of human interaction than those represented in "Home Burial." Perhaps the most frequently quoted and misquoted poem in the volume is "Mending Wall." The opening poem, "Mending Wall" in perfectly colloquial blank verse delineates the important theme of drawing and understanding the boundaries between people. The poem mixes foreboding and tolerance and depicts the mystery of otherness by blurring the distinctions between the natural and the human world. What is the "something . . . that doesn't love a wall"? Is it a human or a natural force, or a combination of both?

> Something there is that doesn't love a wall,
> That sends the frozen-ground-swell under it,
> And spills the upper boulders in the sun;
> And makes gaps even two can pass abreast;

Frost heaves and hunters, nature and culture, and something left unnamed combine to topple parts of the wall that the first-person narrator, whom we might take to be Frost, and his neighbor agree on a certain day to repair. But why do they need a wall between them, asks Frost. The neighbor responds, "Good fences make good neighbors," but with the "mischief of spring" in him, Frost refuses to accept this answer and probes for more:

> "*Why* do they make good neighbors? Is it
> Where there are cows? But here there are
> no cows.
> Before I built a wall I'd ask to know
> What I was walling in or walling out,
> And to whom I was like to give offense.
> Something there is that doesn't love a wall,
> That wants it down."

That something, perhaps, is the need for human companionship and communication, the something that should have breached the barrier between the protagonists of "Home Burial," for instance. The neighbor, however, cannot share Frost's interrogative mood. "Like an old-stone savage armed," the neighbor moves in the "darkness" of his refusal to question received values. Rather than enter into a discussion, he adheres to what Frost realizes is "his father's saying"; he "likes having thought of it so well/ He says again, 'Good fences make good neighbors.'" Frost does not endorse this saying but questions it. The poem advocates knowledge against the blind ignorance of tradition ("I'd ask to know/ What I was walling in or walling out"), and it does so for the sake of human communication. Like most of the other dramatic poems in *North of Boston*, "Mending Wall" stands for dialogue against silence, for breaching (if not wholly breaking down) the barriers of history, ego, and tradition.

RETURN TO AMERICA: THE ESTABLISHED POET

At the close of 1914 Henry Holt and Company had agreed to publish Frost's books in the United States, and he was on the verge of the greatest success any twentieth-century American poet would enjoy. When World War I broke out, Frost borrowed money to return to America with his family, taking along Edward Thomas' fifteen-year-old son Merfyn, who was to visit friends in New Hampshire. In

February 1915 the Frosts and Merfyn arrived in New York where Frost met with his editor at Holt, Alfred Harcourt, who would become a close friend. American journals were now enthusiastically publishing Frost's work; *North of Boston*, just published, garnered excellent reviews including an especially enthusiastic one by Amy Lowell; and *A Boy's Will* would appear in April and also receive favorable notices.

In June, Frost moved to Franconia, New Hampshire, and began to become accustomed to giving the readings and lectures that would occupy much of his time and energy for the rest of his life. In 1916 he accepted a teaching position at Amherst College, to begin in the winter of 1917; after a three-year hiatus (1920–1923) caused by disagreements between him and President Alexander Meiklejohn about the curriculum, Frost taught at least occasionally at Amherst for much of the rest of his life (sometimes spending part of the school year also teaching at the University of Michigan). Frost enjoyed literary celebrity, and as his shyness dissipated he became popular on the lecture circuit. Lecture and reading fees would soon become his largest source of income, though the royalties from his books, especially from collected editions, were substantial.

Mountain Interval, which appeared in November 1916, was not as enthusiastically received as his two earlier books. The reviews were favorable, but critics seemed to have nothing new to say about Frost, and the comments have a perfunctory quality, which might indicate that Frost's achievement was already being taken for granted. W. S. Braithewaite, for example, refers to "that indescribable magic which Mr. Frost evokes from the plain and severe quality of New England life and character"; Harriet Monroe in *Poetry* links him to Edgar Lee Masters; and Sidney Cox in the *New Republic* finds "sincerity" the "fundamental and embracing quality" of Frost's new book. Braithewaite and Monroe see Frost as a regional poet, Cox finds him a moralist, and no one has anything substantive to say about the aesthetic qualities of the poems.

Mountain Interval, unlike *A Boy's Will*, a collection of lyrics, and *North of Boston*, a group of narrative poems, mixes Frost's two predominant genres. Perhaps, as William H. Pritchard has suggested, Frost no longer wished to be read as a "merely lyric or merely narrative writer." In any case all Frost's future books, except for the verse dramas *A Masque of Reason* (1945) and *A Masque of Mercy* (1947) would mix various kinds of poems. *Mountain Interval* contains some of Frost's best poems, including "An Old Man's Winter Night," "The Oven Bird," "The Cow in Apple Time," "Range-Finding," and "The Hill Wife." Two of his most anthologized poems embody the bemused lyric meditation and stark, tragic vision central to Frost's poetics. "The Road Not Taken," written with Edward Thomas in mind, is often misread as a poem advocating nonconformity, but it is really a meditation on the difficulty—perhaps the impossibility—of making an intelligent choice when faced with the unknown. "'Out, Out—'" takes its title from Lady Macbeth's harsh self-reproach, and in a way it too is "a tale/ Told by an idiot, full of sound and fury, / Signifying nothing": Frost's poem—about the death of a boy injured by a saw—seems to be spoken by a moral idiot who draws no conclusions but merely notes that the spectators of the incident, "since they/ Were not the one dead, turned to their affairs." The indifference of the speaker and the other witnesses seems unspeakably cruel, but it simply reiterates what the wife in "Home Burial" means when she notes that "The nearest friends can go/ With anyone to death, comes so far short/ They might as well not try to go at all."

The best-known poem in *Mountain Interval* is "Birches," the last line of which—"One could do worse than be a swinger of birches"—has come to define Frost. (One biography of Frost is even entitled *Robert Frost: A Swinger of Birches.*) If we read "Birches" as an allegory of the playful and heaven-aspiring activity of poetry writing it does indeed define Frost very well. The swinger of birches is a farm boy, far from town, with no other boys to play baseball with. His swinging from the tops of the trees bends them but doesn't bow them the way ice storms do:

> Often you must have seen them
> Loaded with ice a sunny winter morning
> After a rain. They click upon themselves
> As the breeze rises, and turn many-colored
> As the stir cracks and crazes their enamel.
> Soon the sun's warmth makes them shed crystal shells
> Shattering and avalanching on the snow-crust—
> Such heaps of broken glass to sweep away
> You'd think the inner dome of heaven had fallen.
> They are dragged to the withered bracken by the load,
> And they seem not to break; though once they are bowed
> So low for long, they never right themselves:
> You may see their trunks arching in the woods
> Years afterwards, trailing their leaves on the ground
> Like girls on hands and knees that throw their hair
> Before them over their heads to dry in the sun.

Rather than having the ice storm (which Frost identifies with "Truth," a kind of literary naturalism) bend them, however, he prefers to envision the farm boy doing it, so that the adult Frost can imagine adopting the role himself when responsibilities and sorrows press too heavily upon him:

> So was I once myself a swinger of birches,
> And so I dream of going back to be.
> It's when I'm weary of considerations,
> And life is too much like a pathless wood
> Where your face burns and tickles with the cobwebs
> Broken across it, and one eye is weeping
> From a twig's having lashed across it open.
> I'd like to get away from earth awhile
> And then come back to it and begin over.

He must return to earth because "Earth's the right place for love," but the climb "*Toward heaven*" (Frost's emphasis) refreshes, enlightens, and cheers.

In 1917 Edward Thomas was killed by shell fire at the battle of Arras, adding to Frost's sorrows. Frost had been successful in getting Thomas' poetry published in America, which was some consolation, but Thomas was a close friend and Frost never forgot him. In *New Hampshire: A Poem with Notes and Grace Notes* (1923) he would eulogize Thomas in a poem plainly entitled "To E. T.," addressed to its subject and sounding as much like one of Thomas' own poems as Frost's. But the most memorable poem Frost would write of his friend is "Iris by Night" (in *A Further Range*, 1936), which describes an evening walk when "came a moment of confusing lights" as a dazzling spectrum embraced Frost and Thomas. A moonbow, a rare meteorological phenomenon, seemed to consecrate their friendship:

> Then a small rainbow like a trellis gate,
> A very small moon-made prismatic bow,
> Stood closely over us through which to go.
> And then we were vouchsafed the miracle
> That never yet to other two befell
> And I alone of us have lived to tell.
> A wonder! Bow and rainbow as it bent,
> Instead of moving with us as we went,
> (To keep the pots of gold from being found)
> It lifted from its dewy pediment
> Its two mote-swimming many-colored ends,
> And gathered them together in a ring.
> And we stood in it softly circled round
> From all division time or foe can bring
> In a relation of elected friends.

The union depicted here is as permanent as memory itself and yet as fragile as the atmospheric event. Though Frost survives his friend, the ring, like a wedding ring, attests to the mystical solemnity, emotional depth, and duration of the epiphanic moment. As Brad Leithauser remarks in reviewing the Library of America edition of Frost's work in the *New York Review of Books* "Iris by Night" "must be one of the most moving poems ever dedicated to friendship . . . the work of . . . a true friend and a great heart."

Despite the relatively modest success of *Mountain Interval*, Frost's reputation continued to grow during and after the war years. The National Institute of Arts and Letters elected him a member. His play *A Way Out* was published in *The Seven Arts* in 1917 and performed two years later by Amherst students. *Poetry* magazine awarded him a one-hundred-dollar prize for "Snow." He met the other well-known American poets—Sara Teasdale, Vachel Lindsay, Carl Sandburg, Louis Untermeyer, and Amy Lowell—as an equal. Of these, Untermeyer would become an essential friend, correspondent, and promoter of Frost's work, while the others, especially Lowell and Sandburg, would come to seem rivals, though in Sandburg's case a friendly one. But with the publication of only three small collections of poems, some of them written many years before, Frost had already assumed a preeminent role among contemporary American writers, a position he would never lose.

THE 1920s: NEW HAMPSHIRE

In 1920 a dispute that began with Frost's distaste for Stark Young, a popular teacher at Amherst College who was homosexual and particularly opinionated about aesthetics, led to an open dispute with President Meiklejohn. Frost resigned his post at Amherst, sold his farm in Franconia, and bought property in South Shaftsbury, Vermont. Meanwhile his sister Jeanie, who had grown paranoid over the years, was arrested in Portland, Maine, for disturbing the peace. Frost went to Portland and had Jeanie committed to the state mental hospital in Augusta. More encouragingly, to provide him with the financial security to write poetry, Henry Holt began paying Frost one hundred dollars a month as a consulting editor. Meanwhile his fame as a speaker and reader grew, and he made visits to various colleges, including, in 1921, the University of Michigan, where he was offered a one-year fellowship. In October he moved his family to Ann Arbor, where he would live and work for part of the year for some time to come. Ann Arbor would prove to be an especially congenial setting. Frost arranged a lecture series there featuring his favorite colleagues, or rivals, including Amy Lowell, Louis Untermeyer, Carl Sandburg, Vachel Lindsay, and prose writers such as Hamlin Garland and Dorothy Canfield Fisher. The university awarded Frost an honorary M.A. in 1922.

Frost published two books in 1923. *Selected Poems* appeared in March, and *New Hampshire* in November. *New Hampshire,* which brought Frost his first of four Pulitzer Prizes, contains many of his most frequently anthologized poems, including "The Star-Splitter," "The Ax-Helve," "Fire and Ice," "In a Disused Graveyard," "Nothing Gold Can Stay," "The Aim Was Song," "Stopping by Woods on a Snowy Evening," "For Once, Then, Something," "Evening in a Sugar Orchard," "A Hillside Thaw," and "The Need of Being Versed in Country Things." In fact, almost every poem is memorable except the title poem, a long, rambling, self-conscious mock-Horatian eclogue about the state in which Frost had until recently resided and the state of American material well-being.

"For Once, Then, Something" offers a teasing glimpse of the possibilities of transcendence and the likelihood of being self-deluded in searching for the ineffable. Frost at first asserts his right to kneel at well-curbs (the stone rims around the mouths of wells) in such a way as to see himself "in the summer heaven godlike/ Looking out of a wreath of fern and cloud puffs." He admits, however, that "*Once*" he saw something "beyond the picture,/ Through the picture, a something white, uncertain." He cannot identify this something, only attest to its momentary presence. A drip from a fern, a touch of naturalism, obliterates the vision. He toys with the possibilities (and the reader) by asking "What was that whiteness?/ Truth? A pebble of quartz?" but can assert, at last, only that "For once" he saw "something" other than himself. Whether this poem indicts or endorses the Romantic notion that empathic observation of nature can lead to a glimpse of the spiritual ineffable is hard to say.

The playful humor of "For Once, Then, Something" does not negate the serious issue of transcendence. Nor does the more serious tone of "Stopping by Woods on a Snowy Evening" conceal Frost's wit in playing off a jaunty meter and rhyme scheme against a situation of dark intent, one that seems to bring him face to face with oblivion. The emphatic rhyme scheme—*aaba bbcb ccdc dddd*—imposes a stuttering hesitancy on the opening of the poem, a mood of doubt and irresolution in keeping with the situation.

Whose woods these are I think I know.
His house is in the village though;
He will not see me stopping here
To watch his woods fill up with snow.

My little horse must think it queer
To stop without a farmhouse near
Between the woods and frozen lake
The darkest evening of the year.

Yet with the personification of the horse a self-awareness enters the poem, and the mood shifts as the narrator recognizes the loneliness, loveliness, and dark depth before him:

He gives his harness bells a shake
To ask if there is some mistake.
The only other sound's the sweep
Of easy wind and downy flake.

The domestic woodlot, the possession of a neighbor, gives way to a beautiful otherness inimical to the human. To enter the woods, or even to stay very long looking into them, would undo the life the narrator still has before him, and he isn't ready for that:

The woods are lovely, dark and deep,
But I have promises to keep,
And miles to go before I sleep,
And miles to go before I sleep.

The critic Richard Poirier has pointed out that this poem is about ownership—the first line alerts us to this—and the difficulties of self-possession. The ownership of land is a business matter, and the narrator of this poem has business to carry on. But he also needs to be reminded, or to remind himself, that if he does not claim himself fully through consciousness, if he drifts off to sleep in the snowfall, he will lose himself forever to a hypnotic beauty he can never possess.

Another poem that depicts the need to assert our humanity against nature, "On a Tree Fallen across the Road," a Shakespearean sonnet in the first person plural, avoids the seriousness of "Stopping by Woods" by personifying a storm in playful tones and arguing for the inconsequence of natural violence:

The tree the tempest with a crash of wood
Throws down in front of us is not to bar
Our passage to our journey's end for good,
But just to ask us who we think we are.

A fallen tree does not represent a serious challenge to human progress, but in "The Need of Being Versed in Country Things" the burning of a house means an absolute end to human presence in the location. Even so, the natural presence that is there echoes the lost humanity, the "murmur" of birds—phoebes—"more like the sigh we sigh/ From too much dwelling on what has been." In the context of the muted apocalyptic vision of the poem, to be "versed in country things" means to avoid imposing human emotions on the natural world. Speaking of the birds, Frost observes:

For them there was really nothing sad.
But though they rejoiced in the nest they
  kept,
One had to be versed in country things
Not to believe the phoebes wept.

And yet, to retain their human sympathies, the poet and the reader with him have to believe the phoebes wept. The sheer impossibility of avoiding anthropomorphism defines us in the face of an intractable otherness.

"Good-by and Keep Cold" deals with the problem of defining an apt relationship between human beings and nature: specifically, between the poet and his recently planted orchard. Written in anapestic tetrameter (the first foot of each line being a trochee), a difficult and showy meter, "Good-by and Keep Cold" seems at first to be a practical exposition, like one of Virgil's *Georgics*, on the difficulties faced by orchards in winter, when deep steady cold is better than alternating cold and thaw. But it is really about the narrator's need to go about his business, as in "Stopping by Woods," and the need to detach himself from what he can never be part of: "My business awhile is with different trees,/ Less carefully nurtured, less fruitful than these. . . ."

Not every poem in *New Hampshire* deals with the difficulty of understanding the relationship between the human and the natural worlds, however. One of the finest poems Frost ever wrote, "The Witch of Coös," the first part of "Two Witches," is a dramatic dialogue in which a narrator visiting a backwoods farm listens to a woman and her son discuss her supernatural abilities and visions. The story the woman tells is of a deep winter night when she heard a skeleton rise from its grave in the cellar, creep up the stairs and confront her, then continue up to the attic, where presumably it still resides. The narrator of the poem reveals that the woman's lover had been murdered by her now deceased husband, and he refuses to either treat the ambulatory skeleton as a fact or to entirely reject the woman's story. Though the story seems impossible, the woman's manner of telling it is too coherent and playful to suggest insanity. When she admits, over her son's interjected obfuscations, that the skeleton was her lover, killed by her husband, the stark truth seems to complete rather than to contrast with her otherwise improbable story. Though some critics, refusing to take the ghostly narrative seriously, have read this poem as a tale of psychological evasion, it is possible to read it quite the other way around, as a tale honed through many retellings to eventually help the woman face the ugly truth she now confesses. The only fact the narrator, in the concluding lines, can confirm is the name of the dead husband. The stark naming—"Toffile Lajway"—represents everything left unknown. Randall Jarrell in "The Other Robert Frost" claims that " 'The Witch of Coös' is the best thing of its kind since Chaucer," and most readers of Frost would probably agree.

FAMILIAL TRAGEDIES

The title poem of *New Hampshire* meanders. Nevertheless the book as a whole solidified Frost's reputation. Much of the story of the remainder of his life is of countless honors received, dinners attended, readings and lectures given. Still, his domestic life and the need to make money shaped his routine. When Frost began teaching at Ann Arbor, Elinor worried about their being distant from their children, who were now on their own. When Marjorie became seriously ill both Frost and Elinor returned to Pittsfield, where Marjorie and Lesley had started a bookshop, to look after her. Frost successfully concluded his year at Michigan (the first of several), found time to return to Amherst for a lecture, gave talks at Bryn Mawr and Union College, and accepted a new arrangement with Amherst in which he assumed no formal teaching responsibilities. In January 1927 he moved back to Amherst, where five years later he bought a fine house and seemed to settle permanently. He continued to divide his teaching efforts between Amherst and Michigan, traveled and lectured widely, and signed a new contract with Holt that included a royalty increase and monthly payments of two hundred and fifty dollars for a five-year period.

In the late 1920s Frost's children grew up and married, but they did not achieve the stability their parents had. Frost's daughter Irma married John Cone and produced a grandson, Jack, in 1927, but her mental state gradually became unbalanced. Marjorie developed tuberculosis and a heart condition. In 1929 Lesley, married to Dwight Francis, gave birth to her first child, but she divorced her husband in 1931, soon after their daughter Lesley Lee Francis was born. Carol's future wife Lillian, a close friend of Marjorie, also developed tuberculosis and moved to Monrovia, California, for her health. Marjorie, attempting to make a normal life for herself, despite her poor health, met Willard Fraser, an archaeologist, and became engaged to him. The personal and financial difficulties of Frost's children meant he had considerable expenses for travel and for their medical treatment, and he intensified his lecture schedule to raise the needed funds.

The ominous series of difficulties that began in the late 1920s culminated in one of the major tragedies of Frost's life. In 1934 Marjorie, married the year before, gave birth to a daughter and contracted puerperal fever. Frost had her flown to the Mayo Clinic, where despite intensive treatment she died on May 2. After Marjorie's burial in Billings, Montana, Frost brought her husband and baby back to Amherst with him and Elinor. He wrote to Louis Untermeyer, "The noblest of us all is dead and has taken our hearts out of the world with her" (*Selected Letters*). In 1936 Frost privately published *Franconia*, a small volume of Marjorie's poems.

Through these difficult years Frost remained productive as a poet and published three important volumes. In November 1928 *West-Running Brook* appeared, along with a revised *Selected Poems*; in 1930 *Collected Poems* earned him his second Pulitzer Prize; and in 1936 *A Further Range*, his most controversial book, won him his third. Reviews of *West-Running Brook* were favorable, even flattering, but some such as Frederick Pierce's piece in the *Yale Review* (December 1928) struck a note of concern expressing disappointment with "the smallness, limitation, almost barrenness of the theme itself." The "theme," which disturbed some other reviewers too, and would bother more when *A Further Range* appeared, involved Frost's insistent (and to some, socially irresponsible) individualism. Individualism was embodied in the metaphor of the brook too stubborn to flow east as all the nearby brooks did or, even worse, in the figure of "A Lone Striker," who appears in the first poem in *A Further Range*: his idiosyncratic disregard for the necessities of work seemed to mock the labor movement that had become so central to the struggle against the Great Depression.

Certainly Frost is not a poet with a social program; in fact he went out of his way to mock social reformers, claiming to prefer the world exactly as it was, warts and all. In a letter to Kimball Flaccus he wrote, "I wouldn't give a cent to see the world, the United States or even New York made better. I want them just as they are for me to make poetical on paper. I dont ask anything done to them that I dont do to them myself. I'm a mere selfish artist most of the time." But Frost denied himself the role of the reformer because he had a proper sense of his role as an artist. He inadvertently proved the wisdom of this choice when in his later work, after 1940 or so, he assumed the voice of the sage and of the cracker-barrel philosopher, substituting a kind of political folk wisdom for imagery and metaphor and abandoning much of his previous artistry.

In *West-Running Brook*, *A Further Range*, and most of *A Witness Tree* Frost's artistry generally remains at its mature peak. *West-Running Brook*, besides its satirical title poem, a dialogue in which a husband and wife discuss with some acrimony the nature of contraries and beginnings, contains some memorable lyrics, including "Acquainted with the Night," "Once by the Pacific," "Spring Pools," "A Winter Eden," "Sand Dunes," and "Canis Major." The tone of much of the collection, particularly the section originally entitled "Fiat Nox," is grimmer than most of Frost's previous work. "Acquainted with the Night," an unusual sonnet in terza rima except for a final couplet, illustrates the lonely necessity of individualism by dramatizing the singularity of existence:

I have been one acquainted with the night.
I have walked out in rain—and back in rain.
I have outwalked the furthest city light.

I have looked down the saddest city lane.
I have passed by the watchman on his beat
And dropped my eyes, unwilling to explain.

I have stood still and stopped the sound of feet
When far away an interrupted cry
Came over houses from another street,

But not to call me back or say good-by;
And further still at an unearthly height,
One luminary clock against the sky

Proclaimed the time was neither wrong nor right.
I have been one acquainted with the night.

In this dark little drama only the clock that with grim humor proclaims "the time . . . neither wrong nor right" even faintly speaks for Frost's sense of play. As Frank Lentricchia has pointed out: "The terror of loneliness experienced by the self [in this poem]. . . . flows from a fully aware and mature consciousness," and is all the more terrible for it. "Acquainted with the Night" is not merely about the philosophical awareness of individuality but is a genuinely existential confrontation with nothingness.

Yet the social, not the philosophical, stance of Frost's poetry disturbed some critics in the 1930s. When eight years after *West-Running Brook*, *A Further Range* appeared, reviewers still treated Frost's work with respect, even adulation; but some of the most prominent critics dissented on the important issue of the book's political, economic, and social content. Rolfe Humphries, for example, writing in the *New Masses* deplored Frost's "excursion into the field of the political didactic." *News-Week* entitled a review "Frost: He Is Sometimes a Poet and Sometimes a Stump-Speaker" and found the book "disappointing." Newton Arvin, writing in *Partisan Review*, declared Frost a minor poet "on the sandy and melancholy fringes of our actual life."

Politically self-conscious reviewers were disturbed not only by "A Lone Striker" but also by the now famous poem "Two Tramps in Mud Time," which distinguishes between working for necessity and working for pleasure and concludes by arguing that Frost the individualist would not recognize such a distinction. Thus, in the reading of some, the poem declares Frost to be indifferent to social necessities. Referring to the two ways of working the poem concludes:

But yield who will to their separation,
My object in living is to unite
My avocation and my vocation
As my two eyes make one in sight.
Only where love and need are one,
And the work is play for mortal stakes,
Is the deed ever really done
For Heaven and the future's sakes.

Critics might reasonably have objected to so didactic an ending to a poem that contains such images as

A bluebird comes tenderly up to alight
And turns to the wind to unruffle a plume
His song so pitched as not to excite
A single flower as yet to bloom.

The didactic note troubles other poems, too, like "The White-Tailed Hornet," "A Blue Ribbon at Amesbury," "Build Soil," and "A Drumlin Woodchuck." Deeper into the volume, however, appear strong poems like "The Old Barn at the Bottom of the Fogs," "Desert Places," "Design," "Neither Out Far nor In Deep," and "The Figure in the Doorway," all of which further develop the themes of confronting nothingness, the isolation of the individual, and the uncertainty of the relationship between the human and the natural worlds. *A Further Range* is Frost's darkest and most demanding collection, and though some of its grimmer notes may derive from the poet's personal tragedies the book does seem, despite its critics' complaints, a serious—though oblique—response to the economic and social difficulties of the Great Depression, rather than a reflection on merely personal difficulties.

A Further Range won Frost his third Pulitzer Prize in 1937, but his personal troubles continued. That year Elinor underwent surgery for breast cancer; the Frosts traveled to Gainesville, Florida, to spend the winter with Lesley and her children and allow Elinor to recover her strength. However, after a devastating series of heart attacks in March 1938, Elinor died. Frost, stricken with guilt, collapsed and was unable to attend Elinor's cremation. Lesley blamed her father for hastening Elinor's death by forcing her to climb stairs (though living on the second floor was Elinor's idea) and told him he should never have had children. Elinor had been diagnosed many years before with a heart condition that perhaps should have precluded childbirth, so to that extent Lesley was right. The deaths of Elliott and Marjorie, the marital difficulties of Lesley and Irma, and finally the death of Elinor seemed more than either Lesley or her father could bear. Lesley's accusations, whether justified or not, greatly added to his private sufferings.

"THE FIGURE A POEM MAKES"

That June a disheartened and lonely Frost resigned from Amherst College once again, sold his house, and moved back to South Shaftsbury. Kathleen Morrison, known as Kay, whom Frost had known for several years, invited him to visit friends in West Dover, Vermont, with her. Frost became infatuated and asked Morrison to leave her husband, Theodore Morrison, a lecturer at Harvard, and marry him. Though she refused, she agreed to become his secretary and arrange his lectures and readings. She performed this service for the rest of his life. With the publication of Jeffrey Meyers' biography *Robert Frost* (1996), this relationship, which had been described by most of Frost's previous biographers as platonic, came under fuller scrutiny. Meyers graphically explored the sexual relationship between Frost and Morrison, which had remained entirely secret until partly exposed by the publication of Robert Spangler Newdick's biography *Newdick's Season of Frost* (1976). The secrecy, maintained through Morrison's lifetime, came about largely because Lawrance Roger Thompson, Frost's major biographer, also had an affair with Morrison, and the ensuing complications seemed to him best concealed, though he detailed the evidence in his unpublished notes.

Yet the nature of the relationship between Frost and Morrison seems, in retrospect, plainly delineated in Frost's poetry. "The Silken Tent," a love poem Frost wrote for Morrison, is vividly sensual and suggests how she balanced her love obligations. A seamless one-sentence sonnet, the poem embodies Morrison "as in a field a silken tent," which is stirred by a summer breeze and sways, bound not by a "single cord" but "loosely bound/ By countless silken ties of love and thought/ To everything on earth the compass round." Only when one tie goes "slightly taut" does she feel at all confined. Though the poem may simply signify Morrison's generally rich engagement with the world, it may also represent her embroilment in numerous love affairs; the "capriciousness of summer air," her cheerful promiscuity; the "slightest bondage," her apparently unconfining marriage.

Despite the stress of their relationship, Morrison's presence made the rest of Frost's life less lonely and depressing than it might have been. Carol Frost committed suicide in the house in South Shaftsbury in 1940, shooting himself with a hunting rifle while his son Prescott slept upstairs. Irma by 1947 had deteriorated so badly that Frost had her committed to the New Hampshire State mental hospital. Writing and teaching and lecturing through these difficult years of declining health, Frost required both practical assistance and emotional support, and Morrison offered both.

"The Silken Tent" was the first poem, after two epigraphs, in *A Witness Tree*, which appeared in 1942 and won Frost his fourth Pulitzer Prize. The first fourteen poems form a sequence working backward in time and level of experience from the ecstasy of "The Silken Tent" through the dark natural sublimities of "Come In" and "The Most of It" to the willful sexual cruelty of "The Subverted Flower" and the allegorical narrative (about a "stolen lady") of "The Discovery of the Madeiras." Some of these poems are among Frost's very best lyrics, but despite the celebratory "Silken Tent" the vision of the universe they project, like that of "Design," is a difficult and challenging one.

In 1939 Frost published "The Figure a Poem Makes," his most famous prose statement, as a preface to a new edition of his collected poems. In the essay he argues that a poem begins in delight and ends in wisdom. But "delight" and "wisdom" seem inadequate terms to frame poems like "Come In" and "The Most of It." These poems find the natural world inimical to human needs and desires, but they offer in their graceful unfolding a compensatory beauty. For example, a stanza from "Come In" reads:

> Far in the pillared dark
> Thrush music went—
> Almost like a call to come in
> To the dark and lament.

Like "Stopping by Woods," "Come In" tempts the speaker with a beguiling darkness that he refuses on the grounds that he has not been asked and would not "come in . . . even if asked." In "The Most of It" someone finding himself alone in the universe calls across the landscape—across a lake—hears only the echo of his voice, and receives no "original response," except once, when an "embodiment" crashes through a rockfall, splashes through the lake, and in swimming toward him reveals itself "as a great buck . . . / Pushing the crumpled water up ahead." This indifferent though beautiful creature, the poem concludes, "was all"—meaning it was either utterly inadequate or wonderfully, totally adequate but unacceptable to the lone person who wants "counter-love," which the natural world will never give him.

None of the poems in *A Witness Tree* are as garrulous and clumsy as "Build Soil," the "Political Pastoral" in *A Further Range* that justifiably irritated some reviewers. But except for "Trespass" the poems following "The Quest of the Purple-Fringed" display a serious diminution of Frost's powers. A lack of subtlety, a reduced technique—heavy-handed rhymes and clumsy rhythms—and a didactic certainty, already present in the weaker poems of *A Further Range*, spoil much of Frost's late work. Though he would publish two more collections, as well as his two "masques," only one major poem remained to be written. This was the masterpiece "Directive," which appeared in *Steeple Bush* (1947) and redeemed an otherwise unprepossessing book. Jarrell, in reviewing it in the *New York Times* remarked that "most of the poems in [*Steeple Bush*] merely remind you, by their persistence in the mannerisms of what was genius, that they are productions of somebody who once, and somewhere else, was a great poet." Nonetheless he remarks of "Directive" that "there are weak places in the poem, but they are nothing beside so much longing, tenderness, and passive sadness." Later in his revised version of the review, the essay "To the Laodiceans," Jarrell quotes "Directive" in its entirety and comments that "it shows the coalescence of three of Frost's obsessive themes, those of isolation, of extinction, and of the final limitations of man."

"Directive" invites the reader to withdraw from "all this now too much for us" and follow a "guide . . . / Who only has at heart your getting lost" into a region of abandoned villages and rutted stony roads to find a site (perhaps where Frost and his family once lived) where lie the shattered dishes of a children's playhouse and a cellar hole "Now slowly closing like a dent in dough." Here the guide offers a drink from "A broken drinking goblet like the Grail," and a toast, "Drink and be whole again beyond confusion." This poem of redemption in memory both mocks and honors the rituals through which salvation traditionally comes. Robert Lowell calls "Directive" a journey "to the destroyed homestead of [Frost's] early marriage." It is a sad and beautiful poem and the truest ending to Frost's poetic life.

LAST WRITINGS

A Masque of Reason (1945) and *A Masque of Mercy* (1947) are not Jonsonian masques but resemble the radio plays popular at the time that they were written. Both masques received some very severe reviews (and some favorable ones); both are talky, marred by unsuccessful humor and unconvincing profundities. In *Reason* a couple who turn out to be Job and his wife carry on a rather arch discussion with God in which the role of the wife seems to be to represent the underlying mystery of the universe, while in *Mercy* Jonah appears as a refugee (a "poor, poor swallowable little man," one character calls him) whose fear of God, reflected in the other characters, reveals the paradoxical nature of our conceptions of divinity. The first masque enlarges upon the Old Testament story; the second pits the Old Testament notion of harsh divinity against the New Testament's emphasis on mercy (a key character in *Mercy* is named Paul). Both masques suffer from self-consciously metaphysical dialogue and lack of drama, but in dealing with issues of religious concern (Frost was skeptical about faith) they serve as somewhat interesting afterwords to the long career in poetry that precedes them.

The last decades of Frost's life were eventful. Continuing to teach at Dartmouth, Harvard, and Amherst again (this time with a lifetime appointment), Frost traveled extensively, even on a U.S. State Department visit to Brazil, where Elizabeth Bishop was impressed by his lecture. In 1957 he made his third trip to England and received honorary degrees from both Oxford and Cambridge universities. On his return, although he had objected to the award of the 1948 Bollingen Prize to Ezra Pound for *The Pisan Cantos*, Frost materially participated in freeing Pound from his confinement at St. Elizabeths Hospital where Pound had been sent when found unfit to stand trial for treason. Frost's involvement in Pound's situation led to his playing a larger public role. In 1961 he read a poem at the presidential inauguration of John F. Kennedy. In 1962 Frost traveled to Russia at the invitation of the State Department and met with Premier Nikita Khrushchev, with whom he talked for an hour and a half. Unfortunately he spoke unguardedly (and not entirely honestly) to the press on his return, and this strained his friendship with Kennedy.

In the Clearing (1962), Frost's last book, contains a few sharp epigrams and the long autobiographical poem "Kitty Hawk," which is written in a clumsy meter varying from dimeter to trimeter. "The Draft Horse" is a terse and frightening mystery, "Pod of the Milkweed" a witty meditation, and "Questioning Faces" a single startling and dramatic image:

> The winter owl banked just in time to pass
> And save herself from breaking window
> glass.
> And her wings straining suddenly aspread
> Caught color from the last of evening red
> In a display of underdown and quill
> To glassed-in children at the window sill.

The "evening red," suggesting the crimson of disaster that would have occurred if the owl had not "banked in time," enriches this picture with Frost's characteristic sense of the doubleness of metaphor. Beyond a few strong poems, however, *In the Clearing* only faintly echoes the poet's former voice. The reviews were generally respectful, but the most honest one may have been in the *Wisconsin Library Bulletin*, which noted that Frost's new poems were "closer to jingles than to the memorable poetry we associate with his name." In December Frost learned he had prostate and bladder cancer. After a series of pulmonary embolisms he died in his eighty-ninth year on January 29, 1963. Following a private memorial service in Appleton Chapel at Harvard and a public one at Johnson Chapel, Amherst College, Frost's ashes were buried beside Elinor's in the Frost family plot in Old Bennington, Vermont.

Since Frost's death, dozens of books and hundreds of articles on his work and life have appeared, most notably Lawrance Roger

Thompson's three-volume biography, which almost ruined Frost's reputation by portraying him as a petty, malevolent man obsessed with personal ambitions. Since then, other biographical and critical studies, especially William H. Pritchard's 1984 biography, have greatly modified that picture, and Frost's reputation as a poet has grown large enough to outweigh concern with his personal shortcomings. Frost the man was surely imperfect, but along with William Butler Yeats and Thomas Hardy he is one of the greatest twentieth-century poets to write in traditional prosodic forms. His best poems are as well-known and widely admired as any in the English language. Critical interest in Frost's work continues to grow.

Selected Bibliography

WORKS OF ROBERT FROST

POETRY

A Boy's Will. London: David Nutt, 1913; New York: Henry Holt, 1915.

North of Boston. London: David Nutt, 1914; New York: Henry Holt, 1914.

Mountain Interval. New York: Henry Holt, 1916.

New Hampshire: A Poem with Notes and Grace Notes. New York: Henry Holt, 1923.

West-Running Brook. New York: Henry Holt, 1928.

A Further Range. New York: Henry Holt, 1936.

A Witness Tree. New York: Henry Holt, 1942.

A Masque of Reason. New York: Henry Holt, 1945.

Steeple Bush. New York: Henry Holt, 1947

A Masque of Mercy. New York: Henry Holt, 1947.

In the Clearing. New York: Holt, Rinehart, and Winston, 1962.

COLLECTIONS

Selected Poems. New York: Henry Holt, 1923. Revised, 1928. Again revised, 1934.

Collected Poems. New York: Holt, 1930. Revised 1939.

Selected Poems. London: Jonathan Cape, 1936. (Contains introductory essays by W. H. Auden, C. Day Lewis, Paul Engle, and Edwin Muir.)

Complete Poems of Robert Frost. New York: Henry Holt, 1949.

Aforesaid. New York: Henry Holt, 1951.

Selected Poems. Harmondsworth, England: Penguin Books, 1955.

Selected Poems. New York: Holt, Rinehart, and Winston, 1963. (Includes an introduction by Robert Graves.)

The Poetry of Robert Frost: The Collected Poems, Complete and Unabridged. Edited by Edward Connery Lathem. New York: Holt, Rinehart, and Winston, 1969.

Robert Frost: Poetry and Prose. Edited by Edward Connery Lathem and Lawrance Thompson. New York: Holt, Rinehart, and Winston, 1972.

Collected Poems, Prose & Plays. Edited by Richard Poirier and Mark Richardson. New York: Library of America, 1995.

CORRESPONDENCE AND OTHER PROSE WRITINGS

The Letters of Robert Frost to Louis Untermeyer. Edited by Louis Untermeyer. New York: Holt, Rinehart, and Winston, 1963.

Robert Frost and John Bartlett: The Record of a Friendship. Edited by Margaret Bartlett Anderson. New York: Holt, Rinehart, and Winston, 1963.

Robert Frost: Farm-Poultryman. Edited by Edward Connery Lathem and Lawrance Thompson. Hanover, N.H.: Dartmouth Publications, 1963.

Selected Letters of Robert Frost. Edited by Lawrance Thompson. New York: Holt, Rinehart, and Winston, 1964.

Interviews with Robert Frost. Edited by Edward Connery Lathem. New York: Holt, Rinehart, and Winston, 1966.

Selected Prose of Robert Frost. Edited by Hyde Cox and Edward Connery Lathem. New York: Holt, Rinehart, and Winston, 1966.

Family Letters of Robert and Elinor Frost. Edited by Arnold E. Grade. Albany: State University of New York Press, 1972. Foreword by Lesley Frost.

Robert Frost on Writing. Edited by Elaine Barry. New Brunswick, N.J.: Rutgers University Press, 1973.

Prose Jottings of Robert Frost: Selections from his Notebooks and Miscellaneous Manuscripts. Edited by Edward Connery Lathem and Hyde Cox. Lunenberg, Vt.: Stinehour, 1982.

Stories for Lesley. Edited by Roger D. Sell. Charlottesville: University Press of Virginia, 1984. (Illustrated by Warren Chappell.)

BIBLIOGRAPHIES AND CONCORDANCES

Greiner, Donald J. *The Merrill Checklist of Robert Frost*. Columbus, Ohio: C. E. Merrill, 1969.

Lathem, Edward Connery. *A Concordance to the Poetry of Robert Frost*. New York: Holt Information Systems, 1971.

———. *Robert Frost 100*. Boston: Godine, 1974.

Lentricchia, Frank, and Melissa Christensen Lentricchia. *Robert Frost: A Bibliography, 1913–1974*. Metuchen, N.J.: Scarecrow, 1976.

Van Egmond, Peter. *The Critical Reception of Robert Frost*. Boston: G. K. Hall, 1974.

———. *Robert Frost: A Reference Guide, 1974–1990*. Boston: G. K. Hall, 1991.

BIOGRAPHICAL STUDIES

Cox, Sidney. *A Swinger of Birches: A Portrait of Robert Frost*. New York: New York University Press, 1957.

Evans, William R. *Robert Frost and Sidney Cox: Forty Years of Friendship*. Hanover, N.H.: University Press of New England, 1981.

Francis, Lesley Lee. *The Frost Family's Adventure in Poetry: Sheer Morning Gladness at the Brim*. Columbia: University of Missouri Press, 1994.

Frost, Lesley. *New Hampshire's Child: The Derry Journals of Lesley Frost*. Albany: State University of New York Press, 1969.

Gould, Jean. *Robert Frost: The Aim Was Song*. New York: Dodd, Mead, 1964.

Lathem, Edward Connery, and Lawrance Thompson. *Robert Frost and the Lawrence, Massachusetts, High School Bulletin: The Beginning of a Literary Career*. New York: Grolier Club, 1966.

Mertins, Louis. *Robert Frost: Life and Talks—Walking*. Norman: University of Oklahoma Press, 1965.

Meyers, Jeffrey. *Robert Frost*. Boston: Houghton Mifflin, 1996.

Newdick, Robert Spangler. *Newdick's Season of Frost: An Interrupted Biography of Robert Frost*. Albany: State University of New York Press, 1976.

Pritchard, William H. *Frost: A Literary Life Reconsidered*. New York: Oxford University Press, 1984.

Sergeant, Elizabeth Shepley. *Robert Frost: The Trial by Existence*. New York: Holt, Rinehart, and Winston, 1960.

Thompson, Lawrance. *Robert Frost: The Early Years, 1874–1915*. New York: Holt, Rinehart, and Winston, 1966.

———. *Robert Frost: The Years of Triumph, 1915–1938*. New York: Holt, Rinehart, and Winston, 1970.

Thompson, Lawrance, and R. H. Winnick. *Robert Frost: The Later Years, 1938–1963*. New York: Holt, Rinehart, and Winston, 1976.

Walsh, John Evangelist. *Into My Own: The English Years of Robert Frost, 1912–1915*. New York: Grove Press, 1988.

CRITICAL STUDIES

BOOKS

Bagby, George F. *Frost and the Book of Nature*. Knoxville: University of Tennessee Press, 1993.

Bromwich, David. *A Choice of Inheritance: Self and Community from Edmund Burke to Robert Frost*. Cambridge: Harvard University Press, 1989.

Brower, Reuben. *The Poetry of Robert Frost: Constellations of Intention*. New York: Oxford University Press, 1963.

Burnshaw, Stanley. *Robert Frost Himself*. New York: Braziller, 1986.

Cady, Edwin Harrison, and Louis J. Budd, eds.*On Frost: The Best from American Literature*. Durham, N.C.: Duke University Press, 1991.

Committee on the Frost Centennial of the University of Southern Mississippi, ed. *Frost: Centennial Essays*. Jackson: University Press of Mississippi, 1974.

Cook, Reginald Lansing. *Robert Frost: A Living Voice*. Amherst: University of Massachusetts Press, 1974.

Cox, James M. ed. *Robert Frost: A Collection of Critical Essays*. Englewood Cliffs, N.J.: Prentice-Hall, 1962.

Cramer, Jeffrey S. *Robert Frost among His Poems: A Literary Companion to the Poet's Own Biographical Contexts and Associations*. Jefferson, N.C.: McFarland, 1996.

D'Avanzo, Mario L. *A Cloud of Other Poets: Robert Frost and the Romantics*. Lanham, Md.: University Press of America, 1991.

Gerber, Philip L., ed. *Critical Essays on Robert Frost*. Boston: G. K. Hall, 1982.

———. *Robert Frost*. Boston: Twayne, 1982.

Greiner, Donald J. *Robert Frost: The Poet and His Critics*. Chicago: American Library Association, 1974.

Hadas, Rachel. *Form, Cycle, Infinity: Landscape Imagery in the Poetry of Robert Frost*. Lewisburg, Pa.: Bucknell University Press, 1985.

Holland, Norman Norwood. *The Brain of Robert Frost: A Cognitive Approach to Literature*. New York: Routledge, 1988.

Kearns, Katherine. *Robert Frost and a Poetics of Appetite*. New York: Cambridge University Press, 1994.

Kemp, John C. *Robert Frost and New England: The Poet as Regionalist*. Princeton: Princeton University Press, 1979.

Lentricchia, Frank. *Robert Frost: Modern Poetics and the Landscapes of Self*. Durham, N.C.: Duke University Press, 1975.

Monteiro, George. *Robert Frost and the New England Renaissance*. Lexington: University Press of Kentucky, 1988.

Morrison, Kathleen. *Robert Frost: A Pictorial Chronicle*. New York: Holt, Rinehart, and Winston, 1974.

Munson, Gorham Bert. *Robert Frost: A Study in Sensibility and Good Sense*. New York: George H. Doran, 1927.

Oster, Judith. *Toward Robert Frost: The Reader and the Poet*. Athens: University of Georgia Press, 1991.

Poirier, Richard. *Robert Frost: The Work of Knowing*. New York: Oxford University Press, 1977.

Squires, Radcliffe. *The Major Themes of Robert Frost*. Ann Arbor: University of Michigan Press, 1963.

Tharpe, Jac, ed. *Frost: Centennial Essays II*. Jackson: University Press of Mississippi, 1976.

———, ed. *Frost: Centennial Essays III*. Jackson: University Press of Mississippi, 1978.

Thompson, Lawrance. *Fire and Ice: The Art and*

Thought of Robert Frost. New York: Henry Holt, 1942.

Thornton, Richard, ed. *Recognition of Robert Frost: Twenty-Fifth Anniversary*. New York: Henry Holt, 1937.

Wilcox, Earl J., ed. *Robert Frost: The Man and the Poet*. Rock Hill, S.C.: Winthrop College, 1981.

ESSAYS AND REVIEWS

Anonymous. "Frost: He Is Sometimes a Poet and Sometimes a Stump-Speaker." *News-Week*, May 30, 1936, p. 40.

Anonymous. Review of *In the Clearing*. *Wisconsin Library Bulletin* 58: 240 (July–August 1962).

Arvin, Newton. "A Minor Strain." *Partisan Review* 3: 27–28 (June 1936).

Bagby, George F. "The Promethean Frost." *Twentieth-Century Literature* 38, no. 1: 1–19 (Spring 1992).

Bell, Vereen. "Robert Frost and the Nature of Narrative." *New England Review and Bread Loaf Quarterly* 8, no. 1: 70–78 (Autumn 1985).

Benoit, Raymond. "An American Hierophany: The Wood-Pile in Hawthorne and Frost." *Arizona Quarterly* 44, no. 2: 22–27 (Summer 1988).

Boroff, Marie. "Sound Symbolism as Drama in the Poetry of Robert Frost." *PMLA* 107, no. 1: 131–144 (January 1992).

Braithewaite, W. S. "Fifteen Important Volumes of Poems Published in 1916," in his *Anthology of Magazine Verse for 1916 and Year Book of American Poetry*. New York: Laurence J. Gomme, 1916. P. 247.

Brodsky, Joseph. "On Grief and Reason." *New Yorker*, September 26, 1994, pp. 70–78.

Cornett, Michael E. "Robert Frost on Listen America: The Poet's Message to America in 1956." *Papers on Language and Literature* 29, no. 4: 417–435 (Fall 1993).

Cox, Sidney. "The Sincerity of Robert Frost." *New Republic* 12 (August 25, 1917), 109–111.

Dawes, James R. "Masculinity and Transgression in Robert Frost." *American Literature* 65, no. 2: 297–312 (June 1993).

Doreski, William. "Meta-Meditation in Robert Frost's 'The Woodpile,' 'After Apple-Picking,' and 'Directive.'" *Ariel* 23, no. 4: 35–49 (October 1992).

———. "Robert Frost's 'The Census-Taker' and the Problem of Wilderness." *Twentieth Century Literature* 34, no. 1: 30–39 (Spring 1988).

Evans, Oliver H. "'Deeds That Count': Robert Frost's Sonnets." *Texas Studies in Literature and Language* 23, no. 1: 123–137. (Spring 1981).

Francis, Lesley Lee. "Robert Frost and the Majesty of Stones upon Stones." *Journal of Modern Literature* 9, no. 1: 3–26 (Winter 1981–1982).

Heaney, Seamus. "Above the Brim: On Robert Frost." *Salmagundi* nos. 88–89: 275–294 (Fall/Winter 1990–1991).

Hoffman, Daniel. "Robert Frost: The Symbols a Poem Makes." *Gettysburg Review* 7, no. 1: 101–112 (Winter 1994).

Humphries, Rolfe. "A Further Shrinking." *New Masses*, August 1, 1936, pp. 41–42.

Jarrell, Randall. "Tenderness and Passive Sadness." *New York Times Book Review*, June 1, 1947, p. 4. Reprinted in his *Kipling, Auden & Co: Essays and Reviews 1935–1964*. New York: Farrar, Straus, 1980, pp. 140–142.

———. "The Other Frost" and "To the Laodiceans." In his *Poetry and the Age*. New York: Knopf, 1953, pp. 28–36, 37–69.

———. "Robert Frost's 'Home Burial.'" In his *The Third Book of Criticism*. New York: Farrar, Straus, 1969, pp. 191–234.

Leithauser, Brad. "Great Old Modern." *New York Review of Books*, August 8, 1996, pp. 40–43.

Lowell, Robert. "New England and Further." In his *Collected Prose*, edited by Robert Giroux. New York: Farrar, Straus & Giroux, 1987, pp. 179–212.

Monroe, Harriet. "Frost and Masters," *Poetry* 9 (January 1917), 202.

Pierce, Frederick. "Three Poets Against Philistis." *Yale Review* 18: 364–366 (December 1928).

Richardson, Mark. "Robert Frost and the Motives of Poetry." *Essays in Literature* 20, no. 2: 273–291 (Fall 1993).

Scott, Mark. "Andrew Lang's 'Scythe Song' Becomes Robert Frost's 'Mowing': Frost's Practice of Poetry." *Robert Frost Review* 30–38 (Fall 1991).

Sheehy, Donald G. "(Re)Figuring Love: Robert Frost in Crisis, 1938–1942." *New England Quarterly* 63, no. 2: 179–231 (June 1990).

Special Robert Frost Sections. *South Carolina Review* no. 19 (Summer 1987); no. 21 (Fall 1988).

Trilling, Lionel. "A Speech on Robert Frost: A Cultural Episode." In James M. Cox, *Robert Frost: A Collection of Critical Essays*. Englewood Cliffs, N.J.: Prentice-Hall, 1962. Pp. 151–158.

ALLEN GINSBERG
(1926–1997)

JAMES MERSMANN

IN 1855 IN "Song of Myself," Walt Whitman promised he would "become undisguised and naked" and "permit to speak at every hazard, / Nature without check with original energy." Almost exactly 100 years after Whitman's startling personal declaration of independence, Allen Ginsberg stood before a lively crowd of friends at the Six Gallery in San Francisco and passionately declaimed a new song of the self, a poem that had to be howled instead of sung, about a self that had to be retrieved from madness before it could be celebrated. Whereas Whitman could proclaim and celebrate a transcendent self in a healthy universe ("Clear and sweet is my soul, and clear and sweet is all that is not my soul"), Ginsberg had first to confess and reclaim a perverted and nearly annihilated self from the ravages of an insane world: "I saw the best minds of my generation destroyed by madness, starving hysterical naked, / dragging themselves through the negro streets at dawn looking for an angry fix, / angelheaded hipsters burning for the ancient heavenly connection to the starry dynamo in the machinery of night. . . ." "Howl" created a shock wave in American poetry and culture, but it was only a first noisy step in Allen Ginsberg's lifelong struggle to "become undisguised and naked" and to "permit to speak at every hazard" his own nature, however strange.

"Ginsberg, this poem 'Howl' will make you famous in San Francisco," shouted Jack Kerouac after that historic first reading in 1955. "No," corrected San Francisco poet-patriarch Kenneth Rexroth, "this poem will make you famous from bridge to bridge." But "Howl" made Ginsberg famous around the world. Without "Howl" and the notoriety it received when it was ill-advisedly seized and prosecuted as an obscene book by U. S. Customs and San Francisco police in 1956, Ginsberg's other poems might never have been published. Almost surely Ginsberg would never have burgeoned so grandly as public personality-guru-prophet-paterfamilias-spokesman for several generations of beats, hippies, war protestors, environmentalists, and counterculturists of various sorts.

"Howl" is a volcanic eruption, a breakthrough in the cultural crust, a turning point in the life of the poet and American poetry. It is an "eli eli lamma lamma sabactahani saxophone cry" of the "suffering of America's naked mind for love" and a passionate throwing-off of the guilt and self-hatred imposed by a culture whose proper image is Moloch, that ancient Hebrew deity who demanded blood sacrifices of the young.

But while "Howl" purports to speak for a mid-1950's generation of American youth suffering in a "lacklove" nightmare of "robot apartments" and "demonic industries," such a generation did not actually emerge until the Vietnam war years in the middle 1960's. If poets are, as Ezra Pound claimed, "the antennae of the race," then Ginsberg's antennae need not have been uncommonly long to have described the '60's *zeitgeist* a mere ten years early; but in fact "Howl" is a uniquely personal poem dealing primarily with the poet's own past. While a few of the relative clauses of the single long sentence of part I do refer to a narrow circle of friends (Peter Orlovsky, Jack Kerouac, Carl Solomon, Herbert Huncke, Lucien Carr, William Burroughs, and Neal Cassady), most are thinly veiled autobiography. It is Ginsberg himself

> who passed through universities with
> radiant cool eyes hallucinating Arkansas
> and Blake-light tragedy among the
> scholars of war,
> who were [was] expelled from the academies
> [Columbia] for crazy & publishing
> obscene odes on the windows of the
> skull,
>
> . . .
>
> who studied Plotinus Poe St. John of the
> Cross telepathy and bop kaballa because
> the cosmos instinctively vibrated at their
> [his] feet in Kansas, . . .
> who thought they were [he was] only mad
> when Baltimore [Harlem] gleamed in
> supernatural ecstasy,
>
> . . .
>
> who lost their [his] loveboys to the three old
> shrews of fate . . .
>
> . . .
>
> who were [was] burned alive in their [his]
> innocent flannel suits on Madison avenue
> amid blasts of leaden verse . . .
>
> . . .
>
> who journeyed to Denver, who died in
> Denver, who came back to Denver &
> waited in vain, . . .
>
> . . .
>
> who dreamt and made incarnate gaps in
> Time & Space through images
> juxtaposed, . . .
> to recreate the syntax and measure of poor
> human prose and stand before you
> speechless and intelligent and shaking
> with shame, rejected yet confessing out
> the soul. . . .

"Howl" is not, then, about the best minds of a generation but about the "majestic flaws" of Ginsberg's own mind. "Howl" is a poem of pathology, and the pathology was at least as much private as public. Assuredly, there was madness enough in the complacent 1950's, but it was usually corked tight. The tongue tied in our mouth began to be loosened in Ginsberg's primarily because Moloch had visited him more terribly.

In separate prefaces to *Howl and Other Poems* (1956) and *Empty Mirror, Early Poems* (1961), William Carlos Williams speaks of Ginsberg's poetry as a trip through hell and marvels that Ginsberg ever survived to write a book of poems. If we are ever adequately to understand a poetry so unabashedly confessional and obsessed, we will have to look unblinkingly at the private hell that Ginsberg has had to live through.

Allen Ginsberg was born in Paterson, New Jersey, the son of Louis and Naomi Ginsberg, on June 3, 1926. His father, a high school English teacher with modest poetic talents in the tradition of Longfellow and Whittier, was a man of fairly orthodox and limited mind. His mother, a Russian emigrée and a political activist in her youth, became irrevocably insane during Ginsberg's formative years. According to his own frank and compassionate portrait of her in *Kaddish and Other Poems, 1958–1960* (1961), she was a paranoid schizophrenic who believed she was in danger from assassins and was spied upon and plotted against by Stalinists, Hitlerians, and members of her own family:

> 'Allen, you don't understand—it's ever since those 3 big sticks up my back—they did something to me in Hospital, they poisoned me, they want to see me dead—3 big sticks, 3 big sticks—
>
> 'The Bitch! Old Grandma! Last week I saw her, dressed in pants like an old man, with a sack on her back, climbing up the brick side of the apartment
>
> 'On the fire escape, with poison germs, to throw on me—at night—maybe Louis is helping her—he's under her power—'

In the home, her careless nakedness and seemingly seductive conduct became a source of severe conflict and obsession for her son:

> One time I thought she was trying to make
> me come lay her—flirting to herself at sink—

> lay back on huge bed that filled most of the room, dress up round her hips, big slash of hair, scars of operations, pancreas, belly wounds, abortions, appendix, stitching of incisions pulling down in the fat like hideous thick zippers— ragged long lips between her legs—

The boy is "revolted a little, not much—seemed perhaps a good idea to try—know the Monster of the Beginning Womb—Perhaps—that way. Would she care? She needs a lover."

Numerous poems connect Ginsberg's fear of women with obsessive memories of his mother—"I can't stand these women all over me / smell of Naomi," he writes in "Mescaline"—and the only set of asterisks in "Howl" ("With mother finally ******,") almost implores the reader to infer actual incest.

At age twelve Ginsberg had the traumatic experience of escorting his screaming, hallucinating mother on a five-hour bus trip to a Lakewood, New Jersey, rest home. Returning to Paterson alone late at night, Ginsberg "Went to bed exhausted, wanting to leave the world (probably that year / newly in love with R——— my high school mind hero. . . ."

Ginsberg later followed "R———" to Manhattan and Columbia University, where he met and confessed his love for Jack Kerouac. The heterosexual Kerouac, who was playing on the Columbia football team at the time,

> . . . was very handsome, very beautiful, and mellow—mellow in the sense of infinitely tolerant, like Shakespeare or Tolstoy or Dostoevsky, infinitely understanding. . . . his tolerance gave me *permission* to open up and talk. . . . He wasn't going to hit me. He wasn't going to reject me, really, he was going to accept my soul with all its throbbings and sweetness and worries and dark woes and sorrows and heartaches and joys and glees and mad understanding of mortality. . . .

But, if we are to believe the myth that Ginsberg builds everywhere in his supposedly naked poetry, it was with Neal Cassady that Ginsberg began an exuberant odyssey of heroic love.

However, it is not heroic love that the early Cassady-Ginsberg correspondence reveals but a tense and often brutal symbiosis. Cassady, the irrepressible, fun-loving, fast-moving "cocksman and Adonis of Denver" in Ginsberg's poems and Kerouac's novels, is here quite out of his element—self-conscious, nervous, defensive, and clearly not telling the whole truth. He is troubled that he doesn't feel for Allen the genuine love that Ginsberg so desperately needs; he fears that he may be unable to love anyone; he tries to talk himself into believing this "objectivity of emotionality" has enabled him "to move freely in each groove as it came" and thus proves he is not dangerously and parasitically dependent on Allen: "I've brought this out so you can see an example of my lack of compulsive, emotional need for anyone." Ginsberg is the soul-genius who will educate and sensitize Neal's spirit; but the more experienced Cassady is in the driver's seat physically and is scarcely able to conceal a patronizing attitude toward the tortured young man who "trembles" for love ("Love & Kisses, my boy, opps!, excuse, I'm not Santa Claus am I? Well then, just—Love & Kisses").

When the inevitable break finally came at the end of 1947 (after Ginsberg had "journeyed to Denver," "died in Denver," and come "back to Denver & waited in vain"), Allen abjectly begged Neal for the love he so desperately believed in and needed:

> You know you are the only one who gave me love that I wanted and never had. . . . What must I do for you to get you back? I will do anything. Any indecencies any revelations any creation, any miseries, will they please you. . . . I mean to bend my mind that knows it can destroy you to any base sordid level of adoration and masochistic abnegation that you desire or taunt me with. . . . I hate & fear you so much that I will do anything to win your protection again, and your mercy.
>
> I am lonely, Neal, alone, and always I am frightened. I need someone to love me and kiss me & sleep with me; I am only a child and have the mind of a child. . . . I have always been obedient respectful, I have ad-

> justed my plans to yours, my desires to your own pattern, and now I do ask—I pray—please neal, my neal, come back to me, don't waste me, don't leave me. I don't want to suffer any more, I have had my mind broken open over and over before, I have been isolate and loveless always. I have not slept with anyone since I saw you not because I was faithful but because I am afraid and I know no one. I will always be afraid I will always be worthless, I will always be alone till I die and I will be tormented long after you leave me.

Such letters illuminate Ginsberg's poetry more than any number of interviews and critical analyses. This isolation, fear, self-disgust, and extraordinary hunger for love lie everywhere at the heart of his work.

After the break with Cassady, Ginsberg endured long months of severe depression and isolation alone in a Harlem apartment. His friends were all temporarily out of touch—Burroughs was in Mexico, Huncke in jail, Kerouac holed up on Long Island writing a novel, and Cassady in California about to get married. Ginsberg's mother had once again been incarcerated in a mental hospital. In the midst of this dark night of the soul, unable to act, near catatonia or suicide, Ginsberg was masturbating in his bed one afternoon, idly looking over William Blake's "Sick Rose" and "Ah, Sunflower," when he suddenly began to understand the poems and simultaneously "heard a very deep earthen grave voice in the room," which he immediately assumed was Blake's own voice. It was as if God spoke tenderly to his son: Ginsberg's body "felt *light,* and a sense of cosmic consciousness, vibrations, understanding, awe, and wonder and surprise." Looking out the window, he "saw into the depths of the universe, by looking simply into the ancient sky. The sky suddenly seemed very *ancient.* And this was the very ancient place that he [Blake] was talking about, the sweet golden clime, I suddenly realized that *this* existence was *it*!" Ginsberg saw the "living hand" in the blue of the sky and the craftsmanship of the carved cornices of Harlem, and understood that "existence itself was God." This was the initiation into consciousness that he was born for, and he vowed that he would "never forget, never renig [sic], never deny. Never deny the voice no, never *forget* it, don't get lost mentally wandering in other spirit worlds or American or job worlds or advertising worlds or war worlds or earth worlds."

But Ginsberg does seem to forget, or at least repeatedly to mistranslate and misapply the Blakean message that this world is the "sweet golden clime." Instead of turning to love of the world, Ginsberg turned to the quest of the mystical experience itself and to the use of drugs as "obviously a technique for experimenting with consciousness." In an early poem (1948–1952) of *Empty Mirror* ("The Terms in Which I Think of Reality"), Ginsberg reminds himself that "Time is Eternity" and that a first step toward adjusting to "Reality" is "realizing how real / the world is already." But although he can view the flux and variety of the world as marvelous and will in time learn to be its skillful cataloger (never with Whitman's expansive joy), the world is so full of unpleasant detail that he is "overwhelmed" and turns to "dream again of Heaven." The inescapable fact for Ginsberg is that "the world is a mountain / of shit" and the human predicament is unfortunate at best:

> Man lives like the unhappy
> whore on River Street who
> in her Eternity gets only
>
> a couple of bucks and a lot
> of snide remarks in return
> for seeking physical love
>
> the best way she knows how,
> never really heard of a glad
> job or joyous marriage or
>
> a difference in the heart:
> or thinks it isn't for her,
> which is her worst misery.

Among Ginsberg's special miseries was his arrest and prosecution in 1948 as an accomplice to Huncke, drug addict and thief, who had moved in with the hospitable student and used his New York apartment to stash stolen goods. Ginsberg managed to escape a jail sentence by pleading insanity (he had talked to Blake and seen God!) and spending eight months in the Columbia Psychiatric Institute.

The poems of Ginsberg's troubled early years (1948–1952) are gathered in *Empty Mirror* (1961) and *The Gates of Wrath; Rhymed Poems* (1972). The rhymed poems of the latter show us not the wild madman-prophet-orgiast of "Howl" and later poetry, but the Columbia honor student and English major, the clean-shaven, youthful Dr. Jekyll desperately busy keeping Mr. Hyde locked in the basement with meter and rhyme. They are neither very honest nor very good poems.

Among them are several written to Neal Cassady. Carefully avoiding gender pronouns and explicit sexuality, they speak in all-too-familiar love-poem abstractions and clichés—"my heart was broken in your care; /I never suffered love so fair" ("A Western Ballad"). When they do deal in particulars, as in "Do We Understand Each Other?" they reveal a twenty-two-year-old poet who is as silly as a thirteen-year-old:

> My love was at the wheel,
> And in and out we drove.
> My own eyes were mild.
> How my love merrily
> Dared the other cars to rove:

Sexual content is disguised and anesthetized by polysyllabic abstraction and contorted syntax, as in "A Lover's Garden":

> As seconds on the clock do move,
> Each marks another thought of love;
> Thought follows thought, and we devise
> Each minute to antithesize,
> Till, as the hour chimes its tune,
> Dialectic, we commune.
>
> The argument our minds create
> We do, abed, substantiate. . . .

Considering the repression and dishonesty of such poems, it is easy to understand Ginsberg's subsequent turn to a spontaneous poetics that refuses revision and seeks to record the "naked activity" of the mind. "Now if you are thinking of 'form' or even the 'well made poem' or a sonnet when you're lying on the couch, you'll never say what you have on your mind."

In a few poems truth threatens to break through as a "shroudy stranger" or "shadow." According to Carl Jung, there is in each of us an archetypal "darker brother" who must be recognized and embraced if we are to achieve psychic health and wholeness. In contemporary Western culture, that shadow or repressed self is almost always associated with the body and the libido; the "bright self" or public persona is usually associated with the head and rational faculties. The shadow figures in Ginsberg's poems are beyond his understanding and control, and seem full of unconscious contents relating to his ambivalent feelings about his own body.

Ginsberg consciously connects the "stranger" who haunts his dreams with the voice of the Blake visions, with the presence of God, and with his own desire to die. Thus the Blake of the auditory hallucinations sometimes seems to be Ginsberg's alter ego, one who asks the young poet in "Psalm" to convert the energy of his Harlem pentecost into substance or "bone."

> I saw it here,
> The Miracle, which no man knows entire,
> Nor I myself. But shadow is my prophet,
> I cast a shadow that surpasses me,
> And I write, shadow changes into bone. . . .

Sometimes the shadow seems to be the Divine One hiding inside Ginsberg and looking out through his eyes: "What a sweet dream! to be some incorruptible / Divinity, corporeal without a name, / Suffering metamorphosis of flesh" ("Psalm"). While both of these interpretations of the dream shadow point Ginsberg toward the need to accept his life in the real world, he characteristically strays into longing for death because he "cannot go be wild / or harken back to shape of child" ("Ode: My 24th Year"). Though the Harlem vision told him *this was it,* he persists in "Psalm" in wanting the *it* without the *this*:

> Ah, but to have seen the Dove of still
> Divinity come down in silken light of
> summer sun
> In ignorance of the body and bone's
> madness.

Given Ginsberg's desire to pass from the world into pure vision or pure voice, and given his desperate and frustrated hunger for physical tenderness and love, it is perhaps inevitable that the dream figures should suggest the homoerotic attractiveness of death. The dream stranger in "A Dream" is sometimes a pale boy with beautiful hair and eyes "Walking in a winding sheet, / As fair as was my own disguise" who invites the dreamer to follow him safely "through the grave":

> "And we will walk the double door
> That breaks upon the ageless night,
> Where I have come, and must once more
> Return, and so forsake the light."
>
> The darkness that is half disguised
> In the Zodiac of my dream
> Gazed on me in his bleak eyes. . . .

Ginsberg is both attracted and frightened, tempted and repulsed by those bleak eyes. Either suicide or homosexuality means death; death by one is but a means of avoiding death by the other. Ginsberg would rather die than live with that dark self, but death and that self already seem inextricably fused. Sometimes, as in "The Shrouded Stranger," it appears as a nightstalker with reddened eye who follows old men and young boys and peeps in at windows ready to take with him anyone who would succumb to his strange attraction:

> Maid or dowd or athlete proud
> May wanton with me in the shroud
> Who'll come lay down in the dark with me
> Belly to belly and knee to knee
> Who'll look into my hooded eye
> Who'll lay down under my darkened thigh?

Ginsberg's dreams are haunted because he cannot accept the dark self that his unfortunate childhood created in him but which society will not bless. As late as 1963, in "The Change: Kyoto-Tokyo Express," he admits that he has always denied his "own shape's loveliness" and felt his sexual desire "to be horrible instead of Him." Thus despite the dream stranger's attractive connection to Blake or God, or death, Ginsberg wrestled with him as a fearful adversary who "holds me in his keep / and seeks the bones that he must find"; who "cries out in my name; / he struggles for my writhing frame" ("The Voice of Rock").

If the early rhymed poems conceal Ginsberg, the more prosaic journal jottings of *Empty Mirror* reveal him. These are not poems so much as desperate notes to the self:

> I feel as if I am at a dead
> end and so I am finished.
> All spiritual facts I realize
> are true but I never escape
> the feeling of being closed in
> and the sordidness of self,
> the futility of all that I
> have seen and done and said.
> Maybe if I continued things
> would please me more but now
> I have no hope and I am tired.

In these last lines and elsewhere Ginsberg urges himself to adjust and "make a home in wilderness" ("A Desolation"), but he can experience life only as "A Meaningless Institution" wherein he has been given "a bunk in an enormous ward / surrounded by hundreds of weeping, / decaying men and women," and abandoned without friends or instructions. No matter how much he lectures himself as he does in "Metaphysics" ("This is the one and only / firmament; therefore /it is the absolute world. / There is no other world. / The circle is complete. / I am living in Eternity. / The ways of this world / are the ways of

Heaven"), he cannot make his peace with "ruinous, vile, dirty Time." In "Walking home at night" he thinks of himself

> in company with obscure
> Bartlebys and Judes,
> cadaverous men,
> shrouded men, soft white
> fleshed failures creeping
> in and out of rooms like
> myself. Remembering
> my attic, I reached
> my hands to my head and hissed
> "Oh, God how horrible!"

Oppressed by his sense of how ill he is, Ginsberg wonders in "Marijuana Notation" "Is it this strange / for everybody?" In "I Have Increased Power" he sees that his illness comes from having "no active life / in realworld"; his "dreamworld and realworld / become more and more / distinct and apart," but the real world contains no "consummation forseeable / in ideal joy or passion." "Tonite all is well" shows Ginsberg at the verge of breakdown:

> . . . I am ill,
> I have become physically and
> spiritually impotent in my madness this
> month.
> I suddenly realized that my head
> is severed from my body. . . .

For Ginsberg and for all of us, this is a key perception. Ginsberg's may be a private pathology bordering on clinical hebephrenic schizophrenia, but it is shared to a greater or lesser degree by nearly everyone living in a highly systematized technological urban culture. It is closely related to the "dissociation of sensibility" that T. S. Eliot described in Western culture a half-century earlier, and which has become an increasingly important subject for a multitude of poets as widely different as John Crowe Ransom ("Painted Head"), Gary Snyder ("Milton by Firelight"), and Robert Bly ("A Man Writes to Part of Himself" and all of his work).

Ginsberg's head has been severed from his body. The result, inevitably, is both spiritual and physical impotence, because all potency or power requires a yin-yang admixture or dynamic interchange. Moreover, such a "horizontal" cleavage does not occur without a "vertical," or lateral, bifurcation of the self as well. The "head" in Ginsberg is split between his consuming focus on intuitive mystical experience (Blake, God, eternity—"the ancient heavenly connection to the starry dynamo") and his rigidly patterned superego posing as the rational, thinking self (the machinery in "the machinery of night"); the "body" is torn between the seething shadow of repressed feeling and its nearly catatonic shell, the practical self paralyzed in an empty, meaningless life. The dismembered Ginsberg cannot translate or convert his direct intuitive knowledge from the Blake visions into action or affection in the real world; his reason tells him "all spiritual facts are true," but they are inert and without mana; his feelings are condemned by his superego and fill him with disgust; and his sensations and practical abilities are numbed by the falseness of his life in the nine-to-five world. These mutilated, alienated "selves" roughly correspond to the four functions of the Jungian mandala (intuition, thinking, feeling, sensation); but the unifying fifth or "transcendent function," the Self at the center, is missing. That is the Self that Whitman sang, joining body and soul, outer and inner, good and evil, male and female, animal and angel, in an erotic and mystical union.

Ginsberg is "at a dead end," torn apart, one of the hollow men. He has no Self, and thus it is that the *Empty Mirror* is empty. The gods of his head and the daemons of his body are in conflict: the Old Testament, judging Father struggles against the benevolent "living hand" of the Blake visions; the dionysiac shadow is "burned alive" in the "flannel suit" of the market-research analyst. The superego and the id, the visionary and the "responsible" citizen are all in arms against one another. It should be no surprise, then, that "war" emerges as the primary metaphor of all of Ginsberg's poetry and that his poetry can best be understood as a life-long search for the missing center, for the Self or Soul or Sacred Heart that bridges the gaps between mind and body, Eternity and Time. It is of course the classic work of poetry to put the severed self together again, to show that the Self and the world are the body of God, the Incarnate Word, and that the Self is not separate from but coextensive with the natural world. That precisely was Whitman's glorious achievement in "Song of Myself."

In only one of Ginsberg's early "East Coast" poems does he find enough strength or enough self to confront and challenge the "realworld." In "Paterson" (1949) the line lengthens and the breath deepens. The poem moves as if the poet is at last on his feet, pacing his tenement room in anger, choosing for a change to condemn marketplace America rather than himself. Why should he try to fit in? What, after all, does he "want in these rooms papered with visions of money?" Why should he enter that "war" for such a "prize! the dead prick of commonplace obsession, / harridan vision of electricity at night and daylight misery of thumb-sucking rage" (a rather unpleasant portrait not only of the business world but of married life). He would rather go mad, take drugs, suffer any kind of crucifixion, "rather crawl on my naked belly over the tincans of Cincinnati; / rather drag a rotten railroad tie to a Golgotha in the Rockies." Here at last is the first tentative sound of the angry "Hebraic-Melvillean bardic" voice that will break forth in fury in "Howl." It is also the moment when Ginsberg begins to embrace the "beatness" and "beatitude" that comes from accepting one's failure to fit in and "make it" within the acceptable patterns and values of the dominant culture. Ginsberg has tried mightily to be straight and "normal" ("to tame the hart / and wear the bear"), but he has not succeeded. For more than twenty years he has blamed himself, introjecting the guilt for his unhappiness. In "Paterson" he looks outside himself to notice the enemy in the culture at large.

In 1953 Ginsberg abandoned the emotionally dark environs of New York and New Jersey to travel, via Cuba and Yucatan, to a fresh beginning in San Francisco. Within the next year several important events radically altered his life. The first of these was his meeting with Peter Orlovsky, who is the subject of "Malest Cornifici Tuo Catullo" (*Reality Sandwiches, 1953–60*) and who would become his life companion:

> I'm happy, Kerouac, your madman Allen's finally made it: discovered a new young cat, and my imagination of an eternal boy walks on the streets of San Francisco, handsome, and meets me in cafeterias and loves me. Ah don't think I'm sickening. You're angry at me. For all of my lovers? It's hard to eat shit, without having visions; when they have eyes for me it's like Heaven.

Ginsberg is still perhaps not equal to love (Peter is too easily lost in the "they" of the last line), but he is clearly in love with being loved, and the physical tenderness and attention seem to validate and energize him. Nevertheless, he continues to seek escape from the everyday world (which he perceives as "eating shit") through visions and sex, and he fears and assumes the negative judgment of Kerouac. Ginsberg cannot accept the world or himself. In his own mind he is still really "meat-creephood." If the Moloch of "Howl," part II, is a "heavy judger of men," then Moloch exists as much inside Ginsberg as outside him. He is not only the reification of "mind" in the nation, but is also the disapproving father, Louis Ginsberg in Paterson, New Jersey, and the superego of Allen Ginsberg himself. But the relationship with Peter Orlovsky is the beginning of Moloch's overthrow.

The second event that freed Ginsberg to write "Howl" is the session with a psychiatrist who, Ginsberg claims, "gave me the authority, so to speak, to be myself." (As James Breslin has noted, Ginsberg had not been able to give himself that permission.) He had previously consulted with a long procession of analysts, Freudians, Reichians, Jungians, Adlerians, and Sullivanians. After multiple sessions exploring Ginsberg's unhappiness, this psychiatrist asked simply, "What would you like to do? What is your desire really?" Ginsberg was almost too embarrassed to say. What he wanted to do was quit his job and never work again, to keep living with someone, "maybe even a man," and give himself completely to exploring visions and relationships. (In other words, to be lazy, immoral, and a failure in the eyes of the Father.) The psychiatrist's answer was simply, "Well, why don't you?" Ginsberg did. The result was "Howl."

Ginsberg arranged to be fired from his job so that he could collect unemployment, moved into an apartment with Orlovsky, and one long weekend, with the aid of amphetamines and peyote, began to wail. "Howl" cannot be imitated. It has to be lived and suffered. It is not a creation of art but an *event* in the life of a man. It is a therapeutic disburdening, a shucking off and breaking free of guilt and self-hatred, an attempt to retrieve and affirm a self that had all but disappeared. It is a personal "confessing out the soul" and a cultural cleansing as well, because it named and to a degree exorcised some of the madness growing in everyone since the Industrial Revolution.

In part II of "Howl" Ginsberg turns on his accuser; in open rebellion against the Father, he names and confronts the monster-God-machine who bashes open the skulls and eats up the brains and imagination of its children:

> Moloch whose mind is pure machinery!
> Moloch whose blood is running money!
> Moloch whose fingers are ten armies!
> Moloch whose breast is a cannibal
> dynamo! Moloch whose ear is a smoking
> tomb!
> Moloch whose eyes are a thousand blind
> windows! Moloch whose skyscrapers
> stand in the long streets like endless
> Jehovahs! Moloch whose factories dream
> and croak in the fog! Moloch whose
> smokestacks and antennae crown the
> cities!
> Moloch whose love is endless oil and stone!
> Moloch whose soul is electricity and
> banks! Moloch whose poverty is the
> specter of genius! Moloch whose fate is a
> cloud of sexless hydrogen! Moloch whose
> name is the Mind!

In the face of such a vicious God, the first and perhaps only act of affirmation available to us is to commit ourselves in friendship and sympathy to a fellow victim. This Ginsberg does in part III in a litany of assurances to Carl Solomon, who had been his fellow inmate at Rockland State Mental Hospital:

> I'm with you in Rockland
> where we hug and kiss the United States
> under our bedsheets the United States
> that coughs all night and won't let us
> sleep
> I'm with you in Rockland
> where we wake up electrified out of the
> coma by our own souls' airplanes roaring
> over the roof they've come to drop
> angelic bombs the hospital illuminates
> itself imaginary walls collapse O skinny
> legions run outside O starry-spangled
> shock of mercy the eternal war is here
> O victory forget your underwear we're
> free

In the love of these madmen-victims for each other, there is even a little tenderness left over for the body of Moloch himself, for the United States who is otherwise a rather sickly lay. And once the war against desire and the Self has been abandoned, the soul's weapons can be turned outward to the war against "walls" and repressions, and the Self can forget its underwear and be innocently naked. (It is as if the emaciated legions of Buchenwald and Auschwitz were suddenly liberated by Ginsberg's poetic air raid against der Führer.)

In "Footnote to Howl" (functionally "Howl," part IV), Ginsberg celebrates his escape from the concentration camps of Moloch and sings a long litany of praise proclaiming the holiness of all things: "Holy time in eternity holy eternity in time holy the clocks in space holy the fourth dimension holy the fifth International holy the Angel in Moloch!" Ginsberg's embrace of "time in eternity . . . eternity in time" seems genuine here, as if for the moment his life with Orlovsky and his permission to be himself have lifted him to new self-acceptance and a sense of well-being. The poem and "Footnote" form a kind of *Divine Comedy* in which Ginsberg descends through the agonies of hell to face and name the satanic God wedged at the center of the vortex, before ascending the holy mountain of purgatory through his healing sympathy with Carl Solomon. The "Footnote" is the *Paradiso* of the piece, where Ginsberg seems to have achieved a new level of at-one-ment.

"Howl" is easily Ginsberg's most important, passionate, and unified poem. Likewise, the nine shorter poems in *Howl and Other Poems* (1956) are generally superior to his later work.

In "Sunflower Sutra" for example, Ginsberg is able to forget himself long enough to see with clear eyes "the gray Sunflower poised against the sunset, crackly bleak and dusty with the smut and smog and smoke of olden locomotives in its eye— / corolla of bleary spikes pushed down and broken like a battered crown, seed fallen out of its face, soon-to-be-toothless mouth of sunny air, . . ." and can recognize its besmutted but beautiful blossom as an image of his own soul, which had once thought it was "an impotent dirty old locomotive" instead of a flower. "—We're not our skin of grime, we're not our dread bleak dusty imageless locomotive, we're all beautiful golden sunflowers inside. . . ." This is for the poet not a trite preachment but an exciting discovery; there is a becoming innocence and boyish fascination caught in the spontaneous spill of language that names the trash and litter of urban ash heaps and finds an inextinguishable truth growing adamantly among it.

In "America" too, the poet has gained enough emotional distance to attack the country's faults with humor, mimicking the foolishness of the public and the government and recognizing himself as a strange outsider with considerably different thoughts and "national resources": "My national resources consist of two joints of marijuana millions of genitals an unpublishable private literature that goes 1400 miles an hour and twenty-five-thousand mental institutions." Ginsberg faults his country for its greed, mechanization, xenophobia, gullibility, exaggerated seriousness, puritanical morality, and enslavement to *Time* magazine, but pretends to take the country's fears and programs seriously and vows that he, too, had "better get right down to the job" and put his "queer shoulder to the wheel." Anyone who can thus attack evil is no longer so helplessly its victim.

Even the insatiable hunger and preoccupation with physical love seem quieted and disciplined in this volume. In contrast to his later work, "Song" is almost understated:

> The warm bodies
>   shine together
> in the darkness,
>   the hand moves
> to the center
>   of the flesh,
> the skin trembles
>   in happiness
> and the soul comes
>   joyful to the eye—
>
> yes, yes,
>   that's what
> I wanted,
>   I always wanted,
> I always wanted,
>   to return
> to the body
>   where I was born.

Whereas the "return to the body" that seems to be sought in other volumes is a retreat to infancy and the womb, an escape from life, here it seems almost a Whitmanesque realization of the body electric.

The long lines of *Howl and Other Poems* mark a second major shift in Ginsberg's poetics. Beginning before Columbia and continuing into the early 1950's, Ginsberg had been fascinated with formally rhymed and metered poetry imitative of Donne, Marvell, Shakespeare, and others. As a boy he had accompanied his father to meetings of the Poetry Society of America and heard "mostly old ladies and second-rate poets" praise Longfellow while denouncing Pound, Eliot, and Williams. "*Their* highwater mark was, I guess, Edwin Arlington Robinson, 'Eros Turannos' was considered, I guess, the great highwater mark of twentieth-century poetry." According to Ginsberg, his poetic education did not fare much better at Columbia. There the "supreme literary touchstones" were John Crowe Ransom and Allen Tate. The values were those defined by the New Criticism. Whitman "was considered like a creep." Pound was taught only as a "freak-out," and William Carlos Williams, who lived a few miles away from Ginsberg, was almost completely unknown.

Williams was known to his fellow townsman, however. Ginsberg showed him his rhymed poems and was told that "in this mode perfection is basic" and these were not perfect. Williams advised the young poet to become a more careful and detailed observer and to record what he saw more simply and honestly. Looking back over his journals, Ginsberg discovered that there were such poems hidden in his jottings. The best of these discoveries is "The Brick Layer's Lunch Hour" (*Empty Mirror*), describing a young workman whom Ginsberg had watched from his apartment window. The poem shows Ginsberg's talents of observation and is refreshingly clean of the self-consciousness and concern of his other early poems. But all of the prosy short-line poems in *Empty Mirror* also show that Ginsberg had very little feel for "the variable foot" and poetic line of Williams. Moreover, while these clumsily divided short lines might contain the feelings of the moribund East Coast poet, they could not contain the volatile emotions of the more robust Ginsberg of the West Coast.

Although the more expansive, confessional impulse had always been strong in Ginsberg, he had never felt free to indulge it: "The beginning of the fear in me was, you know, what would my father say to something I would write." The spill of long lines in "Howl" was possible because Ginsberg never intended his father or any other judgers to see it ("I wouldn't want my daddy to see what was in there. About my sex life. . . ."): "I suddenly turned aside in San Francisco, unemployment compensation leisure, to follow my romantic inspiration—Hebraic-Melvillean bardic breath. I thought I wouldn't write a *poem,* but just write what I wanted to without fear, let my imagination go, open secrecy, and scribble magic lines from my real mind—sum up my life—something I wouldn't be able to show anybody, write for my own soul's ear and a few other golden ears."

One of the "few other golden ears" he was writing for was Jack Kerouac, who Ginsberg knew would hear "the long saxophone-like chorus lines . . . taking off from his own inspired prose line really a new poetry." Ginsberg was also shaping his sounds to ear echoes of Illinois Jacquet's "Can't Get Started," Lester Young's "89 choruses of *Lady Be Good,*" as described by Kerouac, and "an extreme rhapsodic wail I once heard in a madhouse."

The long line of "Howl" and Ginsberg's later poetry has its literary origins in William Blake's "Marriage of Heaven and Hell," Christopher Smart's "Jubilate Agno," and Whitman's *Leaves of Grass;* but it is also explained in part by physiology—the "neural impulses" and "the breathing and the belly and the lungs" of a poet whose "movement" and "feeling is for a big long clanky statement"; and perhaps in part by abnormal psychology—the oral and anal erotic's enjoyment of explosive purgations (see Edmund Wilson's "Morose Ben Jonson").

Subsequent volumes of poetry indicate that the wholeness or atone-ment of *Howl and Other Poems* is at best only temporary and at worst perhaps more illusory than real. The seemingly unified self that speaks in these poems may be only a more simplified self, one in which the warring elements have suddenly been reduced from four to two. By abandoning his market research job and "straight" lifestyle, and by repudiating the mental Moloch, Ginsberg has cut away one half of the fragmented self ("sensation" and "thinking"), leaving only the mystic and the "darker brother" ("intuition" and "feeling"). Ginsberg has rejected the systematized moral world of mind and the organized practical world of work. What is left in too much of his later poetry is a Ginsberg who is interested in pure consciousness or pure meat, sainthood or sex, vision or venery. In this he is no different than in *The Gates of Wrath or Empty Mirror,* except that there his energy level is down, his movement slow, and his ambience small; after *Howl and Other Poems* his energy is high, his speed rocketing, and his orbit is the world. While I cannot agree with Reed Whittemore that the "Howl" stage of Ginsberg's career is calamitous, or anything other than healthy for poetry and American culture, it is easy to share some of his other concern that

> . . . this second stage in the Ginsberg saga has been even more calamitous than the "Howl" stage. The first had the genuineness of anger and despair about it—it was home grown and home felt—but the second has been clouded by great expectations, expectations that Ginsberg himself sometimes manages to temper with solid observations and with his striking death-obsession, but that his devotees infallibly leave raw: nirvana in the pad, nightly, forever. There is terror for me in their misconceptions of what inner fantasy-life can make of the stony world; and Ginsberg is one of the breeders of that terror. Saintly he may indeed be as a private sinner—I do not question his private credentials—but he has also been a most influential loudmouth, an eccentric evangelist for an apocalyptic faith (and aesthetic) that has in my opinion competed pretty well with Moloch in mind-destroying.

Only twice again in a long, prolific career does Ginsberg approach the power and significance of "Howl," and in each case—"Kaddish" and "Wichita Vortex Sutra"—he is pushed to powerful utterance by overwhelming emotions. Ginsberg's genius lies not in his craft (of which he claims to have none) but in the authenticity of his feelings.

In the title poem of *Kaddish and Other Poems* the poet who had still felt a need to camouflage his biography behind the "best minds" of his generation in "Howl" confronts himself and his subject with an honesty that is at once brutal and compassionate. The first two long sections of "Kaddish" are meditations on death (and life) as well as stream-of-memory narrative detailings of his mother's madness and death. Death is "that remedy all singers dream of," a release from the dream where we are all trapped "sighing, screaming . . . buying and selling pieces of phantom. . . .

> Ai! ai! we do worse! We are in a fix! And
> you're out, Death let you out, Death had
> the Mercy, you're done with your
> century, done with God, done with the
> path through it—Done with yourself at
> last—Pure—Back to the Babe dark
> before your Father, before us all— . . ."

But in spite of "all the accumulations of life, that wear us out," our tortured existences are significant, almost even beautiful, when seen with the intensity of Ginsberg's love for his mother:

> to have been here, and changed, like a tree,
> broken, or flower—fed to the ground—
> but mad, with its petals, colored,
> thinking Great Universe, shaken, cut in
> the head, leaf stript, hid in an egg crate
> hospital, cloth wrapped, sore—freaked in
> the moon brain, Naughtless.
> No flower like that flower, which knew
> itself in the garden, and fought the
> knife—lost. . . .

A pivotal image in the poem (and for Ginsberg's life) lies in a letter written by his mother just before her death: "—2 days after her death I got her letter— / Strange Prophecies anew! She wrote—'The key is in the window, the key is in the sunlight at the window—I have the key—Get married Allen don't take drugs—the key is in the bars, in the sunlight in the window.'" Paradoxically, Ginsberg's mad mother may indeed have had the key for him, a symbolical insight going well beyond the advice to give up drugs and homosexuality. The key is not in the bright sky or the darkness of the room but at the threshold where light enters the material house. But for Ginsberg the bars that stripe and pattern the light have become Moloch, bars that imprison and separate the visionary and erotic self.

"The Lion for Real" offers a humorous account of Ginsberg's predicament after the Blake visions—the difficulty of telling his analyst and friends about the divine lion in his Harlem room. "To Aunt Rose" is a sympathetic identification with another lonely, buried self. The short-lined "Europe! Europe!" and the prophetic long-lined "Death to Van Gogh's Ear!" build on the war metaphor and continue the attack on Moloch. Most of the remaining poems of *Kaddish and Other Poems* are written under the influence of drugs—nitrous oxide, ayahausco, LSD, mescaline. Though their message may be (as Ginsberg claims) to "widen the area of consciousness," they do little to widen the reader's.

"Scribbled secret notebooks, and wild typewritten pages, for yr own joy" promises the subtitle-epigraph of *Reality Sandwiches, 1953–60* (1963), a book more interesting as autobiography than as poetry. It reveals both the before "Howl" and after "Howl" Ginsberg—the former a love-starved, death-obsessed businessman pondering escape in death or "the total isolation of the bum" ("Over Kansas," 1954), the latter a nostalgic isolatee walking "in the timeless sadness of existence," looking at his "own face streaked with tears in the mirror / of some window," feeling a "tenderness" toward everything but cut off from ordinary people and ordinary life by his lack of desire to own the bonbons and dresses and "Japanese lampshades of intellection" that are at the busy but empty heart of American culture ("My Sad Self," 1958).

"On Burroughs' Work" is an important early statement of Ginsberg's developing poetics, an insistence (influenced by both Burroughs and Kerouac) that poetry become an honest and spontaneous transcript of consciousness, "purest meat and no symbolic dressing," a naked lunch of reality sandwiches without any kind of lettuce to "hide the madness."

"My Alba" (1953) also contains an early and brilliant example of image juxtaposition that Ginsberg had learned from the paintings of Paul Cézanne. Studying Cézanne in 1949, Ginsberg "suddenly got a strange shuddering impression looking at his canvases, partly the effect when someone pulls a venetian blind, reverses the venetian—there's a sudden shift, a flashing that you see in Cézanne's canvases." The flash was a moment when the two-dimensional plane of the canvas seemed to shift into three dimensions and the juxtaposed planes of color suddenly became solid-space objects; in that flash Ginsberg could see through the canvas into cosmic space and feel a sensation like that of his Blake hallucinations. He later discovered that Cézanne had spoken about his attempt to "*reconstitute the petites sensations*" or flashes of perception that he got from nature after his senses had become so refined that he could stand on a hill and merely by moving his head half an inch "the composition of the landscape was totally changed." For Cézanne, this *petite sensation* was the experience of *pater omnipotens aeterna Deus.*

Just as Cézanne worked in two-dimensional planes and trusted to the perceptual leap of the viewer to create the deep space of the painting and the experience of *pater omnipotens aeterna Deus,* so Ginsberg hoped that by simple juxtaposition of disparate images, he might prompt the reader's perception to leap the gap between words and see through the poem to God. Such an intention is behind the "hydrogen jukebox" and "winter midnight smalltown street-light rain" in "Howl," and the "mad locomotive riverbank sunset Frisco hilly tincan evening sit-down vision" of "Sunflower Sutra." But the technique also seems to justify "the unexplainable, unexplained nonperspective line," Ginsberg's jamming together of longer bits, disconnected phrases, glimpses, fragments, subjects in a single poem, separating or joining them only by dashes, line breaks, or open spaces instead of the usual grammatical and logical connections. For all its other virtues, the technique does not work as Ginsberg intended. His poetry seems to have very little success at this mystical flicking of venetian blinds or opening the reader's senses to the immediate apprehension of God. But the technique is a marvelously effective shorthand and can flash the mind with brilliant cultural silhouettes. The "hydrogen jukebox" of "Howl," for example, is a wonderfully radioactive image, throwing off a frenzy of implication and backlighting a huge moral, political, and emotional landscape reaching from the Pentagon to the Six Gallery.

But an earlier and perhaps even stronger example of this Cézanne technique is found in "My Alba," where Ginsberg regrets the five years he wasted in Manhattan as advertising copyist and market researcher with "mental / sliderule and number / machine" deceiving "multitudes / in vast conspiracies / deodorant battleships." The multiple resonances of "deodorant battleships" are too rich for exploration here, but the startling juxtaposition compresses volumes of commentary on the connections between Madison Avenue, war, deception, greed, prudery, fear and hatred of the body, and national paranoia. It also carries the intensity of Ginsberg's repugnance for a world he experienced primarily as an attack on his own flesh.

Planet News: 1961–1967 (1968) contains "Wichita Vortex Sutra," a poem comparable in power to "Howl" and "Kaddish." It is a vehement protest against the war in Vietnam and a concentration of Ginsberg's continuing poetic attack on Western culture's perpetual war against the flesh. The war that Ginsberg finds most intolerable is the "war on Man, the war on Woman," the war of "cold" more destructive than the international cold war, the mentality that would freeze the blood and desire: "the imposition of a vast mental barrier on everybody, a vast antinatural psyche. A hardening, a shutting off of the perception of desire and tenderness which everybody *knows* and which is the very structure of . . . the atom!" The perception of this "imposition" is not new, nor is the war against it. It is essentially the battleground defined by Blake and the romantics, broadened beautifully by Whitman, D.H. Lawrence, E.E. Cummings, and others. But Ginsberg's outcry is more anguished, his anger more personal, his own foot caught in the trap most painfully.

As early as "Paterson" (1949) and "My Alba," Ginsberg had described the Madison Avenue-Wall Street world as a "war." He expanded the metaphor in "Howl," where those stalking-horse "best minds" were "burned alive in their innocent flannel suits on Madison Avenue amid blasts of leaden verse & the tanked-up clatter of the iron regiments of fashion & the nitroglycerine shrieks of the fairies of advertising & the mustard gas of sinister intelligent editors. . . ." Ginsberg sees society as a vast, violent conspiracy of greed, repression, and control that sears the soul and mutilates the flesh as surely as flamethrowers and fragmentation bombs.

In "Death to Van Gogh's Ear!" (1958) Ginsberg shouts like Cassandra against an unhearing "war-creating Whore of Babylon bellowing over Capitols and Academies! / Money! Money! Money!" The moans of the poet's soul go unheard because "they" are too busy "fighting in fiery offices, on carpets of heartfailure, screaming and bargaining with Destiny / fighting the Skeleton with sabres, muskets, buck teeth, indigestion, bombs of larceny, whoredom, rockets, pederasty, / back to the wall to build up their wives and apartments, lawns, suburbs, fairydoms. . . ." Other poems, such as "Europe! Europe!" (1958), depict this "war" as one overwhelming international industry, cowing everyone into meek underground crowds of creeps and perishing saints, mistreated lacklove whores, neglected spouses, hardened children with calcified senses:

> electricity scares downtown
> radio screams for money
> police light on TV screens
> laughs at dim lamps in
> empty rooms tanks crash
> thru bombshell no dream
> of man's joy is made movie
> think factory pushes junk
> autos tin dreams of Eros
> mind eats its flesh in

geekish starvation and no
man's fuck is holy for
man's work is most war

Here as everywhere where war is the subject or the metaphor, the lines rush the reader with the noisy broken rhythms of armed attack. The conspiracy is obviously to stun and annihilate all genuine Eros and sell it back to the mutilated self as think-factory junk and tin dreams.

In Western culture the "mind eats its flesh in / geekish starvation," and despite Ginsberg's claim in "The Green Automobile" (1953) that he had "cashed a great check in my skull bank / to found a miraculous college of the body," he has been among the most terribly wounded casualties of the "war." Ginsberg's body-hatred is visible everywhere in the poems, both where he confesses it and where he professes its opposite. "Oh how wounded, how wounded" exclaimed a holy man the first time he saw Ginsberg. The idiopathic hunger for tenderness and love in Ginsberg's poems is so extreme because Ginsberg has found it difficult to grant himself that love; and the persistent virulence of his attack against the warmakers is a projection of his unfinished struggle to excise the cruel Moloch from his own head.

Just as Ginsberg's "darker brother" rose in rebellion against Moloch in "Howl," so does the god of orgy, Dionysus, frequently overthrow the god of war in Ginsberg's dreams and poems. Thus in "To an Old Poet in Peru" (1960) Ginsberg prophesies the dying man a reward "Brighter than a mask of hammered gold / Sweeter than the joy of armies naked / fucking on the battlefield." In other poems, the war-fear-law-moneymakers (the U.S. Congress, President Lyndon Johnson, J. Edgar Hoover, Francis Cardinal Spellman) are accused of not sleeping with their wives, having shriveled testicles or shamefully tiny penises, while favored revolutionaries like Chairman Mao are cited for their genital blessings ("*Che Guevara has a big cock / Castro's balls are pink—*").

"Who Be Kind To" (1965) is both a childlike plea and a Buddhalike benevolence that urges us all to "be kind to" the "lackloves of Capitals & Congresses" and the "Statue destroyers & tank captains, unhappy / murderers in Mekong & Stanleyville" so that a "new kind of man" might "come to his bliss" and "end the cold war he has borne / against his own kind flesh / since the days of the snake." The days of the snake are not merely the days after the Fall in Eden (the birthday of good and evil, judgment, reason, polarity, righteousness, schizophrenia, dyads, and binary computers), but especially the days since the culture has become dominated by science, industry, and abstraction ("Moloch whose name is the Mind"), by the "mind-snake" that threatens to engulf the Buddha of Mercy like those snaky banyan roots in *Ankor Wat* (1968) that enclose the sacred temple in an inexorable death grip. The mind abstracts, forgets the realities of suffering and desiring flesh: "Man cannot long endure the hunger of the cannibal abstract" ("Death to Van Gogh's Ear!").

In "Wichita Vortex Sutra" the abstractions and lies of language are as much a target as is America's participation in the Vietnam conflict. The poem, like so much of Ginsberg's later work, is "composed" by speaking into a tape recorder while traveling cross-country. But unlike so many "Poems of These States" in *The Fall of America: 1965–1971* (1972) that randomly notate the passing phenomena almost as if a videotape camera were mounted on the car fender, Ginsberg is selective, noticing primarily the examples of language that swirl before his senses here in the heart of the nation—language from television, newspapers, magazines, radios, billboards, railway boxcars, grain elevators, department stores, street signs, songs, news conferences, and "N-B-C-B-S-U-P-A-P-I-N-S-L-I-F-E." Words are the poet's tool, his magic, but the words that swirl around Ginsberg are meant not to reveal truth but to manipulate and conceal it. It is language that has designs on its audience, language originating in greed, smug pride, blind patriotism, chamber of commerce boosterism, political and military dishonesty. He enters this vortex of language as a poet and prophet, as representative of the living Word, but language has been so abused that he is "almost in tears to know / how to speak the right language—." He sees himself almost as a Christ, as the savior longing to speak a healing language of forgiveness and love. "Joy, I am I/ the lone One singing to myself / God come true—." His call is to come back out of the wars of money and power and language to the erotic, ecstatic body:

Come lovers of Lincoln and Omaha,
hear my soft voice at last
As Babes need the chemical touch of flesh
in pink infancy
lest they die Idiot returning to
Inhuman—
Nothing—
So, tender lipt adolescent girl, pale youth,
give me back my soft kiss
Hold me in your innocent arms,
accept my tears as yours to harvest
. . .
No more fear of tenderness, much delight in
weeping, ecstasy
in singing, laughter rises that confounds
staring Idiot mayors
and stony politicians eyeing
Thy breast,
O Man of America, be born!

The antiword or opposite language is the language of news headlines that claim "*Vietnam War Brings Prosperity*" and "*Rusk Says Toughness / Essential for Peace*"; of Senator John Stennis, who urges "Bomb China's 200,000,000"; of General Maxwell Taylor and newscasts that repeat "Vietcong losses leveling up three five zero zero / per month" like "the latest quotation in the human meat market—"; of Secretary of Defense Robert S. McNamara who made "A bad guess" about the number of troops that would be needed to handle the war. Ginsberg builds the tide of incoming language to a rhythmic, hysterical chant: "Put it this way on the radio / Put it this way in television language / Use the words / language, language: / 'A bad guess.' " Ginsberg's extraordinary success in capturing the insanity of such language makes painfully clear what most American poets were discovering about Vietnam: that it was a war on language, as all wars inevitably are. As far back as the Peloponnesian War, Thucydides had noticed how war corrupted language because the ordinary meanings of words were changed to fit man's actions: when man's actions were noble, so was *his* language; when ignoble, his language was prostituted to lie and ennoble his actions. Ginsberg's poem makes us feel the tragedy of language once used for alchemy and transformation, for sacrament and atonement, now used for greed and power by mad and inept sorcerers:

Communion of bum magicians
congress of failures from Kansas &
Missouri
working with the wrong equations
Sorcerer's Apprentices who lost control of
the simplest broomstick in the world:
Language

Both the Vietnam war and the language war are part of the larger war of Apollo and Dionysus in America's lopsided culture. In a brilliant visual and historical metaphor, Ginsberg imagines a spreading tornado of violence spiraling outward from the symbolic and geographical heart of the nation, Wichita's Hotel Eaton:

Carry Nation began the war on Vietnam
here with an angry smashing axe
attacking Wine—
Here fifty years ago, by her violence
began a vortex of hatred that defoliated the
Mekong Delta—
Proud Wichita! vain Wichita
cast the first stone!—

The allusion to the Hebrews who were about to stone the woman taken in adultery suggests once more that war and most human misery flow from *judgment* (Moloch the heavy judger of men), from the blind righteousness of those who have forgotten or denied their own flesh. Ginsberg writes as one who has himself cringed and trembled before such stones of judgment all his life.

If the black-magic language of politicians and generals can create war, then an opposite language of love spoken fervently enough by a sufficient poet ought to have power to bring the war to a halt. Thus Ginsberg is not indulging in literary or symbolic gesture when he declares an end to the war but is raising a prophetic voice in the linguistic wilderness, calling on "all powers of the imagination," all Gods, Seraphim, Prophets, shamans, and holy men of all time and space, and invoking the magic power of the Word: "I lift my voice aloud, / make Mantra of American language now, / pronounce the words beginning my own millennium, / I here declare the end of the War!" Though Ginsberg's serious act of language was largely smiled at by both supporters and detractors at the time, it is perhaps his one act of extraordinary genius. In a time and place where no one believed in such powers (but where they were nevertheless negatively at work), Ginsberg possessed the single imagination remaining in Moloch that was "crazy" enough to take language and poetry seriously.

The long series of cross-country car-plane-bus-train tape-recorder compositions, "Poems of These States," constitutes the bulk of *The Fall of America: 1965–1971* (1972), winner of the National Book Award. As a tribute to Ginsberg's life and work, the award is well deserved; as witness to the excellence of the poetry in *The Fall of America,* the award is of less certain probity. The poems are largely transcripts of the "movie of the mind" and the passing show outside the window. Ginsberg's notations are precise but undiscriminating; he gives us the face of the nation but as an ant crawling across Mt. Rushmore might give us the face of Washington, with every pebble, pimple, and scar: cornstalks standing in the fields, smoking factories, dead rabbits on the highway, road signs, junkyards, hamburger stands, polluted streams, tail-lights, hogs in the sun. And interspersed with these objects of the passing landscape are the myriad "objects" of the media-mind-body-scape: radio evangelists, ax murders in Cleveland, Sunday comics, leg pains, sexual reminiscences, self-congratulations on having given up smoking, Vatican pronouncements, bits of myth, racial tensions, newscasts, international politics, Bob Dylan songs, vomiting, the war in Southeast Asia, assassinations, depleted natural resources, and everything that a man of Ginsberg's mind and history might think, feel, hear, see, taste, touch, remember, and imagine.

These notations become random lists rather than Whitmanesque catalogs. There is no recognition that the phenomenal world and the self are one and the same thing. Ginsberg does not "assume" the world or put it on like flesh as Whitman does. He is "out of the game," not "both in and out of the game watching and wondering at it" like his predecessor. The window does not connect but cuts him off, insulates him from a world that is bulging with insane clutter. Ginsberg is Isaiah as a nonparticipant, and steadily losing energy.

That Ginsberg should relate to the self and the world differently than Whitman is not a criticism of Ginsberg but a revelation of his time and culture. Both poets are representative—I want to say symptomatic—of the human possibility and human circumstance in their time. Ginsberg cannot participate or enter in, because the "game" has begun to have such devastating implications. Whereas Whitman could put the Self together by naming the particulars of the world, for Ginsberg too much of the self is already fragmented and lost in those multitudinous crowdings of things outside the window and inside the head, as if the self needed to be defended from, rather than joined with, the world. Where Whitman could reach out to touch the Oversoul, Ginsberg's reach touches everywhere the stony face of the monster god.

Most of the last half of *The Fall of America* is a section titled "Ecologues of These States 1969–1971." The poems are both "ecologues" (bucolic and shepherdly meditations centered at Ginsberg's farm in Cherry Valley, New York) and "eco-logues," words for the ecology and the mother that is earth. They show a tiring poet withdrawing from the world, wondering "Who can prophesy Peace, or vow Futurity for any but armed insects." The Molochians seem unstoppable in their power and greed, their killing of whales and polluting of streams: "murder of great little fish same as self besmirchment short hair thought control, / mace-repression of gnostic street boys identical with DDT extinction of Bald Eagle—." (Again the underlying implication is that the self and the world ought to be One, but because we are severed from our own bodies we are cut off from the world; hatred of self equals the abuse of nature.)

The calmest and sanest poem in *The Fall of America* is "Ecologue," where the details of the road are replaced by those of the farm—heifer, billy goat, windmill, moon,

& last week one Chill night
                    summer disappeared—
little apples in old trees red,
        tomatoes red & green on vines,
green squash huge under leafspread,
        corn thick in light green husks,
sleepingbag wet with dawn dews
        & that one tree red at woods' edge!

Sanity grows in Ginsberg and in the poem because there is genuine work for the hands and the mind, things to be done, participated in: "Shelf the garage! / Where stack lumber handy to eye? / Electric generator money? Where keep mops in Wintertime?"

If *The Fall of America* saw "Death on All Fronts," *Mind Breaths: Poems 1972–1977* (1977) also carries titles like "Yes and It's Hopeless." Ginsberg seems a second time to have been defeated by the "world," as he was in 1954; he is not twice-born, but twice-beat, and this time he is left even more humble, gentle, and "beatific" than before. Although we have come to like the man behind them, most of these poems are so poor they will not bear discussion. They are written by a man who has given up his prophetic and messianic role and does not believe he can change anything. The fervor has fled. Mostly he is writing because it has become a habit.

One of the few good poems of *Mind Breaths* is the title poem, where Ginsberg sits in his newly discovered *vipasyana* meditation, paying attention to the space into which his breath flows. In a manner evocative of Whitman's grand, slow flights of the imagination across the national landscape, Ginsberg follows his moving breath out into the world. This too is a notation poem, but it is an imagined and much less bumpy ride than the car-plane-bus-train compositions—the lines flow even and slow like the calm breathing of the poet. The moving breath does not merely pass by but surrounds and laves and participates with its objects; and the poem and self seem whole and unified because the breath circles the globe and returns to the breather, who is thus encompassed with a single breath/world.

A second worthy poem of *Mind Breaths,* "Sad Dust Glories," is separately published with six additional poems in *Sad Dust Glories: Poems Written Work Summer in Sierra Woods* (1975). In these, as in "Ecologue," Ginsberg gathers grace from the work of his hands, through the physical labor that has been missing in his life. He is helping to build a cabin in the Sierras on land near Gary Snyder's home and relishes the new pleasure of being

        virtuous tired
glasses slipping off
        my blurry nose
hitting the shining steel
        mushroom head
First time a chisel
        in my hand—

He feels a new sense of self, wonders who he is "wandering / in this forest building / a house," he who has never worked or planted—"Words my seeds." But now he is caught up in the new body rhythms and sensations: "Work! Work! Work! This / inspiration / proves I have dreamed" ("Energy Vampire"). The Sierras and the work tie Ginsberg at last to the here and now, to the "realworld":

Could you be here?
Really be here
    and forget the void?

I am, it's peaceful, empty,
filled with green Ponderosa
swaying parallel tops
fan like needle circles
glittering haloed
in sun that moves slowly
lights up my hammock
heats my face skin
and knees.

Ginsberg's best poems succeed brilliantly and his worst fail utterly because of his poetics of "First Thought, Best Thought" and "Mind is Shapely, Art is Shapely." Because he sought self-revelation instead of poem-as-made-object, Ginsberg stopped revising poems or making clear discriminations between poems and other kinds of language jotted in journals, spoken into tape recorders, written in letters to friends, or hallucinated on drugs. Following the lead of Kerouac, Ginsberg "got into" the "existential thing of writing conceived of as an irreversible action or statement, that's unrevisable and unchangeable once it's made." This finally leads to the rejection of distinctions between life and art, and to the idea that "everything we do is art." Because there can be no craft in the usual sense, no working over of the poems, the poem's quality depends indeed on how shapely the poet's mind happens to be at the moment the poem gets made. Shapely mind usually coincides with authentic passion, as in Ginsberg's best work—"Howl," "Kaddish," "Wichita Vortex Sutra," and a few others where strong feelings lift him above his obsessive ego concerns and psychological debilities; but the great bulk of his work is neither shapely nor impassioned.

Ginsberg believes that the proper subject of poetry is the "action of the mind," and the only craft is in learning to observe the mind and "flashlight" its activity. If the poetic rendering is faithful to the motions and rhythms of the poet's mind and body, it should stir similar motion and feeling in the reader. Ginsberg admits that when such rendering is truly spontaneous, "I don't know whether it even makes sense sometimes. Sometimes I do know it makes complete sense, and I start crying." His desire is to "write during a prophetic illuminative seizure" where he would be in a "state of such complete blissful consciousness that any language emanating from that state will strike a responsive chord of blissful consciousness from any other body into which the words enter and vibrate." Ginsberg is obviously not a poet of ideas but of emotional states; one who sees poetry as "a form of meditation or introspective yoga," a sacrament where one pays complete attention and tries to record and communicate moments of "high epiphanous Mind." But as with his ideas about Cézanne, Ginsberg's theory does not work in practice (readers report few "high epiphanous" moments); instead, Ginsberg's spontaneous compositions communicate not the mystical experience but the naked man, sometimes profound, sometimes beatific, often boring and silly, often obsessed and polymorphously perverse. Ginsberg admits that he is only rarely blessed with "the heat of some truthful tears" and that usually he is "just diddling away."

Ginsberg was greatly excited by Kerouac's idea that future literature would consist of what people actually wrote rather than what they deceived people into thinking they wrote after they revised later on: "And I saw opening up this whole universe where people wouldn't be able to lie any more!" But, as is too often the case, Ginsberg's enthusiasm is exaggerated and illogical. One can tell lies all day without ever revising a word. Honesty has to come at some deeper level. What is logically implied, however, is that Ginsberg believes any control over the mind is dishonest, that thinking is not something a man does but that does him; he is not a thinker but a vehicle for thoughts that think through him like ticker tape. Thus to insist on art as an unedited "actual movie of the mind" is to insist that the active thinker step aside from the task of sorting and discriminating among the images of half-formed thoughts that stream through him, and to embrace and record them all as of equal validity. This apparently carries over, too, into one's life—all actions are equally significant so long as they are spontaneous, not controlled by that Moloch whose name is the mind. In "Today" (1964) Ginsberg tells of such "significant" actions: "I rode in a taxi! / I rode a bus, ate hot Italian Sausages, Coca Cola, a chiliburger, Kool-Aid I drank— / All day I did things!" And after various and random thoughts of fascism, Buster Keaton, Samuel Beckett, pink shirts, Kali-Ma, "vaginal jelly rubber instruments" discovered in his parents' closet, and the note—"Also today bit by a mosquito (to be precise, toward dawn)"—the poem swells to its climax for Ginsberg: "I took a crap once this day—How extraordinary it all goes! recollected, a lifetime! / Imagine writing autobiography what a wealth of Detail to enlist! / I see the contents of future magazines— . . ." Unbelievable as it may seem, this is more serious than ironic, more program than parody. The literature of the future, then, is to be autobiography—and autobiography that refuses to make discriminatory judgments among the events of our lives. But again, the logical result of such thinking is not. a new literature but the end of literature. Where art and literature exactly duplicate life and are identical with it, they are no longer necessary. It is not merely that everyone could write his own book, but that there would be no use for books at all; and where all thinking and utterance is a "transcript of consciousness" as ticker tape, there is no longer a need for language at all. Such a literature is ultimately a literature of silence. That is one way to silence Moloch, but it is an extravagant one.

At the very least Ginsberg's poetics lead toward a literature of "om," the universal sound containing all possible sounds that, by containing all particulars, erases all particulars. Ginsberg's poetry includes everything and, except for a few great poems, fades in the reader's memory to a great blur of static or background hum.

Ginsberg's poetics are another aspect of his reluctance to deal with the exigencies of time and the responsibilities of his own humanness (which is not at all to say that he is not among the most generous and decent of men). Anything less than a completely open, spontaneous poetics requires the imposition of order and the making of judgments. Not only is judgment an attribute of Moloch, but the imposition of order slows down the motion of the mind and threatens to bring it to a dead stop. A fear of stasis, of ossification, obviously haunted all of the "Dharma Bums" and "On the Roaders" of the 1950's and 1960's who sought to keep constantly on the move and at high speed. As Randall Patrick McMurphy (R. P. M.) of Ken Kesey's *One Flew Over the Cuckoo's Nest* (1962) knew so well, the moment a person stands still Big Nurse and The Combine (additional aliases for Moloch) are at him with their institutional thermometers. William Burroughs, too, had written Ginsberg that "The most dangerous thing to do is to stand still." The defining quality in Kerouac's prose style ("how you decide to 'rush' yr statement determines the rhythm") and Ginsberg's poetics is speed. (In his essay on projective verse, Charles Olson had also advised "get on with it, keep moving, keep in, speed," and his motives, too, were to escape the drying cement of the rational mind.) But random perpetual motion, whether physical or mental, is not conducive to wholeness or humanness. Randall Patrick McMurphy finally has to accept "commitment" and confront Big Nurse. But Ginsberg has not wanted to deal with this complex "real world" inside or outside of the head. He sees that world of patterns and judgments as a threat of death by ossification, and usually seeks to escape it by climbing into a cloud or diving into bed, seeking the patternless purities of disembodied vision or mindless sexuality. He avoids what Joseph Campbell would call the "death of petrifact" by fleeing to the opposite "death of chaos." These very choices seem embodied in the images of "Paterson" where Ginsberg refuses the paralysis of Madison Avenue and opts for a death of chaos (in eros, ecstasy, and motion), "rolling over the pavements and highways / by the bayoux and forests and derricks leaving my flesh and my bones hanging on the trees."

Ginsberg clearly has a problem focusing his energies on the "world between." His attention characteristically slips to either side of the rich world of daily human interchange and work. When asked if he ever contemplated writing an epic poem, his first reactions take the familiar leap and dive: "Yeah, but it's just . . . ideas, that I've been carrying around for a long time. One thing which I'd like to do sooner or later is write a long poem which is a narrative and description of all the visions I've ever had. . . . And another idea I had was to write a big long poem about everybody I ever fucked or slept with." In another interview, while discussing his theories of spontaneous composition and the importance of telling the truth no matter what archetypal thought comes into our minds, Ginsberg's first example of an "archetypal thought" is "I want to fuck my mother." A few minutes later he realizes his example might be shocking enough to "wave a red flag in front of understanding" so he substitutes another: "I want to go to heaven." (Is this another of the child-man's ways of saying I want to be touched and held by my mother or by my father?)

What this adds up to is a poetry with four basic contents: the poetry of vision (almost always involving drug use); the poetry of sex (usually frenzied and obsessive); the poetry of the "world between" as mind-movie or passing show; and the poetry of prophecy against Moloch. And running through all of these, but most especially in the last, is the reiterated plea for tenderness and love. But only in Ginsberg's most recent and new poetry of physical work do these four isolated poetries draw together in a more satisfying and stable harmony.

At Cherry Valley and in the Sierras, Ginsberg has at last found some measure of the Soul or Sacred Heart or Self that he has searched for and misunderstood most of his life. He found it not in drugs or sex but in the physical body and the physical world of work that combines intuition and sensation and tames the darker brother into quiet thoughtfulness.

In a tiny poem of *Empty Mirror* Ginsberg had claimed "I made love to myself / in the mirror, kissing my own lips, / saying, 'I love myself, /I love you more than anybody.'" And in the neurotic dis-ease of "Sather Gate Illumination" in 1956, he urgently reiterated his self love ("I believe you are lovely, my soul, soul of Allen, Allen— / and you so beloved, so sweetened, so recalled to your true loveliness, / your original nude breathing Allen"). Methinks he doth protest too much. Years later, after an obsessive search for vision through drugs, and after traveling around the world and consulting holy men who urged him to emphasize the human and to "let your own heart be your guru," Ginsberg became a devotee of the Sacred Heart and announced that he had at last "Come sweetly / now back to my Self as I was—" ("The Change: Kyoto-Tokyo Express," 1963). However, Ginsberg persisted in understanding the "pure delight" and "very lovely doctrine" of the Sacred Heart as teaching that the way to wholeness and bliss "is to give yourself, completely, to your heart's desire," an interpretation that once again dismissed every kind of control and rational discipline. But of course the doctrine of the Sacred Heart has no such easy implications and is much more closely allied to the idea of a difficult struggle to mediate and to love the freckled Incarnation of the Divine in the material world.

Immediately after his Blakean hallucinations in Harlem in 1948, Ginsberg had rushed to his bookcase with a suddenly doubled comprehension to reread St. John of the Cross and Plato and "Plotinus on the Alone." But Ginsberg admitted, "The Plotinus I found more difficult to interpret." A central doctrine in Plotinus is, I believe, that the Soul or Heart is the intermediary between pure spirit and pure matter, between *eidos* and sensation. For Plato, too, the Heart related to the warrior class that stood between the philosopher-kings (head) and the laborers, women, and children (body/genitals). Soul reaches upward toward intellect and divine forms to bring them more surely into embodiment and influence in matter, and reaches downward into the variety and massiveness of matter to lift it upward toward the *nous* and unity. Soul is not lost in the Many, nor does it reside in the One. It is mediator, operating at the level of discursive thought, exerting a rigorous self-discipline by which we awake from the alienation of our lower state and rise again to a knowledge of our true selves. But because in our time Moloch has invaded and occupied the whole area of rigorous moral and intellectual self-discipline and changed the heart (the *cour*-age) of the warrior into the metal of tanks and money, he has in a very literal way robbed Ginsberg of his Heart and Soul, his Selfhood. The "world between" matter and spirit belongs to the monster god, who allows modern men only two possibilities—to become mechanical hollow men who have forgotten the ecstasies of vision and sex; or to become crazy, schizophrenic, head-and-body-severed poets who have "consciousness without a body," "millions of genitals," and "an unpublishable private literature that goes 1400 miles an hour and twenty-five-thousand mental institutions."

Ginsberg was the first of the crowd of writers who emerged in the 1950's and 1960's as "confessional poets"—Sylvia Plath, Anne Sexton, Robert Lowell, John Berryman, Dianne Wakoski, and others—who to a surprising degree share similar backgrounds and psychological problems involving an eroded self-image, compulsive behavior and imagery, death obsession, attempted or actual suicide, time spent in rehabilitative alcoholic and mental institutions, a splitting or doubling of the self in poetic figures, and the traumatic early loss of a parent through madness, abandonment, suicide, or death. These common characteristics should make it clear that "confessional poetry" is not after all merely another movement or school, like the Black Mountain, New York, or Deep Imagist, but an efflorescence of decay, the growing shine of the perishing republic.

There has been a tremendous surface complexity and activity in Ginsberg's life, and indeed he has been more important as an active public figure than as a maker of poems. By the general public he has perhaps been variously viewed as dangerous, obscene, quixotic, or silly; as an advocate and user of drugs; as a leader in the Vietnam war protest; as a mantra-chanting peacemaker, riot-calmer, and holy man; but for a large segment of the aroused population he has stood as a representative of poetry as an art that will not be put to sleep or truckle under to the dull viciousness of "business as usual."

Ginsberg has never been a poet of idea or of craft. His only craft has been emotional honesty; his single "idea" has been tenderness—its scarcity, denial, necessity, beauty, and blessedness. He has crisscrossed the United States, traveled the world, organized the Human Be-In at Berkeley, swallowed peyote and LSD, testified before congressional committees, quieted the rioters at the Democratic National Convention in 1968, "om'd" the judge at the Chicago Seven trial, led the movement of resistance to the Vietnam war, read and taught in colleges, consulted with holy men, adopted Eastern philosophies, chanted mantras, sat in meditation (he has "pried through strata, . . . counsel'd with doctors and calculated close"; he has "wept and fasted, wept and prayed"); and after all this his one wisdom is honesty, his one virtue is compassion.

As a poet his voice has been prophetic and loud (and finally ignored by those most in need of prophecy). His greatest power has come from the magnitude of his own suffering and his own psychological infirmities. These infirmities are multiple and severe, and can be documented everywhere in his poetry. They make him seem "a deliberately shocking, bourgeois-baiting celebrator of a kind of sexuality which the most enlightened post-Freudian man-of-the-world finds it difficult to condone" (Leslie Fiedler); and account for an imagery of sexual behavior that is "hysterically frenzied, suggesting a compulsive search for love and acceptance through ceaselessly self-defeating, external, almost automatic activity" (M. L. Rosenthal). What Rosenthal sees as "a childishly aggressive vocabularity of obscenity" sometimes seems almost a case of pathological coprolalia or Tourette's Syndrome.

But while these sexual obsessions are a recurring infection in the poems, it is paradoxically just this extraordinary and insatiable hollowness and compulsive hunger for love that makes Ginsberg such a formidable opponent to Moloch, and makes us realize how "lacklove" and devoid of tenderness the culture has become. In the war between Moloch and the flesh, Ginsberg is no loudmouth-know-it-all-stateside-civilian but a veteran of the trenches with a gaping stomach wound. His power is what he shows us about the truth of that war. It is hardly a sufficient response to dismiss Ginsberg's poetry as a poetry of neurosis without looking to the neurotic ambience or understanding that a neurotic poetry is the most telling criticism of the culture. The pathology is personal, but not merely personal. Ginsberg is in this sense truly "the biographer of his time" (Helen Vendler).

Like Whitman, when Ginsberg gives us his book of poems, he gives us not a book but a man. Not a pretty man, but a man. Ginsberg may be Whitman as Quasimodo, but he is a modern-day Whitman nonetheless. His song is the Song of the Modern Self, twisted to the point of perversion, eroded almost to the point of invisibility. Ginsberg's great contribution as poet and man has been to confess for us his own need and to raise for us his own uniquely personal *eli eli lamma lamma* sabactahani cry of the naked mind for love.

Selected Bibliography

WORKS OF ALLEN GINSBERG

POETRY

Howl and Other Poems, (San Francisco: City Lights Books, 1956).

Kaddish and Other Poems, 1958–1960, (San Francisco, City Lights Books, 1961).

Empty Mirror, Early Poems, (New York: Totem Press/ Corinth Books, 1961).

Reality Sandwiches, 1953–60, (San Francisco: City Lights Books, 1963).

Wichita Vortex Sutra, (San Francisco: Coyote Books, 1967).

T. V. Baby Poems, (New York: Grossman/Orion Press, 1968).

Ankor Wat, (London: Fulcrum Press, 1968).

Airplane Dreams; Compositions from Journals, (Toronto: Anansi, 1968) (San Francisco: City Lights Books, 1969).

Planet News: 1961–1967, (San Francisco: City Lights Books, 1968).

The Gates of Wrath; Rhymed Poems: 1948–1952, (Bolinas, Calif.: Grey Fox Press, 1972).

The Fall of America: Poems of These States, 1965–1971, (San Francisco: City Lights Books, 1972).

Iron Horse, (Toronto: Coach House Press, 1972) (San Francisco: City Lights Books, 1974).

Sad Dust Glories: Poems Written Work Summer in Sierra Woods, (Berkeley, Calif.: Workingman's Press, 1975).

Mind Breaths: Poems 1972–1977, (San Francisco: City Lights Books, 1977).

Collected Poems 1947–1980, (New York: Harper and Row, 1984).

PROSE JOURNALS, INTERVIEWS, CORRESPONDENCE

"Notes for Howl and Other Poems," *The New American Poetry, 1945–1960* edited by Donald M. Allen (New York: Grove Press, 1960) 414–18.

The Yage Letters, (San Francisco: City Lights Books, 1963) Written with William S. Burroughs.

"The Art of Poetry VIII," *Paris Review* no. 37: 13–55 (Spring 1966).

Indian Journals: March 1962–May 1963, (San Francisco: Dave Haselwood/City Lights Books, 1970).

"A Talk with Allen Ginsberg," *Partisan Review,* 38 no. 3: 289–309 (1971).

Allen Verbatim: Lectures on Poetry, Politics, Consciousness, edited by Gordon Ball (New York: McGraw-Hill, 1974).

As Ever: The Collected Correspondence of Allen Ginsberg and Neal Cassady, (Berkeley, Calif.: Creative Book Arts, 1974).

"Craft Interview with Allen Ginsberg," In *The Craft of Poetry,* edited by William Packard (Garden City, N.Y.: Doubleday, 1974) 53–78.

Gay Sunshine Interview, (Bolinas, Calif.: Grey Fox Press, 1974).

The Visions of the Great Rememberer, (Amherst, Mass.: Mulch Press, 1974).

Chicago Trial Testimony, (San Francisco: City Lights Books, 1975).

Journals: Early Fifties Early Sixties, edited by Gordon Ball (New York: Grove Press, 1977).

BIOGRAPHICAL AND CRITICAL STUDIES

Breslin, James, "Allen Ginsberg: The Origins of 'Howl' and 'Kaddish.'," *Iowa Review,* 8, no. 2: 82–107 (Spring 1977).

Carroll, Paul, *The Poem in Its Skin,* (Chicago: Follett, 1968) pp. 81–108.

Dowden, George, *A Bibliography of Works by Allen Ginsberg: October, 1943 to July 1, 1967,* (San Francisco: City Lights Books, 1971).

Davie, Donald, "On Sincerity: From Wordsworth to Ginsberg," *Encounter,* 31, no. 4: 61–66 (October 1968).

Fiedler, Leslie, *Partisan Review,* "Master of Dreams: The Jew in a Gentile World," 34: 339–56 (Summer 1967).

Hahn, Stephen, "The Prophetic Voice of Allen Ginsberg," *Prospects: Annual of American Cultural Studies* 2: 527–67, (1976).

Heffernan, James A., "Politics and Freedom: Refractions of Blake in Joyce Cary and Allen Ginsberg," *Romantic and Modern: Revaluations of Literary Tradition,* edited by George Bornstein (Pittsburgh: Pittsburgh University Press, 1977) pp. 177–95.

Hoffman, Steven K., "Lowell, Berryman, Roethke, and Ginsberg: Communal Poetry," *Literary Review,* 22 no. 3: 329–41 (Spring 1979).

Howard, Richard., *Alone With America,* (New York: Atheneum, 1969) pp. 145–52.

Hunsberger, Bruce, "Kit Smart's Howl," *Wisconsin Studies in Contemporary Literature,* 6: 34–44 (Winter 1965).

Kramer, Jane, *Allen Ginsberg in America,* (New York: Random House, 1969).

Kramer, Jane, "Paterfamilias," 2 pts. (*New Yorker,* August 17, 1968) 32–73; (August 24, 1968) pp. 38–91.

Merrill, Thomas F., *Allen Ginsberg,* (New York: Twayne, 1969).

Mersmann, James F., *Out of the Vietnam Vortex: A Study of Poets and Poetry Against the War,* (Lawrence: University Press of Kansas, 1974) pp. 31–75.

Parkinson, Thomas F., ed. *A Casebook on the Beat,* (New York: Crowell, 1961).

Portugés, Paul, *The Visionary Poetics of Allen Ginsberg,* (Santa Barbara, Calif.: Ross-Erikson, 1978).

Rosenthal, Macha L., *The New Poets: American and British Poetry Since World War II,* (New York: Oxford University Press, 1967) pp. 89–112.

Rosenthal, Macha L., *The Modern Poets: A Critical Introduction,* (New York: Oxford University Press, 1960).

Simpson, Louis, *A Revolution of Taste,* (New York: Macmillan, 1978) pp. 43–82.

Tytell, John, *Naked Angels: The Lives and Literature of the Beat Generation,* (New York: McGraw-Hill, 1976).

Vendler, Helen, Review of *Planet News. New York Times Book Review,* (August 31, 1969) p. 8.

Whittemore, Reed, "From 'Howl' to OM," *New Republic,* (July 25, 1970) pp. 17–18.

THOMAS GRAY

(1716–1771)

R.W. KETTON-CREMER

I

THOMAS GRAY WAS born in the City of London on 26 December 1716, the son of a scrivener of comfortable means. He was a delicate child and the only one of a large family who survived infancy. His father was a morose and at times violent man who bullied his wife unmercifully and kept her so short of money that she was obliged to run a milliner's shop.

From this uneasy home life the boy was removed to Eton at an early age. He was extremely happy there, and the beauty and tradition of his surroundings made an ineffaceable impression upon him. His closest friends were Horace Walpole, a son of Prime Minister Robert Walpole, and Richard West, whose father was a distinguished lawyer. They were delicate, studious, and precocious boys like himself.

At the age of eighteen, Gray was sent to Peterhouse College, Cambridge, but left in 1738 without taking a degree. The next year he accompanied Walpole on the grand tour and spent the best part of two years in France and Italy. In 1741 he quarreled violently with Walpole and returned home alone. The next year he was deprived of his other intimate friend by the death of West.

At the end of 1742, Gray returned to Peterhouse and lived mainly at Cambridge for the rest of his life. He resided at the college, quietly pursuing his studies and taking advantage of the intellectual amenities of a university, but he was never a fellow and never took any part in tutoring, lecturing, or other academic duties. He spent considerable periods away from Cambridge, sometimes at Stoke Poges in Buckinghamshire, where his mother had settled, sometimes in modest social activities in London (he and Walpole were reconciled in 1744), sometimes in sightseeing tours in various parts of the country. It was a way of life that suited his limited income and his unadventurous disposition. He read and studied incessantly. Classical literature, medieval history, architecture, natural history, and botany were only a few of his interests. But he studied for himself alone, and scarcely anything remains, apart from a vast accumulation of notes, to attest to his profound and varied scholarship.

By nature Gray was retiring, fastidious, overly careful of his health, somewhat affected in manner and speech. He never married, and apart from a passing attraction to a young woman of fashion, Henrietta Speed, his emotions were deflected into channels of friendship. Toward the end of his life, he was disconcerted by the violence of his feelings for a young Swiss visitor to England, Charles-Victor de Bonstetten. Otherwise he seems to have accepted the mischance of his temperament with entire decorum.

In 1756, as a result of a practical joke based on his fear of fire, attempted by some undergraduates, he moved from Peterhouse to Pembroke College. In 1768 he was appointed professor of modern history; but he never delivered any lectures, and he treated the office, despite some occasional prickings of conscience, as a sinecure. He died after a short illness on 30 July 1771.

It had been a lifetime of reading, of reflection, of essentially uncreative study and research, diversified by little outward incident. But occasionally, at long and unpredictable intervals, Gray was impelled to write poetry. He was very conscious of the fitfulness of his inspiration and its brief duration. "Whenever the humour takes me," he wrote, "I will write, because I like it; and because I like myself better when I do. If I do not write much, it is because I cannot." No English poet of his stature has produced so small a body of work. The whole of the poetry that he published in his lifetime amounted to less than one thousand lines, and little more was found among his papers after his death. But this handful of poems exerted a powerful influence on his contemporaries and his immediate successors; and one of them, "Elegy Written in a Country Churchyard," ranks among the supreme poems not only of its century but of all English literature.

II

Apart from a few translations, all of Gray's earliest poems were in Latin, a language that he handled with remarkable ease and grace. His first English poem, "Ode on the Spring," was written in May 1742. He had barely completed it when he heard the news of the death of Richard West. This bereavement only served to enhance the mood of creative activity that possessed him at this time and was so seldom to be repeated. During the next three months he wrote "Ode on a Distant Prospect of Eton College," "Hymn to Adversity," and a sonnet on the death of West. He also mourned West in some Latin lines, outstanding in their intensity of feeling and beauty of expression, that he proposed to include in his ambitious philosophical poem "De principiis cogitandi." But he never completed or even resumed this work and, indeed, never wrote in Latin again.

There was no trace of diffidence or inexperience in Gray's first English poems. From the outset his technical accomplishment was perfect. "Ode on the Spring" is primarily a descriptive poem, an evocation of the sights and sounds of the Buckinghamshire countryside. But the two closing stanzas bring a sudden change of mood. The poet, following a train of thought suggested by a half-remembered passage of Matthew Green's, points an unexpected moral and introduces a personal, indeed an autobiographical, note. He has been observing the insects, the bees and gnats and butterflies, as they revel in the sunshine, and pitying the brevity of their life and happiness. Thereupon the insects, in their turn, reply to the lonely, obscure, and uncompanioned poet:

> Methinks I hear in accents low
> The sportive kind reply:
> Poor moralist! and what art thou?
> A solitary fly!
> Thy Joys no glittering female meets,
> No hive hast thou of hoarded sweets,
> No painted plumage to display:
> On hasty wings thy youth is flown;
> Thy sun is set, thy spring is gone—
> We frolick, while 'tis May.

In the other poems of this memorable summer, written after the shock of West's death, an even stronger note of personal experience and of private emotion is everywhere noticeable. "Ode on a Distant Prospect of Eton College" ostensibly contrasts the carefree years of boyhood with the anxieties, passions, infirmities, frustrations, and disasters of mature life. But in fact Gray is recalling in every line the happiness of his own schooldays, secure in the friendship of Walpole and West, and lamenting his present state, with Walpole apparently hopelessly estranged and West lost to him forever. Four stanzas portray that vanished contentment, "the sunshine of the breast"; four describe the varied and tragic fates in store for the "little victims" as the pitiless years take their toll; and the final stanza reveals resignation and almost reconcilement:

To each his suff'rings: all are men,
Condemn'd alike to groan;
The tender for another's pain,
Th' unfeeling for his own.
Yet ah! why should they know their fate?
Since sorrow never comes too late,
And happiness too swiftly flies.
Thought would destroy their paradise.
No more: where ignorance is bliss,
'Tis folly to be wise.

In "Hymn to Adversity" the same mood persists:

The gen'rous spark extinct revive,
Teach me to love and to forgive

is surely a reference to his estrangement from Walpole. But in this poem his fear of life, the dread of what the future might hold in store for him, the whole burden of what his age knew as melancholy and ours prefers to describe as angst, have almost overshadowed the anguish of his grief for West. In the "Sonnet on the Death of Richard West," on the other hand, that grief is expressed with intensity and concentration. "My lonely anguish melts no heart, but mine"—such was the measure of his sadness.

III

These months of creative inspiration and intense personal sorrow may also have seen the beginnings of the poem eventually known as "Elegy Written in a Country Churchyard." Some critics believe that a substantial portion of the "Elegy" was completed in 1742 and the years immediately following. There can be no doubt that the emotional mood of the poem was deeply influenced by West's death, but I am inclined to think that, except perhaps for some of the opening lines, it was written at a considerably later date and probably over a long stretch of time—that it was, in fact, an example of "emotion recollected in tranquillity."

At the end of 1742, Gray returned to Cambridge and embarked on the scheme of life that has already been described and that he did not substantially alter to the end of his days. Each summer he passed many weeks at his mother's house at Stoke Poges; and there, during his slow, contemplative walks about the fields and lanes, he stored in his memory those country sights and sounds, those sober musings upon the human lot, that were the material of the "Elegy." The progress of its composition will always remain uncertain. We know only that between 1742 and 1750 this quiet scholar, this academic and solitary man, achieved a poem that was to become an enduring part of the English heritage.

The opening stanzas conjure up the solemnity and mystery of evening, the slow advance of dusk over the countryside.

The Curfew tolls the knell of parting day,
The lowing herd wind slowly o'er the lea,
The plowman homeward plods his weary
    way,
And leaves the world to darkness and to me.

Now fades the glimmering landscape on the
    sight,
And all the air a solemn stillness holds,
Save where the beetle wheels his droning
    flight,
And drowsy tinklings lull the distant folds;
    . . .

This eloquence, this faultless music of words, is sustained throughout the poem. It sounds in every line of the succession of stanzas in which Gray meditates upon the fate of those who lie "beneath those rugged elms, that yew-tree's shade." He had watched the laborers of Stoke Poges at work in the fields and woods, had admired their skill in the handling of plow and ax and scythe; and he contrasts their obscure destiny with the range of opportunity, for good or evil, that lay open to those whose lot was less restricted by circumstance.

Let not Ambition mock their useful toil,
Their homely joys, and destiny obscure;
Nor Grandeur hear with a disdainful smile
The short and simple annals of the poor.

The boast of heraldry, the pomp of pow'r,
And all that beauty, all that wealth e'er gave,
Awaits alike th' inevitable hour.
The paths of glory lead but to the grave.

. . .

Perhaps in this neglected spot is laid
Some heart once pregnant with celestial fire;
Hands, that the rod of empire might have sway'd,
Or wak'd to extasy the living lyre.

But Knowledge to their eyes her ample page
Rich with the spoils of time did ne'er unroll;
Chill Penury repress'd their noble rage,
And froze the genial current of the soul.

. . .

Th' applause of list'ning senates to command,
The threats of pain and ruin to despise,
To scatter plenty o'er a smiling land,
And read their hist'ry in a nation's eyes,

Their lot forbad: nor circumscrib'd alone
Their growing virtues, but their crimes confin'd;
Forbad to wade through slaughter to a throne,
And shut the gates of mercy on mankind,

The struggling pangs of conscious truth to hide,
To quench the blushes of ingenuous shame,
Or heap the shrine of Luxury and Pride
With incense kindled at the Muse's flame.

At one stage of its composition, the "Elegy" consisted of eighteen stanzas, of which this was the last, together with the following additional stanzas, which brought the poem to a climax and a close.

The thoughtless World to Majesty may bow
Exalt the brave, & idolize success
But more to Innocence, their Safety owe
Than Power & Genius e'er conspired to bless

And thou, who mindful of the unhonour'd Dead
Dost in these Notes their artless Tale relate
By Night & lonely Contemplation led
To linger in the gloomy Walks of Fate,

Hark how the sacred Calm that broods around
Bids ev'ry fierce tumultuous Passion cease
In still small accents whis'pring from the Ground
A grateful Earnest of eternal Peace

No more with Reason & thyself at Strife
Give anxious Cares & endless Wishes room
But thro' the cool sequester'd Vale of Life
Pursue the silent Tenour of thy Doom.[1]

In this form the "Elegy" was a perfect artistic whole, its reasoning and emotion moving in unbroken harmony from the opening to the close. Some critics view Gray's subsequent recasting as a regrettable afterthought. Walter Savage Landor, for example, spoke of the new conclusion, the three stanzas of the epitaph, as a tin kettle tied to the poem's tail. The reader would do well to compare the earlier with the final version and form an independent judgment, for Gray in due course made some drastic alterations and additions. He canceled the four stanzas just quoted, preserving only a few fragments that he incorporated into his new work. In place of sober resignation, the comfort of "the sacred Calm that broods around," he introduced a sudden note of loneliness, almost of anguish:

For who to dumb Forgetfulness a prey,
This pleasing anxious being e'er resign'd,
Left the warm precincts of the cheerful day,
Nor cast one longing ling'ring look behind?

He sounded a still more personal note when he brought into the foreground

. . . thee, who mindful of th' unhonour'd Dead
Dost in these lines their artless tale relate—

1. These lines appear only in the manuscript of the "Elegy" in the library of Eton College, and are quoted here exactly as they appear in that manuscript.

the figure of the poet himself. He dies; he is buried beside those other dead whose humble lives he had described; and the poem closes now with his "Epitaph," which must also be regarded as Gray's summing up of his own life and his own beliefs:

Here rests his head upon the lap of Earth
A Youth to Fortune and to Fame unknown.
Fair Science frown'd not on his humble birth,
And Melancholy marked him for her own.

Large was his bounty, and his soul sincere,
Heav'n did a recompence as largely send:
He gave to Mis'ry all he had, a tear,
He gain'd from Heav'n ('twas all he wish'd) a friend.

No farther seek his merits to disclose,
Or draw his frailties from their dread abode,
(There they alike in trembling hope repose),
The bosom of his Father and his God.

Alfred Tennyson once spoke of the "Elegy's" "divine truisms that make us weep." Its reflections upon fame and obscurity, ambition and destiny, have indeed become truisms. But in the eighteenth century the poem burst upon the England of King George II, line after noble line, stanza after majestic stanza, with a novel and extraordinary impact. Of one passage Samuel Johnson wrote: "I have never seen the notions in any other place; yet he that reads them here, persuades himself that he has always felt them." Gray gave expression to thoughts that lay deep in the consciousness of all Englishmen—thoughts about their history and traditions, the religion in which they put their trust, the landscapes they knew and loved, the tranquil continuity of village life in an age when the majority of the nation were still country dwellers. And as the century advanced, a century of development and expansion that was to prove so momentous, the "Elegy" became the representative poem of its age. The fastidious, and hypochondriacal recluse had spoken for the English people.

The "Elegy" was running in General James Wolfe's mind a few years later in Canada, on the day before his victory and his death. It has been present in the minds of countless other men and women from that time to this, at moments of crisis in their lives or during hours of quiet reflection. It is probably still the most popular and the best-loved poem in English, the poem that has most surely reached the heart of the ordinary man. As Johnson said—and it should be remembered that Johnson disliked Gray and persistently undervalued the rest of his poetry—the "Elegy" "abounds with images which find a mirrour in every mind, and with sentiments to which every bosom returns an echo."

IV

The "Elegy" was published in 1751, almost by accident. Manuscript copies had been circulated without Gray's sanction, and it was necessary to hurry it out at short notice in order to forestall its piratical printing in a magazine. Its enthusiastic reception somewhat disconcerted the author. His newfound celebrity brought no alteration to his way of life, and he made no attempt to derive advantage from his popular success. Its most important personal consequence, perhaps, was the friendship of two neighbors at Stoke, the Dowager Viscountess Cobham and her young relation Henrietta Speed. Gray described their first encounter in a delightful piece of burlesque poetry, "A Long Story." Walpole once said, with great truth, "Gray never wrote anything easily but things of humour: humour was his natural and original turn." "A Long Story" was all grace and lightheartedness, an entirely gay and happy poem, with its gentle self-mockery and its affectionate portrait of Miss Speed:

To celebrate her eyes, her air—
Coarse panegyricks would but teaze her.
Melissa is her *nom de guerre*.
Alas, who would not wish to please her?

"A Long Story" was a private joke, written for the amusement of Gray's friends. But his next productions were the two great Pindaric odes, "The Progress of Poesy" and "The Bard," which were very much intended for a public audience. Eminent writers are often apt to place unexpected and somewhat disconcerting values upon their own performances; and Gray regarded these two odes, rather than his masterpiece the "Elegy," as the works by which he hoped to be remembered. Youth was now behind him; the youthful sentiments, the personal longings and regrets that lingered in the "Elegy," were to have no place here. He intended the Pindaric odes to be the crown of his poetic maturity.

For almost a century English poets had been producing odes—Abraham Cowley's "Pindariques" are an example—modeled on the odes of Pindar, although no poet until Gray, William Congreve apart, had followed Pindar's structure with absolute fidelity. It was the content, not the form, of these two odes that bewildered his contemporaries. In the first, "The Progress of Poesy," Gray set himself to glorify the poet's calling; and he did so with an exaltation, an allusiveness, and at times an obscurity that render some of its passages difficult even to the instructed reader of today. The notes, which he refused to furnish for the first edition, explain the purport of each stanza and the more recondite of his allusions, but his contemporaries were not accustomed to this rhapsodical and almost incantatory poetry, and remained perplexed. Yet surely some prelude of the romantic revival, some foreshadowing of Samuel Taylor Coleridge and John Keats, is sounded in such a passage as

> In climes beyond the solar road,
> Where shaggy forms o'er ice-built
> mountains roam,
> The Muse has broke the twilight-gloom
> To chear the shiv'ring Native's dull abode.
> And oft, beneath the od'rous shade
> Of Chili's boundless forests laid,
> She deigns to hear the savage Youth repeat
> In loose numbers wildly sweet
> Their feather-cinctur'd Chiefs, and dusky
> Loves. . . .
> (II.2)

The second ode, "The Bard," portrays a traditional episode during the final subjugation of Wales by the English forces. Gray was deeply versed in English history and had recently made some study of Welsh poetry and prosody. The conclusion of the poem, after hanging fire for some time, was inspired by the strains of a blind Welsh harper who happened to visit Cambridge. Most of the stanzas are supposed to be uttered by the bard, who cursed the invading English monarch and his posterity, and who foresaw the time when the prophecies of Merlin and Taliesin would be fulfilled and a Welsh dynasty, in the persons of the Tudor sovereigns, would rule once more over the whole island of Britain. At times during its composition, Gray was seized with a fervor of inspiration that seldom visited him, and during which, as he said later, "I felt myself the bard."

The poem is full of splendid rhetoric, of color and movement and pageantry. It is also heavy with obscurity. Gray lived so intimately in English history that he filled his stanzas with cryptic personifications, the She-wolf of France and the agonizing King, the meek Usurper and the bristled Boar, whose identity evaded—and, were it not for the footnotes, would still evade—the ordinary reader. Many critics, with Johnson at their head, have pointed out the faults of "The Bard" and its companion—incomprehensibility, overelaboration, "glittering accumulations of ungraceful ornaments." But no other writer of the eighteenth century could have achieved the force and eloquence of the penultimate stanza, with its radiant picture of the first Queen Elizabeth:

> Girt with many a Baron bold
> Sublime their starry fronts they rear;
> And gorgeous Dames, and Statesmen old
> In bearded majesty, appear.
> In the midst a Form divine!
> Her eye proclaims her of the Briton-Line;
> Her lyon-port, her awe-commanding face,
> Attemper'd sweet to virgin-grace.
> What strings symphonious tremble in the
> air,

What strains of vocal transport round her
play!
Hear from the grave, great Taliesin, hear;
They breathe a soul to animate thy clay.
Bright Rapture calls, and soaring, as she
sings,
Waves in the eye of Heav'n her many-
colour'd wings.
(III.2)

The Pindaric odes were written in the early 1750's, one of the periods during which, to quote Walpole's words, "Gray was in flower." During these same years he worked on a third poem, never completed, that might have held a very high place among his writings. William Mason gave it the title "Ode on the Pleasure Arising from Vicissitude." The surviving stanzas show that it was to be a poem in his earlier manner, with a strongly personal note, in contrast with the Pindaric odes, which were almost wholly objective. There is a similar contrast between the rhetorical splendor of the Pindarics and the limpid freshness, the almost Wordsworthian simplicity, of this unfinished work.

New-born flocks in rustic dance
Frisking ply their feeble feet.
Forgetful of their wintry trance
The birds his presence greet.
But chief the Sky-lark warbles high
His trembling thrilling ecstasy
And, less'ning from the dazzled sight,
Melts into air and liquid light.
. . .
Yesterday the sullen year
Saw the snowy whirlwind fly;
Mute was the musick of the air,
The Herd stood drooping by:
Their raptures now that wildly flow,
No yesterday, nor morrow know;
'Tis Man alone that Joy descries
With forward and reverted eyes.
(9–16; 21–28)

The Pindaric odes were published in 1757, as the first fruits of Walpole's private press at Strawberry Hill. Gray looked upon them as the summit of his poetic achievement, and was deeply anxious that they should be well received. But he disregarded the warnings of his friends and printed them without notes or any form of explanation to help the reader. Largely as the result of this, their reception was by no means enthusiastic. A fire of criticism, both public and private, was directed against the obscurity of their content and the loftiness of their style. Their admirers, though influential, were few; and altogether Gray was bitterly disappointed. This sense of disappointment, and indeed of frustration, was permanent. Apart from a single poem—written primarily from a sense of duty—he never produced another major work. He withdrew from the contest and devoted his life ever more completely to scholarship and private study.

V

Gray's youth had been steeped in classical learning, and his years in Italy had enhanced his love of ancient Greece and Rome. But in middle age he began to feel the lure of a very different world. The Norns, and not the Sirens, were calling him now. Instead of the sun-drenched Mediterranean landscape or the quiet scenes of the English countryside, he explored the haunted mists of the Celtic and Scandinavian past. His Welsh studies had already borne fruit in "The Bard." He read deeply in early Norse poetry, history, and legend; and in 1760 he was among the first to welcome "Ossian," the alleged translations from ancient Highland poetry produced by James Macpherson. He could never feel quite satisfied as to their genuineness, and he was no more impressed than anyone else by the shifty figure of Macpherson. But the Ossian poems held for him a mystery, a magic and wild romance that he had hitherto sought in vain. "I am gone mad about them," he wrote, "*extasié* with their infinite beauty."

One of Gray's projects, never fulfilled, was a history of English poetry, in the early chapters of which he proposed to include some renderings of the poetry of the Welsh and of the ancient Norse. His next productions were intended as a part of this scheme. "The Descent of Odin" and "The Fatal Sisters" were translations, by way of an intermediate Latin version, from Icelandic originals. He also translated four fragments of varying length from the Welsh, of which "The Triumphs of Owen" alone was published in his lifetime. This group of poems has little real significance today; but to those of Gray's contemporaries who had fallen, as he had, under the spell of northern romanticism, their appeal was profound. "Noble incantations," Walpole called them, and they played their part in the furtherance of the romantic revival not only in England, but throughout continental Europe, where Gray came to be widely read.

Apart from these translations and certain occasional verses, Gray wrote absolutely nothing between 1757 and 1769. His moods of inspiration has always been fitful and ill-sustained, but this prolonged silence was unquestionably due in great measure to his disappointment over the reception of the Pindaric odes. The occasional verses were mainly satirical in intent, those "things of humour" that he wrote so easily. Few of them have survived; there is good reason to think that others were suppressed by his own caution or by the discretion of his executor, William Mason. "The Candidate" was a savage and brilliant squib inspired by the circumstances of a disputed election for the high stewardship at Cambridge. Still more impressive is the poem that he wrote after visiting the eccentric villa built on the North Foreland by Henry Fox, first Lord Holland, a discredited politician whose career he had long watched with deep disapproval.

> Old, and abandon'd by each venal friend,
> Here Holland took the pious resolution
> To smuggle some few years, and strive to mend
> A broken character and constitution.
>
> On this congenial spot he fix'd his choice,
> Earl Goodwin trembled for his neighbouring sand;
> Here seagulls scream and cormorants rejoice,
> And mariners, though shipwreck'd, dread to land.
>
> Here reign the blust'ring North and blighting East,
> No tree is heard to whisper, bird to sing,
> Yet Nature cannot furnish out the feast,
> Art he invokes new horrors still to bring.
>
> Now mould'ring fanes and battlements arise,
> Arches and turrets nodding to their fall,
> Unpeopled palaces delude his eyes,
> And mimick desolation covers all.
>
> "Ah!" said the sighing peer, "had Bute been true,
> Nor Shelburne's, Rigby's, Calcraft's friend-ship vain,
> Far other scenes than these had blest our view,
> And realiz'd the ruins that we feign.
>
> Purg'd by the sword and beautified by fire,
> Then had we seen proud London's hated walls;
> Owls might have hooted in St. Peter's choir,
> And foxes stunk and litter'd in St. Paul's."

In 1768 the professorship of modern history was bestowed on Gray by the duke of Grafton, who had lately become chancellor of the university, and the grateful poet felt it his duty to write an ode to be performed at the ceremonial installation of the duke in the following year. Since the ode was to be set to music, it was designed in the irregular form of a cantata, with sections of uneven length allotted to various soloists and to the chorus. Gray had no personal acquaintance with Grafton and was much attacked and ridiculed for his praises of this highly unpopular figure. Nevertheless the "Installation Ode"[2] was a genuine rekindling of the flame of poetry that had lain so long dormant within him. It is full of striking passages and lines, and at times it is less a paean in praise of the new chancellor than an expression of Gray's gratitude and *pietas* toward the university itself. This was impressively shown when he conjured up the

2. The title appears as "Ode for Music" in R. Lonsdale's edition of the *Poetical Works*, the standard.

majestic procession of its founder and benefactors, in a passage comparable with the noblest in the Pindaric odes:

> But hark! the portals sound, and pacing
>   forth
> With solemn steps and slow
> High Potentates and Dames of royal birth
> And mitred Fathers in long order go:
> Great *Edward* with the lillies on his brow
> From haughty *Gallia* torn,
> And sad *Chatillon,* on her bridal morn
> That wept her bleeding Love, and princely
>   *Clare,*
> And *Anjou's* Heroine, and the paler Rose,
> The rival of her crown, and of her woes,
> And either *Henry* there,
> The murther'd Saint, and the majestick
>   Lord,
> That broke the bonds of *Rome.*
> (Their tears, their little triumphs o'er,
> Their human passions now no more,
> Save Charity, that glows beyond the tomb).
>   (35–50)

Such, in the last of his poems, was Gray's tribute of homage and farewell to Cambridge, where he had passed so many tranquil years.

VI

Gray was described after his death by an enthusiastic friend as "perhaps the most learned man in Europe." Such superlatives are, of course, futile. It is sufficient to say that he was a man of exceptionally wide culture and interests. But none of his major projects—the annotation of Plato, the edition of Strabo, the history of English poetry—came to anything at all. He read and annotated and filled huge notebooks with extracts; he drew up lists and catalogs and pedigrees; Walpole told a friend that "Mr. Gray often vexed me by finding him heaping notes on an interleaved Linnaeus, instead of pranking on his lyre." Such occupations were his barriers against melancholy, his refuge from the depression that so often weighed upon his spirits. "To be employed is to be happy," he wrote, and "to find oneself business is the great art of life."

But Gray has a second claim upon the attention of posterity. He was one of the supreme letter writers of his century, the peer of Horace Walpole and William Cowper. He may seldom have touched his lyre, and then with difficulty and reluctance; but throughout his life he was able to express himself in his private letters to his friends with unfailing ease, clarity, and grace. They begin during his undergraduate days at Cambridge and end only a week or two before his death. They can portray landscape and natural beauty in a manner almost unique in the eighteenth century; they contain some of the most intelligent literary criticism of the time; they are often gay and colloquial, irradiated with a humor usually gentle but occasionally angry and sardonic; they are full of perception and sympathy, and sometimes of deep emotion. In them the story of Gray's life is unfolded, for the comprehending reader, in a manner that makes nonsense of Matthew Arnold's celebrated contention that "Gray never spoke out."

The quality of Gray's letters can best be illustrated by a few brief examples. In nothing was, he more original, more ahead of his time, than in his appreciation of the splendors of mountain scenery. When the ordinary traveler was still averting his eyes from the horrid spectacle of the Alps, Gray in his twenty-third year was anticipating Jean Jacques Rousseau and William Wordsworth. "In our little journey up to the Grande Chartreuse," he wrote in 1739, "I do not remember to have gone ten paces without an exclamation, that there was no restraining: Not a precipice, not a torrent, not a cliff, but is pregnant with religion and poetry. There are certain scenes that would awe an atheist into belief, without the help of other argument." Thirty years later he was writing of English mountains:

> In the evening walk'd alone down to the Lake by the side of *Crow Park* after sunset and saw the solemn colouring of night draw on, the last gleam of sunshine fading away on the hilltops, the deep serene of the water, and

> the long shadows of the mountains thrown across them, till they nearly touch'd the hithermost shore. At distance heard the murmur of many waterfalls not audible in the daytime. Wish'd for the moon, but she was *dark to me and silent, hid in her vacant interlunar cave.*

For his humor, directed so often against himself, a letter may be chosen in which Gray has been discussing his melancholy, his ennui, the spell of indolence that the life of Cambridge was casting over his soul. The prevailing spirit of the place, he wrote, was the spirit of laziness.

> Time will settle my Conscience, Time will reconcile me to this languid Companion: we shall smoke, we shall tipple, we shall doze together. We shall have our little Jokes, like other People, and our long Stories; Brandy will finish what Port begun; and a month after the Time you will see in some Corner of a *London Evening Post,* "Yesterday, died the Revnd. Mr. John Grey, Senior-Fellow of Clare-Hall, a facetious Companion, and well-respected by all that knew him. His death is supposed to be occasion'd by a Fit of an Apoplexy, being found fall'n out of Bed with his Head in the Chamber-Pot."

Gray's understanding of the sorrows of others is revealed in the beautiful letter to William Mason at the time of his wife's death.

> I break in upon you at a moment, when we least of all are permitted to disturb our Friends, only to say, that you are daily and hourly present to my thoughts. If the *worst* be not yet past: you will neglect and pardon me. But if the last struggle be over: if the poor subject of your long anxieties be no longer sensible to your kindness, or to her own sufferings: allow me (at least in idea, for what could I do, were I present, more than this?) to sit by you in silence, and pity from my heart, not her, who is at rest; but you, who lose her. May He, who made us, the Master of our pleasures, and of our pains, preserve and support you!

Finally, to show the depth of emotion in Gray's own nature, a passage may be quoted from one of his letters to Bonstetten, written a year before he died and shortly after that delightful, if not wholly deserving, young man had returned to his native Switzerland.

> I am return'd, my dear Bonstetten, from the little journey I had made into Suffolk without answering the end proposed. The thought, that you might have been with me there, has embitter'd all my hours. Your letter has made me happy; as happy as so gloomy, so solitary a Being as I am is capable of being. I know and have too often felt the disadvantages I lay myself under, how much I hurt the little interest I have in you, by this air of sadness so contrary to your nature and present enjoyments; but sure you will forgive, tho' you can not sympathize with me. It is impossible for me to dissemble with you. Such as I am, I expose my heart to your view, nor wish to conceal a single thought from your penetrating eyes.—All that you say to me, especially on the subject of Switzerland, is infinitely acceptable. It feels too pleasing ever to be fulfill'd, and as often as I read over your truly kind letter, written long since from London, I stop at these words: *La mort qui peut glacer nos bras avant qu'ils soient entrelacés.*

VII

Gray stands as the dominant poetic figure of the middle decades of the eighteenth century. It was a barren time, and he had few competitors. He wrote, moreover, to please himself, without the smallest notion of founding a school, or attracting a following, or achieving publicity of any kind. Nevertheless, although a poet of limited and fastidious output, he exerted a deep influence upon the age in which he lived.

Gray thus influenced his age, and at the same time he was in harmony with it. He was a good European, sensitive to the main trends of contemporary culture, at a time when that culture was becoming to some extent international, when educated people in France and England, Germany and Sweden and Russia, were beginning to think along much the same lines. He had seen the remains of classical antiquity with his own eyes. His travels had given him knowledge and appreciation of all that was best in music, painting, and sculpture. His poems were full of reminiscences of other languages and other literatures, living and dead—Homer and Vergil and Lucretius, Dante and Petrarch, William Shakespeare and John Milton. And in later life his interest in Scandinavian and Celtic legend, which consorted so well with his love of wild and rugged landscape, made him a precursor of the romantic revival that was to sweep across Europe like a flood.

But however great the admiration that was lavished upon Gray's other poems by his contemporaries, and whatever the degree of enjoyment that may be derived from them today, the "Elegy"' remains a work apart. It stands as an extraordinary and isolated phenomenon, a poem that can move us today exactly as it moved our forefathers. That was Gray's achievement, and it is unique in English literature.

Selected Bibliography

BIBLIOGRAPHY

Northup, C. S., *A Bibliography,* (New Haven, 1917) the standard work, listing also all writings about Gray to 1917; *An Elegy Written in a Country Church Yard,* F. G. Stokes, ed. (Oxford, 1929) contains detailed bibliographical descriptions of the early editions to 1771; Starr, H. W., *A Bibliography, 1917–1951,* (Philadelphia, 1953) a continuation of Northup's *Bibliography* to 1951.

COLLECTED EDITIONS

Poems, (London, 1768) supervised by the poet—R. Foulis' handsome ed. was published at Glasgow the same year; W. Mason, ed. *The Poems,* (York, 1775); T. J. Mathias, ed. *The Works,* 2 vols. (London, 1814); J. Mitford, ed. *The Works,* 2 vols. (London, 1816); J. Mitford, ed. *The Works,* 4 vols. (London, 1835–1837) the Aldine ed., with a volume of correspondence added in 1843; E. Gosse, ed. *The Works,* 4 vols. (London, 1884); A. Lane Poole, ed. *The Poetical Works,* (London, 1917) rev. by L. Whibley (London, 1937) with the poetical works of Collins, in the Oxford Standard Authors series; W. T. Williams and G. H. Vallins, eds. *Gray, Collins and Their Circle,* (London, 1937); L. Whibley, ed. *Poems,* Oxford (1939); H. W. Starr and J. R. Hendrickson, eds. *Complete Poems,* (London, 1966) the Oxford English Texts series; A. Johnston, ed. *Selected Poems,* (London, 1967) with poems of William Collins; R. Lonsdale, ed. *Poems,* (London, 1969) the Annotated English Poets series; J. Crofts, ed. *Poetry and Prose,* (Oxford, 1971) the Clarendon English series; *Poems,* (London, 1973) facs. by Scolar Press of 1768 ed.; J. Reeves, ed. *Complete English Poems,* (London, 1973) the Poetry Bookshelf series; R. Lonsdale, ed. *Poetical Works,* (London, 1977) with poetical works of William Collins, the Oxford Standard Authors series.

SEPARATE WORKS

"Ode on a Distant Prospect of Eton College," (London, 1747); "An Elegy Wrote in a Country Church Yard," (London, 1751) the text in the first quarto, with all the variants of the early ed., is given in Stokes's ed. (see above under "Bibliography"). The title was changed ("Wrote" to "Written") and the "Red-breast stanza" added in the third quarto, published 14 March 1751, a month after the first. (The stanza was dropped in 1753.) Facsimiles have been made of the three holograph MSS (British Museum; Eton College; Pembroke College, Cambridge), the latest being of the Eton by the Augustan Reprint Society, G. Sherburn, ed. (London, 1951); *Designs by Mr. R. Bentley for Six Poems by Mr. T. Gray,* (London, 1753) a finely printed and illustrated folio ed. of some textual interest; *Odes,* (Strawberry Hill, Middlesex, 1757); "Ode Performed in the Senate House at Cambridge," (Cambridge, 1769); L. Whibley, ed. "Ode on the Pleasure Arising from Vicissitude," (London, 1933).

LETTERS

The Correspondence of Thomas Gray and William Mason, J. Mitford, ed. (London, 1853); *Letters,* D. C. Tovey, ed. 3 vols. (London, 1900–1912); *The Correspondence of Gray, Walpole, West and Ashton,* P. Toynbee, ed. 2 vols. (Oxford, 1915); *Correspondence,* P. Toynbee and L. Whibley, eds. 3 vols. (Oxford, 1935) repr. (1971) in the Oxford Reprint series; W. S. Lewis, G. L. Lam, and C. H. Bennett, eds. *Walpole's Correspondence with Gray, West and Ashton,* (New Haven, 1948) vols. XIII-XIV of the Yale ed. of Walpole's correspondence; *Selected Letters,* J. W. Krutch, ed. (New York, 1952).

BIOGRAPHICAL AND CRITICAL STUDIES

Mason, W., "Memoirs of the Life and Writings of Mr. Gray," (York, 1775) prefixed to his ed. of the poems; *Lives of the English Poets,* Johnson, S., 4 vols. (London, 1781) vol. IV contains Johnson's account of Gray—the best modern ed. is by G. B. Hill, 3 vols. (Oxford, 1905); Gosse, E., *Gray,* (London, 1882); Arnold, M., *Essays in Criticism: Second Series,* (London, 1888) contains a discussion of Gray; Tovey, D. C., *Gray and His Friends: Letters and Relics,* (Cambridge, 1890); Norton, C. E., *The Poet Gray as a Naturalist,* (Boston, 1903); Cook, A. S., *A Concordance to the English Poems,* (Boston, 1908); Martin, R., *Chronologie de la vie et de l'oeuvre de Thomas Gray,* (Toulouse, 1931) and *Essai sur Thomas Gray,* (Paris, 1934); Empson, W., *Some Versions of Pastoral,* (London, 1935) contains an interesting interpretation of the "Elegy"; Jones, W. Powell, *Thomas Gray, Scholar,* (Cambridge, Mass., 1937); Tillotson, G., *Essays in Criticism and Research,* (Cambridge, 1942) contains the essay "Gray's Letters" Cecil, Lord David, *Poets and Story-Tellers,* (London, 1945) includes the Warton Lecture (1945) "The Poetry of Thomas Gray"; Brooks, C., *The Well Wrought Urn,* (New York, 1948) contains the essay "Gray's Storied Urn"; Cecil, Lord David, *Two Quiet Lives,* (London, 1948); Ketton-Cremer, R. W., *Thomas Gray: A Biography,* (Cambridge, 1955) the standard life; Roberts, S. C., *Doctor Johnson and Others,* (Cambridge, 1958) includes the W. P. Ker Memorial Lecture (Glasgow, 1952) "Thomas Gray of Pembroke,"; Fukuhara, R., *Essays on Thomas Gray,* (Tokyo, 1960) mainly in Japanese but contains some useful essays in English; Tillotson, G., *Augustan Studies,* (London, 1961) contains essays on "Ode on the Spring," and "Ode on the Death of a Favourite Cat", *From Sensibility to Romanticism: Essays Presented to F. A. Pottle,* (Oxford, 1965) contains I. Jack's "Gray's 'Elegy' Reconsidered".

Seamus Heaney

(b. 1939)

GREGORY A. SCHIRMER

SEAMUS HEANEY WAS born the year W. B. Yeats died—a notable coincidence, given that Heaney was eventually to be regarded, both inside and outside Ireland, as the most important Irish poet writing after Yeats. Also in that year, 1939, W. H. Auden (in an elegy on Yeats) made the peculiarly modern observation that "poetry makes nothing happen," a statement that few poets in Auden's wake—and certainly not Heaney—have been able to dismiss without at least some second thoughts. Indeed, for Heaney, an Ulsterman, the question of the value of the poetic enterprise has been particularly pressing; he has watched his literary career develop alongside a steady escalation of sectarian violence in his native Northern Ireland, and while it is one thing to make claims for the validity of art, to justify giving your life to writing poems, in a time of relatively low political voltage, it is quite another to do so when men, women, and children are being killed almost daily in your backyard.

As Yeats had done before him, Heaney has consistently made those claims, and much of his poetry—arguably the best of it—embodies with conviction and candor the poet's struggle to come to terms with urgent political and social realities without compromising the integrity of his art, and without abandoning his faith in art's ability to get at human truths lying beneath the surface of everyday events. In an essay in which he describes T. S. Eliot writing poems in the middle of the bombing of London during World War II, Heaney clearly elucidates that belief in the efficacy of art, a belief that inspires and informs almost all his poetry:

> Here is the great paradox of poetry and of the imaginative arts in general. Faced with the brutality of the historical onslaught, they are practically useless. Yet they verify our singularity, they strike and stake out the ore of self which lies at the base of every individuated life. In one sense the efficacy of poetry is nil—no lyric has ever stopped a tank. In another sense, it is unlimited. It is like the writing in the sand in the face of which accusers and the accused are left speechless and renewed. (*The Government of The Tongue*, p. 107)

This view of the relationship between art and the world requires, among other things, aesthetic distance. Heaney's ability to stand back from the violent conflict between Catholic and Protestant, nationalist and unionist, probably owes more than a little to the circumstances of his life, especially his early years. He was born on 13 April 1939, the oldest of nine children of a Catholic couple, Margaret and Patrick Heaney, living on a farm called Mossbawn, in County Derry, about thirty miles northwest of Belfast. By Heaney's account, the community was a cheerfully mixed one, with Catholics and Protestants living "in proximity to and in harmony with one another." Even the local geography encouraged what Heaney referred to as his capacity for "a kind of double awareness of division": To the west of Mossbawn lay a walled and wooded demesne and a community with the British name of Castledawson; to the east lay bogland, a mysterious, treacherous, powerfully alluring tract of swamp that ran up to the west bank of the river Bann and a village with the distinctly Irish name of Toome. It is no accident that much of Heaney's poetry is rooted in this landscape. For Heaney it represents more than the locale of his childhood memories; it embodies in a highly concrete form many of the political, religious, and cultural divisions that have come to preoccupy his art.

From St. Columb's College in Londonderry, a boarding school to which he won a scholarship in 1951, Heaney went to Queen's University in Belfast, where he was an undergraduate from 1957 to 1961 and where his interest in poetry first began to flower. At Queen's, Heaney read widely in both English and Irish literature and published (under the pen name *Incertus*) some poems in the university's literary magazine. The year after he graduated, while doing postgraduate work at St. Joseph's College of Education in Belfast, Heaney came to know the English writer Philip Hobsbaum, who had recently come to Queen's to teach and organized a group of young poets, including Derek Mahon and Michael Longley, of which Heaney soon became an active part. In August 1965 he married Marie Devlin, a schoolteacher from County Tyrone. During the next few years, while teaching at a secondary school in Belfast and later as lecturer at St. Joseph's, Heaney began placing poems in journals, and in 1966 Faber and Faber brought out his first full-length book of poems, *Death of a Naturalist,* to considerable acclaim. Heaney spent most of the next six years teaching at Queen's and writing. His two sons, Michael and Christopher, were born in 1966 and 1968, respectively. Another book, *Door into the Dark,* appeared in 1969, and a third, *Wintering Out,* in 1972, both of which greatly enhanced Heaney's steadily rising reputation.

In the academic year 1970–1971, Heaney was a guest lecturer at the University of California, Berkeley, a move that proved to be the first step toward a more or less permanent exile from his native Ulster. The decision to go to Berkeley came less than a year after the civil rights movement on behalf of Ulster Catholics had erupted into violence. In California Heaney found an equally charged political atmosphere and, more important, he became convinced there by what he saw among anti-Vietnam War activists that poetry need not be alienated from politics. As he said later in an interview:

> I could see a close connection between the political and cultural assertions being made at that time by the minority in the north of Ireland and the protests and consciousness-raising that were going on in the Bay Area. And the poets were a part of this and also, pre-eminently, part of the protest against the Vietnam war. So that was probably the most important influence I came under in Berkeley, that awareness that poetry was a force, almost a mode of power, certainly a mode of resistance. ("An Interview with Seamus Heaney," *Ploughshares,* p. 20)

A year after his return from California, Heaney and his wife moved with their two sons from Belfast to a house in a rural area of County Wicklow, south of Dublin, known as Glanmore. It was a momentous move in several ways. First, Heaney was giving up the security of his teaching post at Queen's and committing his life fully to writing poetry. Second, he was quite consciously making himself into an exile. The move was seen by some of his fellow Ulstermen as a betrayal, but in Heaney's view it was a necessary break, giving him the distance he needed to write and to think about his writing. The four years in Glanmore were, Heaney later wrote, "an important growth time when I was asking myself questions about the proper function of poets and poetry and learning a new commitment to the art." That new commitment led to two important books, each of which, in different ways, confronted the crisis that Heaney had left behind in Belfast—*North,* published in 1975, and *Field Work,* published in 1979.

In 1976, Heaney and his family, which now included a daughter, Catherine Ann, born at Glanmore three years earlier, moved to Dublin, where he had been teaching since 1975 at Caryfort College, a teacher-training institution. Heaney also, in these years, began strengthening the connection with the United States begun during his year at Berkeley, giving frequent readings in America. In 1981 he resigned his post at Caryfort, and a year later accepted a one-semester-a-year position at Harvard University. In 1984, Heaney was appointed Boylston Professor of Rhetoric and Oratory at Harvard, and he began dividing his time between Dublin and Cambridge. In 1984 he published *Sweeney Astray,* a translation of a Middle Irish romance, and *Station Island,* his sixth collection of poems. Another collection, *The Haw Lantern,* appeared in 1987. In 1989 Heaney was elected Professor of Poetry at Oxford University.

In the 1980's Heaney published two collections of critical essays—*Preoccupations: Selected Prose, 1968–1978* (1980) and *The Government of the Tongue: The 1986 T. S. Eliot Memorial Lectures and Other Critical Writings* (1988)—in which he defines the essentially Romantic poetics that underlies his art. For Heaney, the composition of a poem is a matter of "listening," of "a wise passiveness, a surrender to the energies that spring within the center of the mind" (*Preoccupations,* p. 63). It cannot, therefore, be willed, and cannot be dictated to by specific events, political or otherwise. "The fact is," Heaney writes, "that poetry is its own reality, and no matter how much a poet may concede to the narrative pressures of social, moral, political and historical reality, the ultimate fidelity must be to the demands and promise of the artistic event" (*Government,* p. 101). And so the poet must find ways of engaging the world around him in his work without sacrificing that "ultimate fidelity." In "Feeling into Words," a lecture given in 1974, five years after the outbreak of violence in Ulster, Heaney said that political pressures had forced him to realize that his art could not turn its back on what was happening in the streets of Belfast and Londonderry; but what he needed, he said, was not polemical arguments but "images and symbols adequate to our predicament":

> I felt it imperative to discover a field of force in which, without abandoning fidelity to the processes and experience of poetry . . . it would be possible to encompass the perspectives of humane reason and at the same time to grant the religious intensity of the violence its deplorable authenticity and complexity. (*Preoccupations,* pp. 56–57)

That "authenticity and complexity" is the poet's domain; his aim must be, Heaney says, to reach down and back into his country's history, psychology, and mythology to uncover all the forces "implicit in the terms Irish Catholic and Ulster Protestant."

DEATH OF A NATURALIST

Heaney's first book, published three years before the Ulster violence began in earnest, carries few traces of those forces. The poems in *Death of a Naturalist* describe Heaney's experiences growing up in Mossbawn, and do so, for the most part, neutrally. Standing behind many of them is the twentieth-century Irish poet Patrick Kavanagh, to whom Heaney has acknowledged a large debt. Kavanagh's commitment to writing about his own postage stamp of ground, a piece of land in rural County Monaghan not far in distance or character from the County Derry of Heaney's childhood, made it possible, Heaney said, for him to focus with confidence on the experiences and landscapes of his upbringing. Heaney once said that Kavanagh, more than any other Irish poet, including Yeats, gave all writers coming after him "permission to dwell without cultural anxiety among the usual landmarks of your life." Heaney's evocations of those landmarks differ from Kavanagh's, however, in their Keatsian sensuousness, their richness of sound and image. Here, for example, is a description, taken from the title poem of *Death of a Naturalist,* of a flax dam:

> All year the flax-dam festered in the heart
> Of the townland; green and heavy headed
> Flax had rotted there, weighted down by
>   huge sods.

Daily it sweltered in the punishing sun.
Bubbles gargled delicately, bluebottles
Wove a strong gauze of sound around the
  smell.

The rich, fecund atmosphere of the dam is felt here partly in the irregular, heavily stressed lines, and in a medley of internal sound patterns, alliterative and assonantal ("flax-dam festered," "heavy headed," "rotted" and "weighted," "strong gauze, and "sound around," among others).

There is something of the musical irregularities of Gerard Manley Hopkins lurking in such passages—and Heaney had read and admired Hopkins at Queen's University: ". . . when I first put pen to paper at university, what flowed out was what flowed in, the bumpy alliterating music, the reporting sounds and ricocheting consonants typical of Hopkins's verse"—but the English poet most important to Heaney's early work is Wordsworth. For one thing, as the title of the volume suggests, *Death of a Naturalist* is very much concerned with the destruction of youthful illusion, and can in fact be read as a rural Irish version of Wordsworth's notion of the necessary fall from innocence into experience. But Wordsworth and the Romantics are also crucial to Heaney's poetry because of their theories of poetry. In "The Diviner," Heaney takes a phenomenon of the rural life he knew as a child and transforms it into a metaphor for a Romantic concept of poetic inspiration:

Cut from the green hedge a forked hazel
  stick
That he held tight by the arms of the V:
Circling the terrain, hunting the pluck
Of water, nervous, but professionally

Unfussed. The pluck came sharp as a sting.
The rod jerked down with precise
  convulsions,
Spring water suddenly broadcasting
Through a green aerial its secret stations.

The bystanders would ask to have a try.
He handed them the rod without a word.
It lay dead in their grasp till nonchalantly
He gripped expectant wrists. The hazel
  stirred.

The connection here between poet and diviner—felt particularly in that final rhyme between "word" and "stirred"—embodies a thoroughly Romantic aesthetic. As Heaney once said in discussing this poem, the poet, like the diviner, makes "contact with what lies hidden" and makes "palpable what was sensed or raised." Moreover, the comparison argues for a Wordsworthian passivity on the part of the poet—he grips the wrists of others "nonchalantly," for example—and for the Romantic notion of the poet as a chosen vessel; only the diviner has the mysterious power to find the water.

Death of a Naturalist also introduces another, somewhat similar metaphor for the process of poetic creation, and this one informs much of Heaney's later work. In the first poem in the book, "Digging," Heaney defends his work as a poet by describing it as his version of the cutting of turf done by the men in his family before him:

The cold smell of potato mould, the squelch
  and slap
Of soggy peat, the curt cuts of an edge
Through living roots awaken in my head.
But I've no spade to follow men like them.

Between my finger and my thumb
The squat pen rests.
I'll dig with it.

At this point in Heaney's career, what the Romantic poet-as-archaeologist is likely to find is more individual than communal, more personal than public, as the final poem in the volume, "Personal Helicon," asserts: "I rhyme / To see myself, to set the darkness echoing."

Nonetheless, there are signs in *Death of a Naturalist* of more political concerns. The most ambitious poem in the volume, "At a Potato Digging," explores the relationship between present and past, specifically the past of the Great Famine of the 1840's, in which thousands of Irish died or emigrated when the potato crop failed for several consecutive years. This is a highly charged chapter in Ireland's long and troubled history—the English were (and, in some quarters, still are) blamed for much of the suffering—and Heaney uses the historical perspective to unearth certain cultural fears and attitudes, as well as to make the more general point about how current values, especially in Ireland, are inevitably shaped by the past. After a characteristically vivid description of harvested potatoes,

"Native
to the black hutch of clay
where the halved seed shot and clotted
these knobbed and slit-eyed tubers seem
the petrified hearts of drills"

the poem shifts to the past, relying on the phrase "live skulls, blind-eyed," used to describe the potatoes, as a fulcrum:

Live skulls, blind-eyed, balanced on
wild higgeldy skeletons
scoured the land in 'forty-five,
wolfed the blighted root and died.

. . .

Stinking potatoes fouled the land,
pits turned pus into filthy mounds:
and where potato diggers are
you still smell the running sore.

The ground here, like the landscape in a number of Heaney's later bog poems, is a cultural and political memory bank, a constant reminder of a history of injustice and suffering. And so, when the poem returns to the present, the relative prosperity of the contemporary potato farmer is made to seem precarious, shadowed by a disastrous past that is evoked in certain words and images associated with death and starvation, and so with the famine:

Under a gay flotilla of gulls
The rhythm deadens, the workers stop.
Brown bread and tea in bright canfuls
Are served for lunch. Dead-beat, they flop

Down in the ditch and take their fill,
Thankfully breaking timeless fasts;
Then, stretched on the faithless ground,
  spill
Libations of cold tea, scatter crusts.

DOOR INTO THE DARK

There are flaws in *Death of a Naturalist,* most of them the result of overwriting—of loading each rift with too much ore, of working too hard for the image that will shock (from "Waterfall": "water goes over / Like villains dropped screaming to justice"). Some of this is ironed out in Heaney's next book, *Door into the Dark.* The descriptions of rural life in Heaney's native County Derry tend to be somewhat sparer and more streamlined in this book, the lines less clogged with heavy stresses. In "Gone," for example, Heaney describes an absence rather than a presence, a place left uninhabited and therefore incomplete, all of which is reflected in the way that the poem resists the completeness of full rhyme and the stability of regular stanzas:

Green froth that lathered each end
Of the shining bit
Is a cobweb of grass-dust.
The sweaty twist of the bellyband
Has stiffened, cold in the hand
And pads of the blinkers
Bulge through the ticking.
Reins, chains and traces
Droop in a tangle.

His hot reek is lost.
The place is old in his must.

He cleared in a hurry
Clad only in shods
Leaving this stable unmade.

Similarly, the strain of violent sexuality that runs through a number of Heaney's nature poems in *Death of a Naturalist* is often tempered in *Door into the Dark,* usually by a gentle, wry sense of humor. In "Rite of Spring," Heaney playfully describes in sexual terms that are anything but threatening the process of thawing a frozen pump by wrapping it with straw and then setting the straw on fire:

> . . . then a light
> That sent the pump up in flame.
> It cooled, we lifted her latch,
> Her entrance was wet, and she came.

And there is an erotic tenderness in "Undine" that is hard to find anywhere in *Death of a Naturalist.* This poem retells a myth about a water spirit who has to marry a human and have a child by him before she can be human; and even though Heaney's version of the legend clearly suggests some kind of parallel between political and sexual conquest, it is finally a poem celebrating the union it describes:

> He slashed the briars, shovelled up grey silt
> To give me right of way in my own drains
> And I ran quick for him, cleaned out my rust.
>
> He halted, saw me finally disrobed,
> Running clear, with apparent unconcern.
> Then he walked by me. I rippled and I
> churned
>
> Where ditches intersected near the river
> Until he dug a spade deep in my flank
> And took me to him. I swallowed his trench
>
> Gratefully, dispersing myself for love
> Down in his roots, climbing his brassy
> grain—
> But once he knew my welcome, I alone
>
> Could give him subtle increase and
> reflection.
> He explored me so completely, each limb
> Lost its cold freedom. Human, warmed to
> him.

At the same time, a darkly introspective strain can be discerned in *Door into the Dark.* There is a poem, for example, entitled "Dream," in which Heaney describes himself driving a billhook into someone's skull; there is "The Forge," in which the image of the poet-as-diviner in *Death of a Naturalist* is replaced by that of poet-as-blacksmith, creating in darkness ("All I know is a door into the dark"); there is a poem entitled "Shoreline," in which Heaney sees the Irish consciousness as haunted by the nightmare of invasion:

> A tide
> Is rummaging in
> At the foot of all fields,
> All cliffs and shingles.
> Listen. Is it the Danes,
> A black hawk bent on the sail?
> Or the chinking Normans?

And, last but hardly least, there is the final poem in the collection, "Bogland"—Heaney's first bog poem—in which the landscape of the bog is presented as a memory bank holding all the past in its watery embrace, and threatening to open a door into places unknown and terrifying:

> We have no prairies
> To slice a big sun at evening—
> Everywhere the eye concedes to
> Encroaching horizon,
>
> Is wooed into the cyclops' eye
> Of a tarn. Our unfenced country
> Is bog that keeps crusting
> Between the sights of the sun.
>
> . . .
>
> They'll never dig coal here,
>
> Only the waterlogged trunks
> Of great firs, soft as pulp.
> Our pioneers keep striking
> Inwards and downwards,
>
> Every layer they strip
> Seems camped on before.
> The bogholes might be Atlantic seepage.
> The wet centre is bottomless.

In "Feeling into Words" Heaney described "Bogland" as a poem that laid down "an answering Irish myth" (*Preoccupations,* p. 55) to the legend of the American frontier—significantly, a vertical rather than a horizontal myth. But it was not until after the violence in Northern Ireland erupted that he was able to carry this idea an important step further, to use this notion of the bog as a means of unearthing in his poetry the cultural attitudes and values that lay beneath the terrible daily events that, as a poet born and brought up in Ulster, he could not ignore.

WINTERING OUT

The difference between 1969, the year *Door into the Dark* was published, and 1972, when his next collection, *Wintering Out,* appeared, is registered forcefully in the dedicatory poem to *Wintering Out*. Here the pastoral landscape of Heaney's childhood, evoked so vividly in his first two books, gives way to one of war:

This morning from a dewy motorway
I saw the new camp for the internees:
a bomb had left a crater of fresh clay
in the roadside, and over in the trees

machine-gun posts defined a real stockade.
There was that white mist you get on a tow
ground
and it was déjà-vu, some film made
of Stalag 17, *a bad dream with no sound.*

Is there a life before death? That's
chalked up
on a wall downtown. Competence with
pain,
coherent miseries, a bite and sup,
we hug our little destiny again.

In *Wintering Out,* Heaney approaches this terrain of pain and misery along two principal routes—one linguistic, one metaphoric—each of which enables him to confront the violence while maintaining the integrity of his art.

Having grown up in an area both Protestant and Catholic, unionist and nationalist, Heaney understands full well the political depth charges buried in language—in the choice of one word over another, in the way the same word might be pronounced. In *Wintering Out,* Heaney re-views the places of his childhood through a linguistic lens, and thereby politicizes the landscape. As he said in an interview, "*Wintering Out* tries to insinuate itself into the roots of the political myths by feeling along the lines of language." And so the village of Toome, to the east of Mossbawn, emerges in this book more as a linguistic event than as a geographical one:

My mouth holds round
the soft blastings,
Toome, Toome,
as under the dislodged

slab of the tongue
I push into a souterrain
prospecting what new
in a hundred centuries'

loam, flints, musket-balls,
fragmented ware,
torcs and fish-bones
till I am sleeved in

alluvial mud that shelves
suddenly under
bogwater and tributaries,
and elvers tail my hair.
("Toome")

Heaney is fully aware of the political implications of this kind of linguistic prospecting. The replacement of Irish by English as Ireland's principal language represents a crucial kind of conquest because it facilitates the erosion of Irish culture and traditions. Heaney does not, however, recommend turning back the clock of politics or of language. For better or worse, English is the modern Irish poet's language, and he must find ways to use the tongue of the conqueror to validate and maintain the heritage that it threatens. As he says in "A New Song":

But now our river tongues must rise
From licking deep in native haunts
To flood, with vowelling embrace,
Demesnes staked out in consonants.

If these lines argue for some kind of acceptance of English as Ireland's language—even some kind of "embrace" of those linguistic demesnes marked by consonants rather than vowels—they also, on a more strictly political level, insist that it is not realistic to assume that centuries of British presence in Ireland can be dismissed with the sweep of a hand, or of a hand grenade.

Wintering Out contains the first of Heaney's poems in which bogland is used metaphorically to interpret the conflict in Northern Ireland. In 1969, Heaney came across a photograph of a man from the Iron Age whose body was found preserved in the bogs of Jutland. The photograph appeared in a book entitled *The Bog People* (1969), and its author, P. V. Glob, argued that many of the bodies found strangled or with cut throats in the peat bogs of Jutland were victims of ritual sacrifices to an earth goddess, killed and buried each year to ensure the fertility of the land in the coming spring. For Heaney, as he later said in "Feeling into Words," the parallels with the political tradition of blood sacrifice in Ireland were striking:

> Taken in relation to the tradition of Irish political martyrdom for that cause whose icon is Kathleen Ni Houlihan, this is more than an archaic barbarous rite: it is an archetypal pattern. And the unforgettable photographs of these victims blended in my mind with photographs of atrocities, past and present, in the long rites of Irish political and religious struggles. (*Preoccupations*, pp. 57–58)

These correspondences came together in "The Tollund Man," a poem in which Heaney connects the Irish political tradition of blood sacrifice to a long history of fanaticism going back to the primitive Jutes, and suggests, chiefly through images of the victims, that this kind of ritualistic faith leads to sterility, not fertility:

> I could risk blasphemy,
> Consecrate the cauldron bog
> Our holy ground and pray
> Him to make germinate
>
> The scattered, ambushed
> Flesh of labourers,
> Stockinged corpses
> Laid out in the farmyards,
>
> Tell-tale skin and teeth
> Flecking the sleepers
> Of four young brothers, trailed
> For miles along the lines.

Like many of Heaney's poems about the North, "The Tollund Man" also turns a critical eye on its author, exploring with candor his own ambiguous position. At the end of the poem, Heaney concedes that as an Irishman he cannot help but identify to some extent with the violence and its motives, even though he is appalled by it. Imagining driving through Jutland, he sees himself as both alienated and implicated: "Out there in Jutland / In the old man-killing parishes / I will feel lost, / Unhappy and at home."

Heaney later said that when he wrote "The Tollund Man," he realized that it represented an important development in his work:

> I had a sense of crossing a line really, that my whole being was involved in the sense of—the root sense—of religion. . . . And that was a moment of commitment not in the political sense but in the deeper sense of your life, committing yourself to something. I think that brought me a new possibility of seriousness in the poetic enterprise. ("An Interview with Seamus Heaney," *Ploughshares*, p. 20)

NORTH

That new possibility reached its full flowering in Heaney's fourth book of poems, *North*, which contains a series of poems in which the metaphor of the bog is used to delve into Ireland's rich, tumultuous past, and to exhume attitudes and values that explain, insofar as explanations are possible, the violence in contemporary Ulster. The bog poems in *North* see that violence as part of a long line of atrocity stretching back into the dimness of ancient history, and thus as a manifestation of a deep-seated human need to resort to bloodshed in the name of one cause or another.

In "The Grabaulle Man," for example, Heaney presents an arresting image of the body of a victim found in the bogs of Jutland—"The head lifts / the chin is a visor / raised above the vent / of his slashed throat / that has tanned and toughened"—and uses it to explore the human capacity for transforming such victims into political martyrs or heroes. Heaney also worries in this poem about how the artist can transform reality, sometimes in similarly disconcerting ways. For him, the Grabaulle Man, whom he first encountered in a photograph, has become "perfected in my memory," a product of his imagination. That abstracted image needs, Heaney says, to be weighed against the brutal reality of the victim's actual death and, more to the point, against "the actual weight / of each hooded victim, / slashed and dumped" in contemporary Northern Ireland.

This notion that the poet, like the political partisan, may be guilty of remaking reality for his own purpose is part of the self-reflexive doubt that runs through much of Heaney's writing about the North. Heaney's moral ambiguity about his responsibilities is perhaps nowhere more movingly expressed than in "Punishment," a poem in which the body of a Viking adulteress dug up from the bog, still bearing the marks of her public disgrace, is connected with the contemporary practice of tarring and feathering Ulster Catholic girls caught going out with British soldiers:

> Little adulteress,
> before they punished you
>
> you were flaxen-haired,
> undernourished, and your
> tar-black face was beautiful.
> My poor scapegoat,
>
> I almost love you
> but would have cast, I know,
> the stones of silence.
> I am the artful voyeur
>
> of your brain's exposed
> and darkened combs,
> your muscles' webbing
> and all your numbered bones:
>
> I who have stood dumb
> when your betraying sisters,
> cauled in tar,
> wept by the railings,
>
> who would connive
> in civilized outrage
> yet understand the exact
> and tribal, intimate revenge.

Part of Heaney's self-questioning here has to do with his commitment to writing poems about the North rather than taking some more obviously relevant action—with being, as he says, an "artful voyeur" of the catastrophe. But the poem is also concerned with the broader ambivalence explored in "The Tollund Man." On the one hand, from the perspective of "civilized outrage," Heaney abhors the violence and cruelty. On the other, he understands, in his bones, the feelings that lie behind it; as an Irishman—and as a human being—he cannot help but identify with that desire for "a tribal, intimate revenge."

North is divided into two sections, a division that proves significant in the development of Heaney's poetry. At the end of the first section of the book, in a poem titled "Hercules and Antaeus," Heaney retells the classical story of how Hercules defeated Antaeus by holding him up, keeping him from the ground that nourished him:

> Hercules lifts his arms
> in a remorseless V,
> his triumph unassailed
> by the powers he has shaken
>
> and lifts and banks Antaeus
> high as a profiled ridge,
> a sleeping giant,
> pap for the dispossessed.

This can be read as a version of the conquest of Ireland by England, of the destruction of the dark, vertical, earth-nourished culture of the Irish at the hands of the more rational, more "enlightened" culture of the English; robbed of its contact with the soil, the Irish tradition becomes "a sleeping giant" or, worse, "pap for the dispossessed." For Heaney, however, this myth had an additional significance; it represented an attempt on his part to put behind him the vertical, archaeological poetry of the first part of his career, and to try to establish for himself a more open, more socially conscious, more public voice. As he said in an interview, Hercules for him "represents the possibility of the play of intelligence," and he was at this time looking in his own work for "an intonation that could be called public," a voice that is "set *out* . . . a voice that could *talk out* as well as go into a trance" ("Seamus Heaney," *Viewpoints: Poets in Conversation,* p. 70).

That new Hercules voice sounds distinctly in the second part of *North.* "Whatever You Say Say Nothing," for example, is informed by the same self-criticism at work in "The Grabaulle Man" and "Punishment," but in this poem Heaney's questions about the efficacy of his art are expressed directly, even colloquially, and the richly suggestive metaphor of the bog is replaced by direct references to the seventeenth-century Battle of the Boyne:

> Christ, it's near time that some small leak
> was sprung
>
> In the great dykes the Dutchman made
> To dam the dangerous tide that followed
> Seamus.
> Yet for all this art and sedentary trade
> I am incapable. The famous
>
> Northern reticence, the tight gag of place
> And times: yes, yes. Of the "wee six" I sing
> Where to be saved you only must save face
> And whatever you say, you say nothing.

The tone here is uncharacteristically acerbic, but that note of candid, critical self-examination informs much of Heaney's poetry in the late 1970's and 1980's. In the last poem of *North,* "Exposure," Heaney directs that inquiring gaze at his decision to move to Wicklow in 1972. To some extent, the poem can be read as a defense of that move—Heaney says that he is "neither internee nor informer"—but the poem ends in genuine doubt about the morality of his choosing to leave Ulster behind him, and about what he might have lost, as a poet, by doing so:

> I am neither internee nor informer;
> An inner émigré, grown long-haired
> And thoughtful; a wood-kerne
> Escaped from the massacre,
> Taking protective colouring
> From bole and bark, feeling
> Every wind that blows;
>
> Who, blowing up these sparks
> For their meagre heat, have missed
> The once-in-a-lifetime portent,
> The comet's pulsing rose.

FIELD WORK

Whatever misgivings Heaney might have entertained when he was writing *North,* the move to Glanmore and the full commitment to writing proved to be, at least for his readers, good decisions. Heaney's next collection, *Field Work*—a book very much tied, as its title suggests, to Heaney's experience in Glanmore—was received by many critics as his most accomplished book by far. It also carried Heaney considerably forward in his attempt to develop a more Herculean poetics. In an interview conducted the year *Field Work* was published, Heaney said, "I remember writing a letter to Brian Friel [the Irish playwright] just after *North* was published, saying I no longer wanted a door into the dark—I want a door into the light" ("An Interview with Seamus Heaney," *Ploughshares,* p. 20). In the remarkably flexible and open voice that characterizes most of the poems in it, and in Heaney's willingness to speak directly and often autobiographically about events in the North, *Field Work* clearly opens that door.

Heaney's response to the Ulster violence in this book takes the form largely of elegies written about people he knew. Although this approach might be seen as a means of sidestepping unqualified political commitment—and Heaney does seem to be taking his cue in these poems from Yeats's observation in "Easter 1916" that the poet's role in such matters is chiefly "To murmur name upon name"—the form of the elegy provides Heaney with a way of writing about the pressing political and social realities of his native Ulster while maintaining the aesthetic distance from outright advocacy that he sees as necessary for the poet. This need for poetic independence is itself the theme of several of the elegies in *Field Work.* In perhaps the most moving of them, "Casualty," Heaney identifies his poetic self with a Catholic fisherman named Louis O'Neill, who was killed when he violated a curfew in Belfast. The curfew was imposed by Catholics in mourning for thirteen men shot to death by British paratroopers; O'Neill was killed, in other words, not because of any political actions on his part but because he ignored restrictions placed on his individual freedom in the name of political necessity—placed there by his own "side" in the conflict.

Heaney's admiration for the fisherman rests on O'Neill's willingness to follow his own instincts, but characteristically, when he describes the scene of O'Neill's death, he asks a question that clearly interrogates his own instincts to steer clear of political advocacy in his art: "How culpable was he / That last night when he broke / Our tribe's complicity?" Nonetheless, Heaney insists that the poet must aim for some point beyond the day-to-day conflict. At the end of the poem, the scene of O'Neill's funeral dissolves into a memory of a fishing expedition that Heaney and O'Neill once took together, a memory in which Heaney both defines his essentially Romantic aesthetics (the poet, like the fisherman, hauls "off the bottom" and must surrender to rhythms and feelings that are "working you"), and affirms his faith in the need for the poet to follow his instincts "well out" and "beyond" the press of daily events:

> I missed his funeral,
> Those quiet walkers
> And sideways talkers
> Shoaling out of his lane
> To the respectable
> Purring of the hearse . . .
> They move in equal pace
> With the habitual
> Slow consolation
> Of a dawdling engine,
> The line lifted, hand
> Over fist, cold sunshine
> On the water, the land
> Banked under fog: that morning
> I was taken in his boat,
> The screw purling, turning
> Indolent fathoms white,
> I tasted freedom with him.
> To get out early, haul
> Steadily off the bottom,
> Dispraise the catch, and smile
> As you find a rhythm
> Working you, slow mile by mile,
> Into your proper haunt
> Somewhere, well out, beyond . . .

In the years before Robert Lowell's death in 1977, Lowell and Heaney became well acquainted, and when Lowell died, Heaney wrote an elegy for him in which Lowell becomes the vehicle for Heaney's faith in the independence and integrity of art. From Heaney's point of view, he and Lowell had much in common; just as Heaney's writing had been inevitably shaped by the sectarian violence in Ulster, so Lowell had had to fashion his art in the context of the Vietnam War and a range of powerful political and social forces, some of which Heaney had observed during the year he spent at Berkeley at the beginning of the 1970's. "You drank America / like the heart's / iron vodka," Heaney says in "Elegy," but what he most admired about Lowell was his unwavering commitment, in the face of personal and public catastrophe, to "promulgating art's / deliberate, peremptory / love and arrogance."

If Kavanagh can be seen as an important influence in Heaney's early poems, Lowell strongly affected Heaney's work in the late 1970's and 1980's. That influence is most distinctly felt in the "Glanmore Sonnets," a sequence of ten poems in *Field Work* in which Heaney, taking Lowell's late sonnets as his model, defends his commitment to art, particularly to the new voice, something like Lowell's, that he is working to establish. The second sonnet, for example, drawing on the same kind of colloquial but compressed diction and rhythms observable in Lowell's sonnets, and written in the same autobiographical mode, describes this position:

Then I landed in the hedge-school of
Glanmore
And from the backs of ditches hoped to
raise
A voice caught back off slug-horn and slow
chanter
That might continue, hold, dispel, appease:
Vowels ploughed into other, opened ground,
Each verse returning like the plough turned
round.

By the time *Field Work* was published, the Wicklow experiment was over. Also, Heaney had lived through a decade in which his native Ulster was racked by sectarian violence—a situation that again and again had tested his commitment to being a poet. If the poems of *Field Work* may be taken as a reliable barometer, Heaney emerged from that test with a strengthened faith in his art; it is there in his elegy to Lowell, in the "Glanmore Sonnets," and, perhaps most movingly, in a poem titled "The Harvest Bow," set in the rural County Derry of his childhood. The poem opens with a description of Heaney's father tying a harvest bow from strands of straw, one of the local rituals that both defined a sense of place for Heaney and harkened back to a long tradition of lore and superstition, of magic and poetry:

As you plaited the harvest bow
You implicated the mellowed silence in you
In wheat that does not rust
But brightens as it tightens twist by twist
Into a knowable corona,
A throwaway love-knot of straw.

Like a poem or a story, the harvest bow opens a path for memory and imagination to travel. The middle of the poem recalls Heaney as a child out walking with his father, "You with a harvest bow in your lapel," a memory that leads to a final affirmation of a thoroughly Romantic faith in art's capacity to evoke the reality of the spirit, and thereby make something happen:

The end of art is peace
Could be the motto of this frail device
That I have pinned up on our deal dresser—
Like a drawn snare
Slipped lately by the spirit of the corn
Yet burnished by its passage, and still warm.

SWEENEY ASTRAY

This trust in art's authority, and the corresponding commitment to artistic independence, are major themes of Heaney's poetry in the 1980's. If the Tollund man or the Grabaulle man is the dominating figure in much of Heaney's work in the 1970's, in the following decade it is Mad Sweeney, the poet-hero of a Middle Irish romance and, for Heaney, a powerful symbol of poetic freedom. The story of Sweeney, which surfaced in Ireland in written form sometime between the thirteenth and sixteenth centuries, is one of rebellion against the establishment: Sweeney, a king, is put under a curse by a saint after preventing the construction of a church in his kingdom, and is transformed through the curse into a birdlike creature condemned to wander in exile and apparent madness. In his exile, Sweeney discovers that he has a gift for poetry, and much of the tale consists of the poems about Ireland that he writes in his wanderings.

This tale has been used by several modern Irish writers—most notably Flann O'Brien in his comic metafictional novel *At Swim-Two-Birds*—to explore the relationship between the artist and society. While he was living in Wicklow, Heaney worked on his translation of the story, publishing it in Ireland as *Sweeney Astray* in 1983. In his introduction he makes clear the ways in which, as a contemporary poet from Ulster living out of Ulster, he identifies with the figure of Mad Sweeney. "Insofar as Sweeney is also a figure of the artist," he says, "displaced, guilty, assuaging himself by his utterance, it is possible to read the work as an aspect of the quarrel between free creative imagination and the constraints of religious, political, and domestic obligation."

STATION ISLAND

This quarrel is at the center of Heaney's most important book of the 1980's, *Station Island,* arguably one of the most ambitious and accomplished collection of poems that he has published. The book is divided into three sections: a collection of various lyrics; a twelve-poem sequence entitled "Station Island" and based on a famous religious pilgrimage made by Irish Catholics; and a group of poems collected under the heading "Sweeney Redivivus" and spoken in the voice of a contemporary Sweeney. Several of the lyrics in the first section of the book explore the conflict between "free creative imagination" and the political obligations arising from the violence in Ulster, concluding with the same ambiguity and self-doubt that color much of Heaney's earlier work concerned with this question. In "Sandstone Keepsake," for example, Heaney depicts himself, in a clearly self-deprecating way, as inhabiting a world of illusion, alienated from social and political realities. The poem recalls an evening when he was out wading in an estuary across from a soldiers' camp:

> Anyhow, there I was with the wet red stone
> in my hand, staring across at the watch-
> towers
> from my free state of image and allusion,
> swooped on, then dropped by trained
> binoculars:
>
> a silhouette not worth bothering about,
> out for the evening in scarf and waders
> and not about to set times wrong or right,
> stooping along, one of the venerators.

An even less forgiving self-indictment occurs in the eighth section of "Station Island," describing an imagined encounter between Heaney, on his pilgrimage to Lough Derg, and the ghost of a cousin killed in the Ulster fighting and remembered earlier in a poem in *Field Work* titled "The Strand at Lough Beg." That poem opens with an epigraph taken from Dante's *Purgatorio,* and in "Station Island," Heaney turns this back on himself with a vengeance. The cousin tells him:

> You confused evasion and artistic tact.
> The Protestant who shot me through the
> head
> accuse directly, but indirectly, you
> who now atone perhaps upon this bed
> for the way you whitewashed ugliness and
> drew
> the lovely blinds of the *Purgatorio*
> and saccharined my death with morning
> dew.

If Heaney seems in some ways to be atoning in "Station Island" for such poetic sins, on the whole this dream version of the actual pilgrimage that Irish Catholics have been making to Lough Derg for centuries to atone for their sins describes a renewed and strengthened faith in his art, and in his commitment to maintaining the aesthetic distance that he sees as necessary to it. On his imagined pilgrimage, Heaney meets a series of ghosts from his past and from the tradition of Irish literature—among others, a man named Simon Sweeney from his childhood (another version of Mad Sweeney), the Irish novelist William Carleton (whose "Lough Derg Pilgrim" is a centerpiece of nineteenth-century satire on Catholic superstition), Patrick Kavanagh, and James Joyce. Most of them advise him to steer clear of what Joyce's Stephen Dedalus describes as the nets of nationality, language, and religion. "Stay clear of all processions!" old Simon Sweeney tells Heaney just as he feels himself being swept up in the crowd of pilgrims heading for Lough Derg (section 1). Carleton, authorized by his own Sweeney-like rebellion against conventionality—both in his life and in his art—reminds Heaney that, for the artist, all experience must be seen as secondary; looking around at the pilgrims, he says, "All this is like a trout kept in a spring / or maggots sewn in wounds—/ another life that cleans our element" (section 2).

Appropriately enough, it is Joyce—the exile who rebelled against nationality, language, and religion and then spent his life writing about them from a distance—who gets the last word in "Station Island." He begins by telling Heaney that "Your obligation / is not discharged by any common rite." "That subject people stuff is," in Joyce's view, "a cod's game, / infantile, like your peasant pilgrimage." His final piece of advice—and the last voice that Heaney hears in "Station Island"—blends Joycean references to signatures and circles with Heaney's archaeological imagery of soundings, searches, and probes to make a powerful appeal for the kind of artistic authority and independence that, for Heaney and many other modern writers, Joyce is a model of:

> You lose more of yourself than you redeem
> doing the decent thing. Keep at a tangent.
> When they make the circle wide, it's time
> to swim
>
> out on your own and fill the element
> with signatures on your own frequency,
> echo soundings, searches, probes,
> allurements,
>
> elver-gleams in the dark of the whole sea.
> (section 12)

That Heaney was listening to these voices, especially Joyce's, is evident in the "Sweeney Redivivus" section of *Station Island.* In a strikingly postmodern gesture, Heaney produces in these poems still another version of the Sweeney story that he translated and published as *Sweeney Astray,* this time written in the idiom of contemporary speech, and with Sweeney and Heaney more obviously, and sometimes quite overtly, merged into one figure of the contemporary poet. In "The First Flight," the reborn Sweeney unambiguously pictures himself as having escaped those Joycean nets that Heaney sees as threatening to the poet's independence and integrity, and he does so in terms that obviously invoke Heaney's situation as an Ulster-born poet confronted with the conflict in Northern Ireland:

> I was mired in attachment
> until they began to pronounce me
> a feeder off battlefields
>
> so I mastered new rungs of the air
> to survey out of reach
> their bonfires on hills, their hosting
>
> and fasting, the levies from Scotland
> as always, and the people of art
> diverting their rhythmical chants
>
> to fend off the onslaught of winds
> I would welcome and climb
> at the top of my bent.

"The Cleric" retells the story of Mad Sweeney's reaction to the saint's attempts to build a church in his kingdom but, again, its language and implications are distinctly contemporary:

> If he had stuck to his own
> cramp-jawed abbesses and intoners
> dibbling round the enclosure,
>
> his Latin and blather of love,
> his parchments and scheming
> in letters shipped over water—
>
> but no, he overbore
> with his unctions and orders,
> he had to get in on the ground.

Heaney's attitudes toward the Irish Catholicism of his upbringing are considerably more moderate than Sweeney's are here—he once said in an interview, "I've never felt any need to rebel or do a casting-off of God or anything like that"—but at the end of this poem, Sweeney and Heaney merge completely again, this time in an assertion of how the poet may achieve independence through confrontation with opposition, with those forces of "religious, political, and domestic obligation" that seem so powerfully ranged against his art. Sweeney here argues that even though it may seem that he has lost his battle with the saint, it was the struggle that enabled him to see the importance of his ultimate commitment to poetic freedom:

> History that planted its standards
> on his gables and spires
> ousted me to the marches

of skulking and whingeing.
Or did I desert?
Give him his due, in the end

he opened my path to a kingdom
of such scope and neuter allegiance
my emptiness reigns at its whim.

If this is Mad Sweeney recrowned as poet rather than political ruler, it is also Heaney crowned as a contemporary Irish poet, an artist of "neuter allegiance" who reigns by virtue of his "emptiness," his refusal to permit the political demands of the moment to control his art. And if there is a Yeatsian swell to the last line, it is one to which Heaney has, by this time in his career, earned every right.

Given Heaney's views on the precarious status and nature of art, that version of the poet as ruler, however high it may ride on the winds of Yeatsian self-confidence, cannot reign without qualification. *Station Island* does not end with it; the book instead concludes with the decidedly less ebullient image of the poet searching for inspiration, waiting for the spirit to "raise a dust / in the font of exhaustion" ("On the Road").

THE HAW LANTERN

And it is that image which characterizes much of the atmosphere of *The Haw Lantern* (1987). Heaney was forty-eight when this book was published, and many of the poems in it are clearly the work of someone who has, in his life and art, been increasingly forced to confront loss. At the center of the book—in much the same way the "Glanmore Sonnets are at the center of *Field Work*—is a sequence of sonnets titled "Clearances," written in response to the death of Heaney's mother in 1984. These poems offer moving testimony to Heaney's relationship with his mother and to his grief at her passing, but they are also, in the self-reflexive manner of much of his writing, concerned with the relationship between his mother's death and his writing about his mother's death. More specifically, they have to do with the question of how art is able to convert absence into presence, to create an artificial reality out of the loss of an actual one. In the final poem of the sequence, Heaney gets at this question by recalling a chestnut tree that he had planted when he was a child and that has since been cut down. The loss of the tree—like the loss of his mother—leaves a real vacuum, but in the hands of the artist that absence is made palpable, and the poem seeks to provide access to a spiritual reality made possible by a physical loss. What is empty is also, for the artist, "utterly a source":

I thought of walking round and round a
   space
Utterly empty, utterly a source
Where the decked chestnut tree had lost its
   place
In our front hedge above the wallflowers.

. . .

Deep planted and long gone, my coeval
Chestnut from a jam jar in a hole,
Its heft and hush become a bright nowhere,
A soul ramifying and forever
Silent, beyond silence listened for.

Poems like this clearly break new ground for Heaney, whose work tends to be deeply rooted in actual landscapes. In the essay "The Placeless Heaven: Another Look at Kavanagh," Heaney describes this new concern with the poetic evocation of the spiritual by comparing the early, realistic rural poems of Patrick Kavanagh with the spiritually inclined verse that Kavanagh, after recovering from what was thought to be a terminal illness, wrote late in his career. Heaney specifically talks about the image of the chestnut tree in the final sonnet of "Clearances":

> . . . all of a sudden, a couple of years ago, I began to think of the space where the tree had been or would have been. In my mind's eye I saw it as a kind of luminous emptiness, a warp and waver of light, and once again, in a way that I find hard to define, I began to identify with that space just as years before I had identified with the young tree.

> Except that this time it was not so much a matter of attaching oneself to a living symbol of being rooted in the native ground; it was more a matter of preparing to be unrooted, to be spirited away into some transparent, yet indigenous afterlife. The new place was all idea, if you like; it was generated out of my experience of the old place but it was not a topographical location. It was and remains an imagined realm, even if it can be located at an earthly spot, a placeless heaven rather than a heavenly place. (*Covernment,* p. 3–4)

This is a richly Romantic passage, one showing that Wordsworth's importance for Heaney has become, if anything, even greater in his later work than it was in his earlier. In a poem titled "Hailstones," Heaney uses a distinctly Wordsworthian moment, or "spot of time," to evoke the idea of this placeless heaven that he sees as the rightful province of the poet. This poem, an important one for tracking recent changes in Heaney's poetics, opens with a striking metaphor for the notion of art as a process that is constantly consuming the experience on which it builds, constantly creating an absence by transforming the terms of experience into the terms of art:

> I made a small hard ball
> of burning water running from my hand
>
> just as I make this now
> out of the melt of the real thing
> smarting into its absence.

The poem concludes with a decidedly Romantic memory of a prophetic moment just after the end of a hail shower, a moment through which Heaney insists on art's capacity to create beauty and perfection out of the bleakly ordinary and transient:

> . . . there you had
> the truest foretaste of your aftermath—
> in that dilation
>
> when the light opened in silence
> and a car with wipers going still
> laid perfect tracks in the slush.

Much of *The Haw Lantern* is concerned with how art makes perfect tracks in the slush of experience, and an important part of that experience for Heaney is the political situation in contemporary Northern Ireland. In "From the Frontier of Writing," Heaney focuses on the process of artistic creation—in this case an experience connected to the Ulster violence—and he insists on the value of that process. In a postmodern gesture, the poem provides two versions of the same event: being stopped by soldiers at a roadblock. The first, supposedly the immediate, realistic account before the event is filtered through memory and imagination, underscores the feeling of emptiness or absence that the experience engendered:

> and everything is pure interrogation
> until a rifle motions and you move
> with guarded unconcerned acceleration—
>
> a little emptier, a little spent
> as always by that quiver in the self,
> subjugated, yes, and obedient.

In the second version of the incident, that loss is converted into gain through the power of the imagination to remake reality ("So you drive on to the frontier of writing / where it happens again"). The result is not subjugation but a kind of freedom:

> And suddenly you're through, arraigned yet
> freed,
> as if you'd passed from behind a waterfall
> on the black current of a tarmac road
>
> past armour-plated vehicles, out between
> the posted soldiers flowing and receding
> ike tree shadows into the polished
> windscreen.

Art's ability to re-create experience is also investigated in *The Haw Lantern* through an exploration of allegory, fantasy, and parable. Even a listing of some of the titles in this volume indicates this interest in the wide variety of transforming forms that the artist has to hand: "Parable Island," "From the Republic of

Conscience," "From the Land of the Unspoken," "The Song of the Bullets," "From the Canton of Expectation," "The Mud Vision," "The Riddle." In a number of these poems, Heaney specifically examines the political realities of contemporary Ireland through these deliberately distorting lenses (from "The Land of the Unspoken": "We are a dispersed people whose history / is a sensation of opaque fidelity"; from "Parable Island": "Although they are an occupied nation / and their only border is an inland one / they yield to nobody in their belief / that the country is an island"). "The Mud Vision," a characteristically self-doubting poem, questions whether the visionary power of poetry can have much effect on the real world. In this poem, Heaney imagines the routine of contemporary life in Ireland disrupted by the sudden appearance of a vision, "as if a rose window of mud / Had invented itself out of the glittery damp, / . . . sullied yet lucent." This symbol of spiritual possibility, or at least of radical societal reformation, is never understood, however; and when it fades, it leaves behind nothing but ignorance:

> One day it was gone and the east gable
> Where its trembling corolla had balanced
> Was starkly a ruin again, with dandelions
> Blowing high up on the ledges, and moss
> That slumbered on through its increase. As
> cameras raked
> The site from every angle, experts
> Began their *post factum* jabber and all of us
> Crowded in tight for the big explanations.
> Just like that, we forgot that the vision was
> ours,
> Our one chance to know the incomparable
> And dive to a future. What might have been
> origin
> We dissipated in news. The clarified place
> Had retrieved neither us nor itself . . .

For Heaney, it seems, there must always be some nagging doubts about the worth of those clarified places that his art makes. At the very least, he is too much a postmodern poet not to be constantly scrutinizing himself and his work, constantly worrying about whether, in the end, poetry can make anything happen. In the title poem of *The Haw Lantern,* Heaney settles on a somewhat unlikely image to convey this postmodern need for the artist to monitor himself tirelessly; the poem describes the hawthorn berry as taking the form of Diogenes and his lantern, ever on the search for "one just man." It is a passage that says much about Heaney's own efforts to be both a poet and a just man:

> But sometimes when your breath plumes in
> the frost
> it takes the roaming shape of Diogenes
> with his lantern, seeking one just man;
> so you end up scrutinized from behind the
> haw
> he holds up at eye-level on its twig,
> and you flinch before its bonded pith and
> stone,
> its blood-prick that you wish would test and
> clear you,
> its pecked-at ripeness that scans you, then
> moves on.

Given who he is and the world in which he lives, it seems unlikely that Heaney can ever finally be tested and cleared. At the heart of his poetry is both a faith in the efficacy of his art and the need for constant reexamination of that faith. And if this is a process that seems to have no end, it is also one that perhaps identifies the position of the poet in contemporary society. Moreover, there is certainly much to admire in the candor and courage with which Heaney puts himself through the process, and in his unwavering if never wholly unqualified belief that poetry can make something happen, even if that something is not always immediately clear, not always even visible.

Selected Bibliography

COLLECTED WORKS

Selected Poems: 1965–1975, (London, 1980), reprinted as *Poems: 1965–1975* (New York, 1980); *Preoccupations: Selected Prose 1968–1978,* (London and New York, 1980); *The Government of the Tongue: The*

1986 T.S. Eliot Memorial Lectures and Other Critical Writings, (London, 1988; New York, 1989); *Selected Poems: 1966–1987,* London New York (1990).

SEPARATE WORKS

Death of a Naturalist, (London and New York, 1966); *Door into the Dark,* (London and New York, 1969); *Wintering Out,* (London, 1972; New York, 1973); *Stations,* (Belfast, 1975), a sequence of prose poems; *North,* (London, 1975; New York, 1976); *Field Work,* (London and New York, 1979); *Sweeney Astray,* (London and New York, 1984); *Station Island,* (London, 1984; New York, 1985); *The Haw Lantern,* (London and New York, 1987).

EDITED WORKS, INTRODUCTIONS, AND ANTHOLOGIES

Soundings: An Annual Anthology of New Irish Poetry, edited by Heaney, (Belfast, 1972); *Soundings II,* edited by Heaney, (Belfast, 1974); MacLaverty, M., *Collected Short Stories,* introduction by Heaney, (Dublin, 1978); *The Rattle Bag: An Anthology of Poetry,* edited by Heaney and T. Hughes, (London, 1982); *The Essential Wordsworth,* edited by Heaney, (New York, 1988).

UNCOLLECTED ESSAYS AND REVIEWS

"Out of London: Ulster's Troubles," (*New Statesman,* July 1, 1966); "Old Derry's Walls," (*The Listener,* October 24, 1968); "Celtic Fringe, Viking Fringe," (*The Listener,* August 21, 1969); "Delirium of the Brave," (*The Listener,* November 27, 1969).

"King of the Dark," (*The Listener,* February 5, 1970); "King Conchobar and His Knights," (*The Listener,* March 26, 1970); "Views," (*The Listener,* December 31, 1970) essay on living in Berkeley; "Seamus Heaney Praises Lough Erne," (*The Listener,* February 4, 1971); "A Poet's Childhood," (*The Listener* November 1971); "The Trade of an Irish Poet," (*The Guardian,* May 25, 1972); "Deep as England," (*Hibernia,* December 1, 1972); "Mother Ireland," (*The Listener,* December 7, 1972); "Lost Ulsterman," (*The Listener,* April 26, 1973); "Land-Locked," (*Irish Press,* June 1, 1974); "Summoning Lazarus," (*The Listener,* June 6, 1974); "John Bull's Other Island," (*The Listener,* September 29, 1977).

"Treely and Rurally," *Quarto* 9 (August 1980); "English and Irish," (*The Times Literary Supplement,* October 24, 1980); "On Current Unstated Assumptions About Poetry," (*Critical Inquiry,* Summer 1981); "Envies and Identifications: Dante and the Modern Poet," *Irish University Review* 15 (Spring 1985); " 'Place and Displacement': Recent Poetry from Northern Ireland," *The Wordsworth Circle* 16 (Spring 1985); "Place, Pastness, Poems: A Triptych," *Salmagundi* no. 68–69 (Fall-Winter 1985–1986); "The Glamour of Craig Raine," *Ploughshares* 13 no. 4 (1987); "The Pre-Natal Mountain: Vision and Irony in Recent Irish Poetry," *The Georgia Review* 42 (Fall 1988).

INTERVIEWS

"Poets on Poetry," (*The Listener,* November 8, 1973); Cooke, H., "Interview," (*The Irish Times,* December 28, 1973); Walsh, C., "The Saturday Interview," (*The Irish Times,* December 6, 1975); "Interview," in M. Begley *Rambles in Ireland,* (Old Greenwich, Conn., 1977); Deane, S., "Unhappy and at Home," *The Crane Bag* 1, no. 1, (1977); Randall, J., "An Interview with Seamus Heaney," *Ploughshares* 5, no. 3, (1979); Druce, R., "Raindrops on a Thorn: Interview with Seamus Heaney," *Dutch Quarterly Review of Anglo-American Letters* 9, no. 1, (1979); Silverlight, J., "Brooding Images," (*The Observer,* November 11, 1979); Deane, S., "Talk with Seamus Heaney," (*The New York Times Book Review,* December 2, 1979).

Haffenden, J., "Seamus Heaney," *Viewpoints: Poets in Conversation,* (London, 1981); Kinahan, F., "An Interview with Seamus Heaney," *Critical Inquiry* 8, (Spring 1982); "An Interview with Seamus Heaney," *An Gael* 3, no. 1, (1985); Beisch, J., "An Interview with Seamus Heaney," *The Literary Review: An International Journal of Contemporary Writing* Fairleigh Dickinson University 29, no. 1, (1986).

CRITICAL STUDIES

Buttel, R., *Seamus Heaney,* (Lewisburg, Pa., 1975); T. Curtis, ed., *The Art of Seamus Heaney,* (Bridgend, Wales, 1982); Morrison, B., *Seamus Heaney,* (London and New York, 1982); Annwn, D., *Inhabited Voices: Myth and History in the Poetry of Geoffrey Hill, Seamus Heaney and George Mackay Brown,* (Frome, U.K., 1984); Johnston, D., *Irish Poetry After Joyce,* Notre Dame, Ind. Mountrath, (Ireland, 1985) contains chapter on Kavanagh and Heaney; H. Bloom, ed., *Modern Critical Views: Seamus Heaney,* (New Haven, 1986); Corcoran, N., *Seamus Heaney,* (London and Boston, 1986); Garratt, R. F., *Modern Irish Poetry: Tradition and Continuity from Yeats to Heaney,* (Berkeley and Los Angeles, 1986); J. Genet, comp., *Studies on Seam us Heaney,* (Caen, France, 1987); Foster, T., *Seamus Heaney,* (Boston, 1989); Tamplin, R., *Seamus Heaney,* Milton Keynes, (U.K. and Philadelphia, 1989); Burris, S., *The Poetry of Resistance: Seamus Heaney and The Pastoral Tradition,* (Columbus, Ohio, 1990).

GERARD MANLEY HOPKINS
(1844–1889)

GRAHAM STOREY

INTRODUCTION AND EARLY POEMS

JUDGED BY THE lives of most English nineteenth-century poets. Gerald Manley Hopkins' life was outwardly uneventful. He was born on 28 July 1844 into a prosperous and cultivated home near London and spent his boyhood in Hampstead. He received a conventional middle-class education that culminated in four, mainly very happy, years at Balliol College, Oxford, where he took first classes in classics. His conversion to Roman Catholicism in 1866 was much more of a crisis to his family, teachers, and friends than it would be today. Two years later he entered the Society of Jesus, and after the rigorous Jesuit training, he spent the remainder of his relatively short life (he died on 8 June 1889) carrying out the mission and teaching duties of a Jesuit priest.

This outward life—much of it inevitably isolated—conceals the remarkable intensity of his inner life, of his solitary experience, an intensity that, transmuted into poetry, has moved and excited a vast number of twentieth-century readers. Hopkins' admirers are, I think, most impressed by his remarkable technical originality, by his constant innovations in language, rhythm, and syntax, and by the exhilarating sense of freedom such experimenting brings. For this, they are fully willing to face the linguistic difficulties that inevitably arise. They are impressed too by his energy, both aesthetic and intellectual; by the fineness and self-exactingness of his mind; by his remarkable sensitivity to detail, to the minutiae of nature (a sensitivity that he shares particularly with Samuel Taylor Coleridge); and by his power to express extremes of feeling, uncharted—or not so courageously charted—by other Victorian poets. Few poets have communicated so strongly both excitement at natural beauty and its opposite, intimate knowledge of the terrors of despair. Hopkins above all communicates the mystery of selfhood, both of the experiencing self and of the objects experienced. All of his poetry is religious; but it appeals strongly to an immense number of readers who do not share his faith.

The canon of Hopkins' mature poems is small: between the end of 1875, the year of "The Wreck of the Deutschland," his first great mature poem, and his death in 1889, he wrote only forty-nine finished poems. The poems and fragments that he wrote as an undergraduate, following a few as a schoolboy, are in fact more numerous, but their chief interest now is in showing how excitedly he responded to other poets, particularly to the young John Keats. Hopkins' three earliest known poems, "The Escorial," which won a school prize when he was only fifteen, "A Vision of the Mermaids" (which he illustrated with a pen-and-ink drawing), and "Winter with the Gulf Stream" (published in Once a Week on 14 February 1863, when he was eighteen—one of the few poems published in his lifetime), all show his absorption of Keats. It is Keatsian color that enriches the envisioned mermaids:

clouds of violet glow'd
On prankèd scale; or threads of carmine, shot
Thro' silver, gloom'd to a blood-vivid clot.[1]

Later undergraduate poems chart the religious doubts that led to the crisis of his conversion; and many of these poems again draw for their tone on accepted Victorian models: Christina Rossetti, John Henry Cardinal Newman, Matthew Arnold. Such absorption—or, in some cases, clear imitation—makes the totally new and original voice of "The Wreck" all the more remarkable. Two of the early poems, of 1865 and 1866, are particularly interesting for the light they throw on Hopkins' inner conflicts and hopes. Both the symbolism of "The Alchemist in the City" and the alchemist's sense of isolation and wasted effort point to a similar sense of separateness and failure in Hopkins himself. "The Habit of Perfection" ("Elected Silence, sing to me") asks for a total denial of the senses, but it expresses the senses, in their imagined denial, with a sensuousness that is still Keatsian:

O feel-of-primrose hands, O feet
That want the yield of plushy sward. . . .

That sharp clash of sensuousness (with its intimate grasp on nature) and asceticism is perhaps the most striking characteristic of the young Hopkins' temperament.

Some of Hopkins' undergraduate essays—in particular, the longest of them, "On the Origin of Beauty: A Platonic Dialogue" (1865), which owes much to John Ruskin—show how consciously he was now searching for an aesthetic of his own. "The Probable Future of Metaphysics," written two years later, goes beyond both Ruskin and Walter Pater (who had been his tutor): a belief in Platonic "Ideal Forms" behind every form in nature is now the only alternative to "a philosophy of flux." Hopkins was now moving to the two famous terms he coined the following year in some notes on the early Greek philosopher Parmenides: "inscape" and "instress." Their importance for him was both philosophical and aesthetic; they pointed again to Plato's Ideal Forms; and they provided the objective criteria for both the beauty and reality that he was seeking. "Inscape" he used to denote the distinctive pattern that expresses an object's inner form, gives it its selfhood. "Instress" he used in two senses: (1) for the energy that "upholds" an object's inscape, gives it its essential being, and (2) for the force that the inscape exerts on the perceiver. How important these concepts were for his mature poetry a letter to his friend Robert Bridges of 15 February 1879 shows explicitly:

> But as air, melody, is what strikes me most of all in music and design in painting, so design, pattern or what I am in the habit of calling "inscape" is what I above all aim at in poetry.[2]

Not only do his poems aim at "catching" the inscapes of things ("I caught this morning morning's minion . . ."), but the individual poem itself is an inscape; a pattern of sound and shape as well as of meaning.

Ironically (as it must seem to us now), while Hopkins was developing his all-important poetic criteria, he was writing no poetry. In May 1868, the month in which he made his decision to become a Jesuit, he decided both to burn the poems he had already written ("Slaughter of the innocents" is his 11 May journal entry)[3] and to write no more, "as not belonging to my profession" (as he later told Canon Richard Watson Dixon). Little now unknown was probably destroyed, but his self-imposed poetic silence was kept for over seven years. Instead, his powers of minute observation, his constant search for distinctive beauty, went into the journal he kept faith-

1. All poems are quoted from W. H. Gardner and N. H. MacKenzie, eds., *Poems of Gerard Manley Hopkins*, 4th ed. (Oxford, 1967).

2. All letters to Robert Bridges are quoted from C. C. Abbott, ed., *The Letters of Gerard Manley Hopkins to Robert Bridges*, rev. ed. (London, 1955).

3. See H. House, ed., *The Journals and Papers of Gerard Manley Hopkins*, 2nd ed., completed by G. Storey (London, 1959), pp. 537–539. All quotations from the journals are taken from this ed.

fully from 1866 to 1875. The journal is in a great many ways a workshop for the poems that were to follow it.

But to persuade himself that the writing of poetry would not interfere with his vocation as a priest, Hopkins needed far more than aesthetic justification. He needed a spiritual fiat, a conviction that, as a poet, he could serve God. It was this that the Spiritual Exercises of St. Ignatius Loyola, the meditations that are the central study and practice of every Jesuit, undoubtedly provided. We know what a profound effect they had on him. His most important spiritual writing was the beginning of a commentary on them; its opening, the celebration of selfhood, is his finest piece of sustained prose. Ignatius' favorite image, of the Jesuit as Christ's dedicated soldier, pervades many of his poems. The opening section of "The Wreck of the Deutschland" was inspired by his first experience of the *Exercises* as a novice seven years before. And, for Hopkins, they gave the most compelling of all reasons to rededicate himself as a poet. "Man was created to praise," the *Spiritual Exercises* open; in "Further Notes" on that opening Foundation Exercise, Hopkins wrote: "This world then is word, expression, views of God. . . . the world, man, should after its own manner give God being in return for the being he has given it." The poet, then, has his own place in this sacramental view of nature: the "being" he renders back to God is not only himself but the poem he has created, in its distinctive form another of God's works.

Moreover, in August 1872, while studying philosophy at Stonyhurst, Hopkins discovered the thirteenth-century Franciscan philosopher John Duns Scotus.

> At this time, I had first begun to get hold of the copy of Scotus on the Sentences in the Baddely library and was flush with a new stroke of enthusiasm. It may come to nothing or it may be a mercy from God. But just then when I took in any inscape of the sky or sea I though of Scotus. (journal, August 1872)

Hopkins' enthusiasm was justified. Duns Scotus believed in the "principle of individuation," that the mind could come to know the universal (the *summum* of all medieval philosophy) through apprehending an individual object's "this-ness" (*haecceitas*) and that such apprehensions ultimately reveal God. Hopkins had intuitively believed this earlier, as a famous journal entry shows:

> I do not think I have every seen anything more beautiful than the bluebell I have been looking at. I know the beauty of our Lord by it. It[s inscape] is [mixed of][4] strength and grace. (journal, 18 May 1870)

Duns Scotus gave philosophical and, above all, religious support for Hopkins' own theories of inscape and instress. It is not surprising that several of the mature poems show Duns Scotus' strong influence and that one, "Duns Scotus's Oxford" (1879), is a deeply felt tribute to him.

"THE WRECK OF THE DEUTSCHLAND"

In December 1875, when Hopkins read the account of the wreck of the *Deutschland* and the Rector of St. Beuno's, with whom he was studying theology, told him that "he wished someone would write a poem on the subject," he was ready to break his seven years' poetic silence. What is remarkable is that the poem he wrote should be so utterly different from all the poems he had written before—in language, rhythm, and structure. "The Wreck of the Deutschland" displays all his technical innovations, already in their most sustained form. Of these, the best-documented is his use of "sprung rhythm," of which, explaining the origins of "The Wreck" to Canon Dixon on 5 October 1878, he wrote: "I had long had haunting my ear the echo of a new rhythm which now I realized on paper."[5] But he had

4. Hopkins brackets.

5. All letters to Canon Dixon are quoted from C. C. Abbott, ed., *The Correspondence of Gerard Manley Hopkins and R. W. Dixon*, rev. ed (London, 1965).

been equally concerned over the past two years with poetic language and, above all, its attainment of stress and emphasis: this had been the main subject of lectures on rhetoric he had given, as part of his training, at Manresa House, Roehampton, in 1873–1874. And the excitement of being sent to St. Beuno's, of learning Welsh, and of reading Welsh classical poetry undoubtedly played its part. In the letter to Dixon already quoted, he went on to mention "certain chimes suggested by the Welsh poetry I had been reading (what they called *cynghanedd*)." So an extraordinary confidence in a quite new poetic technique came together with a conviction that he now had a spiritual fiat for writing poetry again, and the result was one of the great religious poems in the English language.

"The Wreck of the Deutschland," Hopkins' longest and, for many, his greatest work, is at once an occasional poem—the central stanzas follow very closely the reports of the wreck in the *Times* (London), 8–13 December 1875—a religious ode, celebrating God's mastery and mercy; and a deeply personal spiritual autobiography: "What refers to myself in the poem is all strictly and literally true and did all occur," Hopkins told Bridges; "nothing is added for poetical padding." It is a complex and difficult poem, and a brief summary may help toward the understanding necessary for its great rewards.

Part I (stanzas 1–10) gives us Hopkins' own spiritual crisis: first, the agony of his own "shipwreck," as he submits to God's mastery ("Thou mastering me/God!"), then the grace of God's mercy, mediated to him through Christ's presence in the Communion (the second half of stanza 3). God's mastery and mercy are developed now almost as in a fugue: first, experienced personally in stanzas 4 ("I am soft sift/ In an hourglass") and 5 ("I kiss my hand/To the stars"), then as the paradox of Christ's Incarnation and Passion (stanzas 6 and 7), which demands our acceptance in the striking image of a ripe sloe bursting in our mouths. Stanzas 9 and 10 bring the two qualities together:

> Make mercy in all of us, out of us all
> Mastery, but be adored, but be adored King.

In their asking for "wrecking" and "storm," the fulfillment of God's double purpose, they link up with part II.

Part II (stanza 11 to the end) gives us the narrative of the shipwreck and of "the tall nun," introduced by stanza 11, proclaiming the inevitability of death ("The sour scythe cringe, and the blear share come") and ending with a prayer to Christ that completes and deepens the theme of part I. The sailing of the *Deutschland* from Bremen, the storm, and the wreck of the ship on the Kenitsh Knock occupy only six stanzas (12–17); the tall nun is dramatically introduced at the end of stanza 17 ("a lioness arose breasting the babble"); and after four stanzas (20–23) describing the nuns' exile and their dedication to the martyred St. Francis, we reach the center of the poem in stanza 24, the tall nun's cry, "O Christ, Christ, come quickly.'" In the next three stanzas Hopkins puts forward, only to reject, possible motives for her cry. It was not that she wished to become more like "her lover" Christ, nor that she wanted a martyr's crown in heaven, nor even that she was driven to ask for ease by the "electrical horror" of the storm. No, it was the daily burden of a life of constant self-sacrifice ("The jading and jar of a cart,/Time's tasking") that made her cry out (stanza 27). Stanza 28, the climax of the poem, gives us the true meaning of the nun's cry: the ellipses ("But how shall I . . . make me room there . . .") show that it is all but inexpressible. The nun has seen Christ himself walking across the water. He will take her to him. Stanza 29 praises her for her understanding. In uttering the cry, the word kept within her, she has, as it were, given Christ a new birth: hence the significance of this night being the eve of the feast of the Immaculate Conception (stanza 30). There is yet a further miracle: the nun's cry has providently startled the lost sheep, the other passengers, the "Comfortless unconfessed," back to the fold—is not "the shipwreck than a harvest?" (stanza 31). The next two stanzas renew Hopkins' praise of

God's mastery and mercy, the theme of part I, and the poem ends with two prayers. The first is to Christ, to "burn" anew, having "royally" reclaimed "his own," and the second is to the tall nun, "Dame, at our door/Drowned," to intercede in heaven for the return of Christ of England.

What gives such a poem, written in two formal parts and thirty-five eight-line stanzas, its compelling sense of unity is, above all, its symbolism. The suffering of the tall nun in the shipwreck (part II) mirrors Hopkins' own spiritual suffering in his "shipwreck" (part I); both ultimately mirror Christ's suffering and Crucifixion, so that the poem ends as a paean of praise to Christ himself. T. K. Bender, in *Gerard Manley Hopkins: The Classical Background* (1966), went further and, claiming that Hopkins wrote in the tradition of Pindar, the greatest of the Greek writers of odes, saw him, like Pindar, as holding the poem together through the power of an unstated by key image. The image he sees us unifying the poem is that of water, with its double powers of healing and destruction. The destruction, in a shipwreck poem, we expect, but few poets have given to the sea the almost apocalyptic power that Hopkins gives to it here:

> And the sea fling-flake, black-backed in the
>   regular blow,
> Sitting Eastnortheast, in cursed quarter, the
>   wind;
>   Wiry and white-fiery and whirlwind-
>   swivelled snow
> Spins to the widow-making unchilding
>   unfathering deeps.
>   (st. 13)

Yet, at the same time, the sea brings the five martyred nuns to their salvation; they

>   Are sisterly sealed in wild waters,
> To bathe in his fall-gold mercies, to breathe
>   in his all-fire glances.
>   (st. 23)

Throughout the rest of the poem, water, the flushing of liquid, melting are images of divine mercy and help:

> Stroke and a stress that stars and storms
>   deliver,
> That guilt is hushed by, hearts are flushed
>   by and melt—
>   (st. 6)

And, in the great vision of Christ's return to earth, in the penultimate stanza, the analogy is again with water, a refreshing shower:

> Not a dooms-day dazzle in his coming nor
>   dark as he came;
>   Kind, but royally reclaiming his own;
> A released shower, let flash[6] to the shire,
>   not a lightning of fire hard-hurled.
>   (st. 34)

The image of water, then, as Bender says, seems to be a key symbol that points to the poem's ultimate subject, the paradox of suffering.

But, if such use of imagery was traditional, Hopkins' use of language and sprung rhythm was daringly experimental. The sprung rhythm shocked his friend Robert Bridges, an orthodox prosodist ("the dragon in the gate," he later called "The Wreck" in his edition of Hopkins' poems); and it was too much for Fr. Henry Coleridge, editor of the Jesuit journal *The Month*, who, as Hopkins said, "dared not publish" the poem. Sprung rhythm, in fact, was vital to what Hopkins was trying to do in poetry by employing speech rhythms to give the words their maximum sound-impact and stress. He explained it to Canon Dixon very simple: "To speak shortly, it consists in scanning by accents or stresses alone, without any account of the number of syllables, so that a foot may be one strong syllable or it may be many light and one strong" (5 October 1878). In a later letter (27 February 1879) he was simpler still: "This then is the essence of sprung rhythm: *one stress makes one foot*, no matter how many or few the syllables."

The stressing throughout "The Wreck" is the same except that in part I the first line of each stanza has two stresses and in part II three; thereafter the number of stresses in

6. Here in its meaning "as a rush of water."

each stanza is 3-4-3-5-5-4-6. As Harold Whitehall showed convincingly in an essay in *The Kenyon Critics* (1937), most of Hopkins' distinctive poetic devices—alliteration, internal rhyming, "chiming" of consonants—all that he defended as achieving "more brilliancy, starriness, quain, margaretting," help us to know which are the strong stresses (Whitehall suggested that this was in fact their main purpose). We quickly see how, as Hopkins intended, they both "fetch out" the meaning (his own phrase) and intensify it. The stressing of stanza 2, for example, is an integral part of the spiritual crisis as Hopkins reexperiences it:

> I did say yes
> O at lightning and lashed rod;
> Thou heardst me truer than tongue confess
> Thy terror, O Christ, O God;
> Thou knowest the walls, altar and hour and night
> The swoon of a heart that the sweep and the hurl of thee trod
> Hard down with a horror of height:
> And the midriff astrain with learning of, laced with fire of stress.

The terror of that is strongly physical too: "a heart . . . trod/Hard down," "the midriff astrain": the strong stresses reenact the violence, and they almost compel us to read the words aloud as Hopkins pleaded to Bridges again and again to do: "Take breath and read it with the ears, as I always wish to be read, and my verse becomes all right." For Hopkins, poetry, like every art, had to have its proper "performance." As he wrote much later (1885) to his youngest brother Everard: "poetry, the darling child of speech, of lips and spoken utterance . . . must be spoken; *till it is spoken it is not performed*, it does not perform, it is not itself."

The shock of "The Wreck" to Bridges, and no doubt to Fr. Coleridge, too, was not only its new rhythm but its language. Hopkins was equally aware of what he was aiming to do here. He wrote to Bridges on 14 August 1879:

> For it seems to me that the poetical language of an age shd. be the current language heightened, to any degree heightened and unlike itself, but not (I mean normally: passing freaks and graces are another thing) an obsolete one. This is Shakespeare's and Milton's practice and the want of it will be fatal to Tennyson's Idylls and plays, to Swinburne, and perhaps to Morris.

The reference to Shakespeare is as important as the comment on his contemporaries. From "The Wreck" onward, Hopkins' use of language *is* Shakespearean: he employs the resources of words to their utmost, makes them work urgently and physically. The words, as he claimed, are "current"; they are also, as he allowed, too, "to any degree heightened" to make their dramatic effect.

For Milton, and particularly for Milton's prosody, Hopkins had the highest possible admiration. "His achievements are quite beyond any other English poet's perhaps any modern poet's," he wrote to Bridges on 3 April 1877; and to Dixon the following year (5 October): "His verse as one reads it seems something necessary and eternal. . . . I have paid a good deal of attention to Milton's versification and collected his later rhythms. . . . I found his most advanced effects in the *Paradise Regained* and, lyrically, in the *Agonistes*." Milton's verse remained a constant subject in Hopkins' letters to both Bridges and Dixon; and it is clear that, as a highly conscious innovator himself, he derived immense encouragement from the poet he saw as the greatest innovator in English prosody.

In stanza 27 of "The Wreck," Hopkins finds, after several attempts, the true reason for the tall nun's cry of "O Christ, Christ, come quickly":

> No, but it was not these.
> The jading and jar of the cart,
> Time's tasking, it is fathers that asking for ease
> Of the sodden-with-its-sorrowing heart,
> Not danger, electrical horror; then further it finds

> The appealing of the Passion is tenderer
> in prayer apart:
> Other, I gather, in measure her mind's
> Burden, in wind's burly and beat of
> endragonèd seas.

The key words here were, and are, in current use (though "electrical" was audacious in 1875); the alliteration and assonance of "jading and jar," "Time's tasking," and "sodden-with-its-sorrowing" heighten and deepen an experience, grounded in the difficulties of a life of constant self-sacrifice, that Hopkins knew only too well.

Rhythm, language, and the inner relationship between the two parts of the poem give "The Wreck" its sense of unity. But critics have been worried by two apparent digressions: stanzas 20–23, describing the birthplace of the five nuns and their relationship to St. Francis, and the final stanza, asking the drowned nun to pray for the conversion (or reconversion) of England to Rome. "The Wreck of the Deutschland" is both a profoundly Catholic and a daringly apocalyptic poem. The exile of the nuns from Germany under the anti-Catholic Falck Laws, their martyrdom in the wreck, even their number, five, mirroring St. Francis' five stigmata, are all central to the poem's true subject, the paradox that suffering brings salvation. The final stanza extends the miracle of the tall nun's vision to the prayed-for miracle of England's conversion. It was Elisabeth Schneider, in "*The Wreck of the Deutschland*: A New Reading" (1966), who first claimed that, for Hopkins, the tall nun actually *saw* Christ as a miraculous presence—hence the virtual impossibility of expressing her experience at the poem's climax:

> But how shall I . . . make me room
> there:
> Reach me a . . . Fancy, come faster—
> Strike you the sight of it? look at it
> loom there,
> Thing that she . . . There then! the
> Master,
> *Ipse*, the only one, Christ, King, Head:
> He was to cure the extremity where he
> had cast her;
> Do, deal, lord it with living and dead;
> Let him rid, her pride, in his triumph,
> despatch and have done with his doom
> there.
> (st. 28)

Christ has come to the tall nun at the climax of the storm; the poem's ultimate prayer—made through her intercession—is that this should prophesy his second coming, to restore England to his flock. The worship of Christ in the magnificently chiming and interlocking final two lines completes His dominant presence throughout the whole poem:

> Pride, rose, prince, hero of us, high-priest,
> Our hearts' charity's hearth's fire, our
> thoughts' chivalry's throng's Lord.
> (st. 35)

POEMS, 1877–1882

Hopkins followed "The Wreck of the Deutschland" with ten sonnets, all written in Wales ("Always to me a mother of Muses") during 1877, his final year at St. Beuno's, leading up to his ordination that September. They include some of his best-known and best-loved poems: "God's Grandeur," "The Starlight Night," "The Windhover," "Hurrahing Harvest." A stanza from part I of "The Wreck," "I Kiss my hand/To the stars" (stanza 5), provides the key to the most exultant of them: the finding, "instressing," of God's mystery in the wonders of nature. In a sense, then, these are poems of meditation, celebrating the created world in all its beauty and wildness—and in all its detailed texture and color—as embodying God; and Louis Martz, in *The Poetry of Meditation* (1954), has claimed that Hopkins belongs to that great seventeenth-century tradition. What is peculiar to Hopkins is the astonishing energy with which, time and again, the meditation is made to lead to a call for spiritual action.

"The Starlight Night," the second of these sonnets (dated 24 February 1877), embodies just this pattern. The octet gives us all the beauty of the star world, its order ("bright boroughs," "circle-citadels"), mystery, and movement (like rippling leaves or doves in flight). It also insists on the excitement with which we should experience it:

> Look at the stars! look, look up at the skies!
> O look at all the fire-folk sitting in the air!

There is an excitement intensified by the imperatives and exclamations and by the use of a sprung line:

> Look at the | stars! | look, look | up at the
> skies!

Then the sestet insists on the action we must take to make all this beauty our own:

> Buy then! bid then!—What?—Prayer,
> patience, alms, vows.

The reward, moreover, is even higher—"within-doors house/The shocks [the sheaves of the harvest]" . . . "Christ and his mother" and all the saints.

"God's Grandeur," the sonnet written the day before, introduces a new note, the shaming contrast between the beauty of nature and man's sin or ugliness. The sonnet begins exultantly:

> The world is charged with the grandeur of
> God.

It moves to one of Hopkins' most intimate, movingly vulnerable apprehensions of nature's secret life:

> There lives the dearest freshness deep down
> things.

But in between there is the cry against man's instinct to spoil (it loses none of its strength by going back to William Blake and William Wordsworth), emphasized by the lines' repetition and assonance:

> Generations have trod, have trod, have trod;
> And all is seared with trade; bleared,
> smeared with toil;
> And wears man's smudge, and shares
> man's smell: the soil
> Is bare now, nor can foot feel, being shod.

It is a note we hear in several more poems: in another of this group of sonnets, "The Sea and The Skylark," written of Rhyl, the North Welsh sea resort, the lark's pure and fresh song shames "this shallow and frail town"; in "Duns Scotus's Oxford," Oxford's "base and brickish skirt" confounds "Rural rural keeping—folk, flocks, and flowers"; and in "Ribblesdale" (1882), industrialist man, "heir/To his own selfbent so bound," thoughtlessly spoils "They lovely dale."

In "Pied Beauty" ("Glory be to God for dappled things—") Hopkins brings together all the "dappled" distinctive life he so loved—particularly the multitudinous detail of color, texture, and shape:

> For skies of couple-colour as a brinded cow;
> For rose-moles all in stipple upon trout
> that swim;
> Fresh-firecoal chestnut-falls; finches' wings;

then in the final two lines he puts them in their proper created order and calls for the action that, alone for him, can save his and our souls:

> He fathers-forth whose beauty is past change:
> Praise him.

Such an ending points to the inadequacy of T. S. Eliot's description of Hopkins as essentially a "nature-poet."

The two most exultant of these sonnets of 1877 are "The Windhover," written in May, and "Hurrahing in Harvest," written the following September, three weeks before his ordination. Hopkins later described "The Windhover" to Bridges as "the best thing I ever wrote." Despite the controversies about its meaning, almost all readers of Hopkins have agreed on is poetic greatness. The octet wonderfully catches every movement of the kestrel in his soaring and gliding flight; sprung rhythm and imagery (the riding-school, the "skate's heel") add to his beauty and power. But the dedication" To Christ our Lord," added by Hopkins, is all-important. "I caught," the sonnet's opening words—"I caught this morning morning's minion"—shows Hopkins seizing the inscape of kestrel; but the images from chivalry ("minion," "kingdom," "dauphin"), taken from the great meditation on the kingdom of Christ in the *Spiritual Exercises*, make it clear that he sees too the presence of Christ in the bird's beauty and mastery, the "achieve of, the mastery of the thing!"

The meaning of the sestet and of "My heart in hiding" from the end of the octet (line 7) has aroused continuing controversy. Some critics, notably I. A. Richards and William Empson, have seen "My heart in hiding" as a cry of envy for the sensuous life symbolized by the kestrel; and they interpret the whole poem as one of inner friction, a subconscious conflict between priest and poet. Conflict there must certainly be in any life of self-sacrifice, and "The Wreck of the Deutschland" shows how intensely Hopkins had dedicated himself to that life. But he never wavered in his vocation, and an unforgettable phrase he used to his agnostic friend Alexander Baillie on 10 April 1871 shows what the Jesuit life meant to him: "this life here [at Stonyhurst] though it is hard is God's will for me as I most intimately know, which is more than violets knee-deep."[7] Hopkins had dedicated himself to the "hidden life"; and the two key images of the sonnet's final three lines stress ("No wonder of it") that the heart dedicated to such service ultimately shines brightest. The "shéer plód" (Hopkins' own stress marks) of the horse makes the ploughshare shine down the furrow ("sillion"); and the "bluebleak embers" of the dying fire, as they split apart, blaze out gold and orange-red. The final line, "Fall, gall themselves, and gash gold-vermillion," suggests strongly Christ's three cries on His way to the Crucifixion.

7. C. C. Abbott, ed., *Further Letters of Gerard Manley Hopkins* (London, 1938).

This still leaves the sonnet's crux, the meaning of "Buckle" in the second line of the sestet:

> Brute beauty and valour and act, oh, air,
> pride, plume, here
> Buckle! AND the fire that breaks from thee
> then, a billion
> Times told lovelier, more dangerous, O my
> chevalier!

Acceptance of the life of self-sacrifice must support its commonest meaning of "collapse, give way under strain"; and the "AND" (thus capitalized) points to the paradox that, though the kestrel's plumage apparently crumples as it swoops down, the light that flashes from it is then at its loveliest. *This* is the paradox of sacrifice. But, as several critics have pointed out, the kestrel's wings do *not* in fact crumple as it dives. "Buckle" has in fact two other meanings: (a) "fasten, buckle on" (*transitive*) and (b) "grapple, prepare for action" (*intransitive*). If either of these was intended, the mood of "buckle" is imperative. In (a) the cry is to Christ, to buckle on to his heart ("here"—stressed in the line) the kestrel's beauty and power; in (b) the cry is to the kestrel's qualities themselves, to come to his heart and prepare themselves for action. It is part of the richness and tension of the poem that no one of these meanings totally and certainly excludes the other two.

"Hurrahing in Harvest" was the outcome, Hopkins wrote to Bridges, "of half an hour of extreme enthusiasm as I walked alone one day from fishing in the Elwy." Hopkins' rapture is intense but precise; the vision is of "our Saviour" Himself, present in the cornfields. Such a presence needs one of his most daring and original images to express it—"as a stallion stalwart, very-violet-sweet!" (we remember the "violets knee-deep" of his letter to Baillie); and its force on him, the beholder, a final, most striking image of immense physical and spiritual energy:

> The heart réars wíngs bold and bolder
> And hurls for him, O half hurls earth for
> him off under his feet.

The moment of understanding, the experience's "instress," has been transformed into pure, visionary activity.

"Spring," written in May 1877, shows us another of nature's "inscapes" that most moved Hopkins, its "wildness and wet," as he called it in the later poem "Inversnaid." Here we have

> When weeds, in wheels, shoot long and
> lovely and lush . . .

("wheels," in particular, is exact—their coiling shape—and exuberant. But the sestet first questions the scene's meaning:

> "What is all this juice and all this joy?"

And then, characteristically, Hopkins transforms it to innocent human beauty—"Innocent mind and Mayday in girl and boy"—and sees it as threatened:

> . . . Have, get, before it cloy,
> Before it cloud, Christ, lord, and sour with
> sinning.

This feeling for innocence threatened by corruption is the major theme of a group of poems inspired by Hopkins' experiences as a priest: "The Handsome Heart" and "The Bugler's First Communion," both written at Oxford in 1879 when he was serving at St. Aloysius' Church; and "Brothers," based on a scene that touched him at Mount St. Mary's College, Chesterfield (where he was "subminister" in 1877–1878), but not completed until 1880. With "Felix Randal," written in April 1880 at Liverpool, where he was priest at St. Francis Xavier's, these are almost his only poems describing incidents in his relations with others. Poetically, the first three seem to have obvious weaknesses; if some readers have been drawn to their delicacy and pathos, others have dismissed them as indulgent and sentimental. And the main reason for such reservations, if we share them, is that, in terms of what we are accustomed to from Hopkins, the incidents they recount—a boy's "gracious answer," a bugler's first Communion, a man's response to his younger brother's acting—seem too simple; we miss the urgency and complexity of the poems about himself. But we cannot miss the ardor of the prayers that end the first two:

> . . . Only . . . On that path you pace
> Run all your race, O brace sterner that
> strain!
> ("The Handsome Heart")

> Recorded only, I have put lips on pleas
> Would brandle[8] adamantine heaven with
> ride and jar, did Prayer go disregarded:
> Forward-like, but however, and like[9]
> favourable heaven heard these.
> ("The Bugler's First Communion")

Nor the sudden, happy recognition of the goodness of human nature that ends "Brothers":

> There dearly thén, deárly,
> Dearly thou canst be kind.

The sonnet "Felix Randal" ("Felix Randal the farrier, O is he dead then? my duty all ended") is a far greater poem: to many it is one of Hopkins' most memorable. More powerfully than in any of his other poems, it brings together priest and poet. It is concerned with an adult, not children—a blacksmith, one of his Liverpool flock, who has just died. It is an elegy but the strong feeling it contains goes both ways. Hopkins' ministrations have comforted Felix, but the blacksmith's need of them has equally comforted Hopkins:

> This seeing the sick endears them to us, us
> too it endears

Hopkins makes Felix's attraction for him quite clear ("his mould of man, big-boned and

8. Shake.
9. Mostly likely.

hardy-handsome"); and as this becomes the accepted love of and for the priest at the sick-bed, the poet can address Felix directly and through his imagination conjure up Felix's marvelously boisterous life in the past:

> How far from then forethought of, all thy
> more boisterous years,
> When thou at the random grim forge,
> powerful amidst peers,
> Didst fettle for the great grey drayhorse his
> bright and battering sandal!

Meanwhile, the year before, at Mount St. Mary's College, Hopkins had written his second long narrative poem, "The Loss of the Eurydice." Like "The Wreck of the Deutschland," it is an occasional poem: the *Eurydice* had just foundered off the Isle of Wight and many details of the disaster are taken from reports in the *Times* (London), 25–27 March 1878. Like "The Wreck," it is an explicitly religious poem; Hopkins sees the wreck, with its loss of three hundred young lives, as an analogy for England's lapse from Roman Catholicism. But there the resemblances end. It is a much simpler poem than "The Wreck," with none of the urgency or complexity of his own close spiritual involvement. This lack of complexity is underlined by the far simpler prosodic structure: four-line stanzas, each line bearing three stresses. "The scanning runs on without break to the end of the stanza, so that each stanza is rather one long line rhymed in passage than four lines with rhymes at the end," runs a note Hopkins added to his manuscript. But the rhymes "in passage" make, at times, considerable demands on us:

> Some asleep unawakened, all unwarned,
> eleven fathoms fallen
> (st. 1)

> But what black Boreas wrecked her? he
> Came equipped, deadly-electric
> (st. 6)

There is not the powerful symbolism of "The Wreck" to give "The Eurydice" that kind of unity. But the description of the storm itself—the sudden quickening of the language, the alliteration, the stresses of the sprung rhythm—suggests an apocalyptic violence:

> A beetling baldbright cloud thorough
> England
> Riding: there did storms not mingle? and
> Hailropes hustle and grind their
> Heavengravel? wolfsnow, worlds of it, wind
> there?
> (st. 7)

The picture of the young drowned sailor is as good as anything Hopkins did in its kind:

> Look, foot to forelock, how all things suit! he
> Is strung by duty, is strained to beauty
> And brown-as-dawning-skinned
> With brine and shine and whirling wind.
> (st. 20)

And stanzas 22–26, in which he contemplates the loss of young life and equates it with England's lapse from Rome, show, movingly, Hopkins' real concern:

> Only the breathing temple and fleet
> Life, this wildworth blown so sweet,
> These daredeaths, ay this crew, in
> Unchrist, all rolled in ruin—
> (st. 24)

The prayer that ends the poem—like that which ends "The Wreck" and so many of the poems of this period—shows how intensely Hopkins hopes, through his poetry, to awaken men to God's providence:

> But to Christ lord of thunder
> Crouch; lay knee by earth low under:
> (st. 28)

Oxford, where Hopkins was a priest at St. Aloysius' Church from December 1878 to October 1879, proved an exceptionally fruitful place and time for his poetry. In all, he wrote nine poems there—besides the two already discussed, "Binsey Poplars," "Duns Scotus's

Oxford," "Henry Purcell," "The Candle Indoors," "Morning, Midday, and Evening Sacrifice," "Andromeda," and "Peace." Of these, many would claim "Henry Purcell" to be among his finest—if most difficult—sonnets. Both it and, expectedly, "Duns Scotus's Oxford," owe a great deal to Scotus. The latter poem is more than attribute; in its celebration of the distinctiveness of Oxford, its *haecceitas* ("Towery city and branchy between towers"), it followed Scotist principles; hence the despair that Scotus' own city, where he traditionally both studied and taught, should have betrayed its past beauty:

> Thou hast a base and brickish skirt there, sours
> That neighbour-nature thy grey beauty is grounded
> Best in; . . .

Yet, for Hopkins, Scotus' presence still haunts Oxford; and the sonnet ends with a moving and heartfeld acknowledgement of what he owes to him:

> Yet ah! this air I gather and I release
> He lived on; these weeds and waters, these walls are what
> He haunted who of all men most sways my spirits to peace;
>
> Of reality the rarest-veinèd unraveller . . .

That last phrase, in its giving to Scotus true insight into the reality of things, links closely with "Henry Purcell," written the following month, and particularly with the important epitaph Hopkins gave to it: that Purcell's music has "uttered in notes the very make and species of man as created both in him and in all men generally."

"Henry Purcell," then, again both explores and celebrates distinctiveness; not only the genius of Purcell's music but, ultimately through that music, of "the very make and species of man," of selfhood itself:

> It is the forègd feature finds me; it is the rehearsal
> Of own, of abrúpt sélf there so thrusts on, so throngs the ear.

This is the essence of Purcell's music: "forgèd" has the force of being beaten out on the anvil, beaten to the right shape, to utter Purcell's "abrúpt sélf" (the stress marks are Hopkins' own). The sestet then seeks to find an exact analogy in nature to bring this insight home, and Hopkins finds it in one of his boldest and most majestic images, that of the "great stormfowl":

> . . . so some great stormfowl, whenever he has walked his while
>
> The thunder-purple seabeach, plùmed purple-of-thunder,
> If a wuthering of his palmy snow-pinions scatter a colossal smile
> Off him, but meaning motion fans fresh our wits with wonder.

The image is difficult, as Robert Bridges found the whole sonnet. But, because of that, Hopkins explained the meaning of almost every phrase in letters to him; and, as he showed, the analogy between Purcell and the "great stormfowl" is an exact one: "It is as when a bird thinking only of soaring spreads its wings: a beholder may happen then to have his attention drawn by the act to the plumage displayed" (4 January 1883). In the same way, Purcell, in his music, shows us unawares its distinctive ("archespecial") beauty. It is one of the poems Hopkins most like himself ("one of my very best pieces," he told Bridges); and its richness and complexity (especially of the final image) fully justify the prosodic innovation he made in it: it is his first sonnet in alexandrines, six-feet lines with a stress to each foot—a meter to which he returned in "Felix Randal."

A third sonnet, "As kingfishers catch fire," given neither title nor date by Hopkins, is an even stronger expression of the belief he shared with Duns Scotus in the fulfilling of individuality. The striking similarity of its imagery to a passage from his December 1881 commentary on the *Spiritual Exercises* suggests that Hopkins may have written it at Roehampton, during his tertianship, a period of renewal after the horrors of his missions in Liverpool and Glasgow. It is a very much simpler sonnet than "Henry Purcell"; but its simplicity is that of absolute confidence, as he moves from the "selving" (his own word) of animate and even inanimate objects—kingfishers, dragonflies, stones, bells—to the "selving" of "the just man" who, by fulfilling himself, becomes, through grace, another Christ:

> Acts in God's eyes what in God's eye he
> is—
> Chríst. For Christ plays in ten thousand
> places,
> Lovely in limbs, and lovely in eyes not his
> To the Father through the features of men's
> faces.

But another note enters increasingly the poems he wrote, after his ten months at Oxford, in Lancashire, either in Liverpool, while serving at St. Francis Xavier's, or at Stonyhurst, where he taught classics for two years, 1882–1884. It is a strong sense of transience, a conviction that the beauty he so loved in the world would pass, however, cherished. Almost ten years earlier, on 17 April 1873, when an ash tree was felled in the garden at Stonyhurst, he had recorded in his journal:

> . . . there came at that moment a great pang and I wished todie and not to see the inscapes of the world destroyed anymore.

It is this feeling of wretchedness at the loss of natural beauty that gives such poignancy to "Binsey Poplars"—felled while he was in Oxford in 1879, a poignancy transmuted by the musical repetitions:

> Ten or twelve, only ten or twelve
> Strokes of Havoc únselve
> The sweet especial scene,
> Rural scene, a rural scene,
> Sweet especial rural scene.

During this period, Hopkins was beginning to write music, mostly airs to his own, Bridges', and Canon Dixon's poems.[10] To some degree, as in this poem, the clear musical concern, while seeming to intensify the feeling, also serves to transmute it, to make it more bearable. This is certainly the effect of the first part of "The Leaden Echo and the Golden Echo," the Maiden's song from his projected verse drama "St. Winefred's Well," written at Stonyhurst in October 1882, of which he wrote to Dixon on 23 October 1886: "I never did anything more musical." Both parts employ musical repetition more than any other poem Hopkins wrote. "The Leaden Echo" ends on the key word "despair" conjured up by the passing of beauty, but its repetition again seems to transmute, to distance it; while "The Golden Echo," although finding the only answer, for Hopkins, to mortal beauty's loss:

> Give beauty back, beauty, beauty, beauty,
> back to God, beauty's self and beauty's
> giver.

still has two lines that face personal feelings head on, in words and rhythm that seem frighteningly undistanced:

> O then, weary then why should we tread? O
> why are we
> so haggard at the heart, so care-coiled, care
> killed,
> so fagged, so flashed, so cogged, so cumbered,
> When the thing we freely fórfeit is kept
> with finders a care. . . .

Those two lines alone of the comparatively few poems of 1880–1882 seem to look forward uncompromisingly to the later poems of desolation. But almost all of them have some sense of loss, of blight, of "unselving" (to use Hopkins' own word from "Binsey Poplars"), even though that is far from the total—or even major—tone of the poem. Much the

10. For a full account of Hopkins as musician, see H. House and G. Storey, eds., *The Journals and Papers of Gerard Manley Hopkins* (Oxford, 1959), pp. 457–497.

most delicate and subtle of them—indeed one of the most delicate and subtle of all Hopkins' poems—is "Spring and Fall," addressed to a young child ("Márgarét, are you grieving/ Over Goldengrove uneaving?"), composed on his way back from Lydiate, in Lancashire, to Liverpool, in September 1880. The sharp but gentle questioning goes to the roots of all sorrow; and one phrase in particular shows Hopkins' skill in using the full resources of words:

> Though worlds of wranwood leafmeal lie;

where "wan" fuses both "dismal" and, as an obsolete prefix, "deficient" or "lost." The end of the poem is perhaps the finest expression we have of Hopkins' belief in the true wisdom of the heart and the spirit ("ghost"):

> Nor mouth had, no nor mind, expressed
> What heart heard of, ghost guessed:
> It is the blight man was born for,
> It is Margaret you mourn for.

Two other poems, written in the autumns of 1881 and 1882, are, at first sight and sound, celebrations, though in very different moods, of the countryside Hopkins so loved—"Inversnaid" of the Scottish Highlands, "Ribblesdale" of the Lancashire dale in which Stonyhurst College lies. But each ends with a warning not to destroy such inscapes. "Inversnaid" describers the movement of the Scottish burn so happily and excitedly that we might miss the sudden menace of the whirlpool:

> Of a pool so pitchblack, féll-frówning,
> It rounds and rounds Despair to drowning.

And no one can miss Hopkins' cry in the final stanzas:

> What would the world be, once bereft
> Of wet and of wildness? Let them be left,
> O let them be left, wildness and wet;
> Long live the weeds and the wilderness yet.

just as no one can miss Hopkins' fear, in the sestet of "Ribblesdale," that man, "the heir/ To his own selfbent so bound," will despoil "Thy lovely dale."

POEMS OF DESOLATION, 1884–1885

The very intensity of the six "terrible sonnets" (as Bridges called them) of 1885—one of them, as Hopkins told Bridges, "written in blood" (17 May 1885) —has led many to believe that the entire five years of Hopkins' time in Dublin—from February 1884, when he took up his appointment as Professor of Greek at University College and Fellow of the Royal University of Ireland, to his death on 8 June 1889 from typhoid—were years of unrelieved wretchedness. This is not confirmed by the other poems he wrote in Ireland: the other two sonnets of 1885—"To what serves Mortal Beauty?" and "The Soldier"—and most of the varied poems, some unfinished, he wrote from 1887 to within six weeks of his death. Nor is it shown by Hopkins' other remarkably wide-ranging signs of intellectual energy, including his projected books on Homer and on "the Dorian Measure or on Rhythm in general" (of which virtually nothing, sadly, remains); letters to Bridges on prosody and John Milton; to R. W. Dixon, on Dixon's own poems and on poetry in general; to Coventry Patmore, giving him detailed criticism for a new edition of his *Collected Poems*; and to his old friend Alexander Baillie on possible early relations between Egypt and Greece. In addition, he was writing a lot of music, and in the year before his death, he began drawing again.

But there can be no doubt of the paralyzing desolation that Hopkins felt in the winter of 1884 (to which the first drafts of "Spelt from Sybil's Leaves" belong) and for more than a year afterward. The "terrible sonnets" themselves document his feelings of isolation, of intense inner struggle, and paradoxically (since they are, to many readers, his finest sonnets), of frustration at his inability to create. Many factors certainly contributed to such feelings: bad health and nervous depression, increased by the strain on his eyes of almost continuous reading of examination papers; his sense of being an exile, exacerbated by the Irish nationalism he detested. And, perhaps, there were less conscious conflicts: the residual, and perhaps for him, inevitable conflict between priest and poet; the suppression of strong, possibly homosexual, feelings; and, most likely, the exaggeration, in his search for sanctity, of the distinction between his "affective" will, his love of beauty (including poetic beauty), and his "elective will," his desire for duty and holiness (an explanation put forward very convincingly by Fr. Christopher Devlin in *The Sermons and Devotional Writings of Gerard Manley Hopkins*, 1959).

"Spelt from Sybil's Leaves," to which Hopkins returned during the first six months of 1885, shows his powers at their finest. It is the only one of his sonnets to use an eight-stress line (marked by a strong caesura after four stresses); he described it to Bridges as "the longest sonnet ever made" and wrote to him on 11 December 1886:

> Of this long sonnet above all remember what applies to all my verse, that it is, as living art should be, made for performance and that its performance is not reading with the eye but loud, leisurely, poetical (not rhetorical) recitation, with long rests, long dwells on the rhyme and other marked syllables, and so on. This sonnet shd. be almost sung: it is most carefully timed in *tempo rubato* [irregular rhythm].

It is a poem of prophecy, of warning, drawing its title from both Vergil's Cumaen Sybil, who guided Aeneas to the underworld (*Aeneid* 6), and the *Dies irae*, "The Day of Wrath," of the Roman Catholic Burial Mass: "As David and the Sybil testify . . . what terror shall affright the soul when the judge comes."[11] In the terrible description of the war within, with which it ends:

> . . . a rack
> Where, selfwrung, selfstrung, sheathe- | and
> shelterless, |
> thóughts against thoughts ín groans grínd,

it prophesies the major theme of the six "terrible sonnets"; but its warning is much more comprehensive. The analogy of the haunting picture of the descent of night, in the first half of the sonnet, is the ending of all "selving," of all the "dappled things" Hopkins loved, of all distinctiveness:

> For earth | her being was unbound; her
> dapple is at an end, as-
> tray or aswarm, all throughther, in throngs;
> self ín | self steepèd and páshed—qúite
> Disremembering, dísmémbering | áll now. . . .

What is deeply impressive in the poem is not only the power of each analogy, each set of images, but the felt exactitude of their parallelism. The straining of evening to be night *becomes* the total blanketing-out of earth's individual features, now lit only by the last rays of the dying sun ("Her fond yellow hornlight wound to the west"); the loss of each object's true shape and meaning, its inscape ("self in self steepèd and páshed") *becomes*—the warning is in line 7 ("Heart, you round me right/With")—the nightmare alternative, where the trees have the shape of dragons and the "bleak light" the texture of a Damascene-worked sword. And this again is "Óur tale," the dire prophecy of the poem's title: once we let earth's multiplicity go—her "once skéined strained véined varíety"—once we attempt to reduce life to absolute moral judgment—"black, white; | right, wrong"—we shall experience the self-torturing, selfwringing rack of the poem's last line. But the final analogy carries the direst warning: "párt, pen, páck" referees to Christ's separation of the sheep from the goats at the Last Judgment (Matt. 25: 31–33). On one level, fear of this judgment lies behind the image in the final line of unprotected conscience on the rack, from which there can be no escape.

Hopkins' description of "Sibyl's Leaves" to Bridges as "living art . . . made for perfor-

11. Paul L. Mariani has also shown how close the poem is to some of Hopkins' Retreat notes for the meditation on Hell from the *Spiritual Exercises* (*A Commentary on the Complete Poems of Gerard Manley Hopkins* ([Ithaca, N. Y., 1970], pp. 199 ff.).

mance"—his totally justified pride in it as a sonnet—must strongly modify our sense of its apparently bleak pessimism. "To what serves Mortal Beauty?" written during a retreat at Clongowes on 23 August 1885—very near in time to the final draft of "Sibyl's Leaves"—shows how gracefully and relaxedly Hopkins could treat the conflict that Fr. Christopher Devlin has suggested is central to the desolate sonnets of this year, his "affective will," his love of beauty, versus his "elective will," his duty to God. The famous story of Pope Gregory the Great sending Augustine to convert England, after seeing the handsome English slaves ("*Non Angli sed Angeli*"),[12] is one example of the higher use of mortal beauty:

> Those lovely lads once, wet-fresh | windfalls of war's storm,
> How then should Gregory, a father, | have gleanèd else from swarmèd Rome?
> But God to a nation | dealt that day's dear chance.

The sonnet's ending, the hope to "Merely meet" mortal beauty and to wish for it, as for all outward beauty, spiritual beauty, "God's better beauty, grace," presents the Christian "use" of beauty and does so with no sign of conflict or strain.

A sense of strain is dominant in the six desolate (although in differing degrees) sonnets that, insofar as we can date them, were written in 1885, the strain, above all, of isolation, of feeling deserted by God, of being certain that his creative capacity was dead. But we cannot miss either the energy, the determination to resist despair, or the authenticity, the equal determination to be utterly true to his own feelings, however self-tortured and self-torturing. Formally, these sonnets are the antitheses of "Spelt from Sybil's Leaves": the language is stark, bare, stripped, to express the essentials of the experience recorded, the resultant pitch of concentration a powerful new rhetoric.

12. Not Angles, but Angels."

Our only keys to dating them are letters and retreat notes. We know Hopkins' state of mind in the spring of 1885 from a letter to Alexander Baillie: his constitutional melancholy, he wrote, was becoming

> . . . more distributed, constant, and crippling. . . . when I am at the worst, though my judgment is never affected, my state is much like madness.

But two letters to Bridges help us to identify and date the sonnets themselves. In May 1885 Hopkins wrote to him, "I have after long silence written two sonnets, which I am touching: if ever anything was written in blood one of these was." And in September of the same year, "I shall shortly have some sonnets to send you, five or more. Four of these came like inspirations unbidden and against my will." Bridges thought the sonnet "written in blood" was "Carrion Comfort"; the more desolate "No worst, there is none," written on the same manuscript page as a revised version of "Carrion Comfort," seems more likely.[13] There can be little doubt that the "five or more" sonnets mentioned in the September letter—neither these nor the one "written in blood" were in fact sent to Bridges—were the "terrible sonnets" and thus very probably written in 1885.

"Carrion Comfort" has the greatest energy of these sonnets. It is generated at once in the opening line, in the refusal to "feast" on despair:

> Not, I'll not, carrion comfort, Despair, not feast on thee;

(there are three more repeated "nots" in the first quatrain). The energy is increased by all the physical images of wrestling, and it is felt strongly again in the successive questions Hopkins asks of his terrible and mysterious adversary. The "underthought" of the sonnet

13. Norman MacKenzie has recently argued for "I wake and feel" as being the most likely in *A Reader's Guide to G. M. Hopkins* (London, 1981), pp. 171–172.

(Hopkins' own word for the "often only half realised" source of a poem's images) combines the Book of Job with Gen. 32: 24–30, Jacob's wrestling with God; but, in turn, the adversary becomes Christ the winnower and finally Christ the Master. By kissing His rod and hand, Hopkins seems to have recovered: "my heart lo! lapped strength, stole joy, would laugh, chéer," But the sonnet ends on an agonizedly questioning note: the only certainty now is that the initial struggle with despair has become a wrestling bout with God Himself, scrupulously and bitterly documented:

> That night, that year
> Of now done darkness I wretch lay
> wrestling with
> (my God!) my God.

The poem "No worst, there is none" creates—or re-creates—an extraordinarily intense sense of physical and mental pain, mainly through imagery, sound, and rhythm, but also through an "underthought" that combines the most intense works of suffering, all of which Hopkins knew intimately: the Book of Job (the "whirlwind"), Aeschylus' *Prometheus Bound* (Prometheus chained to his mountain), *King Lear* (the sonnet's final two lines). In the very first line, "Pitched past pitch of grief" suggests an inexpressible degree of pain; "More pangs . . . schooled at forepangs, wilder wring" turns the grief into something horrifyingly active. The image of the lowing herd of cattle turns the pain into sorrow; but the anvil wincing and singing and Fury's shrieking force the sense of physical pain on us again and turn the screw tighter. Throughout the octet, repetitions and sound accentuate the experience; a mark that Hopkins made in his manuscript connecting "sorrow" with "an" in line 6, thus putting four of the line's five stresses on "áge-old anvil wince and sing," shows how sprung rhythm could "fetch out" his meaning.

The sestet begins with one of Hopkins' most striking images, painfully relevant to the states of nearmadness he described in his letters:

> O the mind, mind has mountains; cliffs of
> fall
> Frightful, sheer, no-man-fathomed. Hold
> them cheap
> May who ne'er hung there. . . .

It ends with clear references to the Book of Job, *King Lear*, and *Macbeth* that not only deepen the experience but universalize it. After the intense pain of the sonnet, the resigned acceptance of the final line seems the only course left open:

> all
> Life death does end and each day dies with
> sleep.

"To seem the stranger lies my lot" records both Hopkins' loneliness as a Roman Catholic in Ireland and his conviction that he can no longer create. The power of the first ten lines is that of direct, simple statement: his grief is poignant, but restrained. That restraint makes the clotted movement of lines 11–13, mirroring his bewildered frustration, the more powerful:

> . . . Only what word
> Wisest my heart breeds dark heaven's
> baffling ban
> Bars or hell's spell thwarts. . . .

Many years ago F. R. Leavis compared these lines to Macbeth's speech, "My thought, whose murder yet is but fantastical," as a "rendering of the very movement of consciousness";[14] and the judgment still holds. Hopkins' bafflement is at his inability to create (seen, as so often in this period, as a natural sexual process: "my heart breeds"); and, as we know from his letters, this sense of frustration extended to all his activities, musical and scholarly as well as poetic. Whether we read the sonnet's last sad phrase, "a lonely began," as a verb following an omitted relative pronoun or as a coined noun, its economy and poignancy fit perfectly the tone of the whole sonnet' its honesty demands our respect.

14. *New Bearings in English Poetry* (London, 1921), p. 170.

"I wake and feel the fell of dark" is, for most readers, probably the most desolate of these sonnets. The multiple meanings of the opening image, "the fell of dark" ("animal hide," "fierce," and "having fallen" are perhaps the key ones), dominate the octet.[15] All of them powerfully suggest the physical oppressiveness of the night's experience and carry that oppressiveness back, as the "black hoürs" "mean years, mean life." The image of "dead" (i.e., undelivered) letters sent to an unhearing God completes the sense of total lostness.

The sestet adds physical nausea to Hopkins' state: "gall" is poison as well as bitterness. In line 11 the bones, blood, and flesh that he praised God for binding in him in the first stanza of "The Wreck of the Deutschland" are now part of God's curse on him:

> Bones built in me, flesh filled, blood
> brimmed the curse.

There are two ambiguities in the sonnet's last three lines. Either "selfyeast" or "a dull dought" can be the subject of "Selfyeast of spirit a dull dough sours": either way, the right, healthy process—the leavening of body by spirit—has been soured, perverted. The second ambiguity should not be there: both theology and the syntax of the final two lines assert that the agonies of the demand in hell must be worse than his. Yet the doubt persists: "but worse" *could* mean that his torments were worse than theirs. The possibility of that is an index of the sonnet's authenticity:

> With witness I speak this.

We believe Hopkins is at his lowest ebb; and in the final two of these Dublin sonnets, "Patients, hard thing!" and "My own heart let me more have pity on," we can readily believe that at last some light has dawned for him. In each he seeks a way out of his misery; but in neither does he belittle the difficulties. The prayer for patients is totally realistic; it means he must continue to endure, to accept "war" and "wounds" and, worse still, the inner conflicts, the grating and bruising of his heart on itself. But patience offers consolations absent from the more tormented sonnets. Like ivy, "Natural heart's ivy," she "masks/Our ruins of wrecked past purpose" (the "beginnings of things, ever so many, which it seems to be might well have been done, ruins and wrecks," as Hopkins described his many unfinished projects in a letter to Baillie); and there, in an image of ivy's purple berries and liquid-green leaves, at once precise and hauntingly beautiful,

> . . . she basks
> Purple eyes and seas of liquid leaves all day.
> ("Patience, hard thing!")

But the final emblem of patience is God Himself. It is He who distills kindness, as a bee distills honey, and fills His honeycomb with it, "and that comes those ways we know."

The description of his own state in the octet of "My own heart let me more have pity on" is more complex and superbly, if difficulty, rendered. Hopkins knows that his torment is self-caused and at that stage is sure that there is no way out. The dense syntax and imagery perfectly mirror his bewilderment:

> I cast for comfort I can no more get
> By groping round my comfortless, then blind
> Eyes in their dark can day or thirst can find
> Thirst's all-in-all in all a world of wet.

We have to understand "world" after "comfortless," so as to parallel "dark" in the next line, and to appreciate that thirst itself seeks water (as the Ancient Mariner did, surrounded by the sea) just as blindness seeks light. As with Shakespeare and the seventeenth-century metaphysical poets, the effort forces us to share the writer's experience.

But the tone of the sestet, like that of the sonnet's first two lines, is self-reproaching, more relaxed, has even a touch of humor:

15. Norman MacKenzie has discussed the many possible meanings of "fell" in *Hopkins* (Edenburgh, 1968), pp. 88–90.

> Soul, self; come, poor Jackself, I do advise
> You, jaded, let be . . .

Bewilderment has now become self-exhortation: "leave comfort root-room" (let it expand like a plant); "let joy size" (let it grow—at God's will); trust unpredictable moments happiness. The final coined verb ("as skies/ Betweenpie mountains": as patches of sky seen between them dapple the mountains) suggests, in its very idiosyncrasy, at least a momentary restoration of Hopkins' faith in his own creativity.

FINAL POEMS, 1887–1889

Most of the poems that Hopkins wrote in the last two years of his life—including the unfinished "Epithalamion"—show, despite his often harrowing letters, how poetically alive he was until his final illness. They also show his constant technical experimentation. Of his three extended sonnets with codas, only one, "Toms' Garland" (September 1887), his one attempt to write a political poem "upon the Unemployed," did not work as he had hoped: he had to confess to Bridges that it was "in point of execution very highly wrought, too much so, I am afraid"; and most modern readers have agreed with him. Each of the other two, "Harry Ploughman" and "That Nature is a Heraclitean Fire," totally justifies, in its own individual way, Hopkins' experimenting. But during the same period he was also deliberately reverting almost to the opposite style, to the "Miltonic plainness and severity" that he told Bridges he had aimed at in "Andromeda," written almost ten years earlier at Oxford. It is this experiment in style, his admiration for John Dryden, "the most masculine of our poets" as he put it, and his hope "to be more intelligible, smoother, and less singular" (letter to Bridges, 25 September 1888) that lie behind the other sonnets of these two years, however different their concerns: "St. Alphonsus Rodriquez," "Thou art indeed just, Lord," and "To R. B.," his last poem, written six weeks before his death and addressed to Bridges. The fourth of these sonnets, "The Shepherd's Brow" (3 April 1889), Bridges excluded from the canon as "thrown off one day in a cynical mood." It is in fact the last of five full drafts; but a note of something near hysteria in its despair makes it, as a poem, much less impressive than either the earlier desolate sonnets or the three "plainer" sonnets of Hopkins' last year.

On 6 November 1887 Hopkins wrote to Bridges of "Harry Ploughman," written at Dromore two months before: "I want Harry Ploughman to be a vivid figure before the mind's eye; if he is not that the sonnet fails." On 11 October, he had written to Bridges that the sonnet was "altogether for recital not for perusal" and its rhythm was "very highly studied." He also thought that the sonnet was a "very good one." It is in fact an astonishingly vivid picture of a ploughman in action, "fetched out" by the sprung rhythm (in one of the two manuscripts Hopkins gives seven "reading-marks" to help the reader)[16] and by the five extra "burden-lines" (which Hopkins thought might be recited by a chorus). The octet—increased to eleven lines by the three "burden-lines"—gives us Harry himself, as Hopkins saw or imagined him in his strength and almost sculptured handsomeness:

> Hard as hurdle arms, with a broth of goldish
> flue,
> Breathed round; the rack of ribs; the scooped
> flank . . .

The bodily details accumulate; but they form a unity, the vital inscape of a man ready for action, all his limbs perfectly disciplined:

> By a grey eye's head steered well, one crew,
> fall to;
> Stand at stress. . . .

Hence the dominant images of the serving sailor or soldier: "one crew," "as at a rollcall, rank," "His sinew-service."

16. Reproduced in *The Poems of Gerard Manley Hopkins*, 4th ed., p. 293.

In the sestet the ploughing itself takes over; and now plough and ploughman, his curls lifted and laced by the wind, his feet racing behind the ploughshare and the upturned shining earth, form a new unity, the inscape of work well done. Ploughing as a symbol of work has a long history, both pagan and Christian; and Hopkins greatly admired one contemporary painting of it, Frederick Walker's *The Plough* (Royal Academy, 1870), which he thought "a divine work" (letter to Dixon, 30 June 1886).[17]

The poem's syntax throughout is difficult, as Hopkins himself confessed to Bridges, and words are used in unusual senses, demanding a leap of understanding from the reader, to make—as they do—the maximum impact. The two word-coinages in line 16, "Churlsgrace, too, child of Amansstrength" (the first from "churl," peasant), sum up the two qualities, grace and strength, that have combined to create this powerfully active figure.

"That Nature is a Heraclitean Fire and of the Comfort of the Resurrection" was written on 26 July 1888, near Dublin, "one windy bright day between floods," Hopkins told Dixon. Both technically and imaginatively it is one of his finest sonnets, fully justifying its great length (it is in alexandrines and has three codas). Hopkins was pleased with what he called its distillation of "early Greek philosophical thought," but prouder of its originality: "The effect of studying masterpieces is to make me admire and do otherwise," he wrote to Bridges two months after its composition.

Heraclitus (*ca.* 535 B.C.–*ca.* 475 B.C.) believed that all nature would ultimately resolve itself into fire. Everything was in a state of flux; not even man's body or soul could escape destruction. This relentless process is the subject of the central section of the sonnet's three sections, lines 10–16. But before this, the sonnet's opening section, lines 1–9, gives us one of Hopkins' most dynamic, excited pictures of nature in movement: racing clouds, light, and boisterous wind play together in apparent abandon: "Heaven-roysterers, in gay gangs they throng." Then, suddenly, Hopkins sees them as part of the Heraclitean process; the wind turns the floods into earth and ooze; then all, as in Heraclitus, becomes fire:

> . . . Million-fuelèd, nature's bonfire burns on.

But man's toiling footprints have been obliterated, too, leading Hopkins to the dramatic change of tone in the second section, as he contemplates the loss of man's mind and soul, communicated in three highly expressive word-coinages: man's "firedint," the spark his being gives out; his "Manshape," his inscape or essence; his "disserval" being, his individual selfhood. All these "death blots black out"; all traces of his precious individuality "vastness blurs and time beats level."

But the change of tone in the final section is more dramatic still. "Enough! the Resurrection" is, for Hopkins, a complete answer to Heraclitus. There is no balking of man's frailties and almost comic inadequacies: he is still "This Jack, joke, poor potsherd, patch, matchwood," but Christ has promised his ultimate survival; he is therefore, too, "immortal diamond." The echo of the last short line makes certainty, for Hopkins, more certain.

"Epithalamion," Hopkins' unfinished ode for his youngest brother Everard's wedding in April 1888, deserves to be better known. It was only a collection of fragments that Bridges, with the greatest skill, put together; and there is little success in the faltering attempt at the end to make the scene, of the boys bathing, apply allegorically to marriage—or indeed in the rather absurd picture of the "listless stranger" (Hopkins himself?) undressing and taking off his boots. But there are marvelous lines that communicate to the full Hopkins' joy in re-creating such a remembered scene and his technical skills in doing so. Of the boys bathing:

> With dare and with downdolphinry and
> bellbright bodies huddling out,

17. It is reproduced in R. K. R. Thornton, ed., *All My Eyes See: The Visual World of G. M. Hopkins* (Sunderland, 1975), p. 105.

Are earthworld, airworld, waterworld
thorough hurled, all by turn and turn
about;

of the pool, surrounded by his favorite trees:

Fairyland; silk-beech, scrolled ash, packed
sycamore, wild wychelm, hornbeam
fretty overstood
By. Rafts and rafts of flake leaves light, dealt
so, painted on the air, . . .

And of the strangely shaped rocks that we know, from his journal and some of his drawings, he was so found of:

. . . a coffer, burly all of blocks
Built of chancequarrièd, selfquainèd, hoar-
huskèd rocks
And the water warbles over into, filleted
with glassy grassy quicksilvery shivès and
shoots. . . .

However diverse the concern, of the three "plain" sonnets written in Ireland during his last year, they share certain new qualities of tone. They are, in form and meter, a return to tradition after the long, experimental sonnets they follow. Letters to Bridges, sending him earlier, finally rejected drafts of "St. Alphonsus Rodriquez," show how deliberate this return was; and one comment on it, however ironically framed, shows how desperate he was to be understood: "The sonnet (I Say it snorting) aims at being understood." He called its sestet "both pregnant and exact"; the near-classical claim is justified by all three sonnets. They are also, all three, very personal, related intimately to his spiritual trials and, above all, to what he felt keenly and, as the poems themselves show, wrongly as poetic sterility. And to objectivity that personal tone, to give it a new, quiet dignity, they have, each of them in different ways, a near-ironic self-awareness.[18]

18. Paul L. Mariani, in his *Commentary on the Complete Poems,* stresses the irony (including "The Shepherd's Brow" in his discussion) and claims that "these last sonnets amount to a new direction in lyrical poetry," (pp. 299, 316).

"St. Alphonsus Rodriguez" was "written to order" in autumn 1888 in honor of a recently canonized sixteenth-century Jesuit hall porter in Majorca. The quiet irony comes from the clear identification of his own state in Dublin, apparently fruitless and inactive, with that of Alphonsus. The sonnet celebrates "the war within" as against the outward martyrdom of "exploit," the inner trials Alphonsus suffered:

Those years and years . . . of world without
event
That in Majorca Alfonso watched the door.

The God "who, with trickling increment, / Veins violets," is the God he trusts, despite his sense of aridity, to bring him slowly but firmly to fulfillment.

In "Thou art indeed just, Lord" (17 March 1889), that trust is sorely tried. The epigraph, from Jer. 12:1, "Why do the ways of the wicked prosper?" partly paraphrased in the sonnet's opening three lines, is bitter enough: Hopkins' tone, emphasized by the repeated "Sir," turns it into a dignified plea. The poignant picture of returning spring in the sestet—"fretty chervil," "fresh wind," and nesting birds—contrasted with his own sense of sterility reinforces the personal bitterness: the image of the straining eunuch comes in both a latter to Bridges and a private retreat-note of the same year. But the prayer of the final line,

Mine, O thou Lord of life, send my roots
rain

in which the "Mine" must surely govern both "lord of life" and "roots," both reacknowledges God's power over him and at least posits a new intimacy between them. The cry of sterility has produced one of his most beautifully structured and tonally delicate sonnets.

Hopkins' last poem, "To R. B.," dated 22 April 1889, six weeks before his death, and sent to Bridges with his last letter to him, again laments his flagging inspiration. But bitterness is now muted. What we have instead is a confident control of the Conception and birth image in the octet and the perfect mirroring of the explanation of his "un-creativity" in the movement and sound of the last four lines:

> O then if in my lagging lines you miss
>
> The roll, the rise, the carol, the creation,
> My winter world, that scarcely breathes that bliss
> Now, yields you, with some sighs, our explanation.

JOURNAL AND LETTERS

Hopkins kept a journal from May 1866, his third year at Oxford, to February 1875, six months after he had begun studying theology at St. Beuno's College in North Wales. It has been of great use to biographers in giving details of outward events—and some more inward events—in Hopkins' life: the exact day, so far as he could record it, of his conversion; his feelings about the various Jesuit institutions in which he lived during his training; two occasions on which he broke down when hearing passages from the lives of Catholics read aloud; the first time he read Duns Scotus and its effect on him.

But its greatest interest is that it covers all but the last ten months of his seven years' "poetic silence," for it was Hopkins' journal that became the outlet for his remarkable powers of observation and for his hypersensitive response to the minutiae of nature. Its most vivid writing is therefore a splendid gloss on the mature poems that were to follow: the trees, skies, clouds, mountains, rushing water, rocks, flowers that were to become the subjects and images of so many of the poems are all recorded here. The journal is full of "wildness and wet," "the weeds and the wilderness. "It is also full of unusual words—dialect, archaic, sometimes coined—which he sought out, as in his poems, to express the inscapes that gave him such delight: "brindled and hatched," "knopped," "pelleted," "ruddled" (of clouds); "dappled with big laps and flowers-in-damask" (of the sun in rain); "They look like little gay jugs by shape when they walk, strutting and jod-jodding with their heads" (of pigeons), to cite only a few. It is in the journal that we have almost all the explicit examples of "inscape" and "instress," used for objects in nature, paintings, even buildings, from 1868 onward: "Query has not Giotto the instress of loveliness" (27 June 1868, on a visit to the National Gallery) is the first; "Swiss trees are, like English, well inscaped—in quains [coigns, wedge-shaped blocks]" (7 July 1868, in Switzerland), the second.

The comments on contemporary paintings in the journal are extremely interesting.[19] Like Ruskin, Hopkins made notes on the exhibitions he visited: during the nine years covered by the journal he went whenever he could to the main exhibitions of the Royal Academy, the National Gallery, and the Society of Painters in Water-Colours, as well as to two special loan exhibitions of National Portraits. On all these he made notes, sometimes only jottings, as well as commenting on them in letters. As we might expect, a great many paintings are judged in terms of their inscape (or instress) or lack of it. As an undergraduate, he had greatly admired the Pre-Raphaelities; the painters in whom he took the most delight or critical interest during these years were Sir John Everett Millais, Frederick Leighton, Frederick Walker, Sir Lawrence Alma-Tadema, and the sculptor Sir Hamo Thornycroft. In 1863, as an undergraduate, he had described Millais as "the greatest English painter, one of the greatest of the world." At the Royal Academy exhibition in May and June 1874 he is more critical, but still highly appreciative:

> Millais—*Scotch Firs; "The silence that is in the lonely woods"*—No such thing, instress absent, firtrunks ungrouped, four or so pairing but not markedly, true bold realism but

19. They are the subject of a chapter by Norman White in *All My Eyes See: The Visual World of G. M. Hopkins*, pp. 89–106, that reproduces many of the paintings that particularly interested Hopkins.

> quite a casual install of woodland with casual heathertufts, broom with black beanpods and so on, but the master shewn in the slouch and toss-up of the firtreehead in near background, in the tufts of fir-needles, and in everything. So too *Winter Fuel: "Bare ruined choirs"* etc—almost no sorrow of autumn; a rawness (though I felt this less the second time), unvelvety papery colouring, especially in raw silver and purple birchstems, crude rusty cartwheels, aimless mess or minglemangle of cut underwood in under-your-nose foreground; aimlessly posed truthful child on shaft of cart; but then most masterly Turner-like outline of craggy hill, silver-streaked with birchtrees, which fielded in an equally masterly rust-coloured young oak, with strong curl and seizure in the dead leaves. (journal, 23 May 1874)

Such a passage illustrates well the vigor, observation, and freshness of the best of Hopkins' journal-writing; it also shows the search for significant detail and for the unusual word in which to capture it that will play such a part in his mature poems.

Hopkins' letters fill three volumes, all edited by C. C. Abbott. There are letters to his undergraduate friends, including the famous letter to Alexander Baillie of 10 September 1864 on the "three kinds" of poetic language; much later letters to Baillie on possible early relations between Egypt and Greece; letters to his family, mainly to his mother; both sides of his correspondence with two fellow poets, Canon R. W. Dixon and Coventry Patmore; and letters to his most intimate friend, the future poet laureate, Robert Bridges. These three contemporary poets, however, much they may have lacked understanding of Hopkins' own poetry—and particularly of his technical innovations—were his only regular readers in his lifetime: his "public," as he called Bridges. The letters to Dixon and Patmore are mainly interesting for the detailed comments on poetry utterly different from Hopkins' own: they show what a meticulous and sympathetic critic Hopkins was. And it is in his letters to Dixon that we find the explanation for Hopkins' seven years' poetic silence, when he became a Jesuit; the account of how "The Wreck of the Deutschland" came to be written; the clearest explanation of sprung rhythm; and his antipathy after the Jesuit *Month*'s rejection of both "The Wreck" and "The Loss of the Eurydice" toward further attempts at publication.

But it is the letters to Bridges that reveal most of Hopkins as a man and add considerably to his stature both as a poet and as a critic, perhaps almost as much as the letters of Keats, whom Hopkins so persistently admired, add to his stature. Dixon was twelve years older than Hopkins, Patmore twenty-two: in a Victorian ambience, that gap made the letters between them necessarily formal. Hopkins and Bridges were the same age, undergraduates at Oxford together, and by 1865 close friends. Despite Bridges' dislike of Roman Catholicism and his lack of sympathy with Hopkins' poetic experiments, they remained close friends to the end of Hopkins' life. For Hopkins, the friendship was vital. After he had become a Jesuit, they met only about a dozen times. Hence the reliance on letters; there are 172 (including a few cards) of Hopkins'; Bridges destroyed his own letters after his friend's death.

Hopkins' letters make wonderful reading. The best of them are vivid, candid, spontaneous, and often sharply comic. They show his capacity to laugh at himself, which we would hardly have expected from the poems. A great many of them, as we would expect, discuss in detail his own and Bridges' poems. Frequently under attack for "obscurities" and "eccentricities," Hopkins is often on the defensive: but the line-by-line explanations he consequently gave Bridges provide the best running commentary we have on his poetry (a commentary often used in earlier sections of this essay). It is to Bridges' questioning of individual effects that we owe some of Hopkins' best-known defenses of both his practice and poetic beliefs:

> Why do I employ sprung rhythm at all? Because it is the nearest to the rhythm of prose, that is the native and natural rhythm of

> speech, the least forced, the most rhetorical and emphatic of all possible rhythms. . . . (21 August 1877)

The above letter was written after Bridges had called the verse of "The Wreck of the Deutschland" "presumptious [*sic*] jugglery."

> To do the Eurydice any kind of justice you must not slovenly read it with the eyes but with your ears, as if the paper were declaiming it at your. For instance the line "she had come from a cruise training seamen" read without stress and declaim is mere Lloyd's Shipping Intelligence; properly read it is quite a different thing. Stress is the life of it. (21 May 1878)

He answered Bridges' charge of "queerness" against the first three lines of the sestet of "The Lantern out of Door."

> . . . as air, melody, is what strikes me most of all in music and design in painting, so design, pattern or what I am in the habit of calling "inscape" is what I above all aim at in poetry. Now it is the virtue of design, pattern, or inscape to be distinctive and it is the vice of distinctiveness, to become queer. This vice I cannot have escaped. (15 February 1879)

> This leads me to say that a kind of touchstone of the highest or most living art is seriousness; not gravity but the being in earnest with your subject—reality. (1 June 1886)

In his criticism of Bridges' own poems, so unlike his own, Hopkins is generous, meticulous, exact in both praise and dispraise. He can be sharp when he wants to be:

> "Disillusion" does exist, as typhus exists and the Protestant religion. The same "brutes" say "disillusion" as say "standpoint" and "preventative" and "equally as well" and "to whomsoever shall ask." (26 January 1881)

And his affection never blurs what he sees as blemishes in character:

> You seem to want to be told over again that you have genius and are a poet and your versus beautiful. . . . You want perhaps to be told more in particular. I am not the best to tell you, being biassed by love, and yet I am too. . . . If I were not your friend I should wish to be the friend of the man who wrote your poems. (22 October 1879)

But there is a great deal more than criticism of each other's poetry in these letters. The two friends shared many other interests: the classics, Milton, music, language, prosody, contemporary writers and painters. Hopkins writes on all of them, sharply and individually. Above all, he can write of his feelings when he most needed a confidant in his last five difficult years in Dublin.

Bridges has been much criticized: for his delay of thirty years in publishing the poems (which he scrupulously kept); for the charges of obscurity and lapses of taste he leveled at some of them in his preface, when he finally edited them in 1918; and for his often tactlessly expressed dislike of Hopkins' Roman Catholicism. Almost all modern readers and critics, with one or two noted exceptions (recorded in the bibliography), are firmly on Hopkins' side. What these letters show, besides the remarkable distinctiveness of a far-ranging mind fully engaged in whatever it touched, is how essential Bridges was to Hopkins' emotional stability; and how important poetry, the other "vocation," remained to the dedicated Jesuit priest.

A final point must be made. Hopkins could never have been accepted as a major poet by his own contemporaries: his innovations were too extreme, his aims—to the temper of his time—too independent. Only comparatively few readers were ready for him in 1918: Bridges' edition of his poems (750 copies only) took twelve years to sell. He has had no obvious followers. But from the 1930's onward his impact has been immense in many countries of the world. His technical innovations in rhythm and language have been endlessly debated and almost universally admired. The challenge he offers appeals strongly to the twentieth-century reader. In this important regard, the thirty years' delay in publication of his poems has in fact worked in Hopkins' favor.

Selected Bibliography

BIBLIOGRAPHY

The Kenyon Critics, *Gerard Manley Hopkins: A Critical Symposium* (Norfolk, Conn, 1945, repr. New York, 1975), contains a bibliography; Charney, M., "A Bibliographical Study of Hopkins Criticism, 1918–1949," *Thought*, 25 (June 1950), 297–326; Cohen, E. H., *Works and Criticism of Gerard Manley Hopkins: A Comprehensive Bibliography* (Washington, D.C., 1969); G. Watson, ed. *The New Cambridge Bibliography of English Literature*, vol. III (Cambridge, 1969), entry for Hopkins by G. Storey; Dunne, T., *Gerard Manley Hopkins: A Comprehensive Bibliography* (Oxford, 1976). Note: The Hopkins Research Bulletin carried annual bibliographies, 1970–1976.

COLLECTED WORKS

Poems of Gerard Manley Hopkins, R. Bridges, ed. (Oxford, 1918), with preface and notes; C. Williams, ed. *Poems of Gerard Manley Hopkins*, 2nd ed. (Oxford, 1930), with additional poems and a critical intro.; W. H. Gardner, ed. *Poems of Gerard Manley Hopkins*, 3rd ed. (Oxford, 1948), with notes and a biographical intro.; W. H. Gardner and N. H. MacKenzie, eds. *Poems of Gerard Manley Hopkins*, 4th ed. (Oxford, 1967; repr. 1970), with additional notes, a foreward on the revised text, and a new biographical and critical intro, the authoritative ed., incorporating all known poems and fragments.

LETTERS AND JOURNALS

C. C. Abbott, ed. *The Letters of Gerard Manley Hopkins to Robert Bridges* (Oxford, 1936; rev. ed. 1955); C. C. Abbott, ed. *The Correspondence of Gerard Manley Hopkins and R. W. Dixon* (Oxford, 1935; rev. ed. London, 1955); H. House, ed. *The Note-Books and Papers of Gerard Manley Hopkins* (Oxford, 1937), with notes and a preface by House, the first publication of Hopkins' early notebooks and journal, with a selection of devotional writings and drawings; C. C. Abbott, ed. *Further Letters of Gerard Manley Hopkins* (Oxford, 1938; enl. 2nd ed. 1956), contains letters to Hopkins' family and friends, and his correspondence with Coventry Patmore; H. House, ed. *The Journals and Papers of Gerard Manley Hopkins*, 2nd ed., rev. and enl., and completed by G. Storey (Oxford, 1959), contains Hopkins' full journal, music, and a large selection of his drawings; C. Devlin, S.J., ed. *The Sermons and Devotional Writings of Gerard Manley Hopkins* (Oxford, 1959), contains all of Hopkins' known spiritual writings with Fr. Devlin's intros.

SEPARATE WORKS

"Winter with the Gulf Stream," *Once a Week*, 8 (February 14, 1863), p. 210; "Barnfloor and Winepress," in *Union Review*, 3 (1865), p. 579; A. H. Miles, ed. *The Poems and the Poetry of the Century* (London, 1893), vol. VIII contains eleven poems by Hopkins (including a partial text of "A Vision of the Mermaids"), with a short intro. by R. Bridges; Beeching, H. C., sel. and arr. *Lyra Sacra* (London, 1895), contains five poems by Hopkins; R. Bridges, ed. *The Spirit of Man* (London, 1916), contains six poems by Hopkins (including partial texts of "Spring and Fall" and "The Habit of Perfection" and stanza 1 of "The Wreck of the Deutschland," as amended by Bridges).

SELECTED WORKS

W. H. Gardner, ed. *Poems and Prose of Gerard Manley Hopkins* (London, 1953; rev. ed. 1969); J. Pick, ed. *A Hopkins Reader* (Oxford, 1953; rev. and enl. ed. Garden City, N.Y., 1966); J. Reeves, ed. *Selected Poems of Gerard Manley Hopkins* (London, 1953; ppbk. ed. 1967); G. Storey, ed. *Hopkins: Selections* (Oxford, 1967); N. H. MacKenzie, ed. *Poems by Gerard Manley Hopkins* (London, 1974), Folio Society.

BIOGRAPHICAL AND CRITICAL STUDIES

Brégy, K., "Gerard Hopkins: An Epitaph and an Appreciation," *Catholic World*, 88 (January 1909), pp. 433–447, one of the first critical essays written from a strong Catholic viewpoint; Keating, J., "Impressions of Father Gerard Hopkins, S.J.," in the *Month*, 114 (July, August and September 1909), pp. 59–68, 151–160, and 246–258, early biographical essays; Richards, I. A., "Gerard Hopkins," in the *Dial* (New York), 81, (September 1926), pp. 195–203, highly influential early critical essay; Empson, W., *Seven Types of Ambiguity* (London, 1930), contains two important sections on Hopkins; Lahey, G. F., S.J., *Gerard Manley Hopkins* (Oxford, 1930), the first biography; Leavis, F. R., *New Bearings in English Poetry* (London, 1932; repr. 1950), contains an important and appreciative chapter on Hopkins; Phare, E., *The Poetry of Gerard Manley Hopkins* (Cambridge, 1933); Kelly, B., *The Mind and Poetry of Gerard Manley Hopkins* (Ditchling, 1935; repr. New York, 1971); *New Verse*, 14 (April 1935), contains essays on Hopkins by Bremond, A., Devlin, C., Griffith, L. W., Grigson, G., House, H., MacNeice, L., and Madge, C.

Daiches, D., *Poetry and the Modern World* (Chicago, 1940), contains a section on Hopkins; Pick, J., *Gerard*

Manley Hopkins: Priest and Poet (Oxford, 1942; rev. ppbk. ed. 1966); Gardner, W. H., *Gerard Manley Hopkins (1844–1899): A Study of Poetic Idiosyncrasy in Relation to Poetic Tradition*, 2 vols. (London, 1944 and 1949; rev ed. Oxford, 1966), the fullest, if discursive, critical study of Hopkins as a poet; The Kenyon Critics, *Gerard Manley Hopkins: A Critical Symposium* (Norfolk, Conn., 1945; repr. New York 1973), contains essays by M. McLuhan, H. Whitehall, J. Miles, A. Warren, R. Lowell, and A. Mizener; Holloway, M. M., *The Prosodic Theory of Gerard Manley Hopkins* (Washington, D.C., 1947); Peters, W. A. M., S.J., *Gerard Manley Hopkins: A Critical Essay Towards the Understanding of His Poetry* (Oxford, 1948; repr. 1970), stresses the effects on Hopkins' poetry of his theories of inscape; Weyand, N., S.J. and R. V. Schoder, S.J. eds., *Immortal Diamond* (London, 1949), contains essays by twelve Jesuit critics; Leavis, F. R., *The Common Pursuit* (London, 1952), contains an influential ch. on Hopkins; Davie, D., *Purity of Diction in English Verse* (London, 1952; 2nd ed. 1967), contains "Hopkins as a Decadent Critic," including some strictures on his language; Hartman, G. H., *The Unmediated Vision* (New Haven, Conn., 1954), contains an essay on Hopkins; Martz, L. L., *The Poetry of Meditation* (New Haven, Conn., 1954; rev. ed. 1962), shows Hopkins' debt to this tradition; Grigson, G., *Gerard Manley Hopkins* (London, 1955), for the British Council, Writers and Their Work, no. 59 (rev. ed., 1962), a particularly perceptive study on Hopkins as a nature-poet; Heuser, A., *The Shaping Vision of Gerard Manley Hopkins* (Oxford, 1958).

Downs, D. A., *Gerard Manley Hopkins: A Study of His Ignation Spirit* (London, 1960), stresses the sacramental nature of Hopkins' poetry; Ritz, J.-G., *Robert Bridges and Gerard Hopkins, 1863–1889: A Literary Friendship* (Oxford, 1960); Boyle, R., S.J., *Metaphor in Hopkins* (Chapel Hill, N.C., 1961), includes a detailed analysis of "The Windhover"; Winters, Y., *The Function of Criticism* (London, 1962), repr. his well-known attack on Hopkins from the *Hudson Review* (1949); Bender, T. K., *Gerard Manley Hopkins: The Classical Background and Critical Reputation of His Work* (Baltimore, 1966); G. H. Hartman, ed. *Hopkins: A Collection of Critical Essays* (Englewood Cliffs, N.J., 1966), includes essays by M. McLuhan, J. Wain, F. R. Leavis, F. O. Matthiessen, A. Warren, W. J. Ong, and others; Lees, F. N., *Gerard Manley Hopkins* (New York, 1966); Schneider, E. W., "The Wreck of the Deutschland: A New Reading," in *PMLA* (March 1966), 110–122; McChesney, D., *A Hopkins Commentary* (London, 1968), detailed commentary on the main poems; MacKenzie, N. H., *Hopkins* (Edinburgh, 1968), Writers and Critics series, an excellent general intro.; Schnieder, E. W., *The Dragon in the Gate: Studies in the Poetry of G. M. Hopkins* (Berkeley, 1968); Thomas, A., S.J., *Hopkins the Jesuit: The Years of Training* (Oxford, 1969), based on Jesuit archives, contains a previously unpublished journal kept by Hopkins while he was a Jesuit novice.

Mariani, P. L., *A Commentary on the Complete Poems of Gerard Manley Hopkins* (Ithaca, N.Y., 1970); Ball, P. M., *The Science of Aspects: The Changing Role of Fact in the Work of Coleridge, Ruskin and Hopkins* (London, 1971); Sulloway, A. G., *Gerard Manley Hopkins and the Victorian Temper* (London, 1972); Fulweiler, H. W., *Letters from the Darkling Plain: Language and the Grounds of Knolwedge in the Poetry of Arnold and Hopkins* (Columbia, Missouri, 1972); Thornton, R. K. R., *Gerard Manley Hopkins: The Poems* (London, 1973), a short, helpful intro. in the Studies in English Literature series; M. Bottrall, ed. *Gerard Manley Hopkins: Poems—A Casebook* (London, 1975), contains essays by H. Read, T. S. Eliot, H. House, G. Grigson, E. Jennings, P. A. Wolfe, and others; P. Milward, S.J. (text) and R. V. Schoder, S.J. (photographs), *Landscape and Inscape: Vision and Inspiration in Hopkins's Poetry* (London, 1975); R. K. R. Thornton, ed. *All My Eyes See: The Visual World of G. M. Hopkins* (Sunderland, 1975), examines the visual aspect of Hopkins' life, illus. by his own, his brothers', and his contemporaries' work; P. Milward, S.J., and R. V. Schoder, S.J., eds. *Readings of "The Wreck": Essays in Commemoration of the Centenary of G. M. Hopkins' "The Wreck of the Deutschland,"* (Chicago, 1976); Bergonzi, B., *Gerard Manley Hopkins* (London, 1977), an up-to-date, succinct biography in the Masters of World Literature series; Milroy, J., *The Language of Gerard Manley Hopkins* (London, 1977); Robinson, J., *In Extremity: A Study of Gerard Manley Hopkins* (Cambridge, 1978); MacKenzie, N. H., *A Reader's Guide to G. M. Hopkins* (London, 1981). Note: Periodicals containing valuable regular contributions about Hopkins include *The Hopkins Research Bulletin* (1970–1976) and *The Hopkins Quarterly* (1974–), Guelph, Ontario. The Hopkins Society Annual Lectures, (1970–), are distributed to its members by the Society.